THE NORTON ANTHOLOGY OF

WORLD
LITERATURE

FOURTH EDITION

VOLUME A

THE NORTON ANTHOLOGY OF

WORLD LITERATURE

FOURTH EDITION

MARTIN PUCHNER, *General Editor*
HARVARD UNIVERSITY

SUZANNE AKBARI
UNIVERSITY OF TORONTO

WIEBKE DENECKE
BOSTON UNIVERSITY

BARBARA FUCHS
UNIVERSITY OF CALIFORNIA, LOS ANGELES

CAROLINE LEVINE
CORNELL UNIVERSITY

PERICLES LEWIS
YALE UNIVERSITY

EMILY WILSON
UNIVERSITY OF PENNSYLVANIA

VOLUME A

W. W. NORTON & COMPANY | New York · London

W. W. Norton & Company has been independent since its founding in 1923, when William Warder Norton and Mary D. Herter Norton first published lectures delivered at the People's Institute, the adult education division of New York City's Cooper Union. The firm soon expanded its program beyond the Institute, publishing books by celebrated academics from America and abroad. By midcentury, the two major pillars of Norton's publishing program—trade books and college texts—were firmly established. In the 1950s, the Norton family transferred control of the company to its employees, and today—with a staff of four hundred and a comparable number of trade, college, and professional titles published each year—W. W. Norton & Company stands as the largest and oldest publishing house owned wholly by its employees.

Editor: Peter Simon
Associate Editor: Gerra Goff
Project Editor: Christine D'Antonio
Manuscript Editor: Mike Fleming
Managing Editor, College: Marian Johnson
Managing Editor, College Digital Media: Kim Yi
Production Manager: Sean Mintus
Media Editor: Carly Fraser-Doria
Media Project Editor: Cooper Wilhelm
Assistant Media Editor: Ava Bramson
Editorial Assistant, Media: Joshua Bianchi
Marketing Manager, Literature: Kimberly Bowers
Art Direction: Rubina Yeh
Book Design: Jo Anne Metsch
Permissions Manager: Megan Schindel
Permissions Clearer: Margaret Gorenstein
Photo Editor: Catherine Abelman
Composition: Westchester Book Services
Manufacturing: Thomson Reuters

Permission to use copyrighted material is included in the backmatter of this book.

Library of Congress Cataloging-in-Publication Data

Names: Puchner, Martin, 1969- editor. | Akbari, Suzanne Conklin, editor. | Denecke, Wiebke, editor. | Fuchs, Barbara, 1970- editor. | Levine, Caroline, 1970- editor. | Lewis, Pericles, editor. | Wilson, Emily R., 1971- editor.
Title: The Norton anthology of world literature / Martin Puchner, general editor ; Suzanne Akbari, Wiebke Denecke, Barbara Fuchs, Caroline Levine, Pericles Lewis, Emily Wilson.
Description: Fourth edition. | New York : W. W. Norton & Company, [2018] | Includes bibliographical references and index.
Identifiers: LCCN 2017060699| ISBN 9780393602814 (pbk. : v. A) | ISBN 9780393602821 (pbk. : v. B) | ISBN 9780393602838 (pbk. : v. C) | ISBN 9780393602845 (pbk. : v. D) | ISBN 9780393602852 (pbk. : v. E) | ISBN 9780393602869 (pbk. : v. F)
Subjects: LCSH: Literature—Collections.
Classification: LCC PN6014 .N66 2018 | DDC 808.8—dc23 LC record available at https://lccn.loc.gov/2017060699

ISBN 978-0-393-60281-4 (pbk.)

W. W. Norton & Company, Inc., 500 Fifth Avenue, New York, NY 10110-0017
wwnorton.com
W. W. Norton & Company Ltd., 15 Carlisle Street, London W1D 3BS

3 4 5 6 7 8 9 0

Contents

ANCIENT ATHENIAN DRAMA

SPEECH, WRITING, AND POETRY / 1071

III. EARLY CHINESE LITERATURE AND THOUGHT   1305

Preface

They arrive in boats, men exhausted from years of warfare and travel. As they approach the shore, their leader spots signs of habitation: flocks of goats and sheep, smoke rising from dwellings. A natural harbor permits them to anchor their boats so that they will be safe from storms. The leader takes an advance team with him to explore the island. It is rich in soil and vegetation, and natural springs flow with cool, clear water. With luck, they will be able to replenish their provisions and be on their way.

In the world of these men, welcoming travelers is a sacred custom, sanctioned by the gods themselves. It is also good policy among seafaring people. Someday, the roles may very well be reversed: today's host may be tomorrow's guest. Yet the travelers can never be certain whether a particular people will honor this custom. Wondering what to expect, the thirteen men enter one of the caves dotting the coastline.

The owner isn't home, but the men enter anyway, without any compunction. There are pens for sheep and goats, and there is plenty of cheese and milk, so the men begin eating. When the owner returns, they are terrified, but their leader, boldly, asks for gifts. The owner is not pleased. Instead of giving the intruders what they demand, he kills two of them and eats them for dinner. And then two more the next day. All the while, he keeps the men trapped in his cave.

A wily man, the leader devises a scheme to escape. He offers the owner wine, enough to make him drunk and sleepy. Once he dozes off, the men take a staff that they have secretly sharpened and they plunge it into the owner's eye, blinding him. Without sight, he cannot see the men clinging to the undersides of his prized sheep as they stroll, one by one, out of the cave to graze, and cleverly the men cling only to the male sheep, not the females, which get milked.

*   *   *

This story of hospitality gone wrong comes from *The Odyssey*, one of the best-known works in all of world literature. We learn of this strange encounter of Greek soldiers with the one-eyed Cyclops named Polyphemus from Odysseus, the protagonist of the epic, when he recounts his exploits at the court of another host, the king of the Phaeacians. Unsurprisingly, Polyphemus isn't presented in the best light. Odysseus describes the Cyclopes as a people without a "proper" community, without agriculture, without hospitality. Is Odysseus, who has been wined and dined by his current host, trying to curry favor with the king of the Phaeacians by telling him how terribly he was treated by these non-Greek others? Reading the passage closely, we can see that Polyphemus and the other Cyclopes are adroit makers of cheese, so they can't be all that lazy. When the blinded Polyphemus cries out for help, his associates come to help him as a matter of course, so they don't live quite as isolated from one another as Odysseus claims. Even though Odysseus asserts that Polyphemus is godless, the land is blessed by the gods with fertility, and Polyphemus's divine father comes to his aid when he prays. Odysseus says that the Cyclopes lack laws and custom, yet we are also shown the careful, regular, customary way that Polyphemus takes care of his household. In a touching scene toward the end of his encounter with Odysseus, after he is blinded, Polyphemus speaks gently and respectfully to his favorite ram, so he can't be all that monstrous. The one-eyed giants assist one another, they are shepherds and artisans, and they are capable of kindness. The passage's ambiguities suggest that perhaps it was partly Odysseus's fault that this encounter between cultures went so badly. Were he and his companions simply travelers badly in need of food, or were they looters hoping to enrich themselves? The passage suggests that it's a matter of narrative perspective, from whose point of view the story is told.

Scenes of hospitality (or the lack thereof) are everywhere in world literature, and questions about hospitality, about the courtesies that we owe to strangers and that strangers owe to us (whether we are guests or hosts), are as important today as they were in the ancient world. Although many writers and thinkers today are fond of saying that our era is the first "truly global" one, stories such as this episode from Homer's *Odyssey* remind us that travel, trade, exile, migration, and cultural encounters of all kinds have been features of human experience for thousands of years.

The experience of reading world literature, too, is a form of travel—a mode of cultural encounter that presents us with languages, cultural norms, customs, and ideas that may be unfamiliar to us, even strange. As readers, each time we begin to read a new work, we put ourselves in the role of a traveler in a foreign land, trying to understand its practices and values and hoping to feel, to some degree and in some way, connected to and welcome among the people we meet there. *The Epic of Gilgamesh*, for example, takes its readers on a tour of Uruk, the first large city in human history, in today's Iraq, boasting of its city walls, its buildings and temples with their stairways and foundations, all made of clay bricks. Like a tour guide, the text even lets its readers inspect the city's clay pits, over one square mile large, that provided the material for this miraculous city made from clay. The greatest marvel of them all is of course *The Epic of Gilgamesh* itself, which was inscribed on clay tablets—the first monument of literature.

Foundational Texts

From its beginnings, *The Norton Anthology of World Literature* has been committed to offering students and teachers as many complete or substantially represented texts as possible. This Fourth Edition emphasizes the importance of *foundational* texts as never before by offering new translations of some of the best-known and most-loved works in the history of world literature. *The Epic of Gilgamesh* stands first in line of these foundational texts, which capture the story of an entire people, telling them where they came from and who they are. Some foundational texts become an object of worship and are deemed sacred, while others are revered as the most consequential story of an entire civilization. Because foundational texts inspire countless retellings—as Homer did for the Greek tragedians—these texts are reference points for the entire subsequent history of literature.

Perhaps no text is more foundational than the one with which we opened this preface: Homer's *Odyssey*. In this Fourth Edition, we feature *The Odyssey* in a new translation by our classics editor, Emily Wilson. This version captures the fast pace and rhythmic regularity of the original and offers a fresh perspective on cultural encounters such as the one between Odysseus and Polyphemus that is described above. Astonishingly, Wilson's translation is the first translation of *The Odyssey* into English by a woman. For centuries, commentators have remarked that *The Odyssey* is unusually attuned to the lives of women, especially in its portrait of Odysseus's wife, Penelope, a compelling and powerful character who cunningly holds a rowdy group of suitors at bay. Wilson's translation pays special attention to the poem's characterization of this remarkable woman, who is every bit as intriguing as the "complicated man" who is the eponymous hero of the tale. Other female characters, too, are given a new voice in this translation. For example, Helen, wife of the Greek king Menelaus and (according to legend) possessor of "the face that launched a thousand ships," is revealed through Wilson's translation to speak of herself not as a "whore" for whose sake so many young Greek men fought, suffered, and died (as she does in most other translations) but instead as a perceptive, clever person, onto whom the Greeks, already eager to fight the Trojans, projected their own aggressive impulses: "They made my face the cause that hounded them," she says. The central conflicts of the epic, the very origin of the Trojan War, appear here in a startling new light.

We are also delighted to feature a new translation of the great Indian epic *The Mahabharata* by Carole Satyamurti, whose modern retelling captures the careful, patterned language of the original by rendering it in a fluent blank verse, a form familiar in English literature from Shakespeare to Wordsworth and also used in Wilson's *Odyssey*, a form particularly suitable to narrative. Readers used to older prose versions will find that the quest for honor and fame at the heart of this epic comes across as never before.

These two examples highlight an exciting dimension of our emphasis on new translations. The first several volumes of this anthology have always been dominated by male voices because men enjoyed privileged access to literacy and cultural influence in the centuries prior to modernity. Our focus on new translations has allowed us to introduce into these volumes many female voices—the voices of translators. So, for example, we present Homer's *Iliad* in a new translation by Caroline Alexander, Sophocles' *Antigone* in a recent translation by Ruby Blondell, and Euripides' *Medea* in a new, specially commissioned translation by Sheila H. Murnaghan, and we continue to offer work in the first volumes translated by female translators such as Laura Gibbs (Aesop's *Fables*), Dorothy Gilbert (Marie de France's *Lais*), Sholeh Wolpé (*The Conference of the Birds*), Wendy Belcher (*Kebra Nagast*), Sheila Fisher (Chaucer's *Canterbury Tales*), Rosalind Brown-Grant (Christine de Pizan's *Book of the City of Ladies*), and Pauline Yu (Wang Wei's poetry), among others. This commitment to featuring the work of female translators extends beyond these early centuries as well, for example in the brilliant new translation by Susan Bernofsky of a foundational text of literary modernity—Kafka's *Metamorphosis*. The result throughout the anthology is that these works now speak to today's readers in new and sometimes surprising ways.

Our emphasis in this edition on new translations is based on and amplifies the conviction expressed by the original editors of this anthology over fifty years ago: that world literature gains its power when it travels from its place of origin and speaks to people in different places. While purists sometimes insist on studying literature only in the original language, a dogma that radically shrinks what one can read, world literature not only relies on translation but actually thrives on it. Translation is a necessity; it is what enables a worldwide circulation of literature. It also is an art. One need only think of the way in which translations of the Bible shaped the history of Latin or English or German. Translations are re-creations of works for new readers. This edition pays keen attention to translation, featuring dozens of new translations that make classic texts newly readable and capture the originals in compelling ways. With each choice of translation, we have sought a version that would spark a sense of wonder while still being accessible to a contemporary reader.

Among other foundational texts presented in new translations and selections is the Qur'an, in a verse translation that is the product of a collaboration between M. A. Rafey Habib, a poet, literary scholar, and Muslim, and Bruce Lawrence, a renowned scholar of Islam. Their team effort captures some of the beauty of this extraordinary, and extraordinarily influential, sacred text. Augustine's *Confessions* are newly presented in a version by Peter Constantine, and Dante's *Inferno* is featured in the long-respected and highly readable translation by the American poet John Ciardi.

We have also maintained our commitment to exciting epics that deserve wider recognition such as the Maya *Popol Vuh*, the East African *Kebra Nagast*, and the *Sunjata*, which commemorates the founding of a West African empire in the late Middle Ages. Like *The Odyssey* and *The Mahabharata*, *Sunjata* was transmitted for centuries in purely oral form. But while *The Odyssey* was written down around 800 B.C.E. and *The Mahabharata* several hundred years later, the *Sunjata* was written down only in the twentieth century. We feature it here in a new prose translation by David C. Conrad, who personally recorded this version from a Mande storyteller, Djanka Tassey Condé, in 1994. In this way, *Sunjata* speaks to the continuing importance of oral storytelling, the origin of all foundational epics, from South Asia via Greece and Africa to Central America. Throughout the anthology, we remind readers that writing has coexisted with oral storytelling since the invention of literature and that it will continue to do so in the future.

A Network of Stories

In addition to foundational texts, we include in this edition a great number of story collections. The origins of this form of literature reach deep into the ancient world, as scribes collected oral stories and assembled them in larger works. We've substantially increased our offerings from what is undoubtedly the most famous of these collections, *The Thousand and One Nights*, to give readers a better sense of the intricate structure of this work, with its stories within stories within stories, all neatly framed by the overarching narrative of Shahrazad, who is telling them to her sister and the king to avoid being put to death. What is most notable about these story collections is how interconnected they are. Stories travel with striking ease from one collection to the next, appearing in *The Jataka*, one of the oldest Indian story collections framed by the

Buddha, and the *Pañcatantra*, an Indian collection put together for the education of princes, to *The Thousand and One Nights*, and, in Greece, Aesop's *Fables*. There existed a continent-spanning network of stories that allowed storytellers and scribes to recycle and reframe what they learned in ever new ways; it proved so compelling that later writers, from Marie de France to Chaucer, borrowed from it frequently. To give readers a sense of these connections, we have rethought our selection of stories by including those that appear in different collections, allowing readers to track the changes that occur when a story is told by the Buddha, by Shahrazad, or on a pilgrimage to Canterbury Cathedral.

Expanded Selections

Along with our focus on making foundational texts and story collections fresh and accessible, we have pruned the overall number of authors and were therefore able to increase our offerings from major texts that feature in many world literature courses. *Don Quixote* now includes the compelling "Captive's Tale," in which Cervantes draws on his own experiences as a slave in Algiers, where he spent five years after having been captured by pirates. Sor Juana Inés de la Cruz, whose significance is steadily increasing, is now represented by an additional selection from her mystery play, *The Divine Narcissus*, in Edith Grossman's elegant translation. Other major texts with increased selections include Machiavelli's *Prince* and, in the twentieth century, Lu Xun, who now can be introduced to students as the author not only of *Diary of a Madman* but also of *Ah Q—The Real Story*.

Despite this focus on foundational texts, story collections, and other major works, there are plenty of entirely new texts in this Fourth Edition. The Spanish Renaissance tale *The Abencerraje* tells of a Moorish knight who is taken prisoner by a Christian on his wedding day. Ultimately his captor relents and allows the knight to marry his beloved. This enormously popular tale speaks of the complex relations between Christianity and Islam in the early modern era and is featured here in a new translation by our Renaissance editor, Barbara Fuchs. Equally exciting is our representation of Korean literature. The *Tale of Hong Kiltong*, a story of a Korean Robin Hood endowed with magical powers, is a classic that we paired with excerpts from Lady Hyegyŏng's memoirs, which chronicle with deep psychological insight the horror and violence at the Korean royal court. These older Korean texts are complemented by a modern writer, Park Wansuh, whose work reflects the upheavals of the twentieth century on the Korean peninsula, from Japanese occupation and the Korean War to economic development. One of the first women to achieve critical success in modern Korea, Park offers readers keen insight into Korea's modern struggles.

We are particularly excited to now close the anthology with a story by the Nigerian writer Chimamanda Ngozi Adichie called "The Headstrong Historian," which, since its publication in 2008, has already become a favorite in world literature classrooms. This compact work introduces us to three generations of Nigerians as they navigate a complicated series of personal and cultural displacements. A thought-provoking exploration of the complex results of cultural contact and influence, this probing, searching journey seemed to us the most fitting conclusion to the anthology's survey of 4,000 years of literature.

Cultural Contact

Odysseus's encounter with the Cyclopes speaks not only to hospitality but also to the theme of cultural contact more generally. The earliest civilizations—those that invented writing and hence literature—sprang up where they did because they were located along strategic trading and migration routes. Contact was not just something that happened between fully formed cultures but something that made these cultures possible in the first place.

Committed to presenting the anthology's riches in a way that conveys this central fact of world literature, we have created sections that encompass broad contact zones—areas of intense trade in peoples, goods, art, and ideas where the earliest literatures emerged and intermingled. One of these is the Mediterranean Sea, whose central importance we visualize with four new maps. It was not just a hostile environment that could derail a journey home, as it did for Odysseus, or where nontravelers, like Polyphemus, might encounter violent invaders willing to attack and steal; it was also a connecting tissue, allowing for intense contact around its harbors. Medieval maps of the Mediterranean pay tribute to this fact: so-called portolan charts show a veritable mesh of lines connecting hundreds of ports. For this edition, we have further emphasized these contact zones, the location of intense conflict (including Cervantes's experience as a slave in North Africa) as well as friendly exchange. In a similar manner, the two major traditions of East Asia—China and Japan—are presented in the context of the larger region, including our new emphasis on Korea.

The importance of cultural contact and encounter is expressed not just in the overall organization of the anthology and the selection of material; it is also made visible in clusters of texts on the theme of travel and conquest, giving students access to documents related to travel, contact, trade, and conflict. For not all travel was voluntary. People traveled to escape wars and famine, plagues and environmental disasters. They were abducted, enslaved, and trafficked. Beginning with the early modern era, European empires dominated global politics and economics and accelerated the pace of globalization by laying down worldwide trade routes and communication networks, but old empires, such as China, continued to be influential as well. We added more material to our cluster "At the Crossroads of Empire," including a letter by Machemba, a chief in East Africa under German colonial control, and Mark Twain's trenchant soliloquy of Belgian King Leopold defending his brutal rule in Congo.

To these expanded clusters, we added a new one, "Poetry and Politics," which includes the Polish national poet Adam Mickiewicz and Latin American poet Rubén Darío's *To Roosevelt*, a powerful reminder of the crucial role poetry played in the gaining of national independence across the world. Poets captured the aspirations of nations and often enshrined those aspirations in national anthems, which also led us to include the Puerto Rican national anthem (one poet included in our anthology, Rabindranath Tagore, wrote not one but two national anthems, of both India and Bangladesh).

In the same volume, we also enhanced our cluster "Realism across the Globe," which traces one of the most successful global literary movements, one that found expression in France, Britain, Russia, Brazil, Mexico, and Japan. In keeping with our commitment to frequently taught authors, we increased our selection of Chekhov and present Tolstoy's *Death of Ivan Ilyich* in a new, acclaimed translation by Peter Carson.

The Birth of World Literature

In 1827, a provincial German writer, living in small-town Weimar, recognized that he was in the privileged position of having access not only to European literature but also to literature from much further afield, including Persian poetry, Chinese novels, and Sanskrit drama. The writer was Johann Wolfgang von Goethe, and in 1827, he coined a term to capture this new force of globalization in literature: "world literature." (We now include the "prologue" to Goethe's play *Faust*, which he wrote after encountering a similar prologue in the classical Sanskrit play *Śhakuntalā*, also included in the anthology.)

Since 1827, for less than 200 years, we have been living in an era of world literature. This era has brought many lost masterpieces back to life, including *The Epic of Gilgamesh*, which was rediscovered in the nineteenth century, and the *Popol Vuh*, which languished in a library until well into the twentieth century. Other works of world literature weren't translated and therefore didn't begin to circulate outside their sphere of origin until the last 200 years, including *The Tale of Genji*. With more literature becoming more widely available than ever before, Goethe's vision of world literature has become a reality today.

In presenting world literature from the dawn of writing to the early twenty-first century, and from oral storytelling to literary experiments of the avant-garde, this anthology raises the question not only of what world literature is but also of the nature of literature itself. We call attention to the changing nature of literature with thematic clusters on literature in the early volumes, to give students and teachers access to how early writers from different cultures thought about literature. But the changing role and nature of literature are visible in the anthology as a whole. Greek tragedy and comedy are experienced by modern students as literary genres, encountered in written texts; but for the ancient Athenians, they were primarily dramas, experienced live in an outdoor theater in the context of a religious and civic ritual. Other texts, such as the Qur'an or the Bible, are sacred pieces of writing, central to many people's religious faith, while others appreciate them primarily or exclusively as literature. Some texts, such as those by Laozi or Plato or Kant, belong in philosophy, while others, such as the Declaration of Independence, are primarily political documents. Our modern conception of literature as imaginative literature, as fiction, is very recent, about 200 years old. We have therefore opted for a much-expanded conception of literature that includes creation myths, wisdom literature, religious texts, philosophy, political writing, and fairy tales in addition to poems, plays, and narrative fiction. This answers to an older definition of literature as writing of high quality or of great cultural significance. There are many texts of philosophy or religion or politics that are not remarkable or influential for their literary qualities and that would therefore have no place in an anthology of world literature. But the works presented here do: in addition to or as part of their other functions, they have acquired the status of literature.

This brings us to the last and perhaps most important question: When we study the world, why study it through its literature? Hasn't literature lost some of its luster for us, we who are faced with so many competing media and art forms? Like no other art form or medium, literature offers us a deep history of human thinking. As our illustration program shows, writing was invented not for the composition of literature but for much more mundane purposes, such as the recording of ownership, contracts, or astronomical observations. But literature is writing's most glorious by-product. Literature can be reactivated with each reading. Many of the great architectural monuments of the past are now in ruins. Literature, too, often has to be excavated, as with many classical texts. But once a text has been found or reconstructed it can be experienced as if for the first time by new readers. Even though many of the literary texts collected in this anthology are at first strange, because they originated so very long ago, they still speak to today's readers with great eloquence and freshness. No other art form can capture the human past with the precision and scope of literature because language expresses human consciousness. Language shapes our thinking, and literature, the highest expression of language, plays an important role in that process, pushing the boundaries of what we can think and how we think it. This is especially true with great, complex, and contradictory works that allow us to explore different narrative perspectives, different points of view.

Works of world literature continue to elicit strong emotions and investments. The epic *Rāmāyana*, for example, plays an important role in the politics of India, where it has been used to bolster Hindu nationalism, just as the *Bhagavad-Gītā* continues to be a moral touchstone in the ethical deliberation about war. The so-called religions of the book, Judaism, Christianity, and Islam, make our selections from their scriptures a more than historical exercise as well. China has recently elevated the sayings of Confucius, whose influence on Chinese attitudes about the state had waned in the twentieth century, creating Confucius Institutes all over the world to promote Chinese culture in what is now called New Confucianism. World literature is never neutral. We know its relevance precisely by the controversies it inspires.

There are many ways of studying other cultures and of understanding the place of our own culture in the world. Archaeologists can show us objects and buildings from the past and speculate, through material remains, how people in the past ate, fought, lived, died, and were buried; scientists can date layers of soil. Literature is capable of something much more extraordinary: it allows us a glimpse into the imaginative lives, the thoughts and feelings of humans from thousands of years ago or living halfway around the world. This is the true magic of world literature as captured in this anthology, our shared human inheritance.

About the Fourth Edition

New Selections and Translations

Following is a list of the new translations, selections, and works in the Fourth Edition, in order:

translation of *The Divine Comedy*, newly included, supplemented by two additional translations from Canto 3 of *Inferno* by Clive James and Mark Musa • A new translation of *Kebra Nagast* by Wendy Belcher and Michael Kleiner, including a new chapter, "About How King Solomon Swore an Oath to the Queen" • Seven new tales from *The Thousand and One Nights*: "[The Story of the Porter and the Three Ladies]," "[The First Dervish's Tale]," "[The Second Dervish's Tale]," "[The Tale of the Envious and the Envied]," "[The Third Dervish's Tale]," "[The Tale of the First Lady]," and "[The Tale of the Second Lady]" • "The Nun's Priest's Tale" from *The Canterbury Tales* • Three new tales from the *Pañcatantra*: "The Bird with Golden Dung" and "The Ass in the Tiger Skin" translated by Arthur W. Ryder and "The Ass without Ears or a Heart" translated by Patrick Olivelle • New selections from *The Tale of Genji*: "Sakaki: A Branch of Sacred Evergreens," "Maboroshi: Spirit Summoner," "Hashihime: The Divine Princess at Uji Bridge," "Agemaki: A Bowknot Tied in Maiden's Loops," "Yadoriki: Trees Encoiled in Vines of Ivy," and "Tenarai: Practicing Calligraphy"

VOLUME C

A new prose translation of *Sunjata: A West African Epic of the Mande* by David C. Conrad • New selections from *The Prince*: "[Liberality and Parsimony]," "[Love and Fear]," "[Dissimulation]," "[Contempt and Hatred]," "[Princely Devices; Fortresses]," "[The Excellent Prince]," "[Flatterers]," and "[The Princes of Italy]" • "The Abencerraje" translated by Barbara Fuchs, Larissa Brewer-García, and Aaron J. Ilika • A new selection from *Don Quixote*, "[A Story of Captivity in North Africa, Told to Don Quixote at the Inn]" • A revised *Fuenteovejuna* translated by G. J. Racz

VOLUME D

A new translation of "What Is Enlightenment?" by Mary C. Smith • A new translation of Sor Juana Inés de la Cruz's work translated by Edith Grossman, including three new sonnets, "[O World, why do you wish to persecute me?]," "[I adore Lisi but do not pretend]," and "[Because you have died, Laura, let affections]," as well as *Loa* to the Mystery Play *The Divine Narcissus: An Allegory* translated by Edith Grossman • Hŏ Kyun's "The Tale of Hong Kiltong" translated by Marshall R. Pihl • A selection from Lady Hyegyŏng's *The Memoirs of Lady Hyegyŏng* translated by JaHyun Kim Haboush

VOLUME E

A new selection from *Faust*, "Prelude in the Theatre" • Machemba's "Letter to Major von Wissmann" translated by Robert Sullivan and Sarah Lawall • A selection from Mark Twain's "King Leopold's Soliloquy" • A new cluster, "Poetry and Politics," including four new works, Adam Mickiewicz's "The Prisoner's Return" translated by Jerzy Peterkiewicz and Burns Singer, Speranza's (Lady Jane Wilde's) "A Lament for the Potato" and "The Exodus," and Lola Rodríguez de Tió's "The Song of the Borinquen" translated by José Nieto, as well as the new translation of "Guantanamera" by Elinor Randall • A new translation of *The Death of Ivan Ilyich* by Peter Carson • A new translation of "The Cane" by Margaret Jull Costa • José López Portillo y Rojas's "Unclaimed Watch" translated by Roberta H. Kimble • Anton Chekhov's "The Lady with the Dog" translated by Ivy Litvinov

VOLUME F

A new translation of *The Metamorphosis* by Susan Bernofsky • Lu Xun's "Ah Q—The Real Story" translated by William A. Lyell • Eric Bentley's translation, new to this edition, of Pirandello's *Six Characters in Search of an Author* • A new translation of "The Dancing Girl of Izu" by J. Martin Homan • Jorge Luis Borges's "The Library of Babel" translated by James E. Irby • M. D. Herder Norton's translations of Rainer Maria Rilke's poems, newly included • A new translation of "Lament for Ignacio Sánchez Mejías" by Pablo Medina • A new translation of "Matryona's Home" by Michael Glenny • Derek Walcott's "Sea Grapes" • Park Wansuh's "Mother's Hitching Post, Part 2" • Yu Hua's "On the Road at Eighteen" • Chimamanda Ngozi Adichie's "The Headstrong Historian"

Resources for Students and Instructors

Norton is pleased to provide students and instructors with abundant resources to make the teaching and study of world literature an even more interesting and rewarding experience.

We are pleased to launch the new *Norton Anthology of World Literature* website, found at digital.wwnorton.com/worldlit4pre1650 (for volumes A, B, C) and digital.wwnorton.com/worldlit4post1650 (for volumes D, E, F). This searchable and sortable site contains thousands of resources for students and instructors in one centralized place at no additional cost. Following are some highlights:

- A series of eight brand-new video modules are designed to enhance classroom presentation and spark student interest in the anthology's works. These videos, conceived of and narrated by the anthology editors, ask students to consider why it is important for them to read and engage with this literature.
- Hundreds of images—maps, author portraits, literary places, and manuscripts—are available for student browsing or instructor download for in-class presentation.
- Several hours of audio recordings are available, including a 10,000-term audio glossary that helps students pronounce the character and place names in the anthologized works.

The site also provides a wealth of teaching resources that are unlocked with an instructor's log-in:

- "Quick read" summaries, teaching notes, discussion questions, and suggested resources for every work in the anthology, from the much-praised *Teaching with* The Norton Anthology of World Literature: *A Guide for Instructors*
- Downloadable Lecture PowerPoints featuring images, quotations from the texts, and lecture notes in the notes view for in-class presentation

In addition to the wealth of resources in *The Norton Anthology of World Literature* website, Norton offers a downloadable Coursepack that allows instructors to easily add high-quality Norton digital media to online, hybrid, or lecture courses—all at no cost. Norton Coursepacks work within existing learning management systems; there's no new system to learn, and access is free and easy. Content is customizable and includes over seventy reading-comprehension quizzes, short-answer questions, links to the videos, and more.

Acknowledgments

The editors would like to thank the following people, who have provided invaluable assistance by giving us sage advice, important encouragement, and help with the preparation of the manuscript: Sara Akbari, Alannah de Barra, Wendy Belcher, Jodi Bilinkoff, Daniel Boucher, Freya Brackett, Psyche Brackett, Michaela Bronstein, Rachel Carroll, Sookja Cho, Kyeong-Hee Choi, Amanda Claybaugh, Lewis Cook, David Damrosch, Dick Davis, Burghild Denecke, Amanda Detry, Anthony Domestico, Megan Eckerle, Marion Eggert, Merve Emre, Maria Fackler, Guillermina de Ferrari, Alyssa Findley, Karina Galperín, Stanton B. Garner, Kimberly Dara Gordon, Elyse Graham, Stephen Greenblatt, Sara Guyer, Langdon Hammer, Emily Hayman, Iain Higgins, Paulo Lemos Horta, Mohja Kahf, Peter Kornicki, Paul W. Kroll, Peter H. Lee, Sung-il Lee, Lydia Liu, Bala Venkat Mani, Ann Matter, Barry McCrea, Alexandra McCullough-Garcia, Rachel McGuiness, Jon McKenzie, Mary Mullen, Djibril Tamsir Niane, Johann Noh, Felicity Nussbaum, Andy Orchard, John Peters, Michael Pettid, Daniel Taro Poch, Daniel Potts, Megan Quigley, Payton Phillips Quintanilla, Catherine de Rose, Imogen Roth, Katherine Rupp, Ellen Sapega, Jesse Schotter, Stephen Scully, Kyung-ho Sim, Sarah Star, Brian Stock, Tomi Suzuki, Joshua Taft, Sara Torres, J. Keith Vincent, Lisa Voigt, Kristen Wanner, Emily Weissbourd, Karoline Xu, Yoon Sun Yang, and Catherine Vance Yeh.

All the editors would like to thank the wonderful people at Norton, principally our editor Pete Simon, the driving force behind this whole undertaking, as well as Marian Johnson (Managing Editor, College), Christine D'Antonio and Kurt Wildermuth (Project Editors), Michael Fleming (Copyeditor), Gerra Goff (Associate Editor), Megan Jackson (College Permissions Manager), Margaret Gorenstein (Permissions), Catherine Abelman (Photo Editor), Debra Morton Hoyt (Art Director; cover design), Rubina Yeh (Design Director), Jo Anne Metsch (Designer; interior text design), Adrian Kitzinger (cartography), Agnieszka Gasparska (timeline design), Carly Fraser-Doria (Media Editor), Ava Bramson (Assistant Editor, Media), Sean Mintus (Production Manager), and Kim Bowers (Marketing Manager, Literature). We'd also like to thank our Instructor's Guide authors: Colleen Clemens (Kutztown University), Elizabeth Watkins (Loyola University New Orleans), and Janet Zong (Harvard University).

This anthology represents a collaboration not only among the editors and their close advisers but also among the thousands of instructors who teach from the anthology and provide valuable and constructive guidance to the publisher and editors. *The Norton Anthology of World Literature* is as much their book as it is ours, and we are grateful to everyone who has cared enough about this anthology to help make it better. We're especially grateful to the professors of world literature who responded to an online survey in 2014, whom we have listed below. Thank you all.

Michelle Abbott (Georgia Highlands College), Elizabeth Ashworth (Castleton State College), Clinton Atchley (Henderson State University), Amber Barnes (Trinity Valley Community College), Rosemary Baxter (Clarendon College), Khani Begum (Bowling Green State University), Joyce Boss (Wartburg College), Floyd Brigdon (Trinity Valley Community College), James Bryant-Trerise (Clackamas Community College), Barbara Cade (Texas College), Kellie Cannon (Coastal Carolina Community College), Amee Carmines (Hampton University), Farrah Cato (University of Central Florida), Brandon Chitwood (Marquette University), Paul Cohen (Texas State University), Judith Cortelloni (Lincoln College), Randall Crump (Kennesaw State University), Sunni Davis (Cossatot Community College), Michael Demson (Sam Houston State University), Richard Diguette (Georgia Perimeter College, Dunwoody), Daniel Dooghan (University of Tampa), Jeff Doty (West Texas A&M University), Myrto Drizou (Valdosta State University), Ashley Dugas (Copiah-Lincoln Community College), Richmond Eustis (Nicholls State University), David Fell (Carroll Community College), Allison Fetters (Chattanooga State Community College), Francis Fletcher (Folsom Lake College), Kathleen D. Fowler (Surry Community College), Louisa Franklin (Young Harris College), James Gamble (University of Arkansas), Antoinette Gazda (Averett University), Adam Golaski (Central Connecticut State University), Anissa Graham (University of North Alabama), Eric Gray (St. Gregory's University), Jared Griffin (Kodiak College), Marne Griffin (Hilbert College), Frank Gruber (Bergen Community College), Laura Hammons (Hinds Community College), Nancy G. Hancock (Austin Peay State University), C. E. Harding (Western Oregon University), Leslie Harrelson (Dalton State College), Eleanor J. Harrington-Austin (North Carolina Central University), Matthew Hokom (Fairmont State University), Scott Hollifield (University of Nevada, Las Vegas), Catherine Howard (University of Houston, Downtown), Jack Kelnhofer (Ocean County College), Katherine King (University of California, Los Angeles), Pam Kingsbury (University of North Alabama), Sophia Kowalski (Hillsborough Community College), Roger Ladd (University of North Carolina at Pembroke), Jameela Lares (University of Southern Mississippi), Susan Lewis (Delaware Technical Community College), Christina Lovin (Eastern Kentucky University), Richard Mace (Pace University), Nicholas R. Marino (Borough of Manhattan Community College, CUNY), Brandi Martinez (Mountain Empire Community College), Kathy Martinez (Sandhills Community College), Matthew Masucci (State College of Florida), Kelli McBride (Seminole State College), Melissa McCoy (Clarendon College), Geoffrey McNeil (Notre Dame de Namur University), Renee Moore (Mississippi Delta Community College), Anna C. Oldfield (Coastal Carolina University), Keri Overall (Texas Woman's University), Maggie Piccolo (Rutgers University), Oana Popescu-Sandu (University of Southern Indiana), Jonathan Purkiss (Pulaski Technical College), Rocio Quispe-Agnoli (Michigan State University), Evan Radcliffe (Villanova University), Ken Raines (Eastern Arizona College), Jonathan Randle (Mississippi College), Kirk G. Rasmussen (Utah Valley University), Helaine Razovsky (Northwestern State University of Louisiana), Karin Rhodes (Salem State University), Stephanie Roberts (Georgia Military College), Allen Salerno (Auburn University), Shannin Schroeder (Southern Arkansas University), Heather Seratt (University of Houston,

Downtown), Conrad Shumaker (University of Central Arkansas), Edward Soloff (St. John's University), Eric Sterling (Auburn University Montgomery), Ron Stormer (Culver-Stockton College), Marianne Szlyk (Montgomery College), Tim Tarkington (Georgia Perimeter College), Allison Tharp (University of Southern Mississippi), Diane Thompson (Northern Virginia Community College), Sevinc Turkkan (College at Brockport, State University of New York), Verne Underwood (Rogue Community College), Patricia Vazquez (College of Southern Nevada), William Wallis (Los Angeles Valley College), Eric Weil (Elizabeth City State University), Denise C. White (Kennesaw State University), Tamora Whitney (Creighton University), Todd Williams (Kutztown University of Pennsylvania), Bertha Wise (Oklahoma City Community College), and Lindsey Zanchettin (Auburn University).

THE NORTON ANTHOLOGY OF

WORLD

LITERATURE

FOURTH EDITION

VOLUME A

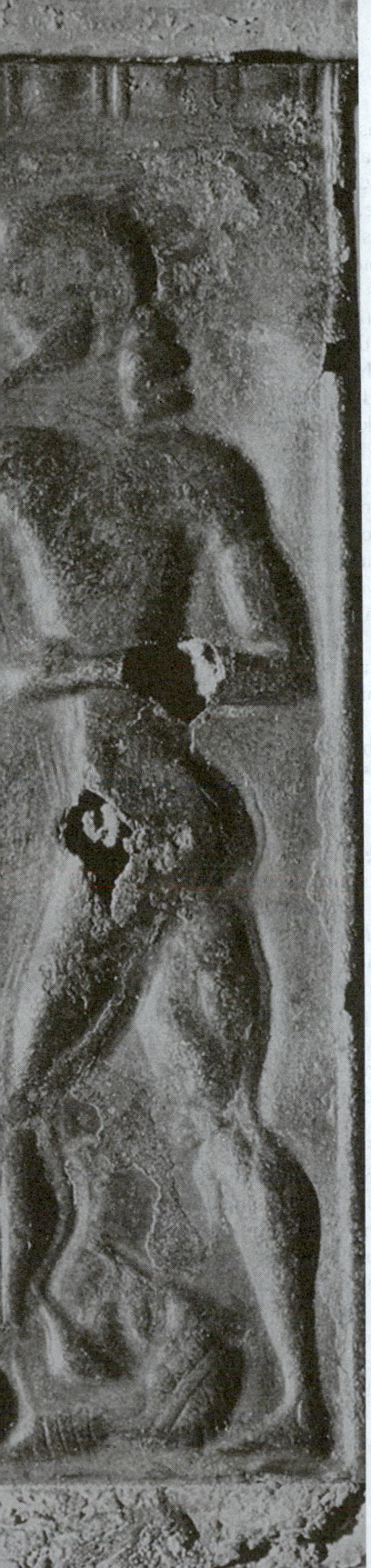

I

Ancient Mediterranean and Near Eastern Literature

THE INVENTION OF WRITING AND THE EARLIEST LITERATURES

The word *literature* comes from the Latin for "letters." "Oral literature" is therefore a contradiction in terms. Most modern Westerners assume that literature is something we read in books; it is, by definition, written language. But people told stories and sang songs long before they had any means to record them. Oral types of poetry and storytelling are quite different from those produced by writing, and it is difficult for us, living in an age dominated by printed and digital language, to imagine a world where nobody could read or write. Preliterate societies had different intellectual values from our own. We tend to think that a "good" story or essay is one that is neatly organized, original, and free from obvious repetition; we think of clichés as a mark of bad writing. But people without literacy tend to love stock phrases, traditional sayings, and proverbs. They are an essential mechanism by which cultural memory is preserved. Before writing, there was no such thing as an "author"—a single individual who, all alone, creates a text to be experienced by a solitary, silent reader. Instead, poets, singers, and

King Priam asks Achilles for the body of his son, Hector. From an archaic Greek bronze relief, ca. 570–560 B.C.E.

storytellers echoed and manipulated the old tales and the inherited wisdom of their people.

Of course, without either writing or recording equipment, all oral storytelling is inevitably lost. The tales that were told before there was writing cannot be collected in any anthology. But they left their mark on the earliest works of written literature—and many subsequent ones as well. As one would expect, literacy did not take hold all at once; the transition was partial and gradual, and in much of the ancient world, poetry and storytelling were less closely associated with written texts than they are for us. **Plato**'s ***Phaedrus*** gives us some indication that the ancient Athenians were conscious of the enormous cultural change involved in the invention of writing. Nostalgia for the days before literacy continued into the later ancient world. By the time of the early Roman Empire—whose culture was much more literate than that of classical Athens—poets could make self-conscious efforts to imitate oral gestures, as when **Virgil**, writing his ultraliterate epic, the *Aeneid*, pretends to be an oral poet: "Wars and a man I sing."

Writing was not originally invented to preserve literature. The earliest written documents we have contain commercial, administrative, political, and legal information. It was in the region of the Tigris and Euphrates rivers, Mesopotamia (which means "the place between the rivers"), that writing was first developed; the earliest texts date from around 3300 to 2990 B.C.E. The characters of this writing were inscribed on tablets of wet clay with a pointed stick; the tablets were then left in the sun to bake hard. The characters are pictographic: the sign for *ox* looks like an ox head and so on. The bulk of the texts are economic—lists of food, textiles, and cattle. But the script is too primitive to handle anything much more complicated than lists, and by 2800 B.C.E. scribes began to use the wedge-shaped end of the stick to make marks rather than the pointed end to draw pictures. The resulting script is known as cuneiform, from the Latin word *cuneus*, "a wedge." By 2500 B.C.E. cuneiform was used for many things beyond administrative lists: the texts preserved historical events and even, finally, literature. It was on clay tablets and in cuneiform script that the great Sumerian epic poem ***Gilgamesh*** was written down. This writing system was not, however, designed for a large reading public. Each sign denoted a syllable—consonant plus a vowel—which meant that the reader had to be familiar with a large number of signs. Furthermore, the same sign often represented two or more different sounds, and the same sound could be represented by several different signs. It is a script that could be written and read only by experts, the scribes, who often proudly recorded their own names on the tablets.

The writing system invented by the Egyptians was even more eso-

An administrative tablet from Mesopotamia, ca. 3100–2900 B.C.E.

teric than cuneiform. It is called hiero-glyphic, an adjective formed from the Greek words for "sacred" and "carving." Although it appears on many different materials, its most conspicuous and con-tinuous use was for inscriptions carved on temple walls and public monuments. It was pictographic, like the earliest Sumerian script, but the pictures were more elaborate and artistic. Unlike the Sumerian pictographs, they were not replaced by a more efficient system; the pictures remained in use for the walls of temples and tombs, while more cursive versions of hieroglyphics—the hieratic and demotic scripts—were developed for faster writing. But the Egyptians soon developed their system to include signs standing for sounds, as well as for single objects: for instance, the same sign could mean either "house," *pr*, or simply the sound *pr*. This was only one of many complications that made even the modi-fied versions of the script a difficult medium of communication for anyone not trained in its intricacies. It is no won-der that one of the frequent figures to appear in Egyptian sculpture and paint-ing is the professional scribe, his legs tucked underneath him, his writing material in his lap, and his brush in his hand.

There was one ancient writing system that, unlike cuneiform and hieroglyphic, survived, in modified forms, until the present day. It was developed by the Phoenicians, a Semitic trading people. The script consisted of twenty-two simple signs for consonantal sounds. Through trade, the Phoenician script spread all over the Mediterranean. It was adopted by the ancient Hebrews, among others. The obvious advantage of this system was that it was so easy to learn. But there was still one area of inefficiency in this system: the absence of any notation for the vowels made for ambiguity. We still do not know, for example, what the vowel sounds were in the sacred name of God, often called the Tetragrammaton ("Four Letters"). In our alphabet the name is written as YHWH. The usual surmise is Jahweh (*yá-way*), but for a long time the traditional English-language version was Jehovah.

One thing was needed to make the script fully efficient: signs for the vowels. This was the contribution of the Greeks, who, in the eighth or possibly the ninth century B.C.E., adopted the Phoenician script for their own language, but used for the vowels some Phoenician signs that stood for consonantal combinations not native to Greek. They took over (but soon modified) the Phoenician letter shapes and also their names: *alpha*, a meaningless word in Greek, represents the original *aleph* ("ox"), and *beta* repre-sents the original *beta* ("house"). The Greeks admitted their indebtedness; Greek myths told the story of Cadmus, king of Tyre, who taught the Greeks how to write, and, as the historian Herodotus tells us, the letters were called Phoeni-cian. The Romans, who adapted the Greek alphabet for their own language, carved their inscriptions on stone in the same capital letters that we still use today.

ANCIENT NEAR EASTERN AND MEDITERRANEAN CULTURES

Modern, postindustrial societies depend, economically, on machines and sources of energy to power them. We use com-plex devices to produce food and clothes, to build roads and cities, to excavate nat-ural resources (such as oil and coal), to construct nonnatural materials (such as plastics), to get from place to place, and to communicate with others across the globe: by phone, television, computers, and the Internet. In the ancient world, most of these machines did not yet exist. Though metal was mined and worked, there was no heavy industry as we know it. Coal and oil were not exploited for energy. War galleys were propelled by sail and human oarsmen; armies moved, sometimes vast distances, on foot. People therefore relied far more heavily on the kind of natural resources that can be easily accessed by human labor: no ancient city could be built far from fresh water and fertile soil on which to grow crops and graze animals for meat and wool. Where we use machines and fossil fuel, all the advanced civilizations of the ancient world depended for their existence on slaves, who worked the land; took care of animals and children; dug the mines; built houses, temples, pyramids, and cities; manufactured household goods (ranging from basic tableware to decorative artwork); performed housework; and provided entertainment. Modern Western societies exploit natural resources and harness them by using the cheap human labor available in less "developed" countries; most of the time, we do not even think about the people who make our clothes, phones, or cars or

about the energy it takes to produce them and dispose of them. Similarly, elite ancient Hebrews, Greeks, and Romans seem to have taken slaves almost entirely for granted. The existence of ancient slavery should remind us not to idealize ancient cultures (even those of the "great Western tradition") and to remember how easily human beings, ourselves included, can be blinkered about the forms of injustice and exploitation that are essential to their cultural existence.

Because ancient societies depended on the proximity of natural resources, especially well-irrigated, fertile soil, the first civilizations of the Mediterranean basin developed in two regions that were particularly receptive to agriculture and animal husbandry. These areas were the valley of the Nile, where annual floods left large tracts of land moist and fertile under the Egyptian sun, and the valleys of the Euphrates and Tigris rivers, which flowed through the Fertile Crescent, a region centered on modern Iraq. Great

A relief from the Palace of Sargon, from the eighth century B.C.E. It shows the transport of large logs propelled by human rowers.

THE ANCIENT MIDDLE EAST

| 0 | 200 | 400 | 600 | 800 | 1000 kilometers |

| 0 | 100 | 200 | 300 | 400 | 500 | 600 miles |

cities—Thebes and Memphis in Egypt and Babylon and Nineveh in the Fertile Crescent—came into being as centers for the complicated administration of the irrigated fields. Supported by the surplus the land produced, they became centers also for government, religion, and culture.

Later, from the second millennium B.C.E. onward, more cultures developed around the Mediterranean, including those of the Hebrews, the Greeks, and the Romans. These societies remained distinct from one another, and each included many separate social groups; we should be wary of generalizing about what "people in antiquity" believed or did. But it does make sense to consider the ancient Mediterranean and Near East as a single, albeit complex, unit, because there were large-scale cultural exchanges between these various peoples as a result of trade, colonization, and imperialism.

Greek sculpture and architecture of the seventh century B.C.E., for instance, owes a heavy debt to Egypt, and striking similarities between Greek and Middle Eastern myths are probably the result of Mesopotamian influence.

Most ancient cultures were polytheistic (they believed in many gods); and since crosscultural religious influence was common, gods from one place were often reinvented in another. Ancient texts that emphasize a single deity over all others are rare: the most important exceptions to the polytheistic rule are the Egyptian *Great Hymn to the Aten*, composed at a time when the Egyptian monarchy was developing a new cult to the sun god; and the Hebrew Bible, which featured the singular and "jealous" god who is now worshipped by many of the world's populations. But neither of these texts suggests that other gods do not exist—only that the creator deity is by far the most important and powerful. The **Hebrew Bible** is also unusual in suggesting, in the Ten Commandments, that religious observance is closely connected with the observance of a code of behavior; ethics and religion were not necessarily linked in the ancient world, and gods of ancient literature often behave in obviously immoral ways. In many ancient cultures, religious practice ("orthopraxy") was more important than religious belief ("orthodoxy"). Religion involved a shared set of rituals and practices that united a community in shared activities such as festivals and song; few ancient cultures would have understood the idea of a religious "creed" (a formal statement outlining the specific beliefs of a particular religious community, to which all members must subscribe). Cult practices were often highly localized. We should, then, be wary of assuming that the stories about gods that appear in ancient literary texts are necessarily a record of the religious beliefs of a whole culture. Myths circulated in many different forms, changing from one place and time to another; in most ancient cultures, composing alternative stories about the gods does not seem to have been regarded as "heretical," as it might seem to a modern Jewish, Christian, or Muslim reader.

THE GREEKS

The origin of the peoples who eventually called themselves Hellenes is still a mystery. The language they spoke belongs clearly to the Indo-European family (which includes the Germanic, Celtic, Italic, and Sanskrit language groups), but many of the ancient Greek words and place names have terminations that are definitely not Indo-European—the word for "sea" (*thalassa*), for example. The Greeks of historic times

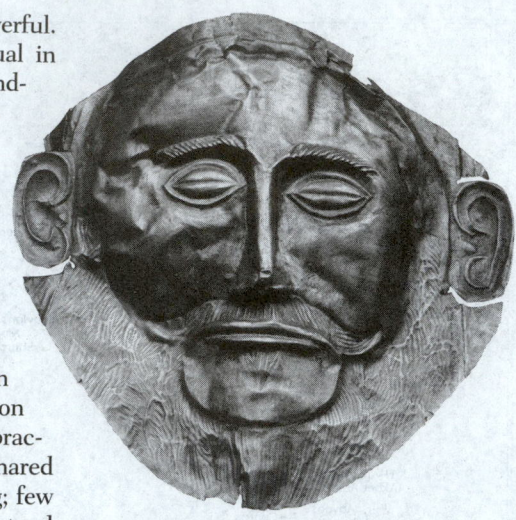

A gold "death mask" from Mycenae, ca. 1550–1500 B.C.E., sometimes referred to as the "mask of Agamemnon."

were presumably a blend of native tribes and Indo-European invaders.

In the second millennium B.C.E., a brilliant culture called Minoan, after the mythical king Minos, flourished on the large island of Crete. It was centered around enormous palace structures, and the citadel of Mycenae and the palace at Pylos show that mainland Greece, in that same period, had a comparably rich culture that included knowledge of a writing system called Linear B. But sometime in the last century of the millennium, the great palaces were destroyed by fire. With them disappeared not only the arts and skills that had created Mycenaean wealth, but even the system of writing. For the next few hundred years, the Greeks were illiterate and so no written evidence survives for this time, known as the Dark Ages of Greece. During this period, the Greeks developed the oral tradition of poetry that would culminate in the ***Iliad*** and the ***Odyssey***.

The Dark Ages ended in the eighth century B.C.E., when Greece again became literate—but with a quite different alphabet, borrowed, as noted earlier, from the Phoenicians. Greece was still highly fragmented, made up of many small independent cities. These were known as "city-states" (a rendering of the Greek term *polis*, from which we get "politics"), because they were independent political and economic entities—not, like modern cities, ruled by a centralized national government. The geography of Greece—a land of mountain barriers and scattered islands—encouraged this fragmentation. The cities differed from each other in their customs, political constitutions, and even dialects: they were rivals and fierce competitors with one another. In the eighth and seventh centuries B.C.E., Greeks founded many new cities all over the Mediterranean coast, including some along the coast of Asia Minor. Many of these new outposts of Greek

civilization experienced a faster economic and cultural development than the older cities of the mainland. It was in the cities founded on the Asian coast that the Greeks adapted to their own language the Phoenician system of writing, adding signs for the vowels to create their alphabet. The Greeks probably first used their new written language for commercial records and transactions, but as literacy became more widespread all over the Greek world in the course of the seventh century B.C.E., treaties and political decrees were inscribed on stone, and literary works were written on rolls of paper made from the Egyptian papyrus plant.

In the sixth century B.C.E., the Persian Empire dominated the Middle East and the eastern Mediterranean Sea, eventually becoming one of the largest empires in the ancient world. Millions of

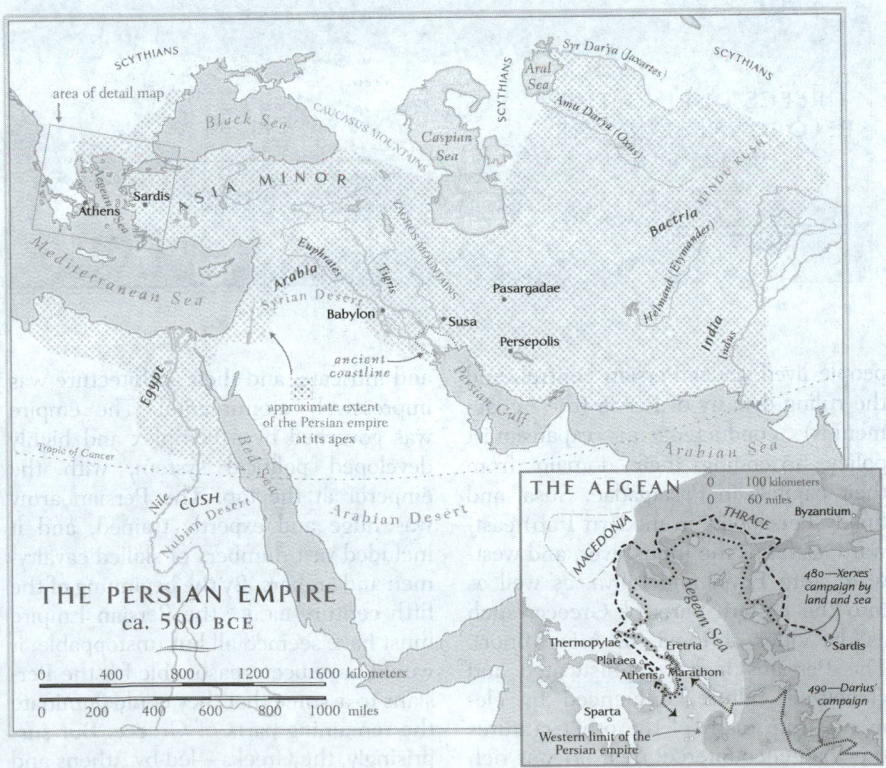

THE PERSIAN EMPIRE
ca. 500 BCE

THE AEGEAN

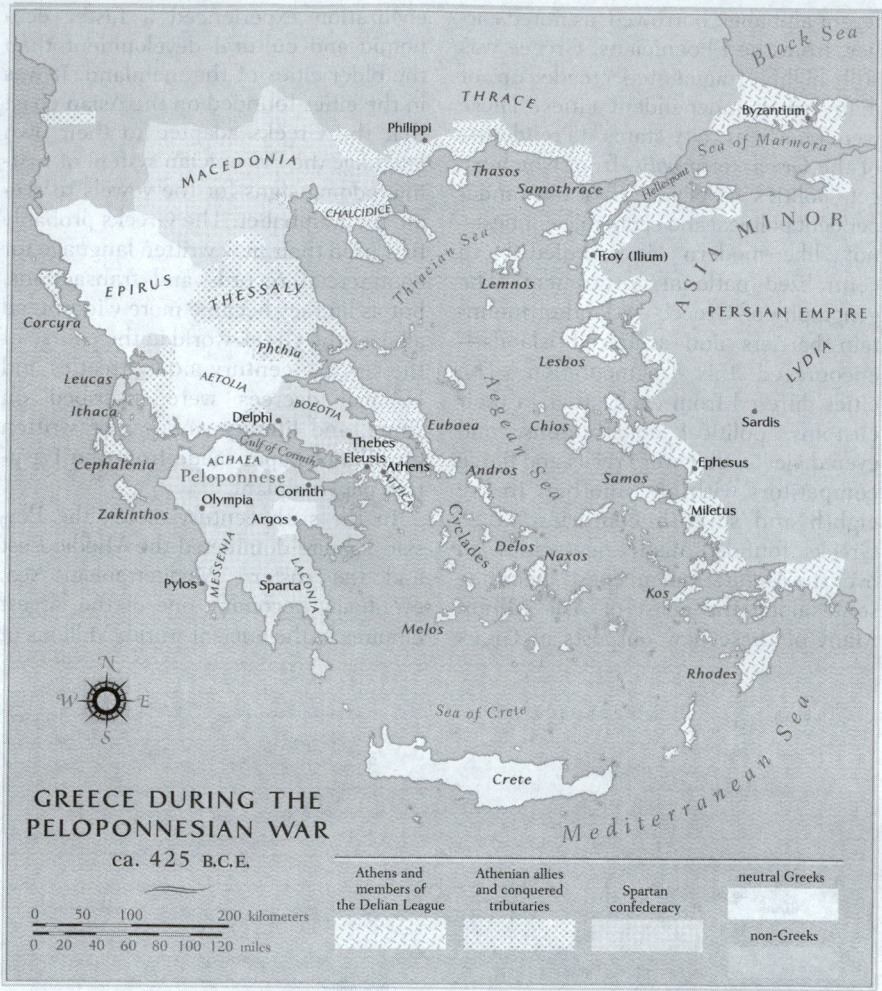

GREECE DURING THE PELOPONNESIAN WAR
ca. 425 B.C.E.

0   50   100   200 kilometers

0 20 40 60 80 100 120 miles

Athens and members of the Delian League

Athenian allies and conquered tributaries

Spartan confederacy

neutral Greeks

non-Greeks

people lived under Persian control, and the ruling dynasty of Persia (the Achaemenids) conducted an expansionist policy, extending their domain from their capitals in Pasargadae, Susa, and finally Persepolis (in modern Iran) eastward, as far as the Indus river, and westward, into Egypt and Libya, as well as into the eastern parts of Greece, such as the cities of Ionia (in Asia Minor). The Persians had a sophisticated and globalized culture, influenced by elements from many of the other cultures they had encountered; their art was rich and intricate, and their architecture was impressively monumental. The empire was governed by a complex and highly developed political system, with the emperor at the top. The Persian army was huge and expertly trained, and it included vast numbers of skilled cavalrymen and archers. By the beginning of the fifth century B.C.E., the Persian Empire must have seemed all but unstoppable; it would have been reasonable for the Persians to assume that they could dominate the remaining parts of Greece. But surprisingly, the Greeks—led by Athens and

A contemporary artist's reconstruction of the Acropolis in fifth-century Athens.
The Parthenon temple is the large structure near the top of the image.

Sparta—managed to repel repeated Persian invasions in the years 490 to 479 B.C.E., winning decisive land and sea battles at Marathon, Salamis, and Plataea. Their astonishing victories over Persia boosted the confidence of the Greek cities in the fifth century. In the wake of this success, the Athenians produced their most important literary and cultural achievements.

Sparta was governed by a ruling elite, an oligarchy ("rule of the few") that used strict military discipline to maintain control over a majority underclass. By contrast, Attica—the city-state of which Athens was the leading city—was at this time a democracy, one of the first such states in the world. *Democracy*, which means "rule by the people," did not imply that all adult inhabitants had the chance to vote; "the people" were a small subset of the population, since women, slaves, and metics (resident aliens) were all excluded from the rights of citizenship.

The citizens of Attica in the fifth century B.C.E. probably numbered only about thirty thousand, while the total population may have been ten times that. Slaves had no rights at all; they were the property of their masters. Women, even freeborn women, could not own property, hold office, or vote. The elite women of Athens had less autonomy than those in most Greek city-states, including Sparta (where women were allowed to exercise outside in the gymnasium); in Athens, they were expected to remain inside the house except for funerals and religious festivals, and were rarely seen by men other than their husbands or male relatives. Moreover, even among citizens who participated in civic life on a roughly equal political footing, there were marked divisions between rich and poor, and between the rural peasant and the city dweller. Still, Athenian democracy represented a bold achievement of civic equality for those who belonged. Since the voting population was so small, it was possible for the city to function as a direct, not representational, democracy: any citizen could attend assembly meetings and vote directly on the issues at hand, rather than electing a representative to vote in his place.

Athens' power lay in the fleet that had played such a decisive role in the struggle against Persia. The city rapidly became the leader of a naval alliance that included most of the islands of the Aegean Sea and many Greek cities on the coast of Asia Minor. This alliance, formed to defend Greece from Persia, soon became an empire, and Athens, with its formidable navy, received an annual tribute from its "allies." Unlike Athens, Sparta was rigidly conservative in government and policy. Because the individual citizen was reared and trained by the state for the state's business, war, the Spartan land army was superior to any other in Greece, and the Spartans controlled, by direct rule or through alliances, a majority of the city-states in the Peloponnese. Athens and Sparta, allies in the war of liberation against Persia, became enemies when the external danger was eliminated. As the years went by, war between the two Greek powers came to be accepted as inevitable by both sides, and in 431 B.C.E. it began. The war ended in 404 B.C.E. with the total defeat of Athens.

During the fifth century, Athens changed culturally and politically, as the self-confidence roused by Persian victories, and celebrated by monumental displays of civic pride (such as the famous Parthenon temple to the city's patron goddess, Athena, completed in 438 B.C.E.), gave way to increasing social tensions and anxieties during the war years. But throughout this century, Athenian democracy provided its citizens with a cultural and intellectual environment that was without precedent in the ancient world. In the sixth century, Greeks on the Ionian coast had already begun to develop new, protoscientific ideas, alternatives to the old myths about how the world was made and how it functioned. Now many of the most original thinkers and writers from all over the Greek world began to gather in Athens. This time marked the beginning of new ways of thinking in many different areas. Greek doctors began to ask new questions about how the body works, including how environmental factors (such as climate and diet) affect health, and they supported their theories by observation. The first anthropological historian, **Herodotus**, analyzed and described how one culture differs from another (focusing on differences among Greeks, Persians, and Egyptians), while the first political historian, Thucydides, showed how economic and political factors could combine to cause war. These years marked the dawning of prose literature, in medicine, history, and philosophy. The fifth century was also the great age of Athenian theater: both tragedy and comedy developed and flourished at this time, and drama provided an essential outlet for the cultural confusions of the age.

Literary and intellectual changes accompanied changes in the ways that elite young men were educated. Throughout the Greek world, during the fifth century and beyond, children's education was based on the poems of Homer; Greek boys learned the tales of the *Iliad* and the *Odyssey* along with the alphabet, often from an educated slave tutor; sections of these poems were also performed by trained actors (rhapsodes) as adult entertainment. But in the fifth century the education of elite adolescent boys changed. Intellectuals immigrating to Athens from other Greek cities catered to a new demand for their services as teachers to train young men for public life, especially for the art of public speaking. These professional tutors, or Sophists ("wisdom teachers"), taught the techniques of rhetoric, as well as more specialized subjects like government, ethics, literary criticism, and even astronomy.

The Sophists were popular, and many parents were willing to spend large sums to have their sons trained by them. But the new educational methods, combined with the new intellectual trends sweeping the city, resulted in a generation gap. Older men felt that the new teachers had corrupted their sons and led them to question the value of traditional religious beliefs and practices. These fathers saw the intellectual developments of the fifth century as morally destructive; some feared the corrosion of moral certainty when teachers made claims, like that of the Sophist Protagoras, that "Man is the measure of all things." The most famous of the Sophists, in his own day as well as later, was Socrates. Socrates was in some ways an unusual Sophist: unlike the majority of these teachers, he was an Athenian citizen, not an immigrant from another city; and, unlike other Sophists, he seems to have demanded no fee for his teaching. But we should not be too quick to accept the sharp distinction that his pupil and defender, Plato, made between the (supposedly fraudulent) Sophists and the (genuinely philosophical) Socrates. Contemporaries—including the comedian

A mosaic from a villa in Pompeii from ca. 100 B.C.E. depicts a philosophical discussion in the Academy of Plato.

A detail from a mosaic (dating from ca. 80 B.C.E.) discovered in Pompeii that shows Alexander the Great on horseback in battle.

Aristophanes, who wrote a play attacking Socrates' dangerous sophistry (*Clouds*)—made no such distinction. Socrates's interests and methods seemed to overlap with those of other wisdom teachers: like Protagoras, he investigated ethics, politics, and truth through "dialectics," a method of question and answer—although, unlike Protagoras, he apparently believed in the possibility of true goodness. Still, his extraordinary mind and personality made him by far the most influential intellectual of his time, and—largely through the work of his most brilliant student, Plato—Socrates became the starting point for all later Western philosophy.

In the last quarter of the fifth century B.C.E., the whole traditional basis of individual conduct, which had been concern for the unity and cohesion of the city-state, was undermined. "In peace and prosperity," says Thucydides, "both states and individuals are actuated by higher motives; . . . but war, which takes away the comfortable provision of daily life, is a hard master, and tends to assimilate men's characters to their conditions." Growing aggressive in their desperation, the Athenians were aware that they were faring badly in the war and launched a disastrous naval campaign in Sicily (413 B.C.E.), in which many ships were lost and many men lost their freedom and their lives. Unstable political conditions followed, leading to a short-lived oligarchic revolution at home (411 B.C.E.). The war dragged on for another seven years, until finally Athens, her last fleet gone, surrendered to the Spartans. A pro-Spartan antidemocratic regime, the Thirty Tyrants, was installed but soon overthrown. Athens became a democracy again, but the confidence and unity of its great age were gone forever. One of the first actions of the new democratic government was to execute Socrates, who had been associated with disgraced former leaders Alcibiades and Critias and whose "corruption of the young" and unusual religious beliefs must have seemed to represent everything the city wanted to forget.

In the fourth century B.C.E., the Greek city-states became involved in constant internecine warfare. Politically and economically bankrupt, they fell under the power of Macedon in the north, whose king, Philip, combined a ferocious energy with a cynicism that enabled him to take full advantage of the disunity of the city-states. Greek liberty ended at the battle of Chaeronea in 338 B.C.E., and Philip's son Alexander inherited a powerful army and political control of all Greece. He led his Macedonian and Greek armies against Persia, and in a few brilliant campaigns became master of an empire that extended into Egypt in the south and to the borders of India in the east. He died at Babylon in 323 B.C.E., and his empire broke up into a number of independent kingdoms ruled by his generals; modern scholars refer to the period that followed (323–146 B.C.E.) as the Hellenistic age. One of these generals, Ptolemy, founded a Greek dynasty that ruled Egypt until after the Roman conquest and ended only with the death of Cleopatra in 30 B.C.E. The results of Alexander's fantastic achievements were surprisingly durable. Into the newly conquered territories came thousands of Greeks who wished to escape from the political futility and economic crisis of the homeland. Wherever they went, they took with them their language, their culture, and their most characteristic buildings—the gymnasium and the theater. The great Hellenistic cities, though now part of kingdoms, grew out of the earlier city-state model and continued many of the city-state's civic and political institutions. At Alexandria, in Egypt, the Ptolemies formed a Greek library to preserve the texts of Greek literature for the scholars who studied and edited them, a school of Greek poetry flourished, and Greek geographers and mathematicians made new advances in science. The Middle East became, as far as the cities were concerned, a Greek-speaking region; and when, some two or three centuries later, the first accounts of the life and teaching of Jesus of Nazareth were recorded, they were written in the simple vernacular Greek known as *koine* ("the common language"), on which the cultural homogeneity of the whole area was based.

ROME

When Alexander died in 323 B.C.E., the city of Rome was engaged in a struggle for control of the surrounding areas. By the middle of the third century B.C.E., Rome dominated most of the Italian peninsula. Expansion southward brought Rome into collision with Carthage, a city in North Africa that was then the greatest power in the western Mediterranean. Two protracted wars resulted (264–241 and 218–201 B.C.E.), and it was only at the end of a third, shorter war (149–146 B.C.E.) that the Romans destroyed their great rival. The second Carthaginian (or Punic) War was particularly hard fought, both in Spain and in Italy itself. The Carthaginian general Hannibal made a spectacular crossing of the Alps, and remained in the peninsula for years, while Rome's southern Italian allies defected to Carthage and had to be slowly won over again. Rome, however, emerged from these wars not merely victorious but a world power. The next two decades saw frequent wars—in Spain, in Greece, and in Asia Minor—that laid the foundations of the Roman Empire.

Unlike Athens, Rome was never a democracy. Instead, from around 509 B.C.E.—when, according to legend, the last tyrannical king of Rome had been overthrown—the state was governed by a complex political system (which changed and developed over time) known as a republic. Power was shared among several different official groups of people, which included the Senate, a body that controlled money and administration, traditionally dominated by the upper classes; the Assemblies, gathered from the people, including lower-class or "plebeian" citizens; and elected officials called Magistrates, the most important of whom were the two Consuls, elected

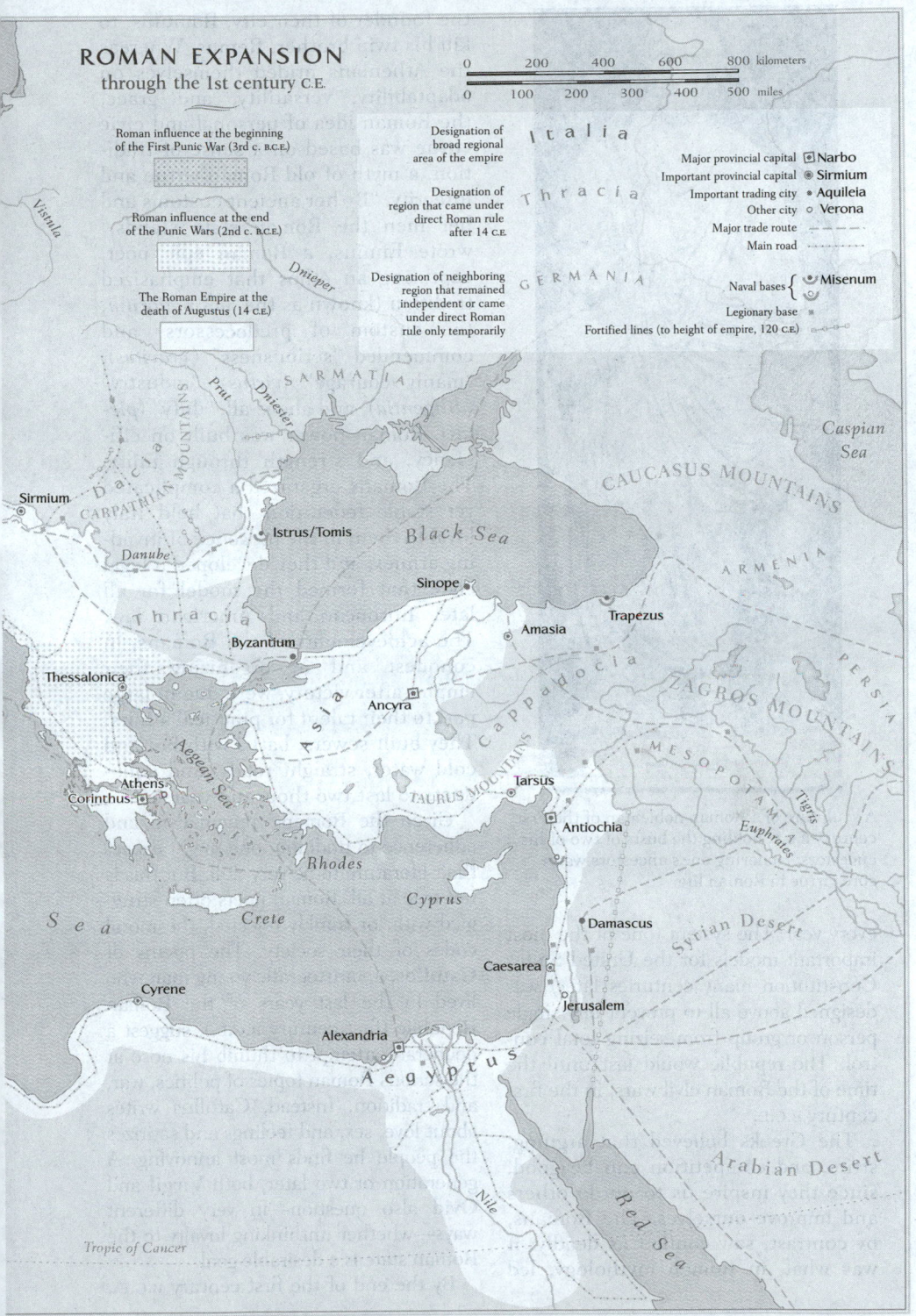

ROMAN EXPANSION
through the 1st century C.E.

0   200   400   600   800 kilometers
0 100 200 300 400 500 miles

Roman influence at the beginning
of the First Punic War (3rd c. B.C.E.)

Roman influence at the end
of the Punic Wars (2nd c. B.C.E.)

The Roman Empire at the
death of Augustus (14 C.E.)

Designation of
broad regional
area of the empire

Designation of
region that came under
direct Roman rule
after 14 C.E.

Designation of neighboring
region that remained
independent or came
under direct Roman
rule only temporarily

Major provincial capital ⬚ Narbo
Important provincial capital ◉ Sirmium
Important trading city ● Aquileia
Other city ○ Verona
Major trade route – – –
Main road – – –

Naval bases { Misenum
Legionary base ▪
Fortified lines (to height of empire, 120 C.E.)

Vistula

Italia

Thracia

GERMANIA

Dnieper

Prut

Dniester

SARMATIA

Dacia

CARPATHIAN MOUNTAINS

Sirmium

Danube

Caspian Sea

CAUCASUS MOUNTAINS

Istrus/Tomis

Black Sea

ARMENIA

Sinope

Trapezus

Amasia

PERSIA

Byzantium

ZAGROS MOUNTAINS

Thracia

Thessalonica

Asia

Ancyra

Cappadocia

MESOPOTAMIA

Athens
Corinthus

Aegean Sea

TAURUS MOUNTAINS

Tarsus

Tigris

Euphrates

Antiochia

Rhodes

Cyprus

Crete

Damascus

Syrian Desert

Sea

Caesarea

Cyrene

Jerusalem

Alexandria

Aegyptus

Arabian Desert

Nile

Red Sea

Tropic of Cancer

A sculpture of a Roman nobleman of the first century B.C.E. holding the busts of two of his ancestors. Honoring one's ancestors was a core virtue in Roman life.

the founder of their city, Romulus, to kill his twin brother, Remus. Whereas the Athenians prided themselves on adaptability, versatility, and grace, the Roman idea of personal and civic virtue was based on a sense of tradition, a myth of old Roman virtue and integrity. "By her ancient customs and her men the Roman state stands," wrote Ennius, a Roman epic poet, capturing an ethos that emphasized tradition (known as the *mos maiorum*, the custom of predecessors) and commended "seriousness" (*gravitas*), "manly courage" (*virtus*), "industry" (*diligentia*), and above all, "duty" (*pietas*). Roman power was built on efficiency, and strength through unity. The Romans organized a complicated yet stable federation that held Italy loyal to them in the presence of invading armies, and they developed a legal code that formed the model for all later European and American law. The achievements of the Romans, in conquest and in organizing their empire after victory, were due in large part to their talent for practical affairs. They built sewers, baths with hot and cold water, straight roads, and aqueducts to last two thousand years.

Given the Romans' pragmatism and adherence to tradition, one might expect their literature to be very dull. But this is not true at all. Roman poets often struggled with, or frankly rejected, the moral codes of their society. The poems of **Catullus**, an aristocratic young man who lived in the last years of the Roman Republic (first century B.C.E.), suggest a deliberate attempt to thumb his nose at the serious Roman topics of politics, war, and tradition. Instead, Catullus writes about love, sex, and feelings and satirizes the people he finds most annoying. A generation or two later, both **Virgil** and **Ovid** also question—in very different ways—whether unthinking loyalty to the Roman state is a desirable goal.

By the end of the first century B.C.E.,

every year. The system (one of the most important models for the United States Constitution many centuries later) was designed above all to prevent any single person or group from seizing total control. The republic would last until the time of the Roman civil wars, in the first century B.C.E.

The Greeks believed that arguing, strife, and competition can be good, since they inspire us to outdo others and improve ourselves. The Romans, by contrast, saw conflict as deadly: it was what, in Roman mythology, led

Rome was the capital of an empire that stretched from the Straits of Gibraltar to Mesopotamia and the frontiers of Palestine, and as far north as Britain. While Greek history began with the epics of Homer (instrumental in creating a sense of Greek national identity that transcended the divisions of the many city-states), the Romans had conquered half the known world before they began to write. Latin literature started with a translation of the *Odyssey*, made by a Greek prisoner of war; and, with the exception of satire, the model was always Greek. Roman authors borrowed wholesale from Greek originals, not furtively but openly and proudly, as a tribute to the source. But this frank acknowledgment of indebtedness should not blind us to the fact that Latin literature is original, and sometimes profoundly so. Catullus translated the Greek lyric poet **Sappho**, but he added to her evocation of agonizing jealousy a distinctively Roman anxiety about idleness. Ovid retold Greek myths, making them funnier by giving them a Roman rhetorical punch. Virgil based his epic, the *Aeneid*, on Homer, but he chose as his theme the coming of the Trojan prince Aeneas to Italy, where he was to found a city from which, in the fullness of time, would come "the Latin race . . . and the high walls of Rome."

The institutions of the Roman city-state proved inadequate for world government. The second and first centuries B.C.E. were dominated by civil war fought by various factions vying for power: generals against senators and populists against aristocrats. Coalitions were formed, but each proved unstable. Julius Caesar, a successful Roman general, seized power (although he refused the title "king"); but he was assassinated in 44 B.C.E. by a party hoping to restore the old system of shared rule. More years of civil war followed, until finally, in 31 B.C.E., Julius's adoptive nephew, Octavian—who later titled himself Augustus—managed to defeat the ruler of the eastern half of the empire, Mark Antony, along with Antony's ally and lover, Cleopatra, queen of Egypt. Augustus played his hand carefully, claiming that he was restoring the Republic; but he assumed primary control of the state and became the first in the long line of Roman emperors.

For the next two hundred years, the successors of Augustus, the Roman emperors, ruled the Mediterranean and Middle Eastern world. The empire covered a vast area that included Britain, France, all southern Europe, the Middle East, and the whole of North Africa. Some native inhabitants in all these areas were killed by the Romans; others were enslaved; many, both slave and free, were Romanized, acculturated into the norms of the Roman people. Roman culture stamped this whole area of the world in ways that can still be discerned today: the Romans built roads, cities, public baths, and theaters, and they brought their literature and language—Latin—to the provinces they ruled. All modern Romance languages, including Spanish, French, and Italian, developed from the language spoken throughout the Roman Empire.

But controlling so many people, in so many different areas, from the central government in Rome was difficult and expensive. It could not be done forever. Marcus Aurelius (121–180 C.E.), who in his spare time wrote a beautiful book of thoughts about his struggle to live a good life (the *Meditations*), was the first emperor to share his power with a partner; this was the first official recognition that the empire was too big to be ruled by one man. The Romans fought a long losing battle against invading tribes from the north and east. When it finally fell, the empire left behind it the idea of the world-state, later adopted by the medieval church, which ruled from the same center, Rome, and which claimed a spiritual authority as great as the secular authority it replaced.

CREATION AND THE COSMOS

Cosmogonies—stories about how the world began—have been told by almost every culture in the world. They help people define their place in the universe, embedding the specifics of one human culture within a wider, "cosmic" pattern. The Greek word *cosmos* implies order and beauty, as well as universe: to compose a "cosmogony" is to describe how the world came to be a beautiful and well-ordered place. The genre includes some of the earliest texts in all surviving literature. These texts give us an idea of how human beings in premodern civilizations tried to make sense of their world, and how they answered questions that still puzzle scientists, philosophers, poets, and theologians today. Where does the world come from? What is it made of? Is there an order or pattern or purpose in the universe, or do things happen at random? Did a god or gods create or arrange the world? How did life on earth begin? How did human beings come into existence? Has there always been evil? If not, how did wickedness and conflict first begin?

These questions are profound, but the answers offered by ancient texts may strike modern readers as primitive or naive. Early cosmogonies provide mythical stories, involving divine personifications, instead of scientific theories (such as the big bang) about the

beginnings and composition of the cosmos. But we should take these stories as a provocation to think harder about what "scientific" thinking really is. How are our beliefs about atomic particles different from ancient beliefs about the power of earth and sky? Clearly, the bards and poets who told most of these stories were not interested in conducting verifiable or falsifiable experiments to find out how the world works. In that sense, they were "unscientific." But it does not follow that they were unsophisticated in their thinking. The authors of the earliest surviving texts were already responding in complex ways to a long set of oral and written traditions.

Nor were these stories immediately supplanted by later ways of thinking and writing. Mythological traditions about the origins of the universe inspired the beginnings of science and informed later discussions of philosophy, history, and theology. The work of the early Greek thinkers who are often seen as the first scientists—the "pre-Socratics"—includes some critique of traditional theology and myth; **Xenophanes**, for instance, suggested that **Homer** and **Hesiod** (whose *Theogony* includes the earliest Greek myths about the origins of the gods) are both "impious" in their depiction of the gods committing adultery. The earliest "scientific" or "philosophical" thought still belongs to the tradition of Hesiod, although entities like "water," "fire," "air," and "mind" are substituted for the named deities who appeared in the archaic texts (like Gaia or Uranus). Much later, the Roman

A detail from the Hellenistic altar of Pergamon, ca. 164–156 B.C.E., that shows the giant Alcyoneus being forcibly separated from the earth goddess, Gaia, by Athena.

philosopher-poet **Lucretius** challenges the idea that we need to imagine divine creators for the (purely material) world, but he makes extensive poetic use of the cosmological tradition even as he rejects it.

This selection includes a range of texts, from the Babylonian creation epic *Enuma Elish* and the archaic Greek *Theogony*, through fragments of Ionian "pre-Socratic" philosophy, and on to the poetry of Lucretius. The continuity of mythical elements across the Babylonian, Greek, and Roman cultures—including the story of divine creation followed by a massive flood—suggests that the ancient Mediterranean world had a common heritage.

Ancient cosmogonies do not usually begin with creation *ex nihilo* ("from nothing"). Rather, they present some kind of primeval matter—often personified forms of earth, sky, and water—from which the world took shape; the Akkadian epic *Enuma Elish* begins by imagining a time before the heaven and earth had names, and the text tells a story of progressively more-detailed processes of naming. In several stories, such as *The Epic of Gilgamesh*, the separation of heaven and earth and their ensuing reunion fuel the creation of humankind and the development of civilization. These works also trace the ways that human life has changed since it began. The change may be presented, as in the **Hebrew Bible** and in the Greek myths of the Golden Age recorded by Hesiod, as a fall from a state of innocence and grace. Alternatively, contemporary culture may be imagined as an improvement on an old, primitive life, as in the Greek myth of Prometheus, who brought fire and technology to helpless humanity. Both these mythical patterns—the idea of decline and the idea of progress—are essential to the way that human beings imagine themselves and their place in the world.

The notion of a whole world is a relatively new one in human history. There is no word for the universe as one entity in Sumerian or Akkadian—the languages spoken by the most ancient Mesopotamian peoples (from the sixth millennium B.C.E. onward). Rather, the universe is conceived as a combination of several constituents and designated by terms such as *An-Ki* ("Heaven-Earth"). But even in these cultures, there was a developing notion of what the *Enuma Elish* calls "the entirety of all of everything." In trying to imagine the whole world, ancient peoples tended, naturally enough, to see their own place as the center and then construct stories about what might lie above, below, and beyond.

Cosmogonies frequently contain a political dimension. Descriptions of the great creator god may, by analogy, praise a human ruler who has an intimate relationship with his divine equivalent. These texts often feature stories of a primeval struggle between different generations of the gods, a "theomachy" (battle of the gods): in several cases, a younger male god (Marduk in the Babylonian stories, Zeus in the Greek myths) manages to destroy, castrate, or enslave the dominant figures of an earlier regime. This kind of story can be seen as the triumph of male power over an earlier time, imagined as matriarchal; as a prototype for how successful human rulers can replace warring factions or oligarchies; or as a mirror of the usual struggles in human families, in which the younger generation always, in the end, takes over from the older. Creation stories may also help establish the centrality of a particular place or culture within the whole world. For instance, by suggesting that the Babylonian deity Marduk played the most important part in the creation of humanity, the Babylonian poem *Enuma Elish* presents Babylon as the most important culture.

A modern impression made from an Akkadian seal from ca. 2200 B.C.E. depicting the sun god riding a boat with a dragon head—suggesting how the civilized god has defeated and co-opted the forces of chaos (the dragon).

Cosmogonies tend to classify the world in a hierarchical structure. The upper world is the home of gods; the lower world, beneath the earth, is often a place of death, demons, gods, and ancestral spirits. The center of the world—in Egypt, Babylon, Israel, Greece, or Rome—is the most habitable area, suitable for humans; beyond it lie less hospitable lands, as well as the ocean, which most ancient Mediterranean peoples imagined as an endless expanse of water surrounding the whole mass of land. The terms in which people imagined creation and the gods varied with the landscape they inhabited. In the largely cloudless desert climate of Egypt, the night sky was particularly clear, and sunrise, along with the disappearance of the stars, was dramatic; in Egyptian texts, the creator god (sometimes presented as the only god that matters—an apparent precursor to monotheistic gods) is closely linked to the sun. In Mesopotamian, Greek, and Hebrew texts, by contrast, we find less emphasis on the sun and more attention paid to the sky in general and especially to water as the element from which everything comes—and to which things may eventually return. Water is sometimes the source of all life; Apsu, the fresh-water ocean, appears as the "begetter of the gods" in *Enuma Elish*.

The Greek man often known as the first philosopher, **Thales**, theorized that the whole world is made of water. But water—especially salt water—is also a locus for fear of the unknown, of the unpredictable, and of the gods' wrath. The story of Noah's flood is paralleled by several other flood myths from the ancient Mediterranean. In *Gilgamesh* (Tablet XI), the earth is conceived as a giant mountain emerging out of the primeval waters. In *Enuma Elish,* the ocean turns into a monster that has to be defeated by Marduk.

Poetic accounts of cosmogony played an important part in literature throughout antiquity: they are not confined to the distant past. Composing stories about cosmic creation was intimately related to thinking about human acts of creation. Creation stories are meditations on the act of making, and we should remember that the Greek word for poetry, *poesis*, primarily means "making." Often some of the most self-aware works of literature, these stories raise questions about how human and divine agency relate to one another when we make up worlds. How do stories get shaped into a satisfying and beautiful arrangement? Is there a perfect or only partial analogy between the ordering of the cosmos and the ordering of a literary text?

THE GREAT HYMN TO THE ATEN

ca. 1350 B.C.E.

Inscribed prominently at the entrance to the tomb of an important official in the new capital city of el-Amarna, this hymn celebrates the sun as creator and sustainer of the world and emphasizes the close connection between the god and his human counterparts, the king (Amenhotep IV) and queen (Nefertiti). The king initiated a religious and political revolution when he exclusively promoted the cult of the sun god, Aten, built a new capital, and changed his name to Akhenaten, which means "He who is effective for Aten." For a decade or two the old pantheon with numerous gods was neglected in favor of a new, singular creator god. Some scholars have seen the cult of Aten as an early type of monotheism, although this is much debated. The peaceful and lyrical tone of the hymn is at odds with the violence accompanying the changes that Akhenaten introduced, which were rejected within a few years of his death, when Egyptians abandoned the new capital, destroyed the king's monuments, and tried to erase his name from their society's memory.

Akhenaten and his family make an offering to Aten, the sun god.

The Great Hymn to the Aten[1]

Adoration of *Re-Harakhti-who-rejoices-in-lightland*[2] *In-his-name-Shu-who-is-Aten,* living forever; the great living Aten who is in jubilee, the lord of all that the Disk encircles, lord of sky, lord of earth, lord of the house-of-Aten[3] in Akhet-Aten; (and of) the King of Upper and Lower Egypt, who lives by Maat, the Lord of the Two Lands,[4] *Neferkheprure,*[5] *Sole-one-of-Re*; the Son of Re who lives by Maat,[6] the Lord of Crowns, *Akhenaten,* great in his lifetime; (and) his beloved great Queen, the Lady of the Two Lands, *Nefer-nefru-Aten Nefertiti,* who lives in health and youth forever. The Vizier, the Fanbearer on the right of the King, ——— Ay; he says:

Splendid you rise in heaven's lightland,
O living Aten, creator of life!
When you have dawned in eastern lightland,
You fill every land with your beauty.[7]
You are beauteous, great, radiant,   5
High over every land;
Your rays embrace the lands,
To the limit of all that you made.
Being Re, you reach their limits,
You bend them for the son whom you love;   10
Though you are far, your rays are on earth,
Though one sees you, your strides are unseen.

When you set in western lightland,[8]
Earth is in darkness as if in death;
One sleeps in chambers, heads covered,   15
One eye does not see another.
Were they robbed of their goods,
That are under their heads,
People would not remark it.
Every lion comes from its den,   20
All the serpents bite;
Darkness hovers, earth is silent,
As their maker rests in lightland.

1. Translated by Miriam Lichtheim.
2. The translation uses "lightland" for the Egyptian *akhet,* more often rendered "horizon." In the vision of Akhenaten, lightland was primarily on the east, where the sun rose. The two phrases in italics make up the formal name of Akhenaten's god, generally referred to as "(the) Aten." They are written in cartouches like kings' names.
3. Both the temple of the Aten in Akhet-Aten and the whole city as the god's estate.
4. A standard title of Egyptian kings. The Two Lands are Upper and Lower Egypt.
5. The name Akhenaten took when ascending the throne, before he initiated his revolution;

it means "the perfect one of the manifestations of Re." Nefer-nefru-Aten is a comparable name given exceptionally to Akhenaten's queen, Nefertiti: "the perfect one of the perfection/beauty of Aten."
6. The most typical epithet of Akhenaten, who used the central Egyptian concept of Maat ("truth, order, justice") without clearly distinguishing it from its traditional meanings.
7. "Beauty" also means "presence."
8. Contrary to traditional Egyptian belief, the west, the normal abode of the dead, is seen in purely negative terms, as night and the absence of the god's protection.

Earth brightens when you dawn in lightland,
When you shine as Aten of daytime;   25
As you dispel the dark,
As you cast your rays,
The Two Lands are in festivity.
Awake they stand on their feet,
You have roused them;   30
Bodies cleansed, clothed,
Their arms adore your appearance.
The entire land sets out to work,
All beasts browse on their herbs;
Trees, herbs are sprouting,   35
Birds fly from their nests,
Their wings greeting your ka.[9]
All flocks frisk on their feet,
All that fly up and alight,
They live when you dawn for them.   40
Ships fare north, fare south as well,
Roads lie open when you rise;
The fish in the river dart before you,
Your rays are in the midst of the sea.

Who makes seed grow in women,   45
Who creates people from sperm;
Who feeds the son in his mother's womb,
Who soothes him to still his tears.
Nurse in the womb,
Giver of breath,   50
To nourish all that he made.
When he comes from the womb to breathe,
On the day of his birth,
You open wide his mouth,
You supply his needs.
When the chick in the egg speaks in the shell,   55
You give him breath within to sustain him;
When you have made him complete,
To break out from the egg,
He comes out from the egg,   60
To announce his completion,
Walking on his legs he comes from it.

How many are your deeds,
Though hidden from sight,
O Sole God beside whom there is none![1]   65
You made the earth as you wished, you alone,
All peoples, herds, and flocks;

---

9. *Ka* normally means the generative principle transmitted through the generations. Here
it seems to mean simply the god's manifestation of himself in the sunrise.

1. This could mean either that no god can be
compared with the Aten/Re or that he is the
only god.

All upon earth that walk on legs,
All on high that fly on wings,
The lands of Khor and Kush,[2]   70
The land of Egypt.
You set every man in his place,
You supply their needs;
Everyone has his food,
His lifetime is counted.   75
Their tongues differ in speech,
Their characters likewise;
Their skins are distinct,
For you distinguished the peoples.

You made Hapy in dat,[3]   80
You bring him when you will,
To nourish the people,
For you made them for yourself.
Lord of all who toils for them,
Lord of all lands who shines for them,   85
Aten of daytime, great in glory!
All distant lands, you make them live,
You made a heavenly Hapy descend for them;
He makes waves on the mountains like the sea,
To drench their fields and their towns.   90
How excellent are your ways, O Lord of eternity!
A Hapy from heaven for foreign peoples,
And all lands' creatures that walk on legs,
For Egypt the Hapy who comes from dat.

Your rays nurse all fields,   95
When you shine they live, they grow for you;
You made the seasons to foster all that you made,
Winter to cool them, heat that they taste you.
You made the far sky to shine therein,
To behold all that you made;   100
You alone, shining in your form of living Aten,
Risen, radiant, distant, near.
You made millions of forms from yourself alone,
Towns, villages, fields, the river's course;
All eyes observe you upon them,   105
For you are the Aten of daytime on high.

2. Syria in the north and Sudan in the south.
3. Hapy is the inundation of the Nile, essential to life in Egypt; dat is Egyptian for "underworld," from which the inundation could be considered to emerge. Other lands that do not have the inundation must be content with rain as an equivalent from the sky; this is then characterized as another Hapy.

[. . .]⁴

You are in my heart,
There is no other who knows you,
Only your son, *Neferkheprure, Sole-one-of-Re,*
Whom you have taught your ways and your might.   110
Those on earth come from your hand as you made them,
When you have dawned they live,
When you set they die;
You yourself are lifetime, one lives by you.
All eyes are on your beauty until you set,   115
All labor ceases when you rest in the west;
When you rise you stir everyone for the King,
Every leg is on the move since you founded the earth.
You rouse them for your son who came from your body,
The King who lives by Maat, the Lord of the Two Lands,   120
Neferkheprure, Sole-one-of-Re,
The Son of Re who lives by Maat, the Lord of crowns,
Akhenaten, great in his lifetime;⁵
(And) the great Queen whom he loves, the Lady of the Two Lands,
Nefer-nefru-Aten Nefertiti, living forever.   125

---

4. A broken and obscure passage omitted by
the translator.
5. A special epithet adopted by Akhenaten.

Nefertiti's epithet "living forever" is a standard
one applied to both kings and queens.

THE BABYLONIAN CREATION EPIC
(*ENUMA ELISH*)

Enuma Elish ("When on high"), titled from the opening words of the poem, is an Akkadian poem that may have originated as early as the eighteenth century B.C.E. (although some have dated it to the twelfth century B.C.E.). Even this ancient story combined several other, much earlier cosmogonies, from Sumerian, Old Akkadian, and West Semitic cultures, that told of the warrior god's struggle against the primeval female sea monster (Tiamat). The narrative structure of our text reflects a clear agenda: the author gives pride of place to the Babylonian god, Marduk, whose temple in Babylon becomes the religious and political center of the world. The story traces the world's creation: from the two primary personifications of ocean (fresh and salt, Apsu and Tiamat) out of which emerge the earliest gods—who fight against the fresh ocean, the father-figure Apsu, when he wants to destroy them and restore primeval silence. Then Marduk, the creator god, kills Tiamat and from her body fashions the world; he establishes the first city, Babylon, where he has his cosmic home in the Esagila temple. Marduk's father, Ea, creates the first humans out of the blood of Qingu, Tiamat's consort and general, and these are to serve the gods' many needs. Finally, Marduk creates the netherworld, providing a mythical space for human existence after death.

From The Babylonian Creation Epic (*Enuma Elish*)[1]

From *Tablet I*

When on high no name was given to heaven,
Nor below was the netherworld called by name,
Primeval Apsu was their progenitor.
And matrix-Tiamat was she who bore them all,[2]
They were mingling their waters together,   5
No canebrake was intertwined nor thicket matted close.[3]
When no gods at all had been brought forth,
Nor called by names, none destinies ordained,
Then were the gods formed within the(se two).

* * *

---

1. Translated by and with footnotes adapted from Benjamin R. Foster.
2. Before anything existed in the world, Mother Ocean, Tiamat, and Fresh Water, Apsu, mingled to produce the first pairs of gods.
3. Nothing divided or covered the waters.

From *Tablet V*

Marduk creates Babylon as the terrestrial counterpart to Esharra, abode of the gods in heaven. The gods are to repose there during their earthly sojourns.

Marduk made ready to speak and said
(These) words to the gods his fathers,
"Above Apsu, the azure dwelling,
"As a counterpart to Esharra, which I built for you,
"Below the firmament, whose grounding I made firm.   5
"A house I shall build, let it be the abode of my pleasure.
"Within it I shall establish its holy place.
"I shall appoint my (holy) chambers.
        I shall establish my kingship.
"When you go up from Apsu to assembly,
"Let your stopping places be here, before your assembly.[4]   10
"When you come down from heaven to [assembly],
"Let your stopping places be there to receive all of you.
"I shall call [its] name [Babylon],
        Houses of the Great Gods,[5]
"We shall all hold fe[stival]s with[in] it."
When the gods his fathers heard what he commanded,   15
They [. . .]
"Over all things that your hands have created,
"Who has [authority, save for you]?
"Over the earth that you have created,
"Who has [authority, save for] you?   20
"Babylon, to which you have given name,
"Make our [stopping place] there forever."

*   *   *

From *Tablet VI*

The rebellious gods are offered a general pardon if they will produce their leader. They produce Qingu, claiming that he started the war. He is sacrificed, and his blood is used to make a human being.

When [Mar]duk heard the speech of the gods,
He was resolving to make artful things:
He would tell his idea to Ea,[6]
What he thought of in his heart he proposes,
"I shall compact blood, I shall cause bones to be,   5
"I shall make stand a human being, let 'Man' be its name.

4. When the gods or their cult images traveled to Babylon, they could stay in chambers at Marduk's temple.
5. Original meaning of the name Babylon.
6. Before this text was written, creation in the Mesopotamian tradition was usually attributed to the Mother Goddess and Ea (or Enki), the god of wisdom and magic. In order to insert Marduk, the Babylonian city god, into this tradition, the text credits Marduk with giving Ea the idea for creating humankind.

THE BABYLONIAN CREATION EPIC | 31

"I shall create humankind,
"They shall bear the gods' burden that those may rest.
"I shall artfully double the ways of the gods:
"Let them be honored as one but divided in twain."[7]   10
Ea answered him, saying these words,
He told him a plan to let the gods rest,
"Let one, their brother, be given to me,
"Let him be destroyed so that people can be fashioned.
"Let the great gods convene in assembly,   15
"Let the guilty one be given up that they may abide."
Marduk convened the great gods in assembly,
He spoke to them magnanimously as he gave the command,
The gods heeded his utterance,
As the king spoke to the Anunna-gods (these) words,   20
"Let your first reply be the truth!
"Do you speak with me truthful words!
"Who was it that made war,
"Suborned Tiamat and drew up for battle?
"Let him be given over to me, the one who made war,   25
"I shall make him bear his punishment, you shall be released."
The Igigi, the great gods answered him,
To Lugaldimmerankia, counsellor of all the gods, their lord,
"It was Qingu who made war,
"Suborned Tiamat and drew up for battle."   30
They bound and held him before Ea.
They imposed the punishment on him and shed his blood.
From his blood he made humankind.
He imposed the burden of the gods and exempted the gods.
After Ea the wise had made humankind,   35
They imposed the burden of the gods on them!
That deed is beyond comprehension.
By the artifices of Marduk did Nudimmud create!

> *Marduk divides the gods of heaven and netherworld.*
> *The gods build Esagila, Marduk's temple in Babylon*

Marduk the king divided the gods,
The Anunna-gods, all of them, above and below,   40
He assigned to Anu[8] for duty at his command.
He set three hundred in heaven for (their) duty,
A like number he designated for the ways of the netherworld:
He made six hundred dwell in heaven and netherworld.
After he had given all the commands,   45
And had divided the shares of the Anunna-gods
      of heaven and netherworld,
The Anunna-gods made ready to speak.
To Marduk their lord they said,

7. Reference to the two main divisions of the Mesopotamian pantheon: the supernatural "Anunna-gods" and the infernal "Igigi-gods."
8. The sky god who is supreme in the pantheon but remote from human affairs. The ancient city-state Uruk, where the great hero Gilgamesh was king, was known for its temple to Anu.

"Now, Lord, you who have liberated us.
"What courtesy may we do you?
"We will make a shrine, whose name will be a byword,
"Your chamber that shall be our stopping place,
  we shall find rest therein.
"We shall lay out the shrine, let us set up its emplacement,
"When we come (to visit you), we shall find rest therein."
When Marduk heard this,   55
His features glowed brightly, like the day,
"Then make Babylon the task that you requested,
"Let its brickwork be formed, build high the shrine."
The Anunna-gods set to with hoes,
One (full) year they made its bricks.   60
When the second year came,
They raised the head of Esagila,[9] the counterpart to Apsu,
They built the upper ziggurat of Apsu,
For Anu-Enlil-Ea[1] they founded his [. . .] and dwelling,
He took his seat in sublimity before them,   65
Its pinnacles were facing toward the base of Esharra.
After they had done the work of Esagila,
All the Anunna-gods devised their own shrines.

     *   *   *

Marduk is made supreme god. Anshar gives him a second name, Asalluhi. Anshar
explains Marduk's role among gods and men with respect to this second name.

After Anu had ordained the destinies of the bow,[2]
He set out the royal throne
  that stood highest among the gods,
Anu had him sit there, in the assembly of the gods.   70
Then the great gods convened,
They made Marduk's destiny highest, they prostrated themselves.
They laid upon themselves a curse (if they broke the oath),
With water and oil they swore, they touched their throats.[3]   75
They granted him exercise of kingship over the gods,
They established him forever
  for lordship of heaven and netherworld.
Anshar[4] gave him an additional name, Asalluhi,
"When he speaks, we will all do obeisance,
"At his command the gods shall pay heed.   80

     *   *   *

9. Wordplay on the name of Marduk's temple, which means "house whose head is high."
1. Here three major gods of the Mesopotamian pantheon probably stand for the powerful Marduk.
2. Right before this passage, Marduk's bow is made into a star constellation by the god Anu.

3. A slashing gesture people performed when taking an oath to show what should happen to those who break it.
4. God of the second generation after the creator couple Tiamat and Apsu. Anshar, "Whole Heaven," is coupled with Kishar, "Whole Earth."

Beginning of the explanation of Marduk's fifty names. Names 1–9 are those borne by Marduk prior to this point in the narrative. Each of them is correlated with crucial points in the narrative as follows: his birth, his creation of the human race to provide for the gods, his terrible anger but his willingness to spare the rebellious gods, his proclamation by the gods as supreme among them, his organization of the cosmos, his saving the gods from danger, his sparing the gods who fought on the side of Tiamat, but his killing of Tiamat and Qingu, and his enabling the gods to proceed with the rest of what is narrated.

"Let us pronounce his fifty names,
"That his ways shall be (thereby) manifest, his deeds likewise(?):
    MARDUK!
"Who, from his birth, was named by his forefather Anu,
"Establisher of pasture and watering place,
    who enriches (their) stables,
"Who by his Deluge weapon subdued the stealthy ones,   85
"Who saved the gods his forefathers from danger.
"He is indeed the Son, the Sun,
    the most radiant of the gods,
"They shall walk in his brilliant light forever.
"On the people whom he made,
    creatures with the breath of life,
"He imposed the gods' burden, that those be released.   90
"Creation, destruction, absolution, punishment:
"Each shall be at his command, these shall gaze upon him.
"MARUKKA shall he be,
    the god who created them (humankind),
"Who granted (thereby) the Anunna-gods contentment,
    who let the Igigi-gods rest.
"MARUTUKKU shall be the trust of his land,
    city, and people,   95
"The people shall heed him forever."
The rest of the fifty names of Marduk follow here.

*   *   *

From *Tablet VII*

Composition and purpose of this text, its approval by Marduk.

They must be grasped: the "first one"[5] should reveal (them),
The wise and knowledgeable should ponder (them) together,
The master should repeat, and make the pupil understand.
The "shepherd," the "herdsman" should pay attention,[6]

---

5. As in other Mesopotamian mythical stories, this part explains how the text originated and how it should be used by later ages. The "first one" probably refers to somebody who recites or "reveals" the text during a religious cere- mony. This epilogue emphasizes the sacredness of the text—approved by Marduk himself— which should not be changed by future generations.
6. "Shepherd" is a metaphor for king.

He must not neglect the Enlil of the gods, Marduk, 5
So his land may prosper and he himself be safe.
His word is truth, what he says is not changed,
Not one god can annul his utterance.
If he frowns, he will not relent,
If he is angry, no god can face his rage. 10
His heart is deep, his feelings all encompassing,
He before whom crime and sin must appear for judgment.
The revelation (of the names) that the "first one"
        discoursed before him (Marduk),
He wrote down and preserved for the future to hear,
The [wo]rd of Marduk who created the Igigi-gods, 15
[His/Its   ] let them [   ], his name let them invoke.
Let them sound abroad the song of Marduk,
How he defeated Tiamat and took kingship.

HESIOD

late eighth century B.C.E.

The *Theogony* and *Works and Days* are composed in the same meter and come from the same period as the Homeric epics—the late eighth century B.C.E. The *Theogony*, which means "birth of the gods," begins with the story of how the poem itself came into being, when the Muses inspired the poet Hesiod on Mount Helicon. The text tells how the Olympian gods, ruled by Zeus, emerged out of the earlier generations: Earth and Sky (Gaia and Ouranos) gave birth to the Titans, who were finally overthrown by Zeus. Hesiod also includes several stories about the prehistory of humanity, which address the origins of technology, sin, and suffering. These include the story of Prometheus, a clever Titan who tricked Zeus and stole fire from heaven to give to mankind; Zeus punished Prometheus with eternal pain and punished humanity by creating woman as a "tempting snare / from which men cannot escape." In *Works and Days*, a poem that combines mythical stories with injunctions about how to live, work, farm, and sail, Hesiod gives a different, somewhat less misogynistic version of the myth, in which a woman (Pandora, or "All Gifts") does not represent evil but accidentally brings evil into the world. Hesiod then offers yet another account of how suffering came to the world, this time without invoking gender at all: humans gradually degenerated, from the age of gold to the age of iron, in which we now live.

From Theogony[1]

I begin my song with the Helikonian Muses whose domain
is Helikon, the great god-haunted mountain;
their soft feet move in the dance that rings
the violet-dark spring and the altar of mighty Zeus.
They bathe their lithe bodies in the water of Permessos   5
or of Hippokrene or of god-haunted Olmeios.
On Helikon's peak they join hands in lovely dances
and their pounding feet awaken desire.
From there they set out and, veiled in mist,
glide through the night and raise enchanting voices   10
to exalt aegis-bearing Zeus and queenly Hera,[2]
the lady of Argos who walks in golden sandals;
gray-eyed Athena, daughter of aegis-bearing Zeus,
and Phoibos Apollon and arrow-shooting Artemis.
They exalt Poseidon, holder and shaker of the earth,   15
stately Themis and Aphrodite of the fluttering eyelids,
and gold-wreathed Hebe and fair Dione.[3]
And then they turn their song to Eos, Helios, and bright Selene,[4]
to Leto, Iapetos, and sinuous-minded Kronos,[5]
to Gaia, great Okeanos,[6] and black Night,   20
and to the holy race of the other deathless gods.
It was they who taught Hesiod beautiful song
as he tended his sheep at the foothills of god-haunted Helikon.
Here are the words the daughters of aegis-bearing Zeus,
the Muses of Olympos, first spoke to me.   25
"Listen, you country bumpkins, you pot-bellied blockheads,
we know how to tell many lies that pass for truth,
and when we wish, we know to tell the truth itself."
So spoke Zeus's daughters, masters of word-craft,
and from a laurel in full bloom they plucked a branch,   30
and gave it to me as a staff, and then breathed into me
divine song, that I might spread the fame of past and future,
and commanded me to hymn the race of the deathless gods,
but always begin and end my song with them.
Yet, trees and rocks are not my theme. Let me sing on!   35
Ah, my heart, begin with the Muses who hymn father Zeus
and in the realm of Olympos gladden his great heart;
with sweet voices they speak of things that are
and things that were and will be, and with effortless smoothness
the song flows from their mouths. The halls of father Zeus   40

1. Translated by Apostolos N. Athanassakis. *Theogony* means "birth of the gods" or "divine generation."
2. Zeus and Hera are the king and queen of the gods.
3. All gods and goddesses. Apollon, god of poetry, and Artemis, goddess of the hunt, are twins; Poseidon, brother of Zeus, causes earthquakes; Themis is goddess of justice (her name means "right" or "lawfulness"); Aphrodite is goddess of sexual desire; *Hebe* means "youth"; Dione is the mother of Aphrodite.
4. Personifications of dawn, sun, and moon.
5. Leto is the mother of Apollo and Artemis; Iapetos and Kronos are Titans (children of the earth and sky).
6. Earth and Ocean.

the thunderer shine with glee and ring, filled with voices
lily-soft and heavenly, and the peaks of snowy Olympos
and the dwellings of the gods resound. With their divine voices
they first sing the glory of the sublime race of the gods
from the beginning, the children born to Gaia and vast Ouranos[7]   45
and of their offspring, the gods who give blessings.
Then they sing of Zeus, father of gods and men—
they begin and end their song with him
and tell of how he surpasses the other gods in rank and might.
And then again the Olympian Muses and daughters of aegis-bearing Zeus   50
hymn the races of men and of the brawny Giants,
and thrill the heart of Zeus in the realm of Olympos.
Mnemosyne,[8] mistress of the Eleutherian hills,
lay with father Zeus and in Pieria gave birth to the Muses
who soothe men's troubles and make them forget their sorrows.   55
Zeus the counselor, far from the other immortals, leaped
into her sacred bed and lay with her for nine nights.
And when, as the seasons turned, the months waned,
many many days passed and a year was completed,
she gave birth to nine daughters of harmonious mind,   60
carefree maidens whose hearts yearn for song;
this was close beneath the highest peak of snowy Olympos,
the very place of their splendid dances and gracious homes.
The Graces and Desire dwell near them and take part
in their feasts. Lovely are their voices when they sing   65
and extol for the whole world the laws
and wise customs of all the immortals.
Then they went to Olympos, delighting in their beautiful voices
and their heavenly song. The black earth resounded with hymns,
and a lovely beat arose as they pounded their feet   70
and advanced toward their father, the king of the sky
who holds the thunderbolt that roars and flames.
He subdued his father, Kronos, by might and for the gods
made a fair settlement and gave each his domain.
All this was sung by the Olympian Muses,   75
great Zeus's nine daughters whose names are
Kleio, Euterpe, Thaleia, Melpomene,
Terpsichore, Erato, Polymnia, Ourania,
and Kalliope, preeminent by far,
the singers' pride in the company of noble kings.[9]   80
And if the daughters of great Zeus honor a king
cherished by Zeus and look upon him when he is born,
they pour on his tongue sweet dew
and make the words that flow from his mouth honey-sweet,
and all the people look up to him as with straight justice   85

---

7. Ouranos (Uranus) is Sky.
8. Memory.
9. The nine Muses preside over nine arts: Kleio over history, Euterpe over music, Thaleia over comedy, Melpomene over tragedy, Terpsichore over dance, Erato over lyric poetry, Polymnia over choral poetry, Ourania over astronomy, and Kalliope over epic.

he gives his verdict and with unerring firmness
and wisdom brings some great strife to a swift end.
This is why kings are prudent, and when in the assembly
injustice is done, wrongs are righted
by the kings with ease and gentle persuasion.   90
When such a king comes to the assembly he stands out;
yes, he is revered like a god and treated with cheerful respect.
Such is the holy gift the Muses give men.
The singers and lyre players of this earth
are descended from the Muses and far-shooting Apollon,   95
but kings are from the line of Zeus. Blessed is the man
whom the Muses love; sweet song flows from his mouth.
A man may have some fresh grief over which to mourn,
and sorrow may have left him no more tears, but if a singer,
a servant of the Muses, sings the glories of ancient men   100
and hymns the blessed gods who dwell on Olympos,
the heavy-hearted man soon shakes off his dark mood, and oblivion
soothes his grief, for this gift of the gods diverts his mind.
Hail, daughters of Zeus! Grant me the gift of lovely song!
Sing the glories of the holy gods to whom death never comes,   105
the gods born of Gaia and starry Ouranos,
and of those whom dark Night bore, or briny Pontos[1] fostered.
Speak first of how the gods and the earth came into being
and of how the rivers, the boundless sea with its raging swell,
the glittering stars, and the wide sky above were created.   110
Tell of the gods born of them, the givers of blessings,
how they divided wealth, and each was given his realm,
and how they first gained possession of many-folded Olympos.
Tell me, O Muses who dwell on Olympos, and observe proper order
for each thing as it first came into being.   115
Chaos[2] was born first and after it came Gaia
the broad-breasted, the firm seat of all
the immortals who hold the peaks of snowy Olympos,
and the misty Tartaros[3] in the depths of broad-pathed earth
and Eros,[4] the fairest of the deathless gods;   120
he unstrings the limbs and subdues both mind
and sensible thought in the breasts of all gods and all men.
Chaos gave birth to Erebos[5] and black Night;
then Erebos mated with Night and made her pregnant
and she in turn gave birth to Ether[6] and Day.   125
Gaia now first gave birth to starry Ouranos,
her match in size, to encompass all of her,
and be the firm seat of all the blessed gods.
She gave birth to the tall mountains, enchanting haunts
of the divine nymphs who dwell in the woodlands;   130
and then she bore Pontos, the barren sea with its raging swell.

---

1. Sea.
2. In Greek, "chaos" suggests a gap or chasm,
not necessarily disorder.
3. An abyss beneath the earth.

4. Sexual desire.
5. Darkness.
6. The upper part of the sky.

All these she bore without mating in sweet love. But then
she did couple with Ouranos to bear deep-eddying Okeanos,
Koios and Kreios, Hyperion and Iapetos,
Theia and Rheia, Themis and Mnemosyne, 135
as well as gold-wreathed Phoibe and lovely Tethys.
Kronos, the sinuous-minded, was her last-born,
a most fearful child who hated his mighty father.
Then she bore the Kyklopes, haughty in their might,
Brontes, Steropes, and Arges of the strong spirit, 140
who made and gave to Zeus the crushing thunder.
In all other respects they were like gods,
but they had one eye in the middle of their foreheads;
their name was Kyklopes because of this single
round eye that leered from their foreheads, 145
and inventive skill and strength and power were in their deeds.
Gaia and Ouranos had three other sons, so great
and mighty that their names are best left unspoken,
Kottos, Briareos, and Gyges, brazen sons all three.
From each one's shoulders a hundred invincible arms 150
sprang forth, and from each one's shoulders atop the sturdy trunk
there grew no fewer than fifty heads;
and there was matchless strength in their hulking frames.
All these awesome children born of Ouranos and Gaia
hated their own father from the day they were born, 155
for as soon as each one came out of the womb,
Ouranos, with joy in his wicked work, hid it
in Gaia's womb and did not let it return to the light.
Huge Gaia groaned within herself
and in her distress she devised a crafty and evil scheme. 160
With great haste she produced gray iron
and made a huge sickle and showed it to her children;
then, her heart filled with grief, she rallied them with these words:
"Yours is a reckless father; obey me, if you will,
that we may all punish your father's outrageous deed, 165
for he was first to plot shameful actions."
So she spoke, and fear gripped them all; not one of them
uttered a sound. Then great, sinuous-minded Kronos
without delay spoke to his prudent mother:
"Mother, this deed I promise you will be done, 170
since I loathe my dread-named father.
It was he who first plotted shameful actions."
So he spoke, and the heart of giant Earth was cheered.
She made him sit in ambush and placed in his hands
a sharp-toothed sickle and confided in him her entire scheme. 175
Ouranos came dragging with him the night, longing for Gaia's love,
and he embraced her and lay stretched out upon her.
Then his son reached out from his hiding place and seized him
with his left hand, while with his right he grasped
the huge, long, and sharp-toothed sickle and swiftly hacked off 180
his father's genitals and tossed them behind him—
and they were not flung from his hand in vain.

Gaia took in all the bloody drops that spattered off,
and as the seasons of the year turned round
she bore the potent Furies and the Giants, immense,   185
dazzling in their armor, holding long spears in their hands,
and then she bore the Ash Tree Nymphs of the boundless earth.
As soon as Kronos had lopped off the genitals with the sickle
he tossed them from the land into the stormy sea.
And as they were carried by the sea a long time, all around them   190
white foam rose from the god's flesh, and in this foam a maiden
was nurtured. First she came close to god-haunted Kythera
and from there she went on to reach sea-girt Cyprus.
There this majestic and fair goddess came out, and soft grass
grew all around her soft feet. Both gods and men   195
call her Aphrodite, foam-born goddess, and fair-wreathed Kythereia;
Aphrodite because she grew out of *aphros,* foam, that is,
and Kythereia because she touched land at Kythera.
She is called Kyprogenes, because she was born
in sea-girt Cyprus, and Philommedes, fond of a man's genitals,   200
because to them she owed her birth. Fair Himeros[7] and Eros
became her companions when she was born and when she joined the gods.
And here is the power she has had from the start
and her share in the lives of men and deathless gods:
from her come young girls' whispers and smiles and deception   205
and honey-sweet love and its joyful pleasures.
But the great father Ouranos railed at his own children
and gave them the nickname Titans, Overreachers,
because he said they had, with reckless power, overreached him
to do a monstrous thing that would be avenged someday.   210
Night gave birth to hideous Moros and black Ker[8]
and then to Death and Sleep and to the brood of Dreams.

* * *

From Works and Days[1]

This is why Zeus devised sorrows and troubles for men.
He hid fire. But Prometheus, noble son of Iapetos,[2]
stole it back for man's sake from Zeus, whose counsels are many.
In the hollow of a fennel stalk he slipped it away,
unnoticed by Zeus, who delights in thunder.   5
So the cloud-gatherer in anger said to him:
"Son of Iapetos, craftiest of all,
you rejoice at tricking my wits and stealing the fire
which will be a curse to you and to the generations that follow.

7. Longing.
8. Doom and Fate.
1. Translated by Apostolos N. Athanassakis.
Early in the poem, Hesiod urges his addressee
to work hard; this passage explains why humans

cannot simply live a life of ease.
2. Iapetos is a Titan, a child of the Earth
and Sky, part of the generation of divine
beings that preceded Zeus and the other
Olympians.

The price for the stolen fire will be a gift of evil 10
to charm the hearts of all men as they hug their own doom."
This said, the father of gods and men roared with laughter.
Then he ordered widely acclaimed Hephaistos[3] to mix earth with water
with all haste and place in them human voice
and strength. His orders were to make a face 15
such as goddesses have and the shape of a lovely maiden;
Athena was to teach her skills and intricate weaving,
and golden Aphrodite[4] should pour grace round her head,
and stinging desire and limb-gnawing passion.
Then he ordered Hermes[5] the pathbreaker and slayer of Argos 20
to put in her the mind of a bitch and a thievish nature.
So he spoke, and they obeyed lord Zeus, son of Kronos.
Without delay the renowned lame god fashioned from earth,
through Zeus's will, the likeness of a shy maiden,
and Athena, the gray-eyed goddess, clothed her and decked her out. 25
Then the divine graces and queenly Persuasion
gave her golden necklaces to wear, and the lovely-haired Seasons
stood round her and crowned her with spring flowers.
Pallas Athena adorned her body with every kind of jewel,
and the Slayer of Argos—Hermes the guide—through the will 30
of Zeus whose thunder roars placed in her breast
lies, coaxing words, and a thievish nature.
The gods' herald then gave her voice and called this woman
Pandora[6] because all the gods who dwell on Olympos
gave her as a gift—a scourge for toiling men. 35
Now when the Father finished his grand and wily scheme
he sent the glorious Slayer of Argos and swift messenger
to bring the gift of the gods to Epimetheus,[7]
who did not heed Prometheus's warning never to accept
a gift from Olympian Zeus, but send it back, 40
for fear that some evil might befall mortals.
First he accepted it and then saw the evil in it.
Earlier, human tribes lived on this earth
without suffering and toilsome hardship
and without painful illnesses that bring death to men— 45
a wretched life ages men before their time—
but the woman with her hands removed the great lid of the jar
and scattered its contents, bringing grief and cares to men.
Only Hope stayed under the rim of the jar
and did not fly away from her secure stronghold, 50
for in compliance with the wishes of cloud-gathering Zeus
Pandora put the lid on the jar before she could come out.
The rest wander among men as numberless sorrows,

3. God associated with technological skill and craftsmanship.
4. The goddess of sexual desire. Athena is the goddess of handicrafts and wisdom.
5. Messenger god, who killed the many-eyed

monster Argos.
6. The name means "all gift."
7. Brother of Prometheus. *Prometheus* suggests "forethought"; *Epimetheus*, "hindsight."

since earth and sea teem with miseries.
Some diseases come upon men during the day, and some   55
roam about and bring pains to men in the silence of night
because Zeus the counselor made them mute.
So there is no way to escape the designs of Zeus.
I will give you the pith of another story—if you wish—
with consummate skill. Treasure this thought in your heart: 60
men and gods have a common descent.
At first the immortals who dwell on Olympos
created a golden race of mortal men.
That was when Kronos was king of the sky,
and they lived like gods, carefree in their hearts,   65
shielded from pain and misery. Helpless old age
did not exist, and with limbs of unsagging vigor
they enjoyed the delights of feasts, out of evil's reach.
A sleeplike death subdued them, and every good thing was theirs;
the barley-giving earth asked for no toil to bring forth   70
a rich and plentiful harvest. They knew no constraint
and lived in peace and abundance as lords of their lands,
rich in flocks and dear to the blessed gods.
But the earth covered this race,
and they became holy spirits that haunt it,   75
benign protectors of mortals that drive harm away
and keep a watchful eye over lawsuits and wicked deeds,
swathed in misty veils as they wander over the earth.
They are givers of wealth by kingly prerogative.
The gods of Olympos made a second race   80
—a much worse one—this time of silver,
unlike the golden one in thought or looks.
For a hundred years they were nurtured by their prudent mothers
as playful children—each a big baby in his house—
but when they grew up and reached adolescence   85
they lived only for a short while, plagued by the pains
of foolishness. They could not refrain from reckless violence
against one another and did not want to worship the gods
and on holy altars perform sacrifices for them,
as custom differing from place to place dictates.   90
In time Zeus, son of Kronos, was angered and buried them
because they denied the blessed Olympians their due honors.
The earth covered this race, too;
they dwell under the ground and are called blessed mortals—
they are second but, still, greatly honored.   95
Zeus the father made a third race of mortals,
this time of bronze, not at all like the silver one.
Fashioned from ash trees, they were dreadful and mighty
and bent on the harsh deeds of war and violence;
they ate no bread and their hearts were tough as steel.   100
No one could come near them, for their strength was great
and mighty arms grew from the shoulders of their sturdy bodies.
Bronze were their weapons, bronze their homes,
and bronze was what they worked—there was no black iron then.

With their hands they worked one another's destruction   105
and they reached the dank home of cold Hades
nameless. Black death claimed them for all their fierceness,
and they left the bright sunlight behind them.
But when the earth covered this race, too,
Zeus, son of Kronos, made upon the nourishing land   110
yet another race—the fourth one—better and more just.
They were the divine race of heroes, who are called
demigods; they preceded us on this boundless earth.
Evil war and dreadful battle wiped them all out,
some fighting over the flocks of Oidipous   115
at seven-gated Thebes, in the land of Kadmos,
others over the great gulf of the sea in ships
that had sailed to Troy for the sake of lovely-haired Helen;
there death threw his dark mantle over them.
Yet others of them father Zeus, son of Kronos, settled at earth's ends,   120
apart from men, and gave them shelter and food.
They live there with hearts unburdened by cares
in the islands of the blessed, near stormy Okeanos,
these blissful heroes for whom three times a year
the barley-giving land brings forth full grain sweet as honey.   125
I wish I were not counted among the fifth race of men,
but rather had died before, or been born after it.
This is the race of iron. Neither day nor night
will give them rest as they waste away with toil
and pain. Growing cares will be given them by the gods,   130
and their lot will be a blend of good and bad.
Zeus will destroy this race of mortals
when children are born gray at the temples.
Children will not resemble their fathers,
and there will be no affection between guest and host   135
and no love between friends or brothers as in the past.
Sons and daughters will be quick to offend their aging parents
and rebuke them and speak to them with rudeness
and cruelty, not knowing about divine retribution;
they will not even repay their parents for their keep—   140
these law-breakers—and they will sack one another's city.
The man who keeps his oath, or is just and good,
will not be favored, but the evildoers and scoundrels
will be honored, for might will make right and shame will vanish.
Base men will harm their betters with words   145
that are crooked and then swear they are fair.
And all toiling humanity will be blighted by envy,
grim and strident envy that takes its joy in the ruin of others.
Then Shame and Retribution will cover their fair bodies
with white cloaks and, leaving men behind,   150
will go to Olympos from the broad-pathed earth
to be among the race of the immortals, while grief and pain
will linger among men, whom harm will find defenseless.

EARLY GREEK PHILOSOPHY[1]
seventh through fifth centuries B.C.E.

The earliest "scientific" thinkers of ancient Greece are known as the pre-Socratics, because historians have often seen a sharp break between their interests—mostly in the physical structure of matter—and those of philosophers after Socrates, who concentrated above all on ethics. Most of the thinkers quoted here lived in the Greek-speaking cities of Ionia, in modern Turkey. Unfortunately, we have access to the words and ideas of these people only in "fragments," which usually means that they were quoted or paraphrased by much later ancient authors. But it is clear, even from these fragmentary sources, that their ideas were revolutionary. Thales of Miletus (ca. 624–546 B.C.E.) was the first to suggest that the world is made of a single underlying substance, which he theorized was water. Thales made various mathematical discoveries and was probably the first person to predict a solar eclipse, in 585 B.C.E. Heraclitus (ca. 535–475 B.C.E.) was known for his obscurity in antiquity, but he seems to have theorized that change is the fundamental principle of the universe, which operates by a continual process of opposites turning into each other. Empedocles (ca. 490–430), a Greek living in Sicily, created a simplified version of this idea:

he suggested that the world works by a combination of love and strife, so that the four elements—air, earth, fire, and water—are constantly being conjoined and separated from one another. Anaxagoras (500–428 B.C.E.) came up with another variant on this idea, suggesting that the parts of the universe are in a constant process of separation and mixture, controlled by an underlying principle of intelligence, or mind. A little later in the fifth century B.C.E., the Greek atomists would develop the (startlingly modern) idea that the basic building blocks of matter are not fire, water, air, or earth but atoms and empty space (the void).

It is difficult to tell how shocking all these new theories were in the Greek world. There are stories about Anaxagoras being tried for impiety, but these are late and unreliable. Many Greeks in the sixth and fifth centuries B.C.E. seem to have been ready for a wide range of new speculations about the nature of the universe. Moreover, even the pre-Socratic speculators themselves seem often to have thought their new views were perfectly compatible with the old religious ideas about how the universe was made. Thales said that the world is made of water; but he also said, "Everything is full of gods."

---

1. All selections translated by Jonathan Barnes.

Thales[2]

Most of the first philosophers thought that principles in the form of matter were the only principles of all things. For they say that the element and first principle of the things that exist is that from which they all are and from which they first come into being and into which they are finally destroyed, its substance remaining and its properties changing. . . . There must be some nature—either one or more than one—from which the other things come into being, it being preserved. But as to the number and form of this sort of principle, they do not all agree. Thales, the founder of this kind of philosophy, says that it is water (that is why he declares that the earth rests on water). He perhaps came to acquire this belief from seeing that the nourishment of everything is moist and that heat itself comes from this and lives by this (for that from which anything comes into being is its first principle)—he came to his belief both for this reason and because the seeds of everything have a moist nature, and water is the natural principle of moist things.

Heraclitus[3]

Heraclitus of Ephesus is most clearly of this opinion [i.e. that everything will change into fire]. He holds that there is a world which is eternal and a world which is perishing, and he is aware that the created world is the former in a certain state. Now that he recognized that the world which is uniquely characterized by the totality of substance is eternal, is evident when he says:

The world, the same for all, neither any god nor any man made; but it was always and is and will be, fire ever-living, kindling in measures and being extinguished in measures.

And that he believed it to be generated and destructible is indicated by the following words:

Turnings of fire: first, sea; of sea, half is earth, half lightning-flash.

—He says in effect that, by reason and god which rule everything, fire is turned by way of air into moisture, the seed, as it were, of creation, which he calls sea; and from this, again, come earth and heaven and what they contain. He shows clearly in the following words that they are restored again and become fire:

Sea is dissolved and measured into the same proportion that existed at first.

And the same holds for the other elements.

---

2. None of Thales's own writings survive. This passage is an account of his views, and those of the other "first philosophers," by the much later (fourth century B.C.E.) philosopher Aristotle.

3. Heraclitus's work survives only through quotations and citations by later writers. This passage was written by a prominent Christian writer from the second century C.E., Clement of Alexandria (ca. 150–215 C.E.). Since Clement lived some seven hundred years after Heraclitus, he had a very different perspective on theology and creation; but his testimony is valuable because he must have read Heraclitus's book—which is now lost. The lines in italics are apparently direct quotations from Heraclitus, while those in regular font summarize his views.

Empedocles[4]

I will tell a two-fold story. At one time they grew to be one alone
from being many, and at another they grew apart again to be
   many from being one.
Double is the generation of mortal things, double their passing away:
one is born and destroyed by the congregation of everything,
the other is nurtured and flies apart as they grow apart again.   5
And these never cease their continual change,
now coming together by Love all into one,
now again all being carried apart by the hatred of Strife.
<Thus insofar as they have learned to become one from many>[5]
and again become many as the one grows apart,   10
to that extent they come into being and have no lasting life;
but insofar as they never cease their continual change,
to that extent they exist forever, unmoving in a circle.
   But come, hear my words; for learning enlarges the mind.
As I said before when I revealed the limits of my words,   15
I will tell a two-fold story. At one time they grew to be one alone
from being many, and at another they grew apart again to be
   many from being one—
fire and water and earth and the endless height of air,
and cursed Strife apart from them, balanced in every way,
and Love among them, equal in length and breadth.   20
Her you must regard with your mind: do not sit staring with your eyes.
She is thought to be innate also in the limbs of mortals,
by whom they think thoughts of love and perform deeds of union,
calling her Joy by name and Aphrodite,
whom no one has seen whirling among them—   25
no mortal man. Listen to the course of my argument, which does
   not deceive:
these are all equal and of the same age,
but they hold different offices and each has its own character;
and in turn they come to power as time revolves.
And in addition to them nothing comes into being or ceases.   30

Anaxagoras[6]

Mind is something infinite and self-controlling, and it has been mixed with no
thing but is alone itself by itself. For if it were not by itself but had been mixed
with some other thing, it would share in all things, if it had been mixed with
any. For in everything there is present a share of everything, as I have said earlier,
and the things commingled with it would have prevented it from controlling
anything in the way in which it does when it is actually alone by itself. For it is

---

4. This passage from Empedocles' poem "On Nature" is quoted by a philosophical writer from the fifth century C.E., Simplicius.

5. The angle brackets mean that this line may not belong in the original poem.

6. This passage is also quoted by Simplicius.

the finest of all things and the purest, and it possesses all knowledge about everything, and it has the greatest strength. And mind controls all those things, both great and small, which possess soul. And mind controlled the whole revolution, so that it revolved in the first place. And first it began to revolve in a small area, and it is revolving more widely, and it will revolve yet more widely. And mind recognizes all the things which are commingling and separating off and dissociating. And mind arranged everything—what was to be and what was and what now is and what will be—and also this revolution in which revolve the stars and the sun and the moon and the air and the ether which are separating off. But the revolution itself made them separate them off. And the dense is separating off from the rare, and the hot from the cold, and the bright from the dark, and the dry from the wet. And there are many shares of many things, but nothing completely separates off or dissociates one from another except mind. All mind, both great and small, is alike. Nothing else is alike, but each single thing is and was most patently those things of which it contains most.

LUCRETIUS

ca. 55 B.C.E.

The epic *On the Nature of Things*, by Lucretius (ca. 99–55 B.C.E.), is the only surviving work of an Epicurean Roman poet. Epicurus was a Greek philosopher who lived in the fourth and third centuries B.C.E. and whose philosophy emphasizes tranquility or peace of mind as the primary goal of human life. Epicureans believed that false beliefs—about the origins and nature of the universe and about death—and false fears about the gods are the primary sources of human anxiety. They were not atheists, but they denied that the gods played any part in the creation or direction of the universe; instead, the gods lived at the edge of the universe, in a state of perfect peace to which humans should aspire. Lucretius argues that the workings of the world that most humans falsely ascribe to divine intervention can all be explained in material terms; matter is composed of atoms, which are in a constant state of random motion, and this in itself is sufficient to explain the phenomena that we see around us. One of the most challenging aspects of Lucretius's work is the interplay between the scientific and the poetic, and between the materialist and the mythological. For instance, Lucretius denies that the gods direct the world, yet he begins his poem with a beautiful, moving description of how the goddess Venus controls every aspect of life on earth.

From On the Nature of Things[1]

From *Book I*

Mother of Romans, delight of gods and men,
Sweet Venus,[2] who under the wheeling signs of heaven
Rouse the ship-shouldering sea and the fruitful earth
And make them teem—for through you all that breathe
Are begotten, and rise to see the light of the sun;   5
From you, goddess, the winds flee, from you and your coming
Flee the storms of heaven; for you the artful earth
Sends up sweet flowers, for you the ocean laughs
And the calm skies shimmer in a bath of light.
And now, when the gates are wide for spring and its splendor   10
And the west wind, fostering life, blows strong and free,
Pricked in their hearts by your power, the birds of the air
Give the first sign, goddess, of you and your entering;
Then through the fertile fields the love-wild beasts
Frolic, and swim the rapids (so seized with your charm   15
They eagerly follow wherever you may lead);
Yes, across seas and mountains and hungering rivers
And the leaf-springing homes of the birds and the greening fields,
Into all hearts you strike your lure of love
That by desire they propagate their kinds.   20
And since it is you alone who govern the birth
And growth of things, since nothing without you
Can be glad or lovely or rise to the shores of light,
I ask you to befriend me as I try
To pen these verses *On the Nature of Things*   25
For my friend Memmius[3] whom you, goddess, have ever
Caused to excel, accomplished in all things.
All the more, goddess, grant them lasting grace!
In the meantime let the savage works of war
Rest easy, slumbering over land and sea.   30
For you alone can bless us mortal men
With quiet peace; Mars, potent of arms, holds sway
In battle, but surrenders at your bosom,
Vanquished by the eternal wound of love.
There, his chiseled neck thrown back, he gapes at you,   35
Goddess, and feeds his greedy eyes with love;
He reclines; his spirit lingers upon your lips.
Melting about him, goddess, as he rests
On your holy body, pour from your lips sweet nothings,
Seeking, renowned one, quiet peace for Rome.   40
For I cannot work with a clear mind while my country

---

1. Translated by Anthony M. Esolen.
2. Roman counterpart of the Greek goddess Aphrodite; goddess of sex and mother of Aeneas, founder of Rome. The opening of the poem is surprising, since Epicurean philosophers like Lucretius did not normally believe in the usual myths about the gods.
3. A Roman orator and apparently Lucretius's patron.

Suffers, nor can the illustrious scion of
The Memmian house neglect the common good.[4]

For by necessity the gods above
Enjoy eternity in highest peace,   45
Withdrawn and far removed from our affairs.
Free of all sorrow, free of peril, the gods
Thrive in their own works and need nothing from us,
Not won with virtuous deeds nor touched by rage.

Then withdraw from cares and apply your cunning mind   50
To hear the truth of reasoned theory,
That the verses I give you, arranged with diligent love,
You will not scorn before you understand.
I open for you by discussing the ultimate law
Of the gods and sky; I reveal the atoms, whence   55
Nature creates and feeds and grows all things
And into which she resolves them when they are spent;
"Matter," "engendering bodies," "the seeds of things"
Are other terms for atoms which I use
In setting forth their laws; and "first beginnings"—   60
For from these elements all the world is formed.

When before our eyes man's life lay groveling, prostrate,
Crushed to the dust under the burden of Religion
(Which thrust its head from heaven, its horrible face
Glowering over mankind born to die),   65
One man, a Greek, was the first mortal who dared
Oppose his eyes, the first to stand firm in defiance.[5]
Not the fables of gods, nor lightning, nor the menacing
Rumble of heaven could daunt him, but all the more
They whetted his keen mind with longing to be   70
First to smash open the tight-barred gates of Nature.
His vigor of mind prevailed, and he strode far
Beyond the fiery battlements of the world,
Raiding the fields of the unmeasured All.
Our victor returns with knowledge of what can arise,   75
What cannot, what law grants each thing its own
Deep-driven boundary stone and finite scope.
Religion now lies trampled beneath our feet,
And we are made gods by the victory.[6]

You hear these things, and I fear you'll think yourself   80
On the road to evil, learning the fundamentals
Of blasphemy. Not so! Too often Religion
Herself gives birth to evil and blasphemous deeds.

---

4. The poem must have been composed during one of the many Roman civil wars, which
dominated the first century B.C.E.
5. The Greek was the philosopher Epicurus.

6. The translation here is a little loose; in fact,
Lucretius would be reluctant to equate humans
with gods. The original literally means "Victory
makes us equal with the sky."

At Aulis, for instance:[7] the pride of the Greek people,
The chosen peers, defiled Diana's altar   85
With the shameful blood of the virgin Iphigenia.
As soon as they tressed her hair with the ritual fillet,
The tassels spilling neatly upon each cheek,
And she sensed her grieving father beside the altar
With the acolytes nearby, hiding the knife,   90
And countrymen weeping to look upon her—mute
With fear, she fell to her knees, she groped for the earth.
Poor girl, what good did it do her then, that she
Was the first to give the king the name of "father"?
Up to the altar the men escorted her, trembling;   95
Not so that when her solemn rites were finished
She might be cheered in the ringing wedding-hymn,
But filthily, at the marrying age, unblemished
Victim, she fell by her father's slaughter-stroke
To shove his fleet off on a *bon voyage!*   100
Such wickedness Religion can incite!

* * *

From *Book V*[8]

Just so, don't think that the holy seats of the gods
Are found in any region of the world.
Our minds can hardly see, remote from sense,
The slender substance of their deities.
As they ever elude the touch and the strike of our hands   5
They cannot touch a thing that we can touch.
A thing can't touch if it's not touchable.
Therefore their dwellings also must be different
From ours, and be as subtle as their bodies.
I'll prove this to you later, at some length.   10
Further, to say that for man's sake the gods
Wished to prepare this glorious world, and therefore
It's only right to praise their handiwork
And think it will be deathless and eternal—
Shocking, that what the gods in their timeless wisdom   15
Founded for mankind to outlast the ages
You should ever shake from its base by any force,
Pound it with words and topple it—Memmius, to
Invent such errors and paste them one to the next
Is stupid. What gain can our grateful hearts bestow   20
Upon the blessed immortal gods, that they
Might take one step to act on our behalf?

7. At Aulis, when the Greek ships gathered
to sail against Troy, they found themselves
becalmed. The priest Calchas said that Diana
(Artemis in the Greek pantheon) was angry
and could be appeased only if the Greek leader,
Agamemnon, killed his daughter Iphigeneia.

8. In this much later passage, Lucretius explains
why we should not accept the mythological
stories about the gods and their creation of the
world (like those found in Hesiod). He is not
arguing that gods do not exist but, rather, that
they do not intervene in human affairs.

What innovation after such long peace
Can lure them on to wish to change their lives?
Only someone whom the old order thwarted   25
Takes joy in a new one; but if nothing irksome
Has ever befallen you down the beautiful ages,
What could enkindle a love for novelty?
Their lives, I suppose, lay sunk in sorrow and darkness
Until there dawned the birthday of the world?   30
And what did it hurt, that *we* had not been made?
Now whoever's been born, he ought to want to stay
Alive, so long as pleasures keep their charm.
But for him who's never tasted the love of life—
Never been on the roster—what harm, in not being born?   35
The model, moreover, first planted in their minds
For the very idea of man and the birth of the world,
Where did they get it? How could they see what to make?
How could they ever find out about first-beginnings,
What those might make when you shuffle their order, if   40
Nature herself had given them no peek?
But many atoms jumbled in many ways,
Spurred on by blows through the endless stretch of time,
Are launched and driven along by their own weight
And come together and try all combinations,   45
Whatever their assemblies might create;
No wonder then, if into such arrangements
They happen also to fall, the tracks that would
Bring forth and still restore the universe.
But if I knew nothing of atoms, of what they were,   50
Still from the very ways of the heavens, from many
Other things I could name, I'd dare to assert
And prove that not for us and not by gods
Was this world made. There's too much wrong with it!
To start, what the vast sweep of the sky vaults over,   55
Mountains take up the lion's share and forests
Full of wild beasts, and sloughs and rocky cliffs
And the sea that holds the headlands far apart.
Worse, torrid heat and the constant fall of snow
Remove from mortals two-thirds of the earth.   60
And what's left to farm, Nature, through her own force,
Would choke with briars; man's strength must stand against it,
Inured to groan over the iron mattock,
To scratch a life by leaning hard at the plow.
The clods are rich, but the plow must turn them over,   65
Loosen and work them, prod them to give birth;
Crops won't spring up in the air all by themselves.
And now that our hard work has paid off in crops,
Breaking into leaf and flower over the fields,
The sun in the sky will scorch them in its rage   70
Or sudden storms will kill, or frost and ice,
Or the blasts of bullying winds will batter them down.
And the wild beasts that set your hairs to bristle,

Hostile to man, on the land, in the sea—why should
Nature create and feed them? Or why should the seasons 75
Bring pestilence? Why should early Death come stalking?
And then, a baby, tossed up like a mariner by
Fierce waves, lies naked on the beach, dumb, helpless
To save its life, when Nature has spilled it out
Of the clench of its mother's womb to the shores of light, 80
And fills the place with wailing—as is proper
For one whom so much suffering awaits.
But the various flocks and cattle and beasts grow up
And don't need rattles, or the kindly wet-nurse
Teasing with her sweet broken baby talk; 85
Don't need to change their clothes for the changing sky;
They need no weapons or high walls to guard
Their own, for the earth herself and artful Nature
Bring forth abundantly for all their needs.

First of all, since the stuff of earth and water, 90
And the soft breath of the air and the brilliant fire,
The four that make this universe,[9] are all
Composed of bodies that are born and die,
We must conclude the world is born, and dies.

For in fact, whatever we see whose parts and members 95
Are of a form to suffer birth and death,
Invariably these things must also die
And be born. Then since I see that the world's chief parts
And members are destroyed, and then reborn,
Surely the heavens and earth must also have 100
A time of origin and time of death.

Don't think that for my own sake in these questions
I've hustled it in as given that earth and fire
Die, and been sure of the death of water and air,
Claiming they'd all be born and grow again. 105
For starters, a good part of the earth, parched
By the relentless sun, stampeded under,
Is breathed forth in a wraith of floating dust
Which high winds scatter in the atmosphere.
And part of the soil is called to wash away 110
In storms, and the streams shave close and gnaw the rocks.
Besides, whatever the earth feeds and grows
Is restored to earth. And since she surely is
The womb of all things and their common grave,
Earth must dwindle, you see, and take on growth again. 115

9. It was commonly believed that the physical world is composed of four elements: earth, air,
fire, and water.

Ancient Egyptian Literature

Ancient Egypt has one of the world's oldest literary traditions. The only others that can match its antiquity and longevity are those of ancient Mesopotamia, China, and India. Stretching over almost three millennia, from perhaps as early as 2700 B.C.E. to the Common Era, the texts that emerged from ancient Egypt display a remarkable range of themes, genres, and styles: biographical inscriptions honoring the dead from tombs, stone stelae, and statues; hymns to the gods; accounts of travel adventures; laments of life and loss; wisdom texts advising future generations on how to live a good life in a flawed world; passionate love poetry; fantastic tales; and satirical fables.

For much of the Common Era, the literature of ancient Egypt was virtually unknown. Except for a few motifs and narratives that passed into Greek and from there into medieval European texts, the Egyptian literary tradition disappeared in the late fourth century C.E., and hieroglyphs, the "sacred engraved signs" of the Egyptian writing system, as the Greeks called them, could not be read. It was not until the nineteenth century that European scholars deciphered the forgotten language and gradually recovered Egypt's written heritage, including the rich body of its literature. We can now appreciate something of the variety, subtlety, and depth of that tradition and through it imagine the lives of kings and court officials, priests and scribes, merchants, and even peasants. Had the Egyptians set their writings down on durable clay tablets, as did their contemporaries in Mesopotamia, rather than on the fragile papyrus that they used, perhaps more works would have survived the ages. As it is, the fragments we know of and have been able to translate provide an exciting glimpse into one of the world's great civilizations.

THE ORAL AND WRITTEN IN EGYPTIAN LITERARY CULTURE

Egyptian texts were written in successive forms of the ancient Egyptian language, a member of the Afroasiatic-language family that was distantly related to ancient Semitic languages such as Hebrew and Akkadian. The classical form of the language is Middle Egyptian, written from about 2000 B.C.E. onward; although Middle Egyptian continued to be used as an elevated literary language, it was partly displaced by Late Egyptian (ca. 1300–900 B.C.E.), and later by Demotic (ca. 650 B.C.E.–third century C.E.). For most of its history, Egyptian was written in two main scripts: the more ceremonial and elaborate hieroglyphic script and the cursive form using ink on papyrus, called "hieratic" or "priestly writing" by the Greeks, which was used for everyday affairs and for religious texts.

Literacy was restricted to elites in ancient Egypt; perhaps as few as one in a hundred people could read and write. Thus, literature was not a medium for broad consumption by reading but was enjoyed mostly through oral delivery. Skillful speech was highly valued. The *Instruction of Ptahhotep,* a wisdom text, states that "perfect speech is more hidden than malachite, yet it is found with the maidservants at the millstones." The frequent appearance of storytellers in texts shows that the Egyptians saw written compositions as part of a culture of oral performance. Their great pleasure in wordplay, alliteration, and repetition—features that come to the fore in oral recitation—is another indicator of the connection between writing and performance.

The earliest longer texts come from the Old Kingdom in the third millennium B.C.E. Inscriptions carved in the tombs of high-ranking officials praise the moral worth of their occupants and sometimes tell of memorable events in their lives. They are in metrical form and carefully crafted. Thousands of such texts survive from the three millennia of ancient Egyptian history, and they constitute the largest category of continuous composition surviving from ancient Egypt. Also from the Old Kingdom come the Pyramid Texts, such as the *Cannibal Spell for King Unis,* which were carved in the burial apartments of the kings and some queens from about 2325 B.C.E. onward.

THE CLASSICAL PERIODS OF EGYPTIAN LITERATURE

Kings of the Middle Kingdom (ca. 1940–1650 B.C.E.) expanded the use of writing and scribal schools. The first great period of Egyptian literature, which formed part of this development, saw the production of tales, wisdom texts, dialogues, and complaints. These genres employ complex imaginary settings and narrative frames such as cycles of stories. This fictional literature set the standard for later times, which looked back in awe to the Middle Kingdom, considering it the classical age of Egyptian literature. *The Tale of Sinuhe*, a story of an ancient Egyptian's life abroad in Palestine and Syria and his triumphant return home, is the most elaborate example of these tales and features in our selections.

During the New Kingdom era (ca. 1500–1000 B.C.E.), motifs deriving from the Near East became more prominent in Egyptian literature, part of a larger cosmopolitanism that resulted from Egypt's active relations with other countries. A bold affirmation of this life and its pleasures appears in a new genre of the New Kingdom, short poems performed at social gatherings, poems in praise of city life, and "harpist's songs," depicted as being performed by harpists, which meditate on the next life. In defiance of Egypt's traditional lavish tomb culture, some of these poems claim that constructing a monumental tomb with expensive grave goods is worthless and that one should instead enjoy this life on earth to the full. The passionate love poems featured in our selections appear only during the New Kingdom and are another expression of a forceful embracing of pleasures in this life.

THE LATE PERIOD
(CA. 1000–30 B.C.E.)

The first millennium B.C.E. Egypt brought major upheavals to Egyptian society and literature. Egypt lost its imperial power and became the target of foreign invasions: as Nubians, Assyrians, Persians, and Alexander the Great's Macedonians swept through Egypt, ruling dynasties, the ethnic make-up of society, and religious beliefs and literary production changed drastically. Finally, in 30 B.C.E., Egypt lost its political independence; when Roman armies conquered the country, Queen Cleopatra, its last independent ruler, notoriously committed suicide by snakebite, and Egypt became a province of the Roman Empire.

Against this backdrop of foreign invasion and political instability, some literature of the Late Period carries more somber tones. For example, some autobiographical inscriptions now contain passages of intense grief. We can see this in our selections from the *Stela of Taimhotep*, a remarkable composition in which the dead woman Taimhotep narrates her life and concludes with shattering lyrics lamenting the desolation that awaits us after death.

The new form of written Egyptian, Demotic, which first appeared around 650 B.C.E., was used for literary compositions into the third century C.E. Literature in the classical language, modeled on the style of the Middle and New Kingdoms, continued to be transmitted, while Demotic developed new themes and longer tales. In our selections, a brilliant example of the elaborate character of Late Period narratives is *Setne Khamwas and Naneferkaptah*, a fantastic tale that involves magic, divine books that can kill, the obsessive search for ancient magical texts, grave robberies,

and embarrassing dreams in the king's presence. In the Late Period, Egyptians could situate their fictional tales in many different earlier periods, and they took full advantage of this possibility.

Egypt is one of the world's great civilizations. Its culture faded during the third century C.E. and became overshadowed by the Hellenistic and Roman cultures that increasingly permeated Egypt's society. By that date, Egyptian literature had flourished for three millennia, three times longer than the most ancient European literary traditions today. With its fabulous age and rich record of innovation, Egypt's literature uniquely showcases the dynamics of change over time. It humbles us as we think about whether and how the world's literary traditions stand the test of time.

THE TALE OF SINUHE
nineteenth century B.C.E.

Popular and preserved in many copies, *The Tale of Sinuhe* is one of the most elaborate of all Middle Kingdom tales. Although it circulated in manuscript form as a text for reading aloud, it has the form of an autobiographical inscription that would have adorned the tomb of the speaker, the courtier Sinuhe. Sinuhe tells the remarkable story of his escape from home, trials and triumphs abroad, and glorious return. He flees from Egypt as a young man during the political crisis surrounding the royal succession in the early twelfth dynasty. When the dynasty's founder, King Amenemhat I (ca. 1940–1910 B.C.E.) dies, Sinuhe is accompanying the king's son Senwosret I on a military campaign. Fearing that he

might become a victim of infighting, he deserts the army and settles in Palestine and Syria, where he spends his adult life making a successful career and living in prosperity. But, as he advances in years, his yearning to return to his homeland makes him accept a pardon from King Senwosret. After a dramatic encounter between the king and the former deserter, Sinuhe is accepted back into the Egyptian court, dies, and is buried in high honors. Sinuhe's story is a moving meditation on exile and home, life's patterns of adversity and success, royal mercy, and the nature and value of Egyptian identity. It speaks evocatively to our world today, where so many people experience displacement, exile, and the challenges of conflicting identities.

The Tale of Sinuhe[1]

The Patrician and Count,[2]
Governor of the Sovereign's Domains in the Syrian lands,
the True Acquaintance of the King, whom he loves,
the Follower, Sinuhe says,
'I was a Follower who followed his lord,   5
a servant of the Royal Chambers[3]
and of the Patrician Lady,[4] the greatly praised,
the Queen of Senwosret in Khnemsut,
the Princess of Amenemhat in Qanefru,
Nefru, the blessed lady.   10

REGNAL YEAR 30, MONTH 3 OF THE INUNDATION SEASON, DAY 7:[5]
The God ascended to his horizon;
the Dual King Sehotepibre
mounted to heaven,
and was united with the sun,   15
the divine flesh mingling with its creator.
The Residence was in silence,[6]
hearts were in mourning,
the Great Portal was shut,
the entourage was bowed down,   20
and the patricians were in grief.

Now his Majesty had sent out an expedition to the Libyan land,[7]
with his eldest son at its head,
the Perfected God[8] Senwosret;
but now he was returning, having carried off Libyan captives   25
and all sorts of cattle without number.
The Friends of the Court[9]
sent to the western border
to inform the prince
of the affair which had happened in the Audience Hall.[1]   30

1. Translated by Richard B. Parkinson.
2. Sinuhe's first two titles attribute to him the highest standing among the Egyptian elite. The title "Governor" is otherwise unknown and probably fictitious. "Follower" is used for servants, including someone of high rank who serves royalty.
3. The private apartments of the king and his family.
4. The first element in the title sequence of Nefru, the queen of Senwosret I; "Khnemsut" is a name for that king's pyramid complex. The queen is said to be the daughter of King Amenemhat I; Qanefru is the name of his pyramid complex.
5. The date formula is written in red, both to mark a significant event and in imitation of administrative documents. The next five lines give a poetic narration of the death of Amenemhat I, in which he is taken up to heaven like a

bird. "Dual King" is a title that evokes the two principal aspects of kingship. "Sehotepibre" is the throne name Amenemhat took on accession, in addition to the birth name that he retained.
6. The "Residence" is both the royal-palace complex and its surrounding town. The "Great Portal" is the principal entrance to the palace, which features again near the end of the tale. People are "bowed down" in a pose of mourning.
7. Probably an area near the Mediterranean coast to the west of the Nile delta.
8. A standard title of kings that indicates that they assumed the role of a junior god when they took the throne.
9. A formal title for members of a king's close entourage.
1. The official hall in which the king received visitors. The "affair" is the king's death, probably through assassination.

On the road the messengers found him.
They reached him at nightfall.
Not a moment did he wait;
the falcon flew off with his followers,[2]
without informing his expedition.
Now, when the royal children
accompanying him on this expedition were sent to,
one of them was summoned.
Now, when I was standing on duty,
I heard his voice as he spoke,
as I was a little way off.
My heart staggered, my arms spread out;
trembling fell on every limb.
I removed myself, leaping,
to look for a hiding place.
I put myself between two bushes,
until the traveller had parted from the road.

I travelled southwards.[3]
I did not plan to reach this Residence,
expecting strife would happen;
I did not think to live after him.
I went across Lake Maaty in the region of the Sycomore.
I came to the Isle of Sneferu.
I passed a day on the edge of a field.
When it was daylight again, I made an early start.
I met a man standing in my way.
He saluted me, though I was afraid of him.
When it was supper-time,
I had arrived at Cattle-Quay.

I crossed in a rudderless barge[4]
blown by the west wind.
I passed east of Iaku,
above Lady of the Red Mountain.
I gave my feet a northwards path,
and I reached The Walls of the Ruler,
made to beat back the Syrians.
I crouched down in a bush
for fear of being seen by the watcher
on duty upon the wall.

2. "Falcon" alludes to the description of
Amenemhat flying up to heaven, while the
mention of his entourage as "followers"
alludes to Sinuhe's description of himself as a
"Follower." Here, the king as falcon is a metaphor for swift travel, not for ascent to heaven.
3. Sinuhe moves down the Nile delta to its
apex, some way north of the royal residence
and a suitable place to cross the Nile. The

places named may be in the region of the great
pyramids of Giza.
4. Boats would have their rudders removed to
discourage theft. Metaphorically, the rudderless barge is a state that lacks leadership. After
crossing the river, Sinuhe moves north along
the eastern edge of the Nile delta to its northeast frontier fortifications.

I travelled in the night-time.[5]
When it was dawn I had reached Peten.
I alighted on an island of Kemur.
Thirst's attack overtook me,
and I was scorched, my throat parched.
I said, "This is the taste of death."
But I lifted up my heart, and gathered my limbs together,
as I heard the noise of cattle lowing, caught sight of Syrians,
and a leader of theirs, who had once been
in Egypt, recognized me.

Then he gave me water,
while he boiled milk for me.
I went with him to his tribe,
and what they did was good.
Country gave me to country.
I set out for Byblos; I got to Qedem.[6]
I had spent half a year there,
when Amunenshi carried me off.
He was the ruler of upper Retjenu,
and he told me, "You'll be happy with me,
for you'll hear the speech of Egypt."
He said this, knowing my character
and having heard of my understanding,
and the Egyptians who were with him there
had vouched for me.

Then he said to me, "Why did you come here?
Has anything happened in the Residence?"
Then I said to him, "It's that the Dual King Sehotepibre
has gone to the horizon,
and how this all happened is unknown."
But I spoke in half-truths.[7]
"I have come from the expedition to the Libyan land:
it was reported to me, and my heart failed
and carried me off on the ways of flight.
I had not been talked of, and my face had not been spat upon;
I had heard no reproaches; my name had not been heard
      in the herald's mouth.
I do not know what brought me to this country—it is like a
      plan of God."
Then he said unto me, "So how is that land
without him—that worthy God,
fear of whom is throughout the countries

70

75

80

85

90

95

100

105

110

5. Sinuhe has passed the wall and is in marshland just east of the border. He is found by
nomads, who offer him standard desert hospitality.
6. Byblos is a city on the Lebanon coast
with which Egypt had longstanding relations.
Qedem, which is a region rather than a specific

place, is probably inland to the east. Upper
Retjenu is perhaps in the same general area.
The presence of Egyptians in Amunenshi's
entourage implies that his polity is quite large.
7. This is the first of several passages in which
Sinuhe explores his own motivation for his
flight.

like Sekhmet's in a plague year?"[8]
I spoke thus to him, answering him,
"Indeed, his son has already entered the palace,[9]
and has taken up his father's inheritance.
Now, he is a God who is peerless,[1]   115
before whom no other exists.
He is a lord of understanding, excellent of plans, effective of orders;
coming and going are by his command.
He subjugates the countries.
His father stayed within his palace,   120
and he reported to him that what he had ordained was done.[2]

Now, he is a hero, active with his strong arm,
a champion without compare,
seen descending on barbarians, approaching the combat.
He curbs horns, weakens hands;   125
his foes cannot marshall troops.
He is vengeful, a smasher of foreheads;[3]
close to him no one can stand.
He is far-striding, destroying the fugitive;
there is no end for the man who shows him his back.   130
He is firm-hearted at the moment of forcing retreat.
He turns back again and again; he shows not his own back.
He is stout-hearted, seeing the masses;
he allows no rest around his heart.

He is bold, descending on Easterners;[4]   135
his joy is to plunder barbarians.
As soon as he takes up his shield, he tramples;
he needs no second blow to slay.
None can escape his arrow, none draw his bow.
As before the power of the Great One,   140
barbarians flee before him.
Having foreseen the end, he fights heedless of all else.

He is a lord of kindness, great of sweetness.
Through love he has conquered.
His city loves him more than its own members;   145
it rejoices at him more than at its God.
Men and women pass by, exulting at him.
He is a king, who conquered in the egg,
his eyes on it from birth.

---

8. Sekhmet is the lioness goddess of disease, but also of healing.

9. Senwosret I had probably been co-regent with Amenemhat for ten years, a hitherto unprecedented arrangement that is perhaps glossed over here.

1. For the next forty lines, Sinuhe pronounces a seemingly standardized eulogy of the king as

defender of Egypt and provider for his people.

2. Another likely allusion to the co-regency.

3. This evokes the icon of the king of Egypt smiting foreheads of enemies with a mace, which was known through its use on seals and other portable works of art.

4. These include Amunenshi, whom Sinuhe is addressing.

He makes those born with him plentiful. 150
He is unique, God-given.
How joyful this land, since he has ruled!
He extends its borders.

He will conquer southern lands, without yet considering
    northern countries.
He was begotten to strike Syrians, to trample Sand-farers. 155
Send to him, let him know your name,[5]
as a man far from his Majesty who enquires!
He will not fail to do good
for a country that will be loyal to him."

And he said unto me, "Well, Egypt is certainly happy, 160
knowing of his success.
But look, you are here,
and you will stay with me; I shall do you good."[6]
He placed me at the head of his children.
He joined me to his eldest daughter. 165
He had me make my choice of his country,
from the choicest of what was his,
on his border with another country.
It was a good land,
called Iaa.[7] 170
Figs were in it, and grapes;
its wine was more copious than its water;
great its honey, plentiful its moringa-oil,
with all kinds of fruit on its trees.
Barley was there, and emmer, and numberless were its 175
    cattle of all kinds.[8]
Now, what came to me as a favourite was great.
He appointed me the ruler of a tribe
of the choicest of his country.

Provisions and strong drinks were made for me,
with wine as a daily supply, and cooked flesh, 180
and roast fowl, as well as wild game.
They would snare and lay it all out for me,
as well as the catch of my own hounds.
Many sweets were made for me,
with milk in every cooked dish.[9] 185

5. Sinuhe finally adjusts what he says in order to relate it to Amunenshi.
6. Amunenshi's reply deflates the rhetoric of Sinuhe's speech.
7. The name of this area is known from lists of foreign places dating from about four hundred years after the *Tale of Sinuhe*, but perhaps deriving from knowledge of the text. It is uncertain whether Iaa is an invented locality or a real one.
8. The landscape is described as settled and agricultural, but later allusions make it appear seminomadic. "Moringa-oil" is the standard culinary oil of ancient Egypt.
9. A probable piece of local color that has parallels in more recent Middle Eastern cuisine and likely relates to Jewish prohibitions against mixing milk and meat.

I spent many years there,[1]
and my children became heroes,
each man subjugating his tribe.
The messenger who went north and south to the Residence[2]
would tarry for me. I would make all men tarry.   190
I would give water to the thirsty,[3]
and I returned the wanderer to his path and rescued the robbed.
The Syrians who became so bold[4]
as to resist the countries' rulers—I countered their movements.
This ruler of Retjenu   195
would have me do many missions
as the commander of his army.
Every country for which I set out,
I made my attack on it,
and it was driven from its grasslands and wells;   200
I plundered its cattle and carried off its inhabitants,
and their food was taken away.
I killed the people in it with my strong arm, my bow,
my movements, and my excellent plans.

In his heart I attained high regard;   205
he loved me, knowing my valour.
He placed me at the head of his children, having seen the
      strength of my arms.
A hero of Retjenu came
to provoke me in my tent;[5]
he was a peerless champion, who had subjugated all the land.   210
He said he would fight with me, he planned to rob me,
and thought to plunder my cattle, on the advice of his tribe.
That ruler conferred with me;
I spoke thus, "I do not know him.[6]
So am I some ally of his, to walk around in his camp?   215
Or does this mean that I've opened his private quarters,
      overturned his stockade?
It is resentment at seeing me do your missions.

How like am I to a bull of the roaming cattle in the midst
      of another herd,
whom the bull of that little herd attacks,
whom that long-horned bull is charging!   220

1. Sinuhe appears to stay about a generation in Iaa, but the tale's chronology is not very precise.
2. This alludes to diplomatic traffic and reminds the audience of the Egyptian speakers mentioned earlier in the text.
3. This is a standard good deed performed by members of the Egyptian elite; the next couple of actions are adjusted to the local context.
4. The "Syrians" are members of the numerous smaller local polities that are subordinate to "rulers." Sinuhe acts as general for Amunenshi ("This ruler of Retjenu," as the Syrian region was traditionally known), but the following passage gives him an almost royal role as a conqueror and defender of territory.
5. The "hero of Retjenu" is a local strongman. Sinuhe is presented here as living in a nomadic encampment.
6. Sinuhe's elaborate speech here is modeled on public rhetoric. Its depiction of the fight for status compares human beings to cattle and suggests that Sinuhe has been wrongly accused of trying to get at the hero's women.

Can an inferior ever be loved as a superior?
No barbarian can ever ally with a Delta man;[7]
what can establish the papyrus on the mountain?
Does that bull want to fight,
or does that champion bull want to sound a retreat   225
in terror of being equalled?

If he has the will to fight, let him speak his wish!
Does God not know what He has fated,
or does He know how it stands?"
When it was night I strung my bow and tried my arrows,[8]   230
sharpened my sword and polished my weapons.
When it was dawn, all Retjenu had come,
having incited its tribes and gathered its neighbouring
    countries,
for it had planned this fight; and yet every breast burned for me,
the wives jabbered, and every heart was sore for me,   235
saying, "Is there another man mighty enough to fight him?"

Then his shield, his axe,
his armful of javelins fell to me:
after I had escaped his weapons and made them pass by me,
with his arrows spent in vain,   240
one after the other,
he approached me, and I shot him;
my arrow stuck in his neck,
he cried out, and fell on his face.
I felled him with his own axe,   245
and gave my war cry on his back,
while every Asiatic[9] was bellowing.
To Montu[1] I gave praises,
while his supporters mourned for him.
This ruler Amunenshi   250
took me into his arms.
Then I carried off his property and plundered his cattle.
What he planned to do to me, I did to him;
I seized what was in his tent, and stripped his camp.
With this I became great, and grew copious of wealth,   255
and grew plentiful of cattle.

For now God has acted so as to be gracious to one with
    whom He was offended,[2]

---

7. Barbarians, who are generally nomads, are especially incompatible with the sedentary delta inhabitants. In the converse case, "papyrus," the habitat of which is the marshland of the Nile delta, cannot grow on a mountain.
8. Having been challenged by the hero, Sinuhe prepares to fight him. The duel is a spectacle for the whole region, in which Sinuhe is perceived as the underdog.

9. An archaic term here for local Syrians.
1. The god of war, who guides kings in battle.
2. A renewed meditation on Sinuhe's motivation for flight, which leads here into a lyrical celebration of his success, followed at once by a sense of loss because he is abroad. This long passage is presented as something like a soliloquy.

whom He led astray to another country.
Today, He is satisfied.
A fugitive takes flight because of his surroundings;
    but my reputation is in the Residence.   260
A creeping man creeps off because of hunger;
    but I give bread to my neighbour.
A man leaves his land because of nakedness;
    but I have bright linen, white linen.
A man runs off because of the lack of someone to send;
    but I am plentiful of serfs.
Good is my house, spacious my dwelling place,
    and memory of me is in the palace.
Whatever God fated this flight   265
—be gracious, and bring me home!
Surely You will let me see the place where my heart still stays!
What matters more than my being buried
in the land where I was born?
This is my prayer for help, that the good event befall,
that God give me grace!   270
May He act in this way, to make well the end of someone
    whom He made helpless,
His heart sore for someone He compelled
to live in a foreign country!
Does this mean that He is so gracious today as to hear the
    prayer of someone far off
who shall then turn from where he has roamed the earth   275
to the place from which he was carried away?
May the king of Egypt be gracious to me,[3]
that I may live on his grace!
May I greet the Mistress of the Land who is in his palace,
and hear her children's messages!   280
So shall my limbs grow young again, for now old age has fallen:
weakness has overtaken me,
my eyes are heavy, and my arms weak;
my legs have ceased to follow, and my heart is weary;
I am near to dying.   285
May they lead me to the cities of eternity![4]
May I follow the Lady of All,
and then she shall tell me that all is well with her children!
May she pass eternity above me![5]

Now the Majesty of the Dual King Kheperkare was told   290
about the state of affairs in which I was.
And his Majesty sent to me,
with bounty of royal giving,

---

3. Sinuhe turns to thinking of the king and then of the queen mother, whom he used to serve.
4. The king and his family should provide for Sinuhe in death. In some periods kings donated monumental tombs to key members of the elite.

5. The queen mother, the "Lady of All," is assimilated to the sky goddess, Nut, who is in turn thought of as the lid of the coffin in which Sinuhe wishes to be laid to rest. In myth Nut is the ancestress of the king of Egypt.

to gladden the heart of this humble servant
like any ruler of a country,
and the royal children who were in his palace let me hear
their messages.[6]

Copy of the Decree Brought to this Humble Servant[7]
about his Being Brought Back to Egypt:
"Horus Living-of-Incarnations;
Two Ladies Living-of-Incarnations;
Golden Horus Living-of-Incarnations;
Dual King Kheperkare;
Son of Re Senwosret
—may he live for all time and eternity!
Royal Decree to the Follower Sinuhe:
Look, this decree of the king is brought to you
to inform you that your roving through countries,
going from Qedem to Retjenu,
country giving you to country,
was at the counsel of your own heart.[8]
What had you done, that you should be acted against?
You had not cursed, that your speech should be punished.
You had not spoken in the officials' council, that your
utterances should be opposed.
This idea carried off your heart—
it was not in my heart against you.
This your Heaven, who is in my palace, endures
and flourishes in the kingship of the land
today as she did before,
and her children are in the Audience Hall.

You will store up the wealth given by them,
and live on their bounty.[9]
Return to Egypt!
And you will see the Residence where you grew up,
kiss the earth at the Great Portal,[1]
and join the Friends.
For today you have already begun to be old, have lost your virility,
and have in mind the day of burial,
the passing to blessedness.

6. The royal children should now be mature adults; here the tale condenses events.
7. The heading to the king's letter to Sinuhe is written in red to mark its significance. Royal communications are known as "decrees" rather than "letters." The full five-part titulary of Senwosret I as king and a line of good wishes follow the heading. The heading of the decree is then repeated in abbreviated form.
8. The king attributes responsibility for flight to Sinuhe himself. The next three lines are sub-

tly different from Sinuhe's earlier statement to Amunenshi that no one had sought to accuse or pursue him.
9. This implies that the queen mother and royal children would provide the resources to maintain Sinuhe on his return.
1. The ceremonial entrance to the royal-palace complex, where both foreigners and Egyptians were expected to prostrate themselves and kiss the earth.

A night vigil will be assigned to you, with holy oils[2]
and wrappings from the hands of Tayet.
A funeral procession will be made for you on the day of
    joining the earth,
with a mummy case of gold,
a mask of lapis lazuli,
a heaven over you,[3] and you placed in a hearse,
with oxen dragging you,
and singers going before you.
The dance of the Oblivious ones[4] will be done at the mouth
    of your tomb-chamber,
and the offering-invocation recited for you;
sacrifices will be made at the mouth of your offering-chapel,
and your pillars will be built of white stone
in the midst of the royal children's.
Your death will not happen in a foreign country;
Asiatics will not lay you to rest;
you will not be put in a ram's skin[5] when your coffin is made.
This is too long to be roaming the earth!
Think of your corpse—and return!"
As I stood in the middle of my tribe, this decree reached me.
It was read to me and I prostrated myself,
I touched the earth
and scattered it on my chest;
I roved round my camp, shouting and saying,
"How can this be done for a servant
whose heart led him astray to strange countries?
So good is the kindness which saves me from death!
Your spirit will let me make my end
with my limbs at home!"

Copy of the Reply to this Decree:
"The servant of the palace, Sinuhe says,
'Most happy welcome!
Concerning this flight which your humble servant[6] made in
    his ignorance:
It is your spirit, Perfected God, Lord of the Two Lands,
which is loved by the Sungod, and favoured by Montu Lord
    of Thebes;
Amun Lord of the Throne of the Two Lands,[7]

(line numbers: 330, 335, 340, 345, 350, 355, 360)

---

2. A brief allusion to mummification and attendant rituals. Tayet is the goddess of weaving.
3. A canopy placed over the mummy in its
coffin for the funeral procession.
4. A dance known from tomb reliefs of the third
millennium, and a mark of the highest status.
5. A typical burial for a nomad. From an Egyptian perspective, Syrians are nomads who have
uncouth burial practices.
6. Letter writers term themselves "(humble)
servants"; the king's decree and Sinuhe's reply
are thus an exchange of letters.

7. Amun was the dynastic god of the twelfth
dynasty. The other deities named are a group
relating to Thebes followed by gods of the east,
where Sinuhe is, and gods of foreign lands.
Sopdu-Neferbau-Semseru is a form of an eastern Delta god that is otherwise unknown. The
Lady of Imet is Wadjet, the serpent deity whose
figure was worn as a protective emblem on the
king's crown. Wereret is a form of Hathor, and
Punt is a real but also semimythical land bordering the southern Red Sea.

Sobek-Re, Horus, Hathor,
Atum and his company of Gods, 365
Sopdu-Neferbau-Semseru the eastern Horus,
the Lady of Imet—may she enfold your head!—
the divine Council upon the Flood,
Min-Horus in the midst of the countries,
Wereret Lady of Punt, 370
Nut, Haroeris-Re,
and all the Gods of the Homeland and the islands of the Sea—
may they give life and dominion to your nostrils,
endow you with their bounty,
and give you eternity without limit, 375
all time without end!
May fear of you resound in lands and countries,
with the circuit of the sun curbed by you![8]
This is the prayer of a humble servant for his lord,
who saves from the West. 380
The lord of perception, perceiver of the people,[9]
perceives as the Majesty of the Court[1]
what your humble servant was afraid to say—
it is like an unrepeatably great matter.
O great God, equal of the Sungod in understanding 385
    someone who willingly serves him!
Your humble servant is in the hand of him who enquires after him:
these things are placed at your disposal.
Your Majesty is Horus the conqueror;
your arms are mighty against all lands.
Now, may your Majesty command that he be made to bring 390
    the Meki man from Qedem,[2]
the settler from out of Keshu,
and the Menus man from the lands of the Fenkhu.
They are rulers who are well known,
who live by love of you.
Without calling Retjenu to mind—it is yours, even like your hounds! 395

This flight which your humble servant made—
I had not planned it. It was not in my heart.[3]
I had not thought of it. I know not what parted me from
    my place.
It was like the nature of a dream,
like a Delta man seeing himself in Elephantine,[4] 400

8. The sun encircles the known world, which the king of Egypt can claim to dominate.
9. The king's perception, which is comparable with that of the Sungod, is his most valuable quality for the elite, because through it he knows what they need.
1. The palace and the king's entourage are personified manifestations of the king himself.
2. Three local rulers are mentioned, from different parts of Syria. "Meki man" and "Menus man" are terms for rulers, following a usage known from Near Eastern texts of the same general period.
3. This is Sinuhe's final presentation of the reasons for his flight, adapted here to exalt the status of the king.
4. The southernmost town of Egypt, in a narrow stretch of land surrounded by desert. "Marshy lagoons" contrast strongly with the landscape of the south.

a man of the marshy lagoons in Southern Egypt.
I had no cause to be afraid; no one had run after me.
I had heard no reproaches; my name had not been heard in
     the herald's mouth.
Only—that shuddering of my limbs,
my feet hastening,   405
my heart overmastering me,
the God who fated this flight dragging me away!
I was not presumptuous before,
for a man respects him who is acknowledged by his land,
and the Sungod has put respect for you throughout the land,   410
and terror of you in every country.
Whether I am at home,
whether I am in this place—
it is you who veils this horizon of mine.
The sun shines for love of you;[5]   415
the water of the river
is drunk when you wish;
the air of heaven
is breathed when you say.

Your humble servant will hand over to the chicks[6]   420
which your humble servant has begotten in this place.
A journey has been made for your humble servant!
May your Majesty do as you desire!
Men live on the breath of your giving:
may the Sungod, Horus, and Hathor love   425
these your noble nostrils,
which Montu Lord of Thebes desires
to live for all time!'"
I was allowed to spend a day in Iaa,
handing over my property to my children;   430
my eldest son was in charge of my tribe,
and all my property was his—
my servants, all my cattle,
my fruit, and all my orchard trees.
This humble servant then came southwards,   435
and I halted at the Ways of Horus.[7]
The commander there who was in charge of the garrison
sent a message to the Residence to inform them.

And his Majesty caused a worthy Overseer of the Peasants
     of the Royal Household to come,
accompanied by laden boats,   440
and bearing bounty of royal giving
for the Syrians who had come with me,

5. The section concludes with a brief lyrical passage evoking the idea that even foreigners depend
on the king of Egypt for the air they breathe.
This is taken up again in the next passage.
6. The family Sinuhe has raised in exile. The

letter concludes with an abbreviated mention
of the deities under whom Senwosret I rules.
7. The end of the route across North Sinai from
Palestine, where a fortress marked the Egyptian
frontier at the northeast corner of the Nile delta.

leading me to the Ways of Horus;
and I announced each one by his name.[8]
Every serving man was at his duty.   445
I set sail,
with kneading and brewing beside me,
until I reached the harbour of Itj-tawi.[9]
When it was dawn, very early,[1]
they came and summoned me;   450
ten men coming,
ten men going,
ushering me to the palace.

I touched the ground between the sphinxes,[2]
as the royal children stood in the portal, receiving me;   455
and the Friends who usher to the Pillared Hall
were showing me the way to the Audience Hall.
I found his Majesty on the great throne
in the portal of electrum.[3]
Then I was stretched out prostrate,[4]   460
unconscious of myself in front of him,
while this God was addressing me amicably.
I was like a man seized in the dusk,
my soul had perished, my limbs failed,
my heart was not in my body.   465
I did not know life from death.

And his Majesty said to one of these Friends,
"Raise him up, let him speak to me!"
And his Majesty said, "Look, you have returned after
     roaming foreign countries,
after flight has made its attack on you;   470
you are now elderly, and have reached old age.
Your burial is no small matter;
you will not be laid to rest by barbarians.
Act against yourself, act against yourself no more!
You did not speak when your name was announced—   475
are you afraid of punishment?"[5]
I answered this with the answer of a frightened man:
"What does my lord say to me, that I can answer?

8. This passage presents the reception of a diplomatic mission. The Syrians have provided safe passage to Sinuhe; it is not stated whether they too continue by boat to the Residence.
9. The name of the twelfth-dynasty royal residence, perhaps near Lisht to the south of ancient Memphis.
1. In antiquity business probably followed the natural rhythm of the day. Here, the association with dawn also suggests a new beginning and integration with the king's role as manifestation of the Sungod on earth.
2. Protective sphinx statues would be set up

beside the entrance gateway to the palace complex.
3. The king probably sits in a niche. Electrum is a white alloy of gold and silver; the area may either have been painted white or gilded with electrum.
4. Overawed, Sinuhe loses consciousness as he prostrates himself before the king. The following passage echoes Sinuhe's earlier sense of being near death when he left Egypt and was rescued by nomads.
5. The king acts the part of an angry god.

For this is no disrespect towards God, but is a terror
which is in my body like that which created the fated flight.[6]   480
Look, I am in front of you, and life is yours;
may your Majesty do as he desires!"

And the royal children were ushered in,
and his Majesty said to the Queen,
"Look, Sinuhe has returned as an Asiatic,   485
an offspring of the Syrians!"
She gave a very great cry,[7]
and the royal children shrieked as one.
And they said unto his Majesty,
"Is it really he,   490
sovereign, my lord?"
And his Majesty said, "It is really he."
Now they had brought with them their necklaces,[8]
their rattles and their sistra.
And they presented them to his Majesty: 495
"Your hands upon this beauty, enduring king,
these insignia of the Lady of Heaven!
May the Golden One give life to your nostrils,
the Lady of Stars enfold you!
South-crown fares north, North-crown south,[9]   500
joined and made one
in the words of your Majesty,
on whose brow the uraeus is placed!

You have delivered the poor from evil.
So may the Sungod, Lord of the Two Lands, be gracious to you!   505
Hail to you, as to the Lady of All!
Slacken your bow, withdraw your shaft![1]
Give breath to him who suffocates!
Give back the good we give on this good day—[2]
present us with North Wind's Son,[3]   510
the barbarian born in the Homeland!
Through fear of you he took flight,
through terror of you he left the land.

6. Sinuhe makes one last allusion to the motivation for his flight. In the next line he evokes
the conception that a man's life depends on the
king, who in turn receives it from the Sungod.
7. This evokes the role of goddesses in rituals,
often acted by women, in which they ululate.
The royal children's "shriek" is probably both
childish and a reference to ritual shouting.
8. The text mentions three ritual instruments
(one of them a necklace), used in the cult of
the goddess Hathor, with whom the queen is
identified. "Sistra" (singular *sistrum*) are a special type of metallic rattle. Hathor's role is to
pacify the angry Sungod. The following song
names Hathor as the "Golden One"; she is also
the "Lady of Stars."

9. The two principal crowns of the king represent the halves of the country and are united
in the double crown on the king's head. The
"uraeus" is the fire-spitting protective snake
that identifies the king and was alluded to earlier as the Lady of Imet.
1. The king takes on the role of the creator god
Atum, who sometimes holds a bow and arrow.
2. The "good we give" is their ritual presentation of the emblems of Hathor.
3. A pun on the name of *Sinuhe* that refers to
his exile in Syria, to the north of Egypt, while
evoking the breeze that alleviates the heat in
Egypt. Sinuhe's own name has occurred only
twice in the text.

A face that has seen your face shall not pale!
An eye that has gazed at you shall not fear!"   515

And his Majesty said, "He shall not fear,
he shall not gibber in terror!
He will be a Friend among the officials,
and he will be appointed amongst the entourage.
Proceed to the Robing Chamber to attend on him!"   520
I went forth from the Audience Hall,
with the royal children giving me their hands.
And afterwards, we went through the Great Portal.[4]
I was appointed to the house of a prince,[5]
with costly things in it, with a bathroom in it   525
and divine images of the horizon,[6]
with treasures from the Treasury in it,
clothes of royal linen,
myrrh and kingly fine oil,
with officials whom the king loved in every room,   530
and every serving man at his duty.

The years were made to pass from my limbs;
I became clean-shaven, and my hair was combed.
A load was given back to the foreign country,[7]
and clothes back to the Sand-farers.   535
I was clad in fine linen;
I was anointed with fine oil.
I slept in a bed.
I returned the sand to those who are upon it
and the tree oil to those smeared with it.   540

I was given the house of a Governor,
such as belongs to a Friend.
Many craftsmen were building it,
all its trees were freshly planted.
Meals were brought to me from the palace,[8]   545
three and four times a day,
as well as what the royal children gave,
without making a moment's ceasing.
A pyramid of stone was built for me,[9]
in the midst of the pyramids.   550
The masons who construct the pyramid measured out its foundations;

4. Sinuhe and the royal children leave the palace complex after his audience with the king.
5. This is the first specific mention of a male child of the king. The description of his house is probably close to that of a palace.
6. It is not clear what this line refers to. The "horizon" is the place of sunrise, also a euphemism for the tomb. Perhaps houses belonging to the royal family had wall paintings. Only kingly buildings would have had images of deities.
7. The dirt from Syria is washed off Sinuhe. A couple of variants of this idea follow. "Tree oil" is seen as inferior and foreign.
8. Dependence on central kitchens appears to have been common in the ancient world. Sinuhe does not seem to receive a household of his own servants.
9. No pyramid of a nonroyal person is known from this period. Either the word for "pyramid" is used with a broader meaning or the description is hyperbolic.

the draughtsman drew in it;
the overseer of sculptors carved in it;
the overseer of the works which are in the burial grounds
    busied himself with it.
All the equipment to be put in a tomb shaft—   555
its share of these things was made.
I was given funerary priests;[1]
a funerary demesne was made for me,
with fields in it and a garden in its proper place,
as is done for a Chief Friend.   560
My image was overlaid with gold,[2]
and its kilt with electrum.
It is his Majesty who has caused this to be done.
There is no other lowly man for whom the like was done.
I was in the favours of the king's giving,   565
until the day of landing came.'[3]

So it ends, from start to finish,[4]
as found in writing.

---

1. Sinuhe receives an endowment to support and continue his mortuary cult after death and burial. At the same time, the "garden" implies that this is a place of delight to which his spirit could return from the next world.
2. No gilded statue of a nonroyal person is known; gilding seems to have been reserved for the gods and the king. This is another instance of likely hyperbole, as is implied by the next two lines. As he dies and is buried, Sinuhe's status becomes higher even than that of a normal member of the elite.
3. A euphemism for death. Since most travel in Egypt was by boat, one "landed" on the other side after death.
4. A short note by the copyist, known as a colophon, written in red at the end of the text.

EGYPTIAN LOVE POEMS[1]
ca. 1300–1100 B.C.E.

Although love poetry must have existed in oral form in earlier periods, love poems only survive on papyri, potsherds, and flakes of limestone from the later part of the New Kingdom. Looking at the women musicians and nearly nude girls singing and dancing in the paintings on tomb walls, we can imagine that love songs were performed with music and dance at banquets. Composed in rather informal, at times graphic language, similar texts were also used in the cult of goddesses and in praise of royal women. Egyptian love poetry shows striking parallels with love poetry of other Near Eastern traditions, such as the somewhat later Song of Songs in the **Hebrew Bible**.

1. All selections translated by Michael V. Fox.

The lovers in the poems are young and often not yet free from parental supervision. As a gesture of endearment, they address each other as "brother" and "sister," words that have a broad meaning in ancient Egyptian. Roughly half of the poems are spoken by the girl, and half by the boy. (A small group, not represented in this selection, gives the words of the garden tree in whose shade the girl and boy have a tryst.) Many poems imagine situations in which the lovers might meet and make themselves attractive to each other: by going into the water to retrieve a fish—an erotic symbol—the girl, for example, can make her dress transparent and expose her charms. Many of the poems brim with imagery of the pleasures of desire and sex, but some also remind us how fleeting love can be: in one poem the girl worries, after the lovers have spent the night together, that the boy is now more interested in breakfast than in staying with her.

The Beginning of the Song That Diverts the Heart

(*Girl*)
How beautiful is your beloved,[2]
    the one adored of your heart,
        when she has returned from the meadow!
My beloved, my darling,
    my heart longs for your love—   5
        all that you created!
I say to you:
    See what happened!
I came ready to trap birds,
    my snare in one hand,   10
my cage in the other,
    together with my mat.[3]
All the birds of the land Punt[4]
    have descended on Egypt,
        anointed with myrrh.   15
The first to come
    takes my bait.
Its fragrance comes from Punt,
    its claws full of balm.[5]
My heart desires you.   20
    Let us release it[6] together.
I am with you, I alone,
    to let you hear the sound of my call,[7]
        for my lovely myrrh-anointed one.

2. In the original, this is literally "your sister." *Sister* and *brother* are frequent terms of affection in the Egyptian love songs. The terms imply intimacy, not consanguinity.
3. Perhaps to be placed as a cover over the birdcage.
4. A region bordering on the southern Red Sea from which aromatics came, as well as an ideal location known as "God's Land."

5. Or "its claws are caught by the balm." (The Egyptian can be read as a double entendre.) Birds were sometimes trapped by pitch smeared on a tree.
6. "It" is the "bait" mentioned before. This probably refers to the fulfilment of sexual desire.
7. Fowlers imitated bird calls to lure birds to the trap.

You are here with me,
    as I set the snare. 25
Going to the field is pleasant (indeed)
    for one who loves it.[8]

[My god, my Lotus . . .]

(Girl)
My god, my lotus . . .[1]
The north wind blows . . .
    How pleasant it is to go to the river. . . .
My heart longs to go down
    to bathe before you, 5
that I may show you my beauty
    in a tunic of the finest royal linen,
drenched in fragrant oils,
    my hair plaited in reeds.
I'd go down to the water with you,
    and come out to you carrying a red fish,[2] 10
        which feels just right in my fingers.
I'd set it before you,
    while gazing at your beauty.
O my hero, my beloved,
    come and see me! 15

(Boy)
My beloved's love
    is over there, on the other side,
The river surrounds my body.[3]
    The flood waters are powerful in this season,
        and a crocodile waits on the sandbank. 5
Yet I went down to the water
    to wade through the flood,
        my heart brave in the channel.
I found the crocodile to be like a mouse,[4]
    and the surface of the water like dry land to my feet. 10
It is her love
    that makes me strong.
        She casts a water spell for me!
I see my heart's beloved
    standing right before me! 15

---

8. Just what "it" refers to is vague, perhaps intentionally so. Is it bird trapping? Lovemaking?
1. The lotus was the most important Egyptian flower, whose aroma was held to excite the senses. The "north wind" is the breeze that makes the heat bearable and brings the breath of life.
2. A tilapia, a well-known erotic symbol that was also used as an amulet made of red stone.
3. He has—at least in imagination—stepped into the Nile, braving its dangers to reach the girl on the other side.
4. This alludes to tales of magic in which a magician can turn a tiny figure into a crocodile and vice versa.

(*Boy*)
My beloved has come,
     my heart rejoices,
          my arms are open to embrace her.
My heart is as happy in its place
     as a fish in its pond.
O night, you are mine forever,   5
     since my lady came to me!

[I wish I were her Nubian maid]

(*Boy*)
I wish I were her Nubian maid,
     her attendant in secret,
          as she brings her a bowl of mandragoras.[1]
It is in her hand,
     while she gives pleasure.   5
In other words:
she would grant me
     the hue of her whole body.[2]

(*Boy*)
I wish I were the laundryman
     of my beloved's clothes,
          for even just a month!
I would be strengthened
     by grasping the garments   5
          that touch her body.
For I would be washing out the moringa oils[3]
     that are in her kerchief.
Then I'd rub my body
     with her castoff garments,   10
          and she . . .
O how I would be in joy and delight,
     my body vigorous!

(*Boy*)
I wish I were her little signet ring,
     the keeper of her finger!
I would see her love[4]
     each and every day,
And I would steal her heart.   5

---

1. The mandragora fruit was thought to be an aphrodisiac. It was also an erotic symbol, both for its flower and probably for its long taproot.
2. In the boy's fantasy, he is a maidservant in the girl's bedchamber. He would offer fruit while the girl gave him pleasure. That is to say, she would let him see her naked.
3. Moringa oil was the normal ancient Egyptian oil, and evidently could be perfumed.
4. Her capacity to inspire love.

[I passed close by his house]

Sixth Stanza[1]

(*Girl*)
I passed close by his house,
    and found his door ajar.
My beloved was standing beside his mother,
    and with him all his brothers and sisters.
Love of him captures the heart   5
    of all who walk along the way—
a precious youth without peer,
    a lover excellent of character!
He gazed at me when I passed by,
    but I must exult alone.   10
How joyfully does my heart rejoice, my beloved,
    since I first saw you!
If only mother knew my heart
    she would go inside for a while.
        O Golden One,[2] put that in her heart!   15
Then I could hurry to my beloved
    and kiss him in front of everyone,
        and not be ashamed because of anyone.
I would be happy to have them see
    that you know me,   20
        and would hold festival to my Goddess.
My heart leaps up to go forth
    that I may gaze on my beloved.
How lovely it is to pass by![3]

[Seven whole days]

Seventh Stanza

(*Boy*)
Seven whole days[1] I have not seen my beloved.
Illness has invaded me,
    my limbs have grown heavy,
        and I barely sense my own body.
Should the master physicians come to me,   5
    their medicines could not ease my heart.
The lector priests[2] have no good treatment,
    because my illness cannot be diagnosed.
But if someone tells me, "Here she is!"—that will revive me.
    Her name—that is what will get me up.   10

---

1. This poem and the next are excerpted from a set of numbered stanzas.
2. Hathor, the goddess of love.
3. Each stanza in this seven-stanza song starts and ends by punning on a word. In Egyptian *six* and *pass by* sound alike.

1. The number seven is used because this is the seventh stanza. Ancient Egypt did not have a seven-day week.
2. Specialists in religious and magical texts. Here the term means "magicians."

The coming and going of her messengers—
    that's what will revive my heart.
More potent than any medicine is my beloved for me;
    more powerful than the *Physician's Manual*.
Her coming in from outside is my amulet.[3]   15
    If I see her, I'll become healthy.
If she but gives me a glance, my limbs will regain vigor.
    If she speaks, I'll grow strong.
If I hug her, she'll drive illness from me.
    But she has been gone for seven days.   20

[Am I not here with you?]

(*Girl*)
Am I not here with you?
    Then why have you set your heart to leave?
        Why don't you embrace me?
Has my deed come back upon me?
If you seek to caress my thighs.   5
Is it because you are thinking of food
    that you would go away?
        Or because you are a slave to your belly?
Is it because you care about clothes?
    Well, I have a bedsheet!   10
Is it because you are hungry that you would leave?
    Then take my breasts
        that their gift may flow forth to you.
Better a day in the embrace of my beloved
    than thousands on thousands anywhere else!   15

3. *Amulet* also means "well-being," and both senses apply here.

SETNE KHAMWAS AND NANEFERKAPTAH (SETNE 1)

ca. 250 B.C.E.

The protagonist of *Setne Khamwas and Naneferkaptah*, and of another relatively well-preserved tale from the Ptolemaic period (332–30 B.C.E.), is based on the legendary son of the famous ruler Ramses II (ca. 1279–1213 B.C.E.). Prince Khamwas was high priest of the god Ptah of Memphis and restored many ancient monuments. The fictional character is a magician who spends time in the old tombs of the necropolis and in that way is comparable with his historical model. He is both a warning to others that one's ambitions should not overreach what is proper for human beings and a figure of fun, because his misjudgments get him into ridiculous situations.

The magic at the core of the Setne Khamwas tales had been a theme of Egyptian stories for at least fifteen hundred years. Egyptian magicians and healers were famous throughout the ancient Near East, and several motifs in the Setne tales have parallels in other ancient literatures, showing that they belonged to a wider literary world of the Near East and the ancient Mediterranean.

Setne Khamwas and Naneferkaptah is set in the time of Ramses II, a thousand years before the tale was composed, but that period is made into the frame for yet older events, narrated by the deceased Ahwere, a king's daughter who had married her own brother, Naneferkaptah. Naneferkaptah had stolen the magic book of the god Thoth and had paid for this misdeed with the lives of his wife and son, driving him to suicide. Setne narrowly succeeds in stealing the same book from the tomb of Naneferkaptah, but then thinks he is being driven to commit terrible crimes by the beautiful woman Tabubu, with whom he desires to have sex. He finally suffers deep humiliation before Ramses II himself, which leads Setne to accept his father's advice and replace the book in the tomb. The tale should be set against the reality that almost all ancient tombs that contained anything of value were robbed, often while or very soon after the corpse was buried. It invites its audience to reflect on the dangers of obsessions with the past and the supernatural and on the importance of accepting the limits of a human lifetime.

Setne Khamwas and Naneferkaptah[1]

The lost beginning may be reconstructed as follows:

Prince Khamwas, son of King Ramses II and high priest of Ptah at Memphis, was a very learned scribe and magician who spent his time in the study of ancient monuments and books. One day he was told of the existence of a book of magic written by the god Thoth himself and kept in the tomb of a prince named Naneferkaptah (Na-nefer-ka-ptah), who had lived in the distant past and was buried somewhere in the vast necropolis of Memphis. After a long search, Prince Khamwas, accompanied by his foster brother Inaros, found the tomb of Naneferkaptah and entered it. He saw the magic book, which radiated a strong light, and tried to seize it. But the spirits of Naneferkaptah and of his wife Ahwere rose up to defend their cherished possession.

Ahwere and her son Merib were not buried in this Memphite tomb but rather in distant Coptos, where they had lost their lives. But the spirit of Ahwere was with her husband at this critical moment, and she now stood before Prince Khamwas and told him how her husband had acquired the magic book and how they had all paid for it with their lives. She begins her story by relating that she and Naneferkaptah had been brother and sister and the only children of a Pharaoh named Mernebptah. They had loved each other very

---

1. Translated by Miriam Lichtheim.

much and had wanted to marry. But Pharaoh wished to marry his son to the daughter of a general and his daughter to the son of a general. In her anguish Ahwere had asked the steward of Pharaoh's palace to plead with Pharaoh on her behalf. The steward had done so and Pharaoh had become silent and distressed. To the steward's question, why he was distressed, Pharaoh answered:

(Here begins the story on page 3 of the papyrus)

"It is you who distress me. If it so happens that I have only two children, is it right to marry the one to the other? I will marry Naneferkaptah to the daughter of a general, and I will marry Ahwere to the son of another general, so that our family may increase!"

When the time came for the banquet to be set before Pharaoh, they came for me and took me to the banquet. But my heart was very sad and I did not have my former looks. Pharaoh said to me: "Ahwere, was it you who sent to me with those foolish words, 'Let me marry [Naneferkaptah, my] elder [brother]'?"

I said to him: "Let me marry the son of a general, and let him marry the daughter of another general, so that our family may increase!" I laughed and Pharaoh laughed.[2]

[When the steward of the palace came] Pharaoh [said to him]: "Steward, let Ahwere be taken to the house of Naneferkaptah tonight, and let all sorts of beautiful things be taken with her."

I was taken as a wife to the house of Naneferkaptah [that night, and Pharaoh] sent me a present of silver and gold, and all Pharaoh's household sent me presents. Naneferkaptah made holiday with me, and he entertained all Pharaoh's household. He slept with me that night and found me [pleasing. He slept with] me again and again, and we loved each other.

When my time of purification came I made no more purification. It was reported to Pharaoh, and his heart was very happy. Pharaoh had many things taken [out of the treasury] and sent me presents of silver, gold, and royal linen, all very beautiful. When my time of bearing came, I bore this boy who is before you, who was named Merib. He was entered in the register of the House of Life.[3]

[It so happened that] my brother Naneferkaptah [had no] occupation on earth but walking on the desert of Memphis, reading the writings that were in the tombs of the Pharaohs and on the stelae of the scribes of the House of Life and the writings that were on [the other monuments, for his zeal] concerning writings was very great.

After this there was a procession in honor of Ptah,[4] and Naneferkaptah went into the temple to worship. As he was walking behind the procession, reading the writings on the shrines of the gods, [an old priest saw] him and laughed. Naneferkaptah said to him: "Why are you laughing at me?" He said: "I am not laughing at you. I am laughing because you are reading writings that have no [importance for anyone]. If you desire to read writings, come to me and I will

2. His laughter, which has parallels in tales of the world of the gods, signifies that he has been won over. His initial reluctance to let Ahwere marry her brother is part of a wider issue, because only kings could marry immediate kin, and such marriages are known from only a few periods.
3. An institution attached to temples where texts were copied and scribes were trained, some of them both in everyday handwritten scripts and in the hieroglyphic display script. Princes were typically literate, but the focus here is more on ability to use magical texts than on general literacy.
4. The principal god of Memphis, whose temple was at the center of the city.

have you taken to the place where that book is that Thoth wrote with his own hand, when he came down following the other gods.[5] Two spells are written in it. When you [recite the first spell you will] charm the sky, the earth, the netherworld, the mountains, and the waters. You will discover what all the birds of the sky and all the reptiles are saying. You will see the fish of the deep [though there are twenty-one divine cubits[6] of water] over [them]. When you recite the second spell, it will happen that, whether you are in the netherworld or in your form on earth, you will see Pre appearing in the sky with his Ennead, and the Moon in its form of rising."[7]

[Naneferkaptah said to him]: "As he (the king) lives, tell me a good thing that you desire, so that I may do it for you, and you send me to the place where this book is!"

The priest said to Naneferkaptah: "If you wish to be sent [to the place where this book is] you must give me a hundred pieces of silver for my burial, and you must endow me with two priestly stipends tax free."

Naneferkaptah called a servant and had the hundred pieces of silver given to the priest. He added the two stipends and had [the priest] endowed with them [tax free].

The priest said to Naneferkaptah: "The book in question is in the middle of the water of Coptos[8] in a box of iron. In the box of iron is a box of [copper. In the box of copper is] a box of juniper wood. In the box of juniper wood is a box of ivory and ebony. In the box of ivory and ebony is a [box of silver. In the box of silver] is a box of gold, and in it is the book. [There are six miles of] serpents, scorpions, and all kinds of reptiles around the box in which the book is, and there is [an eternal serpent around] this same box."

When the priest had thus spoken to Naneferkaptah, he did not know where on earth he was.[9] He came out of the temple, he told [me everything that had happened to him]. He [said] to me: "I will go to Coptos, I will bring this book, hastening back to the north again." But I chided the priest, saying: "May Neith[1] curse you for having told him these [dreadful things! You have brought] me combat, you have brought me strife. The region of Thebes,[2] I now find it [abhorrent]." I did what I could with Naneferkaptah to prevent him from going to Coptos; he did not listen to me. He went to [Pharaoh and told] Pharaoh everything that the priest had said to him.

Pharaoh said to him: "What is that [you want]?" He said to him: "Let the ship of Pharaoh be given to me with its equipment. I will take Ahwere [and her boy Merib] to the south with me. I will bring this book without delay."

---

5. Thoth is the god of wisdom and of writing and is strongly associated with magic. He "goes down following the gods" because he is the secretary of the sungod and his entourage as such follows behind them.

6. About thirty-five feet.

7. The West is the realm of the dead. *Pre* is the later form of the name of the sungod, Re. Ennead is the principal group of nine deities associated with the sungod.

8. This appears in later sections to be reached up the Nile. If it is a stretch of water near Coptos, it would have to be a small lake. Otherwise it might be the Red Sea, several days' journey from Coptos through the eastern desert of Egypt.

9. He was dazzled by what the priest said. The same idiom is used later when Setne encounters an exceedingly beautiful woman.

1. Neith is a major goddess of the area of Memphis and of the Nile delta.

2. The southern part of Upper Egypt. Coptos is a little to the north of Thebes. Ahwere knows that Naneferkaptah's mission can bring no good, and her dislike of Thebes—an attitude typical of people from the area of Memphis—is prescient.

The ship of Pharaoh was given [him] with its equipment. We boarded it, we set sail, we arrived [at Coptos]. It [was announced] to the priests of Isis of Coptos and the chief priest of Isis. They came down to meet us, hastening to meet Naneferkaptah, and their wives came down to meet me. [We went up from the shore and went into] the temple of Isis and Harpocrates.[3] Naneferkaptah sent for an ox, a goose, and wine. He made burnt offering and libation before Isis of Coptos and Harpocrates. We were taken to a very beautiful house [filled with all good things].

Naneferkaptah spent four days making holiday with the priests of Isis of Coptos, and the wives of the priests of Isis made holiday with me. When the morning of our fifth day came. Naneferkaptah had [much] pure [wax brought] to him. He made a boat filled with its rowers and sailors. He recited a spell to them, he made them live, he gave them breath, he put them on the water. He filled the ship of Pharaoh with sand, [he tied it to the other boat]. He [went] on board, and I sat above the water of Coptos, saying: "I shall learn what happens to him."

He said to the rowers: "Row me to the place where that book is!" [They rowed him by night] as by day. In three days he reached it. He cast sand before him, and a gap formed in the river. He found six miles of serpents, scorpions, and all kinds of reptiles around [the place where the book was]. He found an eternal serpent around this same box. He recited a spell to the six miles of serpents, scorpions, and all kinds of reptiles that were around the box, and did not let them come up. [He went to the place where] the eternal serpent was. He fought it and killed it. It came to life again and resumed its shape. He [fought it again, a second time, and killed it; it came to life again. He [fought it again, a third] time, cut it in two pieces, and put sand between one piece and the other.[4] [It died] and no longer resumed its shape.

Naneferkaptah went to the place where the box was. [He found it was a box of] iron. He opened it and found a box of copper. He opened it and found a box of juniper wood. He opened it and found a box of ivory and ebony. [He opened it and found a box of] silver. He opened it and found a box of gold. He opened it and found the book in it. He brought the book up out of the box of gold.

He recited a spell from it; [he charmed the sky, the earth, the netherworld, the] mountains, the waters. He discovered what all the birds of the sky and the fish of the deep and the beasts of the desert were saying. He recited another spell; he saw [Pre appearing in the sky with his Ennead], and the Moon rising, and the stars in their forms. He saw the fish of the deep, though there were twenty-one divine cubits of water over them. He recited a spell to the [water; he made it resume its form].

[He went on] board, he said to the rowers: "Row me back to the place [I came] from." They rowed him by night as by day. He reached me at the place where I was; [he found me sitting] above the water of Coptos, not having drunk nor eaten, not having done anything on earth, and looking like a person who has reached the Good House.[5]

I said to Naneferkaptah: ["Welcome back! Let me] see this book for which we have taken these [great] pains!" He put the book into my hand. I recited one spell from it; I charmed the sky, the earth, the netherworld, the mountains, the

3. Harpocrates was Horus's name as a child god, son of Osiris and Isis.
4. This was a standard way of magically stop-ping a snake from coming back to life.
5. The embalmers' workshop. Naneferkaptah appears as if dead from his exertions.

waters. I discovered what all the birds of the sky and the fish of the deep and the beasts were saying. I recited another spell; I saw Pre appearing in the sky with his Ennead. I saw the Moon rising, and all the stars of the sky in their forms. I saw the fish of the deep, though there were twenty-one divine cubits of water over them.

As I could not write[6]—I mean, compared with Naneferkaptah, my brother, who was a good scribe and very wise man—he had a sheet of new papyrus brought to him. He wrote on it every word that was in the book before him. He soaked it in beer, he dissolved it in water. When he knew it had dissolved, he drank it and knew what had been in it.[7]

We returned to Coptos the same day and made holiday before Isis of Coptos and Harpocrates. We went on board, we traveled north, we reached a point six miles north of Coptos.

Now Thoth had found out everything that had happened to Naneferkaptah regarding the book, and Thoth hastened to report it to Pre, saying: "Learn of my right and my case against Naneferkaptah, the son of Pharaoh Mernebptah![8] He went to my storehouse; he plundered it; he seized my box with my document. He killed my guardian who was watching over it!"[9] He was told: "He is yours together with every person belonging to him." They sent a divine power from heaven, saying: "Do not allow Naneferkaptah and any person belonging to him to get to Memphis safely!"

At a certain moment the boy Merib came out from under the awning of Pharaoh's ship, fell into the water, and drowned. All the people on board cried out. Naneferkaptah came out from his tent, recited a spell to him, and made him rise up, though there were twenty-one divine cubits of water over him. He recited a spell to him and made him relate to him everything that had happened to him, and the nature of the accusation that Thoth had made before Pre.[1]

We returned to Coptos with him. We had him taken to the Good House. We had him tended, we had him embalmed like a prince and important person. We laid him to rest in his coffin in the desert of Coptos. Naneferkaptah, my brother, said: "Let us go north, let us not delay, lest Pharaoh hear the things that have happened to us and his heart become sad because of them." We went on board, we went north without delay.

Six miles north of Coptos, at the place where the boy Merib had fallen into the river, I came out from under the awning of Pharaoh's ship, fell into the river, and drowned. All the people on board cried out and told Naneferkaptah. He came out from the tent of Pharaoh's ship, recited a spell to me, and made me rise up, though there were twenty-one divine cubits of water over me. He had me brought up, recited a spell to me, and made me relate to him everything that had happened to me, and the nature of the accusation that Thoth had made before Pre.

He returned to Coptos with me. He had me taken to the Good House. He had me tended, he had me embalmed in the manner of a prince and very

6. Ahwere is not literate, but simply having the magic manuscript in her hands makes her able to read it and use its formulas.
7. By drinking the dissolved ashes of the inscribed papyrus, Naneferkaptah assimilates its contents.
8. A form of the name of Merneptah, the suc-

cessor of Ramses II and a brother of the historical Setne Khamwas.
9. The snake that protected the chest with the papyrus.
1. Merib had learned of Thoth's complaint, presumably after he had drowned.

important person. He laid me to rest in the tomb in which the boy Merib was resting. He went on board, he went north without delay.

Six miles north of Coptos, at the place where we had fallen into the river, he spoke to his heart saying: "Could I go to Coptos and dwell there also? If I go to Memphis now and Pharaoh asks me about his children, what shall I say to him? Can I say to him, 'I took your children to the region of Thebes; I killed them and stayed alive, and I have come to Memphis yet alive'?"

He sent for a scarf of royal linen belonging to him, and made it into a bandage; he bound the book, placed it on his body, and made it fast. Naneferkaptah came out from under the awning of Pharaoh's ship, fell into the water, and drowned. All the people on board cried out, saying: "Great woe, sad woe! Will he return, the good scribe, the learned man whose like has not been?"

Pharaoh's ship sailed north, no man on earth knowing where Naneferkaptah was. They reached Memphis and sent word to Pharaoh. Pharaoh came down to meet Pharaoh's ship; he wore mourning and all the people of Memphis wore mourning, including the priests of Ptah, the chief priest of Ptah, the council, and all Pharaoh's household. Then they saw Naneferkaptah holding on to the rudders of Pharaoh's ship through his craft of a good scribe. They brought him up and saw the book on his body.

Pharaoh said: "Let this book that is on his body be hidden."[2] Then said the council of Pharaoh and the priests of Ptah and the chief priest of Ptah to Pharaoh: "Our great lord—O may he have the lifetime of Pre—Naneferkaptah was a good scribe and a very learned man!" Pharaoh had them give him entry into the Good House on the sixteenth day, wrapping on the thirty-fifth, burial on the seventieth day. And they laid him to rest in his coffin in his resting place.

These are the evil things that befell us on account of this book of which you say, "Let it be given to me." You have no claim to it, whereas our lives on earth were taken on account of it!

Setne takes the book

Setne said to Ahwere: "Let me have this book that I see between you and Naneferkaptah, or else I will take it by force!" Naneferkaptah rose from the bier and said: "Are you Setne, to whom this woman has told these dire things and you have not accepted them? The said book, will you be able to seize it through the power of a good scribe, or through skill in playing draughts with me? Let the two of us play draughts for it!" Said Setne, "I am ready."

They put before them the game board with its pieces, and they both played. Naneferkaptah won one game from Setne. He recited a spell to him, struck his head with the game-box that was before him, and made him sink into the ground as far as his legs. He did the same with the second game. He won it from Setne, and made him sink into the ground as far as his phallus. He did the same with the third game, and made him sink into the ground as far as his ears. After this Setne was in great straits at the hands of Naneferkaptah.

2. The scroll and Naneferkaptah's skill as a magician have enabled his drowned body to become attached to the yacht's rudders and be transported underwater to Memphis. He knew that he would not escape drowning.

Setne called to his foster-brother Inaros, saying: "Hasten up to the earth and tell Pharaoh everything that has happened to me; and bring the amulets of my father Ptah[3] and my books of sorcery." He hastened up to the earth and told Pharaoh everything that had happened to Setne. Pharaoh said: "Take him the amulets of his father Ptah and his books of sorcery." Inaros hastened down into the tomb. He put the amulets on the body of Setne, and he jumped up in that very moment. Setne stretched out his hand for the book and seized it. Then, as Setne came up from the tomb, light went before him, darkness went behind him, and Ahwere wept after him, saying: "Hail, O darkness! Farewell, O light! Everything that was in the tomb has departed!" Naneferkaptah said to Ahwere: "Let your heart not grieve. I will make him bring this book back here, with a forked stick in his hand and a lighted brazier on his head!"[4]

Setne came up from the tomb and made it fast behind him, as it had been. Setne went before Pharaoh and related to him the things that had happened to him on account of the book. Pharaoh said to Setne: "Take this book back to the tomb of Naneferkaptah like a wise man, or else he will make you take it back with a forked stick in your hand and a lighted brazier on your head." Setne did not listen to him. Then Setne had no occupation on earth but to unroll the book and read from it to everyone.

Setne and Tabubu

After this it happened one day that Setne was strolling in the forecourt of the temple of Ptah. Then he saw [a woman] who was very beautiful, there being no other woman like her in appearance. She was beautiful and wore many golden jewels, and maid servants walked behind her as well as two men servants belonging to her household. The moment Setne saw her, he did not know where on earth he was. He called his man servant, saying: "Hasten to the place where this woman is, and find out what her position is." The man servant hastened to the place where the woman was. He called to the maid servant who was following her and asked her, saying, "What woman is this?" She told him: "It is Tabubu, the daughter of the prophet of Bastet, mistress of Ankhtawi.[5] She has come here to worship Ptah, the great god."

The servant returned to Setne and related to him every word she had said to him. Setne said to the servant: "Go, say to the maid. 'It is Setne Khamwas, the son of Pharaoh Usermare,[6] who has sent me to say, 'I will give you ten pieces of gold—spend an hour with me. Or do you have a complaint of wrongdoing? I will have it settled for you. I will have you taken to a hidden place where no one on earth shall find you.'"[7]

The servant returned to the place where Tabubu was. He called her maid and told her. She cried out as if what he said was an insult. Tabubu said to the

---

3. Ptah is Setne's "father" because Setne is high priest of Ptah, like the son of Ramses II after whom his character is modeled.
4. This image, which occurs again later, is modeled on the hieroglyph for a defeated enemy or on pictures of the dead being punished in the next world. In either case, Setne will have failed very visibly.

5. Bastet was one of the goddesses of Memphis. Prophets were high-ranking priests. The temple of Bastet was in a northwestern quarter of the city named Ankhtawi.
6. The throne name of Ramses II.
7. Setne says he will pay Tabubu for sex and, should she object and accuse him, he will go ahead and rape her.

servant: "Stop talking to this foolish maid; come and speak with me." The servant hastened to where Tabubu was and said to her: "I will give you ten pieces of gold; spend an hour with Setne Khamwas, the son of Pharaoh Usermare. If you have a complaint of wrongdoing, he will have it settled for you. He will take you to a hidden place where no one on earth shall find you."

Tabubu said: "Go, tell Setne, 'I am of priestly rank, I am not a low person. If you desire to do what you wish with me, you must come to Bubastis, to my house. It is furnished with everything, and you shall do what you wish with me, without anyone on earth finding me and without my acting like a low woman of the street.'"

The servant returned to Setne and told him everything she had said to him. He said, "That suits (me)!" Everyone around Setne was indignant.

Setne had a boat brought to him. He went on board and hastened to Bubastis. When he came to the west of the suburb he found a very lofty house that had a wall around it, a garden on its north, and a seat at its door. Setne asked, "Whose house is this?" They told him, "It is the house of Tabubu." Setne went inside the wall. While he turned his face to the storehouse in the garden they announced him to Tabubu. She came down, took Setne's hand, and said to him: "By the welfare of the house of the prophet of Bastet, mistress of Ankhtawi, which you have reached, it will please me greatly if you will take the trouble to come up with me."

Setne walked up the stairs of the house with Tabubu. He found the upper story of the house swept and adorned, its floor adorned with real lapis-lazuli and real turquoise. Many couches were in it, spread with royal linen, and many golden cups were on the table. A golden cup was filled with wine and put into Setne's hand. She said to him, "May it please you to eat something." He said to her, "I could not do that." Incense was put on the brazier; ointment was brought to him of the kind provided for Pharaoh. Setne made holiday with Tabubu, never having seen anyone like her.

Setne said to Tabubu: "Let us accomplish what we have come here for." She said to him: "You will return to your house in which you live. I am of priestly rank; I am not a low person. If you desire to do what you wish with me you must make for me a deed of maintenance and of compensation in money for everything, all goods belonging to you." He said to her: "Send for the schoolteacher." He was brought at once. He made for her a deed of maintenance and of compensation in money for everything, all goods belonging to him.

At this moment one came to announce to Setne, "Your children are below." He said, "Let them be brought up." Tabubu rose and put on a garment of royal linen. Setne saw all her limbs through it, and his desire became even greater than it had been before. Setne said: "Tabubu, let me accomplish what I have come here for!" She said to him: "You will return to your house in which you live. I am of priestly rank: I am not a low person. If you desire to do what you wish with me, you must make your children subscribe to my deed. Do not leave them to contend with my children over your property." He had his children brought and made them subscribe to the deed.

Setne said to Tabubu: "Let me accomplish what I have come for!" She said to him: "You will return to your house in which you live. I am of priestly rank; I am not a low person. If you desire to do what you wish with me, you must have your children killed. Do not leave them to contend with my children over your property." Setne said: "Let the abomination that came into your head be done to them." She had his children killed before him. She had them thrown down from the window to the dogs and cats. They ate their flesh, and he heard them as he drank with Tabubu.

Setne said to Tabubu: "Let us accomplish what we have come here for! All the things that you have said, I have done them all for you." She said to him: "Come now to this storehouse." Setne went to the storehouse. He lay down on a couch of ivory and ebony, his wish about to be fulfilled. Tabubu lay down beside Setne. He stretched out his hand to touch her, and she opened her mouth wide in a loud cry. Setne awoke in a state of great heat, his phallus in a[8] [. . .] and there were no clothes on him at all.

At this moment Setne saw a noble person borne in a litter, with many men running beside him, and he had the likeness of Pharaoh. Setne was about to rise but could not rise for shame because he had no clothes on. Pharaoh said: "Setne, what is this state that you are in?" He said: "It is Naneferkaptah who has done it all to me!" Pharaoh said: "Go to Memphis; your children want you; they stand in their rank before Pharaoh." Setne said to Pharaoh: "My great lord—O may he have the lifetime of Pre—how can I go to Memphis with no clothes on me at all?" Pharaoh called to a servant who was standing by and made him give clothes to Setne. Pharaoh said: "Setne, go to Memphis; your children are alive; they stand in their rank before Pharaoh."

Setne returns the book

When Setne came to Memphis he embraced his children, for he found them alive. Pharaoh said to Setne: "Was it a state of drunkenness you were in before?" Setne related everything that had happened with Tabubu and Naneferkaptah. Pharaoh said: "Setne, I did what I could with you before, saying, 'They will kill you if you do not take this book back to the place you took it from.' You have not listened to me until now. Take this book back to Naneferkaptah, with a forked stick in your hand and a lighted brazier on your head."

When Setne came out from before Pharaoh, there was a forked stick in his hand and a lighted brazier on his head. He went down into the tomb in which Naneferkaptah was. Ahwere said to him: "Setne, it is the great god Ptah who has brought you back safely." Naneferkaptah laughed, saying, "It is what I told you before." Setne greeted Naneferkaptah, and he found one could say that Pre was in the whole tomb.[9] Ahwere and Naneferkaptah greeted Setne warmly.

Setne said: "Naneferkaptah, is there any matter which is shameful?" Naneferkaptah said: "Setne, you know that Ahwere and her son Merib are in Coptos; here in this tomb they are through the craft of a good scribe.[1] Let it be asked of you to undertake the task of going to Coptos and [bringing them] here."

When Setne had come up from the tomb, he went before Pharaoh and related to Pharaoh everything that Naneferkaptah had said to him. Pharaoh

8. The text is corrupted here.
9. The return of the scroll has filled the tomb

with light.
1. Scribes were the traditional magicians.

said: "Setne, go to Coptos, bring Ahwere and her son Merib." He said to Pharaoh: "Let the ship of Pharaoh and its equipment be given to me."

The ship of Pharaoh and its equipment were given to him. He went on board, he set sail, he reached Coptos without delay. It was announced to the priests of Isis of Coptos, and the chief priest of Isis. They came down to meet him, they conducted him to the shore.

He went up from it, he went into the temple of Isis of Coptos and Harpocrates. He sent for an ox, a goose, and wine, and made burnt offering and libation before Isis of Coptos and Harpocrates. He went to the desert of Coptos with the priests of Isis and the chief priest of Isis. They spent three days and three nights searching in all the tombs on the desert of Coptos, turning over the stelae of the scribes of the House of Life, and reading the inscriptions on them. They did not find the resting place in which Ahwere and her son were.

When Naneferkaptah found that they did not find the resting place of Ahwere and her son Merib, he rose up as an old man, a very aged priest, and came to meet Setne. When Setne saw him he said to the old man: "You have the appearance of a man of great age. Do you know the resting place in which Ahwere and her son Merib are?" The old man said to Setne: "My great-grandfather said to my grandfather, 'The resting place of Ahwere and her son Merib is at the south corner of the house of the [chief of police].'"

Setne said to the old man: "Perhaps there is some wrong that the chief of police did to you, on account of which you are trying to have his house torn down?" The old man said to Setne: "Have a watch set over me, and let the house of the chief of police be demolished. If they do not find Ahwere and her son Merib under the south corner of his house, let punishment be done to me."

They set a watch over the old man, and they found the resting place of Ahwere and her son Merib under the south corner of the house of the chief of police. Setne let the two noble persons[2] enter into Pharaoh's ship. He had the house of the chief of police built as it had been before. Naneferkaptah let Setne learn the fact that it was he who had come to Coptos, to let them find the resting place in which Ahwere and her son Merib were. Setne went on board Pharaoh's ship. He went north and without delay he reached Memphis with all the people who were with him. When it was announced before Pharaoh, he came down to meet the ship of Pharaoh. He let the noble persons enter into the tomb in which Naneferkaptah was. He had it closed over them all together.

Colophon

This is the complete text, a tale of Setne Khamwas and Naneferkaptah, and his wife Ahwere and her son Merib. It was copied by _____ in year 15, first month of winter.[3]

---

2. *Noble* is an ancient word that came to mean "mummy" in later periods. The mummies of Ahwere and Merib are carried in solemn procession onto the ship.
3. The text was copied during the Ptolemaic

Period (a Hellenistic dynasty established in Egypt by generals of Alexander the Great) under King Ptolemy II, III, or IV, whose years 15 correspond to 271, 232, and 207 B.C.E., respectively.

STELA OF TAIMHOTEP

42 B.C.E.

This stela, which has been known since the beginnings of Egyptology in the early nineteenth century, tells the life story of Taimhotep, the second wife of Psherenptah, the high priest of the ancient capital Memphis, near modern Cairo. Taimhotep died in 42 B.C.E., and her husband followed her at the end of the next year. They belonged to a large priestly family that was prominent for more than two centuries. One of the few known inscriptions that tell of women's lives, Taimhotep's biography is composed in elaborately phrased Classical Egyptian, displaying an extraordinary command of a form of the language that had been current almost two thousand years earlier. The first two thirds (omitted from the selection here) speak about her traditional role as a woman, which was essentially to bear a male heir for her husband, whose titles and achievements fill much of the text. The last part starts with her death and continues with a remarkable group of poems pronounced from the beyond, depicting the next world as a terrible place and centering on Taimhotep's desperate yearning for water, a pressing concern for those buried in desert tombs. These poems were probably sung during funeral ceremonies as a dramatic outpouring of grief.

Stela of Taimhotep[1]

Year 10, month 2 of Emergence,[2] day 16
was the day on which I died.

There placed me my husband[3]—the priest of Ptah,
priest of Osiris, lord of Rosetau,
priest of the Dual King, Lord of the Two Lands,
Ptolemy, true of voice,[4]
keeper of secrets in the house of Ptah,
keeper of secrets in sky, earth, and underworld,
keeper of secrets in Rosetau,
keeper of secrets in Rutiset,[5]
chief controller of craftsmen, Psherenptah—in the West.
He performed for me all the rites for an effective mummy.
He buried me in a perfect burial.
He deposited my corpse in his tomb in the area of Rutiset.

1. Translated and with footnotes by John Baines.
2. The middle season of the three in the ancient Egyptian calendar. This date computes to 15 February 42 B.C.E. Taimhotep died at the age of thirty, not particularly young in the ancient context.
3. Psherenptah performed the funeral rituals for Taimhotep in person. "Rosetau" is a traditional name for a necropolis, particularly that of Memphis. Psherenptah's priesthood of

Osiris, the god of the dead, was the relevant one for the funeral among the many he held.
4. Psherenptah was also priest of the mortuary cult of Ptolemy XII Neos Dionysos (known as Auletes [80–51 B.C.E.]). The culturally Greek ruler Ptolemy, whose capital was Alexandria, bears traditional Egyptian kingly titles.
5. Rutiset is the most ancient and hallowed area of the necropolis of Memphis, modern North Saqqara.

The stela of Taimhotep.

Oh my brother,[6] my husband,   15
my companion, great controller of craftsmen:
may your heart not tire in drinking and eating,
drunkenness and sexual pleasure.
Spend a perfect day and follow your heart[7] all the time.
Do not place care in your heart.   20

Years taken upon earth are good.
As for the West, it is a land of sleeping in darkness.[8]
It is dire to dwell in for those who are there.
Those who sleep in their cloth wrappings,[9]
they do not awaken to see their kin.   25
They do not see their fathers and their mothers;
their hearts miss their wives and their children.

The water of life that is for everyone therein, it is thirst before me;[1]
it comes to the one who is upon earth, but it is thirst for me.
Water is beside me,   30
but I do not know the place where it is,
since I came to this wadi.[2]

6. A term of endearment between spouses. Taimhotep is speaking to Psherenptah from the next world.
7. A traditional phrase meaning "do what you want."
8. The dead are supposed to be reborn to dwell in light. Taimhotep denies this.
9. Mummies were wrapped in multiple layers of cloth. Rituals performed on the mummy were supposed to enable the deceased to leave the mummy and move freely. Here the effectiveness of the ritual is denied.
1. Taimhotep can see water but cannot reach it.
2. The tomb is located in a dry depression in the desert.

Give me the water that is gone
so that I may say to myself: "my body is not far from water."[3]
Set my face to the north wind,   35
at the edge of the water.
Perhaps then my heart will be assuaged in its suffering.

As for death, "Come" is his name:[4]
everyone whom he summons, they come to him at once,
their hearts terror-struck in fear of him.   40
No one looks toward him among gods and humans;
the great ones among them like the small.

His finger is not repulsed from anyone he wishes to touch.
He snatches the son from his mother,
while the old man wanders in his path.   45
All the fearful plead before him;[5]
he does not turn his face to them; he does not come to the
      one who beseeches him.
He does not listen to the one who extols him;
he does not look at the one who gives to him
gifts of all sorts.   50

Oh all who reach this desert place,[6] be fearful for me,
burn incense for me on the flame,
make libations at every festival of the West.

The scribe, one who makes live,[7] wise man,
keeper of secrets in the house of gold and in Tjenenet,[8]   55
the priest Harimhotep,
son of the priest Khaihap, true of voice,
born of Herankh.

---

3. Taimhotep imagines the effect of receiving a libation in the next world—a theme to which she returns—while also evoking an ideal location where there is both water and the coveted north wind, which brings cool air and makes the heat bearable. Scenes where the deceased receive libations by pools are common in the decoration of tombs and stelae.
4. Death is imagined as a malicious demon. This idea is known also from images.
5. Death is like a god who would hear prayers, but he does not heed them.
6. People were expected to visit the tombs of their relatives and might also perform offering formulas at other tombs. Taimhotep addresses passersby in the necropolis. Making libations is the core ritual act that will guarantee water to the deceased.
7. This is a title of a sculptor. The last lines identify the person who made the stela and perhaps composed its text. He was a kinsman of Taimhotep.
8. The "house of gold" was a treasury and craft workshop attached to temples. Tjenenet was an ancient temple in Memphis.

THE EPIC OF GILGAMESH

ca. 1900–250 B.C.E.

he Epic of Gilgamesh is the greatest work of ancient Mesopotamia and one of the earliest pieces of world literature. The story of its main protagonist, King Gilgamesh, and his quest for immortality touches on the most fundamental questions of what it means to be human: death and friendship, nature and civilization, power and violence, travel adventures and homecoming, love and sexuality. Because of the appeal of its central hero and his struggle with the meaning of culture in the face of human mortality, the epic spread throughout the ancient Near East and was translated into various regional languages during the second millennium B.C.E. As far as we know, no other literary work of the ancient world spread so widely across cultures and languages. And yet, after a long period of popularity, *Gilgamesh* was forgotten, seemingly for good: after circulating in various versions for many centuries, it vanished from human memory for over two thousand years. Its rediscovery by archaeologists in the nineteenth century was a sensation and allows us to read a story that for many centuries was known to many cultures and people throughout the Near East but has come down to us today only by chance on brittle clay tablets.

KING GILGAMESH AND HIS STORY

Gilgamesh was thought to be a priest-king of the city-state of Uruk in southern Mesopotamia, the lands around the rivers Euphrates and Tigris in modern-day Iraq. He probably ruled around 2700 B.C.E. and was remembered for the building of Uruk's monumental city walls, which were ten kilometers (six miles) long and fitted with nine hundred towers; portions of these walls are still visible today. We will never know for sure how the historical king compares to the epic hero Gilgamesh. But soon after his death, he was venerated as a great king and judge of the Underworld. In the epic he appears as "two-thirds . . . divine" and "one-third . . . human," the offspring of Ninsun, a goddess in the shape of a wild cow, and a human father named Lugalbanda. By some accounts, *Gilgamesh* means "the offspring is a hero," or, according to another etymology, "the old man is still a young man."

Gilgamesh was not written by one specific author but evolved gradually over the long span of a millennium. The earliest story of Gilgamesh appears around 2100 B.C.E. in a cycle of poems in the Sumerian language. Sumerian is the earliest Mesopotamian language. It is written in cuneiform script—wedge-shaped characters incised in clay or stone—and has no connection to any other known language. About six hundred years after Gilgamesh's death, kings of the third dynasty of Ur, another Mesopotamian city-state, claimed descent from the legendary king of Uruk and enjoyed hearing of the great deeds of Gilgamesh at court; the earliest cycle of Gilgamesh poems was written for these rulers. As in the later epic, in the Sumerian cycle of poems Gilgamesh is a powerful king and an awe-inspiring warrior. Gilgamesh's shattering realization that he will die and can attain immortality only by making a name for himself appears already in this earliest version of the Gilgamesh story, where he exclaims:

> I have peered over the city wall,
> I have seen the corpses floating in
> the river's water.
> So too it will come to pass for me,
> so it will happen to me . . .
> Since no man can avoid life's end,
> I would enter the mountain land
> and set up my name.

The Sumerian poetry cycle became the basis for the old version of *Gilgamesh,* written in Babylonian, a variant of the Akkadian language—a transnational written language that was widely used throughout the ancient Near East. The traditional Babylonian epic version of *Gilgamesh,* which adapted the Sumerian poems into a connected narrative, circulated for more than fifteen hundred years. It was read widely from Mesopotamia to Syria, the Levant, and Anatolia and was translated into non-Mesopotamian languages such as Hittite, the language of an empire that controlled Turkey and northern Syria in the latter half of the second millennium B.C.E.

The definitive revision of the epic is attributed to a Babylonian priest and scholar named Sin-leqi-unninni. He lived around 1200 B.C.E., and by his time King Gilgamesh had been dead for about fifteen hundred years. He carefully selected elements from the older traditions, inserted new plot elements, and added a preface to the epic. His version, included here in translation, is divided into eleven chapters recorded on eleven clay tablets. New fragments of *Gilgamesh* continue to surface from archaeological excavations; some pieces are still missing, and some passages are fragmentary and barely legible, but thanks to the painstaking work of scholars of ancient Mesopotamia we can today read an extended, gripping narrative.

THE WORLD'S OLDEST EPIC HERO

The Gilgamesh of the epic is an awe-inspiring, sparkling hero, but at first also the epitome of a bad ruler: arrogant, oppressive, and brutal. As the epic begins, the people of Uruk complain to the Sumerian gods about Gilgamesh's overbearing behavior, and so the gods create the wild man Enkidu to confront Gilgamesh. While Gilgamesh is a mixture of human and divine, Enkidu is a blend of human and wild animal, though godlike in his own way. He is raised by beasts in the wilderness and eats what they eat. When he breaks hunters' traps for the sake of his animal companions he becomes a threat to human society and Gilgamesh decides to tame him with the attractions of urban life and civilization: for seven days Enkidu makes love to a harlot (prostitute), sent out for the purpose, and at her urging he takes a cleansing bath and accepts clothing and a first meal of basic human foodstuff, bread and beer. Shamhat, the prostitute, leads him to the city of Uruk. Although he and Gilgamesh are at first bent on competing with each other, they quickly develop a deep bond of friendship.

Their friendship established, Gilgamesh proposes to Enkidu the first of their epic adventures: to travel to the great Cedar Forest and slay the giant Humbaba, who guards the forest for the harsh god Enlil. With the blessing of the sun god Shamash they succeed, and they cut down some magnificent trees that they float down the Euphrates River to Mesopotamia. But their violent act has its consequence: the dying giant curses them and Enlil is enraged. Their second adventure leads to a yet more ambiguous success, which will set in motion the tragic end of their friendship. Gilgamesh, cleansed from battle and radiant in victory, attracts the desire of Ishtar, goddess of love and warfare. Instead of politely resisting her advances, Gil-

This modern impression of an ancient cylinder seal shows a bearded hero, kneeling and raising an outstretched lion above his head.

gamesh makes the fatal error of chiding her for her fickle passions and known cruelty toward her lovers, and heaps insults on the goddess. Scandalized by Gilgamesh's accusations, she unleashes the Bull of Heaven against the two friends, and it wreaks havoc in Uruk. After the heroic duo kills the Bull of Heaven, a council of the gods convenes to avoid further disaster. In a gap in the text, the gods decide that Gilgamesh and Enkidu have gone too far; one of them must die. The lot falls to Enkidu, because Gilgamesh is the king.

Enkidu's death brings Gilgamesh face to face with mortality. He mourns for Enkidu bitterly for seven days and nights and only when a worm creeps out of the corpse's nose does he accept that his friend is dead. Terrified that he too will die, Gilgamesh forsakes the civilized world to find the one human being known to have achieved immortality: Utanapishtim, survivor of the Great Flood. Like Enkidu in his days as a wild man, Gilgamesh roams the steppe, disheveled and clad in a lionskin, and sets out on a quest to ask Utanapishtim

for the secret of eternal life. He braves monsters, runs along the sun's path under the earth at night, encounters a mysterious woman who keeps a tavern at the edge of the world, passes a garden of jeweled trees, crosses the waters of death, and finally arrives at the doorstep of Utanapishtim and his wife. Utanapishtim's dramatic account of their experience and survival of the flood resembles the biblical story of Noah and the Great Flood in Genesis. At his wife's request, Utanapishtim gives Gilgamesh the chance to attain immortality by eating a magic plant, but he is afraid to try it and a serpent steals the magic plant and gains the power of immortality for itself. In the end Gilgamesh returns to Uruk, empty-handed. Although in the final moments of the epic he proudly surveys the mighty city walls of his making, he is a profoundly changed man.

AN ANCIENT EPIC

The word *epic* is originally Greek and refers to a long poem narrating important historical or cosmic events in

elevated language and involving a pan-
oramic sweep of action and a cast of
protagonists who straddle the human
and divine worlds. Some epics, like
Homer's *Iliad*, tell of the foundation or
destruction of civilizations or cities, featuring noisy battle scenes, in which the
heroes can prove their strength, wisdom,
and understanding of the workings of
the divine order. Other epics, like **Homer's** *Odyssey*, focus on the travels and
adventures of a central protagonist.
Greek epics usually invoke the Muses,
goddesses in charge of the arts and a
poet's inspiration, who inform the poets
of past events and the world of the gods.
Epics often include long speeches, in
which protagonists remember past
events or justify future actions. And they
rely heavily on the repetition of lines
with variation and on a rhetoric of parallels and contrasts. Scholars of Homeric
epic have argued that repetition and formulaic expression helped the bards to
remember and recite extensive story-
lines and pointed to the poems' oral
and performative roots.

Gilgamesh shares a few fundamental
features with Greek epic. True, there
was no concept in Mesopotamia corresponding to the Western literary genre
"epic," and *Gilgamesh* has no equivalent to the strict hexameter of Greek
epic. A verse line in *Gilgamesh* is not
defined by a fixed number of syllables
or stresses but varies in length, which
can only be inferred by context, such
as patterns of parallelism. Still, in contrast to the literary works of other civilizations of the ancient world that had
no epic, like China and East Asia, *Gilgamesh* can be considered part of a
larger Near Eastern and Mediterranean
epic tradition. Although *Gilgamesh* was
only translated into cuneiform languages and never directly entered the
epic repertoire of alphabet languages
like Greek, it shared with the Greek
tradition a number of classically epic
motifs. In Achilles' mourning for his

friend Patroclus (in Homer's *Iliad*) we
can recognize Gilgamesh's desperation
at the loss of Enkidu. Just as Gilgamesh
finally returns to Uruk after challenging adventures, Odysseus (in Homer's
Odyssey) returns to Ithaca from the
Trojan War in the guise of a destitute
stranger after performing dangerous
feats. In *Gilgamesh* and Greek epics,
scenes featuring councils of the gods
who decide the fate of their heroes
reflect religious beliefs about the inter-
section between human limitations
and divine powers but are also astute
plot devices that sharpen the profile of
the heroes and their ways of confronting divine antagonism. We can see a
parallel to the wiliness of the Greek
gods and their personal preferences in
the opposition of Shamash and Enlil,
in particular in Enlil's argument that
Enkidu should be sacrificed and Gilgamesh spared.

In contrast to the orally rooted Homeric epic, *Gilgamesh* was from the outset conceived as a literary work. With its
elevated style, geometrically parallel
phrases, and moments of complex word
play, *Gilgamesh* was addressed to the
sophisticated ears and minds of scholars
and members of the royal court. We
know that it was used in Babylonian
schools to teach literature. This hypothesis is further supported when we look
at the nuanced use of speech registers in
the epic's portrayal of its protagonists.
Utanapishtim speaks in an obscure
archaic style that befits a sage from
before the Great Flood, and he has a solemn way of rolling and doubling his
consonants. The goddess Ishtar appears
in an unfavorable light, talking like a
low-class streetwalker. In contrast,
Shamhat, the prostitute who brings
Enkidu to the city, speaks with unexpected eloquence and distinction.

Shamhat is a thought-provoking example of the several powerful female protagonists in *Gilgamesh*. Much of what
Gilgamesh accomplishes is ultimately

due to women: his mother's pleas with the sun god Shamash allow him to kill Humbaba; the wife of the scorpion monster persuades her husband to give Gilgamesh entrance to the tunnel leading to the jeweled garden; and the mysterious woman he finds at the end of the world, the tavern keeper Siduri, helps him find Utanapishtim, whose wife persuades her husband to give Gilgamesh the plant of rejuvenation. In some of Gilgamesh's encounters there are touches of wit and parody. It is stunning to find this blend of epic grandeur and comic sobriety in the world's earliest epic. Part of the epic's subtlety is invisible today, because we know so much less about the historical and literary context of *Gilgamesh* than we know about the context of Greek epic. Still, the glimpses we get show the sophistication of the early Mesopotamian states and the art of literary narrative they developed.

Like Mesopotamian civilization and its cuneiform writing system, *Gilgamesh* eventually disappeared. In the seventh century B.C.E., when an invading force of ancient Iranian people called Medians sacked Nineveh, one of the capitals of the Assyrian Empire, copies of the epic written on clay tablets, which had been preserved in the palace library of Ashurbanipal, the last great Assyrian king (reigned 668–627 B.C.E.), vanished in the destruction. Although the epic did not disappear

completely and still circulated until the third century B.C.E., it was only rediscovered in the 1850s, when an English explorer, Austen Henry Layard, dug up thousands of tablets from the site at Nineveh. They were later deciphered at the British Museum in London, and when the young curator George Smith made the stunning discovery that this epic contained a version of the biblical story of the flood, which had hitherto been considered unique to the book of Genesis, this challenged conceptions about the origin of biblical narrative. *Gilgamesh* was suddenly propelled into the canon of world literature.

The Epic of Gilgamesh took shape many centuries before the Greeks and Hebrews learned how to write, and it circulated in the Near East and Levant long before the book of Genesis and the Homeric epics took shape. The rediscovery of the names of the gods and humans who people the epic and of the history of the cities and lands in which they lived is a gradual, ongoing process. And the meaning of the epic itself is tantalizingly ambiguous. Has Gilgamesh succeeded or failed in his quest? What makes us human? Can civilization bring immortality? Whatever we decide to believe, the story of Gilgamesh and his companion Enkidu, of their quest for fame and immortality, speaks to contemporary readers with an urgency and immediacy that makes us forget just how ancient it is.

The Epic of Gilgamesh[1]

Tablet I

He who saw the wellspring, the foundations of the land,
Who knew the ways, was wise in all things,
Gilgamesh, who saw the wellspring, the foundations of the land,
He knew the ways, was wise in all things,
He it was who inspected holy places everywhere,   5

---

1. Translated by and with footnotes adapted from Benjamin R. Foster.

Full understanding of it all he gained,
He saw what was secret and revealed what was hidden,
He brought back tidings from before the flood,
From a distant journey came home, weary, at peace,
Engraved all his hardships on a monument of stone,   10
He built the walls of ramparted Uruk,[2]
The lustrous treasury of hallowed Eanna!
See its upper wall, whose facing gleams like copper,
Gaze at the lower course, which nothing will equal,
Mount the stone stairway, there from days of old,   15
Approach Eanna, the dwelling of Ishtar,
Which no future king, no human being will equal.
Go up, pace out the walls of Uruk,
Study the foundation terrace and examine the brickwork.
Is not its masonry of kiln-fired brick?   20
And did not seven masters lay its foundations?
One square mile of city, one square mile of gardens,
One square mile of clay pits, a half square mile of Ishtar's dwelling,
Three and a half square miles is the measure of Uruk!
Search out the foundation box of copper,   25
Release its lock of bronze,
Raise the lid upon its hidden contents,
Take up and read from the lapis tablet
Of him, Gilgamesh, who underwent many hardships.
Surpassing all kings, for his stature renowned,   30
Heroic offspring of Uruk, a charging wild bull,
He leads the way in the vanguard,
He marches at the rear, defender of his comrades.
Mighty floodwall, protector of his troops,
Furious flood-wave smashing walls of stone,   35
Wild calf of Lugalbanda, Gilgamesh is perfect in strength,
Suckling of the sublime wild cow, the woman Ninsun,[3]
Towering Gilgamesh is uncannily perfect.
Opening passes in the mountains,
Digging wells at the highlands' verge,   40
Traversing the ocean, the vast sea, to the sun's rising,
Exploring the furthest reaches of the earth,
Seeking everywhere for eternal life,
Reaching in his might Utanapishtim the Distant One,
Restorer of holy places that the deluge had destroyed,   45
Founder of rites for the teeming peoples,
Who could be his like for kingly virtue?
And who, like Gilgamesh, can proclaim, "I am king!"
Gilgamesh was singled out from the day of his birth,

---

2. City-state ruled by King Gilgamesh. It was the largest city of Mesopotamia at the time and among its important temples featured Eanna, a sanctuary for the goddess of love and warfare, Ishtar.
3. Lugalbanda, Gilgamesh's father, was an earlier king of Uruk. His mother was Ninsun, a goddess called "the wild cow."

Two-thirds of him was divine, one-third of him was human!   50
The Lady of Birth drew his body's image,
The God of Wisdom brought his stature to perfection.

He was perfection in height,
Ideally handsome

In the enclosure of Uruk he strode back and forth,   55
Lording it like a wild bull, his head thrust high.
The onslaught of his weapons had no equal.
His teammates stood forth by his game stick,
He was harrying the young men of Uruk beyond reason.
Gilgamesh would leave no son to his father,   60
Day and night he would rampage fiercely.
This was the shepherd of ramparted Uruk,
This was the people's shepherd,
Bold, superb, accomplished, and mature!
Gilgamesh would leave no girl to her mother!   65
The warrior's daughter, the young man's spouse,
Goddesses kept hearing their plaints.
The gods of heaven, the lords who command,
Said to Anu:[4]

    You created this headstrong wild bull in ramparted Uruk,   70
    The onslaught of his weapons has no equal.
    His teammates stand forth by his game stick,
    He is harrying the young men of Uruk beyond reason.
    Gilgamesh leaves no son to his father!
    Day and night he rampages fiercely.   75
    This is the shepherd of ramparted Uruk,
    This is the people's shepherd,
    Bold, superb, accomplished, and mature!
    Gilgamesh leaves no girl to her mother!

The warrior's daughter, the young man's spouse,   80
Anu kept hearing their plaints.

[Anu speaks.]

    Let them summon Aruru,[5] the great one,
    She created the boundless human race.
    Let her create a partner for Gilgamesh, mighty in strength,
    Let them contend with each other, that Uruk may have peace.   85

They summoned the birth goddess, Aruru:

    You, Aruru, created the boundless human race,
    Now, create what Anu commanded,

---

4. The sky god who is supreme in the pantheon but remote from human affairs. Uruk

was known for its temples for Anu and Ishtar.
5. Goddess of birth.

To his stormy heart, let that one be equal,
Let them contend with each other, that Uruk may have peace.   90

When Aruru heard this,
She conceived within her what Anu commanded.
Aruru wet her hands,
She pinched off clay, she tossed it upon the steppe,
She created valiant Enkidu in the steppe,   95
Offspring of potter's clay, with the force of the hero Ninurta.[6]
Shaggy with hair was his whole body,
He was made lush with head hair, like a woman,
The locks of his hair grew thick as a grainfield.
He knew neither people nor inhabited land,   100
He dressed as animals do.
He fed on grass with gazelles,
With beasts he jostled at the water hole,
With wildlife he drank his fill of water.

A hunter, a trapping-man,   105
Encountered him at the edge of the water hole.
One day, a second, and a third he encountered him at the edge
   of the water hole.
When he saw him, the hunter stood stock-still with terror,
As for Enkidu, he went home with his beasts.
Aghast, struck dumb,   110
His heart in a turmoil, his face drawn,
With woe in his vitals,
His face like a traveler's from afar,
The hunter made ready to speak, saying to his father:

My father, there is a certain fellow who has come
   from the uplands,   115
He is the mightiest in the land, strength is his,
Like the force of heaven, so mighty is his strength.
He constantly ranges over the uplands,
Constantly feeding on grass with beasts,
Constantly making his way to the edge of the water hole.   120
I am too frightened to approach him.
He has filled in the pits I dug,
He has torn out my traps I set,
He has helped the beasts, wildlife of the steppe, slip
   from my hands,
He will not let me work the steppe.   125

His father made ready to speak, saying to the hunter:

My son, in Uruk dwells Gilgamesh,
There is no one more mighty than he.
Like the force of heaven, so mighty is his strength.

6. A god of agriculture and war. Son of Enlil.

Take the road, set off towards Uruk,   130
Tell Gilgamesh of the mightiness-man.
He will give you Shamhat the harlot, take her with you,
Let her prevail over him, instead of a mighty man.
When the wild beasts draw near the water hole,
Let her strip off her clothing, laying bare her charms.   135
When he sees her, he will approach her.
His beasts that grew up with him on the steppe will deny him.

Giving heed to the advice of his father,
The hunter went forth.
He took the road, set off towards Uruk,   140
To the king, Gilgamesh, he said these words:

> There is a certain fellow who has come from the uplands,
> He is mightiest in the land, strength is his,
> Like the force of heaven, so mighty is his strength.
> He constantly ranges over the uplands,   145
> Constantly feeding on grass with his beasts,
> Constantly making his way to the edge of the water hole.
> I am too frightened to approach him.
> He has filled in the pits I dug,
> He has torn out my traps I set,   150
> He has helped the beasts, wildlife of the steppe, slip
>   from my hands,
> He will not allow me to work the steppe.

Gilgamesh said to him, to the hunter:

> Go, hunter, take with you Shamhat the harlot,
> When the wild beasts draw near the water hole,   155
> Let her strip off her clothing, laying bare her charms.
> When he sees her, he will approach her,
> His beasts that grew up with him on the steppe will deny him.

Forth went the hunter, taking with him Shamhat the harlot,
They took the road, going straight on their way.   160
On the third day they arrived at the appointed place.
Hunter and harlot sat down to wait.
One day, a second day, they sat by the edge of the water hole,
The beasts came to the water hole to drink,
The wildlife came to drink their fill of water.   165
But as for him, Enkidu, born in the uplands,
Who feeds on grass with gazelles,
Who drinks at the water hole with beasts,
Who, with wildlife, drinks his fill of water,
Shamhat looked upon him, a human-man,   170
A barbarous fellow from the midst of the steppe:

> There he is, Shamhat, open your embrace,
> Open your embrace, let him take your charms!
> Be not bashful, take his vitality!

When he sees you, he will approach you,   175
Toss aside your clothing, let him lie upon you,
Treat him, a human, to woman's work!
His wild beasts that grew up with him will deny him,
As in his ardor he caresses you!

Shamhat loosened her garments,   180
She exposed her loins, he took her charms.
She was not bashful, she took his vitality.
She tossed aside her clothing and he lay upon her,
She treated him, a human, to woman's work,
As in his ardor he caressed her.   185
Six days, seven nights was Enkidu aroused, flowing into Shamhat.
After he had his fill of her delights,
He set off towards his beasts.
When they saw him, Enkidu, the gazelles shied off,
The wild beasts of the steppe shunned his person.   190
Enkidu had spent himself, his body was limp,
His knees stood still, while his beasts went away.
Enkidu was too slow, he could not run as before,
But he had gained reason and expanded his understanding.

He returned, he sat at the harlot's feet,   195
The harlot gazed upon his face,
While he listened to what the harlot was saying.
The harlot said to him, to Enkidu:

    You are handsome, Enkidu, you are become like a god,
    Why roam the steppe with wild beasts?   200
    Come, let me lead you to ramparted Uruk,
    To the holy temple, abode of Anu and Ishtar,
    The place of Gilgamesh, who is perfect in strength,
    And so, like a wild bull, he lords it over the young men.

As she was speaking to him, her words found favor,   205
He was yearning for one to know his heart, a friend.
Enkidu said to her, to the harlot:

    Come, Shamhat, escort me
    To the lustrous hallowed temple, abode of Anu and Ishtar,
    The place of Gilgamesh, who is perfect in strength,   210
    And so, like a wild bull, he lords it over the young men.
    I myself will challenge him, I will speak out boldly,
    I will raise a cry in Uruk: I am the mighty one!
    I am come forward to alter destinies!
    He who was born in the steppe is mighty, strength is his!   215

[Shamhat speaks.]

    Come then, let him see your face,
    I will show you Gilgamesh, where he is I know full well.
    Come then, Enkidu, to ramparted Uruk,
    Where fellows are resplendent in holiday clothing,

Where every day is set for celebration,   220
Where harps and drums are played.
And the harlots too, they are fairest of form,
Rich in beauty, full of delights,
Even the great gods are kept from sleeping at night!
Enkidu, you who have not learned to live,   225
Oh, let me show you Gilgamesh, the joy-woe man.
Look at him, gaze upon his face,
He is radiant with virility, manly vigor is his,
The whole of his body is seductively gorgeous.
Mightier strength has he than you,   230
Never resting by day or night.
O Enkidu, renounce your audacity!
Gilgamesh is beloved of Shamash,
Anu, Enlil, and Ea broadened his wisdom.[7]
Ere you come down from the uplands,   235
Gilgamesh will dream of you in Uruk.

[*The scene shifts to Uruk.*]

Gilgamesh went to relate the dreams, saying to his mother:

Mother, I had a dream last night:
There were stars of heaven around me,
Like the force of heaven, something kept falling upon me!   240
I tried to carry it but it was too strong for me,
I tried to move it but I could not budge it.
The whole of Uruk was standing by it,
The people formed a crowd around it,
A throng was jostling towards it,   245
Young men were mobbed around it,
Infantile, they were groveling before it!
[I fell in love with it], like a woman I caressed it,
I carried it off and laid it down before you,
Then you were making it my partner.   250

The mother of Gilgamesh, knowing and wise,
Who understands everything, said to her son,
Ninsun the wild cow, knowing and wise,
Who understands everything, said to Gilgamesh:

The stars of heaven around you,   255
Like the force of heaven, what kept falling upon you,
Your trying to move it but not being able to budge it,
Your laying it down before me,
Then my making it your partner,
Your falling in love with it, your caressing it like a woman,   260

---

7. Shamash was god of the sun and of ora-   god of wisdom and magic, is known for his
cles, overseeing matters of justice and right   beneficence to the human race.
dealing; Enlil was supreme god on earth; Ea, a

Means there will come to you a strong one,
A companion who rescues a friend.
He will be mighty in the land, strength will be his,
Like the force of heaven, so mighty will be his strength.
You will fall in love with him and caress him like a woman.   265
He will be mighty and rescue you, time and again.

He had a second dream,
He arose and went before the goddess, his mother,
Gilgamesh said to her, to his mother:

> Mother, I had a second dream.   270
> An axe was thrown down in a street of ramparted Uruk,
> They were crowding around it,
> The whole of Uruk was standing by it,
> The people formed a crowd around it,
> A throng was jostling towards it.   275
> I carried it off and laid it down before you,
> I fell in love with it, like a woman I caressed it,
> Then you were making it my partner.

The mother of Gilgamesh, knowing and wise,
Who understands everything, said to her son,   280
Ninsun the wild cow, knowing and wise,
Who understands everything, said to Gilgamesh:

> My son, the axe you saw is a man.
> Your loving it like a woman and caressing it,
> And my making it your partner   285
> Means there will come to you a strong one,
> A companion who rescues a friend,
> He will be mighty in the land, strength will be his,
> Like the strength of heaven, so mighty will be his strength.

Gilgamesh said to her, to his mother: 290

> Let this befall according to the command of the great
>   counselor Enlil,
> I want a friend for my own counselor,
> For my own counselor do I want a friend!

Even while he was having his dreams,
Shamhat was telling the dreams of Gilgamesh to Enkidu,   295
Each was drawn by love to the other.

Tablet II

While Enkidu was seated before her,
Each was drawn by love to the other.
Enkidu forgot the steppe where he was born,
For six days, seven nights Enkidu was aroused and flowed
    into Shamhat.

The harlot said to him, to Enkidu:

> You are handsome, Enkidu, you are become like a god,
> Why roam the steppe with wild beasts?
> Come, let me lead you to ramparted Uruk,
> To the holy temple, abode of Anu,
> Let me lead you to ramparted Uruk,   10
> To hallowed Eanna, abode of Ishtar,
> The place of Gilgamesh, who is perfect in strength,
> And so, like a wild bull, he lords it over the people.
> You are just like him,
> You will love him like your own self.   15
> Come away from this desolation, bereft even of shepherds.

He heard what she said, accepted her words,
He was yearning for one to know his heart, a friend.
The counsel of Shamhat touched his heart.
She took off her clothing, with one piece she dressed him,   20
The second she herself put on.
Clasping his hand, like a guardian deity she led him,
To the shepherds' huts, where a sheepfold was,
The shepherds crowded around him,
They murmured their opinions among themselves: 25

> This fellow, how like Gilgamesh in stature,
> In stature tall, proud as a battlement.
> No doubt he was born in the steppe,
> Like the force of heaven, mighty is his strength.

They set bread before him,   30
They set beer before him.
He looked uncertainly, then stared,
Enkidu did not know to eat bread,
Nor had he ever learned to drink beer!
The harlot made ready to speak, saying to Enkidu: 35

> Eat the bread, Enkidu, the staff of life,
> Drink the beer, the custom of the land.

Enkidu ate the bread until he was sated,
He drank seven juglets of the beer.
His mood became relaxed, he was singing joyously,   40
He felt lighthearted and his features glowed.
He treated his hairy body with water,
He anointed himself with oil, turned into a man,
He put on clothing, became like a warrior.
He took his weapon, hunted lions,   45
The shepherds lay down to rest at night.
He slew wolves, defeated lions,
The herdsmen, the great gods, lay down to sleep.
Enkidu was their watchman, a wakeful man,
He was tall.   50

He was making love with Shamhat.
He lifted his eyes, he saw a man.
He said to the harlot:

> Shamhat, bring that man here!
> Why has he come?
> I will ask him to account for himself. 55

The harlot summoned the man,
He came over, Enkidu said to him:

> Fellow, where are you rushing?
> What is this, your burdensome errand? 60

The man made ready to speak, said to Enkidu:

> They have invited me to a wedding,
> Is it not people's custom to get married?
> I have heaped high on the festival tray
> The fancy dishes for the wedding. 65
> People's veils are open for the taking.
> For Gilgamesh, king of ramparted Uruk,
> People's veils are open for the taking!
> He mates with the lawful wife,
> He first, the groom after. 70
> By divine decree pronounced,
> From the cutting of his umbilical cord, she is his due.[8]

At the man's account, his face went pale.

Enkidu was walking in front, with Shamhat behind him.

When he entered the street of ramparted Uruk, 75
A multitude crowded around him.
He stood there in the street of ramparted Uruk,
With the people crowding around him.
They said about him:

> He is like Gilgamesh in build,
> Though shorter in stature, he is stronger of frame. 80
> This man, where he was born,
> Ate the springtime grass,
> He must have nursed on the milk of wild beasts.

The whole of Uruk was standing beside him, 85
The people formed a crowd around him,
A throng was jostling towards him,
Young men were mobbed around him,
Infantile, they groveled before him.

---

8. This means that by his birthright Gilgamesh can take brides on their wedding nights, then leave them to their husbands.

In Uruk at this time sacrifices were underway,   90
Young men were celebrating.
The hero stood ready for the upright young man,
For Gilgamesh, as for a god, the partner was ready.
For the goddess of lovemaking, the bed was made,
Gilgamesh was to join with the girl that night.   95

Enkidu approached him,
They met in the public street.
Enkidu blocked the door to the wedding with his foot,
Not allowing Gilgamesh to enter.
They grappled each other, holding fast like wrestlers,   100
They shattered the doorpost, the wall shook.
Gilgamesh and Enkidu grappled each other,
Holding fast like wrestlers,
They shattered the doorpost, the wall shook!
They grappled each other at the door to the wedding,   105
They fought in the street, the public square.
It was Gilgamesh who knelt for the pin, his foot on the ground.
His fury abated, he turned away.
After he turned away,
Enkidu said to him, to Gilgamesh: 110

> As one unique did your mother bear you,
> The wild cow of the ramparts, Ninsun,
> Exalted you above the most valorous of men!
> Enlil has granted you kingship over the people.

They kissed each other and made friends.   115

[*Gilgamesh speaks.*]

> Enkidu has neither father nor mother,
> His hair was growing freely,
> He was born in the steppe.

Enkidu stood still, listening to what he said,
He shuddered and sat down.   120
Tears filled his eyes,
He was listless, his strength turned to weakness.
They clasped each other,
They joined hands.

Gilgamesh made ready to speak,   125
Saying to Enkidu:

> Why are your eyes full of tears,
> Why are you listless, your strength turned to weakness?

Enkidu said to him, to Gilgamesh:

> Cries of sorrow, my friend, have cramped my muscles,   130
> Woe has entered my heart.

Gilgamesh made ready to speak,
Saying to Enkidu:

> There dwells in the forest the fierce monster Humbaba,
> You and I shall kill him   135
> And wipe out something evil from the land.

Enkidu made ready to speak,
Saying to Gilgamesh:

> My friend, I knew that country
> When I roamed with the wild beasts.
> The forest is sixty double leagues in every direction,   140
> Who can go into it?
> Humbaba's cry is the roar of a deluge,
> His maw is fire, his breath is death.
> Why do you want to do this?   145
> The haunt of Humbaba is a hopeless quest.

Gilgamesh made ready to speak,
Saying to Enkidu:

> I must go up the mountain forest,
> I must cut a cedar tree   150
> That cedar must be big enough
> To make whirlwinds when it falls.

Enkidu made ready to speak,
Saying to Gilgamesh:

> How shall the likes of us go to the forest of cedars, my friend?   155
> In order to safeguard the forest of cedars,
> Enlil has appointed him to terrify the people,
> Enlil has destined him seven fearsome glories.[9]
> That journey is not to be undertaken,
> That creature is not to be looked upon.   160
> The guardian of [. . .], the forest of cedars,
> Humbaba's cry is the roar of a deluge,
> His maw is fire, his breath is death.
> He can hear rustling in the forest for sixty double leagues.
> Who can go into his forest?   165
> Adad is first and Humbaba is second.
> Who, even among the gods, could attack him?
> In order to safeguard the forest of cedars,
> Enlil has appointed him to terrify the people,
> Enlil has destined him seven fearsome glories.   170
> Besides, whosoever enters his forest is struck down by disease.

---

9. It was believed that divine beings were surrounded by an awe-inspiring radiance. In the older versions of *Gilgamesh*, this radiance was considered removable, like garments or jewelry.

Gilgamesh made ready to speak,
Saying to Enkidu:

> Why, my friend, do you raise such unworthy objections?
> Who, my friend, can go up to heaven?   175
> The gods dwell forever in the sun,
> People's days are numbered,
> Whatever they attempt is a puff of air.
> Here you are, even you, afraid of death,
> What has become of your bravery's might?   180
> I will go before you,
> You can call out to me, "Go on, be not afraid!"
> If I fall on the way, I'll establish my name:
> "Gilgamesh, who joined battle with fierce Humbaba" they'll say.
>
> You were born and grew up on the steppe,   185
> When a lion sprang at you, you knew what to do.
> Young men fled before you
>
> You speak unworthily,
> How you pule! You make me ill.
> I must set my hand to cutting a cedar tree,   190
> I must establish eternal fame.
> Come, my friend, let's both be off to the foundry,
> Let them cast axes such as we'll need.

Off they went to the craftsmen,
The craftsmen, seated around, discussed the matter.   195
They cast great axes,
Axe blades weighing 180 pounds each they cast.
They cast great daggers,
Their blades were 120 pounds each,
The cross guards of their handles thirty pounds each.   200
They carried daggers worked with thirty pounds of gold,
Gilgamesh and Enkidu bore ten times sixty pounds each.

Gilgamesh spoke to the elders of ramparted Uruk:

> Hear me, O elders of ramparted Uruk,
> The one of whom they speak   205
> I, Gilgamesh, would see!
> The one whose name resounds across the whole world,
> I will hunt him down in the forest of cedars.
> I will make the land hear
> How mighty is the scion of Uruk.   210
> I will set my hand to cutting a cedar,
> An eternal name I will make for myself!

The elders of ramparted Uruk arose,
They responded to Gilgamesh with their advice:

> You are young, Gilgamesh, your feelings carry you away,   215
> You are ignorant of what you speak, flightiness has taken you,

You do not know what you are attempting.
We have heard of Humbaba, his features are grotesque,
Who is there who could face his weaponry?
He can hear rustling in the forest for sixty double leagues.   220
Who can go into it?
Humbaba's cry is the roar of a deluge,
His maw is fire, his breath is death.
Adad is first and Humbaba is second.
Who, even among the gods, could attack him?   225
In order to safeguard the forest of cedars,
Enlil has appointed him to terrify the people,
Enlil has destined him seven fearsome glories.
Besides, whosoever enters his forest is struck down by disease.

When Gilgamesh heard the speech of his counselors,   230
He looked at his friend and laughed:

    Now then, my friend, do you say the same:
    "I am afraid to die"?

Tablet III

The elders spoke to him, saying to Gilgamesh:

    Come back safely to Uruk's haven,
    Trust not, Gilgamesh, in your strength alone,
    Let your eyes see all, make your blow strike home.
    He who goes in front saves his companion,   5
    He who knows the path protects his friend.
    Let Enkidu walk before you,
    He knows the way to the forest of cedars,
    He has seen battle, been exposed to combat.
    Enkidu will protect his friend, safeguard his companion,   10
    Let him return, to be a grave husband.[1]
    We in our assembly entrust the king to you,
    On your return, entrust the king again to us.

Gilgamesh made ready to speak,
Saying to Enkidu: 15

    Come, my friend, let us go to the sublime temple,
    To go before Ninsun, the great queen.
    Ninsun the wise, who is versed in all knowledge,
    Will send us on our way with good advice.

---

1. "Grave husband" plays on the words for "bride" and "interment" (grave); the phrase seems to portend Enkidu's death.

Clasping each other, hand in hand,   20
Gilgamesh and Enkidu went to the sublime temple,
To go before Ninsun, the great queen.
Gilgamesh came forward and entered before her:

    O Ninsun, I have taken on a noble quest,
    I travel a distant road, to where Humbaba is,   25
    To face a battle unknown,
    To mount a campaign unknown.
    Give me your blessing, that I may go on my journey,
    That I may indeed see your face safely again,
    That I may indeed reenter joyfully the gate of ramparted Uruk,   30
    That I may indeed return to hold the festival for the new year,
    That I may indeed celebrate the festival for the new year twice over.
    May that festival be held in my presence, the fanfare sound!
    May their drums resound before you!

Ninsun the wild cow heard them out with sadness,   35
The speeches of Gilgamesh, her son, and Enkidu.
Ninsun entered the bathhouse seven times,
She bathed herself in water with tamarisk and soapwort.[2]
She put on a garment as beseemed her body,
She put on an ornament as beseemed her breast,   40
She set [. . .] and donned her tiara.
She climbed the stairs, mounted to the roof terrace,
She set up an incense offering to Shamash.
She made the offering, to Shamash she raised her hands in prayer:

    Why did you endow my son Gilgamesh with a restless heart?   45
    Now you have moved him to travel
    A distant road, to where Humbaba is,
    To face a battle unknown,
    To mount an expedition unknown.
    Until he goes and returns,   50
    Until he reaches the forest of cedars,
    Until he has slain fierce Humbaba,
    And wipes out from the land the evil thing you hate,
    In the day, when you traverse the sky,
    May Aya,[3] your bride, not fear to remind you,   55
    "Entrust him to the watchmen of the night."

    While Gilgamesh journeys to the forest of cedars,
    May the days be long, may the nights be short,
    May his loins be girded, his arms strong!
    At night, let him make a camp for sleeping,   60
    Let him make a shelter to fall asleep in.
    May Aya, your bride, not fear to remind you,

2. A medicinal plant used in cleansing and
magic.
3. Goddess of dawn and wife of Shamash, the
sun god, often called upon in prayers to intercede with her husband.

When Gilgamesh, Enkidu, and Humbaba meet,
Raise up for his sake, O Shamash, great winds against Humbaba,
South wind, north wind, east wind, west wind, moaning wind,   65
Blasting wind, lashing wind, contrary wind, dust storm,
Demon wind, freezing wind, storm wind, whirlwind:
Raise up thirteen winds to blot out Humbaba's face,
So he cannot charge forward, cannot retreat,
Then let Gilgamesh's weapons defeat Humbaba.   70
As soon as your own [radiance] flares forth,
At that very moment heed the man who reveres you.
May your swift mules [. . .] you,
A comfortable seat, a bed is laid for you,
May the gods, your brethren, serve you your favorite foods,   75
May Aya, the great bride, dab your face with the fringe of her
      spotless garment.

Ninsun the wild cow made a second plea to Shamash:

O Shamash, will not Gilgamesh [. . .] the gods for you?
Will he not share heaven with you?
Will he not share tiara and scepter with the moon?   80
Will he not act in wisdom with Ea in the depths?
Will he not rule the human race with Irnina?[4]
Will he not dwell with Ningishzida[5] in the Land of No Return?

[*Ninsun apparently inducts Enkidu into the staff of her temple.*]

After Ninsun the wild cow had made her plea,
Ninsun the wild cow, knowing and wise, who understands everything,   85
She extinguished the incense, [she came down from the roof terrace],
She summoned Enkidu to impart her message:

Mighty Enkidu, though you are no issue of my womb,
Your little ones shall be among the devotees of Gilgamesh,
The priestesses, votaries, cult women of the temple.   90

She placed a token around Enkidu's neck:

As the priestesses take in a foundling,
And the daughters of the gods bring up an adopted child,
I herewith take Enkidu, as my adopted son,
may Gilgamesh treat him well.   95

His dignitaries stood by, wishing him well,
In a crowd, the young men of Uruk ran along behind him,

---

4. Another name for Ishtar and a local form
of the goddess.

5. Literally "Lord of the Upright Tree," a
netherworld deity.

While his dignitaries made obeisance to him:

> Come back safely to Uruk's haven!
> Trust not, Gilgamesh, in your strength alone,   100
> Let your eyes see all, make your blow strike home.
> He who goes in front saves his companion,
> He who knows the path protects his friend.
> Let Enkidu walk before you,
> He knows the way to the forest of cedars.   105
> He has seen battle, been exposed to combat.
> Enkidu will protect his friend, safeguard his companion,
> Let him return, to be a grave husband.
> We in our assembly entrust the king to you,
> On your return, entrust the king again to us.   110

The elders hailed him,
Counseled Gilgamesh for the journey:

> Trust not, Gilgamesh, in your own strength,
> Let your vision be clear, take care of yourself.
> Let Enkidu go ahead of you,   115
> He has seen the road, has traveled the way.
> He knows the ways into the forest
> And all the tricks of Humbaba.
> He who goes first safeguards his companion,
> His vision is clear, he protects himself.   120
> May Shamash help you to your goal,
> May he disclose to you what your words propose,
> May he open for you the barred road,
> Make straight the pathway to your tread,
> Make straight the upland to your feet.   125
> May nightfall bring you good tidings,
> May Lugalbanda stand by you in your cause.
> In a trice accomplish what you desire,
> Wash your feet in the river of Humbaba whom you seek.
> When you stop for the night, dig a well,   130
> May there always be pure water in your waterskin.[6]
> You should libate cool water to Shamash
> And be mindful of Lugalbanda.

Tablet IV

At twenty double leagues they took a bite to eat,
At thirty double leagues they made their camp,
Fifty double leagues they went in a single day,
A journey of a month and a half in three days.
They approached Mount Lebanon.   5
Towards sunset they dug a well,
Filled their waterskin with water.

---

6. Travelers carried drinking water in leather bags.

Gilgamesh went up onto the mountain,
He poured out flour for an offering, saying.

    O mountain, bring me a propitious dream!   10

Enkidu made Gilgamesh a shelter for receiving dreams,
A gust was blowing, he fastened the door.
He had him lie down in a circle of flour,
And spreading out like a net, Enkidu lay down in the doorway.
Gilgamesh sat there, chin on his knee.   15
Sleep, which usually steals over people, fell upon him.
In the middle of the night he awoke,
Got up and said to his friend:

    My friend, did you not call me? Why am I awake?
    Did you not touch me? Why am I disturbed?   20
    Did a god not pass by? Why does my flesh tingle?
    My friend, I had a dream,
    And the dream I had was very disturbing.

The one born in the steppe,
Enkidu explained the dream to his friend: 25

    My friend, your dream is favorable,
    The dream is very precious as an omen.
    My friend, the mountain you saw is Humbaba,
    We will catch Humbaba and kill him,
    Then we will throw down his corpse on the field of battle.   30
    Further, at dawn the word of Shamash will be in our favor.

At twenty double leagues they took a bite to eat,
At thirty double leagues they made their camp,
Fifty double leagues they went in a single day,
A journey of a month and a half in three days.   35
They approached Mount Lebanon.
Towards sunset they dug a well,
They filled their waterskin with water.
Gilgamesh went up onto the mountain,
He poured out flour for an offering, saying: 40

    O mountain, bring me a propitious dream!

Enkidu made Gilgamesh a shelter for receiving dreams,
A gust was blowing, he fastened the door.
He had him lie down in a circle of flour,
And spreading out like a net, Enkidu lay down in the doorway.   45
Gilgamesh sat there, chin on his knee.
Sleep, which usually steals over people, fell upon him.
In the middle of the night he awoke,

Got up and said to his friend:

> My friend, did you not call me? Why am I awake?   50
> Did you not touch me? Why am I disturbed?
> Did a god not pass by? Why does my flesh tingle?
> My friend, I had a second dream,
> And the dream I had was very disturbing.
> A mountain was in my dream, an enemy.   55
> It threw me down, pinning my feet,
> A fearsome glare grew ever more intense.
> A certain young man, handsomest in the world, truly handsome he was,
> He pulled me out from the base of the mountain,
> He gave me water to drink and eased my fear,   60
> He set my feet on the ground again.

The one born in the steppe,
Enkidu explained the dream to his friend:

> My friend, your dream is favorable,
> The dream is very precious as an omen.   65
> My friend, we will go [. . .]
> The strange thing was Humbaba,
> Was not the mountain, the strange thing, Humbaba?
> Come then, banish your fear.

At twenty double leagues they took a bite to eat,   70
At thirty double leagues they made their camp,
Fifty double leagues they went in a single day,
A journey of a month and a half in three days.
They approached Mount Lebanon.
Towards sunset they dug a well,   75
They filled their waterskin with water.
Gilgamesh went up onto the mountain,
He poured out flour as an offering, saying:

> O mountain, bring me a propitious dream!

Enkidu made Gilgamesh a shelter for receiving dreams,   80
A gust was blowing, he fastened the door.
He had him lie down in a circle of flour,
And spreading out like a net, Enkidu lay down in the doorway.
Gilgamesh sat there, chin on his knee.
Sleep, which usually steals over people, fell upon him.   85
In the middle of the night he awoke,
Got up and said to his friend:

> My friend, did you not call me? Why am I awake?
> Did you not touch me? Why am I disturbed?
> Did a god not pass by? Why does my flesh tingle?   90
> My friend, I had a third dream,
> And the dream I had was very disturbing.

The heavens cried out, the earth was thundering,
Daylight faded, darkness fell,
Lightning flashed, fire shot up,   95
The flames burgeoned, spewing death.
Then the glow was dimmed, the fire was extinguished,
The burning coals that were falling turned to ashes.
You who were born in the steppe, let us discuss it.

Enkidu [explained], helped him accept his dream,   100
Saying to Gilgamesh:

[*Enkidu's explanation is mostly lost, but perhaps it was that the volcanolike
explosion was Humbaba, who flared up, then died.*]

Humbaba, like a god [. . .]
[. . .] the light flaring [. . .]
We will be victorious over him.
Humbaba aroused our fury,   105
we will prevail over him.
Further, at dawn the word of Shamash will be in our favor.

At twenty double leagues they took a bite to eat,
At thirty double leagues they made their camp.
Fifty double leagues they went in a single day,   110
A journey of a month and a half in three days.
They approached Mount Lebanon.[7]
Towards sunset they dug a well,
They filled their waterskin with water.
Gilgamesh went up onto the mountain,   115
He poured out flour as an offering, saying:

O mountain, bring me a propitious dream!

Enkidu made Gilgamesh a shelter for receiving dreams,
A gust was blowing, he fastened the door.
He had him lie down in a circle of flour,   120
And spreading out like a net, Enkidu lay down in the doorway.
Gilgamesh sat there, chin on his knee.
Sleep, which usually steals over people, fell upon him.
In the middle of the night he awoke,

My friend, did you not call me? Why am I awake?   125
Did you not touch me? Why am I disturbed?
Did a god not pass by? Why does my flesh tingle?
My friend, I had a [fourth] dream,
The dream I had was very disturbing.
My friend, I saw a fourth dream,   130
More terrible than the other three.

---

7. Mountain ranges along the Mediterranean coast of present-day Lebanon.

I saw the lion-headed monster-bird Anzu[8] in the sky.
He began to descend upon us, like a cloud.
He was terrifying, his appearance was horrible!
His maw was fire, his breath death.   135

[*Enkidu explains the fourth dream.*]

The lion-headed monster-bird Anzu who descended upon us, like a cloud,
Who was terrifying, whose appearance was horrible,
Whose maw was fire, whose breath was death,
Whose dreadful aura frightens you.
The young man you saw was mighty Shamash.   140

[*It is not clear how many dreams there were in all though one version refers to
five. A poorly preserved manuscript of an old version includes the following
dream that could be inserted here, as portions of it are fulfilled in
Tablet VI.*]

I was grasping a wild bull of the steppe!
As it bellowed, it split the earth,
It raised clouds of dust, blotting out the sky.
I crouched down before it,
It seized my hands, pinioned my arms.   145
Someone pulled me out,
He stroked my cheeks, he gave me to drink from his waterskin.

[*Enkidu explains the dream.*]

It is the god, my friend, to whom we go,
The wild bull was no enemy at all,
The wild bull you saw is Shamash, the protector,   150
He will take our hands in need.
The one who gave you water to drink from his waterskin
Is your god who proclaims your glory, Lugalbanda.
We should rely on one another,
We will accomplish together a deed unheard of in the land.   155

[*Something has happened to discourage Gilgamesh, perhaps an unfavorable
oracle. Shamash comes to their aid with timely advice, just before they hear
Humbaba's cry.*]

[*Before Shamash his tears flowed down*]:

Remember, stand by me, hear [my prayer],
Gilgamesh, scion of [ramparted Uruk]!

8. Monstrous bird with the head of a lion. He appears in a mythological story, where he steals
power from the god Enlil but is defeated in battle by Enlil's son Ninurta.

Shamash heard what he said,
From afar a warning voice called to him from the sky: 160

> Hurry, confront him, do not let him go off into the forest,
> Do not let him enter the thicket!
> He has not donned all of his seven fearsome glories,
> One he has on, six he has left off!

They charged forward like wild bulls. 165
He let out a single bloodcurdling cry,
The guardian of the forest shrieked aloud,
Humbaba was roaring like thunder.

Gilgamesh made ready to speak,
Said to Enkidu: 170

> Humbaba [. . .]
> We cannot confront him separately.

Gilgamesh spoke to him, said to Enkidu:

> My friend, why do we raise such unworthy objections?
> Have we not crossed all the mountains? 175
> The end of the quest is before us.
> My friend knows battle,
> You rubbed on herbs, you did not fear death,
> Your battle cry should be dinning like a drum!
> Let the paralysis leave your arm, let weakness quit your knees, 180
> Take my hand, my friend, let us walk on together!
> Your heart should be urging you to battle.
> Forget about death,
> He who marches first, protects himself,
> Let him keep his comrade safe! 185
> Those two will have established fame down through the ages.

The pair reached the edge of the forest,
They stopped their talk and stood there.

Tablet V

They stood at the edge of the forest,
They gazed at the height of the cedars,
They gazed at the way into the forest.
Where Humbaba would walk, a path was made,
Straight were the ways and easy the going. 5
They saw the cedar mountain, dwelling of the gods, sacred to the
    goddess Irnina.
On the slopes of that mountain, the cedar bears its abundance,
Agreeable is its shade, full of pleasures.
The undergrowth is tangled, the [thicket] interwoven.

[In older versions, they begin to cut trees and Humbaba hears the noise. In the standard version, they meet Humbaba first.]

Humbaba made ready to speak, saying to Gilgamesh: 10

> How well-advised they are, the fool Gilgamesh and the yokelman!
> Why have you come here to me?
> Come now, Enkidu, small-fry, who does not know his father,
> Spawn of a turtle or tortoise, who sucked no mother's milk!
> I used to see you when you were younger but would not go near you.   15
> Had I killed the likes of you, would I have filled my belly?
> You have brought Gilgamesh before me,
> You stand there, a barbarian foe!
> I should cut off your head, Gilgamesh, throat and neck,
> I should let cawing buzzard, screaming eagle, and vulture feed
>   on your flesh.   20

Gilgamesh made ready to speak, saying to Enkidu:

> My friend, Humbaba's features have grown more grotesque,
> We strode up like heroes to vanquish him.

Enkidu made ready to speak, saying to Gilgamesh:

> Why, my friend, do you raise such unworthy objections?   25
> How you pule! You make me ill.
> Now, my friend, this has dragged on long enough.
> The time has come to pour the copper into the mold.
> Will you take another hour to blow the bellows,
> An hour more to let it cool?   30
> To launch the flood weapon, to wield the lash,
> Retreat not a foot, you must not turn back,
> Let your eyes see all, let your blow strike home!

[In the combat with Humbaba, the rift valley of Lebanon is formed by their circling feet.]

He struck the ground to confront him.
At their heels the earth split apart,   35
As they circled, the ranges of Lebanon were sundered!
The white clouds turned black,
Death rained down like fog upon them.
Shamash raised the great winds against Humbaba,
South wind, north wind, east wind, west wind, moaning wind,   40
Blasting wind, lashing wind, contrary wind, dust storm,
Demon wind, freezing wind, storm wind, whirlwind:
The thirteen winds blotted out Humbaba's face,
He could not charge forward, he could not retreat.
Then Gilgamesh's weapons defeated Humbaba.   45

Humbaba begged for life, saying to Gilgamesh:

You were once a child, Gilgamesh, you had a mother who bore you,
You are the offspring of Ninsun the wild cow.
You grew up to fulfill the oracle of Shamash, lord of the mountain:
"Gilgamesh, scion of Uruk, is to be king."   50

O Gilgamesh, spare my life!
Let me dwell here for you [as your . . .],
Say however many trees you [require . . .],
For you I will guard the myrtle wood [. . .].

Enkidu made ready to speak, saying to Gilgamesh: 55

My friend! Do not listen to what Humbaba says,
Do not heed his entreaties!

[*Humbaba is speaking to Enkidu.*]

You know the lore of my forest,
And you understand all I have to say.
I might have lifted you up, dangled you from a twig at the entrance
    to my forest,   60
I might have let cawing buzzard, screaming eagle, and vulture feed
    on your flesh.
Now then, Enkidu, mercy is up to you,
Tell Gilgamesh to spare my life!

Enkidu made ready to speak, saying to Gilgamesh:

My friend! Humbaba is guardian of the forest of cedars,   65
Finish him off for the kill, put him out of existence.
Humbaba is guardian of the forest of cedars,
Finish him off for the kill, put him out of existence,
Before Enlil the foremost one hears of this!
The great gods will become angry with us,   70
Enlil in Nippur, Shamash in Larsa.[9]
Establish your reputation for all time:
"Gilgamesh, who slew Humbaba."

May the pair of them never reach old age!
May Gilgamesh and Enkidu come across no graver friend to bank on![1]   75

9. Nippur and Larsa are cities in Babylonia with important temples to Enlil and Shamash, respectively.
1. This is one of the elaborate, sometimes obscure wordplays in *Gilgamesh*. In Humbaba's curse, *cross* sounds like *friend* and *bank* echoes *grave*, so that the giant's words can mean either "May they not cross water safely to the opposite bank" or "May they not find a friend to rely on."

[*An old version contains the following exchange between Gilgamesh and Enkidu concerning the seven fearsome glories of Humbaba.*]

Gilgamesh said to Enkidu:

> Now, my friend, let us go on to victory!
> The glories will be lost in the confusion,
> The glories will be lost and the brightness will [. . .].

Enkidu said to him, to Gilgamesh: 80

> My friend, catch the bird and where will its chicks go?
> Let us search out the glories later,
> They will run around in the grass like chicks.
> Strike him again, then kill his retinue.

[*Gilgamesh kills Humbaba. In some versions he has to strike multiple blows before the monster falls.*]

Gilgamesh heeded his friend's command,   85
He raised the axe at his side,
He drew the sword at his belt.
Gilgamesh struck him on the neck,
Enkidu, his friend, [. . .].
They pulled out [. . .] as far as the lungs,   90
He tore out the [. . .],
He forced the head into a cauldron.
[. . .] in abundance fell on the mountain,
He struck him, Humbaba the guardian, down to the ground.
His blood [. . .]   95
For two leagues the cedars [. . .].
He killed the glories with him.
He slew the monster, guardian of the forest,
At whose cry the mountains of Lebanon trembled,
At whose cry all the mountains quaked.   100
He slew the monster, guardian of the forest,
He trampled on the broken [. . .],
He struck down the seven glories.
The battle net [. . .], the sword weighing eight times sixty pounds,
He took the weight of ten times sixty pounds upon him,   105
He forced his way into the forest,
He opened the secret dwelling of the supreme gods.
Gilgamesh cut down the trees,
Enkidu chose the timbers.
Enkidu made ready to speak, said to Gilgamesh: 110

> You killed the guardian by your strength,
> Who else could cut through this forest of trees?
> My friend, we have felled the lofty cedar,
> Whose crown once pierced the sky.
> I will make a door six times twelve cubits high, two times twelve
>   cubits wide,   115

One cubit shall be its thickness,
Its hinge pole, ferrule, and pivot box shall be unique.[2]
Let no stranger approach it, may only a god go through.
Let the Euphrates bring it to Nippur,
Nippur, the sanctuary of Enlil. 120
May Enlil be delighted with you,
May Enlil rejoice over it!

They lashed together a raft
Enkidu embarked
And Gilgamesh [. . .] the head of Humbaba. 125

Tablet VI

He washed his matted locks, cleaned his head strap,
He shook his hair down over his shoulders.
He threw off his filthy clothes, he put on clean ones,
Wrapping himself in a cloak, he tied on his sash,
Gilgamesh put on his kingly diadem. 5
The princess Ishtar coveted Gilgamesh's beauty:

Come, Gilgamesh, you shall be my bridegroom!
Give, oh give me of your lusciousness!
You shall be my husband and I shall be your wife.
I will ready for you a chariot of lapis and gold, 10
With golden wheels and fittings of gemstones,
You shall harness storm demons as if they were giant mules.
Enter our house amidst fragrance of cedar,
When you enter our house,
The splendid exotic doorsill shall do you homage, 15
Kings, nobles, and princes shall kneel before you,
They shall bring you gifts of mountain and lowland as tribute.
Your goats shall bear triplets, your ewes twins,
Your pack-laden donkey shall overtake the mule,
Your horses shall run proud before the wagon, 20
Your ox in the yoke shall have none to compare!

Gilgamesh made ready to speak,
Saying to the princess Ishtar:
What shall I give you if I take you to wife?
Shall I give you a headdress for your person, or clothing?
Shall I give you bread or drink? 25
Shall I give you food, worthy of divinity?
Shall I give you drink, worthy of queenship?
What would I get if I marry you?
You are a brazier that goes out when it freezes, 30

---

2. Mesopotamian doors did not use hinges but were made of a panel attached to a post. It was this post, or "hinge pole," that rotated when the door was opened or closed, some- times on a piece of metal, or "ferrule," at the bottom. The top of the post was cased or enclosed so the hinge pole would not slip off its pivot point.

A flimsy door that keeps out neither wind nor draught,
A palace that crushes a warrior,
A mouse that gnaws through its housing,
Tar that smears its bearer,
Waterskin that soaks its bearer,   35
Weak stone that undermines a wall,
Battering ram that destroys the wall for an enemy,
Shoe that pinches its wearer!
Which of your lovers lasted forever?
Which of your heroes went up to heaven?   40
Come, I call you to account for your lovers:
He who had jugs of cream on his shoulders and [. . .] on his arm,
For Dumuzi,[3] your girlhood lover,
You ordained year after year of weeping.
You fell in love with the brightly colored roller bird,   45
Then you struck him and broke his wing.
In the woods he sits crying "My-wing!"
You fell in love with the lion, perfect in strength,
Then you dug for him ambush pits, seven times seven.
You fell in love with the wild stallion, eager for the fray,   50
Whip, goad, and lash you ordained for him,
Seven double leagues of galloping you ordained for him,
You ordained that he muddy his water when he drinks,
You ordained perpetual weeping for his mother, divine Silili.
You fell in love with the shepherd, keeper of herds,   55
Who always set out cakes baked in embers for you,
Slaughtered kids for you every day.
You struck him and turned him into a wolf,
His own shepherd boys harry him off,
And his own hounds snap at his heels!   60
You fell in love with Ishullanu,[4] your father's gardener,
Who always brought you baskets of dates,
Who daily made your table splendid.
You wanted him, so you sidled up to him:
"My Ishullanu, let's have a taste of your vigor!   65
Bring out your member, touch our sweet spot!"
Ishullanu said to you,
"Me? What do you want of me?
Hath my mother not baked? Have I not eaten?
Shall what I taste for food be insults and curses?   70
In the cold, is my cover to be the touch of a reed?"
When you heard what he said,
You struck him and turned him into a scarecrow,
You left him stuck in his own garden patch,
His well sweep goes up no longer, his bucket does not descend.   75

---

3. Shepherd god. He was a youthful lover of
Ishtar, who let him be taken to the netherworld when she had to provide a substitute for
herself.

4. According to a Sumerian myth, Ishtar
seduced a gardener named Ishullanu whom she
then sought to kill.

As for me, now that you've fallen in love with me, you will treat me
  like them!
When Ishtar heard this,
Ishtar was furious and went up to heaven,
Ishtar went sobbing before Anu, her father,
Before Antum, her mother, her tears flowed down: 80

> Father, Gilgamesh has said outrageous things about me,
> Gilgamesh's been spouting insults about me,
> Insults and curses against me!

Anu made ready to speak,
Saying to the princess Ishtar: 85

> Well now, did you not provoke the king, Gilgamesh,
> And so Gilgamesh spouted insults about you,
> Insults and curses against you?

Ishtar made ready to speak,
Saying to Anu, her father: 90

> Well then, Father, pretty please, the Bull of Heaven,
> So I can kill Gilgamesh on his home ground.
> If you don't give me the Bull of Heaven,
> I'll strike [. . .] to its foundation,
> I'll raise up the dead to devour the living,   95
> The dead shall outnumber the living!

Anu made ready to speak,
Saying to the princess Ishtar:

> If you insist on the Bull of Heaven from me,
> Let the widow of Uruk gather seven years of chaff,
> Let the farmer of Uruk raise seven years of hay.   100

Ishtar made ready to speak,
Saying to Anu, her father:

> The widow of Uruk has gathered seven years of chaff,
> The farmer of Uruk has raised seven years of hay.   105
> With the Bull of Heaven's fury I will kill him!

When Anu heard what Ishtar said,
He placed the lead rope of the Bull of Heaven in her hand,
Ishtar led the Bull of Heaven away.

When it reached Uruk,   110
It dried up the groves, reedbeds, and marshes,
It went down to the river, it lowered the river by seven cubits.
At the bull's snort, a pit opened up,
One hundred young men of Uruk fell into it.
At its second snort, a pit opened up,   115
Two hundred young men of Uruk fell into it.

At its third snort, a pit opened up,
Enkidu fell into it, up to his middle.
Enkidu jumped out and seized the bull by its horns,
The bull spewed its foam in his face,   120
Swished dung at him with the tuft of its tail.
Enkidu made ready to speak,
Saying to Gilgamesh:

> I have seen, my friend, the strength of the Bull of Heaven,
> So knowing its strength, I know how to deal with it.   125
> I will get around the strength of the Bull of Heaven,
> I will circle behind the Bull of Heaven,
> I will grab it by the tuft of its tail,
> I will set my feet on its [. . .],
> Then you, like a strong, skillful slaughterer,   130
> Thrust your dagger between neck, horn, and tendon!

Enkidu circled behind the Bull of Heaven,
He grabbed it by the tuft of its tail,
He set his feet on its [. . .],
And Gilgamesh, like a strong, skillful slaughterer,   135
Thrust his dagger between neck, horn, and tendon!

After they had killed the Bull of Heaven,
They ripped out its heart and set it before Shamash.
They stepped back and prostrated themselves before Shamash,
Then the two comrades sat down beside each other.   140
Ishtar went up on the wall of ramparted Uruk,
She writhed in grief, she let out a wail:

> That bully Gilgamesh who demeaned me, he's killed the Bull of Heaven!

When Enkidu heard what Ishtar said,
He tore off the bull's haunch and flung it at her: 145

> If I could vanquish you, I'd turn you to this,
> I'd drape the guts beside you!

Ishtar convened the cult women, prostitutes, harlots,
She set up a lament over the haunch of the bull.

Gilgamesh summoned all the expert craftsmen,   150
The craftsmen marveled at the massiveness of its horns,
They were molded from thirty pounds each of lapis blue,
Their outer shell was two thumbs thick!
Six times three hundred quarts of oil, the capacity of both,
He donated to anoint the statue of his god, Lugalbanda.   155
He brought them inside and hung them up in his master bedroom.

They washed their hands in the Euphrates,
Clasping each other, they came away,

Paraded through the streets of Uruk.
The people of Uruk crowded to look upon them.   160
Gilgamesh made a speech
To the servant-women of his palace:

> Who is the handsomest of young men?
> Who is the most glorious of males?
> Gilgamesh is the handsomest of young men!   165
> Gilgamesh is the most glorious of males!
> She at whom we flung the haunch in our passion,
> Ishtar, she has no one in the street to satisfy her.

Gilgamesh held a celebration in his palace.
The young men slept stretched out on the couch of night.   170
While Enkidu slept, he had a dream.

Tablet VII

My friend, why were the great gods in council?

Enkidu raised,
spoke to the door as if it were human:[5]

> O bosky door, insensate,
> Which lends an ear that is not there,
> I sought your wood for twenty double leagues,   5
> Till I beheld a lofty cedar.
> No rival had your tree in the forest.
> Six times twelve cubits was your height, two times twelve cubits was
>   your width,
> One cubit was your thickness,   10
> Your hinge pole, ferrule, and pivot box were unique.
> I made you, I brought you to Nippur, I set you up.
> Had I known, O door, how you would requite me,
> And that this your goodness towards me [. . .],
> I would have raised my axe, I would have chopped you down,   15
> I would have floated you as a raft to the temple of Shamash,
> I would have set up the lion-headed monster-bird Anzu at its gate,
> Because Shamash heard my plea
> He gave me the weapon to kill Humbaba.
> Now then, O door, it was I who made you, it was I who set you up.   20
> I will tear you out!
> May a king who shall arise after me despise you,
> May he alter my inscription and put on his own![6]

5. Because there is a gap in the text, it is unclear why Enkidu curses the door so violently. Since it is made of cedar wood from the forest, it might embody the adventure that results in Enkidu's death.

6. These concluding words of Enkidu's curse of the cedar door parody traditional Mesopotamian inscriptions affixed to monuments, which called the wrath of the gods upon anyone who damaged, removed, or usurped the monument.

He tore out his hair, threw away his clothing.

When he heard out this speech, swiftly, quickly his tears flowed down,   25
When Gilgamesh heard out Enkidu's speech, swiftly, quickly, his tears
   flowed down.

Gilgamesh made ready to speak, saying to Enkidu:

> My friend, you are rational but you say strange things,
> Why, my friend, does your heart speak strange things?
> The dream is a most precious omen, though very frightening,   30
> Your lips are buzzing like flies.
> Though frightening, the dream is a precious omen.
> The gods left mourning for the living,
> The dream left mourning for the living,
> The dream left woe for the living!   35
> Now I shall go pray to the great gods,
> I will be assiduous to my own god, I will pray to yours,
> To Anu, father of the gods,
> To Enlil, counselor of the gods,
> I will make your image of gold beyond measure.   40
> You can pay no silver, no gold can you [. . .],
> What Enlil commanded is not like the [. . .] of the gods,
> What he commanded, he will not retract.
> The verdict he has scrivened, he will not reverse nor erase.
> People often die before their time.   45

At the first glimmer of dawn,
Enkidu lifted his head, weeping before Shamash,
Before the sun's fiery glare, his tears flowed down:

> I have turned to you, O Shamash, on account of the precious days
>   of my life,
> As for that hunter, the entrapping-man,   50
> Who did not let me get as much life as my friend,
> May that hunter not get enough to make him a living.
> Make his profit loss, cut down his take,
> May his income, his portion evaporate before you,
> Any wildlife that enters his traps, make it go out the window!   55

When he had cursed the hunter to his heart's content,
He resolved to curse the harlot Shamhat:

> Come, Shamhat, I will ordain you a destiny,
> A destiny that will never end, forever and ever!
> I will lay on you the greatest of all curses,   60
> Swiftly, inexorably, may my curse come upon you.
> May you never make a home that you can enjoy,
> May you never caress a child of your own,
> May you never be received among decent women.
> May beer sludge impregnate your lap,   65
> May the drunkard bespatter your best clothes with vomit.

May your swain prefer beauties,
May he pinch you like potter's clay.
May you get no alabaster,
May no table to be proud of be set in your house.   70
May the nook you enjoy be a doorstep,
May the public crossroads be your dwelling,
May vacant lots be your sleeping place,
May the shade of a wall be your place of business.
May brambles and thorns flay your feet,   75
May toper and sober slap your cheek.[7]
May riffraff of the street shove each other in your brothel,
May there be a brawl there.
When you stroll with your cronies, may they catcall after you.
May the builder not keep your roof in repair,   80
May the screech owl roost in the ruins of your home.
May a feast never be held where you live.

May your purple finery be expropriated,
May filthy underwear be what you are given,
Because you diminished me, an innocent,   85
Yes me, an innocent, you wronged me in my steppe.

When Shamash heard what he said,
From afar a warning voice called to him from the sky:

O Enkidu, why curse Shamhat the harlot,
Who fed you bread, fit for a god,   90
Who poured you beer, fit for a king,
Who dressed you in a noble garment,
And gave you handsome Gilgamesh for a comrade?
Now then, Gilgamesh is your friend and blood brother!
Won't he lay you down in the ultimate resting place?   95
In a perfect resting place he will surely lay you down!
He will settle you in peaceful rest in that dwelling sinister,
Rulers of the netherworld will do you homage.
He will have the people of Uruk shed bitter tears for you,
He will make the pleasure-loving people burdened down for you,   100
And, as for him, after your death, he will let his hair grow matted,
He will put on a lion skin and roam the steppe.

When Enkidu heard the speech of the valiant Shamash,
His raging heart was calmed,
his fury was calmed: 105

Come, Shamhat, I will ordain you a destiny,
My mouth that cursed you, let it bless you instead.
May governors and dignitaries fall in love with you,
May the man one double league away slap his thighs in excitement,
May the man two double leagues away let down his hair.   110

7. That is, may anyone hit her, drunk or not.

May the subordinate not hold back from you, but open his trousers,
May he give you obsidian, lapis, and gold,
May ear bangles be your gift.
To the man whose wealth is secure, whose granaries are full,
May Ishtar of the gods introduce you,   115
For your sake may the wife and mother of seven be abandoned.

Enkidu was sick at heart,
He lay there lonely.
He told his friend what weighed on his mind:

My friend, what a dream I had last night!   120
Heaven cried out, earth made reply,
I was standing between them.
There was a certain man, his face was somber,
His face was like that of the lion-headed monster-bird Anzu,
His hands were the paws of a lion,   125
His fingernails were the talons of an eagle.
He seized me by the hair, he was too strong for me,
I hit him but he sprang back like a swing rope,
He hit me and capsized me like a raft.
Like a wild bull he trampled me,   130
"Save me, my friend!"—but you did not save me!
He trussed my limbs like a bird's.
Holding me fast, he took me down to the house of shadows,
    the dwelling of hell,
To the house whence none who enters comes forth,
On the road from which there is no way back,   135
To the house whose dwellers are deprived of light,
Where dust is their fare and their food is clay.
They are dressed like birds in feather garments,
Yea, they shall see no daylight, for they abide in darkness.
Dust lies thick on the door and bolt,   140
When I entered that house of dust,
I saw crowns in a heap,
There dwelt the kings, the crowned heads who once ruled the land,
Who always set out roast meat for Anu and Enlil,
Who always set out baked offerings, libated cool water from
    waterskins.   145
In that house of dust I entered,
Dwelt high priests and acolytes,
Dwelt reciters of spells and ecstatics,[8]
Dwelt the anointers of the great gods,
Dwelt old King Etana[9] and the god of the beasts,   150
Dwelt the queen of the netherworld, Ereshkigal.[1]

---

8. Reciters of spells were learned scholars, while prophets, or "ecstatics," were people who spoke in a trance without having studied their words. Ecstatics were sometimes social outcasts or people without education.

9. Ancient king who was said to have flown up to heaven on an eagle to find a plant that would help him and his wife have a child.
1. Queen of the netherworld and jealous sister of the goddess Ishtar.

Belet-seri,[2] scribe of the netherworld, was kneeling before her,
She was holding a tablet and reading to her,
She lifted her head, she looked at me:
"Who brought this man?"   155
I who went with you through all hardships,
Remember me, my friend, do not forget what I have undergone!
My friend had a dream needing no interpretation.

The day he had the dream, his strength ran out.
Enkidu lay there one day, a second day he was ill,   160
Enkidu lay in his bed, his illness grew worse.
A third day, a fourth day, Enkidu's illness grew worse.
A fifth, a sixth, a seventh,
An eighth, a ninth, a tenth day,
Enkidu's illness grew worse.   165
An eleventh, a twelfth day,
Enkidu lay in his bed.
He called for Gilgamesh, roused him with his cry:

My friend laid on me the greatest curse of all!
I feared the battle but will die in my bed,   170
My friend, he who falls quickly in battle is glorious.

[*Enkidu dies.*]

Tablet VIII

At the first glimmer of dawn,
Gilgamesh lamented his friend:

Enkidu, my friend, your mother the gazelle,
Your father the wild ass brought you into the world,
Onagers raised you on their milk,
And the wild beasts taught you all the grazing places.   5
The pathways, O Enkidu, to the forest of cedars,
May they weep for you, without falling silent, night and day.
May the elders of the teeming city, ramparted Uruk, weep for you,
May the crowd who blessed our departure weep for you.   10
May the heights of highland and mountain weep for you,
May the lowlands wail like your mother.
May the forest of balsam and cedar weep for you,
Which we slashed in our fury.
May bear, hyena, panther, leopard, deer, jackal,   15
Lion, wild bull, gazelle, ibex, the beasts and creatures of the steppe,
    weep for you.[3]
May the sacred Ulaya River[4] weep for you, along whose banks we once
    strode erect,
May the holy Euphrates weep for you,
Whose waters we libated from waterskins.

---

2. Literally "Lady of the Steppe," scribe and bookkeeper in the netherworld.
3. This refers to an episode that does not appear in the extant portions of the epic.
4. Karun River in the southwest of modern Iran.

May the young men of ramparted Uruk weep for you,   20
Who watched us slay the Bull of Heaven in combat.
May the plowman weep for you at his plow,
Who extolled your name in the sweet song of harvest home.
May they weep for you, of the teeming city of Uruk,
Who exalted your name at the first [. . .].   25
May the shepherd and herdsman weep for you,
Who held the milk and buttermilk to your mouth,
May the nurse weep for you,
Who treated your rashes with butter.
May the harlot weep for you,   30
Who massaged you with sweet-smelling oil.
Like brothers may they weep for you,
Like sisters may they tear out their hair for your sake.
Enkidu, as your father, your mother,
I weep for you bitterly.   35

Hear me, O young men, listen to me,
Hear me, O elders of Uruk, listen to me!
I mourn my friend Enkidu,
I howl as bitterly as a professional keener.
Oh for the axe at my side, oh for the safeguard by my hand,   40
Oh for the sword at my belt, oh for the shield before me,
Oh for my best garment, oh for the raiment that pleased me most!
An ill wind rose against me and snatched it away!
O my friend, swift wild donkey, mountain onager, panther of the steppe,
O Enkidu my friend, swift wild donkey, mountain onager, panther
    of the steppe!   45
You who stood by me when we climbed the mountain,
Seized and slew the Bull of Heaven,
Felled Humbaba who dwelt in the forest of cedar,
What now is this sleep that has seized you?
Come back to me! You hear me not.   50

But, as for him, he did not raise his head.
He touched his heart but it was not beating.
Then he covered his friend's face, like a bride's.
He hovered round him like an eagle,
Like a lioness whose cubs are in a pitfall,   55
He paced to and fro, back and forth,
Tearing out and hurling away the locks of his hair,
Ripping off and throwing away his fine clothes like something foul.

At the first glimmer of dawn,
Gilgamesh sent out a proclamation to the land: 60

Hear ye, blacksmith, lapidary,[5] metalworker, goldsmith, jeweler!
Make an image of my friend,
Such as no one ever made of his friend!

5. Gem carver.

I will lay you down in the ultimate resting place,
In a perfect resting place I will surely lay you down.   65
I will settle you in peaceful rest in that dwelling sinister,
Rulers of the netherworld will do you homage.
I will have the people of Uruk shed bitter tears for you,
I will make the pleasure-loving people burdened down for you,
And, as for me, now that you are dead, I will let my hair grow matted,   70
I will put on a lion skin and roam the steppe!

He slaughtered fatted cattle and sheep, heaped them high for his friend,
They carried off all the meat for the rulers of the netherworld.
He displayed in the open for Ishtar, the great queen,
Saying: "May Ishtar, the great queen, accept this,   75
May she welcome my friend and walk at his side."

He displayed in the open for Ninshuluhha,[6] housekeeper of the
    netherworld,
Saying: "May Ninshuluhha, housekeeper of the crowded netherworld,
    accept this,
May she welcome my friend and walk at his side.
May she intercede on behalf of my friend, lest he lose courage."   80
The obsidian knife with lapis fitting,
The sharpening stone pure-whetted with Euphrates water,
He displayed in the open for Bibbu, meat carver of the netherworld,
Saying: "May Bibbu, meat carver of the crowded netherworld,
    accept this,
Welcome my friend and walk at his side."   85

Tablet IX

Gilgamesh was weeping bitterly for Enkidu, his friend,
As he roamed the steppe:

Shall I not die too? Am I not like Enkidu?
Oh woe has entered my vitals!
I have grown afraid of death, so I roam the steppe.
Having come this far, I will go on swiftly
Towards Utanapishtim,[7] son of Ubar-Tutu.   5
I have reached mountain passes at night.
I saw lions, I felt afraid,
I looked up to pray to the moon,
To the moon, beacon of the gods, my prayers went forth: 10
"Keep me safe!"

---

6. A netherworld deity in charge of ritual washing.
7. Akkadian name for the sage who, together with his wife, survived the Great Flood and became immortal. He resembles the biblical Noah and his name literally means "He Found Life." He is called "Ziusudra" in Sumerian and "Ullu" in Hittite.

[At night] he lay down, then awoke from a dream.
He rejoiced to be alive.
He raised the axe at his side,   15
He drew the sword from his belt,
He dropped among them like an arrow,
He struck the lions, scattered, and killed them.

[*Gilgamesh approaches the scorpion monsters who guard the gateway to the
sun's passage through the mountains.*]

The twin peaks are called Mashum.
When he arrived at the twin peaks called Mashum,   20
Which daily watch over the rising and setting of the sun,
Whose peaks thrust upward to the vault of heaven,
Whose flanks reach downward to hell,
Where scorpion monsters guard its gateway,
Whose appearance is dreadful, whose venom is death,   25
Their fear-inspiring radiance spreads over the mountains,
They watch over the sun at its rising and setting,
When Gilgamesh saw their fearsomeness and terror,
He covered his face.
He took hold of himself and approached them.   30

The scorpion monster called to his wife:

    This one who has come to us, his body is flesh of a god!

The wife of the scorpion monster answered him:

    Two-thirds of him is divine, one-third is human.

The scorpion monster, the male one, called out,   35
To Gilgamesh, scion of the gods, he said these words:

    Who are you who have come this long way?

[*The scorpion monster apparently warns Gilgamesh that he has only twelve
hours to get through the sun's tunnel before the sun enters it at nightfall.*]

The scorpion monster made ready to speak, spoke to him,
Said to Gilgamesh, [scion of the gods]:

    Go, Gilgamesh!   40

He opened to him the gateway of the mountain,
Gilgamesh entered the mountain.
He heeded the words of the scorpion monster,
He set out on the way of the sun.

When he had gone one double hour,   45
Dense was the darkness, no light was there,
It would not let him look behind him.
When he had gone two double hours,
Dense was the darkness, no light was there,
It would not let him look behind him.   50
When he had gone three double hours,
Dense was the darkness, no light was there,
It would not let him look behind him.
When he had gone four double hours,
Dense was the darkness, no light was there,   55
It would not let him look behind him.
When he had gone five double hours,
Dense was the darkness, no light was there,
It would not let him look behind him.
When he had gone six double hours,   60
Dense was the darkness, no light was there,
It would not let him look behind him.
When he had gone seven double hours,
Dense was the darkness, there was no light,
It would not let him look behind him.   65
When he had gone eight double hours, he rushed ahead,
Dense was the darkness, there was no light,
It would not let him look behind him.
When he had gone nine double hours, he felt the north wind,
Dense was the darkness, there was no light,   70
It would not let him look behind him.
When he had gone ten double hours,
The time for the sun's entry was drawing near.
When he had gone eleven double hours, just one double hour was left,
When he had gone twelve double hours, he came out ahead of the sun!   75
He had run twelve double hours, bright light still reigned!
He went forward, seeing the trees of the gods.
The carnelian bore its fruit,
Like bunches of grapes dangling, lovely to see,
The lapis bore foliage,   80
Fruit it bore, a delight to behold.

[*The fragmentary lines that remain continue the description of the wonderful grove.*]

Tablet X

[*Gilgamesh approaches the tavern of Siduri, a female tavern keeper who lives at the end of the earth. This interesting personage is unknown outside this poem, nor is it clear who her clientele might be in such a remote spot.*]

Siduri[8] the tavern keeper, who dwells at the edge of the sea,
For her was wrought the cuprack,[9] for her the brewing vat of gold,
Gilgamesh made his way towards her,
He was clad in a skin,
He had flesh of gods in his body.   5
Woe was in his vitals,
His face was like a traveler's from afar.
The tavern keeper eyed him from a distance,
Speaking to herself, she said these words,
She debated with herself: 10

> This no doubt is a slaughterer of wild bulls!
> Why would he make straight for my door?

At the sight of him the tavern keeper barred her door,
She barred her door and mounted to the roof terrace.
But he, Gilgamesh, put his ear to the door,   15
He lifted his chin.

Gilgamesh said to her, to the tavern keeper:

> Tavern keeper, when you saw me why did you bar your door,
> Bar your door and mount to the roof terrace?
> I will strike down your door, I will shatter your doorbolt,   20

Gilgamesh said to her, to the tavern keeper:

> I am Gilgamesh, who killed the guardian,
> Who seized and killed the bull that came down from heaven,
> Who felled Humbaba who dwelt in the forest of cedars,
> Who killed lions at the mountain passes.   25

The tavern keeper said to him, to Gilgamesh:

> If you are indeed Gilgamesh, who killed the guardian,
> Who felled Humbaba who dwelt in the forest of cedars,
> Who killed lions at the mountain passes,
> Who seized and killed the bull that came down from heaven,   30
> Why are your cheeks emaciated, your face cast down,
> Your heart wretched, your features wasted,
> Woe in your vitals,
> Your face like a traveler's from afar,

8. Literally "Maiden" in Hurrian, a language of northern Syria and northern Mesopotamia that was not related to Sumerian or Akkadian.

9. Some Mesopotamian drinking cups were conical, with pointed bottoms, so they were set on a wooden rack to hold them up.

Your features weathered by cold and sun,   35
Why are you clad in a lion skin, roaming the steppe?

Gilgamesh said to her, to the tavern keeper:

My cheeks would not be emaciated, nor my face cast down,
Nor my heart wretched nor my features wasted,
Nor would there be woe in my vitals,   40
Nor would my face be like a traveler's from afar,
Nor would my features be weathered by cold and sun,
Nor would I be clad in a lion skin, roaming the steppe,
But for my friend, swift wild donkey, mountain onager, panther
   of the steppe,
But for Enkidu, swift wild donkey, mountain onager, panther
   of the steppe,   45
My friend whom I so loved, who went with me through every hardship,
Enkidu, whom I so loved, who went with me through every hardship,
The fate of mankind has overtaken him.
Six days and seven nights I wept for him,
I would not give him up for burial,   50
Until a worm fell out of his nose.
I was frightened.
I have grown afraid of death, so I roam the steppe,
My friend's case weighs heavy upon me.
A distant road I roam over the steppe,   55
My friend Enkidu's case weighs heavy upon me!
A distant road I roam over the steppe,
How can I be silent? How can I hold my peace?
My friend whom I loved is turned into clay,
Enkidu, my friend whom I loved, is turned into clay!   60
Shall I too not lie down like him,
And never get up forever and ever?

[*An old version adds the following episode.*]

After his death I could find no life,
Back and forth I prowled like a bandit in the steppe.
Now that I have seen your face, tavern keeper,
May I not see that death I constantly fear!   65

The tavern keeper said to him, to Gilgamesh:

Gilgamesh, wherefore do you wander?
The eternal life you are seeking you shall not find.
When the gods created mankind,
They established death for mankind,   70
And withheld eternal life for themselves.
As for you, Gilgamesh, let your stomach be full,
Always be happy, night and day.
Make every day a delight,   75
Night and day play and dance.
Your clothes should be clean,

Your head should be washed,
You should bathe in water,
Look proudly on the little one holding your hand, 80
Let your mate be always blissful in your loins,
This, then, is the work of mankind.

Gilgamesh said to her, to the tavern keeper:

What are you saying, tavern keeper?
I am heartsick for my friend. 85
What are you saying, tavern keeper?
I am heartsick for Enkidu!

[*The standard version resumes.*]

Gilgamesh said to her, to the tavern keeper:

Now then, tavern keeper, what is the way to Utanapishtim?
What are its signs? Give them to me. 90
Give, oh give me its signs!
If need be, I'll cross the sea,
If not, I'll roam the steppe.

The tavern keeper said to him, to Gilgamesh:

Gilgamesh, there has never been a place to cross, 95
There has been no one from the dawn of time who could ever cross
   this sea.
The valiant Shamash alone can cross this sea,
Save for the sun, who could cross this sea?
The crossing is perilous, highly perilous the course,
And midway lie the waters of death, whose surface is impassable. 100
Suppose, Gilgamesh, you do cross the sea,
When you reach the waters of death, what will you do?
Yet, Gilgamesh, there is Ur-Shanabi,[1] Utanapishtim's boatman,
He has the Stone Charms with him as he trims pine trees in the forest.
Go, show yourself to him, 105
If possible, cross with him, if not, then turn back.

[*Gilgamesh advances and without preamble attacks Ur-Shanabi and smashes
the Stone Charms.*]

When Gilgamesh heard this,
He raised the axe at his side,
He drew the sword at his belt,
He crept forward, went down towards them, 110
Like an arrow he dropped among them,
His battle cry resounded in the forest.
When Ur-Shanabi saw the shining [. . .],
He raised his axe, he trembled before him,

---

1. Servant of Utanapishtim, ferryman who crosses the ocean and the waters of death.

But he, for his part, struck his head [. . .] Gilgamesh,   115
He seized his arm [. . .] his chest.
And the Stone Charms, the protection . . . of the boat,
Without which no one crosses the waters of death,
He smashed them and threw them into the broad sea,
Into the channel he threw them, his own hands foiled him,   120
He smashed them and threw them into the channel!

Gilgamesh said to him, to Ur-Shanabi:

> Now then, Ur-Shanabi, what is the way to Utanapishtim?
> What are its signs? Give them to me,
> Give, oh give me its signs!   125
> If need be, I'll cross the sea,
> If not, I'll roam the steppe.

Ur-Shanabi said to him, to Gilgamesh:

> Your own hands have foiled you, Gilgamesh,
> You have smashed the Stone Charms, you have thrown them into
>   the channel.   130

[*An old version has the following here.*]

> The Stone Charms, Gilgamesh, are what carry me,
> Lest I touch the waters of death.
> In your fury you have smashed them,
> The Stone Charms, they are what I had with me to make the crossing!
>
> Gilgamesh, raise the axe in your hand,   135
> Go down into the forest, cut twice sixty poles each five times twelve
>   cubits long,
> Dress them, set on handguards,
> Bring them to me.

When Gilgamesh heard this,
He raised the axe at his side,   140
He drew the sword at his belt,
He went down into the forest, cut twice sixty poles each five times
    twelve cubits long,
He dressed them, set on handguards,
He brought them to him.
Gilgamesh and Ur-Shanabi embarked in the boat,   145
They launched the boat, they embarked upon it.
A journey of a month and a half they made in three days!
Ur-Shanabi reached the waters of death,
Ur-Shanabi said to him, to Gilgamesh:

> Stand back, Gilgamesh! Take the first pole,   150
> Your hand must not touch the waters of death,
> Take the second, the third, the fourth pole, Gilgamesh,
> Take the fifth, sixth, and seventh pole, Gilgamesh,

Take the eighth, ninth, and tenth pole, Gilgamesh,
Take the eleventh and twelfth pole, Gilgamesh.   155

With twice sixty Gilgamesh had used up the poles.
Then he, for his part, took off his belt,
Gilgamesh tore off his clothes from his body,
Held high his arms for a mast.
Utanapishtim was watching him from a distance,   160
Speaking to himself, he said these words,
He debated to himself:

> Why have the Stone Charms, belonging to the boat, been smashed,
> And one not its master embarked thereon?
> He who comes here is no man of mine.   165

[*In the fragmentary lines that follow, Gilgamesh lands at Utanapishtim's wharf
and questions him.*]

Utanapishtim said to him, to Gilgamesh:

> Why are your cheeks emaciated, your face cast down,
> Your heart wretched, your features wasted,
> Woe in your vitals,
> Your face like a traveler's from afar,   170
> Your features weathered by cold and sun,
> Why are you clad in a lion skin, roaming the steppe?

Gilgamesh said to him, to Utanapishtim:

> My cheeks would not be emaciated, nor my face cast down,
> Nor my heart wretched, nor my features wasted,   175
> Nor would there be woe in my vitals,
> Nor would my face be like a traveler's from afar,
> Nor would my features be weathered by cold and sun,
> Nor would I be clad in a lion skin, roaming the steppe,
>
> But for my friend, swift wild donkey, mountain onager, panther
>   of the steppe,   180
> But for Enkidu, my friend, swift wild donkey, mountain onager, panther
>   of the steppe,
> He who stood by me as we ascended the mountain,
> Seized and killed the bull that came down from heaven,
> Felled Humbaba who dwelt in the forest of cedars,
> Killed lions at the mountain passes,   185
> My friend whom I so loved, who went with me through every hardship,
> Enkidu, whom I so loved, who went with me through every hardship,
> The fate of mankind has overtaken him.
> Six days and seven nights I wept for him,
> I would not give him up for burial,   190
> Until a worm fell out of his nose.
> I was frightened.
> I have grown afraid of death, so I roam the steppe,

My friend's case weighs heavy upon me.
A distant road I roam over the steppe,   195
My friend Enkidu's case weighs heavy upon me!
A distant path I roam over the steppe,
How can I be silent? How can I hold my peace?
My friend whom I loved is turned into clay,
Enkidu, my friend whom I loved, is turned into clay!   200
Shall I too not lie down like him,
And never get up, forever and ever?

Gilgamesh said to him, to Utanapishtim:

So it is to go find Utanapishtim, whom they call the "Distant One,"
I traversed all lands,   205
I came over, one after another, wearisome mountains,
Then I crossed, one after another, all the seas.
Too little sweet sleep has smoothed my countenance,
I have worn myself out in sleeplessness,
My muscles ache for misery,   210
What have I gained for my trials?
I had not reached the tavern keeper when my clothes were worn out,
I killed bear, hyena, lion, panther, leopard, deer, ibex, wild beasts
     of the steepe,
I ate their meat, I [. . .] their skins.
Let them close behind me the doors of woe,   215
Let them seal them with pitch and tar.

Utanapishtim said to him, to Gilgamesh:

Why, O Gilgamesh, did you prolong woe,
You who are formed of the flesh of gods and mankind,
You for whom the gods acted like fathers and mothers?   220
When was it, Gilgamesh, you [. . .] to a fool?

You strive ceaselessly, what do you gain?
When you wear out your strength in ceaseless striving,
When you torture your limbs with pain,
You hasten the distant end of your days.   225
Mankind, whose descendants are snapped off like reeds in a canebrake!
The handsome young man, the lovely young woman, death [. . .]
No one sees death,
No one sees the face of death,
No one hears the voice of death,   230
But cruel death cuts off mankind.
Do we build a house forever?
Do we make a home forever?
Do brothers divide an inheritance forever?
Do disputes prevail in the land forever?   235
Do rivers rise in flood forever?
Dragonflies drift downstream on a river,
Their faces staring at the sun,
Then, suddenly, there is nothing.

The sleeper and the dead, how alike they are! 240
They limn not death's image,
No one dead has ever greeted a human in this world.
The supreme gods, the great gods, being convened,
Mammetum, she who creates destinies, ordaining destinies with them,
They established death and life, 245
They did not reveal the time of death.

Tablet XI

Gilgamesh said to him, to Utanapishtim the Distant One:

As I look upon you, Utanapishtim,
Your limbs are not different, you are just as I am.
Indeed, you are not different at all, you are just as I am!
Yet your heart is drained of battle spirit, 5
You lie flat on your back, your arm idle.
You then, how did you join the ranks of the gods and find eternal life?

Utanapishtim said to him, to Gilgamesh:

I will reveal to you, O Gilgamesh, a secret matter,
And a mystery of the gods I will tell you. 10
The city Shuruppak,[2] a city you yourself have knowledge of,
Which once was set on the bank of the Euphrates,
That aforesaid city was ancient and gods once were within it.
The great gods resolved to send the deluge,
Their father Anu was sworn, 15
The counselor the valiant Enlil,
Their throne-bearer Ninurta,
Their canal-officer Ennugi,[3]
Their leader Ea was sworn with them.
He repeated their plans to the reed fence: 20
"Reed fence, reed fence, wall, wall!
Listen, O reed fence! Pay attention, O wall!
O Man of Shuruppak, son of Ubar-Tutu,
Wreck house, build boat,
Forsake possessions and seek life, 25
Belongings reject and life save!
Take aboard the boat seed of all living things.
The boat you shall build,
Let her dimensions be measured out:
Let her width and length be equal, 30
Roof her over like the watery depths."
I understood full well, I said to Ea, my lord:
"Your command, my lord, exactly as you said it,
I shall faithfully execute.

2. City in Babylonia reputed to antedate the flood, long abandoned at the time the epic was written.

3. Minor deity in charge of water courses.

What shall I answer the city, the populace, and the elders?"   35
Ea made ready to speak,
Saying to me, his servant:
"So, you shall speak to them thus:
'No doubt Enlil dislikes me,
I shall not dwell in your city.   40
I shall not set my foot on the dry land of Enlil,
I shall descend to the watery depths and dwell with my lord Ea.
Upon you he shall shower down in abundance,
A windfall of birds, a surprise of fishes,
He shall pour upon you a harvest of riches,   45
In the morning cakes in spates,
In the evening grains in rains.'"

At the first glimmer of dawn,
The land was assembling at the gate of Atrahasis:[4]
The carpenter carried his axe,   50
The reed cutter carried his stone,
The old men brought cordage,
The young men ran around,
The wealthy carried the pitch,
The poor brought what was needed.   55
In five days I had planked her hull:
One full acre was her deck space,
Ten dozen cubits, the height of each of her sides,
Ten dozen cubits square, her outer dimensions.[5]
I laid out her structure, I planned her design: 60
I decked her in six,
I divided her in seven,
Her interior I divided in nine.
I drove the water plugs into her,
I saw to the spars and laid in what was needful.   65
Thrice thirty-six hundred measures of pitch I poured in the oven,
Thrice thirty-six hundred measures of tar I poured out inside her.
Thrice thirty-six hundred measures basket-bearers brought
    aboard for oil,
Not counting the thirty-six hundred measures of oil that the offering
    consumed,
And the twice thirty-six hundred measures of oil that the boatbuilders
    made off with.   70
For the builders I slaughtered bullocks,
I killed sheep upon sheep every day,
Beer, ale, oil, and wine
I gave out to the workers like river water,
They made a feast as on New Year's Day,   75

4. Literally "Super-wise," another Akkadian name of the immortal flood hero Utanapishtim.
5. The proportions of the boat suggest stan- dard measures of both ship building and the construction of ziggurats, pyramidal temple towers.

I dispensed ointment with my own hand.
By the setting of Shamash,[6] the ship was completed.
Since boarding was very difficult,
They brought up gangplanks, fore and aft,
They came up her sides two-thirds of her height.   80
Whatever I had I loaded upon her:
What silver I had I loaded upon her,
What gold I had I loaded upon her,
What living creatures I had I loaded upon her,
I sent up on board all my family and kin,   85
Beasts of the steppe, wild animals of the steppe, all types of skilled
    craftsmen I sent up on board.
Shamash set for me the appointed time:
"In the morning, cakes in spates,
In the evening, grains in rains,
Go into your boat and caulk the door!"   90
That appointed time arrived,
In the morning cakes in spates,
In the evening grains in rains,
I gazed upon the face of the storm,
The weather was dreadful to behold!   95
I went into the boat and caulked the door.
To the caulker of the boat, to Puzur-Amurri the boatman,
I gave over the edifice, with all it contained.

At the first glimmer of dawn,
A black cloud rose above the horizon.   100
Inside it Adad[7] was thundering,
While the destroying gods Shullat and Hanish[8] went in front,
Moving as an advance force over hill and plain.
Errakal[9] tore out the mooring posts of the world,
Ninurta[1] came and made the dikes overflow.   105
The supreme gods held torches aloft,
Setting the land ablaze with their glow.
Adad's awesome power passed over the heavens,
Whatever was light was turned into darkness.
He flooded the land, he smashed it like a clay pot!   110
For one day the storm wind blew,
Swiftly it blew, the flood came forth,
It passed over the people like a battle,
No one could see the one next to him,

6. The references to Shamash here and below suggest that in some now lost version of this story, Shamash, the god of justice, rather than Ea, the god of wisdom, warned Utanapishtim of the flood and told him how much time he had to build his ship. This substitution of one god for the other might be due to Shamash's role in the epic as protector of Gilgamesh. In the oldest account of the Babylonian story of the flood, Ea sets a timing device, apparently a water clock, to inform Utanapishtim of the time left before the onset of the deluge.
7. God of thunder.
8. Gods of destructive storms.
9. God of death.
1. God of war.

The people could not recognize one another in the downpour.   115
The gods became frightened of the deluge,
They shrank back, went up to Anu's highest heaven.
The gods cowered like dogs, crouching outside.
Ishtar screamed like a woman in childbirth,
And sweet-voiced Belet-ili[2] wailed aloud: 120
"Would that day had come to naught,
When I spoke up for evil in the assembly of the gods!
How could I have spoken up for evil in the assembly of the gods,
And spoken up for battle to destroy my people?
It was I myself who brought my people into the world,   125
Now, like a school of fish, they choke up the sea!"
The supreme gods were weeping with her,
The gods sat where they were, weeping,
Their lips were parched, taking on a crust.
Six days and seven nights   130
The wind continued, the deluge and windstorm leveled the land.
When the seventh day arrived,
The windstorm and deluge left off their battle,
Which had struggled, like a woman in labor.
The sea grew calm, the tempest stilled, the deluge ceased.   135

I looked at the weather, stillness reigned,
And the whole human race had turned into clay.
The landscape was flat as a rooftop.
I opened the hatch, sunlight fell upon my face.
Falling to my knees, I sat down weeping,   140
Tears running down my face.
I looked at the edges of the world, the borders of the sea,
At twelve times sixty double leagues the periphery emerged.
The boat had come to rest on Mount Nimush,[3]
Mount Nimush held the boat fast, not letting it move.   145
One day, a second day Mount Nimush held the boat fast, not letting
     it move.
A third day, a fourth day Mount Nimush held the boat fast, not letting
     it move.
A fifth day, a sixth day Mount Nimush held the boat fast, not letting
     it move.

When the seventh day arrived,
I brought out a dove and set it free.   150
The dove went off and returned,
No landing place came to its view, so it turned back.
I brought out a swallow and set it free,
The swallow went off and returned,
No landing place came to its view, so it turned back.   155

2. A goddess of birth, who in one version of the flood story was said to have collaborated with the god Ea in creating the human race.

3. High peak sometimes identified with Pir Omar Gudrun in Kurdistan. Landing place of the ark in the Gilgamesh epic.

I brought out a raven and set it free,
The raven went off and saw the ebbing of the waters.
It ate, preened, left droppings, did not turn back.
I released all to the four directions,
I brought out an offering and offered it to the four directions.   160
I set up an incense offering on the summit of the mountain,
I arranged seven and seven cult vessels,
I heaped reeds, cedar, and myrtle in their bowls.
The gods smelled the savor,
The gods smelled the sweet savor,   165
The gods crowded round the sacrificer like flies.

As soon as Belet-ili arrived,
She held up the great fly-ornaments that Anu had made
     in his ardor:
"O gods, these shall be my lapis necklace, lest I forget,
I shall be mindful of these days and not forget, not ever!   170
The gods should come to the incense offering,
But Enlil should not come to the incense offering,
For he, irrationally, brought on the flood,
And marked my people for destruction!"
As soon as Enlil arrived,   175
He saw the boat, Enlil flew into a rage,
He was filled with fury at the gods:
"Who came through alive? No man was to survive destruction!"
Ninurta made ready to speak,
Said to the valiant Enlil: 180
"Who but Ea could contrive such a thing?
For Ea alone knows every artifice."

Ea made ready to speak,
Said to the valiant Enlil:
"You, O valiant one, are the wisest of the gods,   185
How could you, irrationally, have brought on the flood?
Punish the wrongdoer for his wrongdoing,
Punish the transgressor for his transgression,
But be lenient, lest he be cut off,
Bear with him, lest he [. . .].   190
Instead of your bringing on a flood,
Let the lion rise up to diminish the human race!
Instead of your bringing on a flood,
Let the wolf rise up to diminish the human race!
Instead of your bringing on a flood,   195
Let famine rise up to wreak havoc in the land!
Instead of your bringing on a flood,
Let pestilence rise up to wreak havoc in the land!
It was not I who disclosed the secret of the great gods,
I made Atrahasis have a dream and so he heard the secret   200
     of the gods.
Now then, make some plan for him."
Then Enlil came up into the boat,

Leading me by the hand, he brought me up too.
He brought my wife up and had her kneel beside me.
He touched our brows, stood between us to bless us: 205
"Hitherto Utanapishtim has been a human being,
Now Utanapishtim and his wife shall become like us gods.
Utanapishtim shall dwell far distant at the source of the rivers."
Thus it was that they took me far distant and had me dwell at the
    source of the rivers.
Now then, who will convene the gods for your sake,   210
That you may find the eternal life you seek?
Come, come, try not to sleep for six days and seven nights.

As he sat there on his haunches,
Sleep was swirling over him like a mist.
Utanapishtim said to her, to his wife: 215

Behold this fellow who seeks eternal life!
Sleep swirls over him like a mist.

[*Utanapishtim's wife, taking pity on Gilgamesh, urges her husband to awaken
him and let him go home*].

His wife said to him, to Utanapishtim the Distant One:

Do touch him that the man may wake up,
That he may return safe on the way whence he came,   220
That through the gate he came forth he may return to his land.

Utanapishtim said to her, to his wife:

Since the human race is duplicitous, he'll endeavor to dupe you.
Come, come, bake his daily loaves, put them one after another by his
    head,
Then mark the wall for each day he has slept.   225

She baked his daily loaves for him, put them one after another by his head,
Then dated the wall for each day he slept.
The first loaf was dried hard,
The second was leathery, the third soggy,
The crust of the fourth turned white,
The fifth was gray with mold, the sixth was fresh,   230
The seventh was still on the coals when he touched him, the man woke up.

Gilgamesh said to him, to Utanapishtim the Distant One:

Scarcely had sleep stolen over me,
When straightaway you touched me and roused me.   235

Utanapishtim said to him, to Gilgamesh:

Up with you, Gilgamesh, count your daily loaves,
That the days you have slept may be known to you.

The first loaf is dried hard,
The second is leathery, the third soggy,   240
The crust of the fourth has turned white,
The fifth is gray with mold,
The sixth is fresh,
The seventh was still in the coals when I touched you and
    you woke up.

Gilgamesh said to him, to Utanapishtim the Distant One: 245

What then should I do, Utanapishtim, whither should I go,
Now that the Bereaver has seized my flesh?
Death lurks in my bedchamber,
And wherever I turn, there is death!

Utanapishtim said to him, to Ur-Shanabi the boatman: 250

Ur-Shanabi, may the harbor offer you no haven,
May the crossing point reject you,
Be banished from the shore you shuttled to.
The man you brought here,
His body is matted with filthy hair,   255
Hides have marred the beauty of his flesh.
Take him away, Ur-Shanabi, bring him to the washing place.
Have him wash out his filthy hair with water, clean as snow,
Have him throw away his hides, let the sea carry them off,
Let his body be rinsed clean.   260
Let his headband be new,
Have him put on raiment worthy of him.
Until he reaches his city,
Until he completes his journey,
Let his garments stay spotless, fresh and new.   265

Ur-Shanabi took him away and brought him to the washing place.
He washed out his filthy hair with water, clean as snow,
He threw away his hides, the sea carried them off,
His body was rinsed clean.
He renewed his headband,   270
He put on raiment worthy of him.
Until he reached his city,
Until he completed his journey,
His garments would stay spotless, fresh and new.

Gilgamesh and Ur-Shanabi embarked on the boat,   275
They launched the boat, they embarked upon it.
His wife said to him, to Utanapishtim the Distant One:

Gilgamesh has come here, spent with exertion,
What will you give him for his homeward journey?

At that he, Gilgamesh, lifted the pole,   280
Bringing the boat back by the shore.

Utanapishtim said to him, to Gilgamesh:

> Gilgamesh, you have come here, spent with exertion,
> What shall I give you for your homeward journey?
> I will reveal to you, O Gilgamesh, a secret matter,   285
> And a mystery of the gods I will tell you.
> There is a certain plant, its stem is like a thornbush,
> Its thorns, like the wild rose, will prick [your hand].
> If you can secure this plant, [. . .]

No sooner had Gilgamesh heard this,   290
He opened a shaft, flung away his tools.
He tied heavy stones to his feet,
They pulled him down into the watery depths.
He took the plant though it pricked his hand.
He cut the heavy stones from his feet,   295
The sea cast him up on his home shore.

Gilgamesh said to him, to Ur-Shanabi the boatman:

> Ur-Shanabi, this plant is cure for heartache,
> Whereby a man will regain his stamina.
> I will take it to ramparted Uruk,   300
> I will have an old man eat some and so test the plant.
> His name shall be "Old Man Has Become Young-Again-Man."
> I myself will eat it and so return to my carefree youth.

At twenty double leagues they took a bite to eat,
At thirty double leagues they made their camp.   305

Gilgamesh saw a pond whose water was cool,
He went down into it to bathe in the water.
A snake caught the scent of the plant,
Stealthily it came up and carried the plant away,
On its way back it shed its skin.   310

Thereupon Gilgamesh sat down weeping,
His tears flowed down his face,
He said to Ur-Shanabi the boatman:

> For whom, Ur-Shanabi, have my hands been toiling?
> For whom has my heart's blood been poured out?   315
> For myself I have obtained no benefit,
> I have done a good deed for a reptile!
> Now, floodwaters rise against me for twenty double leagues,
> When I opened the shaft, I flung away the tools.
> How shall I find my bearings?   320
> I have come much too far to go back, and I abandoned the boat on
>   the shore.

At twenty double leagues they took a bite to eat,
At thirty double leagues they made their camp.

When they arrived in ramparted Uruk,
Gilgamesh said to him, to Ur-Shanabi the boatman:　　　　325

> Go up, Ur-Shanabi, pace out the walls of Uruk.
> Study the foundation terrace and examine the brickwork.
> Is not its masonry of kiln-fired brick?
> And did not seven masters lay its foundations?
> One square mile of city, one square mile of gardens,　　330
> One square mile of clay pits, a half square mile of Ishtar's dwelling,
> Three and a half square miles is the measure of Uruk!

THE HEBREW BIBLE

ca. 1000–300 B.C.E.

The sacred writings of the ancient Hebrew people are arguably the world's most influential texts. They have remained the sacred text of Judaism and have inspired two other major world religions: Christianity and Islam. Because these texts have been so influential in human affairs, and have become central to so many people's core religious beliefs, they are not often read in the same way as "literary" texts. But studying the books of the Hebrew Bible as literature—paying close attention to their narrative techniques, their imagery, characterization, and point of view—is not incompatible with religious faith. Close reading enriches our understanding and appreciation of these texts as supremely important cultural and historical documents, for readers of any religious background or belief.

The Hebrew Bible encompasses a rich variety of texts from different periods, composed in both poetry and prose. One of the obvious differences between the Bible and most works of "literature"—such as **Aeschylus**'s *Agamemnon* or **Virgil**'s *Aeneid*—is that no single human hand composed the whole Bible, or even the whole of Genesis or Job. Traditionally, Moses is thought to have been the author of the first five books of the Bible and also, according to some traditions, the book of Job. But modern Bible scholars agree that these books, in their current form, must have been woven together from several different earlier sources. This theory explains the otherwise puzzling fact that there are often odd contradictions and repetitions in the narrative. For example, God tells Noah to take two of every kind of animal into the ark; but a little later, the Lord tells Noah to take seven pairs of each animal. The simplest explanation for this kind of discrepancy is that the text we have is a collage built of several earlier narratives, put together, or "redacted," into a single master story. Many scholars believe that it is possible to distinguish between the different original strands, each of which has its distinct stylistic features and perspectives on the narrative. For instance, one strand of the text is identified by the name that it uses for God, *YHWH* (a personal name for the Hebrew god: in English, *Jehovah*, and hence the strand is called *J*); in another strand (dubbed *E*), God is called *Elohim* (which comes from the standard Semitic term for any god, *el*).

The various sources have been put together with great skill, and the result is a text of extraordinary literary, philosophical, and theological richness. The lengthiest selections included here are abridged versions of the books of Genesis and Job. Perhaps the most important element running through the two is a complex ethical concern with how human suffering and prosperity come about and what role God plays in shaping human lives. The books resist easy answers to these questions. We might expect that God would simply punish wrongdoers and reward the righteous; and indeed, he does punish Adam and Eve for their disobedience. But often the relation between human behavior and divine favor is shown to be deeply mysterious. God favors Abel over Cain, blesses Noah and Abraham over all other humans, seems to pay more attention to Isaac than Ishmael, favors Jacob over Esau and Joseph over his brothers, and blesses the Hebrew people over all other inhabitants of the Middle East; but in none of these cases are we given an explanation, let alone a moral justification. Moreover, God allows even his favorites, such as Jacob, Joseph, and Job, to suffer terrible hardship before restoring them to prosperity. The book of Job brings this issue explicitly to the forefront. God's ways are mysterious, and instead of reinforcing a simple moral (like "Be good and God will bless you"), the Bible constantly undercuts it. But throughout these texts, we see that God's power is the major force in all of human history.

It is no accident that the book of Genesis—unlike other ancient creation stories—begins not with earth, sky, and sea but with God himself, the originator of everything.

GENESIS

The first book of the Bible takes its name from the Greek word for "origin" or "birth"—*genesis*. The book tells a story of how the world, and the human race, came into existence; how humans first disobeyed God; and how God began to establish a special relationship with a series of chosen men and their families: Noah, Abraham, Isaac, Jacob, and Joseph. The book was probably redacted in the fifth century B.C.E., a period when the people of Judah were in exile in Babylon. One can understand Genesis in this context as an attempt to consolidate Jewish identity in the midst of an alien culture.

The first section (chapters 1–11) recounts "creation history"—God's creation of the world and of humankind, and the development of early human society. Human beings occupy center stage in this account of the world's origin, as they do not in, for example, Mesopotamian and Greek creation stories. This early age is marked especially by God's anger at humanity, from his expulsion of Adam and Eve from Eden to his destruction of the Tower of Babel, which scatters human beings and divides their single language into many languages. God's decision to destroy humanity is presented as a reversal of the original act of creation. The flood mixes together again the waters that were separated on the second day of creation, and it destroys almost all the different kinds of animals created on the fifth and sixth days, together with almost all humans.

But not quite all animals and humans are destroyed. Noah and his family, and the animals taken onto the ark, are spared, because Noah has found favor in God's eyes; Noah's various wives and the chosen animals, it seems, have attracted no particular divine attention but benefit by association with Noah. This dramatic demonstration of God's power and willingness to favor certain members of the human race while destroying others leads to a new beginning. The second part of Genesis (chapters 12–50) moves from humanity in general to the stories of four men and their families: Abraham and his wife, Sarah; Isaac and his wife, Rebekah; Jacob and his wives, Leah and Rachel; and Joseph and his brothers. The transition is marked by God's first declaration of his commitment to the people of Israel. When he tells Noah's descendant Abram (who will be renamed Abraham) to leave his home in Mesopotamia, he declares, "I will make you a great nation and I will bless you and make your name great, and you shall be a blessing." Showing him the land of Canaan, he promises, "To your seed I will give this land." This positive covenant builds on the merely negative promise God has already made to humanity in general: that he will never again destroy the world by flood (chapter 9). Now there is a purpose in history: other peoples will be blessed through the people of Israel, who are chosen for a particularly close relationship with God.

Many complications arise that seem to threaten the fulfillment of the covenant—and add narrative excitement to the story. God has promised "this land" to Abraham's children, but repeatedly, Abraham's descendants—Jacob, and later Joseph and his brothers—must leave the land of their fathers, deferring the hope of a settled home in the promised land. The pattern of exile from home recurs again and again in the book of Genesis and recalls the expulsion of Adam and Eve from the Garden of Eden, while the strife between family members, especially brothers, and the theme of the triumph of a younger brother over an elder, constantly recall the story of Cain and Abel. Repeatedly, we see God's covenant fulfilled in unexpected ways, revealing his power and his surpassing of merely human expectations.

God himself can be seen as the most vivid and complex character of the book of Genesis. He, like the humans made in his image, enjoys an evening stroll through a cool garden; he is willing to scheme and make deals; he has his particular friends and his favorites; and he is capable of emotions: pleasure, hope, anger, and regret. But the human characters in this book, both men and women, are also strikingly vivid. They are people of intense feelings, and their relationships with one another, their loves, hatreds, fears, and desires, are evoked in compelling detail.

It is worthwhile to pay close attention to the way the text brings people's feelings, characters, and motivations to life in just a few simple words. We often seem to be invited to ponder several possible layers of meaning in what people say, as when Abraham loads up Isaac with wood for the fire, takes the cleaver in his hand, and leads him into the mountain. Isaac says simply, "Father!" Is he scared? Does he know what his father plans to do? Does the word fill Abraham himself with guilt and horror? Or is he unshaking in his resolve to obey? A world of family conflict is opened up in the text's simple observations. "And Isaac loved Esau for the game that he brought him, but Rebekah loved Jacob," or "The LORD regarded Abel and his offering but He did not regard Cain and his offering." Reasons for these preferences seem to exist, but they are often deeply hidden.

The tale of Jacob, who is renamed "Israel," is central to this text and forms one of its most gripping story lines. Jacob and Esau are twins who fight each other even in the womb: as shown in Robert Crumb's memorable image, Jacob emerges already grabbing hold of his brother's heel—a detail reminiscent of the everlasting "enmity" between humanity and the serpent, which bites the heels of the children of Adam. As they grow older, the brothers grow ever more different: Esau is a wild, hairy man, while Jacob, the mother's boy, the clever one, likes to stay home. Jacob plays a pair of tricks on his brother, first duping him out of his birthright and then robbing him of his dying father's blessing. Understandably enough, Esau wants to kill him. And yet when Jacob travels away from home, he is granted a vision from God, who promises him protection, the inheritance of the land, and blessing for himself and for his "seed." Why, we may wonder, does God prefer the trickster Jacob over the loyal, filial Esau? Is he rewarded for his brains, which he certainly has in abundance? Or for his unstoppable drive to get ahead, evident even from the womb? Or is it his capacity to love, shown in his relationships with his mother, his favorite wife, and his favorite sons? Is it his willingness to engage directly with God and God's messengers, as when he wrestles with the angel all night and emerges declaring, "I have seen God face to face"? Whatever we decide, it is striking that Jacob, or "Israel," the father of the Jewish people, is presented in such fascinatingly unidealized terms. He is a fully human, rounded, and believable character.

Joseph, the firstborn of Jacob's favorite wife, Rachel, is a very different but equally fascinating character. Whereas Jacob's intelligence is practical, focused on the present—combining an acute ability to judge other people with a keen eye for how to protect and promote himself—Joseph is a dreamer, whose mind can read symbols and look to the future. He has a sense of his own great destiny, confirmed by his dreams, which represent him as the first of all his race. Dreams occupy an interesting middle ground in this story, between internal and external worlds: on the one hand, Joseph's dreams are a clue to his state of mind, his hopes for greatness; on the other, his dreams are a sign of the fact that God has favored him and will set him above his brothers. Like later prophets, Joseph suffers many tribulations. As Pharoah's dream interpreter, Joseph becomes a prototype for the later priests and prophets of Israel: he can discern divine purpose in the signs that remain mysterious to ordinary humans. Joseph's story forms a bridge to the book of Exodus, in which the Hebrew people will need long-term faith in God and in their destiny to survive the years of exile.

Like the *Odyssey*, the book of Genesis is about the search for a homeland, a special place of belonging—although here the quest belongs not to a single man but to a whole people. As in the *Odyssey*, hospitality plays an essential part in the value structure of the text. It is often through human hospitality that God's plan can succeed. Abraham, sitting by his tent flap in the alien land of Mamre, passes a test of his hospitality with flying colors when he offers a lavish feast to the "three men" who turn out to be messengers of the Lord. We see the descendants of Abraham negotiate their relationships with the various other peoples who inhabit the area that God seems to have promised as their inheritance. At the same time, they must try to avoid total assimilation: Isaac insists, for example, that Jacob must not "take a wife from the daughters of Canaan"; in terms of culture, worship, and "seed," the people must remain distinct. Circumcision, which God enjoins on Abraham and his family, marks this male line off from its neighbors. But the story of Joseph illustrates the advantages of at

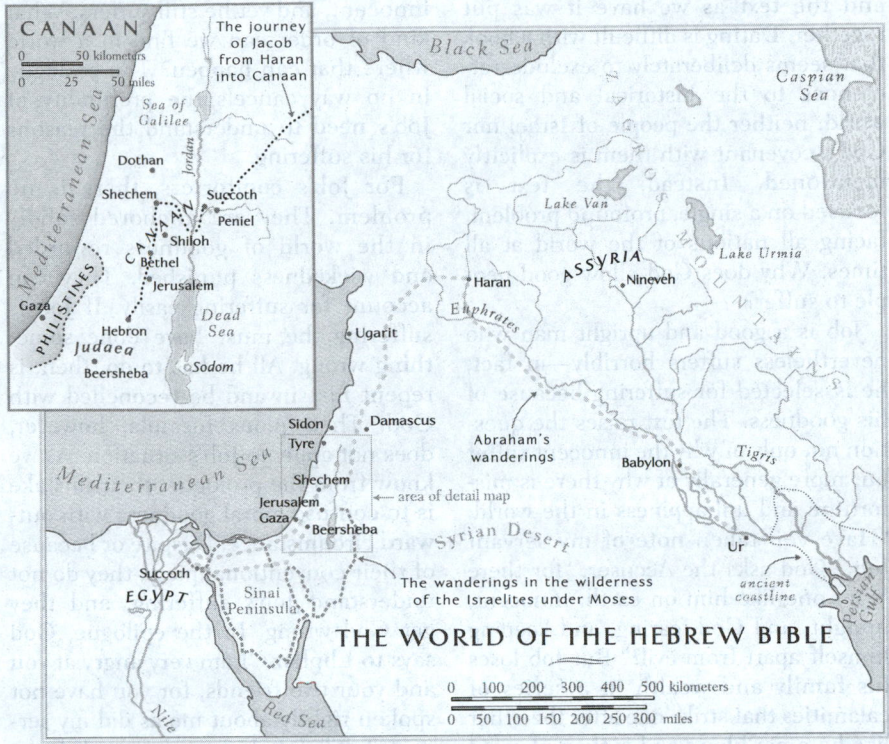

CANAAN

The journey of Jacob from Haran into Canaan

THE WORLD OF THE HEBREW BIBLE

least partial assimilation. Joseph dresses as an Egyptian, marries an Egyptian woman, and has children by her, even as he remembers his family, his father, and the land of his birth; it is, indeed, through his power in the land of Egypt, and his willingness to serve Pharoah, that Joseph manages to save his family and preserve the future of Israel.

EXODUS

After the death of Joseph, the Hebrew people remain in Egypt and multiply, and the Egyptians become increasingly hostile toward this alien population. Moses, along with his brother Aaron, is chosen by God as the savior of the people, the man who will lead them out of slavery and exile and back to their homeland in Canaan. They escape from Egypt, crossing the waters of the Red Sea, which miraculously part to let

them through and then wash back to drown Pharoah and his army. In the wilderness, Moses goes to hear the word of God at the top of Mount Sinai, and the Ten Commandments are revealed to him: ten rules of ethical and religious conduct, to be carved on stone tablets, that will form the basis for the new law of the Hebrew people and their covenant with God.

JOB

The book of Job draws on an ancient folk tale about God and his Accuser (the Hebrew term is "Satan") testing a just man, who finally passes their test. But the biblical story makes this motif into the prose frame for an extraordinary poem recounting Job's conversations with his friends and with God. Perhaps sometime around the fifth century B.C.E., the poem was composed and the text as we have it was put together. Dating is difficult with a book that seems deliberately to exclude references to the historical and social world: neither the people of Israel nor God's covenant with them is explicitly mentioned. Instead, the text is focused on a single, profound problem, facing all nations of the world at all times. Why does God allow good people to suffer?

Job is a good and upright man who nevertheless suffers horribly—in fact, he is selected for suffering because of his goodness. The text raises the question not only of why the innocent suffer but more generally of why there is misfortune and unhappiness in the world. "Have you taken note of my servant Job," God asks the Accuser, "for there is no one like him on earth: innocent, upright, and God-fearing, and keeping himself apart from evil?" But Job loses his family and wealth in a series of calamities that strike one after the other like hammer blows and is then plagued with a horrible disease. In a series of magnificent speeches, he expresses his sense of his own innocence and demands one thing: to understand the reason for his suffering.

From the beginning, we can see a little farther into the problem than Job. In the prologue, the Accuser challenges God's praise of Job by pointing out that Job's goodness has never been tested; it is easy to be righteous in prosperity. Because we see that Job's afflictions originate in a test, we know that there is a reason for his suffering, but we may not find it a valid reason and may feel that Job is the object of sport for higher powers. If so, what we know from the prologue only makes the problem of innocent suffering worse. Alternatively, we can see God's wager as a sign of his respect for Job and his willingness to trust humanity to make good choices and remain faithful no matter what. But the fact remains that Job is

innocent, and yet he still suffers. What kind of order can we find in a world where that can happen? The prologue in no way cancels the profundity of Job's need to understand the reasons for his suffering.

For Job's comforters, there is no problem. They are anchored solidly in the world of goodness rewarded and wickedness punished. They can account for suffering easily. If Job is suffering, he must have done something wrong. All he has to do, then, is repent his sin and be reconciled with God. Their pious formula, however, does not apply to Job's situation. As we know from the prologue, their mistake is to confuse moral goodness with outward circumstance. Despite or because of their conventional piety, they do not understand Job's suffering, and they get God wrong. In the epilogue, God says to Eliphaz, "I am very angry at you and your two friends, for you have not spoken rightly about me as did my servant Job." Job has spoken rightly by insisting on his innocence and not reducing God's ways to a formula. He also avoids identifying goodness with his fortune in life; unlike his friends, Job acknowledges that good people sometimes suffer dreadfully, and he is appalled by it. But he fulfills God's expectations because he does not curse or in any way repudiate him. Instead, Job wants God to meet him face to face. But he is mistaken to think that he and God can meet on such equal terms and that he can get an explanation. In the end, God does speak to him, but only to pose a series of wonderful but entirely unanswerable questions, such as "Where were you when I founded the earth?" There is no reciprocal conversation; Job simply, briefly, acknowledges his error and recognizes the vast, incommensurable greatness of God.

The text culminates in God's magnificent speech from the storm, which ranges over all of creation and its animal life. The contrast with the account of creation in the first chapter of Genesis, which puts human beings at the center, is dramatic. Here there are beasts whose might far surpasses that of humans, who seem just a part of the created world, and the poetry of this speech conveys the awe and mystery that are attributes of God. The book of Job does not explain innocent suffering, but it does leave us with a sense of what we cannot understand.

PSALMS

The book of Psalms is a collection of 150 poems or hymns. Traditionally, King David was imagined as the author, though modern scholars believe that the various poems come from different time periods, some from before Jerusalem was besieged and finally destroyed by the Babylonians (in 587 B.C.E.), while others (such as "By the Rivers of Babylon") were clearly composed afterward, at a time when the Hebrew people were exiled to the city of their conquerors. Most were composed to be used in worship, and they range in theme and mood, from hymns of praise or joyful thanksgiving to desperate songs of lament expressing the sorrows of a people in exile or the bitterness of a person unjustly wronged. The rich, vivid imagery of the Psalms—memorably conveyed in the language of the King James translation, used here—has had an essential influence on the development of literature in English.

A NOTE ON THE TRANSLATION

Except for the Psalms, presented in the King James version, the biblical text given here is from the recent modern translations by Robert Alter. Alter's language is mostly contemporary, but he is conscious of the need to be faithful to the poetic rhythms of the original—

both in the verse of the book of Job and in the rhythmical prose of Genesis (which includes short passages of verse). Far more than other translators, Alter preserves the simple syntax and verbal repetitions of the Hebrew—for instance, by repeating *and* no less than twenty times in the first eight verses of Genesis. The lack of subordination is an essential feature of the original text's style, as are other kinds of word order that Alter tries to imitate in English, like emphatic inversion (God says, "To your seed I will give" rather than "I will give to your seed"). The Bible tells its complex story in a surprisingly small number of words, and nouns may take on greater power through their repetition in a number of different contexts: it is worthwhile to trace, for example, the use of *hand* or *house* or *brother* throughout the book of Genesis. Alter does not manage to retain every repetition or verbal effect of the Hebrew, but the translation comes close to mirroring the Bible's combination of simple, colloquial vocabulary (with occasional uses of archaic or peculiar phrasing) and vivid concrete metaphor. Alter uses *seed*, for example, to reflect the Hebrew imagery, instead of changing it to *children* or *offspring* (as the New Revised Standard Version does).

We also include one chapter of Robert Crumb's graphic-novel version of Genesis. This uses the Alter translation, but brings it to life with striking black-and-white illustrations of the characters and events. The chosen chapter includes one of the genealogical sections, which form an essential element in the Genesis narrative but often make for slow going for modern readers; Crumb's pictures transform the names into a memorable lineup of personalities. His version of the scene in which Jacob tricks Esau out of his birthright is a gripping realization of this emotionally charged story. Reading even a little of Crumb's version is a good reminder of what we may risk forgetting: that the Hebrew Bible is—for all its theological and philosophical profundity—a very entertaining book.

Genesis 1–4[1]

[From Creation to the Murder of Abel]

1. When God began to create heaven and earth, and the earth then was welter and waste[2] and darkness over the deep and God's breath[3] hovering over the waters, God said, "Let there be light." And there was light. And God saw the light, that it was good, and God divided the light from the darkness. And God called the light Day, and the darkness He called Night. And it was evening and it was morning, first day. And God said, "Let there be a vault in the midst of the waters, and let it divide water from water."[4] And God made the vault and it divided the water beneath the vault from the water above the vault, and so it was. And God called the vault Heavens, and it was evening and it was morning, second day. And God said, "Let the waters under the heavens be gathered in one place so that the dry land will appear," and so it was. And God called the dry land Earth and the gathering of waters He called Seas, and God saw that it was good. And God said, "Let the earth grow grass, plants yielding seed of each kind and trees bearing fruit of each kind, that has its seed within it upon the earth." And so it was. And the earth put forth grass, plants yielding seed, and trees bearing fruit of each kind, and God saw that it was good. And it was evening and it was morning, third day. And God said, "Let there be lights in the vault of the heavens to divide the day from the night, and they shall be signs for the fixed times and for days and years, and they shall be lights in the vault of the heavens to light up the earth." And so it was. And God made the two great lights, the great light for dominion of day and the small light for dominion of night, and the stars. And God placed them in the vault of the heavens to light up the earth and to have dominion over day and night and to divide the light from the darkness. And God saw that it was good. And it was evening and it was morning, fourth day. And God said, "Let the waters swarm with the swarm of living creatures and let fowl fly over the earth across the vault of the heavens." And God created the great sea monsters and every living creature that crawls, which the water had swarmed forth of each kind, and the winged fowl of each kind, and God saw that it was good. And God blessed them, saying, "Be fruitful and multiply and fill the water in the seas and let the fowl multiply in the earth." And it was evening and it was morning, fifth day. And God said, "Let the earth bring forth living creatures of each kind, cattle and crawling things and wild beasts of each kind." And so it was. And God made wild beasts of each kind and cattle of every kind and all crawling things on the ground of each kind, and God saw that it was good. And God said, "Let us make a human

---

1. Excerpts from Genesis are translated by Robert Alter. The notes are indebted to Alter's annotations.
2. The translator combines a rare English word (*welter*, meaning chaos, or the turmoil of rolling waves) with *waste* to render a phrase that is very rare in the Hebrew, *tohu wabohu*.
3. The Hebrew word for "breath," *ruah*, may also mean "spirit."
4. The water below the vault, or sky, is the ocean; the water above the vault is the rain.

in our image,[5] by our likeness, to hold sway over the fish of the sea and the fowl of the heavens and the cattle and the wild beasts and all the crawling things that crawl upon the earth.

> And God created the human in his image,
> in the image of God He created him,
> male and female He created them.[6]

And God blessed them, and God said to them, "Be fruitful and multiply and fill the earth and conquer it, and hold sway over the fish of the sea and the fowl of the heavens and every beast that crawls upon the earth." And God said, "Look, I have given you every seed-bearing plant on the face of all the earth and every tree that has fruit bearing seed, yours they will be for food. And to all the beasts of the earth and to all the fowl of the heavens and to all that crawls on the earth, which has the breath of life within it, the green plants for food." And so it was. And God saw all that He had done, and, look, it was very good. And it was evening and it was morning, the sixth day.

2.[7] Then the heavens and the earth were completed, and all their array. And God completed on the seventh day the task He had done, and He ceased on the seventh day from all the task He had done. And God blessed the seventh day and hallowed it, for on it He had ceased from all His task that He had created to do. This is the tale of the heavens and the earth when they were created. On the day the LORD God made earth and heavens, no shrub of the field being yet on the earth and no plant of the field yet sprouted, for the LORD God had not caused rain to fall on the earth and there was no human to till the soil, and wetness would well from the earth to water all the surface of the soil, then the LORD God fashioned the human, humus from the soil,[8] and blew into his nostrils the breath of life, and the human became a living creature. And the LORD God planted a garden in Eden, to the east, and He placed there the human He had fashioned. And the LORD God caused to sprout from the soil every tree lovely to look at and good for food, and the tree of life was in the midst of the garden, and the tree of knowledge, good and evil. Now a river runs out of Eden to water the garden and from there splits off into four streams. The name of the first is Pishon, the one that winds through the whole land of Havilah, where there is gold. And the gold of that land is goodly, bdellium[9] is there, and lapis lazuli. And the name of the second river is Gihon, the one that winds through all the land of Cush. And the name of the third river is Tigris, the one that goes to the east of Ashur. And the fourth river is Euphrates. And the LORD God took the human and set him down in the garden of Eden to till it and watch it. And the LORD God commanded the human, saying, "From

---

5. The Hebrew word for "human" is ʿadam, which also means "dust"; it is not the first man's name, but the noun denoting all humanity. It does not necessarily imply that the human is male.

6. Here and elsewhere in the translation, the indentation marks a shift into a brief passage of verse in the translation, reflecting a shift in the original.

7. This is the beginning of a different account of the Creation, which does not agree in all respects with the first.

8. There is a pun in the Hebrew on ʿadam, "human," and ʿadamah, "humus" or "soil."

9. A fragrant tree.

every fruit of the garden you may surely eat. But from the tree of knowledge, good and evil, you shall not eat, for on the day you eat from it, you are doomed to die." And the LORD God said, "It is not good for the human to be alone, I shall make him a sustainer beside him." And the LORD God fashioned from the soil each beast of the field and each fowl of the heavens and brought each to the human to see what he would call it, and whatever the human called a living creature, that was its name. And the human called names to all the cattle and to the fowl of the heavens and to all the beasts of the field, but for the human no sustainer beside him was found. And the LORD God cast a deep slumber on the human, and he slept, and He took one of his ribs and closed over the flesh where it had been, and the LORD God built the rib He had taken from the human into a woman and He brought her to the human. And the human said:

> "This one at last, bone of my bones
> and flesh of my flesh,
> This one shall be called Woman,
> for from man was this one taken."[1]

Therefore does a man leave his father and his mother and cling to his wife and they become one flesh. And the two of them were naked, the human and his woman, and they were not ashamed.

3. Now the serpent was most cunning of all the beasts of the field that the LORD God had made. And he said to the woman, "Though God said, you shall not eat from any tree of the garden—" And the woman said to the serpent, "From the fruit of the garden's trees we may eat, but from the fruit of the tree in the midst of the garden God has said, 'You shall not eat from it and you shall not touch it, lest you die.'" And the serpent said to the woman, "You shall not be doomed to die. For God knows that on the day you eat of it your eyes will be opened and you will become as gods knowing good and evil." And the woman saw that the tree was good for eating and that it was lust to the eyes and the tree was lovely to look at, and she took of its fruit and ate, and she also gave to her man, and he ate. And the eyes of the two were opened, and they knew they were naked, and they sewed fig leaves and made themselves loincloths.

   And they heard the sound of the LORD God walking about in the garden in the evening breeze, and the human and his woman hid from the LORD God in the midst of the trees of the garden. And the LORD God called to the human and said to him, "Where are you?" And he said, "I heard Your sound in the garden and I was afraid, for I was naked, and I hid." And He said, "Who told you that you were naked? From the tree I commanded you not to eat have you eaten?" And the human said, "The woman whom you gave by me, she gave me from the tree, and I ate." And the LORD God said to the woman, "What is this you have done?" And the woman said, "The serpent beguiled me and I ate." And the LORD God said to the serpent, "Because you have done this,

---

1. "Man" is *ish* in Hebrew; "woman" is *ishshah*.

> Cursed be you
>   of all cattle and all beasts of the field.
> On your belly shall you go
>   and dust shall you eat all the days of your life.
> Enmity will I set between you and the woman,
>   between your seed and hers.
> He will boot your head
>   and you will bite his heel."[2]

To the woman He said,

> "I will terribly sharpen your birth pangs,
>   in pain shall you bear children.
> And for your man shall be your longing,
>   and he shall rule over you."

And to the human He said, "Because you listened to the voice of your wife and ate from the tree that I commanded you 'You shall not eat from it,'

> Cursed be the soil for your sake,
>   with pangs shall you eat from it all the days of your life.
> Thorn and thistle shall it sprout for you
>   and you shall eat the plants of the field.
> By the sweat of your brow shall you eat bread
>   till you return to the soil,
>   for from there were you taken,
> for dust you are
>   and to dust shall you return."

And the human called his woman's name Eve, for she was the mother of all that lives.[3] And the LORD God made skin coats for the human and his woman, and He clothed them. And the LORD God said, "Now that the human has become like one of us, knowing good and evil, he may reach out and take as well from the tree of life and live forever." And the LORD God sent him from the garden of Eden to till the soil from which he had been taken. And He drove out the human and set up east of the garden of Eden the cherubim and the flame of the whirling sword to guard the way to the tree of life.

4. And the human knew Eve his woman and she conceived and bore Cain, and she said, "I have got me a man with the LORD." And she bore as well his brother, Abel, and Abel became a herder of sheep while Cain was a tiller of the soil. And it happened in the course of time that Cain brought from the fruit of the soil an offering to the LORD. And Abel too had brought from the choice firstlings of his flock, and the LORD regarded Abel and his offering but He did not regard Cain and his offering, and Cain was very incensed, and his face fell. And the LORD said to Cain,

---

2. "Boot . . . bite" represents a pun in Hebrew: the word for trampling, or "booting," is repeated to refer to the snake's reaction; it may refer to the snake's hiss just before it bites.

3. The name *Hawah*, Eve, is similar to the verbal root *hayah*, "to live."

"Why are you incensed,
and why is your face fallen?
For whether you offer well,
or whether you do not,
at the tent flap sin crouches
and for you is its longing
but you will rule over it."[4]

And Cain said to Abel his brother, "Let us go out to the field." And when they were in the field, Cain rose against Abel his brother and killed him. And the LORD said to Cain, "Where is Abel your brother?" And he said, "I do not know. Am I my brother's keeper?" And He said, "What have you done? Listen! your brother's blood cries out to me from the soil. And so, cursed shall you be by the soil that gaped with its mouth to take your brother's blood from your hand. If you till the soil, it will no longer give you its strength. A restless wanderer shall you be on the earth." And Cain said to the LORD, "My punishment is too great to bear. Now that You have driven me this day from the soil and I must hide from Your presence, I shall be a restless wanderer on the earth and whoever finds me will kill me." And the LORD said to him, "Therefore whoever kills Cain shall suffer sevenfold vengeance." And the LORD set a mark upon Cain so that whoever found him would not slay him.

And Cain went out from the LORD's presence and dwelled in the land of Nod east of Eden. And Cain knew his wife and she conceived and bore Enoch. Then he became the builder of a city and called the name of the city, like his son's name, Enoch. And Irad was born to Enoch,[5] and Irad begot Mehujael and Mehujael begot Methusael and Methusael begot Lamech. And Lamech took him two wives, the name of the one was Adah and the name of the other was Zillah. And Adah bore Jabal: he was the first of tent dwellers with live-stock. And his brother's name was Jubal: he was the first of all who play on the lyre and pipe. As for Zillah, she bore Tubal-Cain, who forged every tool of copper and iron. And the sister of Tubal-Cain was Naamah. And Lamech said to his wives,

"Adah and Zillah, O hearken my voice,
You wives of Lamech, give ear to my speech.
For a man have I slain for my wound,
a boy for my bruising.
For sevenfold Cain is avenged,
and Lamech seventy and seven."

And Adam again knew his wife and she bore a son and called his name Seth, as to say, "God has granted me[6] other seed in place of Abel, for Cain has killed him." As for Seth, to him, too, a son was born, and he called his name Enosh. It was then that the name of the LORD was first invoked.

---

4. Obscure; it seems to mean something like "Sin shall be eager for you, but you must master it."

5. This is the first of many lists of genealogies in the book of Genesis. Genealogy is one of the major ways in which the text evokes and orders historical time and creates a connection between past and present.

6. The pun in Hebrew is between the name *Shet* and the verb *shat*, "granted."

Genesis 6–9

[Noah and the Flood]

6. And it happened as humankind began to multiply over the earth and daughters were born to them, that the sons of God saw that the daughters of man were comely, and they took themselves wives howsoever they chose.[7] And the LORD said, "My breath shall not abide in the human forever, for he is but flesh. Let his days be a hundred and twenty years."

The Nephilim[8] were then on the earth, and afterward as well, the sons of God having come to bed with the daughters of man who bore them children: they are the heroes of yore, the men of renown.

And the LORD saw that the evil of the human creature was great on the earth and that every scheme of his heart's devising was only perpetually evil. And the LORD regretted having made the human on earth and was grieved to the heart. And the LORD said, "I will wipe out the human race I created from the face of the earth, from human to cattle to crawling thing to the fowl of the heavens, for I regret that I have made them." But Noah found favor in the eyes of the LORD. This is the lineage of Noah—Noah was a righteous man, he was blameless in his time, Noah walked with God—and Noah begot three sons, Shem and Ham and Japheth. And the earth was corrupt before God and the earth was filled with outrage. And God saw the earth and, look, it was corrupt, for all flesh had corrupted its ways on the earth. And God said to Noah, "The end of all flesh is come before me, for the earth is filled with outrage by them, and I am now about to destroy them, with the earth. Make yourself an ark of cypress wood, with cells you shall make the ark, and caulk it inside and out with pitch. This is how you shall make it: three hundred cubits, the ark's length; fifty cubits, its width; thirty cubits, its height. Make a skylight in the ark, within a cubit of the top you shall finish it, and put an entrance in the ark on one side. With lower and middle and upper decks you shall make it. As for me, I am about to bring the Flood, water upon the earth, to destroy all flesh that has within it the breath of life from under the heavens, everything on the earth shall perish. And I will set up my covenant with you, and you shall enter the ark, you and your sons and your wife and the wives of your sons, with you. And from all that lives, from all flesh, two of each thing you shall bring to the ark to keep alive with you, male and female they shall be. From the fowl of each kind and from the cattle of each kind and from all that crawls on the earth of each kind, two of each thing shall come to you to be kept alive. As for you, take you from every food that is eaten and store it by you, to serve for you and for them as food." And this Noah did; as all that God commanded him, so he did.

7. And the LORD said to Noah, "Come into the ark, you and all your household, for it is you I have seen righteous before Me in this generation. Of every clean animal take you seven pairs, each with its mate, and of every animal that is not

---

7. The passage is based on archaic myths (perhaps from an old Hittite tradition) about male gods ("the sons of God") having sex with mortal women.
8. This appears to mean "the fallen ones."

The allusion seems cryptic, perhaps because the monotheistic writer is avoiding explicit discussion of multiple semidivine or divine figures, although the idea of such beings would have been familiar to the ancient reader.

clean, one pair, each with its mate.[9] Of the fowl of the heavens as well seven pairs, male and female, to keep seed alive over all the earth. For in seven days' time I will make it rain on the earth forty days and forty nights and I will wipe out from the face of the earth all existing things that I have made." And Noah did all that the LORD commanded him.

Noah was six hundred years old when the Flood came, water over the earth. And Noah and his sons and his wife and his sons' wives came into the ark because of the waters of the Flood. Of the clean animals and of the animals that were not clean and of the fowl and of all that crawls upon the ground two each came to Noah into the ark, male and female, as God had commanded Noah. And it happened after seven days, that the waters of the Flood were over the earth. In the six hundredth year of Noah's life, in the second month, on the seventeenth day of the month, on that day,

> All the wellsprings of the great deep burst
> and the casements of the heavens were opened.

And the rain was over the earth forty days and forty nights. That very day, Noah and Shem and Ham and Japheth, the sons of Noah, and Noah's wife, and the three wives of his sons together with them, came into the ark, they as well as beasts of each kind and cattle of each kind and each kind of crawling thing that crawls on the earth and each kind of bird, each winged thing. They came to Noah into the ark, two by two of all flesh that has the breath of life within it. And those that came in, male and female of all flesh they came, as God had commanded him, and the LORD shut him in. And the Flood was forty days over the earth, and the waters multiplied and bore the ark upward and it rose above the earth. And the waters surged and multiplied mightily over the earth, and the ark went on the surface of the water. And the waters surged most mightily over the earth, and all the high mountains under the heavens were covered. Fifteen cubits above them the waters surged as the mountains were covered. And all flesh that stirs on the earth perished, the fowl and the cattle and the beasts and all swarming things that swarm upon the earth, and all humankind. All that had the quickening breath of life in its nostrils, of all that was on dry land, died. And He wiped out all existing things from the face of the earth, from humans to cattle to crawling things to the fowl of the heavens, they were wiped out from the earth. And Noah alone remained, and those with him in the ark. And the waters surged over the earth one hundred and fifty days.

8. And God remembered Noah and all the beasts and all the cattle that were with him in the ark. And God sent a wind over the earth and the waters subsided. And the wellsprings of the deep were dammed up, and the casements of the heavens, the rain from the heavens held back. And the waters receded from the earth little by little, and the waters ebbed. At the end of a hundred and fifty days the ark came to rest, on the seventeenth day of the seventh month, on the

---

9. "Clean" and "not clean" refer to the categories of animals that might or might not be sacrificed; it does not refer to dietary restrictions, which came later in the tradition. There is clearly a discrepancy in the narratives here, between the previous chapter's specification of "two of each thing" and this chapter's requirement of "seven pairs."

mountains of Ararat. The waters continued to ebb, until the tenth month, on the first day of the tenth month, the mountaintops appeared. And it happened, at the end of forty days, that Noah opened the window of the ark he had made. And he sent out the raven and it went forth to and fro until the waters should dry up from the earth. And he sent out the dove to see whether the waters had abated from the surface of the ground. But the dove found no resting place for its foot and it returned to him to the ark, for the waters were over all the earth. And he reached out and took it and brought it back to him into the ark. Then he waited another seven days and again sent the dove out from the ark. And the dove came back to him at eventide and, look, a plucked olive leaf was in its bill, and Noah knew that the waters had abated from the earth. Then he waited still another seven days and sent out the dove, and it did not return to him again. And it happened in the six hundred and first year, in the first month, on the first day of the month, the waters dried up from the earth, and Noah took off the covering of the ark and he saw and, look, the surface of the ground was dry. And in the second month, on the twenty-seventh day of the month, the earth was completely dry. And God spoke to Noah, saying, "Go out of the ark, you and your wife and your sons and your sons' wives, with you. All the animals that are with you of all flesh, fowl and cattle and every crawling thing that crawls on the earth, take out with you, and let them swarm through the earth and be fruitful and multiply on the earth." And Noah went out, his sons and his wife and his sons' wives with him. Every beast, every crawling thing, and every fowl, everything that stirs on the earth, by their families, came out of the ark. And Noah built an altar to the LORD and he took from every clean cattle and every clean fowl and offered burnt offerings on the altar. And the LORD smelled the fragrant odor and the LORD said in His heart, "I will not again damn the soil on humankind's score. For the devisings of the human heart are evil from youth. And I will not again strike down all living things as I did. As long as all the days of the earth—

> seedtime and harvest
> and cold and heat
> and summer and winter
> and day and night
> shall not cease."

9. And God blessed Noah and his sons and He said to them, "Be fruitful and multiply and fill the earth. And the dread and fear of you shall be upon all the beasts of the field and all the fowl of the heavens, in all that crawls on the ground and in all the fish of the sea. In your hand they are given. All stirring things that are alive, yours shall be for food, like the green plants, I have given all to you. But flesh with its lifeblood still in it you shall not eat. And just so, your lifeblood I will requite, from every beast I will requite it, and from humankind, from every man's brother. I will requite human life.

> He who sheds human blood
> by humans his blood shall be shed,[1]

1. There is wordplay in the original, between 'adam, "human," and dam, "blood."

> for in the image of God
> He made humankind.
> As for you, be fruitful and multiply,
> swarm through the earth, and hold sway over it."

And God said to Noah and to his sons with him, "And I, I am about to establish My covenant with you and with your seed after you, and with every living creature that is with you, the fowl and the cattle and every beast of the earth with you, all that have come out of the ark, every beast of the earth. And I will establish My covenant with you, that never again shall all flesh be cut off by the waters of the Flood, and never again shall there be a Flood to destroy the earth." And God said, "This is the sign of the covenant that I set between Me and you and every living creature that is with you, for everlasting generations: My bow I have set in the clouds to be a sign of the covenant between Me and the earth, and so, when I send clouds over the earth, the bow will appear in the cloud. Then I will remember My covenant, between Me and you and every living creature of all flesh, and the waters will no more become a Flood to destroy all flesh. And the bow shall be in the cloud and I will see it, to remember the everlasting covenant between God and all living creatures, all flesh that is on the earth." And God said to Noah, "This is the sign of the covenant I have established between Me and all flesh that is on the earth."

And the sons of Noah who came out from the ark were Shem and Ham and Japheth, and Ham was the father of Canaan. These three were the sons of Noah, and from these the whole earth spread out. And Noah, a man of the soil, was the first to plant a vineyard. And he drank of the wine and became drunk, and exposed himself within his tent. And Ham the father of Canaan saw his father's nakedness and told his two brothers outside. And Shem and Japheth took a cloak and put it over both their shoulders and walked backward and covered their father's nakedness, their faces turned backward so they did not see their father's nakedness. And Noah woke from his wine and he knew what his youngest son had done to him.[2] And he said,

> "Cursed be Canaan,
> the lowliest slave shall he be
> to his brothers."[3]

And he said,

> "Blessed be the LORD
> the God of Shem,
> unto them shall Canaan be slave.

---

2. The text leaves it unclear what Ham has done. Perhaps simply seeing his father naked is breaking a taboo.

3. An obvious purpose of this story is to justify the idea that the Israelites, rather than the Canaanites, ought to control the land of Canaan—an important issue in later Israelite history. After antiquity, Noah's three sons were often believed to have been the ancestors of the three supposed racial groups in the world: Japheth was the ancestor of European and Asian peoples, Shem was the ancestor of the Semitic races, and Ham was the ancestor of Africans. This interpretation goes well beyond the text itself and has often been motivated, implicitly or explicitly, by racism.

> May God enlarge Japheth,
> may he dwell in the tents of Shem,
> unto them shall Canaan be slave."

And Noah lived after the Flood three hundred and fifty years. And all the days of Noah were nine hundred and fifty years. Then he died.

From Genesis 11

[*The Tower of Babel*]

11. And all the earth was one language, one set of words. And it happened as they journeyed from the east that they found a valley in the land of Shinar and settled there. And they said to each other, "Come, let us bake bricks and burn them hard." And the brick served them as stone, and bitumen served them as mortar. And they said, "Come, let us build us a city and a tower with its top in the heavens, that we may make us a name, lest we be scattered over all the earth." And the LORD came down to see the city and the tower that the human creatures had built. And the LORD said, "As one people with one language for all, if this is what they have begun to do, now nothing they plot to do will elude them. Come, let us go down and baffle their language there so that they will not understand each other's language." And the LORD scattered them from there over all the earth and they left off building the city. Therefore it is called Babel, for there the LORD made the language of all the earth babble.[4] And from there the LORD scattered them over all the earth.

* * *

From Genesis 12, 17, 18

[*God's Promise to Abraham*]

12. And the LORD said to Abram,[5] "Go forth from your land and your birthplace and your father's house to the land I will show you. And I will make you a great nation and I will bless you and make your name great, and you shall be a blessing. And I will bless those who bless you, and those who damn you I will curse, and all the clans of the earth through you shall be blessed." And Abram went forth as the LORD had spoken to him and Lot went forth with him, Abram being seventy-five years old when he left Haran. And Abram took

---

4. The pun in Hebrew is between *balal*, "to mix" or "to confuse," and the Akkadian place name *Babel* (or *Babylon*), which probably originally meant "gate of heaven." The "tower" is presumably a ziggurat, the type of tall building surrounding temple complexes in many ancient Mesopotamian cultures.

5. Ten generations and hundreds of years have passed since the time of Noah. Abram is a descendant of Noah's son Shem.

Sarai his wife and Lot his nephew and all the goods they had gotten and the folk they had bought in Haran,[6] and they set out on the way to the land of Canaan, and they came to the land of Canaan. And Abram crossed through the land to the site of Shechem, to the Terebinth of Moreh. The Canaanite was then in the land. And the LORD appeared to Abram and said, "To your seed I will give this land." And he built an altar there to the LORD who had appeared to him.

* * *

17. And Abram was ninety-nine years old, and the LORD appeared to Abram and said to him, "I am El Shaddai.[7] Walk in My presence and be blameless, and I will grant My covenant between Me and you and I will multiply you very greatly." And Abram flung himself on his face, and God spoke to him, saying, "As for Me, this is My covenant with you: you shall be father to a multitude of nations. And no longer shall your name be called Abram but your name shall be Abraham, for I have made you father to a multitude of nations.[8] And I will make you most abundantly fruitful and turn you into nations, and kings shall come forth from you. And I will establish My covenant between Me and you and your seed after you through their generations as an everlasting covenant to be God to you and to your seed after you. And I will give unto you and your seed after you the land in which you sojourn, the whole land of Canaan, as an everlasting holding, and I will be their God."

And God said to Abraham, "As for you, you shall keep My commandment, you and your seed after you through their generations."

* * *

18. And the LORD appeared to him in the Terebinths of Mamre[9] when he was sitting by the tent flap in the heat of the day. And he raised his eyes and saw, and, look, three men were standing before him. He saw, and he ran toward them from the tent flap and bowed to the ground. And he said, "My lord, if I have found favor in your eyes, please do not go on past your servant. Let a little water be fetched and bathe your feet and stretch out under the tree, and let me fetch a morsel of bread, and refresh yourselves. Then you may go on, for have you not come by your servant?" And they said, "Do as you have spoken." And Abraham hurried to the tent to Sarah and he said, "Hurry! Knead three *seahs* of choice semolina flour and make loaves."[1] And to the herd Abraham ran and fetched a tender and goodly calf and gave it to the lad, who

6. Slaves. Slavery was a common institution in the ancient Near East. The slave girl Hagar will play an important part in the story, since she is the mother of Abram's first son, Ishmael.
7. *El* means God; the meaning of *Shaddai* is obscure.
8. The names *Abram* and *Abraham* both mean "exalted father." Abram and Sarai (later Sarah) have to change their names, not to gain titles with new meaning but as a sign of

taking on their new roles as instruments of God's purpose.
9. Terebinths are small trees that produce turpentine; the word used here is sometimes interpreted to mean "oak trees." Mamre was the site of a cult shrine to the major Canaanite sky god.
1. A *seah* is a dry measure equal to about thirty cups; three *seahs* is almost five gallons—a lot of food for three people.

hurried to prepare it. And he fetched curds and milk and the calf that had been prepared and he set these before them, he standing over them under the tree, and they ate. And they said to him, "Where is Sarah your wife?" And he said, "There, in the tent." And he said, "I will surely return to you at this very season and, look, a son shall Sarah your wife have," and Sarah was listening at the tent flap, which was behind him. And Abraham and Sarah were old, advanced in years, Sarah no longer had her woman's flow. And Sarah laughed inwardly, saying, "After being shriveled, shall I have pleasure, and my husband is old?" And the LORD said to Abraham, "Why is it that Sarah laughed, saying, 'Shall I really give birth, old as I am?' Is anything beyond the LORD? In due time I will return to you, at this very season, and Sarah shall have a son." And Sarah dissembled, saying, "I did not laugh," for she was afraid. And He said, "Yes, you did laugh."

* * *

From Genesis 21, 22

[Abraham and Isaac]

21. And the LORD singled out Sarah as He had said, and the LORD did for Sarah as He had spoken. And Sarah conceived and bore a son to Abraham in his old age at the set time that God had spoken to him. And Abraham called the name of his son who was born to him, whom Sarah bore him, Isaac.[2] And Abraham circumcised Isaac his son when he was eight days old, as God had charged him. And Abraham was a hundred years old when Isaac his son was born to him. And Sarah said,

> "Laughter has God made me,
> Whoever hears will laugh at me."

* * *

22. And it happened after these things that God tested Abraham. And He said to him, "Abraham!" and he said, "Here I am." And He said, "Take, pray, your son, your only one, whom you love, Isaac, and go forth to the land of Moriah and offer him up as a burnt offering on one of the mountains which I shall say to you." And Abraham rose early in the morning and saddled his donkey and took his two lads with him, and Isaac his son, and he split wood for the offering, and rose and went to the place that God had said to him. On the third day Abraham raised his eyes and saw the place from afar. And Abraham said to his lads, "Sit you here with the donkey and let me and the lad walk ahead and let us worship and return to you." And Abraham took the wood for the offering and put it on Isaac his son and he took in his hand the

2. "He who laughs."

fire and the cleaver, and the two of them went together. And Isaac said to Abraham his father, "Father!" and he said, "Here I am, my son." And he said, "Here is the fire and the wood but where is the sheep for the offering?" And Abraham said, "God will see to the sheep for the offering, my son." And the two of them went together. And they came to the place that God had said to him, and Abraham built there an altar and laid out the wood and bound Isaac his son and placed him on the altar on top of the wood. And Abraham reached out his hand and took the cleaver to slaughter his son. And the LORD's messenger called out to him from the heavens and said, "Abraham, Abraham!" and he said, "Here I am." And he said, "Do not reach out your hand against the lad, and do nothing to him, for now I know that you fear God and you have not held back your son, your only one, from Me." And Abraham raised his eyes and saw and, look, a ram was caught in the thicket by its horns, and Abraham went and took the ram and offered him up as a burnt offering instead of his son. And Abraham called the name of that place YHWH-Yireh, as is said to this day, "On the mount of the LORD there is sight."[3] And the LORD's messenger called out to Abraham once again from the heavens, and He said, "By My own Self I swear, declares the LORD, that because you have done this thing and have not held back your son, your only one, I will greatly bless you and will greatly multiply your seed, as the stars in the heavens and as the sand on the shore of the sea, and your seed shall take hold of its enemies' gate. And all the nations of the earth will be blessed through your seed because you have listened to my voice." And Abraham returned to his lads, and they rose and went together to Beersheba, and Abraham dwelled in Beersheba.

* * *

Genesis 25

[*Esau Spurns His Birthright*]

We give chapter 25 of Genesis in the graphic-novel version by Robert Crumb. The words are based on Robert Alter's translation. Readers are invited to think about how the extra visual material contributes to the text and how these pictures might change one's interpretation of the Bible. We have chosen this chapter partly because it includes one of the many genealogies in Genesis, which are an essential feature of the Hebrew Bible's narrative method but hard for modern readers to appreciate; they are made vivid by Crumb's pictures. Moreover, Crumb's powerful depiction of Rebekah's conversation with the Lord is a good reminder of how important the female characters (the Matriarchs) are in this narrative. The chapter also marks the beginning of the story of Jacob and Esau; illustrations emphasize the textual, visual distinction between the hairy, wild hunter Esau and the smooth-skinned, smooth-talking Jacob.

---

3. The place name means "The Lord (Yaweh) sees" or "The Lord is seen."

Chapter 25

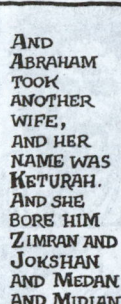

AND ABRAHAM TOOK ANOTHER WIFE, AND HER NAME WAS KETURAH. AND SHE BORE HIM ZIMRAN AND JOKSHAN AND MEDAN AND MIDIAN AND ISHBAK AND SHUAH.

AND JOKSHAN BEGOT SHEBA AND DEDAN. AND THE SONS OF DEDAN WERE THE ASHURIM AND THE LETUSHIM AND THE LEUMMIM. AND THE SONS OF MIDIAN WERE EPHAH AND EPHER AND ENOCH AND ABIDA AND ELDAAH. ALL THESE WERE THE DESCENDANTS OF KETURAH.

AND ABRAHAM GAVE EVERYTHING HE HAD TO ISAAC. AND TO THE SONS OF HIS CONCUBINES ABRAHAM GAVE GIFTS WHILE HE WAS STILL ALIVE, AND SENT THEM AWAY FROM ISAAC, HIS SON, EASTWARD, TO THE LAND OF THE EAST.

AND THESE ARE THE DAYS OF THE YEARS OF THE LIFE OF ABRAHAM, WHICH HE LIVED: 175 YEARS. AND ABRAHAM BREATHED HIS LAST AND DIED AT A RIPE OLD AGE, OLD AND SATED WITH YEARS, AND HE WAS GATHERED TO HIS KINFOLK.

AND ISAAC AND ISHMAEL, HIS SONS, BURIED HIM IN THE MACHPELAH CAVE IN THE FIELD OF EPHRON, SON OF ZOHAR THE HITTITE, WHICH FACES MAMRE, THE FIELD THAT ABRAHAM HAD BOUGHT FROM THE HITTITES. THERE ABRAHAM WAS BURIED, WITH SARAH, HIS WIFE.

AND IT CAME TO PASS AFTER THE DEATH OF ABRAHAM THAT GOD BLESSED HIS SON ISAAC, AND ISAAC SETTLED NEAR BEER-LAHAI-ROI.

AND THIS IS THE LINEAGE OF ISHMAEL, SON OF ABRAHAM WHOM HAGAR, THE EGYPTIAN, SARAH'S SLAVE-GIRL, BORE TO ABRAHAM. AND THESE ARE THE NAMES OF THE SONS OF ISHMAEL ACCORDING TO THEIR LINEAGE...

NEBAIOTH, THE FIRSTBORN OF ISHMAEL...

AND KEDAR...

AND ADBEEL...

AND MIBSAM...

AND MISHMA...

AND DUMA...

AND MASSA...

HADAD...

AND TEMA...

JETUR...

NAPHISH...

AND KEDMAH.

THESE ARE THE SONS OF ISHMAEL, AND THESE ARE THEIR NAMES, BY THEIR TOWNS AND BY THEIR STRONGHOLDS, TWELVE CHIEFTAINS ACCORDING TO THEIR CLANS.

AND THESE ARE THE YEARS OF THE LIFE OF ISHMAEL: 137 YEARS. AND HE BREATHED HIS LAST AND DIED AND HE WAS GATHERED TO HIS KINFOLK. AND THEY RANGED FROM HAVILAH TO SHUR, WHICH FACES EGYPT, AND TILL YOU COME TO ASSHUR.

AND THIS IS THE LINEAGE OF ISAAC, SON OF ABRAHAM. ABRAHAM BEGOT ISAAC. AND ISAAC WAS FORTY YEARS OLD WHEN HE TOOK AS WIFE REBEKAH, DAUGHTER OF BETHUEL THE ARAMEAN FROM PADDAN-ARAM, SISTER OF LABAN THE ARAMEAN. AND ISAAC PLEADED WITH THE LORD ON BEHALF OF HIS WIFE, FOR SHE WAS BARREN.

IN THE FACE OF ALL HIS KIN HE WENT DOWN.

4. Rebekah's question is terse and open to interpretation. It may be elliptical (perhaps "Why am I . . . even having these babies?"), or it may imply, "Why me?"

Genesis 27

[*Jacob and Esau*]

27. And it happened when Isaac was old, that his eyes grew too bleary to see, and he called to Esau his elder son and said to him, "My son!" and he said, "Here I am." And he said, "Look, I have grown old; I know not how soon I shall die. So now, take up, pray, your gear, your quiver and your bow, and go out to the field, and hunt me some game, and make me a dish of the kind that I love and bring it to me that I may eat, so that I may solemnly bless you before I die." And Rebekah was listening as Isaac spoke to Esau his son, and Esau went off to the field to hunt game to bring.

And Rebekah said to Jacob her son, "Look, I have heard your father speaking to Esau your brother, saying, 'Bring me some game and make me a dish that I may eat, and I shall bless you in the LORD's presence before I die.' So now, my son, listen to my voice, to what I command you. Go, pray, to the flock, and fetch me from there two choice kids that I may make them into a dish for your father of the kind he loves. And you shall bring it to your father and he shall eat, so that he may bless you before he dies." And Jacob said to Rebekah his mother, "Look, Esau my brother is a hairy man and I am a smooth-skinned man. What if my father feels me and I seem a cheat to him and bring on myself a curse and not a blessing?" And his mother said, "Upon me your curse, my son. Just listen to my voice and go, fetch them for me." And he went and he fetched and he brought to his mother, and his mother made a dish of the kind his father loved. And Rebekah took the garments of Esau her elder son, the finery that was with her in the house, and put them on Jacob her younger son, and the skins of the kids she put on his hands and on the smooth part of his neck. And she placed the dish, and the bread she had made, in the hand of Jacob her son. And he came to his father and said, "Father!" And he said, "Here I am. Who are you, my son?" And Jacob said to his father, "I am Esau your firstborn. I have done as you have spoken to me. Rise, pray, sit up, and eat of my game so that you may solemnly bless me." And Isaac said to his son, "How is it you found it this soon, my son?" And he said, "Because the LORD your God gave me good luck." And Isaac said to Jacob, "Come close, pray, that I may feel you, my son, whether you are my son Esau or not." And Jacob came close to Isaac his father and he felt him and he said, "The voice is the voice of Jacob and the hands are Esau's hands." But he did not recognize him for his hands were, like Esau's hands, hairy, and he blessed him. And he said, "Are you my son Esau?" And he said, "I am." And he said, "Serve me, that I may eat of the game of my son, so that I may solemnly bless you." And he served him and he ate, and he brought him wine and he drank. And Isaac his father said to him, "Come close, pray, and kiss me, my son." And he came close and kissed him, and he smelled his garments and he blessed him and he said, "See, the smell of my son is like the smell of the field that the LORD has blessed.

> May God grant you
> > from the dew of the heavens and the fat of the earth,
> > and abundance of grain and drink.
> May peoples serve you,
> > and nations bow before you.

> Be overlord to your brothers,
>> may your mother's sons bow before you.
> Those who curse you be cursed,
>> and those who bless you, blessed."

And it happened as soon as Isaac finished blessing Jacob, and Jacob barely had left the presence of Isaac his father, that Esau his brother came back from the hunt. And he, too, made a dish and brought it to his father and he said to his father, "Let my father rise and eat of the game of his son so that you may solemnly bless me." And his father Isaac said, "Who are you?" And he said, "I am your son, your firstborn, Esau." And Isaac was seized with a very great trembling and he said, "Who is it, then, who caught game and brought it to me and I ate everything before you came and blessed him? Now blessed he stays." When Esau heard his father's words, he cried out with a great and very bitter outcry and he said to his father, "Bless me, too, Father!" And he said, "Your brother has come in deceit and has taken your blessing." And he said,

> "Was his name called Jacob
>> that he should trip me now twice by the heels?
> My birthright he took,
>> and look, now, he's taken my blessing."

And he said, "Have you not kept back a blessing for me?"

And Isaac answered and said to Esau, "Look, I made him overlord to you, and all his brothers I gave him as slaves, and with grain and wine I endowed him. For you, then, what can I do, my son?" And Esau said to his father, "Do you have but one blessing, my father? Bless me, too, Father." And Esau raised his voice and he wept. And Isaac his father answered and said to him,

> "Look, from the fat of the earth be your dwelling
>> and from the dew of the heavens above.
> By your sword shall you live
>> and your brother shall you serve.
> And when you rebel
>> you shall break off his yoke from your neck."

And Esau seethed with resentment against Jacob over the blessing his father had blessed him, and Esau said in his heart, "As soon as the time for mourning my father comes round, I will kill Jacob my brother." And Rebekah was told the words of Esau her elder son, and she sent and summoned Jacob her younger son and said to him, "Look, Esau your brother is consoling himself with the idea he will kill you. So now, my son, listen to my voice, and rise, flee to my brother Laban in Haran, and you may stay with him a while until your brother's wrath subsides, until your brother's rage against you subsides and he forgets what you did to him, and I shall send and fetch you from there. Why should I be bereft of you both on one day?" And Rebekah said to Isaac, "I loathe my life because of the Hittite women! If Jacob takes a wife from Hittite women like these, from the native girls, what good to me is life?"

From Genesis 28

[*Jacob's Dream*]

28. * * * And Jacob left Beersheba and set out for Haran. And he came upon a certain place and stopped there for the night, for the sun had set, and he took one of the stones of the place and put it at his head and he lay down in that place, and he dreamed, and, look, a ramp was set against the ground with its top reaching the heavens, and, look, messengers of God were going up and coming down it. And, look, the LORD was poised over him and He said, "I, the LORD, am the God of Abraham your father and the God of Isaac. The land on which you lie, to you I will give it and to your seed. And your seed shall be like the dust of the earth and you shall burst forth to the west and the east and the north and the south, and all the clans of the earth shall be blessed through you, and through your seed. And, look, I am with you and I will guard you wherever you go, and I will bring you back to this land, for I will not leave you until I have done that which I have spoken to you." And Jacob awoke from his sleep and he said, "Indeed, the LORD is in this place, and I did not know." And he was afraid and he said,

> "How fearsome is this place!
> This can be but the house of God,
>   and this is the gate of the heavens."

And Jacob rose early in the morning and took the stone he had put at his head, and he set it as a pillar and poured oil over its top. And he called the name of that place Bethel, though the name of the town before had been Luz. And Jacob made a vow, saying, "If the LORD God be with me and guard me on this way that I am going and give me bread to eat and clothing to wear, and I return safely to my father's house, then the LORD will be my God. And this stone that I set as a pillar will be a house of God, and everything that You give me I will surely tithe it to You."

From Genesis 29

[*Rachel and Leah*]

29. And Jacob lifted his feet and went on to the land of the Easterners. And he saw and, look, there was a well in the field, and, look, three flocks of sheep were lying beside it, for from that well they would water the flocks, and the stone was big on the mouth of the well. And when all the flocks were gathered there, they would roll the stone from the mouth of the well and would water the sheep and put back the stone in its place on the mouth of the well. And Jacob said to them, "My brothers, where are you from?" And they said, "We are from Haran." And he said to them, "Do you know Laban son of Nabor?" And they said, "We know him." And he said to them, "Is he well?" And they said, "He is well, and, look, Rachel his daughter is coming with the sheep." And he said, "Look, the day is still long. It is not time to gather in the herd. Water the sheep and take them to graze." And they said, "We cannot until all the flocks have gathered and the stone is rolled from the mouth of the well and we water the sheep." He was still speaking with them when Rachel came with her father's sheep, for she was a shepherdess. And it happened when Jacob saw Rachel daughter of Laban his mother's brother and the sheep of Laban his mother's brother that he stepped forward and rolled the stone from the mouth of the well and watered the sheep of Laban his mother's brother. And Jacob kissed Rachel and lifted his voice and wept. And Jacob told Rachel that he was her father's kin, and that he was Rebekah's son, and she ran and told her father. And it happened, when Laban heard the report of Jacob his sister's son, he ran toward him and embraced him and kissed him and brought him to his house. And he recounted to Laban all these things. And Laban said to him, "Indeed, you are my bone and my flesh."

And he stayed with him a month's time, and Laban said to Jacob, "Because you are my kin, should you serve me for nothing? Tell me what your wages should be." And Laban had two daughters. The name of the elder was Leah and the name of the younger Rachel. And Leah's eyes were tender, but Rachel was comely in features and comely to look at, and Jacob loved Rachel. And he said, "I will serve seven years for Rachel your younger daughter." And Laban said, "Better I should give her to you than give her to another man. Stay with me." And Jacob served seven years for Rachel, and they seemed in his eyes but a few days in his love for her. And Jacob said to Laban, "Give me my wife, for my time is done, and let me come to bed with her." And Laban gathered all the men of the place and made a feast. And when evening came, he took Leah his daughter and brought her to Jacob, and he came to bed with her. And Laban gave Zilpah his slavegirl to Leah his daughter as her slavegirl. And when morning came, look, she was Leah. And he said to Laban, "What is this you have done to me? Was it not for Rachel that I served you, and why have you deceived me?" And Laban said, "It is not done thus in our place, to give the younger girl before the firstborn. Finish out the bridal week of this one and we shall give you the other as well for the service you render me for still another seven years." And so Jacob did. And when he finished out the bridal week of the one, he gave him Rachel his daughter as wife. And Laban gave to Rachel his daughter Bilhah his slavegirl as her slavegirl. And he came to bed with Rachel, too, and, indeed, loved Rachel more than Leah, and he served him still another seven years.

* * *

From Genesis 31

[Jacob's Flight Back to Canaan]

31. And he[5] heard the words of Laban's sons, saying, "Jacob has taken everything of our father's, and from what belonged to our father he has made all this wealth." And Jacob saw Laban's face and, look, it was not disposed toward him

5. Jacob.

as in time past. And the LORD said to Jacob, "Return to the land of your fathers and to your birthplace and I will be with you."

* * *

From Genesis 32

[Jacob Is Renamed Israel]

32. * * * And he rose on that night and took his two wives and his two slave-girls and his eleven boys and he crossed over the Jabbok ford. And he took them and brought them across the stream, and he brought across all that he had. And Jacob was left alone, and a man wrestled with him until the break of dawn. And he saw that he had not won out against him and he touched his hip-socket and Jacob's hip-socket was wrenched as he wrestled with him. And he said, "Let me go, for dawn is breaking." And he said, "I will not let you go unless you bless me." And he said to him, "What is your name?" And he said, "Jacob." And he said, "Not Jacob shall your name hence be said, but Israel, for you have striven with God and men, and won out." And Jacob asked and said, "Tell your name, pray." And he said, "Why should you ask my name?" and there he blessed him. And Jacob called the name of the place Peniel, meaning, "I have seen God face to face and I came out alive." And the sun rose upon him as he passed Penuel[6] and he was limping on his hip. Therefore the children of Israel do not eat the sinew of the thigh which is by the hip-socket to this day, for he had touched Jacob's hip-socket at the sinew of the thigh.

From Genesis 33

[Jacob and Esau Reconciled]

33. And Jacob raised his eyes and saw and, look, Esau was coming, and with him were four hundred men. And he divided the children between Leah and Rachel, and between the two slavegirls. And he placed the slavegirls and their children first, and Leah and her children after them, and Rachel and Joseph[7] last. And he passed before them and bowed to the ground seven times until he drew near his brother. And Esau ran to meet him and embraced him and fell upon his neck and kissed him, and they wept. And he raised his eyes and saw the women and the children and he said, "Who are these with you?" And he said, "The children with whom God has favored your servant." And the slave-girls drew near, they and their children, and they bowed down. And Leah, too, and her children drew near, and they bowed down, and then Joseph and Rachel drew near and bowed down. And he said, "What do you mean by all this camp I have met?" And he said, "To find favor in the eyes of my lord." And Esau said, "I have much, my brother. Keep what you have." And Jacob said, "O, no, pray, if I have found favor in your eyes, take this tribute from my hand,

---

6. "Penuel" is an alternate spelling of "Peniel." It is not clear why the text uses both.   7. Joseph is the first-born son of Rachel and Jacob.

for have I not seen your face as one might see God's face, and you received me in kindness? Pray, take my blessing that has been brought you, for God has favored me and I have everything." And he pressed him, and he took it.

* * *

Genesis 37, 39–45

[The Story of Joseph]

37. And Jacob dwelled in the land of his father's sojournings, in the land of Canaan. This is the lineage of Jacob—Joseph, seventeen years old, was tending the flock with his brothers, assisting the sons of Bilhah and the sons of Zilpah, the wives of his father. And Joseph brought ill report of them to their father. And Israel loved Joseph more than all his sons, for he was the child of his old age, and he made him an ornamented tunic.[8] And his brothers saw it was he their father loved more than all his brothers, and they hated him and could not speak a kind word to him. And Joseph dreamed a dream and told it to his brothers and they hated him all the more. And he said to them, "Listen, pray, to this dream that I dreamed. And, look, we were binding sheaves in the field, and, look, my sheaf arose and actually stood up, and, look, your sheaves drew round and bowed to my sheaf." And his brothers said to him, "Do you mean to reign over us, do you mean to rule us?" And they hated him all the more, for his dreams and for his words. And he dreamed yet another dream and recounted it to his brothers, and he said, "Look, I dreamed a dream again, and, look, the sun and the moon and eleven stars were bowing to me." And he recounted it to his father and to his brothers, and his father rebuked him and said to him, "What is this dream that you have dreamed? Shall we really come, I and your mother and your brothers, to bow before you to the ground?" And his brothers were jealous of him, while his father kept the thing in mind.

And his brothers went to graze their father's flock at Shechem. And Israel said to Joseph, "You know, your brothers are pasturing at Shechem. Come, let me send you to them," and he said to him, "Here I am." And he said to him, "Go, pray, to see how your brothers fare, and how the flock fares, and bring me back word." And he sent him from the valley of Hebron and he came to Shechem. And a man found him and, look, he was wandering in the field, and the man asked him, saying, "What is it you seek?" And he said, "My brothers I seek. Tell me, pray, where are they pasturing?" And the man said, "They have journeyed on from here, for I heard them say, 'Let us go to Dothan.'" And Joseph went after his brothers and found them at Dothan. And they saw him from afar before he drew near them and they plotted against him to put him to death. And they said to each other, "Here comes that dream-master! And so now, let us kill him and fling him into one of the pits and we can say, a vicious beast has devoured him, and we shall see what will come of his dreams." And Reuben heard and came to his rescue and said, "We must not take his life." And Reuben said to them, "Shed no blood! Fling him into this pit in the wilder-

---

8. Sometimes translated as a "coat of many colors," but the text does not actually mention color. It is probably a fancy garment with appliqués sewn on.

ness and do not raise a hand against him"—that he might rescue him from their hands to bring him back to his father. And it happened when Joseph came to his brothers that they stripped Joseph of his tunic, the ornamented tunic that he had on him. And they took him and flung him into the pit, and the pit was empty, there was no water in it. And they sat down to eat bread, and they raised their eyes and saw and, look, a caravan of Ishmaelites was coming from Gilead, their camels bearing gum and balm and ladanum[9] on their way to take down to Egypt. And Judah said to his brothers, "What gain is there if we kill our brother and cover up his blood? Come, let us sell him to the Ishmaelites and our hand will not be against him, for he is our brother, our own flesh." And his brothers agreed. And Midianite merchantmen passed by and pulled Joseph up out of the pit and sold Joseph to the Ishmaelites for twenty pieces of silver, and they brought Joseph to Egypt.[1] And Reuben came back to the pit and, look, Joseph was not in the pit, and he rent his garments, and he came back to his brothers, and he said, "The boy is gone, and I, where can I turn?" And they took Joseph's tunic and slaughtered a kid and dipped the tunic in the blood, and they sent the ornamented tunic and had it brought to their father, and they said, "This we found. Recognize, pray, is it your son's tunic or not?" And he recognized it, and he said, "It is my son's tunic.

> A vicious beast has devoured him,
> Joseph is torn to shreds!"

And Jacob rent his clothes and put sackcloth round his waist and mourned for his son many days. And all his sons and all his daughters rose to console him and he refused to be consoled and he said, "Rather I will go down to my son in Sheol mourning,"[2] and his father keened for him.

But the Midianites had sold him into Egypt to Potiphar, Pharaoh's courtier, the high chamberlain.

39. And Joseph was brought down to Egypt, and Potiphar, courtier of Pharaoh, the high chamberlain, an Egyptian man, bought him from the hands of the Ishmaelites who had brought him down there. And the LORD was with Joseph and he was a successful man, and he was in the house of his Egyptian master. And his master saw that the LORD was with him, and all that he did the LORD made succeed in his hand, and Joseph found favor in his eyes and he ministered to him, and he put him in charge of his house, and all that he had he placed in his hands. And it happened from the time he put him in charge of his house and of all he had, that the LORD had blessed the Egyptian's house for Joseph's sake and the LORD's blessing was on all that he had in house and field. And he left all that he had in Joseph's hands, and he gave no thought to anything with him there save the bread he ate. And Joseph was comely in features and comely to look at.

And it happened after these things that his master's wife raised her eyes to Joseph and said, "Lie with me." And he refused. And he said to his master's

---

9. A type of resin used in perfume and medicine.
1. The text here combines two different stories: that Joseph's brothers took him out of the pit and sold him to the Ishmaelites and that

Midianite merchants found him and sold him. The second version seems to be part of an attempt to retell the story in a way that exonerates Reuben.
2. Sheol is the land of the dead.

wife, "Look, my master has given no thought with me here to what is in the house, and all that he has he has placed in my hands. He is not greater in this house than I, and he has held back nothing from me except you, as you are his wife, and how could I do this great evil and give offense to God?" And so she spoke to Joseph day after day, and he would not listen to her, to lie by her, to be with her. And it happened, on one such day, that he came into the house to perform his task, and there was no man of the men of the house there in the house. And she seized him by his garment, saying, "Lie with me." And he left his garment in her hand and he fled and went out. And so, when she saw that he had left his garment in her hand and fled outside, she called out to the people of the house and said to them, saying, "See, he has brought us a Hebrew man to play with us. He came into me to lie with me and I called out in a loud voice, and so, when he heard me raise my voice and call out, he left his garment by me and fled and went out." And she laid out his garment by her until his master returned to his house. And she spoke to him things of this sort, saying, "The Hebrew slave came into me, whom you brought us, to play with me. And so, when I raised my voice and called out, he left his garment by me and fled outside." And it happened, when his master heard his wife's words which she spoke to him, saying, "Things of this sort your slave has done to me," he became incensed. And Joseph's master took him and placed him in the prison-house, the place where the king's prisoners were held.

And he was there in the prison-house, and God was with Joseph and extended kindness to him, and granted him favor in the eyes of the prison-house warden. And the prison-house warden placed in Joseph's hands all the prisoners who were in the prison-house, and all that they were to do there, it was he who did it. The prison-house warden had to see to nothing that was in his hands, as the Lord was with him, and whatever he did, the Lord made succeed.

40. And it happened after these things that the cupbearer of the king of Egypt and his baker gave offense to their lord, the king of Egypt. And Pharaoh was furious with his two courtiers, the chief cupbearer and the chief baker. And he put them under guard in the house of the high chamberlain, the prison-house, the place where Joseph was held. And the high chamberlain assigned Joseph to them and he ministered to them, and they stayed a good while under guard.

And the two of them dreamed a dream, each his own dream, on a single night, each a dream with its own solution—the cupbearer and the baker to the king of Egypt who were held in the prison-house. And Joseph came to them in the morning and saw them and, look, they were frowning. And he asked Pharaoh's courtiers who were with him under guard in his lord's house, saying, "Why are your faces downcast today?" And they said to him, "We dreamed a dream and there is no one to solve it." And Joseph said to them, "Are not solutions from God? Pray, recount them to me." And the chief cupbearer recounted his dream to Joseph and said to him, "In my dream—and look, a vine was before me. And on the vine were three tendrils, and as it was budding, its blossom shot up, its clusters ripened to grapes. And Pharaoh's cup was in my hand. And I took the grapes and crushed them into Pharaoh's cup and I placed the cup in Pharaoh's palm." And Joseph said, "This is its solution. The three tendrils are three days. Three days hence Pharaoh will lift up your head and restore you to your place, and you will put Pharaoh's cup in his hand, as you used to do when you were his cupbearer. But if you remember I was with you once it goes well for you, do me the kindness, pray, to mention me to Pharaoh and bring me out of this house. For indeed I was stolen from the land of the Hebrews, and here, too, I have done nothing that I should have been put in the pit." And the chief baker saw that he had solved well, and he said to Joseph, "I, too, in my dream—and look, there were three openwork baskets on my head, and in the topmost were all sorts of food for Pharaoh, baker's ware, and birds were eating from the basket over my head." And Joseph answered and said, "This is its solution. The three baskets are three days. Three days hence Pharaoh will lift up your head from upon you and impale you on a pole and the birds will eat your flesh from upon you."

And it happened on the third day, Pharaoh's birthday, that he made a feast for all his servants, and he lifted up the head of the chief cupbearer and the head of the chief baker in the midst of his servants. And he restored the chief cupbearer to his cupbearing, and he put the cup in Pharaoh's hand; and the chief baker he impaled—just as Joseph had solved it for them. But the chief cupbearer did not remember Joseph, no, he forgot him.

41. And it happened at the end of two full years that Pharaoh dreamed, and, look, he was standing by the Nile. And, look, out of the Nile came up seven cows, fair to look at and fat in flesh, and they grazed in the rushes. And, look, another seven cows came up after them out of the Nile, foul to look at and meager in flesh, and stood by the cows on the bank of the Nile. And the foul-looking meager-fleshed cows ate up the seven fair-looking fat cows, and Pharaoh awoke. And he slept and dreamed a second time, and, look, seven ears of grain came up on a single stalk, fat and goodly. And, look, seven meager ears, blasted by the east wind, sprouted after them. And the meager ears swallowed the seven fat and full ears, and Pharaoh awoke, and, look, it was a dream. And it happened in the morning that his heart pounded, and he sent and called in all the soothsayers of Egypt and all its wise men, and Pharaoh recounted to them his dreams, but none could solve them for Pharaoh. And the chief cup-bearer spoke to Pharaoh, saying, "My offenses I recall today. Pharaoh had been furious with his servants and he placed me under guard in the house of the high chamberlain—me and the chief baker. And we dreamed a dream on the same night, he and I, each of us dreamed a dream with its own solution. And there with us was a Hebrew lad, a slave of the high chamberlain, and we recounted to him and he solved our dreams, each of us according to his dream he solved it. And it happened just as he had solved it for us, so it came about—me he restored to my post and him he impaled."

And Pharaoh sent and called for Joseph, and they hurried him from the pit, and he shaved and changed his garments and came before Pharaoh. And Pharaoh said to Joseph, "I dreamed a dream and none can solve it, and I have heard about you that you can understand a dream to solve it." And Joseph answered Pharaoh, saying, "Not I! God will answer for Pharaoh's well-being." And Pharaoh spoke to Joseph: "In my dream, here I was standing on the bank of the Nile, and, look, out of the Nile came up seven cows fat in flesh and fair in feature, and they grazed in the rushes. And, look, another seven cows came up after them, gaunt and very foul-featured and meager in flesh, I had not seen their like in all the land of Egypt for foulness. And the meager, foul cows ate up the first seven fat cows, and they were taken into their bellies and you could not tell that they had come into their bellies, for their looks were as foul as before, and I woke. And I saw in my dream, and, look, seven ears of grain came up on a single stalk, full and goodly. And, look, seven shriveled, meager ears, blasted by the east wind, sprouted after them. And the meager ears swallowed the seven goodly ears, and I spoke to my soothsayers and none could tell me the meaning." And Joseph said to Pharaoh, "Pharaoh's dream is one. What God is about to do He has told Pharaoh. The seven goodly cows are seven years, and the seven ears of grain are seven years. The dream is one. And the seven meager and foul cows who came up after them are seven years, and the seven meager ears of grain, blasted by the east wind, will be seven years of famine. It is just as I said to Pharaoh: what God is about to do He has shown Pharaoh. Look, seven years are coming of great plenty through all the land of Egypt. And seven years of famine will arise after them and all the plenty will be forgotten in the land of Egypt, and the famine will ravage the land, and you will not be able to tell there was plenty in the land because of that famine afterward, for it will be very grave. And the repeating of the dream to Pharaoh two times, this means that the thing has been fixed by God and God is hastening to do it. And so, let Pharaoh look out for a discerning, wise man and set him over the land of Egypt. Let Pharaoh do this: appoint overseers for the land and muster the land of Egypt in the seven years of plenty. And let them collect all the food of these good years that are coming and let them pile up grain under Pharaoh's hand, food in the cities, to keep under guard. And the food will be a reserve for the land for the seven years of famine which will be in the land of Egypt, that the land may not perish in the famine." And the thing seemed good in Pharaoh's eyes and in the eyes of his servants. And Pharaoh said to his servants, "Could we find a man like him, in whom is the spirit of God?" And Pharaoh said to Joseph, "After God has made known to you all this, there is none as discerning and wise as you. You shall be over my house, and by your lips all my folk shall be guided. By the throne alone shall I be greater than you." And Pharaoh said to Joseph, "See, I have set you over all the land of Egypt." And Pharaoh took off his ring from his hand and put it on Joseph's hand and had him clothed in fine linen clothes and placed the golden collar round his neck. And he had him ride in the chariot of his viceroy, and they called out before him *Abrekh*,[3] setting him over all the land of Egypt. And Pharaoh said to Joseph, "I am Pharaoh! Without you no man shall raise hand or foot in all the land of Egypt." And Pharaoh called Joseph's name Zaphenath-Paneah, and he gave him Asenath daughter of Potiphera, priest of On, as wife, and Joseph went out over the land of Egypt.

And Joseph was thirty years old when he stood before Pharaoh king of Egypt, and Joseph went out from Pharaoh's presence and passed through all the land of Egypt. And the land in the seven years of plenty made gatherings. And he collected all the food of the seven years that were in the land of Egypt and he placed food in the cities, the food from the fields round each city he placed within it. And Joseph piled up grain like the sand of the sea, very much, until he ceased counting, for it was beyond count.

And to Joseph two sons were born before the coming of the year of famine, whom Asenath daughter of Potiphera priest of On bore him. And Joseph called

---

3. Evidently an Egyptian word, perhaps meaning "Make way!"

the name of the firstborn Manasseh, meaning, God has released me from all the debt of my hardship, and of all my father's house. And the name of the second he called Ephraim, meaning, God has made me fruitful in the land of my affliction.

And the seven years of the plenty that had been in the land of Egypt came to an end. And the seven years of famine began to come, as Joseph had said, and there was famine in all the lands, but in the land of Egypt there was bread. And all the land of Egypt was hungry and the people cried out to Pharaoh for bread, and Pharaoh said to all of Egypt, "Go to Joseph. What he says to you, you must do." And the famine was over all the land. And Joseph laid open whatever had grain within and sold provisions to Egypt. And the famine grew harsh in the land of Egypt. And all the earth came to Egypt, to Joseph, to get provisions, for the famine had grown harsh in all the earth.

42. And Jacob saw that there were provisions in Egypt, and Jacob said to his sons, "Why are you fearful?" And he said, "Look, I have heard that there are provisions in Egypt. Go down there, and get us provisions from there that we may live and not die." And the ten brothers of Joseph went down to buy grain from Egypt. But Benjamin, Joseph's brother, Jacob did not send with his brothers, for he thought, Lest harm befall him.

And the sons of Israel came to buy provisions among those who came, for there was famine in the land of Canaan. As for Joseph, he was the regent of the land, he was the provider to all the people of the land. And Joseph's brothers came and bowed down to him, their faces to the ground. And Joseph saw his brothers and recognized them, and he played the stranger to them and spoke harshly to them, and said to them, "Where have you come from?" And they said, "From the land of Canaan, to buy food." And Joseph recognized his brothers but they did not recognize him. And Joseph remembered the dreams he had dreamed about them, and he said to them, "You are spies! To see the land's nakedness you have come." And they said to him, "No, my lord, for your servants have come to buy food. We are all the sons of one man. We are honest. Your servants would never be spies." And he said to them, "No! For the land's nakedness you have come to see." And they said, "Twelve brothers your servants are, we are the sons of one man in the land of Canaan, and, look, the youngest is now with our father, and one is no more." And Joseph said to them, "That's just what I told you, you are spies. In this shall you be tested—by Pharaoh! You shall not leave this place unless your youngest brother comes here. Send one of you to bring your brother, and as for the rest of you, you will be detained, and your words will be tested as to whether the truth is with you, and if not, by Pharaoh, you must be spies!" And he put them under guard for three days. And Joseph said to them on the third day, "Do this and live, for I fear God. If you are honest, let one of your brothers be detained in this very guardhouse, and the rest of you go forth and bring back provisions to stave off the famine in your homes. And your youngest brother you shall bring to me, that your words may be confirmed and you need not die." And so they did. And they said each to his brother, "Alas, we are guilty for our brother, whose mortal distress we saw when he pleaded with us and we did not listen. That is why this distress has overtaken us." Then Reuben spoke out to them in these words: "Didn't I say to you 'Do not sin against the boy,' and you would not listen? And now, look, his blood is requited." And they did not know that Joseph understood, for there was an interpreter between them. And he turned away from them and wept and returned to them and spoke to them, and he took Simeon from them and placed him in fetters before their eyes.

And Joseph gave orders to fill their baggage with grain and to put back their silver into each one's pack and to give them supplies for the way, and so he did for them. And they loaded their provisions on their donkeys and they set out from there. Then one of them opened his pack to give provender to his donkey at the encampment, and he saw his silver and, look, it was in the mouth of his bag. And he said to his brothers, "My silver has been put back and, look it's actually in my bag." And they were dumbfounded and trembled each before his brother, saying, "What is this that God has done to us?" And they came to Jacob their father, to the land of Canaan, and they told him all that had befallen them, saying, "The man who is lord of the land spoke harshly to us and made us out to be spies in the land. And we said to him, 'We are honest. We would never be spies. Twelve brothers we are, the sons of our father. One is no more and the youngest is now with our father in the land of Canaan.' And the man who is lord of the land said to us, 'By this shall I know if you are honest: one of your brothers leave with me and provisions against the famine in your homes take, and go. And bring your youngest brother to me that I may know you are not spies but are honest. I shall give you back your brother and you can trade in the land.'" And just as they were emptying their packs, look, each one's bundle of silver was in his pack. And they saw their bundles, both they and their father, and were afraid. And Jacob their father said to them, "Me you have bereaved. Joseph is no more and Simeon is no more, and Benjamin you would take! It is I who bear it all." And Reuben spoke to his father, saying, "My two sons you may put to death if I do not bring him back to you. Place him in my hands and I will return him to you." And he said, "My son shall not go down with you, for his brother is dead, and he alone remains, and should harm befall him on the way you are going, you would bring down my gray head in sorrow to Sheol."

43. And the famine grew grave in the land. And it happened when they had eaten up the provisions they had brought from Egypt, that their father said to them, "Go back, buy us some food." And Judah said to him, saying, "The man firmly warned us, saying, 'You shall not see my face unless your brother is with you.' If you are going to send our brother with us, we may go down and buy you food, but if you are not going to send him, we will not go down, for the man said to us, 'You shall not see my face unless your brother is with you.'" And Israel said, "Why have you done me this harm to tell the man you had another brother?" And they said, "The man firmly asked us about ourselves and our kindred, saying, 'Is your father still living? Do you have a brother?' And we told him, in response to these words. Could we know he would say, 'Bring down your brother?'" And Judah said to Israel his father, "Send the lad with me, and let us rise and go, that we may live and not die, neither we, nor you, nor our little ones. I will be his pledge, from my hand you may seek him: if I do not bring him to you and set him before you, I will bear the blame to you for all time. For had we not tarried, by now we could have come back twice." And Israel their father said to them, "If it must be so, do this: take of the best yield of the land in your baggage and bring down to the man as tribute some balm and some honey, gum and ladanum, pistachio nuts and almonds. And double the silver take in your hand, and the silver that was put back in the mouths of your bags bring back in your hand. Perhaps it was a mistake. And your brother take, and rise and go back to the man. And may El Shaddai grant you mercy before the man, that he discharge to you your other brother, and Benjamin. As for me, if I must be bereaved, I will be bereaved."

And the men took this tribute and double the silver they took in their hand, and Benjamin, and they rose and went down to Egypt and stood in Joseph's presence. And Joseph saw Benjamin with them and he said to the one who was over his house, "Bring the men into the house, and slaughter an animal and prepare it, for with me the men shall eat at noon." And the man did as Joseph had said, and the man brought the men to Joseph's house. And the men were afraid at being brought to Joseph's house, and they said, "Because of the silver put back in our bags the first time we've been brought, in order to fall upon us, to attack us, and to take us as slaves, and our donkeys." And they approached the man who was over Joseph's house, and they spoke to him by the entrance of the house. And they said, "Please, my lord, we indeed came down the first time to buy food, and it happened when we came to the encampment that we opened our bags and, look, each man's silver was in the mouth of his bag, our silver in full weight, and we have brought it back in our hand, and we have brought down more silver to buy food. We do not know who put our silver in our bags." And he said, "All is well with you, do not fear. Your God and the God of your father has placed treasure for you in your bags. Your silver has come to me."[4] And he brought Simeon out to them. And the man brought the men into Joseph's house, and he gave them water and they bathed their feet, and he gave provender to their donkeys. And they prepared the tribute against Joseph's arrival at noon, for they had heard that there they would eat bread. And Joseph came into the house, and they brought him the tribute that was in their hand, into the house, and they bowed down to him to the ground. And he asked how they were, and he said, "Is all well with your aged father of whom you spoke? Is he still alive?" And they said, "All is well with your servant, our father. He is still alive." And they did obeisance and bowed down. And he raised his eyes and saw Benjamin his brother, his mother's son, and he said, "Is this your youngest brother of whom you spoke to me?" And he said, "God be gracious to you, my son." And Joseph hurried out, for his feelings for his brother overwhelmed him and he wanted to weep, and he went into the chamber and wept there. And he bathed his face and came out and held himself in check and said, "Serve bread." And they served him and them separately and the Egyptians that were eating with him separately, for the Egyptians would not eat bread with the Hebrews, as it was abhorrent to Egypt. And they were seated before him, the firstborn according to his birthright, the youngest according to his youth, and the men marveled to each other. And he had portions passed to them from before him, and Benjamin's portion was five times more than the portion of all the rest, and they drank, and they got drunk with him.

44. And he charged the one who was over his house, saying, "Fill the men's bags with as much food as they can carry, and put each man's silver in the mouth of his bag. And my goblet, the silver goblet, put in the mouth of the bag

4. I.e., "I have been paid."

of the youngest, with the silver for his provisions." And he did as Joseph had spoken. The morning had just brightened when the men were sent off, they and their donkeys. They had come out of the city, they were not far off, when Joseph said to the one who was over his house, "Rise, pursue the men, and when you overtake them, say to them, 'Why have you paid back evil for good? Is not this the one from which my lord drinks, and in which he always divines?[5] You have wrought evil in what you did.'" And he overtook them and spoke to them these words. And they said to him, "Why should our lord speak words like these? Far be it from your servants to do such a thing! Why, the silver we found in the mouth of our bags we brought back to you from the land of Canaan. How then could we steal from your master's house silver or gold? He of your servants with whom it be found shall die, and, what's more, we shall become slaves to our lord." And he said, "Even so, as by your words, let it be: he with whom it be found shall become a slave to me, and you shall be clear." And they hurried and each man set down his bag on the ground and each opened his bag. And he searched, beginning with the oldest and ending with the youngest, and he found the goblet in Benjamin's bag. And they rent their garments, and each loaded his donkey and they returned to the city.

And Judah with his brothers came into Joseph's house, for he was still there, and they threw themselves before him to the ground. And Joseph said to them, "What is this deed you have done? Did you not know that a man like me would surely divine?" And Judah said, "What shall we say to my lord? What shall we speak and how shall we prove ourselves right? God has found out your servants' crime. Here we are, slaves to my lord, both we and the one in whose hand the goblet was found." And he said, "Far be it from me to do this! The man in whose hand the goblet was found, he shall become my slave, and you, go up in peace to your father." And Judah approached him and said, "Please, my lord, let your servant speak a word in my lord's hearing and let your wrath not flare against your servant, for you are like Pharaoh. My lord had asked his servants, saying, 'Do you have a father or brother?' And we said to my lord, 'We have an aged father and a young child of his old age, and his brother being dead, he alone is left of his mother, and his father loves him.' And you said to your servants, 'Bring him down to me, that I may set my eyes on him.' And we said to my lord, 'The lad cannot leave his father. Should he leave his father, he would die.' And you said to your servants, 'If your youngest brother does not come down with you, you shall not see my face again.' And it happened when we went up to your servant, my father, that we told him the words of my lord. And our father said, 'Go back, buy us some food.' And we said, 'We cannot go down. If our youngest brother is with us, we shall go down. For we cannot see the face of the man if our youngest brother is not with us.' And your servant, our father, said to us, 'You know that two did my wife bear me. And one went out from me and I thought, O, he's been torn to shreds, and I have not seen him since. And should you take this one, too, from my presence and harm befall him, you would bring down my gray head in evil to Sheol.' And so, should I come to your servant, my father, and the lad be not with us, for his life is bound to the lad's, when he saw the lad was not with us, he would die, and your servants would bring down the gray head of your servant, our father, in sorrow to Sheol. For your servant became pledge for the lad to my father, saying, 'If I do

---

5. Predicts the future from the appearance of liquid in the cup.

not bring him to you, I will bear the blame to my father for all time.' And so, let your servant, pray, stay instead of the lad as a slave to my lord, and let the lad go up with his brothers. For how shall I go up to my father, if the lad be not with us? Let me see not the evil that would find out my father!"

45. And Joseph could no longer hold himself in check before all who stood attendance upon him, and he cried, "Clear out everyone around me!" And no man stood with him when Joseph made himself known to his brothers. And he wept aloud and the Egyptians heard and the house of Pharaoh heard. And Joseph said to his brothers, "I am Joseph. Is my father still alive?" But his brothers could not answer him, for they were dismayed before him. And Joseph said to his brothers, "Come close to me, pray," and they came close, and he said, "I am Joseph your brother whom you sold into Egypt. And now, do not be pained and do not be incensed with yourselves that you sold me down here, because for sustenance God has sent me before you. Two years now there has been famine in the heart of the land, and there are yet five years without plowing and harvest. And God has sent me before you to make you a remnant on earth[6] and to preserve life, for you to be a great surviving group. And so, it is not you who sent me here but God, and He has made me father to Pharaoh and lord to all his house and ruler over all the land of Egypt. Hurry and go up to my father and say to him, 'Thus says your son Joseph: God has made me lord to all Egypt. Come down to me, do not delay. And you shall dwell in the land of Goshen[7] and shall be close to me, you and your sons and the sons of your sons and your flocks and your cattle and all that is yours. And I will sustain you there, for yet five years of famine remain—lest you lose all, you and your household and all that is yours.' And, look, your own eyes can see, and the eyes of my brother Benjamin, that it is my very mouth that speaks to you. And you must tell my father all my glory in Egypt and all that you have seen, and hurry and bring down my father here." And he fell upon the neck of his brother Benjamin and he wept, and Benjamin wept on his neck. And he kissed all his brothers and wept over them. And after that, his brothers spoke with him.

And the news was heard in the house of Pharaoh, saying, "Joseph's brothers have come." And it was good in Pharaoh's eyes and in his servants' eyes. And Pharaoh said to Joseph, "Say to your brothers: 'This now do. Load up your beasts and go, return to the land of Canaan. And take your father and your households and come back to me, that I may give you the best of the land of Egypt, and you shall live off the fat of the land.' And you, charge them: 'This now do. Take you from the land of Egypt wagons for your little ones and for your wives, and convey your father, and come. And regret not your belongings, for the best of all the land of Egypt is yours.'"

And so the sons of Israel did, and Joseph gave them wagons, as Pharaoh had ordered, and he gave them supplies for the journey. To all of them, each one, he gave changes of garments, and to Benjamin he gave three hundred pieces of silver and five changes of garments. And to his father he sent as follows: ten donkeys conveying from the best of Egypt, and ten she-asses conveying grain and bread and food for his father for the journey. And he sent off his brothers and they went, and he said to them, "Do not be perturbed on the journey."

---

6. I.e., "to ensure a posterity for you."   7. The Nile delta.

And they went up from Egypt and they came to the land of Canaan to Jacob their father. And they told him, saying, "Joseph is still alive," and that he was ruler in all the land of Egypt. And his heart stopped, for he did not believe them. And they spoke to him all the words of Joseph that he had spoken to them, and he saw the wagons that Joseph had sent to convey him, and the spirit of Jacob their father revived. And Israel said, "Enough! Joseph my son is still alive. Let me go see him before I die."

From Genesis 46, 47

[Jacob Travels to Egypt]

46. And Israel journeyed onward, with all that was his, and he came to Beersheba, and he offered sacrifices to the God of his father Isaac. And God said to Israel through visions of the night, "Jacob, Jacob," and he said, "Here I am." And He said, "I am the god, God of your father. Fear not to go down to Egypt, for a great nation I will make you there. I Myself will go down with you to Egypt and I Myself will surely bring you back up as well, and Joseph shall lay his hand on your eyes." And Jacob arose from Beersheba, and the sons of Israel conveyed Jacob their father and their little ones and their wives in the wagons Pharaoh had sent to convey him. And they took their cattle and their substance that they had got in the land of Canaan and they came to Egypt, Jacob and all his seed with him. His sons, and the sons of his sons with him, his daughters and the daughters of his sons, and all his seed, he brought with him to Egypt.

* * *

And Joseph harnessed his chariot and went up to meet Israel his father in Goshen, and appeared before him and fell on his neck, and he wept on his neck a long while. And Israel said to Joseph, "I may die now, after seeing your face, for you are still alive."

* * *

47. * * * And Joseph settled his father and his brothers and gave them a holding in the land of Egypt in the best of the land, in the land of Rameses, as Pharaoh had commanded. And Joseph sustained his father and his brothers and all his father's household with bread, down to the mouths of the little ones.

* * *

From Genesis 50

[The Death of Joseph]

50. * * * And Joseph dwelled in Egypt, he and his father's household, and Joseph lived a hundred and ten years. And Joseph saw the third generation of sons from Ephraim, and the sons, as well, of Machir son of Manasseh were born on Joseph's knees. And Joseph said to his brothers, "I am about to die, and God will surely single you out and take you up from this land to the land He promised to Isaac and to Jacob." And Joseph made the sons of Israel swear, saying, "When God indeed singles you out, you shall take up my bones from this place." And Joseph died, a hundred and ten years old, and they embalmed him and he was put in a coffin in Egypt.

From Exodus 19–20[1]

[Moses Receives the Law]

19. On the third new moon of the Israelites' going out from Egypt, on this day did they come to the Wilderness of Sinai. And they journeyed onward from Rephidim and they came to the Wilderness of Sinai, and Israel camped there over against the mountain. And Moses had gone up to God, and the LORD called out to him from the mountain, saying, "Thus shall you say to the house of Jacob, and shall you tell to the Israelites: 'You yourselves saw what I did to Egypt, and I bore you on the wings of eagles[2] and I brought you to Me. And now, if you will truly heed My voice and keep My covenant, you will become for Me a treasure among all the peoples, for Mine is all the earth. And as for you, you will become for Me a kingdom of priests and a holy nation.' These are the words that you shall speak to the Israelites."

And Moses came and he called to the elders of the people, and he set before them all these words that the LORD had charged him. And all the people answered together and said, "Everything that the LORD has spoken we shall do." And Moses brought back the people's words to the LORD. And the LORD said to Moses, "Look, I am about to come to you in the utmost cloud, so that the people may hear as I speak to you, and you as well they will trust for all time." And Moses told the people's words to the LORD. And the LORD said to Moses, "Go to the people and consecrate them today and tomorrow, and they shall wash their cloaks. And they shall ready themselves for the third day, for on the third day the LORD will come down before the eyes of all the people on Mount Sinai. And you shall set bounds for the people all around, saying, 'Watch yourselves not to go up on the mountain or to touch its edge. Whosoever touches the mountain is doomed to die. No hand shall touch him,[3] but He shall surely be stoned or be shot, whether beast or man, he shall not live. When the ram's horn blasts long, they[4] it is who will go up the mountain.'" And Moses came down from the mountain to the people, and he consecrated the people, and they washed their cloaks. And he said to the people, "Ready yourselves for three days. Do not go near a woman."[5] And it happened on the third day as it turned morning, that there was thunder and lightning and a heavy cloud on the mountain and the sound of the ram's horn, very strong, and

1. Translated by Robert Alter, to whose notes some of the following annotations are indebted.
2. A metaphor for salvation. "What I did to Egypt" refers to the plagues that afflicted Egypt and to the destruction of the Egyptian army, as it pursued the departing Israelites, at the Red Sea.
3. Whoever violates the ban on touching the mountain will be impure and an outcast from the community. Therefore he has to be killed at a distance, with stones or arrows.
4. I.e., Moses and Aaron.
5. Sexual abstinence and the washing of clothes were methods of ritual purification.

all the people who were in the camp trembled. And Moses brought out the people toward God from the camp and they stationed themselves at the bottom of the mountain. And Mount Sinai was all in smoke because the LORD had come down on it in fire, and its smoke went up like the smoke from a kiln, and the whole mountain trembled greatly. And the sound of the ram's horn grew stronger and stronger. Moses would speak, and God would answer him with voice.[6] And the LORD came down on Mount Sinai, to the mountaintop, and the LORD called Moses to the mountaintop, and Moses went up. And the LORD said to Moses, "Go down, warn the people, lest they break through to the LORD to see and many of them perish. And the priests, too, who come near to the LORD, shall consecrate themselves,[7] lest the LORD burst forth against them." And Moses said to the Lord, "The people will not be able to come up to Mount Sinai, for You Yourself warned us, saying, 'Set bounds to the mountain and consecrate it.'" And the LORD said to him, "Go down, and you shall come up, you and Aaron[8] with you, and the priests and the people shall not break through to go up to the LORD, lest He burst forth against them." And Moses went down to the people and said it to them.

20. And God spoke all these words, saying: "I am the LORD your God Who brought you out of the land of Egypt, out of the house of slaves. You[9] shall have no other gods beside Me. You shall make you no carved likeness and no image of what is in the heavens above or what is on the earth below or what is in the waters beneath the earth. You shall not bow to them and you shall not worship them, for I am the LORD your God, a jealous god, reckoning the crime of fathers with sons, with the third generation and with the fourth, for My foes and doing kindness to the thousandth generation for My friends and for those who keep My commands. You shall not take the name of the LORD your God in vain, for the LORD will not acquit whosoever takes His name in vain. Remember the sabbath day to hallow it. Six days you shall work and you shall do your tasks, but the seventh day is a sabbath to the LORD your God. You shall do no task, you and your son and your daughter, your male slave and your slavegirl and your beast and your sojourner who is within your gates. For six days did the LORD make the heavens and the earth, the sea and all that is in it, and He rested on the seventh day. Therefore did the LORD bless the sabbath day and hallow it. Honor your father and your mother, so that your days may be long on the soil that the LORD your God has given you. You shall not murder. You shall not commit adultery. You shall not steal. You shall not bear false witness against your fellow man. You shall not covet your fellow man's wife, or his male slave, or his slavegirl, or his ox, or his donkey, or anything that your fellow man has."

And all the people were seeing the thunder and the flashes and the sound of the ram's horn and the mountain in smoke, and the people saw and they drew back and stood at a distance. And they said to Moses, "Speak you with us that we may hear, and let not God speak with us lest we die." And Moses said to the

---

6. I.e., with words.

7. I.e., they are to purify themselves and remain at the bottom of the mountain as the rest of the people do.

8. Moses' closest companion and in an early tradition his brother; Aaron was Israel's first

High Priest.

9. Here and throughout this passage, the Hebrew text uses the singular of "you" (formulations of law elsewhere in the Hebrew Bible use the plural). The commandments are thus addressed to each person individually.

people, "Do not fear, for in order to test you God has come and in order that His fear be upon you, so that you do not offend." And the people stood at a distance, and Moses drew near the thick cloud where God was.

* * *

From Job[1]

1. A man there was in the land of Uz[2] Job, his name. And the man was blameless and upright and feared God and shunned evil. And seven sons were born to him, and three daughters. And his flocks came to seven thousand sheep and three thousand camels and five hundred yokes of cattle and five hundred she-asses and a great abundance of slaves. And that man was greater than all the dwellers of the East. And his sons would go and hold a feast, in each one's house on his set day, and they would call to their sisters to eat and drink with them. And it happened when the days of the feast came round, that Job would send and consecrate them and rise early in the morning and offer up burnt offerings according to the number of them all. For Job thought, Perhaps my sons have offended and cursed God in their hearts. Thus would Job do at all times.

And one day, the sons of God[3] came to stand in attendance before the LORD, and the Adversary,[4] too, came among them. And the LORD said to the Adversary, "From where do you come?" And the Adversary answered the LORD and said, "From roaming the earth and walking about in it." And the LORD said to the Adversary, "Have you paid heed to my servant Job, for there is none like him on earth, a blameless and upright man, who fears God and shuns evil?" And the Adversary answered the LORD and said, "Does Job fear God for nothing? Have You not hedged him about and his household and all that he has all around? The work of his hands You have blessed, and his flocks have spread over the land. And yet, reach out Your hand, pray, and strike all he has. Will he not curse You to Your face? And the LORD said to the Adversary, "Look, all that he has is in your hands. Only against him do not reach out your hand." And the Adversary went out from before the LORD's presence.

And one day, his sons and his daughters were eating and drinking wine in the house of their brother, the firstborn. And a messenger came to Job and said, "The cattle were plowing and the she-asses grazing by them, and Sabeans fell upon them and took them, and the lads they struck down by the edge of the sword, and I alone escaped to tell you." This one was still speaking when another came and said, "God's fire fell from the heavens and burned among the sheep and the lads and consumed them, and I alone escaped to tell you." This one was still speaking when another came and said, "Chaldaeans set out in three bands and pounced upon the camels and took them, and the lads they struck down by the edge of the sword." This one was still speaking when another came and said,

1. Translated by Robert Alter, to whom some of the following notes are indebted.
2. *'Uts* (Uz) means "counsel," or "advice," so the story takes place in an unreal, fabulous landscape: the Land of Counsel.
3. This phrase reflects a premonotheistic idea of a family or council of gods.

4. "The Adversary," or "the satan" (*hasatan* in the original), means a person, thing, or set of circumstances that is an obstacle to someone. It does not mean "devil"; the modern connotations of evil are absent from the original word, and clearly this "satan" is part of God's court.

"Your sons and your daughters were eating and drinking wine in the house of their brother, the firstborn. And, look, a great wind came from beyond the wilderness and struck the four corners of the house, and it fell on the young people, and they died. And I alone escaped to tell you." And Job rose and tore his garment and shaved his head and fell to the earth and bowed down.[5] And he said,

> "Naked I came out from my mother's womb,
>   and naked shall I return there.
> The LORD has given and the LORD has taken.
>   May the LORD's name be blessed."

With all this, Job did not offend, nor did he put blame on God.

2. And one day, the sons of God came to stand in attendance before the LORD, and the Adversary, too, came among them to stand in attendance before the LORD. And the LORD said to the Adversary, "From whence do you come?" And the Adversary answered the LORD and said, "From roaming the earth and walking about in it." And the LORD said to the Adversary, "Have you paid heed to My servant Job, for there is none like him on earth, a blameless and upright man, who fears God and shuns evil and still clings to his innocence, and you incited Me against him to destroy him for nothing." And the Adversary answered the LORD and said, "Skin for skin![6] A man will give all he has for his own life. Yet, reach out, pray, your hand and strike his bone and his flesh. Will he not curse You to Your face?" And the LORD said to the Adversary, "Here he is in your hands. Only preserve his life." And the Adversary went out from before the LORD's presence. And he struck Job with a grievous burning rash from the soles of his feet to the crown of his head. And he took a potsherd to scrape himself with, and he was sitting among the ashes. And his wife said to him, "Do you still cling to your innocence? Curse God and die." And he said to her, "You speak as one of the base women would speak. Shall we accept good from God, too, and evil we shall not accept?" With all this, Job did not offend with his lips.

And Job's three companions heard of all this harm that had come upon him, and they came, each from his place—Eliphaz the Temanite and Bildad the Shuhite and Zophar the Naamathite, and they agreed to meet to grieve with him and to comfort him. And they lifted up their eyes from afar and did not recognize him, and they lifted up their voices and wept, and each tore his garment, and they tossed dust on their heads toward the heavens. And they sat with him on the ground seven days and seven nights, and none spoke a word to him, for they saw that the pain was very great.

3. Afterward, Job opened his mouth and cursed his day. And Job spoke up and he said:

> Annul the day that I was born
>   and the night that said, "A man is conceived."
> That day, let it be darkness.
>   Let God above not seek it out,

---

5. Gestures of mourning.
6. An obscure proverb, perhaps meaning that

Job will truly suffer only once pain touches his own skin.

nor brightness shine upon it. 5
Let darkness, death's shadow, foul it,
  let a cloud-mass rest upon it,
  let day-gloom dismay it.
That night, let murk overtake it.
  Let it not join in the days of the year, 10
  let it not enter the number of months.
Oh, let that night be barren,
  let it have no song of joy.
Let the day-cursers hex it,
  those ready to rouse Leviathan.[7] 15
Let its twilight stars go dark.
  Let it hope for day in vain,
  and let it not see the eyelids of dawn.
For it did not shut the belly's doors
  to hide wretchedness from my eyes. 20
Why did I not die from the womb,
  from the belly come out, breathe my last?
Why did knees welcome me,
  and why breasts, that I should suck?
For now I would lie and be still, 25
  would sleep and know repose
with kings and the councilors of earth,
  who build ruins for themselves,
or with princes, possessors of gold,
  who fill their houses with silver. 30
Or like a buried stillbirth I'd be,
  like babes who never saw light.
There the wicked cease their troubling,
  and there the weary repose.
All together the prisoners are tranquil, 35
  they hear not the taskmaster's voice.
The small and the great are there,
  and the slave is free of his master.
Why give light to the wretched
  and life to the deeply embittered, 40
who wait for death in vain,
  dig for it more than for treasure,
who rejoice at the tomb,
  are glad when they find the grave?
—To a man whose way is hidden, 45
  and God has hedged him about.
For before my bread my moaning comes,
  and my roar pours out like water.
For I feared a thing—it befell me,
  what I dreaded came upon me. 50
I was not quiet, I was not still,
  I had no repose, and trouble came.

7. Leviathan is a sea monster, representing chaos in Canaanite mythology. The "day-cursers" are magicians.

4. And Eliphaz spoke out and he said:

If speech were tried against you, could you stand it?
   Yet who can hold back words?
Look, you reproved many,
   and slack hands you strengthened.
The stumbler your words lifted up,   5
   and bended knees you bolstered.
But now it comes to you and you cannot stand it,
   it reaches you and you are dismayed.
Is not your reverence your safety,
   your hope—your blameless ways?   10
Recall, pray: what innocent man has died,
   and where were the upright demolished?
As I have seen, those who plow mischief,
   those who plant wretchedness, reap it.
Through God's breath they die,   15
   before his nostrils' breathing they vanish.
The lion's roar, the maned beast's sound—
   and the young lions' teeth are smashed.
The king of beasts dies with no prey,
   the whelps of the lion are scattered.   20
And to me came a word in secret,
   and my ear caught a tag-end of it,
in musings from nighttime's visions
   when slumber falls upon men.
Fear called to me, and trembling,   25
   and all my limbs it gripped with fear.
And a spirit passed over my face,
   made the hair on my flesh stand on end.
It halted, its look unfamiliar,
   an image before my eyes,   30
     stillness, and a sound did I hear:
Can a mortal be cleared before God,
   can a man be made pure by his Maker?
Why, His servants He does not trust,
   His agents He charges with blame.   35
All the more so, the clay-house dwellers,
   whose foundation is in the dust,
     who are crushed more quickly than moths.
From morning to eve they are shattered,
   unawares they are lost forever.   40
Should their life-thread be broken within them,
   they die, and without any wisdom.

5. Call out, pray: will any answer you,
   and to whom of the angels will you turn?
For anger kills a fool,
   and the simple, envy slays.
I have seen a fool striking root—   5
   all at once his abode I saw cursed.

His children are distant from rescue
　and are crushed in the gate—none will save.
Whose harvest the hungry eat
　and from among thorns they take it away,　10
　and the thirsty pant for their wealth.
For crime does not spring from the dust,
　nor from the soil does wretchedness sprout.
But man is to wretchedness born
　like sparks flying upward.　15
Yet I search for El[8]
　and to God I make my case,
Who does great things without limit
　wonders beyond all number,
Who brings rain down on the earth　20
　and sends water over the fields.
Who raises the lowly on high—
　the downcast are lifted in rescue.
Thwarts the designs of the cunning,
　and their hands do not perform wisely.　25
He entraps the wise in their cunning,
　and the crooked's counsel proves hasty.
By day they encounter darkness,
　as in night they go groping at noon.
He rescues the simple from the sword,　30
　and from the hand of the strong, the impoverished,
and the indigent then has hope,
　and wickedness clamps its mouth shut.
Why, happy the man whom God corrects.
　Shaddai's reproof do not spurn!　35
For He causes pain and binds the wound,
　He deals blows but His hands will heal.
In six straits He will save you,
　and in seven harm will not touch you.
In famine He redeems you from death,　40
　and in battle from the sword.
From the scourge of the tongue you are hidden,
　and you shall fear not assault when it comes.
At assault and starvation you laugh,
　and the beasts of the earth you fear not.　45
With the stones of the field is your pact,
　the beasts of the field leagued with you.
And you shall know that your tent is peaceful,
　probe your home and find nothing amiss.
And you shall know that your seed is abundant,　50
　your offspring like the grass of the earth.
You shall come to the grave in vigor,
　as grain-shocks mount in their season.
Look, this we have searched, it is so.
　Hear it, and you—you should know.　55

8. God.

6. And Job spoke out and he said:

Could my anguish but be weighed,
  and my disaster on the scales be borne,
they would be heavier now than the sand of the sea.
  Thus my words are choked back.
For Shaddai's arrows are in me—   5
  their venom my spirit drinks.
    The terrors of God beset me.
Does the wild ass bray over his grass,
  the ox bellow over his feed?[9]
Is tasteless food eaten unsalted,   10
  does the oozing of mallows have savor?[1]
My throat refuses to touch them.
  They resemble my sickening flesh.
If only my wish were fulfilled,
  and my hope God might grant.   15
If God would deign to crush me,
  loose His hand and tear me apart.
And this still would be my comfort,
  I shrink back in pangs—he spares not.
    Yet I withhold not the Holy One's words.   20
What is my strength, that I should hope,
  and what my end that I should endure?
Is my strength the strength of stones,
  is my flesh made of bronze?
Indeed, there is no help within me,   25
  and prudence is driven from me.
The blighted man's friend owes him kindness,
  though the fear of Shaddai he forsake.
My brothers betrayed like a wadi,[2]
  like the channel of brooks that run dry.   30
They are dark from the ice,
  snow heaped on them.
When they warm, they are gone,
  in the heat they melt from their place.
The paths that they go on are winding,   35
  they mount in the void and are lost.
The caravans of Tema looked out,[3]
  the convoys of Sheba awaited.
Disappointed in what they had trusted,
  they reached it and their hopes were dashed.   40
For now you are His.
  You see panic and you fear.

---

9. Rhetorical questions. The idea is that animals do not complain when fed appropriately,
and, by analogy, humans do not complain
unless they are truly suffering.
1. The tasteless food may be literal (Job cannot
eat because he is too upset), or metaphorical.

2. A desert ravine, which is full of water only
in the rainy season; when summer comes, it
runs dry.
3. For water, continuing the image of the dried-
up *wadi*.

Did I say, Give for me,
   and with your wealth pay a ransom for me,
and free me from the hands of the foe,   45
   from the oppressors' hands redeem me?
Instruct me—as for me, I'll keep silent,
   and let me know where I went wrong.
How forceful are honest words.
   Yet what rebuke is the rebuke by you?   50
Do you mean to rebuke with words,
   treat the speech of the desperate as wind?
Even for the orphan you cast lots,
   and haggle for your companion.
And now, deign to turn toward me.   55
   To your face I will surely not lie.
Relent, pray, let there be no injustice.
   Relent. I am yet in the right.
Is there injustice on my tongue?
   Does my palate not taste disasters?   60

7. Does not man have fixed service on earth,
   and like a hired worker's his days?
Like a slave he pants for shade,
   like a hired worker he waits for his pay.
Thus I was heir to futile moons,   5
   and wretched nights were allotted to me.
Lying down, I thought, When shall I rise?—
   Each evening, I was sated with tossing till dawn.
My flesh was clothed with worms and earth-clods,
   my skin rippled with running sores.   10
My days are swifter than the weaver's shuttle.
   They snap off without any hope.
Recall that my life is a breath.
   Not again will my eyes see good.
The eye of who sees me will not make me out.   15
   Your eyes are on me—I am gone.
A cloud vanishes and goes off.
   Thus, who goes down to Sheol[4] will not come up.
He will not return to his home.
   His place will not know him again.   20
As for me, I will not restrain my mouth.
   I would lament with my spirit in straits
      I would speak when my being is bitter.
Am I Yamm[5] or am I the Sea Beast,
   that You should put a watch upon me?   25
When I thought my couch would console me,
   that my bed would bear my lament,
You panicked me in dreams
   and in visions you struck me with terror.

4. The land of the dead.
5. Yamm is the sea god in Canaanite mythology, also known as Leviathan; he was subdued by Baal, the weather god, whom Job here associates with his own God.

And my throat would have chosen choking,   30
  my bones—death.
I am sickened—I won't live forever.
  Let me be, for my days are mere breath.
What is man that You make him great
  and that You pay heed to him?   35
You single him out every morning,
  every moment examine him.
How long till You turn away from me?
  You don't let me go while I swallow my spit.[6]
What is my offense that I have done to You,   40
  O Watcher of man?
Why did You make me Your target,
  and I became a burden to You?
And why do You not pardon my crime
  and let my sin pass away?   45
For soon I shall lie in the dust.
  You will seek me, and I shall be gone.

8. And Bildad the Shuhite spoke out and he said,

How long will you jabber such things?—
  the words of your mouth, one huge wind.
Would God pervert justice,
  would Shaddai pervert what is right?
If your children offended Him,   5
  He dispatched them because of their crime.
If you yourself sought out God,
  and pleaded to Shaddai,
if you were honest and pure,
  by now He would rouse Himself for you,   10
    and would make your righteous home whole.
Then your beginning would seem a trifle
  and your latter day very grand.
For ask, pray, generations of old,
  take in what their fathers found out.   15
For we are but yesterday, unknowing,
  for our days are a shadow on earth.
Will they not teach you and say to you,
  and from their heart bring out words?
Will papyrus sprout with no marsh,   20
  reeds grow grand without water?
Still in its blossom, not yet plucked,
  before any grass it will wither.
Thus is the end of all who forget God,
  and the hope of the tainted is lost.   25
Whose faith is mere cobweb,
  a spider's house his trust.

6. I.e., not even for a second.

He leans on his house and it will not stand,
 he grasps it and it does not endure.
—He is moist in the sun,   30
 and his tendrils push out in his garden.
Round a knoll his roots twist,
 on a stone house they take hold.
If his place should uproot him
 and deny him—"I never saw you,"   35
why, this is his joyous way,
 from another soil he will spring.
Look, God will not spurn the blameless,
 nor hold the hand of evildoers.
He will yet fill your mouth with laughter   40
 and your lips with a shout of joy.
Your foes will be clothed in disgrace,
 and the tent of the wicked gone.

9. And Job spoke out and he said

Of course, I knew it was so:
 how can man be right before God?
Should a person bring grievance against Him,
 He will not answer one of a thousand.
Wise in mind, staunch in strength,   5
 who can argue with Him and come out whole?
He uproots mountains and they know not,
 overturns them in His wrath.
He makes earth shake in its setting,
 and its pillars shudder.   10
He bids the sun not to rise,
 and the stars He seals up tight.
He stretches the heavens alone
 and tramples the crests of the sea.
He makes the Bear and Orion,   15
 the Pleiades and the South Wind's chambers.
He performs great things without limit
 and wonders without number.
Look, He passes over me and I do not see,
 slips by me and I cannot grasp Him.   20
Look, He seizes—who can resist Him?
 Who can tell him, "What do You do?"
God will not relent his fury.
 Beneath him Rahab's[7] minions stoop.
And yet, as for me, I would answer Him,   25
 would choose my words with Him.
Though in the right, I can't make my plea.
 I would have to entreat my own judge.
Should I call out and He answer me,
 I would not trust Him to heed my voice   30

7. Another name for the sea monster (Baal, or Leviathan).

Who for a hair would crush me
    and make my wounds many for nought.
He does not allow me to catch my breath
    as He sates me with bitterness.
If it's strength—He is staunch,   35
    and if it's justice—who can arraign Him?
Though in the right, my mouth will convict me,
    I am blameless, yet He makes me crooked.
I am blameless—I know not myself,
    I loathe my life.   40
It's all the same, and so I thought:
    the blameless and the wicked He destroys.
If a scourge causes death in an instant,
    He mocks the innocent's plight.
The earth is given in the wicked man's hand,   45
    the face of its judges He veils.
        If not He—then who else?
And my days are swifter than a courier.
    They have fled and have never seen good,
slipped away like reed ships,   50
    like an eagle swooping on prey.
If I said, I would forget my lament.
    I would leave my grim mood and be gladdened,
I was in terror of all my suffering.
    I knew You would not acquit me.   55
I will be guilty.
    Why should I toil in vain?
Should I bathe in snow,
    make my palms pure with lye,
You would yet plunge me into a pit,   60
    and my robes would defile me.
For He is not a man like me that I might answer Him,
    that we might come together in court.
Would there were an arbiter between us,
    who could lay his hand on us both,   65
who could take from me His rod,
    and His terror would not confound me.
I would speak, and I will not fear Him,
    for that is not the way I am.

10. My whole being loathes my life.
Let me give vent to my lament.
    Let me speak when my being is bitter.
I shall say to God: Do not convict me.
    Inform me why You accuse me.   5
Is it good for You to oppress,
    to spurn Your own palms' labor,
        and on the council of the wicked to shine?
Do You have the eyes of mortal flesh,
    do You see as man would see?   10
Are Your days like a mortal's days,

Your years like the years of a man,
that You should search out my crime
   and inquire for my offense?
You surely know I am not guilty,   15
   but there is none who saves from Your hand.
Your hands fashioned me and made me,
   and then You turn round and destroy me!
Recall, pray, that like clay You worked me,
   and to the dust You will make me return.   20
Why, You poured me out like milk
   and like cheese You curdled me.
With skin and flesh You clothed me,
   with bones and sinews entwined me.
Life and kindness you gave me,   25
   and Your precepts my spirit kept.
Yet these did You hide in Your heart;
   I knew that this was with You:
If I offended, You kept watch upon me
   and of my crime would not acquit me.   30
If I was guilty, alas for me,
   and though innocent, I could not raise my head,
      sated with shame and surfeited with disgrace.
Like a triumphant lion You hunt me,
   over again wondrously smite me.   35
You summon new witnesses against me
   and swell up your anger toward me—
      vanishings and hard service are mine.
And why from the womb did You take me?
   I'd breathe my last, no eye would have seen me.   40
As though I had not been, I would be.
   From belly to grave I'd be carried.
My days are but few—let me be.
   Turn away that I may have some gladness
before I go, never more to return,   45
   to the land of dark and death's shadow,
the land of gloom, thickest murk,
   death's shadow and disorder,
      where it shines thickest murk.

11. And Zophar the Naamathite spoke out and he said:
Shall a swarm of words be unanswered,
   and should a smooth talker be in the right?
Your lies may silence folk,
   you mock and no one protests.   5
And you say: my teaching is spotless,
   and I am pure in your eyes.
Yet, if only God would speak,
   and He would open His lips against you,
would tell you wisdom's secrets,   10
   for prudence is double-edged.
      And know, God leaves some of your crime forgotten.

Can you find what God has probed,
  can you find Shaddai's last end?
Higher than heaven, what can you do,   15
  deeper than Sheol, what can you know?
Longer than earth is its measure,
  and broader than the sea.
Should He slip away or confine or assemble,
  who can resist Him?   20
For He knows the empty folk,
  He sees wrongdoing and surely takes note.
And a hollow man will get a wise heart
  when a wild ass is born a man.
If you yourself readied your heart   25
  and spread out your palms to Him,
if there is wrongdoing in your hands, remove it,
  let no mischief dwell in your tents.
For then you will raise your face unstained,
  you will be steadfast and will not fear.   30
For you will forget wretchedness,
  like water gone off, recall it.
And life will rise higher than noon,
  will soar, will be like the morning.
And you will trust, for there is hope,   35
  will search, and lie secure.
You will stretch out, and none make you tremble,
  and many pay court to you.
And the eyes of the wicked will pine,
  escape will be lost to them,   40
    and their hope—a last gasp of breath.

12. And Job spoke up and he said:
Oh yes, you are the people,
  and with you wisdom will die!
But I, too, have a mind like you,
  I am no less than you,   5
    and who does not know such things?
A laughing-stock to his friend I am,
  who calls to his God and is answered,
    a laughing-stock of the blameless just man.
The smug man's thought scorns disaster,   10
  readied for those who stumble.
The tents of despoilers are tranquil,
  provokers of God are secure,
    whom God has led by the hand.
Yet ask of the beasts, they will teach you,   15
  the fowl of the heavens will tell you,
or speak to the earth, it will teach you,
  the fish of the sea will inform you.
Who has not known in all these
  that the LORD's hand has done this?   20
In Whose hand is the breath of each living thing,

and the spirit of all human flesh.
Does not the ear make out words,
   the palate taste food?
In the aged is wisdom,   25
   and in length of days understanding.
With Him are wisdom and strength,
   He possesses counsel and understanding.
Why, He destroys and there is no rebuilding,
   closes in on a man, leaves no opening.   30
Why, He holds back the waters and they dry up,
   sends them forth and they turn the earth over.
With Him is power and prudence,
   His the duped and the duper.
He leads counselors astray   35
   and judges He drives to madness.
He undoes the sash of kings
   and binds a loincloth round their waist.
He leads priests astray,
   the mighty He misleads.   40
He takes away speech from the trustworthy,
   and sense from the elders He takes,
He pours forth scorn on princes,
   and the belt of the nobles He slackens,
lays bare depths from the darkness   45
   and brings out to light death's shadow,
raises nations high and destroys them,
   flattens nations and leads them away,
stuns the minds of the people's leaders,
   makes them wander in trackless wastes—   50
they grope in darkness without light,
   He makes them wander like drunken men.

13. Why, my eye has seen all,
   my ear has heard and understood.
As you know, I, too, know.
   I am no less than you.
Yet I would speak to Shaddai,   5
   and I want to dispute with God.
And yet, you plaster lies,[8]
   you are all quack-healers.
Would that you fell silent,
   and this would be your wisdom.   10
Hear, pray, my dispute,
   and to my lips' pleas listen closely.
Would you speak crookedness of God,
   and of Him would you speak false things?
Would you be partial on His behalf,   15
   would you plead the case of God?
Would it be good that He probed you,

8. An idiom also found in the Psalms; the idea is that the truth is "plastered over" with lies.

as one mocks a man would you mock Him?
He shall surely dispute with you
    if in secret you are partial.   20
Will not His majesty strike you with terror,
    and His fear fall upon you?
Your pronouncements are maxims of ash,
    your word-piles, piles of clay.
Be silent before me—I would speak,   25
    no matter what befalls me.
Why should I bear my flesh in my teeth,
    and my life-breath place in my palm?
Look, He slays me, I have no hope.
    Yet my ways I'll dispute to His face.   30
Even that becomes my rescue,
    for no tainted man comes before Him.
Hear, O hear my word
    and my utterance in your ear.
Look, pray, I have laid out my case,   35
    I know that I am in the right.
Who would make a plea against me?
    I would be silent then, breathe my last.
Just two things do not do to me,
    then would I not hide from Your presence.   40
Take Your palm away from me,
    and let Your dread not strike me with terror.
Call and I will reply,
    or I will speak, and answer me.
How many crimes and offenses have I?   45
    My offense and my wrong, inform me.
Why do You hide Your face,
    and count me Your enemy?
Would You harry a driven leaf,
    and a dry straw would You chase,   50
that You should write bitter things against me,
    make me heir to the crimes of my youth?
And You put my feet in stocks,
    watch after all my paths,
        on the soles of my feet make a mark.[9]   55

And man wears away like rot,
    like a garment eaten by moths.

14. Man born of woman,
    scant of days and sated with trouble,
like a blossom he comes forth and withers,
    and flees like a shadow—he will not stay.
Even on such You cast Your eye,   5
    and me You bring in judgment with You?
[Who can make the impure pure?

---

9. Probably a reference to branding or tattooing done to mark out a criminal.

No one.]¹
Oh, his days are decreed,
    the number of his months are with You,   10
       his limits You fixed that he cannot pass.
Turn away from him that he may cease,
    until he serves out his day like a hired man.
For a tree has hope:
    though cut down, it can still be removed,   15
       and its shoots will not cease.
Though its root grow old in the ground
    and its stock die in the dust,
from the scent of water it flowers,
    and puts forth branches like a sapling.   20
But a strong man dies defeated,
    man breathes his last, and where is he?
Water runs out from a lake,
    and a river is parched and dries up,
but a man lies down and will not arise,   25
    till the sky is no more he will not awake
       and will not rouse from his sleep.
Would that You hid me in Sheol,
    concealed me till Your anger passed,
       set me a limit and recalled me.   30
If a man dies will he live?
    All my hard service days I shall hope
       until my vanishing comes.
Call out and I shall answer you,
    for the work of Your hand You should yearn.   35
For then You would count my steps,
    You would not keep watch over my offense.
My crime would be sealed in a packet,
    You would plaster over my guilt.
And yet, a falling mountain crumbles,   40
    a rock is ripped from its place.
Water wears away stones,
    its surge sweeps up the dust of the earth,
       and the hope of man You destroy.
You overwhelm him forever, and he goes off,   45
    You change his face and send him away.
If his sons grow great, he will not know.
    And should they dwindle, he will not notice them.
But the flesh upon him will ache,
    his own being will mourn for him.   50

*   *   *

29. And Job again took up his theme and he said:
Would that I were as in moons of yore,
    as the days when God watched over me,

---

1. This verse is bracketed because it is metrically too short; many scholars think it does not
belong in the text.

when He shined his lamp over my head,
    by its light I walked in darkness,   5
as I was in the days of my prime—
    God an intimate of my tent,
when Shaddai still was with me,
    all around me my lads;
when my feet bathed in curds   10
    and the rock poured out streams of oil,
when I went out to the city's gate,
    in the square I secured my seat.[2]
Lads saw me and took cover,
    the aged arose, stood up.   15
Noblemen held back their words,
    their palm they put to their mouth.
The voice of the princes was muffled,
    their tongue to their palate stuck.
When the ear heard, it affirmed me,   20
    and the eye saw and acclaimed me.
For I would free the poor who cried out,
    the orphan with no one to help him.
The perishing man's blessing would reach me,
    and the widow's heart I made sing.   25
Righteousness I donned and it clothed me,
    like a cloak and a headdress, my justice.
Eyes I became for the blind,
    and legs for the lame I was.
A father I was for the impoverished,   30
    a stranger's cause I took up.
And I cracked the wrongdoer's jaws,
    from his teeth I would wrench the prey.
And I thought: In my nest I shall breathe my last,
    and my days will abound like the sand.   35
My root will be open to water,
    and dew in my branches abide,
My glory renewed within me,
    and my bow ever fresh in my hand.
To me they would listen awaiting   40
    and fall silent at my advice.
At my speech they would say nothing further,
    and upon them my word would drop.
They waited for me as for rain,
    and gaped open their mouths as for showers.   45
I laughed to them—they scarcely trusted—
    but my face's light they did not dim.
I chose their way and sat as chief,
    I dwelled like a king in his brigade
        when he comforts the mourning.   50

---

2. The square just inside the city gate was the town's meeting place; having a seat there would be a sign of status.

30. And now mere striplings laugh at me
    whose fathers I spurned
        to put with the dogs of my flock.
The strength of their hands—what use to me?
    From them the vigor has gone: 5
In want and starvation bereft
    they flee to desert land,
        the darkness of desolate dunes,
plucking saltwort from the bush,
    the roots of broomwood their bread.   10
From within they are banished—
    people shout over them as at thieves.
In river ravines they encamp,
    holes in the dust and crags.
Among bushes they bray,   15
    beneath thornplants they huddle.
Vile creatures and nameless, too,
    they are struck from the land.
And now I become their taunt,
    I become their mocking word.   20
They despised me, were distant to me,
    and from my face they did not spare their spit.
For my bowstring they loosed and abused me,
    cast off restraint toward me.
On the right, raw youths stand up,   25
    they make me run off
        and pave against me their roadways of ruin.
They shatter my path,
    my disaster devise,
        and none helps me against them.   30
Like a wide water-burst they come,
    in the shape of a tempest they tumble.
Terror rolls over me,
    pursues my path like the wind,
        and my rescue like a cloud passes on.   35
And now my life spills out,
    days of affliction seize me.
At night my limbs are pierced,
    and my sinews know no rest.
With great power He seizes my garment,   40
    grabs hold of me at the collar.
He hurls me into the muck,
    and I become like dust and ashes.
I scream to You and You do not answer,
    I stand still and You do not observe me.   45
You become a cruel one toward me,
    with the might of Your hand You hound me.
You bear me up, on the wind make me straddle,
    break me apart in a storm.
For I know You'll return me to death,   50
    the meetinghouse of all living things.

But one would not reach out against the afflicted
  if in his disaster he screamed.
Have I not wept for the bleak-fated man,
  sorrowed for the impoverished?   55
For I hoped for good and evil came.
  I expected light and darkness fell.
My innards seethed and would not be still,
  days of affliction greeted me.
In gloom did I walk, with no sun,   60
  I rose in assembly and I screamed.
Brother I was to the jackals,
  companion to ostriches.[3]
My skin turned black upon me,
  my limbs were scorched by drought.   65
And my lyre has turned into mourning,
  my flute, a keening sound.

31. A pact I sealed with my eyes—
  I will not gaze on a virgin.
And what is the share from God above,
  the portion from Shaddai in the heights?
Is there not ruin for the wrongdoer,   5
  and estrangement for those who do evil?
Does He not see my way,
  and all my steps count?
Have I walked in a lie,
  has my foot hurried to deceit?   10
Let Him weigh me on fair scales,
  that God know my blamelessness.
If my stride has strayed from the way,
  and my heart gone after my eyes,
    or the least thing stuck to my palms,   15
let me sow and another shall eat,
  my offspring torn up by the roots.
If my heart was seduced by a woman,
  and at the door of my friend I lurked,
let my wife grind for another   20
  and upon her let others crouch.[4]
For that is lewdness,
  and that is a grave crime.
For it is fire that consumes to Perdition,
  and in all my yield eats the roots.   25
If I spurned the case of my slave
  or my slavegirl, in their brief against me,
what would I do when God stands up,
  and when He assays it, what would I answer?
Why, my Maker made him in the belly,   30
  and formed him in the selfsame womb.

---

3. Known for their loud, mournful cries.
4. The "grinding" and "crouching" are implicit metaphors for sex.

Did I hold back the poor from his desire
    or make the eyes of the widow pine?
Did I eat my bread alone,
    and an orphan not eat from it?   35
For from my youth like a father I raised him,
    and from my mother's womb I led him.
If I saw a man failing, ungarbed,
    and no garment for the impoverished,
did his loins not then bless me,   40
    and from my sheep's shearing was he not warmed?
If I raised my hand against an orphan,
    when I saw my advantage in the gate,
let my shoulder fall out of its socket
    and my arm break off from its shaft.   45
For ruin from God is my fear,
    and His presence I cannot withstand.
If I made gold my bulwark,
    and fine gold I called my trust,
if I rejoiced that my wealth was great   50
    and that abundance my hand had found,
if I saw light when it gleamed
    and the moon gliding grand,
and my heart was seduced in secret,
    and my hand caressed my mouth,   55
this, too, would be a grave crime,
    for I would have denied God above.[5]
If I rejoiced at my foe's disaster,
    and exulted when harm found him out—
yet I did not let my mouth offend   60
    to seek out his life in an oath.
Did the men of my tent ever say,
    "Would that we were never sated of his flesh"?
The sojourner did not sleep outside.
    My doors to the wayfarer I opened.   65
Did I hide like Adam my wrongdoings,
    to bury within me my crime,
that I should fear the teeming crowd,
    and the scorn of clans terrify me,
        fall silent and keep within doors?   70
Would that I had someone to hear me out.
    Here's my mark—let Shaddai answer me,
    and let my accuser indict his writ.
I would bear it upon my shoulder,
    bind it as a crown upon me.   75
The number of my steps I would tell Him,
    like a prince I would approach him.
If my soil has cried out against me,
    and together its furrows wept,

---

5. Apparently refers to idolatrous worship of the sun and moon.

if I ate its yield without payment,   80
  and drove its owners to despair,
instead of wheat let nettles grow,
  and instead of barley, stinkweed.

Here end the words of Job.

               *   *   *

38. And the LORD answered Job from the whirlwind and He said:
  Who is this who darkens counsel
    in words without knowledge?
  Gird, pray, your loins like a man,
    that I may ask you, and you can inform Me.
  Where were you when I founded earth?   5
    Tell, if you know understanding.
  Who fixed its measures, do you know,
    or who stretched a line upon it?
  In what were its sockets sunk,
    or who laid its cornerstone,   10
  when the morning stars sang together,
    and all the sons of God shouted for joy?
  Who hedged the sea in with doors,
    when it gushed forth from the womb,
  when I made cloud its clothing,   15
    and thick mist its swaddling bands?
  I made breakers upon it My limit,
    and set a bolt with double doors.
  And I said, "Thus far come, no further,
    here halt the surge of your waves."   20
  Have you ever commanded the morning,
    appointed the dawn to its place,
  to seize the earth's corners,
    that the wicked be shaken from it?
  It turns like sealing clay,   25
    takes color like a garment,
  and their light is withdrawn from the wicked,
    and the upraised arm is broken.
  Have you come into the springs of the sea,
    in the bottommost deep walked about?   30
  Have the gates of death been laid bare to you,
    and the gates of death's shadow have you seen?
  Did you take in the breadth of the earth?
    Tell, if you know it all.
  Where is the way that light dwells,   35
    and darkness, where is its place,
  that you might take it to its home
    and understand the paths to its house?
  You know, for were you born then,
    and the number of your days is great!   40
  Have you come into the storehouse of snow,
    the storehouse of hail have you seen,

which I keep for a time of strife,
 for a day of battle and war?
By what way does the west wind fan out,   45
 the east wind whip over the earth?
Who split a channel for the torrent,
 and a way for the thunderstorm,
to rain on a land without man,
 wilderness bare of humankind,   50
to sate the desolate dunes
 and make the grass sprout there?
Does the rain have a father,
 or who begot the drops of dew?
From whose belly did the ice come forth,   55
 to the frost of the heavens who gave birth?
Water congeals like stone,
 and the face of the deep locks hard.
Can you tie the bands of the Pleiades,
 or loose Orion's reins?   60
Can you bring constellations out in their season,
 lead the Great Bear and her cubs?
Do you know the laws of the heavens,
 can you fix their rule on earth?
Can you lift your voice to the cloud,   65
 that the water-spate cover you?
Can you send lightning bolts on their way,
 and they will say to you, "Here we are!"?
Who placed in the hidden parts wisdom,
 or who gave the mind understanding?   70
Who counted the skies in wisdom,
 and the jars of the heavens who tilted,
when the dust melts to a mass,
 and the clods cling fast together?
Can you hunt prey for the lion,   75
 fill the king of beast's appetite,
when it crouches in its den,
 lies in ambush in the covert?
Who readies the raven's prey
 when its young cry out to God   80
  and stray deprived of food?

39. Do you know the mountain goats' birth-time,
 do you mark the calving of the gazelles?
Do you number the months till they come to term
 and know their birthing time?
They crouch, burst forth with their babes,   5
 their young they push out to the world.
Their offspring batten, grow big in the wild,
 they go out and do not return.
Who set the wild ass free,
 and the onager's reins who loosed,   10

whose home I made in the steppes,
   his dwelling-place flats of salt?
He scoffs at the bustling city,
   the driver's shouts he does not hear.
He roams mountains for his forage,   15
   and every green thing he seeks.
Will the wild ox want to serve you,
   pass the night at your feeding trough?
Bind the wild ox with cord for the furrow,
   will he harrow the valleys behind you?   20
Can you rely on him with his great power
   and leave your labor to him?
Can you trust him to bring back your seed,
   gather grain on your threshing floor?
The ostrich's wing joyously beats.   25
   Is the pinion, the plume like the stork's?
For she leaves her eggs on the ground,
   and in the dust she lets them warm.
And she forgets that a foot can crush them,
   and a beast of the field stomp on them—   30
harsh, abandons her young to a stranger,
   in vain her labor, without fear.
For God made her forgetful of wisdom,
   and He did not allot her insight.
Now on the height she races,   35
   she scoffs at the horse and its rider.
Do you give might to the horse,
   do you clothe his neck with a mane?
Do you make his roar like locusts—
   his splendid snort is terror.   40
He churns up the valley exulting,
   in power goes out to the clash of arms.
He scoffs at fear and is undaunted,
   turns not back before the sword.
Over him rattles the quiver,   45
   the blade, the javelin, and the spear.
With clamor and clatter he swallows the ground,
   and ignores the trumpet's sound.
At the trumpet he says, "Aha,"
   and from afar he scents the fray,   50
     the thunder of captains, the shouts.
Does the hawk soar by your wisdom,
   spread his wings to fly away south?
By your word does the eagle mount
   and set his nest on high?   55
On the crag he dwells and beds down,
   on the crest of the crag his stronghold.
From there he seeks out food,
   from afar his eyes look down.
His chicks lap up blood,   60
   where the slain are, there he is.

40. And the LORD answered Job and He said:
Will he who disputes with Shaddai be reproved?
   Who argues with God, let him answer!
And Job answered the LORD and he said:
Look, I am worthless. What can I say back to You?   5
   My hand I put over my mouth.
Once have I spoken and I will not answer,
   twice, and will not go on.
And the LORD answered Job from the whirlwind and He
   said:
Gird, pray, your loins like a man.   10
   Let me ask you, and you will inform Me.
Will you indeed overthrow My case,
   hold Me guilty, so you can be right?
If you have an arm like God's,
   and with a voice like His you can thunder,   15
put on, pray, pride and preeminence,
   and grandeur and glory don.
Let loose your utmost wrath,
   see every proud man, bring him low.
See every proud man, make him kneel,   20
   tramp on the wicked where they are.
Bury them in the dust together,
   shut them up in the grave.
And I on my part shall acclaim you,
   for your right hand triumphs for you.   25
Look, pray: Behemoth[6] whom I made with you,
   grass like cattle he eats.
Look, pray: the power in his loins,
   the virile strength in his belly's muscles.
He makes his tail stand like a cedar,   30
   his balls' sinews twine together.
His bones are bars of bronze,
   his limbs like iron rods.
He is the first of the ways of God.
   Let his Maker draw near him with His sword!   35
For the mountains offer their yield to him,
   every beast of the field plays there.
Underneath the lotus he lies,
   in the covert of reeds and marsh.
The lotus hedges him, shades him,   40
   the brook willows stand around him.
Look, he swallows a river at his ease,
   untroubled while Jordan pours into his mouth.
Could one take him with one's eyes,
with barbs pierce his nose?   45

---

6. The Hebrew word *behemot* simply means "beasts"; the description suggests a mythologized version of the hippopotamus, an animal the poet had presumably never seen.

Could you draw Leviathan[7] with a hook,
  and with a cord press down his tongue?
Could you put a lead-line in his nose,
  and with a fish-hook pierce his cheek?
Would he urgently entreat you,   50
  would he speak to you gentle words?
Would he seal a pact with you,
  that you take him as lifelong slave?
Could you play with him like a bird,
  and leash him for your young women?   55
Could hucksters haggle over him,
  divide him among the traders?
Could you fill his skin with darts,
  and a fisherman's net with his head?
Just put your hand upon him—   60
  you will no more recall how to battle.

41. Look, all hope of him is dashed,
  at his mere sight one is cast down.
No fierce one could arouse him,
  and who before him could stand up?
Who could go before Me in this I'd reward,   5
  under all the heavens he would be mine.
I would not keep silent about him,
  about his heroic acts and surpassing grace.
Who can uncover his outer garb,
  come into his double mail?   10
Who can pry open the doors of his face?
  All around his teeth is terror.
His back is rows of shields,
  closed with the tightest seal.
Each touches against the next,   15
  no breath can come between them.
Each sticks fast to the next,
  locked together, they will not part.
His sneezes shoot out light,
  and his eyes are like the eyelids of dawn.   20
Firebrands leap from his mouth,
  sparks of fire fly into the air.
From his nostrils smoke comes out,
  like a boiling vat on brushwood.
His breath kindles coals,   25
  and flame comes out of his mouth.
Strength abides in his neck,
  and before him power dances.
The folds of his flesh cling together;
  hard-cast, he will not totter.   30
His heart is cast hard as stone,

7. The mythical Canaanite sea monster, here associated with the crocodile.

cast hard as a nether millstone.[8]
When he rears up, the gods are frightened,[9]
   when he crashes down, they cringe.
Who overtakes him with sword, it will not avail,   35
   nor spear nor dart nor lance.
Iron he deems as straw,
   and bronze as rotten wood.
No arrow can make him flee,
   slingstones for him turn to straw.   40
Missiles are deemed as straw,
   and he mocks the javelin's clatter.
Beneath him, jagged shards,
   he draws a harrow over the mud.
He makes the deep boil like a pot,   45
   turns sea to an ointment pan.
Behind him glistens a wake,
   he makes the deep seem hoary.
He has no match on earth,
   made as he is without fear.   50
All that is lofty he can see.
   He is king over all proud beasts.

42. And Job answered the LORD and he said:
   I know You can do anything,
      and no devising is beyond You.
   "Who is this obscuring counsel without knowledge?"[1]
      Therefore I told but did not understand,
         wonders beyond me that I did not know.   5
   "Hear, pray, and I will speak
      Let me ask you, that you may inform me."
   By the ear's rumor I heard of You,
      and now my eye has seen You.
   Therefore do I recant,   10
      And I repent in dust and ashes.

And it happened after the LORD had spoken these words to Job, that the LORD said to Eliphaz the Temanite: "My wrath has flared against you and your two companions because you have not spoken rightly of Me as did My servant Job. And now, take for yourselves seven bulls and seven rams and go to My servant Job, and offer a burnt-offering for yourselves, and Job My servant will pray on your behalf. To him only I shall show favor, not to do a vile thing to you, for you have not spoken rightly of Me as did my servant Job. And Eliphaz the Temanite and Bildad the Shuhite and Zophar the Naamathite went out and did according to all that the LORD had spoken to them, and the LORD showed favor to Job. And the LORD restored Job's fortunes when he prayed for

8. Flour was ground between two stones; the bottom one would have to be particularly hard, to withstand the pressure.
9. "Gods" = a sign that the text is not mono-theistic. Job believes that his Lord is the best

and strongest but not the only god.
1. I.e., giving advice in ignorance of the facts. The line is a quotation of the Lord's words to Job.

his companions, and the LORD increased twofold all that Job had. And all his male and female kinfolk and all who had known him before came and broke bread with him in his house and grieved with him and comforted him for all the harm that the LORD had brought on him. And each of them gave him one kesitah[2] and one golden ring. And the LORD blessed Job's latter days more than his former days, and he had fourteen thousand sheep and six thousand camels and a thousand yoke of oxen and a thousand she-asses. And he had seven sons and three daughters. And he called the name of the first one Dove and the name of the second Cinnamon and the name of the third Horn of Eye-shade.[3] And there were no women in the land so beautiful as Job's daughters. And their father gave them an estate among their brothers. And Job lived a hundred and forty years after this, and he saw his children and his children's children, four generations. And Job died, aged and sated in years.

Psalm 8[1]

1. O Lord our Lord, how excellent is thy name in all the earth! who hast set thy glory above the heavens.

2. Out of the mouth of babes and sucklings hast thou ordained strength because of thine enemies, that thou mightest still the enemy and the avenger.

3. When I consider thy heavens, the work of thy fingers, the moon and the stars, which thou hast ordained;

4. What is man, that thou art mindful of him? and the son of man, that thou visitest him?

5. For thou hast made him a little lower than the angels, and hast crowned him with glory and honour.

6. Thou madest him to have dominion over the works of thy hands; thou hast put all things under his feet:

7. All sheep and oxen, yea, and the beasts of the field;

8. The fowl of the air, and the fish of the sea, and whatsoever passeth through the paths of the seas.

9. O Lord our Lord, how excellent is thy name in all the earth!

Psalm 19

1. The heavens declare the glory of God; and the firmament sheweth his handywork.

2. Day unto day uttereth speech, and night unto night sheweth knowledge.

3. There is no speech nor language, where their voice is not heard.

4. Their line is gone out through all the earth, and their words to the end of the world. In them hath he set a tabernacle for the sun,

---

2. A valuable coin.
3. A substance used for eye makeup.

1. The text of the Psalms is that of the King James version.

5. Which is as a bridegroom coming out of his chamber, and rejoiceth as a strong man to run a race.

6. His going forth is from the end of the heaven, and his circuit unto the ends of it: and there is nothing hid from the heat thereof.

7. The law of the Lord is perfect, converting the soul: the testimony of the Lord is sure, making wise the simple.

8. The statutes of the Lord are right, rejoicing the heart: the commandment of the Lord is pure, enlightening the eyes.

9. The fear of the Lord is clean, enduring for ever: the judgments of the Lord are true and righteous altogether.

10. More to be desired are they than gold, yea, than much fine gold: sweeter also than honey and the honeycomb.

11. Moreover by them is thy servant warned: and in keeping of them there is great reward.

12. Who can understand his errors? cleanse thou me from secret faults.

13. Keep back thy servant also from presumptuous sins; let them not have dominion over me: then shall I be upright, and I shall be innocent from the great transgression.

14. Let the words of my mouth, and the meditation of my heart, be acceptable in thy sight, O Lord, my strength, and my redeemer.

Psalm 23

1. The Lord is my shepherd; I shall not want.

2. He maketh me to lie down in green pastures: he leadeth me beside the still waters.

3. He restoreth my soul: he leadeth me in the paths of righteousness for his name's sake.

4. Yea, though I walk through the valley of the shadow of death, I will fear no evil: for thou art with me; thy rod and thy staff they comfort me.

5. Thou preparest a table before me in the presence of mine enemies: thou anointest my head with oil; my cup runneth over.

6. Surely goodness and mercy shall follow me all the days of my life: and I will dwell in the house of the Lord for ever.

Psalm 104

1. Bless the Lord, O my soul. O Lord my God, thou art very great; thou art clothed with honour and majesty.

2. Who coverest thyself with light as with a garment: who stretchest out the heavens like a curtain:

3. Who layeth the beams of his chambers in the waters: who maketh the clouds his chariot: who walketh upon the wings of the wind:

4. Who maketh his angels spirits; his ministers a flaming fire:

5. Who laid the foundations of the earth, that it should not be removed for ever.

6. Thou coveredst it with the deep as with a garment: the waters stood above the mountains.

7. At thy rebuke they fled; at the voice of thy thunder they hasted away.

8. They go up by the mountains; they go down by the valleys unto the place which thou hast founded for them.

9. Thou hast set a bound that they may not pass over; that they turn not again to cover the earth.

10. He sendeth the springs into the valleys, which run among the hills.

11. They give drink to every beast of the field: the wild asses quench their thirst.

12. By them shall the fowls of the heaven have their habitation, which sing among the branches.

13. He watereth the hills from his chambers: the earth is satisfied with the fruit of thy works.

14. He causeth the grass to grow for the cattle, and herb for the service of man: that he may bring forth food out of the earth;

15. And wine that maketh glad the heart of man, and oil to make his face to shine, and bread which strengtheneth man's heart.

16. The trees of the Lord are full of sap; the cedars of Lebanon, which he hath planted;

17. Where the birds make their nests: as for the stork, the fir trees are her house.

18. The high hills are a refuge for the wild goats; and the rocks for the conies.

19. He appointed the moon for seasons: the sun knoweth his going down.

20. Thou makest darkness, and it is night: wherein all the beasts of the forest do creep forth.

21. The young lions roar after their prey, and seek their meat from God.

22. The sun ariseth, they gather themselves together, and lay them down in their dens.

23. Man goeth forth unto his work and to his labour until the evening.

24. O Lord, how manifold are thy works! in wisdom hast thou made them all: the earth is full of thy riches.

25. So is this great and wide sea, wherein are things creeping innumerable, both small and great beasts.

26. There go the ships: there is that leviathan, whom thou hast made to play therein.

27. These wait all upon thee; that thou mayest give them their meat in due season.

28. That thou givest them they gather: thou openest thine hand, they are filled with good.

29. Thou hidest thy face, they are troubled: thou takest away their breath, they die, and return to their dust.

30. Thou sendest forth thy spirit, they are created: and thou renewest the face of the earth.

31. The glory of the Lord shall endure for ever: the Lord shall rejoice in his works.

32. He looketh on the earth, and it trembleth: he toucheth the hills, and they smoke.

33. I will sing unto the Lord as long as I live: I will sing praise to my God while I have my being.

34. My meditation of him shall be sweet: I will be glad in the Lord.

35. Let the sinners be consumed out of the earth, and let the wicked be no more. Bless thou the Lord, O my soul. Praise ye the Lord.

Psalm 137

1. By the rivers of Babylon,[1] there we sat down, yea, we wept, when we remembered Zion.

2. We hanged our harps upon the willows in the midst thereof.

3. For there they that carried us away captive required of us a song; and they that wasted us required of us mirth, saying, Sing us one of the songs of Zion.

4. How shall we sing the Lord's song in a strange land?

5. If I forget thee, O Jerusalem, let my right hand forget her cunning.

6. If I do not remember thee, let my tongue cleave to the roof of my mouth; if I prefer not Jerusalem above my chief joy.

7. Remember, O Lord, the children of Edom[2] in the day of Jerusalem; who said, Rase it, rase it, even to the foundation thereof.

8. O daughter of Babylon, who art to be destroyed; happy shall he be, that rewardeth thee as thou hast served us.

9. Happy shall he be, that taketh and dasheth thy little ones against the stones.

1. On the Euphrates River. Jerusalem was captured and sacked by the Babylonians in 586 B.C.E. The Hebrews were taken away into cap-

tivity in Babylon.
2. The Edomites helped the Babylonians capture Jerusalem.

HOMER

eighth century B.C.E.

The *Iliad* and the *Odyssey* tell the story of the clash of two great civilizations, and the effects of war on both the winners and the losers. Both poems are about the Trojan War, a mythical conflict between a coalition of Greeks and the inhabitants of Troy, a city in Asia Minor. These are the earliest works of Greek literature, composed almost three thousand years before our time. Yet they are rich and sophisticated in their narrative techniques, and they provide extraordinarily vivid portrayals of people, social relationships, and feelings, especially our incompatible desires for honor and violence, and for peace and a home.

HISTORICAL CONTEXTS

The earliest Greek-speaking people were the Myceneans, whose culture probably inspired the Trojan legends. About 2000 B.C.E., they began building big, fortified cities around central palaces in the south of Greece. The Myceneans had a form of writing now known as "Linear B"—not an alphabet but a "syllabary" (in which a symbol corresponds to each syllable, not to each letter)—as well as a centralized, tightly controlled economy and sophisticated artistic and architectural traditions. The metal they used for weapons, armor, and tools was predominantly bronze, and their time is therefore known as the Bronze Age.

After dominating the region for about six hundred years, Mycenean civilization came to an end around 1200 B.C.E. Archaeological investigations suggest that the great cities were burnt or destroyed at this time, perhaps by invasion or war. The next few hundred years are known as the Dark Ages of Greece: people seem to have been less wealthy, and the cultural knowledge of the Myceneans, including the knowledge of writing, was lost.

Greeks of this time spoke many different dialects and lived in small towns and villages scattered across a wide area. They did not regain their knowledge of reading or writing until an alphabet, invented by a trading people called the Phoenicians, was adopted in the eighth century B.C.E.

One might think that an illiterate society could have nothing like "literature," a word based on the Latin for "letters" (*litterae*). In the centuries of Greek illiteracy, however, there developed a thriving tradition of oral poetry, especially on the Ionian coast, in modern-day Turkey. Travelling bards told tales of the lost age of heroes who fought with bronze, and of the great cities besieged and destroyed by war. The Homeric poems make use of folk memories of a real conflict or conflicts between the Mycenean Greeks and inhabitants of one or more cities in Asia Minor. The world of Homer is neither historical in a modern sense nor purely fictional. Through poetry, the Greeks of the Dark Ages created and preserved their own past.

Oral poets in ancient Greece used a traditional form (a six-beat line called hexameter), fitting their own riffs into the rhythm, with musical accompaniment. They also relied on common themes, traditional stories, traditional characters, traditional descriptors (such as "swift Achilles" or "black ships"), phrases that fit the rhythm of the line, and even whole scenes that follow a set pattern, such as the way a warrior gets dressed or the way that meals are prepared. Fluent poetic ad-libbing is very difficult; these techniques gave each performer a structure, so that stories and lines did not have to be generated entirely on the spot. We know that the tradition of this type of composition must have gone back hundreds of years, because the *Iliad* and the *Odyssey* include details that would have been anachronistic by the time these poems were written down, such as the use of bronze weapons: by the eighth century, soldiers fought with iron. Details from different periods are jumbled together, so that even in the eighth century B.C.E. the heroic, mythic world of the Homeric poems must have seemed quite distant from everyday reality. In addition, the poems mix different Greek dialects, the speech of many different areas in the Greek-speaking world, into a language unlike anything anyone ever actually spoke.

There is an ancient tradition that the *Iliad* and the *Odyssey* were both composed by a blind, illiterate singer from the island of Chios, named Homer. But many scholars—in antiquity and today—have suspected that this story is more legend than fact, and it is quite possible that there was no such person as "Homer."

It is hard to understand the relation between the heroic poetry composed and sung by illiterate bards in archaic Greece, and the written texts of the *Odyssey* and the *Iliad*. The question is made all the more difficult because the poems are far longer than most instances of oral poetic performance, including that of the oral poets living in the former Yugoslavia, who were studied by classicists in the twentieth century as the closest living analogy to ancient Greek bards. Good bards may be able to keep going for an hour or two: in the Homeric poems themselves, there are accounts of singers performing for a while after dinner. But a complete performance of either of these poems would have lasted at least twenty hours. This is much too long for an audience to sit through in an evening. It would also have been difficult for any poet, even a genius, to compose at this length without the use of writing. Perhaps, then, these poems are the work of an oral poet, or poets, who became literate. Or perhaps they represent a collaboration between one or more oral poets, and a scribe. In any case, soon after the Greeks developed their alphabet, they found a way to preserve their oral tradition in two monumental written poems.

These works make use of tradition in strikingly original ways, creating just two coherent stories out of the mass of legends that surrounded the Trojan War. They are long poems about heroes, a genre that later came to be called *epic*—from the Greek for "story" or "word." Throughout the ancient world, for hundreds of years to come, everybody knew the *Iliad* and the *Odyssey*. The poems were performed aloud, illustrated in paintings on vases or on walls, read, learned by heart, remembered, reworked, and imitated by everyone in the Greek and Roman worlds, from the Athenian tragedians to the Roman poet **Virgil**.

THE *ILIAD*

The title *Iliad* suggests a work about the Trojan War, since *Ilias* is another name for Troy. Greek readers or listeners would have been familiar with the background myths. Paris, a prince of Troy, son of King Priam, had to judge which of three goddesses should be awarded a golden apple: Athena, goddess of wisdom; Hera, the queen of the gods and thus a representative of power; or Aphrodite, goddess of sexual desire. He chose Aphrodite, and as his reward she gave him the most beautiful woman in the world, Helen of Sparta, to be his wife. Unfortunately, Helen already had a husband: Menelaos (or Menelaus in the Latin spelling), king of Sparta and brother of the powerful general Agamemnon. When Paris took Helen with him back to Troy from Mycenae, Agamemnon and Menelaos mustered a great army, a coalition drawn from many Greek cities, including the great heroes Achilles, the fastest runner and best fighter, and Odysseus, the cleverest of the Greeks. So began a war that lasted ten years, until Odysseus finally devised a stratagem to enter the city walls of Troy. He built a wooden horse, filled it with Greek warriors, and tricked the Trojans into taking the horse into the city. After nightfall, the Greek soldiers leaped from the horse and killed the male inhabitants, captured the women, and razed the city to the ground.

Surprisingly, none of these events play any part in the main narrative of the *Iliad*, which begins when the war is already in its tenth year and ends before the capture of the city. Moreover, the central focus is not on the conflict between Greeks and Trojans, but on a conflict among the Greek commanders. The first word of the *Iliad* is "Wrath," and the wrath of Achilles—first against his comrade Agamemnon, and only later against the enemy Trojans—is the central subject of the poem. In Greek, the word used is *menis*, a term otherwise applied only to the wrath of the gods. Achilles' rage is an extraordinary thing, which sets him apart from the rest of humanity—Greeks and Trojans. The poem tells how Achilles, the greatest Greek hero and the son of a goddess, becomes alienated from his society, how his anger against the Greeks shifts into an inhuman aggression against the Trojans, and how he is at last willing to return to the human world.

The *Iliad* is about war, honor, and aggression. There are moments of graphic violence, when we are told exactly where the point of a spear or sword penetrates vulnerable human flesh: as when Achilles' friend Patroclus throws his spear at another warrior, Sarpedon, and catches him "where the lungs close in around the beating heart"; or when Hector rams his spear into Patroclus, "into his lower flank, and drove the bronze point through"; or when Achilles' spear "went utterly through the soft neck" of Hector but "did not sever the windpipe." The precise anatomical detail reminds us how vulnerable these warriors are, because they have mortal bodies—in contrast to the gods, who may participate in battle but can never die.

The plot deals with the exchange or ransoming of human bodies. Achilles' anger at Agamemnon is roused by a quarrel about who owns Briseïs, a young woman Achilles has seized as a prize of war but whom Agamemnon takes as recompense for the loss of his own captive woman, Chryseïs. The story also hinges on the ownership of dead male bodies: the corpses, in turn, of Sarpedon, Patroclus, and Hector. War seems to produce its own kind of economy, a system of exchange: a live woman for a dead warrior, one life for another, or death for undying fame.

The *Iliad* is a violent poem, and, on one level, the violence simply contributes to the entertainment: it is exciting to hear or read about slaughter. But it would be a mistake to see the *Iliad* as pure military propaganda. At times, the poem brings out the terrible pity of war: the city of Troy will be ruined, the people killed or enslaved, and the poet looks back with regret to "the days of peace, before the Greeks came." Some similes compare the violence on the battlefield to the events of the world of peace, where people can plow their fields, build their homes, and watch their sheep. But these similes may suggest that violence and the threat of pain and death are facts of life: even when people are at peace, there is murder, and lions or wolves leap into the fold to kill the sheep.

Within the narrow world of the battlefield, Homer's vividly imagined characters have choices to make. They cannot choose, like gods, to avoid death; but they can choose how they will die. The poem itself acknowledges that the exchange of honor for death may seem inadequate. After Agamemnon has treated him dishonorably,

Achilles begins to question the whole heroic code and its system of trading death for glory: "For not worth my life is all they say I lion used to possess," he declares, since prizes of honor can always be replaced but "the life of a man does not come back." Unlike the other fighters, Achilles knows for sure—thanks to the goddess Thetis, his mother—that remaining at Troy will mean his death. But all the warriors of the *Iliad* are conscious that in fighting they risk their own deaths. Achilles' choices—to fight and die soon, in this war, or go home and live a little longer—are therefore a starker version of the decision faced by all who fight.

Fascinatingly, the *Iliad* makes the Trojans as fully human as the Greeks. The Trojan hero, Hector, seems to many readers the most likeable character in the poem, fighting not for vengeance but to protect his wife and their infant son. One of the most touching moments comes as Hector says goodbye to his tearful wife before going into battle; a deep tenderness connects Hector and his family—in contrast to the more shallow associations of the Greeks with their female prisoners of war. As Hector reaches

Achilles (left) slays Hector. From a red-figured volute-krater (a large ceramic wine decanter), ca. 500–480 B.C.E.

down to kiss his son, the child screams, frightened at seeing his father in his helmet. The parents laugh together, and Hector takes off the helmet so the baby will not be scared as he swings him in his arms. The moment is both heartwarming and chilling, since we know—and his wife knows—that this devoted father will never see his son again; the baby is right to be frightened, since he will soon be hurled headlong from the city walls by the victorious Greeks.

The *Iliad* culminates in an astonishing encounter, between Priam, king of Troy, and Achilles, who has killed his son Hector. Priam goes to plead with Achilles to return his son's body, and the two enemies end up sitting together, each weeping for those they have lost. The experience of grief is common to all humans, even those who kill each other in war. The major contrast drawn by the *Iliad* is not between Greek and Trojan, but between the humans and the immortal gods. The gods play an important role in the action of the poem, sometimes intervening to cause or prevent a hero's death or dishonor. We are told at the beginning that there is a connection between all the deaths caused by Achilles' wrath and the will of Zeus: the whole action of the poem happened as "the will of Zeus was accomplished." But the presence of the gods does not turn the human characters into puppets, controlled only by the gods or by fate. Human characters are never forced by gods to act out of character. Rather, human action and divine action work together, and the gods provide a way of talking about the elements of human experience that are otherwise incomprehensible.

Moreover, the presence of the gods—like the similes—makes us particularly aware of what is distinctive about human life in war. In the world

of the gods, there are conflicts about hierarchy, just as there are on earth: sometimes the lesser gods refuse to recognize the authority of Zeus, just as some Greek chieftains sometimes refuse to bow to Agamemnon. But on Olympus, all quarrels end in laughter and drinking, not death. The most important fact about all the warriors in the *Iliad* is that they die. Moreover, before death humans have to face grief, dishonor, loss, and pain—experiences that play little or no part in any god's life. Achilles in his wrath refuses to accept the horror of loss: loss of honor, and the loss of his dearest friend, Patroclus. His anger can end, and he can eat again, only when his heart becomes "enduring," and he realizes that all humans, even the greatest warriors, have to endure unendurable loss and keep on living. The *Iliad* provides a bleak but inspiring account of human suffering as a kind of power that the gods themselves cannot achieve.

THE *ODYSSEY*

The *Odyssey*, which is included in its entirety in this anthology, has a special place in the study of world literature, since it deals explicitly with the relationship between the people we know and those who are strange to us. It is about a journey that spans most of the world as it was known to Greeks at the time, and deals with issues that any student of world literature must confront, including the place of literature and memory in the formation of cultural identity. The poem shows us, in depth and in detail, the complex relationships between one Westerner, a Greek man, and the other cultures that he encounters—not in war, but in the course of a long journey, where the worst enemies may be found inside his own household. The poem tells the story of Odysseus's homecoming from Troy, tracing his reclamation of a household from which he has been absent for the past twenty years. It is a gripping and varied tale, which includes fantasy and magic but also focuses on domestic details and on the human need for a family and a home.

The *Odyssey* is set after the *Iliad*, and was probably produced a little later, since it seems deliberately to avoid repeating anything that had been included in the *Iliad*, and fills in many important details that had been absent from the other poem—including allusions to the actual fall of Troy, and its aftermath. The *Odyssey* creates a different but complementary vision of the Trojan War, showing how the Greeks faced further danger in the long voyage back to Greece, and in their return to homes from which they had been absent for many years.

In the Greek original, the first word of the *Odyssey*—our first clue to the poem's subject—is *andra* ("a man"). One man, Odysseus himself, is the center of the poem, in a way that no single hero, not even Achilles, is the center of the *Iliad*. The journey from war to peace requires different skills from those needed on the battlefield, and through the figure of Odysseus the poem shows us what those skills might be. He has strength and physical courage, but he also has brains: the "clear rascal" is the smartest of those who fought at Troy. He is famously adaptable, a "man who can adapt to anything," able to deal with any eventuality, no matter how difficult or unexpected. He has psychological strength, an ability both to endure and to inflict pain without flinching; more than once, the poem connects the name *Odysseus* with the Greek word for "to be angry" or "hate" (*odyssomai*): Odysseus is the man hated by the god Poseidon. He has the patience and self-restraint required to bide his time until the moment comes for him to reveal himself to his household. Most of all, he has the will to go home, and to restore his home to its proper order. It is no accident that Odysseus's favorite weapon is not the sword or the spear but the bow, which shoots from a distance at the target of his choosing.

"Man" is also the subject of the *Odyssey* in a broader sense, because the poem has a particular interest in the diversity of cultures and ways of life. The *Iliad* is set almost exclusively on the battlefield of Troy, and is focused on the relationships among the aristocratic male warriors. By contrast, the *Odyssey* shows us a multitude of distinct worlds and cultures, including nonhuman cultures. Odysseus spends years on the luxurious island of the nymph Calypso; he encounters the sweetly singing Sirens, the monster Scylla, and the Lotus-eaters; and he disembarks on the island of the sun, with its tempting, delicious cattle, and of the witch Circe, who can turn men to pigs. He is almost killed on the island of the shepherd-giants, the Cyclopes, and he is welcomed in the magical land of Phaeacia, where fruits ripen all season long, and where he meets the king, the queen, and the princess, Nausicaa, who is out to do laundry and play ball with her girlfriends, while daydreaming about her future husband. The many cultures of the poem include both the exotic and the ordinary.

Even in the Greek world, we are given glimpses of several distinct ways of life. The rich land of Sparta, ruled by Menelaus (or Menelaos) and his retrieved wife, the beautiful, sophisticated Helen, with her elaborate embroidery and her narcotics, contrasts with the poor island of Ithaca, Odysseus's homeland, which is too stony to raise horses or plentiful crops. In Ithaca, we see the lives of women as well as men; of old Laertes, Odysseus's father, as well as his insecure young son, Telemachus; and of the poor as well as the rich—including the old nurse who washes Odysseus and the pig-keeper, Eumaeus, who gives him shelter. In showing multiple encounters between the Greek hero and people who are very different from him, the Homeric poem invites us to think about how we ought to behave toward people who are not the same as ourselves.

The *Odyssey* is particularly concerned with the laws of hospitality, which in Greek is *xenia*—a word that covers the whole relationship between guests and hosts, and between strangers and those who take them in. Hospitality is the fundamental criterion for civilized society in this poem. Cultures may vary in other respects, but any good society will accommodate the wanderer as a guest. Odysseus encounters many strange peoples in the course of his journey. Some, like the goddess Calypso, are almost too welcoming: she invites him into her home and her bed, and keeps him there even when he longs to go home. Odysseus acknowledges that Calypso is far more beautiful than his own wife and that her island is more lush than his own stony homeland; but, movingly, he still wants to go back. This poem deals with the fundamental desire we feel for our own people and our own place, not because they are better than any other, but simply because they are ours. Similarly, Odysseus rejects the possibility of starting his life over in the hospitable land of the Phaeacians. The monstrous one-eyed Cyclops, Polyphemus, is a grotesque counterpart to the good Phaeacian hosts: instead of welcoming and feeding his guests, the Cyclops wants to eat them for dinner. This encounter is a reminder of how

distinctive, and sometimes unheroic, are the skills Odysseus needs to survive the journey home. Heroes in battle, in the *Iliad*, are always concerned that their names be remembered in times to come. But Odysseus defeats Polyphemus—whose name suggests "Much-named"—by denying his own name, calling himself "Noman." The journey home has to trump even Odysseus's heroic identity.

At times, Odysseus's own men transgress the norms of hospitality, as when they kill the cattle of the Sun, which they have been expressly forbidden to touch. We see further variations on the theme of hospitality in the visits that Odysseus's son, Telemachus, pays to his father's friends. The account in the first four books of Telemachus' activities—short journeys to visit uncles, cousins, and kinsmen in the surrounding neighborhood— may seem oddly inconsequential, and even unheroic. But a great deal of the *Odyssey*'s attraction lies in the way it values the little details of human relationships and human feelings over grand tales of honor and killing in war.

Hospitality is tested most severely when Odysseus arrives as a stranger back in his own home. The suitors have seized control of his house and are abusing his unwitting hospitality, in his absence, by courting his wife, devouring his food and drink, and ruining his property. There are repeated references in the *Odyssey* to the nightmare double of Odysseus's return: the homecoming of Agamemnon, who came back from Troy only to be killed in his bath by his wife, Clytemnestra, and her lover, Aegisthus. Zeus, the king of the gods, insists at the beginning of the poem that Aegisthus is hated by the gods, and he praises Agamemnon's son, Orestes, who avenges his father's death by killing the adulterous murderer.

First-time readers may be surprised that the wanderings of Odysseus, across the sea from Troy back to his stony Greek homeland, Ithaca, occupy only a short part of the whole poem. In the second half of the poem, beginning at book 13, Odysseus is back home in Ithaca. But his journey is only half complete. He arrives home as a stranger, disguised as a poor beggar. The act of homecoming seems to require several stages, beyond merely reaching a geographic location. Odysseus comes up with multiple tales to explain his presence in Ithaca; he uses his many disguises to test the loyalty of those he meets—and, as in the encounter with Polyphemus, he must show enormous self-control in his willingness to suppress his identity, at least temporarily. Throughout the poem, Odysseus has a particularly close affinity with poets and storytellers; he himself narrates his wanderings to the Phaeacians, and, once back on Ithaca, he tells a series of false stories about who he is and where he comes from. Controlling and multiplying stories is one of the most important ways in which Odysseus is a person who can "always find solutions"; he is able to see the multiplicity of the world and constantly to redefine his own place in it.

In the course of his homecoming, Odysseus passes a series of tests, and creates more tests of his own. He must show his mastery of weapons (such as the strong-bow) and his knowledge of the people who make up his household. Odysseus has to win the peace by reconnecting with each loyal member of his home: his servants, his son, his father, and—most memorably—his wife, Penelope. He tests her loyalty by refusing to reveal himself to her right away. But she shows herself a perfect match for her trickster husband, putting him to yet another test. When it is bedtime, she asks the servant to bring out the bed—the bed that, as only Odysseus himself could know, is formed from a tree growing right through the house; if Odysseus were an imposter, he would think the bed could be moved. The immovable bed is, of course, an image for the permanence of Penelope and Odysseus's marriage. When they talk in the bed that night after sex, a simile suggests that now, at last, both Odysseus and Penelope have come home; he, weeping, and she, clinging to him, are like sailors saved from drowning, "Grateful to be alive, they crawl to land." The image first seems to apply to Odysseus, and then to Penelope—a shift that suggests the dynamic intimacy between husband and wife.

The *Odyssey* has elements we associate with many other types of literature: romance, folklore, heroism, mystery, travelers' tales, magic, military exploits, and family drama. It is a text that can be enjoyed on any number of levels: as a feminized version of epic—a heroic story focused not on men fighting wars, but a journey home; as a love story; as a fantasy about fathers, sons, and patriarchy; as an account of Greek identity; as a work of primitive anthropology; as a meditation on cultural difference; as a morality tale; or as a pilgrim's progress. As the first word indicates, this is a poem about humanity. An extraordinarily rich work, as multilayered and intelligent as its hero, the *Odyssey* is enjoyable on first reading, and worth rereading over and over again.

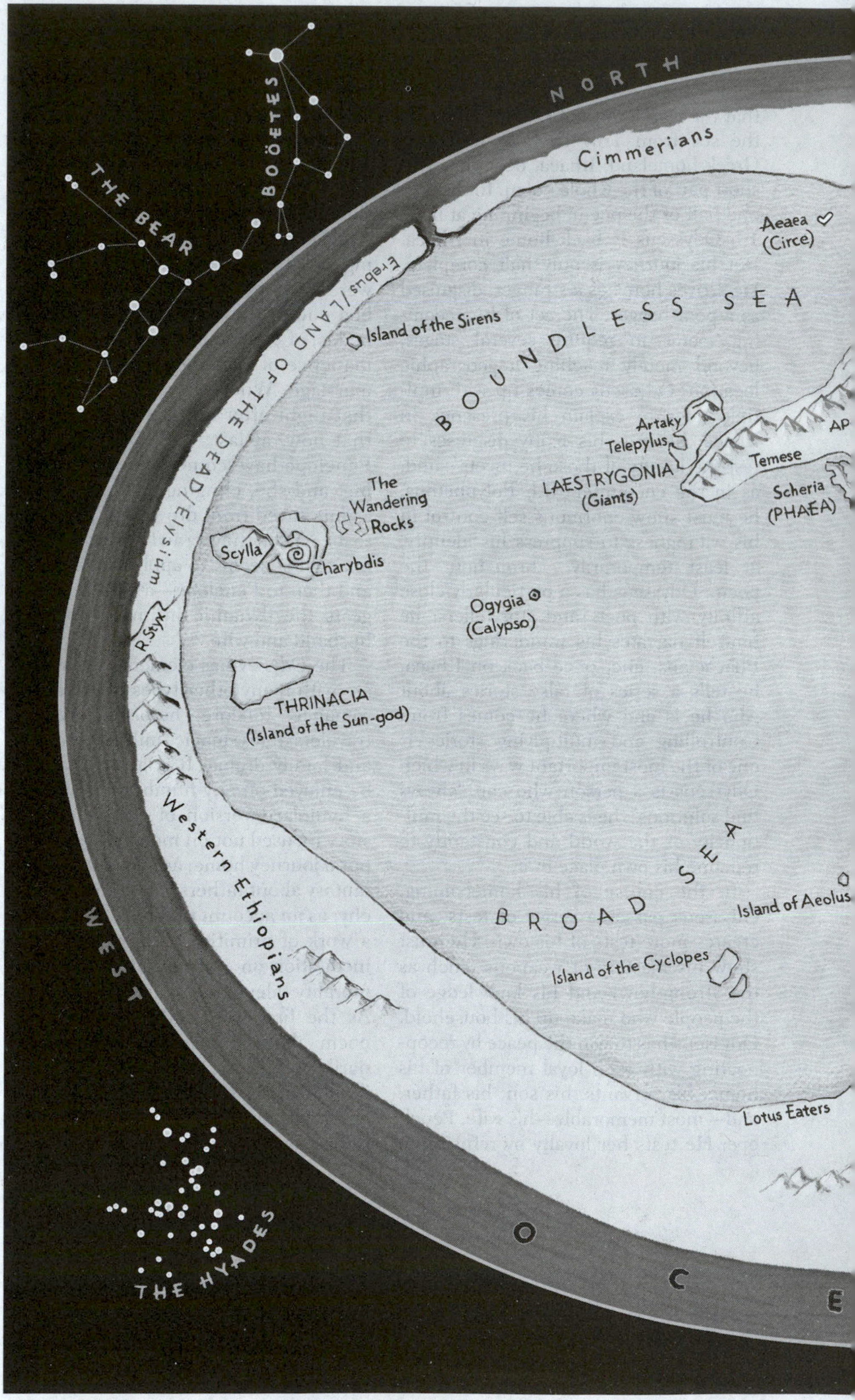
NORTH
BOÖETES
THE BEAR
Cimmerians
Aeaea
(Circe)
BOUNDLESS SEA
Erebus/LAND OF THE DEAD/Elysium
Island of the Sirens
Artaky
Telepylus
LAESTRYGONIA
(Giants)
Temese
Scheria
The
Wandering
Rocks
Scylla
Charybdis
Ogygia
(Calypso)
R. Styx
THRINACIA
(Island of the Sun-god)
Western Ethiopians
BROAD SEA
Island of Aeolus
Island of the Cyclopes
WEST
Lotus Eaters
THE HYADES
O C E

The
World
of
The
Odyssey

THE PLEIADES

EOS/THE DAWN

E A S T

Abii

Phasis

Eastern Ethiopians

Mt
Olympus

T H R A C E

Cicones

PHRYGIA

Solymi

Mt Ossa

Lemnos

•Troy

Mt Pelion

Gyrae

ulichium

Chios

Same

Asteris

Mycenae
Sparta
Pylos

Psyria

P H O E N I C I A

aca

Ortygia

Cyprus

Zacynthus

Cape Malea

Sidon•

Cythera

Crete

G R E A T   S E A

Pharos

Erembi

R. Nile/Aegyptus

E
G
Y
P
T

Thebes•

L I B Y A

Pygmies

ORION

A

N

SOUTH

THE DOG

Crete

R. Jardan

[Cydonians]

Knossos Amnisus
[Pelasgians]
Gortyn
Phaestus

Dia

KILOMETERS 50 100
MILES 30 60

T H R A C E

Cicones
Ismarus

Samothrace

Hellespont

Lemnos
[Sintians]

Tenedos

Troy/Ilium

Mt
Olympus

Lesbos

Pergamum

R. Hermu

R. Maces

Scyros

Cape
Mimas

Smyrna

Psara

Euboea

Chios

Ephesus

Athens

Samos

R. Me

Miletus

Argos

Delos

Halica

Cape
Geraestus

?Dia (Naxos)

Sparta

Rhod

The
AEGEAN
and
ASIA MINOR

Crete

(M E D I T E R

KILOMETERS 0 50 100 200
MILES 0 30 60 120

(B L A C K   S E A)

Sinope

[Amazons]

R. Lycus

P H R Y G I A

R. Halys

R. Sangarius

Kanesh

Hittites

Salt Lake

R. Pyramus

R. Sarus

TAURUS MTS

Tarsus

R. Calycadnus

Aleppo

[Solymi]

LYCIA

SOLYMA MTS

P
H
O
E
N
I
C
I
A

Cyprus

Paphos

Damascus

Sidon

N E A N   S E A)

R. Apsus

MAC

IONIAN (

EPIRUS

R. Thyamis

(Corcyra/Corfu)

[Pelasgians]

Dodona •

THESPROTIA

R. Pe

Ephyra •

R. Acheron

R. Arachthus

IONIAN SEA)

R. Achelous

Nericus

AETO

Dulichium
(Leukas)

Taphos
Taphian
Islands

Ithaca

Needle
(Echinades)
Islands

Mt Neriton

Chalcis

CEPHALLENIA

Same

Zacynthus

PELC

MAINLAND GREECE

KILOMETERS
0   50   100

MILES
0   30   60

THRACE

R. Axius

NIA

R. Haliacmon

PIERIA

Mt
mpus

HESSALY

Larissa

MAGNESIA

Mt Ossa

Pherae   Iolcos

Mt Pelion

Phylace

Myrmidons]
PHTHIA

Lemnos

(A E G E A N   S E A)

Scyros

DORIS

Aegae

E U B O E A

Mt Parnassus
Panopeus

tho/Delphi   Orchomenus Lake
Copais   Thebes

Aulis

Euboea

BOEOTIA

ulf of Corinth)

A T T I C A

Athens

NNESE

Dulichium
(Leukas)

Taphos

Taphian
Islands

Rithron Cove
Mt Neriton
Ithaca Needle
(Echinades)
Islands

CEPHALLENIA

Same

(I O N I A N   S E A)

Zacynthus

A C H A E A

Epians

Elis
R. Peneus

Mt Erymanthus

ELIS

A R C A D I A

Phaea

Olympia

R. Alpheus

[Cauconians]

MESSENIA

Messene

Pherae

Pylos

The
PELOPONNESE

KILOMETERS   0   50   100
MILES   0   30   60

EUBOEA

Mt Parnassus
Pytho/Delphi
Lake Copais
Euboea
Aulis
Thebes
[Cadmians]
peresia (Aegira)
Marathon
Eleusis
Megara
Athens
ATTICA
Salamis
Cyllene
Corinth
Mycenae
ARGO
Epidaurus
Argos
Cape Geraestus
Cape Sounion
(MIRTOAN SEA)
ACEDAEMON
parta
US MTS
Cape Malea
Cythera

From THE ILIAD[1]

BOOK I

[The Wrath of Achilles]

Wrath—sing, goddess,[2] of the ruinous wrath of Peleus' son Achilles
that inflicted woes without number upon the Achaeans,
hurled forth to Hades many strong souls of warriors
and rendered their bodies prey for the dogs,
for all birds, and the will of Zeus was accomplished;   5
sing from when they two first stood in conflict—
Atreus' son, lord of men, and godlike Achilles.
      Which of the gods, then, set these two together in conflict, to fight?
Apollo, son of Leto and Zeus; who in his rage at the king
raised a virulent plague through the army; the men were dying   10
because the son of Atreus dishonored the priest Chryses.[3]
For he came to the Achaeans' swift ships
bearing countless gifts to ransom his daughter,
holding in his hands on a golden staff the wreaths of Apollo
who strikes from afar, and beseeched all the Achaeans—   15
but mostly the two sons of Atreus, marshalers of men:
      "Sons of Atreus and you other strong-greaved Achaeans,
may the gods who have homes on Olympus grant you
to plunder the city of Priam,[4] and reach your home safely;
release to me my beloved daughter, take instead the ransom,   20
revering Zeus' son who strikes from afar—Apollo."
      Then the rest of the Achaeans all shouted assent,
to respect the priest and accept the splendid ransom;
but this did not please the heart of Atreus' son Agamemnon,
and violently he sent him away and laid a powerful warning upon him: 25
"Let me not find you, old man, near our hollow ships,
either loitering now or coming again later,
lest the god's staff and wreath not protect you.
The girl I will not release; sooner will old age come upon her
in our house, in Argos,[5] far from her homeland,   30
pacing back and forth by the loom and sharing my bed.
So go, do not make me angry, and you will return the safer."
      Thus he spoke; and the old man was afraid and obeyed his word,
and he went in silence along the shore of the tumultuous sea.
And going aside, the old man fervently prayed   35
to lord Apollo, whom lovely-haired Leto bore:
"Hear me, God of the silver bow, you who stand over Chryse
and Killa most holy, you whose might rules Tenedos,[6]

---

1. Translated by Caroline Alexander.
2. Calliope, the muse who inspires epic poetry.
3. Chryses is from the town of Chryse near Troy. The Greeks had captured his daughter when they sacked Thebes (see below) and had given her to Agamemnon as his share of the booty.
4. Troy; Priam is its king. Olympus is the mountain in northern Greece that was supposed to be the home of the gods.
5. Agamemnon's home in the northeastern Peloponnesus, the southern part of mainland Greece.
6. An island off the Trojan coast. Like Chryse, Killa is a town near Troy.

God of Plague;[7] if ever I roofed over a temple that pleased you,
or if ever I burned as sacrifice to you the fatty thighbones   40
of bulls and of goats[8]—grant me this wish:
May the Danaans[9] pay for my tears with your arrows."

    Thus he prayed, and Phoebus Apollo heard him,
and set out from the heights of Olympus, rage in his heart,
with his bow on his shoulders and his hooded quiver;   45
the arrows clattered on his shoulders as he raged,
as the god himself moved; and he came like the night.
Then far from the ships he crouched, and let loose an arrow—
and terrible was the ring of his silver bow.
First he went after the mules and sleek dogs,   50
but then, letting fly a sharp arrow, he struck at the men themselves,
and the crowded pyres of the dead burned without ceasing.

    Nine days the shafts of the god flew through the army,
and on the tenth Achilles summoned the people to assembly;
the goddess of the white arms, Hera,[1] put this in his mind,   55
for she was distressed for the Danaans, since she saw them dying.
And when they were gathered together and assembled,
Achilles of the swift feet stood and addressed them:
"Son of Atreus, I now think that, staggering back,
we shall go home again—if we escape death that is—   60
if after all war and plague alike are to rout the Achaeans;
but come—let us ask some seer, or priest,
or even an interpreter of dreams, for a dream, too, is from Zeus,
who may tell us why Phoebus Apollo is so greatly angered,
if perhaps he faults our vows and sacrifice,   65
and whether receiving the burnt fat of sheep, of goats without blemish,
he may somehow be willing to avert our destruction."

    Thus Achilles spoke and sat down. Then stood among them
Calchas the son of Thestor, far the most eminent of bird-seers,
who knew things that are, and things to come, and what had gone
    before,   70
and had guided the ships of the Achaeans to Troy,
through his divination, which Phoebus Apollo gave him.
He in his wisdom spoke and addressed them:
"O Achilles, dear to Zeus, you bid me state the reason
for the wrath of Apollo, the lord who strikes from afar.   75
Then I will speak, but you listen closely and swear an oath to me
that in good earnest you will stand by me in word and strength of hand;
for I well know that I will anger a man who
has great power over the Argives, and whom the Achaeans obey.
For a king has the upper hand when he is angered with a
    base-born man;   80
if he does swallow his anger for that day,
yet he also holds resentment for later, until he brings it to fulfillment,
within his breast. You now declare whether you will protect me."

7. Apollo.
8. In sacrifice to Apollo.
9. The Greeks. Homer also calls them Achaeans and Argives.
1. Sister and wife of Zeus; she was hostile to
the Trojans and therefore favored the Greeks.

Then answering him Achilles of the swift feet spoke:
"Take courage, and speak freely of any omen you know;   85
for by Apollo beloved of Zeus, to whom you, Calchas,
pray when you reveal the gods' omens to the Danaans,
no man while I live and see light upon this earth
will lay heavy hands upon you by the hollow ships—
none of all the Danaans, not even if you speak of Agamemnon,   90
who now makes claim to be far the best man in the army."
    And then the blameless priest took courage and spoke:
"It is not with prayer, nor with sacrifice that he finds fault,
but for the sake of his priest, whom Agamemnon dishonored,
and did not release his daughter, and did not accept the ransom—   95
for that reason the god who shoots from afar has sent these sufferings,
   and will send yet more;
nor will he drive this foul plague away from the Danaans
until we give back the dark-eyed girl to her dear father
without price, without ransom, and lead a holy sacrifice
to Chryse; propitiating him in this way we might persuade him."   100
    Thus speaking he sat down; and then rose among them
the warrior son of Atreus, wide-ruling Agamemnon,
greatly distressed, his darkening heart consumed with rage,
his eyes like gleaming fires.
Glaring, he first addressed Calchas: 105
    "Prophet of evil, never yet have you spoken anything good for me,
always to prophesy evil is dear to your heart.
You have never spoken nor yet accomplished any good word;
and now you speak in assembly of the Danaans, declaiming god's will—
that for this reason, you say, the Archer who shoots from afar causes their
   affliction—   110
because I was not willing to accept his splendid ransom
for the girl Chryseïs,[2] since I greatly desire to have her
at home; for I prefer her to Clytemnestra,
my wedded wife, as she is not inferior to her,
not in figure or bearing, nor even in disposition or handiwork.   115
Yet, even so, I am willing to give her back—if this is for the best.
I wish my men to be safe rather than perish.
But make ready another prize at once, so that I alone
of the Achaeans am not unrecompensed, since that is not fitting.
For all of you are witness that my own prize goes elsewhere."   120
    Then answered him swift-footed, godlike Achilles:
"Most honored son of Atreus, of all men most covetous of possessions,
how then can the great-hearted Achaeans give you a prize?
We do not know of any great common store laid up anywhere,
but those things we carried from the cities, these have been distributed— 125
and it is not fitting to go about gathering these things again from the men.
But no, relinquish the girl to the god now; we Achaeans
will pay you back three times, four times over, if ever Zeus
gives us the well-walled city of Troy to plunder."
    Then answering him spoke powerful Agamemnon: 130

2. Daughter of Chryses.

"Do not in this way, skilled though you be, godlike Achilles,
try to trick me, for you will not outwit nor persuade me.
Or do you intend—while you yourself have a prize—that I just sit here
without one—are you ordering me to give the girl back?
No, either the great-hearted Achaeans will give me a prize   135
suited to my wishes, of equal value—
or if they do not give one, then I myself will go and take
either your own prize, or that of Ajax, or I will
take and carry away the prize of Odysseus;[3] and whomever I visit will be
    made angry;
but we shall consider these things later.   140
For now, come, let us drag one of our dark ships to the bright salt sea,
and assemble in it suitable rowers, and place the sacrifice in it,
and take on the girl herself, Chryseïs of the lovely cheeks;
and let there be one man in command, some man of counsel,
either Ajax or Idomeneus,[4] or noble Odysseus,   145
or you, son of Peleus, most terrifying of all men,
you might reconcile to us Apollo who works from afar, and perform
    the sacrifice."
            Then looking at him from under his brows swift-footed Achilles
    spoke:
"O wrapped in shamelessness, cunning in spirit—
how can any man of the Achaeans obey your words with good heart,   150
to journey with you or join men in violent battle?
For it was not on account of Trojan warriors I came
to wage battle here, since to me they are blameless—
never yet have they driven off my cattle, or my horses,
nor ever in Phthia,[5] where the rich earth breeds warriors,   155
have they destroyed my harvest, since there is much between us,
both shadowy mountains and clashing sea.
But we followed you, O great shameless one, for your pleasure,
to win recompense for Menelaos[6] and for you, dog-face,
from the Trojans; none of this do you pause to consider or care for.   160
And now you boast you will personally take my prize from me,
for which I suffered much hardship, which the sons of the Achaeans
    gave me!
Never do I receive a prize equal to yours when the Achaeans
sack some well-settled city of the Trojans;
it is my hands that conduct the greater part of furious war,   165
yet when it comes to division of the spoils
yours is the far greater prize, and I bearing some small thing, yet also
    prized,
make my way to my ships, wearied with fighting.
Now I am going to Phthia, since it is far better
to go home with my curved ships, and I do not intend   170
to stay here dishonored, hauling up riches and wealth for you."

3. Ajax, son of Telamon, was the bravest of
the Greeks after Achilles; Odysseus the most
crafty of the Greeks.
4. King of Crete and a prominent leader on
the Greek side.

5. Achilles' home in northern Greece.
6. Agamemnon's brother. The aim of the
expedition against Troy was to recover his wife,
Helen, who had left with with Paris, a son of
Priam.

Then Agamemnon lord of men answered him:
"Run, then, if your spirit so moves you. Nor will I
beg you to stay here for my sake. Other men stand by me,
who will pay me honor, and especially all-devising Zeus.   175
You are most hateful to me of the kings cherished by Zeus;
always contention is dear to you, and fighting and battles.
If you are so very powerful, a god doubtless gave this to you.
Go home with your ships and your companions—
be lord of the Myrmidons;[7] of you I take no account,   180
nor do I care that you are angered. But I promise you this:
As Phoebus Apollo robs me of Chryseïs,
whom I will send away, on my ship, with my companions—
so I will take Briseïs[8] of the pretty cheeks,
yes, your prize, going myself to your hut, so that you will discern   185
how much I am your better and so another man will be loath
to speak as my equal, openly matching himself with me."

    So he spoke. And anguish descended upon the son of Peleus
and the heart in his rugged breast debated two ways,
whether he should draw the sharp sword by his side   190
and scatter the men and slay and despoil the son of Atreus,
or check his anger and restrain his spirit.
While he churned these things through his heart and mind,
as he was drawing from its sheath his great sword, Athena[9] came to him
down from heaven; for Hera the goddess with white arms dispatched her,   195
who in her heart loved and cared for both men alike.
She came up behind and grabbed the son of Peleus' tawny hair,
appearing to him alone, and none of the others saw her.
Thunderstruck, Achilles turned behind him and at once recognized
Pallas Athena; for her eyes gleamed terribly.   200
And addressing her, he spoke winged words:
"Why do you come again, daughter of Zeus who wields the aegis?
Is it to witness the outrage of Agamemnon, the son of Atreus?
But I state openly to you, and I think that it will be accomplished,
that by these insolent acts he will shortly lose his life."   205

    Then the gleaming-eyed goddess addressed him:
"From heaven I have come to stop your anger, if you will heed me;
Hera the white-armed goddess sent me forth,
who in her heart loves and cares for you both alike.
Come, leave off this contention, stay your hand on your sword,   210
but rather cut him with words, telling him how things will be.
For I will tell you this, and it will be accomplished;
someday you will have three times as many shining gifts
because of this outrage; restrain yourself and obey me."

    Then in reply Achilles of the swift feet addressed her: 215
"I must obey the word of you both, goddess,

---

7. The contingent led by Achilles.
8. A captive woman who had been awarded to Achilles.
9. A goddess, daughter of Zeus, and a patron of human ingenuity and resourcefulness, whether exemplified by handicrafts (such as carpentry or weaving) or cunning in dealing with others. One of her epithets is Pallas. Like Hera, she sided with the Greeks in the war.

enraged in spirit though I am; for so is it better.
If a man heeds the gods, then they also listen to him."
He spoke and checked his powerful hand on the silver sword hilt
and back into the sheath thrust the great sword, nor did he disobey   220
the word of Athena. Then she was gone to Olympus,
to the house of Zeus who wields the aegis and the company of the other
  gods.
      And the son of Peleus once more with menacing words
addressed Agamemnon, and he did not hold back his anger:
"Wine-besotted, you who have the eyes of a dog and the heart of a deer,   225
never do you have courage to gear up for battle with your people,
nor go on ambush with the best of the Achaeans;
to you that is as death.
Far better it is, all through the broad army of the Achaeans,
to seize the gifts of the man who speaks against you.   230
King who feeds upon your people, since you rule worthless men;
otherwise, son of Atreus, this now would be your last outrage.
But I say openly to you, and I swear a great oath to it—
yes, by this scepter,[1] that never again will put forth leaves and shoots
when once it has left behind its stump in the mountains,   235
nor will it flourish again, since the bronze axe has stripped it round,
leaf and bark; and now in turn the sons of the Achaeans
busy with justice carry it around in their hands, they who
safeguard the ordinances of Zeus—this will be my great oath:
someday a yearning for Achilles will come upon the sons of the
  Achaeans,   240
every man; then nothing will save you, for all your grief,
when at the hands of man-slaying Hector[2]
dying men fall in their multitude; and you will rip the heart within you,
raging that you paid no honor to the best of the Achaeans."
      Thus spoke the son of Peleus, and hurled the gold-studded   245
scepter to the ground, and sat down,
while the son of Atreus raged on the other side. Then between them rose
  Nestor,
the sweet-sounding, the clear speaker from Pylos,[3]
whose voice flowed from his tongue more sweetly than honey.
In his time two generations of mortal men had already   250
perished, those who were born and raised with him in days of old,
in sacred Pylos, and he was ruler among the third generation.
With kindly thoughts to both he advised and addressed them:
      "Oh look now, surely great trouble comes to the land of the
  Achaeans!
Surely Priam and the sons of Priam would be gladdened   255
and the rest of the Trojans greatly rejoiced in heart
if they were to learn you two were fighting over all this—
you who surpass the Danaans in counsel, who surpass them in fighting!

---

1. A wooden staff that symbolized authority.
It was handed by a herald to whichever leader
rose to speak in an assembly as a sign of his
authority to speak.

2. Son of Priam; he was the foremost warrior
among the Trojans.
3. A territory on the western shore of the
Peloponnesus.

But hearken; you are both younger than me.
For once upon a time I banded with better   260
men even than you, and never did they slight me.
Never yet have I seen, nor shall see such men—
Peirithoös and Dryas, shepherd of his people,
and Kaineus and Exadios and Polyphemos like a god.[4]   264
These were raised to be strongest of earthly men;   266
they were the strongest and they fought with the strongest—
the Centaurs who lie in the mountains—and terribly they slaughtered
    them.
And yet with these men I kept company, coming from Pylos,
far away, from a distant land; for they summoned me.   270
And I fought by myself, I alone; against these men no
mortal now upon earth could fight.
And yet they marked my counsels and heeded my word.
Now you two heed me, since it is better to do so.
You should not, great though you are, deprive him of the girl,   275
but let her be, as it was to him the sons of the Achaeans gave her as prize;
nor you, son of Peleus, venture to contend face-to-face
with your king, since the king bearing the scepter partakes of
a very different honor, and is he to whom Zeus has given distinction.
And if you are the stronger man, and the mother who bore you a
    goddess,[5]   280
yet is this one more powerful, since he rules over more men.
Son of Atreus, restrain your spirit; for I—yes, I—
entreat you to relinquish your anger with Achilles, who is for all
Achaeans the great wall of defense against this evil war."
        Then in turn lord Agamemnon spoke: 285
"Indeed all these things, old sir, you rightly say;
but this man wants to be above all other men;
he wants to be lord over all, to rule all,
to give orders to all—which I think that one man at least will not obey.
And if the eternal gods have made him a spearman   290
they do not on that account appoint him to speak insults."
        Interrupting, godlike Achilles answered him:
"May I be called a coward and of no account
if I submit to you in everything you should say.
Give such orders to other men, but do not act as master to me.   295
For I do not think it likely I will obey you.
And I will tell you something else and put it away in your mind—
I will not fight for the girl with strength of hand,
not with you, nor with any other man, since you who take her from me
    also gave her.
But of other possessions beside my ships, swift and dark,   300

---

4. Heroes of an earlier generation. These are
the Lapiths from Thessaly in northern Greece.
At the wedding of Peirithoös, the mountain-
dwelling centaurs (half human, half horse)
got drunk and tried to rape the women who
were present. The Lapiths killed them after a
fierce fight. The line numbers here account

for lines that were omitted by the translator
because they may not belong to the next.
5. The sea nymph Thetis, who was married to
the mortal Peleus (Achilles' father). She later
left him and went to live with her father, Nereus,
in the depths of the Aegean Sea.

of these you can take nothing lifted against my will.
And I invite you to try, so that these men too will know—
very quickly will your dark blood gush round my spear."
       Having fought like this with words, blow for blow,
they both stood, and broke up the assembly by the ships of the Achaeans.   305
Peleus' son went to his shelter and balanced ships
with the son of Menoetius[6] and his companions.
But the son of Atreus then drew a swift ship down to the sea,
and chose twenty rowers to go in her, and put on board the sacrificial
   hecatomb
for the god, and fetching Chryseïs of the lovely cheeks   310
put her on board; and resourceful Odysseus came on as leader.
       Then, embarked, they sailed upon the watery way,
and the son of Atreus charged the men to purify themselves.
They cleansed themselves and cast the impurities into the sea,
and to Apollo they made perfect sacrificial hecatombs   315
of bulls and goats along the shore of the murmuring sea;
and the savor rose to heaven amid a swirl of smoke.
       So they attended to these tasks throughout the army; but
   Agamemnon did not
leave off the quarrel, in which he first threatened Achilles,
but spoke to Talthybios and Eurybates,   320
who were heralds and ready henchmen:
"Go to the shelter of Peleus' son Achilles;
take by the hand Briseïs of the lovely cheeks and lead her away.
And if he does not give her up, I myself will take her,
coming in force, and it will be the worse for him."   325
       So saying, he sent them forth, and enjoined on them a harsh
   command.
And they two went unwilling along the shore of the murmuring sea,
and came to the camp and ships of the Myrmidons.
They found Achilles by his shelter and dark ship,
sitting; and he did not rejoice to see them.   330
The two stood in fear and awe of the king,
and neither addressed him, nor questioned.
But Achilles understood in his heart, and spoke to them:
       "Hail heralds, messengers of Zeus, as also of men—
come close; you are not to blame in my eyes, but Agamemnon,   335
who sends you two forth on account of the girl Briseïs.
But come, Patroclus, descended from Zeus, bring out the girl
and give her to these two to take away. And let them both be witnesses
before the blessed gods and mortal men alike,
and before him, this stubborn king, if ever hereafter   340
other men need me to ward off shameful destruction.
For he surely raves in his ruinous heart,
and knows not to look ahead as well as behind
as to how the Achaeans shall fight in safety beside the ships."
       Thus he spoke and Patroclus obeyed his beloved companion,   345
and from the shelter led Briseïs of the lovely cheeks,

6. Patroclus, Achilles' closest friend.

and gave her to be taken away. And straightway the heralds left for the
   ships of the Achaeans.
She the young woman, unwilling, went with them. But Achilles,
weeping, quickly slipping away from his companions, sat
on the shore of the gray salt sea, and looked out to depths as dark as
   wine;   350
again and again, stretching forth his hands, he prayed to his beloved
   mother:
"Mother, since you bore me to be short-lived as I am,
Olympian Zeus who thunders on high ought to
grant me at least honor; but now he honors me not even a little.
For the son of Atreus, wide-ruling Agamemnon   355
has dishonored me; he keeps my prize, having seized it, he personally
   taking it."
        So he spoke, shedding tears, and his lady mother heard him
as she sat in the depths of the salt sea beside her aged father.
At once she rose from the clear salt sea, like mist,
and sat before him as he wept,   360
and caressed him with her hand, and spoke to him and said his name:
"Child, why do you cry? What pain has come to your heart?
Speak out, don't hide it, so that we both know."
        Groaning deeply, Achilles of the swift feet spoke to her:
"You know; why should I recount these things to you who know them all? 365
We came to Thebes, the holy city of Eëtion;[7]
we sacked it and brought everything here.
The sons of the Achaeans fairly divided the things among them,
and to the son of Atreus they gave out Chryseïs of the lovely cheeks.
Then Chryses, a priest of Apollo who strikes from afar,   370
came to the swift ships of the bronze-clad Achaeans
bearing untold ransom to set free his daughter,
holding in his hands the wreaths of Apollo who strikes from afar
on a golden staff, and beseeched all the Achaeans,
but mostly the two sons of Atreus, marshalers of men.   375
Then all the rest of the Achaeans shouted assent,
to respect the priest and take the splendid ransom;
but this did not please the heart of Atreus' son Agamemnon,
but violently he drove him away and laid a strong injunction upon him.
And in anger the old man went back; and Apollo   380
heard him when he prayed, since he was very dear to him,
and he let fly an evil arrow against the Argives; and now the men
died in quick succession as the arrows of the god ranged
everywhere through the broad army of the Achaeans. But then a seer
possessed of good knowledge publicly declared to us the wishes of the
   god who works his will.   385
Straightway I led in urging that the god be appeased;
but then anger seized the son of Atreus, and suddenly rising to speak
he declared aloud a threat, which is now fulfilled.

7. Eëtion was king of the Cilicians in Asia
Minor and father of Hector's wife, Andromache. "Thebes" (or Thebe): the Cilicians' capital city, not the Greek or Egyptian city of the
same name.

For the dark-eyed Achaeans are sending the girl on a swift ship
to the town of Chryse, taking gifts for lord Apollo; 390
just now the heralds set out from my shelter leading
the daughter of Briseus, whom the sons of the Achaeans gave to me.
But you, if you have the power, defend your son;
go to Olympus and petition Zeus, if ever in any way
in word or in deed you delighted the heart of Zeus. 395
For many times in the halls of my father I have heard you
boast when you said that from the dark-clouded son of Cronus,
alone among immortals, you warded off shameful destruction,
at that time when the other Olympians sought to bind him—
Hera and Poseidon[8] and Pallas Athena; 400
but you coming to him, goddess, released his bonds,
swiftly summoning to high Olympus the Hundred-Handed One,
whom the gods call Briareos the Strong—but all men call
Aigaion—he in turn is stronger than his father;[9]
and this one seated himself beside the son of Cronus, rejoicing in his
    glory. 405
And the blessed gods trembled before him, and did no more binding.
Now remind Zeus of these things, seat yourself beside him and clasp his
    knees
and see if he might be willing to aid the Trojans,
and to pen the Achaeans around the sterns of their ships and the sea,
dying, so that all may have profit of their king, 410
and he will know, Atreus' son, wide-ruling Agamemnon,
his delusion, when he paid no honor to the best of the Achaeans."
    Then Thetis answered him, with tears flowing down:
"Ah me, my child, why did I, bitter in childbearing, raise you?
Would that you sat by your ships without tears, without pain, 415
for indeed your measure of life is so very small, not long at all.
And now you are at once short-lived and unlucky beyond all men;
so I bore you to an unworthy fate in my halls.
To speak your request to Zeus who hurls the thunderbolt
I myself shall go to Olympus of the deep snow; perhaps he will heed me. 420
But you stay now by your fast-running ships,
nurse your wrath at the Achaeans, and leave off the war entirely.
Zeus went yesterday to the river of Ocean among the blameless
    Aethiopians,[1]
to attend a feast, and all the gods accompanied him.
On the twelfth day he will come back to Olympus, 425
and then at that time I will go for you to the bronze-floored house
    of Zeus,
and I will clasp his knees in supplication, and I think I will persuade him."
    Then speaking thus she went away and left him there,
angered in his heart on account of the fair-belted woman,
whom they were taking by force against his will. And Odysseus 430

---

8. Brother of Zeus and god of the sea.
9. Aigaion's father is Uranus, the Sky, husband of Earth and the first divine ruler. He was overthrown by his son Cronus, who in turn was overthrown by his son Zeus.
1. A people believed to live at the extreme edges of the world. Ocean was thought of as a river that encircled the earth.

was drawing near the town of Chryse, bearing the sacred hecatomb.
When they had come inside the deep harbor,
they furled the sails, and placed them in the dark ship,
and deftly lowering the mast by the forestays, laid it in the mast-gallows,
and rowed her to her mooring under oars;   435
then they threw the anchor stones, and made fast the stern lines,
and themselves disembarked into the broken surf,
and disembarked the hecatomb for Apollo, who strikes from afar;
and Chryseïs disembarked from the seagoing ship.
Then leading her to the altar resourceful Odysseus   440
placed her in her father's hands and addressed him:
"O Chryses, Agamemnon, lord of men, dispatched me
to lead your child to you and to perform sacred hecatombs to Phoebus
on behalf of the Danaans, so that we might propitiate lord Apollo,
who has now sent sufferings, much lamented, upon the Argives."   445
        So speaking, he placed her in the priest's arms, and he, rejoicing,
    received
his beloved daughter; and the men swiftly set up the splendid hecatomb
    for the god
in good order around the well-built altar,
then they washed their hands and took up the barley for scattering.
And Chryses prayed aloud for them, lifting his hands: 450
"Hear me, thou of the silver bow, you who stand over Chryse
and Killa most holy, you whose might rules Tenedos,
surely once before this you heard me when I prayed;
honoring me you smote hard the host of the Achaeans.
Now, as once before, fulfill this wish for me;   455
now this time ward shameful destruction from the Danaans."
Thus he spoke praying, and Phoebus Apollo heard him.
        Then when they had prayed and thrown the scattering barley
    before them,
they first drew back the heads of the sacrificial animals and cut their
    throats, and flayed them,
and cut out the thighbones and covered them over with fat   460
they had made into double folds, and placed raw flesh upon them;
the old man burned these on a cleft-stick and over them poured in libation
dark-gleaming wine; and the youths beside him held sacrificial forks in
    hand.
Then when the thighbones had been consumed by fire and they had
    tasted the entrails,
they cut up the other parts and pierced them through on spits   465
and roasted them with care, and then drew off all the pieces.
And when they had ceased their work and prepared their meal,
they feasted, nor did any man's appetite lack his due portion.
And when they had put away desire for eating and drinking,
the young men filled mixing bowls brimful with wine,   470
and after pouring libations in each cup, distributed it to all;
then all day long they sought the favor of the god in dance and song,
the young Achaean men beautifully singing a hymn of praise,
celebrating the god who works from afar; and the god rejoiced in his
    heart as he listened.

When the sun sank and dusk came on,   475
then they laid down to sleep by the stern lines of their ship;
and when dawn, born of the morning, shone forth her fingers of rosy light,
then they sailed out for the broad army of the Achaeans.
And to them Apollo who works from afar sent a following wind.
They stepped the mast and spread the glistening sails,   480
and the wind blew gusts in the middle of the sail, and around
the cutwater the bow-wave, shimmering dark, sang loud as the ship
     proceeded.
She swept over the swell, making her course.
And when they arrived at the broad army of the Achaeans,
they dragged the dark ship ashore   485
high on the sand, and splayed long struts beneath,
and themselves scattered to their ships and shelters.
          But, he, sitting idle by his fast-running ships, remained full of
     wrath—
the Zeus-descended son of Peleus,[2] Achilles of the swift feet;
never did he go to the assembly where men win glory,   490
never to war, but consumed his own heart,
biding his time there; yet he yearned for the war shout and battle.
          But when at length the twelfth dawn arose,
then all the gods who live forever went to Olympus
together, with Zeus as their leader; and Thetis did not neglect her son's 495
directives, and she rose from the heaving surface of the sea,
and at dawn ascended to towering Olympus.
She found the far-thundering son of Cronus sitting apart from the others
on the topmost peak of ridged Olympus;
and she sat before him and clasped his knees   500
with her left hand, and with her right took hold of him beneath
     his chin,[3]
and in supplication addressed lord Zeus, the son of Cronus:
"Father Zeus, if ever among the immortals I helped you
by word or by deed, accomplish this wish for me:
honor my son, who was born short-lived beyond all men,   505
and yet now the lord of men Agamemnon has
dishonored him; he holds his prize, having seized it, he personally taking it.
Do you now revenge him, Olympian Zeus, all-devising;
give strength to the Trojans until that time the Achaeans
recompense my son and exalt him with honor."   510
          So she spoke; but Zeus who gathers the clouds did not answer her,
but sat silent a long while. And as she had clasped his knees, so Thetis
now held on, clinging closely, and beseeched him again:
"Promise me faithfully, and nod your assent,
or refuse me—you have nothing to fear—so that I may learn   515
how much I am of all gods the most dishonored."
          Greatly troubled, Zeus who gathers the clouds addressed her:
"This is a deadly business, when you set me up to quarrel

2. Peleus was the son of Aeacus, son of Zeus.
3. She takes on the posture of the suppliant, which physically emphasizes the desperation and urgency of her request. Zeus was, above all other gods, the protector of suppliants.

with Hera, when she will harass me with words of abuse.
As it is, she is always quarreling with me in the presence of the
    immortal gods,   520
and maintains, as you know, that I help the Trojans in battle.
Now go back, lest Hera notice anything;
I will make these matters my concern, to bring them to accomplishment.
Come, I will my bow my head for you, so that you may be convinced;
for among immortals this is the greatest   525
testament of my determination; for not revocable, nor false,
nor unfulfilled is anything to which I have bowed my head."
The son of Cronus spoke, and nodded with his blue-black brows,
the ambrosial mane of the lord god swept forward
from his immortal head; and he shook great Olympus.   530
            Thus the two parted after conspiring; and she
sprang into the deep salt sea from shining Olympus,
and Zeus went to his home; and all the gods rose as a body
from their seats before their father; nor did any dare
remain seated as he approached, but all stood to meet him.   535
So he took his seat there upon his throne; nor did Hera
fail to perceive at a glance that silver-footed
Thetis, the daughter of the old man of the sea, had conspired with him.
Straightway she addressed Zeus, the son of Cronus, with taunting
    words:
"Which of the gods now, O cunning schemer, has conspired with you?   540
Always you love being away from me, mulling over your secrets
to make your decisions. Never yet to me
have you willingly dared state what you are thinking."
            Then the father of gods and men answered her:
"Hera, do not hope to know all my thoughts;   545
they will be hard for you, although you are my wife.
However, that which is fitting for you to hear, no other,
of gods or men, will know before you;
but that which I may wish to consider apart from the gods—
do not press me about each and every thing, nor make inquiry."   550
            Then answered him the ox-eyed lady Hera:
"Most dread son of Cronus, what sort of word have you spoken?
Certainly before now I have neither pressed you, nor made inquiry,
and entirely without interference you devise whatever you want.
But now my heart is terribly afraid lest   555
silver-footed Thetis, daughter of the old man of the sea, won you over;
for at dawn she came to your side and clasped your knees.
And I suspect you pledged faithfully to her that you would honor
Achilles, and destroy many by the ships of the Achaeans."
            Then in answer Zeus who gathers the clouds addressed her: 560
"What possesses you? You always suspect something, I never get
    past you.
Nonetheless, you can accomplish nothing at all, but will only be
further from my heart—and it will be the worse for you.
If this is the way things are—then you may be sure this is the way that
    pleases me.
Sit down and be silent, and obey my word,   565

lest the gods in Olympus, as many as there are, be of no avail to you
　against me
as I close in, when I lay my unassailable hands upon you."
　　　Thus he spoke and the ox-eyed lady Hera was afraid,
and she sat down in silence, bending her own heart into submission;
and throughout the house of Zeus the heavenly gods were troubled.　570
To them Hephaestus,[4] famed for his art, began to speak,
comforting his dear mother, white-armed Hera:
"To be sure this will be a deadly business, not to be borne,
if you two quarrel this way for the sake of mortals,
carrying on this jabbering among the gods; nor　　　　　　　575
will there be any pleasure from our noble feast if unseemliness prevails.
I advise my mother, sensible as she is,
to be agreeable to our dear father Zeus, so that our father
will not reproach us again, and throw our feast into disorder.
For what if the Olympian wielder of lightning wished to　　　580
blast us from our seats—for he is much the strongest.
Rather address him with gentle words;
then straightway will the Olympian be favorable to us."
　　　Thus he spoke, and springing to his feet placed a
　double-handled cup
in his dear mother's hands, and addressed her:　　　　　　585
"Endure, my mother, and restrain yourself, distressed though you be,
lest, dear as you are, I with my own eyes see you
struck down; then for all my grief I will have no power
to help you; for it is painful to oppose the Olympian.
For at another time before this, when I was trying to ward him
　from you,　　　　　　　　　　　　　　　　　　　　590
he grabbed me by the foot and cast me from the threshold of heaven;
the whole day I drifted down, and as the sun set
I dropped on Lemnos,[5] and there was but little life still in me.
It was there the Sintian men quickly ministered to me after my fall."
　　　So he spoke and Hera, goddess of the white arms, smiled　595
and smiling accepted the cup from her son's hand.
Then to all the other gods, serving to the right,
he poured sweet nectar[6] like wine, drawing from a mixing bowl;
and unquenchable laughter broke out among the blessed gods
as they watched Hephaestus bustling through the halls.　　　600
　　　Then all day long until the sun went down,
they feasted, nor was the appetite of any stinted of fair portion—
nor stinted of the beautifully wrought lyre, which Apollo held,
or of the Muses, who sang, one following the other, with lovely voice.
Then when the sun's bright light went down,　　　　　　605
they left to go to bed, each in his own house,
where the famous crook-legged god,
Hephaestus, had made a house for each with skillful understanding.
Olympian Zeus, wielder of lightning, went to his bed

---

4. The lame god of fire and the patron of crafts-
people, especially metalworkers.
5. An island in the Aegean Sea, inhabited by

the Sintians.
6. The drink of the gods.

where he was wont to retire when sweet sleep came to him;   610
here mounting his bed, he went to sleep, with Hera of the golden
   throne beside him.

Summary   The Greeks, in spite of Achilles' withdrawal, continue to fight. They do not
suffer excessively from Achilles' absence; on the contrary, they press the Trojans so hard that
Hector, the Trojan leader, after rallying his men, returns to the city to urge the Trojans to offer
special prayers and sacrifices to the gods.

From BOOK VI

[Hector Returns to Troy]

* * *

      And Hector called to the Trojans, shouting loud: 110
"High-spirited Trojans and allies far-renowned,
be ready men and defend the city from outrage,
so that I may go to Ilion[7] and speak with
the elder counselors and our wives
to pray to the divine ones, and promise hecatombs."   115
So speaking Hector of the shimmering helm departed;
the black oxskin of his shield struck him at both neck and ankles,
the rim which ran on the edge of his bossed shield.
      Then Glaukos the son of Hippolochos and the son of Tydeus
came together in the space between both armies, straining to fight   120
And when they had advanced almost upon each other,
Diomedes[8] of the war cry first addressed the other:
"Who are you, brave friend, of men consigned to death?
For I have never seen you in battle where men win glory
before this time, but now striding far in front of all men   125
in your bold courage, you stand to wait my long-shadowed spear—
and they are sons of brokenhearted men, who face my might.
But if you are one of the immortals come down from heaven,
I would not go to battle with the gods of heaven.
For not long, not long at all, did the son of Dryas live, powerful
   Lykourgos,[9]   130
who competed with the gods of heaven;
who in time past drove the nurses of raving Dionysus[1]
down the mountain slopes of holy Nysa, and all of them as one
scattered their sacred staffs to the ground, when struck by the cattle goad
that man-slaughtering Lykourgos wielded. And Dionysus, fleeing,   135
plunged beneath a wave of the salt sea, and Thetis took him, terrified,
in her embrace; for powerful trembling held him at the man's bellowing.
Then the gods who live at ease were enraged with Lykourgos,
and the son of Cronus struck him blind; nor was he still long
for life, once he incurred the hatred of all immortal gods.   140

---

7. Another name for Troy.
8. One of the foremost Greek leaders, son of
Tydeus. "Glaukos": a Trojan ally, from Lycia in
Asia Minor.

9. King of Thrace, a half-wild region along the
north shore of the Aegean Sea.
1. God of the vine.

So I would not wish to do battle with the blessed gods.
But if you are a man, of mortals who eat the fruit of worked land,
draw near, so that you may more swiftly arrive at death's border."
        And in turn the glorious son of Hippolochos addressed him:
"Great-hearted son of Tydeus, why do you ask my lineage?   145
As a generation of leaves, so is the generation of men.
The wind scatters some leaves to the ground, but the forest grows
    others
that flourish and in the time of spring come to succeed them;
so a generation of men either grows, or it dies.
But if you indeed wish to learn these things, so as to know well   150
my family's lineage, many men know of it.
There is a city, Ephyre,[2] in a corner of horse-pasturing Argos,
where Sisyphus ruled, who was born most cunning of men,
Sisyphus the son of Aeolus; he fathered a son, Glaukos;
then Glaukos fathered blameless Bellerophon.   155
And to Bellerophon the gods gave beauty and also attractive
manliness; but Proitos intended evil things against him in his heart,
and since he was more powerful by far, he drove Bellerophon from
    the land
of Argives; since Zeus had subjugated them beneath Proitos' scepter.
For the wife of Proitos, regal Anteia, was mad   160
to lie with him in secret love; but she did not
persuade wise-thinking Bellerophon, for he was noble-hearted.
So speaking a lie, she addressed king Proitos:
'May you die, O Proitos, or kill Bellerophon,
who desired to lie in love with me, I who was not willing.'   165
So she spoke; and anger seized the king at what he heard.
Yet he refrained from killing Bellerophon, for in his heart he felt shame
    to do so,
but sent him to Lycia, and gave him baneful signs,
scratching on a folded tablet many destructive things,
and instructed him to show them to his father-in-law, so that that he
    might die.   170
And Bellerophon went to Lycia under blameless escort of the gods.
And when he came to Lycia and the flowing river Xanthos,[3]
the lord of wide Lycia honored him graciously;
for nine days he gave him hospitality and sacrificed nine cattle.
But when the tenth dawn shone forth her rosy fingers of light,   175
then it was he questioned him and asked to see the symbols,
whatever it was he had brought with him from his son-in-law Proitos.
And when he was given his son-in-law's evil message,
first he ordered Bellerophon to slay the invincible Chimaira;
a thing of divine origin, not of men,   180
a lion in front, its hind part a serpent, and its middle a goat,
breathing forth a fearsome raging blaze of fire.
But Bellerophon killed it, following signs from the gods.
Second, he now fought the legendary Solymi;

2. An old name for Corinth, a city in the north-   3. A river in Lycia.
east Peloponnesus.

it was, he used to say, the most violent battle of men he entered.   185
The third time, he killed the man-battling Amazons.
And then the king contrived another cunning trick for him as he returned;
choosing the best men from wide Lycia
he set an ambush. But it was these men who did not return back home,
for blameless Bellerophon slew them all.   190
And when the king perceived that he was from the noble lineage of a god,
he detained Bellerophon there, and indeed offered him his daughter,
and gave him half of all his royal honor;
and the Lycians cut out a plot of land surpassing all others,
a beautiful plot, with orchards and tilled fields, for him to enjoy.   195
And the king's daughter bore three children to wise Bellerophon,
Isandros and Hippolochos and Laodameia.
And with Laodameia Zeus all-devising lay,
and she bore godlike Sarpedon of the bronze armor.
But when Bellerophon too became hateful to all gods,   200
he wandered alone across the Aleian plain,
consuming his own heart, avoiding the paths of men,
and his son Isandros was killed by Ares, insatiate of war,
as he fought the glorious Solymi,
and Artemis of the golden reins killed his daughter in anger.   205
And Hippolochos begot me, and I say I am born of him;
he sent me to Troy, and gave many directives to me,
always to be best and to be better than all others,
not to disgrace the line of my fathers, who were far the best
in Ephyre and in broad Lycia.   210
Of such descent and blood do I claim to be."
            So he spoke; and Diomedes of the war cry rejoiced.
He fixed his spear in the nourishing earth,
then with friendly words addressed the shepherd of the people:
"Now then, surely you are my guest friend from my father's side of
      long ago;   215
for noble Oineus once received blameless Bellerophon
as guest friend in his halls, detaining him for twenty days.
They even gave to each other splendid gifts of friendship;[4]
Oineus gave a war-belt bright with crimson,
and Bellerophon a two-handled cup of gold;   220
and I left it in my home when setting forth;
I do not remember Tydeus, since I was still small
when he left me, that time the Achaean people perished at Thebes.[5]
Now therefore I am guest friend to you in the heart of Argos,
as you to me in Lycia, whenever I should come to their country.   225
Let us avoid each other's spears, even in the thick of battle;
for there are many Trojans and their famed allies for me
to kill, whom god might put in my hands, or let me catch with my feet,

4. It was customary for guest-friends to exchange gifts.
5. Tydeus was one of the seven heroes who attacked Thebes. They were led by Oedipus's son Polynices, who was attempting to dislodge his brother, Eteocles, from the kingship. The brothers killed each other, and the rest of the seven also perished. Diomedes, along with the sons of the other champions, later sacked Thebes.

and in turn many Achaeans are there for you to kill, whomever of them
   you can.
Let us exchange armor with each other, so that these others here   230
will know that we claim to be guest friends from our fathers."
       Having so spoken, they both leapt from their chariots
and took each other's hands and pledged their trust.
But Zeus the son of Cronus took away the wits from Glaukos,
who exchanged with Diomedes son of Tydeus armor   235
of gold for that of bronze, a hundred oxen's value for nine.
       But as Hector came to the Scaean gates and rampart,
the wives and daughters of the Trojans ran to surround him,
asking about their sons and brothers and kinsmen and
their husbands; but he urged them to pray to the gods,   240
each woman in turn; for woes had been bound upon many.
       When he came to the sumptuous house of Priam
built with its smooth-wrought colonnades—within it
were fifty chambers of polished stone,
close built to one another; where the sons   245
of Priam slept beside their wedded wives;
on the other side, facing them inside the courtyard, were his daughters'
twelve roofed chambers of polished stone,
close built to one another; where the sons-in-law
of Priam slept beside their modest wives—   250
there Hector's mother,[6] giver of kindness, came to meet him,
leading Laodike, the most outstanding in beauty of her daughters,
and clung to him with her hand and spoke to him and said his name:
"Child, why have you come, leaving the reckless fighting?
Truly, the sons of the Achaeans, of cursed name, have worn you out   255
with their battling round the city, and your spirit has impelled you to
   come here,
to lift your hands to Zeus in supplication from the high place of the city.
But wait, while I bring you wine, honey-sweet,
for you to make libation to Zeus the father and the immortals
first, and then yourself have enjoyment, should you drink it.   260
Wine greatly strengthens the spirit in a weary man,
as you have been wearied protecting your people."
       And then great Hector of the shimmering helm answered her:
"Do not to me offer up wine, sweet to the spirit, my lady mother,
lest you sap my limbs of strength, and I forget my courage.   265
And I shrink from pouring a libation of dark-gleaming wine to Zeus
with unwashed hands; a man cannot pray to the son of Cronus
of the dark clouds spattered with blood and gore.
But you to the temple of Athena of the Spoils
go with burnt offerings, summoning the elder women,   270
and place a robe, one which seems to you to be the loveliest and most
   ample
in your house, and which is most precious to you,
and place this on the knees of the statue of Athena of the lovely hair;
and pledge to sacrifice to her in the temple twelve young cows,

6. Hecuba.

yearlings, unbroken, if she would have mercy   275
on the city and on the wives of the Trojans and their infant children,
if she would ward off the son of Tydeus from holy Ilion—
savage spearman, violent master of the rout.
But you go to the temple of Athena of the Spoils,
and I will seek after Paris,[7] to summon him,   280
if he should choose to hear me speak. Would that the earth
would gape to swallow him on the spot. For the Olympian has raised him to
   be a great affliction
to the Trojans and to great-hearted Priam and to his children.
If I could see him on his way down into the house of Hades,
I would declare my heart had forgotten sorrow."   285
      So he spoke; and his mother going to the house called for
her handmaids, and they gathered the elder women throughout the city.
And she herself went down into the scented chamber,
where were robes of intricate design, the work of women of Sidon
whom Alexandros,[8] godlike in beauty, himself   290
led from Sidon, sailing upon the wide deep sea
on that journey, on which he brought away high-born Helen.
Taking up one of these, Hecuba carried it as a gift to Athena,
the robe that was most beautiful in decorations and the largest,
which gleamed like a star; it had been lying beneath the others.   295
Then she set out on her way, and many women elders went with her.
      And when they came to the temple of Athena on the citadel height,
Theano of the lovely cheeks opened the doors for them,
the daughter of Kisseus, wife of Antenor breaker of horses;
for the Trojans had appointed her priestess of Athena.   300
With a wailing cry, all the women raised their hands to Athena;
and taking the robe, Theano of the lovely cheeks
lay it on the knees of the statue of lovely haired Athena;
and praying, she entreated the daughter of mighty Zeus:
"Lady, Athena protector of the city, shining of goddesses,   305
break the spear of Diomedes, and grant that he
drop headlong before the Scaean gates,
so we will now, without delay, sacrifice to you in your temple twelve
   young cows,
yearlings, unbroken, if you would have mercy
on the city and on the wives of the Trojans and their infant children."   310
Thus she spoke beseeching; but Pallas Athena turned away her head.
      So the women were praying to the daughter of almighty Zeus;
but Hector went to the house of Alexandros,
a thing of beauty, which he himself had built by men who were the
   very best
craftsmen in Troy's rich-soiled land,   315
and who built for him a sleeping chamber, hall and courtyard
close by that of Priam and Hector, on the citadel height.
Therein entered Hector, beloved by Zeus, and in his hand

---

7. Hector's brother, whose seduction and abduction of Helen, the wife of Menelaos, caused the war.

8. Another name for Paris. "Sidon": A Phoenician city on the coast of what is now Lebanon.

he held his spear of eleven cubits length; before him gleamed
the bronze point of the spear shaft, round which ran a golden binding
   ring.   320
He found Alexandros in his splendid chamber handling his armor,
his shield and breastplate, and turning over his curved bow;
Argive Helen was sitting with her serving women,
and directing her maids' fine handwork.
And seeing him, Hector reviled him with contemptuous words:[9]   325
"Unnatural man, it is not good to store this anger in your heart.
Men are perishing about the city and steep walls
as they do battle, and it is on your account the battle shout and war
blaze all around this city; you would confront another man
were you to see him anywhere hanging back from hated war.   330
Up now; lest the town is soon made hot by enemy fire."
      In turn godlike Alexandros addressed him:
"Hector, since you fairly rebuke me, nor beyond what is fair,
on this account I will speak to you, and you mark and hear me.
It was not so much in anger and resentment of the Trojans   335
I was sitting in my room; no, I wished to yield myself to grief.
Just now, my wife was coaxing me with gentle words,
urging me into battle. And it seems to me too that this
will be better; victory shifts from man to man.
But come, wait a bit, let me put on the armor of Ares;   340
or go, and I will come after; I expect I'll catch you up."
      So he spoke, and Hector of the shimmering helm said nothing
   to him.
But Helen addressed him softly:
"Brother-in-law of me, an evil-thinking dog who strikes cold fear,
would that on the day when first my mother gave me birth,   345
some foul-weather storm of wind carrying me had borne me
to a mountain or a swelling wave of the tumultuous sea,
where the wave would have swept me away before these deeds had
   happened.
But since the gods have so decreed these evils,
then would I were the wife of a better man,   350
a man who knew what righteous blame was and the many reproaches
   that men make.
But the wits of this man here are not steady now, nor will they be
hereafter; and I think that he will reap the fruit of this.
But come now, come in and take your seat upon this stool,
brother-in-law, since the toil of fighting has mostly stood astride
   your heart   355
because of me, a dog, and Alexandros' infatuation,
we on whom Zeus has laid this evil fate, so that even after this
there will be songs of us for men to come."
      Then answered her great Hector of the shimmering helm:

9. In book 3, Paris fought with Menelaos in single combat to settle the war. He was about to lose when Aphrodite spirited him off to his house in Troy, where she then persuaded Helen to join him. In book 4, fighting broke out again when the Trojan archer Pandaros, on Athena's advice, wounded Menelaos.

"Do not have me sit, Helen, for all your love; you will not persuade me.   360
For my spirit has already set me to defend
the Trojans, who have great longing for me when I am away.
But you rouse this one, and let him hurry,
so that he might catch me up while inside the city.
For my part I am going home, so that I may see   365
my household and my beloved wife and little son.
For I do not know whether, returning once more to them, I will come
    back again,
or if, already now, the gods will defeat me beneath the hands of the
    Achaeans."
        So speaking, Hector of the shimmering helm departed;
and quickly he reached his well-established home.   370
But he did not find white-armed Andromache in his halls,
for she with her child and fair-robed attendant
had taken her stand upon the tower, weeping and shedding tears.
And when Hector did not find his blameless wife,
he paused upon the threshold as he was going, and spoke among the
    servants: 375
"Come, maids, and tell me clearly;
where has white-armed Andromache gone from the hall?
To some house of my sisters, or of my brothers' fair-robed wives,
or has she set out for the temple of Athena, where the other
Trojan women with lovely hair propitiate the dread goddess?"   380
And in turn his ready housekeeper addressed him:
"Hector, since you strongly bid me speak the truth,
it is not to some house of your sisters, or of your brothers' fair-robed
    wives,
nor has she set out for the temple of Athena, where the other
Trojan women with lovely hair propitiate the dread goddess,   385
but she has gone to the great tower of Ilion, because she heard
the Trojans are worn down, and that Achaean strength is great,
by now she has arrived at the tower in urgent haste
like a madwoman; the nurse with her carries the baby."
        The housekeeper spoke, and Hector ran from the house   390
back the same way through the well-built streets.
When he arrived at the Scaean gates, having crossed the great city,
there where he intended to pass through to the plain,
there his worthy wife came to meet him, running,
Andromache, daughter of great-hearted Eëtion—   395
Eëtion, who once lived below wooded Plakos,
in Thebes below Mount Plakos, ruling the Cilician men;
his daughter was held as wife by bronze-armored Hector.
She met him then, and her attendant came with her,
the child held against her breast, tender-hearted, just a baby,   400
the cherished only child of Hector, beautiful like a star,
whom Hector used to call Scamandrios,[1] but all others
Astyanax, lord of the city; for his father alone protected Ilion.
        And looking at his child in silence, Hector smiled,

---

1. After the Trojan river Scamander.

but Andromache came and stood close to him shedding tears 405
and clung to him with her hand and spoke to him and said his name:
"Inhuman one, your strength will destroy you, and you take no pity
on the child and young one, or on me who have no future, who will
   soon be
bereft of you; the Achaeans will soon kill you,
the whole of them rushing in attack. And for me it would be better 410
with you lost to go down beneath the earth; for no other
comfort will there be hereafter, when you meet your fate,
but grief. I have no father or lady mother;
it was godlike Achilles who slew my father,
when he sacked the well-established town of the Cilicians, 415
high-gated Thebes, and killed Eëtion;
yet he did not strip his body, for in his heart he thought it shameful,
but he cremated him with his decorated war-gear,
and heaped a burial mound over. And around it elms were grown
by nymphs of the mountains, daughters of Zeus who wields the
   aegis. 420
And they who were my seven brothers in our halls,
they all on a single day entered the house of Hades;
all of them swift-footed godlike Achilles slew
as they watched over their shambling cattle and white sheep.
And my mother, who was queen under wooded Plakos, 425
when he led her here with the rest of his plunder,
he set her free again, accepting untold ransom;
and, in the hall of her father, Artemis[2] who showers arrows struck
   her down.
Hector, so you are father to me, and honored mother,
and my brother, and you are my strong husband. 430
So have pity now and stay here by the ramparts,
do not make your child fatherless, your wife a widow.
Station your men by the wild fig tree, where the city is
easiest to scale and the walls can be overrun.
Three times they came there and tested it, the best men 435
with the two Aiantes and illustrious Idomeneus,
and with the sons of Atreus and Tydeus' daring son;
perhaps some seer, well skilled, told them of it,
or it was their own spirit that urged and compelled them."
      And great Hector of the shimmering helm answered her: 440
"Surely, all these things concern me too, my wife; but greatly
I would dread what they would think, the Trojans and the Trojan women
   with their trailing robes,
if like a coward I should shirk away from fighting.
My spirit does not allow me, for I have learned to be brave
always and to fight among the front rank of Trojans, 445
winning great glory for my father, and for me.
But I know this well in my mind and in my heart;
there will some time be a day when holy Ilion is destroyed,
and Priam and the people of Priam of the fine ash-spear;

---

2. Virgin goddess of the hunt, dispenser of natural and painless death to women.

but it is not the coming suffering of the Trojans that so much
    distresses me,   450
nor of Hecuba herself, nor of lord Priam,
nor of my many and brave brothers who
will fall in dust at the hands of enemy men,
so much as distress for you, when some bronze-armored Achaean
leads you off in tears, taking away your day of freedom.   455
And in Argos you will work the loom for another woman,
and carry water from the spring of Messeïs or Hypereia
time and again under compulsion, and necessity will lie harsh
    upon you.
And one day someone seeing you shedding tears may say:
'This is the wife of Hector, who used to be best of the horse-breaking
    Trojans   460
in waging battle, at that time when men fought round Ilion.'
So one day someone may speak; and for you the pain will be new again,
bereft of such a husband to ward off the day of slavery.
But may the heaped earth cover me over dead
before I ever hear your cry as you are dragged away."   465
        So speaking, shining Hector reached out for his son;
but the child turned away, back to the breast of his fair-belted nurse,
crying, frightened at the sight of his own father,
struck with terror seeing the bronze helmet and crest of horsehair,
nodding dreadfully, as he thought, from the topmost of the helmet.   470
They burst out laughing, his dear father and lady mother.
At once shining Hector lifted the helmet from his head,
and placed it, gleaming, on the earth;
then he rocked his beloved son in his arms and kissed him,
and prayed aloud to Zeus and to the other gods: 475
"Zeus, and you other gods, grant now that this child too,
my son, will become, even as I am, conspicuous among Trojans,
likewise skilled in courage, and rule Ilion in strength.
And one day may someone say of him, 'this man is far better than his
    father'
as he returns from war, and may he bear back bloodstained spoils of
    armor,   480
having killed an enemy man, and his mother's heart rejoice."
        So speaking he placed in the hands of his beloved wife
his son; and she took him to her perfumed breast,
laughing as she cried. And her husband took pity, watching,
and with his hand he caressed her and spoke to her and said her name: 485
"Foolish one, do not, I beg you, distress your heart too much.
No man against fate will hurl me to Hades;
for no man, I think, escapes destiny,
not the cowardly, nor the brave, once he is born.
But go to the house and tend to your work,   490
to your loom and distaff, and direct your handmaids
to ply their work; war is the concern of men,
all men, and me most of all, who live in Ilion."
        So speaking, shining Hector took up his helmet
crested with horsehair; and his beloved wife went home,   495

turning to look back all the while, letting the full tears fall.
Soon she reached the well-established home
of man-slaying Hector, and inside found her many
handmaids; and she stirred all of them to lamentation.
They lamented Hector in his own house while he was yet alive; 500
for they did not think that he would come home again,
returned from war, escaping the might and hands of the Achaeans.

Nor did Paris linger in his high-roofed house,
but when he had put on his glorious armor, elaborate in bronze,
then he sped through the city, confident in the swiftness of his feet. 505
As when a horse confined to a stall, fed on barley at the manger,
breaking his tether runs with pounding feet across the plain
to immerse himself in the fair-flowing waters of his accustomed river,
triumphant, and he holds his head high, his mane
streaming about his shoulders; emboldened by his beauty, 510
his knees bear him lightly to the pasture and places horses love;
so Paris, son of Priam, from the heights of Pergamos[3]
set out radiant in his armor like the sun,
laughing out loud, his swift feet carrying him. Quickly
he found shining Hector, his brother, as he was about 515
to turn from the place where he had spoken fondly with his wife.

Godlike Alexandros addressed him first:
"Elder brother of mine, to be sure I have delayed you as you hurried
by my tarrying, I did not come in proper time, as you were urging."
Answering him spoke Hector of the shimmering helm: 520
"Strange one, no man who is fair
could slight your work in battle, since you are brave;
but you hang back by choice and are not willing. And for that I
grieve deep in my heart, when I hear insults about you
from the Trojans, who suffer much hardship on your account. 525
But let us go. We will redress these matters later, if ever Zeus
grants us to dedicate in our halls a feast bowl of freedom
to the heavenly gods who live forever,
after driving out of Troy the strong-greaved[4] Achaeans."

Summary The Trojans rally successfully and go on the offensive. They drive the Greeks
back to the light fortifications they have built around their beached ships. The Trojans light their
watchfires on the plain, ready to deliver the attack in the morning.

From BOOK VIII

[*The Tide of the Battle Turns*]

* * *

And they in high confidence between the lines of battle
sat down the night long, and their many fires blazed.
As when in heaven stars about the bright moon 555

---

3. The citadel of Troy.
4. I.e., with bronze greaves (the shin protectors of Homeric warriors).

shine conspicuous, when the upper air turns windless,
and all the peaks and jutting cliffs are shown,
and valleys, and from heaven above the boundless bright air is rent with
    light
and all the stars are seen, and the shepherd's heart rejoices,
so between the ships and streams of Xanthos   560
in such multitude shone the watchfires of the Trojans' burning, before
    Ilion.
A thousand fires were burning on the plain, and by each one
sat fifty men in the glow of fire's gleaming;
and the horses munched their white barley and their grain
standing beside their chariots as they awaited Dawn on her fair throne.   565

BOOK IX

[*The Embassy to Achilles*]

So the Trojans held their guard; but preternatural Panic,
handmaid of cold Flight, held the Achaeans,
and all the best of them were stricken with grief too great to bear.
As dual winds rouse the fish-filled sea,
Northern Boreas and Zephyros from the West,[5] both blowing from
    Thrace,   5
coming on a sudden; and the wave massed to darkness
rises in a crest, and far along the salt sea it scatters seaweed—
so was the spirit rent in the breasts of the Achaeans.
        And the son of Atreus, stricken at heart with great grief,
went back and forth commanding the clear-voiced heralds   10
to summon by name each man to the assembly,
but with no hue and cry, and he himself went to work with the foremost.
They took their seat in the assembly, stricken; and Agamemnon
stood up, streaming tears like a dark-water spring,
which down sheer rock streams somber water;   15
so groaning deeply he addressed his words to the Argives:
"O friends, leaders and protectors of the Argives—
greatly has Zeus the son of Cronus bound me in grievous deception,
hard he is, who at one time promised me and gave assurance
that I would return home after sacking well-walled Troy.   20
Now he has devised an evil deceit and bids me
go back to Argos dishonored, since I have destroyed a multitude of men.
This, it seems, must please Zeus, supreme in might,
who has brought to ruin the citadels of many cities,
and will destroy yet more; for his is the greatest power.   25
But come—let us all be persuaded to do as I say;
let us flee with our ships to our beloved homeland,
for we will not ever take Troy of the wide ways."
        So he spoke, and all the men were hushed in silence;
for a long time the sons of the Achaeans were quiet with sorrow.   30
At length Diomedes of the war cry addressed him:

5. The north and west winds, respectively.

"Son of Atreus, I will first combat your folly,
which is one's right, my lord, in the assembly; and do you not be angered.
You first reviled my courage before the Danaans,
you said that I was unwarlike and a coward;[6] all these things   35
the Argives know, both young and old.
To you the son of devious Cronus gave half measure;
he granted that by your scepter you would be honored beyond all men,
but courage he did not give you, which is the greatest power.
What possesses you? Do you really suppose that the sons of Achaeans
    are so   40
unwarlike and cowardly, as you declare?
But if your own spirit is set on departing,
go—the way lies open, your ships stand by the sea,
those so many ships that followed you from Mycenae;[7]
but the rest of the long-haired Achaeans will remain,   45
until we sack Troy. Come! Let even they
flee in their ships to the beloved fatherland,
we two, I and Sthenelos,[8] will fight until we learn firsthand
the fated end of Ilion; for it was with god we came."

        So he spoke; and all the sons of the Achaeans shouted assent,   50
in admiration of the word of Diomedes breaker of horses.
And standing among them the horseman Nestor addressed them:
"Son of Tydeus, in war you are strong beyond all,
and in council you are best among all your age.
No man of all the Achaeans will slight your word,   55
nor speak against it; but your words have not reached a conclusion.
How young you are yet—you might even be my son,
the youngest by birth—but you talk good sense to
the Argive kings, for what you say is proper.
But come, I who claim to be older than you,   60
I will speak plainly and thoroughly. No man can
discredit my word, not even lord Agamemnon;
without tribe, lawless, without home is that man,
who desires cold-blooded war among his own people.
Let us yield now to night's darkness   65
and prepare our meals; let the guards each
camp out along the ditch dug outside the wall.
On the young men I lay all these charges. And then,
son of Atreus, do you take the lead; for you are the most kingly;
make a banquet for the senior leaders. It is fitting for you, it is not
    unseemly;   70
your shelters are full of wine that Achaean ships
bring every day from Thrace across the broad high sea.
All hospitality is yours—you are lord of many—
and when a multitude is assembled, listen to that man who gives the best
counsel. Very great is the need of all Achaeans   75
for good and shrewd counsel, when close by their ships the enemy
burn their many watchfires; who could take joy in this?

6. This insult was voiced during Agamemnon's   7. The city near Argos that Agamemnon ruled.
review of his forces before the battle (book 4).   8. Diomedes' companion.

This is the night that will either destroy the army or save it."
     So he spoke; and they listened closely and obeyed.
Forth the guards hastened under arms   80
mustered about Nestor's son Thrasymedes, shepherd of the people,
and about Askalaphos and Ialmenos, sons of Ares,
and about Meriones and Aphareus and Deïpyros and
about the son of Kreion, shining Lykomedes.
Seven leaders of the guards there were, and with each a hundred   85
young men proceeded grasping long spears in their hands.
On arrival, they settled in the space between the ditch and rampart,[9]
and there they kindled fires, and each prepared his meal.
     And the son of Atreus led the Achaeans' senior leaders in a body
into his shelter, and before them set a hearty feast;   90
and they reached out their hands to the good things set ready before them.
And when they had put away desire for eating and drinking,
the old man taking the lead began to weave his plan to them,
Nestor, whose counsel in time past had proved best,
he in his wisdom spoke and addressed them: 95
"Most glorious son of Atreus, lord of men Agamemnon,
with you I will end, with you begin, since over many
men are you lord and Zeus has put into your hand
both scepter and tradition, that you might take counsel in their interest.
Therefore you beyond others should speak out what you have to say,
    and also listen,   100
and even fulfill the advice of another, when the spirit moves him
to speak some word for good; for whatever he may begin will depend
    on you.
So then, I will speak as it seems best to me.
Nor shall any other man have in mind counsel better than this,
such as I have turned in mind both in the past and still now—   105
turned since that time when you, O descended from Zeus, went and took
the girl Briseïs from the shelter of Achilles, for all his anger,
not at all in accordance with our counsel; for I did indeed
strongly dissuade you; but you, yielding to your great-hearted fury,
dishonored the best of men, one whom the very gods esteem;   110
for you have taken and hold his prize. Still, even now
let us consider how we might, making atonement, win him over
with propitiatory gifts and gentle words."
     Then answered him the lord of men, Agamemnon:
"Old one, not at all falsely have you recounted my delusion—   115
I was struck with delusion, I myself make no denial. Worth many
warriors is the man whom Zeus loves in his heart,
as now he honors this one, and brings defeat to the Achaean people.
But since I was struck with delusion, guided by my wretched sense,
I am willing to make amends and to offer untold recompense.   120
To all of you I will enumerate the illustrious gifts:
seven tripods[1] untouched by fire, ten talents of gold,

---

9. In book 7, the Greeks built this rampart and dug the ditch in front of it to protect their ships, which were threatened by the Trojans.

1. Three-footed kettles; such metal equipment was rare and highly valued.

twenty gleaming cauldrons, twelve horses—
muscular, bearers of prizes, who won contests with their speed of feet.
A man would not be bereft of possessions,   125
nor lacking in valuable gold, who owned as much
as the single-hoofed horses have won for me in prizes.
And I will give seven women, skilled in flawless works of hand,
women of Lesbos,[2] whom, when he himself took strong-founded Lesbos,
I selected, who in beauty surpass all tribes of women;   130
these I will give to him, and among them will be the one I took away,
the daughter of Briseus. And more—I will swear a great oath
that I never mounted her bed and lay with her,
which is the custom of humankind, of men and of women.
These things, all of them, will be his at once; and if later   135
the gods grant us to sack the great city of Priam,
let him heap his ship with gold and bronze in abundance,
coming in when we Achaeans divide among ourselves the spoils;
and let he himself chose twenty Trojan women,
who, after Helen of Argos, are most beautiful.   140
And if we return to Achaean Argos, nurturer of tilled fields,
he will be my son-in-law, and I will honor him equally with Orestes,[3]
who, late-born to me, was raised in great luxury.
I have three daughters in my well-built halls,
Chrysothemis and Laodike and Iphianassa;   145
of these, let him take which he will as his own, without bride-price,
to the house of Peleus; and I will give bride-gifts with her,
a great many, such as no man has yet bestowed upon his daughter.
Seven citadels I will give to him, well-inhabited,
Kardamyle and Enope and grassy Hire,   150
sacred Pherai and Antheia of the deep meadows,
and lovely Aipeia and Pedasos with its vines.
All are near the sea, on the border of sandy Pylos,
and in them dwell men who are rich in sheep and rich in cattle,
who will honor him with gifts as they would a god,   155
and who under scepter of his rule will fulfill his prospering laws.
These things I will accomplish for him if he gives over his anger.
Let him give way—Hades is implacable and unyielding;
and therefore is for mortal men most hateful of all the gods—
let him submit to me, since I am the greater king   160
and since I claim myself to be in age the elder."
      Then answered him the Gerenian horseman Nestor:
"Most glorious son of Atreus, lord of men Agamemnon,
the gifts you offer lord Achilles cannot now be slighted;
come, let us dispatch chosen men, who with all swiftness   165
will go to the shelter of Peleus' son Achilles.
Come now, those men I select, let them do as I say.
Let Phoinix[4] beloved of Zeus lead first of all,
and then great Ajax and godlike Odysseus;

---

2. A large island off the coast of present-day Turkey.

3. Agamemnon's son.

4. He is especially suited for this embassy because he was tutor to the young Achilles.

and let the heralds Odios and Eurybates follow with them.   170
Bring water for their hands, bid them speak no word of ill omen,
so that we may conciliate Zeus son of Cronus, that he might take pity."
         So he spoke, and what he said found favor with all,
and without delay the heralds streamed the water over their hands,
the young men filled mixing bowls brimful with wine,   175
and after preparing libations in each cup, distributed it to all.
Then when they had poured offering and drunk as much as their spirit
    desired,
they set out from the shelter of Agamemnon son of Atreus.
And to them the Gerenian horseman Nestor gave many instructions
looking encouragingly at each, but most of all at Odysseus,   180
to endeavor to win over the blameless son of Peleus.
         And the two groups went along the shore of the tumultuous sea,
making many prayers to the god who holds the earth
that they might readily persuade the proud heart of Aeacides.[5]
And so they came to the shelters and ships of the Myrmidons,   185
and found him delighting his heart in a pure-toned lyre,
exquisitely wrought, with a bridge of silver upon it,
which he won from spoils when he lay waste the city of Eëtion.
With this he was delighting his spirit and singing of the glorious deeds
    of men;
Patroclus by himself was sitting opposite in silence,   190
watchfully awaiting Aeacides, for when he would break off his singing.
And they came forward, godlike Odysseus leading the way,
and stood before him. In amazement Achilles sprang up,
lyre in hand, leaving the place where he was sitting;
so likewise Patroclus rose, when he saw the men.   195
And greeting them Achilles of the swift feet spoke:
"Welcome; surely you come as dear friends—indeed there is great need—
who are dearest to me, even in anger, of the Achaeans."
So speaking godlike Achilles led them closer,
and seated them on divans and shimmering carpets.   200
And at once he addressed Patroclus who was standing near:
"Set up a larger mixing bowl, son of Menoetius,
and mix stronger wine, and prepare a cup for each man;
for these beneath my roof are my dearest friends."
         So he spoke, and Patroclus obeyed his beloved companion.   205
He threw down a great meat-block by the light of the fire,
and placed on it the back of a sheep and of a fat goat,
and the chine of a fattened pig rich with lard;
Automedon[6] held the board for him, and godlike Achilles carved.
And these he deftly cut up and pierced through on spits,   210
and the son of Menoetius, a man like a god, made the fire burn big.
Then when the fire had burned down and its flame was extinguished,
spreading the embers, he arranged the spits above them,
lifting and placing them upon the andirons, and sprinkled holy salt.
And when he had roasted the meat and heaped it on chargers,   215

5. Another name for Achilles. "The god who   **6.** Achilles' charioteer.
holds the earth": Poseidon, god of the sea.

Patroclus took bread to distribute around the table
in fine baskets, but Achilles distributed the meat.
And he himself sat facing godlike Odysseus
by the opposite wall, and to the gods he bade
Patroclus, his companion, make offering; and he into the fire cast the
    first cuts.[7]   220
Then they reached out their hands to the good things set ready before
    them.
        And when they had put away desire for eating and drinking,
Ajax nodded to Phoinix; and godlike Odysseus perceived him,
and filling a cup with wine he pledged Achilles:
"To your happiness, Achilles; we do not lack fair share of feasting,   225
both in the shelter of Agamemnon son of Atreus,
and now even here; there is abundance to satisfy the spirit
for us to dine on. But our work of concern is not fair feasts,
but destruction too great to behold, beloved of Zeus,
is what we fear; it is in doubt whether we will save our well-benched
    ships,   230
or they will be destroyed, if you do not arm yourself in might.
Hard by the ships and defensive wall they have pitched camp,
the high-spirited Trojans and their far-renowned allies,
blazing many fires throughout the army, and no longer, they say,
will they be restrained, but will fall upon our black ships.   235
Zeus the son of Cronus shows them favorable omens
of lightning; Hector in the great exultation of his strength
rages uncontrollably—trusting in Zeus, he respects neither
man nor god, but overpowering fury has entered in him.
He prays that shining dawn will show forth swiftly;   240
for he threatens to hack the stern-posts from the ships
and destroy them in ravenous fire, and slaughter
the Achaeans beside the ships when they are roused by smoke.
These things I fear terribly in my heart, lest the gods
accomplish these threats for him, and then our fate would be   245
to perish in Troy, far from the horse-grazed pastures of Argos.
Rise up! if you are minded even at this late hour to save
Achaea's sons in their extremity from the Trojan onslaught.
For you too there will be grief in time after, nor is there any means
to find remedy once evil is accomplished; before that take thought   250
how you might ward off from the Danaans their day of evil.
        "O my friend, surely your father Peleus gave you instruction
on that day, when he sent you from Phthia to Agamemnon:
'My child, strength of body Athena and Hera will give you,
if that is their will, but your great-hearted spirit is for you   255
to restrain within your breast; friendship is far better;
desist from strife that creates only evil, and they will honor you more,
youths and elders of the Argives alike.'
So the old man instructed you, and you have forgotten. But even now
stop, give up this heart-grieving anger; and Agamemnon   260
will give you gifts in compensation, if you desist this anger;

---

7. The portion of meat reserved for the gods.

come now, hear me, and I will enumerate for you
all the gifts in his shelter Agamemnon promises to you;
seven tripods untouched by fire, ten talents of gold,
twenty gleaming cauldrons, twelve horses—   265
muscular, bearers of prizes, who won contests with speed of their feet.
A man would not lack possessions,
nor would he be lacking in valuable gold, who owned as much
as Agamemnon's horses have won in prizes with their feet.
He will give seven women, skilled in flawless works of hand,   270
women of Lesbos, whom, when you took strong-founded Lesbos,
he selected, who in beauty then surpassed all tribes of women;
these he will give to you, and among them will be the one he took away
    before,
the daughter of Briseus. And more—he will swear a great oath,
that he never mounted her bed and lay with her,   275
which is the custom, my lord, both of men and of women;
these things, all of them, will be yours at once; and if later
the gods grant us to sack the great city of Priam,
heap your ship with gold and bronze in abundance,
coming in when we Achaeans divide among ourselves the spoils;   280
and chose for yourself twenty Trojan women,
who, after Helen of Argos, are most beautiful.
And if we return to Achaean Argos, nurturer of tilled fields,
you can be his son-in-law, and he will honor you equally with Orestes,
who, late-born to him, was raised in great luxury.   285
He has three daughters in his well-built halls,
Chrysothemis and Laodike and Iphianassa;
of these, take which you will as your own, without bride-price,
to the house of Peleus; and he will give bride-gifts with her,
a great many, such as no man has yet bestowed upon his daughter.   290
Seven citadels he will give to you, well-inhabited,
Kardamyle and Enope and grassy Hire,
sacred Pherai and Antheia of the deep meadows,
and lovely Aipeia and Pedasos with its vines.
All are near the sea, on the border of sandy Pylos,   295
and in them dwell men who are rich in sheep and rich in cattle,
who will honor you with gifts as they would a god,
and who under scepter of your rule will fulfill your prospering laws.
These things he will accomplish for you if you give over your anger.
        "But if the son of Atreus has become more hateful, even to the
    bottom of your heart,   300
he and his gifts, then on all the other Achaean forces
have pity, those worn to extremity throughout the army, who honor you
like a god; surely in their eyes you would win very great glory.
For you might kill even Hector, since he would close upon you
in the grip of his deadly madness, seeing that he claims there is no man
    his equal   305
of Danaans whom our ships brought to this place."
        Then answering him spoke Achilles of the swift feet:
"Zeus-descended son of Laertes, Odysseus of many stratagems,
I must speak out what I have to say without care for consequence,

how I will now decide and thus how it will be accomplished,   310
so that you do not sit around me murmuring now from one side, now
   from another;
for hateful to me as the gates of Hades is that man,
who hides one thing in his mind, but says another;
and it is I who will say how it seems best to me.
I think neither Atreus' son Agamemnon will persuade me,   315
nor the other Danaans, since it seems there is no thanks
for doing battle against enemy men without respite, forever;
the fate is the same if a man hangs back, and if he battles greatly,
in equal honor are both coward and warrior;
and they die alike, both the man who has done nothing and he who has
   accomplished many things.   320
Nor is there any profit for me, because I have endured affliction at heart,
ever staking my life to do combat.
As a bird to her unfledged young brings
in her mouth whatever she catches, but for herself it goes badly,
so I too have passed many sleepless nights,   325
and come through many blood-soaked days of fighting,
doing battle with men who fight for their own wives.
Twelve cities of men I have sacked from my ships,
and eleven, I say, on foot throughout Troy's rich-soiled land;
and from all these I carried off as spoil many treasures, valuable
   treasures,   330
and would take and give them all to Agamemnon
the son of Atreus; and he hanging back beside his swift ships
accepted them, and would distribute little, and hold on to much.
Other prizes of honor he doled out to the noble men and to the kings;
theirs remain unplundered; mine alone of the Achaeans   335
he took away, and holds the bride fitted to my heart. Let him lie with her
and take his pleasure. But why must the Argives be at war with
the Trojans? Why did the son of Atreus assemble and lead
an army here? Was it not for Helen of the lovely hair?
Do the sons of Atreus alone of mortal men love their wives?   340
No, for any man who is decent and wise
loves her who is his own and cares for her, as I too loved
this one from my heart, spear-won though she be.
And now since he has taken my prize from my hands and cheated me,
let him not test me who know him too well—he will not persuade me—   345
but, Odysseus, let him ponder with you and the other kings
how to stave off from his ships consuming fire.
To be sure, he has done a great deal of work without me;
he has now even built a wall, and driven a trench around it,
broad and long, and planted stakes inside;   350
but not even so will he be able to withstand the strength
of man-slaying Hector; but so long as I was fighting among the Achaeans,
Hector was not minded to stir up battle beyond the wall,
but used to come only so far as the Scaean gates and oak tree.
There once he stood up to me alone, and barely escaped my onslaught.   355
   "Now, since I am not willing to do battle with shining Hector,
tomorrow having made holy sacrifice to Zeus and all the gods,

and heaping full my ships, after I have drawn them down to the salt sea—
you will see for yourself, if you should wish to and if these things
   interest you,
at very early morn, riding the fish-filled Hellespont,   360
my ships, and in them men eager to row;
and if the illustrious Earth-Shaker should grant fair passage,
on the third day I shall arrive at Phthia of the rich soil.
A great many possessions are there for me, which I left behind when I
   came on this ruinous journey,
and from here I shall lead away more gold and ruddy bronze   365
and fair-belted women, and gray iron,
as much as was assigned to me; but the prize of honor, though he gave me,
that lord Agamemnon in his towering outrage has taken back,
the son of Atreus. State all these things to him, as I direct,
openly, so that other Achaeans too will scorn him   370
if, as I have no doubt, he still hopes to cheat some one of the Danaans,
ever covered as he is in shamelessness; nor would he,
dog though he is, dare to look me in the face.
I will no longer join him in counsel, nor in deed;
for he has cheated me outright and sinned against me; let him not ever
   again   375
deceive me with words; enough for him. Let him go his cursed way
without hindrance; for Zeus all-devising has snatched his wits from him.
        "His gifts are hateful to me. I hold him at the value of a splinter.
Not if he gave me ten and twenty times as much
as he now owns, and if more were to come from other quarters,   380
not as much as is brought into Orchomenos,[8] or Egyptian
Thebes, where the greatest abundance of wealth lies stored in houses,
and which has a hundred gates, and through each two hundred
men march forth with horse and chariot,
not if he were to give me as many gifts as there are grains of dust or sand, 385
not even then would Agamemnon persuade my heart,
before he pays me back all this heart-grieving outrage.
I will not marry a daughter of Agamemnon son of Atreus,
not if she rivals golden Aphrodite in beauty,
and in skill matches Athena the gleaming-eyed;   390
not even so will I marry her. Let him acquire another one of the
   Achaeans,
someone who is befitting him and is more kingly.
For if the gods preserve me so long and I reach my home,
then Peleus himself will seek out a woman for me;
there are many Achaean women throughout Hellas and Phthia,[9]   395
daughters of noble men who defend high cities;
of these whichever I like I will make my beloved wife.
There time and again my strong spirit was set upon
a wife, wooed and wedded, a wife suited to me,

---

8. A city in central Greece, northwest of The- all of Greece, in Homer it refers to a region
bes; it was one of the most important Greek cit- next to Achilles' home district of Phthia. Both
ies from the Bronze Age onward. are in northern Greece.
9. Although Hellas later became the name for

to enjoy the wealth that aged Peleus acquired.   400
For not worth my life is all they say
Ilion used to possess, the well-settled high city,
in those days before, in peacetime, before there came the sons of the
   Achaeans,
not all that Phoebus Apollo the archer's
stone threshold contains in rocky Pytho.[1]   405
Cattle and fat sheep are carried off as plunder,
tripods are for the getting and tawny high-headed horses;
but the life of a man does not come back, not by plunder
nor by possession, once it passes the barrier of his teeth.
For my mother tells me, the goddess Thetis of the silver feet,   410
that two fates carry me to death's end;
if I remain here to fight around the city of the Trojans,
my return home is lost, but my glory will be undying;
but if I go home to the beloved land of my father,
outstanding glory will be lost to me, but my life will be long,   415
nor will death's end come on me swiftly.
And I would advise the rest of you
to make sail for home, since you will never see the fated end
of lofty Ilion; for sure it is that over it far-thundering Zeus
stretches his protective hand, and its people are now bold.   420
      "But you go to the Achaean nobles
and openly declare my message, for this is the privilege of counselors,
so they will think out in their minds some other better plan,
which might save their ships and the army of the Achaeans
by their hollow ships, since this plan of theirs is not feasible   425
that they have now devised while my wrath raged.
Let Phoinix remain here and sleep with us,
so that he may come with my ships to our beloved fatherland
tomorrow, if he wishes; I will not take him by force."
      So he spoke, and all the men were hushed in silence   430
amazed at his words; for he had spoken very powerfully.
At length Phoinix the aged horseman addressed him,
bursting forth in tears; for he feared greatly for the ships of the Achaeans:
"If now you ponder going home, shining Achilles,
and you do not intend in any way at all to defend the swift ships   435
from obliterating fire, because rage has assailed your heart,
how, then, apart from you, dear child, could I be left here
on my own? With you the aged horseman Peleus dispatched me
on that day when he sent you from Phthia to Agamemnon,
a child, knowing nothing of indiscriminate war,   440
nor of speaking in assembly, where men develop distinction;
for that reason he sent me out to teach you all these things,
to be both a speaker of words and a performer of deeds.
So therefore, dear child, I would not willingly be left behind
away from you, not if a very god should give me promise   445
to scrape old age away and render me fresh flourishing with youth,

---

1. Apollo's oracular shrine at Delphi. Its wealth consisted of offerings made to the god by grateful
worshippers.

as I was when I first left Hellas, the land of lovely women,
fleeing the hostility of my father, Amyntor son of Ormenos,
who was enraged with me on account of his mistress, she of the fine hair,
whom he lay with in love, and dishonored his wife, 450
my mother; she constantly begged me, at my knees,
to have intercourse with the mistress, so that she would hate the old man.
I obeyed her and did this; my father immediately suspecting
prayed and prayed for a curse upon me, and called upon the loathsome
    Furies,²
that he might never set upon his knees any dear child 455
born of me; and the gods fulfilled his curse,
both Zeus of the underworld and dread Persephone.³
I was ready to kill him with a sharp bronze sword;
but some one of the immortal gods turned my wits, who put me in mind
of people's opinion and the censure of mankind, 460
that among the Achaeans I might not be called a parricide.
Then no longer at all could the spirit in my chest be restrained
to wander along our halls, with my father angered;
true it is that many times kinsmen and cousins living around
restrained me with their pleas there in the halls; 465
many fat sheep and shambling twist-horned cattle
they slaughtered, many pigs luxuriant with fat
were singed and stretched across the fire of Hephaestus,
and much wine was drunk from the vats of the old man;
nine nights they kept watch close about me, 470
and taking turns they held guard, nor ever did the fires go out—
one beneath the entrance of the well-guarded courtyard,
the other in the alcove before my bedroom doors.
But when the tenth night came upon me with its murky darkness,
then I smashed the close-fitted doors of my chamber, 475
went out, and leapt over the courtyard wall
easily, escaping notice of the men on guard and household women.
Then I fled far away, through Hellas' wide country,
and arrived at Phthia of the rich soil, mother of flocks,
into the house of lord Peleus; and he willingly received me 480
and loved me, as a father loves his child,
his only child late-born to many properties;
and he made me rich, and gave me as a gift the rule of many people,
and I lived on the border of Phthia, ruling the Dolopes.
And you I made as great as you are, godlike Achilles, 485
loving you from my heart, for with no other man were you willing
to go out to the feast, nor would you eat in your own halls
before I settled you on my knees,
and cutting the meat first, gave you your fill and held the wine to your lips.
Many times you soaked through the tunic on my breast 490
spewing forth wine in your troublesome childish way.
So I suffered much for you and labored much,
with this in mind—that the gods would not create any offspring for me

---

2. Avenging spirits, particularly concerned   3. Wife of Hades (the "Underworld Zeus").
with crimes committed by kin against kin.

of my own; but you, godlike Achilles, I tried to make my son,
so that you might one day defend me from abject ruin. 495

     "Come, Achilles, master your great spirit; you must not keep
your heart without pity. And even the gods themselves can be turned,
although their majesty and honor and strength are even greater;
but with burnt sacrifices and prayers of propitiation
and libation and the savor of burnt offerings men turn them around 500
by praying, whenever some man has transgressed and strayed.
For Prayers of Penitence exist, daughters of great Zeus,
halting and grimacing and with squinting eyes,
their concern is to follow blind Delusion.
Delusion—she is strong and swift of foot, and thus 505
far outstrips all Prayers, and over every land she gets ahead
to trip up men; but Prayers of Penitence make amends thereafter.
The man who respects these daughters of Zeus when they approach,
him they greatly help and heed him as he prays;
but the man who spurns and rigidly rejects them, 510
then they go and pray to Zeus the son of Cronus
that Delusion follow him, so that thwarted by his blindness, he is punished.
Come, Achilles, you too grant that honor come to Zeus' daughters,
honor that bends the will of other, even noble, men.
If the son of Atreus were not bringing gifts and naming gifts to follow, 515
but continued to make violent outrage,
I would not bid you cast off your wrath
to defend the Argives, despite their need.
But now he both offers many things forthwith, and promises more later,
and has dispatched the best men to make supplication 520
chosen throughout the Achaean army, men who to you yourself
are dearest of the Argives; do not slight their word,
nor their journey; before, your anger was not blameworthy.

     "Thus also in days of old, we have heard the famous deeds of
    warrior men
when swelling anger seized them; 525
they were open to gifts and were moved by words.
I myself remember this deed of long ago, it is nothing new,
it was like this, I will tell it among you, all my friends;
the Curetes and the Aetolians, steadfast in battle, were fighting
around the city of Calydon,⁴ and killing each other, 530
the Aetolians defending lovely Calydon, Oineus' city,
the Curetes straining to sack it in war.
For it happened that Artemis of the golden throne had stirred up evil
    among them
in anger,⁵ as Oineus made no offering of first fruits to her
on the high ground of his orchard—the other gods shared in sacrificial
    hecatombs, 535
but to her alone, the daughter of great Zeus, he had not offered sacrifice.

---

4. A city in northwestern Greece. The Curetes and Aetolians were the local tribes, once allied but at odds in this story.
5. The Greek text says, ambiguously, "had cursed them." Possibly Artemis cursed both Aetolians and Curetes, since Oeneus was king of the Aetolian city Calydon.

Either he had forgotten or he had not thought of it, in the great delusion
 of his heart.
In her anger, she, child of Zeus who showers arrows,
incited a wild boar, foaming mad, with flashing tusks,
who did much evil to Oineus' orchard, as boars do;   540
many the tree he hurled to the ground, trunks and all, great trees
with their very roots and the blossoms of their fruit.
Meleager the son of Oineus killed it,
having gathered the hunting men of many cities
and their dogs; for in truth he could not have killed it with few; 545
so great it was, it brought many to the sorrow of the funeral pyre.
And then over its body the goddess incited much uproar and cry for battle,
concerning the head of the boar and its bristled hide,
between the Curetes and the great-hearted Aetolians.
   Then so long as Meleager beloved of Ares went to battle, 550
so long things went badly for the Curetes, nor could they
stand their ground outside the wall,[6] for all their numbers;
but when anger entered Meleager, anger that also swells
in the breasts of other men, even those of good understanding and
 shrewd mind,
why then, angered in his heart at his own mother Althaia   555
he lay apart with his wedded wife, beautiful Cleopatra,
the daughter of Marpessa—she of the slender ankles, the child of Euenos
and of Idas, who was the strongest of men upon earth
at that time, and even raised his bow against lord
Phoebus Apollo for the sake of this maiden with slender ankles— 560
after that, within their home her father and lady mother
used to call her name Halcyon, for her
mother shared the halcyon's fate, the sorrowing sea bird,
weeping, because Phoebus Apollo who works from afar had snatched
 her daughter away;
it was with this Cleopatra that Meleager lay brooding on his
 heart-grieving rage,   565
raging at his mother's curses, because she
in anguish over his slaying of her brother,[7] made prayer again and again
 to the gods,
again and again beating the nourishing earth with her hands,
calling on Hades and dread Persephone,
sitting bent-kneed, her bosom soaked with tears,   570
to send death to her child; and Erinys who walks in darkness
heard her from the nether dark of Erebus,[8] and her heart is implacable.
   "And soon around the gates arose the roar of the Curetes, the din
of towers being assailed; and the Aetolian elders beseeched Meleager,
and sent the gods' noblest priests   575

---

6. The Greek text says only "the wall"—probably not Calydon's wall, since the Curetes
should be attacking that city. It may be the wall
of Pleuron, the Curetes' city. Or, as one commentator has suggested, the wall could be one
built by the besieging Curetes around their
encampment outside Calydon, as the Greeks
have done at Troy.

7. In the course of the battles Meleager had
killed one of his mother's brothers.

8. The underworld. "Erinys": a Fury, or avenging spirit.

to come out and defend them, pledging a great reward:
wherever lay the richest field in lovely Calydon,
there they urged him to take for himself a piece of land, of surpassing
   beauty,
and mark off from the common lot fifty acres,
one half for vineyards, one half open field for plowing.   580
Again and again the aged horseman Oineus entreated him,
standing on the threshold of his high-roofed chamber,
shaking the fitted doors, pleading with his son,
time and again his sisters and lady mother
entreated him; but he denied them vehemently; time and again did his
   companions,   585
who were the most devoted and dearest to him of all men;
but not even so did they win over the heart in his breast,
until that moment when his chamber was hammered with close blows,
   and the Curetes
were scaling the walls and setting fire to the great city.
And then his fair-belted wife supplicated Meleager   590
as she wept, and went through everything for him,
all the sufferings that come to those whose city is taken;
they kill the men and fire reduces the city to dust,
strangers lead off the children and slender-waisted women.
And as Meleager heard tell of these evil deeds, his heart was stirred,   595
and he went and clad his body in his glittering armor.
So he beat back from the Aetolians their day of evil,
yielding to his own heart; but they never paid him the gifts,
the many splendid and welcome gifts—and he averted the evil to no end.
     "But you Achilles, do not think such things in your mind, nor let
   some dark spirit   600
turn you that way, dear one; it would be less worthy
to defend the ships once they are burning. But come while there are gifts;
the Achaeans will honor you like a god.
But if without gifts you enter the man-destroying battle,
you will no longer be so honored, for all you beat back the war."   605
     Then answering him, Achilles of the swift feet spoke:
"Phoinix, old father, cherished by Zeus, in no way do I have need
of such honor—I think I am honored by the just measure of Zeus,
which would keep me by the curved ships, as long as life's breath
remains in my breast and my knees have motion.   610
And I will tell you something else and put it away in your mind;
do not confound my heart with your weeping and groaning,
carrying favor for the warrior son of Atreus; you should not
hold him so dear, lest you become hateful to me who love you.
It is fitting for you to join me to trouble him who troubles me.   615
Rule equally with me, and share half my honor.
These men will take my message, but you stay and take your rest
on a soft bed here; when the dawn shows forth
we will consider whether we will return with our men, or stay."
     He spoke, and he motioned silently with his brows to Patroclus   620
to smooth the snug bed for Phoinix, so that with all speed
the others would think of going back from his shelter. And Ajax

the godlike son of Telamon spoke his word among them:
"Zeus-descended son of Laertes, Odysseus of many stratagems,
let us go; for it does not seem to me that fulfillment of our mandate   625
will be accomplished on this journey. We must report his word without
    delay,
unfavorable even as it is, to the Danaans,
who surely await us now. But Achilles
has made savage the great-hearted spirit in his breast,
he is hard, and turns his back on that friendship of companions   630
for which we honored him beyond all others by the ships,
pitiless; a man will accept payment even from his brother's killer
or for his dead child,
and the man who has paid much in penalty remains there, in his
    country,
and the heart and the proud spirit of the other is checked,   635
by accepting recompense. But in your breast the gods have placed
an implacable, a baneful spirit, for the sake of a single
girl; and now we offer you seven, exceptional, the best,
and many other things besides. Gentle your heart,
respect your house; we are under your roof   640
from all the multitude of the Danaans, and beyond all others,
as many as the Achaeans are, yearn to be closest and dearest to you."

    And answering him Achilles of the swift feet spoke:
"Ajax, son of Telamon descended from Zeus, leader of the people,
you seem in a way to speak everything after my mind,   645
but my heart swells with rage when I recall those things—
how in the presence of the Argives he degraded me,
the son of Atreus, as if I were some worthless vagabond.
But all of you go and speak my message openly—
that I shall have no thought again of bloodstained war   650
until the son of brilliant Priam, shining Hector,
reaches the ships and shelters of the Myrmidons,
killing Argives, and smokes the ships with smoldering fire;
about my shelter and dark ship
I think, Hector, eager though he be for war, will be stopped."   655

        So he spoke. And the men each having taken up a double-
    handled cup
and having poured libations beside the ships went back, and Odysseus led.
And Patroclus bade the companions and servant women
lay out a snug bed for Phoinix forthwith;
and they in obedience lay out the bed as he commanded,   660
with fleeces and a covering cloth and fine nubbed linen.
There the old man lay down and awaited the shining dawn;
but Achilles slept in the inner recess of his well-built shelter,
and with him lay a woman, one he had taken from Lesbos,
the daughter of Phorbas, Diomede of the lovely cheeks;   665
and on the other side lay Patroclus, and by him
fair-belted Iphis, whom godlike Achilles gave him
when he took steep Scyros, the high city of Enyeus.

        And when the others appeared inside the son of Atreus' shelter,
then with cups of gold uplifted the sons of the Achaeans pledged them,   670

rising to their feet, one after the other, and made interrogation.
And first to make inquiry was the lord of men Agamemnon:
"Come, tell me, O illustrious Odysseus, great pride of the Achaeans,
will he beat back the blazing fire from our ships,
or did he refuse, and does rage still have hold of his great-hearted
   spirit?" 675
       Then in turn much-enduring godlike Odysseus addressed him:
"Most glorious son of Atreus, lord of men Agamemnon;
the man is unwilling to quench his rage, but is all the more
filled with wrath, and rejects you and your gifts.
And he urges you yourself to consult among the Argives 680
how you might save your ships and the army of the Achaeans.
He himself threatened when dawn shows forth
to haul his well-benched double-ended ships to the sea;
and he said he would advise the rest of us
to make sail for home, 'since you will never see the fated end 685
of lofty Ilion; for sure it is that over it far-thundering Zeus
stretches his protective hand, and its people are now bold.'
Thus he spoke; and these men are here to confirm this, who came with me,
Ajax and the two heralds, both men of good sense.
But Phoinix the old man sleeps there, as he urges, 690
in order that he may follow with him in his ships to their beloved
   fatherland
tomorrow, if he chooses; for he will not take him by force."
       So he spoke, and all the men were hushed in silence
amazed at his words; for he had spoken very powerfully.
For a long time the sons of the Achaeans were quiet with sorrow. 695
At length Diomedes of the war cry addressed them:
"Most glorious son of Atreus, lord of men Agamemnon;
you should not have beseeched the blameless son of Peleus
offering endless gifts. He is a proud man as it is;
but now you have inclined him all the more to pride. 700
Come, let him be, either he will go
or he will stay. Then he will fight again, whenever
the spirit in his own breast bids him and god urges.
But come, for so I speak, and let us all be persuaded;
let us now take rest in sleep having satisfied our hearts with 705
food and wine, for this is our strength and courage;
but when Dawn the beautiful shows forth a finger of rosy light,
swiftly array men and horses before the ships,
urging them on, and yourself fight in the front lines."
So he spoke, and all the princes assented, 710
in admiration of the word of Diomedes breaker of horses.
Then when they had poured libations, each man went to his shelter
where they laid themselves to rest and took the gift of sleep.

Summary   After Achilles' refusal, the situation of the Greeks worsens rapidly. Agamemnon, Diomedes, and Odysseus are all wounded. The Trojans breach the stockade and fight beside the ships. Patroclus tries to bring Achilles to the aid of the Greeks, but the most he can obtain is permission for himself to fight, clad in Achilles' armor, at the head of the Myrmidons.

From BOOK XVI

[Patroclus Fights and Dies]

* * *

And when Sarpedon[9] saw his loose-robed Lycian comrades
broken at the hands of Patroclus, son of Menoetius,   420
he called out, addressing the godlike Lycians:
"For shame, O Lycians! Whither do you flee? Now be swift to fight.
For I will go forth to meet this man,[1] so that I may learn
who this is who holds sway over us and has worked so much evil
on the Trojans, since the knees of many men, brave men, he has
   unstrung."   425
     He spoke and leapt from his chariot in his armor to the ground;
and from the other side Patroclus leapt from his chariot, when he saw him.
And as great birds of prey, hook-clawed, bent-beaked,
screaming loud on a high rock go to battle,
so these, screaming, charged at one another.   430
     And seeing them the son of devious Cronus pitied them,
and he spoke to Hera, his sister and his wife:
"Alas for me that Sarpedon, dearest of men to me,
is destined to be broken by the hand of Patroclus son of Menoetius.
My heart is inclined two ways in my breast as I debate this,   435
whether snatching him alive from tearful battle
I should set him down in the rich country of Lycia,
or now beat him down at the hands of Menoetius' son."
     Then answered him ox-eyed lady Hera:
"Most dread son of Cronus, what kind of word have you spoken?   440
This mortal man, long ago consigned to his allotted fate—
you wish to release him from the hard-sorrow death?
Do so; but not all the other gods will approve.
And something else I will tell you, and you put it away in your mind—
if you should send Sarpedon to his home alive,   445
take care, lest some other of the gods should also wish
to send his beloved son away from the ferocious combat.
For around the great city of Priam there are fighting many
sons of the immortals; you will arouse a terrible rancor in them.
But if he is dear to you, and your heart feels pity,   450
then let him in this ferocious combat
be killed at the hands of Menoetius' son Patroclus,
but when his soul and his life force have left him,
send Death and gentle Sleep[2] to carry him
until they come to the country of broad Lycia,   455
where his brothers and his kinsmen will bury him
with a tomb and marking stone, for this is the honor of the dead."
     So she spoke; and the father of gods and of men did not disobey.
But to the earth he rained drops of blood

9. King of Lycia in Asia Minor, son of Zeus and
a mortal woman; he is a Trojan ally (for his genealogy, see his cousin Glaukos's account in his
speech to Diomedes in book 6, lines 155–217).

1. He is referring to Patroclus, who has
returned to the battle wearing Achilles' armor.
2. The brother of Death, according to the
Greeks.

honoring his beloved son, whom Patroclus was to   460
destroy in Troy's rich soil, far from the land of his father.
     And when they had advanced almost upon each other,
then Patroclus struck illustrious Thrasydemos,
who was the good henchman of his lord Sarpedon,
in the lower belly, and unstrung his limbs.   465
And Sarpedon attacking second missed Patroclus
with his shining spear, but struck the horse Pedasos[3]
on the right shoulder with the spear; and he crashed down, gasping out
   his life,
and collapsed in the dust screaming, and his life-spirit flew away.
And the paired horses wheeled apart, the yoke groaned, their reins   470
were tangled, since their trace horse lay in the dust.
But spear-famed Automedon found an end to this;
drawing his fine-edged sword from beside his sturdy thigh,
darting forward with swift skill, he cut away the trace;
and the two horses righted themselves, and were pulled on course by
   the reins.   475
     And again the two men came together in heart-devouring strife.
And again Sarpedon missed with his shining spear,
and over Patroclus' left shoulder the spear-point
passed, nor struck him. But then Patroclus attacked with his bronze-
   headed spear;
and from his hand the shaft did not fly in vain,   480
but struck, there where the lungs close in around the beating heart;
Sarpedon fell as when an oak falls, or white poplar,
or stately pine that in the mountains timbering men
fell with fresh-whetted axes to make a ship;
so he lay stretched out before his chariot and horses,   485
roaring, clutching at the bloodied dust.
As when a lion coming among a herd slaughters a fiery, great-hearted
bull among the shambling cattle,
and it dies groaning under the lion's jaws,
so at the hands of Patroclus did the leader of the shield-bearing
   Lycians   490
rage as he lay dying, and called by name his beloved comrade:
"Glaukos old friend, warrior among men, now you must
be a spearman and brave warrior;
if you are quick, let bitter war be your desire.
Before all else, range everywhere to rouse the Lycian leaders   495
to go to battle round Sarpedon;
and then you yourself fight for me with your bronze spear.
For I will be a disgrace and a rebuke for you
all your days through if the Achaeans
strip the armor from me, fallen among the gathering of their ships.   500
Hold on strongly, and rally all the people."
     Then as he was so speaking, the end that is death covered

3. The third (or "trace") horse that ran alongside the pair pulling Patroclus's chariot to help
it maneuver. The other two horses are immortal, given by the gods to Achilles' father Peleus.
In the next lines, they shy away from contact
with death.

his nose and eyes. Patroclus stepping with his heel upon his chest
yanked his spear from the flesh, and the lungs followed with it;
so he drew forth the man's soul and his spear-point together.　　　　505
And the Myrmidons kept hold of Sarpedon's panting horses,
as they strained for flight, free of their master's chariot.
　　　　But a dreadful grief descended on Glaukos as he heard Sarpedon's
　　voice,
and his heart was stirred, because he was not able to defend him.
Taking his own arm with his hand he pressed it; for his wound bore
　　hard　　510
upon him where Teucer, warding off harm from his companions,
had struck him with his arrow as he rushed the high rampart.[4]
And praying, Glaukos addressed Apollo who shoots from afar:
"Hear me, lord, you who are somewhere in the rich land of Lycia,
or in Troy; for you are able, wherever you are, to hear　　515
a man in distress, as distress comes to me now.
For I have this mighty wound, and my arm
is pierced around with sharp pain, nor can I staunch the blood,
and my shoulder is heavy beneath it;
I cannot hold my spear steady, nor can I join in battle　　520
going among my enemies. And the best of men has perished,
Sarpedon, son of Zeus—who did not defend his own son.
But you, lord,[5] heal this powerful wound for me,
calm the pains, and give me strength, so that
summoning my Lycian companions I stir them to do battle,　　525
and myself fight about the body of the man who has died."
　　　　So he spoke praying, and Phoebus Apollo heard him;
at once he stopped the pains, and from the grievous wound
he staunched the dark blood, and cast strength in his spirit.
And Glaukos knew this within his heart and he rejoiced,　　530
because the great god had heard his praying at once.
First, ranging everywhere he roused the Lycian leaders
to go to battle round Sarpedon;
and then with long strides he went among the Trojans,
to Poulydamas the son of Panthoös, and shining Agenor,　　535
then to Aeneas and to Hector of the brazen helm.
And standing close to him he spoke winged words:
"Hector, now do you take no thought at all of your allies,
who for your sake, far from their friends and fatherland,
waste away their lives, but you are unwilling to fight for them.　　540
Sarpedon lies dead, lord of the spear-bearing Lycians,
who protected broad Lycia with his just judgment and strength;
brazen Ares has broken him with his spear at the hands of Patroclus.
Come, friends, take your stand by him, feel shame in your heart
lest they strip his armor away, and maltreat his body,　　545
they the Myrmidons, in anger that so many Danaans have died,
those whom we killed by their swift ships with our spears."

---

4. The wall erected by the Greeks to protect their ships and breached by the Trojans. "Teucer": an archer on the Greek side, half- brother of Ajax.
5. Apollo, who inflicted the plague in book 1, is also the god of healing.

So he spoke, and there swept the Trojans, head to foot, a wave
  of grief,
uncontainable, unrelenting, since Sarpedon had been a support of
  their city,
outlander though he was; for with him many   550
troops had followed, and he had been preeminent in waging battle.
And in pressing haste they made straight for the Danaans; and leading
  them
was Hector, angered for Sarpedon. But the Achaeans
were rallied by Patroclus, the rugged-hearted son of Menoetius;
and he first addressed the two Aiantes,[6] both already burning to do
  battle: 555
"Aiantes, now let it be your desire to fight
as such as you were among men before, or yet better.
The man lies dead who first leapt upon the Achaeans' ramparts,
Sarpedon. Come, let us see if we can mutilate and shame him and seize
the armor from his shoulders to bear away; and any one of his
  companions   560
who defends the body, let us beat him down with our pitiless bronze."
So he spoke, but they already burned to fight them off.
      And when the men on both sides had strengthened their ranks,
Trojans and Lycians and Myrmidons and Achaeans
met to fight about the body of the man who died,   565
shouting fearfully; and the arms of the men rang loud.
And Zeus spread a deadly darkness on the ferocious combat,
so that over his beloved son there would be deadly toil of fighting.
      The Trojans first pushed back the dark-eyed Achaeans;
then not the worst among the Myrmidons was struck—   570
shining Epeigeus, the son of great-hearted Agakles,
who ruled in well-settled Boudeion
in time before; but after slaying his noble cousin
he had come as suppliant to Peleus and Thetis of the silver feet;
and they sent him to accompany Achilles, breaker of men,   575
to Ilion of the horses, to wage battle with the Trojans.
This man shining Hector struck, as he took hold of Sarpedon's body,
on the head with a boulder; and the whole of his head within its strong
  helmet
was cleaved in two; and he dropped face forward
upon the corpse, and death which shatters the spirit seeped
  around him.   580
      And grief descended on Patroclus for his dead companion,
and he made straight through the frontlines like a swift hawk,
who sets to scattered flight the daws and starlings;
so rider Patroclus, straight for the Lycians
you rushed, and for the Trojans, your heart enraged over your
  companion.   585

---

6. Or "Ajaxes." Of the two Greek warriors with this name, the son of Telamon was among the most outstanding fighters at Troy; the less distinguished son of Oïleus still played a promi- nent role in battle (and, according to poetry outside the *Iliad*, in the sack of Troy). They are sometimes found fighting together.

And he struck Sthenelaos, the dear son of Ithaimenes,
on his neck with a boulder, and smashed the tendons from it.
Then the frontline fighters and shining Hector fell back;
as far as a cast is made of a long hunting javelin,
which a man hurls forth making trial of his strength, either in contest   590
or also in war when his life-shattering enemies press close,
so far did the Trojans give way, and the Achaeans push them.

    Then Glaukos, leader of the shield-bearing Lycians, was first
to turn, and he killed great-hearted Bathykles,
the beloved son of Chalkon, who making his home in Hellas   595
was outstanding in prosperity and wealth among the Myrmidons;
this man Glaukos, turning suddenly, stabbed with his spear in the middle
of his chest, just as the other in pursuit was catching him,
and he fell with a thud. Crushing grief took hold of the Achaeans
as the brave man fell; but the Trojans rejoiced greatly,   600
and running up they stood about him in a throng; nor did the Achaeans
forget their courage, but bore their fury straight toward them.

    Then in turn Meriones[7] slew a Trojan commander,
Laogonos, the bold son of Onetor, who was priest of Idaean[8]
Zeus, and was honored like a god by the people;   605
this man Meriones struck below the jaw and ear, and swiftly his spirit
left his limbs, and the hateful darkness took him.
And Aeneas let fly a bronze-tipped spear at Meriones,
for he hoped to strike him as he strode forward under cover of his shield;
but Meriones looking straight ahead dodged the bronze spear-point,   610
for he ducked forward, and the long spear-shaft
was fixed in the earth behind him, the butt-end quivering;
then mighty Ares took away its force.   613
And Aeneas was angered in heart and called out:[9]   616
"Meriones, my spear would surely have put swift end to you for good,
dancer though you be, had I only hit you."[1]
Then spear-famed Meriones answered him in return:
"Aeneas, hard it is for you, for all your strength,   620
to quench the life of every man who comes against you
to defend himself; yes, even you are mortal.
And if I too should chance to strike you dead center with sharp bronze,
even strong as you are and trusting in your strength of hand,
you would soon give glory to me and your soul to Hades."   625
So he spoke; but the brave son of Menoetius rebuked him:
"Meriones, why do you, a good warrior, utter these things?
Old friend, it is not by abusive words the Trojans
will give way from the corpse; the earth will bury many a man before
    that.
For the sum of war lies in strength of hands, the sum of words in
    council;   630
therefore there is no need to pile up words, but to do battle."

---

7. A warrior from Crete on the Greek side.
8. Of Ida, a high mountain near Troy where
Zeus had a cult (and from which he watches
the fighting on the plain).

9. The line numbers here account for lines
that were omitted by the translator because
they may not belong in the text.
1. In Homer, dancing is the opposite of warfare.

So speaking he led on, and the other followed with him, a man like a god.
     And as the clangor of woodcutting men is raised
in the glens of a mountain, and is heard from far away,
so from the wide-wayed earth arose the pounding of men's   635
bronze and strong-made ox-hide shields,
as they stabbed at one another with their swords and double-edged spears,
Nor would even a clear-sighted man still recognize godlike Sarpedon,
since with blood and dust and missile shafts
he was covered from his head right down to the bottom of his feet;   640
and always the men thronged about his corpse, as when flies
in a sheepfold buzz about pails over-full of milk
in the season of spring, when milk soaks the buckets;
so they thronged about the corpse; nor ever did Zeus
turn his shining eyes from the ferocious combat,   645
but ever gazed down upon them, and pondered in his heart
many things as he brooded on the slaying of Patroclus,
whether now in the ferocious combat,
right there about godlike Sarpedon, shining Hector
should kill Patroclus with his bronze spear and take the armor from
   his shoulders,   650
or whether for yet more men he should increase the hard toil of war.
And this seemed to him as he considered, to be best—
that the good henchmen of Peleus' son Achilles
one more time should force the Trojans and bronze-helmed Hector
to their city, and snatch the lives of many.   655
And in Hector first he inspired a coward's spirit:
mounting his chariot, Hector turned his team for flight, and bade the
   other
Trojans flee; for he saw how the holy scales of Zeus were balanced.
Then the strong Lycians did not stand firm, but fled,
all of them, when they saw their king struck in the heart   660
lying in a heap of corpses; for many men had dropped upon him,
when the son of Cronus stretched tight the mighty strife of battle.
Then from the shoulders of Sarpedon the Achaeans seized his armor,
bronze, glittering; and this to the hollow ships
the brave son of Menoetius gave his companions to carry.   665
     And then Zeus who gathers the clouds addressed Apollo:
"Come now, beloved Phoebus, take Sarpedon out of range of the flying
weapons and cleanse him of his dark-clouded blood, and
conveying him far away, bathe him in the flowing of a river
and anoint him with ambrosia, and put ambrosial clothing
   round him.   670
And send him forth to be conveyed with swift guards of honor,
Sleep and Death, the twins, who will soon
lay him in broad Lycia's rich country;
there his brothers and his kinsmen will bury him
with a tomb and marking stone, for this is the honor of the dead."   675
     So he spoke, nor did Apollo fail to hearken to his father;
down from the Idaean mountains he descended into the dread field
   of battle,
and straightway lifting godlike Sarpedon out of range of flying weapons,

conveying him far away, he bathed him in the flowing of a river
and anointed him with ambrosia, and put ambrosial clothing
   round him.   680
And he sent him forth to be conveyed with swift guards of honor,
Sleep and Death, the twins, who soon
set him down in broad Lycia's rich country.
      But Patroclus shouting to Automedon to follow with the horses,
made for the Lycians and Trojans, blinded to his great folly—   685
fool; if only he had observed the son of Peleus' command,[2]
he might yet have escaped from the fated evil of dark death.
But the mind of Zeus is ever mightier than the mind of man;
Zeus who puts even a brave man to flight and takes away his victory
easily, but at another time urges him on to battle;   690
Zeus who now put fury in the breast of Patroclus.
      Then who was the first, who was the last you slew,
Patroclus, when the gods summoned you deathward?
Adrestos first, and Autonoös, and Echeklos,
and Perimos the son of Megas, and Epistor, and Melanippos,   695
and then Elasos and Moulios and Pylartes;
these he killed, and the rest turned their thoughts to flight, every man
   of them.
Then would the sons of the Achaeans have taken high-gated Troy
under the hands of Patroclus, as he raged ever forward with his spear,
had not Phoebus Apollo on the strong-built tower   700
taken his stand, with deadly deeds in mind for him, but help for the
   Trojans.
Three times to the angled joint of the high wall went
Patroclus, and three times Apollo smote him back,
batting with immortal hands the shining shield.
But when for the fourth time Patroclus charged like something more
   than human,   705
the god calling out in a voice of dread spoke winged words:
"Give way, Patroclus, seed of Zeus; it is not fated
that the city of the noble Trojans be sacked under your spear,
nor under that of Achilles, he who is greater by far than you."
So he spoke; and Patroclus withdrew a great way back,   710
shunning the wrath of far-shooting Apollo.
      And at the Scaean gates Hector pulled up his single-hoofed horses;
he debated whether, driving through the tumult, he should go to battle
   once again,
or should call for his men to mass within the walls.
And as he thought these things there came up to him Phoebus Apollo, 715
in the likeness of a young and powerful man,
Asios, who was the maternal uncle of horse-breaking Hector,
brother of Hecuba, and son of Dymas,
who dwelt in Phrygia, by the flowing waters of Sangarios.
In likeness to him Apollo son of Zeus addressed him: 720
"Hector, why do you give over fighting? You should not.

<hr />

2. In sending Patroclus into battle, Achilles told him only to chase the Trojans from the Greek ships and not to pursue them all the way back to Troy.

Would I were stronger than you by as much as I am weaker!
Then you would soon regret holding back from war.
But come, drive your strong-hoofed horses against Patroclus,
in hope you might kill him, and Apollo give you great glory." 725
       So speaking he set out again, a god among the fighting throng
  of men,
and shining Hector called to skilled Kebriones
to whip the horses into battle; and Apollo
set out and made his way into the throng, and against the Argives
he launched evil rout, and to the Trojans and to Hector he gave glory. 730
And Hector let the other Danaans go, and did not kill them,
but it was against Patroclus he drove his strong-hoofed horses.
And Patroclus from his side jumped from behind his horses to the
  ground,
holding his spear in his left hand, and with the other he seized a rock
glittering and jagged, which his hand covered over, 735
and with his strength behind it he hurled; he did not long stand in awe
  of the man,
nor was his cast in vain, but he struck Hector's charioteer
Kebriones, a bastard son of worthy Priam,
between his eyes with the sharp rock as he held the horses' reins.
The stone shattered his brows, the bone did not hold, 740
his eyes fell to the ground in the dust
before his feet; and he, like a diver,
dropped from the strong-made chariot, and his spirit left his bones.
And mocking, you addressed him, rider Patroclus:
"How now, truly a most nimble man; how easily he somersaults! 745
No doubt were he also in the fish-filled sea,
this man would fill the bellies of many as he groped for molluscs,
leaping from a ship, even in rough seas;
as now on land he somersaults lightly from his chariot.
To be sure, there are divers among the Trojans too." 750
So speaking he made for the warrior Kebriones
with the spring of a lion, who ravaging a sheepfold
is struck on the chest, and it is his courage that destroys him;
so at Kebriones, Patroclus, did you leap in your fury.
      And from the other side Hector sprang from behind his horses
  to the ground. 755
They two around Kebriones contended like lions
who in mountain heights fight over a slain deer,
both hungry, both with high resolve,
so over Kebriones the two masters of battle,
Patroclus son of Menoetius and shining Hector, 760
strained to cut the flesh of one another with pitiless bronze.
When Hector caught Kebriones by the head, nor would let go,
Patroclus from the other side took hold of his feet; and the rest of the
Trojans and Danaans joined in the ferocious combat.
As the East and South Winds vie with each other 765
in a mountain glen to set the deep woods shaking,
oak and ash and fine-barked cornel
that hurl at each other sharp-pointed boughs

with inhuman roar, crashing as they shatter,
so the Trojans and Achaeans surging toward each other   770
cut their enemy down, nor did either have thought of disastrous flight.
And around Kebriones many sharp spears stuck fast
and feathered arrows springing from their bowstrings,
and many great boulders battered the shields
of the men fighting round him. But Kebriones lay in the whirling dust,   775
a great man in his greatness, unmindful of his horsemanship.
   As long as the sun stood astride the middle heaven,
so long the shafts of both sides found their mark, and the people fell;
but when the sun passed over to the time for unyoking of oxen,
then even beyond fate the Achaeans were the stronger.   780
Away from the flying weapons they dragged the warrior Kebriones,
away from the shouting of the Trojans, and from his shoulders took his
 armor,
and Patroclus with evil intent sprang for the Trojans.
   Three times then he charged at them, swift Ares' equal,
shouting his terrifying cry, and three times he slew nine men;   785
but when for the fourth time he swept against them, like something more
 than human,
then for you, Patroclus, was shown the end of life;
for meeting you in the ferocious combat was Apollo
the dread. Patroclus did not see him as he closed in through the tumult;
for cloaked in thick mist Apollo met him,   790
then stood behind, and struck the back and broad shoulders of Patroclus
with the flat of his hand, so that his eyes spun.
From his head Phoebus Apollo struck the helmet;
and rolling beneath the horses' hooves it rang resounding,
four-horned, hollow-eyed, the horsehair crest defiled   795
with blood and dust. Before this it was forbidden that
the horsehair-crested helmet be defiled by dust,[3]
for it had protected the handsome head and brow of the godlike man
Achilles; but now Zeus gave it to Hector
to wear on his head; but his own death was very near.   800
In Patroclus' hands the long-shadowed spear was wholly shattered,
heavy, massive, powerful, pointed with bronze; from his shoulders
his bordered shield and belt dropped to the ground;
then lord Apollo, son of Zeus, undid his breastplate.
   Confusion seized his wits, his shining limbs were loosed
 beneath him,   805
Patroclus stood stunned. Behind him, in his back, between his shoulders,
a Dardanian man struck with a sharp spear at close range,
Euphorbos son of Panthoös, who surpassed the youths of his own age
in work of spear and horsemanship and speed of feet;
already he had brought down twenty men from behind their horses   810
since first coming with his chariot, to learn the art of war;
he first let fly his spear at you, rider Patroclus,
but did not kill you. And back he ran again, and mingled in the crowd,

---

3. Because it was divinely made, part of the armor given by the gods to Peleus on his marriage
to Thetis.

snatching from your flesh his ash-wood spear, and did not stand to wait,
Patroclus, naked though he was among the fighters.   815
And Patroclus, broken by the blow of the god and by the spear,
tried to retreat into the band of his companions and shun death.
        But Hector, when he saw great-hearted Patroclus
drawing back, when he saw him wounded with sharp bronze,
then through the ranks he closed upon him, and stabbed with
        his spear   820
into his lower flank, and drove the bronze point through;
with a thud Patroclus fell, and his falling brought great anguish on the
        Achaean army.
As when a lion overpowers a tireless boar in spirited combat,
they who on the mountain heights go to battle with high resolve
over a small spring, and both desire to drink,   825
and as the boar gasps hard for breath, the lion beats him down with
        violent strength—
so, having slain so many, the brave son of Menoetius
was stripped of his life by Hector son of Priam at close quarters with
        his spear.
And vaunting over him Hector spoke out winged words:
"Patroclus, surely you thought you would cut down our city,   830
and stripping the Trojan women of their day of freedom
would carry them in ships to your beloved fatherland,
you fool; for in front of them the swift horses of Hector
galloped with outstretched legs to battle, and I with my spear myself
outshone the battle-loving Trojans, I who warded off from them   835
the day of slavery; you the vultures will devour here.
Poor wretch, nor, great though he is, did Achilles rescue you,
who, I suppose, laid many injunctions on you, while he remained and
        you departed:
'Do not return to me, Patroclus, master of horses,
by the hollow ships, before you have ripped man-slaying Hector's   840
bloodied tunic around his breast.'
Thus I suppose he spoke to you, and persuaded your fool's wits."
        Then with little strength you answered him, rider Patroclus:
"Make your great boast now, Hector; for Zeus the son of Cronus
has given you victory and Apollo, they who easily broke me;   845
for they took the armor from my shoulders.
But if twenty such as you had encountered me,
all would have died here broken beneath my spear;
deadly Fate and the son of Leto killed me,
and of men it was Euphorbos; you were third to kill me.   850
And something else I will tell you, and you put it away in your mind—
you yourself will not live long, but already
death and powerful fate stand close beside you,
to be broken at the hands of blameless Achilles Aeacides."
Then the closure of death enveloped him as he was speaking   855
and his soul flying from his limbs started for Hades,
lamenting her fate, abandoning manhood and all its young vigor.
        And shining Hector addressed him, dead though he was:
"Patroclus, why do you now prophesy sheer destruction for me?

Who knows whether Achilles, son of Thetis of the lovely hair,   860
might be stabbed first by my spear, and lose his life?"
So speaking he drew his bronze-pointed spear from the wound,
stepping on Patroclus with his heel, and shoved him on his back away
    from his spear.
            And straightway he went with his spear after Automedon,
the godlike henchman of swift-footed Aeacides,   865
and took aim to strike him; but the swift horses bore Automedon away,
the immortal horses that the gods gave as glorious gifts to Peleus.

Summary   Hector strips Achilles' divine armor from Patroclus's corpse. A fierce fight for
the body itself ends in partial success for the Greeks; they take Patroclus's body but have to
retreat to their camp, with the Trojans at their heels.

BOOK XVIII

[The Shield of Achilles]

So they fought like blazing fire;
but Antilochos[4] went as swift-footed messenger to Achilles.
And he found him in front of his straight-horned ships,
foreboding in his heart those things that now had happened,
and troubled he addressed his own great-hearted spirit: 5
"Ah me, why now are the long-haired Achaeans again
driven to the ships in panicked confusion across the plain?
May the gods not have accomplished evil sufferings for my heart,
as once my mother plainly told me, and said to me
that while I yet lived, the best of Myrmidons   10
at Trojan hands would leave the light of day.
Surely Menoetius' brave son has already died,
stubborn one; and yet I told him that when he had driven off the
    blazing fire
to come back to the ships, not battle in his strength with Hector."
            While he churned these things through his mind and heart,   15
the son of noble Nestor drew close to him
shedding hot tears, and spoke his grievous message:
"Woe to me, son of brilliant Peleus, surely it is a baleful
message you will hear, would that it had never happened.
Patroclus lies dead, and they are fighting round his naked   20
body; for Hector of the shimmering helm has his armor."
            So he spoke; and a dark cloud of grief enveloped Achilles.
Taking with both hands the fire-blackened ashes,
he poured them down upon his head, and defiled his handsome face;
on his fragrant tunic the black ash settled;   25
and he lay outstretched in the dust,

---

4. A son of Nestor. He has been sent to tell Achilles that Patroclus is dead.

a great man in his greatness, and with his own hands he defiled his hair,
   tearing at it.
And the female slaves, whom Achilles and Patroclus had seized as plunder,
stricken at heart cried loud, and ran outside
around brilliant Achilles, and all with their hands   30
beat their breasts, and the limbs of each went slack beneath them;
on his other side Antilochos wept, pouring tears,
holding the hands of Achilles as his noble heart groaned.
For he feared lest Achilles cut his own throat with iron.
      Dreadful were Achilles' cries of grief; his lady mother heard   35
as she sat in the depths of the sea beside her aged father.
Then she wailed in turn; and all the goddesses gathered round her,
who down in the depths of the sea were daughters of Nereus.
There was Glauke, Thaleia and Kymodoke,
Nesaie and Speio, Thoë and ox-eyed Halia,   40
Kymothoë and also Aktaia, and Limnoreia,
Melite, and Iaira, Amphithoë and Agauë,
Doto, Proto and Pherousa, Dynamene,
Dexamene, Amphinome and Kallianeira;
Doris and Panope and illustrious Galateia   45
and Nemertes and Apseudes and Kallianassa;
and Klymene was there and Ianeira and also Ianassa,
Maira and Oreithyia and Amatheia of the lovely hair,
and the others who in the depths of the sea were daughters of Nereus.
And the silvery cave was filled with them; and all together   50
beat their breasts. And Thetis led the lament:
"Hear me, sister Nereids, so that all of you
may know well as you listen, how many are the sorrows in my heart.
Ay me, wretched I am—ay me, unhappy bearer of the noblest son,
since I bore a son, blameless and strong,   55
outstanding among warriors, who shot up like a young shoot,
and having nurtured him like a growing tree on the high ground of an
   orchard
I sent him forth with the curved ships to Ilion,
to go to battle against the Trojans; him I shall not welcome again
returned home into the house of Peleus.   60
So long as he lives and sees the sun's light,
he has sorrow, nor can I help him at all by going to him.
But come, so that I may see my beloved child and hear of
what sorrow has come to him while he stayed away from the fighting."
      So speaking she left the cave; and her sisters went with her   65
in tears, and the swell of the sea broke around them.
And when they reached the rich soil of Troy,
up onto the shore of the sea they went, up one after the other, where
   the ships
of the Myrmidons had been drawn up, close-pressed round swift Achilles.
And his lady mother stood beside him as he groaned deeply,   70
and keenly wailing she held her son's head,
and in lament spoke winged words:
"Child, why do you cry? What sorrow has reached your heart?
Speak out, do not hide it. Those things have been accomplished for you

through Zeus, as at that time before you prayed with uplifted hands,   75
that all the sons of the Achaeans be pinned against the sterns of their
    ships
and for want of you suffer deeds that shamed them."
        Then groaning deeply swift-footed Achilles answered her:
"Mother mine, these things the Olympian indeed fulfilled for me;
but what pleasure do I have in them, since my beloved companion died,   80
Patroclus, whom I revered beyond all companions,
as equal to my own life? I have lost him, and after slaying him Hector
stripped the stupendous armor, a wonder to behold,
a thing of beauty; the armor the gods gave to Peleus as splendid gifts
on that day when they placed you in the bed of a mortal man.   85
Would that you had made your home with the immortal goddesses of
    the sea,
and Peleus had taken to himself a mortal wife.
But as it is, for you too there must be grief immeasurable in heart
for the death of your son, whom you will not receive again
returned to home, since my spirit does not bid me   90
to go on living nor take my part among men, unless, before all else,
Hector, beaten beneath my spear, lose his life,
and pay the penalty for making prey of Menoetius' son Patroclus."
        Then in turn Thetis spoke to him as she shed her tear:
"Then you will die soon, my child, from what you say;   95
for your fate is prepared straightway after Hector's."
Then greatly troubled swift-footed Achilles spoke to her:
"Straightway may I die, since I was not destined to help my companion
as he was killed; and a very long way from his fatherland
he perished, and lacked me to be his defender against harm.   100
Now since I am not returning to my beloved fatherland,
nor was I in any way salvation's light to Patroclus, nor to my other
companions, who have been broken in their number by shining Hector,
but sat beside the ships a useless burden on the earth,
I who am such as no other of the bronze-clad Achaeans   105
is in battle; though in the assembly there are others better—
would that strife perish from gods and men,
and anger, which incites even a man of sense to violence,
and which, far sweeter than dripping honey,
wells like smoke in the breast of men,   110
as Agamemnon lord of men then angered me.
But let us leave these things in the past for all our distress,
subduing the spirit in our own breasts by necessity;
for now I am setting out to find the destroyer of a dear life—
Hector. I will take death at that time when   115
Zeus and the other deathless gods wish to accomplish it.
For even the mighty Heracles[5] did not escape from death,
for all that he was dearest to lord Zeus the son of Cronus,
but fate broke him and the hard anger of Hera;

---

5. The greatest of Greek heroes, the son of
Zeus by a mortal woman; pursued by the jealousy of Hera, he was forced to undertake twelve
great labors and finally died in agony from the
effects of a poisoned garment.

so I too, if the same fate has been prepared for me,   120
shall lie when I have died. But now let me win outstanding glory,
and drive some woman of Troy, or deep-breasted Dardan[6] woman,
wiping with both hands from her soft cheeks
the thick-falling tears, to moan aloud,
and may they know that I stayed too long from fighting.   125
Do not detain me from battle though you love me; you will not
   persuade me."
      Then answered him Thetis of the silver feet:
"Yes, all these things, my child, you have spoken truly; nor is it shameful
to ward off sheer destruction from your afflicted comrades.
Yet your beautiful armor is held among the Trojans,   130
the brazen, glittering armor. Hector of the shimmering helm
exults in this, wearing it on his own shoulders; but I do not think
he will exult in it for long, since his slaughter is near at hand.
But do not enter in the strife of battle
until you see me returned here with your own eyes;   135
for at dawn I shall come back with the rising of the sun
carrying splendid armor from lord Hephaestus."
      Then having so spoken she took herself away from her son,
and turned to speak to her sisters of the sea:
"All of you now make your way into the broad gulf of ocean,   140
to see the old man of the sea and the halls of our father,
and to tell him everything; and I am going to high Olympus,
to the side of Hephaestus, famed for his skill, to see if he might be willing
to give to my son glorious gleaming armor."
So she spoke; and they at once plunged beneath the ocean swell;   145
and she, the goddess Thetis of the silver feet, went again to Olympus,
so that she might carry splendid armor to her beloved son.
      Her feet brought her to Olympus; meanwhile the Achaeans
fleeing with inhuman shouts before man-slaughtering Hector
reached their ships and the Hellespont.   150
But Patroclus—the strong-greaved Achaeans could not drag
the body of Achilles' henchman out from under the flying spears and
   arrow shafts;
for again the Trojan host and horses came upon him,
as did Hector son of Priam, like fire in fighting spirit.
Three times shining Hector seized the body by the feet from behind,   155
determined to drag it off, and shouted loud to spur the Trojans.
And three times the two Aiantes, mantled in their fierce courage,
beat him from the corpse. But steadfastly trusting in his battle prowess
Hector would now spring forth through the press of battle, now again
take his stand and cry aloud, nor fell back at all;   160
but as from a carcass rustic herdsmen fail to drive away
a tawny lion in his great hunger,
so the two Aiantes, fully armed, were not able
to frighten Hector son of Priam from the corpse.
      And indeed he would have dragged it away and won for himself
   glory everlasting,   165

6. Trojan.

had not swift Iris[7] with feet like the wind come to the son of Peleus
as messenger, racing from Olympus with word to prepare for battle,
in secret from Zeus and the other gods; for Hera it was who sent her;
and standing close to him she spoke her winged words:
"Rise up, son of Peleus, most terrifying of men;   170
protect Patroclus, for whose sake the dread fighting
is under way before the ships—they are killing one another,
both those who fight to defend the body of he who died,
and the Trojans who rush to haul it off to windy Ilion.
Above all others shining Hector   175
is bent on dragging it away; and his heart is urgent to impale the head
upon spiked stakes, cut from its tender neck.
Come, rise up, don't lie still; shame be on your heart,
should Patrocluos become a plaything for Trojan dogs.
Yours the dishonor, if he comes mutilated to the dead."   180
        Then answered her swift-footed godlike Achilles:
"Divine Iris, which of the gods sent you as messenger to me?"
Then in turn swift Iris with feet like the wind addressed him:
"Hera sent me, the glorious wife of Zeus;
nor does the high-throned son of Cronus know, nor any other   185
of the immortals, who dwell about snow-clad Olympus."
Then answering her spoke swift-footed Achilles:
"How then am I to go among the tumult? For those others have my
   armor.
And my beloved mother forbade me arm for battle
before I see her coming with my own eyes;   190
for she pledged to bring splendid armor from Hephaestus.
And I do not know who else's illustrious arms I might put on,
unless it be the great shield of Telamonian Ajax.[8]
But he too, I think, is engaged among the frontline fighters,
wreaking havoc with his spear around Patroclus who lies dead."   195
Then in turn swift Iris with feet like the wind addressed him:
"We too well know that they hold your glorious armor.
But go as you are to the ditch and show yourself to the Trojans—
perhaps in dread of you they might retreat from fighting,
the Trojans, and the warrior sons of the Achaeans draw breath   200
in their extremity; for respite in war is brief."
        So speaking swift-footed Iris departed;
and Achilles beloved of Zeus arose. And Athena
cast the tasseled aegis[9] about his mighty shoulders;
she, shining among goddesses, encircled round his head a cloud of   205
gold, and from it blazed bright-shining fire.
And as when smoke rising from a city reaches the clear high air
from a distant island, which enemy men fight round,
and they the whole day long are pitted in hateful warfare

---

7. Goddess of the rainbow and the usual messenger of the gods in the *Iliad*.
8. The son of Telamon, the more famous of
the two heroes named Ajax. His distinctive
attribute in the *Iliad* is a huge shield that covers
his whole body.
9. A tasseled garment or piece of armor that
belonged to Zeus but was often carried by
Athena in poetry and art. It induced panic when
shaken at an enemy.

around their city walls, but with the sun's setting   210
the beacon fires blaze, torch upon torch, and flaring upward
the glare becomes visible to those who live around,
in the hope that they might come with ships as allies against destruction,
so from Achilles' head the radiance reached the clear high air.
And going away from the wall he stood at the ditch, nor did he mix with   215
the Achaeans; for he observed his mother's knowing command.
And standing there he shouted, and from the distance Pallas Athena
cried out too; unspeakable was the uproar he incited in the Trojans.
As when a clarion voice is heard, when cries the trumpet
of life-destroying enemies who surround a city,   220
such then was the clarion voice of Aeacides.
          And when they heard the brazen voice of Aeacides,
the spirit in man each was thrown in turmoil; the horses with their fine
    manes
wheeled their chariots back, for in their hearts they forebode distress
    to come,
and the charioteers were struck from their senses, when they saw the
    weariless   225
terrible fire above the head of Peleus' great-hearted son
blazing; and this the gleaming-eyed goddess Athena caused to blaze.
Three times across the ditch godlike Achilles cried his great cry,
and three times the Trojans and their illustrious allies were thrown in
    panic.
Then and there perished twelve outstanding men   230
upon their own chariots and spears. And the Achaeans
with relief pulled Patroclus out from under the missiles,
and laid him on a litter; and his beloved companions stood around it
weeping, and with them followed swift-footed Achilles
shedding hot tears, when he looked upon his trusted comrade   235
lying on the bier, torn with sharp bronze,
whom he had sent forth with horses and chariots
into war, but did not welcome him returned home again.
          And ox-eyed lady Hera caused the tireless sun
to return, unwilling, into the streams of Ocean;   240
the sun set, and the glorious Achaeans ceased
from the powerful din of battle and all-leveling war.
The Trojans in their turn on the other side, withdrawing from the
mighty combat released their swift horses from under their chariots,
and gathered into assembly before taking thought for supper;   245
and the assembly took place with them standing upright, nor did any
    man dare
to take his seat; for trembling held them all, because Achilles
had appeared; he who for a long time had abandoned the painful battle.
          And to them Poulydamas, wise son of Panthoös,
was first to speak to the assembly; he alone looked both forward and
    behind him;[1]   250
he was Hector's comrade, and born in the same night,
but the one greatly excelled in speech, and the other in the spear;

---

1. I.e., he was a prophet; he knew the past and foresaw the future.

he with wise intent gave counsel to them and spoke:
"Consider well, my friends; I for my part urge
you now to go to the city, and not await the bright dawn   255
on the open plain beside the ships; we are far from our ramparts.
As long as that man harbored wrath at noble Agamemnon,
so long were the Achaeans easier to fight;
I myself used to welcome sleeping by the swift ships at night,
with the hope we would seize these double-ended ships.   260
But now terribly I dread the swift-footed son of Peleus;
such is the reckless might of that one's spirit, he will not wish
to remain upon the plain, in this middle ground where Achaeans and
    Trojans
both share between them battle's fury,
but he will fight for our city and our women.   265
Come, let us go to the city, be persuaded by me; for this is how it will be.
Now ambrosial night has curbed the swift-footed son of Peleus;
but if he finds us here
tomorrow when he rises under arms, well will a man come to know him;
and gladly will he make his way to sacred Ilion—   270
he who escapes; but the dogs and vultures will devour many
of the Trojans—but may this word never come to my hearing.
If you will be persuaded by my words, painful though they are,
this night we will harbor our strength in the place of assembly,
and our high walls and gates and the doors fitted to them—   275
the long, well-honed, barred doors—will guard our city;
and in early morning, having armed in our weapons with the dawn,
we will take up position along the ramparts. The worse for him, if he
    chooses
to come from his ships to do battle around our walls;
he will go back to the ships, when he has given his high-necked horses   280
their fill of running roundabout, as he roams beneath the city walls.
Even his courage will not permit him to storm inside,
nor will he ever sack our city. Before that the sleek dogs will devour him."
        Then looking at him from beneath his brows spoke Hector of the
    shimmering helm:
"Poulydamas, these things you declare are no longer pleasing to me,   285
you who bid us go back to cower down in the city.
Or have you all not had your fill of being penned inside the walls?
In days before, the city of Priam, as all men born of earth
were wont to say, was rich in gold, rich in bronze—
by now the splendid treasures have vanished from our houses,   290
and many possessions went for sale to Phrygia and lovely Maeonia,[2]
since mighty Zeus conceived hatred for us.
And now, at this time when the son of devious Cronus grants me
to win glory by the ships and drive the Achaeans to the sea—
you fool, no longer disclose such thoughts among the people!   295
None of the Trojans will obey you, for I will not allow it.
But come, let us all be persuaded to do as I say.
Take your meal now at your posts throughout the army

2. Countries in Asia Minor allied with Troy.

and be mindful of your watches and each of you be alert;
and whoever of the Trojans is excessively distressed for his
    possessions,   300
let him gather them together and give them to the people to consume
    as common stock;
better that one of them have profit of them than the Achaeans;
and in early morning, having armed in our weapons with the dawn,
by the hollow ships we shall awaken cutting war.
And if in fact Achilles the godlike has stirred himself to action by his
    ships,   305
the worse it will be for him, if he so chooses, for I will not
flee from him out of this grievous war, but I will strongly
face him—we shall see whether he will win great glory, or I.
Enyalios[3] the god of war is impartial; and often he kills the one who kills."

        Thus declared Hector, and the Trojans shouted their applause,   310
the fools, for Pallas Athena took their wits away;
all assented to Hector as he devised disaster,
but none to Poulydamas, who thought out excellent counsel.

        Then they took their meal throughout the army; but the Achaeans
through all the night groaned aloud as they mourned Patroclus.   315
And the son of Peleus led their impassioned lament,
placing his man-slaughtering hands on the breast of his companion,
groaning without ceasing, as a full-maned lion,
whose cubs a hunting man has stolen away
out from the dense forest, and who returning too late is stricken with
    grief,   320
and many is the valley he traverses, following after the footprints of
    the man,
in the hope he would find him in some quarter; for very bitter anger
    holds him;
so groaning deeply Achilles addressed the Myrmidons:
"Alas, alas, empty were the words I let fall that day
as I encouraged the warrior Menoetius within his walls;   325
I said to him that I would bring his son back to Opoeis[4] surrounded in
    glory
after sacking Ilion and receiving a share of the spoils.
But Zeus does not fulfill men's every wish;
for it was fated that we both stain the same earth
here in Troy, since I will not be returning home   330
to be received by old Peleus, the horseman, in his halls,
nor by Thetis my mother, but the earth will cover me here.
But now, Patroclus, since I am following you beneath the earth,
I shall not honor you with funeral rites, until I lay here
the armaments and head of Hector, your slayer, great-hearted one;   335
and before your pyre I shall cut the throats of twelve
noble sons of Troy, in anger for your killing.
In the meanwhile you will lie as you are by my curved ships,

---

3. Another name for Ares.
4. An ancient city near the eastern coast of the   central Greek mainland and home of Menoetius, father of Patroclus.

and around you women of Troy and deep-breasted Dardan women
shall wail for you night and day as they shed their tears,   340
those women whom we ourselves toiled to win by force and the
    long spear
when we two sacked the rich cities of earth-born men."
        So speaking godlike Achilles ordered his companions
to set a great cauldron on its three-legged stand astride the fire, so that
    with all speed
they could wash away the clotted blood from Patroclus;   345
and they set a cauldron for heating bathing water on the blazing fire,
then poured water in it, and took sticks of wood and kindled them
    beneath it.
And the fire caught the belly of the cauldron, and heated the water.
Then when the water had come to boil in the bright bronze,
they washed him and anointed him luxuriantly with oil,   350
and filled in his wounds with seasoned unguents;
and placing him on the bier, they covered him with soft linen
from his head to his feet, and over this with a shining mantle.
        Then nightlong the Myrmidons groaned aloud as around Achilles
of the swift feet they mourned Patroclus.   355
But Zeus addressed Hera, his sister and his wife:
"So once more, you have accomplished things your way, after all, my
    brown-eyed lady Hera,
having roused to action swift-footed Achilles. Surely the long-haired
    Achaeans
must be your own offspring!"
        Then answered him ox-eyed lady Hera: 360
"Most dread son of Cronus, what sort of word have you spoken?
Surely, even a human tries to do what he can for another man,
one who is only mortal, and who does not know so many arts as we;
how then should not I—who claim to be the highest of the goddesses,
both by birth and because I am called your wife,   365
and you are lord of all the immortal gods—
how should I not contrive evil for the Trojans whom I hate?"
        Thus they were speaking such things to one another.
But silver-footed Thetis arrived at the home of Hephaestus,
imperishable, strewn with stars, conspicuous amongst the homes of the
    immortals,   370
made of bronze, which the crippled god had built himself.
And she found him dripping with sweat, twisting back and forth about
    his bellows,
hard at work; for he was forging fully twenty tripods
to stand round the inside wall of his well-built palace.
He placed golden wheels beneath the legs of each,   375
so that of their own accord they might go into the divine assembly
    for him
and then return back to his house again, a wonder to behold.
And they were so far finished, but the elaborate handles were not
affixed; these he was fitting and striking the rivets.
And while he toiled at these things with his skilled understanding,   380
the goddess Thetis of the silver feet approached him;

and Charis[5] of the shining headdress saw her as she was coming forward,
lovely Charis, whom the famed bent-legged god had wed,
and she clasped her hand, and spoke to her and said her name:
"Why, Thetis of the flowing robe, have you come to our house?   385
You are honored and beloved, but you have not come frequently before.
But follow me in, so that I can set all hospitality before you."
        So speaking she, shining among goddesses, led Thetis forward.
Then she settled her on a beautiful elaborate silver chair,
and placed a stool beneath her feet;   390
and she called Hephaestus famed for his art and spoke a word to him:
"Hephaestus, come this way; Thetis has need of something from you."
Then the renowned god of the crooked legs answered her:
"Then surely in our house is a goddess whom I hold in awe and revere.
She saved me, that time I suffered bodily pain when I was made to fall a
    long way   395
by the efforts of my dog-faced mother, who wanted
to hide me away for being lame. At that time I would have suffered many
    cares at heart,
had not Thetis taken me to her bosom,
and Eurynome the daughter of Ocean of the shifting tide.
For nine years with them I forged many intricate objects,   400
brooches and curving spirals for the hair, buds of rosettes and necklaces
in their hollow cave; and all around the boundless currents of the Ocean
with its foam flowed murmuring; nor did any other being
know of this, neither of gods nor of mortal men,
but Thetis and Eurynome knew, they who saved me.   405
Now she has come to our house; therefore I must surely
repay to Thetis of the lovely hair all the value of my life.
But you now set before her fitting hospitality,
while I put away my bellows and all my tools."
        He spoke, and the huge craftsman rose from the anvil block   410
limping, but his shrunken legs moved nimbly beneath him.
He put the bellows aside from the fire, and all the tools
with which he worked he gathered into a silver box.
And with a sponge he wiped around his face and both his arms
and powerful neck and shaggy chest,   415
and he put on a tunic, took up his thick staff, and went out the door,
limping; and supporting their master were attendants
made of gold, which seemed like living maidens.
In their hearts there is intelligence, and they have voice
and vigor, and from the immortal gods they have learned skills.   420
These bustled about supporting their master; and making his halting way
to where Thetis was, he took his seat upon a shining chair,
and clasped her hand, and spoke to her and said her name:
"Why, Thetis of the flowing robe, have you come to our house?
You are honored and beloved, but you have not come frequently before.   425
Speak what you will; my heart compels me to accomplish it,
if I am able to accomplish it, and if it can be accomplished."
        Then Thetis answered him as she let her tears fall:

5. Literally, "Grace" or "Beauty," one of the Three Graces.

"Hephaestus—who of all the goddesses on Olympus,
endures in her heart so many bitter cares,   430
as the griefs Zeus the son of Cronus has given to me beyond all?
Out of all the other goddesses of the sea he made me subject to a mortal
    husband,
Peleus son of Aeacus, and I endured the bed of a mortal man
very much unwilling; he now worn out with bitter age
lies in his halls, but there are other troubles now for me;   435
for he gave me a son to bear and to raise
outstanding among warriors, who shot up like a young shoot,
and having nurtured him like a growing tree on the high ground of an
    orchard
I sent him forth with the curved ships to Ilion,
to go to battle against the Trojans; him I shall not welcome again   440
returned home into the house of Peleus.
So long as he lives and sees the sun's light
he has sorrow, nor can I help him at all by going to him.
The girl, whom the sons of the Achaeans picked out as prize for him,
she it was, from his hands, lord Agamemnon took back;   445
and he has been consuming his heart in grief for her, while the Trojans
pinned the Achaeans against the sterns of their ships, nor
let them go forth from that place; and the Argive elders
beseeched him, and promised many splendid gifts.
At this he refused to ward off their destruction,   450
but then put his own armor about Patroclus,
and sent him to the fighting, and gave a great host with him.
All the day they battled around the Scaean gates;
and surely that same day he would have sacked the city, had not Apollo
killed the brave son of Menoetius as he was wreaking much destruction   455
among the front fighters, and gave glory to Hector.
And it is for this reason I have now come to your knees, to see if you
    would be willing
to give to my short-lived son a shield and crested helmet
and fine greaves with silver fastenings
and a breastplate; for those that were his, his trusted comrade lost   460
when he was beaten down by the Trojans; and my son lies upon the
    ground grieving at heart."
      Then answered her the famous crook-legged god:
"Have courage; do not let these matters be a care to your heart.
Would that I were so surely able to hide him away from death and its
    hard sorrow,
when dread fate comes upon him,   465
as he will have his splendid armor, such as many a man
of the many men to come shall hold in wonder, whoever sees it."
      So speaking he left her there, and went to his bellows;
and he turned them to the fire and gave them their commands to get
    to work.
And all twenty bellows began to blow into the crucibles,   470
from every angle blasting up and forth their strong-blown gusts
for him as he hurried to be now in this place, now again in that,
in whatever manner Hephaestus wished, and accomplished the job.

And he cast on the fire weariless bronze, and tin
and treasured gold and silver; and then 475
he placed his great anvil on his anvil block, and with one hand grasped
his mighty hammer, and with the other grasped his tongs.
　　　And first of all he made a great and mighty shield,
working it intricately throughout, and cast around it a shining rim
of triple thickness, glittering, and from it a silver shield-strap. 480
Five were the layers of the shield itself; and on it
he wrought with knowing genius many intricate designs.
　　　On it he formed the earth, and the heaven, and the sea
and the weariless sun and waxing moon,
and on it were all the wonders with which the heaven is ringed, 485
the Pleiades and Hyades and the might of Orion,
and Arctos the Bear,[6] which men name the Wagon,
and which always revolves in the same place, watchful for Orion,
and alone has no part in the baths of Ocean.
　　　And on it he made two cities of mortal men, 490
both beautiful; and in one there were weddings and wedding feasts,
and they were leading the brides from their chambers beneath the gleam
　　of torches
through the city, and loud rose the bridal song;
and the young men whirled in dance and in their midst
the flutes and lyres raised their hubbub; and the women 495
standing in their doorways each watched in admiration.
And the people were thronged into the place of meeting; and there
　　a dispute
had arisen, and two men were contending about the blood price
for a man who had been killed. The one was promising to pay all,
declaring so to the people, but the other refused to accept a thing; 500
and both desired the resolution be taken to a judge;
the people spoke out for both sides, favoring one or the other,
and heralds were holding the people in check. The elders
were sitting upon seats of polished stone in a sacred circle,
and holding in their hands the staves of the heralds with their ringing
　　voices; 505
to these the two sides next rushed, and in turn the elders each gave
　　judgment.
And there lay in their midst two talents of gold,
to give to him who might speak the straightest judgment among them.
　　　But around the other city lay two armies of men,
shining in their armor. And they were torn between two plans, 510
either to sack the city, or to divide everything equally with its people,
as much wealth as the lovely town held within.
But the city was not yielding, and the men were secretly arming for
　　ambush.
And their beloved wives and little children stood guard upon the
　　ramparts

6. Ursa Major, or the Big Dipper, which never
descends below the horizon (i.e., into Ocean).
The Pleiades, Hyades, and Orion are all clusters
of stars, or constellations. Orion was a giant
hunter of Greek mythology.

with those men whom old age held,   515
but the other men set forth; and Ares led them and Pallas Athena,
both made in gold, and the clothing on them was golden,
magnificent and mighty with their armor, like very gods,
standing out apart; and beneath them the people were smaller.
And when these arrived at the place where it seemed to them good for
   ambush,   520
on the river, at the watering place for all the grazing herds,
there they sat down, covered in their gleaming bronze.
And at a distance from them, their two lookouts were in position
waiting for when they might see sheep and twist-horned cattle;
and these soon came in sight, with two herdsmen following with them   525
taking pleasure in their flute, and did not at all foresee the plot.
And catching sight of them ahead, the men in ambush ran toward them,
and swiftly, on both sides, cut off the herds of cattle and splendid flocks
of white-wooled sheep, and killed the shepherds for good measure.
But the other men, when they heard the great uproar from the cattle   530
as they were sitting before the place of meeting, they at once mounted
   behind their high-stepping
horses and went after them in pursuit. They reached the place swiftly,
and having arrayed the battle, began fighting by the riverbanks,
smiting one another with their bronze-headed spears.
And Strife was joining the throng of battle, and Tumult, and painful
   Death,   535
holding now a living man new-wounded, now one unharmed,
now dragging a man who had died by his feet through the press of battle;
and Death wore around her shoulders a cape crimsoned with the blood
   of men.
And they dashed in battle and fought like living men,
dragging away the bodies of those slain by one another.   540
          And on the shield he made a soft fallow field—fertile worked land
broad and thrice-plowed; and on it many plowmen
were driving their yoked teams of oxen turning up and down the field.
And when they came to the furrow end, after turning around,
then would a man come up to give into their hands a cup of   545
honey-sweet wine; and they would turn back along the row,
eager to reach the turning place of the deep fallow field.
And the earth darkened behind them, like land that has been plowed,
made of gold though it was; a wonder indeed was that which was
   wrought.
          And on the shield he placed a royal estate; and there the laborers   550
were reaping, sharp sickles in their hands.
Some sheaths were thickly falling to the ground along the row,
others the sheaf binders bundled with bands.
Three binders stood by; but behind them
children were gathering handfuls, carrying them in their arms,   555
constantly nearby. And among them the king, in silence,
staff in hand, stood near the line rejoicing in his heart.
And to one side heralds were readying a feast beneath an oak,
dressing the great ox they had slaughtered. And the women
were scattering quantities of white barley for the workers as a meal.   560

And on the shield he put a great vineyard heavy with clumps
    of grapes,
a thing of beauty, all in gold, and the dark clusters were along it.
And it was set up on vine poles of solid silver;
and on either side he drove a ditch of blue enamel, and around it a fence
of tin. One path alone was on it,   565
on which grape bearers made their way, when they gathered in the
    vineyard.
Maidens and young men with the giddy hearts of youth
carried the honey-sweet crop in woven baskets;
and in their midst a boy played his clear-sounding lyre
with enchantment, and beautifully sang to it the mournful harvest
    song   570
in his soft voice. And the others beating time all together
with song and cries followed, skipping with their feet.
        And on it he made a herd of straight-horned cattle,
and the cows were made of gold and tin,
and lowing they hastened from the farmyard to their pasture,   575
beside a rushing river, beside the waving reeds.
Golden herdsmen accompanied the cattle,
four in all, and nine sleek dogs followed at their feet;
but two dread lions held a bellowing bull
among the foremost cattle; and he lowing loudly   580
was being dragged away, and the dogs and sturdy youths followed
    after him.
And the two lions tearing open the great bull's hide
were gulping down the entrails and dark blood; at a loss,
the herdsmen set the swift dogs in pursuit, urging them on,
but they shrank from biting the lions,   585
and standing very close bayed and stayed away.
        And on the shield the famed crook-legged god made a meadow,
a great meadow for white-fleeced sheep lying in a lovely glen,
and farmsteads and huts for the shepherds and their folds.
And on it the famed crook-legged god made a patterned place for
    dancing,   590
like that which once in broad Knossos
Daedalus created for Ariadne[7] of the lovely hair.
There the unwed youths and maidens worth many oxen as their bridal
    price
were dancing, holding each other's hands at the wrist;
and the girls were wearing finest linen, and the youths wore   595
fine-spun tunics, soft shining with oil.
And the girls wore lovely crowns of flowers, and the youths were
    carrying
golden daggers from their silver sword-belts.
And now the youths with practiced feet would lightly run in rings,
as when a crouching potter makes trial of the potter's wheel   600

7. Daughter of Minos, king of Crete. Daedalus was the prototypical craftsman who built
the labyrinth to house the Minotaur and who

escaped from Crete on wings with his son
Icarus. Knossus was the site of Minos's great
palace.

fitted to his hand, to see if it speeds round;
and then another time they would run across each other's lines.
And a great crowd stood around the stirring dance
filled with delight; and among them two acrobats, 604/5
leaders of the dance, went whirling through their midst.
    And Hephaestus set on it the great might of the river Ocean,
along the outmost edge of the thick-made shield.
    And when he had made the great and massive shield,
then he wrought a breastplate for Achilles more resplendent than the
   light of fire, 610
and he made a helmet for him, strong and fitted to his temples,
a thing of beauty, intricately wrought, and set a gold crest on it;
and then he made greaves for him of pliant tin.
    And when the famed crook-legged god had made all the armor
   with his toil,
lifting it up he set it before the mother of Achilles; 615
and she like a hawk leapt down from snowy summit of Olympus,
carrying the glittering armor from Hephaestus.

Summary   Achilles finally accepts gifts of restitution from Agamemnon, as he refused to do earlier. His return to the fighting brings terror to the Trojans and turns the battle into a rout in which Achilles kills every Trojan that crosses his path. As he pursues Agenor, Apollo tricks him by rescuing his intended victim (he spirits him away in a mist) and assumes Agenor's shape to lead Achilles away from the walls of Troy. The Trojans take refuge in the city, all except Hector.

BOOK XXII

[*The Death of Hector*]

So those who had fled terrorized like fawns into the city
dried off their sweat and drank and slaked their thirst,
slumped on the splendid ramparts. The Achaeans, however,
drew near the walls with shields inclined against their shoulders;
and there ruinous fate bound Hector to stand his ground, 5
before the Scaean gates of Ilion.
    Now Phoebus Apollo hailed Peleion:
"Why, son of Peleus, do you chase me, with those swift feet,
you a mortal, I an undying god? You must not yet know
that I am divine, you rage after me so furiously! 10
Is it of no concern, this business with the Trojans, whom you scattered
   in fear—
who are by now cowering in the city, while you slope off here?
You will never kill me; I am not marked by fate."
Then greatly stirred, swift-footed Achilles answered him:
"You have thwarted me, most malevolent of all the gods, you who strike
   from afar, 15
turning me here away from the city walls; otherwise many would
have bitten the dirt before they arrived at Ilion.
Saving them, you have robbed me of great glory,
lightly, without fear of retribution;

I would pay you back, if that power were in me."   20
So speaking, he made toward the city, intent on great things,
straining like a prizewinning horse who with his chariot
runs effortlessly, stretching over the plain—
so swiftly did Achilles move his feet and knees.

    And old Priam first beheld him with his eyes   25
as, shining like a star, Achilles streaked across the plain,
the star that comes at summer's end,[8] its clear gleaming
in the milky murk of night displayed among the multitude of stars—
the star they give the name Orion's Dog;
most radiant it is, but it makes an evil portent,   30
and brings great feverish heat on pitiful mortal men—
just so did his bronze breastplate shine about Achilles running.
The old man cried out and hammered his head with his hands,
lifting them on high; crying mightily he called,
imploring his beloved son; for before the gates Hector   35
continued to stand firm, intent on combat with Achilles.
To him the old man called piteously, reaching out his hands:
"Hector, for my sake, do not wait for this man
on your own, without allies, lest you straightway meet your fate,
broken by Peleion; since he is so much stronger,   40
he is pitiless; would that he were as dear to the gods
as he is to me—in short order would the dogs and vultures devour him
as he lay dead; and bitter pain would leave my heart.
This is the man who has bereaved me of many sons, brave sons,
killing them, or selling them to far-off islands.   45
Even now there are two, Lykaon and Polydoros,
whom I cannot see in the city of the cowering Trojans,
sons whom Altes' daughter Laothoë[9] bore me, a queen among women.
If they are alive somewhere among the army, then
I will ransom them for bronze or gold; all this is inside—   50
old, illustrious Altes endowed his daughter richly.[1]
But if they have already died and are in the house of Hades,
this is anguish to my heart and to their mother, we who bore them;
but to the rest of the people, it will be anguish shorter lived
than if you also should die, broken by Achilles.   55
Come inside the walls, my child, that you may save the
Trojan men and Trojan women, do not make a gift of glory to
the son of Peleus, who will rob you of your very life.
And on me—wretched, still feeling—have pity,
born to ill fate, whom on the threshold of old age father Zeus, son of
    Cronus,   60
will blight with my hard fate, when I have seen
the destruction of my sons, the abduction of my daughters,
my chambers ravaged, and innocent children

8. Sirius, or the Dog Star, the brightest star in
the constellation Canis Major. In Greece it rises
in late summer, the hottest time of the year.
9. Laothoë was one of Priam's wives. Achilles

killed Polydorus and Lykaon in the fighting
outside the city (books 20 and 21).
1. The dowry of Laothoë, Altes' daughter.

hurled to the ground in the terror of battle;
my daughters-in-law abducted by the wicked hands of Achaean men,　65
and I myself, last of all, at my very gates, my dogs
will rip raw, when some man with sharp bronze,
stabbing or casting, will strip the spirit from my limbs—
the dogs I raised in my halls and fed at my table as guardians of my gates,
these, maddened by the drinking of my blood,　70
will sprawl in my doorway. All is seemly for the young man
slain in war, torn by sharp bronze,
laid out dead; everything is honorable to him in death, whatever shows.
But when the dogs defile the white head and white beard
and the private parts of a dead old man—　75
this is most pitiable for wretched mortals."
So the old man spoke, and pulled his white hair with his hands,
tearing it from his head. But he did not persuade the heart of Hector.
　　　Now in turn his mother wailed, raining tears,
and loosening her robe, with a hand she exposed her breast　80
and raining tears addressed him with winged words:
"Hector, my child, be moved by this and have pity on me,
if ever I used to give you my breast to soothe you—
remember those times, dear child, defend yourself against this deadly man
from inside the walls; don't stand as champion against him,　85
my stubborn one. If he cuts you down, I will surely never
mourn you on your deathbed, dear budding branch, whom I bore,
nor will your worthy wife. But a long way from us
by the ships of the Achaeans the running dogs will eat you."
　　　Thus both of them weeping addressed their dear son,　90
repeatedly beseeching. But they did not persuade the heart of Hector,
and he awaited Achilles, who was looming huge as he drew near.
As a snake by its hole in the mountains waits for a man,
having eaten evil poisons, and a deadly anger comes upon it,
and it shoots a stinging glance, coiled by its hole,　95
so Hector keeping his spirit unquelled did not retreat,
but having leaned his shining shield against the jutting tower,
in agitation he spoke to his great-hearted spirit:
"Oh me, if I enter the gates and walls
Poulydamas will be the first to reproach me,　100
who bade me lead the Trojans to the city
that baneful night when Achilles the godlike rose,
but I was not persuaded. It would have been far better if I had.
Now since I have destroyed my people by my recklessness,
I dread the Trojan men and the Trojan women with their trailing robes,　105
lest some other man more worthless than me say:
'Hector, trusting in his strength, destroyed his people'—
thus they will speak. It would be far better, then, for me
to confront Achilles, either to kill him and return home,
or to die with honor at his hands, before my city.　110
But what if I put aside my studded shield
and my strong helmet, leaned my spear against the walls,
and going out alone approached noble Achilles,
and pledged to him Helen and the possessions with her?

All those things—as much as Alexandros carried away to Troy   115
in his hollow ships, which was the beginning of our quarrel—
to give to the sons of Atreus to lead away; and in addition
to divide everything else with the Achaeans, whatever this city holds,
and after that to make a formal oath with the Trojan council
not to hide anything, but to divide it all, equally[2]—   120
but why does my heart debate these things?   122
I could set forth to meet him and he not pity me,
nor even respect me, but kill me naked as I was,
as if I were a woman, since I would have put off my armor.   125
It is not now possible from rock or oak, in the country way,
to chatter to him those things that a girl and youth
chatter to each other, a girl and youth—
no, it is better to engage with him straightway;
we shall see to whom the Olympians give glory."   130

      Thus his thoughts churned as he waited, and Achilles drew near,
equal to the war god, the helmet-shaking warrior,
brandishing his Pelian ash-wood spear above his right shoulder,
terrifying. The bronze glinted around him like the flare
of blazing fire or the sun rising.   135
And as he watched him, trembling took hold of Hector; and he could no
   longer endure
there to stand his ground, but left the gates behind and, terrified, he ran.
The son of Peleus charged for him, trusting in the swiftness of his feet;
as a mountain hawk, lightest of all things on wings,
easily swoops after a terror-stricken dove,   140
which, away from under, flees, but crying sharply near
he swoops continuously and his spirit drives him to take her;
so Achilles flew straight for him, ravenous, and Hector fled
under the walls of Troy, working his swift knees.

      By the watch place and the wild fig tree twisted by wind,   145
always away from the walls, along the wagon path they ran
and reached the two fair-flowing streams, where the two springs
gush forth from the whirling waters of Scamander.[3]
One flows with warm water, enveloping steam
rises from it as if from a burning fire.   150
The other even in summer runs as cold as hail,
or snow water, or ice that forms from water.
Near to these there are the broad washing hollows
of fine stone, where their lustrous clothes
the Trojan wives and their beautiful daughters washed,   155
in those days before, in peacetime, before there came the sons of the
   Achaeans.
By this place they ran, one fleeing, the other behind pursuing;
outstanding was he who fled ahead—but far better he who pursued him
swiftly; since it was not for a sacral animal, nor for an oxhide
they contended, prizes in the races of men—   160

2. The line numbers here account for lines that were omitted by the translator because they may
not belong to the text.
3. One of the two rivers in the plain of Troy.

but they ran for the life of Hector breaker of horses.
As when prizewinning single-hoofed horses
tear around the turning post—a great prize awaits,
a tripod, or woman, in those games held when a man has died—
so three times around the city of Priam they whirled   165
in the swiftness of their feet, and all the gods looked on.
To them the father of men and gods spoke the first word:
"Alas; it is a dear man whom my eyes see
pursued around the wall; my heart grieves
for Hector, who has burned many thigh cuts of sacral oxen to me,   170
both on the summit of Ida of the many glens, and at other times
on the heights of his citadel. But now godlike Achilles
pursues him in the swiftness of his feet around the city of Priam.
But come, you gods, consider and take counsel
whether we shall save him from death, or   175
noble though he is, break him at the hands of Achilles son of Peleus."
Then the gleaming-eyed goddess Athena answered him:
"O father of the bright thunderbolt and black clouds, what have you said?
This man who is mortal, consigned long ago to fate—
you want to take him back and free him from the harsh sorrow of death?   180
Do so; but not all the other gods will approve."
In answer, Zeus who gathers the clouds addressed her:
"Take heart, Tritogeneia,[4] dear child. I did not now
speak in earnest, and I mean to be kind to you.
Act in whatever way your mind inclines, nor hold back any longer."   185
So speaking, he urged Athena, who had been eager even before;
and she went, slipping down from the peaks of Olympus.
Relentlessly, swift Achilles kept driving Hector panicked before him,
as when a dog in the mountains pursues a deer's fawn
that he has started from its bed through glens and dells;   190
and though, cowering in fright, it eludes him beneath a thicket,
the dog runs on, tracking it steadily, until he finds it—
so Hector could not elude Achilles of the swift feet.
Each time he made to dash toward the Dardanian gates,
under the well-built tower,   195
in the hope that men from above might defend him with thrown missiles,
each time did Achilles, outstripping him, turn him back
toward the plain, and he himself sped ever by the city.
As in a dream a man is not able to pursue one who eludes him,
nor is the other able to escape, nor he to pursue,   200
so Achilles for all the swiftness of his feet was not able to lay hold of
Hector, nor Hector to escape.
How then could Hector have eluded his fated death
had not Apollo for that last and final time joined closely with him
to rouse his spirit and make swift his knees?
And shining Achilles was shaking his head at his men,   205
nor allowed them to let their sharp spears fly at Hector,
lest whoever making the throw claim glory, and himself come second.
But when for the fourth time they came to the springs,

4. Another name for Athena.

then Zeus the father leveled his golden scales,
and placed in them two portions of death that brings enduring grief,   210
that of Achilles and that of Hector breaker of horses;
he lifted them, holding by the middle; and the measured day of Hector sank,
headed to Hades, and Phoebus Apollo abandoned him.

    Then the gleaming-eyed goddess Athena came up to the son of
  Peleus
and standing near addressed him with winged words: 215
"Now I hope, illustrious Achilles, beloved of Zeus,
to carry honor for us two back to the Achaean ships,
after breaking Hector, insatiable though he be for battle;
he can no longer get clear of us,
not if Apollo the Far-Shooter should suffer countless trials for
  his sake,   220
groveling before Father Zeus who wields the aegis.
But you now stop and catch your breath, while I
make my way to Hector and convince him to fight man-to-man."
Thus spoke Athena, and Achilles obeyed and rejoiced in his heart,
and stood leaning on his bronze-flanged ash-wood spear.   225

    She left him and came up to shining Hector
in the likeness of Deïphobos,[5] in form and steady voice.
Standing close, she spoke winged words:
"My brother, swift Achilles presses you hard,
pursuing you around the city of Priam in the swiftness of his feet.   230
Come; let us take our stand and standing firm defend ourselves."

    Then great Hector of the shimmering helm addressed her in turn:
"Deïphobos, even before you were far dearest to me
of my brothers, those sons whom Hecuba and Priam bore.
Now I am minded to honor you even more in my heart—   235
you who dared for my sake, when you saw me with your eyes,
to quit the walls where the others remain inside."

    Then the gleaming-eyed goddess Athena spoke to him:
"My brother, our father and lady mother implored me greatly,
entreating in turn, and the companions about them,   240
to remain there—for so great is the dread of all;
but my inner spirit was harrowed with impotent grief.
But now let us two press straight forward and go to battle,
and let there be no restraint of our spears, so that we shall see if Achilles,
killing us both, will bear our bloodied arms   245
to his hollow ships, or if he will be broken by your spear."
Thus spoke Athena and with cunning led him on.

    And when they had advanced almost upon each other
great Hector of the shimmering helm spoke first:
"No longer, son of Peleus, shall I flee from you, as before   250
I fled three times around the great city of Priam, nor could then endure
to withstand your charge. But now my spirit stirs me
to hold firm before you. I will kill you, or be killed.
But come, let us take an oath upon our gods, for they
will be the best witnesses and protectors of agreements.   255

5. Hector's brother.

I will not, outrageous though you are, dishonor you if Zeus grants me
to endure, and I take your life.
But when I have stripped you of your splendid armor, Achilles,
I will give your body back to the Achaeans; and do you the same."
        Then looking at him from beneath his brows, Achilles of the
    swift feet spoke: 260
"Hector, doer of unforgettable deeds—do not to me propose agreements.
As there are no pacts of faith between lions and men,
nor do wolves and lambs have spirit in kind,
but they plot evil unremittingly for one another,
so it is not possible that you and I be friends, nor for us two   265
will there be oaths; before that time one of us falling
will sate with his blood the shield-bearing warrior god.
Recollect your every skill. Now the need is very great
to be a spearman and brave warrior.
There will be no further escape for you, but soon Pallas Athena   270
will break you by my spear. Now you will pay in one sum
for all the sorrows of my companions, those whom you killed, raging
    with your spear."
        He spoke, and balancing his long-shadowed spear, he let it fly.
But, holding it in his sight as it came at him, shining Hector avoided it,
for as he watched, he crouched, and the bronze spear flew over   275
and stuck in the earth; but Pallas Athena snatched it up
and gave it back to Achilles, escaping the notice of Hector, shepherd of
    the people.
And Hector addressed the noble son of Peleus:
"You missed! It was not, then, godlike Achilles,
from Zeus you knew my fate—you only thought you did;   280
and you turn out to a glib talker, cunning with words—
fearing you, you thought I would forget my strength and valor—
but you will not fix your spear in my back as I flee,
but drive it through my breast as I come at you,
if a god grants this. Now in your turn dodge my spear,   285
bronze-pointed; would that you carried the whole of it in your flesh.
Then would this war be the lighter to bear for the Trojans,
with you dead. For you are their greatest evil."
        He spoke, and balancing his long-shadowing spear, he let it fly,
and hurled at the middle of the son of Peleus' shield, nor did he miss;   290
but the spear glanced off the shield, for a long way. And Hector was angry
that his swift cast flew from his hand in vain,
and he stood dejected, nor did he have any other ash-shafted spear.
Raising his great voice he called Deïphobos of the pale shield
and asked for his long spear—but Deïphobos was not near him.   295
        And Hector understood within his heart and spoke aloud:
"This is it. The gods summon me deathward.
I thought the warrior Deïphobos was by me,
but he is inside the walls and Athena has tricked me.
Hateful death is very near me; it is no longer far away,   300
nor is there escape. And for some long time this has been pleasing
to Zeus and to Zeus' son who shoots from afar, who before this
protected me willingly enough. Yet now destiny has caught me.

Let me not die without a struggle and ingloriously,
but while doing some great thing for even men to come to hear of." 305
So speaking he drew his sharp sword
that hung down by his side, huge and strong-made,
and collecting himself he swooped like a high-flying eagle,
an eagle that plunges through lowering clouds toward the plain
to snatch a soft lamb or a cowering hare; 310
so Hector swooped brandishing his sharp sword.
But Achilles charged, his spirit filled with
savage passion. Before his breast he held his covering shield,
beautiful and intricately wrought, and nodded with his shining
four-ridged helmet; splendid horsehair flowed about it 315
of gold, which Hephaestus had set thickly around the helmet crest.
As a star moves among other stars in the milky murk of night,
Hesperus the Evening Star, the most beautiful star to stand in heaven,
so the light shone from the well-pointed spearhead that Achilles
was shaking in his right hand, bent upon evil for Hector, 320
surveying his handsome flesh, where it might best give way.
The rest of his body was held by brazen armor,
the splendid armor he stripped after slaying strong Patroclus—
but at that point where the collarbone holds the neck from the shoulders
  there showed
his gullet, where death of the soul comes swiftest; 325
and at this point shining Achilles drove with his spear as Hector strove
  against him,
and the spearhead went utterly through the soft neck.
Heavy with bronze though it was, the ash-spear did not sever the windpipe,
so that he could speak, making an exchange of words.
He fell in the dust. And shining Achilles vaunted: 330
"Hector, you surely thought when you stripped Patroclus
that you were safe, and you thought nothing of me as I was absent—
pitiable fool. For standing by, his far greater avenger,
I remained behind by the hollow ships—
I who have broken the strength of your knees. You the dogs and birds 335
will rip apart shamefully; Patroclus the Achaeans will honor with funeral
  rites."
Then with little strength Hector of the shimmering helm
  addressed him:
"By your soul, by your knees, by your parents,
do not let the dogs devour me by the ships of the Achaeans,
but take the bronze and abundance of gold, 340
the gifts my father and lady mother will give you;
give my body back to go home, so that
the Trojans and the Trojan wives will give my dead body its portion of
  the fire."
Then looking at him from under his brows Achilles of the swift
  feet answered:
"Do not, you dog, supplicate me by knees or parents. 345
Would that my passion and spirit would drive me
to devour your hacked-off flesh raw, such things you have done;
so there is no one who can keep the dogs from your head,

not if they haul here and weigh out ten times and twenty times
the ransom, and promise more,   350
not if Dardanian Priam seeks to pay your weight in gold,
not in any way will your lady mother
mourn you laid out upon your bier, the child she bore;
but the dogs and the birds will devour you wholly."
    Then, dying, Hector of the shimmering helm addressed him: 355
"Knowing you well, I divine my fate; nor will I persuade you.
Surely, the soul in your breast is iron.
Yet now take care, lest I become the cause of the god's wrath against you,
on that day when Paris and Phoebus Apollo
destroy you, great warrior though you be, at the Scaean gates."   360
Then the closure of death enveloped him as he was speaking,
and his soul flying from his limbs started for Hades,
lamenting her fate, abandoning manhood and all its young vigor.
    But shining Achilles addressed him, dead though he was:
"Lie dead. I will take death at that time when   365
Zeus and the other deathless gods wish to accomplish it."
He spoke and pulled his bronze spear from the dead body
and laying it aside he stripped the bloodied armor from Hector's
    shoulders.
But the other sons of the Achaeans ran up around him
and admired Hector's physique and beauty,   370
nor was there a man who stood by him without inflicting a wound.
And thus each would speak, looking at his neighbor:
"Well, well; he is softer to handle, to be sure,
this Hector, than when he torched our ships with blazing fire."
Thus they would speak, and stabbed him as they stood by.   375
    But when shining Achilles of the swift feet had stripped Hector
    of his armor,
he stood amid the Achaeans and pronounced winged words:
"O friends, leaders and counselors of the Achaeans;
since the gods gave me this man to be broken,
who committed evil deeds, more than all the other Trojans together,   380
come, let us go under arms and scout around the city
so that we may learn the disposition of the Trojans, what they have in
    mind,
whether they will abandon their high city now this man is dead,
or desire to remain, although Hector is no longer with them—
but why does my spirit recite these things?   385
There lies by the ships a dead man, unmourned, unburied—
Patroclus. I shall not forget him as long as I am
among the living and my own knees have power in them.
And if other men forget the dead in Hades,
I will remember my beloved companion even there.   390
But come now, Achaean men, singing a victory song
let us return to our hollow ships, and bring him along.
We have achieved great glory; we have slain shining Hector,
whom the Trojans worshipped throughout their city as a god."
    He spoke, and conceived a shocking deed for shining Hector;   395
behind both feet he pierced the tendon

between the heel and ankle and fastened there oxhide straps,
and bound him to his chariot and let the head drag along.
Lifting his glorious armor, Achilles mounted his chariot,
and whipped the horses to begin, and they two, not unwilling, took off.   400
A cloud of dust rose as Hector was dragged, his blue-black hair
fanning around him, his head lolling wholly in the dust
that before was handsome; so Zeus gave him to his enemies
to be defiled in the land of his own fathers.

His head was wholly befouled by dust; and now his mother   405
ripped her hair and flung her shining veil
far away, shrieking her grief aloud as she looked on her child.
His beloved father cried out pitiably and around them the people
were gripped by wailing and crying throughout the city—
it was as if the whole of   410
lofty Ilion, from its topmost point, were consumed with fire.
With difficulty the people restrained old Priam in his grief
as he strove to go forth from the Dardanian gates.
Thrashing in the muck, he entreated all,
calling off each man by name: 415
"Hold off, friend, for all your care for me, and let me
leave the city to go to the ships of the Achaeans.
I will entreat this reckless man of violent deeds,
if somehow he may respect my age and pity
my years. Even his father is of such years,   420
Peleus, who bore him and raised him to be the destruction
of the Trojans; and beyond all men he has inflicted hardship on me.
For so many of my flourishing sons he killed,
but for all my grief, I did not mourn as much for all of them
as for this one, bitter grief for whom will carry me down to the house of
    Hades—   425
Hector. Would that he died in my arms.
We would have glutted ourselves with crying and weeping,
his mother, she, ill-fated woman who bore him, and I."
Thus he spoke lamenting; and thereupon the people mourned.

And Hecuba led the Trojan women in passionate lament: 430
"My child, I am nothing. Why should I live now, grievously suffering,
when you are dead? You who were night and day
my triumph through the city, a blessing to all,
to the Trojans and the Trojan women throughout the city, who
    received you
like a god; for to them you were, indeed, their glory,   435
while you lived; and now death and fate have overtaken you."

Thus she spoke, crying. But Hector's wife knew nothing.
For no trusty messenger had come to her
announcing that her husband remained outside the walls,
and she was weaving at her loom in the corner of her high-roofed house   440
a crimson cloak of double-thickness, and working intricate figures in it.
She called through the house to her attendants with the lovely hair
to set a great tripod over the fire, so
there would be a warm bath for Hector, when he returned home from
    battle—

poor wretch, she did not know that far from all baths   445
gleaming-eyed Athena had broken him at the hands of Achilles.
Then she heard the keening and groaning from the tower
and her limbs shook, and the shuttle fell to the ground,
and she called back to her maids with the beautiful hair:
"Come, both of you follow me; I will see what trouble has happened.   450
I hear the voice of Hector's worthy mother,
the heart in my own breast leaps to my mouth, my limbs beneath me
are rigid; something evil is come near the sons of Priam.
May this word not come to my hearing; but terribly
I fear that shining Achilles has cut my bold Hector   455
from the city on his own, and driving him toward the plain
has stopped him of that fateful ardor
that possessed him, since he never remained in the ranks of men,
but rushed far to the front, yielding in his courage to no one."

   So speaking she raced through the hall like a madwoman,   460
her heart shaking; and her two maids ran with her.
But when she reached the tower and the crowd of men,
she stood on the wall, staring around her; and saw him
dragged before the city. Swift horses
dragged him, unconcernedly, to the hollow ships of the Achaeans.   465
Dark night descended over her eyes,
she fell backward and breathed out her soul;
far from her head she flung her shining headdress,
the diadem and cap and the braided binding,
and the veil, which golden Aphrodite gave her   470
on that day when Hector of the shimmering helm led her
out of the house of Eëtion, when he gave countless gifts for her dowry.
In a throng around her stood her husband's sisters and his brothers' wives,
who supported her among themselves, as she was stricken to the point of
   death.

   But when then she regained her breath and the strength in her
   breast was collected,   475
with gulping sobs she spoke with the Trojan women:
"Hector, I am unlucky. For we were both born to one fate,
you in Troy, in the house of Priam,
and I in Thebes, under forested Plakos,
in the house of Eëtion, who reared me when I was still young,   480
ill-fated he, I of bitter fate. I wish that he had not begotten me.
Now you go to the house of Hades in the depths of the earth,
leaving me in shuddering grief,
a widow in your house. The child is still only a baby,
whom we bore, you and I, both ill-fated. You will   485
be, Hector, no help to him, now you have died, nor he to you.
For even if he escapes this war of the Achaeans and all its tears,
there will always be for him pain and care hereafter.
Other men will rob him of his land;
the day of orphaning cuts a child off entirely from those his age;   490
he is bent low in all things, his cheeks are tearstained.
In his neediness, the child approaches his father's companions,
he tugs one by the cloak, another by his tunic;

pitying him, one of them offers him a little cup
and he moistens his lips, but he does not moisten his palate.   495
But a child blessed with both parents will beat him away from the feast,
striking him with his hands, reviling him with abuse:
'Get away—your father does not dine with us'—
and crying the boy comes up to his widowed mother—
Astyanax; who before on his father's knees   500
used to eat only marrow and the rich fat of sheep,
then when sleep took him and he left off his childish play,
he would slumber in bed in his nurse's embrace,
in his soft bedding, his heart filled with cheery thoughts.
Now he will suffer many things, missing his dear father—   505
'Astyanax'—'little lord of the city'—whom the Trojans called by this name,
for you alone, Hector, defended their gates and long walls.
Now beside the curved ships, away from your parents,
the writhing worms devour you when the dogs have had enough
of your naked body; yet there are clothes laid aside in the house,   510
finely woven, beautiful, fashioned by the hands of women.
Now I will burn them all in a blazing fire,
for they are no use to you, you are not wrapped in them—
I will burn them to be an honor to you in the sight of the Trojan men and
Trojan women."
So she spoke, crying, and the women in response mourned.   515

Summary   Achilles buries Patroclus, and the Greeks celebrate the dead hero's fame with
athletic games, for which Achilles gives the prizes.

BOOK XXIV

[Achilles and Priam]

The games were dispersed, and the men scattered to go
each to his own swift ship. And they began to think about their meal
and giving themselves over to the pleasure of sweet sleep; but Achilles
wept still, remembering his beloved companion, nor did sleep,
who masters all, take hold of him, but he turned himself this side and that   5
yearning for the manly strength and noble spirit of Patroclus,
and remembered with yearning all he been through with him and all the
    woes he had suffered,
running through dangerous waves and the conflicts of men.
Recalling these things he let the warm tears fall,
as he lay now on his side, now again   10
on his back, and now face down; then starting up
he would wander in distraction along the salt-sea shore. He came to know
the dawn as she appeared over the sea and shore;
and when he had yoked his swift horses to his chariot,
he would tie Hector behind the chariot so as to drag him;   15
and after dragging him three times around the tomb of Menoetius' dead son
he would rest again in his shelter, and leave Hector
stretched in the dust upon his face. But Apollo warded off from Hector's
    flesh

all disfigurement, pitying the mortal man,
dead though he was, and covered him wholly round   20
with his golden aegis, so that Achilles would not tear the skin away as he
    dragged him.
        So in his rage Achilles kept outraging glorious Hector;
and as they watched, the blessed gods took pity on the son of Priam,
and kept urging sharp-sighted Hermes, Slayer of Argos, to steal him away.
And this found favor with all other gods, but not with Hera,   25
nor with Poseidon, nor with the gleaming-eyed maiden Athena,
for their hatred persisted, as at the start, for sacred Ilion,
and the people of Priam, because of the folly of Alexandros
who insulted the goddesses, when they came to his shepherd's steading,
and gave the nod to her, the goddess whose gift to him was ruinous lust.[6]   30
        But when at length the twelfth dawn rose since Hector's death,
then it was that Phoebus Apollo addressed the immortals:
"You gods are relentless, destroyers of men! Did Hector never
burn as offerings to you the thighbones of oxen and of goats without
    blemish?
And now, dead though he is, you cannot bring yourselves to rescue him,   35
for his wife to look on, for his mother, for his child,
and for his father and his people, who would with all speed
burn him upon a pyre and honor him with funeral rites;
but you gods choose to abet murderous Achilles,
in whose breast the heart knows no justice,   40
nor does his purpose bend, but his skill is in savage things, like a lion,
who giving way to his great strength and bold heart
goes for the flocks of men, to snatch his feast.
So Achilles has destroyed pity, nor has he shame,
which does great harm to men but also profits them.   45
A man surely is likely to lose someone even dearer—
a brother born of the same womb, or his own son—
but having wept and mourned, he lets it go;
for the Fates placed an enduring heart within mankind;
but Achilles, after he has stripped brilliant Hector of his life,   50
fastens him to his chariot and drags him round the tomb of his
    companion.
This is neither good for Achilles, nor is it worthy;
let him beware lest, noble though he be, we gods be angered with him.
For in his rage he outrages the senseless earth."
        Then in anger white-armed Hera addressed him: 55
"This speech of yours, you of the silver bow, might be justified
if you gods hold Achilles and Hector in the same honor.
But Hector is mortal and sucked at the breast of a woman,
while Achilles is born of a goddess, one whom I myself
nurtured and reared and gave as wife to her husband,   60
to Peleus, who was exceedingly dear to the immortals' hearts;
and all you gods took part in the wedding. And you among them
partook of the feast, lyre in hand, you companion of evil, faithless forever."
        Then answering her spoke Zeus who gathers the clouds:

6. Aphrodite, whom Paris judged more beautiful than Athena and Hera because he found the
bribe that she offered him—Helen—the most attractive.

"Hera, do not be angered with the gods.   65
The men will not have the same honor; yet Hector too
was dearest to the gods of all mortal men in Ilion.
For so he was to me, since he never failed to offer pleasing gifts;
my altar was never lacking its fair share of sacrifice,
of libation and the savour of burnt offering; for this honor is our due.   70
But as for stealing bold Hector away, let that go, it is in no way possible
without Achilles' notice, for always
his mother is at his side night and day alike;
but perhaps one of the gods would summon Thetis to my presence,
so that I could speak a close word to her, so that Achilles would   75
accept gifts from Priam and release Hector for ransom."

So he spoke; and storm-footed Iris sprang up to take his message.
Between Samothrace and rugged Imbros[7]
she leapt into the dark sea; and the sea groaned about her;
she sped to the depths of the sea like a leaden weight,   80
which mounted upon a piece of field-ox horn
goes bearing death to the fish who eat its carrion bait.
She found Thetis in a hollow cave; and gathered round her were
the other goddesses of the sea, and she in the middle
was weeping for the fate of her blameless son, who was destined   85
to perish in the rich soil of Troy, far from his fatherland.
Standing close, swift-footed Iris addressed her:
"Rise up, Thetis; Zeus whose counsels are unfailing, summons you."
Then the goddess Thetis of the silver feet answered her:
"What does he, the great god, command of me? I dread   90
mingling with the immortals; for I have sorrows without end within
    my heart.
Yet I will go, his word will not be in vain, whatever he might say."

So speaking the shining among goddesses took her blue-black
veil; and than this there is no darker garment;
and she set out, and swift Iris with feet like the wind led the way   95
before her; and on either side the waves of the sea parted for them.
Going up onto the shore, they darted to heaven;
and they found the far-thundering son of Cronus, and gathered round him
were sitting all the other blessed gods who live forever.
Then beside Zeus the father Thetis took her seat, which Athena yielded
    to her.   100
Hera placed a beautiful cup of gold into her hands
and spoke kindly words; and Thetis gave it back after drinking.

Then to them the father of gods and men began his speech:
"You have come to Olympus, divine Thetis, despite your cares,
bearing grief that cannot be forgotten in your heart; I know this.   105
But even so I will tell you the reason for which I have called you here.
For nine days a quarrel has arisen among the immortals
concerning Hector's body and Achilles, sacker of cities.
They urge sharp-sighted Hermes, Slayer of Argos, to steal the body away.
I however grant this honor to Achilles,   110
safeguarding your respect and loving friendship for time after:

7. Islands in the northeast Aegean Sea.

go quickly to the army and lay a charge upon your son;
tell him the gods are angry,[8] and that I beyond all
immortals am provoked to rage, because in his madman's heart
he holds Hector beside his curved ships, nor has surrendered him—   115
and that perhaps in fear of me he would give Hector back.
And I will dispatch Iris to great-hearted Priam, to tell him
to obtain the release of his dear son by going to the ships of the Achaeans,
and to bear gifts for Achilles, which would soften his heart."
      So he spoke; nor did the goddess Thetis of the silver feet
    disobey,   120
and she left, darting down from the heights of Olympus,
and made her way to her son's shelter; inside she found him
groaning without cessation; around him his close companions
busily attended to him and readied the morning meal;
a great fleecy sheep had been slain by them in the shelter.   125
His lady mother sat down close beside him,
and stroked his hand, and spoke to him and said his name:
"My child, how long will you devour your heart
in weeping and grieving, mindful neither of food
nor bed? Indeed, it is good to lie with a woman   130
in lovemaking; you will not be living long with me, but already
death stands close beside you and powerful destiny.
Now, mark me at once; I bring a message for you from Zeus;
he says the gods are angry with you, and that he beyond all
immortals is provoked to rage, because in your madman's heart   135
you hold Hector beside your curved ships nor have surrendered him.
But come, give him up, and accept ransom for his body."
      Then answering her spoke swift-footed Achilles:
"Let the man appear who would bring the ransom and bear the body,
if the Olympian himself in earnest bids."   140
      So they, amid the gathering of ships, mother and son,
were speaking many things, winged words, to one another;
and the son of Cronus dispatched Iris into holy Ilion:
"Come, swift Iris, leave this Olympian seat
and bear a message to great-hearted Priam inside Ilion,   145
that he ransom his beloved son, going to the ships of the Achaeans,
and that he bear gifts for Achilles, which would soften his heart,
he alone, and let no other man of Troy go with him.
A herald may accompany him, some older man, who can drive
the mules and the strong-wheeled wagon, to bring back   150
to the city the dead man, whom godlike Achilles killed.
And let no thought of death trouble his heart, nor any fear;
for we will have Hermes, Slayer of Argos, accompany him as escort,
who will lead him, conducting him until he comes to Achilles.
And when he has led him inside Achilles' shelter,   155
Achilles himself will not kill him and he will restrain all others;
for he is not witless, nor thoughtless, nor without morals,
but with great kindness he will have mercy on the suppliant."
      So he spoke; and storm-footed Iris sprang up to take his message.

---

8. Suppliants were under the protection of the gods, especially of Zeus.

And she came to the house of Priam, and there was met with crying
   and lamentation;   160
the sons sitting about their father inside the courtyard
stained their garments with their tears, and among them the old man
was wrapped in his mantle, molded to it; much dung
was round about the neck and head of the old man,
which wallowing in he had scraped up with his own hands.   165
All through his house his daughters and the wives of his sons wailed
   in grief,
remembering those men who in such numbers and nobility
lay dead, having lost their lives at Argive hands.
And Iris, messenger of Zeus, stood by Priam and addressed him,
speaking softly; and trembling seized his limbs: 170
"Have courage in your heart, Priam son of Dardanos, nor fear at all.
For I do not come to you here bearing evil,
but with good intentions; for I am a messenger to you from Zeus,
who though far away takes great thought for and pities you.
The Olympian bids you redeem brilliant Hector by ransom,   175
and bring gifts to Achilles, which would soften his heart,
you alone, and let no other man of Troy go with you.
A herald may accompany you, some older man, who can drive
the mules and the strong-wheeled wagon, to bring back
to the city the dead man, whom godlike Achilles killed.   180
And do not let any thought of death trouble your heart, nor any fear;
for Hermes, Slayer of Argos, will follow with you as escort,
and will lead you, conducting you until he comes to Achilles.
But when he has led you inside Achilles' shelter,
Achilles himself will not kill you and will restrain all others;   185
for he is not witless, nor thoughtless, nor without morals,
but with great kindness he will have mercy on a suppliant."
      Then so speaking, Iris of the swift feet departed;
and Priam ordered his sons to prepare the strong-wheeled mule-drawn
   wagon
and to fasten upon it a wicker carrier.   190
And he went down into his storeroom, high-roofed
and fragrant with cedar, which held his many precious things.
And he called to his wife Hecuba and spoke to her:
"My poor wife, from Zeus an Olympian messenger came to me,
and bids me ransom our beloved son, going to the ships of the Achaeans, 195
to bring gifts to Achilles, which would soften his heart.
Come and tell me this—how to your mind does this seem to be?
For terribly does my spirit urge me, and my heart,
to go there to the ships, inside the broad army of the Achaeans."
      So he spoke; and his wife cried out and answered him in a word: 200
"Alas for me, where have your wits departed, for which you were
famed before, among even those from other lands, as well as those you ruled?
How can you wish to go to the Achaean ships alone,
into the sight of a man who killed your many and your noble
sons? Your heart is iron.   205
For if he sets eyes upon you, and seizes you,
ravening and faithless man as he is, he will not have pity on you,

nor will he in any way respect your standing. No, let us weep now
as we sit far from Hector in our halls; thus it seems powerful Destiny
spun her fated thread[9] for him at his very birth, when I myself brought
   him to life, 210
to glut swift-footed dogs far from his parents
beside a violent man, whose liver I wish I could take hold of,
burying my teeth into its middle to eat; then would there be revenge
for my son, since he was not killed as he played the coward,
but as he took his stand in defense of the Trojans and the deep-breasted 215
Trojan women, taking thought of neither flight nor shelter."

     And old Priam, godlike, spoke to her again:
"Do not delay me in my wish to go, nor yourself,
in my own halls, be a bird of ill omen; you will not persuade me.
For if any other person on earth had commanded me, 220
the smoke-watching seers, or priests,
we would have said it was a lie and we would turn our backs on it;
but as it is, since I myself heard the god and looked her in the face,
I am going, and her word will not be in vain. And if it is my fate
to die beside the ships of the bronze-clad Achaeans, 225
then so I wish it; let Achilles slay me at once
after I have clasped in my arms my son, when I have put away all
   desire for weeping."

     He spoke, and opened up the fine covers of his chests.
There he drew out twelve splendid robes,
and twelve single-folded woolen cloaks, and as many blankets, 230
as many mantles of white linen, and as many tunics too,
and he weighed and brought out ten full talents of gold,
and brought out two gleaming tripods, and four cauldrons,
and he brought out a splendid cup, which Thracian men gave to him
when he went to them on a mission, a magnificent possession; not 235
even this did the old man withhold, as he desired with all his heart
to ransom back his beloved son. And the Trojans, all,
he kept away from his covered halls, reviling them with shaming words:
"Be gone, outrages, disgraces; is there no weeping
in your own homes, that you have come to trouble me? 240
Or do you think it too little, that Zeus the son of Cronus has given me
   suffering,
destroying my best of sons? But you will come to know what this
   means too;
for you will be all the easier for the Achaeans
to kill now my son has died. But
before I behold with my own eyes my city sacked and ravaged, 245
may I enter in the house of Hades."

     He spoke, and drove the men off with his staff; and they went out
before the old man's urgency. And to his own sons he shouted rebuke,
railing at Helenos and Paris and brilliant Agathon
and Pammon and Antiphonos and Polites of the war cry 250
and Deïphobos and Hippothoös, too, and noble Dios.
To these nine, the old man, shouting his threats, gave orders:

9. Fate or the Fates were often pictured as spinning the thread of a person's life.

"Make haste, worthless children, my disgraces. I would the pack of you
together had been slain by the swift ship instead of Hector.
Woe is me, fated utterly, since I sired the best sons   255
in broad Troy, but I say not one of them is left,
Mestor the godlike and Troilos the chariot fighter
and Hector, who was a god among men, nor did he seem to be
the son of mortal man, but of a god.
War destroyed these men, and all these things of shame are left,   260
the liars and dancers, and heroes of the dance floor,
snatchers of lambs and kids in their own land.
Will you all not prepare a wagon for me at once,
and place all these things in it, so that we can go upon our way?"
        So he spoke; and they trembling before the old man's threats   265
lifted out the strong-wheeled wagon for the mule,
a beautiful thing, newly made, and fastened the wicker carrier on it,
and took down from its peg the mule yoke
made of boxwood and with a knob upon it, well-fitted with rings to guide
    the reins;
and they brought out the yoke strap of nine cubits length together with
    the yoke.   270
Then they fitted the yoke skillfully onto the well-polished wagon pole,
at the front end, and cast the ring over its peg,
and they bound the thong three times on each side to the knob, and then
secured it with a series of turns, and tucked the end under.
And carrying it from the storeroom they piled onto the polished wagon   275
the vast ransom for the head of Hector.
They yoked the mules, strong-footed, working in harness,
which in time before the Mysians[1] gave as glorious gifts to Priam.
And for Priam they led under the yoke the horses that the old man,
keeping them for himself, tended at their well-polished manger.   280
        So the herald and Priam were having the animals yoked in the
high-roofed house, a flurry of thoughts in their minds.
And Hecuba with stricken heart drew near them,
carrying in her right hand in a cup of gold
wine that is sweet to the mind, so that they might set out after making
    libation.   285
She stood before the horses, and spoke to Priam and said his name:
"Here, pour an offering to Zeus the father, and pray that you come home,
back from the enemy men, since your heart drives you
to the ships, although I do not wish it.
Come, pray then to the son of Cronus of the black cloud   290
on Ida, who looks down upon the whole of Troy,
and ask for a bird of omen, the swift messenger that for him
is most prized of birds and whose strength is greatest,
to fly to the right, so that you yourself, marking it with your eyes,
may go trusting in it to the ships of the Danaans of swift horses.   295
But if far-thundering Zeus does not send you his messenger,
I would surely not then urge or bid you,
go to the Argive ships, for all you are determined."
        Then answering her spoke godlike Priam:

1. A people of central Asia Minor.

"O my woman, I will not disobey what you demand;   300
for it is good to raise one's hands to Zeus, that he might have mercy."
He spoke, and the old man called on the handmaid attendant
to pour clean water on their hands; and the maid came up beside him
holding in her hands both a water bowl and pouring jug.
And after washing his hands, Priam took the cup from his wife.   305
Then standing in the middle of his court he prayed, and poured a wine
   libation
as he looked toward the heavens, and lifting his voice he spoke:
"Father Zeus, ruling from Mount Ida, most glorious and greatest,
grant that I come as one welcomed to the shelter of Achilles and that he
   pity me.
And send a bird, your swift messenger, which for you yourself   310
is most prized of birds and whose strength is greatest,
to fly to the right, so that I myself, marking it with my eyes,
may go trusting in it to the ships of the Danaans of swift horses."

     So he spoke in prayer, and Zeus all-devising heard him,
and he sent at once an eagle, the surest omen of winged birds,   315
the dusky hunter men call the darkly-spangled one.
As wide as the door of a lofty room is made
in the house of a wealthy man, strong-fitted with bolts,
so wide were its wings on either side; and it appeared to them
on the right as it swept through the city. And seeing it they   320
rejoiced, and the spirit in the breasts of all was lifted.

     Then in haste the old man mounted his polished chariot,
and drove out of the gateway and echoing colonnade.
In front, drawing the four-wheeled wagon, went the mules,
which skillful Idaios the herald was driving; then the horses behind,   325
which the old man as he guided urged with his whip swiftly on
through the city. And all his dear ones followed with him
lamenting greatly, as if he were going to his death.

     Then when they descended from the city and reached the plain,
the rest, turning back, returned to Ilion,   330
the sons and the husbands of his daughters; but the two men did not
   escape the notice
of far-thundering Zeus as they came into view upon the plain, and he
   pitied the old man as he saw him
and swiftly spoke to Hermes his dear son:
"Hermes, it pleases you beyond all other gods
to act as man's companion,[2] and you listen to whomever you will;   335
go now, and lead Priam to the hollow ships of the Achaeans
in such a way that none of the other Danaans sees him,
no one notices, until he arrives at the shelter of the son of Peleus."

     So he spoke; nor did the messenger, the Slayer of Argos, disobey.
Straightway he bound beneath his feet his splendid sandals   340
immortal, golden, which carried him over the water
and over the boundless earth with the breath of the wind;

---

2. Among his many functions, Hermes is an escort to travelers (in particular, he guides the souls of the dead to the underworld). He is also a trickster and will put the guards at the Greek wall to sleep so that Priam can pass through.

he took up his wand, with which he charms the eyes
of whichever men he wishes, and rouses them again when they have
   slumbered;
and taking this in his hands the mighty Slayer of Argos flew away.   345
Swiftly he arrived at Troy and at the Hellespont;
then he set out in the likeness of a noble youth
with his first beard, which is when early manhood is most graceful.
    And when Priam and Idaios had driven beyond the great burial
   mound of Ilos,[3]
then they brought the mules and horses to a stand at the river,   350
so they could drink; for dusk by now had come upon the earth.
And as he looked, the herald caught sight of Hermes
drawing close from nearby, and raising his voice he spoke to Priam:
"Take care, son of Dardanos; there is need for a cautious mind.
I see a man, and I think we two will soon be torn to pieces.   355
Come, let us flee with the horses, or if not
let us take hold of his knees and beg, in the hope that he have mercy."
    So he spoke; and the old man's mind was in turmoil, and he was
   dreadfully afraid,
and the hair stood up on his bent limbs,
and he stood stupefied. But the Runner himself drawing near   360
and taking the old man's hand, inquired of him and addressed him:
"Whither, father, do you guide your mules and horses so
through the ambrosial night, when other mortal men are sleeping?
Do you have no fear of the Achaeans, who breathe fury,
hostile men and your enemy, who are near?   365
If any one of them should see you leading so much treasure
through the black fast-moving night, what then would be your plan?
You yourself are not young, and this man who attends you is too old
for driving men away, who might step forth in violence.
But I will do nothing to harm you, and will keep any other man   370
from you who would; for I liken you to my own father."
    Then old Priam, like a god, answered him:
"These things are much as you say, dear child.
But still one of the gods has surely stretched his hands above me,
who sent such a lucky wayfarer as you to fall in with me,   375
for such is your build and wonderful beauty,
and you have good sense in your mind; yours are blessed parents."
    Then in turn the messenger and Slayer of Argos addressed him:
"Yes, all these things, old man, you rightly say.
But come and tell me this and relate it exactly;   380
either you are sending away somewhere your many fine possessions
to men in other lands, so that they stay there safe for you,
or you are all abandoning sacred Ilion
in fear; for such a man, the best, has fallen,
your son; for he held nothing back in fight with the Achaeans."   385
    Then old Priam, like a god, answered him:
"Who are you, my good friend, and who are your parents?
How well you tell the fate of my unhappy son."

---

3. Priam's grandfather. The tomb was a landmark on the Trojan plain.

Then in turn the messenger and Slayer of Argos addressed him:
"You test me, old man, when you ask of brilliant Hector.   390
The man whom many times I saw with my own eyes
in battle where men win glory, and when he drove the Argives
to the ships and kept killing them as he slashed with his sharp bronze
   sword.
We stood by looking on in wonder; for Achilles
did not permit us to join the fight, being angered with the son of Atreus.   395
For I am a companion-in-arms of Achilles, and the same well-made ship
   brought us both.
I come from the Myrmidons, and my father is Polyktor.
He is a wealthy man, but he is old now, just as you;
He has six sons, and I am his seventh;
having shaken lots among us, it fell to me to follow here.   400
And now I have come to the plain from the ships; for at dawn
the dark-eyed Achaeans will deploy for battle round the city.
For these men have grown impatient sitting around, nor can the
Achaean kings restrain them in their eagerness for war."
     Then old Priam, like a god, answered him: 405
"If you are a companion of Peleus' son Achilles,
come and tell me the whole truth,
whether my son is still by the ships, or whether Achilles
has cut him limb from limb and already thrown him to his dogs."
     Then in turn the messenger and Slayer of Argos addressed him: 410
"O old man, the dogs have not eaten him at all, nor the birds,
but he lies there still beside Achilles' ship
among the shelters, just as he was. It is now the twelfth day
he has been lying, and his body has not decayed at all, nor have the worms
gnawed at him, which consume men slain in battle.   415
It is true Achilles drags him heedlessly around the tomb
of his companion, when the bright dawn shows forth,
but does not disfigure him; you yourself would wonder at this, going there,
how he lies fresh like the dew, and he is wholly cleansed of blood,
there is no stain anywhere; all the wounds have closed together,   420
all the wounds that he was struck; for many men drove their bronze
   weapons into him.
So do the blessed gods care for your noble son
although he is dead, since he was very dear to their hearts."
     So he spoke; and the old man rejoiced, and answered with a word:
"O child, surely it is a good thing to give the immortals   425
their proper gifts, since never did my son—if ever he was—
forget in his halls the gods who hold Olympus;
they remembered in turn these offerings even in his fated death.
But come and accept this beautiful two-handled cup from me,
and give me your protection, and with the gods escort me,   430
until I come to the shelter of the son of Peleus."
     Then in turn the messenger and Slayer of Argos addressed him:
"You make trial of my youth, old man, but you will not persuade me,
who bid me accept your gifts behind Achilles' back.
I fear him and in my heart I shrink   435
to rob him, lest something evil befall me later.

But with all kindness I would be your escort even should we go all the way
to famous Argos, whether by swift ship, or accompanying you on foot;
and no man would fight with you, making light of your escort."

      He spoke and springing onto the horse-drawn chariot the
   Runner   440
swiftly took the whip and reins into his hands,
and breathed a brave spirit into the mules and horses.
And when they reached the fortifications of the ships and the ditch—
the watch guards were just beginning to busy themselves with their
   meals—
then the messenger Argeïphontes[4] poured sleep upon them   445
all, and straightway opened the gates and pushed back the bolts,
and led in Priam and the glorious gifts upon the wagon.

      And when they came before the towering quarters of the son of
   Peleus—
which the Myrmidons had built for their lord,
cutting logs of fir, and thatched it above   450
after gathering bristling reeds from the meadow;
and all around it they built for their lord a great courtyard
with close-set stakes; a single bolt made of fir secured its door,
a bolt that three Achaean men would drive shut,
and three men would draw the great bolt back from its door,   455
three other men, but Achilles would drive it shut even on his own—
there Hermes the Runner opened it for the old man,
and brought inside the illustrious gifts for the swift-footed son of Peleus.
He descended from behind the horses to the ground and spoke:
"Old sir, I, a divine god, came to your aid;   460
I am Hermes; for my father sent me to accompany you as escort.
Yet I shall be quick to go back, nor will I enter into Achilles' sight;
for it would be cause for anger
should a mortal man entertain a god in this way, face-to-face.
But you go in and take hold of the knees of the son of Peleus;   465
and make your prayer in the name of his father and his mother of the
   lovely hair and his son, so that you stir his heart."

      Thus speaking, Hermes departed for high Olympus.
And Priam leapt from behind his horses to the ground,
and left Idaios there; and he remained   470
guarding the mules and horses. The old man went straight toward the
   quarters,
where Achilles beloved of Zeus would always sit, and found him
inside; his companions were sitting apart; two alone,
the warrior Automedon and Alkimos, companion of Ares,
were busy by him. He had just finished his meal,   475
eating and drinking, and the table still lay beside him.
Unseen by these men great Priam entered, then standing close
with his arms he clasped Achilles' knees and kissed the
terrible man-slaughtering hands, which had killed his many sons.
As when madness closes tight upon a man who, after killing someone 480
in his own land, arrives in the country of others,

4. Literally, "Argos-slayer," another name for Hermes.

at a rich man's house, and wonder grips those looking on,
so Achilles looked in wonder at godlike Priam,
and the others in wonder, too, looked each toward the other.

    And in supplication Priam addressed him: 485
"Remember your father, godlike Achilles,
The same age as I, on the ruinous threshold of old age.
And perhaps those who dwell around surround him and
bear hard upon him, nor is there anyone to ward off harm and
   destruction.
Yet surely when he hears you are living   490
he rejoices in his heart and hopes for all his days
to see his beloved son returning from Troy.
But I am fated utterly, since I sired the best sons
in broad Troy, but I say not one of them is left.
Fifty were my sons, when the sons of the Achaeans came;   495
nineteen were born to me from the womb of the same mother,
and the rest the women in my palace bore to me.
Of these furious Ares has made slack the knees of many;
he who alone was left to me, he alone protected our city and those inside it,
him it was you lately killed as he fought to defend his country,   500
Hector. And for his sake I come now to the ships of the Achaeans
to win his release from you, and I bear an untold ransom.
Revere the gods, Achilles, and have pity upon me,
remembering your father; for I am yet more pitiful,
and have endured such things as no other mortal man upon the earth,   505
drawing to my lips the hands of the man who killed my son."

    So he spoke; and he stirred in the other a yearning to weep for
  his own father,
and taking hold of his hand he gently pushed the old man away.
And the two remembered, the one weeping without cessation for
man-slaughtering Hector as he lay curled before Achilles' feet,   510
and Achilles wept for his own father, and then again for
Patroclus; and the sound of their lament was raised throughout the hall.

    But when godlike Achilles had taken his fill of lamentation
and the yearning had gone from his breast and very limbs,
he rose suddenly from his seat, and raised the old man by the hand,   515
pitying his gray head and gray beard,
and lifting his voice he addressed him with winged word:
"Poor soul, surely you have endured much evil in your heart.
How did you dare to go to the Achaean ships alone,
into the sight of a man who killed your many and your noble   520
sons? Your heart is iron.
But come and seat yourself upon the chair, and let us leave these sorrows
lying undisturbed within our hearts, grieving though we are;
for there is no profit in grief that numbs the heart.
For thus have the gods spun the thread of destiny for wretched mortals,   525
that we live in sorrow; and they themselves are free from care.
For two urns lie stored on the floor of Zeus
full of such gifts as he gives, one of evil, the other of good.
Should Zeus who delights in thunder bestow mixed lots upon a man,
he will sometimes meet with evil, another time with good;   530

but should he give to a man only from the urn of woe, he renders him the
    object of abuse,
and grinding distress drives him across the shining earth,
and he roams, esteemed by neither gods nor mortals.
Thus to Peleus too the gods gave shining gifts
from his birth; for he surpassed all men   535
in happiness and wealth, and was lord of the Myrmidons,
and to him, mortal though he was, they gave a goddess as his wife;
but to even him god gave evil, since
in his halls was born no line of lordly sons,
but he begot a single all-untimely child; nor do I care for him   540
as he grows old, since very far from my fatherland
I sit at Troy, afflicting you and your children.
And you, old man, we have heard, were blessed in time before;
as much as Lesbos, seat of Makar, contains out there within its boundaries,
and Phrygia inland and the boundless Hellespont,   545
all these, they say, old man, you surpassed in sons and wealth.
But since the gods of heaven have brought this misery to you,
there is forever fighting and the killing of men about your city.
Bear up, nor mourn incessantly in your heart;
for you will accomplish nothing in grieving for your son,   550
nor will you raise him from the dead; before that happens you will suffer
    yet another evil."

       Then old Priam, like a god, answered him:
"Do not have me sit upon a chair, god-cherished one, while Hector
lies in your shelters unburied, but quick as you can
release him, so that I may see him with my eyes, and you accept the
    many gifts   555
of ransom, which we bring for you. And have enjoyment of them, and may
you return to your fatherland, since from the first you spared me."[5]   557

       Then looking at him from under his brows swift-footed Achilles
    spoke: 559
"Provoke me no further, old man; for I myself am minded   560
to release Hector to you; from Zeus my mother came to me as messenger,
she who bore me, daughter of the old man of the sea.
I recognize, Priam, in my mind, and it does not escape me,
that some one of the gods led you to the Achaeans' swift ships;
for no mortal man, not even a young man in his prime, would dare   565
to come to our camp; nor could he have slipped by the watch guards, nor
    could he
easily force back the bolts of our doors.
Therefore do not now stir my heart further in its sorrows,
lest, old man, I do not spare even yourself within my shelter,
suppliant though you be, but transgress the commands of Zeus."   570

       Thus he spoke; and the old man was afraid and obeyed his word.
And the son of Peleus like a lion sprang out the door of his shelter,
and not alone; with him followed his two henchmen,
the warrior Automedon and Alkimos, whom beyond all other companions
Achilles honored after Patroclus died.   575

5. The line numbers here account for lines that were omitted by the translator because they may
not belong in the text.

They released the horses and mules from under their yokes,
and led in the herald, crier to the old man,
and they seated him upon a bench; and from the strong-wheeled wagon
they lifted the boundless ransom for the body of Hector.
But they left two fine-spun robes and a tunic,   580
so Achilles could wrap the body and give it to be carried home.
And summoning his maids, Achilles ordered them to wash the body and
    anoint it,
after taking it to a place apart, so that Priam should not see his son,
for fear the old man might not keep his anger hidden in his anguished heart
on seeing his son, and might stir Achilles' own heart to violence   585
and he kill Priam, and transgress the commands of Zeus.
And when then the maids had washed and anointed the body with oil,
they put around it the beautiful robe and tunic,
and Achilles himself lifted it and placed it upon a bier,
then his companions with him lifted this onto the polished wagon.   590
And Achilles groaned, and called his dear companion's name:
"Do not, Patroclus, be angered with me, if you should learn,
though you be in the house of Hades, that I released shining Hector
to his father, since the ransom he gave me was not unworthy.
And I in turn will give you a portion of it, as much as is fitting."   595

          He spoke, and godlike Achilles went back into his shelter,
and took his seat on the richly wrought chair, from which he had risen,
against the far wall, and spoke his word to Priam:
"Your son has been released to you, old man, as you bade,
and lies upon a bier; and with the dawn's appearance,   600
you will see yourself when you take him. But now let us not forget our
    supper.
For even Niobe[6] of the lovely hair did not forget her food,
she whose twelve children were destroyed in her halls,
six daughters, and six sons in the prime of manhood.
The sons Apollo slew with his silver bow   605
in his anger with Niobe, and Artemis who showers arrows slew the
    daughters,
because Niobe equalled herself to Leto of the lovely cheeks—
for she would boast that Leto bore two children, while she herself had
    borne many.
So two only though they were, they destroyed the many.
And for nine days they lay in their own blood, nor was there anyone   610
to give them burial; for the son of Cronus had turned the people into stone.
Then on the tenth day the heavenly gods gave them burial,
and Niobe bethought herself of food, when she was worn out with weeping.
And now among the rocks somewhere, in the lonely mountains
of Sipylos, where they say are the sleeping places of the immortal   615
nymphs who race beside the river Achelous,
there, stone though she is, she broods upon the cares sent her from the
    gods.[7]

---

6. Wife of Amphion, one of the two founders
of the great Greek city of Thebes.
7. The legend of Niobe being turned into stone
is thought to have had its origin in a rock face of

Mount Sipylus (in Asia Minor) that resembled a
woman who wept inconsolably for the loss of
her children. The Achelous River runs near
Mount Sipylus.

But come, and let us two, illustrious old sir, take thought
of food. For you may weep for your dear son again
when you have brought him into Ilion; he will be the cause of many
　　tears."　　　　　　　　　　　　　　　　　　　　　　　　　　620
　　　　　　He spoke, and springing to his feet swift Achilles, with a cut to
　　the throat,
slaughtered a shining white sheep; his companions flayed it and with skill
　　prepared it properly.
They sliced the flesh skillfully and pierced it on spits
and roasted it with care, and then drew off all the pieces.
Automedon took bread to distribute around the table　　　　　625
in fine baskets; but Achilles distributed the meat;
and they reached out their hands to the good things set ready before them.
And when they had put away desire for eating and drinking,
then did Priam son of Dardanos look in wonder at Achilles,
how massive he was, what kind of man; for he was like the gods to
　　look upon;　　　　　　　　　　　　　　　　　　　　　　　630
and Achilles looked in wonder at Dardanian Priam,
gazing on his noble face and listening to his words.
　　　　　　But when they had their fill of looking upon each other,
then old Priam the godlike addressed Achilles first:
"Let me go to bed now quickly, god-cherished one, so that　　635
we may have solace when we lie down beneath sweet sleep.
For not yet have my eyes closed beneath my lids,
from the time my son lost his life at your hands,
but always I groaned in lament and brooded on my sorrows without
　　measure,
wallowing in dung in the enclosure of my court.　　　　　　640
But now I have tasted food and let gleaming wine
down my throat; before I had tasted nothing."
　　　　　　He spoke; and Achilles ordered the companions and servant women
to set out a bed under cover of the porch and to throw upon it
splendid crimson blankets to lie upon, and to spread rugs over them,　　645
and to place woolen cloaks on top of all to cover them.
And the maids went from the hall bearing torches in their hands,
and working in haste soon spread two beds.
Then bantering, Achilles of the swift feet addressed Priam:
"Sleep outside, old friend, for fear one of the Achaean　　　650
leaders come suddenly upon us here, who forever
devise their counsels beside me, as is right and proper.
If one of them were to see you through the swift black night,
he would at once make it known to Agamemnon, shepherd of the people,
and there would be delay in the surrender of the body.　　　655
But come and tell me this and relate it exactly;
how many days do you desire to give funeral rites to shining Hector—
for so long I will wait and hold back the army."
　　　　　　Then old Priam the godlike answered him:
"If then you are willing for me to accomplish Hector's funeral,　　660
by doing as follows, Achilles, you would give me a kindness.
For you know how we are penned within the city, and it is a long way
to bring wood from, the mountains; for the Trojans are greatly afraid;

nine days we would mourn him in our halls,
and on the tenth we would bury him and the people would feast,   665
and on the eleventh day we would make a tomb for him:
and on the twelfth we shall go to war, if indeed we must."
    Then in turn swift-footed godlike Achilles addressed him:
"These things, old Priam, will be as you ask;
I will suspend the war for such time, as you command."   670
And so speaking he took hold of the old man's right hand
by the wrist, lest he have any fear in his heart.
    Then they lay down to sleep there in the forecourt of the shelter,
the herald and Priam, a flurry of thoughts in their minds.
But Achilles slept in the inner recess of his well-built shelter,   675
and Briseïs of the lovely cheeks lay at his side.
    So the other gods as well as chariot-fighting men
slept through the night, overcome by soft slumber,
but sleep did not lay hold of Hermes the runner
as he turned over in his heart how he might send king Priam   680
from the ships unnoticed by the hallowed watchers of the gate.
And he stood above Priam's head and addressed him with his words:
"Old man, surely you have no thought of any evil, seeing how you sleep
in the midst of enemy men, since Achilles spared you.
And now you have won release of your beloved son, and gave many
    things for him;   685
but your sons who were left behind would give yet three times
as much ransom for you alive, should Agamemnon
the son of Atreus recognize you, and all the Achaeans."
So he spoke; and the old man was afraid, and woke up his herald.
Then Hermes yoked the mules and horses for them,   690
and himself drove swiftly through the camp; nor did anyone see.
    But when they reached the crossing of the fair-flowing stream,[8]   692
then Hermes departed for high Olympus;   694
and Dawn robed in saffron spread over all the earth;   695
the men with lamentation and groaning drove the horses on
to the city, and the mules carried the corpse. No man
saw them at first, nor any fair-belted woman,
but then Cassandra,[9] like to golden Aphrodite,
having gone up to the height of Pergamos, saw her beloved father   700
standing in the chariot and the herald and city crier;
and then she saw Hector lying upon the bier drawn by the mules.
She wailed her grief aloud, then cried out to the whole city:
"Look upon Hector, men and women of Troy! Come,
if ever before you used to rejoice when he returned alive from battle,   705
since he was the great joy of the city and all its people."
    So she spoke; nor did any man remain there in the city
nor any woman; uncontrollable grief seized all;
close by the gates they met Priam as he brought Hector's body;
at the front his beloved wife and lady mother ripped their hair in grief   710

---

8. The line numbers here account for lines that were omitted by the translator because they may not belong in the text.

9. Daughter of Priam and Hecuba; she was a prophetess and foretold the fall of Troy, but was cursed by Apollo to be disbelieved.

for him, lunging at the strong-wheeled wagon,
to touch his head; and the throng surrounded him weeping.
And for the whole day long until the sun's going down they would have
mourned Hector, pouring their tears before the gates,
had not the old man spoken among them from the chariot: 715
"Make way for me to pass with the mules; later
you can sate yourselves with weeping, when I have brought him home."
So he spoke; and they stood aside and made way for the wagon.
        And when they had brought him into the illustrious house, then
they laid him upon a fretted bed, and set beside it singers,   720
leaders of the dirges, who sang their mournful dirge song,
and the women keened in response.
        And white-armed Andromache led the lament among them,
holding in her arms the head of horse-breaking Hector:
"My husband, you were lost from life while young, and are leaving me
    a widow   725
in your halls; and the child is still just a baby,
whom we bore, you and I, ill-fated both, nor do I think
he will reach young manhood; before that this city
will be wholly ravaged; for you its watchman have perished, who used to
    guard it,
who protected its devoted wives and tender children.   730
They soon will be carried away in the hollow ships,
and I with them; and you then, my child, either you will follow with me,
and there do work unworthy of you
toiling for a harsh master—or some Achaean man
seizing you by the arm will hurl you from the ramparts, unhappy death,[1]   735
in his anger, one whose brother, perhaps, Hector slew,
or his father or even his son, since so many of the Achaeans
gripped the broad earth in their teeth at Hector's hands.
For your father was no gentle man in sad battle;
therefore the people mourn him through the city,   740
and cursed is the grief and lamentation you have laid upon your parents,
Hector. And to me beyond all others will be left painful sorrow;
for you did not reach out your hands to me from your bed as you were dying,
nor did you speak some close word to me, which I might always
remember through the nights and days as I shed my tears."   745
So she spoke, crying, and the women in response mourned.
        And Hecuba led them next in the passionate lament:
"Hector, far the dearest to my heart of all my sons,
while you were alive you were dear to the gods,
who now care for you even in your fated lot of death.   750
Other sons of mine Achilles of the swift feet would sell,
whomever he captured, beyond the murmuring salt sea,
into Samothrace, into Imbros and sea-spattered Lemnos;
but he plucked your soul from you with his tapered bronze spear,
and dragged you again and again around the tomb of his companion   755
Patroclus, whom you slew—nor did he raise him from the dead so doing—
yet now you lie as fresh as dew, unsullied in my halls,

---

1. Astyanax was, in fact, hurled from Troy's walls after the city fell.

like one whom Apollo of the silver bow
approaches and kills with his gentle arrows."
So she spoke weeping, and stirred unceasing wailing.   760
      Then third among the women, Helen led the lament:
"Hector, far dearest to my heart of all my husband's brothers;
too true, my husband is Alexandros of godlike beauty,
who led me to Troy; would that I had died before;
for this is now the twentieth year for me   765
since I set out from there and forsook my fatherland,
but never yet did I hear a harsh or abusive word from you,
but if someone else would revile me in these halls,
one of my husband's brothers, or his sisters, or one of my fine-robed
   sisters-in-law,
or my husband's mother—but my husband's father was like a kind
   father always—   770
you with soothing words would restrain them
with your gentle nature and kind speech.
Therefore I weep, grieving at heart, for you and for me, ill-fated, together;
for no longer is there anyone else in broad Troy
to be kind or friend to me, but all shudder at me."   775
So she spoke crying, and in response all the great multitude moaned.
      Then old Priam spoke his word among the people:
"Men of Troy, now fetch timber to the city. Have no fear in your heart
of cunning ambush by the Argives; for Achilles,
as he sent me from the black ships, gave orders thus,   780
that he would do no harm before the twelfth dawn comes."
So he spoke; and the men yoked the oxen and mules to the wagons,
and soon they were gathered before the city.
      For nine days they brought an immense pile of timber;
and when at length the tenth dawn showed, bringing light to mortals,   785
then, shedding tears, they carried forth bold Hector.
On the very top of the pyre they placed his body, and on it flung the fire.
      And when Dawn born of the morning showed forth her fingers
   of rosy light,
then around the pyre of illustrious Hector the people gathered;[2]   789
first they extinguished the burning pyre with dark-gleaming wine   791
entirely, all that retained the fire's strength; and then
his brothers and his comrades picked out his white bones
as they wept, and the swelling tears fell from their cheeks.
And taking the bones they placed them in a golden box,   795
after covering them round with soft purple cloth;
swiftly they placed these in a hollowed grave, and covered it
from above with great stones set close together.
Lightly they heaped up the burial mound—lookouts were set all round,
lest the strong-greaved Achaeans should attack before—   800
and when they had piled up the mound they started back. Then
having come together they duly gave a glorious feast
in the house of Priam, king nurtured by Zeus.
Thus they tended the funeral of Hector, breaker of horses.

---

2. The line numbers here account for lines that were omitted by the translator because they may
not belong in the text.

The Odyssey[1]

BOOK I

The Boy and the Goddess

Tell me about a complicated man.[2]
Muse, tell me how he wandered and was lost
when he had wrecked the holy town of Troy,
and where he went, and who he met, the pain
he suffered in the storms at sea, and how   5
he worked to save his life and bring his men
back home. He failed to keep them safe; poor fools,
they ate the Sun God's cattle,[3] and the god
kept them from home. Now goddess, child of Zeus,[4]
tell the old story for our modern times.   10
Find the beginning.

    All the other Greeks
who had survived the brutal sack of Troy
sailed safely home to their own wives—except
this man alone. Calypso,[5] a great goddess,
had trapped him in her cave; she wanted him   15
to be her husband. When the year rolled round
in which the gods decreed he should go home
to Ithaca, his troubles still went on.
The man was friendless. All the gods took pity,
except Poseidon's[6] anger never ended   20
until Odysseus was back at home.
But now the distant Ethiopians,
who live between the sunset and the dawn,
were worshipping the Sea God with a feast,
a hundred cattle and a hundred rams.   25
There sat the god, delighting in his banquet.
The other gods were gathered on Olympus,
in Father Zeus'[7] palace. He was thinking
of fine, well-born Aegisthus, who was killed
by Agamemnon's famous son Orestes.[8]   30
He told the deathless gods,

       "This is absurd,
that mortals blame the gods! They say we cause

---

1. Translated by Emily Wilson.
2. Odysseus, who is not named until several lines later.
3. The sun god Hyperion was, in Greek mythology, a Titan, one of the generation of gods that preceded the Olympians. The story of how Odysseus' men ate the cattle of the sun will be told in book 12.
4. The muse.
5. Daughter of the Titan Atlas, who holds up

the sky.
6. Poseidon is the god of the sea, brother of Zeus.
7. Zeus is the king of the gods.
8. Agamemnon was killed on his return home by the usurper Aegisthus, with the help of Agamemnon's adulterous wife, Clytemnestra. Orestes, Agamemnon and Clytemnestra's son, killed his mother and Aegisthus.

their suffering, but they themselves increase it
by folly. So Aegisthus overstepped:
he took the legal wife of Agamemnon,   35
then killed the husband when he came back home
although he knew that it would doom them all.
We gods had warned Aegisthus; we sent down
perceptive Hermes,[9] who flashed into sight
and told him not to murder Agamemnon   40
or court his wife; Orestes would grow up
and come back to his home to take revenge.
Aegisthus would not hear that good advice.
But now his death has paid all debts."

                                               Athena[1]
looked at him steadily and answered, "Father,   45
he did deserve to die. Bring death to all
who act like him! But I am agonizing
about Odysseus and his bad luck.
For too long he has suffered, with no friends,
sea all around him, sea on every side,   50
out on an island where a goddess lives,
daughter of fearful Atlas, who holds up
the pillars of the sea, and knows its depths—
those pillars keep the heaven and earth apart.
His daughter holds that poor unhappy man,   55
and tries beguiling him with gentle words
to cease all thoughts of Ithaca; but he
longs to see even just the smoke that rises
from his own homeland, and he wants to die.
You do not even care, Olympian!   60
Remember how he sacrificed to you
on the broad plain of Troy beside his ships?
So why do you dismiss Odysseus?"[2]

"Daughter!" the Cloud God said, "You must be joking,
since how could I forget Odysseus?   65
He is more sensible than other humans,
and makes more sacrifices to the gods.
But Lord Poseidon rages, unrelenting,
because Odysseus destroyed the eye
of godlike Polyphemus, his own son,   70
the strongest of the Cyclopes—whose mother,
Thoösa, is a sea-nymph, child of Phorcys,[3]
the sea king; and she lay beside Poseidon
inside a hollow cave. So now Poseidon
prevents Odysseus from reaching home   75

9. Messenger god.
1. Goddess of wisdom, who favors Odysseus.
2. The word in the original for Zeus hostile

treatment of Odysseus (*odyssao*) is reminiscent
of the name "Odysseus."
3. A minor sea god. "Cyclopes": one-eyed giants.

but does not kill him. Come then, we must plan:
how can he get back home? Poseidon must
give up his anger, since he cannot fight
alone against the will of all the gods."

Athena's eyes lit up and she replied,   80
"Great Father, if the blessed gods at last
will let Odysseus return back home,
then hurry, we must send our messenger,
Hermes the giant-slayer. He must swoop
down to Ogygia right away and tell   85
the beautiful Calypso we have formed
a firm decision that Odysseus
has waited long enough. He must go home.
And I will go to Ithaca to rouse
the courage of his son, and make him call   90
a meeting, and speak out against the suitors
who kill his flocks of sheep and longhorn cattle
unstoppably. Then I will send him off
to Pylos and to Sparta, to seek news
about his father's journey home, and gain   95
a noble reputation for himself."

With that, she tied her sandals on her feet,
the marvelous golden sandals that she wears
to travel sea and land, as fast as wind.
She took the heavy bronze-tipped spear she uses   100
to tame the ranks of warriors with whom
she is enraged. Then from the mountain down
she sped to Ithaca, and stopped outside
Odysseus' court, bronze spear in hand.
She looked like Mentes now, the Taphian leader,[4]   105
a guest-friend. There she found the lordly suitors
sitting on hides—they killed the cows themselves—
and playing checkers. Quick, attentive house slaves
were waiting on them. Some were mixing wine
with water in the bowls, and others brought   110
the tables out and wiped them off with sponges,
and others carved up heaping plates of meat.
Telemachus was sitting with them, feeling
dejected. In his mind he saw his father
coming from somewhere, scattering the suitors,   115
and gaining back his honor, and control
of all his property. With this in mind,
he was the first to see Athena there.
He disapproved of leaving strangers stranded,
so he went straight to meet her at the gate,   120
and shook her hand, and took her spear of bronze,
and let his words fly out to her.

---

4. The Taphians were an island people from the Ionian Sea. "Mentes": a friend of Odysseus.

"Good evening,
stranger, and welcome. Be our guest, come share
our dinner, and then tell us what you need."

He led her in, and Pallas followed him.   125
Inside the high-roofed hall, he set her spear
beside a pillar in a polished stand,
in which Odysseus kept stores of weapons.
And then he led her to a chair and spread
a smooth embroidered cloth across the seat,   130
and pulled a footstool up to it. He sat
beside her on a chair of inlaid wood,
a distance from the suitors, so their shouting
would not upset the stranger during dinner;
also to ask about his absent father.   135
A girl brought washing water in a jug
of gold, and poured it on their hands and into
a silver bowl, and set a table by them.
A deferential slave brought bread and laid
a wide array of food, a generous spread.   140
The carver set beside them plates of meat
of every kind, and gave them golden cups.
The cup boy kept on topping up the wine.
The suitors sauntered in and sat on chairs,
observing proper order,[5] and the slaves   145
poured water on their hands. The house girls brought
baskets of bread and heaped it up beside them,
and house boys filled their wine-bowls up with drink.
They reached to take the good things set before them.
Once they were satisfied with food and drink,   150
the suitors turned their minds to other things—
singing and dancing, glories of the feast.
A slave brought out a well-tuned lyre and gave it
to Phemius, the man the suitors forced
to sing for them. He struck the chords to start   155
his lovely song.

      Telemachus leaned in
close to Athena, so they would not hear,
and said,

      "Dear guest—excuse my saying this—
these men are only interested in music,
a life of ease. They make no contribution.   160
This food belongs to someone else, a man
whose white bones may be lying in the rain
or sunk beneath the waves. If they saw him

5. There may be an implication here that the
suitors seat themselves according to some
kind of rank, with the more important ones
taking a more honorable position.

return to Ithaca, they would all pray
for faster feet, instead of wealth and gold   165
and fancy clothes. In fact, he must have died.
We have no hope. He will not come back home.
If someone says so, we do not believe it.
But come now, tell me this and tell the truth.
Who are you? From what city, and what parents?   170
What kind of ship did you here arrive on?
What sailors brought you here, and by what route?
You surely did not travel here on foot!
Here is the thing I really want to know:
have you been here before? Are you a friend   175
who visited my father? Many men
came to his house. He traveled many places."

Athena's clear bright eyes met his. She said,
"Yes, I will tell you everything. I am
Mentes, the son of wise Anchialus,   180
lord of the Taphians, who love the oar.
I traveled with my ship and my companions
over the wine-dark sea to foreign lands,
with iron that I hope to trade for copper
in Temese. My ship is in the harbor   185
far from the town, beneath the woody hill.
And you and I are guest-friends through our fathers,
from long ago—Laertes[6] can confirm it.
I hear that fine old man no longer comes
to town, but lives out in the countryside,   190
stricken by grief, with only one old slave,
who gives him food and drink when he trails back
leg-weary from his orchard, rich in vines.
I came because they told me that your father
was here—but now it seems that gods have blocked   195
his path back home. But I am sure that he
is not yet dead. The wide sea keeps him trapped
upon some island, captured by fierce men
who will not let him go. Now I will make
a prophecy the gods have given me,   200
and I think it will all come true, although
I am no prophet. He will not be gone
much longer from his own dear native land,
even if chains of iron hold him fast.
He will devise a means of getting home.   205
He is resourceful. Tell me now—are you
Odysseus' son? You are so tall!
Your handsome face and eyes resemble his.
We often met and knew each other well,
before he went to Troy, where all the best   210

6. Odysseus' father.

leaders of Argos sailed in hollow ships.
From that time on, we have not seen each other."

Telemachus was careful as he answered.
"Dear guest, I will be frank with you. My mother
says that I am his son, but I cannot   215
be sure, since no one knows his own begetting.
I wish I were the son of someone lucky,
who could grow old at home with all his wealth.
Instead, the most unlucky man alive
is said to be my father—since you ask."   220

Athena looked at him with sparkling eyes.
"Son of Penelope, you and your sons
will make a name in history, since you are
so clever. But now tell me this. Who are
these banqueters? And what is the occasion?   225
A drinking party, or a wedding feast?
They look so arrogant and self-indulgent,
making themselves at home. A wise observer
would surely disapprove of how they act."

Telemachus said moodily, "My friend,   230
since you have raised the subject, there was once
a time when this house here was doing well,
our future bright, when he was still at home.
But now the gods have changed their plans and cursed us,
and cast my father into utter darkness.   235
If he had died it would not be this bad—
if he had fallen with his friends at Troy,
or in his loved ones' arms, when he had wound
the threads of war to end. The Greeks would then
have built a tomb for him; he would have won   240
fame for his son. But now, the winds have seized him,
and he is nameless and unknown. He left
nothing but tears for me. I do not weep
only for him. The gods have given me
so many other troubles. All the chiefs   245
of Same, Zacynthus, Dulichium,
and local lords from rocky Ithaca,
are courting Mother, wasting our whole house.
She does not turn these awful suitors down,
nor can she end the courting. They keep eating,   250
spoiling my house—and soon, they will kill me!"

Athena said in outrage, "This is monstrous!
You need Odysseus to come back home
and lay his hands on all those shameless suitors!
If only he would come here now and stand   255
right at the gates, with two spears in his hands,
in shield and helmet, as when I first saw him!

Odysseus was visiting our house,
drinking and having fun on his way back
from sailing in swift ships to Ephyra   260
to visit Ilus. He had gone there looking
for deadly poison to anoint his arrows.
Ilus refused, because he feared the gods.
My father gave Odysseus the poison,
loving him blindly. May Odysseus   265
come meet the suitors with that urge to kill!
A bitter courtship and short life for them!
But whether he comes home to take revenge,
or not, is with the gods. You must consider
how best to drive these suitors from your house.   270
Come, listen carefully to what I say.
Tomorrow call the Achaean[7] chiefs to meeting,
and tell the suitors—let the gods be witness—
'All of you, go away! To your own homes!'
As for your mother, if she wants to marry,   275
let her return to her great father's home.
They will make her a wedding and prepare
abundant gifts to show her father's love.
Now here is some advice from me for you.
Fit out a ship with twenty oars, the best,   280
and go find out about your long-lost father.
Someone may tell you news, or you may hear
a voice from Zeus, best source of information.
First go to Pylos, question godlike Nestor;
from there, to Sparta; visit Menelaus.[8]   285
He came home last of all the Achaean heroes.
If you should hear that he is still alive
and coming home, put up with this abuse
for one more year. But if you hear that he
is dead, go home, and build a tomb for him,   290
and hold a lavish funeral to show
the honor he deserves, and give your mother
in marriage to a man. When this is done,
consider deeply how you might be able
to kill the suitors in your halls—by tricks   295
or openly. You must not stick to childhood;
you are no longer just a little boy.
You surely heard how everybody praised
Orestes when he killed the man who killed
his famous father—devious Aegisthus?   300
Dear boy, I see how big and tall you are.
Be brave, and win yourself a lasting name.
But I must go now, on my speedy ship;
my friends are getting tired of waiting for me.
Remember what I said and heed my words."   305

7. Greek.
8. Brother of Agamemnon, husband of Helen,

the woman whose abduction by Paris caused
the Trojan War.

Telemachus was brooding on her words,
and said, "Dear guest, you were so kind to give me
this fatherly advice. I will remember.
I know that you are eager to be off,
but please enjoy a bath before you go,   310
and take a gift with you. I want to give you
a precious, pretty treasure as a keepsake
to mark our special friendship."

                 But the goddess
Athena met his gaze and said, "Do not
hold me back now. I must be on my way.   315
As for the gift you feel inspired to give me,
save it for when I come on my way home
and let me give you presents then as well
in fair exchange."

               With that, the owl-eyed goddess
flew away like a bird, up through the smoke.   320
She left him feeling braver, more determined,
and with his father even more in mind.
Watching her go, he was amazed and saw
she was a god. Then godlike, he went off
to meet the suitors.

               They were sitting calmly,   325
listening to the poet, who sang how
Athena cursed the journey of the Greeks
as they were sailing home from Troy. Upstairs,
Penelope had heard the marvelous song.
She clambered down the steep steps of her house,   330
not by herself—two slave girls came with her.
She reached the suitors looking like a goddess,
then stopped and stood beside a sturdy pillar,
holding a gauzy veil before her face.
Her slave girls stood, one on each side of her.   335
In tears, she told the holy singer,

                 "Stop,
please, Phemius! You know so many songs,
enchanting tales of things that gods and men
have done, the deeds that singers publicize.
Sing something else, and let them drink in peace.   340
Stop this upsetting song that always breaks
my heart, so I can hardly bear my grief.
I miss him all the time—that man, my husband,
whose story is so famous throughout Greece."

Sullen Telemachus said, "Mother, no,   345
you must not criticize the loyal bard
for singing as it pleases him to sing.

Poets are not to blame for how things are;
Zeus is; he gives to each as is his will.
Do not blame Phemius because he told   350
about the Greek disasters. You must know
the newest song is always praised the most.
So steel your heart and listen to the song.
Odysseus was not the only one
who did not come back home again from Troy.   355
Many were lost. Go in and do your work.
Stick to the loom and distaff. Tell your slaves
to do their chores as well. It is for men
to talk, especially me. I am the master."

That startled her. She went back to her room,   360
and took her son's uneasy words to heart.
She went upstairs, along with both her slaves,
and wept there for her dear Odysseus,
until Athena gave her eyes sweet sleep.
Throughout the shadowy hall the suitors clamored,   365
praying to lie beside her in her bed.
Telemachus inhaled, then started speaking.

"You suitors, you are taking this too far.
Let us enjoy the feast in peace. It is
a lovely thing to listen to a bard,   370
especially one with such a godlike voice.
At dawn, let us assemble in the square.
I have to tell you this—it is an order.
You have to leave my halls. Go dine elsewhere!
Eat your own food, or share between your houses.   375
Or if you think it easier and better
to ruin one man's wealth, and if you think
that you can get away with it—go on!
I call upon the gods; Zeus will grant vengeance.
You will be punished and destroyed, right here!"   380

He spoke, and they began to bite their lips,
shocked that Telemachus would dare to speak
so boldly. But Antinous replied,

"Telemachus, the gods themselves have taught you
such pride, to talk so big and brash in public!   385
May Zeus the son of Cronus never grant you
your true inheritance, which is the throne
of Ithaca."

              His mind alert and focused,
Telemachus replied, "Antinous,
you will not like this, but I have to say,   390
I hope Zeus does give me the throne. Do you
deny it is an honorable thing

to be a king? It brings the household wealth,
and honor to the man. But there are many
other great chiefs in sea-girt Ithaca,   395
both old and young. I know that. One of them
may seize the throne, now that Odysseus
has died. But I shall be at least the lord
of my own house and of the slaves that he
seized for my benefit."

                  Eurymachus   400
replied, "Telemachus, the gods must choose
which of us will be king of Ithaca.
But still, I hope you keep your own possessions,
and rule your house. May no man drive you out,
and seize your wealth, while Ithaca survives.   405
Now, friend, I want to ask about the stranger.
Where was he from, what country? Did he say?
Where is his place of birth, his native soil?
Does he bring news your father will come home?
Or did he come here for some other purpose?   410
How suddenly he darted off, not waiting
for us to meet him. Yet he looked important."

The boy said soberly, "Eurymachus,
my father is not ever coming home.
I do not listen now to any gossip,   415
or forecasts from the psychics whom my mother
invites to visit us. The stranger was
my father's guest-friend Mentes, son of wise
Anchialus, who rules the Taphians,
the people of the oar."

                Those were his words,   420
but in his mind he knew she was a god.
They danced to music and enjoyed themselves
till evening, then they went back home to sleep.
Telemachus' bedroom had been built
above the courtyard, so it had a view.   425
He went upstairs, preoccupied by thought.
A loyal slave went with him, Eurycleia,
daughter of Ops; she brought the burning torches.
Laertes bought her many years before
when she was very young, for twenty oxen.   430
He gave her status in the household, equal
to his own wife, but never slept with her,
avoiding bitter feelings in his marriage.
She brought the torches now; she was the slave
who loved him most, since she had cared for him   435
when he was tiny. Entering the room,
he sat down on the bed, took off his tunic,
and gave it to the vigilant old woman.

She smoothed it out and folded it, then hung it
up on a hook beside his wooden bed,   440
and left the room. She used the silver latch
to close the door; the strap pulled tight the bolt.
He slept the night there, wrapped in woolen blankets,
planning the journey told him by Athena.

BOOK 2

A Dangerous Journey

The early Dawn was born; her fingers bloomed.
Odysseus' well-beloved son
jumped up, put on his clothes, and strapped his sword
across his back, and tied his handsome sandals
onto his well-oiled feet. He left the room   5
looking just like a god.

           He quickly told
the clear-voiced heralds they must call the Greeks
to council. Soon the men, their long hair flowing,
were gathered all together in the square.
Telemachus arrived, bronze sword in hand,   10
not by himself—two swift dogs came with him.
Athena poured a heavenly grace upon him.
The elders let him join them, and he sat
upon his father's throne. The first to speak
was wise Aegyptius, a bent old soldier.   15
His darling son, the spear-man Antiphus,
had sailed with Lord Odysseus to Troy;
the Cyclops killed him in his cave and made him
his final course at dinner. This old father
had three sons left. One teamed up with the suitors—   20
Eurynomus. The others spent their time
working the farm. But still the father mourned
the son whom he had lost. He spoke in tears.

"People of Ithaca, now hear my words.
We have not met in council since the day   25
Odysseus departed with his ships.
Who called us? Someone old or young? And why?
Has he found out an army is approaching?
Or does he have some other piece of news
which he would like to share with all of us?   30
I think he is a helpful, decent man.
I hope that Zeus rewards his good intentions!"

Odysseus' loving son felt glad,
and eagerly got up to speak and stood
among them, in the center of the group.   35
The competent official, named Pisenor,

passed him the speaking-stick; he held it up,
and first addressed Aegyptius.

                    "Here, sir!
Now look no further for the man you seek.
I called the meeting. I am in deep trouble.   40
I have no information of an army
that might attack us, nor do I have news
of any other danger to our people.
I need help for myself. My family
has suffered two disasters. First I lost   45
my father, who was kind to you as if
you also were his sons. Now, even worse,
my house is being ripped apart; my wealth
will soon be gone! The sons of all the nobles
have shoved inside my house to court my mother,   50
against her wishes. They should go and ask
Icarius her father to provide
a dowry, and choose who should be her husband.
They are too scared. Instead, they haunt our house
day after day, and kill our cows and pigs   55
and good fat goats. They feast and drink red wine,
not caring if they waste it all. There is
no man to save the house—no man like him,
Odysseus. I cannot fight against them;
I would be useless. I have had no training.   60
But if I had the power, I would do it!
It is unbearable, what they have done!
They ruined my whole house! It is not fair!
You suitors all should feel ashamed! Consider
what others in the neighborhood will think!   65
And also be afraid! The angry gods
will turn on you in rage; they will be shocked
at all this criminal behavior!
I beg you, by Olympian Zeus, and by
the goddess who presides in human meetings: 70
Justice! But never mind. Friends, leave me be,[1]
and let me cry and suffer by myself.
Or did Odysseus, my warlike father,
deliberately do harm to our own side?
Is that why you seem set on hurting me,   75
encouraging these suitors? Oh, if only
you Ithacans would eat my stock yourselves!
If you did that, I soon would get revenge;
I would come through the town and keep demanding,
until it all got given back. But now,   80
you make me so unhappy! This is pointless!"

---

1. Telemachus switches from addressing the suitors to addressing the general population of
Ithaca.

He stopped, frustrated, flung the scepter down,
and burst out crying. Everyone was seized
by pity. No one spoke; they hesitated
to answer him unkindly. Then at last   85
Antinous began.

      "Telemachus,
you stuck-up, wilful little boy! How dare you
try to embarrass us and put the blame
on us? We suitors have not done you wrong.
Go blame your precious mother! She is cunning.   90
It is the third year, soon it will be four,
that she has cheated us of what we want.
She offers hope to all, sends notes to each,
but all the while her mind moves somewhere else.
She came up with a special trick: she fixed   95
a mighty loom inside the palace hall.
Weaving her fine long cloth, she said to us,
'Young men, you are my suitors. Since my husband,
the brave Odysseus, is dead, I know
you want to marry me. You must be patient;   100
I have worked hard to weave this winding-sheet
to bury good Laertes when he dies.
He gained such wealth, the women would reproach me
if he were buried with no shroud. Please let me
finish it!' And her words made sense to us.   105
So every day she wove the mighty cloth,
and then at night by torchlight, she unwove it.
For three long years her trick beguiled the Greeks.
But when the fourth year's seasons rolled around,
a woman slave who knew the truth told us.   110
We caught her there, unraveling the cloth,
and made her finish it. This is our answer,
so you and all the Greeks may understand.
Dismiss your mother, let her father tell her
to marry anyone his heart desires.   115
Athena blessed her with intelligence,
great artistry and skill, a finer mind
than anyone has ever had before,
even the braided girls of ancient Greece,
Tyro, Alcmene, garlanded Mycene—   120
none of them had Penelope's understanding.
But if she wants to go on hurting us,
her plans are contrary to destiny.
We suitors will keep eating up your wealth,
and livelihood, as long as she pursues   125
this plan the gods have put inside her heart.
For her it may be glory, but for you,
pure loss. We will not go back to our farms
or anywhere, until she picks a husband."

Telemachus insisted, breathing hard,   130
"Antinous, I cannot force my mother
out of the house. She gave me birth and raised me.
My father is elsewhere—alive or dead.
If I insist my mother has to leave,
Icarius will make me pay the price,   135
and gods will send more trouble; if she goes,
Mother will rouse up Furies[2] full of hate
to take revenge, and everyone will curse me.
I will not. If you feel upset, you go!
Out of my house! Stop eating all my food!   140
Devour each other's property, not mine!
Or do you really think it right to waste
one person's means of life, and go scot-free?
Then try it! I will call the deathless gods!
May Zeus give recompense some day for this!   145
You will die here, and nobody will care!"

Then Zeus, whose voice resounds around the world,
sent down two eagles from the mountain peak.
At first they hovered on the breath of wind,
close by each other, balanced on their wings.   150
Reaching the noisy middle of the crowd,
they wheeled and whirred and flapped their mighty wings,
swooping at each man's head with eyes like death,
and with their talons ripped each face and neck.[3]
Then to the right they flew,[4] across the town.   155
Everyone was astonished at the sight;
they wondered in their hearts what this could mean.
Old Halitherses, son of Mastor, spoke.
More than the other elders, this old leader
excelled at prophecy and knew the birds.[5]   160
He gave them good advice.

                        "Now Ithacans,
listen! I speak especially for the suitors.
Disaster rolls their way! Odysseus
will not be absent from his friends for long;
already he is near and sows the seeds   165
of death for all of them, and more disaster
for many others in bright Ithaca.
We have to form a plan to make them stop.
That would be best for them as well by far.
I am experienced at prophecy;   170
my words came true for him, that mastermind,
Odysseus. I told him when he left

2. Spirits of vengeance.
3. The original may mean "at each other's faces and necks," or more likely, "ripping at their own faces and necks."
4. Signs on the right side were supposed to be lucky.
5. Prophets observed bird flight in order to predict the future or interpret the will of the gods.

for Troy with all the Argives, he would suffer
most terribly, and all his men would die,
but in the twentieth year he would come home,   175
unrecognized. Now it is coming true."

Eurymachus, the son of Polybus,
replied, "Old man, be off! Go home and spout
your portents to your children, or it will
be worse for them. But I can read these omens   180
better than you can. Many birds go flying
in sunlight, and not all are meaningful.
Odysseus is dead, away from home.
I wish that you had died with him, to stop
your forecasts! You are making this boy angry,   185
hoping that he will give your household gifts.
But let me tell you this, which will come true.
You may know many ancient forms of wisdom,
but if you tease this boy and make him angry,
he will be hurt, and never get to act   190
on any of these prophecies of yours.
And, old man, we will make you pay so much
your heart will break, your pain will cut so deep.
I will advise Telemachus myself,
in front of everyone, to send his mother   195
back to her father's family, to fix
her wedding, and the gifts a well-loved daughter
should have. Unless he does that, we will never
cease from this torturous courtship. We are not
afraid of anyone, much less this boy   200
with his long speeches, nor your pointless portents.
They will not come to pass and they will make you
hated. His house will be devoured, and payback
will never come, as long as she frustrates
our hopes of marriage. Meanwhile, we will wait   205
in daily hope, competing for the prize,
not seeking other women as our wives."

Telemachus, his mind made up, replied,
"All right, Eurymachus, and all of you.
I will not talk about this anymore.   210
The gods and all of you already know.
Just let me have a ship and twenty men
to make a journey with me, out and back,
to Sparta and to sandy Pylos, seeking
news about when my father may come home.   215
I may hear it from somebody, or from
a voice from Zeus—it often happens so.
If I find out my father is alive
and coming home, I will endure this pain
for one more year. But if I hear that he   220
is dead, I will come home to my own land,

and build a tomb and hold the funeral rites
as he deserves, and I will give my mother
to a new husband."

                    He sat down, and up
stood Mentor. When Odysseus sailed off,   225
this was the friend he asked to guard his house
and told the slaves to look to him as master.
Mentor addressed the crowd.

                    "Now Ithacans!
Listen! This changes everything! Now kings
should never try to judge with righteousness   230
or rule their people gently. Kings should always
be cruel, since the people whom he ruled
as kindly as a father, have forgotten
their King Odysseus. I do not blame
the suitors' overconfidence, rough ways   235
and violence, in eating up his household;
they risk their lives, supposing that the master
will never come back home. But I do blame
you others, sitting passive, never speaking
against them, though you far outnumber them."   240

Leocritus, Euenor's son, replied,
"Mentor, for shame! You must have lost your mind!
Fool, telling us to stop our banqueting!
You could not fight us; we outnumber you.
Even if Ithacan Odysseus   245
came back and found us feasting in his house,
and tried to drive us out, his wife would get
no joy of his return, no matter how
she misses him. If he tried fighting solo
against us, he would die a cruel death.   250
So what you said was nonsense. Anyway,
we must disperse, and everyone get busy.
Mentor and Halitherses, since you are
old comrades of his father, you can guide
Telemachus' journey. I suspect   255
he will not manage to go anywhere;
he will just wait in Ithaca for news."

The crowd broke up; the Ithacans went home;
the suitors, to Odysseus' house.

Telemachus slipped out and at the beach   260
he dipped his hands in salty gray seawater,
and asked Athena,

                    "Goddess, hear my prayer!
Just yesterday you came and ordered me

to sail the hazy sea and find out news
of my long-absent father's journey home.   265
The Greeks are wasting everything, especially
these bullying, mean suitors."

                              Then Athena
came near him with the voice and guise of Mentor,
and spoke to him with words that flew like birds.
"Telemachus, you will be brave and thoughtful,   270
if your own father's forcefulness runs through you.
How capable he was, in word and deed!
Your journey will succeed, if you are his.
If you are not his son, his true-born son,
I doubt you can achieve what you desire.   275
And it is rare for sons to be like fathers;
only a few are better, most are worse.
But you will be no coward and no fool.
You do possess your father's cunning mind,
so there is hope you will do all these things.   280
Forget about those foolish suitors' plans.
They have no brains and no morality.
They do not know black doom will kill them all,
and some day soon: their death is near at hand.
You will achieve the journey that you seek,   285
since I will go with you, just like a father.
I will equip a good swift ship for you.
Now go back home to where those suitors are,
and get provisions. Pack them in containers:
some wine in jars, and grain, the strength of men,   290
in sturdy skins. And I will go through town,
calling for volunteers to come with us.
There are a lot of ships in Ithaca,
both new and old. I will select the best one;
we will equip her quickly and sail fast,   295
far off across the sea."

                              So spoke the goddess,
daughter of Zeus. Telemachus obeyed.
His heart was troubled as he went back home.
He found the arrogant suitors in the hall,
skinning some goats and charring hogs for dinner.   300
Antinous began to laugh. He called him,
and seized his hand and spoke these words to him.

"Telemachus, you are being so pigheaded!
Why not put all your troubles from your heart?
Come eat and drink with me, just as before.   305
You know the Greeks will fix it all for you.
They will select a ship and crew, and soon
you will reach Pylos, where you hope to hear
word of your father."

But the boy was wary,
and said, "Antinous, I cannot eat;   310
I have no peace or joy when I am with
you selfish suitors. Is it not enough
that you destroyed my rich inheritance
when I was just a little boy? But now
I have grown bigger, and I got advice   315
from other people, and my heart wells up
with courage. I will try to bring down doom
on your heads here at home or when I go
to Pylos. Yes, I really will go there,
as passenger, although I do not own   320
a ship or have a crew—because of you!"[6]

He snatched his hand away. But as they feasted,
the suitors started mocking him and jeering.
With sneers they said,

                    "Oh no! Telemachus
is going to kill us! He will bring supporters   325
from Pylos or from Sparta—he is quite
determined! Or indeed he may be fetching
some lethal poisons from the fertile fields
of Ephyra, to mix up in our wine-bowl
and kill us all!"

                    Another proud young man   330
said, "Well, who knows, perhaps he will get lost
in that curved ship, and die, so far away
from all his family—just like his father.
And what a pity that would be for us!
Then we would have to share out all his wealth,   335
and give away the house itself to her—
his mother, and the man who marries her."

The boy went downstairs, to his father's storeroom,
wide and high-roofed, piled high with gold and bronze
and clothes in chests and fragrant olive oil.   340
Down there the jars of vintage wine were stored,
which held the sweet, unmixed and godlike drink,
lined in a row against the wall, in case
weary Odysseus came home at last.
The double doors were locked and closely fitted.   345
A woman checked the contents, night and day,
guarding it all with great intelligence,
and that was Eurycleia, child of Ops.
He called her to the chamber and addressed her.

6. Telemachus has seen through Antinous'
false promise that the Greeks will provide a
ship, and he is suggesting that, if he had not
been deprived of his inheritance by the suitors, he would already have the means for his
journey without having to rely on others.

"Nanny, please pour sweet wine in jugs for me,   350
the second best one, not the one you keep
for when the poor unlucky king escapes
from evil fate and death, and comes back home.
Fill up twelve jugs with wine for me, and pour me
some twenty pounds of fine-milled barley-groats,   355
all packed in sturdy leather bags. Load up
all these provisions secretly. At nightfall,
I will come here and get them, when my mother
has gone upstairs to go to sleep. I am
leaving for Sparta and for sandy Pylos,   360
to learn about my father's journey home."

At that his loving nurse began to wail,
and sobbed,

                  "Sweet child! What gave you this idea?
Why do you want to go so far? You are
an only child, and dearly loved! The king,   365
Odysseus, is gone, lost, far from home,
and they will plot against you when you leave,
scheming to murder you and share this wealth.
Stay with us, we who love you! Do not go
searching for danger out on restless seas!"   370

Telemachus decisively replied,
"Nanny, you need not worry. Gods have blessed
this plan. But promise me you will not tell
Mother, until she notices me gone.
Say nothing for twelve days, so she will not   375
start crying; it would spoil her pretty skin."

At that the old nurse swore a mighty oath
by all the gods that she would keep the secret,
and then she drew the wine for him in jars,
and poured the barley-groats in well-stitched bags.   380
Telemachus returned to see the suitors.

Meanwhile, bright-eyed Athena had a plan.
Resembling Telemachus, she went
all through the city, standing by each man,
and urged them to assemble by the ship   385
at night, and asked the son of Phronius,
Noëmon,[7] for his speedy ship; he promised
to give it gladly. Then the sun went down
and all the streets grew dark. The goddess dragged
the ship into the water, and she loaded   390
the necessary tackle for a journey.
Right at the beach's farthest end the goddess

---

7. Both names suggest wisdom or mindfulness.

stood and assembled good strong men as crew;
she coached each one. Then, eyes ablaze with plans,
she went back to Odysseus' house,   395
and poured sweet sleep upon the drunken suitors.
She struck them and their cups fell from their hands.
Disguised as Mentor both in looks and voice,
she called the boy out from the mighty hall,
and looked intently in his face, and said,   400

"Telemachus, your crew of armored men
is ready at the oar for your departure.
Come on! No time to waste! We must be gone!"

So speaking, Pallas quickly led the boy;
he followed in the footsteps of the goddess.   405
They went down to the seashore and the ship,
and found the long-haired sailors on the beach.
Inspired and confident, Telemachus
called out,

                "My friends! Come on, let us go fetch
the rations; they are ready in the hall.   410
But quietly—my mother does not know,
nor do the other women, except one."

And so he led them, and they followed him.
They loaded everything upon the decks;
Odysseus' son instructed them,   415
and then embarked—Athena led the way.
She sat down in the stern, and next to her
Telemachus was sitting. Then the crew
released the ropes and boarded, each at oar.
Athena called a favorable wind,   420
pure Zephyr whistling on wine-dark sea.
Telemachus commanded his companions
to seize the rigging; so they did, and raised
the pine-wood mast inside the rounded block,
and bound it down with forestays round about,   425
and raised the bright white sails with leather ropes.
Wind blew the middle sail; the purple wave
was splashing loudly round the moving keel.
The goddess rode the waves and smoothed the way.
The quick black ship held steady, so they fastened   430
the tackle down, and filled their cups with wine.
They poured libations to the deathless gods,
especially to the bright-eyed child of Zeus.
All through the night till dawn the ship sailed on.

BOOK 3

An Old King Remembers

Leaving the Ocean's streams,[1] the Sun leapt up
into the sky of bronze,[2] to shine his light
for gods and mortals on the fertile earth.
Telemachus arrived in Pylos, where
the Pylians were bringing to the beach   5
black bulls for blue Poseidon, Lord of Earthquakes.
There were nine pews, five hundred men on each,
and each group had nine bulls to sacrifice.
They burned the thigh-bones for the god, and ate
the innards. Then the Ithacans arrived,   10
took down their sails, dropped anchor and alighted.
The goddess with the flashing eyes, Athena,
first led Telemachus onshore, then spoke.

"Do not be shy, Telemachus. You sailed
over the sea to ask about your father,   15
where the earth hides him, what his fate might be.
So hurry now to Nestor, lord of horses.
Learn what advice he has in mind for you.
Supplicate him yourself, and he will tell you
the truth; he is not one to tell a lie."   20

Telemachus replied, "But Mentor, how
can I approach and talk to him? I am
quite inexperienced at making speeches,
and as a young man, I feel awkward talking
to elders."

      She looked straight into his eyes,   25
and answered, "You will work out what to do,
through your own wits and with divine assistance.
The gods have blessed you in your life so far."

So Pallas spoke and quickly led him on;
he followed in the footsteps of the goddess.   30

They reached the center of the town, where Nestor
was sitting with his sons and his companions,
putting the meat on spits and roasting it
for dinner. When they saw the strangers coming,
they all stood up with open arms to greet them,   35
inviting them to join them. Nestor's son
Pisistratus shook hands and sat them down,

---

1. The ocean was imagined as a vast river
running round the landmass of the world.
2. The word used in the original, *polychalkos*,
translates literally as "of much bronze," which

could mean that the gods in heaven are well-
supplied with bronze implements, or that the
sky is solid and firm, like bronze, or that it is
bright and shiny.

spreading soft fleeces on the sand beside
his father and his brother, Thrasymedes.
He served them giblets and he poured some wine   40
into a golden cup, and raised a toast
to Pallas, child of Zeus the Aegis-Lord.

"Now guest, give prayers of thanks to Lord Poseidon,
and pour libations for the god. This feast
is in his honor; pay him proper dues.   45
Then give the boy the cup of honeyed wine,
so he can offer to the deathless gods
libations. Everybody needs the gods.
I give the golden chalice to you first,
because the boy is younger, more my age."   50

He put the cup of sweet wine in her hand.
Athena was impressed with his good manners,
because he rightly gave it first to her.
At once she made a heartfelt prayer.

                                        "Poseidon!
O Shaker of the Earth, do not refuse   55
to grant our prayer; may all these things come true.
Bring fame to Nestor and his sons, and grant
gifts to the Pylians, as recompense
for this fine sacrifice.[3] And may the quest
for which we sailed here in our swift black ship   60
succeed, and may we come home safe again."

She made her prayer come true all by herself.
She gave Telemachus the splendid cup
with double handle, and his prayer matched hers.
And then they cooked the outer parts of meat,   65
and helped themselves to pieces, sharing round
the glorious feast, till they could eat no more.
Then first Gerenian Nestor,[4] horse-lord, spoke.

"Now that our guests are satisfied with food,
time now to talk to them and ask them questions.   70
Strangers, who are you? Where did you sail from?
Are you on business, or just scouting round
like pirates on the sea, who risk their lives
to ravage foreign homes?"

                            Telemachus
was thoughtful but not shy. Athena gave him   75
the confidence deep in his heart to ask

---

3. Athena literally says a "hecatomb," a sacrifice at which a hundred oxen were supposed to
be killed.

4. Gerenia is a town in Messenia where Nestor
took refuge when Heracles was attacking Pylos;
Nestor was the sole survivor of his generation.

about his absent father, and to gain
a noble reputation for himself.

"Great Nestor, son of Neleus," he said,
"You ask where I am from. I will be frank.   80
I come from Ithaca, beneath Mount Neion,
and I am here on private, family business.
I came to gather news about my father,
long-suffering Odysseus. They say
he fought with you to sack the town of Troy.   85
We know the place where all the other men
who battled with the Trojans lost their lives.
But Zeus still keeps Odysseus' fate
in darkness; no one knows where he was lost.
Maybe some hostile men killed him on land,   90
or he was drowned in Amphitrite's waves.[5]
I beg you, tell me, did you see him die
with your own eyes? Or have you any news
about where he may be? He must be lost.
His mother surely bore him for misfortune.   95
You need not sweeten what you say, in pity
or from embarrassment. Just tell me straight
what your eyes saw of him, my noble father.
If ever he made promises to you
and kept his word at Troy, in times of trouble,   100
remember those times now. Tell me the truth!"

Gerenian Nestor, horse-lord, answered him,
"Dear boy, you call to mind how much we suffered,
with strong, unyielding hearts, in distant lands
when we were sailing over misty seas,   105
led by Achilles on a hunt for spoils,
and when we fought around the mighty city
of Priam. Our best warriors were killed.
Ajax lies dead there, and there lies Achilles;
there lies his godlike friend and guide, Patroclus;   110
my own strong, matchless son lies dead there too,
Antilochus, who fought and ran so well.
More pain, more grief—our sufferings increased.
Who could recount so many, many losses?
If you stayed here five years and kept on asking   115
how many things the fighters suffered there,
you would get bored and go back home again
before the story ended. Nine long years
we schemed to bring them down, and finally
Zeus made our plots succeed. Odysseus,   120
your father, if you really are his son—
well, no one dared to try to equal him
in cleverness. That man was always best

5. Amphitrite is a sea goddess; the name is used here as metonymy for the sea itself.

at every kind of trick. And seeing you,
I am amazed at how you talk like him.   125
One would not think so young a man could do it.
Well, back in Troy, Odysseus and I
always agreed in councils, with one mind.
We gave the Argives all the best advice.
After we conquered Priam's lofty town,   130
a god dispersed the ships of the Achaeans.
Zeus planned a bitter journey home for us,
since some of us had neither sense nor morals.
Gray-eyed Athena, daughter of the Thunder,
became enraged and brought about disaster.[6]   135
She set the sons of Atreus to fight
each other. Hastily, they called the people
at sunset, not observing proper norms.[7]
The men arrived already drunk on wine;
the brothers told them why they called the meeting.   140
Then Menelaus said that it was time
to sail back home across the open sea.
But Agamemnon disagreed entirely.
He wanted them to stay and sacrifice[8]
to heal the sickness of Athena's wrath—   145
pointless! He did not know she would not yield.
The minds of the immortals rarely change.
So those two stood and argued angrily,
and with a dreadful clash of arms the Greeks
leapt up on two opposing sides. We slept   150
that eerie night with hearts intent on hatred
against each other—since Zeus meant us harm.
At dawn one group of us dragged down our ships
into the sea piled high with loot and women,
while half the army still remained there, stationed   155
with Agamemnon, shepherd of the people.
My friends and I set sail with all good speed—
a god had made the choppy sea lie calm.
We came to Tenedos and sacrificed,
praying to get back home—but Zeus refused;   160
the cruel god roused yet more strife among us.
Your father's plans were always flexible:
his men turned round their prows and sailed right back
to make their peace again with Agamemnon.
But I assembled all my fleet, and fled—   165
I understood some god must mean us harm.
Then Diomedes roused his men to come,
and ruddy Menelaus quickly sailed

6. Ajax raped the Trojan prophet Cassandra
(daughter of Priam) in a temple to Athena;
Nestor alludes to this violation but never spells it
out. The pollution of her temple is what caused
the unappeasable rage of Athena and Zeus.

7. The suggestion is that the Greeks will inevitably be tired and drunk if called to a meeting
at the wrong time, after dinner.
8. Literally, to perform a hecatomb—a sacrifice of multiple animals at once.

to meet with us on Lesbos, and we pondered
our long sea journey. Should we travel north, 170
go past the rocks of Chios to our left,
to Psyria, or under Chios, passing
blustery Mimas?[9] So we prayed for signs.
The god told us to cross the open sea
towards Euboea, to escape disaster. 175
A fair wind whistled and our ships sped on
across the journey-ways of fish, and landed
at nightfall in Geraestus.[1] To Poseidon
we offered many bulls, since we had crossed
safely across wide waters. The fourth day 180
the men of Diomedes moored their ships
at Argos; I kept going on, to Pylos.
The wind the god had sent kept holding strong
the whole way home. So, my dear boy, I have
no news about what happened next. I do not 185
know which of them has died and who is safe.
But I can tell you what I heard while sitting
here in my halls. You ought to know. They say
Achilles' son led home the Myrmidons,[2]
and Philoctetes[3] came back home with glory. 190
And Idomeneus[4] led back his crew
to Crete; no man of his who had survived
the war was lost at sea. And Agamemnon?
You must have heard, though you live far away.
Aegisthus murdered him! But he has paid 195
a bitter price. How fortunate the dead man
had left a son to take revenge upon
the wicked, scheming killer, that Aegisthus,
who killed Orestes' father. My dear boy,
I see that you are tall and strong. Be brave, 200
so you will be remembered."

             Thoughtfully
Telemachus replied, "Your Majesty,
King Nestor, yes. Orestes took revenge.
The Greeks will make him famous through the world
and into future times. I wish the gods 205
would grant me that much power against those men
who threaten and insult me—those cruel suitors!
The gods have not yet granted us this blessing,
my father and myself. We must endure."

---

9. The latter is the longer but safer route, with less open sea.

1. Geraestus was the most southern part of Euboea.

2. The Myrmidons are a Thessalian tribe and Achilles' men in the *Iliad*. Neoptolemus (also known as Pyrrhus) was Achilles' son; he led the tribe after his father's death.

3. Philoctetes was a hero with a wounded foot that never healed; his bow was essential in the final destruction of Troy.

4. Idomeneus is a Cretan king; he will appear later, in Odysseus' false tales of traveling in Crete.

Gerenian Nestor, lord of horses, answered,   210
"Dear boy, since you have brought the subject up,
I have been told about your mother's suitors,
how badly they are treating you at home.
But do you willingly submit to it?
Or has a god's voice led the townspeople   215
to hate you? Well, who knows, perhaps one day
he[5] will come home and take revenge, alone,
or with an army of the Greeks. If only
Athena loved you, as she used to care
for glorious Odysseus at Troy   220
when we were doing badly. I have never
seen gods display such favor as she gave
when she stood by your father. If she helped you
with that much love, the suitors would forget
their hopes for marriage."

            Then Telemachus   225
replied, "My lord, I doubt that this will happen.
I am surprised you have such confidence.
I would not be so hopeful, even if
the gods were willing."

            Then the goddess spoke.
"Telemachus, what do you mean? A god   230
can easily save anyone, at will,
no matter what the distance. I would rather
suffer immensely, but then get home safe,
than die on my return like Agamemnon,
murdered by his own wife, and by Aegisthus.   235
But death is universal. Even gods
cannot protect the people that they love,
when fate and cruel death catch up with them."

Telemachus said apprehensively,
"Mentor, this is upsetting. Change the subject.   240
He has no real chance now of getting home.
The gods have fenced him round with death and darkness.
Let me ask Nestor something else—he is
wiser and more informed than anyone.
They say he ruled for three whole generations.   245
He looks to me like some immortal god.
So Nestor, son of Neleus, tell me truly,
how did the great King Agamemnon die?
And where was Menelaus? Was he lost,
away from Greece, when that Aegisthus dared   250
to kill a king, a better man than him?
How did that wicked trickster's plot succeed?"

---

5. "He" must be Odysseus.

Gerenian Nestor, lord of horses, answered,
"I will tell everything—though you can guess
what would have happened if fair Menelaus   255
had found Aegisthus living in his halls
on his return. And even when he died,
no one would bury him; he lay upon
the open plain without a tomb and far
from town for birds and dogs to eat. No Greek   260
would mourn that monster. While we fought and labored
at Troy, this layabout sat safe in Argos,
seducing Clytemnestra, noble wife
of Agamemnon. For a while, she scorned
his foul suggestions, since her heart was good.   265
Moreover, when her husband went to Troy,
he left a poet, ordered to protect her.
But finally Fate forced the queen to yield.
Aegisthus left the poet to be eaten
by birds, abandoned on a desert island.   270
He led the woman back to his own house
by mutual desire, and then he made
numerous offerings on holy altars
of animals and lovely gold and cloth:
he had succeeded far beyond his hopes.   275

And meanwhile, I left Troy with Menelaus;
we sailed together, best of friends. We reached
the holy cape of Athens, Sounion.
There Phoebus with his gentle arrows shot
and killed the pilot, Phrontis, as he held   280
the ship's helm as she sped along. No man
knew better how to steer through any storm,
so Menelaus stopped to bury him
with proper rites. At last he sailed again
across the wine-dark sea; but as his ships   285
rushed round the craggy heights of Malea,
far-seeing Zeus sent curses on his journey,
pouring out screaming winds and giant waves
the size of mountains—splitting up the fleet.
Some ships were hurled to Crete, to River Jardan,   290
where the Cydonian people have their homes.
There steep rock rises sheer above the sea
near Gortyn in the misty deep; south winds
drive mighty waves towards the left-hand crag,
and push them west to Phaestus;[6] one small rock   295
restrains the massive currents. All the ships
were smashed by waves against those rocks. The men
were almost drowned. Five other dark-prowed ships
were blown by wind and sea away to Egypt.
There Menelaus gathered wealth and gold   300

6. Phaestus and Gortyn were cities in Crete.

and drifted with his ships through foreign lands.
Meanwhile at home, Aegisthus had been plotting.
He killed the son of Atreus and seized
control of rich Mycenae, where he reigned
for seven years. But in the eighth, Orestes   305
came to destroy him. He returned from Athens,
and killed his father's murderer, then called
the Argives to a funeral, a feast
for clever, scheming, cowardly Aegisthus
whom he had killed, and his own hated mother.   310
That very day, rambunctious Menelaus
arrived with all his ships crammed full of treasure.
The moral is, you must not stay away
too long, dear boy, when those proud suitors lurk
inside your house. They may divide your wealth   315
among themselves and make your journey useless.
But I suggest you go to Menelaus.
He recently returned from lands so distant
no one would even hope to get home safe
once driven by the winds so far off course,   320
over such dangerous, enormous seas.
Birds migrate there and take a year or more
to travel back. Go visit him by ship
with your own crew. Or if you would prefer,
you can go there by land—here is a carriage.   325
My sons can guide you all the way to Sparta,[7]
to Menelaus. Ask him for the truth.
He will not lie; he is an honest man."

The sun went down and darkness fell. The goddess,
bright-eyed Athena, spoke to them.

                                        "King Nestor,   330
your speech was good and your advice was sound.
But now slice up the tongues and pour the wine
for Lord Poseidon and the other gods
before we rest—time now to go to bed.
The light is fading and it is not right   335
to linger at a banquet in the dark."

The people listened to Athena's words.
The house slaves poured fresh water on their hands,
and boys filled up the mixing bowls with wine,
and poured it into cups, and first prepared   340
the sacrifice. They threw tongues on the fire,
then sprinkled wine, then each man drank his fill.
Then Zeus' daughter and the godlike boy

---

7. Nestor lavishly suggests that multiple sons will accompany Telemachus; however, as it turns out, only one of Nestor's sons, Pisistratus, goes with the Ithacan.

both rose to go together to their ship.
But Nestor called to stop them.

              "Zeus forbids it!   345
And all the other gods who live forever!
You cannot leave my house for your swift ship
as if I were a poor and ragged man
with so few beds and blankets in his home
that neither he nor guests can sleep in comfort.   350
I have soft quilts and blankets in abundance.
The darling son of great Odysseus
must not sleep on the ship's deck, while I live!
Not while my sons remain here in my house,
ready to welcome anyone who visits."   355

The bright-eyed goddess answered him, "Old friend,
you are quite right. Telemachus should do
just as you say. That is a better plan.
He will stay here tonight and go to sleep
in your fine palace. But I must go back   360
to tell the crew the news and keep them strong.
You see, I am the oldest in our party.
The rest are younger men, close friends together,
the same age as our brave Telemachus.
I will sleep there beside the hollow ship.   365
At dawn I have important obligations:
to visit with the great Cauconians.
The boy can be your guest. Then send him off
escorted by your son. Give him a carriage,
drawn by your strongest and most nimble horses." 370

Bright-eyed Athena flew away, transformed
into an ossifrage.[8] Astonishment
seized all the people watching, even Nestor.
He seized Telemachus' hand and said,

"Dear boy, I am now sure that you will be   375
a hero, since the gods are on your side
at your young age. This was a god, none other
than great Athena, true-born child of Zeus,
who also glorified your noble father.
Goddess, be kind to us as well, and grant   380
honor to me, my good wife, and our sons.
Now I will sacrifice a yearling heifer,
broad-browed and still unyoked, and gild her horns
with gold to bless your journey."

              So he spoke,
and Pallas heard his prayer. Gerenian Nestor   385

---

8. A type of vulture, also known as a lammergeier.

led them and led his sons and sons-in-law
inside his own magnificent great hall.
When they were all inside, he seated them
on benches and on chairs arranged in order,
and he himself mixed up the bowl for them   390
of sweet delicious wine. He had preserved it
eleven years. The slave girl opened it,
pulling the lid off. As the old man mixed,
he prayed and poured libations for Athena.

They all poured also, then they drank their fill,   395
then each went home to sleep in his own chamber.
Nestor the horseman made a special bed
right there for his dear friend, the warrior's son:
a camp bed on the echoing portico,
beside Pisistratus, the only son   400
not living with a wife but still at home.
Nestor himself slept by his wife, the queen,
in a secluded corner of the palace.

When newborn Dawn appeared with rosy fingers,
the horse-lord Nestor jumped up out of bed,   405
and hurried down towards the polished stones
that stood outside his palace,[9] bright with oil.
There Neleus used to give godlike advice,
until Fate took him and he went to Hades,
and Nestor, guardian of the Greeks, took over   410
the scepter. From their rooms his sons arrived
to throng around him: Echephron and Stratius,
Aretus, Perseus, great Thrasymedes,
and strong Pisistratus the sixth. They brought
godlike Telemachus to sit with them.   415
Nestor spoke first.

        "Dear sons, now hurry up,
fulfil my wishes. First we must appease
Athena, who revealed herself to me
during the holy feast. Now one of you
must run down to the fields to choose a cow;   420
let herdsmen drive her back here. And another,
go to Telemachus' ship and bring
the men—leave only two behind. Another
must bring Laerces here, who pours the gold,
so he can gild the heifer's horns. You others,   425
stay here together. Tell the girls inside
to cook a royal feast, and set out seats,
put wood around the altar, and clear water."

9. The stones that mark Nestor's judgment seat have been anointed with oil, a mark of their
sanctity.

At that, the sons all got to work. The cow
was brought up from the field. The crew arrived   430
from the swift, solid ship. The goldsmith came
with all the bronze tools useful for his trade—
hammer and anvil and well-crafted tongs—
and worked the gold. Athena came to take
the sacrifice. King Nestor gave the gold;   435
the craftsman poured it on the horns, to make
a lovely offering to please the goddess.
Stratius and Echephron together led
the heifer by the horns. Aretes came
and brought a water bowl adorned with flowers,   440
and in his other hand, a box of grain.
Strong Thrasymedes stood nearby and held
a sharpened axe, prepared to strike the cow.
Perseus held the blood-bowl. Nestor started
to sprinkle barley-groats and ritual water,   445
and as he threw the hairs into the fire
he said prayers to Athena.[1] When the rites
were finished, mighty Thrasymedes struck.
The axe sliced through the sinews of the neck.
The cow was paralyzed. Then Nestor's daughters   450
and his sons' wives, and his own loyal queen,
Eurydice, began to chant. The men
hoisted the body, and Pisistratus
sliced through her throat.[2] Black blood poured out. The life
was gone. They butchered her, cut out the thighs,   455
all in the proper place, and covered them
with double fat and placed raw flesh upon them.[3]
The old king burned the pieces on the logs,
and poured the bright red wine. The young men came
to stand beside him holding five-pronged forks.   460
They burned the thigh-bones thoroughly and tasted
the entrails, then carved up the rest and skewered
the meat on pointed spits, and roasted it.

Meanwhile, Telemachus was being washed
by Nestor's eldest daughter, Polycaste.   465
When she had washed and rubbed his skin with oil
she dressed him in a tunic and fine cloak
and he emerged; his looks were like a god's.
He sat by Nestor, shepherd of the people.

1. Before sacrifice, one washed one's hands and sprinkled barley grains on the victim and the altar to ensure that the sacrifice was legitimate. It was then traditional to cut a few hairs from the victim's head, as Nestor does, to make the animal no longer inviolate before it dies.

2. The animal had to be held up, facing the gods, while its neck was slit; the blood would then be collected in the designated bowl.

3. The thigh bones were presented to the god, covered with a double layer of fat and then with little pieces of the rest of the raw carcass on top.

The meat was roasted and drawn off the spits. 470
They sat to eat, while trained slaves served the food,
pouring the wine for them in golden cups.
After their hunger and their thirst were gone,
Gerenian Nestor, horse-lord, started talking.

"My sons, now bring two horses with fine manes 475
and yoke them to the carriage, so our guest
can start his journey."

               They obeyed at once,
and quickly latched swift horses to the carriage.
One of the house girls brought out food and wine
and delicacies fit to feed a king. 480
Telemachus got in the lovely carriage;
Pisistratus, the son of Nestor, followed,
and sat beside him, taking up the reins,
and whipped the horses. Eagerly they flew
off for the open plain, and left the town. 485
All day they ran and made the harness rattle.
At sunset when the streets grew dark, they came
to Pherae, to the home of Diocles,
son of Ortilochus; Alpheus was
his grandfather. They spent the night as guests. 490
When rosy-fingered Dawn came bright and early,
they yoked the horses to the painted carriage,
and drove out from the gate and echoing porch.
At a light touch of whip, the horses flew.
Swiftly they drew towards their journey's end, 495
on through the fields of wheat, until the sun
began to set and shadows filled the streets.

BOOK 4

What the Sea God Said

They came to Sparta, land of caves and valleys,
and drove to Menelaus' house. They found him
hosting a wedding feast for many guests
to celebrate his children's marriages.
In Troy he had declared that he would give 5
his daughter to Achilles' son,[1] who ruled
the Myrmidons. Now he was sending her,
with dowry gifts of horse-drawn chariots;
the gods had made the marriage come to pass.
And he was welcoming a Spartan bride, 10
Alector's daughter, for his well-loved son,
strong Megapenthes, mothered by a slave.
The gods had given Helen no more children
after the beautiful Hermione,

---

1. I.e., Neoptolemus, son of Achilles and the princess Deidamia.

image of Aphrodite all in gold. 15
Neighbors and family were feasting gladly
under the king's high roof. The bard was singing
and strumming, and two acrobats were spinning
and leading them in dance. Telemachus
and Nestor's son stopped by the palace doors 20
and held their horses. Menelaus' guard,
Eteoneus, ran out and saw them there,
and then hurried back inside to tell his master.

"Your Majesty, there are two men outside,
strangers who seem like sons of Zeus. Please tell me, 25
should we take off the harness from their horses?
Or send them off to find another host?"

Flushed Menelaus shouted angrily,
"You used to have some brains!
Now you are talking like a silly child. 30
We two were fed by many different hosts
before returning home. As we may hope
for Zeus to keep us safe in future times,
untack their horses! Lead them in to dine!"

So Eteoneus rushed out from the palace, 35
and ordered other slaves to follow him.
They freed the sweating horses from their yoke
and tied them by the manger, which they filled
with emmer that they mixed with bright white barley.
They leaned the carriage up against the wall 40
and led their guests inside the godlike house.
The boys looked round the palace in amazement:
the lofty halls of famous Menelaus
shone like the dazzling light of sun or moon.
When they had satisfied their eyes with staring, 45
they went to take a bath in polished tubs.
The slave girls helped them wash and rubbed them down
in olive oil, then dressed them in wool cloaks
and tunics, and then seated them beside
the son of Atreus, King Menelaus. 50
A house girl brought a basin made of silver,
and water in a golden jug. She poured it
over their hands to wash, then set a table
of polished wood beside them, and a humble
slave girl brought bread and many canapés, 55
a lavish spread. The carver carried platters
with every kind of meat, and set before them
cups made of gold. Then ruddy Menelaus
welcomed them both and told them,

                                    "Help yourselves!
Enjoy the food! When you have shared our meal, 60

we will begin to ask you who you are.
Your fathers must be scepter-bearing kings;
the sons of peasants do not look like you."

With that, he took the dish of rich roast meat,
cut from the back, which was his special meal,   65
and offered it to them. They reached their hands
to take the food set out in front of them.
After their thirst and hunger had been sated,
Telemachus turned round to Nestor's son,
ducking his head so no one else could hear.   70

"Pisistratus! Dear friend, do you see how
these echoing halls are shining bright with bronze,
and silver, gold and ivory and amber?
It is as full of riches as the palace
of Zeus on Mount Olympus! I am struck   75
with awe." When Menelaus heard his words,
he spoke to them in turn—his words flew out.

"No mortal, my dear boys, can rival Zeus.
His halls and home and property are deathless.
Some man may match my wealth; or maybe not.   80
I suffered for it. I was lost, adrift
at sea for eight long years. I traipsed through Cyprus,
Phoenicia, Egypt, Ethiopia,
Sidon and Araby, and Libya,
where lambs are born with horns—their ewes give birth   85
three times a year. The master and his slave
have milk and cheese and meat; the flock provides
sweet milk year round. But while I wandered there
accumulating wealth, someone crept in
and killed my brother; his own scheming wife   90
betrayed him. I can take no joy in all
my wealth. Whoever they may be, your fathers
have surely told you how much I have suffered!
I lost my lovely home, and I was parted
for many years from all my splendid riches.   95
I wish I had stayed here, with just a third
of all the treasure I have now acquired,
if those who died at Troy, so far away
from Argive pastures, were alive and well.
I sit here in my palace, mourning all   100
who died, and often weeping. Sometimes tears
bring comfort to my heart, but not for long;
cold grief grows sickening. I miss them all,
but one man most. When I remember him,
I cannot eat or sleep, since no one labored   105
like him—Odysseus. His destiny
was suffering, and mine the endless pain
of missing him. We do not even know

if he is still alive—he has been gone
so long. His faithful wife and old Laertes   110
must grieve for him, and young Telemachus,
who was a newborn when he went away."

These words roused in the boy a desperate need
to mourn his father. Tears rolled down his face
and splashed down on the ground. He lifted up   115
his cloak to hide his eyes. But Menelaus
noticed and wondered whether he should wait
until the boy first spoke about his father,
or ask. As he was hesitating, Helen
emerged from her high-ceilinged, fragrant bedroom,   120
like Artemis, who carries golden arrows.
Adraste set a special chair for her,
Alcippe spread upon it soft wool blankets,
and Phylo brought a silver sewing basket,
given to her by Alcandre, the wife   125
of Polybus, who lived in Thebes, in Egypt,
where people have extraordinary wealth.
He gave two silver tubs to Menelaus,
a pair of tripods and ten pounds of gold.
His wife gave other lovely gifts for Helen: 130
a golden spindle and this silver basket
on wheels; the rims were finished off with gold.
Phylo, her girl, brought out that basket now,
packed full of yarn she had already spun.
A spindle wound around with purple wool   135
was laid across it. She sat down and put
her feet upon a stool, and asked her husband,

"Do we know who these men are, Menelaus,
who have arrived here in our house? Shall I
conceal my thoughts or speak? I feel compelled   140
to say, the sight of them amazes me.
I never saw two people so alike
as this boy and Telemachus, the son
of spirited Odysseus, the child
he left behind, a little newborn baby,   145
the day the Greeks marched off to Troy, their minds
fixated on the war and violence.
They made my face the cause that hounded them."

High-colored Menelaus answered, "Wife,
I saw the likeness too. Odysseus   150
had hands like those, those legs, that hair, that head,
that glancing gaze. And when I spoke just now
about Odysseus and all the things
he suffered for my sake, the boy grimaced,
and floods of tears were rolling down his cheeks;   155
he raised his purple cloak to hide his eyes."

Pisistratus, the son of Nestor, spoke.
"King Menelaus, you are right. This is
that warrior's true-born son, just as you said.
But he is shy and feels he should not speak   160
too boldly in your presence right away.
Your voice is like a god's to us. Lord Nestor
sent me to guide him here. He longed to see you
to get some news from you or some advice.
A son whose father is away will suffer   165
intensely, if he has no man at home
to help him. In the absence of his father,
Telemachus has no one to protect him."

Then Menelaus answered, "So the son
of my dear friend, who worked so hard for me,   170
has come here to my house! I always thought
that I would greet that friend with warmth beyond
all other Argives, if Zeus let us sail
home with all speed across the sea. I would have
brought him from Ithaca, with all his wealth,   175
his son and people, and bestowed on him
a town in Argos, driving out the natives
from somewhere hereabouts under my rule.
We would have constantly spent time together.
Nothing would have divided us in love   180
and joy, till death's dark cloud surrounded us.
But I suppose the god begrudged our friendship,
and kept that poor, unlucky man from home."

His words made everybody want to cry.
Helen was weeping, as was Menelaus.   185
Pisistratus' eyes were full of tears
for irreplaceable Antilochus,[2]
killed by the noble son of shining Dawn.
Mindful of him, he spoke with words like wings.

"King Menelaus, when we spoke of you   190
back home in our own halls, my father Nestor
always declared you are exceptional
for common sense. So listen now to me.
I disapprove of crying during dinner.
Dawn will soon come; weep then. There is no harm   195
in mourning when a person dies; it is
the only honor we can pay the dead—
to cut our hair and drench our cheeks with tears.
I had a brother named Antilochus,
one of the bravest fighters in the army,   200
a sprinter and a warrior. He died.

2. Antilochus was a son of Nestor (so brother to Pisistratus), killed at Troy by Memnon, son of
the goddess Dawn.

I never got to meet him or to see him.
Perhaps you did?"

King Menelaus answered,
"My friend, you speak just as a wise man should,
like somebody much older than yourself.   205
You show your father's wisdom in your speech.
A lineage is easy to discern
when Zeus spins out a life of happiness,
in marriage and in offspring. So he gave
good luck to Nestor all his life; he aged   210
at home in comfort, and his sons are wise
and skillful spear-men. Yes, we will stop crying
and turn our minds to dinner once again.
Let them pour water on our hands. At dawn,
Telemachus and I can talk at length."   215

At that Asphalion, the nimble house slave
of mighty Menelaus, poured the water
over their hands. They helped themselves to food
from laden tables. Then the child of Zeus,
Helen, decided she would mix the wine   220
with drugs to take all pain and rage away,
to bring forgetfulness of every evil.
Whoever drinks this mixture from the bowl
will shed no tears that day, not even if
her mother or her father die, nor even   225
if soldiers kill her brother or her darling
son with bronze spears before her very eyes.
Helen had these powerful magic drugs
from Polydamna, wife of Thon, from Egypt,
where fertile fields produce the most narcotics: 230
some good, some dangerous. The people there
are skillful doctors. They are the Healer's people.[3]
She mixed the wine and told the slave to pour it,
and then she spoke again.

                              "Now Menelaus,
and you two noble sons of noble men,   235
Zeus gives us good and bad at different times;
he has the power. Sit here then and eat,
and I will entertain you with a story.
Enjoy it; it is fitting to the times.
I cannot tell of all the challenges   240
steadfast Odysseus has undergone.
But I will tell you what that brave man did
at Troy, when the Achaeans were in trouble.
He beat himself and bruised his body badly
and put a ragged cloak on, like a slave,   245

---

3. The Healer, Paieon, is the doctor to the gods. He was later identified with Apollo.

then shuffled through the enemy city streets.
In his disguise he seemed a poor old beggar,
hardly a man to sail with the Achaeans.
He crept through Troy like that, and no one knew him
except for me. I saw through his disguise   250
and questioned him. He was too smart to talk,
acting evasive. But I washed and scrubbed him
with oil and dressed him, and I swore an oath
that I would not reveal him to the Trojans
before he had got back to his own camp.   255
He told me all the things the Greeks were planning.
On his way back, he used his long bronze sword
to slaughter many Trojans, and he brought
useful intelligence to tell the Greeks.
The Trojan women keened in grief, but I   260
was glad—by then I wanted to go home.
I wished that Aphrodite had not made me
go crazy when she took me from my country,
and made me leave my daughter and the bed
I shared with my fine, handsome, clever husband."   265

And Menelaus said,

            "Yes, wife, quite right.
I have been round the world, and I have met
many heroic men and known their minds.
I never saw a man so resolute
as that Odysseus. How tough he was!   270
And what impressive fortitude he showed
inside the Wooden Horse! We fighters lurked
inside, to bring destruction to the Trojans.
You came there too. Some spirit who desired
to glorify the Trojans urged you on.   275
Godlike Deiphobus was following you.[4]
Three times you went around the hollow belly,
touching the hiding place, and calling on
us Greeks by name; you put on different voices
for each man's wife. Then I and Diomedes   280
and good Odysseus, inside the horse,
heard you call out to us, and we two wanted
to go out, or to answer from in there.
Odysseus prevented us from going.
Then all the other sons of the Achaeans   285
were quiet; Anticlus still wished to answer.
Odysseus' hands clamped shut his mouth
and saved us all. He held him there like that,
until Athena led you far away."

---

4. There was a legend that Helen married Deiphobus, another son of Priam, after the death of Paris.

Weighing these words, Telemachus replied,   290
"But Menelaus, all this makes it worse!
My father's courage could not save his life,
even if he had had a heart of iron.
So now, show us to bed. We need the comfort
of being lulled into a sweet deep sleep."   295

Then Argive Helen told her girls to spread
beds on the porch and pile on them fine rugs
of purple, and lay blankets over them,
with woolly covers on the very top.
The girls went out with torches in their hands   300
and made the beds. A slave led out the guests.
Telemachus and Nestor's handsome son
slept in the front room; Menelaus slept
far back inside the lofty house. Beside him
lay marvelous Helen, in her flowing gown.   305

Soon Dawn was born, her fingers bright with roses.
Gruff Menelaus jumped up out of bed,
got dressed and strapped his sharp sword to his shoulder,
then tied his sandals on his well-oiled feet.
He went out of his bedroom like a god,   310
approached Telemachus, and spoke to him.

"What need has brought you here, Telemachus,
to Sparta, over such expanse of sea?
Private or public business? Tell me truly!"

Telemachus inhaled and then replied,   315
"King Menelaus, son of Atreus,
I came in search of news about my father.
My house is being eaten up; our wealth
is ruined. My whole home is full of men
who mean me harm—my mother's loutish suitors.   320
Each day they kill more sheep, more longhorn cattle.
So I am begging you, here on my knees,
tell me the dreadful news, if he is dead!
Perhaps you saw it with your eyes, or heard
tales of his travels. He was surely born   325
to suffer in extraordinary ways.
Please do not try to sweeten bitter news
from pity; tell me truly if you saw him,
and how he was. If my heroic father
ever helped you at Troy when things were bad,   330
keep that in mind right now, and tell the truth."

Flushed, Menelaus shouted out in anger,
"Damn them! Those cowards want to steal the bed
of one whose heart is braver than their own.
As when a deer lays down two newborn fawns,   335

still sucklings, in the lair of some strong lion,
and goes to look for pasture, over slopes
and grassy valleys; when the lion comes back
to his own bed, he brings down doom on them—
so will Odysseus upon those men.   340
O Father Zeus, Athena, and Apollo,
I pray he is as strong as when he stood
to wrestle Philomeleides, on Lesbos,
and hurled him to the ground, and we all cheered.
So may Odysseus attack the suitors.   345
May all their lives be brief, their weddings cursed!
As for your questions, I will not deceive you.
I will not hide a single word I heard
from that old sea god Proteus. Although
I longed to come back home, away from Egypt,   350
the gods prevented me, since I had failed
to offer perfect hecatombs. They always
desire obedience. There is an island
out in the sea beside the coast of Egypt,
named Pharos. If a clear wind blows your ship,   355
it takes all day to travel to that island.
Its harbor has good anchorage, and there
men draw dark water up, and then launch off
to sea. But I was held for twenty days
by gods. No winds appeared to guide my ships   360
across the water's back. All our supplies
would have been gone, and all our hope; but then
a goddess, Eidothea, pitied me—
the child of Proteus, the old sea god.
She met me pacing sadly all alone.   365
My men were off around the island, fishing
with hooks, as usual—hunger pinched their bellies.
She stood beside me and she spoke to me.
'Stranger, are you so foolish that you choose
to give up, and take pleasure in your pain?   370
There is no end in sight; you have been stuck
here on this island for so long. Your men
grow weak at heart.' I answered her and said,
'Whoever you may be—for sure a goddess—
I tell you I am trapped against my will.   375
I must have sinned against the deathless gods
who live in heaven. Please explain which spirit
is blocking me from going home across
the teeming sea. Gods must know everything.'
That shining goddess answered me at once,   380
'Stranger, I will be frank with you. A deathless
old sea god haunts this place, named Proteus
of Egypt, who can speak infallibly,
who knows the depths of seas, and serves Poseidon.
They say he is the one who fathered me.   385
If you can somehow lie in wait and catch him,

he will explain how you can get back home,
plotting your path where fish leap through the waters.
And if you wish it, prince, he will explain
what happened in your home, both good and bad, 390
while you were gone on this long, painful journey.'
Those were her words. I answered, 'Tell me, please,
how I can trap this ancient god, so he
will not see me too soon, and get away.
It is not easy for a man to catch 395
a god.' The goddess answered me at once,
'Stranger, I will instruct you thoroughly.
When the sun hits the midpoint of the sky,
the old god bobs above the salty water;
the breath of Zephyr hides him in dark shade. 400
He goes to take his nap inside the caves.
Around him sleep the clustering seals, the daughters
of lovely Lady Brine.[5] Their breath smells sour
from gray seawater, pungent salty depths.
Select the three best men you have on board, 405
and when dawn breaks, I will take all of you
down to the shore, and set you in a line.
Let me explain the old god's tricks. He will
first count the seals and walk around among them.
When he has counted them and checked them all, 410
he lies down in the middle, like a shepherd
among his flock of sheep. When you observe
him sleeping, gather all your force and strength,
and hold him there, despite his desperate struggles.
In trying to escape, he will change shape 415
to every animal on earth, and then
water and holy fire. You must hold fast
unshaken, and press harder; keep him down.
At last he will assume again the form
in which he went to sleep, and he will speak 420
and question you. Then, warrior, release
your forceful hold on that old god, and ask him
which god is angry with you, and the way
to cross the fish-filled waters and go home.'
With that she sank beneath the deep sea waves. 425
I went down to the ships upon the sand.
My heart was surging in me as I walked.
Arriving at the ships and at the shore,
we made our meal. Then came immortal night;
we went to sleep beside the water's edge. 430
When Dawn appeared, her fingers bright with flowers,
I walked beside the spreading sea, along
the dunes, and prayed intensely to the gods.

5. The obscure word translated here suggests
something like "daughter of the salty sea"; it
is elsewhere an epithet of Thetis, mother of
Achilles, but here seems to imply a different sea
goddess.

Then I chose out my three most trusted men.
The goddess dove down deep inside the sea   435
and brought four sealskins up from underwater,
new-flayed—to help her plot against her father.
She scooped out hiding places in the sand,
and sat to wait. We came right up to her.
She laid us in a row, and put a skin   440
on each. It would have been a dismal hideout,
stinking of salt-bred seals. Who would lie down
to rest beside a creature from the sea?
But she brought sweet ambrosia to save us.
She very kindly put it in our nostrils,   445
to take away the stench of seal. We waited
all morning, apprehensively. And then
out of the sea there rose a pod of seals;
they lay along the shore. At noon the god
emerged above the waves. He went among   450
his fatted seals and counted out their number.
He counted us among the first of them,
suspecting nothing. Then he lay down too.
With a great shout we pounced on him and grabbed him.
The old god still remembered all his tricks,   455
and first became a lion with a mane,
then snake, then leopard, then a mighty boar,
then flowing water, then a leafy tree.
But we kept holding on: our hearts stood firm.
At last that ancient sorcerer grew tired,   460
and then he asked me, 'Son of Atreus!
What god devised this plan with you and taught you
to lurk and capture me against my will?
What do you want from me?' And I replied,
'Old god, why do you want to throw me off?   465
You know I have been trapped here on this island
for far too long, with no way out; my heart
grows faint. So tell me—gods know everything—
what spirit stops my journey? And how can I
get home across the watery shoals of fish?'   470
At once he answered me and told me this:
'You should have given Zeus and other gods
fine offerings, to speed your journey home
across the wine-dark sea. It is your fate
not to go home or see the ones you love   475
until you go again to Egypt's river,
watered by Zeus, and kill a hundred cows,
to please the deathless gods who live in heaven.
Then they will let you travel where you wish.'
I felt heartbroken that I had to cross   480
the misty sea and go again to Egypt:
a long and bitter journey! But I answered,
'Sir, I will do exactly as you say.
But come now, tell me this, and tell me truly,

did all the Greeks sail safely home by ship,   485
whom Nestor and myself left there in Troy?
Did any meet a dreadful death at sea,
on his own ship, or in familiar arms,
after the war wound up?' When I said this,
at once he answered me and said these words.   490
'O son of Atreus! Why ask me this?
You have no need to know or learn my mind.
When I have told you, you will not be long
able to hold back tears. So many men
were killed, and many left behind at Troy.   495
Just two of all the bronze-clad captains died
while traveling back home; one more perhaps
may be alive, trapped somewhere out at sea.
Ajax was drowned;[6] his ships were sunk. Poseidon
first drove him to the rocks of Gyrae, then   500
rescued him from the sea; he would have lived,
despite Athena's hatred, but he made
a crazy boast—that he survived the waves
against the wishes of the gods. Poseidon
heard his rash words. At once, he seized his trident   505
in mighty hands, and hit the Gyran rock.
One half remained; the other, on which Ajax
sat as he boasted, cracked right off and fell
into the sea, and carried him deep down.
The boundless waves washed over him; he drank   510
the salty brine, and died. But Agamemnon
survived—the goddess Hera saved his fleet.
When he had almost reached the craggy mountain
of Malea, a gust of wind took hold
and bore him over waves where fish were jumping,   515
across the rumbling depths to where all farms
are finished,[7] where Thyestes[8] used to live,
and now his son Aegisthus. After that,
the route was clear: the gods made all winds fair.
Then joyfully he stepped foot in his country,   520
and touched and kissed the earth of his dear home.
He wept hot floods of tears, from happiness.
But from the lookout post the watchman saw him.
Scheming Aegisthus paid that man two talents
of gold to watch all year, so Agamemnon   525
could not slip past unseen, or summon up
his will to fight. The spy rushed off to tell
the King. Aegisthus formed a plan at once.
He chose the twenty best men in the land

6. The Ajax referred to here is Locrian Ajax, also known as Lesser Ajax—not the hero known for his shield and skill in defensive warfare. He had raped Cassandra, the prophet daughter of Priam, in the temple of Athena. Athena was outraged and asked Poseidon to take revenge.

7. This suggests that there are lands beyond the limits of agriculture, and hence, beyond civilized culture.
8. Thyestes was the brother of Atreus, father of Agamemnon and Menelaus.

to lurk in ambush, and he told the house slaves   530
to cook a feast. He rode out on his carriage,
and summoned Agamemnon, who suspected
nothing. Aegisthus killed him over dinner,
just as a person kills an ox at manger.
All of the men who came with him were killed,   535
and all those of Aegisthus; all were killed.'

His story broke my heart, and I sat down
upon the sands and wept. I did not want
to go on living or to see the sun.
I thrashed around and wailed. When I was done,   540
the old sea god spoke words of truth to me.
'Now, son of Atreus, your endless weeping
has gone on long enough. It does no good.
Quickly, go home. You may still find Aegisthus
alive, or else Orestes may have come   545
and killed him; you can join his funeral.'
Those words made me a man again: my heart
was warmed inside, despite my grief. My words
took wings. I said, 'I know now of those two;
but name the third who may be still alive,   550
trapped somewhere in the wide expanse of sea,
or may be dead. I know the news may hurt,
but still I want to hear it.' And he answered,
'It is Laertes' son, the Ithacan.
I saw him crying, shedding floods of tears   555
upon Calypso's island, in her chambers.
She traps him there; he cannot go back home.
He has no boats with oars or crew to row him
across the sea's broad back to his own land.
But Menelaus, it is not your fate   560
to die in Argos. Gods will carry you
off to the world's end, to Elysium.
Those fields are ruled by tawny Rhadamanthus
and life is there the easiest for humans.
There is no snow, no heavy storms or rain,   565
but Ocean always sends up gentle breezes
of Zephyr to refresh the people there.
You gain these blessings as the son-in-law
of Zeus through Helen.' Then the old god sank
beneath the waves. I went back to my ships   570
and godlike men, and as I walked my mind
swirled with my many thoughts. Beside the fleet
we cooked and ate our meal, then holy night
came down; we slept beside the surging water.
When early Dawn appeared and touched the sky   575
with blossom, first we launched the balanced ships
into the salty sea, put up the masts
and fixed the sails, and then the men embarked

and sat on benches neatly, in their lines.
And then at once they struck the sea with oars.   580
We soon reached Egypt's holy rain-fed river.
We docked the ships and sacrificed the oxen.
When I had quenched the anger of the gods,
I built a mound to honor Agamemnon,
for his immortal fame. The gods at last   585
gave me fair wind, and sent me quickly home.
But come now, stay with me here in my palace,
until eleven days or twelve have passed.
Then I will send you off with precious gifts,
three horses and a gleaming chariot.   590
Also a lovely cup so you can pour
gifts to the gods, and always think of me."

Then tactfully Telemachus replied,
"Please do not keep me here so long, my lord.
Indeed, I would be glad to stay a year;   595
I would not even miss my home or parents—
I get such pleasure listening to you.
But my poor friends are surely tired of waiting
in Pylos. You have made me stay too long.
And for a gift, please only give me treasure.   600
You keep your lovely horses here; I cannot
transport them all the way to Ithaca.
You rule these open meadows, rich in clover,
white barley in wide rows, and wheat and grass.
In Ithaca, there are no fields or racetracks.   605
Though it is only fit for goats, we love it
more than horse pasture. Islands out at sea
have no good grazing—ours the least of all."

Then Menelaus smiled and clasped his hand,
and spoke to him in his loud booming voice.   610

"My boy, your words are proof of your good blood.
I will give different gifts, just as you ask.
I will give you the finest piece of treasure
of all the hoard I have piled up at home:
a finely crafted bowl, of purest silver,   615
with gold around the rim. Hephaestus made it,
and Phaedimus the king of Sidon gave it
to me, when I was visiting his house
as I was traveling home. You can have that."

Such was their conversation. Then the guests   620
entered the palace, bringing lamb and wine
that gives one confidence. The girls, all dressed
in pretty scarves, brought bread for them. So went
the feasting in the house of Menelaus.

Meanwhile, outside Odysseus' house,   625
the suitors were as arrogant as usual,
enjoying throwing discuses and spears
out on the playing field. The two chief suitors,
were sitting there: Antinous and godlike
Eurymachus. Just then Noëmon, son   630
of Phronius, approached and asked a question.

"So do we know, Antinous, or not,
whether Telemachus is coming back
from sandy Pylos? He left with my ship.
I need it, to cross over to the fields   635
of Elis, where I have twelve mares with mules
suckling their teats and not yet broken in.
I want to take and train one."

                              They were all
astonished, since they had not thought the boy
was gone to Pylos, but was somewhere near,   640
out with the sheep or pigs. Antinous
said,

          "Tell me true, when did he go? And who
went with him? Did he choose some Ithacans,
or slaves and laborers? It could be either.
And tell me also, did he steal the ship   645
from you by force, or did you give it to him
freely, because he asked?"

                              Noëmon, son
of Phronius, replied, "I gave it freely.
What could I do, when someone so upset
was asking me? A noble boy like that?   650
It would have been ungracious to refuse.
The young men who were with him were high class,
the best in town except ourselves. I saw
Mentor embark as captain—or perhaps
not Mentor but a god who looked like him.   655
This puzzles me, that yesterday at dawn
I saw great Mentor here, though he had gone
to Pylos in the ship."

                              With that, Noëmon
departed for his father's house. Those leaders
were furious. At once they made the suitors   660
stop playing games and sit. Antinous
spoke up with eyes bright as fire, his mind
darkened with anger.

                              "Damn! That stuck-up boy
succeeded in his stupid trip. We thought

he would not manage it. Telemachus   665
has launched a ship and picked an ideal crew,
despite us all! This is the start of worse.
May Zeus destroy his strength before he reaches
manhood. Give me a ship and twenty men,
so I may watch and catch him in the strait   670
in between Ithaca and craggy Same.
A sad end to this journey for his father!"

All of them praised his words, endorsed his plan,
and went inside Odysseus' palace.
Penelope was soon aware of all   675
the suitors' secret plots. The house boy Medon
told her, since he had been outside the courtyard
and he had heard the plans they were devising.
He rushed to tell her. As he stepped inside,
across the threshold, she came up and asked him,   680

"Well, boy, why have those lordly suitors sent you?
To tell godlike Odysseus' girls
to stop their work and make a feast for them?
I hope this is their final meal! I hope
they never gather elsewhere to go courting!   685
You suitors who come crowding here are wasting
Telemachus' wealth! When you were younger
you never paid attention to your fathers
who told you of Odysseus' greatness.
He never spoke or acted without justice,   690
among the people. Lords are mostly biased;
they favor one person and hate another.
But he did not. He did no wrong at all.
Now you! Your wicked deeds and plans are clear.
No gratitude for favors from the past!"   695

Then knowledgeable Medon answered her,
"My Queen, I wish this were the worst of it.
Now they are plotting even greater ruin.
May Zeus ensure it never comes to pass!
The suitors want to kill Telemachus   700
with sharp bronze weapons on his journey home.
He went to sandy Pylos and to Sparta
for word about his father."

                              At the news,
her legs grew weak; her heart sank; she was struck
dumb for a time, her voice blocked as her eyes   705
filled up with tears. At last she answered him,
"But why did my son go away? There was
no need to go on those swift ships that gallop
like horses over miles of salty water.
Did he intend to lose his name as well,   710

and be unknown?"

　　　　　　　And Medon said, "Perhaps
some god or his own heart nudged him to go
to Pylos to find out about his father,
if he will come back home, or if he has
already met his fate." With that, he left her.　　　　　　　715

Grief wrapped around her, eating at her heart.
The house was full of chairs but she could not
bear to sit upright. In her bedroom doorway,
collapsing on the floor, she wept and cried.
Around her all her women, young and old,　　　　　　　720
were whimpering. Voice thick with tears, she sobbed,

"Friends, listen! Zeus has cursed me more than all
the women of my family. Already
I lost my noble, lionhearted husband,
most talented and brave of all the Greeks,　　　　　　　725
whose fame is spread through Greece. And now the winds
have taken my dear son, and no one told me
that he was setting out. Shame on you all!
You knew that he was leaving in that ship!
Not one of you came here to wake me up!　　　　　　　730
If only I had known about his journey,
he would have stayed—no matter how he wanted
to leave—or else have left me dead right here.
Now call old Dolius, my gardener,
the slave who cares for all my trees. My father　　　　　　　735
gave him to me when I came here. Tell him
to hurry off and sit beside Laertes,
and tell him everything; he may decide
to go in tears to plead with those who want
to kill godlike Odysseus' son,　　　　　　　740
his grandson."

　　　　　　　Then the loyal Eurycleia
said, "Lady, sweetheart, even if you take
a sword and kill me, I will tell the truth.
I knew all this. I gave him what he asked for,
bread and sweet wine. He made me swear an oath　　　　　　　745
not to inform you, till twelve days had passed,
or till you heard about it, and you missed him,
so that you would not cry and spoil your beauty.
Now have a bath, get changed into clean clothes,
go with your slave girls upstairs to your room,　　　　　　　750
pray to Athena, child of Zeus the King.
She may save him from death. And do not bother
poor old Laertes; he has pain enough.
I do not think the blessed gods despise

this family; I trust that there will always   755
be one to rule this house and rich estate."

This soothed Penelope. She dried her tears,
and took her bath and got dressed in clean clothes,
then went up to her bedroom with her girls.
She put some barley on a tray and prayed.   760

"Hear me, Athena, tireless child of Zeus,
if my quick-minded husband ever gave you
fat thighs of beef or lamb here in our halls,
remember now and save the son I love.
Protect him from the abuses of those suitors!"   765
She wailed aloud; the goddess heard her prayer.

The suitors made a racket that resounded
all through the palace shadows. They were boasting,
"This queen whom all of us have come here courting
is ready now to marry one of us,   770
and does not even know her son will die!"
They spoke not knowing how things really stood.
Antinous declared to them,

                         "My lords,
you have to stop this bragging! Quiet down,
or those inside will hear it. Now get up   775
in silence. We must go and follow through
the plan we all agreed on in our hearts."
With that, he picked the twenty strongest men.
They went down to the seashore; first of all
they launched the swift black ship in deep saltwater,   780
set up the mast and raised the sails and fit
the oars in proper order in the straps
of leather, then spread out the bright white sails.
With confidence their slaves dealt out the weapons.
They moored high up the stream and disembarked.   785
They ate there, while they waited for the evening.

Penelope lay upstairs in her bedroom,
refusing food and drink, consuming nothing.
She wondered if her fine son would escape
from death, or be brought down by those proud suitors.   790
Her mind was like a lion, caught by humans,
when they are clustering round him in a circle,
trying to trap him; so sweet drowsiness
subdued her and she slept, her limbs relaxed.

Athena, bright-eyed goddess, had a plan.   795
She made a phantom looking like a woman,
Iphthime, child of great Icarius,
the wife of Eumelus who lived in Pherae.

She sent it to Odysseus' house,
to make Penelope feel less distressed   800
and stop her tears of grief. It traveled through
the latch's thong, and in her bedroom stood
above her head, and asked,

                              "Penelope,
Are you asleep? And are you still upset?
The gods who live at ease have no desire   805
for you to weep or worry. Know, your son
is coming home. He has not wronged the gods."
Intelligent Penelope, still sleeping
sweetly inside the gates of dreams, replied,

"Sister, why have you come? Your house is far,   810
and you have never visited before.
You tell me to stop grieving and not feel
the many pains that prickle at my heart.
But long ago I lost my lionhearted
husband, a man more talented than any,   815
famous throughout all Greece. Now my dear son
has sailed off in a ship, though he knows nothing
of hardship and the world; he is a child.
I worry for him more than for his father.
I shudder, I am scared of what may happen,   820
at sea, or in the country that he went to.
He has so many enemies; they plan
to murder him before he reaches home."

The misty phantom answered her, "Have courage.
Let not your heart be troubled or afraid.   825
He has a goddess as his guide—Athena,
a helper many men have prayed to have.
She has great power. Pitying your grief,
she sent me here to tell you all of this."

Careful Penelope replied, "If you   830
are actually a god, with news from gods,
tell me about my husband too, poor man!
Tell if he is alive and sees the sun,
or dead already in the house of Hades!"

The spirit said, "I cannot tell you whether   835
he is alive or dead. It is not good
to speak of things intangible as wind."

With that, the phantom floated through the air
into the breeze. And then Penelope
woke up from sleep, and she was glad at heart,   840
because she dreamed so clearly in the night.

The suitors got on board and sailed across
the water, set on murdering the boy.
There is a rocky island out at sea,
in between Ithaca and craggy Same,   845
called Asteris—quite small but with a harbor
to shelter ships, and there they lurked in ambush.

BOOK 5

From the Goddess to the Storm

Then Dawn rose up from bed with Lord Tithonus,[1]
to bring the light to deathless gods and mortals.
The gods sat down for council, with the great
Thunderlord Zeus. Athena was concerned
about Odysseus' many troubles,   5
trapped by the nymph Calypso in her house.

"Father, and all immortal gods," she said,
"No longer let a sceptered king be kind,
or gentle, or pay heed to right and wrong.
Let every king be cruel, his acts unjust!   10
Odysseus ruled gently, like a father,
but no one even thinks about him now.
The wretched man is stranded on an island;
Calypso forces him to stay with her.
He cannot make his way back to his country.   15
He has no ships, no oars, and no companions
to help him sail across the wide-backed sea.
His son has gone for news of his lost father,
in sandy Pylos and in splendid Sparta;
they plot to kill the boy when he returns!"   20

Smiling at her, Lord Zeus who heaps the clouds
replied, "Ah, daughter! What a thing to say!
Did you not plan all this yourself, so that
Odysseus could come and take revenge
upon those suitors? Now use all your skill: 25
ensure Telemachus comes safely home,
and that the suitors fail and sail away."

Then turning to his son he said, "Dear Hermes,
you are my messenger. Go tell the goddess
our fixed intention: that Odysseus   30
must go back home—he has endured enough.
Without a god or human as his guide,
he will drift miserably for twenty days
upon a makeshift raft, and then arrive

---

1. Dawn's lover, a mortal man whom she made immortal (though not ageless) and brought to live with her in the sky.

at fertile Scheria. The magical   35
Phaeacians will respect him like a god,
and send him in a ship to his dear homeland,
with gifts of bronze and heaps of gold and clothing,
more than he would have brought with him from Troy
if he had come directly, with his share   40
of plunder. It is granted him to see
the ones he loves, beneath his own high roof,
in his own country."

                         Hermes heard these words.
At once he fastened on his feet the sandals
of everlasting gold with which he flies   45
on breath of air across the sea and land;
he seized the wand he uses to enchant
men's eyes to sleep or wake as he desires,
and flew. The god flashed bright in all his power.
He touched Pieria, then from the sky   50
he plunged into the sea and swooped between
the waves, just like a seagull catching fish,
wetting its whirring wings in tireless brine.
So Hermes scudded through the surging swell.
Then finally, he reached the distant island,   55
stepped from the indigo water to the shore,
and reached the cavern where the goddess lived.

There sat Calypso with her braided curls.
Beside the hearth a mighty fire was burning.
The scent of citrus and of brittle pine   60
suffused the island. Inside, she was singing
and weaving with a shuttle made of gold.
Her voice was beautiful. Around the cave
a luscious forest flourished: alder, poplar,
and scented cypress. It was full of wings.   65
Birds nested there but hunted out at sea:
the owls, the hawks, the gulls with gaping beaks.
A ripe and luscious vine, hung thick with grapes,
was stretched to coil around her cave. Four springs
spurted with sparkling water as they laced   70
with crisscross currents intertwined together.
The meadow softly bloomed with celery
and violets. He gazed around in wonder
and joy, at sights to please even a god.
Even the deathless god who once killed Argos[2]   75
stood still, his heart amazed at all he saw.
At last he went inside the cave. Calypso,
the splendid goddess, knew the god on sight:
the deathless gods all recognize each other,
however far away their homes may be.   80

2. One of the standard epithets for Hermes.

But Hermes did not find Odysseus,
since he was sitting by the shore as usual,
sobbing in grief and pain; his heart was breaking.
In tears he stared across the fruitless sea.

Divine Calypso told her guest to sit   85
upon a gleaming, glittering chair, and said,
"Dear friend, Lord Hermes of the golden wand,
why have you come? You do not often visit.
What do you have in mind? My heart inclines
to help you if I can, if it is fated.   90
For now, come in, and let me make you welcome."

At that the goddess led him to a table
heaped with ambrosia, and she mixed a drink:
red nectar.[3] So mercurial Hermes drank
and ate till he was satisfied, and then   95
the diplomat explained why he had come.

"You are a goddess, I a god—and yet
you ask why I am here. Well, I will tell you.
Zeus ordered me to come—I did not want to.
Who would desire to cross such an expanse   100
of endless salty sea? No human town
is near here, where gods get fine sacrifices.
Still, none can sway or check the will of Zeus.
He says the most unhappy man alive
is living here—a warrior from those   105
who fought the town of Priam for nine years
and in the tenth they sacked it and sailed home.
But on the journey back, they wronged Athena.
She roused the wind and surging sea against them
and all his brave companions were destroyed,   110
while he himself was blown here by the waves.
Zeus orders you to send him on his way
at once, since it is not his destiny
to die here far away from those he loves.
It is his fate to see his family   115
and come back home, to his own native land."

Calypso shuddered and let fly at him.
"You cruel, jealous gods! You bear a grudge
whenever any goddess takes a man
to sleep with as a lover in her bed.   120
Just so the gods who live at ease were angry
when rosy-fingered Dawn took up Orion,[4]
and from her golden throne, chaste Artemis
attacked and killed him with her gentle arrows.

---

3. Food of the gods.
4. Orion was a human hunter with whom Dawn fell in love; the huntress goddess, Artemis, shot and killed him.

Demeter with the cornrows in her hair   125
indulged her own desire, and she made love
with Iasion in triple-furrowed fields—
till Zeus found out, hurled flashing flame and killed him.[5]
So now, you male gods are upset with me
for living with a man. A man I saved!   130
Zeus pinned his ship and with his flash of lightning
smashed it to pieces. All his friends were killed
out on the wine-dark sea. This man alone,
clutching the keel, was swept by wind and wave,
and came here, to my home. I cared for him   135
and loved him, and I vowed to to set him free
from time and death forever. Still, I know
no other god can change the will of Zeus.
So let him go, if that is Zeus' order,
across the barren sea. I will not give   140
an escort for this trip across the water;
I have no ships or rowers. But I will
share what I know with him, and gladly give
useful advice so he can safely reach
his home."

         The mediator, Zeus' servant,   145
replied, "Then send him now, avoid the wrath
of Zeus, do not enrage him, or one day
his rage will hurt you." With these words, he vanished.

Acknowledging the edict sent from Zeus,
the goddess went to find Odysseus.   150
She found him on the shore. His eyes were always
tearful; he wept sweet life away, in longing
to go back home, since she no longer pleased him.
He had no choice. He spent his nights with her
inside her hollow cave, not wanting her   155
though she still wanted him. By day he sat
out on the rocky beach, in tears and grief,
staring in heartbreak at the fruitless sea.

The goddess stood by him and said, "Poor man!
Stop grieving, please. You need not waste your life.   160
I am quite ready now to send you off.
Using your sword of bronze, cut trunks and build
a raft, fix decks across, and let it take you
across the misty sea. I will provide
water, red wine, and food, to stop you starving,   165
and I will give you clothes, and send a wind
to blow you safely home, if this is what

5. Demeter, goddess of the harvest, fell in love with Iasion (and in some versions had two sons by
him); Zeus killed him with a thunderbolt.

those sky gods want. They are more powerful
than me; they get their way."

                    Odysseus,
informed by many years of pain and loss,   170
shuddered and let his words fly out at her.
"Goddess, you have some other scheme in mind,
not my safe passage. You are telling me
to cross this vast and terrifying gulf,
in just a raft, when even stable schooners   175
sped on by winds from Zeus would not succeed?
No, goddess, I will not get on a raft,
unless you swear to me a mighty oath
you are not planning yet more pain for me."

At that, divine Calypso smiled at him.   180
She reached out and caressed him with her hand,
saying, "You scalawag! What you have said
shows that you understand how these things work.
But by this earth, and by the sky above,
and by the waters of the Styx[6] below,   185
which is the strongest oath for blessed gods,
I swear I will not plot more pain for you.
I have made plans for you as I would do
for my own self, if I were in your place.
I am not made of iron; no, my heart   190
is kind and decent, and I pity you."

And with those words, the goddess quickly turned
and led the way; he followed in her footsteps.
They reached the cave together, man and goddess.
The chair that Hermes had been sitting on   195
was empty now; Odysseus sat there.
The goddess gave him human food and drink.
She sat and faced godlike Odysseus
while slave girls brought her nectar and ambrosia.
They reached to take the good things set before them,   200
and satisfied their hunger and their thirst.

The goddess-queen began. "Odysseus,
son of Laertes, blessed by Zeus—your plans
are always changing. Do you really want
to go back to that home you love so much?   205
Well then, good-bye! But if you understood
how glutted you will be with suffering
before you reach your home, you would stay here
with me and be immortal—though you might
still wish to see that wife you always pine for.   210

6. River of the underworld.

And anyway, I know my body is
better than hers is. I am taller too.
Mortals can never rival the immortals
in beauty."

        So Odysseus, with tact,
said "Do not be enraged at me, great goddess.   215
You are quite right. I know my modest wife
Penelope could never match your beauty.
She is a human; you are deathless, ageless.
But even so, I want to go back home,
and every day I hope that day will come.   220
If some god strikes me on the wine-dark sea,
I will endure it. By now I am used
to suffering—I have gone through so much,
at sea and in the war. Let this come too."

The sun went down and brought the darkness on.   225
They went inside the hollow cave and took
the pleasure of their love, held close together.

When vernal Dawn first touched the sky with flowers,
they rose and dressed: Odysseus put on
his cloak and tunic, and Calypso wore   230
her fine long robe of silver. Round her waist
she wrapped a golden belt, and veiled her head.
Then she prepared the journey for the man.
She gave an axe that fitted in his grip,
its handle made of finest olive wood;   235
its huge bronze blade was sharp on either side.
She also gave a polished adze. She led him
out to the island's end, where tall trees grew:
black poplar, alder, fir that touched the sky,
good for a nimble boat of seasoned timber.   240
When she had shown him where the tall trees grew,
Calypso, queen of goddesses, went home.
Odysseus began and made good progress.
With his bronze axe he cut down twenty trunks,
polished them skillfully and planed them straight.   245
Calypso brought a gimlet and he drilled
through every plank and fitted them together,
fixing it firm with pegs and fastenings.
As wide as when a man who knows his trade
marks out the curving hull to fit a ship,   250
so wide Odysseus marked out his raft.
He notched the side decks to the close-set frame
and fixed long planks along the ribs to finish.
He set a mast inside, and joined to it
a yardarm and a rudder to steer straight.   255
He heaped the boat with brush, and caulked the sides
with wickerwork, to keep the water out.

Calypso brought him fabric for a sail,
and he constructed that with equal skill.
He fastened up the braces, clews and halyards,   260
and using levers, launched her on the sea.

The work had taken four days; on the fifth
Calypso let him go. She washed and dressed him
in clothes that smelled of incense. On the raft
she put a flask of wine, a bigger flask   265
of water, and a large supply of food.
She sent him off with gentle, lukewarm breezes.
Gladly Odysseus spread out his sails
to catch the wind; with skill he steered the rudder.
No sleep fell on his eyes; he watched the stars,   270
the Pleiades, late-setting Boötes,
and Bear, which people also call the Plow,
which circles in one place, and marks Orion—
the only star that has no share of Ocean.[7]
Calypso, queen of goddesses, had told him   275
to keep the Bear on his left side while sailing.
He sailed the sea for seven days and ten,
and on the eighteenth day, a murky mountain
of the Phaeacian land appeared—it rose
up like a shield beyond the misty sea.   280

Returning from the Ethiopians,
and pausing on Mount Solyma, Poseidon,
Master of Earthquakes, saw the distant raft.[8]
Enraged, he shook his head and told himself,

"This is outrageous! So it seems the gods   285
have changed their plans about Odysseus
while I was absent! He has almost reached
Phaeacia, where it is his destiny
to flee the rope of pain that binds him now.
But I will goad him to more misery,   290
till he is sick of it."

        He gathered up
the clouds, and seized his trident and stirred round
the sea and roused the gusts of every wind,
and covered earth and sea with fog. Night stretched
from heaven. Eurus, Notus, blasting Zephyr   295
and Boreas,[9] the child of sky, all fell
and rolled a mighty wave. Odysseus
grew weak at knees. He cried out in despair,

---

7. The idea is that the Plow (Big Dipper) is the only constellation that stays above the horizon all year round. This is not true in astronomical fact; other constellations also remain visible year round.

8. The Solymi people, and the Solyma mountain, were in Lycia, in eastern Greece; the geography requires the god to have extremely good eyesight, since Odysseus is sailing in the west.
9. The four winds.

"More pain? How will it end? I am afraid
the goddess spoke the truth: that I will have   300
a sea of sufferings before I reach
my homeland. It is coming true! Zeus whirls
the air. Look at those clouds! He agitates
the waves, as winds attack from all directions.
I can hold on to one thing: certain death.   305
Those Greeks were lucky, three and four times over,
who died upon the plain of Troy to help
the sons of Atreus. I wish I had
died that same day the mass of Trojans hurled
their bronze-tipped spears at me around the corpse   310
of Peleus' son.[1] I would have had
a funeral, and honor from the Greeks;
but now I have to die this cruel death!"

A wave crashed onto him, and overturned
the raft, and he fell out. The rudder slipped   315
out of his hands. The winds blew all directions
and one enormous gust snapped off the mast.
The sail and yardarm drifted out to sea.
Then for a long time rushing, crashing waves
kept him submerged: he could not reach the surface.   320
The clothes Calypso gave him weighed him down.
At last he rose and spat the sour saltwater
out of his mouth—it gushed forth in a torrent.
Despite his pain and weakness, he remembered
his raft, and lunged to get it through the waves;   325
he climbed on top of it and clung to life.
The great waves carried it this way and that.
As when the thistles, clumping close together,
are borne across the prairie by the North Wind,
so these winds swept the raft across the sea.   330
The South Wind hurls it, then the North Wind grabs it,
then East Wind yields and lets the West Wind drive it.
But stepping softly, Ino,[2] the White Goddess,
Cadmus' child, once human, human-voiced,
now honored with the gods in salty depths,   335
noticed that he was suffering and lost,
with pity. Like a gull with wings outstretched
she rose up from the sea, sat on the raft
and said,

      "Poor man! Why does enraged Poseidon
create an odyssey[3] of pain for you?   340
But his hostility will not destroy you.
You seem intelligent. Do as I say.

---

1. The reference is to Achilles.
2. Ino was a human girl transformed into a sea
nymph.

3. The original uses a verb that puns on Odysseus' name: *odysat'*, which means "he hated" or "he was angry at."

Strip off your clothes and leave the raft behind
for winds to take away. With just your arms
swim to Phaeacia. Fate decrees that there   345
you will survive. Here, take my scarf and tie it
under your chest: with this immortal veil,
you need not be afraid of death or danger.
But when you reach dry earth, untie the scarf
and throw it out to sea, away from land,   350
and turn away." With that, the goddess gave it,
and plunged back down inside the surging sea,
just like a gull. The black wave covered her.

The hero who had suffered so much danger
was troubled and confused. He asked himself,   355
"Some deity has said to leave the raft.
But what if gods are weaving tricks again?
I will not trust her yet: with my own eyes
I saw the land she said I should escape to,
and it is far away. I will do this: 360
as long as these wood timbers hold together,
I will hang on, however hard it is.
But when the waves have smashed my raft to pieces,
then I will have no choice, and I will swim."

While he was thinking this, the Lord of Earthquakes,   365
Poseidon, roused a huge and dreadful wave
that arched above his head: he hurled it at him.
As when a fierce wind ruffles up a heap
of dry wheat chaff; it scatters here and there;
so were the raft's long timbers flung apart.   370
He climbed astride a plank and rode along
as if on horseback. He took off the clothes
Calypso gave him, but he tied the scarf
around his chest, and dove into the sea,
spreading his arms to swim. The Lord of Earthquakes   375
saw him and nodded, muttering, "At last
you are in pain! Go drift across the sea,
till you meet people blessed by Zeus, the Sky Lord.
But even then, I think you will not lack
for suffering." He spurred his fine-maned horses,   380
and went to Aegae, where he had his home.

Athena, child of Zeus, devised a plan.
She blocked the path of all the other winds,
told them to cease and made them go to sleep,
but roused swift Boreas and smoothed the waves   385
in front of him, so that Odysseus
could reach Phaeacia and escape from death.

Two days and nights he drifted on the waves:
each moment he expected he would die.

But when the Dawn with dazzling braids brought day   390
for the third time, the wind died down. No breeze,
but total calm. As he was lifted up
by an enormous wave, he scanned around,
and saw the shore nearby. As when a father
lies sick and weak for many days, tormented   395
by some cruel spirit, till at last the gods
restore him back to life; his children feel
great joy; Odysseus felt that same joy
when he saw land. He swam and longed to set
his feet on earth. But when he was in earshot,   400
he heard the boom of surf against the rocks.
The mighty waves were crashing on the shore,
a dreadful belching. Everything was covered
in salty foam. There were no sheltering harbors
for ships, just sheer crags, reefs and solid cliffs.   405
Odysseus' heart and legs gave way.
Shaken but purposeful, he told himself,

"Zeus went beyond my hopes and let me see
dry land! I made it, cutting the abyss!
But I see no way out from this gray sea.   410
There are steep cliffs offshore, and all around
the rushing water roars; the rock runs sheer;
the sea is deep near shore; there is no way
to set my feet on land without disaster.
If I attempt to scramble out, a wave   415
will seize and dash me on the jagged rock;
a useless effort. But if I swim on farther,
looking for bays or coves or slanting beaches,
storm winds may seize me once again and drag me,
howling with grief, towards the fish-filled sea.   420
A god may even send a great sea-monster,
the kind that famous Amphitrite[4] rears.
I know Poseidon wants to do me harm."

As he was thinking this, the waves grew big
and hurled him at the craggy shore. His skin   425
would have been ripped away, and his bones smashed,
had not Athena given him a thought.
He grabbed a rock as he was swept along
with both hands, and clung to it, groaning, till
the wave passed by. But then the swell rushed back,   430
and struck him hard and hurled him out to sea.
As when an octopus, dragged from its den,
has many pebbles sticking to its suckers,
so his strong hands were skinned against the rocks.
A mighty wave rolled over him again.   435
He would have died too soon, in misery,

---

4. Wife of Poseidon, representative of the sea; see also 3.91.

without the inspiration of Athena.
He came up from the wave that spewed to shore
and swam towards the land, in search of beaches
with gradual slopes, or inlets from the sea.   440
He swam until he reached a river's mouth
with gentle waters; that place seemed ideal,
smooth and not stony, sheltered from the wind.
He sensed its current; in his heart he prayed,

"Unknown god, hear me! How I longed for you!   445
I have escaped the salt sea and Poseidon.
Even the deathless gods respect a man
who is as lost as I am now. I have
gone through so much and reached your flowing streams.
Pity me, lord! I am your supplicant."   450

The current ceased; the River God restrained
the waves and made them calm. He brought him safe
into the river mouth. His legs cramped up;
the sea had broken him. His swollen body
gushed brine from mouth and nostrils. There he lay,   455
winded and silent, hardly fit to move.
A terrible exhaustion overcame him.
When he could breathe and think again, he took
the goddess' scarf off, and let it go
into the river flowing to the sea;   460
strong currents swept it down and Ino's hands
took it. He crawled on land and crouched beside
the reeds and bent to kiss life-giving earth,
and trembling, he spoke to his own heart.

"What now? What will become of me? If I   465
stay up all wretched night beside this river,
the cruel frost and gentle dew together
may finish me: my life is thin with weakness.
At dawn a cold breeze blows beside the river.
But if I climb the slope to those dark woods   470
and go to rest in that thick undergrowth,
letting sweet sleep take hold of me, and losing
my cold and weariness—wild beasts may find me
and treat me as their prey."

　　　　　　　　　　　But he decided
to go into the woods. He found a place   475
beside a clearing, near the water's edge.
He crawled beneath two bushes grown together,
of thorn and olive.[5] No strong wet wind could blow
through them, no shining sunbeam ever strike them,

---

5. The first bush is either wild olive or fig or evergreen thorn. The olive wood is significant in that it is Athena's tree: the goddess is still watching over her favorite.

no rain could penetrate them; they were growing 480
so thickly intertwined. Odysseus
crept under, and he scraped a bed together,
of leaves: there were enough to cover two
against the worst of winter. Seeing this,
the hero who had suffered for so long 485
was happy. He lay down inside and heaped
more leaves on top. As when a man who lives
out on a lonely farm that has no neighbors
buries a glowing torch inside black embers
to save the seed of fire and keep a source— 490
so was Odysseus concealed in leaves.
Athena poured down sleep to shut his eyes
so all his painful weariness could end.

BOOK 6

A Princess and Her Laundry

Odysseus had suffered. In exhaustion
from all his long ordeals, the hero slept.
Meanwhile, Athena went to the Phaeacians.
This people used to live in Hyperia,
a land of dancing. But their mighty neighbors, 5
the Cyclopes, kept looting them, and they
could not hold out. Their king, Nausithous,
brought them to Scheria, a distant place,
and built a wall around the town, and homes,
and temples to the gods, and plots of land. 10
He went to Hades. Then Alcinous,
who has god-given wisdom, came to power.
Bright-eyed Athena traveled to his palace,
to help Odysseus' journey home.
She went inside the decorated bedroom 15
where the young princess, Nausicaa, was sleeping,
as lovely as a goddess. Slaves were sleeping
outside her doorway, one on either side;
two charming girls with all the Graces' gifts.
The shining doors were shut, but like the wind 20
the goddess reached the bed of Nausicaa,
disguised as her best friend, a girl her age,
the daughter of the famous sailor Dymas.
Sharp-eyed Athena said,

                    "Oh, Nausicaa!
So lazy! But your mother should have taught you! 25
Your clothes are lying there in dirty heaps,
though you will soon be married, and you need
a pretty dress to wear, and clothes to give
to all your bridesmaids. That impresses people,
and makes the parents happy. When day comes, 30

we have to do the laundry. I will come
and help you, so the work will soon be done.
Surely you will not long remain unmarried.
The best young men here in your native land
already want to court you. So at dawn   35
go ask your father for the cart with mules,
to carry dresses, scarves, and sheets. You should
ride there, not walk; the washing pools are far
from town."

        The goddess looked into her eyes,
then went back to Olympus, which they say   40
is where the gods will have their home forever.
The place is never shaken by the wind,
or wet with rain or blanketed by snow.
A cloudless sky is spread above the mountain,
white radiance all round. The blessed gods   45
live there in happiness forevermore.

Then Dawn came from her lovely throne, and woke
the girl. She was amazed, remembering
her dream, and in a fine dress, went to tell
her parents, whom she found inside the hall.   50
Her mother sat beside the hearth and spun
sea-purpled yarn, her house girls all around her.
Her father was just heading out to council
with his renowned advisors, since his people
had called him to a meeting. She stood near him   55
and said,

        "Dear Daddy, please would you set up
the wagon with the big smooth wheels for me,
so I can take my fine clothes to the river
to wash them? They are dirty. And you too
should wear clean clothes for meeting your advisors,   60
dressed in your best to make important plans.
Your five sons also—two of whom are married,
but three are strapping single men—they always
want to wear nice fresh-laundered clothes when they
are going dancing. This is on my mind."   65

She said this since she felt too shy to talk
of marriage to her father. But he knew,
and answered, "Child, I would not grudge the mules
or anything you want. Go on! The slaves
can fit the wagon with its cargo rack."   70

He called the household slaves, and they obeyed.
They made the wagon ready and inspected
its wheels, led up the mules, and yoked them to it.
The girl brought out the multicolored clothes,

and put them on the cart, while in a basket   75
her mother packed nutritious food for her—
a varied meal, with olives, cheese, and wine,
stored in a goatskin. Then the girl got in.
Her mother handed her a golden flask
of oil, to use when she had had her bath.   80
Then Nausicaa took up the whip and reins,
and cracked the whip. The mules were on their way,
eager to go and rattling the harness,
bringing the clothes and girl and all her slaves.
They reached the lovely river where the pools   85
are always full—the water flows in streams
and bubbles up from underneath, to wash
even the dirtiest of laundry. There
they freed the mules and drove them to the river
to graze on honeyed grass beside the stream.   90
The girls brought out the laundry from the cart,
and brought it to the washing pools and trod it,
competing with each other. When the dirt
was gone, they spread the clothes along the shore,
where salt sea washes pebbles to the beach.   95
They bathed and rubbed themselves with olive oil.
Then they sat on the riverbank and ate,
and waited for the sun to dry the clothes.
But when they finished eating, they took off
their head-scarves to play ball. The white-armed princess   100
led them in play—like Artemis the archer,
running across the heights of Taygetus
and Erymanthus; she is glad to run
with boars and fleet-foot deer. The rustic daughters
of Zeus the Aegis King play round about her,   105
while Leto is delighted in her heart,
seeing her daughter far above the rest,
though all are beautiful. So Nausicaa
stood out above them all. But when the girl
was thinking she should head for home and yoke   110
the mules, and pack the laundry up again,
Athena's eyes flashed bright. Odysseus
must wake up, see the pretty girl, and have
an escort to the town of the Phaeacians.
The princess threw the ball towards a slave girl,   115
who missed the catch. It fell down in an eddy;
the girls all started screaming, very loudly.
Odysseus woke up, and thought things over.

"What is this country I have come to now?
Are all the people wild and violent,   120
or good, hospitable, and god-fearing?
I heard the sound of female voices. Is it
nymphs, who frequent the craggy mountaintops,
and river streams and meadows lush with grass?

Or could this noise I hear be human voices?   125
I have to try to find out who they are."

Odysseus jumped up from out the bushes.
Grasping a leafy branch he broke it off
to cover up his manly private parts.
Just as a mountain lion trusts its strength,   130
and beaten by the rain and wind, its eyes
burn bright as it attacks the cows or sheep,
or wild deer, and hunger drives it on
to try the sturdy pens of sheep—so need
impelled Odysseus to come upon   135
the girls with pretty hair, though he was naked.
All caked with salt, he looked a dreadful sight.
They ran along the shore quite terrified,
some here, some there. But Nausicaa stayed still.
Athena made her legs stop trembling   140
and gave her courage in her heart. She stood there.
He wondered, should he touch her knees, or keep
some distance and use charming words, to beg
the pretty girl to show him to the town,
and give him clothes. At last he thought it best   145
to keep some distance and use words to beg her.
The girl might be alarmed at being touched.
His words were calculated flattery.

"My lady, please! Are you divine or human?
If you are some great goddess from the sky,   150
you look like Zeus' daughter Artemis—
you are as tall and beautiful as she.
But if you live on earth and are a human,
your mother and your father must be lucky,
your brothers also—lucky three times over.   155
Their hearts must be delighted, seeing you,
their flourishing new sprout, the dancers' leader.
And that man will be luckiest by far,
who takes you home with dowry, as his bride.
I have seen no one like you. Never, no one.   160
My eyes are dazzled when I look at you.
I traveled once to Delos, on my way
to war and suffering; my troops marched with me.
Beside Apollo's altar sprang a sapling,
a fresh young palm. I gazed at it and marveled.   165
I never saw so magical a tree.
My lady, you transfix me that same way.
I am in awe of you, afraid to touch
your knees. But I am desperate. I came from
Ogygia, and for twenty days storm winds   170
and waves were driving me, adrift until
yesterday some god washed me up right here,
perhaps to meet more suffering. I think

my troubles will not end until the gods
have done their all. My lady, pity me.   175
Battered and wrecked, I come to you, you first—
and I know no one else in this whole country.
Show me the town, give me some rags to wear,
if you brought any clothes when you came here.
So may the gods grant all your heart's desires,   180
a home and husband, somebody like-minded.
For nothing could be better than when two
live in one house, their minds in harmony,
husband and wife. Their enemies are jealous,
their friends delighted, and they have great honor."   185

Then white-armed Nausicaa replied, "Well, stranger,
you seem a brave and clever man; you know
that Zeus apportions happiness to people,
to good and bad, each one as he decides.
Your troubles come from him, and you must bear them.   190
But since you have arrived here in our land,
you will not lack for clothes or anything
a person needs in times of desperation.
I will show you the town. The people here
are called Phaeacians, and I am the daughter   195
of the great King Alcinous, on whom
depends the strength and power of our people."

And then she called her slaves with braided hair.
"Wait, girls! Why are you running from this man?
Do you believe he is an enemy?   200
No living person ever born would come
to our Phaeacia with a hostile mind,
since we are much beloved by the gods.
Our island is remote, washed round by sea;
we have no human contact. But this man   205
is lost, poor thing. We must look after him.
All foreigners and beggars come from Zeus,
and any act of kindness is a blessing.
So give the stranger food and drink, and wash him
down in the river, sheltered from the wind."   210
They stopped, and egged each other on to take
Odysseus to shelter, as the princess,
the daughter of Alcinous, had told them.
They gave him clothes, a tunic and a cloak,
the olive oil in the golden flask,   215
and led him down to wash beside the river.
Odysseus politely said,

                              "Now, girls,
wait at a distance here, so I can wash
my grimy back, and rub myself with oil—
it has been quite a while since I have done it.   220

Please let me wash in private. I am shy
of being naked with you—pretty girls
with lovely hair."

            So they withdrew, and told
their mistress. Then he used the river water
to scrub the brine off from his back and shoulders,   225
and wash the crusty sea salt from his hair.
But when he was all clean and richly oiled,
dressed in the clothes the young unmarried girl
had given him, Athena made him look
bigger and sturdier, and made his hair   230
grow curling tendrils like a hyacinth.
As when Athena and Hephaestus teach
a knowledgeable craftsman every art,
and he pours gold on silver, making objects
more beautiful—just so Athena poured   235
attractiveness across his head and shoulders.
Then he went off and sat beside the sea;
his handsomeness was dazzling. The girl
was shocked. She told her slaves with tidy hair,
"Now listen to me, girls! The gods who live   240
on Mount Olympus must have wished this man
to come in contact with my godlike people.
Before, he looked so poor and unrefined;
now he is like a god that lives in heaven.
I hope I get a man like this as husband,   245
a man that lives here and would like to stay.
But, girls, now give the stranger food and drink!"

She gave her orders and the girls obeyed—
they gave Odysseus some food and drink.
He wolfed the food and drank. He was half starved;   250
it had been ages since he tasted food.
Then white-armed Nausicaa had formed a plan.
Folding the clothes, she packed them in the wagon,
and yoked the mules, and then she climbed inside.
She gave Odysseus some clear instructions.   255

"Stranger, get ready; you must go to town,
and I will have you meet the best of all
our people. You seem smart; do as I say.
While we are passing through the fields and farmlands,
you have to follow quickly with the girls   260
behind the mules, and let me lead the way.
Then we will reach the lofty city wall,
which has a scenic port on either side,
and one slim gate, where curved ships are drawn up
along the road: a special spot for each.   265
The meeting place surrounds Poseidon's shrine,
fitted with heavy stones set deep in earth.

And there the workers make the ships' equipment—
cables and sails—and there they plane the oars.
Phaeacians do not care for archery;   270
their passion is for sails and oars and ships,
on which they love to cross the dark-gray ocean.
The people in the town are proud; I worry
that they may speak against me. Someone rude
may say, 'Who is that big strong man with her?   275
Where did she find that stranger? Will he be
her husband? She has got him from a ship,
a foreigner, since no one lives near here,
or else a god, the answer to her prayers,
descended from the sky to hold her tight.   280
Better if she has found herself a man
from elsewhere, since she scorns the people here,
although she has so many noble suitors.'
So they will shame me. I myself would blame
a girl who got too intimate with men   285
before her marriage, and who went against
her loving parents' rules. But listen, stranger,
I will explain the quickest way to gain
my father's help to make your way back home.
Beside the road there is a grove of poplars;   290
it has a fountain, and a meadow round it.
It is Athena's place, where Father has
his orchard and estate,[1] as far from town
as human voice can carry. Sit down there
and wait until I reach my father's house   295
in town. But when you think I have arrived,
walk on and ask directions for the palace
of King Alcinous, my mighty father.
It will be very easy finding it;
a tiny child could guide you there. It is   300
unlike the other houses in Phaeacia.
Go through the courtyard, in the house and on
straight to the Great Hall. You will find my mother
sitting beside the hearth by firelight,
and spinning her amazing purple wool.   305
She leans against a pillar, slaves behind her.
My father has a throne right next to hers;
he sits and sips his wine, just like a god.
But pass him by, embrace my mother's knees
to supplicate. If you do this, you quickly   310
will reach your home, however far it is,
in happiness. If she is good to you,
and looks upon you kindly in her heart,
you can be sure of getting to your house,
back to your family and native land."   315

---

1. The "estate," *temenos*, is land set apart for a king or a temple precinct.

With that, she used her shining whip to urge
the mules to go. They left the river streams,
and trotted well and clipped their hooves along.
She drove an easy pace to let her slaves
and great Odysseus keep up on foot.   320
The sun was setting when they reached the grove,
the famous sanctuary of Athena.
Odysseus sat in it, and at once
he prayed to mighty Zeus' daughter.

                            "Hear me,
daughter of Zeus! Unvanquished Queen! If ever,   325
when that earth-shaker god was wrecking me,
you helped me—may they pity me and give me
kind welcome in Phaeacia." And Athena
heard him but did not yet appear to him,
respecting her own uncle[2] in his fury   330
against Odysseus till he reached home.

BOOK 7

A Magical Kingdom

Odysseus sat patiently and prayed.
Meanwhile, the fine strong mules conveyed the girl
to town; she reached her father's palace gate.
Her brothers gathered round her like immortals.
They took the harness off the mules and brought   5
the clothes inside. She went to her own room.
Eurymedusa, her old slave, had lit
a fire for her. This woman had been brought
from Apeire by ship, long years before.
The people chose to give her to the king,   10
because they bowed before him like a god.
She used to babysit young Nausicaa,
and now she lit her fire and cooked her meal.

Odysseus walked briskly to the town.
Athena helpfully surrounded him   15
with mist that kept him safe from rude remarks
from people who might ask him who he was.
When he had almost reached the lovely city,
bright-eyed Athena met him, like a girl,
young and unmarried, with a water pitcher.   20
She stopped in front of him. Odysseus
said,

"Child, would you escort me to the house
of King Alcinous, who rules this land?
I have been through hard times. I traveled here

2. Poseidon.

from far away; I am a foreigner,   25
and I know no one who lives here in town
or anywhere round here."

           With twinkling eyes
the goddess answered, "Mr. Foreigner,
I will take you to where you want to go.
The king lives near my father's home. But you   30
must walk in silence. Do not look at people,
and ask no questions. People here are not
too keen on strangers coming from abroad,
although they like to cross the sea themselves.
They know their ships go very fast. Poseidon   35
gave them this gift. Their boats can fly like wings,
or quick as thoughts."

           The goddess led him there.
He followed closely in her skipping steps.
The seafaring Phaeacians did not see him
as he passed through the town, since that great goddess,   40
pigtailed Athena, in her care for him
made him invisible with magic mist.
He was amazed to see the ships and harbors
and meeting places of the noblemen,
and high walls set with stakes on top—a wonder!   45
They reached the splendid palace of the king.
Divine Athena winked at him and said,
"Here, Mr. Foreigner, this is the house
you wanted me to take you to. You will
find them, the king and queen, inside at dinner.   50
Do not be scared; go in. The brave succeed
in all adventures, even those who come
from countries far away. First greet the queen.
Arete is her name.[1] The king and queen
have common ancestry—Nausithous.   55
Eurymedon was long ago the king
over the Giants, who were proud and bad.
He killed them, his own people, and then he
got killed as well. His youngest daughter was
named Periboea. She was very pretty.   60
Poseidon slept with her. She had a child,
Nausithous, and he became the king
here in Phaeacia, and he had two sons,
our King Alcinous, and Rhexenor.
Apollo shot that Rhexenor when he   65
was newly married, with no son. He left
a daughter, our Arete, and her uncle,
Alcinous, made her his wife. No woman
is honored as he honors her. She is

---

1. The name suggests "Prayed for" or "Wanted."

precious to him, her children, and the people.   70
We look at her as if she were a goddess,
and point her out when she walks through our town.
She is extremely clever and perceptive;
she solves disputes to help the men she likes.
If she looks on you kindly in her heart,   75
you have a chance of seeing those you love,
and getting back again to your big house
and homeland."

        So bright-eyed Athena left him.
She went from lovely Scheria, across
the tireless sea, to Marathon and Athens,   80
and went inside Erechtheus' palace.[2]

Odysseus approached the royal house,
and stood there by the threshold made of bronze.
His heart was mulling over many things.
The palace of the mighty king was high,   85
and shone like rays of sunlight or of moonlight.
The walls were bronze all over, from the entrance
back to the bedrooms, and along them ran
a frieze of blue. Gold doors held safe the house.
Pillars of silver rose up from the threshold,   90
the lintel silver, and the handle, gold.
Silver and golden dogs stood at each side,
made by Hephaestus[3] with great artistry,
to guard the home of brave Alcinous—
immortal dogs, unaging for all time.   95
At intervals were seats set in the walls,
right from the doorway to the inner rooms,
with soft embroidered throws, the work of women.
Phaeacian lords and ladies sat upon them,
eating and drinking, since they lacked for nothing.   100
Boys made of gold were set on pedestals,
and they held burning torches in their hands,
lighting the hall at night for those at dinner.
The king had fifty slave girls in his house;
some ground the yellow grain upon the millstone,   105
others wove cloth and sat there spinning yarn,
with fingers quick as rustling poplar leaves,
and oil was dripping from the woven fabric.[4]
Just as Phaeacian men have special talent
for launching ships to sea, the women there   110
are expert weavers, since Athena gave them
fine minds and skill to make most lovely things.
Outside the courtyard by the doors there grows

2. Erechtheus was a legendary king of Athens.
3. God of fire and metalworking.
4. The oil may be from the fabric itself if it is wool, or perhaps the women are applying olive oil to the material to make the weaving easier.

an orchard of four acres, hedged around.
The trees are tall, luxuriant with fruit: 115
bright-colored apples, pears and pomegranate,
sweet figs and fertile olives, and the crop
never runs out or withers in the winter,
nor in the summer. Fruit grows all year round.
The West Wind always blows and makes it swell   120
and ripen: mellowing pear on mellowing pear,
apple on apple, grapes on grapes, and figs.
A fertile vineyard too is planted there.
They use the warmer side, a flattened slope,
for drying grapes in sunshine. They pick bunches   125
and trample them, while unripe clusters open
and shed their blooms, and others turn to purple.
There are two springs: one flows all through the garden,
the other gushes from the courtyard threshold,
towards the palace, and the people draw   130
freshwater. So the gods had blessed the house
of King Alcinous with lovely gifts.
Hardened, long-suffering Odysseus
stood there and stared, astonished in his heart,
then quickly strode across the palace threshold.   135
He found the lordly leaders of Phaeacia
pouring drink offerings for sharp-eyed Hermes,
to whom they give libations before bed.
Odysseus went in the house disguised
in mist with which Athena covered him,   140
until he reached Arete and the king.
He threw his arms around Arete's knees,
and all at once, the magic mist dispersed.
They were astonished when they saw the man,
and all fell silent. Then Odysseus   145
said,

      "Queen Arete, child of Rhexenor,
I have had many years of pain and loss.
I beg you, and your husband, and these men
who feast here—may the gods bless you in life,
and may you leave your children wealth and honor.   150
Now help me, please, to get back home, and quickly!
I miss my family. I have been gone
so long it hurts."

                He sat down by the hearth
among the ashes of the fire. They all
were silent till Echeneus spoke up.   155
He was an elder statesman of Phaeacia,
a skillful orator and learned man.
Wanting to help, he said,

"Alcinous,
you know it is not right to leave a stranger
sitting there on the floor beside the hearth   160
among the cinders. Everyone is waiting
for you to give the word. Make him get up,
and seat him on a silver chair, and order
wine to be poured, so we may make libations
to Zeus the Thunderlord, who loves the needy.   165
The house girl ought to bring the stranger food
out from the storeroom."

So Alcinous
reached for Odysseus' hand, and raised
the many-minded hero from the ashes.
He made Laodamas, his favorite son,   170
vacate his chair so he could sit beside him.
The slave girl brought him water in a pitcher
of gold to wash his hands, and poured it out
over a silver bowl, and fetched a table
of polished wood; a humble slave brought out   175
bread and an ample plateful of the meat.
Half-starved and weak, the hero ate and drank.
Majestic King Alcinous addressed
Pontonous, the wine boy.

"Go and mix
a bowl and serve the wine to all our guests,   180
so we may offer drink to thundering Zeus
who blesses those in need." The boy mixed up
the sweet, delicious wine, and filled the cups
for everyone, with first pour for the gods.
They made the offerings and drank as much   185
as they desired, and then Alcinous
said,

"Listen, lords. Hear what my heart commands.
The feast is over; go home, go to bed.
At dawn, we will call more of our best men,
and host the stranger in our halls, and offer   190
fine sacrifices to the gods, then plan
how we may help his journey, so our guest
may travel quickly, without pain or trouble,
encountering no trouble on the way,
however far away it is, until   195
he reaches home. Once there, he must endure
whatever was spun out when he was born
by Fate and by the heavy ones, the Spinners.[5]
But if he is immortal, come from heaven,

5. The Spinners are imagined in Greek mythology as three old female figures who construct
the thread of human destiny—associated here
with Fate, the "share" allotted to humans in life.

the gods have changed their ways, since in the past   200
they used to show themselves to us directly
whenever we would give them hecatombs.
They sit and eat among us. Even if
just one of us meets them alone, out walking,
they do not hide from us; we are close friends,   205
as are the Giants and Cyclopic peoples."

Odysseus, with careful calculation,
said,

         "No, Alcinous, please think again.
I am not like the deathless gods in heaven.
My height is normal. I look like a human.   210
In pain I am a match for any man,
whoever you may know that suffers most.
I could tell many stories of the dangers
that I have suffered through; gods willed it so.
But let me have my meal, despite my grief.   215
The belly is just like a whining dog:
it begs and forces one to notice it,
despite exhaustion or the depths of sorrow.
My heart is full of sorrow, but my stomach
is always telling me to eat and drink.   220
It tells me to forget what I have suffered,
and fill it up. At dawn tomorrow, help me
to reach my homeland, after all this pain.
May I live out my final days in sight
of my own property and slaves and home."   225

They all agreed the stranger's words made sense,
and that he should be sent back home. They poured
drink offerings to the gods, and drank as much
as they desired, then all went home to bed.
Odysseus was left there in the hall,   230
sitting beside Arete and the godlike
Alcinous. The dishes from the feast
were cleaned up by the slaves. White-armed Arete
had noticed his fine clothes, the cloak and shirt
she wove herself, with help from her slave girls.   235
Her words flew out to him as if on wings.

"Stranger, let me be first to speak to you.
Where are you from? And who gave you those clothes?
I thought you said you drifted here by sea?"

Planning his words with careful skill, he answered,   240
"It would be difficult, Your Majesty,
to tell it all; the gods have given me
so many troubles. I will tell you this.
There is an island, far out in the sea,

Ogygia, where the child of Atlas lives,   245
the mighty goddess with smooth braids, the crafty
Calypso, friend to neither gods nor mortals.
A spirit brought me to her hearth, alone,
when Zeus scooped up my ship and with bright lightning
split it apart across the wine-dark sea.   250
All of my comrades, my brave friends, were killed.
I wrapped my arms around the keel and floated
for ten days. On the tenth black night, the gods
carried me till I reached Ogygia,
home of the beautiful and mighty goddess   255
Calypso. Lovingly she cared for me,
vowing to set me free from death and time
forever. But she never swayed my heart.
I stayed for seven years; she gave me clothes
like those of gods, but they were always wet   260
with tears. At last the eighth year rolled around,
and word came down from Zeus that I must go,
and finally her mind was changed. She sent me
upon a well-bound wooden raft, equipped
with food, sweet wine, and clothes as if for gods,   265
and sent a fair warm wind. I sailed the sea
for seventeen long days; on day eighteen,
the murky mountains of your land appeared,
and I was overjoyed, but more bad luck
was hurled at me. Poseidon roused the winds   270
to block me, and he stirred the sea. I sobbed,
and clung there, going nowhere, till my raft
was smashed to pieces by the massive storm.
But I swam through this gulf of water till
the current brought me here. If I had tried   275
to land at once, I would have been swept back
against the crags. I swam a way away,
until I reached a river mouth, which seemed
a perfect spot for landing: it was sheltered
from wind, and smooth, quite free from rocks. So there   280
I flopped and tried to gather up my strength
until the holy nightfall. Then I crawled
out of the rain-fed river to the bank,
and hid inside the bushes, and I heaped
some leaves to cover me. Some god poured down   285
deep sleep. With heavy heart I slept all night
and through the dawn to noon, beneath the leaves.
Then in the afternoon, when sleep released me,
I woke, and saw girls playing on the beach—
your daughter, like a goddess, and her slaves.   290
I prayed to her. One would not think a girl
as young as her would have so much good sense;
young people are not usually so thoughtful.
She was so kind to me; she gave me food
and wine, and had them wash me in the river,   295

and let me have these clothes. Now I have told you
the truth, no matter what."

            Alcinous
said, "Just one of these things my daughter did
was not correct: she should have brought you here
to us herself, escorted by her slave girls,   300
since you had supplicated first to her."

With careful tact Odysseus replied,
"Your daughter is quite wonderful, great king.
Please do not blame her. She told me to come
here with her slaves, but I was too embarrassed,   305
and nervous. I thought you might get annoyed
at seeing me. We humans on this earth
are apt to be suspicious."

            And the king
replied, "My heart is not the type to feel
anger for no good reason. Moderation   310
is always best. Athena, Zeus, Apollo,
what a congenial man you are! I wish
you would stay here, and marry my own daughter,
and be my son. I would give you a home
and wealth if you would like to stay. If not,   315
we will not keep you here against your will.
May Zeus not have it so! As for your journey,
I give my word that you can go tomorrow.
Lying down, lulled to sleep, you will be rowed
across the peaceful sea until you reach   320
your land and home, or anywhere you want,
even beyond Euboea, which our people
saw when they carried fair-haired Rhadamanthus
to visit Tityus, the son of Gaia.[6]
It is supposed to be the farthest shore   325
on earth, but they were there and back that day,
not even tired. That shows just how fine
my ships are, and my men who stir the sea
with oars."

           At that Odysseus, who had
endured so much, was happy, and he prayed,   330

"O Father Zeus, may everything come true,
just as Alcinous has said. So may
his fame burn bright forever on the earth,
and may I reach my home."

---

6. Rhadamanthus is the mythical son of Zeus
and Europa, closely associated with Crete. The
story of his visit to Tityus is entirely unknown
beyond this passage.

                              Then at these words,
white-armed Arete called to her attendants   335
to put a bed out on the porch and lay
fine purple blankets on it and to spread
covers and woolly quilts across the top.
With torches in their hands they bustled out.
They made the bed up neatly, very fast,   340
then came and called Odysseus.

                              "Now guest,
get up and come outside, your bed is ready."

Odysseus was glad to go to sleep
after his long adventures, on that bed
surrounded by the rustling of the porch.   345
Alcinous was sleeping in his room,
beside his wife, who made their bed and shared it.

BOOK 8

The Songs of a Poet

Soon Dawn appeared and touched the sky with roses.
Majestic, holy King Alcinous
leapt out of bed, as did Odysseus,
the city-sacker. Then the blessed king,
mighty Alcinous, led out his guest   5
to the Phaeacian council by the ships.
They sat there side by side on polished stones.
Meanwhile, Athena walked all through the town,
appearing like the royal messenger.
To help Odysseus' journey home,   10
she stood beside each man in turn and said,

"My lord, come to the meeting place, to learn
about the visitor to our king's home.
Despite his wanderings by sea, he looks
like an immortal god."

                              So she roused up   15
the hearts and minds of each, and soon the seats
of council were filled up; the men assembled.
Seeing Laertes' clever son, the crowd
marveled. Athena poured unearthly charm
upon his head and shoulders, and she made him   20
taller and sturdier, so these Phaeacians
would welcome and respect him, when he managed
the many trials of skill that they would set
to test him. When the people were assembled,
Alcinous addressed them.

                   "Hear me, leaders   25
and chieftains of Phaeacia. I will tell you
the promptings of my heart. This foreigner—
I do not know his name—came wandering
from west or east and showed up at my house.
He begs and prays for help to travel on.   30
Let us assist him, as we have before
with other guests: no visitor has ever
been forced to linger in my house. We always
give them safe passage home. Now let us launch
a ship for her maiden voyage on the water,   35
and choose a crew of fifty-two, the men
selected as the best, and lash the oars
beside the benches. Then return to shore,
and come to my house. Let the young men hurry
to cook a feast. I will provide supplies,   40
plenty for everyone. And I invite
you also, lords, to welcome him with me.
Do not refuse! We also must invite
Demodocus, the poet. Gods inspire him,
so any song he chooses to perform   45
is wonderful to hear."

                 He led the way.
The lords went with him, and the house boy fetched
the bard. The fifty-two select young men
went to the shore, just as the king commanded.
They reached the restless salty sea, and launched   50
the black ship on the depths, set up the mast
and sails, and fastened in the oars, by tying
each to its leather thole-strap,[1] all in order.
They spread the white sails wide, and moored the ship
out in the water. Then the men walked up   55
towards the mighty palace of the king.
The halls and porticoes were thronged with people,
both old and young. To feed his many guests
Alcinous killed twelve sheep, and eight boars
with silver tusks, and two slow-lumbering cows.   60
Skinning the animals, they cooked a feast.
The house boy brought the poet, whom the Muse
adored. She gave him two gifts, good and bad:
she took his sight away, but gave sweet song.
The wine boy brought a silver-studded chair   65
and propped it by a pillar, in the middle
of all the guests, and by a peg he hung
the poet's lyre above his head and helped him
to reach it, and he set a table by him,
and a bread basket and a cup of wine   70
to drink whenever he desired. They all

---

1. Tholes are pins set in the side of a boat to keep the oar in place.

took food. When they were satisfied, the Muse
prompted the bard to sing of famous actions,
an episode whose fame has touched the sky:
Achilles' and Odysseus' quarrel— 75
how at a splendid sacrificial feast,
they argued bitterly, and Agamemnon
was glad because the best of the Achaeans
were quarreling, since when he had consulted
the oracle at Pytho, crossing over 80
the entry stone, Apollo had foretold
that this would be the start of suffering
for Greeks and Trojans, through the plans of Zeus.[2]
So sang the famous bard. Odysseus
with his strong hands picked up his heavy cloak 85
of purple, and he covered up his face.
He was ashamed to let them see him cry.
Each time the singer paused, Odysseus
wiped tears, drew down the cloak and poured a splash
of wine out of his goblet, for the gods. 90
But each time, the Phaeacian nobles urged
the bard to sing again—they loved his songs.
So he would start again; Odysseus
would moan and hide his head beneath his cloak.
Only Alcinous could see his tears, 95
since he was sitting next to him, and heard
his sobbing. So he quickly spoke.

                    "My lords!
We have already satisfied our wish
for feasting, and the lyre, the feast's companion.
Now let us go outside and set up contests 100
in every sport, so when our guest goes home
he can tell all his friends we are the best
at boxing, wrestling, long-jumping, and sprinting."

With that he led the way; the others followed.
The boy took down the lyre from its peg 105
and took Demodocus' hand to lead him
out with the crowd who went to watch the games.
Many young athletes stood there: Acroneüs,
Ocyalus, Elatreus, Nauteus,
Thoön, Anchialus, Eretmeus, 110
Anabesineus and Ponteus,
Prymneus, Proreus, Amphialus,
the son of Polynaus, son of Tecton,[3]
and Naubolus' son, Euryalus,
like Ares, cause of ruin. In his looks 115

2. Apparently the Delphic oracle ("Pytho") told Agamemnon that Troy would be destroyed when the "best of the Achaeans" were quarreling.

3. These names are all invented to suggest the Phaeacians' skill in seafaring.

and strength, he was the best in all Phaeacia,
after Laodamas. Three sons of great
Alcinous stood up: Laodamas,
godlike Clytoneus, and Halius.
First came the footrace. They lined up, then dashed   120
all in an instant, right around the track
so fast they raised the dust up from the field.
Clytoneus was the best by far at sprinting:
he raced past all the others by the length
of a field plowed by mules,[4] and reached the crowd.   125
Next came the brutal sport of wrestling,
in which Euryalus was best. In jumping,
Amphialus excelled. And at the discus,
by far the best of all was Elatreus.
The prince Laodamas excelled at boxing.   130
They all enjoyed the games. When they were over,
Laodamas, Alcinous' son,
said,

     "Now my friends, we ought to ask the stranger
if he plays any sports. His build is strong;
his legs and arms and neck are very sturdy,   135
and he is in his prime, though he has been
broken by suffering. No pain can shake
a man as badly as the sea, however
strong he once was."

     Euryalus replied,
"You are quite right, Laodamas. Why not   140
call out to challenge him yourself?"

     The noble
son of Alcinous agreed with him.
He stood up in the middle of them all
and called Odysseus.

     "Come here!" he said.
"Now you, sir! You should try our games as well,   145
if you know any sports; it seems you would.
Nothing can be more glorious for a man,
in a whole lifetime, than what he achieves
with hands and feet. So try, set care aside.
Soon you will travel, since your ship is launched.   150
The crew is standing by."

     Odysseus
thought carefully—he had a plan. He answered,

---

4. The length of land that could be plowed in a day was a standard unit of measurement. The distance imagined here is probably about 200 feet (an unlikely margin for a race).

"Laodamas, why mock me with this challenge?
My heart is set on sorrow, not on games,
since I have suffered and endured so much   155
that now I only want to get back home.
I sit here praying to your king and people
to grant my wish."

        Euryalus responded
with outright taunting.

        "Stranger, I suppose
you must be ignorant of all athletics.   160
I know your type. The captain of a crew
of merchant sailors, you roam round at sea
and only care about your freight and cargo,
keeping close watch on your ill-gotten gains.
You are no athlete."

        With a scowl, he answered,   165
"What crazy arrogance from you, you stranger!
The gods do not bless everyone the same,
with equal gifts of body, mind, or speech.
One man is weak, but gods may crown his words
with loveliness. Men gladly look to him;   170
his speech is steady, with calm dignity.
He stands out from his audience, and when
he walks through town, the people look at him
as if he were a god. Another man
has godlike looks but no grace in his words.   175
Like you—you look impressive, and a god
could not improve your body. But your mind
is crippled. You have stirred my heart to anger
with these outrageous comments. I am not
lacking experience of sports and games.   180
When I was young, I trusted my strong arms
and was among the first. Now pain has crushed me.
I have endured the agonies of war,
and struggled through the dangers of the sea.
But you have challenged me and stung my heart.   185
Despite my suffering, I will compete."

With that he leapt up, cloak and all, and seized
a massive discus, heavier than that
used by the others. He spun around, drew back
his arm and from his brawny hand he hurled.   190
The stone went humming. The Phaeacians, known
for rowing, ducked down cowering beneath
its arc; it flew beyond the other pegs.
Athena marked the spot. In human guise
she spoke.

"A blind man, stranger, could discern   195
this mark by groping. It is far ahead
of all the others. You can celebrate!
You won this round, and none of them will ever
throw further—or as far!"

                    Odysseus
was thrilled to realize he had a friend   200
to take his side, and with a lighter heart,
he told the young Phaeacians,

                              "Try to match this!
If you can do it, I will throw another,
as far or farther. You have made me angry,
so I will take you on in any sport.   205
Come on! In boxing, wrestling, or sprinting,
I will compete with anyone, except
Laodamas: he is my host. Who would
fight with a friend? A man who challenges
those who have welcomed him in a strange land   210
is worthless and a fool; he spites himself.
But I will challenge any of you others.
Test my ability, let me know yours.
I am not weak at any sport men practice.
I know the way to hold a polished bow.   215
I always was the first to hit my man
out of a horde of enemies, though many
comrades stood by me, arrows taking air.
At Troy, when the Achaeans shot their bows,
the only one superior to me   220
was Philoctetes. Other men who eat
their bread on earth are all worse shots than me.
But I will not compete with super-archers,
with Heracles or Eurytus, who risked
competing with the gods at archery.   225
Apollo was enraged at him and killed him
as soon as he proposed it. He died young
and did not reach old age in his own home.
And I can throw a spear beyond the shots
that others reach with arrows. I am only   230
concerned that one of you may win the footrace:
I lost my stamina and my legs weakened
during my time at sea, upon the raft;
I could not do my exercise routine."

The crowd was silent, but Alcinous   235
said, "Sir, you have expressed, with fine good manners,
your wish to show your talents, and your anger
at that man who stood up in this arena
and mocked you, as no one who understands
how to speak properly would ever do.   240

Now listen carefully, so you may tell
your own fine friends at home when you are feasting
beside your wife and children, and remember
our skill in all the deeds we have accomplished
from our forefathers' time till now. We are   245
not brilliant at wrestling or boxing,
but we are quick at sprinting, and with ships
we are the best. We love the feast, the lyre,
dancing and varied clothes, hot baths and bed.
But now let the best dancers of Phaeacia   250
perform, so that our guest may tell his friends
when he gets home, how excellent we are
at seafaring, at running, and at dancing
and song. Let someone bring the well-tuned lyre
from inside for Demodocus—go quickly!"   255

So spoke the king. The house boy brought the lyre.
The people chose nine referees to check
the games were fair. They leveled out a floor
for dancing, with a fine wide ring around.
The house boy gave Demodocus the lyre.   260
He walked into the middle, flanked by boys,
young and well trained, who tapped their feet performing
the holy dance, their quick legs bright with speed.
Odysseus was wonder-struck to see it.
The poet strummed and sang a charming song   265
about the love of fair-crowned Aphrodite
for Ares, who gave lavish gifts to her
and shamed the bed of Lord Hephaestus, where
they secretly had sex. The Sun God saw them,
and told Hephaestus—bitter news for him.[5]   270
He marched into his forge to get revenge,
and set the mighty anvil on its block,
and hammered chains so strong that they could never
be broken or undone. He was so angry
at Ares. When his trap was made, he went   275
inside the room of his beloved bed,
and twined the mass of cables all around
the bedposts, and then hung them from the ceiling,
like slender spiderwebs, so finely made
that nobody could see them, even gods: 280
the craftsmanship was so ingenious.
When he had set that trap across the bed,
he traveled to the cultured town of Lemnos,
which was his favorite place in all the world.
Ares the golden rider had kept watch.   285
He saw Hephaestus, famous wonder-worker,
leaving his house, and went inside himself;

---

5. Aphrodite, the goddess of sex, was married   Ares, god of war; Helius, the sun god, who
to the god Hephaestus, but had an affair with   sees whatever the sun sees, revealed the truth.

he wanted to make love with Aphrodite.
She had returned from visiting her father,
the mighty son of Cronus; there she sat.   290
Then Ares took her hand and said to her,

"My darling, let us go to bed. Hephaestus
is out of town; he must have gone to Lemnos
to see the Sintians whose speech is strange."

She was excited to lie down with him;   295
they went to bed together. But the chains
ingenious Hephaestus had created
wrapped tight around them, so they could not move
or get up. Then they knew that they were trapped.
The limping god drew near—before he reached   300
the land of Lemnos, he had turned back home.
Troubled at heart, he came towards his house.
Standing there in the doorway, he was seized
by savage rage. He gave a mighty shout,
calling to all the gods,

                        "O Father Zeus,   305
and all you blessed gods who live forever,
look! You may laugh, but it is hard to bear.
See how my Aphrodite, child of Zeus,
is disrespecting me for being lame.
She loves destructive Ares, who is strong   310
and handsome. I am weak. I blame my parents.
If only I had not been born! But come,
see where those two are sleeping in my bed,
as lovers. I am horrified to see it.
But I predict they will not want to lie   315
longer like that, however great their love.
Soon they will want to wake up, but my trap
and chains will hold them fast, until her father
pays back the price I gave him for his daughter.
Her eyes stare at me like a dog. She is   320
so beautiful, but lacking self-control."

The gods assembled at his house: Poseidon,
Earth-Shaker, helpful Hermes, and Apollo.
The goddesses stayed home, from modesty.
The blessed gods who give good things were standing   325
inside the doorway, and they burst out laughing,
at what a clever trap Hephaestus set.
And as they looked, they said to one another,

"Crime does not pay! The slow can beat the quick,
as now Hephaestus, who is lame and slow,   330
has used his skill to catch the fastest sprinter
of all those on Olympus. Ares owes
the price for his adultery." They gossiped.

Apollo, son of Zeus, then said to Hermes,
"Hermes my brother, would you like to sleep   335
with golden Aphrodite, in her bed,
even weighed down by mighty chains?"

                                 And Hermes
the sharp-eyed messenger replied, "Ah, brother,
Apollo lord of archery: if only!
I would be bound three times as tight or more   340
and let you gods and all your wives look on,
if only I could sleep with Aphrodite."

Then laughter rose among the deathless gods.
Only Poseidon did not laugh. He begged
and pleaded with Hephaestus to release   345
Ares. He told the wonder-working god,

"Now let him go! I promise he will pay
the penalty in full among the gods,
just as you ask."

                         The famous limping god
replied, "Poseidon, do not ask me this.   350
It is disgusting, bailing scoundrels out.
How could I bind you, while the gods look on,
if Ares should escape his bonds and debts?"
Poseidon, Lord of Earthquakes, answered him,
"Hephaestus, if he tries to dodge this debt,   355
I promise I will pay."

                           The limping god
said, "Then, in courtesy to you, I must
do as you ask." So using all his strength,
Hephaestus loosed the chains. The pair of lovers
were free from their constraints, and both jumped up.   360
Ares went off to Thrace, while Aphrodite
smiled as she went to Cyprus, to the island
of Paphos, where she had a fragrant altar
and sanctuary. The Graces washed her there,
and rubbed her with the magic oil that glows   365
upon immortals, and they dressed her up
in gorgeous clothes. She looked astonishing.

That was the poet's song. Odysseus
was happy listening; so were they all.
And then Alcinous told Halius   370
to dance with Laodamas; no one danced
as well as them. They took a purple ball
which Polybus the artisan had made them.
One boy would leap and toss it to the clouds;
the other would jump up, feet off the ground,   375

and catch it easily before he landed.
After they practiced throwing it straight upwards,
they danced across the fertile earth, crisscrossing,
constantly trading places. Other boys
who stood around the field were beating time   380
with noisy stomping. Then Odysseus
said,

      "King of many citizens, great lord,
you boasted that your dancers are the best,
and it is true. I feel amazed to see
this marvelous show."

                That pleased the reverend king.   385
He spoke at once to his seafaring people.
"Hear me, Phaeacian leaders, lords and nobles.
The stranger seems extremely wise to me.
So let us give him gifts, as hosts should do
to guests in friendship. Twelve lords rule our people,   390
with me as thirteenth lord. Let us each bring
a pound of precious gold and laundered clothes,
a tunic and a cloak. Then pile them up,
and let our guest take all these gifts, and go
to dinner with them, happy in his heart.   395
Euryalus should tell him he is sorry,
and give a special gift, since what he said
was inappropriate."

             They all agreed,
and each sent back a deputy to fetch
the presents. And Euryalus spoke out.   400

"My lord Alcinous, great king of kings,
I will apologize, as you command.
And I will give him this bronze sword which has
a silver handle, and a scabbard carved
of ivory—a precious gift for him."   405
With that he put the silver-studded sword
into Odysseus' hands; his words
flew out.

      "I welcome you, sir. Be our guest.
If something rude of any kind was said,
let the winds take it. May the gods allow you   410
to reach your home and see your wife again,
since you have suffered so long, far away
from those who love you."

               And Odysseus
said, "Friend, I wish you well. May gods protect you,
and may you never miss the sword you gave me."   415

With that, he strapped the silver-studded sword
across his back, and as the sun went down
the precious gifts were brought to him. The slaves
took them inside Alcinous' house.
The princes piled the lovely things beside   420
the queen, their mother. King Alcinous
led everyone inside and had them sit
on upright chairs. He told Arete,

                              "Wife,
bring out our finest chest, and put inside it
a tunic and a freshly laundered cloak.   425
Set a bronze cauldron on the fire to boil,
so he can take a bath. Then let him see
the precious gifts our noblemen have brought,
and then enjoy the banquet and the song.
I also have a gift: a splendid cup   430
of gold. I hope he always thinks of me
whenever he pours offerings to Zeus
and other gods."

                    Arete told her slaves
to quickly set a mighty pot to warm,
for washing. So upon the blazing flames   435
they set the cauldron and poured water in,
and heaped up wood. The fire licked around
the belly of the tub and warmed the water.
Arete brought from her own room a chest
to give the guest, and packed the gifts inside—   440
the clothes and gold that they had given him;
and she herself put in a cloak and tunic.
She told him,

                "Watch the lid, and tie it closed,
so nobody can rob you as you travel,
when you are lulled to sleep on your black ship."   445

Odysseus, experienced in loss,
took careful note. He shut the lid and tied
a cunning knot that he had learned from Circe.
Then right away the slave girl led him off
towards the bath to wash. He was delighted   450
to see hot water. He had not been bathed
since he had left the home of curly-haired
Calypso, who had taken care of him
as if he were a god. The slave girls washed him,
rubbed oil on him and dressed him in a tunic   455
and fine wool mantle. Freshly bathed, he joined
the men at wine. And there stood Nausicaa,
divinely beautiful, beside a pillar
that held the palace roof. She was amazed
to see Odysseus. Her words flew fast.   460

"Good-bye then, stranger, but remember me
when you reach home, because you owe your life
to me. I helped you first."

                          Odysseus
replied politely, "Nausicaa, may Zeus,
husband of Hera, mighty Lord of Thunder,   465
allow me to go back and see my home.
There I shall pray to you as to a god,
forever, princess, since you saved my life."
With that he went to sit beside the king.

Now they were serving out the food and pouring   470
wine, and the steward led out to the center
Demodocus, the well-respected poet.
He sat him in the middle of the banquet,
against a pillar. Then Odysseus
thought fast, and sliced a helping from the pig,   475
all richly laced with fat. The plate of meat
had plenty left. He told the boy,

                               "Go take
this meat and give it to Demodocus.
Despite my grief, I would be glad to meet him.
Poets are honored by all those who live   480
on earth. The Muse has taught them how to sing;
she loves the race of poets."

                         So the house boy
handed it to Demodocus. He took it
gladly; and everybody took their food.
When they had had enough to eat and drink,   485
the clever mastermind of many schemes
said,

     "You are wonderful, Demodocus!
I praise you more than anyone; Apollo,[6]
or else the Muse, the child of Zeus, has taught you.
You tell so accurately what the Greeks   490
achieved, and what they suffered, there at Troy,
as if you had been there, or heard about it
from somebody who was. So sing the story
about the Wooden Horse, which Epeius
built with Athena's help. Odysseus   495
dragged it inside and to the citadel,
filled up with men to sack the town. If you
can tell that as it happened, I will say
that you truly are blessed with inspiration."

6. God associated with poetry, who carried the lyre.

A god inspired the bard to sing. He started   500
with how the Greeks set fire to their camp
and then embarked and sailed away. Meanwhile,
Odysseus brought in a gang of men
into the heart of Troy, inside the horse.
The Trojans pulled the thing up to the summit,   505
and sat around discussing what to do.
Some said, "We ought to strike the wood with swords!"
Others said, "Drag it higher up and hurl it
down from the rocks!" But some said they should leave it
to pacify the gods. So it would be.   510
The town was doomed to ruin when it took
that horse, chock-full of fighters bringing death
to Trojans. And he sang how the Achaeans
poured from the horse, in ambush from the hollow,
and sacked the city; how they scattered out,   515
destroying every neighborhood. Like Ares,
Odysseus, with Menelaus, rushed
to find Deiphobus' house,[7] and there
he won at last, through dreadful violence,
thanks to Athena. So the poet sang.   520

Odysseus was melting into tears;
his cheeks were wet with weeping, as a woman
weeps, as she falls to wrap her arms around
her husband, fallen fighting for his home
and children. She is watching as he gasps   525
and dies. She shrieks, a clear high wail, collapsing
upon his corpse. The men are right behind.
They hit her shoulders with their spears and lead her
to slavery, hard labor, and a life
of pain. Her face is marked with her despair.   530
In that same desperate way, Odysseus
was crying. No one noticed that his eyes
were wet with tears, except Alcinous,
who sat right next to him and heard his sobs.
Quickly he spoke to his seafaring people.   535

"Listen, my lords and nobles of Phaeacia!
Demodocus should stop and set aside
the lyre, since what he sings does not give pleasure
to everyone. Throughout this heavenly song,
since dinnertime, our guest has been in pain,   540
grieving. A heavy burden weighs his heart.
Let the song end, so we can all be happy,
both guest and hosts. That would be best by far.
This send-off party and these precious gifts,

7. After Paris was killed, Helen was appropri-   Odysseus killed him and mangled his corpse,
ated by Deiphobus, another Trojan prince;   and Menelaus reclaimed his wife.

which we give out of friendship, are for him,   545
our guest of honor. Any man of sense
will treat a guest in need like his own brother.
Stranger, now answer all my questions clearly,
not with evasion; frankness would be best.
What did your parents name you? With what name   550
are you known to your people? Surely no one
in all the world is nameless, poor or noble,
since parents give a name to every child
at birth. And also tell me of your country,
your people, and your city, so our ships,   555
steered by their own good sense, may take you there.
Phaeacians have no need of men at helm
nor rudders, as in other ships. Our boats
intuit what is in the minds of men,
and know all human towns and fertile fields.   560
They rush at full tilt right across the gulf
of salty sea, concealed in mist and clouds.
They have no fear of damages or loss.
But once I heard Nausithous, my father,
say that Poseidon hates us for the help   565
we give to take our guests across the sea,
and that one day a ship of ours would suffer
shipwreck on its return; a mighty mountain
would block our town from sight. So Father said.
Perhaps the god will bring these things to pass   570
or not, as is his will. But come now, tell me
about your wanderings: describe the places,
the people, and the cities you have seen.
Which ones were wild and cruel, unwelcoming,
and which were kind to visitors, respecting   575
the gods? And please explain why you were crying,
sobbing your heart out when you heard him sing
what happened to the Greeks at Troy. The gods
devised and measured out this devastation,
to make a song for those in times to come.   580
Did you lose somebody at Troy? A man
from your wife's family, perhaps her father
or brother? Ties of marriage are the closest
after the bonds of blood. Or else perhaps
you lost the friend who knew you best of all?   585
A friend can be as close as any brother."

BOOK 9

A Pirate in a Shepherd's Cave

Wily Odysseus, the lord of lies,
answered,

          "My lord Alcinous, great king,
it is a splendid thing to hear a poet
as talented as this. His voice is godlike.
I think that there can be no greater pleasure   5
than when the whole community enjoys
a banquet, as we sit inside the house,
and listen to the singer, and the tables
are heaped with bread and meat; the wine boy ladles
drink from the bowl and pours it into cups.   10
To me this seems ideal, a thing of beauty.
Now something prompted you to ask about
my own sad story. I will tell you, though
the memory increases my despair.
Where shall I start? Where can I end? The gods   15
have given me so much to cry about.
First I will tell my name, so we will be
acquainted and if I survive, you can
be my guest in my distant home one day.
I am Odysseus, Laertes' son,   20
known for my many clever tricks and lies.
My fame extends to heaven, but I live
in Ithaca, where shaking forest hides
Mount Neriton. Close by are other islands:
Dulichium, and wooded Zacynthus   25
and Same. All the others face the dawn;
my Ithaca is set apart, most distant,
facing the dark.[1] It is a rugged land,
but good at raising children. To my eyes
no country could be sweeter. As you know,   30
divine Calypso held me in her cave,
wanting to marry me; and likewise Circe,
the trickster, trapped me, and she wanted me
to be her husband. But she never swayed
my heart, since when a man is far from home,   35
living abroad, there is no sweeter thing
than his own native land and family.
Now let me tell you all the trouble Zeus
has caused me on my journey home from Troy.
A blast of wind pushed me off course towards   40
the Cicones in Ismarus.[2] I sacked

1. The suggestion is that Ithaca is farthest west, facing the setting sun ("the darkness"), whereas the other islands are more to the east. It is impossible to reconcile this claim with actual geography.

2. The Cicones, a Thracian people, were allies of Troy. But the passage does not suggest that Odysseus' piracy is motivated by any particular military objective.

the town and killed the men. We took their wives
and shared their riches equally among us.
Then I said we must run away. Those fools
refused to listen. They were drinking wine   45
excessively, and killing sheep and cattle
along the beach. The Cicones called out
to neighbors on the mainland, who were strong
and numerous, and skilled at horseback fighting,
and if need be, on foot. They came like leaves   50
and blossoms in the spring at dawn. Then Zeus
gave us bad luck. Poor us! The enemy
assembled round the ships and fought with swords
of bronze. And while the holy morning light
was bright and strong, we held them off, though they   55
outnumbered us. But when the sun turned round
and dipped, the hour when oxen are released,
the Cicones began to overpower
us Greeks. Six well-armed members of my crew
died from each ship. The rest of us survived,   60
and we escaped the danger. We prepared
to sail away with heavy hearts, relieved
to be alive, but grieving for our friends.
Before we launched the ships, we called aloud
three times to each of our poor lost companions,   65
slaughtered at the hands of Cicones.

The Cloud Lord Zeus hurled North Wind at our ships,
a terrible typhoon, and covered up
the sea and earth with fog. Night fell from heaven
and seized us and our ships keeled over sideways;   70
the sails were ripped three times by blasting wind.
Scared for our lives, we hoisted down the sails
and rowed with all our might towards the shore.
We stayed there for two days and nights, exhausted,
eating our hearts with pain. When bright-haired Dawn   75
brought the third morning, we set up our masts,
unfurled the shining sails, and climbed aboard.
The wind blew straight, the pilots steered, and I
would have come safely home, to my own land,
but as I rounded Malea, a current   80
and blast of wind pushed me off course, away
from Cythera. For nine days I was swept
by stormy winds across the fish-filled sea.
On the tenth day, I landed on the island
of those who live on food from lotus flowers.   85
We gathered water, and my crew prepared
a meal. We picnicked by the ships, then I
chose two men, and one slave to make the third,
to go and scout. We needed to find out
what kind of people lived there on that island.   90
The scouts encountered humans, Lotus-Eaters,

who did not hurt them. They just shared with them
their sweet delicious fruit. But as they ate it,
they lost the will to come back and bring news
to me. They wanted only to stay there,   95
feeding on lotus with the Lotus-Eaters.
They had forgotten home. I dragged them back
in tears, forced them on board the hollow ships,
pushed them below the decks, and tied them up.
I told the other men, the loyal ones,   100
to get back in the ships, so no one else
would taste the lotus and forget about
our destination. They embarked and sat
along the rowing benches, side by side,
and struck the grayish water with their oars.   105

With heavy hearts we sailed along and reached
the country of high-minded Cyclopes,
the mavericks. They put their trust in gods,
and do not plant their food from seed, nor plow,
and yet the barley, grain, and clustering wine-grapes   110
all flourish there, increased by rain from Zeus.
They hold no councils, have no common laws,
but live in caves on lofty mountaintops,
and each makes laws for his own wife and children,
without concern for what the others think.   115
A distance from this island is another,
across the water, slantways from the harbor,
level and thickly wooded. Countless goats
live there but people never visit it.
No hunters labor through its woods to scale   120
its hilly peaks. There are no flocks of sheep,
no fields of plowland—it is all untilled,
unsown and uninhabited by humans.
Only the bleating goats live there and graze.
Cyclopic people have no red-cheeked ships[3]   125
and no shipwright among them who could build
boats, to enable them to row across
to other cities, as most people do,
crossing the sea to visit one another.
With boats they could have turned this island into   130
a fertile colony, with proper harvests.
By the gray shore there lie well-watered meadows,
where vines would never fail. There is flat land
for plowing, and abundant crops would grow
in the autumn; there is richness underground.   135
The harbor has good anchorage; there is
no need of anchor stones or ropes or cables.
The ships that come to shore there can remain
beached safely till the sailors wish to leave

3. Ships were decorated with red at the prow.

and fair winds blow. Up by the harbor head   140
freshwater gushes down beneath the caves.
The poplars grow around it. There we sailed:
the gods were guiding us all through the darkness.
Thick fog wrapped round our ships and in the sky
the moon was dark and clothed in clouds, so we   145
saw nothing of the island. None of us
could see the great waves rolling in towards
the land, until we rowed right to the beach.
We lowered all the sails and disembarked
onto the shore, and there we fell asleep.   150

When early Dawn shone forth with rosy fingers,
we roamed around that island full of wonders.
The daughters of the great King Zeus, the nymphs,
drove out the mountain goats so that my crew
could eat. On seeing them, we dashed to fetch   155
our javelins and bows from on board ship.
We split into three groups, took aim and shot.
Some god gave us good hunting. All twelve crews
had nine goats each, and ten for mine. We sat there
all day till sunset, eating meat and drinking   160
our strong red wine. The ships' supply of that
had not run out; when we had sacked the holy
citadel of the Cicones, we all
took gallons of it, poured in great big pitchers.
We looked across the narrow strip of water   165
at the Cyclopic island, saw their smoke,
and heard the baaing of their sheep and goats.
The sun went down and in the hours of darkness
we lay and slept on shore beside the sea.
But when the rosy hands of Dawn appeared,   170
I called my men together and addressed them.

"My loyal friends! Stay here, the rest of you,
while with my boat and crew I go to check
who those men are, find out if they are wild,
lawless aggressors, or the type to welcome   175
strangers, and fear the gods."

                              With that, I climbed
on board and told my crew to come with me
and then untie the cables of the ship.
Quickly they did so, sat along the benches,
and struck the whitening water with their oars.   180
The journey was not long. Upon arrival,
right at the edge of land, beside the sea,
we saw a high cave overhung with laurel,
the home of several herds of sheep and goats.
Around that cave was built a lofty courtyard,   185
of deep-set stones, with tall pines rising up,

and leafy oaks. There lived a massive man
who shepherded his flocks all by himself.
He did not go to visit other people,
but kept apart, and did not know the ways 190
of custom. In his build he was a wonder,
a giant, not like men who live on bread,
but like a wooded peak in airy mountains,
rising alone above the rest.

                I told
my loyal crew to guard the ship, while I 195
would go with just twelve chosen men, my favorites.
I took a goatskin full of dark sweet wine
that I was given by Apollo's priest,
Maron the son of Euanthes, who lived
inside the shady grove on Ismarus. 200
In reverence to the god, I came to help him,
and save his wife and son. He gave me gifts:
a silver bowl and seven pounds of gold,
well wrought, and siphoned off some sweet strong wine,
and filled twelve jars for me—a godlike drink. 205
The slaves knew nothing of this wine; it was
known just to him, his wife, and one house girl.
Whenever he was drinking it, he poured
a single shot into a cup, and added
twenty of water, and a marvelous smell 210
rose from the bowl, and all would long to taste it.
I filled a big skin up with it, and packed
provisions in a bag—my heart suspected
that I might meet a man of courage, wild,
and lacking knowledge of the normal customs. 215

We soon were at the cave, but did not find
the Cyclops; he was pasturing his flocks.
We went inside and looked at everything.
We saw his crates weighed down with cheese, and pens
crammed full of lambs divided up by age: 220
the newborns, middlings, and those just weaned.
There were well-crafted bowls and pails for milking,
all full of whey. My crew begged, "Let us grab
some cheese and quickly drive the kids and lambs
out of their pens and down to our swift ships, 225
and sail away across the salty water!"
That would have been the better choice. But I
refused. I hoped to see him, and find out
if he would give us gifts. In fact he brought
no joy to my companions. Then we lit 230
a fire, and made a sacrifice, and ate
some cheese, and sat to wait inside the cave
until he brought his flocks back home. He came
at dinnertime, and brought a load of wood

to make a fire. He hurled it noisily   235
into the cave. We were afraid, and cowered
towards the back. He drove his ewes and nannies
inside to milk them, but he left the rams
and he-goats in the spacious yard outside.
He lifted up the heavy stone and set it   240
to block the entrance of the cave. It was
a rock so huge and massive, twenty-two
strong carts could not have dragged it from the threshold.
He sat, and all in order milked his ewes
and she-goats, then he set the lambs to suck   245
beside each bleating mother. Then he curdled
half of the fresh white milk, set that aside
in wicker baskets, and the rest he stored
in pails so he could drink it with his dinner.
When he had carefully performed his chores,   250
he lit a fire, then looked around and saw us.
'Strangers! Who are you? Where did you come from
across the watery depths? Are you on business,
or roaming round without a goal, like pirates,
who risk their lives at sea to bring disaster   255
to other people?'

       So he spoke. His voice,
so deep and booming, and his giant size,
made our hearts sink in terror. Even so,
I answered,

       'We are Greeks, come here from Troy.
The winds have swept us off in all directions   260
across the vast expanse of sea, off course
from our planned route back home. Zeus willed it so.
We are proud to be the men of Agamemnon,
the son of Atreus, whose fame is greatest
under the sky, for sacking that vast city   265
and killing many people. Now we beg you,
here at your knees, to grant a gift, as is
the norm for hosts and guests. Please, sir, my lord:
respect the gods. We are your suppliants,
and Zeus is on our side, since he takes care   270
of visitors, guest-friends, and those in need.'

Unmoved he said, 'Well, foreigner, you are
a fool, or from some very distant country.
You order me to fear the gods! My people
think nothing of that Zeus with his big scepter,   275
nor any god; our strength is more than theirs.
If I spare you or spare your friends, it will not
be out of fear of Zeus. I do the bidding
of my own heart. But are you going far

in that fine ship of yours, or somewhere near?' 280
He spoke to test me, but I saw right through him.
I know how these things work. I answered him
deceitfully.

        'Poseidon, the Earth-Shaker,
shipwrecked me at the far end of your island.
He pushed us in; wind dashed us on the rocks. 285
We barely managed to survive.'

                 But he
made no reply and showed no mercy. Leaping
up high, he reached his hands towards my men,
seized two, and knocked them hard against the ground
like puppies, and the floor was wet with brains. 290
He ripped them limb by limb to make his meal,
then ate them like a lion on the mountains,
devouring flesh, entrails, and marrow bones,
and leaving nothing. Watching this disaster,
we wept and lifted up our hands in prayer 295
to Zeus. We felt so helpless. When the Cyclops
had filled his massive belly with his meal
of human meat and unmixed milk,[4] he lay
stretched out among his flocks. Then thinking like
a military man, I thought I should 300
get out my sword, go up to him and thrust
right through his torso, feeling for his liver.[5]
That would have doomed us all. On second thoughts,
I realized we were too weak to move
the mighty stone he set in the high doorway. 305
So we stayed there in misery till dawn.

Early the Dawn appeared, pink fingers blooming,
and then he lit his fire and milked his ewes
in turn, and set a lamb by every one.
When he had diligently done his chores, 310
he grabbed two men and made a meal of them.
After he ate, he drove his fat flock out.
He rolled the boulder out and back with ease,
as one would set the lid upon a quiver.
Then whistling merrily, the Cyclops drove 315
his fat flocks to the mountain. I was left,
scheming to take revenge on him and hurt him,
and gain the glory, if Athena let me.
I made my plan. Beside the pen there stood
a great big club, green olive wood, which he 320
had cut to dry, to be his walking stick.

---

4. The word for "unmixed" is usually used for wine undiluted with water. The text is making a sort of joke since milk is the equivalent of wine for this usually teetotaling character.
5. He imagines having to move by feel, since the cave is entirely dark.

It was so massive that it looked to us
like a ship's mast, a twenty-oared black freighter
that sails across the vast sea full of cargo.
I went and cut from it about a cubit,   325
and gave it to the men, and ordered them
to scrape it down. They made it smooth and I
stood by and sharpened up the tip, and made it
hard in the blazing flame. The cave was full
of dung; I hid the club beneath a pile.   330
Then I gave orders that the men cast lots
for who would lift the stake with me and press it
into his eye, when sweet sleep overtook him.
The lots fell on the men I would have chosen:
four men, and I was fifth among their number.   335

At evening he drove back his woolly flocks
into the spacious cave, both male and female,
and left none in the yard outside—perhaps
suspecting something, or perhaps a god
told him to do it. He picked up and placed   340
the stone to form a door, and sat to milk
the sheep and bleating goats in turn, then put
the little ones to suck. His chores were done;
he grabbed two men for dinner. I approached
and offered him a cup of ivy wood,   345
filled full of wine. I said,

         'Here, Cyclops! You
have eaten human meat; now drink some wine,
sample the merchandise our ship contains.
I brought it as a holy offering,[6]
so you might pity me and send me home.   350
But you are in a cruel rage, beyond
what anyone could bear. Do you expect
more guests, when you have treated us so rudely?'

He took and drank the sweet delicious wine;
he loved it, and demanded more.

         'Another!   355
And now tell me your name, so I can give you
a present as my guest, one you will like.
My people do have wine; grape clusters grow
from our rich earth, fed well by rain from Zeus.
But this is nectar, god food!'

         So I gave him   360
another cup of wine, and then two more.

---

6. The term used here is usually applied to drink offerings given to the gods.

He drank them all, unwisely. With the wine
gone to his head, I told him, all politeness,

'Cyclops, you asked my name. I will reveal it;
then you must give the gift you promised me,   365
of hospitality. My name is Noman.
My family and friends all call me Noman.'
He answered with no pity in his heart,
'I will eat Noman last; first I will eat
the other men. That is my gift to you.'   370
Then he collapsed, fell on his back, and lay there,
his massive neck askew. All-conquering sleep
took him. In drunken heaviness, he spewed
wine from his throat, and chunks of human flesh.
And then I drove the spear into the embers   375
to heat it up, and told my men, 'Be brave!'
I wanted none of them to shrink in fear.
The fire soon had seized the olive spear,
green though it was, and terribly it glowed.
I quickly snatched it from the fire. My crew   380
stood firm: some god was breathing courage in us.
They took the olive spear, its tip all sharp,
and shoved it in his eye. I leaned on top
and twisted it, as when a man drills wood
for shipbuilding. Below, the workers spin   385
the drill with straps, stretched out from either end.
So round and round it goes, and so we whirled
the fire-sharp weapon in his eye. His blood
poured out around the stake, and blazing fire
sizzled his lids and brows, and fried the roots.   390
As when a blacksmith dips an axe or adze
to temper it in ice-cold water; loudly
it shrieks. From this, the iron takes on its power.
So did his eyeball crackle on the spear.
Horribly then he howled, the rocks resounded,   395
and we shrank back in fear. He tugged the spear
out of his eye, all soaked with gushing blood.
Desperately with both hands he hurled it from him,
and shouted to the Cyclopes who lived
in caves high up on windy cliffs around.   400
They heard and came from every side, and stood
near to the cave, and called out, 'Polyphemus!
What is the matter? Are you badly hurt?
Why are you screaming through the holy night
and keeping us awake? Is someone stealing   405
your herds, or trying to kill you, by some trick
or force?'

     Strong Polyphemus from inside
replied, 'My friends! Noman is killing me
by tricks, not force.'

Their words flew back to him:
'If no one hurts you, you are all alone: 410
Great Zeus has made you sick; no help for that.
Pray to your father, mighty Lord Poseidon.'

Then off they went, and I laughed to myself,
at how my name, the 'no man' maneuver, tricked him.[7]
The Cyclops groaned and labored in his pain,   415
felt with blind hands and took the door-stone out,
and sat there at the entrance, arms outstretched,
to catch whoever went out with the sheep.
Maybe he thought I was a total fool.
But I was strategizing, hatching plans,   420
so that my men and I could all survive.
I wove all kinds of wiles and cunning schemes;
danger was near and it was life or death.
The best idea I formed was this: there were
those well-fed sturdy rams with good thick fleece,   425
wool as dark as violets—all fine big creatures.
So silently I tied them with the rope
used by the giant Cyclops as a bed.
I bound the rams in sets of three and set
a man beneath each middle sheep, with one   430
on either side, and so my men were saved.
One ram was best of all the flock; I grabbed
his back and curled myself up underneath
his furry belly, clinging to his fleece;
by force of will I kept on hanging there.   435
And then we waited miserably for day.

When early Dawn revealed her rose-red hands,
the rams jumped up, all eager for the grass.
The ewes were bleating in their pens, unmilked,
their udders full to bursting. Though their master   440
was weak and worn with pain, he felt the back
of each ram as he lined them up—but missed
the men tied up beneath their woolly bellies.
Last of them all, the big ram went outside,
heavy with wool and me—the clever trickster.   445
Strong Polyphemus stroked his back and asked him,

'Sweet ram, why are you last today to leave
the cave? You are not normally so slow.
You are the first to eat the tender flowers,
leaping across the meadow, first to drink,   450
and first to want to go back to the sheepfold
at evening time. But now you are the last.

7. There is a pun here in the Greek that is   means "nobody" but also "cunning." "Maneu-
impossible to translate into English: *metis*   ver" is designed to hint at the wordplay.

You grieve for Master's eye; that wicked man,
helped by his nasty henchmen, got me drunk
and blinded me. Noman will not escape!   455
If only you could talk like me, and tell me
where he is skulking in his fear of me.
Then I would dash his brains out on the rocks,
and make them spatter all across the cave,
to ease the pain that no-good Noman brought.'   460

With that, he nudged the ram away outside.
We rode a short way from the cave, then I
first freed myself and then untied my men.
We stole his nice fat animals, and ran,
constantly glancing all around and back   465
until we reached the ship. The other men
were glad to see us, their surviving friends,
but wept for those who died. I ordered them
to stop their crying, scowling hard at each.
I made them shove the fleecy flock on board,   470
and row the boat out into salty water.
So they embarked, sat on their rowing benches,
and struck their oar blades in the whitening sea.
When I had gone as far as shouts can carry,
I jeered back,

       'Hey, you, Cyclops! Idiot!   475
The crew trapped in your cave did not belong
to some poor weakling. Well, you had it coming!
You had no shame at eating your own guests!
So Zeus and other gods have paid you back.'

My taunting made him angrier. He ripped   480
a rock out of the hill and hurled it at us.
It landed right in front of our dark prow,
and almost crushed the tip of the steering oar.
The stone sank in the water; waves surged up.
The backflow all at once propelled the ship   485
landwards; the swollen water pushed us with it.
I grabbed a big long pole, and shoved us off.
I told my men, 'Row fast, to save your lives!'
and gestured with my head to make them hurry.
They bent down to their oars and started rowing.   490
We got out twice as far across the sea,
and then I called to him again. My crew
begged me to stop, and pleaded with me.

                'Please!
Calm down! Why are you being so insistent
and taunting this wild man? He hurled that stone   495
and drove our ship right back to land. We thought

that we were going to die. If he had heard us,
he would have hurled a jagged rock and crushed
our heads and wooden ship. He throws so hard!

But my tough heart was not convinced; I was   500
still furious, and shouted back again,

'Cyclops! If any mortal asks you how
your eye was mutilated and made blind,
say that Odysseus, the city-sacker,
Laertes' son, who lives in Ithaca,   505
destroyed your sight.'

            He groaned, 'The prophecy!
It has come true at last! There was a tall
and handsome man named Telemus, the son
of Eurymus, who lived among my people;
he spent his life here, soothsaying for us.   510
He told me that Odysseus' hands
would make me lose my sight. I always thought
a tall and handsome man would visit me,
endowed with strength and courage. But this weakling,
this little nobody, has blinded me;   515
by wine he got the best of me. Come on,
Odysseus, and let me give you gifts,
and ask Poseidon's help to get you home.
I am his son; the god is proud to be
my father. He will heal me, if he wants,   520
though no one else, not god nor man, can do it.'

After he said these words, I answered him,
'If only I could steal your life from you,
and send you down to Hades' house below,
as sure as nobody will ever heal you,   525
even the god of earthquakes.'

            But he prayed
holding his arms towards the starry sky,
'Listen, Earth-Shaker, Blue-Haired Lord Poseidon:
acknowledge me your son, and be my father.
Grant that Odysseus, the city-sacker,   530
will never go back home. Or if it is
fated that he will see his family,
then let him get there late and with no honor,
in pain and lacking ships, and having caused
the death of all his men, and let him find   535
more trouble in his own house.'

            Blue Poseidon
granted his son's prayer. Polyphemus raised
a rock far bigger than the last, and swung,

then hurled it with immeasurable force.
It fell a little short, beside our rudder,   540
and splashed into the sea; the waves surged up,
and pushed the boat ahead, to the other shore.
We reached the island where our ships were docked.
The men were sitting waiting for us, weeping.
We beached our ship and disembarked, then took   545
the sheep that we had stolen from the Cyclops
out of the ship's hold, and we shared them out
fairly, so all the men got equal portions.
But in dividing up the flock, my crew
gave me alone the ram, the Cyclops' favorite.   550
There on the shore, I slaughtered him for Zeus,
the son of Cronus, god of Dark Clouds, Lord
of all the world. I burned the thighs. The god
ignored my offering, and planned to ruin
all of my ships and all my loyal men.   555
So all day long till sunset we were sitting,
feasting on meat and drinking sweet strong wine.
But when the sun went down and darkness fell,
we went to sleep beside the breaking waves.
Then when rose-fingered Dawn came, bright and early,   560
I roused my men and told them to embark
and loose the cables. Quickly they obeyed,
sat at their rowing benches, all in order,
and struck the gray saltwater with their oars.
So we sailed on, with sorrow in our hearts,   565
glad to survive, but grieving for our friends."

BOOK 10

The Winds and the Witch

"We reached the floating island of Aeolus,
who is well loved by all the deathless gods.
Around it, on sheer cliffs, there runs a wall
of solid bronze, impregnable. Twelve children
live with him in his palace: six strong boys,   5
and six girls. He arranged their marriages,
one sister to each brother. They are always
feasting there with their parents, at a banquet
that never ends. By day, the savor fills
the house; the court reverberates with sound.   10
At night they sleep beside the wives they love
on rope beds piled with blankets.

                                            We arrived
at that fine citadel. He welcomed me
and made me stay a month, and asked for news
of Troy, the Argive ships, and how the Greeks   15
went home. I told him everything. At last

I told him he should send me on my way.
So he agreed to help me, and he gave me
a bag of oxhide leather and he tied
the gusty winds inside it. Zeus, the son   20
of Cronus, made him steward of the winds,
and he can stop or rouse them as he wishes.
He bound the bag with shining silver wire
to my curved ship, so no gust could escape,
however small, and he made Zephyr blow   25
so that the breath could carry home our ships
and us. But it was not to be. Our folly
ruined us. For nine days and nights we sailed,
and on the tenth, our native land appeared.
We were so near, we saw men tending fires.   30
Exhausted, I let sweet sleep overcome me.
I had been doing all the steering, hoping
that we would get home sooner if I did.
But while I slept my men began to mutter,
saying the great Aeolus gave me gifts—   35
silver and gold that I was taking home.
With glances to his neighbor, each complained,

'It seems that everybody loves this man,
and honors him, in every place we sail to.
He also has that loot from sacking Troy.   40
We shared the journey with him, yet we come
back home with empty hands. And now Aeolus
has made this friendly gift to him. So hurry,
we should look in the bag, and see how much
is in there—how much silver, how much gold.'   45

That bad idea took hold of them; they did it.
They opened up the bag, and all the winds
rushed out at once. A sudden buffet seized us
and hurled us back to sea, the wrong direction,
far from our home. They screamed and I woke up,   50
and wondered if I should jump off the ship
and drown, or bite my lip, be stoical,
and stay among the living. I endured it,
covered my face, and lay on deck. A blast
of storm wind whooshed the ships back to the island   55
of great Aeolus. They began to weep.
We disembarked and filled our jars with water,
and hungrily the men devoured their dinner.
When they were done, I took one slave with me
and one crew member, back to see Aeolus.   60
He was at dinner with his wife and children.
We entered and sat down beside the doorposts.
Startled, they asked,

'Why are you here again?
You had bad luck? What happened? Surely we
helped you go on your way, and meant for you   65
to reach your homeland, where you wished to go.'

I answered sadly, 'Blame my men, and blame
my stubborn urge to sleep, which ruined us.
Dear friends, you have the power to put things right.'

I hoped these words would soften them, but they   70
were silent. Then the father yelled, 'Get out!
You nasty creature, leave my island! Now!
It is not right for me to help convey
a man so deeply hated by the gods.
You godforsaken thing, how dare you come here?   75
Get out!'

        He roared and drove us from his palace.
Dispirited, we sailed away. The men
grew worn out with the agony of rowing;
our folly had deprived us of fair winds.
We rowed six days and nights; the seventh day   80
we came to Laestrygonia—the town
of Telepylus upon the cliffs of Lamos.[1]
A herdsman there, returning to his home,
can greet another herdsman going out.[2]
A sleepless man could earn a double wage   85
by herding cows, then pasturing white sheep—
the paths of day and night are close together.[3]
We reached the famous harbor, all surrounded
by sheer rock cliffs. On each side, strips of shore
jut out and almost meet, a narrow mouth.   90
No waves rear up in there, not even small ones.
White calm is everywhere. So all the others
harbored their ships inside, crammed close together.
I was the only one who chose to moor
my ship outside the harbor, fastening   95
the cables to a rock a way away.
I disembarked and climbed a crag to scout.
I saw no sign of cattle or of humans,
except some smoke that rose up from the earth.
I picked two men, and one slave as the third,   100
and sent them to find out what people lived
and ate bread in this land. They disembarked
and walked along a smooth path, where the wagons
brought wood down from the mountains to the city.

1. Lamos is the founder of this mythical place.
2. The idea is that in this strange country
herdsmen work around the clock, a day shift
and a night shift.
3. This odd line presumably means that the

nights are almost nonexistent here, as in areas
near the Arctic Circle. Attempts to plot Laestrygonia on a real map have not been convinc-
ing; this is a fictional place, melding several
elements of actual geography.

They met a girl in front of town, out fetching   105
some water. She was heading for the fountain
of Artaky, the whole town's water source.
She was the strapping child of Antiphates,
king of the Laestrygonians. They asked her
about the king and people of the country.   110
She promptly took them to the high-roofed palace
of her own father. When they went inside
they found a woman, mountain-high. They were
appalled and shocked. The giantess at once
summoned the king her husband from the council;   115
he tried to kill my men, and grabbing one
he ate him up. The other two escaped,
back to the ship. The king's shout boomed through town.
Hearing, the mighty Laestrygonians
thronged from all sides, not humanlike, but giants.[4]   120
With boulders bigger than a man could lift
they pelted at us from the cliffs. We heard
the dreadful uproar of ships being broken
and dying men. They speared them there like fish.
A gruesome meal! While they were killing them   125
inside the harbor, I drew out my sword
and cut the ropes that moored my dark-cheeked ship,
and yelling to my men, I told them, 'Row
as fast as possible away from danger!'
They rowed at double time, afraid to die.   130
My ship was lucky and we reached the sea
beyond the overhanging cliffs. The rest,
trapped in the bay together, were destroyed.
We sailed off sadly, happy to survive,
but with our good friends lost. We reached Aeaea,   135
home of the beautiful, dreadful goddess Circe,
who speaks in human languages—the sister
of Aeetes whose mind is set on ruin.
Those two are children of the Sun who shines
on mortals, and of Perse, child of Ocean.[5]   140
Under the guidance of some god we drifted
silently to the harbor, and we moored there.
For two days and two nights we lay onshore,
exhausted and our hearts consumed with grief.
On the third morning brought by braided Dawn,   145
I took my spear and sharp sword, and I ran
up from the ship to higher ground, to look
for signs of humans, listening for voices.
I climbed up to a crag, and I saw smoke
rising from Circe's palace, from the earth   150
up through the woods and thickets. I considered

---

4. The giants were children of Earth, fertilized
by the blood of Uranus after his castration.
5. Perse is one of the many daughters of

Ocean; Aeetes was the cruel king of Colchis,
owner of the Golden Fleece and father of
Medea.

if I should go down and investigate,
since I had seen the smoke. But I decided
to go back down first, to the beach and ship
and feed my men, and then set out to scout.   155
When I had almost reached my ship, some god
took pity on me in my loneliness,
and sent a mighty stag with great tall antlers
to cross my path. He ran down from the forest
to drink out of the river; it was hot.   160
I struck him in the middle of his back;
my bronze spear pierced him. With a moan, he fell
onto the dust; his spirit flew away.
I stepped on him and tugged my bronze spear out,
and left it on the ground, while I plucked twigs   165
and twines, and wove a rope, a fathom's length,
well knotted all the way along, and bound
the hooves of that huge animal. I went
down to my dark ship with him on my back.
I used my spear to lean on, since the stag   170
was too big to be lugged across one shoulder.
I dumped him down before the ship and made
a comforting pep talk to cheer my men.

'My friends! We will not yet go down to Hades,
sad though we are, before our fated day.   175
Come on, since we have food and drink on board,
let us not starve ourselves; now time to eat!'

They quickly heeded my commands, and took
their cloaks down from their faces,[6] and they marveled
to see the big stag lying on the beach.   180
It was enormous. When they finished staring,
they washed their hands and cooked a splendid meal.
So all that day till sunset we sat eating
the meat aplenty and the strong sweet wine.
When darkness fell, we went to sleep beside   185
the seashore. Then the roses of Dawn's fingers
appeared again; I called my men and told them,

'Listen to me, my friends, despite your grief.
We do not know where darkness lives, nor dawn,
nor where the sun that shines upon the world   190
goes underneath the earth, nor where it rises.
We need a way to fix our current plight,
but I do not know how. I climbed the rocks
to higher ground to look around. This is
an island, wreathed about by boundless sea.   195
The land lies low. I saw smoke in the middle,
rising up through the forest and thick bush.'

6. People in Homer cover their faces in grief; the men in this small band of survivors have been grieving the loss of the other eleven ships and their crew members.

At that, their hearts sank, since they all remembered
what happened with the Laestrygonians,
their King Antiphates, and how the mighty   200
Cyclops devoured the men. They wept and wailed,
and shed great floods of tears. But all that grieving
could do no good. I made them wear their armor,
and split them in two groups. I led one,
and made godlike Eurylochus lead the other.   205
We shook the lots in a helmet made of bronze;
Eurylochus' lot jumped out. So he
went with his band of twenty-two, all weeping.
Those left behind with me were crying too.
Inside the glade they found the house of Circe   210
built out of polished stones, on high foundations.
Round it were mountain wolves and lions, which
she tamed with drugs. They did not rush on them,
but gathered around them in a friendly way,
their long tails wagging, as dogs nuzzle round   215
their master when he comes back home from dinner
with treats for them. Just so, those sharp-clawed wolves
and lions, mighty beasts, came snuggling up.
The men were terrified. They stood outside
and heard some lovely singing. It was Circe,   220
the goddess. She was weaving as she sang,
an intricate, enchanting piece of work,
the kind a goddess fashions. Then Polites,
my most devoted and most loyal man,
a leader to his peers, said,

           'Friends, inside   225
someone is weaving on that massive loom,
and singing so the floor resounds. Perhaps
a woman, or a goddess. Let us call her.'

They shouted out to her. She came at once,
opened the shining doors, and asked them in.   230
So thinking nothing of it, in they went.
Eurylochus alone remained outside,
suspecting trickery. She led them in,
sat them on chairs, and blended them a potion
of barley, cheese, and golden honey, mixed   235
with Pramnian wine.[7] She added potent drugs
to make them totally forget their home.
They took and drank the mixture. Then she struck them,
using her magic wand, and penned them in
the pigsty. They were turned to pigs in body   240
and voice and hair; their minds remained the same.

7. A particular type of wine rather than from a particular location; it is described as black and harsh by the medical writer Galen. The same wine is used for the potion made in Nestor's cup, in book 11 of the *Iliad*.

They squealed at their imprisonment, and Circe
threw them some mast and cornel cherries—food
that pigs like rooting for in muddy ground.
Eurylochus ran back to our black ship,   245
to tell us of the terrible disaster
that happened to his friends. He tried to speak,
but could not, overwhelmed by grief. His eyes
were full of tears, his heart was pierced with sorrow.
Astonished, we all questioned him. At last   250
he spoke about what happened to the others.

'Odysseus, we went off through the woods,
as you commanded. In the glade we found
a beautiful tall house of polished stone.
We heard a voice: a woman or a goddess   255
was singing as she worked her loom. My friends
called out to her. She opened up the doors,
inviting them inside. Suspecting nothing,
they followed her. But I stayed there outside,
fearing some trick. Then all at once, they vanished.   260
I sat there for a while to watch and wait,
but none of them came back.'

                At this, I strapped
my silver-studded sword across my back,
took up my bow, and told him, 'Take me there.'
He grasped my knees and begged me tearfully,   265

'No no, my lord! Please do not make me go!
Let me stay here! You cannot bring them back,
and you will not return here if you try.
Hurry, we must escape with these men here!
We have a chance to save our lives!'

                     I said,   270
'You can stay here beside the ship and eat
and drink. But I will go. I must do this.'
I left the ship and shore, and walked on up,
crossing the sacred glades, and I had almost
reached the great house of the enchantress Circe,   275
when I met Hermes, carrying his wand
of gold. He seemed an adolescent boy,
the cutest age, when beards first start to grow.
He took my hand and said,

                  'Why have you come
across these hills alone? You do not know   280
this place, poor man. Your men were turned to pigs
in Circe's house, and crammed in pens. Do you
imagine you can set them free? You cannot.
If you try that, you will not get back home.

You will stay here with them. But I can help you. 285
Here, take this antidote to keep you safe
when you go into Circe's house. Now I
will tell you all her lethal spells and tricks.
She will make you a potion mixed with poison.
Its magic will not work on you because 290
you have the herb I gave you. When she strikes you
with her long wand, then draw your sharpened sword
and rush at her as if you mean to kill her.
She will be frightened of you, and will tell you
to sleep with her. Do not hold out against her— 295
she is a goddess. If you sleep with her,
you will set free your friends and save yourself.
Tell her to swear an oath by all the gods
that she will not plot further harm for you—
or while you have your clothes off, she may hurt you, 300
unmanning you.'

          The bright mercurial god
pulled from the ground a plant and showed me how
its root is black, its flower white as milk.
The gods call this plant Moly.[8] It is hard
for mortal men to dig it up, but gods 305
are able to do everything. Then Hermes
flew through the wooded island, back towards
high Mount Olympus. I went in the house
of Circe. My heart pounded as I walked.
I stood there at the doorway, and I saw her, 310
the lovely Circe with her braided hair.
I called; she heard and opened up the doors
and asked me in. I followed nervously.
She led me to a silver-studded chair,
all finely crafted, with a footstool under. 315
In a gold cup she mixed a drink for me,
adding the drug—she hoped to do me harm.
I sipped it, but the magic did not work.
She struck me with her wand and said,

                     'Now go!
Out to the sty, and lie there with your men!' 320
But I drew my sharp sword from by my thigh
and leapt at her as if I meant to kill her.
She screamed and ducked beneath the sword, and grasped
my knees, and wailing asked me,

                    'Who are you?
Where is your city? And who are your parents? 325

8. Probably an imaginary plant, though the
legend may be connected to the ancient idea
that garlic (which also has a white flower and
dark root) can be used against bad spirits and
vampires.

I am amazed that you could drink my potion
and yet are not bewitched. No other man
has drunk it and withstood the magic charm.
But you are different. Your mind is not
enchanted. You must be Odysseus,   330
the man who can adapt to anything.
Bright flashing Hermes of the golden wand
has often told me that you would sail here
from Troy in your swift ship. Now sheathe your sword
and come to bed with me. Through making love   335
we may begin to trust each other more.'

I answered, 'Circe! How can you command me
to treat you gently, when you turned my men
to pigs, and you are planning to play tricks
in telling me to come to bed with you,   340
so you can take my courage and my manhood
when you have got me naked? I refuse
to come to bed with you, unless you swear
a mighty oath that you will not form plans
to hurt me anymore.'

                              When I said that,   345
at once she made the oath as I had asked.
She vowed and formed the oath, and then at last
I went up to the dazzling bed of Circe.

Meanwhile, four slaves, her house girls, were at work
around the palace. They were nymphs, the daughters   350
of fountains and of groves and holy rivers
that flow into the sea. One set fine cloths
of purple on the chairs, with stones beneath them.
Beside each chair, another pulled up tables
of silver and set golden baskets on them.   355
The third mixed up inside a silver bowl
sweet, cheering wine, and poured it in gold cups.
The fourth brought water, and she lit a fire
beneath a mighty tripod, till it boiled.
It started bubbling in the copper cauldron;   360
she took me to the bathtub, and began
to wash my head and shoulders, using water
mixed to the perfect temperature, to take
my deep soul-crushing weariness away.
After the bath, she oiled my skin and dressed me   365
in fine wool cloak and tunic, and she led me
to a silver-studded well-carved chair, and set
a footstool underneath. Another slave
brought water for my hands, in a gold pitcher,
and poured it over them, to a silver bowl.   370
She set a polished table near. The cook
brought bread and laid a generous feast, and Circe

told me to eat. But my heart was unwilling.
I sat there with my mind on other things;
I had forebodings. Circe noticed me   375
sitting, not touching food, and weighed by grief.
She stood near me and asked, 'Odysseus!
why are you sitting there so silently,
like someone mute, eating your heart, not touching
the banquet or the wine? You need not fear.   380
Remember, I already swore an oath.'

But I said, 'Circe, no! What decent man
could bear to taste his food or sip his wine
before he saw his men with his own eyes,
and set them free? If you are so insistent   385
on telling me to eat and drink, then free them,
so I may see with my own eyes my crew
of loyal men.'

      So Circe left the hall
holding her wand, and opened up the pigsty
and drove them out, still looking like fat boars,   390
large and full grown. They stood in front of her.
Majestic Lady Circe walked among them,
anointing each with some new drug. The potion
had made thick hog-hairs sprout out on their bodies.
Those bristles all flew off and they were men,   395
but younger than before, and much more handsome,
and taller. Then they recognized me. Each
embraced me tightly in his arms, and started
sobbing in desperation. So the house
rang loud with noise, and even she herself   400
pitied them. She came near to me and said,

'Odysseus, you always find solutions.
Go now to your swift ship beside the sea.
First drag the ship to land, and bring your stores
and all your gear inside the caves. Then come   405
back with your loyal men.'

      My heart agreed;
I went down to my swift ship on the shore.
I found my loyal men beside the ship,
weeping and shedding floods of tears. As when
a herd of cows is coming back from pasture   410
into the yard; and all the little heifers
jump from their pens to skip and run towards
their mothers, and they cluster round them, mooing;
just so my men, as soon as they saw me,
began to weep, and in their minds it seemed   415
as if they had arrived in their own home,
the land of rugged Ithaca, where they

were born and raised. Still sobbing, they cried out,

'Oh, Master! We are glad to see you back!
It is as if we had come home ourselves,   420
to Ithaca, our fatherland. But tell us
about how all our other friends were killed.'

I reassured them, saying, 'First we must
drag up the ship to land, and put the stores
and all our gear inside the caves; then hurry,   425
all of you, come with me, and see your friends
inside the goddess Circe's holy house,
eating and drinking; they have food enough
to last forever.'

           They believed my story,
with the exception of Eurylochus,   430
who warned them,

               'Fools! Why would you go up there?
Why would you choose to take on so much danger,
to enter Circe's house, where she will turn us
to pigs or wolves or lions, all of us,
forced to protect her mighty house for her?   435
Remember what the Cyclops did? Our friends
went to his home with this rash lord of ours.
Because of his bad choices, they all died.'

At that, I thought of drawing my long sword
from by my sturdy thigh, to cut his head off   440
and let it fall down to the ground—although
he was close family. My men restrained me,
saying to me, 'No, king, please let him go!
Let him stay here and guard the ship, and we
will follow you to Circe's holy house.'   445

So they went up, away from ship and shore.
Eurylochus did not stay there; he came,
fearing my angry scolding.

              Meanwhile Circe
had freed the other men, and in her house
she gently bathed them, rubbing them with oil.   450
She had them dressed in woolen cloaks and tunics.
We found them feasting in the hall. The men,
seeing each other face to face again,
began to weep; their sobbing filled the hall.
The goddess stood beside me and said,

                      'King,   455
clever Odysseus, Laertes' son,

now stop encouraging this lamentation.
I know you and your men have suffered greatly,
out on the fish-filled sea, and on dry land
from hostile men. But it is time to eat   460
and drink some wine. You must get back the drive
you had when you set out from Ithaca.
You are worn down and brokenhearted, always
dwelling on pain and wandering. You never
feel joy at heart. You have endured too much.'   465

We did as she had said. Then every day
for a whole year we feasted there on meat
and sweet strong wine. But when the year was over,
when months had waned and seasons turned, and each
long day had passed its course, my loyal men   470
called me and said,

                        'Be guided by the gods.
Now it is time to think of our own country,
if you are fated to survive and reach
your high-roofed house and your forefathers' land.'

My warrior soul agreed. So all day long   475
till sunset we kept sitting at the feast
of meat and sweet strong wine. But when the sun
set, and the darkness came, they went to bed
all through the shadowy palace. I went up
to Circe's splendid bed, and touched her knees   480
in supplication, and the goddess listened.

'Circe,' I said, 'fulfill the vow you made
to send me home. My heart now longs to go.
My men are also desperate to leave.
Whenever you are absent, they exhaust me   485
with constant lamentation.'

                        And she answered,
'Laertes' son, great King Odysseus,
master of every challenge, you need not
remain here in my house against your will.
But first you must complete another journey.   490
Go to the house of Hades and the dreadful
Persephone,[9] and ask the Theban prophet,
the blind Tiresias, for his advice.
Persephone has given him alone
full understanding, even now in death.   495
The other spirits flit around as shadows.'

9. Hades is god of the underworld. Persephone is his wife.

That broke my heart, and sitting on the bed
I wept, and lost all will to live and see
the shining sun. When I was done with sobbing
and rolling round in grief, I said to her,   500

'But Circe, who can guide us on this journey?
No one before has ever sailed to Hades
by ship.'

      And right away the goddess answered,
'You are resourceful, King Odysseus.
You need not worry that you have no pilot   505
to steer your ship. Set up your mast, let fly
your white sails, and sit down. The North Wind's breath
will blow the ship. When you have crossed the stream
of Ocean, you will reach the shore, where willows
let fall their dying fruit, and towering poplars   510
grow in the forest of Persephone.
Tie up your ship in the deep-eddying Ocean,
and go into the moldering home of Hades.
The Pyriphlegethon and Cocytus,
a tributary of the Styx, both run   515
into the Acheron. The flowing water
resounds beside the rock. Brave man, go there,
and dig a hole a cubit[1] wide and long,
and round it pour libations for the dead:
first honey-mix,[2] then sweet wine, and the third   520
of water. Sprinkle barley, and beseech
the spirits of the dead. Vow if you reach
the barren land of Ithaca, to kill
a heifer in your halls, the best you have,
uncalved, and you will heap the fire with meat,   525
and offer to Tiresias alone
a ram, pure black, the best of all your flock.
When you have prayed to all the famous dead,
slaughter one ram and one black ewe, directing
the animals to Erebus,[3] but turn   530
yourself away, towards the gushing river.
Many will come. Then tell your men to skin
the sheep that lie there killed by ruthless bronze,
and burn them, with a prayer to mighty Hades
and terrible Persephone. Then draw   535
your sword and sit. Do not let them come near
the blood, until you hear Tiresias.
The prophet will soon come, and he will tell you
about your journey, measured out across
the fish-filled sea, and how you will get home.'   540

1. A unit of measure roughly equivalent to the
length of a human forearm.
2. A mixture of honey with some other substance, perhaps milk.
3. The underworld.

Dawn on her golden throne began to shine,
and Circe dressed me in my cloak and tunic.
The goddess wore a long white dress, of fine
and delicate fabric, with a golden belt,
and on her head, a veil. Then I walked round,   545
all through the house, and called my men. I stood
beside each one, and roused them with my words.

'Wake up! Now no more dozing in sweet sleep.
We have to go. The goddess gave instructions.'

They did as I had said. But even then   550
I could not lead my men away unharmed.
The youngest one—Elpenor was his name—
not very brave in war, nor very smart,
was lying high up in the home of Circe,
apart from his companions, seeking coolness   555
since he was drunk. He heard the noise and bustle,
the movements of his friends, and jumped up quickly,
forgetting to climb down the lofty ladder.
He fell down crashing headlong from the roof,
and broke his neck, right at the spine. His spirit   560
went down to Hades.

        Then I told the others,
'Perhaps you think that you are going home.
But Circe says we have to go towards
the house of Hades and Persephone,
to meet Tiresias, the Theban spirit.'   565

At that, their hearts were broken. They sat down
right there and wept and tore their clothes. But all
their lamentation did no good. We went
down to our speedy ship beside the sea,
despite our grief. We shed abundant tears.   570
Then Circe came and tied up one black ewe
and one ram by the ship, and slipped away,
easily; who can see the gods go by
unless they wish to show themselves to us?"

BOOK 11

The Dead

"We reached the sea and first of all we launched
the ship into the sparkling salty water,
set up the mast and sails, and brought the sheep
on board with us. We were still grieving, weeping,
in floods of tears. But beautiful, dread Circe,   5
the goddess who can speak in human tongues,
sent us a wind to fill our sails, fair wind

befriending us behind the dark blue prow.
We made our tackle shipshape, then sat down.
The wind and pilot guided straight our course.　　　　　　10
The sun set. It was dark in all directions.

We reached the limits of deep-flowing Ocean,
where the Cimmerians live and have their city.
Their land is covered up in mist and cloud;
the shining Sun God never looks on them　　　　　　　15
with his bright beams—not when he rises up
into the starry sky, nor when he turns
back from the heavens to earth. Destructive night
blankets the world for all poor mortals there.
We beached our ship, drove out the sheep, and went　　20
to seek the stream of Ocean where the goddess
had told us we must go. Eurylochus
and Perimedes made the sacrifice.
I drew my sword and dug a hole, a fathom
widthways and lengthways, and I poured libations　　　25
for all the dead: first honey-mix, sweet wine,
and lastly, water. On the top, I sprinkled
barley, and made a solemn vow that if
I reached my homeland, I would sacrifice
my best young heifer, still uncalved, and pile　　　　30
the altar high with offerings for the dead.
I promised for Tiresias as well
a pure black sheep, the best in all my flock.
So with these vows, I called upon the dead.
I took the sheep and slit their throats above　　　　35
the pit. Black blood flowed out. The spirits came
up out of Erebus and gathered round.
Teenagers, girls and boys, the old who suffered
for many years, and fresh young brides whom labor
destroyed in youth; and many men cut down　　　　40
in battle by bronze spears, still dressed in armor
stained with their blood. From every side they crowded
around the pit, with eerie cries. Pale fear
took hold of me. I roused my men and told them
to flay the sheep that I had killed, and burn them,　　45
and pray to Hades and Persephone.
I drew my sword and sat on guard, preventing
the spirits of the dead from coming near
the blood, till I had met Tiresias.

First came the spirit of my man Elpenor,　　　　　50
who had not yet been buried in the earth.
We left his body in the house of Circe
without a funeral or burial;
we were too occupied with other things.
On sight of him, I wept in pity, saying,　　　　　55

'Elpenor, how did you come here, in darkness?
You came on foot more quickly than I sailed.'

He groaned in answer, 'Lord Odysseus,
you master every circumstance. But I
had bad luck from some god, and too much wine   60
befuddled me. In Circe's house I lay
upstairs, and I forgot to use the ladder
to climb down from the roof. I fell headfirst;
my neck was broken from my spine. My spirit
came down to Hades. By the men you left,   65
the absent ones! And by your wife! And father,
who brought you up from babyhood! And by
your son, Telemachus, whom you abandoned
alone at home, I beg you! When you sail
from Hades and you dock your ship again   70
at Aeaea, please, my lord, remember me.
Do not go on and leave me there unburied,
abandoned, without tears or lamentation—
or you will make the gods enraged at you.
Burn me with all my arms, and heap a mound   75
beside the gray salt sea, so in the future
people will know of me and my misfortune.
And fix into the tomb the oar I used
to row with my companions while I lived.'

'Poor man!' I answered, 'I will do all this.'   80

We sat there talking sadly—I on one side
held firm my sword in blood, while on the other
the ghost of my crew member made his speech.
Then came the spirit of my own dead mother,
Autolycus'[1] daughter Anticleia,   85
whom I had left alive when I went off
to holy Troy. On seeing her, I wept
in pity. But despite my bitter grief,
I would not let her near the blood till I
talked to Tiresias. The prophet came   90
holding a golden scepter, and he knew me,
and said,

          'King under Zeus, Odysseus,
adept survivor, why did you abandon
the sun, poor man, to see the dead, and this
place without joy? Step back now from the pit,   95
hold up your sharp sword so that I may drink
the blood and speak to you.'

---

1. Autolycus is Odysseus' maternal grandfather; the name suggests "Wolf Man."

> At that, I sheathed
> my silver-studded sword. When he had drunk
> the murky blood, the famous prophet spoke.

> 'Odysseus, you think of going home   100
> as honey-sweet, but gods will make it bitter.
> I think Poseidon will not cease to feel
> incensed because you blinded his dear son.
> You have to suffer, but you can get home,
> if you control your urges and your men.   105
> Turn from the purple depths and sail your ship
> towards the island of Thrinacia; there
> you will find grazing cows and fine fat sheep,
> belonging to the god who sees and hears
> all things—the Sun God. If you leave them be,   110
> keeping your mind fixed on your journey home,
> you may still get to Ithaca, despite
> great losses. But if you hurt those cows, I see
> disaster for your ship and for your men.
> If you yourself escape, you will come home   115
> late and exhausted, in a stranger's boat,
> having destroyed your men. And you will find
> invaders eating your supplies at home,
> courting your wife with gifts. Then you will match
> the suitors' violence and kill them all,   120
> inside your halls, through tricks or in the open,
> with sharp bronze weapons. When those men are dead,
> you have to go away and take an oar
> to people with no knowledge of the sea,
> who do not salt their food. They never saw   125
> a ship's red prow, nor oars, the wings of boats.
> I prophesy the signs of things to come.
> When you meet somebody, a traveler,
> who calls the thing you carry on your back
> a winnowing fan, then fix that oar in earth   130
> and make fine sacrifices to Poseidon—
> a bull and stud-boar. Then you will go home
> and offer holy hecatombs to all
> the deathless gods who live in heaven, each
> in order. Gentle death will come to you,   135
> far from the sea, of comfortable old age,
> your people flourishing. So it will be.'

> I said, 'Tiresias, I hope the gods
> spin out this fate for me. But tell me this,
> and tell the truth. I saw my mother's spirit,   140
> sitting in silence near the blood, refusing
> even to talk to me, or meet my eyes!
> My lord, how can I make her recognize
> that it is me?'

            At once he made his answer.
'That is an easy matter to explain.   145
Whenever you allow one of these spirits
to come here near the blood, it will be able
to speak the truth to you. As soon as you
push them away, they have to leave again.'

With that, Tiresias, the prophet spirit,   150
was finished; he departed to the house
of Hades. I stayed rooted there in place
until my mother came and drank the blood.
She knew me then and spoke in tones of grief.

'My child! How did you come here through the darkness   155
while you were still alive? This place is hard
for living men to see. There are great rivers
and dreadful gulfs, including the great Ocean
which none can cross on foot; one needs a ship.
Have you come wandering here, so far from Troy,   160
with ship and crew? Have you not yet arrived
in Ithaca, nor seen your wife at home?'

I answered, 'Mother, I was forced to come
to Hades to consult the prophet spirit,
Theban Tiresias. I have not yet   165
come near to Greece, nor reached my own home country.
I have been lost and wretchedly unhappy
since I first followed mighty Agamemnon
to Troy, the land of horses, to make war
upon the people there. But tell me, how   170
was sad death brought upon you? By long illness?
Or did the archer Artemis destroy you
with gentle arrows?[2] Tell me too about
my father and the son I left behind.
Are they still honored as the kings? Or has   175
another taken over, saying I
will not return? And tell me what my wife
is thinking, and her plans. Does she stay with
our son and focus on his care, or has
the best of the Achaeans[3] married her?'   180

My mother answered, 'She stays firm. Her heart
is strong. She is still in your house. And all
her nights are passed in misery, and days
in tears. But no one has usurped your throne.
Telemachus still tends the whole estate   185
unharmed and feasts in style, as lords should do,
and he is always asked to council meetings.

2. Artemis, goddess of hunting and childbirth,   women.
was particularly associated with the deaths of   3. Greeks.

Your father stays out in the countryside.
He will not come to town. He does not sleep
on a real bed with blankets and fresh sheets.   190
In winter he sleeps inside, by the fire,
just lying in the ashes with the slaves;
his clothes are rags. In summer and at harvest,
the piles of fallen leaves are beds for him.
He lies there grieving, full of sorrow, longing   195
for your return. His old age is not easy.
And that is why I met my fate and died.
The goddess did not shoot me in my home,
aiming with gentle arrows. Nor did sickness
suck all the strength out from my limbs, with long   200
and cruel wasting. No, it was missing you,
Odysseus, my sunshine; your sharp mind,
and your kind heart. That took sweet life from me.'

Then in my heart I wanted to embrace
the spirit of my mother. She was dead,   205
and I did not know how. Three times I tried,
longing to touch her. But three times her ghost
flew from my arms, like shadows or like dreams.
Sharp pain pierced deeper in me as I cried,

'No, Mother! Why do you not stay for me,   210
and let me hold you, even here in Hades?
Let us wrap loving arms around each other
and find a frigid comfort in shared tears!
But is this really you? Or has the Queen
sent me a phantom, to increase my grief?'   215

She answered, 'Oh, my child! You are the most
unlucky man alive. Persephone
is not deceiving you. This is the rule
for mortals when we die. Our muscles cease
to hold the flesh and skeleton together;   220
as soon as life departs from our white bones,
the force of blazing fire destroys the corpse.
The spirit flies away and soon is gone,
just like a dream. Now hurry to the light;
remember all these things, so you may tell   225
your wife in times to come.'

                                  As we were talking,
some women came, sent by Persephone—
the daughters and the wives of warriors.
They thronged and clustered round the blood. I wanted
to speak to each of them, and made a plan.   230
I drew my sword and would not let them come
together in a group to drink the blood.
They took turns coming forward, and each told

her history; I questioned each. The first
was well-born Tyro, child of Salmoneus,   235
and wife of Cretheus, Aeolus' son.
She fell in love with River Enipeus,
most handsome of all rivers that pour water
over the earth. She often went to visit
his lovely streams. Poseidon took his form,   240
and at the river mouth he lay with her.
Around them arched a dark-blue wave that stood
high as a mountain, and it hid the god
and mortal woman. There he loosed her belt
and made her sleep. The god made love to her,   245
and afterwards, he took her hand and spoke.

'Woman, be glad about this love. You will
bear glorious children in the coming year.
Affairs with gods always result in offspring.
Look after them and raise them. Now go home;   250
tell no one who I am. But I will tell you.
I am Poseidon, Shaker of the Earth.'
With that he sank beneath the ocean waves.

She brought two sons to term, named Pelias
and Neleus, both sturdy boys who served   255
almighty Zeus; and Pelias' home
was on the spacious dancing fields of Iolcus,
where sheep are plentiful; his brother lived
in sandy Pylos. And she bore more sons,
to Cretheus: Aeson, Pheres, Amythaon   260
who loved war chariots.

                            And after her
I saw Antiope, who said she slept
in Zeus' arms and bore two sons: Amphion
and Zethus, the first settlers of Thebes,
city of seven gates. Strong though they were,   265
they could not live there on the open plain
without defenses.

                    Then I saw Alcmene,
wife of Amphitryon, who by great Zeus
conceived the lionhearted Heracles.
And I saw Megara, proud Creon's child,   270
the wife of tireless Heracles. I saw
fine Epicaste, Oedipus' mother,
who did a dreadful thing in ignorance:
she married her own son. He killed his father,
and married her. The gods revealed the truth   275
to humans; through their deadly plans, he ruled
the Cadmeans in Thebes, despite his pain.
But Epicaste crossed the gates of Hades;

she tied a noose and hung it from the ceiling,
and hanged herself for sorrow, leaving him   280
the agonies a mother's Furies bring.[4]

Then I saw Chloris, who was youngest daughter
of Amphion, who ruled the Minyans
in Orchomenus. She was beautiful,
and Neleus paid rich bride-gifts for her.   285
She was the queen in Pylos, and she bore
Chromius, Nestor, Periclymenus,
and mighty Pero, who was such a marvel
that all the men desired to marry her.
But Neleus would only let her marry   290
a man who could drive off the stubborn cattle
of Iphicles from Phylace. The prophet
Melampus was the only one who tried,
but gods restrained him, cursing him; the herdsmen
shackled him. Days and months went by, the seasons   295
changed as the year went by, until at last
Iphicles set him free as his reward
for prophecy.[5] The will of Zeus was done.
And then I saw Tyndareus' wife,
Leda, who bore him two strong sons: the horseman   300
Castor, and Polydeuces, skillful boxer.
Life-giving earth contains them, still alive.
Zeus honors them even in the underworld.
They live and die alternately, and they
are honored like the gods.[6]

                    And then I saw   305
Iphimedeia, wife of Aloeus,
who proudly said Poseidon slept with her.
She had two sons whose lives were both cut short:
Otus and famous Ephialtes, whom
the fertile earth raised up as the tallest heroes   310
after renowned Orion. At nine years,
they were nine cubits wide, nine fathoms high.
They brought the din of dreadful raging war
to the immortal gods and tried to set
Ossa and Pelion—trees, leaves and all—   315
on Mount Olympus, high up in the sky.
They might have managed it, if they had reached

4. This passage gives a version of the myth
different from that of Sophocles' play, in which
Oedipus' mother is called Jocasta.
5. The prophet Melampus, after his unsuccessful attempt to drive off Iphicles' cattle and
win his daughter's hand, prophesied that Iphicles, who had been impotent, would be able to
have more children. In reward for the good
prophecy, Iphicles set Melampus free.

6. Castor and Polydeuces (also known as Pollux), the twins associated with the constellation Gemini, were given by Zeus the privilege
of being alive on every other day, taking turns.
According to many versions of the myth, Zeus
was actually their father, having seduced Leda
in the guise of a swan (so the twins are brothers
of Helen and Clytemnestra).

full adulthood. Apollo, son of Zeus
by braided Leto, killed them: they were both
dead before down could grow on their young chins,   320
dead before beards could wreathe their naked faces.

Then I saw Phaedra, Procris,[7] and the lovely
daughter of dangerous Minos, Ariadne.
Theseus tried to bring her back from Crete
to Athens, but could not succeed; the goddess   325
Artemis killed her on the isle of Día,
when Dionysus spoke against her.[8] Then
came Maera, Clymene and Eriphyle:
accepting golden bribes, she killed her husband.[9]
I cannot name each famous wife and daughter   330
I saw there; holy night would pass away
before I finished. I must go to sleep
on board the ship beside my crew, or else
right here. I know the gods and you will help
my onward journey."

        They were silent, spellbound,   335
listening in the shadowy hall. White-armed
Arete spoke.

        "Phaeacians! Look at him!
What a tall, handsome man! And what a mind!
He is my special guest, but all of you
share in our rank as lords; so do not send him   340
away too fast, and when he leaves, you must
be generous. He is in need, and you
are rich in treasure, through the will of gods."

The veteran Echeneus, the oldest
man in their company, said, "Our wise queen   345
has hit the mark, my friends. Do as she says.
But first Alcinous must speak and act."

The king said, "Let it be as she has spoken,
as long as I am ruler of this nation
of seafarers. I know our guest is keen   350
to go back home, but let him stay till morning.

<hr/>

7. Phaedra was the elder daughter of Minos, king of Crete, who married Theseus of Athens and fell in love with his son, her stepson, with disastrous results. Procris was the daughter of Erectheus, another king of Athens, who was killed unintentionally by her husband, Cephalus.

8. Ariadne, another daughter of Minos of Crete, helped Theseus through the Cretan labyrinth to kill her half-brother, the Minotaur, and was taken off with him on his ship. In later versions of the legend, Theseus abandoned her, and she was whisked away by Dionysus. This Homeric version implies that she somehow offended Dionysus—it is unclear how, and this story is otherwise unknown.

9. Eriphyle accepted the bribe of a gold necklace to persuade her husband, Amphiaraus, king of Argos, to go on a doomed raid against Thebes.

I will give all his presents then. You men
will all help him, but I will help the most,
since I hold power here."

Odysseus

answered with careful tact, "Alcinous,   355
king over all the people, if you urged me
to stay here for a year before you gave
the parting gifts and sent me on my way,
I would be happy. It would be far better
to reach my own dear home with hands filled full   360
of treasure. So all men would honor me
and welcome me back home in Ithaca."

Alcinous replied, "Odysseus,
the earth sustains all different kinds of people.
Many are cheats and thieves, who fashion lies   365
out of thin air. But when I look at you,
I know you are not in that category.
Your story has both grace and wisdom in it.
You sounded like a skillful poet, telling
the sufferings of all the Greeks, including   370
what you endured yourself. But come now, tell me
if you saw any spirits of your friends,
who went with you to Troy and undertook
the grief and pain of war. The night is long;
it is not time to sleep yet. Tell me more   375
amazing deeds! I would keep listening
until bright daybreak, if you kept on telling
the dangers you have passed."

Odysseus

answered politely, "King Alcinous,
there is a time for many tales, but also   380
a time for sleep. If you still want to hear,
I will not grudge you stories. I will tell you
some even more distressing ones, about
my friend who managed to escape the shrieks
and battle din at Troy but perished later,   385
killed in his own home by an evil wife.
Holy Persephone dispersed the ghosts
of women and they went their separate ways.
The ghost of Agamemnon came in sorrow
with all the rest who met their fate with him   390
inside Aegisthus' house. He recognized me
when he had drunk the blood. He wept out loud,
and tearfully reached out his hands towards me,
desperate to touch. His energy and strength
and all the suppleness his limbs once had   395
were gone. I wept and my heart pitied him.
I cried out,

'Lord of men, King Agamemnon!
How did you die? What bad luck brought you down?
Was it Poseidon rousing up a blast
of cruel wind to wreck your ships? Or were you   400
killed on dry land by enemies as you
were poaching their fat flocks of sheep or cattle,
or fighting for their city and their wives?'

He answered right away, 'King under Zeus,
Odysseus—survivor! No, Poseidon   405
did not rouse up a dreadful blast of wind
to wreck my ship. No hostile men on land
killed me in self-defense. It was Aegisthus
who planned my death and murdered me, with help
from my own wife. He called me to his house   410
to dinner and he killed me, as one slaughters
an ox at manger. What a dreadful death!
My men were systematically slaughtered
like pigs in a rich lord's house for some feast,
a wedding or a banquet. You have seen   415
many cut down in war in thick of battle,
or slaughtered in a combat hand to hand;
but you would grieve with even deeper pity
if you could see us lying dead beneath
the tables piled with food and wine. The floor   420
swam thick with blood. I heard the desperate voice
of Priam's daughter, poor Cassandra,[1] whom
deceitful Clytemnestra killed beside me.
As I lay dying, struck through by the sword,
I tried to lift my arms up from the ground.   425
That she-dog turned away. I went to Hades.
She did not even shut my eyes or close
my mouth. There is no more disgusting act
than when a wife betrays a man like that.
That woman formed a plot to murder me!   430
Her husband! When I got back home, I thought
I would be welcomed, at least by my slaves
and children. She has such an evil mind
that she has poured down shame on her own head
and on all other women, even good ones.'   435

I cried out, 'Curse her! Zeus has always brought
disaster to the house of Atreus
through women. Many men were lost for Helen,
and Clytemnestra[2] formed this plot against you
when you were far away.'

          At once he answered,   440
'So you must never treat your wife too well.

---

1. Cassandra, who had the gift of prophecy
from Apollo, was brought back from Troy as a
prize of war by Agamemnon.
2. Helen and Clytemnestra were sisters.

Do not let her know everything you know.
Tell her some things, hide others. But your wife
will not kill you, Odysseus. The wise
Penelope is much too sensible   445
to do such things. Your bride was very young
when we went off to war. She had a baby
still at her breast, who must be now a man.
He will be glad when you come home and see him,
and he will throw his arms around his father.   450
That is how things should go. My wife prevented
my eager eyes from gazing at my son.
She killed me first. I have a final piece
of sound advice for you—take heed of it.
When you arrive in your own land, do not   455
anchor your ship in full view; move in secret.
There is no trusting women any longer.
But have you any news about my son?
Is he alive? Is he in Orchomenus,
or sandy Pylos, or with Menelaus   460
in Sparta? Surely my fine son Orestes
is not yet dead.'

         I answered, 'Agamemnon,
why ask me this? I do not even know
whether he is alive or dead. It is
pointless to talk of hypotheticals.'   465

Both of us wept profusely, deeply grieving
over the bitter words we spoke. Then came
the spirits of Achilles[3] and Patroclus
and of Antilochus and Ajax,[4] who
was handsomest and had the best physique   470
of all the Greeks, next only to Achilles
the sprinter. And Achilles recognized me
and spoke in tears.

         'My lord Odysseus,
you fox! What will you think of next? How could you
bear to come down to Hades? Numb dead people   475
live here, the shades of poor exhausted mortals.'
I said, 'Achilles, greatest of Greek heroes,
I came down here to meet Tiresias,
in case he had advice for my return
to rocky Ithaca. I have not even   480
returned to Greece, my homeland. I have had
bad luck. But no one's luck was ever better
than yours, nor ever will be. In your life
we Greeks respected you as we do gods,

---

3. Best of the Greek heroes, prominent character in the *Iliad*.

4. Strong Greek hero known for defensive fighting.

and now that you are here, you have great power 485
among the dead. Achilles, you should not
be bitter at your death.'

     But he replied,
'Odysseus, you must not comfort me
for death. I would prefer to be a workman,
hired by a poor man on a peasant farm, 490
than rule as king of all the dead. But come,
tell me about my son. Do you have news?
Did he march off to war to be a leader?
And what about my father Peleus?
Does he still have good standing among all 495
the Myrmidons? Or do they treat him badly
in Phthia and Greece, since he is old
and frail? Now I have left the light of day,
and am not there to help, as on the plains
of Troy when I was killing the best Trojans, 500
to help the Greeks. If I could go for even
a little while, with all that strength I had,
up to my father's house, I would make those
who hurt and disrespect him wish my hands
were not invincible.'

     I answered him, 505
'I have no news to tell about your father,
but I can tell you all about your son,
dear Neoptolemus. I brought him from
Scyros by ship, with other well-armed Greeks.
When we were strategizing about Troy, 510
he always spoke up first and to the purpose,
unmatched except by Nestor and myself.
And when we fought at Troy, he never paused
in the great throng of battle; he was always
fearlessly running forward, and he slaughtered 515
enormous numbers in the clash of war.
I cannot name all those he killed for us.
But with his bronze he cut down Eurypylus,
the son of Telephus, most handsome man
I ever saw, next only to great Memnon. 520
The multitude of Cetians he brought
were also killed, since Priam bribed his mother.[5]
When we, the Argive leaders, were preparing
to climb inside the Wooden Horse, it was
my task to open up and close the door. 525
The other Greek commanders were in tears;
their legs were shaking. Not your handsome boy!
I never saw his face grow pale; he had

---

5. After the death of Achilles, Priam bribed for the Trojans.
Eurypylus' mother to persuade her son to fight

no tears to wipe away. Inside the horse,
he begged me to allow him to jump out.   530
He gripped his sword hilt and his heavy spear,
so desperate to go hurt the Trojans.
At last, when we had sacked the lofty city
of Priam, he embarked weighed down with spoils.
No sharp bronze spear had wounded him at all;   535
he was unhurt by all the skirmishes
endured in war when Ares rages blind.'

After I told him this, Achilles' ghost
took great swift-footed strides across the fields
of asphodel, delighted to have heard   540
about the glorious prowess of his son.

Other dead souls were gathering, all sad;
each told the story of his sorrow. Only
Ajax kept back, enraged because I won
Achilles' armor,[6] when the case was judged   545
beside the ships. The hero's mother, Thetis,
and sons of Troy, and Pallas, gave the arms
to me. I wish I had not won this contest!
For those arms Ajax lies beneath the earth,
whose looks and deeds were best of all the Greeks   550
after Achilles, son of Peleus.
I spoke to him to try to make it up.

'Please, Ajax, son of mighty Telamon,
can you not set aside your rage at me
about those cursed arms? Not even now,   555
in death? The gods made them to ruin us.
You were our tower; what a loss you were!
We Greeks were struck by grief when you were gone;
we mourned as long for you as for Achilles.
Blame nobody but Zeus. He ruined us,   560
in hatred for the army of the Greeks;
and that was why he brought this doom on you.
But listen now, my lord. Subdue your anger.'
He did not answer. He went off and followed
the spirits of the dead to Erebus.   565

Despite his rage, we might have spoken longer
if I had not felt in my heart an urge
to see more spirits. I saw Minos[7] there,
the son of Zeus, who holds the golden scepter
and sits in judgment on the dead. They ask   570
their king to arbitrate disputes, inside
the house of Hades, where the doors are always

---

6. Achilles' sea-goddess mother, Thetis, had   7. Legendary king of Crete.
given him armor crafted by the god Hephaestus.

wide open. I saw great Orion,[8] chasing
across the fields of asphodel the beasts
he killed when living high in lonely mountains,   575
holding his indestructible bronze club.
And I saw Tityus, the son of Gaia,
stretched out nine miles.[9] When Leto, Zeus' lover,
was traveling to Pytho, through the fields
of beautiful Panopeus, he raped her.   580
Two vultures sit on either side of him,
ripping his liver, plunging in his bowels;
he fails to push them off. I saw the pain
of Tantalus, in water to his chin,
so parched, no way to drink. When that old man   585
bent down towards the water, it was gone;
some god had dried it up, and at his feet
dark earth appeared. Tall leafy trees hung fruit
above his head: sweet figs and pomegranates
and brightly shining apples and ripe olives.   590
But when he grasped them with his hands, the wind
hurled them away towards the shadowy clouds.
And I saw Sisyphus in torment, pushing
a giant rock with both hands, leaning on it
with all his might to shove it up towards   595
a hilltop; when he almost reached the peak,
its weight would swerve, and it would roll back down,
heedlessly. But he kept on straining, pushing,
his body drenched in sweat, his head all dusty.
I saw a phantom of great Heracles.   600
The man himself is with the deathless gods,[1]
happy and feasting, with fine-ankled Hebe,[2]
the child of mighty Zeus and golden Hera.
Around his ghost, the dead souls shrieked like birds,
all panic struck. He walked like gloomy night,   605
holding his bow uncased and with an arrow
held on the string. He glowered terribly,
poised for a shot. Around his chest was strapped
a terrifying baldric made of gold,
fashioned with marvelous images of bears,   610
wild boars, and lions with fierce staring eyes,
and battles and the slaughtering of men.
I hope the craftsman who designed this scene
will never make another work like this.
This Heracles at once knew who I was,   615
and full of grief he cried,

---

8. Mythical hunter who was turned into the
constellation Orion.
9. Tityus was a Titan, one of the generation
before the Olympian gods. Gaia is the original
earth goddess.
1. Heracles, a son of Zeus, was supposed to
have been rewarded after all his labors with a
place among the Olympian gods. The confusing suggestion that his phantom is with the
dead, while his real self is with the gods, may
be a reflection of various views about whether
or not Heracles really was apotheosized.
2. "Hebe" means "youth."

'Odysseus!
Master of every circumstance, so you
are also tortured by the weight of fortune
as I was while I lived beneath the sun?
I was a son of Zeus, and yet my pain   620
was infinite. I was enslaved to someone
far less heroic than myself, who laid
harsh labors on me.[3] Once he sent me here
to bring back Cerberus,[4] since he could think
of no worse task for me. I brought the Dog   625
up out of Hades, with the help of Hermes,
and flashing-eyed Athena.'

           He went back
to Hades' house. I stayed, in case more heroes
who died in ancient times should come to me.
I would have seen the noble men I hoped for,   630
Pirithous and Theseus, god-born.[5]
But masses of the dead came thronging round
with eerie cries, and cold fear seized me, lest
the dreadful Queen Persephone might send
the monster's head, the Gorgon,[6] out of Hades.   635
So then I hurried back and told my men
to climb on board the ship and loose the cables.
They did so, and sat down along the benches.
The current bore the ship down River Ocean,
first with the help of oars, and then fair wind."   640

BOOK 12

Difficult Choices

"Our ship sailed out beyond the stream of Ocean,
across the waves of open sea, and came
to Aeaea, home of newborn Dawn, who dances
in meadows with the beams of Helius.
We beached the ship upon the sandy shore,   5
and disembarked, and there we fell asleep
while waiting for bright morning. When Dawn came,
born early, with her fingertips like petals,
I sent my men to Circe's house, to bring
the body of the dead Elpenor. Quickly   10
we chopped the wood and at the farthest headland

---

3. Eurystheus, at the behest of the goddess Hera, laid the labors on Heracles, whom she resented as an illegitimate son of her husband, Zeus.
4. Guard dog of the underworld.
5. Theseus, a son of Poseidon, was a mythic

king of Athens and killer of the Minotaur. Pirithous was his best friend, a son of Zeus; together they went to the underworld, hoping to abduct Persephone.
6. Female monster whose gaze turns onlookers to stone.

we held a funeral for him, and wept
profusely, crying out in grief. We burned
his body and his gear, and built a mound,
and dragged a pillar onto it, and fixed   15
his oar on top—each ritual step in turn.
Circe, the well-groomed goddess, was aware
that we were back from Hades, and she hurried
to meet us with her slaves. They carried bread
and meat and bright red wine. She stood among us,   20
and said,

       'This is amazing! You all went
alive to Hades—you will be twice-dead,
when other people only die one time!
Eat now, and stay here drinking wine all day.
At dawn, sail on. I will explain your route   25
in detail, so no evil thing can stitch
a means to hurt you, on the land or sea.'

I am a stubborn man, but I agreed,
so there we sat and feasted on the meat
and strong sweet wine until the sun went down.   30
When darkness fell, the men slept by the ship.
Then Circe took my hand, and led me off
apart from them, and questioned me in detail.
I told her everything. The lady Circe
replied at last,

       'That quest is over now.   35
So listen, I will give you good instructions;
another god will make sure you remember.
First you will reach the Sirens, who bewitch
all passersby. If anyone goes near them
in ignorance, and listens to their voices,   40
that man will never travel to his home,
and never make his wife and children happy
to have him back with them again. The Sirens
who sit there in their meadow will seduce him
with piercing songs. Around about them lie   45
great heaps of men, flesh rotting from their bones,
their skin all shriveled up. Use wax to plug
your sailors' ears as you row past, so they
are deaf to them. But if you wish to hear them,
your men must fasten you to your ship's mast   50
by hand and foot, straight upright, with tight ropes.
So bound, you can enjoy the Sirens' song.
But if you beg your men to set you free,
they have to tie you down with firmer knots.
I will not give you definite instructions   55
about which route to take when you have sailed
beyond the Sirens. Let your heart decide.

There are two choices, and the first goes through
vast overhanging rocks, which Amphitrite
batters aggressively with mighty waves. 60
The blessed gods call these the Wandering Rocks.
No birds can fly through safe, not even doves,
who bring ambrosia to Zeus. One dove
is always lost in that sheer gulf of stone
and Zeus must send another to restore 65
the number of the flock. No human ship
has ever passed there. When one tries to enter,
the waves and raging gusts of fire engulf
ship timbers and the bodies of the men.
Only the famous *Argo* sailed through there 70
returning from the visit with Aeetes.
The current hurled the ship towards the rocks,
but Hera, who loved Jason, led them safe.[1]
Taking the second way, you meet two rocks:
one reaches up to heaven with its peak, 75
surrounded by blue fog that never clears.
No light comes through there, even in the summer.
No man could climb it or set foot upon it,
even if he had twenty hands and feet.
The rock is sheer, as if it had been polished. 80
Right in the middle lies a murky cave
that faces west, towards dark Erebus.
Steer your ship past it, great Odysseus.
The hollow cave is so high up, no man
could shoot it with an arrow. There lives Scylla, 85
howling and barking horribly; her voice
is puppylike, but she is dangerous;
even a god would be afraid of her.
She has twelve dangling legs and six long necks
with a gruesome head on each, and in each face 90
three rows of crowded teeth, pregnant with death.
Her belly slumps inside the hollow cave;
she keeps her heads above the yawning chasm
and scopes around the rock, and hunts for fish.
She catches dolphins, seals, and sometimes even 95
enormous whales—Queen Amphitrite, ruler
of roaring waters, nurtures many creatures.
No sailors ever pass that way unharmed.
She snatches one man with each mouth from off
each dark-prowed ship. The other rock is near, 100
enough to shoot an arrow right across.
This second rock is lower down, and on it
there grows a fig tree with thick leaves. Beneath,
divine Charybdis sucks black water down.

1. The Greek hero Jason sailed in the *Argo* to get the Golden Fleece from King Aeetes of Colchis. The journey of Jason and the Argonauts was supposed to have taken place a generation before the wanderings of Odysseus. Jason was the favorite of the goddess Hera.

Three times a day she spurts it up; three times   105
she glugs it down. Avoid that place when she
is swallowing the water. No one could
save you from death then, even great Poseidon.
Row fast, and steer your ship alongside Scylla,
since it is better if you lose six men   110
than all of them.'

               I answered, 'Goddess, please,
tell me the truth: is there no other way?
Or I can somehow circumvent Charybdis
and stop that Scylla when she tries to kill
my men?'

             The goddess answered, 'No, you fool!   115
Your mind is still obsessed with deeds of war.
But now you must surrender to the gods.
She is not mortal. She is deathless evil,
terrible, wild and cruel. You cannot fight her.
The best solution and the only way   120
is flight. I am afraid if you take time
to arm beside the rock, she will attack
again with all six heads and take six more.
So row away with all your might, and call
on Scylla's mother, Cratais, Great Force,   125
who bore her as a blight on humankind.
Go fast, before the goddess strikes again.
Then you will reach the island called Thrinacia,
where Helius keeps sheep and many cattle:[2]
fifty per herd, with seven herds in all.   130
They never reproduce or die, and those
who tend them are the smooth-haired goddesses,
Phaethousa and Lampetia, the shining
daughters of Helius by bright Neaira.
She brought them up, then sent them off to live   135
there in remote Thrinacia, to guard
their father's sheep and cattle. If you can
remember home and leave the cows unharmed,
you will at last arrive in Ithaca.
But if you damage them, I must foretell   140
disaster for your ship and for your crew.
Even if you survive, you will return
late and humiliated, having caused
the death of all your men.'

             The golden throne
of Dawn was riding up the sky as Circe   145
concluded, and she strode across her island.
I went back to my ship and roused the men

---

2. Helius and Hyperion are both sun gods, here confused.

to get on board and loose the sternward cables.
Embarking, they sat down, each in his place,
and struck the gray saltwater with their oars.   150
Behind our dark-prowed ship, the dreadful goddess
Circe sent friendly wind to fill the sails.
We worked efficiently to organize
the rigging, and the breeze and pilot steered.
Then with an anxious heart I told the crew,   155

'My friends, the revelations Circe shared
with me should not be kept a secret, known
to me alone. I will share them with you,
and we can die in knowledge of the truth,
or else escape. She said we must avoid   160
the voices of the otherworldly Sirens;
steer past their flowering meadow. And she says
that I alone should hear their singing. Bind me,
to keep me upright at the mast, wound round
with rope. If I beseech you and command you   165
to set me free, you must increase my bonds
and chain me even tighter.'

        So I told them
each detail. Soon our well-built ship, blown fast
by fair winds, neared the island of the Sirens,
and suddenly, the wind died down. Calm came.   170
Some spirit lulled the waves to sleep. The men
got up, pulled down the sails, and stowed them in
the hollow hold. They sat at oar and made
the water whiten, struck by polished wood.
I gripped a wheel of wax between my hands   175
and cut it small. Firm kneading and the sunlight
warmed it, and then I rubbed it in the ears
of each man in his turn. They bound my hands
and feet, straight upright at the mast. They sat
and hit the sea with oars. We traveled fast,   180
and when we were in earshot of the Sirens,
they knew our ship was near, and started singing.

'Odysseus! Come here! You are well-known
from many stories! Glory of the Greeks!
Now stop your ship and listen to our voices.   185
All those who pass this way hear honeyed song,
poured from our mouths. The music brings them joy,
and they go on their way with greater knowledge,
since we know everything the Greeks and Trojans
suffered in Troy, by gods' will; and we know   190
whatever happens anywhere on earth.'

Their song was so melodious, I longed
to listen more. I told my men to free me.

I scowled at them, but they kept rowing on.
Eurylochus and Perimedes stood 195
and tied me even tighter, with more knots.
But when we were well past them and I could
no longer hear the singing of the Sirens,
I nodded to my men, and they removed
the wax that I had used to plug their ears, 200
and untied me. When we had left that island,
I saw a mighty wave and smoke, and heard
a roar. The men were terrified; their hands
let fall the oars—they splashed down in the water.
The ship stayed still, since no one now was pulling 205
the slender blades. I strode along the deck
pausing to cheer each man, then gave a speech
to rally all of them.

        'Dear friends! We are
experienced in danger. This is not
worse than the time the Cyclops captured us, 210
and forced us to remain inside his cave.
We got away that time, thanks to my skill
and brains and strategy. Remember that.
Come on then, all of you, and trust my words.
Sit on your benches, strike the swelling deep 215
with oars, since Zeus may grant us a way out
from this disaster also. Pilot, listen:
these are your orders. As you hold the rudder,
direct the ship away from that dark smoke
and rising wave, and head towards the rock; 220
if the ship veers the other way, you will
endanger us.'

        They promptly followed orders.
I did not mention Scylla, since she meant
inevitable death, and if they knew,
the men would drop the oars and go and huddle 225
down in the hold in fear. Then I ignored
Circe's advice that I should not bear arms;
it was too hard for me. I dressed myself
in glorious armor; in my hands I took
two long spears, and I climbed up on the forecastle. 230
I thought that rocky Scylla would appear
from that direction, to destroy my men.
So we rowed through the narrow strait in tears.
On one side, Scylla; on the other, shining
Charybdis with a dreadful gurgling noise 235
sucked down the water. When she spewed it out,
she seethed, all churning like a boiling cauldron
on a huge fire. The froth flew high, to spatter
the topmost rocks on either side. But when
she swallowed back the sea, she seemed all stirred 240

from inside, and the rock around was roaring
dreadfully, and the dark-blue sand below
was visible. The men were seized by fear.
But while our frightened gaze was on Charybdis,
Scylla snatched six men from the ship—my strongest,   245
best fighters. Looking back from down below,
I saw their feet and hands up high, as they
were carried off. In agony they cried
to me and called my name—their final words.
As when a fisherman out on a cliff   250
casts his long rod and line set round with oxhorn
to trick the little fishes with his bait;
when one is caught, he flings it gasping back
onto the shore—so those men gasped as Scylla
lifted them up high to her rocky cave   255
and at the entrance ate them up—still screaming,
still reaching out to me in their death throes.
That was the most heartrending sight I saw
in all the time I suffered on the sea.

Free from the rocks of Scylla and Charybdis   260
we quickly reached the island of the god,
Hyperion's son Helius, the Sun God.
There were his cattle, with their fine broad faces,
and many flocks of well-fed sheep. While still
out on the sea in my black ship, I heard   265
the lowing of the cattle in their pens,
and bleating of the sheep. I kept in mind
the words of blind Tiresias the prophet
and Circe. Both had given strict instructions
that we avoid the island of the Sun,   270
the god of human joy. I told the men
with heavy heart,

                'My friends, I know how much
you have endured. But listen to me now.
Tiresias and Circe both insisted
we must avoid the island of the Sun,   275
the joy of mortals. They said dreadful danger
lurks there for us. We have to steer our ship
around it.'

                They were quite downcast by this.
Eurylochus said angrily to me,
'You are unfair to us, Odysseus.   280
You may be strong; you never seem to tire;
you must be made of iron. But we men
have had no rest or sleep; we are exhausted.
And you refuse to let us disembark
and cook our tasty dinner on this island.   285
You order us to drift around all night

in our swift ship across the misty sea.
At night, fierce storms rise up and wreck men's ships,
and how can anyone escape disaster
if sudden gusts of wind from south or west   290
bring cruel blasts to break the ship, despite
the wishes of the gods? Let us submit
to evening. Let us stay here, and cook food
beside the ship. At dawn we can embark
and sail the open sea.'

                    That was his speech.   295
The other men agreed, and then I saw
a spirit must be plotting our destruction.
My words flew out.

                    'Eurylochus! You force me
to yield, since I am one and you are many.
But all of you, swear me a mighty oath: 300
if we find any herd of cows, or flock
of sheep, do not be fool enough to kill
a single animal. Stay clear, and eat
the food provided by immortal Circe.'

They swore as I commanded. When they finished   305
making the oath, we set our well-built ship
inside the curving harbor, near freshwater.
The men got out and skillfully cooked dinner.
When they were satisfied with food and drink,
they wept, remembering their dear companions,   310
whom Scylla captured from the ship and ate.
Sweet sleep came down upon them as they cried.
When night was over, when the stars were gone,
Zeus roused a blast of wind, an eerie storm.
He covered earth and sea with fog, and darkness   315
fell down from heaven. When rose-fingered Dawn
appeared, we dragged the ship inside a cave,
a place nymphs danced in, and we moored it there.
I gave a speech to my assembled men.

'My friends, we have supplies on board. Let us   320
not touch the cattle, or we will regret it.
Those cows and fat sheep are the property
of Helius, the great Sun God, who sees
all things, and hears all things.' I told them this.
Reluctantly they yielded. But that month   325
the South Wind blew and never stopped. No other
was ever blowing, only South and East.
While the men still had food and wine, they kept
clear of the cows. They hoped to save their lives.
But when our ship's supplies ran out, the men   330
were forced to hunt; they used their hooks to catch
both fish and birds, whatever they could get,

since hunger gnawed their bellies. I strode off
to pray, in case some god would show me how
to get back home. I left my men behind,   335
and crossed the island, washed my hands, in shelter
out of the wind, and prayed to all the gods.
They poured sweet sleep upon my eyes.

                              Meanwhile,
Eurylochus proposed a foolish plan.
'Listen, my friends! You have already suffered   340
too much. All human deaths are hard to bear.
But starving is most miserable of all.
So let us poach the finest of these cattle,
and sacrifice them to the deathless gods.
If we get home to Ithaca, at once   345
we will construct a temple to the Sun God,
with treasure in it. If he is so angry
about these cows that he decides to wreck
our ship, and if the other gods agree—
I would prefer to drink the sea and die   350
at once, than perish slowly, shriveled up
here on this desert island.'

                       All the others
agreed with him. They went to poach the best
of Helius' cattle, which were grazing
beside the ship. The men surrounded them,   355
and called upon the gods. They had plucked leaves
from oak trees—on the ship there was no barley.[3]
They prayed, then killed them, skinned them, and cut off
the thighs, and covered up the bones with fat,
a double layer, with raw meat on top.   360
They had no wine to pour libations over
the burning offering, but they made do
with water, and they roasted all the innards.
And when the thighs were burned, the entrails sprinkled,
they cut the other meat up into chunks   365
for skewers.

                Sweet sleep melted from my eyes;
I rushed back to the ship beside the shore.
When I was close, the meaty smell of cooking
enfolded me. I groaned, and told the gods,

'O Zeus, and all you deathless gods! You blinded   370
my mind with that infernal sleep. My men
did dreadful things while I was gone.'

                        Meanwhile,
Lampetia in flowing skirts ran off

---

3. Barley is a component of a ritual sacrifice.

to tell the Sun God we had killed his cows.
Enraged, he called the other gods at once.

                                    'Great Zeus,   375
and all you other deathless gods, you must
punish Odysseus' men. They killed
my cattle! I delighted in those cows
all through each day, when I went up to heaven
and when I turned to earth. If they do not   380
repay me, I will sink down into Hades
and bring my bright light only to the dead.'

Zeus answered, 'Helius! Please shine with us
and shine for mortals on life-giving earth.
I will immediately smite their ship   385
with my bright thunderbolt, and smash it up
in fragments, all across the wine-dark sea.'

I heard this from the beautiful Calypso,
who had been told by Hermes.

                              Back on shore
beside my ship, I scolded each of them.   390
It did no good; the cows were dead already.
The gods sent signs—the hides began to twitch,
the meat on skewers started mooing, raw
and cooked. There was the sound of cattle lowing.
For six days my men banqueted on beef   395
from Helius. When Zeus, the son of Cronus,
led in the seventh day, the wind became
less stormy, and we quickly went on board.
We set the mast up and unfurled the sails
and set out on the open sea.

                              When we   400
had left that island, we could see no other,
only the sky and sea. Zeus made a mass
of dark-blue storm cloud hang above our ship.
The sea grew dark beneath it. For a moment
the ship moved on, but then came Zephyr, shrieking, 405
noisily rushing, with torrential tempest.
A mighty gust of wind broke off both forestays;
the tacking was all scattered in the hold.
The mast was broken backwards, and it struck
the pilot in the stern; it smashed his skull.   410
His bones were crushed, his skeleton was smashed.
He fell down like a diver from the deck;
his spirit left his body. At that instant,
Zeus thundered and hurled bolts to strike the ship;
shaken, it filled with sulfur. All the men   415
fell overboard, and they were swept away

like seagulls on the waves beside the ship.
The gods prevented them from reaching home.

I paced on board until the current ripped
the ship's side from the keel. The waves bore off 420
the husk, and snapped the mast. But thrown across it
there was a backstay cable, oxhide leather.
With this I lashed the keel and mast together,
and rode them, carried on by fearsome winds.
At last the tempest ceased, the West Wind lulled. 425
I worried that the South Wind might compel me
to backtrack, to the terrible Charybdis.
All night I was swept backwards and at sunrise
I came back to the dreadful rocks of Scylla
and of Charybdis, gulping salty water, 430
and overshadowed by the fig tree's branches.
I jumped and clutched its trunk, batlike—unable
to plant my feet, or climb. The roots were down
too low; the tall long branches were too high.
So I kept clinging on; I hoped Charybdis 435
would belch my mast and keel back up. She did!
As one who spends the whole day judging quarrels
between young men, at last goes home to eat—
at that same hour, the planks came bobbing up
out of Charybdis. I let go my hands 440
and feet and dropped myself way down to splash
into the sea below, beside the timbers
of floating wood. I clambered onto them,
and used my hands to row myself away,
and Zeus ensured that Scylla did not see me, 445
or else I could not have survived. I drifted
for nine days. On the evening of the tenth,
the gods helped me to reach the island of
the dreadful, beautiful, divine Calypso.
She loved and cared for me. Why should I tell 450
the story that I told you and your wife
yesterday in your house? It is annoying,
repeating tales that have been told before."

BOOK 13

Two Tricksters

After he finished, all were silent, spellbound,
sitting inside the shadowy hall. At last,
Alcinous said,

      "Now, Odysseus,
since you have been my guest, beneath my roof,
you need not wander anymore. You have 5
endured enough; you will get home again.

And all you regulars, my honored friends
who always drink red wine here in my house
and listen to my singer: heed my words.
Our guest has clothes packed up inside a trunk,   10
and other gifts that we have given him.
Each of us now should add a mighty tripod
and cauldron. I will make the people pay
a levy, so that none of us will suffer
from unrewarded generosity."   15

The king's words pleased them all. They went back home
to rest. Then Dawn was born again; her fingers
bloomed, and they hurried back towards the ship
bringing heroic gifts of bronze. The king
embarked and stowed them underneath the beams,   20
to leave room for the crew when they were rowing.
Then all the men went back with him to eat.
The holy king killed sacrificial meat—
a cow to Zeus of dark clouds, son of Cronus,
who rules the world. They burned the thighs and feasted   25
in happiness. The well-respected singer
Demodocus made music in their midst.
But all the while Odysseus kept turning
his head towards the shining sun, impatient
for it to set. He longed to leave. As when   30
a man is desperate for dinnertime
after he spends the whole day with his oxen
dragging the jointed plow across the field,
and welcomes sunset, when he can go home
to eat; his legs are aching on the way—   35
just so Odysseus was glad of sunset.
At once he told the seafaring Phaeacians,
especially Alcinous,

                              "Great king,
and all of you, please send me safely home
with offerings, and thank you. I am grateful   40
to you for giving me my heart's desire:
a passage home, with gifts. I hope the gods
maintain my luck. When I am home, I pray
to find my wife still faultless, and my loved ones
safe. And may you Phaeacians live to bring   45
joy to your wives and children—every blessing.
I pray there is no trouble for your people."

They praised his words and said that they must help
their guest go home, since he had spoken well.
Alcinous addressed his right-hand man.   50
"Pontonous, now mix a bowl of wine;
serve drinks to everybody in the hall,
so we may pray to Zeus and help our guest

back to his homeland."

                 So the steward mixed
a cheering bowl of wine and served them all   55
in turn. Still in their seats, they poured libations
to all the blessed gods that live in heaven.
Godlike Odysseus stood up and put
a double-handled cup into the hands
of Arete. His words flew out to her.   60

"Bless you forever, queen, until old age
and death arrive for you, as for us all.
I will leave now. Be happy in your home
and children, and your people, and your king."

With that, the noble hero crossed the threshold.   65
Alcinous sent out his steward with him
to guide him to the swift ship on the shore.
Arete sent some slave girls too. One brought
a freshly laundered cloak and tunic; one
carried the well-carved chest; the third brought bread   70
and red wine. When they reached the ship, the guides
took all the food and drink and packed it neatly
inside the hold. They spread a sheet and blanket
out on the stern-deck of the hollow ship
so he could sleep there soundly. Climbing on,   75
he lay there quietly. The rowers sat
down on the benches calmly, and then loosed
the cable from the mooring stone. They pulled,
leaning back hard; the oar blades splashed the water.
A sound sweet sleep fell on his eyes, like death;   80
he did not stir. As four fine stallions
rush at the whip and race their chariot
across the track, heads high, an easy canter—
so was the ship's prow raised. The seething waves
of sounding purple sea rushed round the stern   85
as she sped straight ahead. The swiftest bird,
a hawk, could never overtake; she sailed
so fast, and cleaved the waves. She bore a man
whose mind was like the gods', who had endured
many heartbreaking losses, and the pain   90
of war and shipwreck. Now he slept in peace,
and he remembered nothing of his pain.

But when the brightest star that carries news
about the coming Dawn rose up the sky,
the seaborne ship neared land. There is a harbor   95
of Phorcys, ancient sea god, in the district
of Ithaca. On either side of it
there are sheer cliffs that jut across the bay;
they shelter it and keep big waves outside

when storm winds blow. The ships remain in harbor 100
without a tether, once they cross its bounds.
At the bay's head there grows a long-leafed olive,
and near it is a beautiful dark cave,
a holy place of sea-nymphs—Nereids.
Inside are bowls and amphorae of stone, 105
and buzzing bees bring honey. There are looms,
also of stone; the Nymphs weave purple cloth,
sea-purple—it is marvelous to see.
Water is always flowing through. There are
two entrances. The north one is for humans; 110
the south is sacred. People cannot enter
that way—it is the path of the immortals.

They rowed inside the bay; they knew the place
of old. Their arms were pulling at top speed;
the ship was traveling so fast that when 115
she reached dry land, she beached for half her length.
They disembarked, and lifted from the ship
Odysseus, wrapped up in sheets and blankets.
They set him on the sand, still fast asleep.
They unpacked all the presents he was given 120
by the Phaeacian lords to take back home,
thanks to Athena's care. They heaped the things
beside the olive tree, so no one passing
would do them any damage while their owner
was sleeping. Then they rowed away, back home. 125

Poseidon, Lord of Earthquakes, still remembered
his hatred of Odysseus; he asked
Zeus what he meant to do.

                                    "O Father Zeus!
I will lose all my standing with the gods,
since mortals fail to honor me, though these 130
Phaeacians are my very own descendants!
I always said Odysseus would reach
home in the end. I did not take away
that privilege from him, no, not at all,
since you had promised it with your own nod. 135
Their swift ship carried him across the ocean,
and they have set him down in Ithaca
with a magnificent array of gifts:
bronze, heaps of gold and fine-spun clothes, far more
spoils than he ever would have won at Troy 140
if he had got out safely."

                    Storm God Zeus
exclaimed, "Earth-Shaker! How absurd! The gods
do not dishonor you; it would be hard
to disrespect an elder so high-ranking.

If willful humans fail to show respect,   145
then punish them; you always have that power.
Do as you wish!"

        Poseidon answered, "Lord
of Dark Clouds, I have always wanted to.
I held back out of deference to you.
But now, when that fine ship of those Phaeacians   150
comes back from helping him across, I want
to smash it in the sea, and overwhelm
their city with a mountain, to prevent them
from ever guiding travelers again."

The Cloud Lord Zeus said, "Brother, I suggest   155
that while the people in the city watch,
you turn the ship arriving into stone,
still looking like a ship. They will all
be shocked. Then you can surround their town
with a huge mountain."

        Hearing this, Poseidon   160
went to Phaeacian Scheria, and waited.
As the ship sped towards the shore, the god
moved near it, turned it all to stone, and slapped
his palm to make it rooted to the seabed.
He vanished, and the people of Phaeacia,   165
known for their oars and famous ships, began
to ask each other,

        "What? Who fixed that ship
firm in the sea as she was rushing home?
We saw it all!" They could not understand it.
Alcinous addressed the crowd and spoke.   170

"So it is true! My father long ago
said that Poseidon hates us for our habit
of helping travelers get home again;
we got away with it, but he foretold
that one day great Poseidon would destroy   175
a ship on her return from such a journey;
the god would hide our city with a mountain.
And now the old man's words are coming true.
So all of you must listen to me now.
Stop helping visitors to travel onward.   180
We have to sacrifice twelve bulls, handpicked
for Lord Poseidon, so he may show mercy,
and not enfold our city in a mountain."

At this, they were afraid, and they prepared
the bulls, and all the leaders of Phaeacia   185
prayed to Poseidon, standing round the altar.

Meanwhile Odysseus, who had been sleeping
in his own native land of Ithaca,
woke up, but did not recognize the place
from which he had been absent for so long.   190
Pallas Athena cast a mist upon it,
so she could tell him how things stood, and make him
unrecognizable to his own wife
and family and neighbors, till he paid
the suitors back for how they misbehaved.   195
The friendly harbors and the winding paths
and leafy trees were all quite unfamiliar
to their own king. He leapt up to his feet
and looking at his native land, he groaned
and smacked his thighs, and sobbed,

                         "Where am I now?   200
Are those who live here violent and cruel?
Or are they kind to strangers, folks who fear
the gods? Where can I carry all my treasure?
And where can I go wandering? If only
I had remained there in Phaeacia, till   205
I went on to some other mighty king
who might have been my friend and helped me home.
Where can I leave my things? Not here for sure;
they will be stolen. Those Phaeacian lords
were not so trustworthy! They promised me   210
that they would bring me home to Ithaca.
They broke their word and brought me somewhere else.
May Zeus who helps the needy make them pay!
Zeus watches everyone, and punishes
the sinner. Let me count my treasure now—   215
they may have stolen some when they sailed off."

He counted all the tripods, cauldrons, gold
and cloth, but none was missing. Then he paced
beside the loud resounding sea, hunched up
with homesickness and sobbing in his grief.   220
Athena came towards him; she looked like
a shepherd, young and soft-skinned as a prince,
wearing a folded mantle of fine cloth
across her shoulders; on her tender feet
were sandals, and she held a javelin.   225
Odysseus was overjoyed to see her.
He cried,

              "Oh, friend! You are the very first
person that I have met here. Greetings! Please,
be kind, protect my treasure and myself.
I pray to you and supplicate, as if   230
you were a god. I touch your knees; please help me!
And tell me, please, what is this place? An island?

Or is it a peninsula that slopes
towards the sea from fertile mainland fields?
Who lives here?"

          And with twinkling eyes the goddess   235
said, "Stranger, you must be a foreigner
from distant parts, or foolish, since you ask
about this famous country. Many people
know it, from those who live towards the east
under the rising sun, to those out west   240
in lands of gloomy dusk. This is rough country,
not fit for grazing horses, and not spacious,
but not infertile; corn and wine abound here.
The land is always wet with rain and dew.
There are fine water holes, and it is good   245
for raising goats and cattle, and the trees
are varied. Foreigner, I think the name
of Ithaca is even known in Troy,
a land they say is far away from Greece."

Odysseus, who had endured so much,   250
so long, was overjoyed, to hear from her
that he was in his own dear native land.
His words took wings and flew, but he did not
tell her the truth; he bit his story back.
His mind was always full of clever schemes.   255
"Yes, I have heard of Ithaca, although
I come from distant Crete. Now I am here
with all this wealth; I left an equal share
of riches for my children back at home.
I am in exile. On the fields of Crete   260
I killed Orsilochus, the speedy sprinter,
the son of Idomeneus, the king.
I had refused to serve or help his father
at Troy; I led my own men. So the son
wanted to steal the Trojan spoils for which   265
I worked so hard, in war and long sea journeys.
I hid beside the road with one companion,
and as he came back from the countryside,
I ambushed him, and hit him with my spear.
The sky was dark that night, and no one saw me   270
kill him with my sharp sword of bronze. And after
I murdered him, I quickly rowed away
to visit the Phoenicians, and I gave them
a share of loot, which made them very glad.
I told them they should transport me to Pylos,   275
or famous Elis, ruled by the Epeians.
But storm winds drove them off away from there
against their will: they did not mean to trick me.
So swept off course, we came here in the night.
We rowed at top speed into harbor, hungry,   280

but none of us took any thought of dinner.
We disembarked and all lay down right there.
Sweet sleep enfolded me. I was exhausted.
They took my treasure from the ship and set it
beside me as I slept upon the sand.   285
And then they sailed away to well-built Sidon,
and I was left here grieving."

       At his words,
Athena smiled into his eyes. She took
his hand, and changed her body to a woman's:
beautiful, tall, and skilled in all the arts.   290
Her words were light as feathers.

         "To outwit you
in all your tricks, a person or a god
would need to be an expert at deceit.
You clever rascal! So duplicitous,
so talented at lying! You love fiction   295
and tricks so deeply, you refuse to stop
even in your own land. Yes, both of us
are smart. No man can plan and talk like you,
and I am known among the gods for insight
and craftiness. You failed to recognize me: 300
I am Athena, child of Zeus. I always
stand near you and take care of you, in all
your hardships. I made sure that you were welcomed
by the Phaeacians. I have come here now
to weave a plan with you and hide the treasure   305
which, thanks to me, they gave you to take home.
I will reveal the challenges you face
at home. This is your fate, and you must bear it
bravely, not telling any man or woman
that you have finished wandering and come back.   310
Suffer in silence, bear their brutal treatment."

Odysseus, still wary, answered, "Goddess,
even the smartest man may find it hard
to recognize you. You disguise yourself
so many ways. I do know that you helped me   315
during the Trojan War, so long ago.
But when we Greeks had sacked the town of Priam,
and we embarked, and gods dispersed our fleet,
I did not see you there on board my ship,
daughter of Zeus. You gave me no protection.   320
Lost and confused, I waited for the gods
to free me from my pain. I met you later,
in rich Phaeacia, and you spoke to me
comforting words, and led me to the city.
Please, by your father Zeus! I cannot think   325
that this is Ithaca. I must be elsewhere.

You want to fool me and make fun of me.
Tell me the truth! Is this my own dear home?"

With glowing eyes she said, "You always have
such keen intelligence, and that is why   330
I cannot leave you when you need my help.
You have such intuition and such focus.
An ordinary man would rush straight home
to see his wife and children when he reached
his country, after such a journey. You   335
decided not to even ask about them,
until you test your wife. She sits at home,
passing each night in misery, each day
in tears. For my part, I have never doubted.
I felt sure in my heart you would get home,   340
after the loss of all your men. But I
did not want conflict with my father's brother,
Poseidon, who resented you because
you blinded his beloved son.[1] Now I
will show you Ithaca, so you believe.   345
This is the bay of Phorcys, ancient sea god,
and at the head there is an olive tree
with long leaves, and nearby, the shady cave
sacred to nymphs called Nereids, to whom
you sacrificed so many hundred cattle.   350
And here is Neriton, the wooded mountain."

With that, the goddess made the mist disperse.
The land was visible. Odysseus,
after so long a wait and so much pain,
was filled with happiness at last. In joy   355
he kissed the fertile earth of his own country,
then lifted high his arms and prayed,

                                          "O Nymphs!
I never thought I would come back to you,
daughters of Zeus.[2] Accept my loving prayers,
and I will give you gifts, as in the past,   360
if my commander, child of Zeus, is kind
and lets me live and raise my son."

                              Athena
looked straight into his eyes and said, "Be brave.
You need not worry. Let us hurry now
to hide the treasure safely in the cave.   365
And then we must make plans."

1. Polyphemus the Cyclops.
2. The Nereids were sometimes presented as daughters of Poseidon.

The goddess went
down in the murky cave, and looked around
for hiding spots. Odysseus brought in
the presents the Phaeacians gave him—gold,
and tireless bronze and finely woven cloth.   370
Athena set them all inside, and fixed
the door-stone up, and then the two sat down
against the sacred olive and they planned
how to destroy the suitors. Eyes aglow,
Athena said,

      "Great king, Laertes' son,   375
master of plots and plans, Odysseus,
think how to strike the suitors. For three years
they have been lording in your house and courting
your godlike wife with gifts. She always longs
for your return, and grieves. She leads them on   380
with promises and messages to each,
but her mind moves elsewhere."

           Odysseus
cried, "Oh! I would have died like Agamemnon
in my own house, if you had not explained
exactly how things stand. So, goddess, now   385
weave me a strategy to pay them back.
Stand by me, give me courage and the drive
to fight as when I broke the shining crown
of Troy. If you will join me with that zeal
and help me, goddess-queen, I could do battle   390
against three hundred men at once."

          Athena
looked straight at him, clear-eyed. She said, "I will
be with you, truly. Know I stand beside you
as we begin our work. I do believe
the suitors who devour your livelihood   395
will spatter your broad floors with blood and brains.
But now I will disguise you, so no human
can recognize you. I will shrivel up
the fine skin of your supple arms and legs,
ruin your hair, and dress you up in rags,   400
so everyone will shudder, seeing you.
And I will cloud your eyes, to make you seem
ugly to all the suitors, and your wife
and to the son you left at home. Now visit
the swineherd who, though he is just a slave,   405
adores your son and wise Penelope
and is your friend. Go look for him among
the sows who root beside the Corax rock
and near the spring of Arethusa, drinking
black water, eating good nutritious acorns,   410

which fatten pigs. Stay there and sit with him,
and ask him everything. And I will go
to Sparta, where the girls are beautiful,
to fetch Telemachus, the boy you love.
He went to Menelaus, to find out   415
if you are still alive."

                  He asked her sharply,
"But why did you not tell him? You must know
everything. Did you want him suffering
like me, lost out at sea, while others eat
his whole inheritance?"

                  With shining eyes   420
Athena answered, "Come now, do not worry
about the boy. I guided him myself
so that he might win glory by his journey.
He is not suffering. He is away,
sitting and banqueting with Menelaus.   425
The suitors do indeed desire to kill him,
and wait in ambush for him in their ship.
But they will not succeed, I think. The earth
will cover one or more of those who eat
your property."

                  Then with her wand Athena   430
tapped him; his handsome body withered up;
his limbs became arthritic. She bleached out
his hair, and made his skin look old and wrinkled,
and dimmed his fine bright eyes. She turned his clothes
into a tattered cloak and ragged tunic,   435
dirty with soot. She wrapped around his shoulders
a massive leather deerskin, and she gave him
a threadbare tote bag and a walking stick.
Their plans were set; they parted. She went off
to Sparta, to go fetch Telemachus.   440

BOOK 14

A Loyal Slave

Leaving the bay, he hiked the rugged path
through woodland and across the cliffs; Athena
had shown him where to go to find the swineherd.
Of all those in Odysseus' household,
this noble slave cared most about preserving   5
the master's property. Odysseus
found him as he was sitting out on his porch.
His yard was high and visible for miles,
of fieldstones topped with twigs of thorny pear.
He built it in the absence of his master,   10

with no help from Laertes or the mistress.
Around the yard, he set a ring of stakes,
of wood with bark stripped off. Inside the yard,
he made twelve sties all next to one another,
for breeding sows, with fifty in each one.   15
The boars slept outside; there were fewer of them,
because the suitors kept on eating them.
The swineherd let them have the fattest boars;
just three hundred and sixty still remained.
Their captain kept four fierce half-wild dogs   20
to guard the gate. Now he was cutting oxhide
to make himself some sandals. Of his men,
three herded up the pigs, and ran around
in all directions; he had sent the fourth
to town to take a pig to those proud suitors.   25
He had no choice; he had to satisfy
their cravings for fresh meat.

                      Then suddenly
the guard dogs saw Odysseus, and rushed
towards him with loud barks. He kept his head,
and sank down to the ground and dropped his stick. 30
They would have hurt him terribly, and shamed him
on his own property—but acting fast
the swineherd dropped his leatherwork and rushed
to chase the dogs away. He yelled at them
and pelted them with stones to make them scatter.   35
And then he told his master,

                        "My dogs almost
ripped you apart, old man! You would have brought me
shame, when the gods are hurting me already.
I am in mourning for an absent master,
raising his pigs for other men to eat.   40
My lord is lost and maybe even hungry,
in lands where the people speak in foreign tongues—
if he is even still alive, still seeing
the sunlight. Well now, follow me, old man,
fill up on food and wine, then tell me where   45
you come from, and the troubles you have borne."

The noble swineherd heaped up cushy brushwood,
and spread a furry goatskin over it—his own
bed-blanket, thick and warm. Odysseus
sat down and was delighted at this welcome.   50
He said,

                    "May Zeus and all the deathless gods
reward you with your heart's desire, because
you welcomed me so willingly."

And you,
Eumaeus, answered, "One must honor guests
and foreigners and strangers, even those   55
much poorer than oneself. Zeus watches over
beggars and guests and strangers. What I have
to give is small, but I will give it gladly.
Life is like this for slaves: we live in fear,
when younger men have power over us.   60
My real lord is kept from home by gods.
He would have taken care of me, and given
what kindly owners give to loyal slaves:
a house with land, and wife whom many men
would want—as recompense for years of labor   65
which gods have blessed and made to prosper. Master
would have been good to me, if he had stayed
here till old age. He must be dead by now.
Damn Helen and her family! So many
have died for her sake. Master went to Troy,   70
to win back Agamemnon's honor, fighting
the Trojans."

Then he belted up his tunic
and hurried to the pen, and chose two piglets.
Inside he butchered them, singed off the bristles,
chopped up the meat and roasted it on skewers.   75
He set it, piping hot, before his guest,
sprinkling barley on the top. He mixed
wine in an ivy bowl, as sweet as honey,
and then sat down across from him, and urged,
"Now, guest, eat up! This is a poor slave's meal: 80
a suckling pig. The suitors eat the hogs.
Their hearts have no compassion! They ignore
the gods, who watch and hate such crimes and bless
good deeds and justice. Even cutthroat pirates,
who go to plunder other people's lands,   85
seizing the spoils that Zeus has granted them,
and sail home in a ship filled full of treasure—
even they feel the watchful eyes of gods.
These suitors must have heard some god's voice saying,
'Odysseus has died.' So they refuse   90
to go back to their own homes or to arrange
suitable marriages. Instead they sit,
wasting his wealth on feasts. Each night and day
they butcher sheep, not one but dozens of them,
and pour out yet more wine for reckless drinking.   95
Those selfish oafs! My lord was very rich;
no others on the mainland or back here
in Ithaca, nor twenty all combined,
possessed as much. I will list all of it.
Twelve herds of cattle on the mainland, twelve   100
of sheep, and twelve of pigs, and twelve of goats.

He had to hire more laborers to help us.
And out here on the far end of the island,
eleven herds of goats are grazing, watched
by good men. Every day, a herdsman takes   105
whichever goat seems fattest and most healthy
up to the palace. I, who watch these pigs,
must choose the best for them."

                       Odysseus
gratefully wolfed the meat and drank the wine
in silence. He was hatching plots to ruin   110
the suitors. After he had had enough
to eat, he took the wine-cup he had drunk from,
filled it again and gave it to Eumaeus,
who took it gladly. Then Odysseus
said,

     "Friend, who bought you? This rich, noble man   115
that you describe—who is he? You say he
died in the war for Agamemnon's honor.
Perhaps I know him, since he must be famous.
Zeus and the other gods will be aware
if I have seen him and can bring you news.   120
He traveled widely."

                    But the swineherd said,
"His wife and son will not trust travelers
who claim to bring them news. Tramps always lie
to get a meal—they have no cause to tell
the truth. All those who pass through Ithaca   125
go to my mistress spinning foolish tales.
She welcomes them and questions them, while tears
stream from her eyes, and rightly so: a wife
should mourn for her dead husband. Sir, you also
would weave tall tales if you got clothes for it.   130
But in reality, my master's skin
has been ripped off his bones by birds of prey
and dogs; his life is gone. Or he has been
eaten at sea by fish; his bones are lying
upon the beach, heaped high with sand. His death   135
is ruin for us all, especially me,
since I will never have so kind a master,
however far I go, not even if
I go back to the home of my own parents
who gave me birth and brought me up. I wish   140
that I could see them, in my native land.
But I grieve less for my own family
than for Odysseus. I miss him so.
I hesitate to call him by his name,
stranger: I would prefer to call him 'brother,'   145
even when he is far away, because
he loved and cared for me with so much kindness."

Odysseus was self-restrained. He said,
"My friend, you are so adamant, insisting
that he will not come back. You have no faith.   150
But this is no tall tale: I swear to you
Odysseus is on his way. And when
he is in his own house, then I will claim
my prize as messenger—some better clothes.
Till then, I will take nothing, though I need them.   155
I hate like Hades' gates the man who caves
to poverty, and starts to lie. I swear
by Zeus, and by the welcome that you gave me,
and by the hearth of great Odysseus,
where I am going: all this will turn out   160
as I say now. Odysseus will come,
within this very cycle of the moon:
between the waning and the waxing time,
he will come home, and pay back all those here
who disrespect his wife and noble son."   165

You answered him, swineherd Eumaeus, "Sir,
I will not give you this reward, since he
will not come home. Relax and drink. Let us
think about other things. Do not remind me.
My heart is troubled when a person mentions   170
my faithful master. Never mind your oath.
I hope he comes, as do Penelope
and old Laertes and Telemachus.
May it come true. But I cannot forget
my grief for that poor boy, my master's son.   175
Thanks to the gods, he grew up like a tree,
handsome and strong, as if to match his father
when he becomes a man. But somebody
or some god ruined his good sense. He went
to Pylos, seeking news about his father.   180
The suitors lie in wait for when he comes
back home, and soon Arcesius' line[1]
will be wiped out on Ithaca. No more.
They may catch him, or he may get away,
kept safe by Zeus. Now tell me, sir, the truth   185
about your own adventures. Where are you from?
Where do your parents live? Where is your town?
On what boat did you sail here? How did sailors
bring you to Ithaca? And who were they?
I know you did not reach this land by foot."   190

Odysseus said cunningly, "I will
tell you the truth, the whole truth. How I wish
we two could sit at ease here in this cottage,

---

1. Arcesius was Laertes' father; he may have been more prominent in earlier versions of the myth.

and we had food and sweet strong wine to last
as long as we desired, while all the work   195
was done by others! Even if I talked
a whole year, I would not complete the story
of everything the gods have made me suffer.
Proudly I say, I come from spacious Crete,
the son of wealthy Castor Hylacides,   200
whose sons by his main wife were numerous,
raised in his house. My mother was a slave,
bought as a concubine, and yet my father
respected me like all his other sons.
The Cretan people held him in high honor   205
as if he were a god, since he was rich
and had such noble sons. But fate arrived
to take him down to Hades. Then my brothers
selfishly seized his property, and gave
only a tiny part to me, with barely   210
a place to live. But I was not a weakling,
or cowardly in fighting. My great skill
and talent helped me win a wife who had
a decent dowry—all lost now. But you
can see in stubble how the grain once grew,   215
though I am crushed by grief. I have the gift
of courage from Athena and from Ares.
Whenever I chose warriors to ambush
our enemies, I never thought of death.
I leapt out far in front, and ran to catch them   220
and spear them. That was how I was in war.
I did not like farmwork or housekeeping,
or raising children. I liked sailing better,
and war with spears and arrows, deadly weapons.
Others may shudder at such things, but gods   225
made my heart love them. People's preferences
are different. Before the Greeks went off
to march on Troy, I led my troops and fleet
on nine forays, with great success. I had
my pick of all the spoils, and got much more   230
when we shared out the winnings. Soon my house
grew rich; I was a fine, important man
among the Cretans. But far-seeing Zeus
arranged that expedition of disaster,
which made so many men collapse and fall.   235
The people wanted me to sail to Troy
with Idomeneus. We had no choice;
their will was strong, constraining us. We Greeks
fought for nine years, and in the tenth we sacked
the town of Priam, and sailed home. Some god   240
scattered the Greeks, and I was cursed by Zeus.
I stayed for just one month at home, enjoying
my children and my wife and my possessions.
Some impulse made me want to sail to Egypt,

with nine ships and a godlike crew. I rushed   245
to get the fleet prepared and gather up
the men. I paid for many animals,
to kill as sacrifices for the gods
and for the men to cook and eat. We feasted
six days, then on the seventh we embarked   250
and sailed from Crete. A fair north wind was blowing
so we could drift on easily, like floating
downstream. No one got sick, and all our ships
came through undamaged. We sat tight, and let
the wind and pilot guide us over seas.   255
In five days we had reached the river valley
of Egypt; my fleet docked inside the Nile.
I told the loyal men to wait and guard
the ships while I sent scouts to check around
from points of higher ground. But they indulged   260
their own aggressive impulses, and started
willfully doing damage to the fields
of Egypt and enslaved the little children
and women, and they killed the men. The news
soon reached the city; people heard the screaming,   265
and right away at dawn, they all arrived.
The plain was filled with warriors on foot,
and chariots and gleaming bronze, and Zeus,
the Lord of Lightning, caused my men to panic.
They dared not keep on fighting; danger lurked   270
on every side. Then many of my men
were killed with sharp bronze spears; the rest were taken
as slaves to work for them. I wish I too
had died in Egypt! But more pain remained.
Zeus put another plan into my mind.   275
I took my helmet off my head and dropped
my shield and sword, and unarmed I approached
the king. Beside his chariot I grasped
his knees and kissed them. He was merciful;
he kept me safe, and took me home with him,   280
riding his chariot. My eyes were wet.
Many Egyptians were enraged with me,
and tried to kill me with their spears; the king
protected me—he feared the wrath of Zeus,
the god of strangers, who hates wickedness.   285
I stayed there seven years and gained great wealth;
all the Egyptian people gave me gifts.
But in the eighth, an avaricious man
came from Phoenicia. He was good at lying,
skilled and well practiced at exploiting people.   290
He tricked me into going off with him
back to Phoenicia, where he lived. I stayed
a year, but when the hours and days and months
had rolled around again, he made me sail
over the seas to Libya, pretending   295

that I would go with him to do some trading.
His true plan was to sell me for a profit.
I had suspicions, but I climbed on board.
The ship sailed out with fair north wind behind her
from Crete out into open sea. But Zeus   300
planned to destroy the crew. On leaving Crete,
no other land was visible, but only
the sea and sky. Zeus set a dark-blue cloud
across our ship that cast a shadow over
the sea. He thundered and then hurled a bolt   305
of lightning at the ship. The impact whirled
the ship right round and filled her up with sulfur.
The men fell overboard and all were swept
away by waves, like cormorants beside
the dark ship, and gods took away their chance   310
of getting home. But in my desperation
Zeus rescued me. He put the sturdy mast
into my hands. I clung to it and drifted,
propelled by storm winds for nine days. And on
the tenth black night, the rolling waters swept me   315
towards Thesprotia. There the king, named Pheidon,
helped me without expecting recompense
because his son had found me all worn out,
chilled by the morning air. He took my hand,
raised me and led me to his father's house,   320
and dressed me. That was where I heard about
Odysseus—the king said he had been
a guest there on his journey home. The king
showed me the treasure that Odysseus
had gathered: gold and bronze and hard-worked iron.   325
The royal stores contained enough to feed
his family for ten more generations.
Odysseus, the king said, had gone off
to Dodona, to ask the holy oak
what Zeus intended.[2] He had been too long   330
away from fertile Ithaca. He wondered
how best to get back home—in some disguise
or openly. The king then swore to me,
pouring libations, that he had a boat
prepared and crew picked out, to take him back   335
to his dear homeland. But he sent me first;
it happened some Thesprotians[3] were already
sailing towards grain-rich Dulichium.
The king told them to treat me well and take me
to King Acastus. But their hearts preferred   340
to bring me once again to misery.
After the ship was out upon the sea,

---

2. Dodona in Epirus was the seat of the most
ancient oracle of Zeus, where a holy oak was
supposed to deliver the god's voice, perhaps
through rustling leaves.
3. Greek tribe with a friendly relationship to
the Ithacans.

they plotted to enslave me. They stripped off
my cloak and tunic, and tossed me these rags
in which you see me now. And when night fell   345
they came to Ithaca's bright fields, and tied me
tightly with rope and left me on the ship,
and quickly went ashore to get some dinner.
The gods themselves unloosed my bonds; they slipped
easily off. I pulled my ragged clothes   350
over my head, slid down the smooth ship's plank
and plunged chest-forward in the sea. I swam
fast with both arms, and quickly got away.
I came ashore beside a flowering thicket
and huddled there in fear. They stomped around,   355
shouting, but in a while they gave up looking,
and got back on the ship. The gods themselves
hid me with ease, and brought me to this cottage—
a wise man's home—because it is my fate
to stay alive."

               Eumaeus, you replied,   360
"Poor guest! Your tale of woe is very moving,
but pointless; I will not believe a word
about Odysseus. Why did you stoop
to tell those silly lies? I know about
my master's homecoming. The gods detest him;   365
they loathe him, since they did not let him die
at Troy or in his friends' arms, when the war
was winding up, so that the Greeks could build
a mound to glorify him and his son
in times to come. The robber-winds have snatched him.   370
He has no glory now. I am a loner;
I live here with the pigs, and do not go
to town, except when wise Penelope
calls me to share some news. The people cluster
around her, asking questions—some in sorrow   375
about their absent master; others glad
to eat at his expense. I ask no questions,
since an Aetolian fooled me with his lies.[4]
He came to my house, saying he had killed
a man in distant parts and run away.   380
I welcomed him. He said that he had seen
Odysseus with Idomeneus
in Crete, repairing ships that storms had wrecked.
He promised that my lord would come in summer
or harvesttime, made rich by heaps of treasure,   385
his crew complete. A god has brought you here;
but do not try to trick me or make nice
with lies. I will be kind to you, old man,

---

4. Aetolians were a Greek tribe living on the
north coast of the Gulf of Corinth, a mountainous region; they were reputed to be a wild
or primitive people.

not for your stories, but in fear of Zeus,
the god of strangers, and because I feel   390
pity for you."

      But sly Odysseus
answered, "You are too skeptical! Despite
my oath, I see you will not trust me. May
the gods of Mount Olympus be our witness
that if your master ever comes back home   395
to this house, you will give me clothes to wear,
and help me to Dulichium—I want
to go there. But if he does not arrive,
and I am wrong, your slaves can drive me over
the cliff tops, so no other beggar tries   400
to trick you."

      But the upright swineherd answered,
"Yes, guest, I would be praised enormously
among all men, now and in times to come,
if I took you inside and welcomed you,
then murdered you! And doing this,   405
with what clean conscience could I pray to Zeus?
In any case, now it is dinnertime.
My men should come inside, so we can cook
delicious food."

      That was their conversation.
In came the herdsmen, and they drove the pigs   410
into their usual pens to rest; there rose
a mighty din of grunting pigs. The noble
swineherd addressed his men.

      "Bring out the best
pig for our guest, who comes from distant lands.
And let us all enjoy ourselves. We suffer   415
in bitter toil for these white-tusked pigs,
while others eat the food we labor for,
and give us nothing."

      With a keen bronze axe
he chopped the wood. They brought a fattened pig
of five years old and put it on the altar.   420
The swineherd's heart was good: he kept in mind
the gods. He shaved the bristles off its head,
and threw them in the fire, and prayed to all
the gods, that through his ingenuity,
his master would come home. He stretched up   425
tall, and used a piece of oaken firewood
to strike. The life departed, and they slit
the throat and singed the hide, and chopped it up.
The swineherd made an offering of meat,

laid flesh across the fine rich fat, and put it   430
upon the fire with barley-grain on top,
and sliced the rest and put it all on skewers,
and roasted it with care, then drew the meat off
and heaped it high on platters. Next he stood
and served it out in seven equal parts,   435
the first with prayers, for Hermes and the Nymphs,
and then he served the others to the men.
He gave Odysseus the piece of honor,
cut from the spine. His master was delighted,
and said,

       "Eumaeus, may Zeus bless and love you   440
as I do, since you give me such good things."

You answered him, swineherd Eumaeus, "Eat,
dear guest; enjoy it, simple though it is.
Gods give, gods take away, as is their will;
to gods all things are possible."

               With that,   445
he made the sacrifices to the gods,
poured a libation from the bright red wine,
then gave Odysseus, the city-sacker,
the cup. At last the swineherd sat to eat.
Mesaulius served the food—that was the slave   450
bought by Eumaeus in his master's absence,
with no help from his mistress or Laertes.
He traded him from Taphians.[5] They all
reached out to take the good things set before them.
When they had had enough of food and drink,   455
Mesaulius cleared things away; the men
were full of bread and meat, and wanting sleep.
Night fell, a moonless, bitter night. Zeus rained
continually; wet Zephyr blew his hardest.
Odysseus—to test out if Eumaeus   460
was kind enough to take his own cloak off,
or tell another man to do it—said,

"Eumaeus and you others, all of you.
I want to brag a little. I am dizzy,
under the influence of wine, which makes   465
even the wisest people sing and giggle,
and dance, and say things best not spoken. Since
I have begun this blabbering, here goes,
I will be honest. I wish I was young
and strong again! As when we planned an ambush   470
under the walls of Troy—the leading men
were Menelaus and Odysseus,

5. An island people from the Ionian Sea.

and I was chosen as the third commander.
When we had reached the city wall, we lay
in bushes, reeds, and marshes, hiding under   475
our shields. Night fell, harsh and icy cold,
with North Wind and a sleetlike snow, so cold
the ice grew on our weapons. All the others
had cloaks; they slept in comfort, tucked beneath
their shields. But I had foolishly forgotten   480
my cloak and left it, not expecting cold.
I carried just my shield and shining belt.
In the last part of night, as stars were setting,
I went near to Odysseus and nudged him.
He listened to me carefully. I said,   485
'Your Majesty, Odysseus, great general,
I am about to die from this cold weather!
I have no cloak. Some spirit tricked me into
wearing my tunic only; now there is
no way to fix it.' Instantly he thought   490
of this solution. What a strategist
and fighter! Very quietly he whispered,
'Hush now, do not let any of the others
hear you.' He propped his head up on his elbow,
and told them, 'Listen, friends. I had a dream   495
sent by the gods. We moved too far away
from where the ships are. Someone needs to speak
to Agamemnon, shepherd of the people,
and tell him to send more troops here.' At that,
Thoas the son of Andraimon leapt up,   500
took off his purple cloak and sprinted down
towards the ships. I snuggled down in comfort
under his cloak till golden Dawn shone bright.
If only I was young and strong again!
Then one of these pig-keepers on this farm   505
would give a cloak to me, both from respect
and friendship. As it is, they all despise me
for wearing dirty rags."

      Eumaeus, you
replied, "That was a splendid tale, old man!
It worked. You will get all the clothes and things   510
a poor old beggar needs—at least for now.
But in the morning, you will have to put
your old rags on again. We only have
one outfit each, no spares. My master's son
will give you clothes when he arrives, and help you   515
to travel on wherever you desire."

With that, he stood and set a bed for him
beside the fire, and threw on it some skins
of sheep and goats. Odysseus lay down.
Eumaeus tucked him in a big thick cloak,   520

his extra one, for really bitter weather.
Odysseus went to sleep; the young men slept
beside him. But the swineherd did not like
to sleep so distant from the pigs; he started
to leave. Odysseus was glad the slave   525
took good care of his absent master's things.
Eumaeus slung his sharp sword belt across
his well-toned back, and wrapped around himself
his windproof cloak and fine big furry goatskin.
He took a sharpened knife to ward away   530
humans or dogs, and he went off to sleep
out where the pigs with silver tusks were sleeping;
a hanging rock protected them from wind.

BOOK 15

The Prince Returns

Athena went to Sparta, to ensure
the safe return of Prince Telemachus.
She found him with Pisistratus, both lying
on Menelaus' porch, and Nestor's son
was fast asleep, but no sweet slumber held   5
Telemachus. His worries for his father
kept him awake all through god-given night.
Owl-eyed Athena stood by him and said,

"Telemachus, you should no longer travel
so far from home, abandoning your wealth,   10
with greedy men at home. You must watch out;
they may divide and eat up all your wealth,
and make your journey useless. Quickly ask
for help from Menelaus to get home,
so you may find your mother safe and blameless.   15
Her father and her brothers are already
telling her she should wed Eurymachus.
He is the one most generous with gifts
to her and to her father. Do not let her
take any items from the house, without   20
your full consent. You know how women are—
they want to help the house of any man
they marry. When one darling husband dies,
his wife forgets him, and her children by him.
She does not even ask how they are doing.   25
Let your best slave girl watch your property,
until the gods give you your own wife. Also,
I have more news: take note. There is a gang
of suitors lurking in the stream between
your Ithaca and rocky Same, who   30
have plans to kill you on your journey home.
But I suspect that some of those who waste

your wealth will soon be lying under earth.
Now steer your ship far distant from the islands,
and sail both day and night. Some god who guards   35
and watches over you will send fair wind
behind your sails. When you first reach the shore
of Ithaca, your men must drag the ship
up to the town, while you first go and visit
the swineherd, who is better than most slaves.   40
Spend the night there. Tell him to go to town
to tell Penelope that you have come
safely back home from Pylos."

                With these words
the goddess went back up to Mount Olympus.
He woke the son of Nestor with a kick,   45
and said to him,

                "Pisistratus! Go fetch
the horses, get them harnessed to the carriage,
and let us hurry on our way."

                He answered,
"Telemachus, this is impossible,
for us to drive when it is pitch-black night,   50
however eager we may be to travel.
Dawn will come soon. Wait till great Menelaus
comes out to bring us presents in his carriage,
and sends us on our way with friendly words.
A generous host is sure to be remembered   55
as long as his guests live."

                Then all at once
Dawn on her golden throne lit up the sky.
King Menelaus got up from the bed
he shared with fair-haired Helen and approached them.
Seeing him on his way, Telemachus   60
put on his bright white tunic, and then slung
his mighty sword across his sturdy shoulders.
So in a warlike guise, the well-loved son
of godlike King Odysseus stood near
and spoke to Menelaus.

                "Royal son   65
of Atreus, now, please, send me home now,
to my beloved country. My heart yearns
to go back home."

                And Menelaus answered,
"Telemachus, I will not keep you here
if you are truly desperate for home.   70

I disapprove of too much friendliness
and of too much standoffishness. A balance
is best. To force a visitor to stay
is just as bad as pushing him to go.
Be kind to guests while they are visiting,   75
then help them on their way. So friend, remain
just till I fetch some splendid gifts to pile
onto your carriage. Wait till you see them!
I will instruct the women to prepare
a banquet in the hall from our rich stores.   80
Feasting before a long trip brings you honor;
it also makes good sense. And if you want
to have me travel with you all through Greece,
I shall yoke up my horses and escort you
through every town, and everywhere we go   85
we will be given gifts—a fine bronze tripod,
a cauldron, or two mules, or golden cups."

Telemachus replied, "King Menelaus,
I want to go home right away. I have
no one back there to watch my property.   90
I would not want to die while I am searching
for Father, or to lose my wealth at home."

So General Menelaus shouted out
to tell his wife and female slaves to make
a feast from his rich stores. Eteoneus   95
got out of bed and came—he lived nearby.
The general boomed out orders: "Light the fire
and roast the meat!" The slave obeyed. Meanwhile,
his master went inside the fragrant room
containing treasures. Helen went with him,   100
and Megapenthes. There he took a goblet,
two-handled, and he told his son to bring
a silver bowl. And Helen stood beside
the chests in which she kept the special clothes
that she had worked with her own hands. She lifted   105
the most elaborate and largest robe
that shone like starlight under all the rest.
Then they went through the palace till they reached
Telemachus. And fair-haired Menelaus
said to him,

              "May great Zeus, the Lord of Thunder,   110
husband of Hera, make your wish come true—
may you go back home safely. I will give you
the best of all my treasure, as a mark
of deep respect: a bowl of solid silver,
circled with gold; Hephaestus fashioned it.   115
The King of Sidon, Phaedimus, bestowed it

on me when I was at his house, en route
for home. Now take it; it is yours."

                    He gave
the goblet first, and Megapenthes brought
the shining silver bowl and put it down   120
in front of him. Then Helen's lovely cheeks
flushed as she moved in close. She held the robe
and said,

        "Sweet boy, I also have a gift,
crafted by my own hands. Remember Helen
when your own wedding day at last arrives,   125
and let your bride wear this. Until that time,
your mother should take care of it. I wish you
great joy. I hope you reach your well-built home,
and fatherland."

             She handed it to him;
he took it gladly. Prince Pisistratus   130
took all the gifts and packed them in the luggage,
and marveled at them in his heart.

                   The king
led them inside; they sat on chairs. A slave girl
brought out a beautiful gold water pitcher
and silver bowl so she could wash their hands.   135
She set a polished table at their side.
Another lowly girl brought bread and food
of every kind. Boethoedes began
to carve and serve the meat. The king's son poured
the wine for everyone. They helped themselves   140
to all the delicacies spread before them.
When they were satisfied, Telemachus
and Nestor's son strapped on the horses' harness,
and yoked them to the chariot and drove
off from the echoing portico and gate.   145
But Menelaus ran up just behind them,
holding a golden cup of honeyed wine
in his right hand, so they could pour libations
before they left. He stopped in front of them
and spreading wide his arms said,

                    "Boys, good luck!   150
Give Nestor my best wishes—he was always
as kind as any father while we Greeks
were making war in Troy."

                 Telemachus
said carefully, "Yes, king, when we go there
we will pass on what you have said. I hope   155

I may go back to Ithaca and meet
Odysseus—good luck to match my fortune
in all your generosity and kindness."

Then on the right an eagle flew; it held
a big white goose clutched in its claws—a tame one,   160
caught from the yard. The people, men and women,
were running round and yelling after it.
It darted on the right beside the boys,
and flew before their horses. They were all
delighted. Nestor's son was first to speak.   165

"My lord, King Menelaus, what do you think?
Was this a sign sent by some god for us?
Or sent for you?"

           And Menelaus, favorite
of Ares, wondered how he ought to answer.

But Helen cut in first and said, "Now listen,   170
and I will make a prophecy. The gods
have put it in my heart and I believe
it will come true. Just as the eagle flew
down from the mountains where he has his home
with chicks and parents, seizing this tame goose—   175
so will Odysseus, who has been gone
so long and has endured so much, come back
and take revenge. Indeed, he is already
at home and planting ruin for the suitors."

Telemachus replied, "May thundering Zeus   180
fulfill your prophecy at once! If so,
I would bow down to you as to a goddess."

He whipped the horses and they galloped off
through the town center to the open plain.
All day the harness rattled as they ran.   185
But when the sun went down and it grew dark,
they came to Pherae, home of Diocles,
son of Ortilochus, who was the son
of Alpheus. He welcomed them and there
they spent the night. When rosy-fingered Dawn   190
the early-born appeared, they yoked the horses,
climbed in the chariot, and drove away
from the resounding portico and gate.
The horses flew with gusto at the whip.
Soon they were near the rocky town of Pylos.   195
Telemachus then asked Pisistratus,

"Would you do me a favor? We are friends
because our fathers have been friends forever,

and we are age-mates, and this trip has made us
even more intimate. Please do not bring me   200
beyond my ship, but leave me here, in case
the old man forces me to visit him
and be his guest. I long to get back home.
I have to go, and fast."

                         The son of Nestor
wondered how he should best respond. He thought   205
upon reflection he should turn the horses
back to the ship and shore beside the sea.
There he took out the splendid gifts and clothes
and gold from Menelaus, and he packed them
inside the stern, and told Telemachus,   210

"Hurry! Embark now! Get your crew in too,
before I get back home and tell my father
that you are here. I know him; he is stubborn.
He will not let you go; he will come here
to fetch you, and he surely will not leave   215
without you. He will be in such a rage!"

With that, he spurred the horses. Long manes flowing,
they galloped to the citadel of Pylos.
Telemachus gave orders: "Make it all
shipshape, my friends, and get on board, so we   220
can start our journey."

                         Quickly they obeyed
and sat along the benches. As he worked,
with prayers and sacrifices to Athena,
a foreigner approached him, who had killed
a man in Argos and had run away.   225
He was a prophet and descended from
Melampus, who once lived in Pylos, land
of sheep.[1] Melampus had been rich, and owned
a palace, but he left his home, escaping
from Neleus, a proud, important man,   230
who seized all his great wealth while he was trapped
and tortured in the house of Phylacus,
because a Fury put inside his mind
a dangerous obsession with the daughter
of Neleus. He managed to escape,   235
and drove the cattle, lowing loudly, off
from Phylace to Pylos. He avenged

---

1. Melampus, great-grandfather of Theoclymenus, lived in Pylos, and his brother fell in
love with the daughter of Neleus, Pero. Neleus
demanded the herds of Phylacus as the bride-
price; Melampus tried to steal them for his
brother, but he was imprisoned by Phylacus.
He noticed that worms were eating the
wooden beams of his prison and foretold their
fall. Phylacus, impressed at his prophetic talent, released him; he brought the herds to
Neleus, won Pero for his brother, and moved
to Argos.

the wrong that Neleus had done to him,
and brought the woman to his brother's house
as wife, then went to Argos, home of horses,   240
since there it was his destiny to rule
the multitude of Argives, and he had
two strong sons: Mantius, and Antiphates,
who fathered the heroic Oïcles,
whose son was Amphiaraus, the warlord,   245
whom Zeus who holds the aegis and Apollo
adored wholeheartedly. But he did not
live to old age, since he was killed at Thebes,
because his wife took bribes.[2] He had two sons,
Amphilochus and Alcmaeon. The sons   250
of Mantius were Clitus, snatched by Dawn
to join the gods, because he was so handsome,
and Polypheides, whom Apollo gave
the best prophetic skill of any mortal
after Amphiaraus had died. This prophet   255
grew angry with his father, and migrated
to Hyperesia, and there he told
fortunes for everyone. It was his son,
named Theoclymenus, who had approached
Telemachus while he was pouring wine   260
and praying to the gods. The stranger said,

"My friend, I find you making sacrifices.
I beg you, by religion, by the gods,
and by your life and your men's lives: who are you?
Who are your parents? What is your home town?"   265

Telemachus said, "Stranger, I will tell you.
I come from Ithaca; my father is
Odysseus—he was. He must have died
some dreadful death by now. It was for him
I got this ship and crew. I sailed to seek   270
news of my absent father."

                      And the stranger
replied, "I too am far from home. I killed
a man of my own tribe, and he had many
brothers and kinsmen, powerful in Argos,
so I am on the run. They want to kill me.   275
I have been doomed to homelessness. But please,
let me on board your ship. I come to you
in desperation—otherwise I will
surely be killed. Those men are after me."

2. The mythical Theban War was initiated by the two sons of Oedipus, Polyneices and Eteocles, over control of the city. Polyneices bribed Eriphyle with a gold necklace to persuade her husband, Amphiaraus, to join his army, although he was doomed to die if he did so.

Telemachus said, "Yes, you can join us   280
on board our ship. And what we have is yours;
you are our guest."

               He took the stranger's spear,
laid it on deck, then climbed on board himself,
sat at the stern, and had his guest sit down
beside him at the stern. They loosed the ropes.   285
Telemachus gave orders to the men
to seize the tackle; promptly they obeyed,
and raised the wooden mast and fastened it
into the socket, binding it with forestays,
and hauled the white sail up with leather cables.   290
Sharp-eyed Athena sent fair wind that gusted
a wild explosive breath through bright clear sky;
the ship began to race across the sea,
past Crouni and the lovely streams of Chalcis.
The sun went down and all the world was dark.   295
Impelled by wind from Zeus, the ship sped on
past Pheae and they came to famous Elis
ruled by the Epeians; from there they steered
towards the Needle Islands, still unsure
if they would die.

               Meanwhile, Odysseus   300
was having dinner with the noble swineherd
inside the cottage, and the other men
were eating with them. After they were done,
Odysseus began to test the swineherd,
to see if he would be hospitable,   305
and ask him to stay there, out on the farm,
or send him into town. He said,

                    "Eumaeus,
listen, and listen all of you. At dawn
I plan to go to town to beg—I have
no wish to be a burden to you all.   310
I only need directions and a guide
who can go with me. I will roam around
the city on my own, in search of drink
and crusts of bread—so it must be. And if
I reach the house of King Odysseus,   315
I plan to tell Penelope my news,
and mingle with the high and mighty suitors;
they may give me some food from their rich stores.
I could do anything they want at once.
I have the capability, you see.   320
Hermes the messenger, the god who gives
favor and glorifies all human labor,
has blessed me with unrivaled skill in all
domestic tasks: fire-laying, splitting logs,

carving and roasting meat, and pouring wine—   325
I can do all the chores poor people do
to serve the rich."

                But angrily you said,
Eumaeus, "No! Why would you think of this?
You would be killed if you set foot among
that horde of suitors; their aggression reaches   330
the iron sky. And those who wait on them
are not like you. They are young men, well dressed,
with bright clean hair and handsome faces, serving
the bread and wine and meat, piled high upon
their polished tables. Stay here. No one minds   335
your presence—not myself, nor my companions.
And when Odysseus' son arrives,
he will provide a proper cloak and tunic,
and help you travel where your heart desires."

Odysseus, experienced in pain,   340
answered, "I hope Zeus loves you as I do,
since you have saved me from the agonies
of wandering. The worst thing humans suffer
is homelessness; we must endure this life
because of desperate hunger; we endure,   345
as migrants with no home. But since you now
want me to stay and wait for your young master,
tell me about Odysseus' parents.
His father, when he left, was on the threshold
of age. Are they alive still? Have they died?"   350

He answered, "Stranger, I will tell you truly.
Laertes is alive, but he is always
praying to Zeus to let him pass away
in his own home. He feels such desperate grief
about his son and his beloved wife,   355
whose death made him so heartbroken, he aged
before his time. She died a dreadful death,
a death I would not wish for any friend—
grieving her absent son, the famous hero.
While she was still alive, despite her sadness,   360
she used to like to talk and chat with me—
she brought me up herself with her own daughter,
strong, pretty Ctimene, her youngest child.
She raised us both together, treating me
almost as equal, just a little less.   365
And when we came of age, they sent the girl
to Same, for a hefty bridal-price.
The mother dressed me in fine clothes, a cloak
and tunic, tying sandals on my feet,
and sent me to the country. But she still   370
loved me with all her heart. I miss them both.

The blessed gods have made my work here prosper,
so I have had enough to eat and drink
and give to guests. But I hear no good news
about my mistress. Ruin has befallen   375
the house from those invaders. All her slaves
miss talking to their owner, getting gossip,
sharing some food and drink with her, and taking
scraps to the fields with them—the kind of thing
that makes slaves happy."

               And Odysseus   380
exclaimed, "Eumaeus! What a little child
you were when you were taken far from home
and from your parents! Tell me more. Did they
live in a city that was sacked? Or was it
bandits that found you, herding sheep or cows   385
alone? Did they seize hold of you and put you
onto their ship, and sell you for a profit
in this man's house?"

              The swineherd answered him,
"Since you have asked this question, stranger, listen;
enjoy my story, sitting quietly,   390
drinking your wine. These nights are magical,
with time enough to sleep and to enjoy
hearing a tale. You need not sleep too early;
it is unhealthy. Any other man
who feels the need of sleep should go lie down,   395
get up at dawn, have breakfast, and go herd
the master's pigs. But let us, you and I,
sit in my cottage over food and wine,
and take some joy in hearing how much pain
we each have suffered. After many years   400
of agony and absence from one's home,
a person can begin enjoying grief.
I will tell you my story as you ask.
There is an island—you may know it—called
Syria, where the sun turns round, above   405
Ortygia.³ It has few inhabitants,
but it is good land, rich in sheep and wine
and grain; no famine ever hurts those there,
nor any deadly sickness. They grow old,
and with their gentle arrows, Artemis   410
and silver-bowed Apollo cause their death.
The land is split into two provinces;
my father Ctesius was king of both.
Then avaricious merchants came—Phoenicians,

3. The concept is that the sun, like a competi-
tor in a Greek race, turns around on its course
when it reaches the farthest point—presumably
toward the west. The place names here do not
seem to correspond to any real geography.

skilled sailors, with great piles of treasure stored   415
in their black ship. And in my father's house
there was a woman from Phoenicia—tall
and beautiful and skilled in many arts.
Those clever rascals tricked her. One of them
first found her washing clothes beside the ship   420
and lay with her. Sex sways all women's minds,
even the best of them. And then he asked her
where she was from and who she was; she showed him
my father's palace, and she said, 'I am
from Sidon, rich in bronze. I am the daughter   425
of wealthy Arybas; as I was walking
back from the fields one day, some Taphian pirates
kidnapped me, brought me here to this man's house,
and sold me to him, for a tidy sum.'
Her secret lover said, 'Then would you like   430
to go back home with us, and see your parents
and your fine home again? They are alive
and quite rich now.' The woman said, 'Oh, yes,
I would! If all you sailors swear an oath
to bring me safely home.' At that, they swore   435
as she had asked, and made their solemn vows.
And then the woman said, 'You must keep mum,
and none of you can even speak to me
if you bump into me beside the road
or at the water fountain—otherwise   440
someone might tell the old man at the house.
Then he would get suspicious, chain me up,
and plan to have you killed. Remember this,
bear it in mind and do your trading quickly,
and when your ship is full of stores to take   445
back home with you, send news to me, and fast.
I will bring gold with me as well, whatever
wealth I can find to hand. I also want
to give another gift to pay my fare.
I take care of my master's clever son—   450
who always runs around outside with me.
I will bring him on board and he will fetch
a pretty price from foreigners.' With that,
she went back to the palace. For a year
they stayed with us accumulating wealth   455
by trading, and they filled their ship's hold up.
When it was time to go, they sent a man
to tell the woman at my father's house.
He was a very cunning man. He wore
a golden necklace strung with amber beads;   460
the slave girls in the palace and my mother
stared and began to finger it and ask
how much it cost; he nodded to the woman
in silence, and then went back to the ship.
She took me by the hand and led me out   465

into the forecourt, where she found some cups
left on the tables by my father's men
who had been banqueting, and now had gone
to council—they were having a debate.
She took three cups and hid them in her dress   470
and carried them away with her. I followed,
knowing no better. As the sun went down,
we hurried through the dark streets to the harbor.
There was the swift Phoenician ship. They all
embarked, put us on board as well, and sailed   475
over the watery waves; Zeus sent fair wind.
For seven days we sailed and on the eighth,
Artemis struck the woman with her arrows.
She crashed into the ship's hold like a seagull.
They threw her overboard to feed the fish   480
and seals, and I was left there, brokenhearted.
The current carried them to Ithaca,
and then Laertes bought me with his wealth.
That was the way my eyes first saw this land."

Odysseus replied, "My heart is touched   485
to hear the story of your sufferings,
Eumaeus. In the end, though, Zeus has blessed you,
since after going through all that, you came
to live with someone kind, a man who gives you
plenty to eat and drink. Your life is good.   490
But as for me, I am still lost; I trekked
through many towns before I wandered here."

So went their conversation; then they slept
for just a little while; Dawn soon arrived
upon her throne.

       Meanwhile, Telemachus   495
drew near the mainland. Lowering the sail
nimbly, his men took down the mast and rowed
to anchorage. They cast the mooring stones,
and tied the cables from the stern, then climbed
out in the surf, and waded into shore.   500
There they made dinner, mixing bright red wine.
When they had had enough to eat and drink,
the boy said sensibly,

       "You all should drag
the ship towards the town, while I go visit
the herdsmen in the fields of my estate.   505
Then I will come to town, at evening time.
At dawn, I will provide a feast for you
of meat and wine."

Then Theoclymenus
asked him, "But where shall I go, my dear boy?
To whose house? One of those who rule this land?   510
Or should I go at once to your own mother
in your house?"

          And Telemachus replied,
"Well, ordinarily I would invite you.
We are good hosts. But as it is—best not,
for your own sake. I will not be at home,   515
and Mother will not see you; she is weaving
upstairs upon her loom—she does not want
the suitors seeing her. So I suggest
you go to someone else's house: the son
of skillful Polybus, Eurymachus.   520
The Ithacans look at him as a god.
He is the dominant suitor and the keenest
on marrying my mother and acquiring
the riches of Odysseus. Zeus knows
the future, he alone. Eurymachus   525
may die a dreadful death before that marriage."

As he said this, a bird flew on his right:
a hawk, Apollo's messenger. It clutched
a pigeon in its talons; feathers scattered
between the ship and young Telemachus.   530
Then Theoclymenus called him aside
and grasped him by the hand, and said to him,
"Telemachus! Some god has sent this bird
to fly on your right hand. I knew at once
it was a sign. No family in all   535
of Ithaca has greater power; you are
the kings forever."

          He replied, "Oh, stranger!
I hope your words come true! If so, I would
give you so many gifts to show my friendship
that everyone you met would be impressed."   540

And then he told his faithful man, "Piraeus,
you were most trustworthy of those who came
with me to Pylos. Let this stranger come
to your own house, be kind to him and give him
a cordial welcome till I come."

          Piraeus   545
answered, "However long you are away,
I will take care of him."

          And then he climbed
aboard and told the men to come as well,

and loose the cables, which they did, and sat
down on the benches. Then Telemachus   550
tied on his sandals, and took from the deck
his sharp bronze spear. The men untied the ropes
and sailed towards the town, just as the son
of great Odysseus had ordered them.
The boy walked quickly till he reached the farmyard.   555
Hundreds of pigs were there and with them slept
the swineherd who knew how to help his masters.

BOOK 16

Father and Son

At dawn the swineherd and Odysseus
made breakfast, lit the fire, and sent the herdsmen
out with the pigs that they had rounded up.
The dogs, that as a rule would bark at strangers,
were quiet when they saw Telemachus;   5
they panted at him. When Odysseus
saw how they acted, and heard footsteps coming,
he said,

      "Eumaeus, someone must be coming—
a friend or somebody you know—the dogs
are friendly, with no barking. I can hear   10
footsteps."

      He hardly finished, when his son,
his own dear son, was there inside the gate.
Amazed, the swineherd jumped up, letting fall
the cups in which he had been mixing wine;
it spilled. He ran towards his master, kissed   15
his face and shining eyes and both his hands,
and wept. Just as a father, when he sees
his own dear son, his only son, his dear
most precious boy, returned from foreign lands
after ten years of grieving for his loss,   20
welcomes him; so the swineherd wrapped his arms
around godlike Telemachus and kissed him,
as if he were returning from the dead.
With tears still in his eyes he said,

      "Sweet light!
You have come back, Telemachus. I thought   25
that I would never see you anymore,
after you sailed to Pylos. My dear child,
come in, let me enjoy the sight of you
now you are back. Come in! You do not often
come to the countryside to see us herders;   30
you stay in town to watch that evil horde
of suitors."

And Telemachus replied
warily, "Grandpa, yes, I will come in.
I came to see you here with my own eyes,
and hear if Mother still stays in the house,   35
or if some other man has married her
already, and Odysseus' bed
is empty, full of ugly spiderwebs."

The swineherd, the commander, said, "Indeed,
her heart is loyal. She is in your house,   40
weeping by night and sad by day."

                          He took
Telemachus' sword; the boy came in,
crossing the stony threshold, and his father
offered his seat. Telemachus refused,
saying, "You sit there, stranger. I can find   45
a chair around my hut. The slave can help."

Odysseus went back and sat back down.
The swineherd spread fresh brushwood and a fleece
on top, so that Telemachus could sit.
He set the bread in baskets and brought meat,   50
left over from the meal the day before.
He mixed some wine up in a wooden bowl,
and sat down opposite Odysseus.
They reached to take the good things set before them.
When they were satisfied, Telemachus   55
turned to the noble swineherd.

                          "Tell me, Grandpa,
where did this stranger come from? By what route
did sailors bring him here? And who were they?
He surely did not walk to Ithaca!"

Eumaeus answered, "I will tell you, child.   60
He is from Crete. He says he wandered, lost,
through many towns—so some god spun his fate.
Now he has run away from the Thesprotians
who brought him, and arrived here on my farm.
He is all yours, your suppliant, to treat   65
however you desire."

                          Telemachus
said anxiously, "This news of yours, Eumaeus,
is very worrying to me. How can I
invite him to my house? I am too young
to fight back with my fists if someone picks   70
a fight with me. My mother is unsure
if she should stay with me and show respect
towards her husband's bed and public gossip,

and keep on taking care of things at home,
or marry one of them, whichever suitor   75
asserts himself, and brings most lavish gifts.
But since this man has come here, to your house,
I will dress him in fine clothes, cloak and tunic,
and sandals for his feet, and give a sword,
and help him on his way. If you are willing,   80
keep him here in the farmhouse; care for him.
I will send you some clothes and all his food,
so he will be no bother to these men
or you. I will not let him go to meet
the suitors; they are much too violent.   85
I would be mortified if they abused him.
It would be difficult for one man, even
a strong one, to do anything to them.
They are too many."

                    Then Odysseus,
frustrated, said, "My friend, it is my duty   90
to speak out when I hear the dreadful things
those suitors have been doing in your house,
against your will; it breaks my heart. You are
a good man. Tell me, did you choose to let them
bully you? Have the Ithacans been turned   95
against you by some god? Or do you blame
your brothers, who should be a man's supporters
when conflict comes? If only I had youth
to match my will! I wish I were the son
of great Odysseus—or that I were   100
the man himself come home from wandering.
We can still hope. Let someone chop my head off,
if I would not destroy them when I came
inside the palace of Odysseus!
And if I lost—since I am only one   105
against so many—I would rather die
in my own house, than watch such crimes committed!
Strangers dishonored! Slave girls dragged around,
raped in my lovely home! Men wasting wine
and bread—for nothing! For this waiting game!"   110

Telemachus said soberly, "I will
explain the situation to you, stranger.
The Ithacans are not my enemies,
and I do not have brothers I can blame.
Zeus gave my family a single line: 115
Arcesius had just one son, Laertes,
who had Odysseus, his only son,
and he had me, his only son, whom he
left back at home; he had no joy of me.
And now there are so many cruel invaders,   120
   since all the toughest men from all the islands—

from Same and Dulichium and wooded
Zacynthus, and all those who hold command
in rocky Ithaca, have come to court
my mother, wasting all my wealth. She does not   125
refuse the awful prospect of remarriage,
nor can she end the courtship. They keep eating,
consuming my whole house, and soon they may
destroy me too. These things lie with the gods.
Now Grandpa, you must hurry to the queen,   130
and tell her I am safe back home from Pylos.
I will stay here while you tell her—just her;
do not let any others hear the news,
since many people want to plot my death."

Eumaeus, you replied, "I understand.   135
But tell me, on this same trip, should I go
and tell poor old Laertes? For a while
he used to watch the fields and join the slaves
for dinner at the house, when in the mood,
despite his grief for lost Odysseus.   140
But since your ship set sail away to Pylos,
they say he has stopped eating, will not drink,
and does not go to check the fields. He sits,
weeping and sobbing, worn to skin and bone."

Telemachus said calmly, "That is sad;   145
distressing news. But no, leave him alone.
If human wishes could come true, my first
would be to have my father come back home.
Take her your message, hurry back, and do not
trail round the countryside to look for him.   150
Tell Mother she should send a girl in secret
to run to old Laertes with the news."

At that, the swineherd tied his sandals on,
and started off towards the town. Athena
noticed him leaving from the yard, and stood   155
beside him as a woman, tall and skillful,
and beautiful. Odysseus could see her,
standing beside the entrance to the cottage.
Telemachus could not; the gods are not
equally visible to everyone.   160
The dogs could see her but they did not bark.
They whimpered and slunk back across the room
in fear. She raised her eyebrows, with a nod;
he understood and came out, past the wall,
and stood beside her. Then Athena told him,   165

"Odysseus, great strategist, it is
time for your son to know the truth; together
you have to plan how you will kill the suitors.

Then both of you go into town. I will
join you there soon myself; indeed I am   170
itching to fight."

        And then Athena touched him,
using a golden wand, and dressed him up
in fine clean cloak and tunic, and she made him
taller and younger-looking. He became
tanned, and his cheeks filled out, and on his chin   175
the beard grew dark. And so her work was done,
and off she flew. Odysseus went in.
His son was startled and looked down, afraid
in case it was a god. His words flew out.

"Stranger, you look so different from before.   180
Your clothes, your skin—I think that you must be
some god who has descended from the sky.
Be kind to us, and we will sacrifice,
and give you golden treasures. Pity us!"

Long-suffering Odysseus replied,   185
"I am no god. Why would you think such things?
I am your father, that same man you mourn.
It is because of me these brutal men
are hurting you so badly."

        Then he kissed
his son and cried, tears pouring down his cheeks;   190
he had been holding back till then. The boy
did not yet trust it really was his father,
and said,

        "No, you are not Odysseus,
my father; some god must have cast a spell,
to cause me further pain. No mortal man   195
could manage such a thing by his own wits,
becoming old and young again—unless
some god appeared and did it all with ease.
You certainly were old just now, and wearing
those dirty rags. Now you look like a god."   200

Artful Odysseus said sharply, "No,
Telemachus, you should not be surprised
to see your father. It is me; no other
is on his way. I am Odysseus.
I suffered terribly, and I was lost,   205
but after twenty years, I have come home.
As for the way I look—Athena did it.
The goddess can transform me as she likes;
sometimes a homeless beggar, then she makes me
look like a young man, wearing princely clothes.   210

For heavenly gods it is not difficult
to make a mortal beautiful or ugly."

With that, he sat back down. Telemachus
hurled his arms round his father, and he wept.
They both felt deep desire for lamentation,   215
and wailed with cries as shrill as birds, like eagles
or vultures, when the hunters have deprived them
of fledglings who have not yet learned to fly.
That was how bitterly they wept. Their grieving
would have continued till the sun went down,   220
but suddenly Telemachus said,

                              "Father,
by what route did the sailors bring you here,
to Ithaca? And who were they? I know
you did not walk."

                  Odysseus replied,
"Son, I will tell you everything. Phaeacians,   225
famous for navigation, brought me here.
They always help their guests travel onward.
I slept as their ship sped across the ocean;
they set me down on Ithaca, still sleeping.
They brought me marvelous gifts of gold and bronze   230
and clothing, which are lying in a cave,
since gods have willed it so. Athena told me
to come here and make plans with you to kill
our enemies. How many suitors are there?
What kind of men are they? I am well-known   235
for my intelligence, and I will plot
to work out if we two alone can fight them,
or if we might need others helping us."

Telemachus considered, then said, "Father,
I always heard how excellent you are,   240
at fighting with a spear, and making plans.
But what you said just now—it is too much.
We cannot fight, the two of us, against
such strong men, and so many—there are dozens,
not just a handful. Let me tell you quickly   245
the number of the suitors. Fifty-two
came from Dulichium, all top-notch fighters,
who brought six henchmen. Twenty-four men came
from Same, twenty more from Zacynthus,
and from right here on Ithaca came twelve,   250
all strong young men. They have a house boy with them,
named Medon, and a poet, and two slaves
well trained in carving meat. If we attack
when all those men are crowded in the house,
I am afraid you will be paying back   255

their violence at all too high a price.
Think harder: can we find some kind of helper,
willing to fight for us?"

             Odysseus
said, "Do you think Athena and her father,
Zeus, would be strong enough to keep us safe?   260
Would any other help be necessary?"

Telemachus replied, "The ones you mention
are good defenders. They sit high among
the clouds, and they control both men and gods."

The veteran Odysseus replied,   265
"Those two will quickly join the heat of battle
when we begin to grapple with the suitors,
when in my house the god of war is testing
our fighting force and theirs. Go back at dawn,
and join those overconfident young men.   270
The swineherd will escort me into town.
I will again be looking like a beggar.
If they abuse me and you see me suffer,
you must restrain yourself, repress your feelings,
even if they are pelting me with weapons,   275
and even if they grab me by the foot
to hurl me out. Just watch, and keep your temper.
Politely tell them they should stop this folly.
They will ignore you. Truly now their day
of doom is near at hand. Now listen hard.   280
Athena, my best co-conspirator,
will nudge my heart, and I will nod to you.
Then you must find all weapons in the house
that could be used for fighting; go and hide them
away inside the upstairs storage room.   285
And when the suitors ask where they have gone,
fob them off, saying, 'They were near the fire,
so I removed them from the breath of smoke,
since they were getting damaged; they were losing
the luster that they used to have, before   290
Odysseus went off to Troy. Praise Zeus!
I thought of something even more important:
if you get drunk you may start quarreling,
and hurt each other. Then your lovely dinners
and courtship will be ruined. Arms themselves   295
can prompt a man to use them.' Tell them that.
Leave out two swords, two spears, and two thick shields
for you and me to grab before we rush
to ambush them. Athena will bewitch them,
helped by sharp-witted Zeus. And one more thing: 300
if you are my true son, of my own blood,
let no one know that I am in the house.

Laertes and the swineherd must not know,
nor any of the slave girls, and not even
Penelope, until we have determined   305
the women's attitude. We also must
test the male slaves, and see who has respect
and fears me in his heart, and who does not,
and who looks up to you as you deserve."

His glowing son said, "Father, you will see   310
my courage in the moment. I am tough.
But it would take too long to go around
and test each man like that, and all the while,
the suitors would be sitting in your house,
wasting your wealth with heedless partying.   315
So reconsider. I agree you should
find out about the women—which of them
are innocent, and which dishonor you.
However, I have no desire to traipse
around to test the men; we can do that   320
later, if Zeus reveals a sign to you."

Such was their conversation. Then the ship
in which Telemachus had gone to Pylos
docked in the bay of Ithaca's main town.
They disembarked and dragged the ship onto shore.   325
The slaves brought out the splendid gifts and weapons
and took them to the house of Clytius.
A messenger was sent to tell the queen
Telemachus was back in Ithaca,
and that he said that they must come to town,   330
dragging the ship, in case she had been weeping
in her anxiety about her son.
The swineherd and this messenger met up,
on the same mission, to inform the queen.
When both of them arrived, the slave girls clustered   335
around the messenger. He said,

                              "Great queen,
your dear son has come home!"

                              And then the swineherd
took her aside and told her what her son
had ordered him to say. When he was done,
he walked out through the hall and out the courtyard,   340
leaving the palace hall to join his pigs.

The suitors were upset and down at heart.
Eurymachus the son of Polybus
said, "Friends, the journey of this upstart boy
succeeded! We were sure that he would fail.   345
We must launch our best ship, equipped with rowers,

to speed across the ocean to the others
and tell them to come home at once."

His words
were hardly finished when Amphinomus
spotted a ship inside the harbor, pointed   350
away from land; the sails were being furled,
the men were carrying the oars. He laughed
triumphantly and said,

"No need to send
a messenger! They are already back!
Some god has told them, or they saw his ship   355
approaching, but could not catch up with it."

So leaping up, they went down to the seashore,
and dragged the black ship up onto dry land,
and servants proudly brought the weapons out.
They all went crowding to the marketplace,   360
together, and banned any other men
from joining them, both young and old. And then
Antinous addressed them.

"How amazing!
The gods have saved this man from death! For days
our scouts took turns to watch from windy cliffs.   365
And when the sun went down, we never spent
a night on shore, but sailed to wait till Dawn
at sea in ambush for Telemachus,
to make sure we would catch him. Now some god
has brought him home. We need to make new plans   370
to murder him. He must not get away.
He will obstruct our courtship if he lives,
since he is wise to us, and he will plot,
and now the people will be turned against us.
Telemachus will gather them; he must   375
be furious, and he will not postpone
action. He will stand up and tell them how
we planned to murder him, but failed to do so.
When they hear of our crimes, they will condemn us.
We may get hurt or driven from our land,   380
to foreign territories; we must stop it!
Catch him out in the countryside, away
from town, or on the road. Let us rob him,
and share his wealth and property among us—
and let his mother, and whichever man   385
marries her, keep the house. But if you think
it would be better if we let him live,
and keep his father's riches for himself,
we should stop flocking here to waste the wealth
inside his house. We should each go and court her   390

from home, by sending gifts. One day, the lady
will marry, and the lucky man will be
the one who sends the most gifts."

They were silent.
But then Amphinomus, the famous son
of Nisus, spoke. He had come from the wheat fields   395
and pastures of Dulichium, with others.
He was intelligent; Penelope
preferred his speeches over other men's.
Wisely he said,

"My friends, I for my part
have no desire to kill Telemachus.   400
It is a dreadful thing to kill a person
of royal blood. So first we must discover
the gods' intentions. If great Zeus decrees it,
I will kill him myself, and urge you all
to join me. If the gods do not approve,   405
I say we must not do it."

So he spoke,
and they agreed with what he said. They stood,
and went back to Odysseus' house,
and sat on polished chairs.

Penelope
decided she must show herself to these   410
ungentlemanly suitors, since she had
found out about the plot to kill her son—
Medon had heard their plans, and he told her.
Her women at her side, she went downstairs,
into the hall, approached them and then stopped,   415
standing beside the doorpost with a veil
across her face. She told Antinous,

"You are a brute! A sneak! A criminal!
The people say you are the smartest boy
of all those your own age on Ithaca.   420
It is not true. You are insane! How could you
devise a plan to kill Telemachus?
Do you have no respect for ties created
by supplication, which Zeus watches over?
Have you forgotten that your father came here,   425
running in terror from the Ithacans,
who were enraged because he joined the pirates
of Taphos, and was hounding the Thesprotians,
our allies? So the Ithacans were eager
to kill him, rip his heart out, and devour   430
his wealth. Odysseus protected him!
Now you consume your benefactor's wealth,

and court his wife, and try to kill his son,
and you are hurting me! I tell you, stop!
And make the other suitors stop as well."   435

He said, "Penelope, you need not worry.
Put all this from your mind. There is no man
and never will be, who can harm your boy
while I am still alive upon this earth.
I swear to you, if someone tries, my sword   440
will spill his blood! Your city-sacking husband
often would take me on his lap, and give me
tidbits of meat with his own hands, and sips
of red wine. So Telemachus is now
the man I love the most in all the world.   445
The boy is in no danger, not from us—
there is no help for death brought by the gods."

He spoke to mollify her; all the while
he was devising plans to kill her son.
She went up to her light and airy bedroom,   450
and wept for dear Odysseus, her husband,
until Athena gave her eyes sweet sleep.

As evening fell, the swineherd came back home
to find Odysseus. He and his son
had killed a year-old pig and made a meal.   455
Athena came beside Odysseus
and touched him with her wand again to make him
ragged and old, to make sure when the swineherd
came in, he would not recognize his master,
in case he told Penelope the secret.   460

He came inside. Telemachus spoke first.
"Eumaeus, you are back! What is the news
in town? Are those proud suitors in my house,
back from the ambush, or still lurking there
to catch me on my way back home?"

                      Eumaeus   465
answered, "I did not want to trek through town
asking that question. I preferred to share
my news as fast as possible and then
come back. One of your own men went with me,
a messenger; he told your mother first.   470
I saw one more thing: as I passed the hill
of Hermes, right above the town I saw
a ship draw into harbor, full of men
and loaded up with shields and spears. I thought
it could be them, but I cannot be sure."   475

Then Prince Telemachus began to smile
and met his father's eyes; he did not let
Eumaeus see. When they were finished cooking,
they shared the dinner equally, and all
had plenty, then they took the gift of sleep.   480

BOOK 17

Insults and Abuse

When newborn Dawn appeared with hands of flowers,
Telemachus, Odysseus' son,
fastened his handsome sandals on his feet,
took up his sturdy spear that fit his hand,
and headed out. He told the swineherd,

                                      "Grandpa,   5
I must go into town, to see my mother.
Until we meet, I think she will not stop
her lamentations, tears, and bitter sobbing.
Now I need you to take this poor old stranger
to town to beg his supper; any man   10
who feels like it can feed him. I cannot
put up with everyone right now; I have
too many worries. If he gets annoyed,
the worse for him. I always like to tell
the honest truth."

                     Odysseus replied,   15
"My friend, I do not even want to stay.
Beggars should wander round the town and country.
I will get food from charitable people.
I am too old to stay here as a farmhand,
obeying orders from an overseer.   20
This man will take me, as you told him to,
as soon as I have warmed up by the fire.
I only have these rags; the morning frost
may do me in—you say the town is far."

At that, Telemachus strode quickly out,   25
thinking about his plan to hurt the suitors.
And when he reached the royal house, he propped
his spear against a pillar, and went in,
across the stony threshold.

                            Eurycleia
the nurse, was first to notice his arrival,   30
as she was laying fleeces on the chairs.
Weeping, she rushed at him. The other women
owned by strong-willed Odysseus assembled

and kissed Telemachus' head and shoulders
to welcome him. Then wise Penelope   35
came from her bedroom, looking like a goddess,
like Artemis[1] or golden Aphrodite,
and flung her arms around her darling son,
and wept. She kissed his face and shining eyes,
and through her tears her words flew out.

                                  "You came!   40
Telemachus! Sweet light! I was so sure
that I would never see you anymore
after you sailed to Pylos secretly,
not telling me, to get news of your father.
Tell me, what have you seen?"

                              Telemachus   45
said calmly, "Mother, do not try to make me
upset, or stir my feelings. I survived
the danger. Go upstairs and take your bath,
put on clean clothes and take your women with you
into your bedroom. Sacrifice and pray   50
to all the gods, that one day Zeus may grant
revenge. Now I am going into town.
I will invite the stranger who arrived
right after me on Ithaca. I sent him
ahead, with my brave men, and told Piraeus   55
to take him home and treat him with all kindness
until I come."

                    His flying words hit home.
She washed, put on clean clothes, and prayed to all
the gods, and made them lavish sacrifices,
asking that one day Zeus would bring revenge.   60

Telemachus took up his spear and marched
out through the hall, two swift dogs at his side.
Athena poured unearthly grace upon him.
Everyone was amazed to see him coming.
The suitors gathered round and spoke to him   65
in friendly tones; at heart, they meant him harm.
Keeping away from most of them, he joined
Mentor and Antiphus and Halitherses,
who were his father's friends from long ago.
They questioned him in detail. Then Piraeus   70
approached with Theoclymenus, the stranger
whom he had brought through town towards the center.
At once Telemachus set out and rushed

---

1. Artemis, goddess of hunting, was associated with chastity and the moon.

to stand beside the stranger. And Piraeus
spoke first.

      "Telemachus, send women quickly   75
to my house, so I may give back the gifts
that Menelaus gave you."

          But with caution
Telemachus replied,

      "Piraeus, no.
We do not know exactly what will happen,
and if the suitors in my house by stealth   80
should kill me and divide my father's wealth
between themselves, I would prefer that you
enjoy the gifts than any of those men.
And if I kill them, planting doom among them,
bring me the gifts, and we will both be happy."   85

With this, he led the weary stranger back
to his house, where he laid their cloaks across
chairs; they went to bathe. The slave girls washed them,
rubbed them with oil, and dressed them in wool cloaks
and tunics. Then they left the baths and sat   90
on chairs. A girl brought out a golden pitcher
and poured the washing water on their hands,
over a silver bowl. She set a table
beside them, and a humble slave girl brought
a generous array from their rich stores.   95
Penelope was leaning on a chair
beside the door, facing Telemachus,
spinning fine strands of wool. They helped themselves
to food and drink. When they had had enough,
Penelope, preoccupied, spoke up.   100

      "Telemachus, I will go upstairs now,
to lie down on my bed, which has become
a bed of mourning, always stained with tears,
since my Odysseus went off to Troy
with those two sons of Atreus. But you   105
have failed to tell me if you gathered news
about your father's journey home; now tell me,
before the suitors come."

          Telemachus
answered her calmly. "Mother, I will tell you.
We went to Pylos, visiting King Nestor.   110
He made me very welcome in his palace,
under his roof, as if I were his son
returning after many years away.
He cared for me like one of his own sons.

But he said he had not heard anything   115
from anyone about Odysseus,
alive or dead. He sent me on, with horses
and carriage, to the son of Atreus,
great General Menelaus. There I saw
Helen for whose sake, by the will of gods,   120
the Greeks and Trojans suffered through the war.
When Menelaus asked why I had come
to glorious Sparta, I told him the truth
in detail, and he answered, 'Stupid cowards!
The bed they want to lie down in belongs   125
to someone truly resolute. As when
a deer lays down her newborn suckling fawns
inside the leafy den of some fierce lion,
and goes off to the slopes and grassy valleys
to graze. Then he comes back to his own bed   130
and cruelly destroys both little ones.
So will Odysseus destroy them all.
By Father Zeus, Athena, and Apollo,
I pray he is as strong as long ago,
on Lesbos, when he wrestled Philomeleides   135
and hurled him to the ground, and all the Greeks
cheered. May he fight the suitors that same way,
so all of them will find their courtship ends
badly, and their lives soon. And I will answer
your questions frankly, and tell what I learned   140
from the old Sea God, who can tell no lies.
He said he saw him in distress: the nymph
Calypso has him trapped upon her island,
inside her house. He cannot come back home
to his own country, since he has no fleet   145
or crew to row across the sea's broad back.'
That was what famous Menelaus said.
My tasks accomplished, I sailed off. The gods
gave me fair wind which swiftly brought me home."

His story stirred emotions in her heart.   150
Then godlike Theoclymenus spoke up.

"My lady, wife of great Odysseus,
this news is incomplete. I will reveal
the whole truth with a prophecy. I swear
by Zeus and hospitality and by   155
the hearth of great Odysseus, the place
where I have come: he is already here
in Ithaca—at rest or on his way.
He must have learned what bad things they are doing,
and he is plotting ruin for them all.   160
I know because I saw a sign while sitting
on board the ship—I told Telemachus."

Penelope said carefully, "Well, stranger,
I hope this does come true. I would reward you
with so much warmth and generosity   165
that everyone you met would see your luck."
Meanwhile, outside Odysseus' house,
the suitors relished games of darts and discus,
playing outside as usual, with no thought
of others. Then at dinnertime, when flocks   170
of sheep were trekking home from every field,
led by their shepherds, Medon spoke. He was
the suitors' favorite slave boy, whom they always
brought to their feasts.

         "My lords, you have enjoyed
your games. Now come inside to eat. There is   175
no harm in having meals at proper times."

They followed his advice, stood up and went
inside the palace. They spread out their cloaks
over the chairs, and killed plump goats, large rams,
some fatted pigs, and one domestic cow,   180
and cooked them for the feast.

                Odysseus
was making haste to leave the countryside
for town. The swineherd spoke in lordly tones.

"Stranger, my master says that you can come
to town today, as you desire—though I   185
would rather leave you here to watch the farm.
But I am nervous that the master may
reproach me, and a master's curses fall
heavily on a slave. Now we must go.
The hour is late and it will soon get colder;   190
the sun is sinking low."

              Odysseus
answered, "I understand. We can go now;
you lead the way. But if you have a stick,
give it to me to lean on, since I hear
the path is slippery."

            With that, he slung   195
his bag across his shoulders by its string.
It was all tattered, full of holes. Eumaeus
gave him a serviceable stick. They left;
the dogs and herdsmen stayed to guard the farm.
The swineherd led his master into town   200
resembling a poor old beggar, leaning
upon a stick and dressed in dirty rags.

They walked along the stony path, and near
the town, they reached an ornate fountain, flowing
with clear streams, where the people came for water.   205
It had been built by Ithacus, Neritus,
and Polyctor. A circle of black poplars
grew round it, nurtured by the spring. Cool water
poured from the rocks above. There was an altar
built over it in honor of the Nymphs.   210
All passersby made offerings to them.
Melanthius the son of Dolius,
with two more herders, met them there. He was
driving the finest goats to feed the suitors.
On seeing them, he spoke abusively,   215
in brash, offensive language that enraged
Odysseus.

   "One scoundrel leads another!
Makes sense: gods join like things with like. You foul
pig-man, where are you taking this old swine?
A scrounger, who will rub on many doors,   220
demanding scraps, not gifts for warriors.
If you let me have him to guard my farm,
and muck the pens and toss the kids their fodder,
he could drink whey and fatten his stick legs.
But he does not want work. He likes to traipse   225
around the town and beg for chow to stuff
his greedy belly. I predict, if he
reaches the palace of Odysseus,
a mass of hands will hurl stools at his head,
to pelt him through the house and bruise his ribs."   230

With that, he sauntered past him, and lunged out
to kick him on the hip bone. What a fool!
Odysseus was not pushed off the path;
he stood there fixed in place, and wondered whether
to rush at him, armed with his stick, and kill him,   235
or grab him by the ears and push him down
onto the ground. Instead, he braced himself
and kept his temper. When the swineherd saw
Melanthius insulting him, he prayed,
arms high.

   "O Fountain Nymphs, O Zeus' daughters!   240
If ever King Odysseus brought bones
of lamb and goat in luscious fat for you, then now
fulfill my prayer! May spirits guide him home!
My master will put paid to all the bluster
of this rude man, who loafs round town and lets   245
the animals be ruined by bad herders."

Melanthius the goatherd sneered at him,
"Oh, very nice! This dog knows how to talk,

and it has learned some tricks. One day I will
take him by ship and row him far away   250
from Ithaca, and get a heap of treasure
by selling him. I wish Apollo would
shoot silver arrows at Telemachus
today in his own house; or that the suitors
would kill him. I am sure Odysseus   255
is far away and never coming back."

With that, he left them—they were walking slowly,
and he rushed on ahead of them. He went
inside his master's house, and sat among
the suitors, with Eurymachus, his favorite.   260
The slaves brought out a piece of meat for him,
and a submissive house girl brought him bread.
The swineherd and Odysseus went in,
and stood, surrounded by the strumming sound
of the resounding lyre that Phemius   265
was tuning for his song. Odysseus
grabbed at the swineherd's hand and said,

                "Eumaeus!
This is Odysseus' splendid palace.
It could be recognized among a thousand.
The rooms are all connected, and the courtyard   270
is fenced in by a wall with cornices,
and there are sturdy double doors. No man
could break through here. I notice many men
are feasting; I smell meat, and hear the lyre,
which gods have made companion to the feast."   275

Eumaeus answered, "Right! You are perceptive.
Now we must plan. Will you go inside first
to join the suitors, while I stay out here?
Or do you want to wait, and I will go?
But do not stay too long. If someone sees you,   280
you will be pelted, maybe beaten up."

Unflappable Odysseus said, "Yes,
I thought of that. You go, I will stay here.
I have been hit before. I know hard knocks.
I am resilient. I suffered war   285
and being lost at sea. So let this be.
There is no way to hide a hungry belly.
It is insistent, and the curse of hunger
is why we sail across relentless seas,
and plunder other people."

                As they spoke,   290
Argos, the dog that lay there, raised his head
and ears. Odysseus had trained this dog

but with no benefit—he left too soon
to march on holy Troy. The master gone,
boys took the puppy out to hunt wild goats   295
and deer and hares. But now he lay neglected,
without an owner, in a pile of dung
from mules and cows—the slaves stored heaps of it
outside the door, until they fertilized
the large estate. So Argos lay there dirty,   300
covered with fleas. And when he realized
Odysseus was near, he wagged his tail,
and both his ears dropped back. He was too weak
to move towards his master. At a distance,
Odysseus had noticed, and he wiped   305
his tears away and hid them easily,
and said,

        "Eumaeus, it is strange this dog
is lying in the dung; he looks quite handsome,
though it is hard to tell if he can run,
or if he is a pet, a table dog,   310
kept just for looks."

        Eumaeus, you replied,
"This dog belonged to someone who has died
in foreign lands. If he were in good health,
as when Odysseus abandoned him
and went to Troy, you soon would see how quick   315
and brave he used to be. He went to hunt
in woodland, and he always caught his prey.
His nose was marvelous. But now he is
in bad condition, with his master gone,
long dead. The women fail to care for him.   320
Slaves do not want to do their proper work,
when masters are not watching them. Zeus halves
our value on the day that makes us slaves."

With that, the swineherd went inside the palace,
to join the noble suitors. Twenty years   325
had passed since Argos saw Odysseus,
and now he saw him for the final time—
then suddenly, black death took hold of him.

Telemachus first saw the swineherd coming.
He gave a nod to tell him to come over.   330
Glancing around, Eumaeus saw the stool
used by the boy who carved the suitors' meat.
He picked it up and set it down beside
Telemachus' table. There he sat;
the slave boy brought him meat and bread. And then   335
Odysseus approached and stepped inside,
looking like some poor homeless sad old man;

he hobbled on his stick, then slumped himself
down on the ash-wood threshold, leaning back
against the cypress doorpost, which a workman   340
had smoothed and straightened long ago. The boy
summoned the swineherd over, and picked up
a wheat loaf from the basket and as much
meat as his hands could hold, and gave it to him.
He said,

    "Please take this food out to that stranger,   345
and tell him he should walk around the hall
and beg from all the suitors; shame is not
a friend to those in need."

      The swineherd went
and told Odysseus, "Telemachus
gives you this food and says you ought to beg   350
from all these suitors; shame, he says, is not
fitting for those who have to live by handouts."

Odysseus prayed cautiously, "O Zeus,
bless this Telemachus, and may he have
all that his heart desires."

      And with both hands   355
he took the food and set it at his feet,
on top of his old ragged bag, and ate,
and listened to the singer in the hall.
As he was finishing, the music stopped;
the suitors shouted, and Athena stood   360
beside Odysseus, and prompted him
to go among the suitors, begging scraps,
to find out which of them were bad or good—
although she had no thought of saving any
out of the massacre which was to come.   365
He went around and begged from left to right,
holding his hand out, like a practiced beggar.
They gave him food in pity, and they wondered
who this man was and whereabouts he came from.
They asked each other, and Melanthius,   370
the goatherd, said,

    "You suitors of the queen,
listen to me about this stranger here.
I saw this man before; the swineherd brought him.
I know no more; I do not know his background."

Antinous began to scold the swineherd.   375
"Pig-man! You famous idiot! Why did you
bring this man here? Do we not have already
plenty of homeless people coming here

to spoil our feasts? Is it not bad enough
that they crowd round and eat your master's wealth?   380
You had to ask this other one as well?"

Eumaeus, you replied, "Antinous,
you are a lord, but what you say is trash.
Who would invite a stranger from abroad
unless he had the skills to help the people—   385
a prophet, or a doctor, or a builder,
or poet who can sing and bring delight?
No one would ask a beggar; they bring only
their hunger. Out of all the suitors, you
are meanest to the slaves, especially me.   390
But if the prudent queen and godlike prince
still live here in this house, I do not mind."

Telemachus said, "Shush. Antinous
does not deserve an answer. He is always
picking a fight, and goading on the others."   395

Then turning to Antinous, he said,
"You care for me so nicely, like a father!
You told me I should force the stranger out.
May no god make that happen! Go to him
and give him something; I can spare the food.   400
Go on, I tell you! You should pay no heed
to Mother or the other household slaves
belonging to my father. You were not
concerned about them anyway. You want
to gorge yourself, not share with other people."   405

Antinous replied, "You little show-off!
What nasty temper! What an awful comment!
If all the suitors gave the same as me,
this house could keep him checked for three whole months."

He had a footstool underneath the table,   410
for resting his soft feet on while he feasted;
he brandished it. The others all gave food
and filled the beggar's bag. Odysseus
had finished with his test; he could have walked
back to the threshold, no harm done. Instead,   415
he stood beside Antinous and said,

"Friend, give me something. You must be the best
of all the Greeks. You look like royalty,
so you should give more food than all the rest,
and I will make you known throughout the world.   420
I used to be a rich man, with a palace.
When needy beggars came from anywhere,
no matter who they were, I gave them food.

My slaves were numberless, my wealth was great;
I had the life men say is happiness.   425
But Zeus destroyed it all; he wanted to.
He prompted me to travel with some pirates
to Egypt; that long journey spelled my ruin.
I moored my galleys in the River Nile
and told my loyal men to stay and guard them,   430
and sent out scouts to all the lookout points.
But they were too impulsive, and they sacked
the beautiful Egyptian fields, and seized
women and children, and they killed the men.
The screaming reached the town; the people heard,   435
and rushed to come and help; at dawn the plain
was all filled up with foot soldiers and horses
and flashing bronze. Then Zeus, who loves the thunder,
caused panic in my men—disastrous panic.
Danger was all around us, and not one   440
stood firm. The sharp bronze swords killed many men,
and others were enslaved as laborers.
But they gave me to somebody they met,
a foreigner named Dmetor, king of Cyprus.
I came from there. Such is my tale of woe."   445

Antinous replied, "What god imposed
this pest to spoil our feast? Stay over there,
not near my table—or you can get lost!
Get killed in Egypt or enslaved in Cyprus!
You barefaced beggar! You come up to us,   450
and these men give you treats unthinkingly;
we have so much, and people do not mind
sharing another person's wealth."

                              Sharp-witted
Odysseus drew back from him and said,
"You handsome idiot! You would not give   455
a grain of salt from your own house. You sit
enjoying someone else's food, and yet
you will not give a crumb from this great banquet
to me."

              Antinous was furious,
and scowling said, "That does it! You insult me?   460
You lost the chance to leave with dignity!"
He lifted up his stool and hurled it at
Odysseus' right shoulder, near his back.
It did not knock him over; like a rock
he stood there, shook his head, and silently   465
considered his revenge. Then he went back,
sat on the threshold and set down the bag,
all full of food, and told them, "Listen, suitors
of this world-famous queen; I have to speak.

When men are fighting for their own possessions,   470
for cows or sheep, there is no shame in wounds.
But now Antinous has wounded me
because I came here hungry; hunger brings
such suffering to humans. If there are
gods of the poor, or Furies to avenge us,   475
may he be struck by death, instead of marriage!"

He answered, "Stranger, shut up, or be off!
If you keep talking, we young men will drag you
across the palace by your hands and feet
and have you flayed alive!"

                 But all the others   480
reproached Antinous insistently.
"You ought not to have hit a poor old beggar!
If he turns out to be a god from heaven
it will end badly! Gods disguise themselves
as foreigners and strangers to a town,   485
to see who violates their holy laws,
and who is good."

            Antinous ignored
the suitors' words. The blow increased the pain
inside Telemachus' heart, but he
let fall no tears. He calmly shook his head   490
and thought about revenge.

             Penelope
heard what had happened in the hall, and said
to all her slaves,

            "I hope Apollo shoots
Antinous, just as he hit the beggar!"

And old Eurynome replied, "If only   495
our prayers were answered! None of them would live
to see the Dawn ride in upon her throne."

Penelope said, "Yes, dear, they are all
our enemies and mean to do us harm.
Antinous is the worst; he is like death.   500
Some poor old stranger wandered to this house
and asked the men for food, compelled by need.
The others helped him out and filled his bag;
Antinous hurled a footstool at his shoulder."

She had this conversation in her room   505
with her attendants, while Odysseus
was eating dinner. Then she called the swineherd.

"Eumaeus! Have the stranger come to me,
so I may welcome him, and ask if he
has heard or witnessed anything about   510
long-lost Odysseus. The stranger seems
as if he must have traveled far."

                        Eumaeus
replied, "Your Majesty, I wish these men
would quiet down! The tales the stranger tells
would charm your heart. For three days and three nights   515
I had him stay with me. He ran away
from off a ship, and came to my house first;
he started to describe his sufferings,
and had not finished. Like a singer, blessed
by gods with skill in storytelling—people   520
watch him and hope that he will sing forever—
so this man's tale enchanted me. He says
Odysseus and he are old guest-friends
through their forefathers. This man lived in Crete,
the home of Minos,[2] and he traveled here   525
a rambling route, with dangers compassed round.
He says Odysseus is still alive
and near here, in the rich Thesprotian land,
and he is bringing home a pile of treasure."

Penelope said, "Call him over, let him   530
tell me in person, while the suitors have
their fun here in my house or at the doors;
their mood is festive. In their homes they have
untasted food and wine, which their house slaves
devour, while they are flocking to our house   535
each day to slaughter oxen, sheep, and goats,
to feast and drink our wine, with no restraint.
Our wealth is decimated. There is no man
here like Odysseus, who could defend
the house. But if Odysseus comes back   540
to his own native land, he and his son
will soon take vengeance for their violence."

Telemachus sneezed loudly and the noise
resounded through the hall. Penelope
laughed, and she told Eumaeus,

                            "Call the stranger!   545
My son just sneezed at what I said—you heard?
It is a sign of death for all the suitors;
no one can save them from their ruin now.
But listen: if I find this stranger speaking
the truth, give him nice clothes—a cloak and tunic."   550

2. Legendary king of Crete.

At that, the swineherd went and stood beside
Odysseus. His words had wings.

                "Now sir,
Penelope, Telemachus' mother,
has summoned you. She feels impelled to ask
about her husband, painful though it is.   555
If you tell her the truth—and she will know—
you will get clothes; you desperately need them.
And you can ask for food all through the town,
and fill your belly. Anyone who wants
can give you scraps."

             Strong-willed Odysseus   560
answered, "Eumaeus, I will tell the truth,
the whole truth, to Penelope, and soon.
I know about Odysseus; we shared
in suffering. But I am very nervous
about the rowdy suitors. Their aggression   565
touches the iron sky. When I was walking
across the hall just now, quite harmlessly,
that man hurled something at me, and he hurt me.
Telemachus did nothing to protect me,
and nor did anybody else. So now,   570
tell her to stay right there until night falls,
however eager she may be. At dusk,
she can come nearer, sit beside the fire,
and ask about her husband's journey home.
I do have dirty clothes—you know it well,   575
since it was you I came to first for help."
The swineherd headed back; he crossed the threshold,
and sharp Penelope said,

                "Are you not
bringing the traveler? Is something wrong?
Is he too scared or shy? A homeless man   580
can ill afford such shame."

              Eumaeus answered,
"His words were common sense; he wants to stay
out of the suitors' way; they are aggressive.
He says you should stay here until sunset.
It is much better for you too, my queen,   585
to speak to him alone."

             Penelope
replied, "The stranger is no fool at least.
There never were such bullies as these men,
and they intend us harm."

The swineherd went
back to the crowd of suitors, and approached   590
Telemachus, and tucked his head down close,
so no one else would hear. "My friend," he said,
"I have to go and watch the pigs, and all
your property, and mine. You should take care
of everything, but most of all, yourself.   595
Do not get hurt. So many mean you harm.
I pray that Zeus obliterates them all,
before they injure us!"

            Telemachus
answered, "May it be so. First eat, then go;
come back at dawn with animals for meat.   600
The rest is up to me and up to gods."
So then Eumaeus sat down on the stool,
and ate and drank, then went back to his pigs,
leaving the palace full of banqueters.
It was already late, past afternoon;   605
music and dancing entertained the suitors.

BOOK 18

Two Beggars

Then came a man who begged throughout the town
of Ithaca, notorious for greed.
He ate and drank nonstop, so he was fat
but weak, with no capacity for fighting.
The name his mother gave him as a child   5
was Arnaeus, but all the young men called him
Irus, because he was their messenger.[1]
Now this man tried to chase Odysseus
from his own home, and cursed him.

                         "Get away,
old man! Get out! Or else you will be dragged   10
out by the foot! Do you not see the suitors
winking to tell me I must throw you out?
This is embarrassing for me; I must
make you get up right now! Or we must fight!"

Scowling at him, Odysseus said, "Fool!   15
I did not do you wrong or speak against you.
I am not jealous of another beggar
receiving gifts, however much he gets.
This doorway can accommodate us both.
Do not hog all the wealth; it is not yours.   20
You seem to be a homeless man, like me.

---

1. An allusion to the messenger goddess of the rainbow, Iris.

Gods give all mortal blessings. Do not stir me
to fight or lose my temper. I am old
but I will crack your ribs and smash your face
to bloody pulp—then I will have a day   25
of peace tomorrow; you will not return
here to the palace of Odysseus."

Irus the vagabond was furious.
"This greedy pig yaks on like some old woman
scrubbing an oven! I will hurt him, punch him   30
two-fisted, and rip out his teeth, as farmers
pull out the tusks from pigs that damage crops.
Get ready! Let them watch. How could you be
so dumb, to pick a fight with someone younger?"

So on the threshold at the palace doors   35
their furious aggression reached its peak.
Antinous, that saintly lord, incited
the fight and with a chuckle told the suitors,

"My friends! We never had so fine a show
brought to this house before. The gods be thanked,   40
these two are getting ready for a brawl.
Quick, let us goad them on!"

                              They all jumped up,
laughing, and gathered round the ragged beggars.
Antinous addressed them.

                         "Listen, suitors!
Goat stomachs stuffed with fat and blood are roasting   45
over the fire for dinner. Let the beggar
who wins the fight choose one of these and take it;
and he can always eat with us in future,
and we will let no other beggar come
to share our company."

                         They all agreed.   50
The strategist Odysseus deceived them,
saying, "My friends, there is no way a man
as old as me, worn down by suffering,
can fight a younger man. My hunger forces
bad choices, tempting me to take the beating.   55
But swear a mighty oath that none of you
will step up to help Irus out and hit me
roughly with fists and make me lose to him."

All of them swore the oath as he had asked.
The holy prince Telemachus said,

                         "Guest,   60
if your brave spirit urges you to fight

against this challenger, you need not worry
about the others. Anyone who strikes you
will face a multitude. I am your host;
Eurymachus and this Antinous   65
are sensible and they agree with me."

They all consented, and Odysseus
took off his rags and tied them round his waist,
revealing massive thighs and mighty shoulders,
enormous chest and sturdy arms. Athena   70
stood near him and increased his strength, to suit
the shepherd of the people. All the suitors
were flabbergasted, and they said,

                                        "This means
the end of Irus—brought upon himself![2]
What muscles underneath the old man's rags!"   75

Irus was deeply troubled and afraid;
his heart sank. But the house slaves made him gird
his tunic and get ready. He was shaking.
Antinous said,

                                "Haha, you big show-off!
You would be better dead than so afraid   80
of some old man worn down by suffering.
If this man beats you, proving he is stronger,
I will toss you on board a ship and send you
off to King Echetus in mainland Greece,
the lord of cruelty and pain. He will   85
cut off your nose and ears with pitiless bronze,
and then your genitals, and he will give them
raw to his dogs to eat."

                                These words increased
his shakiness. Escorted to the ring,
he stood. Both raised their fists. Odysseus,   90
who had endured so many insults, wondered
if he should hit him hard enough to kill him,
or give him just a tap to knock him down.
A light touch would be best, he thought, in case
the suitors cottoned on. They came to blows.   95
First Irus hit Odysseus' shoulder;
Odysseus punched Irus on his neck
below the ear, and broke his jaw. Red blood
gushed from his mouth, and with a moan he fell,
teeth chattering, legs flailing. Then the suitors   100
threw up their hands to cheer, and died of laughter.
Odysseus seized Irus by the foot,

---

2. Literally, he will be "not-Irus," with an allusion to the name's link to the word for "strong."

dragging him through the gateway to the courtyard,
and propped him by the wall. He put a staff
into his hand, and said,

                "Sit there and keep   105
the dogs and pigs away! You good-for-nothing!
You must not bully visitors and beggars,
or you will suffer even worse than this!"

Then picking up his ragged bag, he slung it
across his shoulders by the strap and sat   110
beside the door again. The suitors went
inside and raised their cups.

                    "May all the gods
and Zeus give you your heart's desire! That Irus
was sponging everywhere, the greedy pig.
You put a stop to him, and we will send him   115
to Echetus, the king of mass destruction."

Odysseus was thrilled to hear this omen.[3]
Antinous set out the big goat's stomach,
stuffed full of blood and fat, in front of him.
Amphinomus provided two bread baskets,   120
and a gold cup of wine, and welcomed him.

"Sir, be our guest, and may your future luck
be good, though now you have so many troubles."
Odysseus replied, his wits about him,
"Amphinomus, you seem intelligent,   125
like Nisus of Dulichium, your father;
I heard about his wealth and excellence,
and that you are his son. You are well-spoken.
Take note of what I say. Of all the creatures
that live and breathe and creep on earth, we humans 130
are weakest. When the gods bestow on us
good fortune, and our legs are spry and limber,
we think that nothing can ever can go wrong;
but when the gods bring misery and pain,
we have to bear our suffering with calm.   135
Our mood depends on what Zeus sends each day.
I once had what most people count as wealth,
great riches. I committed many crimes,
of violence, abuses of my power,
abetted by my brothers and my father.   140
No one should turn away from what is right;
a man should quietly accept whatever

3. The "omen"—an utterance that has reso-   get his heart's desire. They do not know that his
nance for the future undetected by the speaker— desire is to kill them.
is presumably the suitors' wish for Odysseus to

the gods may give. I see how wickedly
the suitors are behaving—wasting wealth
and failing to respect the wife of one   145
who soon will come back to his family
and homeland. Very soon! May spirits guide you
home, so you do not meet him when he comes.
When he confronts the suitors in this hall
there will be blood."

          He poured an offering   150
of sweet wine to the gods, and took a sip,
then passed the cup back to Amphinomus,
who took it, and then paced around the house,
troubled at heart, his head bowed low; he saw
the danger in his mind. But he was not   155
fated to live; Athena had condemned him
to be defeated by Telemachus
with his strong spear. Amphinomus sat down
on the same chair that he sat on before.

Athena, with her gray eyes glinting, gave   160
thoughtful Penelope a new idea:
to let the suitors see her, so desire
would open up inside them like a sail,
and so her son and husband would respect her.
Mysteriously, she laughed, and told her slave,   165

"Eurynome, I have a new desire:
to let the suitors see me, though I hate them.
I also want to give my son advice:
not to spend so much time with those proud men.
They talk impressively, but their intentions   170
are bad."

          Eurynome replied, "My child,
your words make sense. But you should wash and oil
your skin, not go with blotches on your face
to have this conversation with your son.
You should not grieve forever, and your boy   175
is older now. You always begged the gods
to let you see him grown up, with a beard."

Penelope replied with circumspection,
"Eurynome, I know you care for me,
but do not tell me I should wash myself   180
and put on oil. The gods destroyed my beauty
that day my husband left in hollow ships.
Go call my slave girls, Hippodameia
and Autonoe—they must come with me
into the hall. I do not want to go   185
to meet the men alone. It would be shameful."
So the old woman went and called the girls.

Athena's eyes were bright with plans. She poured
sweet sleep onto Penelope, who lay
down on her couch; her joints relaxed; she slept.   190
Athena gave her gifts of godlike power,
to make the men astonished when they saw her.
She put ambrosial beauty on her face,
the kind that Aphrodite, wreathed in myrtle,
uses before she dances with the Graces.[4]   195
She also made her shapelier and taller,
and made her skin more white than ivory.
The goddess left. The girls came in; their talking
woke up the queen. She felt her cheeks and said,

"Despite my bitter grief, a peaceful sleep   200
enveloped me. If only Artemis
would bring me gentle death right now to end
my misery. I waste my life in longing
for my beloved husband, who was good
at everything—the best of the Achaeans."   205

She went down from her sunny room upstairs.
The two slaves went with her. She reached the suitors,
and stood beside the central pillar, holding
her gauzy veil before her face. Her two
trustworthy slaves stood either side of her.   210
The suitors weakened at the knees; desire
bewitched them, and they longed to lie with her.
She spoke to her dear son, Telemachus.

"Telemachus, you are not thinking straight.
When you were still a child, you had good sense.   215
Now you are bigger; you have reached adulthood.
You are so tall and so good-looking now!
People can see you are a rich man's son;
even a foreigner would know at once.
And yet your judgment is askew. What happened,   220
that you allowed a guest to be insulted?
If strangers in our house are so abused,
what then? You will be shamed! Your reputation
will be destroyed!"

    Telemachus replied
with calculated purpose. "Mother, I do not   225
blame you for being angry. In my heart
I do know right and wrong. I used to be
a child; I am not now. But I cannot
even afford to think my own heart's thoughts.
Those evil suitors keep distracting me,   230
and I have no one on my side. This fight

---

4. Three goddesses, associated with beauty, joy, and good feelings.

between the stranger and that beggar Irus
did not turn out as they had wished; the stranger
was much the stronger. Father Zeus! Apollo!
Athena! May the suitors in our house   235
be beaten and bow down their heads, some in
the house, and some outside. May each man's body
grow weak—like Irus, out there at the gate,
sitting with head slumped down, as if he were
intoxicated; he cannot stand up   240
nor go back home. His body is too frail."

And then Eurymachus spoke up and said,
"O Queen Penelope! Wise, prudent daughter
of great Icarius! If all the Greeks
could see you now, there would be far more suitors   245
feasting here in your house, from dawn to dusk,
because no other woman equals you
in beauty, stature, and well-balanced mind."
Penelope replied with caution. "No,
the deathless gods destroyed my looks that day   250
the Greeks embarked for Troy, and my own husband
Odysseus went with them. If he came
and started taking care of me again,
I would regain my good name and my beauty.
I am weighed down by grief. A spirit set   255
so many troubles on me. At the time
that he left Ithaca, my husband grabbed
my wrist, took my right hand, and said to me,
'Now wife, I do not think we armored Greeks
will all come home unharmed from Troy. They say   260
the Trojans are good warriors with arrows
and javelins, and they ride chariots
drawn by swift horses, which can quickly turn
the tide of war, in which so many die.
Some god may bring me home, or I may be   265
captured out there in Troy. I do not know.
You must remember this: my parents need
to be well cared for in our house, as much
as now or more so with me gone away.
When our son's beard has grown, you must get married   270
to any man you choose, and leave your house.'
Those were my husband's words. The time has come;
the night when I must marry is at hand.
Terrible! I am cursed! Zeus took away
my happiness. Another bitter thought   275
oppresses me: it is not right or proper
to court a decent woman in this way,
a rich man's wife, competing for her hand.
They ought to bring fat sheep and cows to feed
my family, and give fine gifts, not eat   280
what is not theirs, and offer nothing back."

Odysseus, who had endured so much,
was happy she was secretly procuring
presents, and charming them with pretty words,
while her mind moved elsewhere.

                 Antinous   285
said, "Wise Penelope, take all the presents
that any of the Greeks would like to bring.
Refusing gifts is not polite. But we
will not go back to our own farms or elsewhere,
until you choose the best of us to marry."   290

They all agreed and sent their men for gifts.
Antinous brought out a splendid robe,
embroidered, with twelve brooches of pure gold
pinned to the fabric. And Eurymachus
gave her a necklace, finely worked in gold   295
set in with amber beads that shone like sunlight.
Two slaves brought earrings from Eurydamas.
They sparkled beautifully, and triple clusters
like berries hung from each. Pisander's slave
brought her a lovely choker, finely made.   300
All of the suitors gave her different gifts.
The queen went upstairs to her room; her slaves
carried the splendid presents. Then the suitors
turned back to watch the dancing and enjoy
the captivating music. They stayed there   305
in pleasure, till black evening came. They set
three braziers to light the whole great hall,
stuffed with dry wood, well seasoned and fresh cut,
combined with kindling. The slave girls owned
by firm Odysseus took turns to light them.   310
The king himself had all his wits about him,
and said,

           "Slave girls! Odysseus, your master,
has been long gone. Go back and sit beside
the queen and comfort her. Spin yarn or comb
the wool. I can provide these men with light.   315
If they decide to stay here till bright Dawn
rides on her lovely throne, I will not be
defeated. I am tough."

             At that, the girls
began to giggle, peeking at each other.
Pretty Melantho, child of Dolius,   320
had been brought up by Queen Penelope,
who gave her toys and treated her just like
a daughter. But Melantho, unconcerned
about Penelope, was sleeping with

Eurymachus. She started to insult   325
Odysseus, and taunt him.

> "Poor old stranger!
You are insane! You did not want to sleep
out in the smithy or the public shelter;
instead, you come here talking high and mighty
among this crowd of men. Are you not scared?   330
Wine may have dulled your senses, or perhaps
you always say such idiotic things.
Has your defeat of Irus made you crazy?
That beggar? Then watch out, a better man
may fight you soon, and punch your face so hard   335
you will be kicked out of this house all drenched
in blood."

> Odysseus scowled back and said,
"You little dog! I will soon go and tell
Telemachus what you have said, so he
can slice you limb from limb!"

> That made the women   340
tremble with fear; they thought he spoke the truth.
They scattered through the house. He took his stand
beside the braziers to keep them lit,
and looked at all the suitors. In his heart
he formed his plans, which soon would be fulfilled.   345

Athena wanted pain to sink down deep
inside Odysseus. She made the suitors
keep taunting him. Eurymachus was jeering
to make the others laugh.

> "Now listen, suitors!
I have an intuition that this man   350
has come into Odysseus' house
through some god's will. His head is shining brightly
under the lanterns' light—perhaps because
he is completely bald!"

> And then he turned
and asked Odysseus, the city-sacker,   355

"Stranger, if I was hiring, would you like
to labor on a distant farm for me?
You would be paid for sure, if you could plant
tall trees, and build stone walls, and I would give you
your meals all year and clothes, including footwear.   360
But you are only skilled at wickedness.
You have no wish to work. You like to beg,
traipsing around to stuff your greedy belly."

Crafty Odysseus said, "How I wish,
Eurymachus, that we could have a contest   365
in springtime in the meadow, when the days
are growing longer; I would have a scythe
of perfect curvature and so would you.
The grass would be abundant; we would test
our skill by working all day long, not eating   370
until late evening. Or if we could plow
using a pair of fine and well-fed oxen,
strong and both equal in their power to pull,
and if we had four acres of good soil,
then you would see if I know how to cut   375
a furrow straight. Or if Zeus suddenly
made war begin tomorrow, and I had
two spears, a shield, and a helmet all of bronze
close-fitted to my head, you would see me
amid the throng of fighters at the front—   380
and you would not hurl insults at my belly.
You act aggressive, and you think you are
a big strong man, because you spend your time
among this tiny group of lowborn louts.
But if Odysseus appeared, the doors—   385
which are quite wide—would start to seem too narrow,
as you were struggling to get away."

Scowling with rage, Eurymachus replied,
"You nasty hobo! I will make you pay
for showing off in front of all of us.   390
You should be scared! The wine has made you stupid,
or maybe you are always talking nonsense;
or you are all puffed up from having won
over the beggar Irus!"

                                    Then he hurled
a footstool at Odysseus, who ducked   395
behind Amphinomus in fear; it hit
the right hand of the slave boy serving wine;
the wine jug fell and clattered on the ground.
The boy fell backwards on the dust and moaned.
The suitors' shouts resounded through the shadows: 400
"Too bad this foreign drifter did not die
before he came here causing all this bother!
These arguments with beggars are disrupting
our banquet; it is spoiling our nice evening.
This silly fuss is dominating things."   405

Telemachus spoke up with dignity.
"Most noble lords! This is insanity.
Perhaps you dined too well, or else some god
is stirring you. Now you have finished dinner,

go home and sleep, whenever you are ready.   410
I will not force you out."

                They bit their lips,
surprised at the self-confidence he showed.
Amphinomus, the famous son of Nisus,
grandson of Lord Aretias, spoke out
to all of them.

           "My friends! What he has said   415
was fair; no one need take offense. Do not
abuse the stranger, nor the slaves who work
in great Odysseus' house. The boy
should fill the cups with wine, so we can pour
libations, then go home. Telemachus   420
can take care of the stranger—after all,
the beggar came to his house."

               They agreed.
And Moulius, the slave Amphinomus
had brought there from Dulichium, mixed wine
for all of them and shared the drinks around.   425
They poured libations to the gods and sipped
the cheering wine. When they had had enough,
each of them went back home, to his own bed.

BOOK 19

The Queen and the Beggar

Odysseus was left there in the hall,
and with Athena, he was hatching plans
for how to kill the suitors. Words flew fast:

"Telemachus, we have to get the weapons
and hide them. When the suitors see them gone   5
and question you, come up with good excuses.
You can explain, 'The soot had damaged them;
when King Odysseus marched off to Troy
their metal gleamed; now they are growing dull.
I put them safe away from all that smoke.   10
Some spirit also warned me if you drink
too much and argue, you could hurt each other,
dishonoring your banquet and your courtship.
Weapons themselves can tempt a man to fight.'"

Telemachus obeyed his father's word.   15
He summoned Eurycleia, and he told her,
"Shut up the women in their rooms, while I
carry my father's weapons to the storeroom.
They have got dirty since my father left

when I was just a little boy. I want   20
to keep them safe, protected from the smoke."

The loving nurse said, "Child, I wish you would
take charge of all the household management
and guard the wealth. Which girl should bring the torch?
You said the slaves were not allowed to walk   25
in front of you."

           He said, "This stranger will.[1]
A man who eats my bread must work for me,
even if he has come from far away."

She made no answer but locked up the doors
that led inside the hall. Odysseus   30
and his bright boy jumped up and got the helmets
and studded shields and pointed spears. Athena
stood by them with a golden lamp; she made
majestic light. Telemachus said,

           "Father,
my eyes have noticed something very strange.   35
The palace walls, the handsome fir-wood rafters
and crossbeams and the pillars high above
are visible, as if a fire were lit.
Some god from heaven must be in the house."

But cautiously Odysseus replied,   40
"Hush, no more questions, discipline your thoughts.
This is the way of gods from Mount Olympus.
You need to go to bed. I will stay here,
to aggravate the slave girls and your mother,
and make her cry, and let her question me."   45
Telemachus went through the hall, lit up
by blazing torches, to his room. Sleep came,
and there he lay till Dawn. Odysseus
stayed in the hall, still plotting with Athena
how to destroy the suitors.

           Then the queen,   50
her wits about her, came down from her room,
like Artemis or golden Aphrodite.
Slaves pulled her usual chair beside the fire;
it was inlaid with whorls of ivory
and silver, crafted by Icmalius,   55
who had attached a footstool, all in one.
A great big fleece was laid across the chair,

---

1. Eurycleia's question implies an assumption   female slave; there is a momentary surprise that
that carrying the light is the job of a woman, a   the answer is a man.

and pensively Penelope sat down.
The white-armed slave girls came and cleared away
the piles of bread, the tables, and the cups,   60
from which the arrogant suitors had been drinking.
They threw the embers from the braziers
onto the floor, and heaped fresh wood inside them
for light and warmth.

        And then Melantho scolded
Odysseus again. "Hey! Stranger! Will you   65
keep causing trouble, roaming round our house
at night and spying on us women here?
Get out, you tramp! Be happy with your meal!
Or you will soon get pelted with a torch!
Be off!"

        Odysseus began to scowl,   70
and made a calculated speech. "Insane!
You silly girl, why are you mad at me?
Because I am all dirty, dressed in rags,
and begging through the town? I have no choice.
That is how homeless people have to live.   75
I used to have a house, and I was rich,
respectable, and often gave to beggars;
I helped whoever came, no matter what.
I had a multitude of slaves, too, and all
the things we count as wealth; the happy life.   80
Zeus ruined it. He must have wanted to.
Girl, may you never lose the rank you have
among the other slave girls—if your mistress
gets angry, or Odysseus arrives.
It might still happen. But if he is dead   85
and never coming back, his son is now
a man, praise be Apollo. He will notice
any misconduct from the women here.
He is a grown-up now."

        Penelope
had listened warily, and now she spoke   90
to scold the slave. "You brazen, shameless dog!
What impudence! I see what you are doing!
Wipe that impertinent expression off!
You knew quite well—I told you so myself—
that I might keep the stranger in the hall   95
to question him about my missing husband.
I am weighed down by grief."

        And then she turned
to tell Eurynome, "Bring out a chair
and put a cushion on it, so this stranger

can sit and talk with me. I want to ask him   100
some questions."

                So the woman brought a chair
of polished wood, and set a cushion on it.
Odysseus knew how to bide his time.
He sat, and circumspect Penelope
began the conversation.

                     "Stranger, first   105
I want to ask what people you have come from.
Who are your parents? Where is your home town?"

Cunning Odysseus said, "My good woman,[2]
no mortal on the earth would speak against you;
your glory reaches heaven. You must be   110
the daughter of a holy king who ruled
a mighty people with good laws; his rule
made the black earth grow wheat and barley; trees
were full of fruit; the sheep had lambs; the sea
provided fish, and people thrived. This is   115
your house. You have the right to question me,
but do not ask about my family
or native land. The memory will fill
my heart with pain. I am a man of sorrow.
I should not sit in someone else's house   120
lamenting. It is rude to keep on grieving.
The slaves, or even you, might criticize
and say my tearfulness is caused by wine."

Penelope said cautiously, "Well, stranger,
the deathless gods destroyed my strength and beauty   125
the day the Greeks went marching off to Troy,
and my Odysseus went off with them.
If he came back and cared for me again,
I would regain my beauty and my status.
But now I suffer dreadfully; some god   130
has ruined me. The lords of all the islands,
Same, Dulichium, and Zacynthus,
and those who live in Ithaca, are courting
me—though I do not want them to!—and spoiling
my house. I cannot deal with suppliants,   135
strangers and homeless men who want a job.
I miss Odysseus; my heart is melting.
The suitors want to push me into marriage,
but I spin schemes. Some god first prompted me
to set my weaving in the hall and work   140
a long fine cloth. I said to all my suitors,

---

2. Here and throughout the book Odysseus addresses Penelope with a word that means both "woman" and "wife."

'Although Odysseus is dead, postpone
requests for marriage till I finish weaving
this sheet to shroud Laertes when he dies.
My work should not be wasted, or the people   145
in Argos will reproach me, if a man
who won such wealth should lie without a shroud.'
They acquiesced. By day I wove the web,
and in the night by torchlight, I unwove it.
I tricked them for three years; long hours went by   150
and days and months, but then, in the fourth year,
with help from my own fickle, doglike slave girls,
they came and caught me at it. Then they shouted
in protest, and they made me finish it.
I have no more ideas, and I cannot   155
fend off a marriage anymore. My parents
are pressing me to marry, and my son
knows that these men are wasting all his wealth
and he is sick of it. He has become
quite capable of caring for a house   160
that Zeus has glorified. And now, you must
reveal your ancestry. You were not born
from rocks or trees, as in a fairy tale."
The master of deception answered, "Wife
of great Odysseus, Laertes' son,   165
why will you not stop asking me about
my family? I will speak, if I must.
But you are making all my troubles worse.
It is the way of things, when someone is
away from home as long as I have been,   170
roaming through many cities, many dangers.
Still, I will tell you what you ask. My homeland
is Crete, a fertile island out at sea.
I cannot count how many people live there,
in ninety cities, and our languages   175
are mixed; there are Achaeans, native Cretans,
and long-haired Dorians and Pelasgians.
Knossos is there, a mighty city where
Minos, the intimate of Zeus, was king
for nine years,[3] and my father was his son,   180
the brave Deucalion, whose other son
was Idomeneus, who sailed to Troy
with the two sons of Atreus.[4] My name
is Aethon,[5] and I am the younger brother.
In Crete, I saw Odysseus, and gave him   185
guest-gifts. A storm had driven him off course
at Malea, and carried him to Crete,
although he yearned for Troy. He narrowly

3. Every nine years, Minos, king of Crete, was
instructed how to rule by his father, Zeus. Deucalion, his son, succeeded him as king.
4. Agamemnon and Menelaus.

5. The name "Aethon" can suggest either
"shining" or "brown." It may suggest foxy tricks,
since the word is applied to the reddish color of
the fox in Pindar (*Olympian* 11.19).

escaped the winds and found a refuge, mooring
his ships in Amnisus, beside the cave   190
of Eileithyia.[6] He came up to town,
and asked to see my brother, who, he said,
was his good friend, a man he much admired.
But Idomeneus had sailed to Troy
ten days before. I asked him and his crew   195
inside and gave them all a lavish welcome;
our stores were ample, and I made the people
bring barley and red wine and bulls to butcher,
to satisfy their hearts. Those noble Greeks
stayed for twelve days; a mighty north wind trapped them,   200
so strong a person could not stand upright;
some spirit must have summoned it to curse them.
But on the thirteenth day, the wind died down;
they sailed away."

       His lies were like the truth,
and as she listened, she began to weep.   205
Her face was melting, like the snow that Zephyr
scatters across the mountain peaks; then Eurus
thaws it, and as it melts, the rivers swell
and flow again.[7] So were her lovely cheeks
dissolved with tears. She wept for her own husband,   210
who was right next to her. Odysseus
pitied his grieving wife inside his heart,
but kept his eyes quite still, without a flicker,
like horn or iron, and he hid his tears
with artifice. She cried a long, long time,   215
then spoke again.

       "Now stranger, I would like
to set a test, to see if you did host
my husband and the men that followed him
in your own house, as you have said. Describe
his clothes, and what he looked like, and his men."   220

Odysseus the trickster said, "My lady,
that would be hard to say—his visit was
so long ago. It has been twenty years.
But I will tell the image in my mind.
Kingly Odysseus wore a purple cloak,   225
of double-folded wool, held fastened by
a golden brooch with double pins, that was
elaborately engraved. In its front paws
a dog held down a struggling dappled fawn.

6. Amnisus is the port of Knossos in Crete. Eileithyia is a goddess associated with childbirth.
7. Zephyr is the West Wind, Eurus the East. The West Wind is imagined as bringing the snow that is melted by the East Wind of springtime.

All those who saw it marveled how the dog   230
could grip the fawn, and how the fawn could kick
its legs and try to get away, though both
were made of gold. I noticed his white tunic
was soft as dried-up onion peel, and shiny
as sunlight. It astonished many women.   235
But note, I do not know if he had brought
these clothes from home, or if a crew member
had given them to him on board the ship,
or some guest-friend. Odysseus had many
dear friends, since very few could match his worth.   240
And I myself gave him a sword of bronze,
a double-folded purple cloak, and tunic
edged with a fringe. I sent him off in glory
when he embarked. He had a valet with him,
I do remember, named Eurybates,   245
a man a little older than himself,
who had black skin, round shoulders, woolly hair,
and was his favorite out of all his crew
because his mind matched his."

                    These words increased
her grief. She knew the signs that he had planted   250
as evidence, and sobbed; she wept profusely.
Pausing, she said, "I pitied you before,
but now you are a guest and honored friend.
I gave those clothes to him that you describe;
I took them from the storeroom, folded them,   255
and clasped that brooch for him. But I will never
welcome him home. A curse sailed on that ship
when he went off to see Evilium—
the town I will not name."[8]

                    He answered shrewdly,
"Your Majesty, Odysseus' wife,   260
stop ruining your pretty skin with tears,
and grieving for your husband, brokenhearted.
I do not blame you; any woman would
mourn for a husband by whom she had children,
even if he were not the kind of man   265
they say your husband was—a godlike hero.
But stop your crying. Listen. I will tell you
a certainty. I will be frank with you.
I heard Odysseus is coming home.
He is alive and near here, in Thesprotia.   270
By hustling, he gained a heap of treasure
that he is bringing home. He lost his ship
at sea, and let his loyal men be killed
when he had left Thrinacia; Helius

---

8. In the original, Penelope coins a compound word suggesting "Bad Troy" (Troy=Ilium).

and Zeus despised Odysseus,[9] because 275
his men had killed the Cattle of the Sun.
So all those men were drowned beneath the waves,
but he himself was clinging to the rudder
and washed up in the land of the Phaeacians,
the cousins of the gods. They honored him 280
as if he were a god himself, and gave him
abundant gifts, and tried to send him home
safely. He would have been here long ago,
but he decided he should travel more
and gather greater wealth. No man on earth 285
knows better how to make a profit. Pheidon,
the king of the Thesprotians, told me this.
He poured libations and he swore to me
there was a ship already launched and crew
all set to take him home. But Pheidon said 290
good-bye to me first, as a ship of theirs
happened to be already on its way
to barley-rich Dulichium. He showed me
the treasure that Odysseus had gained—
enough to feed his children and grandchildren 295
for ten whole generations. Pheidon said
Odysseus had gone to Dodona,
to ask the rustling oak leaves whether Zeus
advised him, after all those years away,
to go home openly or in disguise. 300
I tell you, he is safe and near at hand.
He will not long be absent from his home
and those that love him. I swear this by Zeus,
the highest, greatest god, and by the hearth
where I am sheltering. This will come true 305
as I have said. This very lunar month,
between the waning and the waxing moon
Odysseus will come."

Penelope
said warily, "Well, stranger, I do hope
that you are right. If so, I would reward you 310
at once with such warm generosity
that everyone you met would see your luck.
In fact, it seems to me, Odysseus
will not come home. No one will see you off
with kind good-byes. There is no master here 315
to welcome visitors as he once did
and send them off with honor. Was there ever
a man like him? Now slaves, give him a wash
and make a bed with mattress, woolen blankets

9. The verb here, *odyssomai*, is the same one associated with the name "Odysseus" elsewhere in the poem (for example, 1.63). It means "to be angry at [somebody]" or "to hate," and it is cognate with a noun for "pain" (*odune*).

and fresh clean sheets, to keep him warm till Dawn 320
assumes her golden throne. Then bathe and oil him;
seat him inside the hall, beside my son,
and let him eat. If any of these men
is so corrupt that he would harm our guest,
the worse for him! He will get nowhere here, 325
however much he rages. Stranger, how
could you have evidence that I excel
all other women in intelligence,
if you were kept in rags, your skin all sunburnt,
in my house? Human beings have short lives. 330
If we are cruel, everyone will curse us
during our life, and mock us when we die.
The names of those who act with nobleness
are brought by travelers across the world,
and many people speak about their goodness." 335

But devious Odysseus said, "Wife
of great Odysseus, I started hating
blankets and fine clean sheets the day I rowed
from cloudy, mountainous Crete. I will lie down
as I have spent so many sleepless nights, 340
on some rough pallet, waiting for bright Dawn.
I do not care for footbaths; do not let
any of these slave women in your house
come near my feet, unless there is an old one
whom I can trust, who has endured the same 345
heartbreak and sorrow as myself. If so,
I would not mind if she should touch my feet."

Penelope said thoughtfully, "Dear guest,
how well you speak! No visitor before
who came into my house from foreign lands 350
has ever been so scrupulous. I have
a sensible old woman, who brought up
my husband. She first took him in her arms
from his own mother as a newborn child.
She is quite weak, but she can wash your feet. 355
Get up now, Eurycleia, wash your master's
age-mate.[1] By now, Odysseus himself
must have old wrinkled feet and hands like these.
We mortals grow old fast in times of trouble."

The old slave shed hot tears, and held her hands 360
across her face, and wailed,

---

1. The original has a temporary ambiguity, where the reader or listener may wonder if Penelope has already recognized her husband and may be about to say "your master's . . . feet."

"Oh, child! I am
so useless to you now! Zeus hated you
beyond all other men, although you are
so god-fearing! No human ever burned
so many thigh-bones to the Lord of Thunder,   365
or sacrificed so much to him. You prayed
that you would reach a comfortable old age
and raise your son to be respected. Now
you are the only one who cannot reach
your home. And when that poor Odysseus   370
stays at the palaces of foreign kings,
I think the women slaves are mocking him
as these bad girls are hounding you. You have
refused to let them wash you, to avoid
abuse. But wise Penelope has told me   375
to wash you, and reluctantly I will,
for her sake and for yours—you move my heart.
Now listen. Many strangers have come here
in trouble and distress. But I have never
seen any man whose body, voice, and feet   380
are so much like my master's."

⁣   He replied
shrewdly, "Old woman, everyone who sees
the two of us says we are much alike;
you were perceptive to observe the likeness."

Then the old woman took the shining cauldron   385
used for a footbath, and she filled it up
with water—lots of cold, a splash of hot.
Odysseus sat there beside the hearth,
and hurriedly turned round to face the darkness.
He had a premonition in his heart   390
that when she touched him, she would feel his scar
and all would be revealed. She kneeled beside him,
and washed her master. Suddenly, she felt
the scar. A white-tusked boar had wounded him
on Mount Parnassus long ago. He went there   395
with his maternal uncles and grandfather,
noble Autolycus,[2] who was the best
of all mankind at telling lies and stealing.
Hermes[3] gave him this talent to reward him
for burning many offerings to him.   400
Much earlier, Autolycus had gone
to Ithaca to see his daughter's baby,
and Eurycleia put the newborn child
on his grandfather's lap and said, 'Now name
your grandson—this much-wanted baby boy.'   405
He told the parents, 'Name him this. I am

2. The name "Autolycus" suggests "Wolf Man."   3. Trickster and messenger god.

disliked by many, all across the world,
and I dislike them back.[4] So name the child
'Odysseus.' And when he is a man,
let him come to his mother's people's house,   410
by Mount Parnassus. I will give him treasure
and send him home rejoicing.' When he grew,
Odysseus came there to claim his gifts.
His cousins and Autolycus embraced him,
and greeted him with friendly words of welcome.   415
His grandma, Amphithea, wrapped her arms
around him like a vine and kissed his face
and shining eyes. Autolycus instructed
his sons to make the dinner. They obeyed
and brought a bull of five years old and flayed it,   420
and chopped it all in pieces, and then sliced
the meat with skill and portioned it on skewers
and roasted it with care, and shared it out,
and everybody got the same amount.
The whole day long they feasted, till the sun   425
went down and darkness fell. Then they lay down
and took the gift of sleep. When early Dawn,
the newborn child with rosy hands, appeared,
Autolycus went hunting with his dogs
and with his sons; Odysseus went too.   430
Up the steep wooded side of Mount Parnassus
they climbed and reached its windswept folds. The sun
rose from the calmly flowing depths of Ocean
to touch the fields, just as the hunters came
into a glen. The dogs had dashed in front,   435
looking for tracks. Autolycus' sons
came after, with Odysseus who kept
close to the dogs, and brandished his long spear.
A mighty boar lurked there; its lair was thick,
protected from the wind; the golden sun   440
could never strike at it with shining rays,
and rain could not get in; there was a pile
of fallen leaves inside. The boar had heard
the sound of feet—the men and dogs were near.
Out of his hiding place he leapt to face them,   445
his bristles standing up, his eyes like fire,
and stood right next to them. Odysseus
was first to rush at him, his long spear gripped
tight in his hand. He tried to strike; the boar
struck first, above his knee, and charging sideways   450
scooped a great hunk of flesh off with his tusk,
but did not reach the bone. Odysseus
wounded the boar's right shoulder, and the spear

4. Autolycus uses the same verb, *odussomai*, as in 19.275 which sounds like the name "Odysseus" and can mean either "I am angry at" or "I am the cause of anger (in others)." See also the note to 1.63.

pierced through. The creature howled and fell to earth.
His life flew out. Autolycus' sons   455
bustled around and skillfully bound up
the wound received by great Odysseus,
and stopped the black blood with a charm, and took him
back to their father's house, and nursed him well,
then gave him splendid gifts, and promptly sent him   460
back home to Ithaca, and he was glad.
His parents welcomed him and asked him questions,
wanting to know how he had got the wound.
He told them he was hunting with his cousins
on Mount Parnassus, and a boar attacked him;   465
the white tusk pierced his leg.

                 The old slave woman,
holding his leg and rubbing with flat palms,
came to that place, and recognized the scar.
She let his leg fall down into the basin.
It clattered, tilted over, and the water   470
spilled out across the floor. Both joy and grief
took hold of her. Her eyes were filled with tears;
her voice was choked. She touched his beard and said,

"You are Odysseus! My darling child!
My master! I did not know it was you   475
until I touched you all around your leg."
She glanced towards Penelope, to tell her
it was her husband. But Penelope
did not look back; she could not meet her eyes,
because Athena turned her mind aside.   480
Odysseus grabbed her throat with his right hand
and with the left, he pulled her close and whispered,

"Nanny! Why are you trying to destroy me?
You fed me at your breast! Now after all
my twenty years of pain, I have arrived   485
back to my home. You have found out; a god
has put the knowledge in your mind. Be silent;
no one must know, or else I promise you,
if some god helps me bring the suitors down,
I will not spare you when I kill the rest,   490
the other slave women, although you were
my nurse."

               With calculation, Eurycleia
answered, "My child! What have you said! You know
my mind is firm, unshakable; I will
remain as strong as stone or iron. Let me   495
promise you this: if you defeat the suitors,
I will tell you which women in the palace
dishonor you, and which are free from guilt."

Odysseus already had a plan.
"Nanny, why do you mention them? No need.   500
I will myself make my own observations
of each of them. Be quiet now; entrust
the future to the gods."

     The old nurse went
to fetch more washing water; all the rest
was spilt. She washed and oiled him, and then   505
he pulled his chair beside the fire again,
to warm himself, and covered up his scar
with rags. And carefully Penelope
spoke to him.

    "Stranger, I have one small question
I want to ask you. It will soon be time   510
to lie down comfortably—at least for those
who can enjoy sweet sleep, no matter what.
But I have been afflicted by some god
with pain beyond all measure. In the day,
I concentrate on my work and my women's,   515
despite my constant grief. But when night comes,
and everybody goes to sleep, I lie
crying in bed and overwhelmed by pain;
worries and sorrows crowd into my heart.
As when the daughter of Pandareus,[5]   520
the pale gray nightingale, sings beautifully
when spring has come, and sits among the leaves
that crowd the trees, and warbles up and down
a symphony of sound, in mourning for
her son by Zethus, darling Itylus,   525
whom she herself had killed in ignorance,
with bronze. Just so, my mind pulls two directions—
should I stay here beside my son, and keep
things all the same—my property, my slave girls,
and my great house—to show respect towards   530
my husband's bed and what the people say?
Or should I marry one of them—whichever
is best of all the suitors and can bring
most presents? When my son was immature,
and young, I could not leave my husband's house.   535
He would not let me. Now that he is big
and all grown-up, he urges me to go;
he is concerned that they are eating up
his property. Now how do you interpret

5. Aedon, daughter of Pandareus, king of Crete, married Zethus, king of Thebes, and tried to kill one of the children of his sister-in-law, Niobe, in a fit of jealousy. By mistake, she killed her own son, Itylus (called Itys in other versions of the myth). She was turned into a nightingale, whose song is supposed to be a constant lament for the dead boy.

this dream of mine? I dreamed that twenty geese   540
came from the river to my house, and they
were eating grain and I was glad to see them.
Then a huge eagle with a pointed beak
swooped from the mountain, broke their necks, and killed them.
I wept and wailed, inside the dream; the women   545
gathered around me, and I cried because
the eagle killed my geese. Then he came back
and sitting on the jutting roof-beam, spoke
in human language, to restrain my grief.
'Penelope, great queen, cheer up. This is   550
no dream; it will come true. It is a vision.
The geese are suitors; I was once an eagle,
but now I am your husband. I have come
back home to put a cruel end to them.'
Then I woke up, looked round, and saw the geese   555
still eating grain beside the trough as they
had done before."

                    Odysseus, well-known
for his intelligence, said, "My dear woman,
there is no way to wrest another meaning
out of the dream; Odysseus himself   560
said how he will fulfill it: it means ruin
for all the suitors. No one can protect them
from death."

                    But shrewd Penelope said, "Stranger,
dreams are confusing, and not all come true.
There are two gates of dreams: one pair is made   565
of horn and one of ivory. The dreams
from ivory are full of trickery;
their stories turn out false. The ones that come
through polished horn come true. But my strange dream
did not come out that way, I think. I wish   570
it had, as does my son. The day of doom
is coming that will take me from the house
of my Odysseus. I will arrange
a contest with his axes. He would set them
all in a row, like ship's props. From a distance   575
he shot an arrow through all twelve of them.
I will assign this contest to the suitors.
Whoever strings his bow most readily,
and shoots through all twelve axes, will win me,
and I will follow him. I will be parted   580
from here, this lovely house, my marriage home,
so full of wealth and life, which I suppose
I will remember even in my dreams."

Scheming Odysseus said, "Honored wife
of great Odysseus, do not postpone   585

this contest. They will fumble with the bow
and will not finish stringing it or shooting
the arrow through, before Odysseus,
the mastermind, arrives."

        She chose her words
with care: "If you would sit and entertain me,   590
guest, I would never wish to go to sleep.
But humans cannot stay awake forever;
immortal gods have set a proper time
for everything that mortals do on earth.
I will go up and lie down on my bed,   595
which is a bed of grief, all stained with tears
that I have cried since he went off to see
Evilium, the town I will not name.
I will lie there, and you lie in this house;
spread blankets on the floor, or have the slaves   600
make up a bed."

        With that, she went upstairs,
accompanied by slave girls. In her room,
she cried for her dear husband, till sharp-sighted
Athena poured sweet sleep onto her eyes.

BOOK 20

The Last Banquet

Odysseus was lying at the entrance
on an untreated oxhide, over which
he heaped a pile of fleeces from the sheep
the suitors sacrificed. Eurynome
spread a thick blanket over him. He lay there   5
but did not sleep; his mind was plotting how
to kill the suitors. Then the girls who had
been sleeping with suitors slipped outside,
giggling and happy to be out together.
His heart was roused to rage; he wondered whether   10
to jump at them and slaughter every one,
or let them have one very final night
with those proud suitors—and his heart was barking,
just as a mother dog will stand astride
her little puppies, bristling to fight,   15
if she sees any man she does not know;
so his heart growled inside him; he was shocked
at their behavior. He slapped his chest
and told himself,

        "Be strong, my heart. You were
hounded by worse the day the Cyclops ate   20
your strong companions. But you kept your nerve,

till cunning saved you from the cave; you thought
that you would die there."

                        So his heart held firm
and constant, but he writhed around, as when
a man rotates a sausage full of fat   25
and blood; the huge fire blazes, and he longs
to have the roasting finished. So he squirmed,
this way and that, and wondered how he could
attack the shameless suitors, being one
against a multitude. Athena came   30
from heaven and stood near him, at his head,
resembling a woman, and she said,

"Why are you wide awake, unlucky man?
This is your house, this is your wife inside,
and your own child, the son you hoped to have."   35

Clever Odysseus said, "Goddess, yes,
all that is true. But I am wondering how
I can attack those upstarts, who are always
clustered together, while I am alone.
My biggest fear is this: if you and Zeus   40
help me to kill them, then what? Where can I
run to escape my punishment? You tell me!"

With glinting eyes Athena said, "So stubborn!
Most men trust friends—even weaker, mortal friends,
whose judgment is far worse than mine. I am   45
a goddess, and throughout your many trials,
I have watched over you. If we were ambushed,
surrounded by not one but fifty gangs
of men who hoped to murder us—you would
escape, and even poach their sheep and cows.   50
Now go to sleep. To stay on guard awake
all night is tiring. Quite soon you will
distance yourself,¹ Odysseus, from trouble."

With that, the goddess drenched his eyes with sleep,
then flew back to Olympus. Sleep took hold,   55
relaxed him, and released him from his worries.
Meanwhile, his faithful wife was wide awake,
crying and sitting upright on her bed
against soft pillows. When her sobs subsided,
she prayed.

                    "O Artemis! Majestic goddess!   60
Daughter of Zeus! If only you would shoot
an arrow in my heart and kill me now,

---

1. The word used for "distance yourself" sounds somewhat like the name "Odysseus."

or let a gust of wind take hold of me
and carry me across the misty clouds
and fling me where the waters of the Ocean[2] 65
pour forth and back again, as when the breezes
took up the daughters of Pandareus,
after the gods destroyed their parents, leaving
the daughters orphaned.[3] Aphrodite helped them,
and gave them honey, cheese, and mellow wine, 70
and Hera gave them beauty and good sense,
above all other women; Artemis
increased their height; Athena taught them how
to be most skillful in all handiwork.
Then Aphrodite went to Mount Olympus 75
to ask Zeus, Thunderlord, to grant the girls
good marriages—he knows all things, all fates,
both good and bad. But Harpies seized and forced them
to serve the cruel Furies. May the gods
annihilate me just like them! Or may 80
Artemis strike me dead, with my gaze fixed
upon Odysseus! Let me not make
a lesser husband glad. When someone weeps
all through the day quite overwhelmed by grief,
but sleeps at night, forgetting everything, 85
her pain is bearable. But I am cursed
with nightmares by some god. Last night, a man
was sleeping by me, just like him when he
marched off to war. My heart was cheered; it seemed
a vision, not a dream."

     As she said this, 90
the golden Dawn arrived. Odysseus
heard his wife weeping, and became confused;
he thought that she was standing by his head,
and that she had already recognized him.
He took the cloak and fleece with which he slept, 95
and put them on a chair inside the palace,
and took the oxhide outside to the courtyard,
then raised his arms and prayed.

       "O Father Zeus!
O gods! If you have brought me back on purpose
across dry land and sea to my own home, 100
after you made me suffer all that pain,
let someone inside speak in words of omen,
and Zeus, display another sign outside."

Zeus, Lord of Cunning, heard him, and he thundered
from bright Olympus, high above the clouds; 105

2. Capital "O" Ocean is distinct from regular seas; it is the great waterway that the Greeks imagined ran all the way around the world.

3. Pandareus stole a golden dog made by Hephaestus from a temple of Zeus; the gods punished him, his wife, and his daughters.

Odysseus was happy. Then a woman,
a wheat grinder, inside the house nearby,
spoke words of omen. Twelve slaves worked the mills
to grind the wheat and barley for the king.
The rest had finished and had gone to sleep.   110
The weakest one was still at work. She paused
her mill, and spoke—he heard it as an omen.

"Zeus, king of gods and humans! You made thunder
boom from a cloudless sky—a sign for someone.
Fulfill a poor slave's prayer: that this will be   115
the last day that the suitors dine in style
here in the old king's house. My knees are sore
from this exhausting work of grinding grain
for them. I pray this is their final meal!"

This sign and Zeus' thunder made her master   120
glad, and more certain he would get revenge
on those who did him wrong.

                              The other women
gathered and lit a fire in the hearth.
Godlike Telemachus got out of bed
and dressed, and slung his sword across his back.   125
He tied his sandals on his well-oiled feet,
and took his sharp and sturdy bronze-tipped spear.
Standing across the threshold, he called out
to Eurycleia.

                    "Nanny! Did you women
make sure our guest was honored, with a meal   130
and comfortable bed? Or did he lie there
neglected? This is typical of Mother!
She may be clever, but she acts on whims!
She treats unwanted guests with great respect,
and rudely sends the better ones away."   135

The nurse said tactfully, "Child, do not blame her,
not now. He drank some wine, and chose a chair.
He said he had already had his dinner—
she asked him. And at bedtime, she brought out
a cot, so that the girls could make his bed.   140
Poor destitute old man! He would not take
nice bedding. He slept outside on the porch,
on oxhide and a fleece; we spread a cloak
on top of him."

                    Telemachus marched off
out of the palace, with his sword in hand,
accompanied by two swift dogs, and went   145
down to the meeting place of the Achaeans.

Then noble Eurycleia, child of Ops,
called to the slaves.

        "Now hurry! You girls sweep
the floors and sprinkle them. Spread purple cloths   150
across the chairs. You others, sponge the tables,
and wash the double-handled cups and bowls.
And you, go fetch the water from the spring.
Be quick! They will be coming soon; it is
a festival for all of them today."   155

They listened carefully and followed orders.
Twenty ran off to fetch the dark spring water;
the other well-trained slaves were working hard
around the house. The able-bodied men
came in and chopped the wood. They knew their work.   160
The women got back from the spring, and with them
the swineherd came with three fat pigs—his best.
He penned them in the yard to root around,
and kindly asked Odysseus,

        "My friend,
are they now treating you with more respect,   165
or still abusing you, just as before?"

Odysseus, the cunning strategist,
replied, "Eumaeus, may the gods avenge
these upstarts for their wickedness and schemes!
The scoundrels have abused me in a house   170
which is not theirs! They show no shame!"

            While they
were talking in this way, Melanthius
arrived with two more herders. They were driving
the very fattest she-goats from the flock—
a contribution to the suitors' banquet.   175
He tied the goats up on the portico,
and started picking on Odysseus.

"Stranger! Are you still here, still causing trouble,
with begging and annoying those inside?
I promise you a beating if you stay!   180
Your begging is not welcome! This is not
the only place in Greece where there is food."

Inscrutable Odysseus said nothing;
he bowed his head in silence, contemplating
his murderous plans.

                    The third and final herdsman,   185
Philoetius, an overseer, came
herding fat he-goats and an uncalved heifer,
brought by a ferryman to Ithaca—
the ferries also carry passengers
when anybody needs to get across.   190
Philoetius tied up his animals
outside, and asked the swineherd,

                              "Who is this
new guest who has arrived? Who are his people?
Where is his native land? His ancestry?
Poor man, he has a kingly look; his bearing   195
is like a lord's. When gods spin threads of pain,
even great kings are made to wander far
and suffer greatly."

                    Then he shook his hand
and greeted him. "Good morning, sir! You are
down on your luck; I hope things change for you.   200
No god is more destructive, Zeus, than you!
You are the father of humanity,
but you do not take pity on our pain.
My eyes are wet, my skin is damp with sweat,
as I think of Odysseus. If he   205
still lives and sees the sun, he must be lost,
and dressed in rags like these. Or if he has
already died, oh, Lord Odysseus!
I am so sorry! He entrusted me
with my first herd when I was just a boy,   210
in Cephallenia.[4] His cattle now
are countless; they would not have multiplied
so well for someone else. But now these men
are telling me to drive the cows to them
for food. They do not care about the boy,   215
or tremble at the eyes of watchful gods.
My master has been gone a long time now.
They want to share his wealth among themselves,
and I keep turning over in my mind
that it would not be right to take the cows   220
and go to foreign lands, when master's son
is here. But it is worse to sit and suffer,
just taking care of other people's cattle.
I would have run away and gone to serve
another king; things are unbearable.   225
But I keep hoping my unlucky master
will come back from wherever he may be
and scatter all these suitors in his halls."

---

4. Cephallenia is apparently the name of Ithaca and all the other towns under the dominion of the Ithacan king. It is not, in this text, identical with the modern Ionian island of Cephalonia.

Crafty Odysseus replied, "I see
you are intelligent. So I will swear 230
a solemn oath to you. I vow by Zeus,
and hospitality, and by this hearth,
that while you are still here, Odysseus
will come back home, and if you want, you can
watch as the boys who swagger here are killed." 235

The cowherd answered, "Stranger, may Zeus make
your words come true—and you would see my strength,
and how prepared my hands would be to fight."
Eumaeus also prayed to all the gods
to bring his many-minded master home. 240

As they were talking in this way, the suitors
were planning how to kill Telemachus.
But then an eagle flew high on their left,[5]
holding a wild dove. Amphinomus
said to them, "Friends, this plan of ours, this murder, 245
will fail. So let us think about our banquet."

They all agreed, and went inside the house
of godlike King Odysseus. They spread
cloths on the chairs and sofas, and they killed
large sheep, fat goats, big pigs, and one tame cow. 250
They cooked the innards and divided them,
and mixed the wine in bowls; the swineherd poured it
into the cups. Philoetius served bread
in baskets, and Melanthius passed round
the wine. They helped themselves to all the food. 255

Then thinking carefully, Telemachus
seated Odysseus inside the hall,
beside the stony threshold, and he brought
a table and a stool. He served him meat
and poured a gold cup full of wine, and said, 260

"Now you are sitting here and drinking wine
among them. I will stop them touching you
or mocking you. This is no public house!
Odysseus acquired it for me.
And you there, suitors! Please, no blows or insults. 265
We do not want to start an argument."

They bit their lips, surprised to hear the boy
speaking so boldly, and Antinous,
Eupeithes' son, declared,

5. The left side is unlucky.

"My lords, we must
accept the threats Telemachus has made,   270
annoying though they are. Zeus would not let us
kill him—or else by now we could have stopped
his speechifying in our banquet hall."

Telemachus ignored him, and meanwhile,
the house boys drove one hundred animals   275
through town for sacrifice.[6] The Ithacans
assembled at Apollo's shady grove—
the lord of archery.[7]

                    Inside the house,
the suitors cooked the meat kebabs, took out
the skewers, then divided up the portions—   280
a splendid feast. They served Odysseus
an equal portion with their own; his son,
Telemachus, had ordered them to do so.

But still Athena would not let the suitors
refrain from hurtful insults and abuse,   285
so even deeper bitterness would sink
into the heart of great Odysseus.
One lawless man from Same named Ctesippus,
encouraged by extraordinary wealth,
had come to court Odysseus' wife   290
because he had been absent for so long.
He shouted to the other reckless suitors,

"Listen! This stranger got an equal share,
as is appropriate. It would, of course,
be wrong to disrespect a guest who comes   295
to visit our Telemachus. Let me
give him a welcome gift, so he can give
gifts to the bath attendant or some other
house slave here in the palace."

                                    Then he grabbed
an ox-foot from the basket, and he hurled it   300
towards Odysseus, who smoothly ducked,
bowing his head, and smiled in scornful rage.
The ox-foot struck the wall. Telemachus
scolded Ctesippus.

                    "You were very lucky
you failed to hit the stranger; he avoided   305
the blow himself. I would have thrust my sword

6. A hecatomb—a ritual sacrifice of one hundred animals—may be understood as the sacrifice of any large number, not necessarily one
hundred. There may also be a connection
between the hundred animals and the roughly

one hundred suitors (108 is the usual count),
who are also soon to be killed.
7. Apollo carries a bow; his arrows can bring
plague.

right through your belly, and your father would
have held your funeral, and not your wedding.
So from now on, you all should stay in check,
here in my house. I used to be a child,   310
but now I understand things, good and bad.
I have to watch and put up with all this:
the slaughtered sheep, the food, the wine. It is
hard for a single man to put a stop
to such a multitude. But please back down   315
from your hostility to me. Or if
you do still want to kill me with bronze swords,
go on; I want you to. It would be better
to die, than have to watch you suitors acting
so horribly—abusing strangers, dragging   320
the house girls through my home, molesting them."

They all fell silent. Agelaus spoke.

"My friends, his words are fair. Do not get angry
or argue back with him. Do not abuse
the stranger, or Odysseus' slaves.   325
Telemachus, I offer some advice
to you and to your mother, with respect.
I hope you can accept it. While you thought
your many-minded father would come home,
there was no harm in holding us at bay,   330
and waiting, in case he came back again.
Now it is obvious he will not come.
So boy, sit by your mother, and advise her
to choose the best, most generous of us
to marry; then you can enjoy the wealth   335
left by your father, eat and drink, and she
can go take care of someone else's house."

Telemachus inhaled, then answered, "Yes!
By Zeus and by my father's sufferings—
lost far from Ithaca, or maybe dead—   340
I will cause no delay, and I will tell her
to pick a husband, and I will provide
a lavish dowry. But I am reluctant
to force her if she does not want to go.
May no god make that happen!" So he spoke.   345

Athena turned the suitors' minds; they laughed
unstoppably. They cackled, and they lost
control of their own faces. Plates of meat
began to drip with blood. Their eyes were full
of tears, and they began to wail in grief.   350
The prophet Theoclymenus addressed them.

"What awful thing is happening to you?
Your faces, heads, and bodies are wrapped up

in night; your screams are blazing out like fire.
The ornate palace ceilings and the walls   355
are spattered with your blood. The porch is full
of ghosts, as is the courtyard—ghosts descending
into the dark of Erebus. The sun
has vanished from the sky, and gloomy mist
is all around."

                    At these words, they all laughed.   360
Eurymachus spoke up.

                          "This new arrival
has lost his mind! Quick, fellows, throw him out!
Make him go to the marketplace—he thinks
it is like night in here!"

                         The prophet answered,
"Eurymachus, I will not ask for guides.   365
I have good eyes and ears and feet; my mind
is working perfectly, and I am leaving.
I sense some evil coming for you all,
who sit here in Odysseus' house
tormenting and oppressing other people.   370
Not one of you will get away."

                       With that,
he left the palace and went down to meet
Piraeus, and was welcomed there.

                          The suitors,
with glances at each other, tried to tease
Telemachus by laughing at his guests.   375

"What awful luck you have with visitors!
Here is this dirty beggar, always wanting
more food and wine, who is unskilled in farmwork
or fighting—a mere burden on the earth!
That other one just stood there prophesying!   380
Now listen—I propose a better plan.
Pack up your strangers on a boat as slaves;
send them to Sicily, and make a profit!"
Telemachus ignored the suitors' words,
and watched his father quietly, still waiting   385
for when they should attack the shameless suitors.
The beautiful Penelope had wisely
set up her chair to face them, and she listened
to what each man was saying. They had killed
numerous animals, and made their banquet   390
with laughter. But no dinnertime could be
less welcome than the one the mighty man
and goddess would soon bring them, in revenge,
because they started it and wronged him first.

BOOK 21

An Archery Contest

With glinting eyes, Athena put a thought
into the mind of wise Penelope,
the daughter of Icarius: to place
the bow and iron axes in the hall
of great Odysseus, and set the contest   5
which would begin the slaughter. She went up
to her own room. Her muscular, firm hand
picked up the ivory handle of the key—
a hook of bronze. Then with her slaves she walked
down to the storeroom where the master kept   10
his treasure: gold and bronze and well-wrought iron.
The curving bow and deadly arrows lay there,
given by Iphitus, Eurytus' son,
the godlike man he happened to befriend
at wise Ortilochus' house, far off   15
in Lacedaemon, in Messenia.[1]
Odysseus had gone to claim a debt—
some people of Messenia had come
in rowing boats and poached three hundred sheep
from Ithaca; they took their shepherds too.   20
Laertes and the other older men
had sent Odysseus to fetch them back
when he was still a boy. And Iphitus
had come there for his horses, twelve fine mares,
each suckling a sturdy mule. These horses   25
would later cause his death, when he had gone
to visit Heracles, who welcomed him,
but killed him, so that he could take the horses—[2]
betraying hospitality, and heedless
about the watchful gods. Before all that,   30
when Iphitus first met Odysseus,
he gave this bow to him, inherited
from his own father. And Odysseus
gave Iphitus a sword and spear, to mark
their bond. But Iphitus was dead before   35
the friends could visit one another's houses.
So when Odysseus' black fleet sailed
to war, he did not take the bow, but stored it
in his own house, to use in Ithaca
in memory of his friend.

               The queen had reached   40
the storeroom, and she stepped across the threshold
of polished oak; a skillful carpenter
had set it level, fixed the frame, and built

---

1. Messenia is a town within Lacedaemon, the region around Sparta.

2. Heracles killed Iphitus in a dispute over the mares of Iphitus's father, Eurytus.

the dazzling double doors. She quickly loosed
the door-thong from its hook, pushed in the key   45
and with true aim, thrust back the fastenings.
The fine doors, as the key struck home, began
to bellow as a bull at pasture bellows.
At once, they flew apart. She stepped inside,
onto the pallet where the scented clothes   50
were stored in chests, and reached to lift the bow
down from its hook, still in its shining case.
She sat down on the floor to take it out,
resting it on her lap, and started sobbing
and wailing as she saw her husband's bow.   55
At last, she dried her eyes, and in her arms
picked up the curving bow and quiver, packed
with many deadly arrows, and she went
to meet her arrogant suitors. Slaves lugged out
a hamper with their master's many axes   60
of bronze and iron, for the competition.
The queen came near the suitors, and she stopped
beside a pillar with a filmy veil
across her face. Two slave girls stood with her.
She said,

       "Now listen, lords. You keep on coming   65
to this house every day, to eat and drink,
wasting the wealth of someone who has been
away too long. Your motives are no secret.
You want to marry me. I am the prize.
So I will set a contest. This great bow   70
belonged to godlike King Odysseus.
If anyone can grasp it in his hands
and string it easily, and shoot through all
twelve axes,[3] I will marry him, and leave
this beautiful rich house, so full of life,   75
my lovely bridal home. I think I will
remember it forever, even in
my dreams."

       She told Eumaeus he should set
the bow and pale-gray iron axes up
before the suitors, and in tears the swineherd   80
took them, and did as she had asked. The cowherd
wept also when he saw his master's bow.

Antinous began to scold and taunt them.
He said, "You idiots! You tactless peasants!
So thoughtless, so undisciplined! You fools,   85

3. The mechanics of the axe competition are debated, but it seems most likely that these are axe heads, without handles, with round, drilled holes in the end through which the wooden handle could be inserted. The axe heads are lined up in a row, with the holes all aligned straight. The goal of the contest is to shoot an arrow through all of the holes.

your selfish crying is upsetting her!
Poor lady, she is sad enough already
at losing her beloved husband. Sit
and eat in silence, or go do your wailing
outside, and leave us suitors here to try   90
the deadly contest of the bow. I think
it will be difficult; not one of us
can match Odysseus. I saw him once
in childhood, and I still remember him."

He hoped he would be first to string the bow   95
and shoot through all the axes. But he would
be first to taste an arrow from the hands
of great Odysseus, whom he had mocked,
urging the others on to do the same.

Then Prince Telemachus addressed them all.   100
"Zeus must have made me stupid! My dear mother,
despite her usual common sense, has said
that she will marry someone else and leave
this house. But I am laughing, and my heart
feels foolish gladness. Well, come on, you suitors.   105
You want this prize—a woman unlike any
in holy Pylos, Argos or Mycenae,
or here in Ithaca or on the mainland.
No woman in Achaea is like her.
There is no need for me to praise my mother.   110
You know her worth. So do not make excuses,
do not put off the contest of the bow.
We want to watch. And I will try myself.
If I succeed in stringing it and shooting
all through, I will no longer mind if Mother   115
goes off with someone else, and leaves me here.
Success would prove me man enough to carry
my father's arms."

                          He stood up straight and tall,
tossed off his purple cloak, unstrapped his sword,
and dug a trench to set the axes up,   120
all in a line, and trod the earth down flat.[4]
They were amazed to see him work so neatly,
though he had never seen it done before.
He stood astride the threshold and began
to try the bow. Three times his muscles trembled,   125
straining to draw it back; three times he failed
to string the bow and shoot through all the axes.
He would have tried a fourth time; he was keen
to keep on pulling. But Odysseus

---

4. If the contest is taking place in the feast
hall—which has a finished floor, not dirt—the
earth seems to be brought in and heaped up to
provide a base for the axes.

shook his head, stopping him. Telemachus   130
said,

      "Ugh! It seems that I will always be
too weak and useless. Or perhaps I am
too young and inexperienced at fighting
in self-defense when someone starts a quarrel.
You all are stronger than I am. You try,   135
and we can end the contest."

             With these words,
he set the bow down on the floor, propped up
against the polished, jointed double door,
and tucked the arrow up against the handle.
He sat back down where he had sat before.   140

Antinous called out, "Now, friends, get up,
from left to right, beginning with the man
next to the wine-slave!"

             They agreed. The first
was Leodes, their holy man,[5] who always
sat in the farthest corner, by the wine-bowl.   145
He was the only one who disapproved
of all their bullying. He grasped the bow
and stood astride the threshold, and he tried
to string it, but he failed. His hands were soft,
untrained by labor, and he grew worn out   150
trying to pull it back. He told the suitors,

"My friends, I cannot do it. Someone else
should have a turn. This bow will take away
courage, life-force, and energy from many
noble young men;[6] but better we should die,   155
than live and lose the goal for which we gather
in this house every day. Each man still hopes
for marriage with Odysseus' wife,
Penelope. But if one tries and fails
to string the bow, let him go use his wealth   160
to court some other fine, well-dressed Greek lady.
And after that, Penelope will marry
whichever man can bring most gifts for her—
the man whom fate has chosen."

             With these words,
he set the bow back down, and leaned it up   165

---

5. The holy man is literally a man who performs sacrifices. However, the job description is somewhat fluid, and he also serves as a prophet or diviner.

6. Leodes speaks in prophetic language, per-haps unconsciously. His words could suggest only that the attempt to string the bow will discourage those who fail, but they can also mean that the bow will kill many men.

against the polished, jointed double door,
tucking the pointed arrow by the handle.
Antinous responded with a jeer.

"My goodness, Leodes! What scary words!
All your tough talk has made me really angry.   170
You cannot string the bow, so you are claiming
that it will take the life from proper men.
You surely were not born for archery.
The rest of us are actual warriors;
we will soon string this bow."

                    He told the goatherd,   175
"Melanthius, come on now, light a fire
and pull a chair beside it, with a fleece,
and bring out from the pantry a big hunk
of fat, so we young men can warm the bow,
grease it, and try it, and so end this contest."   180

Melanthius obeyed at once; he lit
a blazing fire, and pulled a chair beside it,
spreading a fleece on top, and brought the wheel
of fat. The young men warmed the bow, but still
they could not string it. They were far too weak.   185
Antinous and Eurymachus, the leaders,
strongest and most impressive of the suitors,
had still not had their turn.

                    Meanwhile the swineherd
and cowherd had both gone outside the house.
Odysseus himself came after them,   190
and when they were outside the gates, beyond
the courtyard, in a friendly voice he said,
"Cowherd and swineherd, I am hesitating
whether to speak out openly; my impulse
is to be frank. What if some god should guide   195
Odysseus, and suddenly, as if
from nowhere, he was here—how would you act?
Would you be with the suitors, or with him?
How are your hearts inclined?"

                    The cowherd said,
"O Father Zeus, please make this wish come true,   200
that he may come! May spirits guide him home!
Then you would see how well-prepared I am
to fight for him!" Eumaeus prayed in turn
that all the gods would bring Odysseus
back home. The man who thought of everything now knew   205
their minds, and said to them,

"I am here now.
I suffered terribly for twenty years,
and now I have come back to my own land.
I see that you two are the only slaves
who welcome my arrival. I have not   210
heard any others praying I would come
back to my home. I promise, if some god
brings down the noble suitors by my hands,
I will give each of you a wife and wealth,
and well-constructed houses, near my own.   215
You two will be Telemachus' brothers.
Now let me show you clearer proof, so you
can know me well and trust me. See my scar,
made by the boar's white tusk, when I had gone
to hunt on Mount Parnassus with my cousins."   220

So saying, he pulled back his rags and showed
the great big scar. They stared and studied it,
then both burst into tears. They threw their arms
around Odysseus, and kissed his face
and hugged him, overjoyed at seeing him.   225
Odysseus embraced them back and kissed them.
They would have wept till sunset, but he stopped them,
and said,

            "Stop now; if someone steps outside
and sees you crying, they may tell the men.
Go in, not both at once but taking turns,   230
first me, then you, then you. And this will be
our sign: when all the noblemen refuse
to let me have the bow and set of arrows,
then you must bring them through the hall, Eumaeus,
and put them in my hands. Command the women   235
to shut up tight the entrance to the hall,
and go to their own quarters; if they hear
men screaming or loud noises, they must not
come out, but stay there quietly, and work.
And you, Philoetius, lock up the gates   240
leading out from the courtyard with the bolt
and put the rope on too. We must move fast."

With that, he went inside, and sat back down
on the same chair he sat on earlier.
Then the two slaves went in. Eurymachus   245
was handling the bow and warming it,
turning it back and forth beside the fire.
But even after that, he could not manage
to string it, and he groaned, and yelled in fury,

"This is disastrous! For all of us!   250
I do not even mind so much about

the marriage. There are lots of other women
on Ithaca, and in the other cities.
But that we should be proven so much weaker
than King Odysseus, that we should fail   255
to string his bow! Our deep humiliation
will be well-known for many years to come!"

Antinous said, "No, Eurymachus,
it will not be like that, as you well know.
No one should shoot a bow today; it is   260
a feast day for Apollo! We should sit
calmly and leave the axe heads standing there.
No one will come and take them. Let the boy
pour wine, so we can make drink offerings,
and leave the bow for now. At dawn, call back   265
Melanthius, to bring the finest goats,
so we can make our offerings to the god,
Apollo, lord of archery, then try
the bow again, and finish up the contest."

They all agreed with him. Attendants poured   270
water to wash their hands, and boys began
to mix the wine in bowls, and poured a serving
in every cup, so they could make libations
and drink. Odysseus, the lord of lies,
had carefully considered how to fool them.   275
He said,

      "Now hear me, suitors of the Queen;
let me reveal the promptings of my heart.
Eurymachus and Lord Antinous,
I ask you specially, because you spoke
so well: now set the bow aside, and turn   280
towards the gods. At dawn, the god will choose
the victor and give him success. For now,
give me the polished bow, so I can try
my strength and find out if my hands still have
the suppleness and vigor of my youth,   285
or if it has been lost in all my years
of homelessness and poverty."

              They bristled,
nervous in case he strung the polished bow.
Antinous said, "Foreigner! You fool!
Are you not grateful that we let you stay here   290
and eat with noblemen like us, and share
our feast, and hear us talk? No other beggars
can hear our conversation. This good wine
has made you drunk. It does have that effect
on those who gulp and fail to pace themselves.   295

Wine even turned the famous Centaur's head.[7]
When Eurytion visited the Lapiths,
inside the house of brave Pirithous
the wine made him go crazy, and he did
terrible things. The warriors were outraged,   300
and dragged him from the house. Their ruthless swords
cut off his ears and cropped his nose right off.
He wandered, still insane and blown about
by gusts of madness. From that day, the Centaurs
and humans have been enemies. His drinking   305
was harmful to himself. If you should string
that bow, it would be worse for you. No man
will treat you kindly in our house. We will
send you by ship to Echetus, the king
of cruelty; you will find no escape.   330
Sit quietly, drink up, and do not quarrel
with younger men."

                    Astute Penelope
said, "No, Antinous, it is not right
to disrespect a guest Telemachus
has welcomed to this house. And do you think   315
that if this stranger's hands were strong enough
to string the bow, he would take me away
to marry him and live with him? Of course not!
He does not even dream of such a thing.
No need to spoil the feast by worrying   320
about such things; there is no need of that."

Eurymachus said, "Shrewd Penelope,
it is indeed unlikely that this man
would marry you. But we would feel ashamed
if some rude person said, 'Those men are weak!   325
They court a fighter's wife, but cannot string
his bow! Some random beggar has shown up
and strung it easily, and shot right through
all of the axes!' They will talk like that,
and we will be humiliated!"

                    Calmly,   330
Penelope replied, "Eurymachus,
people who waste the riches of a king
have lost their dignity. Why fuss at this?
The stranger is quite tall and muscular;
his father must be noble. Go on, give him   335
the bow, and let us watch. I tell you, if
he strings it by the blessing of Apollo,

7. The following passage refers to the famous drunken brawl between the Lapiths, a Thessalian tribe, and the Centaurs, a wild mountain-dwelling people, later imagined as half-human and half-horse.

I will give him a proper cloak and tunic,
fine clothes and sandals, and a two-edged sword
and dagger, sharp enough to ward away   340
both men and dogs, and I will help him go
wherever he desires to go."

                             With quick
intake of breath, Telemachus replied,
"No, Mother, no one has a better right
than I to give the bow to anyone   345
or to refuse it. No one on this island
or out towards the pasturelands of Elis,
and no man in this house can force my hand,
even if I should choose to give the bow
to him to take away. Go up and work   350
with loom and distaff; tell your girls the same.
The bow is work for men, especially me.[8]
I am the one with power in this house."

She was amazed, and went back to her room,
taking to heart her son's assertive words.   355
Inside her bedroom with her girls, she wept
for her dear husband, her Odysseus,
until clear-eyed Athena let her sleep.

Meanwhile, the swineherd lifted up the bow.
The suitors made an uproar.

                          "Dirty pig-man!   360
Where are you taking it? Are you insane?
The dogs you raised yourself will eat you up
when you are out there with your pigs alone,
if we find favor with Apollo and
the other deathless gods."

                          He was afraid,   365
because there were so many people shouting
inside the hall, and set the bow he carried
down on the ground. Telemachus called out,
in forceful tones.

                     "No, Grandpa! Keep on going!
Keep carrying the bow! You will soon see   370
you have to choose which master to obey.
Though I am younger than you, I am stronger;
watch out, or I will chase you to the fields,
pelting your back with stones. I wish I had
an equal edge on all those who invaded   375

---

8. These two lines echo the words of Hector to Andromache in book 6 of the *Iliad*: "War is a job for men, especially me."

my home to court my mother and make mischief.
I would soon throw them out and make them pay!"

At that, the suitors all began to laugh;
their anger at Telemachus was gone.
Eumaeus went across the hall and gave   380
the bow to competent Odysseus.
And then he summoned Eurycleia, saying,

"Telemachus gave orders you must lock
the doors into the hall and tie them fast.
If any of you women hear a noise   385
of screaming men, stay up there in your quarters;
do not come out; keep quiet and keep working."

At that, she held her tongue and locked the doors
that led into the feast-hall. Philoetius
scurried outside to bolt the outer gates   390
that led into the courtyard. On the porch
lay a fresh-knotted cable made of byblos;⁹
with that, he tied the gates, rushed in and sat
back down, and looked towards Odysseus.

The master was already handling   395
the bow and turning it this way and that,
to see if worms had eaten at the horn
while he was gone. The suitors told each other,

"He stares at it as if he were an expert
in bows. He acts the part! Perhaps he has   400
a bow like this at home or plans to make one.
See how this pitiful migrant fingers it!"
One confident young suitor said, "I hope
his future luck will match how well he does
in stringing it!"

                        So he had tricked them all.   405
After examining the mighty bow
carefully, inch by inch—as easily
as an experienced musician stretches
a sheep-gut string around a lyre's peg
and makes it fast—Odysseus, with ease,   410
strung the great bow. He held it in his right hand
and plucked the string, which sang like swallow-song,
a clear sweet note. The suitors, horrified,
grew pale, and Zeus made ominous thunder rumble.
Odysseus, who had so long been waiting,   415
was glad to hear the signal from the son

---

9. A fiber from the papyrus plant, imported to Greece from Egypt, known for its strength.

of double-dealing Cronus.[1] He took up
an arrow, which was lying on the table.
The others were all packed up in the quiver,
soon to be used. He laid it on the bridge,   420
then pulled the notch-end and the string together,
still sitting in his chair. With careful aim,
he shot. The weighted tip of bronze flew through
each axe head and then out the other side.
He told his son,

        "Telemachus, your guest   425
does you a credit. I hit all the targets
and with no effort strung the bow. I am
still strong, despite their jibes about my weakness.
Though it is daytime, it is time to feast;
and later, we can celebrate with music,   430
the joyful part of dinner."

        With his eyebrows
he signaled, and his son strapped on his sword,
picked up his spear, and stood beside his chair,
next to his father, his bronze weapons flashing.

BOOK 22

Bloodshed

Odysseus ripped off his rags. Now naked,
he leapt upon the threshold with his bow
and quiverfull of arrows, which he tipped
out in a rush before his feet, and spoke.

"Playtime is over. I will shoot again,   5
towards another mark no man has hit.
Apollo, may I manage it!"

        He aimed
his deadly arrow at Antinous.
The young man sat there, just about to lift
his golden goblet, swirling wine around,   10
ready to drink. He had no thought of death.
How could he? Who would think a single man,
among so many banqueters, would dare
to risk dark death, however strong he was?
Odysseus aimed at his throat, then shot.   15

1. Cronus, leader of the Titans (divine descendants of Sky and Earth), was persuaded by his
mother, Earth, to castrate his father, Sky, which
he did with a sickle. Sky threatened revenge,
but Cronus killed him and ruled the world with
his sister/wife, Rhea; they were the parents of
most of the Olympian gods. Cronus swallowed
most of them, but Zeus, the sixth child, organized a war against his father, which he won,
and he became king in turn.

The point pierced all the way through his soft neck.
He flopped down to the side and his cup slipped
out of his hand, and then thick streams of blood
gushed from his nostrils. His foot twitched and knocked
the table down; food scattered on the ground.   20
The bread and roasted meat were soiled with blood.
Seeing him fall, the suitors, in an uproar,
with shouts that filled the hall, jumped up and rushed
to search around by all the thick stone walls
for shields or swords to grab—but there were none.   25
They angrily rebuked Odysseus.

"Stranger, you shot a man, and you will pay!
You will join no more games—you have to die!
For certain! You have killed the best young man
in all of Ithaca. Right here, the vultures   30
will eat your corpse." Those poor fools did not know
that he had killed Antinous on purpose,
nor that the snares of death were round them all.

Clever Odysseus scowled back and sneered,
"Dogs! So you thought I would not come back home   35
from Troy? And so you fleeced my house, and raped
my slave girls, and you flirted with my wife
while I am still alive! You did not fear
the gods who live in heaven, and you thought
no man would ever come to take revenge.   40
Now you are trapped inside the snares of death."

At that, pale fear seized all of them. They groped
to find a way to save their lives somehow.
Only Eurymachus found words to answer.

"If it is you, Odysseus, come back,   45
then we agree! Quite right, the Greeks have done
outrageous things to your estate and home.
But now the one responsible is dead—
Antinous! It was all his idea.
He did not even really want your wife,   50
but had another plan, which Zeus has foiled:
to lie in ambush for your son, and kill him,
then seize the throne and rule in Ithaca.
Now he is slain—quite rightly. Please, my lord,
have mercy on your people! We will pay   55
in public, yes, for all the food and drink.
We each will bring the price of twenty oxen,
and pay you all the gold and bronze you want.
Your anger is quite understandable."

Odysseus saw through him; with a glare   60
he told him, "Even if you give me all

your whole inheritance, and even more,
I will not keep my hands away from slaughter
until I pay you suitors back for all
your wickedness. You have two choices: fight,   65
or run away: just try to save your lives!
Not one of you will get away from death."

At that their knees grew weak, their hearts stopped still.
Eurymachus again addressed the suitors.
"My friends, this man will not hold back his hands.   70
Seizing the bow and arrows, he will shoot us
right from that polished threshold, till he kills
each one of us. Be quick, make plans for battle.
Draw out your swords, use tables as your shields[1]
against the deadly arrows. All together,   75
rush at him, try to drive him off the threshold,
and out of doors, then run all through the town,
and quickly call for help. This man will soon
have shot his last!"

                        He drew his sharp bronze sword
and with a dreadful scream he leapt at him.   80
But that same instant, Lord Odysseus
let fly and hit his chest, beside the nipple,
and instantly the arrow pierced his liver.
The sword fell from his hand. He doubled up
and fell across the table, spilling food   85
and wine across the floor. He smashed his head
against the ground, and in his desperate pain
kicked up the chair, and darkness drenched his eyes.

Amphinomus attacked Odysseus.
He drew his sharp sword, hoping he could force him   90
to yield his place. Telemachus leapt in
and thrust his bronze spear through him from behind,
ramming it through his back and out his chest.
Face-first he crashed and thudded to the ground.
Telemachus dashed back—he left his spear   95
stuck in the body; he was terrified
that if he bent to pull it out, some Greek
would jump on him and stab him with a sword.
He ran and quickly reached his loyal father.
He stood beside him and his words flew out.   100

"Now Father, I will fetch a shield for you
and two spears and a helmet made of bronze,
and I will arm myself, and bring more arms
for our two herdsmen, since we all need weapons."

---

1. In the usual arrangement, there were light
side-tables by each diner, rather than a single
larger dining table; the suitors are to pick up
their tables for self-defense.

Odysseus, the master planner, answered,   105
"Run fast while I still have a stock of arrows,
before they force me from the doors—I am
fighting alone up here."

                    His son obeyed.
He hurried to the storeroom for the arms,
and took eight spears, four shields, and four bronze helmets   110
each fitted out with bushy horsehair plumes.
He hurried back to take them to his father,
and was the first to strap the armor on.
The two slaves also armed themselves, and stood
flanking their brilliant, resourceful leader.   115
As long as he had arrows, he kept shooting,
and one by one he picked the suitors off,
inside his own home. Then at last the king
ran out of arrows; he set down his bow
next to the sturdy doorpost, leaning up   120
against the palace walls, all shining white.
He slung the four-fold shield across his shoulders,
and put the well-made helmet on his head.
The crest of horsehair gave a fearsome nod.
He grasped a bronze-tipped spear in either hand.   125

There was a back gate in the castle walls,
providing access to the passageway,
with tightly fitted doors. Odysseus
ordered the noble swineherd to stand there
to guard it—there was only one way out.   130
Agelaus called out to all the suitors.

"Friends, one of us should slip out through that gate
and quickly tell the people, raise alarms.
That soon would put a stop to this man's shooting."

Melanthius the goatherd answered, "No!   135
My lord, that entryway is much too narrow,
and dangerously near the palace doors.
One man, if he was brave, could keep it guarded
against us all. So I will bring you armor
out of the storeroom, which I think is where   140
those two, our enemies, have hidden it."

Melanthius the goatherd climbed up past
the arrow-slits inside the castle walls,
into the chamber. There he took twelve shields,
twelve spears and twelve bronze helmets, each one crested   145
with horsehair. Then he hurried back downstairs
and handed all the weapons to the suitors.

Odysseus could see that they had arms;
their spears were brandished. His heart stopped, his legs

trembled—he was so shocked at their presumption.   150
At once his words flew out to tell his son,

"One of the women, or Melanthius,
is waging war against us, in my house!"

Wisely Telemachus owned up at once.
"Father, it was my fault, I am to blame.   155
I left the heavy storeroom door ajar.
Someone on their side must have kept good watch.
Go there, Eumaeus, shut the door, and see
if any of the women are against us,
or else, as I suspect, Melanthius."   160

Meanwhile, Melanthius was going back
to get more weapons from the room. The swineherd
saw him and told Odysseus,

                              "My lord,
that little sneak, the man we all suspected,
is going to the stores! Odysseus,   165
you always have a plan for what to do:
so should I kill him, as I think is best,
or bring him here to you, so you can punish
his many crimes against you in your house?"

Odysseus already had a plan.   170
"Telemachus and I will keep the suitors
trapped in the hall—however much they rage.
You two, truss up his hands and feet behind him,
drag him inside the storeroom, string him up,
tying a knotted rope high on the column,   175
and hoist him to the rafters. Torture him
with hours of agony before he dies."

His word was their command; they hurried off,
and reached the weaponry. Melanthius
was unaware of them. As he was searching   180
for arms, they stopped on each side of the door
and waited. When he stepped across the threshold,
holding a lovely helmet in one hand,
and in the other hand, a rusty shield,
once carried by Laertes in his youth,   185
but now in storage, with its seams all loose,
the two men jumped on him and grabbed his hair
to drag him in and threw him on the floor,
shaking with fear. They bound his hands and feet
and yanked them painfully behind his back,   190
just as the lord of suffering had told them.
They tied him with a knotted rope and hoisted
his body up the column to the rafters.
Swineherd Eumaeus, you began to mock him:

"Keep watch the whole night through, Melanthius,   195
tucked up in this soft bed—it serves you right!
And wait there for the golden throne of Dawn
leaving the sea, that hour when you would lead
your goats to this house for the suitors' dinner."

There he was left, bound cruelly and stretched.   200
The herdsmen armed themselves and left the room,
shutting the door, and joined their cunning leader.
They stood there on the threshold, tense with purpose,
just four against so many men inside.
The child of Zeus, Athena, came to meet them;   205
her voice and looks resembled those of Mentor.
Odysseus was happy when he saw her,
and said, "Remember our old friendship, Mentor!
I have been good to you since we were boys.
So help me now!" He guessed it was Athena,   210
who rouses armies.

          From the hall, the suitors
shouted their opposition. Agelaus
called, "Mentor, do not let Odysseus
sway you to help him and to fight against us.
I think this is how things will go. When we   215
have killed this father and his son, you will
die also, if you do as you intend,
and pay with your own life for all your plots.
Our bronze will strip your life away from you,
and we will seize whatever you may own   220
and mix it with the loot we get from here.
Your sons will not survive here in these halls,[2]
nor will your wife and daughters still walk free
in Ithaca."

          At that Athena's heart
became enraged, and angrily she scolded   225
Odysseus. "Where is your courage now?
You fought nine years on end against the Trojans,
for white-armed Helen, Zeus' favorite child.[3]
You slaughtered many men when war was raging,
and formed the plan that made the city fall.[4]   230
Now you are home at last, how can you flinch
from being brave and using proper force
against these suitors? Come now, stand by me
and watch how Mentor, son of Alcimus,
will treat your enemies as recompense   235
for all your service."

---

2. It is unclear in the original whether Agelaus is threatening to kill Mentor's sons or only banish them.

3. The original epithet is an unusual one, *eupatereios,* suggesting "well-fathered."

4. The trick of the Wooden Horse.

But she did not grant
decisive victory; she kept on testing
Odysseus' courage, and his son's.
She flew up like a swallow through the smoke
and nestled in the rafters of the roof.   240

Now Agelaus, Demoptolemus,
Eurynomus, Pisander, Amphimedon,
and Polybus were urging on the suitors.
Those were the most heroic of the group
who still survived and battled for their lives: 245
the others were defeated by the bow
and raining arrows. Agelaus told them,

"That Mentor's boasts were empty, friends! He left,
and they are all alone there at the entrance.
Now force this cruel man to stay his hands.   250
Do not hurl spears at him all in a mass,
but you six must shoot first and pray Lord Zeus
we strike Odysseus and win the fight.
Once he is down, the others will be nothing."

The six men threw their spears as he had said;   255
at once Athena made their efforts fail.
One pierced the doorpost of the palace hall,
another hit the closely fitted door,
another's spear of ash and heavy bronze
fell on the wall. The group of four avoided   260
all of the suitors' spears. Odysseus
had waited long enough.

                              "My friends," he said,
"they want to slaughter us and strip our arms!
Avenge my former wrongs, and save your lives!
Now shoot!"

                 They hurled their spears at once and hit.   265
Odysseus killed Demoptolemus;
Telemachus, Euryades; the swineherd
slaughtered Elatus, and the cowherd killed
Pisander. They all fell and bit the earth.
The other suitors huddled in a corner;   270
the four rushed up and from the corpses pulled
their spears. Again the suitors threw their weapons;
again Athena made them fail. One spear
struck at the doorpost, and another pierced
the door; another ash spear hit the wall.   275
Amphimedon's blow grazed Telemachus
right by the wrist: the bronze tore through his skin.
Ctesippus hurled his spear; it only scratched
the swineherd's shoulder, just above his shield,
flew past and fell down on the floor behind him.   280

The competent, sharp-eyed Odysseus
and his companions hurled their piercing spears
into the swarming throng. The city-sacker
skewered Eurydamas; Telemachus
slashed Amphimedon, and the swineherd struck   285
at Polybus; the cowherd sliced right through
Ctesippus' chest, and crowed,

                      "You fool! You loved
insulting us—now you have stopped your boasting.
The gods have got the last word; they have won.
This is a gift to pay you for that kick   290
you gave Odysseus when he walked through
his own house, as a homeless man in need."

Odysseus moved closer with his spear,
and pierced Agelaus; Telemachus
thrust at Leocritus, and drove his bronze   295
into his belly. He fell down headfirst,
face smashed against the floor.

                     Then from the roof
Athena lifted high her deadly aegis.
The frightened suitors bolted through the hall
like cattle, roused and driven by a gadfly   300
in springtime, when the days are getting longer.
As eagles with their crooked beaks and talons
swoop from the hills and pounce on smaller birds
that fly across the fields beneath the clouds;
the victims have no help and no way out,   305
as their attackers slaughter them, and men
watch and enjoy the violence. So these
four fighters sprang and struck, and drove the suitors
in all directions. Screaming filled the hall,
as skulls were cracked; the whole floor ran with blood.   310

Leodes darted up to supplicate
Odysseus; he touched his knees.

                        "Please, mercy!
I did no wrong, I swear, in word or deed
to any of the women in the house.
I tried to stop the suitors, tried to urge them   315
to keep their hands clean, but they would not listen.
Those fools deserved their fate. But I did nothing!
I am a priest—yet I must lie with them.
Will good behavior go unrewarded?"

The calculating hero scowled at him.   320
"If, as you claim, you sacrificed for them,
you must have often prayed here in my hall

that I would not regain the joys of home,
and that my wife would marry you instead,
and bear you children. You will not escape. 325
Suffer and die!"

        Agelaus had dropped
his sword when he was killed. With his strong arm
Odysseus swung, slashed down and sliced right through
the priest's neck, and his head, still framing words,
rolled in the dust.

          The poet Phemius, 330
who had been forced to sing to please the suitors,
was huddling by the back door with his lyre,
anxiously considering his choices:
to slip outside and crouch beneath the altar
of mighty Zeus, the god of home owners, 335
where his old masters burned so many thigh-bones;
or he could run towards Odysseus
and grasp him by the knees and beg for mercy.
He made his mind up: he would supplicate.
He set his hollow lyre on the ground 340
between the mixing bowl and silver chair,
and dashed to take Odysseus' knees,
beseeching him in quivering winged words.

"I beg you, Lord Odysseus! Have mercy!
Think! If you kill me now, you will be sorry! 345
I have the power to sing for gods and men.
I am self-taught—all kinds of song are planted
by gods inside my heart. I am prepared
to sing for you, as if before a god.
Wait, do not cut my throat! Just ask your son! 350
He will explain it was against my will
that I came here to sing to them after dinner.
They were too fierce and they outnumbered me.
I had no choice."

          Then strong Telemachus
turned quickly to his father, saying, "Stop, 355
hold up your sword—this man is innocent.
And let us also save the house boy, Medon.
He always cared for me when I was young—
unless the herdsmen have already killed him,
or he already met you in your rage." 360

Medon was sensible: he had been hiding
under a chair, beneath a fresh cowhide,
in order to escape from being killed.
Hearing these words, he jumped up from the chair,
took off the cowhide and assumed the pose 365

of supplication near Telemachus,
and said,

       "Friend, here I am! Please spare my life!
Your father is too strong, and furious
against the suitors, who skimmed off his wealth
and failed to honor you. Please, talk to him!"   370

Canny Odysseus smiled down and said,
"You need not worry, he has saved your life.
So live and spread the word that doing good
is far superior to wickedness.
Now leave the hall and go outside; sit down,   375
joining the famous singer in the courtyard,
so I can finish what I have to do
inside my house."

            The two men went outside,
and crouched by Zeus' altar, on the lookout
for death at any moment all around.   380

Odysseus scanned all around his home
for any man who might be still alive,
who might be hiding to escape destruction.
He saw them fallen, all of them, so many,
lying in blood and dust, like fish hauled up   385
out of the dark-gray sea in fine-mesh nets;
tipped out upon the curving beach's sand,
they gasp for water from the salty sea.
So lay the suitors, heaped across each other.
Odysseus, still scheming, told his son,   390

"I need to say something to Eurycleia.
Hurry, Telemachus, and bring her here."

Telemachus was glad to please his father.
He pushed the door ajar and called the nurse.
"Nanny, come quick! You have been here for years.   395
You supervise the female palace slaves.
My father has to talk to you; come on!"

She had no words to answer him, but opened
the doors into the great and sturdy hall.
Telemachus went first and led the way.   400
Among the corpses of the slaughtered men
she saw Odysseus all smeared with blood.
After a lion eats a grazing ox,
its chest and jowls are thick with blood all over;
a dreadful sight. Just so, Odysseus   405
had blood all over him—from hands to feet.

Seeing the corpses, seeing all that blood,
so great a deed of violence, she began
to crow. Odysseus told her to stop
and spoke with fluent words.

                "Old woman, no!   410
Be glad inside your heart, but do not shout.
It is not pious, gloating over men
who have been killed. Divine fate took them down,
and their own wicked deeds. They disrespected
all people that they met, both bad and good.   415
Through their own crimes they came to this bad end.
But tell me now about the household women.
Which ones dishonor me? And which are pure?"

The slave who loved her master answered, "Child,
I will tell you exactly how things stand.   420
In this house we have fifty female slaves
whom we have trained to work, to card the wool,
and taught to tolerate their life as slaves.[5]
Twelve stepped away from honor: those twelve girls
ignore me, and Penelope our mistress.   425
She would not let Telemachus instruct them,
since he is young and only just grown-up.
Let me go upstairs to the women's rooms,
to tell your wife—some god has sent her sleep."

The master strategist Odysseus   430
said,

        "Not yet; do not wake her. Call the women
who made those treasonous plots while I was gone."[6]
The old nurse did so. Walking through the hall,
she called the girls. Meanwhile, Odysseus
summoned the herdsmen and Telemachus   435
and spoke winged words to them.

                    "Now we must start
to clear the corpses out. The girls must help.
Then clean my stately chairs and handsome tables
with sponges fine as honeycomb, and water.
When the whole house is set in proper order,   440
restore my halls to health: take out the girls

5. Some scholars think that *doulosune* in this line ("slavery") suggests sexual slavery and that the line (reading *doulosunes apechesthai*) should be interpreted as "to hold off against (sexual) enslavement"—i.e., to resist the kind of advances made by the suitors.

6. The Greek verb *mechanoonto* ("plotted"—with implications of cunning strategy reminiscent of Odysseus himself) suggests that these girls were deliberately hoping to work against their master—a suggestion that goes well beyond Odysseus' evidence.

between the courtyard wall and the rotunda.
Hack at them with long swords, eradicate
all life from them. They will forget the things
the suitors made them do with them in secret,   445
through Aphrodite."

                   Sobbing desperately
the girls came, weeping, clutching at each other.
They carried out the bodies of the dead
and piled them up on top of one another,
under the roof outside. Odysseus   450
instructed them and forced them to continue.
And then they cleaned his lovely chairs and tables
with wet absorbent sponges, while the prince
and herdsmen with their shovels scraped away
the mess to make the sturdy floor all clean.   455
The girls picked up the trash and took it out.
The men created order in the house
and set it all to rights, then led the girls
outside and trapped them—they could not escape—
between the courtyard wall and the rotunda.   460
Showing initiative, Telemachus
insisted,

        "I refuse to grant these girls
a clean death, since they poured down shame on me
and Mother, when they lay beside the suitors."

At that, he wound a piece of sailor's rope   465
round the rotunda and round the mighty pillar,
stretched up so high no foot could touch the ground.
As doves or thrushes spread their wings to fly
home to their nests, but someone sets a trap—
they crash into a net, a bitter bedtime;   470
just so the girls, their heads all in a row,
were strung up with the noose around their necks
to make their death an agony. They gasped,
feet twitching for a while, but not for long.

Then the men took Melanthius outside   475
and with curved bronze cut off his nose and ears
and ripped away his genitals, to feed
raw to the dogs. Still full of rage, they chopped
his hands and feet off. Then they washed their own,
and they went back inside.

                      Odysseus   480
told his beloved nurse, "Now bring me fire
and sulfur, as a cure for evil things,
and I will fumigate the house. And call
Penelope, her slaves, and all the slave girls
inside the house."

She answered with affection,   485

"Yes, dear, all this is good. But let me bring
a cloak and shirt for you. You should not stand here,
your strong back covered only with those rags.
That would be wrong!"

Odysseus, the master

of every cunning scheme, replied, "No, first   490
I need a fire here, to smoke the hall."
His loving slave complied and brought the fire
and sulfur, and Odysseus made smoke,
and fumigated every room inside
the house and yard. Meanwhile, the old nurse ran   495
all through the palace summoning the women.
By torchlight they came out from their apartments,
to greet Odysseus with open arms.
They kissed his face and took him by the hands
in welcome. He was seized by sweet desire   500
to weep, and in his heart he knew them all.

BOOK 23

The Olive Tree Bed

Chuckling with glee, the old slave climbed upstairs
to tell the queen that her beloved husband
was home. Her weak old knees felt stronger now;
with buoyant steps she went and stood beside
her mistress, at her head, and said,

"Dear child,   5

wake up and see! At long last you have got
your wish come true! Odysseus has come!
He is right here inside this house! At last!
He slaughtered all the suitors who were wasting
his property and threatening his son!"   10

But cautiously Penelope replied,
"You poor old thing! The gods have made you crazy.
They have the power to turn the sanest person
mad, or make fools turn wise. You used to be
so sensible, but they have damaged you.   15
Why else would you be mocking me like this,
with silly stories, in my time of grief?
Why did you wake me from the sleep that sweetly
wrapped round my eyes? I have not slept so soundly
since my Odysseus marched off to see   20
that cursed town—Evilium. Go back!
If any other slave comes here to wake me
and tell me all this nonsense, I will send her
back down at once, and I will not be gentle.
Your old age will protect you from worse scolding."   25

But Eurycleia answered with affection,
"Dear child, I am not mocking you. I am
telling the truth: Odysseus is here!
He is the stranger that they all abused.
Telemachus has known for quite some time,   30
but sensibly he kept his father's plans
a secret, so Odysseus could take
revenge for all their violence and pride."

Penelope was overjoyed; she jumped
from bed and hugged the nurse, and started crying.   35
Her words flew fast.

                    "Dear Nanny! If this is
the truth, if he has come back to this house,
how could he have attacked those shameless suitors,
when he is just one man, and there were always
so many crowded in there?"

                              Eurycleia   40
answered, "I did not see or learn the details.
I heard the sound of screaming from the men
as they were killed. We huddled in our room
and kept the doors tight shut, until your son
called me—his father sent him. Then I saw   45
Odysseus surrounded by dead bodies.
They lay on top of one another, sprawled
across the solid floor. You would have been
thrilled if you saw him, like a lion, drenched
in blood and gore. Now they are all piled up   50
out by the courtyard gates, and he is burning
a mighty fire to fumigate the palace,
restoring all its loveliness. He sent me
to fetch you. Come with me, so both of you
can start to live in happiness. You have   55
endured such misery. Your wish came true!
He is alive! He has come home again,
and found you and your son, and he has taken
revenge on all the suitors who abused him."

Penelope said carefully, "Do not   60
start gloating. As you know, my son and I
would be delighted if he came. We all would.
However, what you say cannot be true.
Some god has killed the suitors out of anger
at their abuse of power and their pride.   65
They failed to show respect to visitors,
both good and bad. Their foolishness has killed them.
But my Odysseus has lost his home,
and far away from Greece, he lost his life."

The nurse replied, "Dear child! How can you say   70
your husband will not come, when he is here,
beside the hearth? Your heart has always been
mistrustful. But I have clear evidence!
When I was washing him, I felt the scar
made when the boar impaled him with its tusk.   75
I tried to tell you, but he grabbed my throat
and stopped me spoiling all his plans. Come with me.
I swear on my own life: if I am lying,
then kill me."

      Wise Penelope said, "Nanny,
it must be hard for you to understand   80
the ways of gods, despite your cleverness.
But let us go to meet my son, so I
can see the suitors dead, and see the man
who killed them."

      So she went downstairs. Her heart
could not decide if she should keep her distance   85
as she was questioning her own dear husband,
or go right up to him and kiss his face
and hold his hands in hers. She crossed the threshold
and sat across from him beside the wall,
in firelight. He sat beside the pillar,   90
and kept his eyes down, waiting to find out
whether the woman who once shared his bed
would speak to him. She sat in silence, stunned.
Sometimes when she was glancing at his face
it seemed like him; but then his dirty clothes   95
were unfamiliar. Telemachus
scolded her.

      "Mother! Cruel, heartless Mother!
Why are you doing this, rejecting Father?
Why do you not go over, sit beside him,
and talk to him? No woman in the world   100
would be so obstinate! To keep your distance
from him when he has come back after twenty
long years of suffering! Your heart is always
harder than rock!"

      But thoughtfully she answered,
"My child, I am confused. I cannot speak,   105
or meet his eyes. If this is really him,
if my Odysseus has come back home,
we have our ways to recognize each other,
through secret signs known only to us two."

Hardened Odysseus began to smile.   110
He told the boy,

                              "You must allow your mother
to test me out; she will soon know me better.
While I am dirty, dressed in rags, she will not
treat me with kindness or acknowledge me.
Meanwhile, we must make plans. If someone murders   115
even just one man, even one who had
few friends in his community, the killer
is forced to run away and leave his homeland
and family. But we have killed the mainstay
of Ithaca, the island's best young men.   120
So what do you suggest?"

                    Telemachus
said warily, "You have to work it out.
They say you have the finest mind in all
the world; no mortal man can rival you
in cleverness. Lead me, and I will be   125
behind you right away. And I will do
my best to be as brave as I can be."

Odysseus was quick to form a plan.
He told him, "Here is what I think is best.
The three of you should wash and change your clothes,   130
and make the slave girls go put on clean dresses.
Then let the godlike singer take the lyre
and play a clear and cheerful dancing tune,
so passersby or neighbors hearing it
will think it is a wedding. We must not   135
allow the news about the suitors' murder
to spread too far until we reach the woods
of our estate, and there we can decide
the best path forward offered us by Zeus."

They did as Lord Odysseus had said.   140
They washed and changed their tunics, and the slave girls
prepared themselves. The singer took the lyre,
and roused in them desire to hear sweet music,
and dance. The house resounded with the thump
of beating feet from all the dancing men   145
and girls in pretty sashes. Those outside
who heard the noises said to one another,

"So somebody is marrying the queen
who had so many suitors! Headstrong woman!
She must have lacked the strength to wait it out   150
and keep her husband's house safe till he came."
They spoke with no idea what really happened.

Eurynome the slave woman began
to wash strong-willed Odysseus. She rubbed him
with olive oil, and dressed him in a tunic   155
and handsome cloak. And then Athena poured

attractiveness from head to toe, and made him
taller and stronger, and his hair grew thick
and curly as a hyacinth. As when
a craftsman whom Athena or Hephaestus[1]   160
has trained in metalwork, so he can make
beautiful artifacts, pours gold on silver—
so she poured beauty on his head and shoulders.
After his bath he looked like an immortal.
He sat down in the same chair opposite   165
his wife and said,

    "Extraordinary woman!
The gods have given you the hardest heart.
No other wife would so reject a husband
who had been suffering for twenty years
and finally come home. Well, Nanny, make   170
a bed for me, so I can rest. This woman
must have an iron heart!"

     Penelope
said shrewdly, "You extraordinary man!
I am not acting proud, or underplaying
this big event; yet I am not surprised   175
at how you look. You looked like this the day
your long oars sailed away from Ithaca.
Now, Eurycleia, make the bed for him
outside the room he built himself. Pull out
the bedstead, and spread quilts and blankets on it."   180
She spoke to test him, and Odysseus
was furious, and told his loyal wife,

"Woman! Your words have cut my heart! Who moved
my bed? It would be difficult for even
a master craftsman—though a god could do it   185
with ease. No man, however young and strong,
could pry it out. There is a trick to how
this bed was made. I made it, no one else.
Inside the court there grew an olive tree
with delicate long leaves, full-grown and green,   190
as sturdy as a pillar, and I built
the room around it. I packed stones together,
and fixed a roof and fitted doors. At last
I trimmed the olive tree and used my bronze
to cut the branches off from root to tip   195
and planed it down and skillfully transformed
the trunk into a bedpost. With a drill,
I bored right through it. This was my first bedpost,
and then I made the other three, inlaid
with gold and silver and with ivory.   200

1. Gods associated with skill in handicrafts and technology.

I stretched ox-leather straps across, dyed purple.
Now I have told the secret trick, the token.
But woman, wife, I do not know if someone—
a man—has cut the olive trunk and moved
my bed, or if it is still safe."

                   At that,   205
her heart and body suddenly relaxed.
She recognized the tokens he had shown her.
She burst out crying and ran straight towards him
and threw her arms around him, kissed his face,
and said,

            "Do not be angry at me now,   210
Odysseus! In every other way
you are a very understanding man.
The gods have made us suffer: they refused
to let us stay together and enjoy
our youth until we reached the edge of age   215
together. Please forgive me, do not keep
bearing a grudge because when I first saw you,
I would not welcome you immediately.
I felt a constant dread that some bad man
would fool me with his lies. There are so many   220
dishonest, clever men. That foreigner[2]
would never have got Helen into bed,
if she had known the Greeks would march to war
and bring her home again. It was a goddess
who made her do it, putting in her heart   225
the passion that first caused my grief as well.
Now you have told the story of our bed,
the secret that no other mortal knows,
except yourself and me, and just one slave,
Actoris,[3] whom my father gave to me   230
when I came here, who used to guard our room.
You made my stubborn heart believe in you."

This made him want to cry. He held his love,
his faithful wife, and wept. As welcome as
the land to swimmers, when Poseidon wrecks   235
their ship at sea and breaks it with great waves
and driving winds; a few escape the sea
and reach the shore, their skin all caked with brine.
Grateful to be alive, they crawl to land.
So glad she was to see her own dear husband,   240
and her white arms would not let go his neck.
They would have wept until the rosy Dawn

---

2. The foreigner is Paris, who came from Troy in the Near East to Sparta in Greece.
3. Actoris is mentioned only here, and it is possible that she has died, to be replaced by Eurynome—which would explain why Penelope is sure that Actoris has not told the stranger the secret.

began to touch the sky, but shining-eyed
Athena intervened. She held night back,
restraining golden Dawn beside the Ocean,   245
and would not let her yoke her swift young colts,
Shining and Bright. Odysseus, mind whirling,
said,

    "Wife, we have not come yet to the end
of all our troubles; there are more to come,
many hard labors which I must complete.   250
The spirit of Tiresias informed me,
that day I went inside the house of Hades
to ask about the journey home for me
and for my men. But come now, let us go
to bed together, wife; let us enjoy   255
the pleasure of sweet sleep."

                    Penelope,
who always thought ahead, said, "When you wish.
The bed is yours. The gods have brought you home,
back to your well-built house. But since a god
has made you speak about these future labors,   260
tell me what they involve. I will find out
eventually, and better to know now."

He answered warily, "You really are
extraordinary. Why would you make me tell you
something to cause you pain? It hurts me too,   265
but I will tell the truth, not hide it from you.
Tiresias foretold that I must travel
through many cities carrying an oar,
till I reach men who do not know the sea,
and do not eat their food with salt, or use   270
boats painted red around the prow, or oars,
which are the wings of ships. He said that I
will know I have arrived when I encounter
someone who calls the object on my back
a winnowing fan.[4] Then I must fix my oar   275
firm in the earth, and make a sacrifice
to Lord Poseidon, of a ram and ox
and stud-boar, perfect animals, then come
back home and give a hecatomb to all
the deathless gods who live above the sky.   280
If I do this, I will not die at sea;
I will grow old in comfort and will meet
a gentle death, surrounded by my people,
who will be rich and happy."

                    Sensibly
Penelope said, "If the gods allow you   285

---

4. I.e., the traveler will not recognize an oar, having never seen the sea.

to reach old age in comfort, there is hope
that there will be an end to all our troubles."

They talked like this. Meanwhile, the slaves were working:
Eurynome and Eurycleia laid
soft blankets on the sturdy bed by torchlight.   290
The nurse went off to sleep; Eurynome
picked up the torch and led them to their bed,
then went to her room. Finally, at last,
with joy the husband and the wife arrived
back in the rites of their old marriage bed.   295

Meanwhile, the herdsmen and Telemachus
stopped dancing, made the women stop, and went
to bed inside the darkened house.

                                                And when
the couple had enjoyed their lovemaking,
they shared another pleasure—telling stories.   300
She told him how she suffered as she watched
the crowd of suitors ruining the house,
killing so many herds of sheep and cattle
and drinking so much wine, because of her.
Odysseus told her how much he hurt   305
so many other people, and in turn
how much he had endured himself. She loved
to listen, and she did not fall asleep
until he told it all. First, how he slaughtered
the Cicones, then traveled to the fields   310
of Lotus-Eaters; what the Cyclops did,
and how he paid him back for ruthlessly
eating his men. Then how he reached Aeolus,
who welcomed him and helped him; but it was
not yet his fate to come back home; a storm   315
snatched him and bore him off across the sea,
howling frustration. Then, he said, he came
to Laestrygonia, whose people wrecked
his fleet and killed his men. And he described
the cleverness of Circe, and his journey   320
to Hades to consult Tiresias,
and how he saw all his dead friends, and saw
his mother, who had loved him as a baby;
then how he heard the Sirens' endless voices,
and reached the Wandering Rocks and terrible   325
Charybdis, and how he had been the first
to get away from Scylla. And he told her
of how his crew devoured the Sun God's cattle;
Zeus roared with smoke and thunder, lightning struck
the ship, and all his loyal men were killed.   330
But he survived, and drifted to Ogygia.
He told her how Calypso trapped him there,

inside her hollow cave, and wanted him
to be her husband; she took care of him
and promised she could set him free from death   335
and time forever. But she never swayed
his heart. He suffered terribly, for years,
and then he reached Phaeacia, where the people
looked up to him as if he were a god,
and sent him in a ship back home again   340
to his dear Ithaca, with gifts of bronze
and gold and piles of clothes. His story ended;
sweet sleep released his heart from all his cares.

Athena, bright-eyed goddess, stayed alert,
and when she thought Odysseus had finished   345
with taking pleasure in his wife and sleep,
she roused the newborn Dawn from Ocean's streams
to bring the golden light to those on earth.
Odysseus got up and told his wife,

"Wife, we have both endured our share of trouble: 350
you wept here as you longed for my return,
while Zeus and other gods were keeping me
away from home, although I longed to come.
But now we have returned to our own bed,
as we both longed to do. You must look after   355
my property inside the house. Meanwhile,
I have to go on raids, to steal replacements
for all the sheep those swaggering suitors killed,
and get the other Greeks to give me more,
until I fill my folds. But first I will   360
go to the orchard in the countryside
to see my grieving father. Then at dawn
the news will spread that I have killed the suitors.
Your orders, wife—though you are smart enough
to need no orders—are, go with your slaves   365
upstairs, sit quietly, and do not talk
to anyone."

He armed himself and called
the herdsmen and Telemachus, and told them
to put on armor too—breastplates of bronze.
Odysseus led all of them outside.   370
The light was bright across the earth. Athena
hid them with night and brought them out of town.

BOOK 24

Restless Spirits

Then Hermes called the spirits of the suitors
out of the house. He held the golden wand
with which he casts a spell to close men's eyes

or open those of sleepers when he wants.
He led the spirits and they followed, squeaking   5
like bats in secret crannies of a cave,
who cling together, and when one becomes
detached and falls down from the rock, the rest
flutter and squeak—just so the spirits squeaked,
and hurried after Hermes, lord of healing.   10
On open roads they crossed the Ocean stream,
went past the rock of Leucas and the gates
of Helius the Sun, and skittered through
the provinces of dreams, and soon arrived
in fields of asphodel, the home of shadows   15
who have been worn to weariness by life.

They found Achilles' ghost there, and Patroclus,
and Ajax, the most handsome of the Greeks
after unmatched Achilles. Agamemnon
had just arrived to join them, in deep grief   20
for his own death, and with him came the others
killed by Aegisthus and his bodyguards.
Achilles' ghost spoke first.

                    "O Agamemnon!
Men used to say that out of all the heroes,
Zeus, Lord of Lightning, favored you the most,   25
because you had command of a great army
in Troy where Greeks endured the pain of war.
But death, which no man living can avoid,
was destined to arrive at the wrong time.
If only you had died at Troy and won   30
the glory of your rank as a commander!
All of the Greeks and allies would have built
a tomb for you, and afterwards your son
would have received great honor. As it is,
it was your fate to die a dreadful death."   35

The ghost of Agamemnon answered him,
"Achilles, son of Peleus, you were
lucky to die at Troy, away from Argos.
The finest warriors of Greece and Troy
fought round your corpse and died. You lay a hero,   40
magnificent amid the whirling dust,
your days of driving chariots forgotten.[1]
We fought all day, and would have fought forever,
but Zeus sent winds to stop us. Then we brought you
back to our ships, and laid you on a bier,   45
away from battle, and we bathed your skin

1. Achilles is usually known as "swift-footed," a quick sprinter on foot rather than a horseman or driver of a chariot. The most famous episode in which he uses a chariot is near the end of the *Iliad*, when he drags the body of his slaughtered enemy, Hector, around the walls of Troy—a gesture of brutality that is forgotten in Achilles' own splendid death scene.

in heated water and anointed you
with oil. We wept for you and cut our hair.
Your mother[2] heard the news, and with her nymphs
she came up from the waves. An eerie wailing   50
sounded across the sea. The men began
to tremble, and they would have rushed on board,
if wise old Nestor had not made them stop.
He always had the best advice for us,
and said, 'My lords, stay here. It is his mother,   55
coming with her immortal water nymphs
to find her own dead son.' At this, the Greeks
regained their courage. The old Sea King's daughters
gathered around you weeping, and they dressed you
in clothes of the immortals. All nine Muses   60
sang lamentations in their lovely voices.
No one could keep from crying at the sound,
so moving was their song. The gods and men
were mourning seventeen long nights and days
and then we gave you to the pyre, and killed   65
many fat sheep and cattle for your corpse.
You burned in clothes from gods; you were anointed
with oil and honey. Troops of warriors
on foot and horseback, fully armed, went marching
around your pyre, and made a mighty din.   70
At last Hephaestus' flame consumed your flesh.
When morning came, we gathered your white bones,
Achilles, and anointed them with oil
and unmixed wine. Your mother gave an urn
of gold with double handles, which she said   75
Hephaestus made and Dionysus gave her.
Your white bones lay inside it, Lord Achilles,
mixed with the bones of your dead friend Patroclus.
We laid the urn beside Antilochus,
the friend you most respected after him.   80
The army of Greek warriors assembled,
and with all reverence we heaped a mound
out on the headland by the Hellespont,
large enough to be visible to those
at sea, both now and in the years to come.   85
Your mother asked the gods for splendid prizes
and put them in the midst of an arena,
so the best athletes could compete for them.
You have seen many burials of heroes,
when young men tie their tunics to compete.   90
But you would have been startled at the riches
that silver-footed Thetis brought for you.
You were so dearly loved by all the gods.
You did not lose your name in death. Your fame
will live forever; everyone will know   95

2. Thetis, a sea goddess.

Achilles. As for me, what good was it
that I wound up the war? When I came home
Aegisthus and my wicked, fiendish wife
murdered me. Zeus had planned it."

                 While they talked,
Hermes the guide came near them, with the suitors   100
killed by Odysseus. The two great lords,
astonished at the sight, rushed up to them,
and Agamemnon's spirit recognized
the son of his old friend, Melaneus,
with whom he stayed in Ithaca. He said,   105

"Amphimedon! What happened to you all?
Why have you all come down here to the land
of darkness? You are all so young and strong;
you must have been the best boys in your town.
Maybe Poseidon raised great waves and winds   110
to wreck your fleet? Or were you all attacked
by men on land while you were poaching cows
or flocks of sheep, or fighting for a city
and women? You must tell me! We are friends.
Do you remember when I visited   115
your home, when Menelaus and myself
were trying to persuade Odysseus
to join the fleet and sail with us to Troy?
It took a whole damned month to cross the sea;
we had to work so hard to sway that man,   120
who sacked the city."[3]

               Amphimedon's spirit
answered, "Great General, Agamemnon, yes,
I do remember everything you say.
And I will tell, in every gruesome detail,
the manner of our death. Odysseus   125
was gone for many years. We came to court
his wife, who had no wish to marry us,
but would not tell us no or make an end.
She planned black death for us, and tricked us too.
She set a mighty loom up in the hall,   130
and wove a wide fine cloth, and said to us,
'Young suitors, now Odysseus is dead.
I know that you are eager for the wedding,
but wait till I am finished with this cloth,
so that my weaving will not go to waste.   135

---

3. According to legend, Odysseus tried to get out of going to the Trojan War by feigning madness. The usual story is that he was demonstrating his insanity by plowing his field using a donkey and an ox yoked together (animals with different strides who would not plow well together). Palamedes, a Greek who had come on the embassy with Agamemnon and Menelaus, put the newborn Telemachus in front of the plow, and Odysseus veered away from his son—thus demonstrating his sanity.

It is a shroud for when Laertes dies,
so that the women in the town do not
blame me because a man who gained such wealth
was buried with no winding-sheet.' Her words
convinced us. So by day she wove the cloth,   140
and then at night by torchlight, she unwove it.
For three long years she fooled us; when the hours
and months had passed, the fourth year rolled around,
and then a girl who knew the truth told us;
and we found her unraveling her work.   145
We made her finish it. When she had washed
the marvelous huge sheet, she showed it to us,
bright as the sun or moon. And then some spirit
of ruin brought Odysseus from somewhere
to Ithaca;[4] he went out to the fields,   150
to where the swineherd lived. His own dear son
sailed in his black ship back from sandy Pylos.
The two of them made plans to murder us.
They showed up at the palace—first the boy,
and then Odysseus propped on a stick   155
and dressed in dirty rags. He seemed to be
a poor old homeless man, who suddenly
appeared, led by the swineherd. None of us
could recognize him, even those of us
who were a little older than myself.   160
We hurled insulting words and missiles at him,
and for a while he patiently endured
abuse in his own home. But when the will
of Zeus awakened him, with his son's help,
he put the splendid weapons in the storeroom   165
and locked the door. Then came his cunning plan:
he told his wife to set for us the axes
and bow. The competition meant our doom,
the start of slaughter. None of us could string
the mighty bow—we all were far too weak.   170
But when it was his turn, we shouted out
that nobody should give the bow to him,
no matter what he said. Telemachus
alone insisted that he ought to have it.
At last Odysseus, with calm composure,   175
took it and strung it easily, and shot
all through the iron axes. Then he stood
astride the threshold with a fearsome scowl,
and started shooting fast. His arrow struck
Antinous, our leader. With sure aim   180
he shot his deadly arrows at more men;
those nearest to him fell. It was apparent

---

4. This passage seems to reflect a different version of the story, in which Odysseus arrives on Ithaca at the exact moment that Penelope is forced to finish the weaving, and also other versions in which Odysseus and Penelope collude together to kill the suitors.

some god was helping them. Impelled by rage,
they rushed around the palace killing us
in turn. There was a dreadful noise of screaming   185
and broken skulls; the whole floor ran with blood.
So, Agamemnon, we were killed. Our bodies
still lie unburied in our killer's house.
Our families at home do not yet know.
They need to wash the black blood from our wounds   190
and weep for us and lay our bodies out.
This is the honor due the dead."

                   The ghost
of Agamemnon answered, "Lucky you,
cunning Odysseus: you got yourself
a wife of virtue—great Penelope.   195
How principled she was, that she remembered
her husband all those years! Her fame will live
forever, and the deathless gods will make
a poem to delight all those on earth
about intelligent Penelope.   200
Not like my wife—who murdered her own husband![5]
Her story will be hateful; she will bring
bad reputation to all other women,
even the good ones."

                 So they spoke together,
standing in Hades, hidden in the earth.   205

Meanwhile, Odysseus and his companions
had left the town and quickly reached the farm,
won by Laertes long ago—he fought
hard for it, and his house was there; the slaves,
who had to do his wishes, lived and slept   210
and ate their food in quarters that surrounded
the central house. One was from Sicily,
the old slave woman who took care of him
out in the countryside. Odysseus
spoke to his slaves and to his son.

                 "Go in,   215
choose the best pig and kill it for our dinner.
And I will test my father, to find out
if he will know me instantly on sight,
or not—I have been absent for so long."

At that he gave his weapons to the slaves.   220
They quickly went inside. Odysseus
walked to the fruitful orchard on his quest.
He did not find old Dolius, the steward,

---

5. Clytemnestra.

nor any of his slaves or sons—he had
led them to gather rocks to build dry-walls.   235
Odysseus' father was alone,
inside the well-built orchard, digging earth
to make it level round a tree. He wore
a dirty ragged tunic, and his leggings
had leather patches to protect from scratches.   230
He wore thick gloves because of thorns, and had
a cap of goatskin. He was wallowing
in grief. The veteran, Odysseus,
seeing his father worn by age and burdened
by desperate, heartfelt sorrow, stopped beneath   235
a towering pear tree, weeping. Then he wondered
whether to kiss his father, twine around him,
and tell him that he had come home again,
and everything that happened on the way—
or question him. He thought it best to start   240
by testing him with teasing and abuse.
With this in mind, Odysseus approached him,
as he was digging round the plant, head down.
His famous son stood at his side and said,

"Old man, you know your trade and take good care   245
of this neat garden. Every plant and vine,
and tree—the figs, the pears, the olive trees—
and bed of herbs is nicely tended. But
I have to say something—please do not get
angry at me—you do not take good care   250
of your own self. You are unkempt, old man.
Your skin is rough and dirty and your clothes
are rags. Your master is neglecting you,
although you are not lazy. In your height
and face, you seem a leader, not a slave.   255
You look like someone who would bathe and eat
and sleep on fluffy pillows and fine sheets,
as is appropriate for older people.
But tell me this: whose slave are you? Whose garden
do you take care of? Also, have I come   260
to Ithaca, as somebody I met
was telling me just now? But he was not
a helpful man: when I was asking him
about a friend of mine, an old guest-friend,
whether he is alive or dead in Hades,   265
this fellow would not say, or even listen.
A while ago, in my own native land,
I had a guest to stay with me, who was
my dearest friend of all my visitors.
He said he was from Ithaca, and that   270
Laertes was his father. I had brought him
into my house, and welcomed him with warmth;
I can afford to be quite generous.

I gave him seven heaps of golden treasure,
a bowl made all of silver and inlaid   275
with flowers, twelve unfolded cloaks, and twelve
thick blankets, twelve fine mantles, and twelve tunics.
Also I gave him four well-trained slave women,
beautiful ones, whom he picked out himself."

His father answered through his tears, "Yes, stranger,   280
you have reached Ithaca. But cruel men
have taken over here. You will receive
nothing for all those gifts. If you had found him
still living in this land, he would have matched
your gifts and welcomed you with open arms   285
before he sent you home. Initial kindness
deserves due recompense. But tell me now,
how long is it since that unlucky man
visited you? Your guest was my own son!
Perhaps fish ate him out at sea, so far   290
from home and family; or birds and beasts
ate him on land. His mother did not lay
his body out and weep for him; nor I,
his father; nor Penelope his wife,
a wise and wealthy woman. She has not   295
closed her own husband's eyes or given him
a funeral. The dead deserve this honor.
But tell me now, who are you? From what city?
Who are your parents? Do you have a ship
docked somewhere, which conveyed you here with friends   300
and crew? Or did you sail as passenger
on someone else's ship, which now is gone?"

Lying Odysseus replied, "I will
tell you the truth completely. I am from
Alybas,[6] and I have a palace there.   305
My name is Eperitus; I am son
of King Apheidas, son of Polypemon.
An evil spirit struck me and I came
from Sicily against my will. My ship
is docked away from town. It is five years   310
since poor, unfortunate Odysseus
came to my home. As he was setting out
we saw good omens—birds towards the right—
so we were hopeful we would meet again
as friends, and share more gifts."

                                    At this, a cloud   315
of black grief wrapped itself around Laertes.

6. Alybas is probably a made-up place, perhaps   or "chosen." The fictional father's name, Aphei-
coined by analogy with *alaomai*, "to wander";   das, suggests "Generous," and the grandfather,
ancient scholars thought it was in southern Italy.   Polypemon, "Rich" or "Much Suffering."
The made-up name Eperitus suggests "picked"

He poured two handfuls of the ashy dust
over his gray old head, and started sobbing.
Odysseus felt heart-wrenched to see his own
beloved father in this state; sharp pain   320
pierced through his nostrils.[7] He rushed up to him
and threw his arms around him, kissing him,
and saying,

       "Father! It is me! I have
been gone for twenty years, and now am home,
in my own father's country. Stop your tears.   325
I will explain, though we do not have long.
I killed the suitors in my house; I took
revenge for all the pain they caused."

                     Laertes
answered, "If you are really my own son
Odysseus come home, show me a sign;   330
let me be sure of it."

           Odysseus
was quick to answer. "First, look here: the scar
made by the boar's white tusk when I had gone
to Mount Parnassus. You and Mother sent me,
to see my grandfather, Autolycus,   335
and get the gifts that he had promised me.
Next I will tell you all the trees that grow
in this fine orchard, which you gave to me.
When I was little, I would follow you
around the garden, asking all their names.   340
We walked beneath these trees; you named them all
and promised them to me. Ten apple trees,
and thirteen pear trees, forty figs, and fifty
grapevines which ripen one by one—their clusters
change as the weather presses from the sky,   345
sent down by Zeus."

          At that, Laertes' heart
and legs gave way; he recognized the signs
Odysseus had given as clear proof.
He threw both arms around his ruthless son,
who caught him as he fainted. When his breath   350
and mind returned, he said,

                "O Father Zeus,
you gods are truly rulers of Olympus,
if it is true the suitors have been punished

---

7. The oddly specific physiological detail has
been taken as metaphorical by some commentators, but it seems best to take it as entirely
literal: the sudden welling up of tears puts pressure on the sinuses.

for all the monstrous things they did. But I
am terrified the Ithacans may soon   355
attack us here, and spread the news around
to all the towns of Cephallenia."

Scheming Odysseus said, "Do not fear.
Come to the farmhouse, where I sent my boy
to go with the two herdsmen, to prepare   360
dinner as fast as possible."

                        With this,
the son and father walked towards the house.
They found them serving generous plates of meat
and mixing wine. The slave from Sicily
washed brave Laertes, and she rubbed his skin   365
with olive oil, and wrapped a handsome cloak
around him. Then Athena, standing near,
made him grow taller and more muscular.
When he emerged, Odysseus was shocked
to see him looking like a god. His words   370
flew fast.

          "Oh, Father! You look different!
A god has made you taller and more handsome."

Thoughtful Laertes said, "O Father Zeus,
Athena, and Apollo! If I were
as strong as when I took the sturdy fortress   375
of Nericus, out on the mainland shore,
when I was king of Cephallenia,
I would have stood beside you yesterday,
with weapons on my back, and fought with you
against the suitors who were in our house!   380
I would have brought so many of them down,
you would have been delighted!"

                        So they spoke.
The work of cooking dinner was complete,
and they sat down on chairs and stools, and reached
to take the food. The old slave Dolius   385
approached them with his sons, who had been working.[8]
Their mother, the Sicilian old woman,
had gone to call them. She took care of them,
and also the old man, made weak by age.[9]
They saw Odysseus and stared, then stopped,   390
astonished. But he spoke to reassure them.

8. Dolius is also the father of Melantho and
Melanthius, who were slaughtered by Odysseus, unbeknownst to him.

9. Presumably the old man is Dolius, though
the same slave also cares for old Laertes.

"Old man, sit down and eat. The rest of you,
put your surprise entirely out of mind.
We have been waiting ages; we are eager
to have our dinner here."

              But Dolius   395
ran straight to him with arms outstretched, and took
Odysseus' wrist and kissed his hand,
and let his words fly out.

                 "My friend! You have
come home! We are so very glad to see you!
We never thought this day would come! The gods   400
have brought you here! A heartfelt welcome to you!
I pray the gods will bless you!—Does your wife
know you have come back home? Or should I send
a message?"

           But Odysseus said coolly,
"Old man, she knows already. Do not bother."   405

So Dolius sat back down on his chair.
His sons were also clustering around
their famous owner, Lord Odysseus,
to welcome him and hold him in their arms.
Then they sat down in turn beside their father.   410
They had their meal together in the farmhouse.

Meanwhile, swift Rumor spread the news all through
the city, of the suitors' dreadful murder.
When people heard, they rushed from all directions
towards the palace of Odysseus,   415
with shouts and lamentations. Then they brought
the bodies from the house and buried them.
The ones from distant towns were sent back home
by ship. The mourners gathered in the square,
heartbroken. When the people were assembled,   420
Eupeithes first stood up and spoke to them.
This man was inconsolable with grief
for his dead son Antinous, the boy
Odysseus killed first. His father wept,
tears falling as he spoke.

               "This scheming man,   425
my friends, has done us all most monstrous wrongs.
First, he took many good men off to sail
with him, and lost the ships, and killed the men!
Now he has come and murdered all the best
of Cephallenia. Come on, before   430
he sneaks away to Pylos or to Elis,

we have to act! We will be shamed forever
unless we take revenge on him for killing
our sons and brothers. I would have no wish
to live; I would prefer to die and join   435
the boys already dead. We have to stop them
escaping overseas! Come on, right now!"

He spoke in tears, and pity seized them all.
But Medon and the bard had woken up;
they came outside and stood among the crowd.   440
They all were terrified, and Medon said,

"Now listen, Ithacans. Odysseus
could not have done such things without the help
of gods. I saw a god myself, disguised
as Mentor, sometimes standing at his side,   445
giving him will to fight, and sometimes rushing
all through the hall to make the suitors scatter.
They fell like flies."

                 Pale terror seized them all.
Then Halitherses, an old warrior,
the only one to know both past and future,   450
stood up; he wished them well. He said to them,

"Now hear me, Ithacans. My friends, it was
because of your own cowardice this happened.
You did not listen to me, or to Mentor,
when we were telling you to stop your sons   455
from acting stupidly. They did great wrong,
through their impulsiveness; they skimmed the wealth
of an important man, and disrespected
his wife, believing he would never come.
But listen now. We must not go and fight,   460
or we will bring more ruin on our heads."

At that, some stayed there, huddling together,
but more than half jumped up with shouts. They thought
Eupeithes had the right idea. They rushed
to arms, and strapped their gleaming armor on,   465
and gathered in a mass before the town.
Eupeithes was their leader—to his cost.
He thought he would avenge his murdered son.
In fact, he would not come back home; it was
his fate to die out there.

                    And then Athena   470
spoke to the son of Cronus.

                      "Father Zeus,
highest of powers! Tell what hidden thoughts

lie in you. Will you now make yet more war
and bitter strife, or join the sides in friendship?"

The Gatherer of Clouds replied, "My child,   475
why ask me this? The plan was your idea,
to have Odysseus come take revenge.
Do as you wish. But here is my advice.
He has already punished all the suitors,
so let them swear an oath that he will be   480
the king forever, and let us make sure
the murder of their brothers and their sons
will be forgotten. Let them all be friends,
just as before, and let them live in peace
and in prosperity."

                  Athena was   485
already eager; at these words she swooped
down from Olympus.

                Meanwhile, they had finished
dinner, and battle-scarred Odysseus
said, "Somebody must go and see if they
are coming near." A son of Dolius   490
obeyed and went. As he stepped out, he stood
across the threshold, and he saw them all
near to the house. At once his words took wings.
He told Odysseus,

                "Those men are near!
We have to arm, and fast!"

                They quickly armed.   495
Odysseus, his son and their two slaves
made four, and Dolius had his six sons.
Laertes and old Dolius were also
needed as fighters, though they had gray hair.
When all of them were dressed in gleaming bronze,   500
they opened up the gates and went outside;
Odysseus was leading them. Athena
came near, disguised as Mentor. When he saw her,
weathered Odysseus was glad and turned
towards Telemachus and said,

                "Now, son,   505
soon you will have experience of fighting
in battle, the true test of worth. You must
not shame your father's family; for years
we have been known across the world for courage
and manliness."

Telemachus inhaled,   510
then said, "Just watch me, Father, if you want
to see my spirit. I will bring no shame
onto your family. You should not speak
of shame."

Laertes, thrilled, cried out, "Ah, gods!
A happy day for me! My son and grandson   515
are arguing about how tough they are!"

With glinting eyes, Athena stood beside him
and said, "You are my favorite, Laertes.
Pray to the bright-eyed goddess and her father,
then lift and hurl your spear."

As she said this,   520
Athena breathed great energy inside him.
Laertes quickly raised and hurled the spear,
and struck Eupeithes through his bronze-cheeked helmet,
which did not stop the weapon; it pierced through.
Then with a thud he fell; his armor clanged   525
around him on the ground. Odysseus
charged the front line, his radiant son beside him;
they hacked with swords and curving spears. They would
have killed them all and made sure none of them
could go back home—but then Athena spoke.   530
Her voice held back the fighters.

"Ithacans!
Stop this destructive war; shed no more blood,
and go your separate ways, at once!"

Her voice
struck them with pale green fear and made them drop
their weapons. They were desperate to save   535
their lives, and they turned back towards the city.
Unwavering Odysseus let out
a dreadful roar, then crouched and swooped upon them,
just like an eagle flying from above.
But Zeus sent down a thunderbolt, which fell   540
in front of his own daughter, great Athena.
She looked at him with steely eyes and said,

"Odysseus, you are adaptable;
you always find solutions. Stop this war,
or Zeus will be enraged at you."

He was   545
glad to obey her. Then Athena made
the warring sides swear solemn oaths of peace
for future times—still in her guise as Mentor.

AESOP

ca. 620–564 B.C.E.

When people think of the literature of ancient Greece and
Rome, they hardly ever think of folk
tales. This may be partly because, in the
modern world, Aesop's fables are usually presented as children's literature—
although nobody in antiquity saw them
this way. Moreover, it is tempting to
think of "classical literature" as a particularly elevated type of writing, represented primarily by ancient tragedy
and epic. Aesop's fables, an enjoyable
hodgepodge of funny anecdotes, proverbs, animal stories, and morality tales
from the ancient Greco-Roman world,
form no part of the usual canon. But
this is, in itself, a good reason to read
them. Aesop gives us a window into
ancient culture very different from that
offered by **Homer** or **Sophocles**. These
well-known but noncanonical stories
also provoke us to reconsider our assumptions about what literature is.

Greek tradition gave the name
"Aesop" to the originator of this genre
and constructed a set of legends about
his life. He had supposedly been a slave
and was known for his ugliness and
outspokenness. But there is no reason
to believe that this has any historical
accuracy. Rather, the stories about
Aesop gave the Greeks and Romans a
way of talking about the fable form
itself: it was, like its quasifictional
inventor, lowly, down-to-earth, unpre-
tentious, and fun.

The stories that appear here are
based on a long oral and written tradition and come from a huge range of
written sources. In particular, the
Greek fable tradition seems to have
important links with tales told in Egypt,
India, and the Near East: the Indian

text the *Pañcatantra* and the tales
about the Buddha called *jātakas* seem
to parallel some of the Greek Aesopic
material. For example, the tales of
"The Lion, the Fox, and the Deer" and
the "The Fox, the Donkey, and the
Lion Skin" are both found in the *Pañcatantra*. The fables of "The Eagle and
the Farmer" and "Aesop and the Lamp"
are both paralleled in stories in the
work of the medieval Persian poet
Rumi. The story of "The Fox and the
Raven" is retold by Chaucer in the *Nun
Priest's Tale*. Additionally, Aesop's fables
include references to animals that are
not native to Greece, including the
camel, the elephant, and the dung beetle. These connections are a useful
reminder that Greek and Roman cultures were heavily influenced by those
of their neighbors, and that people from
different nations and communities
shared stories with one another.

Whereas more formal kinds of literature may remain fixed in their written
form, fables live in the mouths of those
who tell them. The ancient Greeks and
Romans probably shared fables over
dinner and drinks; fables were cited by
poets, comedians, philosophers, orators, politicians, and historians throughout classical antiquity and into the
Middle Ages. Fables are used or alluded
to by many classical writers, including
the Greek comedian **Aristophanes**, the
Roman poet **Horace**, and the later
Roman novelist **Apuleius**. **Aristophanes**' *Lysistrata*, for example, alludes
to "The Dung Beetle and the Eagle."
Fables are present from the beginnings
of Greek literature, in the eighth century B.C.E.; the genre is prominent in
the poetry of **Hesiod**, Homer's con-

temporary. We can see the stories of Prometheus and of Pandora, in Hesiod, as kinds of Aesopic fables. The earliest Greek prose collection of fables was probably made around the third century B.C.E., although this has not survived. Many later prose and verse adaptations were made by other ancient writers, including the Roman poet Phaedrus; and new collections of Aesop, with additions from the oral tradition, continued to be made until the thirteenth century C.E. and beyond. Some of the most famous Aesopic fables appear for the first time in the work of medieval Christian monks. Thus, unlike, say, **Virgil's** *Aeneid*, Aesop's fables were not produced by a single author at a single point in time; instead, they were gathered at different times by many authors, from many long-forgotten storytellers.

Many of these stories have an explicit didactic purpose—much more so than most literature. Sometimes a moral is attached to the beginning or end of the fable; sometimes a character in the story points out its implication. Since fables are told and retold many times, their interpretation may change in different tellings. We also find tensions between different fables—just as, in our own tradition, there are contradictions in proverbial wisdom: too many cooks spoil the broth, but many hands make light work. Such tensions illuminate areas of unconscious cultural disagreement.

But as a whole, the fables recommend a consistent set of values. "High" and "serious" kinds of literature, like tragedy and epic, allow us to identify, at least aspirationally, with people whose status is higher than our own; fables, by contrast, evoke characters who are lowly, and often not even human. Fables are aimed at ordinary people, not aristocrats, and often suggest the danger and folly of trying to change one's status in life, create revolution, or usurp the position of one's betters. The fable, then, is usually a conservative genre that reinforces the status quo. These stories recommend honesty and integrity: many stories mock pretentious characters, whose boasts cannot be matched by real achievement, or people whose words do not match reality; we all know what happened to the boy who cried wolf. Fables value kindness and gratitude—as in the famous story of the shepherd who pulls a thorn from a lion's paw—but also, perhaps most important, the kind of street smarts that enable a person to survive, in any circumstances. The cat's single ability, to climb a tree and escape the hounds, outweighs the fox's whole bag of tricks.

First-time readers of the fables may be surprised to discover that they are not all animal stories and that not all of them have explicit, or even implicit, morals. The various collections of Aesopic tales include all kinds of narratives lumped together. Some stories tell how the world came to be as it is—such as the tale of how the tortoise got its shell. Some feature plants or vegetables, or gods, or foolish humans rather than animals. Some attest to weird ancient beliefs about zoology—such as the claim that hyenas are hermaphrodites. Some seem to make no particular claim to moral teaching and function simply as jokes. The first fable included here, "Demades and the Athenians," is a good introduction to how the ancients may have seen the fable. The audience fails to listen when an orator tries to lecture about politics; but as soon as he begins a fable, the crowd is all ears. He launches into a story that sounds like any promising bar joke: "The goddess Demeter, a swallow, and an eel were walking together down the road." But the punch line, in this case, is that there is no punch line; the audience is robbed of its hope for a funny story. This is a fable against fables, but it is also a reminder of the main reason why they were so popular for so many centuries: fables give easy access to pure narrative pleasure. They can appeal to anybody, of any age, in any era.

From Fables[1]

Demades and the Athenians

The orator Demades[2] was trying to address his Athenian audience. When he failed to get their attention, he asked if he might tell them an Aesop's fable. The audience agreed, so Demades began his story. "The goddess Demeter,[3] a swallow, and an eel were walking together down the road. When they reached a river, the swallow flew up in the air and the eel jumped into the water." Demades then fell silent. The audience asked, "And what about the goddess Demeter?" "As for Demeter," Demades replied, "she is angry at all of you for preferring Aesop's fables to politics!"

So it is that foolish people disregard important business in favour of frivolities.

The Onager, the Donkey, and the Driver

An onager saw a donkey standing in the sunshine. The onager approached the donkey and congratulated him on his good physical condition and excellent diet. Later on, the onager saw that same donkey bearing a load on his back and being harried by a driver who was beating the donkey from behind with a club. The onager then declared, 'Well, I am certainly not going to admire your good fortune any longer, seeing as you pay such a high price for your prosperity!'

The Shepherd and the Lion[4]

While he was wandering in the fields, a lion got a thorn stuck in his paw. He immediately went to a shepherd, wagging his tail as he said, "Don't be afraid! I have come to ask your help; I'm not looking for food." The lion then lifted his paw and placed it in the man's lap. The shepherd pulled out the thorn from the lion's paw and the lion went back into the woods. Later on, the shepherd was falsely accused of a crime and at the next public games he was released from jail and thrown to the beasts. As the wild animals rushed upon him from all sides, the lion recognized that this was the same man who had healed him. Once again the lion raised his paw and placed it in the shepherd's lap. When the king understood what had happened, he commanded that the lion be spared and that the gentle shepherd be sent back home to his family.

When a man acts righteously, he can never be defeated by the punishments inflicted on him by his enemies.

The Eagle and the Farmer[5]

An eagle was caught by a farmer, but the farmer let him go when he realized what he had caught. The eagle did not forget this good deed, and when he saw

---

1. Translated by Laura Gibbs.
2. An orator and politician from the 4th century B.C.E.
3. Demeter was a goddess associated with grain and harvest. She was worshipped in a secret cult known as the Eleusinian Mysteries.

4. In another well-known version of this story, the shepherd is called Androcles.
5. A similar story is told of the prophet Muhammad by the Persian poet Rumi (Mathnawi 3.3233ff.).

the farmer sitting under a wall that was on the verge of collapsing, he snatched the bandana from the man's head, wanting to rouse the man from his seat and make him stand up. After the man set off in pursuit, the kindly eagle dropped what he had snatched and thus fully repaid the man's good deed: the man would have been crushed by the wall's collapse if he had stayed there any longer. After a while the man came back to where he had been sitting and found that the upright section of the wall had fallen to the ground.

This fable shows that if anyone does you a favour you must repay them in kind.

The Fox and the Raven[6]

A story about a fox and a raven which urges us not to trust anyone who is trying to deceive us.

The raven seized a piece of cheese and carried his spoils up to his perch high in a tree. A fox came up and walked in circles around the raven, planning a trick. "What is this?" cried the fox. "O raven, the elegant proportions of your body are remarkable, and you have a complexion that is worthy of the king of the birds! If only you had a voice to match, then you would be first among the fowls!" The fox said these things to trick the raven and the raven fell for it: he let out a great squawk and dropped his cheese. By thus showing off his voice, the raven let go of his spoils. The fox then grabbed the cheese and said, "O raven, you do have a voice, but no brains to go with it!"

If you follow your enemies' advice, you will get hurt.

The Boy Who Cried "Wolf"

There was a boy tending the sheep who would continually go up to the embankment and shout, "Help, there's a wolf!" The farmers would all come running only to find out that what the boy said was not true. Then one day there really was a wolf, but when the boy shouted they didn't believe him and no one came to his aid. The whole flock was eaten by the wolf.

The story shows that this is how liars are rewarded: even if they tell the truth, no one believes them.

The Dung Beetle and the Eagle[7]

As he was being chased by an eagle, the hare ran to the dung beetle, begging the beetle to save him. The beetle implored the eagle to respect the hare's asylum, solemnly compelling him by the sacred name of Zeus and pleading with the eagle not to disregard him simply because of his small size. But the eagle brushed the beetle aside with a flick of his wing and grabbed the hare, tearing

---

6. In the Eastern tradition there is a comparable fable that features in Buddhist texts such as the *Jātaka* stories. The Buddhist version features a crow in a tree and a jackal; the jackal praises the crow and the crow rewards him by shaking down fruit from the tree. A painted vase from the Indus Valley Civilization suggests that a similar story, along with the fable of "The Crow and the Water Jar," may have been known there in 2000 B.C.E. or earlier.

7. This fable is cited by Aristophanes in *Lysistrata*, see p. 811.

him to pieces and devouring him. The beetle was enraged and flew off together with the eagle to find the nest in which the eagle kept his eggs. After the eagle was gone, the beetle smashed all the eggs. When the eagle came back, he was dreadfully upset and looked for the creature who had smashed the eggs, intending to tear him to pieces. When it was time for the eagle to nest again, he put his eggs in an even higher place, but the beetle flew all the way up to the nest, smashed the eggs, and went away. The eagle grieved for his little ones and said that this must be the result of some angry plot of Zeus to exterminate the eagle race. When the next season came, the eagle did not feel secure keeping the eggs in his nest and instead went up to Olympus and placed the eggs in Zeus's lap. The eagle said to Zeus, 'Twice my eggs have been destroyed; this time, I am leaving them here under your protection.' When the beetle found out what the eagle had done, he stuffed himself with dung and went straight up to Zeus and flew right into his face. At the sight of this filthy creature, Zeus was startled and leaped to his feet, forgetting that he held the eagle's eggs inside his lap. As a result, the eggs were broken once again. Zeus then learned of the wrong that had been done to the beetle, and when the eagle returned, Zeus said to him, 'It is only right that you have lost your little ones, since you mistreated the beetle!' The beetle said, 'The eagle treated me badly, but he also acted very impiously towards you, O Zeus! The eagle did not fear to violate your sacred name, and he killed the one who had taken refuge with me. I will not cease until I have punished the eagle completely!' Zeus did not want the race of eagles to be wiped out, so he urged the beetle to relent. When his efforts to persuade the beetle failed, Zeus changed the breeding season of the eagles, so that it would take place at a time when the beetles were not found above ground.

The Dog in the Manger

People frequently begrudge something to others that they themselves cannot enjoy. Even though it does them no good, they won't let others have it. Listen to a fable about such an event.

There was a wicked dog lying in a manger full of hay. When the cattle came and wanted to eat, the dog barred their way, baring his teeth. The cattle said to the dog, "You are being very unfair by begrudging us something we need which is useless to you. Dogs don't eat hay, but you will not let us near it." The same thing happened when a dog was holding a bone in his mouth: the dog couldn't chew on the bone that way, but no other dog was able to chew on it either.

The fable shows that it is not easy to avoid envy: with some effort you can try to escape its effects, but it never goes away entirely.

The North Wind and the Sun

The Sun and the North Wind were quarrelling with each other as to which of the two of them would be able to make a man disrobe. The North Wind went first, blowing fiercely against the man. Yet as the man grew colder and colder, he only wrapped himself up more snugly in his cloak, clutching at it tightly so as to keep a firm grip no matter how hard the wind might be blowing. Thus the North Wind did the man no harm at all and failed to make him strip off his clothes. Next, the Sun began to shine upon the man so brightly that the very air of the day grew hotter and hotter. The man immediately took off his cloak and bundled it up on his shoulders.

The fable shows that to take a humble approach is always more effective and practical than making empty boasts.

The Fox and the Cat

Against lawyers and the like.

The fox ran into the cat and asked, "How many tricks and dodges do you know?" The cat replied, "Actually, I don't know more than one." The fox then asked the cat, "What trick is that?" The cat said, "When the dogs are chasing me, I know how to climb trees and escape." The cat then asked the fox, "And how many tricks do you know?" The fox said, "I know seventeen, and that gives me a full bag of tricks! Come with me, and I'll show you my tricks so that the dogs won't be able to catch you." The cat agreed and the two of them went off together. The hunters began to chase them with their dogs, and the cat said, "I hear the dogs; I'm scared." The fox replied, "Don't be afraid! I will give you a good lesson in how to get away." The dogs and the hunters drew nearer. "Well," said the cat, "I'm going to have to leave you now; I want to do my trick." And so the cat jumped up in the tree. The dogs let the cat go and chased the fox until they caught him: one of the dogs grabbed the fox by the leg, another grabbed his belly, another his back, another his head. The cat, who was sitting up high in the tree, shouted, "Fox! Fox! Open up your bag of tricks! Even so, I'm afraid all of them put together are not going to save you from the hands and teeth of those demons!"

The Tortoise and the Hare

The hare laughed at the tortoise's feet but the tortoise declared, "I will beat you in a race!" The hare replied, "Those are just words. Race with me, and you'll see! Who will mark out the track and serve as our umpire?" "The fox," replied the tortoise, "since she is honest and highly intelligent." When the time for the race had been decided upon, the tortoise did not delay, but immediately took off down the race-course. The hare, however, lay down to take a nap, confident in the speed of his feet. Then, when the hare eventually made his way to the finish line, he found that the tortoise had already won.

The story shows that many people have good natural abilities which are ruined by idleness; on the other hand, sobriety, zeal, and perseverance can prevail over indolence.

The Fox and the Grapes

Driven by hunger, a fox tried to reach some grapes hanging high on the vine. Although she leaped with all her strength, she couldn't manage to reach the grapes. As she went away, the fox remarked, "Oh, you aren't even ripe yet! I don't need any sour grapes."

People who speak disparagingly of things that they cannot attain would do well to apply this instructive little story to their own lives.

The Dog, the Meat, and the Reflection[8]

A dog seized some meat from the butcher shop and ran away with it until he came to a river. When the dog was crossing the river, he saw the reflection of the meat in the water, and it seemed much larger than the meat he was carrying. He dropped his own piece of meat in order to try to snatch at the reflection. When the reflection disappeared, the dog went to grab the meat he had dropped but he was not able to find it anywhere, since a passing raven had immediately snatched the meat and gobbled it up. The dog lamented his sorry condition and said, "Woe is me! I foolishly abandoned what I had in order to grab hold of a phantom, and thus I ended up losing both that phantom and what I had to begin with."

This fable is about greedy people who grasp at more than they need.

The Wolf in Sheep's Clothing[9]

You can get into trouble by wearing a disguise.

A wolf once decided to change his nature by changing his appearance, and thus get plenty to eat. He put on a sheepskin and accompanied the flock to the pasture. The shepherd was fooled by the disguise. When night fell, the shepherd shut up the wolf in the fold with the rest of the sheep, and as the fence was placed across the entrance, the sheepfold was securely closed off. But when the shepherd wanted a sheep for his supper, he took his knife and killed . . . the wolf.

Someone who wears a disguise often loses his life and finds that his performance occasions a major catastrophe.

The Fox, the Donkey, and the Lion Skin[1]

A donkey put on the skin of a lion and went around frightening all the animals. The donkey saw a fox and tried to frighten her too, but she had heard his voice first, so she said to the donkey, 'You can be sure that I too would have been afraid, if I had not already heard the sound of your bray.'

Likewise, there are certain ignorant people whose outward affectations give them an air of importance, but their true identity comes out as soon as they open their big mouths.

8. A version of this story is found in the Buddhist tradition, in the *Calladhanuggaha Jātaka*, featuring a jackal who loses his meat to a vulture while trying to get a fish; another version is found in the Indian *Pañcatantra*, with a fox who abandons his meat to hunt chickens and has his meat taken by a kite.
9. This fable, which is not classical, probably originates as a development of a line in the *New Testament*, when Jesus says, "Beware of those who come to you in sheep's clothing, but inside they are ravening wolves" (Matthew 7.15).
1. This story is paralleled in the Eastern tradition, both in the Buddhist *Sihacama-Jātaka* and in the Pañcatantra, book 3, featuring a donkey in a leopard's skin.

The City Mouse and the Country Mouse[2]

A city mouse once happened to pay a visit to the house of a country mouse where he was served a humble meal of acorns. The city mouse finished his business in the country, and by means of insistent invitations he persuaded the country mouse to come pay him a visit. The city mouse then brought the country mouse into a room that was overflowing with food. As they were feasting on various delicacies, a butler opened the door. The city mouse quickly concealed himself in a familiar mouse-hole, but the poor country mouse was not acquainted with the house and frantically scurried around the floorboards, frightened out of his wits. When the butler had taken what he needed, he closed the door behind him. The city mouse then urged the country mouse to sit back down to dinner. The country mouse refused and said, "How could I possibly do that? Oh, how scared I am! Do you think that the man is going to come back?" This was all that the terrified mouse was able to say. The city mouse insisted, "My dear fellow, you could never find such delicious food as this anywhere else in the world." "Acorns are enough for me," the country mouse maintained, "so long as I am secure in my freedom!"

It is better to live in self-sufficient poverty than to be tormented by the worries of wealth.

The Man and the Golden Eggs[3]

A man had a hen that laid a golden egg for him each and every day. The man was not satisfied with this daily profit, and instead he foolishly grasped for more. Expecting to find a treasure inside, the man slaughtered the hen. When he found that the hen did not have a treasure inside her after all, he remarked to himself, "While chasing after hopes of a treasure, I lost the profit I held in my hands!"

The fable shows that people often grasp for more than they need and thus lose the little they have.

The Old Man and His Sons

Among the folk of days gone by, there was a very elderly gentleman who had many sons. When he was about to reach the end of his life, the old man asked his sons to bring to him a bundle of slender rods, if there happened to be some lying about. One of his sons came and brought the bundle to his father. "Now try, with all your might, my sons, to break these rods that have been bound together." They were not able to do so. The father then said, "Now try to break them one by one." Each rod was easily broken. "O my sons," he said, "if you are all of the same mind, then no one can do you any harm, no matter how great his power. But if your intentions differ from one another, then what happened to the single rods is what will happen to each of you!"[4]

---

2. There is version of this fable in the Indian collection, the *Pañcatantra*, not with mice but a thin cat and a fat cat.
3. There are Eastern analogues to this fable. The *Suvannahamsa Jātaka* has a story of a father who dies and is reincarnated as a swan with golden feathers; his widow greedily plucks them

all and there are none left. The *Mahabharata* has a story of wild birds that spit gold and are killed out of spite.
4. A moral to this story reads: "Brotherly love is humanity's greatest good; even the lowly are exalted by it."

Aesop and His Lamp[5]

Once when Aesop happened to be the only slave in his master's household, he was ordered to prepare dinner earlier than usual. He thus had to visit a few houses looking for fire, until at last he found a place where he could light his lamp. Since his search had taken him out of his way along a winding path, he decided to shorten his journey on the way back and go straight through the forum. There amidst the crowds a talkative fellow shouted at him, 'Aesop, what are you doing with a lamp in the middle of the day?' 'I'm just looking to see if I can find a real man', said Aesop, as he quickly made his way back home. If that public nuisance had bothered to give this any thought, he would immediately have understood that as far as old Aesop was concerned, he was not a man at all, but only a pest who was bothering someone who had better things to do.

The Lion, the Fox, and the Deer[6]

There was a lion who had fallen ill and was lying in a stony ravine, his sluggish limbs stretched out upon the ground. A friendly fox kept him company, and one day the lion said to her, 'I suppose you want me to survive, so listen: I've got a craving for the deer who lives in that dense thicket of pines there in the wilds of the forest. At the moment I no longer have the strength to go hunting after deer myself, but if you would agree to lay a trap with that honeyed speech of yours, the deer could be within my grasp.' The sly fox went off and found the deer in the wild woodlands, gambolling in a meadow of tender grass. The fox prostrated herself before the deer and greeted her, saying that she had come to relay some auspicious information. 'As you know,' the fox said, 'the lion is my neighbour, but he is very sick and about to die, so he has been thinking about who will be king of the beasts after he is gone. The boar is an idiot, the bear is lazy, the leopard is impulsive, the tiger is a loner who keeps to himself . . . but he thinks that the deer would make a most worthy ruler, since she has an impressive appearance and lives a long time. And the antlers of the deer can scare away all kinds of snakes, why, the antlers of the deer are like trees, not at all like the horns of a bull! Need I say more? You have been duly elected: you will rule over the beasts of the hills. When that finally happens, O Mistress, remember that it was the fox who was the first to inform you. That is why I came here, and now goodbye, my dear. I need to hurry back to the lion so that he won't be looking for me again; he relies on my advice in absolutely everything. And I think it would be good if you also obeyed that venerable old head. You need to come to his bedside and comfort him in his trouble. Even little things can sway the thoughts of those who are in the last hours of life; the souls of the dying can be seen in their eyes.' This is what the sly fox said to the deer, and the deer's heart swelled at the sound of those deceitful words. She came to the hollow cave of the beast, with no idea of what lay in store for her. The lion recklessly sprang up from his bed and launched a hasty attack, but he only managed to slash the deer's ears with his pointed claws as the

5. This story may be based on a possibly true anecdote about the philosopher Diogenes the Cynic. The same fable is attributed to a "Christian ascetic" in the work of the Persian poet Rumi (*Mathnawi* 5.2887ff.).

6. This is an ancient Greek story, appearing here in an expanded medieval version. The fable also occurs in the Eastern tradition, in book 4 of the *Pañcatantra*.

wretched creature ran straight out of the door and disappeared into the depths of the woods. The fox wrung her hands in frustration, since her efforts had proved utterly futile. As for the lion, he groaned and chewed at thin air, equally beset by both hunger and despair. Once again he summoned the fox and asked her to find yet another trick to use to catch the deer. The fox plumbed the very depths of her cunning and then said, 'This is a difficult task indeed. But nevertheless I will carry out your command!' The fox then set off after the deer, keen as a hound on the trail, devising elaborate traps and all kinds of mischief. Whenever she ran into a shepherd, the fox would ask if he had happened to see a bleeding deer on the run. And when the shepherd had indeed caught a glimpse of the deer, he would point the fox in the right direction. She finally found the deer concealed in the shade, where she had stopped to catch her breath. The fox stood and stared at the deer, eyebrows raised, the very incarnation of shamelessness. A shiver ran down the deer's spine and her legs quivered as she angrily said to the fox, 'Oh you abominable creature! If you dare to come near me or utter so much as a single word, you will live to regret it! Go find some other simpletons that you can outfox; pick someone else to be king and put him on the throne!' But the fox was undaunted and said to the deer, 'Can you really be so mean-spirited? So overcome by fear? So suspicious of your friends? The lion only wanted what was good for you! In an attempt to rouse you from your former idleness, he tugged at your ear, as a father might do on his deathbed. He wanted to bestow on you every precept you would need in order to take charge of such a kingdom, but you could not even withstand the touch of his feeble hand! Instead, you violently turned aside, inflicting a serious wound on yourself. As for the lion, at this moment he is even more upset than you are. Now that he has found you to be so untrustworthy and scatter-brained, he says that the wolf will be appointed king. Alas alack, what a wicked master he will be! What shall I do then? You are the one who has brought these evils upon all of us. But come, you must be more brave in the future and not let yourself be as easily frightened as some sheep from the flock. I swear these things to you by all the leaves on the trees and by every spring of water: I want to serve you and only you! There is nothing hostile about the lion's behaviour; his heartfelt wish is to make you queen of all the animals!' With these coaxing words, the fox persuaded the tawny deer to enter once again into that very abode of death. As soon as the lion had the deer trapped in the depths of his den, he enjoyed a full-course meal, greedily devouring the flesh of the deer, drinking the marrow from her bones, and feasting on her entrails. The fox, meanwhile, stood there waiting; after having delivered the deer, she was craving a share in the spoils. She stealthily grabbed the brains of the deer which had fallen to the ground and gobbled them up: this, then, was the booty which that sly-boots got for her work. The lion, meanwhile, had made an inventory of all the deer's parts, and the brains were nowhere to be found. He searched around his couch and all over the house. Then the fox confounded the truth of the matter and said, 'That deer had no brains, so don't waste your time looking for them. What kind of brains do you expect from a creature who would come not once but twice into the den of a lion?'

SAPPHO

born ca. 630 B.C.E.

Sappho is the only ancient Greek female author whose work survives in more than tiny fragments. She was an enormously talented poet, much admired in antiquity; a later poet called her the "tenth Muse." In the third century B.C.E., scholars at the great library in Alexandria arranged her poems in nine books, of which the first contained more than a thousand lines. But what we have now are pitiful remnants: one (or possibly two) complete short poems, and a collection of quotations from her work by ancient writers, supplemented by bits and pieces written on ancient scraps of papyrus found in excavations in Egypt. Yet these fragments fully justify the enthusiasm of the ancient critics; Sappho's poems (insofar as we can guess at their nature from the fragments) give us the most vivid evocation of the joys and sorrows of desire in all Greek literature.

About Sappho's life we know almost nothing. She was born about 630 B.C.E. on the fertile island of Lesbos, off the coast of Asia Minor, and spent most of her life there. Her poems suggest that she was married and had a daughter—although we should never assume that Sappho's "I" implies autobiography. It is difficult to find any evidence to answer the questions that we most want to ask. Were these poems performed for women only, or for mixed audiences? Was it common for women to compose poetry on ancient Lesbos? How did Sappho's work win acceptance in the male-dominated world of ancient Greece? We simply do not know. We also know frustratingly little about ancient attitudes toward female same-sex relationships. In the nineteenth century, Sappho's poems were the inspiration for the coinage of the modern term *lesbian*. But no equivalent term was used in the ancient world. Sappho's poems evoke a world in which girls lived an intense communal life of their own, enjoying activities and festivals in which only women took part, in which they were fully engaged with one another. Beyond the evidence of the poems themselves, however, little remains to put these works into historical context.

What we do know, and what we must always bear in mind while reading these poems, is that they were composed not to be read on papyrus or in a book but to be performed by a group of dancing, singing women and girls (a "chorus"), to the accompaniment of musical instruments. Other poets of the period composed in the choral genre, including Alcaeus, a male contemporary who was also from Lesbos. The ancient Greek equivalent of the short, nonnarrative literary form we refer to as "lyric poetry" was literally *lyric*: it was sung to the lyre or cithara, ancestors of the modern guitar. It is not really poetry but the lyrics to songs whose music is lost. These songs evoke many vivid actions, emotions, and images, which were presumably dramatized by the dancers, who might well, for example, have acted out the swift journey of Aphrodite's chariot in poem 1 ["Deathless Aphrodite of the spangled mind"], "whipping their wings down the sky."

Sappho's poems were produced almost two hundred years after the Homeric epics, and we can read them as offering a response, and perhaps a challenge, to the (mostly masculine) world of epic. The *Iliad* concentrates on the battlefield, where men fight and die, while the *Odyssey* shows us the struggles of a male warrior to rebuild his homeland in the aftermath of war. By contrast, Sappho's poems focus on women more than men, and on feelings more than actions. Like **Homer**, Sappho often refers to the physical world in vivid detail (the stars, the trees, the flowers, the sunlight), as well as to the Olympian gods, and to mythology. But she interprets these topics very differently. In poem 44, she uses the characters of the *Iliad* but concentrates on the marriage of Hector and Andromache rather than the war. Aphrodite, goddess of love and sex, seems more important to Sappho than Zeus, the father of the gods. Poem 16 offers another reinterpretation of the Trojan War, as a story not about men fighting but about a woman in love: "Helen—left behind / her most noble husband / and went sailing off to Troy." Sappho emphasizes beauty and personal choices, and suggests that love matters more than armies, and more even than home, family, parents, or children.

But Sappho's vision of love is anything but sentimental. Many of these poems evoke intense negative emotions: alienation, jealousy, and rage. In poem 31, for example, the speaker describes her overwhelming feelings as she watches the woman she loves talking to a man: she trembles, her heart races, she feels close to death. The precise clinical detail of the narrator, as she observes herself, adds to the vividness of this account of emotional breakdown. Sappho is able to describe feelings both from the outside and from the inside, and painfully evokes a sense of distance from the beloved—and from herself: "I don't know what I should do. There are two minds in me," she says in a line from a lost poem (51). In poem 58 the speaker is suffering from a different kind of alienation: watching young girls dance and sing, she stands aside, unable to participate, and bitterly regrets the loss of her own youth.

Sappho repeatedly invokes the goddess associated with sexual desire: Aphrodite. It may be tempting to read Aphrodite as simply a personification of the speaker's own desires. But Sappho presents her as a real and terrifying force in the universe, who may afflict the speaker with all the "bittersweet" agony of love, and who may also be invoked—as in poem 1—to serve her rage and aggression, acting as Sappho's own military "ally" in her desire to inflict pain on the girl who has hurt her.

Some passages of Sappho, including the famous account of jealousy, poem 31, were preserved through quotation by other ancient writers. But many of these poems survived only on scraps of papyrus, mostly dug up from the trash-heaps of the ancient Egyptian city of Oxyrhynchus. It is exciting that we have even this much Sappho: much of our present text was discovered as late as the nineteenth century. Poem 58 was discovered (supplementing a known fragment) in 2004 in the papier-mâché-type wrapping used on an Egyptian mummy. The final poems in our selection—the "Brothers" poem and the "Cypris" poem—were made public only in 2014, as a result of a new papyrus discovery. Most of the papyrus finds are torn and crumpled, so that words and whole lines are often missing from the poems. Some of these gaps can be filled in from our knowledge of Sappho's dialect and the strict meter in which she wrote. In poem 16, for instance, at the end of the third stanza and the beginning of the fourth, the mutilated papyrus tells us that someone or something led Helen astray, and there are traces of a word that seems to have described Helen. The name *Cypris* (the "Cyprian One," the love goddess Aphrodite) and phrases that mean "against her will" or "as soon as she saw him [Paris]" would fit the spaces and the meter. Uncertain as these supplements are, they could help determine our understanding of the poem. The publication of the "New Sappho" poems is an exciting reminder that there are new discoveries to be made, even in literature from over three thousand years ago. The new pieces of Sappho have also broadened our understanding of this great poet, who composed her songs about journeys, time, mythology, and family, as well as about love, alienation, and desire.

1[1]

Deathless Aphrodite of the spangled mind,[2]
child of Zeus, who twists lures, I beg you
do not break with hard pains,
    O lady, my heart

but come here if ever before   5
you caught my voice far off
and listening left your father's
    golden house and came,

yoking your car. And fine birds brought you,
quick sparrows[3] over the black earth   10
whipping their wings down the sky
    through midair—

they arrived. But you, O blessed one,
smiled in your deathless face
and asked what (now again) I have suffered and why   15
    (now again) I am calling out

and what I want to happen most of all
in my crazy heart. Whom should I persuade (now again)
to lead you back into her love? Who, O
    Sappho, is wronging you?   20

For if she flees, soon she will pursue.
If she refuses gifts, rather will she give them.
If she does not love, soon she will love
    even unwilling.

Come to me now: loose me from hard   25
care and all my heart longs
to accomplish, accomplish. You
    be my ally.

1. Translated by Anne Carson.
2. Or "of the spangled throne"; the variant manuscripts preserve both readings (in the Greek there is a single letter's difference between them). The word translated here as "spangled" usually refers to a surface shimmering with bright contrasting colors. The reader can choose whether to imagine a goddess seated in splendor on a highly wrought throne or a love goddess whose mind is shifting and fickle.
3. Aphrodite's sacred birds.

2[4]

Come to me here from Crete to this holy
temple, to your delightful grove of apple
trees, where altars smoke
with frankincense.

16

Some say an army of horsemen, others a host of infantry,
others a fleet of ships is the most beautiful thing
on the black earth. But I say
    it's whatever you love.

It's perfectly easy to make this clear   5
to everyone. For she who surpassed
all in beauty—Helen—left behind
    her most noble husband

and went sailing off to Troy,
giving no thought at all to her child   10
or dear parents, but . . .[5]
    led her astray.

. . . for
. . . lightly
. . . reminded me now of Anactoria[6]   15
    who is not here.

I would rather see her lovely walk
and her bright sparkling face
than the chariots of the Lydians[7]
    or infantry in arms.   20

. . . not possible to happen
. . . to pray to share
. . . unexpected

4. This and the following Sappho poems and fragments are translated by Philip Freeman.
5. Ellipses represent places where the papyrus on which the poem is preserved is torn, and words, half-words, or whole lines are missing.
6. Presumably Anactoria is a girlfriend. The name may connote "princess," since *anax* means "leader" or "king." Anactoria was also an alternative name for the city of Miletus, a powerful city-state in Asia Minor.

7. A wealthy and powerful non-Greek people in Asia Minor, with whom Sappho, living in Lesbos just off the coast, is evidently familiar. A generation or so later, the Lydians would be absorbed into the expanding Persian Empire, but in Sappho's time they were at the height of their prosperity.

17

Come close to me, I pray,
Lady Hera, and may your graceful form appear,
you to whom the sons of Atreus prayed,
        those glorious kings,[8]

after they had accomplished many great deeds,   5
first at Troy, then on the sea.
They came to this island, but they could not
        complete their voyage home

until they called on you and Zeus the god of suppliants
and Thyone's lovely child.[9]   10
So now be kind and help me too,
        as in ancient days.

Holy and beautiful . . .
virgin . . .
around . . .   15

to be . . .
to arrive . . .

31[1]

He seems to me equal to gods that man
whoever he is who opposite you
sits and listens close
        to your sweet speaking

and lovely laughing—oh it   5
puts the heart in my chest on wings
for when I look at you, even a moment, no speaking
        is left in me

no: tongue breaks and thin
fire is racing under skin   10
and in eyes no sight and drumming
        fills ears

---

8. The sons of Atreus are Menelaus and Agamemnon. In the *Odyssey* (3.133ff.) we find the story of the brothers quarreling after the fall of Troy, and according to Homer, Menelaus stopped to pray to Zeus on Lesbos while Agamemnon traveled separately. Sappho's poem suggests a different legend, in which both brothers together came to her island, and prayed to Hera and Dionysos (son of Thyone) as well as Zeus.

9. Thyone is the new name given to Dionysos' mortal mother, Semele, after she was rescued from Hades by her son and became an Olympian goddess associated with frenzy.

1. Translated by Anne Carson.

and cold sweat holds me and shaking
grips me all, greener than grass
I am and dead—or almost   15
   I seem to me.

But all is to be dared, because even a person of poverty[2]

44[3]

Cyprus. . . .[4]
the herald came . . .
Idaeus, the swift messenger[5]
". . . and the rest of Asia . . . undying glory.
Hector and his companions are bringing the lively-eyed,   5
graceful Andromache from holy Thebe and ever-flowing
Placia[6] in their ships over the salty sea, along with many golden
 bracelets
and perfumed purple robes, beautifully painted ornaments
and countless silver cups and ivory."
So he spoke. Quickly Hector's dear father[7] rose up   10
and the news spread among his friends in the spacious city.
At once the sons of Ilus[8] yoked mules to the
smooth-running carts, then the whole crowd
of women and maidens with . . . ankles climbed on board.
The daughters of Priam apart . . .   15
the young men yoked horses to chariots . . .
in great style . . .
charioteers . . .
. . . like the gods
. . . holy together   20
set out . . . to Ilium
the sweet-sounding flute and the cithara mingled
and the sound of castanets. Maidens sang a holy song
and a wondrous echo reached to the sky . . .
everywhere in the streets was . . .   25
mixing-bowls and drinking cups . . .
myrrh and cassia and frankincense mingled.

2. The quotation that is our only source for this poem breaks off here, although this looks like the beginning of a new stanza.
3. This and the following Sappho poems and fragments are translated by Philip Freeman. This poem is our only surviving example of Sappho's narrative poetry. It is composed in the same meter as Homer's epics, dactylic hexameter (unlike all Sappho's other surviving work). It tells the story of the wedding of Hector, prince of Troy, and Andromache, characters famous in myth who feature in the *Iliad*. Some scholars believe this poem may have been composed for performance at a wedding.
4. The island of Cyprus was one of the most important cult centers of Aphrodite. It is not clear how the island related to the beginning of the poem, which is lost.
5. Herald of Troy, a character in the *Iliad*.
6. Homeland of Andromache, in central Greece.
7. Priam, king of Troy.
8. The Trojans; Ilus was the legendary founder of Troy, also known as Ilium.

The older women cried out with joy
and all the men erupted in a high-pitched shout
calling on Paean, far-shooting god skilled with the lyre.   30
They sang in praise of godlike Hector and Andromache.

47

Love shook my heart
like a mountain wind falling on oaks.

48

You came and I was longing for you.
You cooled my heart burning with desire.

51

I don't know what I should do. There are two minds in me

55[9]

But when you die you will lie there and there will be no memory
of you nor longing for you after, for you have no share in the roses
of Pieria.[1] But you will wander unseen in the house of Hades,[2]
flying about among the shadowy dead.

58[3]

. . . I pray
. . . now a festival
. . . under the earth
. . . having a gift of honor
. . . as I am now on the earth   5
. . . taking the sweet-sounding lyre
. . . I sing to the reed-pipe

9. This is a quotation from a lost longer poem, apparently addressed to a rich but talentless woman.
1. Birthplace of the Muses.
2. God of the dead.

3. The first part of this poem has been known since 1922 from a fragmentary papyrus, but the second part (beginning ". . . beautiful gifts") was discovered on another papyrus only in 2004.

. . . fleeing
. . . was bitten
. . . gives success to the mouth   10

. . . beautiful gifts of the violet-laden Muses, children
. . . the sweet-sounding lyre dear to song.
. . . my skin once soft is wrinkled now,
. . . my hair once black has turned to white.
My heart has become heavy, my knees   15
that once danced nimbly like fawns cannot carry me.
How often I lament these things—but what can be done?
No one who is human can escape old age.
They say that rosy-armed Dawn once took
Tithonus,[4] beautiful and young, carrying him to the   20
ends of the earth. But in time grey old age still
found him, even though he had an immortal wife.
. . . imagines
. . . might give
I love the pleasures of life . . . and this to me.   25
Love has given me the brightness and beauty of the sun.

94

. . . "I honestly wish I were dead."
Weeping she left me

with many tears and said this:
"Oh, this has turned out so badly for us, Sappho.
Truly, I leave you against my will."   5

And I answered her:
"Be happy and go—and remember me.
for you know how much we loved you.

But if not, I want to remind
you . . .   10
. . . and the good times we had.

For many crowns of violets
and roses and . . .
. . . you put on by my side,

and many woven garlands   15
made from flowers
around your soft throat,

---

4. According to myth, the goddess Dawn fell in
love with a Trojan boy called Tithonus and carried him off to be with her. She made him
immortal but could not make him immune to
old age. In some versions of the myth, he turned
into a cicada, whom the Greeks imagined as
eternally singing—a kind of insect poet.

and with much perfume
costly . . .
fit for a queen, you anointed yourself.   20

And on a soft bed
delicate . . .
you let loose your desire.

And not any . . . nor any
holy place nor . . .   25
from which we were absent.

No grove . . . no dance
. . . no sound

102

Truly, sweet mother, I cannot weave on the loom,
for I am overcome with desire for a boy because of slender Aphrodite.

104

104A

Evening, you gather together all that shining Dawn has scattered.
You bring back the sheep, you bring back the goat, you bring back
    the child to its mother.

104B

. . . most beautiful of all the stars

105[5]

105A

. . . like the sweet apple that grows red on the lofty branch,
at the very top of the highest bough. The apple-pickers have forgotten it
—no, not forgotten, but they could not reach it.

---

5. This and the next fragment may be from wedding songs. Perhaps the bride, a virgin inaccessible to men until marriage, is compared to the apple. The hyacinth may also be a reference to virginity.

105B

. . . like the hyacinth shepherds tread underfoot
in the mountains, and on the ground the purple flower

111[6]

Raise high the roof—
Hymenaeus!
Raise it up, carpenters—
Hymenaeus!
The bridegroom is coming, the equal of Ares,   5
and he's much bigger than a big man.

112

Blessed bridegroom, your wedding has been accomplished
just as you prayed and you have the maiden bride you desired.

Your form is graceful and your eyes . . .
honey-sweet. Love pours over your lovely face . . .
. . . Aphrodite has greatly honored you   5

114

"Virginity, virginity, where have you gone? You've deserted me!"
"Never again will I come to you, never again will I come."

130

Once again limb-loosening Love makes me tremble,
that bittersweet, irresistible creature.

132

I have a beautiful child who is like golden flowers
in form, my beloved Cleis,[7] for whom
I would not take all of Lydia or lovely . . .

6. This and the next two fragments are certainly from wedding songs. Hymenaeus is the
god of marriage.

7. Sadly, nothing more is known about Cleis,
beyond this fragment.

168B

The moon has set
and the Pleiades.[8] It's the middle
of the night and time goes by.
I lie here alone.

The Brothers Poem[9]

But you are always chattering that Charaxus is coming
with a full ship.[1] These things, I suppose, Zeus
knows and all the other gods. But you should not
      worry about them.

Instead send me and ask me to call on   5
and make many prayers to Queen Hera
that Charaxus return here,
    steering his ship,

and find us safe and sound. Everything else,
all of it, let us leave to the gods.   10
For fair weather comes quickly
        from great storms.

Those to whom the king of Olympus[2] wishes
to send a helpful spirit to banish toils,
these will be happy   15
   and rich in blessings.

And we—if someday his head is freed from labor
and Larichus[3] becomes a gentleman of leisure
—may we be delivered quickly
        from great heaviness of heart.   20

The Cypris Poem

How can a person not be so often distressed,
Queen Cypris,[4] about someone
you want so much to make
        your own?

8. A cluster of stars known as the Seven Sisters.
9. The Brothers poem and the Cypris poem that follows were first published in 2014, from a new papyrus find.
1. Charaxus is known from Herodotus as the name of one of Sappho's brothers. He was supposedly a trader in Lesbian wine. This poem is missing the first stanza or two, so the context of the reference is hard to construct.
2. Zeus.
3. Larichus is also a brother of Sappho's, presumably younger than Charaxus.
4. Cypris is Aphrodite, goddess of love and sex. Presumably this is a single stanza from a much longer poem.

ANCIENT ATHENIAN DRAMA

Modern readers usually find Athenian drama easy to appreciate. Aristophanes' physical, earthy humor is still funny today, and his wild fantasies raise political and social questions that are still relevant in modern times. The tragedies of **Aeschylus**, **Sophocles**, and **Euripides** provide compelling stories about human relationships, whose absorbing, often violent or melodramatic plots invite us to think about profound issues, such as the nature of justice, the meaning of suffering, and clashes between family and state and between human and divine perspectives.

But the original performance contexts of Greek drama were radically different from anything modern readers and theatergoers have experienced. The city festivals of Athens, at which all new comedies and tragedies were first performed, involved a mixture of things we usually regard as wholly separate: politics, religion, music, poetry, serious drama, slapstick, open-air spectacles, and dance. For the combination of drama with song and dance, in a popular format performed for large audiences, our closest analogy might be the Broadway musical. Like Greek tragedy, shows such as *Beauty and the Beast* and *The Little Mermaid* update a traditional, mythic story for a contemporary audience. But Broadway shows usually take place indoors, and have no obvious connection to politics or religion. To get a sense of the strangeness of Athenian dramatic festivals, imagine a major public political event, like the inauguration of a new American president,

combine it with a major religious gathering like an evangelical rally, a papal audience, or the Hajj to Mecca, then add to the mix the Cannes Film festival, a Veterans Day march, a Thanksgiving Day parade (with all the floats), and a grand open-air musical event like Woodstock. The resulting hybrid would be a modern equivalent of the two main Athenian religious occasions that included major dramatic performances: the Great Dionysia and the Lernaea. Both festivals included tragedy and comedy, although tragedy was more central to the Dionysia, while comedy played a larger role at the Lernaea.

Both festivals were held in honor of the god Dionysus, who was associated with wine and, more generally, with overturning the rules and conventions of the normal world. Dionysus was a wild figure: he rode a chariot pulled by leopards, dressed in strange, effeminate clothing and an ivy crown, and was accompanied by ecstatic, crazy women (the maenads) and hairy, permanently erect half-goat men called satyrs. The Athenians knew him as an exotic, foreign god who originated somewhere in Asia Minor before being incorporated in the Olympian pantheon. We should remember the subversive, outsider status of this god when reading Athenian drama.

We know very little about the origins of tragedy or comedy. The word *comedy* seems to come from *komos*, a Greek word denoting a drunken procession. Aristotle tells us that *tragedy* (*tragoidia* in Greek) means "goat song," and suggests that the genre originated as part of a ritual in which a goat was sacrificed or offered as a prize. Sometime in the late sixth century B.C.E., rural celebrations in honor of Dionysus became an official, annual part of the urban festival calendar. Originally, the main entertainment was probably choruses of dancers, who sang hymns and competed for prizes; later, some form of tragedy and, later still, comedy were added to the program. Thespis, from whose name we get the term *thespian*—a character about whom we know next to nothing—is traditionally said to have invented tragedy in the year 534 B.C.E. He "stepped out of the Chorus," creating a part for a single actor who could talk back to the chorus. The invention of the individual actor, distinct from the group, was enormously important: it paved the way for the whole subsequent history of Western drama.

Tragedy was something new in the late sixth century, but contests of poetry in performance had long been a part of Athenian culture. At the largest city festival, the Panathenaia ("All-Athenian," in honor of the city's goddess, Athena), performers called rhapsodes recited parts of **Homer**'s *Iliad* and *Odyssey*; the best performers won prizes. The Homeric poems were an essential model for later drama. Aeschylus supposedly called his own work "slices from the feast of Homer." It was not merely the plots of Greek tragedy that were "Homeric," although like the *Iliad* and *Odyssey* many tragedies dealt with the heroes who fought in the Trojan War. Dramatists also learned from Homer how to create vivid dialogue and fast, exciting narrative, as well as sympathy for a range of different characters, Greek and foreigner alike.

Each year at the Great Dionysia, three tragic poets were chosen by the official city governor (the *archon*) to produce a tetralogy of plays for each day's entertainment. Performances began at dawn and included three tragedies, which might or might not concentrate on a

This detail from the so-called Pronomos Vase, painted in the late fifth century B.C.E., depicts actors preparing for a satyr play.

linked set of stories, followed by a lighter play featuring satyrs (a "satyr play"). A rich Athenian citizen put up the money to pay for the costs of each day's performance, including purchase of costumes and masks, and training of the chorus members and actors. These producers prided themselves on their participation, and gloated if the performance they had financed won the competition: at least one backer tried to rig the results by making a night raid to destroy the gold crowns and costumes that had been ordered for his rival's chorus to wear. Before the dramatic performances began, the tribute paid to the city of Athens by her allies was heaped up in the theater for all to see, and the orphans

A contemporary photograph of the remains of the theater of Dionysus in Athens.

of Athenian men killed in war in the previous year marched in front of the audience, wearing armor provided at the expense of the city. Athenian drama itself can be seen as a comparable display, a demonstration to foreigners and to the Athenians themselves of the city's artistic and intellectual riches, as well as a meditation on its vulnerability.

The only complete works of Greek drama that have survived are a small selection of the tragedies of Aeschylus, Sophocles, and Euripides, and a few comedies by Aristophanes. But of course far more people composed plays in this period, some of which were probably excellent; there were other poets—such as Agathon, the tragedian who appears in **Plato**'s *Symposium*—who were awarded first prize in the competitions. We have just the names of most of these other dramatists, along with some titles and some tantalizing fragments.

Similarly, the scripts are all that survive of Greek drama, and wishful thinking leads us to imagine that what we have is the most important part: we tend to think of these plays simply as "literature," words on a page. But the

words must have formed only a small part of the total effect of the original performances. Those sitting in the upper areas of the theater may well not have been able to hear everything, despite the good acoustics of the theater. The music, gestures, costumes, props, and visual effects may well have had a larger impact on most audience members than any individual detail of phrasing. Writing the script was also a tiny part of the work of a dramatist. The poet was also the director, composer, and choreographer of the plays he created; in the earliest days of drama, the poets were probably also actors in their own work. The prizes were not awarded for writing, but for the work of coaching the actors and dancers: the usual phrase to describe what a dramatist does is "to teach a chorus." In 425, when Aristophanes wrote his first play but had it directed by somebody else, the prize was awarded to the director, not the poet.

The theater of Dionysus, where the plays were performed, held at least 13,000 people, perhaps as many as 17,000—a number comparable to the seating available in Madison Square

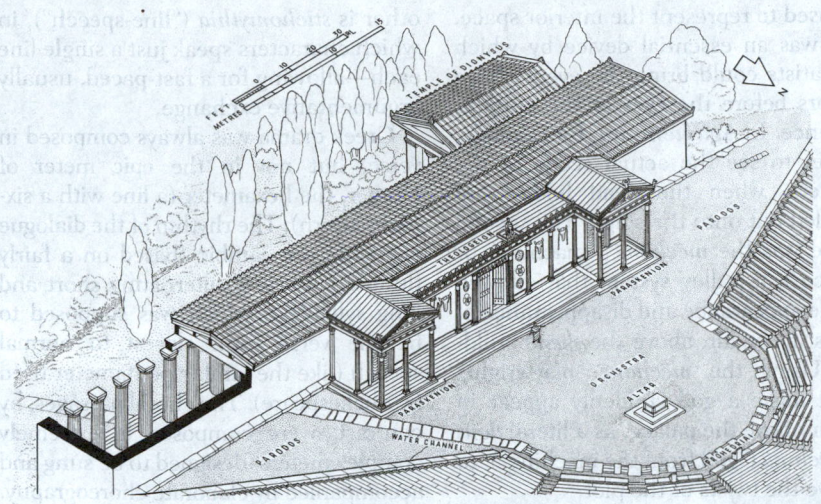

A reconstruction of the Dionysus theater by the theater and architectural scholar Richard Leacroft. An actor stands in the *orchēstra*, while another stands on the roof of the *skēnē*.

Garden. This figure represents a high proportion of the male citizen body, estimated to have been about forty or sixty thousand people—although the total population of Athens, including women, children, foreigners, and slaves, may have been ten times that large.

It is possible that a few women came to the theater in the fifth century; women were almost certainly in attendance by the fourth century. We do not know whether slaves were present. In any case, the majority of the audience consisted of male citizens. In the participatory democracy of fifth-century Athens, the whole citizen body was eligible to participate in policy making, and citizens were accustomed to meet together in public to determine military and domestic policy, at least once a month and usually more often. The structure of the dramatic festival was reminiscent of other political assemblies, where citizens sat to hear speeches on several sides of a case and made their decisions between competing sides.

The theater was an open-air venue, with seating in the round. The central space, called the *orchēstra* (which means "dancing area"), lay at the lowest point of the valley; on the slopes of the hill, spectators sat on wooden benches, surrounding the performance area on three sides. At one end of the *orchēstra* was a wooden platform or stage, with a wooden building on it (the *skēnē*), which could be used to represent whatever interior space was necessary for the play: a palace, a house, a cave, or any other type of structure. There were thus three possible ways for actors to come on and off stage: to the left or right of the stage, or through the doors of the building. Entrances and exits tend to be particularly important in Greek drama, because they took a long time; the audience would have been watching the characters make their way into the playing area before they actually reached the stage. When reading these plays, it is a good idea to pay particular attention to the moments when a new character comes on.

There were also two major structural devices that expanded the possibilities of the playing space. The *ekkuklēma* ("trolley" or "thing that rolls out") was a wooden platform on wheels, which could be trundled out from the central doors of the *skēnē*, and was conventionally used to represent the interior space. This was an essential device by which dramatists could bring the events from indoors before the eyes of the outdoor audience. In *Agamemnon*, for example, we get to see the actual scene of the murders, when the dead bodies are wheeled out onto the stage. The second device was the *mēchanē* ("machine" or "device"), a pulley system that allowed for the appearance and disappearance of actors in the air, above the *skēnē* building. Using the *mēchanē*, playwrights could make a god suddenly appear in the air above the palace, as a literal *deus ex māchinā* ("god from the machine"), to resolve the twists of the plot.

All the actors who performed in Athenian drama were men—including those playing female parts. All actors wore masks. Tragedy and comedy both used a tiny number of actors for the speaking parts. In the first few decades of the century, there were only two actors; later, three actors were used. This meant that the same actors had to play multiple roles, appearing in different masks as the play required. The use of masks, as well as the open-air space, must have necessitated a very different style of acting from that of modern cinema, television, or stage. Facial expressions would have been invisible behind the mask, and were therefore irrelevant; instead, actors must have relied on gestures, body language, and a strongly projected voice.

The dialogue sections of ancient Athenian plays usually show two— occasionally three—characters in confrontation or discussion with one another. Dialogue may be free-flowing and apparently natural. But dramatists made use of two important dialogue techniques. One is the *agon* ("contest" or "struggle"), in which one character makes a long, sometimes legalistic speech, arguing a particular case, and a second character replies with another speech, putting the case against. The

other is *stichomythia* ("line-speech"), in which characters speak just a single line each—allowing for a fast-paced, usually argumentative exchange.

Greek drama was always composed in verse, but not in the epic meter of Homer, the hexameter (a line with a six-part pattern). The rhythm of the dialogue elements was iambic (based on a fairly flexible pattern of alternating short and long syllables), which was supposed to be the verse form closest to normal speech (like the iambic pentameter used by Shakespeare). The choral passages, by contrast, were composed in extremely complex meters, designed to be sung and accompanied by elaborate choreography. Athenian drama thus combined two very different theatrical experiences, interspersing plot-driven, character-heavy dialogue with music, poetry, and dance.

The chorus was composed of twelve—later, fifteen—masked dancers, of whom only one, the "leader," had a speaking role. This group is used in different ways by the different dramatists, and varies radically from play to play. In comedy, the choruses are often nonhuman: Aristophanes, whose plays are frequently named for the chorus, created groups of frogs, birds, wasps, and clouds. The choruses of tragedy are usually more naturalistic; a notable exception is the divine, snake-haired Furies who form the chorus of Aeschylus's *Eumenides*.

The chorus is often a group of inhabitants of the place where the action occurs: it can be used to represent the voice of the ordinary person or the word on the street—although it does not always express common sense, and it frequently fails to get things right. Sometimes the chorus listens sympathetically to the main characters, acting as an internal audience and allowing for the revelation of inner thoughts that might otherwise be hard for the dramatist to bring out. Sometimes, on the other hand, the chorus is either neutral or positively hostile toward the main characters. Choruses can be characters themselves, with their own biases and preoccupations.

The choral songs and dances can allow the dramatist to put the events of the play in a broader perspective: the chorus may take us back in time, looking to earlier events in the same myth, or tracing parallels between this story and others; or it may reflect on the ethical, theological, and metaphysical implications of the events at hand. The poet may also use the chorus to provide a break from the main narrative, a switch to an entirely different mood or perspective. Choral songs can increase the dramatic tension or surprise, as when a cheerful, optimistic song is followed by disaster.

Mutilation and violent death, by murder or suicide, accident, fate, or the gods, are frequent events in Greek tragedy. The threat of violence—which may or may not be averted—provides a strong element in the interest of these plays. But compared to modern television drama or action movies, there is little visible horror. Dead bodies are often displayed onstage, but the actual killing usually takes place offstage. The messenger speech is therefore one of the most important conventions of Athenian drama. Long, vivid, blow-by-blow accounts of offstage disasters allow the audience to imagine and visualize events that the dramatist cannot or will not bring onstage.

Comic poets made up their own plots from scratch, and were able to create stories that combined reality, fantasy, and myth however they chose. Comic poets could depict caricatures of real people—famous politicians, fellow poets like Euripides, or the philosopher Socrates—mixing with made-up characters, as well as with gods and heroes (like Dionysus and Heracles) and personifications (like "The People"). Comedy often made direct references to recent events, and parodied, satirized, or directly attacked the behavior of real contemporary people.

The plots of Greek tragedy, by contrast, focus on a few traditional story patterns, set in the distant past and in non-Athenian city-states: Argos, Thebes, or Troy. But though tragedians used preexisting stories, they felt free, within reason, to shape the myths in their own way; for instance, Aeschylus, Sophocles, and Euripides created very different plays focused on the story of Electra, daughter of the murdered Agamemnon. Tragedy was often relevant in some way to contemporary concerns, but its political and social perspectives are never as explicit as those of comedy.

Since Greek tragedy and comedy were always performed at a religious festival, we might expect these dramas to be more obviously "religious" than they seem at first blush. Comedians often bring gods on stage, but they are not treated in a markedly reverent way: for instance, Dionysus in **Aristophanes'** *Frogs* is a craven coward with a flatulence problem. The power of the gods is usually a more serious issue in tragedy, but even here, modern readers may be surprised at how cruel and unreliable the Greek gods often seem to be. It is perhaps helpful to remember that Athenians of the fifth century—unlike most believers in modern monotheistic religions—saw no necessary connection between religion and morality. Gods are, by definition, immortal and powerful; they need not also be nice. Athenian drama was an act of service to the gods in general, and to Dionysus in particular, because it overturned the everyday world and explored the power of the imagination, showing—in Euripides' words—"how god makes possible the unexpected." By serving the gods, displaying the strange and surprising ways that divine forces operate on human lives, Athenian dramatists were also serving their audiences, creating dramas that were gripping, profound, and unpredictable: qualities that readers still appreciate in these works today.

AESCHYLUS

ca. 524–456 B.C.E.

Aeschylus is the earliest Greek
dramatist whose work survives.
His plays represent the first stage in
the long history of later Western drama.
But Aeschylean tragedy is by no
means primitive or simple. Aeschylus
was a dramatic innovator: his most
important invention was the introduction of the second actor, which created the possibility of conflict between
individuals (rather than simply between
a single actor and the group of the
chorus). This essential move caused
him to be called the "creator of tragedy."
His language, imagery, and stagecraft
are highly sophisticated, his characters are complex and compelling, and
his work invites deep meditation on
relationships between myth and history, men and women, justice and suffering, language and meaning, human
and divine.

LIFE AND TIMES

Aeschylus's life and work were closely
tied up with the changing political situation of Greece in his time. He was
born in the late sixth century, around
524 B.C.E., in the town of Eleusis, in
Attica. The main city of the region was
Athens, a major city-state (*polis*), which
included the rural area outside the city,
as well as the urban downtown. Aeschylus's life was dominated by the strato-
spheric cultural, political, economic,
and military rise of Athens, where he
lived and worked. During this period,
Athens changed its political system
from tyranny to democracy, fought
off foreign invaders against enormous
odds, and grew to become the most

powerful community in the contemporary Mediterranean world.

When Aeschylus was born, Athens
was not yet a democratic state. From 541
to 510, the city was under one-man rule,
dominated by a "tyrant" (a single, powerful ruler; the word in Greek does not
necessarily carry negative connotations).
In 510 B.C.E., after the last tyrant was
ousted from power, Athens became one
of the world's first democracies. From
this time onward, the city was governed
by a fifty-member council, which was
elected by the votes of all citizens. The
majority of the population—including
women, slaves, and resident foreigners—
were not citizens and did not get a vote.
But the shift from tyranny to the new
political system of democracy, which
took place when Aeschylus was around
fifteen years old, was an enormously
significant one. Democracy created a
sense of community and pride among
Athenian citizens, which helped them
band together with other Greek states
against a major military threat: the invading Persian Empire.

Darius the Great, ruler of Persia,
built up the largest empire the world
had yet seen. He subdued many parts
of the Greek world, and in 490 B.C.E.
tried to defeat the remaining cities, in
a fierce battle in the bay of Marathon
near Athens. All Athenian men of
fighting age, including Aeschylus and
his brother, Cynegeirus, gathered in
defense, and, despite being outnumbered at least two to one, the Athenians were the victors. Cynegeirus
was fatally wounded when his arm was
chopped off by an enemy battle-axe,
but Aeschylus lived to tell the tale.

Ten years later, Darius's son Xerxes mustered the Persian forces again, and again invaded Attica. On land, the Greek forces, led by the Spartan general Leonidas and his three hundred men, were slaughtered at Thermopylae. But by sea, in the bay of Salamis, the Athenian navy—probably including Aeschylus—won a decisive victory, sinking hundreds of Persian ships and destroying Xerxes's hope of expanding his father's empire. The battle of Salamis was a turning point in the history of Athens, and arguably in the whole history of later Western culture. After this victory, Athens was free from foreign invasion and eventually became the dominant power in the Greek and Mediterranean worlds.

A few years after Salamis, in 472 B.C.E., Aeschylus produced *Persians*, which is our earliest surviving Greek tragedy. *Persians* focuses on the battle of Salamis, but told from the Persian point of view: it evokes the devastation of Xerxes, his army, his family, and his people as a result of the Greek victory. Aeschylus encourages his audience to sympathize with and weep for the defeated. But he also celebrates Greek victory, and frames it in explicitly ideological terms. Whereas the Persians are subject to the rule of the emperor and his family, the Greeks, led by democratic Athens, are fighting for freedom: they urge each other on with the inspiring cry "Forward, you sons of Hellas! Set your country free!" The trilogy that included *Persians* was awarded first prize at the Great Dionysia, and it established Aeschylus's reputation as the finest tragedian of his day.

Aeschylus was a successful and prolific artist, who composed some ninety tragedies. Many won first prize in the Great Dionysia. Only seven complete plays survive: *Persians, Seven against Thebes, Suppliant Women, Prometheus Bound* (whose authorship has been doubted by some modern scholars),

and the three plays of the *Oresteia: Agamemnon, Libation Bearers,* and *Eumenides.*

Aristophanes' comedy *Frogs*, which was first performed in 405 B.C.E.—some fifty years after Aeschylus's death—provides our most vivid evidence for the tragedian's contemporary reputation. The play features a competition, set in Hades (since both competitors are dead), between Aeschylus and **Euripides**, to decide who is the poet most likely to save the city in times of war. Aeschylus's style is presented as heavy, dignified, nonnaturalistic, and full of strange or archaic turns of phrase, which may be all but incomprehensible. At the same time, he inspires his audiences to feel proud of and fight for their city: anybody witnessing *Persians*, boasts Aeschylus, would be "smitten / with longing for victory over the enemy." But it would be a mistake to see Aeschylus as a simple propagandist. He draws our attention to deep-rooted moral, political, and religious conflicts.

Around 456 B.C.E., two years after the production of what contemporaries agreed was his masterpiece, the *Oresteia*, Aeschylus died in the Greek city of Gela in Sicily, supposedly killed by a falling tortoise. His four-line epitaph celebrates him as a brave patriot, whose finest achievement was his military service on behalf of his country. The lines emphasize his participation in the battle of Marathon against the Persian invasion and make no mention of the fact that he also wrote plays:

> This tomb hides Aeschylus, son of
>   Euphorion,
> the Athenian, who died in fruitful
>   Gela.
> The sacred battlefield of Marathon
>   could tell his famous courage,
> And the long-haired Mede, who
>   knows it well.

THE WORK

Aeschylus's *Agamemnon* is the first play in a trilogy of three linked plays, the *Oresteia,* which was composed and first performed in the year 458 B.C.E. The *Oresteia* is the only complete trilogy we have from ancient Athens. It was clearly a great success: Aeschylus was awarded first prize by the competition judges, and subsequent works by Aeschylus's younger contemporaries, **Sophocles** and Euripides, often refer back to the *Oresteia*.

Agamemnon is the legendary king of Mycenae whose brother, Menelaus, husband of Helen, led the Greek forces in their war against Troy to get Helen back and avenge Menelaus's honor. As *Agamemnon* begins, the king himself is still absent from his home; he has not yet returned from the war. A chorus of twelve old men of Argos evokes the helplessness of those left at home as they wait for news from the war. Then they take us back in time, recalling—in somewhat elliptical fashion—the most important event lying behind the events of the play: Agamemnon's killing of his own daughter, Iphigeneia. It is essential to keep this backstory in our minds as we read the rest of *Agamemnon*. After the abduction of Helen by Paris, the Greek fleet assembled at Aulis, ready to sail to Troy. But the ships were becalmed: no wind came. Calchas, the prophet, then told Agamemnon that he must sacrifice his daughter in order to bring wind to let the fleet sail to Troy. Agamemnon, we are told, had a moment of terrible indecision, but chose, in the end, to kill his own child rather than betray his fleet. The chorus gives us a tear-jerking account of her death: the beautiful young girl, who has often sung at her father's dinner parties, is gagged and slaughtered. The gods send the winds; the ships sail.

Iphigeneia's death is important because it anticipates many of the themes of the play. It is the first of a series of conflicts between a man and a woman, and between different models of justice. Loyalty to family seems irreconcilable with loyalty to the city or the group. This first death of the Trojan War initiates a long series of killings of the innocent and the guilty at Troy, of enemies in battle but also of one family member by another at home.

We may be able to guess that the evils of Aulis will lead to further evils back home in Argos; we may intuit, at least, that this story will not have a happy ending. But it is important to Aeschylus's technique that the threat is oblique, hinted at by symbols and metaphors, and the actual outcome is not revealed until the final scene. Knowledge, in *Agamemnon,* comes slowly, and only at the cost of human suffering. The chorus declares that Zeus himself has established the principle that wisdom comes by suffering: *pathei mathos* (in Greek, *pathos,* suffering, rhymes with *mathos,* learning or wisdom). But the chorus's odes make us face hard questions about how the relationship between suffering and understanding works: whether pain makes people, or societies, better or whether suffering simply teaches us how to suffer. The will of the gods—the most important here being Zeus—remains dark to humans, who struggle to find a moral purpose in the universe.

The atmosphere of the play—mysterious and heavy with foreboding—is created largely through Aeschylus's manipulation of the audience's point of view, and especially through his use of the chorus. This chorus, much more than most Greek choruses, is put in the same position as the audience. Like us, it must watch and wait, and struggle to make sense of events as they unfold. Our identification with the chorus, and with the watchman who begins the play, is increased because the dramatic action of *Agamemnon* happens, as it were, in real time: the performance, like the play, would have begun at dawn.

As always in Greek tragedy, sections of dialogue between characters, and between the chorus and individual characters, alternate with choral sections in much more complex meters, when chorus members danced and sang in the central "dancing space" (*orchēstra*). In *Agamemnon*, the choral songs (or "odes") help put the main story into a larger causal pattern. They look back in time—for instance, to the killing of Iphigeneia and to the abduction of Helen by Paris—and they also search, apparently without much success, for a theological or moral pattern in the strange events they see.

The chorus plays a more central role in *Agamemnon* than in later Greek tragedies, such as **Oedipus the King** or **Medea**. Instead of simply commenting on the actions and dialogue of the characters, the chorus is itself a main character in the play, even at times trying to intervene—as when these old men put up their sticks to try to fight with Clytaemnestra's lover, Aegisthus. By the time he composed *Agamemnon*, Aeschylus had adopted Sophocles' new technique of using three actors, not just two (the model he had worked with earlier in his career); but he does so minimally and rarely uses even two actors at the same time. Most scenes in *Agamemnon* involve dialogue between the chorus and a single character. The central debate between Clytaemnestra and Agamemnon is thrown into sharp relief, because it is so rare in this play that characters speak to each other

rather than to the chorus. There is a particular shock when Cassandra, the Trojan prophetess whom Agamemnon brings home as a concubine, finally speaks, because the audience may not have been expecting the third actor to have a speaking role at all.

When Cassandra does speak, it is in such densely metaphorical language that the chorus cannot understand what she is saying. Only gradually do her words begin to make a kind of sense, as the chorus realizes, too late, that terrible things are happening inside the palace. Cassandra's utterances in this scene are an extreme example of the way that *Agamemnon* as a whole operates. Meaning is conveyed by imagery, and both the audience and the characters onstage struggle to make sense of the hints the gods provide.

Aeschylus also makes his images visible onstage. For instance, when Agamemnon arrives home victorious from Troy, riding a chariot piled high with spoils, the entrance of a chariot, decked out in battle regalia, thundering into the *orchēstra*, must have been a memorable spectacle—and a reminder of the display of real Athenian spoils and tribute that would have taken place a day or two earlier in the festival of Dionysus, in the same space. Clytaemnestra invites her husband to step down from his chariot and walk into the palace on a rich array of scarlet tapestries. Agamemnon is initially reluctant, reminding his wife that he is a Greek man, not a barbarian or a god, and ought not, therefore, to risk the anger of the gods by puffing himself up with excessive regal pomp, and by destroying this beautiful, valuable fabric with his trampling feet. But in a short, brilliantly condensed exchange that uses *stichomythia* (dialogue in which each character speaks only one line at a time), Clytaemnestra overcomes her husband's resistance and persuades him that he should indeed step on the cloths, crushing them as he takes the long walk from the middle of the *orchēstra*, up onto the stage, and inside the palace doors. Located at almost the exact middle of the play, this exchange marks its central turning point. It is the moment when Agamemnon changes from the triumphal conqueror of Troy to the victim in his own home, as he moves from the military space of his chariot down into the domestic space of the palace. The scene provides a visible enactment of several themes from the choral odes, looking both backward, to Aulis, and forward, to the later scenes of the play. The king who walks on blood-red cloths will bathe in real blood inside the house.

The house or palace—represented onstage by the *skēnē*, the wooden stage building at the back of the dancing area—is a particularly important and sinister place in *Agamemnon*; indeed, the most important events in the play are the entrances and exits from the palace. At the opening of the play, we see the watchman stationed on top of the *skēnē*, "like a dog." But his speech hints that, unlike most watchdogs, he has to look out for danger inside the house, even more than from outside. Hard times have come to Argos, and the palace is ruled by the sinister figure of a woman who "maneuvers like a man." In Athenian culture, upper-class women were kept closely inside the house; they rarely went out, except to attend funerals or religious ceremonies. The boldness with which Clytaemnestra repeatedly bursts out of the house—just as much as her strangely outspoken manner—is a sign that she does not behave in an appropriately feminine manner. At the climax of the play, Aeschylus even allows the audience to enter the palace, revealing the area that has—up to this point—been hidden. He uses a stage device called the *ekkuklēma*, the "wheel-out trolley," to move the contents of the *skēnē* out onto the stage, in a final revelation of the inside of that mysterious house.

This is the first play in a trilogy; the other two plays show how the cycle of violence and revenge can continue in future generations but can also be finally resolved, through civic justice, the rule of law, and the reassertion of patriarchal hierarchy. But *Agamemnon* is also a self-contained work, whose narrative moves from darkness to light, from ignorance to revelation, from Troy to Argos, and from male to female power, through a climactic conflict (in the tapestry scene), to a violent and horrifying denouement. *Agamemnon* has the gripping power of any good murder story. The play shows us, with terrible vividness, how one death can lead to another, and it invites us to wonder about divine purposes at work in human lives and whether the killings of war can ever come to a peaceful end.

Agamemnon[1]

CHARACTERS

WATCHMAN
CLYTAEMNESTRA
HERALD
AGAMEMNON
CASSANDRA

AEGISTHUS
CHORUS, *the Old Men of Argos and*
their LEADER
Attendants of Clytaemnestra and of
Agamemnon, bodyguard of Aegisthus

[TIME AND SCENE: *A night in the tenth and final autumn of the Trojan war. The
house of Atreus in Argos. Before it, an altar stands unlit; a* WATCHMAN *on the high
roofs fights to stay awake.*]

WATCHMAN   Dear gods, set me free from all the pain,
the long watch I keep, one whole year awake . . .
propped on my arms, crouched on the roofs of Atreus
like a dog.
      I know the stars by heart,
the armies of the night, and there in the lead   5
the ones that bring us snow or the crops of summer,
bring us all we have—
our great blazing kings of the sky,
I know them, when they rise and when they fall . . .
and now I watch for the light, the signal-fire[2]   10
breaking out of Troy, shouting Troy is taken.
So she commands, full of her high hopes.
That woman[3]—she maneuvers like a man.

And when I keep to my bed, soaked in dew,
and the thoughts go groping through the night   15
and the good dreams that used to guard my sleep . . .
not here, it's the old comrade, terror, at my neck.
I mustn't sleep, no—
     [*Shaking himself awake.*]
          Look alive, sentry.
And I try to pick out tunes, I hum a little,
a good cure for sleep, and the tears start,   20
I cry for the hard times come to the house,
no longer run like the great place of old.

Oh for a blessed end to all our pain,
some godsend burning through the dark—

1. Translated by Robert Fagles, who also wrote
the list of characters and all stage directions
(in italics). No ancient play has these.
2. I.e., the bonfire nearest to Argos, the last in

a chain extending all the way to Troy, each
one visible from the next when fired at night.
3. Clytaemnestra.

[*Light appears slowly in the east; he struggles to his feet and scans it.*]

I salute you!

You dawn of the darkness, you turn night to day—   25
I see the light at last.
They'll be dancing in the streets of Argos⁴
thanks to you, thanks to this new stroke of—

                                        Aieeeeee!

There's your signal clear and true, my queen!
Rise up from bed—hurry, lift a cry of triumph   30
through the house, praise the gods for the beacon,
if they've taken Troy . . .

                        But there it burns,
fire all the way. I'm for the morning dances.
Master's luck is mine. A throw of the torch
has brought us triple-sixes⁵—we have won!   35
My move now—

          [*Beginning to dance, then breaking off, lost in thought.*]

                    Just bring him home. My king,
I'll take your loving hand in mine and then . . .
the rest is silence. The ox is on my tongue.⁶
Aye, but the house and these old stones,
give them a voice and what a tale they'd tell.   40
And so would I, gladly . . .
I speak to those who know; to those who don't
my mind's a blank. I never say a word.

          [*He climbs down from the roof and disappears into the palace through a
          side entrance. A* CHORUS, *the old men of Argos who have not learned the
          news of victory, enters and marches round the altar.*]

CHORUS   Ten years gone, ten to the day
our great avenger went for Priam—   45
    Menelaus⁷ and lord Agamemnon,
two kings with the power of Zeus,
the twin throne, twin sceptre,
Atreus' sturdy yoke of sons
launched Greece in a thousand ships,   50
armadas cutting loose from the land,
armies massed for the cause, the rescue—

---

4. In Homer, Agamemnon, son of Atreus, is king of Mycenae. Later Greek poets, however, referred to his kingdom as Argos or Mycenae, perhaps because the Achaeans in Homer are sometimes called Argives. In 463 B.C.E., just five years before the production of the play, Argos had defeated Mycenae in battle and put an end to the city, displacing the inhabitants or selling them into slavery. Soon after, Argos and Athens entered into an alliance, aimed at Sparta. Since this alliance will be alluded to in

the last play of the trilogy, it is important for Aeschylus to establish the un-Homeric location of the action right at the beginning.
5. The highest throw in the ancient Greek dice game.
6. A proverbial phrase for enforced silence.
7. Another son of Atreus, also a king of Argos and commander of the Greek expedition against Troy. Priam was the king of Troy. His son Paris abducted (or seduced) Menelaus's wife, Helen.

[*From within the palace* CLYTAEMNESTRA *raises a cry of triumph.*]
the heart within them screamed for all-out war!
Like vultures robbed of their young,
    the agony sends them frenzied,   55
soaring high from the nest, round and
round they wheel, they row their wings,
stroke upon churning thrashing stroke,
but all the labor, the bed of pain,
    the young are lost forever.   60
Yet someone hears on high—Apollo,
Pan or Zeus[8]—the piercing wail
these guests of heaven raise,
and drives at the outlaws, late
but true to revenge, a stabbing Fury![9]   65
    [CLYTAEMNESTRA *appears at the doors and pauses with her entourage.*][1]
So towering Zeus the god of guests[2]
drives Atreus' sons at Paris,
all for a woman manned by many
the generations wrestle, knees
grinding the dust, the manhood drains,   70
the spear snaps in the first blood rites
    that marry Greece and Troy.
And now it goes as it goes
and where it ends is Fate.
And neither by singeing flesh   75
nor tipping cups of wine[3]
nor shedding burning tears can you
enchant away the rigid Fury.
    [CLYTAEMNESTRA *lights the altar-fires.*]
We are the old, dishonoured ones,[4]
the broken husks of men.   80
Even then they cast us off,
the rescue mission left us here
to prop a child's strength upon a stick.
What if the new sap rises in his chest?

---

8. The movements of birds are regarded as prophetic signs. Apollo is mentioned perhaps as a prophetic god, Pan as a god of the wild places, Zeus because eagles and vultures were symbolic of his power.

9. This is the first mention of one of these avenging spirits, who will actually appear on stage as the chorus of the final play. Furies are called Erinyes in Greek.

1. There are no stage directions on the manuscript copies of the plays that have come down to us. Here the translator had the queen enter so that she will be visible on stage when the chorus addresses her by name in line 93. Other

scholars, pointing out that in Greek tragedy characters who are offstage are often addressed, disagree, and bring Clytaemnestra on stage only at line 256.

2. Zeus was thought to be particularly interested in punishing those who violated the code of hospitality. Paris had been a guest in Menelaus's house.

3. Neither by burnt sacrifice nor by pouring libations.

4. The general sense of the passage is that only two classes of the male population are left in Argos: those who are too young to fight and those who, like the chorus, are too old.

He has no soldiery in him,   85
    no more than we,
and we are aged past aging,
gloss of the leaf shriveled,
three legs at a time[5] we falter on.
Old men are children once again,   90
    a dream that sways and wavers
into the hard light of day.
                                    But you,
daughter of Leda, queen Clytaemnestra,
what now, what news, what message
drives you through the citadel   95
    burning victims?[6] Look,
the city gods, the gods of Olympus,
gods of the earth and public markets—
all the altars blazing with your gifts!
    Argos blazes! Torches   100
race the sunrise up her skies—
drugged by the lulling holy oils,
    unadulterated,
run from the dark vaults of kings.
    Tell us the news!   105
What you can, what is right—
Heal us, soothe our fears!
Now the darkness comes to the fore,
now the hope glows through your victims,
beating back this raw, relentless anguish   110
    gnawing at the heart.
        [CLYTAEMNESTRA *ignores them and pursues her rituals; they assemble for*
        the opening chorus.]
O but I still have power to sound the god's command at the roads
that launched the kings. The gods breathe power through my song,
    my fighting strength, Persuasion grows with the years—
I sing how the flight of fury hurled the twin command,   115
    one will that hurled young Greece
and winged the spear of vengeance straight for Troy!
The kings of birds to kings of the beaking prows, one black,
    one with a blaze of silver
        skimmed the palace spearhand right   120
    and swooping lower, all could see,
        plunged their claws in a hare, a mother
    bursting with unborn young—the babies spilling,
quick spurts of blood—cut off the race just dashing into life!
Cry, cry for death, but good win out in glory in the end.   125

5. I.e., using a stick, or cane, to support them
when they walk.
6. Clytaemnestra is sacrificing in thanksgiving

for the news of Troy's fall; the chorus does not
know that the news has come via the signal fires.

But the loyal seer of the armies studied Atreus' sons,
two sons with warring hearts—he saw two eagle-kings
   devour the hare and spoke the things to come,[7]
"Years pass, and the long hunt nets the city of Priam,
     the flocks beyond the walls,   130
a kingdom's life and soul—Fate stamps them out.
Just let no curse of the gods lour on us first,
   shatter our giant armor
      forged to strangle Troy. I see
         pure Artemis bristle in pity—   135
            yes, the flying hounds of the Father
slaughter for armies . . . their own victim . . . a woman
trembling young, all born to die—She[8] loathes the eagles' feast!"
Cry, cry for death, but good win out in glory in the end.
   "Artemis, lovely Artemis, so kind   140
to the ravening lion's tender, helpless cubs,
the suckling young of beasts that stalk the wilds—
   bring this sign for all its fortune,
     all its brutal torment home to birth!
I beg you, Healing Apollo, soothe her before   145
her crosswinds hold us down and moor the ships too long,[9]
pressing us on to another victim . . .
   nothing sacred, no
     no feast to be eaten[1]
      the architect of vengeance   150
      [*Turning to the palace.*]
   growing strong in the house
with no fear of the husband
here she waits
the terror raging back and back in the future
     the stealth, the law of the hearth, the mother—   155
      Memory womb of Fury child-avenging Fury!"
So as the eagles wheeled at the crossroads,

---

7. The seer Calchas identified the two eagles ("kings of birds") as symbolic of the two kings and their action as a symbolic prophecy of the destruction of Troy. The two eagles seized and tore a pregnant hare, which meant that the two kings would destroy Troy, thus killing not only the living Trojans but the Trojan generations yet unborn.

8. Artemis, a virgin goddess, patron of hunting, and protectress of wildlife, is angry that the eagles ("the flying hounds") have destroyed a pregnant animal. The prophet fears that she may turn her wrath against the kings whom the eagles represent. "A woman trembling young": just as the eagles kill the hare, the kings will kill Agamemnon's daughter Iphigeneia. The Greek text refers only to the hare, but the translator has made the allusion clear.

9. Calchas foresees the future. Artemis will send unfavorable winds to prevent the sailing of the Greek expedition from Aulis, the port of embarkation. She will demand the sacrifice of Agamemnon's daughter Iphigeneia as the price of the fleet's release. He prays that in spite of its bad aspects, the omen will be truly prophetic— that is, that the Achaeans will capture Troy. He goes on to anticipate and try to avert some of the evils it portends.

1. At an ordinary sacrifice the celebrants gave the gods their due portion and then feasted on the animal's flesh. The word *sacrifice* comes to have the connotation of "feast." There will be no feast at this sacrifice, since the victim will be a human being. The ominous phrase reminds us of a feast of human flesh that has already taken place, Thyestes' feasting on his own children through the trickery of his brother, Atreus.

Calchas clashed out the great good blessings mixed with doom
  for the halls of kings, and singing with our fate
we cry, cry for death, but good win out in glory in the end.   160

    Zeus, great nameless all in all,
    if that name will gain his favor,
      I will call him Zeus.[2]
  I have no words to do him justice,
    weighing all in the balance,   165
    all I have is Zeus, Zeus—
lift this weight, this torment from my spirit,
    cast it once for all.

    He who was so mighty once,[3]
    storming for the wars of heaven,
      he has had his day.   170
And then his son[4] who came to power
  met his match in the third fall
  and he is gone. Zeus, Zeus—
raise your cries and sing him Zeus the Victor!   175
    You will reach the truth:

    Zeus has led us on to know,
  the Helmsman lays it down as law
  that we must suffer, suffer into truth.
We cannot sleep, and drop by drop at the heart   180
  the pain of pain remembered comes again,
  and we resist, but ripeness comes as well.
From the gods enthroned on the awesome rowing-bench[5]
    there comes a violent love.

    So it was that day the king,   185
  the steersman at the helm of Greece,
would never blame a word the prophet said—
swept away by the wrenching winds of fortune
he conspired! Weatherbound we could not sail,
our stores exhausted, fighting strength hard-pressed,   190
and the squadrons rode in the shallows off Chalkis[6]
    where the riptide crashes, drags,

2. It was important, in prayer, to address the divinity by his or her right name: here the chorus uses an inclusive formula—they call on Zeus by whatever name pleases him.
3. Uranus, father of Cronus and grandfather of Zeus, the first lord of heaven. This whole passage refers to a primitive legend that told how Uranus was violently supplanted by his son, Cronus, who was in his turn overthrown by his son, Zeus. This legend is made to bear new meaning by Aeschylus, for he suggests that it is not a meaningless series of acts of violence but a progression to the rule of Zeus, who stands for order and justice. Thus the law of human life that Zeus proclaims and administers—that wisdom comes through suffering—has its counterpart in the history of the establishment of the divine rule.
4. Cronus.
5. The bench of the ship where the helmsman sat.
6. The unruly water of the narrows between Aulis on the mainland and Chalkis on the island of Euboea.

and winds from the north pinned down our hulls at Aulis,
port of anguish . . . head winds starving,
sheets and the cables snapped   195
   and the men's minds strayed,
      the pride, the bloom of Greece
   was raked as time ground on,
ground down, and then the cure for the storm
and it was harsher—Calchas cried,   200
"My captains, Artemis must have blood!"—
   so harsh the sons of Atreus
      dashed their scepters on the rocks,
   could not hold back the tears,

and I still can hear the older warlord saying,   205
"Obey, obey, or a heavy doom will crush me!—
Oh but doom *will* crush me
   once I rend my child,
      the glory of my house—
a father's hands are stained,   210
blood of a young girl streaks the altar.
Pain both ways and what is worse?
Desert the fleets, fail the alliance?
   No, but stop the winds with a virgin's blood,
      feed their lust, their fury?—feed their fury!—   215
Law is law!—
         Let all go well."

And once he slipped his neck in the strap of Fate,
his spirit veering black, impure, unholy,
once he turned he stopped at nothing,
   seized with the frenzy   220
      blinding driving to outrage—
wretched frenzy, cause of all our grief!
Yes, he had the heart
   to sacrifice his daughter!—
to bless the war that avenged a woman's loss,   225
   a bridal rite that sped the men-of-war.

"My father, father!"—she might pray to the winds;
no innocence moves her judges mad for war.
Her father called his henchmen on,
   on with a prayer,   230
      "Hoist her over the altar
like a yearling, give it all your strength!
She's fainting—lift her,
   sweep her robes around her,
but slip this strap in her gentle curving lips . . .   235
   here, gag her hard, a sound will curse the house"—

and the bridle chokes her voice . . . her saffron robes
pouring over the sand
                    her glance like arrows showering
wounding every murderer through with pity
        clear as a picture, live,   240
she strains to call their names . . .
I remember often the days with father's guests
when over the feast her voice unbroken,
     pure as the hymn her loving father
bearing third libations,[7] sang to Saving Zeus—   245
transfixed with joy, Atreus' offspring
       throbbing out their love.

What comes next? I cannot see it, cannot say.
The strong techniques of Calchas do their work.[8]
But Justice turns the balance scales,   250
    sees that we suffer
and we suffer and we learn.
And we will know the future when it comes.
Greet it too early, weep too soon.
    It all comes clear in the light of day.   255
Let all go well today, well as she could want,
       [*Turning to* CLYTAEMNESTRA.]
our midnight watch, our lone defender,
    single-minded queen.
LEADER   We've come,
    Clytaemnestra. We respect your power.
    Right it is to honor the warlord's woman   260
    once he leaves the throne.
                              But why these fires?
    Good news, or more good hopes? We're loyal,
    we want to hear, but never blame your silence.
CLYTAEMNESTRA   Let the new day shine, as the proverb says,
    glorious from the womb of Mother Night.   265
       [*Lost in prayer, then turning to the* CHORUS.]
    You will hear a joy beyond your hopes.
    Priam's citadel—the Greeks have taken Troy!
LEADER   No, what do you mean? I can't believe it.
CLYTAEMNESTRA   Troy is ours. Is that clear enough?
LEADER   The joy of it,
    stealing over me, calling up my tears—   270
CLYTAEMNESTRA   Yes, your eyes expose your loyal hearts.
LEADER   And you have proof?

7. Offerings of wine. At a banquet three libations were poured, the third and last to Zeus
the savior; the last libation was accompanied
by a hymn of praise.

8. This seems to refer to the sacrifice of Iphigeneia. Some scholars take the Greek words to
refer to the fulfillment of Calchas's prophecies.

CLYTAEMNESTRA   I do,
    I must. Unless the god is lying.
LEADER   That,
    or a phantom spirit sends you into raptures.
CLYTAEMNESTRA   No one takes me in with visions—senseless dreams.   275
LEADER   Or giddy rumor, you haven't indulged yourself—
CLYTAEMNESTRA   You treat me like a child, you mock me?
LEADER   Then when did they storm the city?
CLYTAEMNESTRA   Last night, I say, the mother of this morning.
LEADER   And who on earth could run the news so fast?   280
CLYTAEMNESTRA   The god of fire—rushing fire from Ida![9]
    And beacon to beacon rushed it on to me,
    my couriers riding home the torch.
                                    From Troy
    to the bare rock of Lemnos, Hermes' Spur,[1]
    and the Escort winged the great light west   285
    to the Saving Father's face, Mount Athos[2] hurled it
    third in the chain and leaping Ocean's back
    the blaze went dancing on to ecstasy—pitch-pine
    streaming gold like a new-born sun—and brought
    the word in flame to Mount Makistos'[3] brow.   290
    No time to waste, straining, fighting sleep,
    that lookout heaved a torch glowing over
    the murderous straits of Euripos to reach
    Messapion's[4] watchmen craning for the signal.
    Fire for word of fire! tense with the heather   295
    withered gray, they stack it, set it ablaze—
    the hot force of the beacon never flags,
    it springs the Plain of Asôpos, rears
    like a harvest moon to hit Kithairon's[5] crest
    and drives new men to drive the fire on.   300
    That relay pants for the far-flung torch,
    they swell its strength outstripping my commands
    and the light inflames the marsh, the Gorgon's Eye,[6]
    it strikes the peak where the wild goats range[7]—
    my laws, my fire whips that camp!   305
    They spare nothing, eager to build its heat,
    and a huge beard of flame overcomes the headland
    beetling down the Saronic Gulf,[8] and flaring south
    it brings the dawn to the Black Widow's[9] face—

9. The mountain range near Troy. The names
that follow in this speech designate the places
where beacon fires flashed the message of
Troy's fall to Argos. The chain began at Ida.
1. Hermes' cliff is on the island of Lemnos
(off the coast of Asia Minor).
2. On a rocky peninsula in northern Greece.
3. On the island of Euboea off the coast of
central Greece.

4. A mountain on the mainland.
5. A mountain near Thebes.
6. Lake Gorgopis.
7. Mount Aegiplanctus on the Isthmus of
Corinth.
8. The sea.
9. Mount Arachnaeus ("spider") in Argive territory. This is the fire seen by the watchman at
the beginning of the play.

the watch that looms above your heads—and now   310
the true son of the burning flanks of Ida
crashes on the roofs of Atreus' sons!

And I ordained it all.
Torch to torch, running for their lives,
one long succession racing home my fire.
                                    One,   315
first in the laps and last,¹ wins out in triumph.
There you have my proof, *my* burning sign, I tell you—
the power my lord passed on from Troy to me!

LEADER   We'll thank the gods, my lady—first this story,
let me lose myself in the wonder of it all!   320
Tell it start to finish, tell us all.

CLYTAEMNESTRA   The city's ours—in our hands this very day!
I can hear the cries in crossfire rock the walls.
Pour oil and wine in the same bowl,
what have you, friendship? A struggle to the end.   325
So with the victors and the victims—outcries,
you can hear them clashing like their fates.

They are kneeling by the bodies of the dead,
embracing men and brothers, infants over
the aged loins that gave them life, and sobbing,   330
as the yoke constricts their last free breath,
for every dear one lost.
                            And the others,
there, plunging breakneck through the night—
the labor of battle sets them down, ravenous;
to breakfast on the last remains of Troy.   335
Not by rank but the lots of chance they draw,
they lodge in the houses captured by the spear,
settling in so soon, released from the open sky,
the frost and dew. Lucky men, off guard at last,
they sleep away their first good night in years.   340

If only they are revering the city's gods,
the shrines of the gods who love the conquered land,
no plunderer will be plundered in return.
Just let no lust, no mad desire seize the armies²
to ravish what they must not touch—   345
overwhelmed by all they've won!

                    The run for home

---

1. The chain of beacons is compared to a relay race in which the runners carry torches; the last runner (who runs the final lap) comes in first to win.

2. The audience was familiar with the traditional account, according to which Agamemnon and his army failed signally to respect the gods and temples of Troy.

and safety waits, the swerve at the post,[3]
the final lap of the gruelling two-lap race.
And even if the men come back with no offense
to the gods, the avenging dead may never rest—   350
Oh let no new disaster strike! And here
you have it, what a woman has to say.
Let the best win out, clear to see.
A small desire but all that I could want.

LEADER   Spoken like a man, my lady, loyal,   355
full of self-command. I've heard your sign
and now your vision.

    [*Reaching towards her as she turns and re-enters the palace.*]
                Now to praise the gods.
The joy is worth the labor.

CHORUS   O Zeus my king and Night, dear Night,[4]
queen of the house who covers us with glories,[5]   360
you slung your net on the towers of Troy,
neither young nor strong could leap
the giant dredge net of slavery,
    all-embracing ruin.
I adore you, iron Zeus of the guests   365
and your revenge—you drew your longbow
year by year to a taut full draw
till one bolt, not falling short
or arching over the stars,
    could split the mark of Paris!   370

The sky stroke of god!—it is all Troy's to tell,
but even I can trace it to its cause:
god does as god decrees.
    And still some say
that heaven would never stoop to punish men   375
who trample the lovely grace of things
untouchable. How wrong they are!
    A curse burns bright on crime—
        full-blown, the father's crimes will blossom,
           burst into the son's.[6]   380
Let there be less suffering . . .
give us the sense to live on what we need.

---

3. Greek runners turned at a post and came back on a parallel track.
4. Troy fell to a night attack.
5. Probably the moon and stars; an obscure expression in the original.
6. The language throughout this passage is significantly general. The chorus refers to Paris, but everything it says is equally applicable to Agamemnon, who sacrificed his daughter for his ambitions. The original Greek is corrupt (that is, has been garbled in the handwritten tradition) but seems to proclaim the doctrine that the sins of the fathers are visited on the children. So Paris and Agamemnon pay for the misdeeds of their ancestors (as well as their own).

Bastions of wealth
are no defense for the man
who treads the grand altar of Justice   385
down and out of sight.

Persuasion, maddening child of Ruin
overpowers him—Ruin plans it all.
And the wound will smolder on,
     there is no cure,   390
a terrible brilliance kindles on the night.
He is bad bronze scraped on a touchstone:
put to the test, the man goes black.[7]
     Like the boy who chases
          a bird on the wing, brands his city,   395
               brings it down and prays,
but the gods are deaf
to the one who turns to crime, they tear him down.

          So Paris learned:
          he came to Atreus' house
          and shamed the tables spread for guests, 400
               he stole away the queen.

And she left her land *chaos*, clanging shields,
companions tramping, bronze prows, men in bronze,
     and she came to Troy with a dowry, death,   405
strode through the gates
     defiant in every stride,
as prophets of the house[8] looked on and wept,
"Oh the halls and the lords of war,
     the bed and the fresh prints of love.   410
I *see* him, unavenging, unavenged,
the stun of his desolation is so clear—
     he longs for the one who lies across the sea
until her phantom seems to sway the house.

          Her curving images,   415
          her beauty hurts her lord,
          the eyes starve and the touch
               of love is gone,

and radiant dreams are passing in the night,
the memories throb with sorrow, joy with pain . . .   420
     it is pain to dream and see desires
slip through the arms,
     a vision lost forever

---

7. Inferior bronze, adulterated with lead, turns   8. Menelaus's.
black with use.

winging down the moving drifts of sleep."
So he grieves at the royal hearth 425
   yet others' grief is worse, far worse.
All through Greece for those who flocked to war
they are holding back the anguish now,
   you can feel it rising now in every house;
I tell you there is much to tear the heart. 430

         They knew the men they sent,
       but now in place of men
       ashes and urns come back
       to every hearth.[9]

War, War, the great gold-broker of corpses 435
holds the balance of the battle on his spear!
Home from the pyres he sends them,
   home from Troy to the loved ones,
weighted with tears, the urns brimmed full,
   the heroes return in gold-dust,[1] 440
dear, light ash for men; and they weep,
they praise them, "He had skill in the swordplay,"
   "He went down so tall in the onslaught,"
"All for another's woman." So they mutter
in secret and the rancor steals 445
toward our staunch defenders, Atreus' sons.

        And there they ring the walls, the young,
       the lithe, the handsome hold the graves
       they won in Troy; the enemy earth
       rides over those who conquered. 450

The people's voice is heavy with hatred,
now the curses of the people must be paid,
and now I wait, I listen . . .
   there—there is something breathing
under the night's shroud. God takes aim 455
   at the ones who murder many;
the swarthy Furies stalk the man
gone rich beyond all rights—with a twist
   of fortune grind him down, dissolve him
into the blurring dead—there is no help. 460
The reach for power can recoil,
   the bolt of god can strike you at a glance.

---

9. This strikes a contemporary note. In Homer the fallen Achaeans are buried at Troy, but in Aeschylus's Athens the dead were cremated on the battlefield, and their ashes were brought home for burial.

1. I.e., in ashes. The war god is a broker who gives, in exchange for bodies, gold dust (the word used for *bodies* could mean living bodies or corpses).

Make me rich with no man's envy,
neither a raider of cities, no,
nor slave come face to face with life   465
overpowered by another.

[*Speaking singly.*]
—Fire comes and the news is good,
    it races through the streets
but is it true? Who knows?
Or just another lie from heaven?   470
—Show us the man so childish, wonderstruck,
    he's fired up with the first torch,
then when the message shifts
he's sick at heart.

                    —Just like a woman
to fill with thanks before the truth is clear.   475

—So gullible. Their stories spread like wildfire,
    they fly fast and die faster;
rumors voiced by women come to nothing.
LEADER   Soon we'll know her fires for what they are,
her relay race of torches hand-to-hand—   480
know if they're real or just a dream,
the hope of a morning here to take our senses.
I see a herald running from the beach
and a victor's spray of olive shades his eyes
and the dust he kicks, twin to the mud of Troy,   485
shows he has a voice—no kindling timber
on the cliffs, no signal-fires for him.
He can shout the news and give us joy,
or else . . . please, not that.
                    Bring it on,
good fuel to build the first good fires.   490
And if anyone calls down the worst on Argos
let him reap the rotten harvest of his mind.
    [*The* HERALD *rushes in and kneels on the ground.*]
HERALD   Good Greek earth, the soil of my fathers!
Ten years out, and a morning brings me back.
All hopes snapped but one—I'm home at last.   495
Never dreamed I'd die in Greece, assigned
the narrow plot I love the best.
                    And now
I salute the land, the light of the sun,
our high lord Zeus and the king of Pytho[2]—
no more arrows, master, raining on our heads!   500

2. Apollo.

At Scamander's banks we took our share,
your longbow brought us down like plague.[3]
Now come, deliver us, heal us—lord Apollo!
Gods of the market, here, take my salute.
And you, my Hermes,[4] Escort,   505
loving Herald, the herald's shield and prayer!—
And the shining dead[5] of the land who launched the armies,
warm us home . . . we're all the spear has left.

You halls of the kings, you roofs I cherish,
sacred seats—you gods that catch the sun,   510
if your glances ever shone on him in the old days,
greet him well—so many years are lost.
He comes, he brings us light in the darkness,
free for every comrade, Agamemnon lord of men.

Give him the royal welcome he deserves!   515
He hoisted the pickax of Zeus who brings revenge,
he dug Troy down, he worked her soil down,
the shrines of her gods and the high altars, gone!—
and the seed of her wide earth he ground to bits.
That's the yoke he claps on Troy. The king,   520
the son of Atreus comes. The man is blest,
the one man alive to merit such rewards.

Neither Paris nor Troy, partners to the end,
can say their work outweighs their wages now.
Convicted of rapine, stripped of all his spoils,   525
and his father's house and the land that gave it life—
he's scythed them to the roots. The sons of Priam
pay the price twice over.

LEADER   Welcome home
   from the wars, herald, long live your joy.

HERALD   Our joy—
   now I could die gladly. Say the word, dear gods.   530

LEADER   Longing for your country left you raw?

HERALD   The tears fill my eyes, for joy.

LEADER   You too,
   down the sweet disease that kills a man
   with kindness . . .

HERALD   Go on, I don't see what you—

LEADER   Love
   for the ones who love you—that's what took you.

---

3. Compare the opening scene of the *Iliad* (pp. 232–33), where Apollo punishes the Greeks with his arrows (a metaphor for plague).
4. The gods' messenger and patron deity of heralds.
5. The heroes of the past, who are buried in Argos and worshipped.

HERALD   You mean   535
  the land and the armies hungered for each other?
LEADER   There were times I thought I'd faint with longing.
HERALD   So anxious for the armies, why?
LEADER   For years now,
  only my silence kept me free from harm.
HERALD   What,
  with the kings gone did someone threaten you?
LEADER   So much . . .   540
  now as you say, it would be good to die.
HERALD   True, we *have* done well.
  Think back in the years and what have you?
  A few runs of luck, a lot that's bad.
  Who but a god can go through life unmarked?   545
  A long, hard pull we had, if I would tell it all.
  The iron rations, penned in the gangways
  hock by jowl like sheep. Whatever miseries
  break a man, our quota, every sunstarved day.

  Then on the beaches it was worse. Dug in   550
  under the enemy ramparts—deadly going.
  Out of the sky, out of the marshy flats
  the dews soaked us, turned the ruts we fought from
  into gullies, made our gear, our scalps
  crawl with lice.
                    And talk of the cold,   555
  the sleet to freeze the gulls, and the big snows
  come avalanching down from Ida. Oh but the heat,
  the sea and the windless noons, the swells asleep,
  dropped to a dead calm . . .

  But why weep now?   560
  It's over for us, over for them.
  The dead can rest and never rise again;
  no need to call their muster. We're alive,
  do we have to go on raking up old wounds?
  Good-by to all that. Glad I am to say it.   565

  For us, the remains of the Greek contingents,
  the good wins out, no pain can tip the scales,
  not now. So shout this boast to the bright sun—
  fitting it is—wing it over the seas and rolling earth:

  "Once when an Argive expedition captured Troy   570
  they hauled these spoils back to the gods of Greece,
  they bolted them high across the temple doors,
  the glory of the past!"
                    And hearing that,
  men will applaud our city and our chiefs,

and Zeus will have the hero's share of fame— 575
he did the work.
                    That's all I have to say.
LEADER   I'm convinced, glad that I was wrong.
Never too old to learn; it keeps me young.
        [CLYTAEMNESTRA *enters with her women.*]
First the house and the queen, it's their affair,
but I can taste the riches.
CLYTAEMNESTRA   I cried out long ago!⁶— 580
for joy, when the first herald came burning
through the night and told the city's fall.
And there were some who smiled and said,
"A few fires persuade you Troy's in ashes.
Women, women, elated over nothing." 585

You made me seem deranged.
For all that I sacrificed—a woman's way,
you'll say—station to station on the walls
we lifted cries of triumph that resounded
in the temples of the gods. We lulled and blessed 590
the fires with myrrh and they consumed our victims.
        [*Turning to the* HERALD.]
But enough. Why prolong the story?
From the king himself I'll gather all I need.
Now for the best way to welcome home
my lord, my good lord . . .
                    No time to lose! 595
What dawn can feast a woman's eyes like this?
I can see the light, the husband plucked from war
by the Saving God and open wide the gates.

Tell him that, and have him come with speed,
the people's darling—how they long for him. 600
And for his wife,
may he return and find her true at hall,
just as the day he left her, faithful to the last.
A watchdog gentle to him alone,
        [*Glancing towards the palace.*]
                                  savage
to those who cross his path. I have not changed. 605
The strains of time can never break our seal.
In love with a new lord, in ill repute I am
as practiced as I am in dyeing bronze.

That is my boast, teeming with the truth.
I am proud, a woman of my nobility— 610
I'd hurl it from the roofs!

---

6. As the watchman had told her to (line 30).

[*She turns sharply, enters the palace.*]

LEADER   She speaks well, but it takes no seer to know
she only says what's right.

[*The* HERALD *attempts to leave; the* LEADER *takes him by the arm.*]
                       Wait, one thing.
Menelaus, is he home too, safe with the men?[7]
The power of the land—dear king.   615

HERALD   I doubt that lies will help my friends,
in the lean months to come.

LEADER   Help us somehow, tell the truth as well.
But when the two conflict it's hard to hide—
out with it.

HERALD   He's lost, gone from the fleets![8]   620
He and his ship, it's true.

LEADER   After you watched him
pull away from Troy? Or did some storm
attack you all and tear him off the line?

HERALD   There,
like a marksman, the whole disaster cut to a word.

LEADER   How do the escorts give him out—dead or alive?   625

HERALD   No clear report. No one knows . . .
only the wheeling sun that heats the earth to life.

LEADER   But then the storm—how did it reach the ships?
How did it end? Were the angry gods on hand?

HERALD   This blessed day, ruin it with *them*?   630
Better to keep their trophies far apart.

When a runner comes, his face in tears,
saddled with what his city dreaded most,
the armies routed, two wounds in one,
one to the city, one to hearth and home . . .   635
our best men, droves of them, victims
herded from every house by the two-barb whip
that Ares[9] likes to crack,
                    that charioteer
who packs destruction shaft by shaft,
careening on with his brace of bloody mares—   640
When he comes in, I tell you, dragging that much pain,
wail your battle-hymn to the Furies, and high time!

But when he brings salvation home to a city
singing out her heart—
how can I mix the good with so much bad   645

---

7. The relevance of this question and the following speeches lies in the fact that Menelaus's absence makes Agamemnon's murder easier (his presence might have made it impossible) and in the fact that Menelaus is bringing Helen home.
8. For what happened to Menelaus, see *Odyssey* 4 (p. 356).
9. The war god.

and blurt out this?—
                    "Storms swept the Greeks,
and not without the anger of the gods!"

Those enemies for ages, fire[1] and water,
sealed a pact and showed it to the world—
they crushed our wretched squadrons.

                              Night looming,   650
breakers lunging in for the kill
and the black gales come brawling out of the north—
ships ramming, prow into hooking prow, gored
by the rush-and-buck of hurricane pounding rain
by the cloudburst—
                    ships stampeding into the darkness,   655
lashed and spun by the savage shepherd's hand![2]

But when the sun comes up to light the skies
I see the Aegean heaving into a great bloom
of corpses . . . Greeks, the pick of a generation
scattered through the wrecks and broken spars.   660

But not us, not our ship, our hull untouched.
Someone stole us away or begged us off.
No mortal—a god, death grip on the tiller,
or lady luck herself, perched on the helm,
she pulled us through, she saved us. Aye,   665
we'll never battle the heavy surf at anchor,
never shipwreck up some rocky coast.

But once we cleared that sea-hell, not even
trusting luck in the cold light of day,
we battened on our troubles, they were fresh—   670
the armada punished, bludgeoned into nothing.

And now if one of them still has the breath
he's saying we are lost. Why not?
We say the same of him. Well,
here's to the best.
                    And Menelaus?   675
Look to it, he's come back, and yet . . .
if a shaft of the sun can track him down,
alive, and his eyes full of the old fire—
thanks to the strategies of Zeus, Zeus
would never tear the house out by the roots—   680
then there's hope our man will make it home.

---

1. Lightning.
2. The ships were scattered like sheep dispersed by a cruel shepherd.

You've heard it all. Now you have the truth.
  [*Rushing out.*]
CHORUS Who—what power named the name[3] that drove your fate?—
what hidden brain could divine your future,
steer that word to the mark,   685
to the bride of spears,
  the whirlpool churning armies,
    Oh for all the world a Helen!
Hell at the prows, hell at the gates
hell on the men-of-war,   690
from her lair's sheer veils she drifted
  launched by the giant western wind,
   and the long tall waves of men in armor,
huntsmen[4] trailing the oar-blades' dying spoor
slipped into her moorings,   695
  Simois'[5] mouth that chokes with foliage,
    bayed for bloody strife,

for Troy's Blood Wedding Day—she drives her word,
her burning will to the birth, the Fury
late but true to the cause,   700
to the tables shamed
  and Zeus who guards the hearth[6]—
    the Fury makes the Trojans pay!
Shouting their hymns, hymns for the bride
hymns for the kinsmen doomed   705
to the wedding march of Fate.
  Troy changed her tune in her late age,
   and I think I hear the dirges mourning
"Paris, born and groomed for the bed of Fate!"
They mourn with their life breath,   710
  they sing their last, the sons of Priam
  born for bloody slaughter.

  So a man once reared
a lion cub at hall, snatched
from the breast, still craving milk   715
  in the first flush of life.
A captivating pet for the young,
and the old men adored it, pampered it
  in their arms, day in, day out,
like an infant just born.   720
Its eyes on fire, little beggar,
fawning for its belly, slave to food.

---

3. Helen. The name contains the Greek root
hele-, which means "destroy."
4. The Achaean army, which came after her.

5. A river in Troy.
6. I.e., protects the host and guest.

But it came of age
and the parent strain broke out
and it paid its breeders back.   725
   Grateful it was, it went
through the flock to prepare a feast,
an illicit orgy—the house swam with blood,
   one could resist that agony—
      massacre vast and raw!   730
From god there came a priest of ruin,
adopted by the house to lend it warmth.

And the first sensation Helen brought to Troy . . .
call it a spirit
      shimmer of winds dying   735
         glory light as gold
      shaft of the eyes dissolving, open bloom
   that wounds the heart with love.
But veering wild in mid-flight
she whirled her wedding on to a stabbing end,   740
slashed at the sons of Priam—hearthmate, friend to the death,
      sped by Zeus who speeds the guest,
a bride of tears, a Fury.

There's an ancient saying, old as man himself:
men's prosperity   745
      never will die childless,
         once full-grown it breeds.
      Sprung from the great good fortune in the race
   comes bloom on bloom of pain—
insatiable wealth. But not I,   750
I alone say this. Only the reckless act
can breed impiety, multiplying crime on crime,
   while the house kept straight and just
is blessed with radiant children.[7]

      But ancient Violence longs to breed,   755
      new Violence comes
      when its fatal hour comes, the demon comes
      to take her toll—no war, no force, no prayer
      can hinder the midnight Fury stamped
      with parent Fury moving through the house.   760

      But Justice shines in sooty hovels,[8]

---

7. These lines begin with the traditional Greek view that immoderate good fortune (or excellence of any kind beyond the average) is itself the cause of disaster. The chorus, however, rejects this view and states that only an act of evil produces evil consequences.

8. The homes of the poor.

loves the decent life.
From proud halls crusted with gilt by filthy hands
she turns her eyes to find the pure in spirit—
spurning the wealth stamped counterfeit with praise,   765
she steers all things toward their destined end.[9]

[AGAMEMNON *enters in his chariot, his plunder borne before him by his
entourage; behind him, half hidden, stands* CASSANDRA. *The old men press
toward him.*]

Come, my king, the scourge of Troy,
   the true son of Atreus—
How to salute you, how to praise you
neither too high nor low, but hit   770
the note of praise that suits the hour?
So many prize some brave display,
they prefer some flaunt of honor
   once they break the bounds.
When a man fails they share his grief,   775
but the pain can never cut them to the quick.
When a man succeeds they share his glory,
torturing their faces into smiles.
But the good shepherd knows his flock.
When the eyes seem to brim with love   780
   and it is only unction,
he will know, better than we can know.
That day you marshaled the armies
all for Helen—no hiding it now—
I drew you in my mind in black;   785
you seemed a menace at the helm,
   sending men to the grave
to bring her home, that hell on earth.
But now from the depths of trust and love
I say Well fought, well won—   790
   the end is worth the labor!
Search, my king, and learn at last
who stayed at home and kept their faith
and who betrayed the city.[1]

AGAMEMNON   First,
with justice I salute my Argos and my gods,   795
my accomplices who brought me home and won
my rights from Priam's Troy—the just gods.
No need to hear our pleas. Once for all
they consigned their lots to the urn of blood,[2]
they pitched on death for men, annihilation   800

---

9. Here the chorus admits, by implication, that
the poor are less likely to commit evil acts.
1. The chorus tries to warn Agamemnon against
flatterers and dissemblers, but he misses its drift.
2. In an Athenian law court there were
two urns—one for acquittal, one for
condemnation—into which the jurors dropped
their pebbles. (The audience will see them on
stage in the final play of the trilogy.)

for the city. Hope's hand, hovering
over the urn of mercy, left it empty.
Look for the smoke—it is the city's seamark,
building even now.

              The storms of ruin live!
Her last dying breath, rising up from the ashes   805
sends us gales of incense rich in gold.

For that we must thank the gods with a sacrifice
our sons will long remember. For their mad outrage
of a queen we raped their city—we were right.
The beast of Argos, foals of the wild mare,[3]   810
thousands massed in armor rose on the night
the Pleiades went down,[4] and crashing through
their walls our bloody lion lapped its fill,
gorging on the blood of kings.

                 Our thanks to the gods,
long drawn out, but it is just the prelude.   815
    [CLYTAEMNESTRA *approaches with her women; they are carrying dark*
    red tapestries. AGAMEMNON *turns to the* LEADER.]
And your concern, old man, is on my mind.
I hear you and agree, I will support you.
How rare, men with the character to praise
a friend's success without a trace of envy,
poison to the heart—it deals a double blow.   820
Your own losses weigh you down but then,
look at your neighbor's fortune and you weep.
Well I know. I understand society,
the fawning mirror of the proud.

                My comrades . . .
they're shadows, I tell you, ghosts of men   825
who swore they'd die for me. Only Odysseus:
I dragged that man to the wars[5] but once in harness
he was a trace-horse,[6] he gave his all for me.
Dead or alive, no matter, I can praise him.

And now this cause involving men and gods.   830
We must summon the city for a trial,
found a national tribunal. Whatever's healthy,
shore it up with law and help it flourish.
Wherever something calls for drastic cures

---

3. The wooden horse, the stratagem with
which the Greeks captured the city.
4. The setting of a group of stars in the constellation Taurus, late in the fall.
5. Feigning madness to escape going to Troy,
Odysseus was tricked into demonstrating his
sanity.
6. A third horse that ran beside the team
that pulled a chariot; it lent help when special maneuvering was needed, particularly in
making tight turns.

we make our noblest effort: amputate or wield   835
the healing iron, burn the cancer at the roots.

Now I go to my father's house—
I give the gods my right hand, my first salute.
The ones who sent me forth have brought me home.
　　　[*He starts down from the chariot, looks at* CLYTAEMNESTRA, *stops, and offers
　　　up a prayer.*]
Victory, you have sped my way before,   840
now speed me to the last.
　　　[CLYTAEMNESTRA *turns from the king to the* CHORUS.]
CLYTAEMNESTRA　　　　　　　　Old nobility of Argos
gathered here, I am not ashamed to tell you
how I love the man. I am older,
and the fear dies away . . . I am human.
Nothing I say was learned from others.   845
This is my life, my ordeal, long as the siege
he laid at Troy and more demanding.
　　　　　　　　　　　　　　　First,
when a woman sits at home and the man is gone,
the loneliness is terrible,
unconscionable . . .   850
and the rumors spread and fester,
a runner comes with something dreadful,
close on his heels the next and his news worse,
and they shout it out and the whole house can hear;
and wounds—if he took one wound for each report   855
to penetrate these walls, he's gashed like a dragnet,
more, if he had only died . . .
for each death that swelled his record, he could boast
like a triple-bodied Geryon[7] risen from the grave,
"Three shrouds I dug from the earth, one for every body   860
that went down!"
　　　　　　　　　The rumors broke like fever,
broke and then rose higher. There were times
they cut me down and eased my throat from the noose.
I wavered between the living and the dead.
　　　[*Turning to* AGAMEMNON.]

　　　　　　　　　　　　　　　And so
our child is gone, not standing by our side,   865
the bond of our dearest pledges, mine and yours;
by all rights our child should be here . . .
Orestes. You seem startled.
You needn't be. Our loyal brother-in-arms
will take good care of him, Strophios[8] the Phocian.   870

---

7. A monster (eventually killed by Heracles)
who had three bodies and three heads.
8. King of Phocis, a mountainous region near

Delphi. His son, Pylades, accompanies Orestes
when he returns to avenge Agamemnon's
death.

He warned from the start we court two griefs in one.
You risk all on the wars—and what if the people
rise up howling for the king, and anarchy
should dash our plans?
        Men, it is their nature,
trampling on the fighter once he's down.   875
Our child is gone. That is my self-defense
and it is true.
        For me, the tears that welled
like springs are dry. I have no tears to spare.
I'd watch till late at night, my eyes still burn,
I sobbed by the torch I lit for you alone.   880
    [Glancing towards the palace.]
I never let it die . . . but in my dreams
the high thin wail of a gnat would rouse me,
piercing like a trumpet—I could see you
suffer more than all
the hours that slept with me could ever bear.   885

I endured it all. And now, free of grief,
I would salute that man the watchdog of the fold,
the mainroyal,[9] saying stay of the vessel,
rooted oak that thrusts the roof sky-high,
the father's one true heir.
               890
Land at dawn to the shipwrecked past all hope,
light of the morning burning off the night of storm,
the cold clear spring to the parched horseman—
O the ecstasy, to flee the yoke of Fate!

It is right to use the titles he deserves.   895
Let envy keep her distance. We have suffered
long enough.
    [Reaching toward AGAMEMNON.]
        Come to me now, my dearest,
down from the car of war, but never set the foot
that stamped out Troy on earth again, my great one.

Women, why delay? You have your orders.   900
Pave his way with tapestries.[1]
    *[They begin to spread the crimson tapestries between the king and
    the palace doors.]*
              Quickly.
Let the red stream flow and bear him home
to the home he never hoped to see—Justice,
lead him in!
        Leave all the rest to me.

---

9. Upper section of the mainmast.
1. To walk on those tapestries, wall hangings   dyed with the expensive crimson, would be an
   act of extravagant pride.

The spirit within me never yields to sleep.   905
We will set things right, with the god's help.
We will do whatever Fate requires.

AGAMEMNON   There
is Leda's daughter,[2] the keeper of my house.
And the speech to suit my absence, much too long.
But the praise that does us justice,   910
let it come from others, then we prize it.

                                              This—
You treat me like a woman. Groveling, gaping up at me!
What am I, some barbarian[3] peacocking out of Asia?
Never cross my path with robes and draw the lightning.
Never—only the gods deserve the pomps of honor   915
and the stiff brocades of fame. To walk on them . . .
I am human, and it makes my pulses stir
with dread.
                    Give me the tributes of a man
and not a god, a little earth to walk on,
not this gorgeous work.   920
There is no need to sound my reputation.
I have a sense of right and wrong, what's more—
heaven's proudest gift. Call no man blest
until he ends his life in peace, fulfilled.
If I can live by what I say, I have no fear.   925

CLYTAEMNESTRA   One thing more. Be true to your ideals and tell me—
AGAMEMNON   True to my ideals? Once I violate them I am lost.
CLYTAEMNESTRA   Would you have sworn this act to god in a time of terror?
AGAMEMNON   Yes, if a prophet called for a last, drastic rite.
CLYTAEMNESTRA   But Priam—can you see him if he had your success?   930
AGAMEMNON   Striding on the tapestries of God, I see him now.
CLYTAEMNESTRA   And *you* fear the reproach of common men?
AGAMEMNON   The voice of the people—aye, they have enormous power.
CLYTAEMNESTRA   Perhaps, but where's the glory without a little gall?
AGAMEMNON   And where's the woman in all this lust for glory?   935
CLYTAEMNESTRA   But the great victor—it becomes him to give way.
AGAMEMNON   Victory in this . . . war of ours, it means so much to you?
CLYTAEMNESTRA   O give way! The power is yours if you surrender all of
      your own free will to me.
AGAMEMNON   Enough.
If you are so determined—   940
      [*Turning to the women, pointing to his boots.*]
Let someone help me off with these at least.
Old slaves, they've stood me well.
                                     Hurry,
and while I tread his splendors dyed red in the sea,[4]

_____

2. Clytaemnestra. Helen is also a daughter of   3. Foreigner, with negative connotations.
Leda.   4. The dye was made from shellfish.

may no god watch and strike me down with envy
from on high. I feel such shame—   945
to tread the life of the house, a kingdom's worth
of silver in the weaving.

> [*He steps down from the chariot to the tapestries and reveals* CASSANDRA,
> *dressed in the sacred regalia, the fillets, robes and scepter of Apollo.*]

Done is done.

Escort this stranger[5] in, be gentle.
Conquer with compassion. Then the gods
shine down upon you, gently. No one chooses   950
the yoke of slavery, not of one's free will—
and she least of all. The gift of the armies,
flower and pride of all the wealth we won,
she follows me from Troy.

And now,

since you have brought me down with your insistence,   955
just this once I enter my father's house,
trampling royal crimson as I go.

> [*He takes his first steps and pauses.*]

CLYTAEMNESTRA   There is the sea
and who will drain it dry? Precious as silver,
inexhaustible, ever-new, it breeds the more we reap it—
tides on tides of crimson dye our robes blood-red.   960
Our lives are based on wealth, my king,
the gods have seen to that.
Destitution, our house has never heard the word.
I would have sworn to tread on legacies of robes,
at one command from an oracle, deplete the house—   965
suffer the worst to bring that dear life back!

> [*Encouraged,* AGAMEMNON *strides to the entrance.*]

When the root lives on, the new leaves come back,
spreading a dense shroud of shade across the house
to thwart the Dog Star's[6] fury. So you return
to the father's hearth, you bring us warmth in winter   970
like the sun—

And you are Zeus when Zeus

tramples the bitter virgin grape for new wine
and the welcome chill steals through the halls, at last
the master moves among the shadows of his house, fulfilled.

> [AGAMEMNON *goes over the threshold; the women gather up the tapestries*
> *while* CLYTAEMNESTRA *prays.*]

Zeus, Zeus, master of all fullfillment, now fulfill our prayers—   975
speed our rites to their fulfillment once for all!

---

5. Cassandra, daughter of Priam, Agamemnon's share of the human booty from the sack of Troy. She was loved by Apollo, who gave her the gift of prophecy; but when she refused her love to the god, he saw to it that her prophecies, though true, would never be believed until it was too late.
6. Sirius; its appearance in the summer sky marked the beginning of the hot season (the "dog days" of summer).

[*She enters the palace, the doors close, the old men huddle in terror.*]

CHORUS   Why, why does it rock me, never stops,
    this terror beating down my heart,
      this seer that sees it all—
  it beats its wings, uncalled unpaid   980
  thrust on the lungs
  the mercenary song beats on and on
  singing a prophet's strain—
    and I can't throw it off
  like dreams that make no sense,   985
  and the strength drains
  that filled the mind with trust,
  and the years drift by and the driven sand
    has buried the mooring lines
  that churned when the armored squadrons cut for Troy . . .   990
  and now I believe it, I can prove he's home,
    my own clear eyes for witness—

                Agamemnon!

Still it's chanting, beating deep so deep in the heart
this dirge of the Furies, oh dear god,
not fit for the lyre,[7] its own master   995
    it kills our spirit
kills our hopes
and it's real, true, no fantasy—
    stark terror whirls the brain
      and the end is coming   1000
      Justice comes to birth—
I pray my fears prove false and fall
and die and never come to birth!
Even exultant health, well we know,
  exceeds its limits,[8] comes so near disease   1005
it can breach the wall between them.

Even a man's fate, held true on course,
  in a blinding flash rams some hidden reef;
but if caution only casts the pick of the cargo—
one well-balanced cast—   1010
the house will not go down, not outright;[9]
laboring under its wealth of grief
the ship of state rides on.

Yes, and the great green bounty of god,
sown in the furrows year by year and reaped each fall   1015
can end the plague of famine.

---

7. A stringed instrument played on joyful occasions (hence "lyric" poetry).
8. Excess, even in blessings like health, is always dangerous.

9. These lines refer to a traditional Greek belief that the fortunate person could avert the envy of heaven by deliberately getting rid of some precious possession.

But a man's lifeblood
    is dark and mortal.
Once it wets the earth
what song can sing it back?   1020
Not even the master-healer[1]
    who brought the dead to life—
Zeus stopped the man before he did more harm.

Oh, if only the gods had never forged
the chain that curbs our excess,   1025
    one man's fate curbing the next man's fate,
my heart would outrace my song, I'd pour out all I feel—
    but no, I choke with anguish,
        mutter through the nights.
Never to ravel out a hope in time   1030
and the brain is swarming, burning—

[CLYTAEMNESTRA *emerges from the palace and goes to* CASSANDRA,
impassive in the chariot.]

CLYTAEMNESTRA   Won't you come inside? I mean you, Cassandra.
Zeus in all his mercy wants you to share
some victory libations with the house.
The slaves are flocking. Come, lead them   1035
up to the altar of the god who guards
our dearest treasures.
                       Down from the chariot,
no time for pride. Why even Heracles,[2]
they say, was sold into bondage long ago,
he had to endure the bitter bread of slaves.   1040
But if the yoke descends on you, be grateful
for a master born and reared in ancient wealth.
Those who reap a harvest past their hopes
are merciless to their slaves.
                       From us
you will receive what custom says is right.   1045

[CASSANDRA *remains impassive.*]

LEADER   It's *you* she is speaking to, it's all too clear.
You're caught in the nets of doom—obey
if you can obey, unless you cannot bear to.
CLYTAEMNESTRA   Unless she's like a swallow, possessed
of her own barbaric song,[3] strange, dark.   1050
I speak directly as I can—she must obey.
LEADER   Go with her. Make the best of it, she's right.
Step down from the seat, obey her.

---

1. Asclepius, the mythical physician who was so skilled that he finally succeeded in restoring a dead man to life. Zeus struck him with a thunderbolt for going too far.
2. The Greek hero, famous for his twelve labors that rid the earth of monsters, was at one time forced to be the slave to Omphale, an Eastern queen.
3. The comparison of foreign speech to the twittering of a swallow was a Greek commonplace.

CLYTAEMNESTRA   Do it *now*—
I have no time to spend outside. Already
the victims crowd the hearth, the Navelstone,[4]   1055
to bless this day of joy I never hoped to see!—
our victims waiting for the fire and the knife,
and you,
if you want to taste our mystic rites, come now.
If my words can't reach you—
          [*Turning to the* LEADER.]
                          Give her a sign,   1060
one of her exotic handsigns.
LEADER   I think
the stranger needs an interpreter, someone clear.
She's like a wild creature, fresh caught.
CLYTAEMNESTRA   She's mad,
her evil genius murmuring in her ears.
She comes from a *city* fresh caught.   1065
She must learn to take the cutting bridle
before she foams her spirit off in blood—
and that's the last I waste on her contempt!
          [*Wheeling, re-entering the palace. The* LEADER *turns to* CASSANDRA, *who
          remains transfixed.*]
LEADER   Not I, I pity her. I will be gentle.
Come, poor thing. Leave the empty chariot—   1070
Of your own free will try on the yoke of Fate.
CASSANDRA   Aieeeeee! Earth—Mother—
                          Curse of the Earth—Apollo Apollo!
LEADER   Why cry to Apollo?
He's not the god to call with sounds of mourning.
CASSANDRA   Aieeeeee! Earth—Mother—
                          Rape of the Earth—Apollo Apollo!   1075
LEADER   Again, it's a bad omen.
She cries for the god who wants no part of grief.[5]
          [CASSANDRA *steps from the chariot, looks slowly towards the rooftops of the
          palace.*]
CASSANDRA   God of the long road,
Apollo *Apollo* my destroyer—
you destroy me once,[6] destroy me twice—   1080
LEADER   She's about to sense her own ordeal, I think.
Slave that she is, the god lives on inside her.
CASSANDRA   God of the iron marches,
          Apollo *Apollo* my destroyer—
where, where have you led[7] me now? what house—   1085

---

4. An altar of Zeus Herkeios, guardian of the
hearth, which was the religious center of the
home.
5. Apollo (and the Olympian gods in general)
was not invoked in mourning or lamentation.
6. The name *Apollo* suggests the Greek word
apollumi, "destroy." He destroyed her the first

time when he saw to it that no one would
believe her prophecies. "God of the long road":
Apollo Agyieus. This statue, a conical pillar,
was set up outside the door of the house; no
doubt there was one onstage.
7. The Greek word (a form of the verb *agō*)
suggests the god's title Agyieus.

LEADER   The house of Atreus and his sons. Really—
   don't you know? It's true, see for yourself.
CASSANDRA   No . . . the house that hates god,
      an echoing womb of guilt, kinsmen
         torturing kinsmen, severed heads,   1090
   slaughterhouse of heroes, soil streaming blood—
LEADER   A keen hound, this stranger.
   Trailing murder, and murder she will find.
CASSANDRA   See, my witnesses—
      I trust to them, to the babies   1095
         wailing, skewered on the sword,
   their flesh charred, the father gorging on their parts[8]—
LEADER   We'd heard your fame as a seer,
   but no one looks for seers in Argos.
CASSANDRA   Oh no, what horror, what new plot,[9]   1100
   new agony this?—
   it's growing, massing, deep in the house,
      a plot, a monstrous—*thing*
         to crush the loved ones, no,
   there is no cure, and rescue's far away[1] and—   1105
LEADER   I can't read these signs; I knew the first,
   the city rings with them.
CASSANDRA   You, you godforsaken—you'd do *this*?
   The lord of your bed,
   you bathe him . . . his body glistens, then—   1110
      how to tell the climax?—
         comes so quickly, see,
   hand over hand shoots out, hauling ropes—
                  then lunge!
LEADER   Still lost. Her riddles, her dark words of god—
   I'm groping, helpless.
CASSANDRA   No no, look *there*!—   1115
   what's that? some net flung out of hell—
   No, *she* is the snare,
   the bedmate, deathmate, murder's strong right arm!
      Let the insatiate discord in the race
   rear up and shriek "Avenge the victim—stone them dead!"   1120
LEADER   What Fury is this? Why rouse it, lift its wailing
   through the house? I hear you and lose hope.
CHORUS   Drop by drop at the heart, the gold of life ebbs out.
   We are the old soldiers . . . wounds will come
   with the crushing sunset of our lives.   1125
   Death is close, and quick.
CASSANDRA   Look out! *look out*!—
   Ai, drag the great bull from the mate!—

---

8. The feast of Thyestes, who was tricked by
his brother, Atreus, into eating his own children. The story is told by Aegisthus below
(lines 1606–43).

9. Clytaemnestra's murder of Agamemnon.
1. A reference to Menelaus (distant in space)
and Orestes (distant in time).

a thrash of robes, she traps him—
writing—
　　　　black horn glints, twists—
　　　　　　　　　　she gores him through!
　　And now he buckles, look, the bath swirls red—　　　　1130
There's stealth and murder in the cauldron, do you hear?
LEADER　I'm no judge, I've little skill with the oracles,
　　but even I know danger when I hear it.
CHORUS　What good are the oracles to men? Words, more words,
　　and the hurt comes on us, endless words　　　　1135
and a seer's techniques have brought us
terror and the truth.
CASSANDRA　The agony—O I am breaking!—Fate's so hard,
　　and the pain that floods my voice is mine alone.
Why have you brought me here, tormented as I am?　　1140
Why, unless to die with him, why else?
LEADER AND CHORUS　Mad with the rapture—god speeds you on
　　to the song, the deathsong,
like the nightingale[2] that broods on sorrow,
　　mourns her son, her son,　　　　1145
her life inspired with grief for him,
she lilts and shrills, dark bird that lives for night.
CASSANDRA　The nightingale—O for a song, a fate like hers!
　　The gods gave her a life of ease, swathed her in wings,
no tears, no wailing. The knife waits for me.　　1150
They'll splay me on the iron's double edge.
LEADER AND CHORUS　Why?—what god hurls you on, stroke on stroke
　　to the long dying fall?
Why the horror clashing through your music,
　　terror struck to song?—　　　　1155
why the anguish, the wild dance?
Where do your words of god and grief begin?
CASSANDRA　Ai, the wedding, wedding of Paris,
　　death to the loved ones. Oh Scamander,[3]
you nursed my father . . . once at your banks　　1160
　　I nursed and grew, and now at the banks
of Acheron,[4] the stream that carries sorrow,
it seems I'll chant my prophecies too soon.
LEADER AND CHORUS　What are you saying? Wait, it's clear,
　　a child could see the truth, it wounds within,　　1165
　　　Like a bloody fang it tears—
　　I hear your destiny—breaking sobs,
　　　cries that stab the ears.

---

2. Philomela was raped by Tereus, the husband of her sister Procne. The two sisters
avenged themselves by killing Tereus's son,
Itys, and serving up his flesh to Tereus to eat.
Procne was changed into a nightingale mourning for Itys (the name is an imitation of the
sound of the nightingale's song).
3. A Trojan river.
4. One of the rivers of the underworld.

CASSANDRA   Oh the grief, the grief of the city
  ripped to oblivion. Oh the victims, ·   1170
  the flocks my father burned at the wall,
      rich herds in flames . . . no cure for the doom
  that took the city after all, and I,
  her last ember, I go down with her.
LEADER AND CHORUS   You cannot stop, your song goes on—   1175
  some spirit drops from the heights and treads you down
      and the brutal strain grows—
      your death-throes come and come and
      I cannot see the end!
CASSANDRA   Then off with the veils that hid the fresh young
      bride[5]—   1180
  we will see the truth.
  Flare up once more, my oracle! Clear and sharp
  as the wind that blows toward the rising sun,
  I can feel a deeper swell now, gathering head
  to break at last and bring the dawn of grief.   1185

  No more riddles. I will teach you.
  Come, bear witness, run and hunt with me.
  We trail the old barbaric works of slaughter.

  These roofs—look up—there is a dancing troupe
  that never leaves. And they have their harmony   1190
  but it is harsh, their words are harsh, they drink
  beyond the limit. Flushed on the blood of men
  their spirit grows and none can turn away
  their revel breeding in the veins—the Furies!
  They cling to the house for life. They sing,   1195
  sing of the frenzy that began it all,
  strain rising on strain, showering curses
  on the man who tramples on his brother's bed.[6]

  There. Have I hit the mark or not? Am I a fraud,
  a fortune-teller babbling lies from door to door?   1200
  Swear how well I know the ancient crimes
  that live within this house.
LEADER   And if I did?
  Would an oath bind the wounds and heal us?
  But you amaze me. Bred across the sea,
  your language strange, and still you sense the truth   1205
  as if you had been here.
CASSANDRA   Apollo the Prophet
  introduced me to his gift.
LEADER   A *god*—and moved with love?

---

5. At this point, as the meter indicates, Cassandra changes from lyric song, the medium of emotion, to spoken iambic lines, the medium of rational discourse.

6. Thyestes, who seduced the wife of his brother, Atreus.

CASSANDRA   I was ashamed to tell this once,
  but now . . .
LEADER   We spoil ourselves with scruples,   1210
  long as things go well.
CASSANDRA   He came like a wrestler,
  magnificent, took me down and breathed his fire
  through me and—
LEADER   You bore him a child?
CASSANDRA   I yielded,
  then at the climax I recoiled—I deceived Apollo!
LEADER   But the god's skills—they seized you even then?   1215
CASSANDRA   Even then I told my people all the grief to come.
LEADER   And Apollo's anger never touched you?—is it possible?
CASSANDRA   Once I betrayed him I could never be believed.
LEADER   We believe you. Your visions seem so true.
CASSANDRA   Aieeeee!—
  the pain, the terror! the birth-pang of the seer   1220
  who tells the truth—
              it whirls me, oh,
  the storm comes again, the crashing chords!
  Look, you see them nestling at the threshold?
  Young, young in the darkness like a dream,
  like children really, yes, and their loved ones   1225
  brought them down . . .
               their hands, they fill their hands
  with their own flesh, they are serving it like food,
  holding out their entrails . . . now it's clear,
  I can see the armfuls of compassion, see the father
  reach to taste and—
            For so much suffering,   1230
  I tell you, someone plots revenge.
  A lion[7] who lacks a lion's heart,
  he sprawled at home in the royal lair
  and set a trap for the lord on his return.
  My lord . . . I must wear his yoke, I am his slave.   1235
  The lord of the men-of-war, he obliterated Troy—
  he is so blind, so lost to that detestable hellhound
  who pricks her ears and fawns and her tongue draws out
  her glittering words of welcome—
             No, he cannot see
  the stroke that Fury's hiding, stealth, murder.   1240
  What outrage—the woman kills the man!
                What to call
  that . . . monster of Greece, and bring my quarry down?
  Viper coiling back and forth?
            Some sea-witch?—

7. Aegisthus.

Scylla[8] crouched in her rocky nest—nightmare of sailors?
Raging mother of death, storming deathless war against 1245
the ones she loves!

                And how she howled in triumph,
boundless outrage. Just as the tide of battle
broke her way, she seems to rejoice that he
is safe at home from war, saved for her.

Believe me if you will. What will it matter 1250
if you won't? It comes when it comes,
and soon you'll see it face to face
and say the seer was all too true.
You will be moved with pity.

LEADER   Thyestes' feast,
the children's flesh—that I know, 1255
and the fear shudders through me. It's true,
real, no dark signs about it. I hear the rest
but it throws me off the scent.

CASSANDRA   Agamemnon.
You will see him dead.

LEADER   Peace, poor girl!
Put those words to sleep.

CASSANDRA   No use, 1260
the Healer[9] has no hand in this affair.

LEADER   Not if it's true—but god forbid it is!

CASSANDRA   You pray, and they close in to kill!

LEADER   What man prepares this, this dreadful—

CASSANDRA   Man?
You *are* lost, to every word I've said.

LEADER   Yes— 1265
I don't see who can bring the evil off.

CASSANDRA   And yet I know my Greek, too well.

LEADER   So does the Delphic oracle,[1]
but he's hard to understand.

CASSANDRA   His *fire*!—
sears me, sweeps me again—the torture! 1270
Apollo Lord of the Light, you burn,
you blind me—

           Agony!
             She is the lioness,
she rears on her hind legs, she beds with the wolf
when her lion king goes ranging—

                 she will kill me—
Ai, the torture!

           She is mixing her drugs, 1275
adding a measure more of hate for me.

---

8. A human-eating sea monster (see *Odyssey* 12,
pp. 460–61).
9. Apollo.

1. Apollo's oracle; its replies were celebrated
for their obscurity and ambiguity.

She gloats as she whets the sword for him.
He brought me home and we will pay in carnage.

Why mock yourself with these—trappings, the rod,
the god's wreath, his yoke around my throat?   1280
Before I die I'll tread you—
        [*Ripping off her regalia, stamping it into the ground.*]
                                Down, out,
die die die!
Now you're down. I've paid you back.
Look for another victim—I am free at last—
make her rich in all your curse and doom.
        [*Staggering backwards as if wrestling with a spirit tearing at her robes.*]
                                See,   1285
Apollo himself, his fiery hands—I feel him again,
he's stripping off my robes, the Seer's robes!
And after he looked down and saw me mocked,
even in these, his glories, mortified by friends
I loved, and they hated me, they were so blind   1290
to their own demise—
                        I went from door to door,
I was wild with the god, I heard them call me
"Beggar! Wretch! Starve for bread in hell!"

And I endured it all, and now he will
extort me as his due. A seer for the Seer.   1295
He brings me here to die like this,
not to serve at my father's altar. No,
the block is waiting. The cleaver steams
with my life blood, the first blood drawn
for the king's last rites.
        [*Regaining her composure and moving to the altar.*]
                                We will die,   1300
but not without some honor from the gods.
There will come another[2] to avenge us,
born to kill his mother, born
his father's champion. A wanderer, a fugitive
driven off his native land, he will come home   1305
to cope the stones of hate that menace all he loves.
The gods have sworn a monumental oath: as his father lies
upon the ground he draws him home with power like a prayer.

Then why so pitiful, why so many tears?
I have seen my city faring as she fared,   1310
and those who took her, judged by the gods,
faring as they fare. I must be brave.
It is my turn to die.
        [*Approaching the doors.*]

2. Orestes.

I address you as the Gates of Death.
I pray it comes with one clear stroke,   1315
no convulsions, the pulses ebbing out
in gentle death. I'll close my eyes and sleep.

LEADER   So much pain, poor girl, and so much truth,
you've told so much. But if you *see* it coming,
clearly—how can you go to your own death,   1320
like a beast to the altar driven on by god,
and hold your head so high?

CASSANDRA   No escape, my friends,
not now.

LEADER   But the last hour should be savored.

CASSANDRA   My time has come. Little to gain from flight.

LEADER   You're brave, believe me, full of gallant heart.   1325

CASSANDRA   Only the wretched go with praise like that.

LEADER   But to go nobly lends a man some grace.

CASSANDRA   My noble father—you and your noble children.

[*She nears the threshold and recoils, groaning in revulsion.*]

LEADER   What now? what terror flings you back?
Why? Unless some horror in the brain—

CASSANDRA   Murder.   1330
The house breathes with murder—bloody shambles!³

LEADER   No, no, only the victims at the hearth.

CASSANDRA   I know that odor. I smell the open grave.

LEADER   But the Syrian myrrh,⁴ it fills the halls with splendor,
can't you sense it?

CASSANDRA   Well, I must go in now,   1335
mourning Agamemnon's death and mine.
Enough of life!

[*Approaching the doors again and crying out.*]

            Friends—I cried out,
not from fear like a bird fresh caught,
but that you will testify to *how* I died.
When the queen, woman for woman, dies for me,   1340
and a man falls for the man who married grief.
That's all I ask, my friends. A stranger's gift
for one about to die.

LEADER   Poor creature, you
and the end you see so clearly. I pity you.

CASSANDRA   I'd like a few words more, a kind of dirge,   1345
it is my own. I pray to the sun,
the last light I'll see,
that when the avengers cut the assassins down
they will avenge me too, a slave who died,
an easy conquest.

            Oh men, your destiny.   1350

---

3. A slaughterhouse.
4. Incense burned at the sacrifice. Another
interpretation of this line runs, "What you

speak of (that is, the smell of the open grave)
is no Syrian incense, giving splendor to the
palace."

When all is well a shadow can overturn it.
When trouble comes a stroke of the wet sponge,
and the picture's blotted out. And that,
I think that breaks the heart.
     [*She goes through the doors.*]

CHORUS   But the lust for power never dies—   1355
    men cannot have enough.
No one will lift a hand to send it
from his door, to give it warning,
"Power, never come again!"
Take this man: the gods in glory   1360
gave him Priam's city to plunder,
brought him home in splendor like a god.
But now if he must pay for the blood
his fathers shed, and die for the deaths
he brought to pass, and bring more death   1365
to avenge his dying, show us one
    who boasts himself born free
of the raging angel, once he hears—
     [*Cries break out within the palace.*]

AGAMEMNON   Aagh!
Struck deep—the death-blow, deep—

LEADER   Quiet. Cries,
but who? Someone's stabbed—

AGAMEMNON   Aaagh, again . . .   1370
second blow—struck home.

LEADER   The work is done,
you can feel it. The king, and the great cries—
Close ranks now, find the right way out.
     [*But the old men scatter, each speaks singly.*]

CHORUS   —I say send out heralds, muster the guard,
    they'll save the house.

                 —And I say rush in now,   1375
catch them red-handed—butchery running on their blades.

    —Right with you, do something—now or never!

    —Look at them, beating the drum for insurrection.

                     —Yes,
we're wasting time. They rape the name of caution,
their hands will never sleep.

                 —Not a plan in sight.   1380
Let men of action do the planning, too.

    —I'm helpless. Who can raise the dead with words?

    —What, drag out our lives? bow down to the tyrants,
    the ruin of the house?

—Never, better to die
on your feet than live on your knees.

—Wait,   1385
do we take the cries for signs, prophesy like seers
and give him up for dead?

—No more suspicions,
not another word till we have proof.

—Confusion
on all sides—one thing to do. See how it stands
with Agamemnon, once and for all we'll see—   1390

[*He rushes at the doors. They open and reveal a silver cauldron that holds
the body of* AGAMEMNON *shrouded in bloody robes, with the body of* CAS-
SANDRA *to his left and* CLYTAEMNESTRA *standing to his right, sword in
hand. She strides towards the* CHORUS.]

CLYTAEMNESTRA   Words, endless words I've said to serve the moment—
Now it makes me proud to tell the truth.
How else to prepare a death for deadly men
who seem to love you? How to rig the nets
of pain so high no man can overleap them?   1395

I brooded on this trial, this ancient blood feud
year by year. At last my hour came.
Here I stand and here I struck
and here my work is done.
I did it all. I don't deny it, no.   1400
He had no way to flee or fight his destiny—

[*Unwinding the robes from* AGAMEMNON'S *body, spreading them before the
altar where the old men cluster around them, unified as a chorus once again.*]

our never-ending, all embracing net, I cast it
wide for the royal haul, I coil him round and round
in the wealth, the robes of doom, and then I strike him
once, twice, and at each stroke he cries in agony—   1405
he buckles at the knees and crashes here!
And when he's down I add the third, last blow,
to the Zeus who saves the dead beneath the ground
I send that third blow home in homage like a prayer.[5]

So he goes down, and the life is bursting out of him— 1410
great sprays of blood, and the murderous shower
wounds me, dyes me black and I, I revel
like the Earth when the spring rains come down,
the blessed gifts of god, and the new green spear
splits the sheath and rips to birth in glory!   1415

So it stands, elders of Argos gathered here.
Rejoice if you can rejoice—I glory.

5. Like the third libation to Zeus (see p. 642, n. 7).

And if I'd pour upon his body the libation
it deserves, what wine could match my words?
It is right and more than right. He flooded   1420
the vessel of our proud house with misery,
with the vintage of the curse and now
he drains the dregs. My lord is home at last.

LEADER   You appall me, you, your brazen words—
exulting over your fallen king.

CLYTAEMNESTRA   And you,   1425
you try me like some desperate woman.
My heart is steel, well you know. Praise me,
blame me as you choose. It's all one.
Here is Agamemnon, my husband made a corpse
by this right hand—a masterpiece of Justice.   1430
Done is done.

CHORUS   Woman!—what poison cropped from the soil
or strained from the heaving sea, what nursed you,
drove you insane? You brave the curse of Greece.

    You have cut away and flung away and now
the people cast you off to exile,   1435
broken with our hate.

CLYTAEMNESTRA   And now you sentence me?—
you banish *me* from the city, curses breathing
down my neck? But *he*—
name one charge you brought against him then.
He thought no more of it than killing a beast,   1440
and his flocks were rich, teeming in their fleece,
but he sacrificed his own child, our daughter,
the agony I labored into love,
to charm away the savage winds of Thrace.[6]

Didn't the law demand you banish him?—   1445
hunt him from the land for all his guilt?
But now you witness what I've done
and you are ruthless judges.
                            Threaten away!
I'll meet you blow for blow. And if I fall
the throne is yours. If god decrees the reverse,   1450
late as it is, old men, you'll learn your place.

CHORUS   Mad with ambition,
    shrilling pride!—some Fury
crazed with the carnage rages through your brain—
    I can see the flecks of blood inflame your eyes!   1455
But vengeance comes—you'll lose your loved ones,
stroke for painful stroke.

CLYTAEMNESTRA   Then learn this, too, the power of my oaths.
By the child's Rights I brought to birth,

6. Winds from the North (at Aulis).

by Ruin, by Fury—the three gods to whom   1460
I sacrificed this man—I swear my hopes
will never walk the halls of fear so long
as Aegisthus lights the fire on my hearth.
Loyal to me as always, no small shield
to buttress my defiance.
                              Here he lies.   1465
He brutalized me. The darling of all
the golden girls[7] who spread the gates of Troy.
And here his spearprize . . . what wonders she beheld!—
the seer of Apollo shared my husband's bed,
his faithful mate who knelt at the rowing-benches,   1470
worked by every hand.
                              They have their rewards.
He as you know. And she, the swan of the gods
who lived to sing her latest, dying song—
his lover lies beside him.
She brings a fresh, voluptuous relish to my bed!   1475
CHORUS   Oh quickly, let me die—
no bed of labor, no, no wasting illness . . .
bear me off in the sleep that never ends,
      now that he has fallen,
now that our dearest shield lies battered—   1480
   Woman made him suffer,
      woman struck him down.
      Helen the wild, maddening Helen,
      one for the many, the thousand lives
      you murdered under Troy. Now you are crowned   1485
      with this consummate wreath, the blood
      that lives in memory, glistens age to age.
      Once in the halls she walked and she was war,
      angel of war, angel of agony, lighting men to death.

CLYTAEMNESTRA   Pray no more for death, broken   1490
   as you are. And never turn
      your wrath on her, call her
   the scourge of men, the one alone
   who destroyed a myriad Greek lives—
   Helen the grief that never heals.   1495
CHORUS   The *spirit*!—you who tread
   the house and the twinborn sons of Tantalus[8]—
you empower the sisters, Fury's twins
      whose power tears the heart!
Perched on the corpse your carrion raven   1500
      glories in her hymn,

7. In Greek *chryseïdōn*, which recalls the girl   8. Father of Pelops, grandfather of Atreus.
in the first book of the *Iliad* (1.112), Chryseïs,   "Sons": descendants—that is, Agamemnon and
whom Agamemnon said he preferred to Cly-   Menelaus.
taemnestra.

her screaming hymn of pride.
CLYTAEMNESTRA   Now you set your judgment straight,
you summon *him*! Three generations
feed the spirit in the race.   1505
Deep in the veins he feeds our bloodlust—
aye, before the old wound dies
it ripens in another flow of blood.
CHORUS   The great curse of the house, the spirit,
dead weight wrath—and you can praise it!   1510
Praise the insatiate doom that feeds
relentless on our future and our sons.
Oh all through the will of Zeus,
the cause of all, the one who works it all.
What comes to birth that is not Zeus?   1515
Our lives are pain, what part not come from god?

Oh, my king, my captain,
how to salute you, how to mourn you?
What can I say with all my warmth and love?
Here in the black widow's web you lie,   1520
gasping out your life
in a sacrilegious death, dear god,
reduced to a slave's bed,
my king of men, yoked by stealth and Fate,
by the wife's hand that thrust the two-edged sword.   1525

CLYTAEMNESTRA   You claim the work is mine, call me
Agamemnon's wife—you are so wrong.
Fleshed in the wife of this dead man,
the spirit lives within me,
our savage ancient spirit of revenge.   1530
In return for Atreus' brutal feast
he kills his perfect son—for every
murdered child, a crowning sacrifice.
CHORUS   And *you*, innocent of his murder?
And who could swear to that? and how? . . .   1535
and still an avenger could arise,
bred by the fathers' crimes, and lend a hand.
He wades in the blood of brothers,
stream on mounting stream—black war erupts
and where he strides revenge will stride,   1540
clots will mass for the young who were devoured.

Oh my king, my captain,
how to salute you, how to mourn you?
What can I say with all my warmth and love?
Here in the black widow's web you lie,   1545
gasping out your life
in a sacrilegious death, dear god,
reduced to a slave's bed,

my king of men, yoked by stealth and Fate,
by the wife's hand that thrust the two-edged sword.   1550

CLYTAEMNESTRA   No slave's death, I think—
no stealthier than the death he dealt
our house and the offspring of our loins,
    Iphigeneia, girl of tears.
Act for act, wound for wound!   1555
Never exult in Hades, swordsman,
here you are repaid. By the sword
you did your work and by the sword you die.

CHORUS   The mind reels—where to turn?
      All plans dashed, all hope! I cannot think . . .   1560
the roofs are toppling, I dread the drumbeat thunder
the heavy rains of blood will crush the house
      the first light rains are over—
Justice brings new acts of agony, yes,
on new grindstones Fate is grinding sharp the sword of Justice.   1565

Earth, dear Earth,
if only you'd drawn me under
long before I saw him huddled
in the beaten silver bath.
Who will bury him, lift his dirge?   1570
    [*Turning to* CLYTAEMNESTRA.]
You, can you dare *this*?
To kill your lord with your own hand
then mourn his soul with tributes, terrible tributes—
do his enormous works a great dishonor.
This godlike man, this hero. Who at the grave   1575
will sing his praises, pour the wine of tears?
Who will labor there with truth of heart?

CLYTAEMNESTRA   This is no concern of yours.
The hand that bore and cut him down
will hand him down to Mother Earth.   1580
This house will never mourn for him.
    Only our daughter Iphigeneia,
by all rights, will rush to meet him
first at the churning straits,[9]
the ferry over tears—   1585
she'll fling her arms around her father,
pierce him with her love.

CHORUS   Each charge meets counter-charge.
      one can judge between them. Justice.
The plunderer plundered, the killer pays the price.
The truth still holds while Zeus still holds the throne: 1590

9. The river of the underworld over which the dead were ferried.

the one who acts must suffer—
that is law. Who, who can tear from the veins
the bad seed, the curse? The race is welded to its ruin.

CLYTAEMNESTRA   At last you see the future and the truth!   1595
But I will swear a pact with the spirit
born within us. I embrace his works,
cruel as they are but done at last,
    if he will leave our house
in the future, bleed another line   1600
with kinsmen murdering kinsmen.
Whatever he may ask. A few things
are all I need, once I have purged
our fury to destroy each other—
    purged it from our halls.

> [AEGISTHUS *has emerged from the palace with his bodyguard and stands
> triumphant over the body of* AGAMEMNON.]

AEGISTHUS   O what a brilliant day   1605
it is for vengeance! Now I can say once more
there are gods in heaven avenging men,
blazing down on all the crimes of earth.
Now at last I see this man brought down
in the Furies' tangling robes. It feasts my eyes—   1610
he pays for the plot his father's hand contrived.

Atreus, this man's father, was king of Argos.
My father, Thyestes—let me make this clear—
Atreus' brother challenged him for the crown,
and Atreus drove him out of house and home   1615
then lured him back, and home Thyestes came,
poor man, a suppliant to his own hearth,
to pray that Fate might save him.
                    So it did.
There was no dying, no staining our native ground
with *his* blood. Thyestes was the guest,   1620
and this man's godless father—

> [*Pointing to* AGAMEMNON.]

the zeal of the host outstripping a brother's love,
made my father a feast that seemed a feast for gods,
a love feast of his children's flesh.
                        He cuts
the extremities, feet and delicate hands   1625
into small pieces, scatters them over the dish
and serves it to Thyestes throned on high.
He picks at the flesh he cannot recognize,
the soul of innocence eating the food of ruin—
look,

> [*Pointing to the bodies at his feet.*]

that feeds upon the house! And then,   1630

when he sees the monstrous thing he's done, he shrieks,
he reels back head first and vomits up that butchery,
tramples the feast—brings down the curse of Justice:
"Crash to ruin, all the race of Pleisthenes,[1] crash down!"

So you see him, down. And I, the weaver of Justice,   1635
plotted out the kill. Atreus drove us into exile,
my struggling father and I, a babe-in-arms,
his last son, but I became a man
and Justice brought me home. I was abroad
but I reached out and seized my man,   1640
link by link I clamped the fatal scheme
together. Now I could die gladly, even I—
now I see this monster in the nets of Justice.

LEADER   Aegisthus, you revel in pain—you sicken me.
You say you killed the king in cold blood,   1645
singlehanded planned his pitiful death?
I say there's no escape. In the hour of judgment,
trust to this, your head will meet the people's
rocks and curses.

AEGISTHUS   You say! you slaves at the oars—
while the master of the benches cracks the whip?   1650
You'll learn, in your late age, how much it hurts
to teach old bones their place. We have techniques—
chains and the pangs of hunger,
two effective teachers, excellent healers.
They can even cure old men of pride and gall.   1655
Look—can't you see? The more you kick
against the pricks, the more you suffer.

LEADER   You, pathetic—
the king had just returned from battle.
You waited out the war and fouled his lair,   1660
you planned my great commander's fall.

AEGISTHUS   Talk on—
you'll scream for every word, my little Orpheus.[2]
We'll see if the world comes dancing to your song,
your absurd barking—snarl your breath away!
I'll make you dance, I'll bring you all to heel.   1665

LEADER   *You* rule Argos? You who schemed his death
but cringed to cut him down with your own hand?

AEGISTHUS   The treachery was the woman's work, clearly.
I was a marked man, his enemy for ages.
But I will use his riches, stop at nothing   1670
to civilize his people. All but the rebel:
him I'll yoke and break—
no cornfed colt, running free in the traces.

---

1. A name sometimes inserted into the gene-   2. A mythical singer who charmed all nature
alogy of the house of Tantalus.   with his music.

Hunger, ruthless mate of the dark torture-chamber,
trains her eyes upon him till he drops! 1675

LEADER   Coward, why not kill the man yourself?
Why did the woman, the corruption of Greece
and the gods of Greece, have to bring him down?
Orestes—If he still sees the light of day,
bring him home, good Fates, home to kill 1680
this pair at last. Our champion in slaughter!

AEGISTHUS   Bent on insolence? Well, you'll learn, quickly.
At them, men—you have your work at hand!

[*His men draw swords; the old men take up their sticks.*]

LEADER   At them, fist at the hilt, to the last man—

AEGISTHUS   Fist at the hilt, I'm not afraid to die. 1685

LEADER   It's death you want and death you'll have—
we'll make that word your last.

[CLYTAEMNESTRA *moves between them, restraining* AEGISTHUS.]

CLYTAEMNESTRA   No more, my dearest,
no more grief. We have too much to reap
right here, our mighty harvest of despair.
Our lives are based on pain. No bloodshed now. 1690

Fathers of Argos, turn for home before you act
and suffer for it. What we did was destiny.
If we could end the suffering, how we would rejoice.
The spirit's brutal hoof has struck our heart.
And that is what a woman has to say. 1695
Can you accept the truth?

[CLYTAEMNESTRA *turns to leave.*]

AEGISTHUS   But these . . . mouths
that bloom in filth—spitting insults in my teeth.
You tempt your fates, you insubordinate dogs—
to hurl abuse at me, your master!

LEADER   No Greek
worth his salt would grovel at your feet. 1700

AEGISTHUS   I—I'll stalk you all your days!

LEADER   Not if the spirit brings Orestes home.

AEGISTHUS   Exiles feed on hope—well I know.

LEADER   More,
gorge yourself to bursting—soil justice, while you can.

AEGISTHUS   I promise you, you'll pay, old fools—in good time, too! 1705

LEADER   Strut on your own dunghill, you cock beside your mate.

CLYTAEMNESTRA   Let them howl—they're impotent. You and I have
    power now.
We will set the house in order once for all.

[*They enter the palace; the great doors close behind them; the old men
disband and wander off.*]

SOPHOCLES

ca. 496–406 B.C.E.

The seven surviving plays of Sophocles are often considered the most perfect achievement of ancient Athens. They show us people—presented with psychological depth and subtlety—who stand apart from others, on the edges of their social groups. Sophocles invites us to ask what it means to be part of a family, part of a city, part of a team or an army, or part of the human race. Can we choose to embrace or reject our family, friends, and society, or do we have to accept the place to which we were born? Is it a gesture of heroism or folly to take a stand as an outsider? What should we do if forced to choose between our family and a wider social group? Sophocles' thought-provoking and compelling dramas explore themes that are just as relevant today as they were in the fifth century B.C.E., and they provide the classic treatments of mythic figures, such as Oedipus and Antigone, who have been central to later Western culture.

LIFE AND TIMES

Sophocles was a generation younger than **Aeschylus**, and had an unusually long, successful, productive, and apparently happy life. He was born at the start of the fifth century, around 496 B.C.E., in the village of Colonus, which was a short distance north of Athens. His family was probably fairly wealthy—his father may have owned a workshop producing armor, a particularly marketable product at this time of war—and Sophocles seems to have been well educated. An essential element in Greek boys' education at this time was studying the Homeric poems, and Sophocles obviously learned this

lesson well; in later times, he was called the "most Homeric" of the three surviving Athenian tragedians. He was a good-looking, charming boy and a talented dancer. In 480, when he was about fifteen or sixteen, he was chosen to lead a group of naked boys who danced in the victory celebrations for Athens' defeat of the Persian navy at Salamis. The beginning of his public career thus coincided with his city's period of greatest glory and international prestige.

Athens became the major power in the Mediterranean world in the middle decades of the fifth century B.C.E., a period known as the golden or classical age. The most important political figure in the newly dominant city-state was Pericles, a statesman who was also Sophocles' personal friend and who particularly encouraged the arts. Pericles seems to have instituted various legal measures to enable the theater to flourish: for instance, rich citizens were obliged to provide funding for theater productions, and the less wealthy may have had their theater tickets subsidized.

The prosperity of Sophocles' city took a sharp turn for the worse around 431 B.C.E., when the poet would have been in his mid-sixties. The Peloponnesian War, between Athens and Sparta, began at that time and would last until after Sophocles' death. Soon after the outbreak of war, Sophocles' friend Pericles died in a terrible plague that afflicted the whole city. In the last decades of the century, the city became increasingly impoverished and demoralized by war.

Sophocles worked in the Athenian theater all his life. He made some important technical changes in dramatic productions, introducing scene painting and increasing the number of chorus members from twelve to fifteen. His most important innovation was bringing in a third actor (a "tritagonist"). This allowed for three-way dialogues, and for a drama that concentrates on the complex interactions and relationships of individuals with one another. The chorus in Sophocles' dramas became far less central to the plot than it had been in Aeschylus; this is part of the reason why Sophocles' plays may seem more modern to twenty-first century readers and audiences.

Another quality that makes Sophocles particularly accessible to modern readers is his interest in realistic characterization. Sophocles' most memorable characters are intense, passionate, and often larger than life, but always fully human. They frequently adopt positions that seem extreme, but for which they have the best of motives. Sophocles' tragedies ask us to consider when and how it is right to compromise, and to measure the slim divide between concession and selling out. Clashes between stubborn heroism and the voice of moderation are found in all Sophocles' surviving plays.

Contemporaries gave Sophocles' talent its due. He won first prize at the Great Dionysia for the first time in 468 B.C.E., defeating his older rival, Aeschylus; he was still under thirty at the time. Sophocles would defeat Aeschylus several more times in the course of his career. His output was large: he composed over a hundred and twenty plays. The seven that survive include the three Theban plays, dealing with Oedipus and his family: *Oedipus the King*, *Antigone*, and *Oedipus at Colonus*. These were written at intervals of many years, and were never intended to be performed together. The other four surviving tragedies are *Ajax*, about a strongman hero who is driven mad by Athena; *Trachiniae*, about

Heracles' agonizing death at the hands of his jealous wife Deineira (who had thought the poison she gave him was a love potion); *Electra*, which focuses on the unending grief and rage of Agamemnon's daughter after her father's murder; and *Philoctetes*, about the Greek embassy to persuade an embittered, wounded hero to return to battle in Troy. The dating of most of these plays is uncertain, although we know *Philoctetes* is a late play, composed in 409 B.C.E. The judges at the Great Dionysia loved Sophocles' work: he won first prize over twenty times, and never came lower than second.

Sophocles seems to have been equally popular as a person, known for his mellow, easygoing temperament, his religious piety, and his appreciation for the beauty of adolescent boys. We are told that he had "so much charm of character that he was loved everywhere, by everyone." He was friendly with the prominent intellectuals of his day, including the world's first historian, **Herodotus**. He participated in the political activity of the city; he served under Pericles as a treasurer in 443 and 442 B.C.E., and was elected as a general under him in 441. After the Sicilian disaster in 413, in which Athens lost enormous numbers of men and ships, Sophocles—then in his eighties—was one of ten men elected to an emergency group created for policy formation. Sophocles' participation in public life suggests that he was seen as a trustworthy and wise member of the community. Sophocles was married and had five sons, one of whom, Iophon, became a tragedian himself. Sophocles lived to advanced old age and was over ninety when he died.

OEDIPUS THE KING

Many first-time readers of *Oedipus the King* will already know the shocking secret that Oedipus eventually discovers: he killed his father and married his mother, without knowing what he was doing. The mythical background to this play is familiar to readers today, and would have been well known, in its broad outlines, to Sophocles' original audience. This is a drama not of surprise but of suspense: we watch Oedipus uncover the buried truth about himself and his parentage, of which he, unlike us, is ignorant. The mystery, gradually revealed to the spectators in the course of the play, is not what the king has done, but how he will discover what he has done, and how he will respond to this terrible new knowledge.

The legend holds that Laius (Laios), son of Labdacus and king of Thebes, learned long ago from the Delphic oracle (sacred to Apollo) that his son would kill him. When Laius had a son by his wife, Jocasta (Jokasta), he gave the baby to a shepherd to be exposed on Mount Cithaeron. Exposure, a fairly common practice in the ancient world, involved leaving a baby out in some wild place, presumably to die; it allowed parents to dispose of unwanted children without incurring blood guilt. Laius increased the odds against the child's survival by piercing and binding his feet, so there was no chance he could crawl away. But the shepherd felt sorry for the boy and saved him. He was adopted by the childless king and queen of Corinth, Polybus and Merope, and grew up believing himself to be their son.

One day another oracle warned Oedipus that he would kill his father and marry his mother. Oedipus fled Corinth in the direction of Thebes, to avoid this fate. At a place where three paths crossed, he encountered his real father, Laius, without knowing who he was; they quarreled, and Oedipus killed Laius. When he reached Thebes, he found the city oppressed by a dreadful female monster, a Sphinx—part human,

part lion, often also depicted in Greek art with the wings of an eagle and the tail of a snake. The Sphinx refused to let anybody into the city unless they could answer her riddle: "What walks on four legs in the morning, two legs at noon, and three legs in the evening?" She strangled and devoured all travelers who failed to answer the riddle. But Oedipus gave the right answer: "Man." (Human beings crawl on all fours in infancy, walk on two feet in adulthood, and use a cane in old age.) The Sphinx was defeated, and Oedipus was welcomed into the city as a savior. He married the newly widowed queen, Jocasta, and took over the throne.

When Sophocles' play begins, Oedipus has been ruling Thebes successfully for many years, and has four children by Jocasta, two sons and two daughters. But a new trouble is now afflicting the city. Plague has come to Thebes, and the dying inhabitants are searching for the reason why the gods are angry with the city.

The city of Athens suffered a terrible plague in 429 B.C.E., and the play may well have been composed and performed soon afterward—although the dating is uncertain and disputed. Sophocles certainly seems to invite comparisons between the real Athens and the mythical Thebes. Oedipus himself can be seen as a typical fifth-century Athenian: he is optimistic, irascible, self-confident, both pious and skeptical in his attitudes toward religion, and a committed believer in the power of human reason.

In his *Poetics,* the philosopher **Aristotle** describes this play as the finest of all Greek tragedies. It includes two plot patterns that he thought were essential to good drama: a reversal of fortune (*peripeteia*), and a recognition (*anagnorisis*). Aristotle famously cites Oedipus as an example of someone whose fall into misfortune is the result not of bad deeds or evil character, but of some "mistake"—the Greek word is *hamartia*. Later critics applied the quite different concept of a "tragic flaw" to Oedipus, suggesting that we are supposed to see the disastrous events of the drama as somehow the king's own fault. An important consideration against this reading is that in *Oedipus at Colonus*, a later play about the last days of Oedipus, Sophocles makes his hero give a compelling self-defense: "How is my *nature* evil— / if all I did was to return a blow?" There is a clear distinction in Greek thought between moral culpability— which is attached to deliberate, conscious actions—and religious pollution, which may afflict even those who are morally innocent. Readers must decide for themselves how far they think Sophocles goes in presenting his Oedipus as a sympathetic or even admirable figure.

Another popular approach to the play has been to see it as a classic "tragedy of fate," in which a man is brought low by destiny or the gods. Here, we need to distinguish the myth—which can plausibly be seen as a story about the inevitable unfolding of divine will—from Sophocles' treatment of the myth in his play, which suggests a more complex relationship between destiny and human action. Before Sophocles, Aeschylus had produced a trilogy that dealt with the family of Laius and Oedipus. This does not survive, but it is likely that it showed the gradual fulfillment of an inherited curse. In Sophocles' play, our attention is focused less on the original events and their causes (the killing of Laius and the marriage to Jocasta) than on the process by which Oedipus uncovers what he has done.

Sophocles multiplies the number of oracles and messengers in the story, and Apollo—the god associated with prophecy, poetry, and interpretation, as well as with light and the sun—presides over the relentless unfolding of the truth. Oracles are only one of many types of riddling, ambiguous, or ambivalent language used in the play, which is concerned with all kinds of interpretation. Moments of dramatic irony, when the audience hears a meaning of which the speaker is unaware, are another important reminder that words may have more than one sense. For instance, Oedipus vows to fight in defense of Laius "as for my father"— speaking more truly than he knows. The interplay between literal and metaphorical meanings forms another essential technique in the play. Sophocles creates a relationship between literal and metaphorical blindness, between the light of the sun and the light of insight, between Oedipus as "father" of his people and as real father to his own siblings, and between sickness as a physical affliction and as a metaphor for pollution.

The riddle of the Sphinx defines humanity by the number of feet we use at different points in our lives. Sophocles seems to suggest that the name *Oedipus* is closely associated with feet: it can be read either as "Know-Foot" (from the verb *oida*, "to know," and *pous*, "foot"— an appropriate name for the man who solved the Sphinx's riddle), or as "Swell-Foot" (from the verb *oidao*, to swell— a reminder of the baby Oedipus's wounded feet). The first interpretation of his name makes Oedipus seem like an Everyman figure, a representative of all humanity: he is the one who truly understands the human condition. The second reminds us of the ways in which Oedipus is not like us: his feet mark the fact that he was cast out by his parents, rejected from his city, and that he has, unwittingly, done things that seem to make it impossible for him to be part of any human community.

Sigmund Freud famously claimed that the Oedipus myth represents a psychological phenomenon, the "Oedipus complex," which involves the (supposed) desire of all boys to kill their fathers and marry their mothers. But Sophocles' Oedipus does not suffer from Freud's complex: his terrible actions are committed in total ignorance, not through an unconscious desire for patricide or sex with his mother. Another way to think of Sophocles' Oedipus is as a hero who, like Odysseus, struggles to find his way back home after many wanderings and encounters with terrible monsters—but finds himself in a perverted version of the homecoming story, in which the arrival is not the end but the beginning of a nightmare.

A play whose secret you already know might seem unlikely to be interesting. But it is impossible to be bored by *Oedipus the King*. The plot races to its terrible conclusion with the twisting, breakneck pace of a thrilling murder mystery, while the contradictory figure of Oedipus himself—the blind rationalist, the polluted king, the killer of his father, the son and husband of Jocasta, the hunter and the hunted, the stranger in his own home—is a commanding presence who dominates the stage even when he can no longer see.

ANTIGONE

Although funeral practices vary from one culture to another, reverence for the dead and the assumption that we have a responsibility to dispose of corpses in a proper fashion are essential features of all human societies. But Sophocles' *Antigone* explores a situation where the duty to honor and bury the dead seems to conflict with another deep human imperative: the need to create strong community bonds, and to make sharp distinctions between enemies and friends, especially in times of war.

The play was probably composed earlier than *Oedipus the King*, around 442 B.C.E. But it is set at a later point in the chronology of the myth. Oedipus has made his terrible discoveries, and

is dead. His two sons, Eteokles and Polyneices, have fought over the inheritance of the throne of Thebes. While Eteokles had control of Thebes, Polyneices gathered an army, with the help of the king of Argos, and laid siege to the walled city with its seven gates. The brothers eventually faced each other in single combat, and both were killed. *Antigone* begins in the aftermath of this conflict. Eteokles, defender of the city, has been buried with full honor, but the body of Polyneices, as leader of the army that attacked Thebes, still lies outside the city walls. Kreon (the same character as "Creon" in *Oedipus the King*), brother of Oedipus's wife, Jokasta, has now assumed the throne and has issued an edict that the body of the traitor Polyneices must be left unburied.

Several earlier epic narratives and dramas had dealt with the story of Thebes, including Aeschylus's *Seven against Thebes*, which concentrates on the terrible killing of one brother by the other. Sophocles' treatment of the myth was original in a number of important ways. Earlier versions had described Kreon's refusal to bury any of the Argive dead; he was eventually persuaded to do so by the king of Argos. But Sophocles concentrates not on a whole army of dead soldiers but on a single dead brother, and he sets Kreon in conflict not with a fellow king, but with the members of his own family: his son, Haimon, his wife, Eurydike, and his niece, Antigone—characters who were sketchy or nonexistent in earlier versions. Sophocles transforms a story about a clash between two cities into a drama concerned with conflicts between community and family, between man and woman, between young and old, between religious and secular duties, and between the rights of the living and those of the dead. The play shows us a series of oppositions, between values or themes (love and hate, city and family, living and dead) and between characters: Antigone and her sister,

Ismene; Kreon and his son, Haimon; and, above all, Kreon and Antigone.

Antigone often seems to invite us to take sides on points of principle, and many readers find themselves siding more with Antigone than with Kreon. Antigone's decision to bury her brother, a lone woman standing up against the king, seems an obvious instance of "speaking truth to power." Modern readers usually like rebels. Antigone seems, in several scenes of the play, to stand for values we can all cheer for—love, loyalty, and eternal, divine truth—against mere political expediency. She declares, in one inspiring and famous speech, that she opposes Kreon's edict because she chooses to obey the "unwritten and infallible laws" of the gods.

But the play shows us that there is more than one side even to such points of principle as the duty to bury the dead. Sophocles' characters are complex, and neither Antigone nor Kreon can be reduced to a single moral stance. Antigone talks about what she owes to "the dead," as if she were committed to the burial of all family members; but in at least one instance, she suggests that her actions are inspired specifically by her dead brother: a lost husband or child could be replaced, but "with my mother and father both concealed in Hades, no more brothers ever could be born." Antigone's devotion to Polyneices is presented as strange and extreme, almost erotic—in contrast to the moderate position of her sister, Ismene. Antigone's identity as a woman is equally complex. Burying the dead was normally the province of women in Greek society. But Antigone also shows an obsessive preoccupation with the "masculine" values of her own honor and glory, which she refuses to share with anybody. She faces death with courage, and even eagerness; but our final glimpse of her

is as a vulnerable young girl, full of regret at the life she will never live.

Kreon, an equally complex figure, is far more sympathetic than he might seem at first glance. It is a mistake to see him simply as an embodiment of civic, secular law rather than the rights of individuals and the family. Kreon presents himself, not Antigone, as the real defender of family life and of religion. He suggests that Zeus, as the sky god who protects families, will support his attempts to impose order both on his city and on the members of his household: "There is no greater evil than unruliness. It ruins cities and makes households desolate." Yet his debate with his son, Haimon, reminds us that Antigone is not necessarily acting against the values of the city: Kreon, not Antigone, may be the one acting out of "self-will," against the community. Moreover, Kreon's actions are clearly motivated by his own anxieties about his authority—as a ruler, as a father, and as a man. "By no means let a woman get the upper hand," he declares. Similarly, he is shocked by the idea that his son might dare to correct his father. He acknowledges, too late, that his inflexibility has destroyed his home.

The most important theme in *Antigone* is love: both sexual love and love of family. These are represented by two different words in Greek: *eros*, sexual desire, and *philia*, the love that binds us to members of our family and our close friends. Sophocles explores the implications of a traditional Greek ethical rule, that you should "love your friends, and hate your enemies." The play invites us to consider what happens when family members become political enemies: do they remain friends, or not? Is love more important than any ideological or moral principle? Or can love itself be taken too far?

Oedipus the King[1]

CHARACTERS

OEDIPUS, *King of Thebes*
JOCASTA, *His Wife*
CREON, *His Brother-in-Law*
TEIRESIAS, *an Old Blind Prophet*
A PRIEST

FIRST MESSENGER
SECOND MESSENGER
A HERDSMAN
A CHORUS OF OLD MEN OF THEBES

SCENE: *In front of the palace of* OEDIPUS *at Thebes. To the right of the stage near the altar stands the* PRIEST *with a crowd of children.* OEDIPUS *emerges from the central door.*[2]

OEDIPUS   Children, young sons and daughters of old Cadmus,
why do you sit here with your suppliant crowns?[3]
The town is heavy with a mingled burden
of sounds and smells, of groans and hymns and incense;
I did not think it fit that I should hear   5
of this from messengers but came myself,—
I Oedipus whom all men call the Great.
        [*He turns to the* PRIEST.]
You're old and they are young; come, speak for them.
What do you fear or want, that you sit here
suppliant? Indeed I'm willing to give all   10
that you may need; I would be very hard
should I not pity suppliants like these.
PRIEST   O ruler of my country, Oedipus,
you see our company around the altar;
you see our ages; some of us, like these,   15
who cannot yet fly far, and some of us
heavy with age; these children are the chosen
among the young, and I the priest of Zeus.
Within the marketplace sit others crowned
with suppliant garlands, at the double shrine   20
of Pallas and the temple where Ismenus[4]
gives oracles by fire. King, you yourself
have seen our city reeling like a wreck
already; it can scarcely lift its prow
out of the depths, out of the bloody surf.   25
A blight is on the fruitful plants of the earth,
A blight is on the cattle in the fields,
a blight is on our women that no children

1. Translated by David Grene.
2. All stage directions, in italics, are inserted by the translator. Ancient Greek plays do not have these.
3. Branches twined round with wool, carried in ritual to signal that one is at the mercy of another

person. "Cadmus": mythological founder and first king of Thebes.
4. River god of Thebes. "Pallas": warrior goddess, daughter of Zeus; associated with wisdom and technology.

are born to them; a god[5] that carries fire,
a deadly pestilence, is on our town,   30
strikes us and spares not, and the house of Cadmus
is emptied of its people while black Death
grows rich in groaning and in lamentation.
We have not come as suppliants to this altar
because we thought of you as of a god,   35
but rather judging you the first of men
in all the chances of this life and when
we mortals have to do with more than man.
You came and by your coming saved our city,
freed us from tribute which we paid of old   40
to the Sphinx,[6] cruel singer. This you did
in virtue of no knowledge we could give you,
in virtue of no teaching; it was a god
that aided you, men say, and you are held
with the god's assistance to have saved our lives.   45
Now Oedipus, Greatest in all men's eyes,
here falling at your feet we all entreat you,
find us some strength for rescue.
Perhaps you'll hear a wise word from some god,
perhaps you will learn something from a man   50
(for I have seen that for the skilled of practice
the outcome of their counsels live the most).
Noblest of men, go, and raise up our city,
go,—and give heed. For now this land of ours
calls you its savior since you saved it once.   55
So, let us never speak about your reign
as of a time when first our feet were set
secure on high, but later fell to ruin.
Raise up our city, save it and raise it up.
Once you have brought us luck with happy omen;   60
be no less now in fortune.
If you will rule this land, as now you rule it,
better to rule it full of men than empty.
For neither tower nor ship is anything
when empty, and none live in it together.   65

OEDIPUS   I pity you, children. You have come full of longing,
but I have known the story before you told it
only too well. I know you are all sick,
yet there is not one of you, sick though you are,

---

5. The University of Chicago Press's original version of the translation uses capital-G for *god* here, and repeatedly (e.g., again in the other instances of the word in this speech). This has been altered to avoid the implication of monotheism; ancient Greek texts often refer to "a god" or "the god" in the singular, especially when the speaker may not know which of the many gods has been at work.

6. Winged female monster who terrorized Thebes until her riddle was finally answered by Oedipus. The riddle comes in different variants and is never cited by Sophocles, but one common version goes: "What walks on four feet in the morning, two at noon, and three at night?" Oedipus answered, "Man," because humans crawl as babies, walk as adults, and hobble with a stick in old age.

that is as sick as I myself. 70
Your several sorrows each have single scope
and touch but one of you. My spirit groans
for city and myself and you at once.
You have not roused me like a man from sleep;
know that I have given many tears to this, 75
gone many ways wandering in thought,
but as I thought I found only one remedy
and that I took. I sent Menoeceus' son
Creon, Jocasta's brother, to Apollo,
to his Pythian temple,[7] 80
that he might learn there by what act or word
I could save this city. As I count the days,
it vexes me what ails him; he is gone
far longer than he needed for the journey.
But when he comes, then, may I prove a villain, 85
if I shall not do all the god commands.

PRIEST   Thanks for your gracious words. Your servants here
   signal that Creon is this moment coming.

OEDIPUS   His face is bright. O holy Lord Apollo,
   grant that his news too may be bright for us 90
   and bring us safety.

PRIEST   It is happy news,
   I think, for else his head would not be crowned
   with sprigs of fruitful laurel.

OEDIPUS   We will know soon,
   he's within hail. Lord Creon, my good brother, 95
   what is the word you bring us from the god?

      [CREON enters.]

CREON   A good word,—for things hard to bear themselves
   if in the final issue all is well
   I count complete good fortune.

OEDIPUS   What do you mean?
   What you have said so far 100
   leaves me uncertain whether to trust or fear.

CREON   If you will hear my news before these others
   I am ready to speak, or else to go within.

OEDIPUS   Speak it to all;
   the grief I bear, I bear it more for these 105
   than for my own heart.

CREON   I will tell you, then,
   what I heard from the god.
   King Phoebus[8] in plain words commanded us
   to drive out a pollution from our land,

---

7. Apollo is the "god from the shrine of Pytho" (line 175). Pytho was the site of Apollo's oracle, and was also known as Delphi; hence the use of "Delian Healer" in line 178.

8. I.e., Apollo, the god associated with archery, sunlight, poetry, prophecy, healing, and plague. His arrows could cause disease, as they do in the beginning of the *Iliad*.

pollution grown ingrained within the land;   110
drive it out, said the god, not cherish it,
till it's past cure.

OEDIPUS   What is the rite
of purification? How shall it be done?

CREON   By banishing a man, or expiation
of blood by blood, since it is murder guilt   115
which holds our city in this destroying storm.

OEDIPUS   Who is this man whose fate the god pronounces?

CREON   My Lord, before you piloted the state
we had a king called Laius.

OEDIPUS   I know of him by hearsay. I have not seen him.   120

CREON   The god commanded clearly: let someone
punish with force this dead man's murderers.

OEDIPUS   Where are they in the world? Where would a trace
of this old crime be found? It would be hard
to guess where.

CREON   The clue is in this land;   125
that which is sought is found;
the unheeded thing escapes:
so said the god.

OEDIPUS   Was it at home,
or in the country that death came upon him,
or in another country travelling?   130

CREON   He went, he said himself, upon an embassy,
but never returned when he set out from home.

OEDIPUS   Was there no messenger, no fellow traveller
who knew what happened? Such a one might tell
something of use.   135

CREON   They were all killed save one. He fled in terror
and he could tell us nothing in clear terms
of what he knew, nothing, but one thing only.

OEDIPUS   What was it?
If we could even find a slim beginning   140
in which to hope, we might discover much.

CREON   This man said that the robbers they encountered
were many and the hands that did the murder
were many; it was no man's single power.

OEDIPUS   How could a robber dare a deed like this   145
were he not helped with money from the city,
money and treachery?

CREON   That indeed was thought.
But Laius was dead and in our trouble
there was none to help.

OEDIPUS   What trouble was so great to hinder you   150
inquiring out the murder of your king?

CREON   The riddling Sphinx induced us to neglect
mysterious crimes and rather seek solution
of troubles at our feet.

OEDIPUS   I will bring this to light again. King Phoebus   155
    fittingly took this care about the dead,
    and you too fittingly.
    And justly you will see in me an ally,
    a champion of my country and the god.
    For when I drive pollution from the land   160
    I will not serve a distant friend's advantage,
    but act in my own interest. Whoever
    he was that killed the king may readily
    wish to dispatch me with his murderous hand;
    so helping the dead king I help myself.   165

    Come, children, take your suppliant boughs and go;
    up from the altars now. Call the assembly
    and let it meet upon the understanding
    that I'll do everything. God will decide
    whether we prosper or remain in sorrow.   170
PRIEST   Rise, children—it was this we came to seek,
    which of himself the king now offers us.
    May Phoebus who gave us the oracle
    come to our rescue and stay the plague.
        [*Exeunt all but the* CHORUS.]
CHORUS
STROPHE   What is the sweet spoken word of the god from
        the shrine of Pytho rich in gold   175
    that has come to glorious Thebes?
    I am stretched on the rack of doubt, and terror and trembling hold
    my heart, O Delian Healer, and I worship full of fears
    for what doom you will bring to pass, new or renewed in the revolving
        years.
    Speak to me, immortal voice,   180
    child of golden Hope.
ANTISTROPHE   First I call on you, Athene,[9] deathless daughter of Zeus,
    and Artemis,[1] Earth Upholder,
    who sits in the midst of the marketplace in the throne which
        men call Fame,
    and Phoebus, the Far Shooter, three averters of Fate,   185
    come to us now, if ever before, when ruin rushed upon the state,
    you drove destruction's flame away
    out of our land.
STROPHE   Our sorrows defy number;
    all the ship's timbers are rotten;
    taking of thought is no spear for the driving away of the plague.   190
    There are no growing children in this famous land;
    there are no women bearing the pangs of childbirth.
    You may see them one with another, like birds swift on the wing,

9. I.e., Athena.
1. Sister of Apollo; goddess associated with hunting, childbirth, the moon, and protecting the weak.

quicker than fire unmastered,   195
speeding away to the coast of the western god.
ANTISTROPHE   In the unnumbered deaths
  of its people the city dies;
  those children that are born lie dead on the naked earth
  unpitied, spreading contagion of death; and grey-haired mothers
    and wives   200
  everywhere stand at the altar's edge, suppliant, moaning;
  the hymn to the healing god rings out but with it the wailing
    voices are blended.
From these our sufferings grant us, O golden Daughter of Zeus,
  glad-faced deliverance.
STROPHE   There is no clash of brazen shields but our fight is with the
    war god,   205
  a war god ringed with the cries of men, a savage god who burns us;
  grant that he turn in racing course backwards out of our country's
    bounds
  to the great palace of Amphitrite or where the waves of the
    Thracian sea[2]
  deny the stranger safe anchorage.
  Whatsoever escapes the night   210
  at last the light of day revisits;
  so smite the war god, Father Zeus,
  beneath your thunderbolt,
  for you are the Lord of the lightning, the lightning that carries fire.
ANTISTROPHE   And your unconquered arrow shafts, winged by the
    golden corded bow,   215
  Lycean King,[3] I beg to be at our side for help;
  and the gleaming torches of Artemis with which she scours the
    Lycean hills,
  and I call on the god with the turban of gold, who gave his name
    to this country of ours,
  the Bacchic god[4] with the wind-flushed face,
  Evian One, who travel   220
  with the Maenad company,[5]
  combat the god that burns us
  with your torch of pine;
  for the god that is our enemy is a god unhonoured among the gods.
         [OEDIPUS returns.]
OEDIPUS   For what you ask me—if you will hear my words,   225
  and hearing welcome them and fight the plague,
  you will find strength and lightening of your load.
  Hark to me; what I say to you, I say

---

2. Northernmost part of the Aegean Sea where
it borders on Thrace in northern Greece.
"Amphitrite": sea goddess and consort of Poseidon, god of the seas.
3. Common epithet for Apollo.
4. Dionysus, god of wine, theater, and mad-

ness, is closely associated with Thebes, since
his mother, Semele, was a princess of Thebes.
He is called "Evian One" from the traditional
ritual cry made by his followers: "*Evoi! Evoi!*"
5. Dionysus's wild female followers.

as one that is a stranger to the story
as stranger to the deed. For I would not   230
be far upon the track if I alone
were tracing it without a clue. But now,
since after all was finished, I became
a citizen among you, citizens—
now I proclaim to all the men of Thebes: 235
who so among you knows the murderer
by whose hand Laius, son of Labdacus,
died—I command him to tell everything
to me,—yes, though he fears himself to take the blame
on his own head; for bitter punishment   240
he shall have none, but leave this land unharmed.
Or if he knows the murderer, another,
a foreigner, still let him speak the truth.
For I will pay him and be grateful, too.
But if you shall keep silence, if perhaps   245
some one of you, to shield a guilty friend,
or for his own sake shall reject my words—
hear what I shall do then:
I forbid that man, whoever he be, my land,
my land where I hold sovereignty and throne;   250
and I forbid any to welcome him
or cry him greeting or make him a sharer
in sacrifice or offering to the gods,
or give him water for his hands to wash.
I command all to drive him from their homes,   255
since he is our pollution, as the oracle
of Pytho's god proclaimed him now to me.
So I stand forth a champion of the god
and of the man who died.
Upon the murderer I invoke this curse—   260
whether he is one man and all unknown,
or one of many—may he wear out his life
in misery to miserable doom!
If with my knowledge he lives at my hearth
I pray that I myself may feel my curse.   265
On you I lay my charge to fulfill all this
for me, for the god, and for this land of ours
destroyed and blighted, by the god forsaken.

Even were this no matter of god's ordinance
it would not fit you so to leave it lie,   270
unpurified, since a good man is dead
and one that was a king. Search it out.
Since I am now the holder of his office,
and have his bed and wife that once was his,
and had his line not been unfortunate   275
we would have common children—(fortune leaped

upon his head)—because of all these things,
I fight in his defence as for my father,
and I shall try all means to take the murderer
of Laius the son of Labdacus   280
the son of Polydorus and before him
of Cadmus and before him of Agenor.[6]
Those who do not obey me, may the gods
grant no crops springing from the ground they plough
nor children to their women! May a fate   285
like this, or one still worse than this consume them!
For you whom these words please, the other Thebans,
may Justice as your ally and all the gods
live with you, blessing you now and for ever!

CHORUS   As you have held me to my oath, I speak: 290
I neither killed the king nor can declare
the killer; but since Phoebus set the quest
it is his part to tell who the man is.

OEDIPUS   Right; but to put compulsion on the gods
against their will—no man can do that.   295

CHORUS   May I then say what I think second best?

OEDIPUS   If there's a third best, too, spare not to tell it.

CHORUS   I know that what the Lord Teiresias
sees, is most often what the Lord Apollo
sees. If you should inquire of this from him   300
you might find out most clearly.

OEDIPUS   Even in this my actions have not been sluggard.
On Creon's word I have sent two messengers
and why the prophet is not here already
I have been wondering.

CHORUS   His skill apart   305
there is besides only an old faint story.

OEDIPUS   What is it?
I look at every story.

CHORUS   It was said
that he was killed by certain wayfarers.

OEDIPUS   I heard that, too, but no one saw the killer.   310

CHORUS   Yet if he has a share of fear at all,
his courage will not stand firm, hearing your curse.

OEDIPUS   The man who in the doing did not shrink
will fear no word.

CHORUS   Here comes his prosecutor:
led by your men the godly prophet comes   315
in whom alone of mankind truth is native.

[Enter TEIRESIAS, led by a little boy.]

OEDIPUS   Teiresias, you are versed in everything,
things teachable and things not to be spoken,
things of the heaven and earth-creeping things.

6. Cadmus, founder and first king of Thebes, was the son of Agenor. Polydorus was Cadmus's son
and father of Labdacus, who was father of Laius.

You have no eyes but in your mind you know   320
with what a plague our city is afflicted.
My lord, in you alone we find a champion,
in you alone one that can rescue us.
Perhaps you have not heard the messengers,
but Phoebus sent in answer to our sending   325
an oracle declaring that our freedom
from this disease would only come when we
should learn the names of those who killed King Laius,
and kill them or expel from our country.
Do not begrudge us oracles from birds,   330
or any other way of prophecy
within your skill; save yourself and the city,
save me; redeem the debt of our pollution
that lies on us because of this dead man.
We are in your hands; pains are most nobly taken   335
to help another when you have means and power.

TEIRESIAS   Alas, how terrible is wisdom when
it brings no profit to the man that's wise!
This I knew well, but had forgotten it,
else I would not have come here.

OEDIPUS   What is this?   340
How sad you are now you have come!

TEIRESIAS   Let me
go home. It will be easiest for us both
to bear our several destinies to the end
if you will follow my advice.

OEDIPUS   You'd rob us
of this your gift of prophecy? You talk   345
as one who had no care for law nor love
for Thebes who reared you.

TEIRESIAS   Yes, but I see that even your own words
miss the mark; therefore I must fear for mine.

OEDIPUS   For god's sake if you know of anything,   350
do not turn from us; all of us kneel to you,
all of us here, your suppliants.

TEIRESIAS   All of you here know nothing. I will not
bring to the light of day my troubles, mine—
rather than call them yours.

OEDIPUS   What do you mean?   355
You know of something but refuse to speak.
Would you betray us and destroy the city?

TEIRESIAS   I will not bring this pain upon us both,
neither on you nor on myself. Why is it
you question me and waste your labour? I   360
will tell you nothing.

OEDIPUS   You would provoke a stone! Tell us, you villain,
tell us, and do not stand there quietly
unmoved and balking at the issue.

TEIRESIAS   You blame my temper but you do not see[7]   365
   your own that lives within you; it is me
   you chide.

OEDIPUS   Who would not feel his temper rise
   at words like these with which you shame our city?

TEIRESIAS   Of themselves things will come, although I hide them   370
   and breathe no word of them.

OEDIPUS   Since they will come
   tell them to me.

TEIRESIAS   I will say nothing further.
   Against this answer let your temper rage
   as wildly as you will.

OEDIPUS   Indeed I am
   so angry I shall not hold back a jot   375
   of what I think. For I would have you know
   I think you were complotter of the deed
   and doer of the deed save in so far
   as for the actual killing. Had you had eyes
   I would have said alone you murdered him.   380

TEIRESIAS   Yes? Then I warn you faithfully to keep
   the letter of your proclamation and
   from this day forth to speak no word of greeting
   to these nor me; you are the land's pollution.

OEDIPUS   How shamelessly you started up this taunt!   385
   How do you think you will escape?

TEIRESIAS   I have.
   I have escaped; the truth is what I cherish
   and that's my strength.

OEDIPUS   And who has taught you truth?
   Not your profession surely!

TEIRESIAS   You have taught me,
   for you have made me speak against my will.   390

OEDIPUS   Speak what? Tell me again that I may learn it better.

TEIRESIAS   Did you not understand before or would you
   provoke me into speaking?

OEDIPUS   I did not grasp it,
   not so to call it known. Say it again.

TEIRESIAS   I say you are the murderer of the king   395
   whose murderer you seek.

OEDIPUS   Not twice you shall
   say calumnies like this and stay unpunished.

TEIRESIAS   Shall I say more to tempt your anger more?

OEDIPUS   As much as you desire; it will be said
   in vain.   400

TEIRESIAS   I say that with those you love best
   you live in foulest shame unconsciously

---

7. "Temper" in the original Greek is a femi-   the one "that lives within you," i.e., Jocasta.
nine noun, and there is a veiled reference to

and do not see where you are in calamity.

OEDIPUS   Do you imagine you can always talk
like this, and live to laugh at it hereafter?   405

TEIRESIAS   Yes, if the truth has anything of strength.

OEDIPUS   It has, but not for you; it has no strength
for you because you are blind in mind and ears
as well as in your eyes.

TEIRESIAS   You are a poor wretch
to taunt me with the very insults which   410
everyone soon will heap upon yourself.

OEDIPUS   Your life is one long night so that you cannot
hurt me or any other who sees the light.

TEIRESIAS   It is not fate that I should be your ruin,
Apollo is enough; it is his care   415
to work this out.

OEDIPUS   Was this your own design
or Creon's?

TEIRESIAS   Creon is no hurt to you,
but you are to yourself.

OEDIPUS   Wealth, sovereignty, and skill outmatching skill
for the contrivance of an envied life!   420
Great store of jealousy fill your treasury chests,
if my friend Creon, friend from the first and loyal,
thus secretly attacks me, secretly
desires to drive me out and secretly
suborns this juggling, trick-devising quack,   425
this wily beggar who has only eyes
for his own gains, but blindness in his skill.
For, tell me, where have you seen clear, Teiresias,
with your prophetic eyes? When the dark singer,
the Sphinx, was in your country, did you speak   430
word of deliverance to its citizens?
And yet the riddle's answer was not the province
of a chance comer. It was a prophet's task
and plainly you had no such gift of prophecy
from birds nor otherwise from any god   435
to glean a word of knowledge. But I came,
Oedipus, who knew nothing, and I stopped her.
I solved the riddle by my wit alone.
Mine was no knowledge got from birds. And now
you would expel me,   440
because you think that you will find a place
by Creon's throne. I think you will be sorry,
both you and your accomplice, for your plot
to drive me out. And did I not regard you
as an old man, some suffering would have taught you   445
that what was in your heart was treason.

CHORUS   We look at this man's words and yours, my king,
and we find both have spoken them in anger.

We need no angry words but only thought
how we may best hit the god's meaning for us.   450

TEIRESIAS   If you are king, at least I have the right
no less to speak in my defence against you.
Of that much I am master. I am no slave
of yours, but Loxias',[8] and so I shall not
enroll myself with Creon for my patron.   455
Since you have taunted me with being blind,
here is my word for you.
You have your eyes but see not where you are
in sin, nor where you live, nor whom you live with.
Do you know who your parents are? Unknowing   460
you are an enemy to kith and kin
in death, beneath the earth, and in this life.
A deadly footed, double striking curse,
from father and mother both, shall drive you forth
out of this land, with darkness on your eyes,   465
that now have such straight vision. Shall there be
a place will not be harbour to your cries,
a corner of Cithaeron[9] will not ring
in echo to your cries, soon, soon,—
when you shall learn the secret of your marriage,   470
which steered you to a haven in this house,—
haven no haven, after lucky voyage?
And of the multitude of other evils
establishing a grim equality
between you and your children, you know nothing.   475
So, muddy with contempt my words and Creon's!
Misery shall grind no man as it will you.

OEDIPUS   Is it endurable that I should hear
such words from him? Go and a curse go with you!
Quick, home with you! Out of my house at once!   480

TEIRESIAS   I would not have come either had you not called me.

OEDIPUS   I did not know then you would talk like a fool—
or it would have been long before I called you.

TEIRESIAS   I am a fool then, as it seems to you—
but to the parents who have bred you, wise.   485

OEDIPUS   What parents? Stop! Who are they of all the world?

TEIRESIAS   This day will show your birth and will destroy you.

OEDIPUS   How needlessly your riddles darken everything.

TEIRESIAS   But it's in riddle answering you are strongest.

OEDIPUS   Yes. Taunt me where you will find me great.   490

TEIRESIAS   It is this very luck that has destroyed you.

OEDIPUS   I do not care, if it has saved this city.

TEIRESIAS   Well, I will go. Come, boy, lead me away.

OEDIPUS   Yes, lead him off. So long as you are here,

8. Loxias is a title of Apollo.
9. Mountain range near Thebes, where Oedipus was left to die as a baby.

you'll be a stumbling block and a vexation;   495
once gone, you will not trouble me again.

TEIRESIAS   I have said
what I came here to say not fearing your
countenance: there is no way you can hurt me.
I tell you, king, this man, this murderer
(whom you have long declared you are in search of,   500
indicting him in threatening proclamation
as murderer of Laius)—he is here.
In name he is a stranger among citizens
but soon he will be shown to be a citizen
true native Theban, and he'll have no joy   505
of the discovery: blindness for sight
and beggary for riches his exchange,
he shall go journeying to a foreign country
tapping his way before him with a stick.
He shall be proved father and brother both   510
to his own children in his house; to her
that gave him birth, a son and husband both;
a fellow sower in his father's bed
with that same father that he murdered.
Go within, reckon that out, and if you find me   515
mistaken, say I have no skill in prophecy.

    [*Exeunt separately* TEIRESIAS *and* OEDIPUS.]

CHORUS STROPHE   Who is the man proclaimed
  by Delphi's prophetic rock
  as the bloody-handed murderer,
  the doer of deeds that none dare name?   520
Now is the time for him to run
with a stronger foot
than Pegasus[1]
for the child of Zeus leaps in arms upon him
with fire and the lightning bolt,   525
and terribly close on his heels
are the Fates that never miss.

ANTISTROPHE   Lately from snowy Parnassus[2]
  clearly the voice flashed forth,
  bidding each Theban track him down,   530
  the unknown murderer.
In the savage forests he lurks and in
the caverns like
the mountain bull.
He is sad and lonely, and lonely his feet   535
that carry him far from the navel of earth;[3]
but its prophecies, ever living,
flutter around his head.

1. Divine winged horse.
2. Mountain in central Greece near Delphi
and thus sacred to Apollo.

3. Delphi was imagined to be the center of
the earth and hence its navel.

STROPHE   The augur has spread confusion,
  terrible confusion;   540
  I do not approve what was said
  nor can I deny it.
  I do not know what to say;
  I am in a flutter of foreboding;
  I never heard in the present   545
  nor past of a quarrel between
  the sons of Labdacus and Polybus,[4]
  that I might bring as proof
  in attacking the popular fame
  of Oedipus, seeking   550
  to take vengeance for undiscovered
  death in the line of Labdacus.

ANTISTROPHE   Truly Zeus and Apollo are wise
  and in human things all knowing;
  but amongst men there is no   555
  distinct judgment, between the prophet
  and me—which of us is right.
  One man may pass another in wisdom
  but I would never agree
  with those that find fault with the king   560
  till I should see the word
  proved right beyond doubt. For once
  in visible form the Sphinx
  came on him and all of us
  saw his wisdom and in that test   565
  he saved the city. So he will not be condemned by my mind.

      [Enter CREON.]

CREON   Citizens, I have come because I heard
  deadly words spread about me, that the king
  accuses me. I cannot take that from him.
  If he believes that in these present troubles   570
  he has been wronged by me in word or deed
  I do not want to live on with the burden
  of such a scandal on me. The report
  injures me doubly and most vitally—
  for I'll be called a traitor to my city   575
  and traitor also to my friends and you.
CHORUS   Perhaps it was a sudden gust of anger
  that forced that insult from him, and no judgment.
CREON   But did he say that it was in compliance
  with schemes of mine that the seer told him lies?   580
CHORUS   Yes, he said that, but why, I do not know.
CREON   Were his eyes straight in his head? Was his mind right
  when he accused me in this fashion?

4. Polybus is Oedipus's adoptive father, the king of Corinth, husband of Merope.

CHORUS   I do not know; I have no eyes to see
   what princes do. Here comes the king himself.   585
      [*Enter* OEDIPUS.]
OEDIPUS   You, sir, how is it you come here? Have you so much
   brazen-faced daring that you venture in
   my house although you are proved manifestly
   the murderer of that man, and though you tried,
   openly, highway robbery of my crown?   590
   For god's sake, tell me what you saw in me,
   what cowardice or what stupidity,
   that made you lay a plot like this against me?
   Did you imagine I should not observe
   the crafty scheme that stole upon me or   595
   seeing it, take no means to counter it?
   Was it not stupid of you to make the attempt,
   to try to hunt down royal power without
   the people at your back or friends? For only
   with the people at your back or money can   600
   the hunt end in the capture of a crown.
CREON   Do you know what you're doing? Will you listen
   to words to answer yours, and then pass judgment?
OEDIPUS   You're quick to speak, but I am slow to grasp you,
   for I have found you dangerous,—and my foe.   605
CREON   First of all hear what I shall say to that.
OEDIPUS   At least don't tell me that you are not guilty.
CREON   If you think obstinacy without wisdom
   a valuable possession, you are wrong.
OEDIPUS   And you are wrong if you believe that one,   610
   a criminal, will not be punished only
   because he is my kinsman.
CREON   This is but just—
   but tell me, then, of what offense I'm guilty?
OEDIPUS   Did you or did you not urge me to send
   to this prophetic mumbler?
CREON   I did indeed,   615
   and I shall stand by what I told you.
OEDIPUS   How long ago is it since Laius. . . .
CREON   What about Laius? I don't understand.
OEDIPUS   Vanished—died—was murdered?
CREON   It is long,
   a long, long time to reckon.
OEDIPUS   Was this prophet   620
   in the profession then?
CREON   He was, and honoured
   as highly as he is today.
OEDIPUS   At that time did he say a word about me?
CREON   Never, at least when I was near him.
OEDIPUS   You never made a search for the dead man?   625
CREON   We searched, indeed, but never learned of anything.

OEDIPUS   Why did our wise old friend not say this then?

CREON   I don't know; and when I know nothing, I
　usually hold my tongue.

OEDIPUS   You know this much,
　and can declare this much if you are loyal.　　　　　　　　630

CREON   What is it? If I know, I'll not deny it.

OEDIPUS   That he would not have said that I killed Laius
　had he not met you first.

CREON   You know yourself
　whether he said this, but I demand that I
　should hear as much from you as you from me.　　　　　　635

OEDIPUS   Then hear,—I'll not be proved a murderer.

CREON   Well, then. You're married to my sister.

OEDIPUS   Yes,
　that I am not disposed to deny.

CREON   You rule
　this country giving her an equal share
　in the government?

OEDIPUS   Yes, everything she wants　　　640
　she has from me.

CREON   And I, as thirdsman to you,
　am rated as the equal of you two?

OEDIPUS   Yes, and it's there you've proved yourself false friend.

CREON   Not if you will reflect on it as I do.
　Consider, first, if you think anyone　　　　　　　　　　　645
　would choose to rule and fear rather than rule
　and sleep untroubled by a fear if power
　were equal in both cases. I, at least,
　I was not born with such a frantic yearning
　to be a king—but to do what kings do.　　　　　　　　　650
　And so it is with everyone who has learned
　wisdom and self-control. As it stands now,
　the prizes are all mine—and without fear.
　But if I were the king myself, I must
　do much that went against the grain.　　　　　　　　　655
　How should despotic rule seem sweeter to me
　than painless power and an assured authority?
　I am not so besotted yet that I
　want other honours than those that come with profit.
　Now every man's my pleasure; every man greets me;　　660
　now those who are your suitors fawn on me,—
　success for them depends upon my favour.
　Why should I let all this go to win that?
　My mind would not be traitor if it's wise;
　I am no treason lover, of my nature,　　　　　　　　　665
　nor would I ever dare to join a plot.
　Prove what I say. Go to the oracle
　at Pytho and inquire about the answers,

if they are as I told you. For the rest,
if you discover I laid any plot   670
together with the seer kill me, I say,
not only by your vote but by my own.
But do not charge me on obscure opinion
without some proof to back it. It's not just
lightly to count your knaves as honest men,   675
nor honest men as knaves. To throw away
an honest friend is, as it were, to throw
your life away, which a man loves the best.
In time you will know all with certainty;
time is the only test of honest men,   680
one day is space enough to know a rogue.

CHORUS   His words are wise, king, if one fears to fall.
Those who are quick of temper are not safe.

OEDIPUS   When he that plots against me secretly
moves quickly, I must quickly counterplot.   685
If I wait taking no decisive measure
his business will be done, and mine be spoiled.

CREON   What do you want to do then? Banish me?

OEDIPUS   No, certainly; kill you, not banish you.[5]

CREON   I do not think that you've your wits about you.   690

OEDIPUS   For my own interests, yes.

CREON   But for mine, too,
you should think equally.

OEDIPUS   You are a rogue.

CREON   Suppose you do not understand?

OEDIPUS   But yet
I must be ruler.

CREON   Not if you rule badly.

OEDIPUS   O, city, city!

CREON   I too have some share   695
in the city; it is not yours alone.

CHORUS   Stop, my lords! Here—and in the nick of time
I see Jocasta coming from the house;
with her help lay the quarrel that now stirs you.
          [Enter JOCASTA.]

JOCASTA   For shame! Why have you raised this foolish squabbling 700
brawl? Are you not ashamed to air your private
griefs when the country's sick? Go in, you, Oedipus,
and you, too, Creon, into the house. Don't magnify
your nothing troubles.

CREON   Sister, Oedipus,
your husband, thinks he has the right to do   705

5. Two lines omitted here owing to the confusion in the dialogue consequent on the loss of a
third line. In the omitted lines, Oedipus accuses the Chorus of being jealous, and the Chorus
accuses Oedipus of lacking trust.

terrible wrongs—he has but to choose between
two terrors: banishing or killing me.

OEDIPUS He's right, Jocasta; for I find him plotting
with knavish tricks against my person.

CREON That god may never bless me! May I die   710
accursed, if I have been guilty of
one tittle of the charge you bring against me!

JOCASTA I beg you, Oedipus, trust him in this,
spare him for the sake of this his oath to god,
for my sake, and the sake of those who stand here.   715

CHORUS[6] Be gracious, be merciful,
we beg of you.

OEDIPUS In what would you have me yield?

CHORUS He has been no silly child in the past.
He is strong in his oath now.   720
Spare him.

OEDIPUS Do you know what you ask?

CHORUS Yes.

OEDIPUS Tell me then.

CHORUS He has been your friend before all men's eyes; do not cast him   725
away dishonoured on an obscure conjecture.

OEDIPUS I would have you know that this request of yours
really requests my death or banishment.

CHORUS May the Sun god, king of gods, forbid! May I die without god's
blessing, without friends' help, if I had any such thought. But my   730
spirit is broken by my unhappiness for my wasting country; and
this would but add troubles amongst ourselves to the other
troubles.

OEDIPUS Well, let him go then—if I must die ten times for it,
or be sent out dishonoured into exile.   735
It is your lips that prayed for him I pitied,
not his; wherever he is, I shall hate him.

CREON I see you sulk in yielding and you're dangerous
when you are out of temper; natures like yours
are justly heaviest for themselves to bear.   740

OEDIPUS Leave me alone! Take yourself off, I tell you.

CREON I'll go, you have not known me, but they have,
and they have known my innocence.
        [Exit.]

CHORUS Won't you take him inside, lady?

JOCASTA Yes, when I've found out what was the matter.   745

CHORUS There was some misconceived suspicion of a story, and on the
other side the sting of injustice.

JOCASTA So, on both sides?

CHORUS Yes.

JOCASTA What was the story?   750

---

6. The meter changes in the original, marking an increase in emotional intensity, with presumably a different musical accompaniment.

CHORUS   I think it best, in the interests of the country, to leave it where
    it ended.
OEDIPUS   You see where you have ended, straight of judgment
    although you are, by softening my anger.
CHORUS   Sir, I have said before and I say again—be sure that I would have   755
    been proved a madman, bankrupt in sane council, if I should put
    you away, you who steered the country I love safely when she
    was crazed with troubles. God grant that now, too, you may
    prove a fortunate guide for us.
JOCASTA   Tell me, my lord, I beg of you, what was it   760
    that roused your anger so?
OEDIPUS   Yes, I will tell you.
    I honour you more than I honour them.
    It was Creon and the plots he laid against me.
JOCASTA   Tell me—if you can clearly tell the quarrel—
OEDIPUS   Creon says
    that I'm the murderer of Laius.   765
JOCASTA   Of his own knowledge or on information?
OEDIPUS   He sent this rascal prophet to me, since
    he keeps his own mouth clean of any guilt.
JOCASTA   Do not concern yourself about this matter;
    listen to me and learn that human beings   770
    have no part in the craft of prophecy.
    Of that I'll show you a short proof.
    There was an oracle once that came to Laius,—
    I will not say that it was Phoebus' own,
    but it was from his servants—and it told him   775
    that it was fate that he should die a victim
    at the hands of his own son, a son to be born
    of Laius and me. But, see now, he,
    the king, was killed by foreign highway robbers
    at a place where three roads meet—so goes the story;   780
    and for the son—before three days were out
    after his birth King Laius pierced his ankles
    and by the hands of others cast him forth
    upon a pathless hillside. So Apollo
    failed to fulfill his oracle to the son,   785
    that he should kill his father, and to Laius
    also proved false in that the thing he feared,
    death at his son's hands, never came to pass.
    So clear in this case were the oracles,
    so clear and false. Give them no heed, I say;   790
    what god discovers need of, easily
    he shows to us himself.
OEDIPUS   O dear Jocasta,
    as I hear this from you, there comes upon me
    a wandering of the soul—I could run mad.
JOCASTA   What trouble is it, that you turn again   795

and speak like this?

OEDIPUS   I thought I heard you say
that Laius was killed at a crossroads.

JOCASTA   Yes, that was how the story went and still
that word goes round.

OEDIPUS   Where is this place, Jocasta,
where he was murdered?

JOCASTA   Phocis is the country   800
and the road splits there, one of two roads from Delphi,
another comes from Daulia.

OEDIPUS   How long ago is this?

JOCASTA   The news came to the city just before
you became king and all men's eyes looked to you.
What is it, Oedipus, that's in your mind?   805

OEDIPUS   What have you designed, O Zeus, to do with me?

JOCASTA   What is the thought that troubles your heart?

OEDIPUS   Don't ask me yet—tell me of Laius—
How did he look? How old or young was he?

JOCASTA   He was a tall man and his hair was grizzled   810
already—nearly white—and in his form
not unlike you.

OEDIPUS   O god, I think I have
called curses on myself in ignorance.

JOCASTA   What do you mean? I am terrified
when I look at you.

OEDIPUS   I have a deadly fear   815
that the old seer had eyes. You'll show me more
if you can tell me one more thing.

JOCASTA   I will.
I'm frightened,—but if I can understand,
I'll tell you all you ask.

OEDIPUS   How was his company?
Had he few with him when he went this journey,   820
or many servants, as would suit a prince?

JOCASTA   In all there were but five, and among them
a herald; and one carriage for the king.

OEDIPUS   It's plain—its plain—who was it told you this?

JOCASTA   The only servant that escaped safe home.   825

OEDIPUS   Is he at home now?

JOCASTA   No, when he came home again
and saw you king and Laius was dead,
he came to me and touched my hand and begged
that I should send him to the fields to be
my shepherd and so he might see the city   830
as far off as he might. So I
sent him away. He was an honest man,
as slaves go, and was worthy of far more
than what he asked of me.

OEDIPUS   O, how I wish that he could come back quickly!   835

JOCASTA   He can. Why is your heart so set on this?
OEDIPUS   O dear Jocasta, I am full of fears
   that I have spoken far too much; and therefore
   I wish to see this shepherd.
JOCASTA   He will come;
   but, Oedipus, I think I'm worthy too   840
   to know what it is that disquiets you.
OEDIPUS   It shall not be kept from you, since my mind
   has gone so far with its forebodings. Whom
   should I confide in rather than you, who is there
   of more importance to me who have passed   845
   through such a fortune?
   Polybus was my father, king of Corinth,
   and Merope, the Dorian, my mother.
   I was held greatest of the citizens
   in Corinth till a curious chance befell me   850
   as I shall tell you—curious, indeed,
   but hardly worth the store I set upon it.
   There was a dinner and at it a man,
   a drunken man, accused me in his drink
   of being bastard. I was furious   855
   but held my temper under for that day.
   Next day I went and taxed my parents with it;
   they took the insult very ill from him,
   the drunken fellow who had uttered it.
   So I was comforted for their part, but   860
   still this thing rankled always, for the story
   crept about widely. And I went at last
   to Pytho, though my parents did not know.
   But Phoebus sent me home again unhonoured
   in what I came to learn, but he foretold   865
   other and desperate horrors to befall me,
   that I was fated to lie with my mother,
   and show to daylight an accursed breed
   which men would not endure, and I was doomed
   to be murderer of the father that begot me.   870
   When I heard this I fled, and in the days
   that followed I would measure from the stars
   the whereabouts of Corinth—yes, I fled
   to somewhere where I should not see fulfilled
   the infamies told in that dreadful oracle.   875
   And as I journeyed I came to the place
   where, as you say, this king met with his death.
   Jocasta, I will tell you the whole truth.
   When I was near the branching of the crossroads,
   going on foot, I was encountered by   880
   a herald and a carriage with a man in it,
   just as you tell me. He that led the way
   and the old man himself wanted to thrust me

out of the road by force. I became angry
and struck the coachman who was pushing me.   885
When the old man saw this he watched his moment,
and as I passed he struck me from his carriage,
full on the head with his two-pointed goad.
But he was paid in full and presently
my stick had struck him backwards from the car   890
and he rolled out of it. And then I killed them
all. If it happened there was any tie
of kinship twixt this man and Laius,
who is then now more miserable than I,
what man on earth so hated by the gods,   895
since neither citizen nor foreigner
may welcome me at home or even greet me,
but drive me out of doors? And it is I,
I and no other have so cursed myself.
And I pollute the bed of him I killed   900
by the hands that killed him. Was I not born evil?
Am I not utterly unclean? I had to fly
and in my banishment not even see
my kindred nor set foot in my own country,
or otherwise my fate was to be yoked   905
in marriage with my mother and kill my father,
Polybus who begot me and had reared me.
Would not one rightly judge and say that on me
these things were sent by some malignant god?
O no, no, no—O holy majesty   910
of god on high, may I not see that day!
May I be gone out of men's sight before
I see the deadly taint of this disaster
come upon me.

CHORUS   Sir, we too fear these things. But until you see this man face to   915
face and hear his story, hope.

OEDIPUS   Yes, I have just this much of hope—to wait until the herdsman
comes.

JOCASTA   And when he comes, what do you want with him?

OEDIPUS   I'll tell you; if I find that his story is the same as yours, I at least   920
will be clear of this guilt.

JOCASTA   Why—what so particularly did you learn from my story?

OEDIPUS   You said that he spoke of highway *robbers* who killed Laius. Now
if he uses the same number, it was not I who killed him. One man
cannot be the same as many. But if he speaks of a man travelling
alone, then clearly the burden of the guilt inclines towards me.   925

JOCASTA   Be sure, at least, that this was how he told the story. He cannot
unsay it now, for every one in the city heard it—not I alone. But,
Oedipus, even if he diverges from what he said then, he shall
never prove that the murder of Laius squares rightly with the
prophecy—for Loxias declared that the king should be killed by   930

his own son. And that poor creature did not kill him surely,—
for he died himself first. So as far as prophecy goes, henceforward
I shall not look to the right hand or the left.

OEDIPUS   Right. But yet, send someone for the peasant to bring him here;   935
do not neglect it.

JOCASTA   I will send quickly. Now let me go indoors. I will do nothing
except what pleases you.

      [Exeunt.]

CHORUS STROPHE   May destiny ever find me
  pious in word and deed
  prescribed by the laws that live on high: 940
  laws begotten in the clear air of heaven,
  whose only father is Olympus;
  no mortal nature brought them to birth,
  no forgetfulness shall lull them to sleep;
  for the god is great in them and grows not old.   945

ANTISTROPHE   Insolence[7] breeds the tyrant, insolence
  if it is glutted with a surfeit, unseasonable, unprofitable,
  climbs to the rooftop and plunges
  sheer down to the ruin that must be,
  and there its feet are no service.   950
  But I pray that the god may never
  abolish the eager ambition that profits the state.
  For I shall never cease to hold the god as our protector.

STROPHE   If a man walks with haughtiness
  of hand or word and gives no heed   955
  to Justice and the shrines of gods
  despises—may an evil doom
  smite him for his ill-starred pride of heart!—
  if he reaps gains without justice
  and will not hold from impiety   960
  and his fingers itch for untouchable things.
  When such things are done, what man shall contrive
  to shield his soul from the shafts of the god?
  When such deeds are held in honour,
  why should I honour the gods in the dance?[8]   965

ANTISTROPHE   No longer to the holy place,
  to the navel of earth I'll go
  to worship, nor to Abae
  nor to Olympia,[9]
  unless the oracles are proved to fit,   970
  for all men's hands to point at.
  O Zeus, if you are rightly called
  the sovereign lord, all-mastering,

---

7. The word in Greek for "insolence" is *hybris*, which usually connotes violence.

8. The Greek verb used here, *choreuein*, connotes "dance in a chorus," linking the mythi- cal drama to the real theatrical performance.

9. Home to a great sanctuary of Zeus and Hera. "The navel of earth": Delphi. "Abae": oracular site near Thebes.

let this not escape you nor your ever-living power!
The oracles concerning Laius   975
are old and dim and men regard them not.
Apollo is nowhere clear in honour; god's service perishes.

[*Enter* JOCASTA, *carrying garlands.*]

JOCASTA   Princes of the land, I have had the thought to go
to the gods' temples, bringing in my hand
garlands and gifts of incense, as you see.   980
For Oedipus excites himself too much
at every sort of trouble, not conjecturing,
like a man of sense, what will be from what was,
but he is always at the speaker's mercy,
when he speaks terrors. I can do no good   985
by my advice, and so I came as suppliant
to you, Lycaean Apollo,[1] who are nearest.
These are the symbols of my prayer and this
my prayer: grant us escape free of the curse.
Now when we look to him we are all afraid;   990
he's pilot of our ship and he is frightened.

[*Enter* MESSENGER.]

MESSENGER   Might I learn from you, sirs, where is the house of Oedipus?
Or best of all, if you know, where is the king himself?

CHORUS   This is his house and he is within doors. This lady is his wife
and mother of his children.   995

MESSENGER   God bless you, lady, and god bless your household! God
bless Oedipus' noble wife!

JOCASTA   God bless you, sir, for your kind greeting! What do you want
of us that you have come here? What have you to tell us?

MESSENGER   Good news, lady. Good for your house and for your husband. 1000

JOCASTA   What is your news? Who sent you to us?

MESSENGER   I come from Corinth and the news I bring will give you
pleasure.
Perhaps a little pain too.

JOCASTA   What is this news of double meaning?   1005

MESSENGER   The people of the Isthmus will choose Oedipus to be
their king.
That is the rumour there.

JOCASTA   But isn't their king still old Polybus?

MESSENGER   No. He is in his grave. Death has got him.   1010

JOCASTA   Is that the truth? Is Oedipus' father dead?

MESSENGER   May I die myself if it be otherwise!

JOCASTA (*to a servant*)   Be quick and run to the king with the news!
O oracles of the gods, where are you now? It was from this man
Oedipus fled, lest he should be his murderer! And now he is dead, 1015
in the course of nature, and not killed by Oedipus.

[*Enter* OEDIPUS]

OEDIPUS   Dearest Jocasta, why have you sent for me?

1. Apollo was worshipped in rituals on Mount Lycaeon—literally, "Wolf Mountain."

JOCASTA   Listen to this man and when you hear reflect what is the outcome of the holy oracles of the gods.

OEDIPUS   Who is he? What is his message for me?   1020

JOCASTA   He is from Corinth and he tells us that your father Polybus is
dead and gone.

OEDIPUS   What's this you say, sir? Tell me yourself.

MESSENGER   Since this is the first matter you want clearly told:
Polybus has gone down to death. You may be sure of it.   1025

OEDIPUS   By treachery or sickness?

MESSENGER   A small thing will put old bodies asleep.

OEDIPUS   So he died of sickness, it seems,—poor old man!

MESSENGER   Yes, and of age—the long years he had measured.

OEDIPUS   Ha! Ha! O dear Jocasta, why should one   1030
look to the Pythian hearth? Why should one look
to the birds screaming overhead? They prophesied
that I should kill my father! But he's dead,
and hidden deep in earth, and I stand here   1035
who never laid a hand on spear against him,—
unless perhaps he died of longing for me,
and thus I am his murderer. But they,
the oracles, as they stand—he's taken them
away with him, they're dead as he himself is,
and worthless.

JOCASTA   That I told you before now.   1040

OEDIPUS   You did, but I was misled by my fear.

JOCASTA   Then lay no more of them to heart, not one.

OEDIPUS   But surely I must fear my mother's bed?

JOCASTA   Why should man fear since chance is all in all
for him, and he can clearly foreknow nothing?   1045
Best to live lightly, as one can, unthinkingly.
As to your mother's marriage bed,—don't fear it.
Before this, in dreams too, as well as oracles,
many a man has lain with his own mother.   1050
But he to whom such things are nothing bears
his life most easily.

OEDIPUS   All that you say would be said perfectly
if she were dead; but since she lives I must
still fear, although you talk so well, Jocasta.

JOCASTA   Still in your father's death there's light of comfort?   1055

OEDIPUS   Great light of comfort; but I fear the living.

MESSENGER   Who is the woman that makes you afraid?

OEDIPUS   Merope, old man, Polybus' wife.

MESSENGER   What about her frightens the queen and you?

OEDIPUS   A terrible oracle, stranger, from the gods.   1060

MESSENGER   Can it be told? Or does the sacred law
forbid another to have knowledge of it?

OEDIPUS   O no! Once on a time Loxias said
that I should lie with my own mother and
take on my hands the blood of my own father.   1065

And so for these long years I've lived away
from Corinth; it has been to my great happiness;
but yet it's sweet to see the face of parents.
MESSENGER   This was the fear which drove you out of Corinth?
OEDIPUS   Old man, I did not wish to kill my father.   1070
MESSENGER   Why should I not free you from this fear, sir,
since I have come to you in all goodwill?
OEDIPUS   You would not find me thankless if you did.
MESSENGER   Why, it was just for this I brought the news,—
to earn your thanks when you had come safe home.   1075
OEDIPUS   No, I will never come near my parents.
MESSENGER   Son,
it's very plain you don't know what you're doing.
OEDIPUS   What do you mean, old man? For god's sake, tell me.
MESSENGER   If your homecoming is checked by fears like these.
OEDIPUS   Yes, I'm afraid that Phoebus may prove right.   1080
MESSENGER   The murder and the incest?
OEDIPUS   Yes, old man;
that is my constant terror.
MESSENGER   Do you know
that all your fears are empty?
OEDIPUS   How is that,
if they are father and mother and I their son?
MESSENGER   Because Polybus was no kin to you in blood.   1085
OEDIPUS   What, was not Polybus my father?
MESSENGER   No more than I but just so much.
OEDIPUS   How can
my father be my father as much as one
that's nothing to me?
MESSENGER   Neither he nor I
begat you.   1090
OEDIPUS   Why then did he call me son?
MESSENGER   A gift he took you from these hands of mine.
OEDIPUS   Did he love so much what he took from another's hand?
MESSENGER   His childlessness before persuaded him.
OEDIPUS   Was I a child you bought or found when I   1095
was given to him?
MESSENGER   On Cithaeron's slopes
in the twisting thickets you were found.
OEDIPUS   And why
were you a traveller in those parts?
MESSENGER   I was   1100
in charge of mountain flocks.
OEDIPUS   You were a shepherd?
A hireling vagrant?
MESSENGER   Yes, but at least at that time
the man that saved your life, son.
OEDIPUS   What ailed me when you took me in your arms?
MESSENGER   In that your ankles should be witnesses.   1105

OEDIPUS   Why do you speak of that old pain?
MESSENGER   I loosed you;
   the tendons of your feet were pierced and fettered,—
OEDIPUS   My swaddling clothes brought me a rare disgrace.
MESSENGER   So that from this you're called your present name.[2]
OEDIPUS   Was this my father's doing or my mother's?   1110
   For god's sake, tell me.
MESSENGER   I don't know, but he
   who gave you to me has more knowledge than I.
OEDIPUS   You yourself did not find me then? You took me
   from someone else?
MESSENGER   Yes, from another shepherd.   1115
OEDIPUS   Who was he? Do you know him well enough
   to tell?
MESSENGER   He was called Laius' man.
OEDIPUS   You mean the king who reigned here in the old days?
MESSENGER   Yes, he was that man's shepherd.
OEDIPUS   Is he alive   1120
   still, so that I could see him?
MESSENGER   You who live here
   would know that best.
OEDIPUS   Do any of you here
   know of this shepherd whom he speaks about
   in town or in the fields? Tell me. It's time
   that this was found out once for all.   1125
CHORUS   I think he is none other than the peasant
   whom you have sought to see already; but
   Jocasta here can tell us best of that.
OEDIPUS   Jocasta, do you know about this man
   whom we have sent for? Is he the man he mentions?   1130
JOCASTA   Why ask of whom he spoke? Don't give it heed;
   nor try to keep in mind what has been said.
   It will be wasted labour.
OEDIPUS   With such clues
   I could not fail to bring my birth to light.
JOCASTA   I beg you—do not hunt this out—I beg you,   1135
   if you have any care for your own life.
   What I am suffering is enough.
OEDIPUS   Keep up
   your heart, Jocasta. Though I'm proved a slave,
   thrice slave, and though my mother is thrice slave,
   you'll not be shown to be of lowly lineage.   1140
JOCASTA   O be persuaded by me, I entreat you;
   do not do this.
OEDIPUS   I will not be persuaded to let be
   the chance of finding out the whole thing clearly.

---

2. The name "Oedipus" suggests "swollen foot."

JOCASTA   It is because I wish you well that I   1145
   give you this counsel—and it's the best counsel.
OEDIPUS   Then the best counsel vexes me, and has
   for some while since.
JOCASTA   Oedipus, may the god help you!
   God keep you from the knowledge of who you are!
OEDIPUS   Here, someone, go and fetch the shepherd for me;   1150
   and let her find her joy in her rich family!
JOCASTA   O Oedipus, unhappy Oedipus!
   that is all I can call you, and the last thing
   that I shall ever call you.
      [Exit.]
CHORUS   Why has the queen gone, Oedipus, in wild   1155
   grief rushing from us? I am afraid that trouble
   Will break out of this silence.
OEDIPUS   Break out what will! I at least shall be
   willing to see my ancestry, though humble.
   Perhaps she is ashamed of my low birth,   1160
   for she has all a woman's high-flown pride.
   But I account myself a child of Fortune,
   beneficent Fortune, and I shall not be
   dishonoured. She's the mother from whom I spring;
   the months, my brothers, marked me, now as small,   1165
   and now again as mighty. Such is my breeding,
   and I shall never prove so false to it,
   as not to find the secret of my birth.
CHORUS
STROPHE   If I am a prophet and wise of heart
   you shall not fail, Cithaeron,   1170
   by the limitless sky, you shall not!—
   to know at tomorrow's full moon
   that Oedipus honours you,
   as native to him and mother and nurse at once;
   and that you are honoured in dancing by us, as finding favour in   1175
     sight of our king.
   Apollo, to whom we cry, find these things pleasing!
ANTISTROPHE   Who was it bore you, child? One of
   the long-lived nymphs who lay with Pan—
   the father who treads the hills?[3]   1180
   Or was she a bride of Loxias, your mother? The grassy slopes
   are all of them dear to him. Or perhaps Cyllene's king
   or the Bacchants' god that lives on the tops
   of the hills received you a gift from some
   one of the Helicon[4] nymphs, with whom he mostly plays?   1185
     [Enter an old man, led by OEDIPUS' servants.]

---

3. Pan was a countryside god, patron of shepherds.
4. A mountain in Boeotia, supposedly inhabited by the Muses as well as nymphs (female

nature spirits). Dionysus ("the Bacchants' god"),
like Pan and the messenger god, Hermes ("Cyllene's king"), haunted the wild places.

OEDIPUS   If someone like myself who never met him
   may make a guess,—I think this is the herdsman,
   whom we were seeking. His old age is consonant
   with the other. And besides, the men who bring him
   I recognize as my own servants. You   1190
   perhaps may better me in knowledge since
   you've seen the man before.
CHORUS   You can be sure
   I recognize him. For if Laius
   had ever an honest shepherd, this was he.
OEDIPUS   You, sir, from Corinth, I must ask you first,   1195
   is this the man you spoke of?
MESSENGER   This is he
   before your eyes.
OEDIPUS   Old man, look here at me
   and tell me what I ask you. Were you ever
   a servant of King Laius?
HERDSMAN   I was,—   1200
   no slave he bought but reared in his own house.
OEDIPUS   What did you do as work? How did you live?
HERDSMAN   Most of my life was spent among the flocks.
OEDIPUS   In what part of the country did you live?
HERDSMAN   Cithaeron and the places near to it.   1205
OEDIPUS   And somewhere there perhaps you knew this man?
HERDSMAN   What was his occupation? Who?
OEDIPUS   This man here,
   have you had any dealings with him?
HERDSMAN   No—
   not such that I can quickly call to mind.
MESSENGER   That is no wonder, master. But I'll make him 1210
   remember what he does not know. For I know, that he well
   knows the country of Cithaeron, how he with two flocks, I with
   one kept company for three years—each year half a year—from
   spring till autumn time and then when winter came I drove my
   flocks to our fold home again and he to Laius's steadings.   1215
   Well—am I right or not in what I said we did?
HERDSMAN   You're right—although it's a long time ago.
MESSENGER   Do you remember giving me a child
   to bring up as my foster child?
HERDSMAN   What's this?
   Why do you ask this question?
MESSENGER   Look, old man,   1220
   here he is—here's the man who was that child!
HERDSMAN   Death take you! Won't you hold your tongue?
OEDIPUS   No, no,
   do not find fault with him, old man. Your words
   are more at fault than his.
HERDSMAN   O best of masters,
   how do I give offense?   1225

OEDIPUS   When you refuse
  to speak about the child of whom he asks you.

HERDSMAN   He speaks out of his ignorance, without meaning.

OEDIPUS   If you'll not talk to gratify me, you
  will talk with pain to urge you.

HERDSMAN   O please, sir,
  don't hurt an old man, sir.

OEDIPUS [to the servants]   Here, one of you,   1230
  twist his hands behind him.

HERDSMAN   Why, gods help me, why?
  What do you want to know?

OEDIPUS   You gave a child
  to him,—the child he asked you of?

HERDSMAN   I did.
  I wish I'd died the day I did.   1235

OEDIPUS   You will
  unless you tell me truly.

HERDSMAN   And I'll die
  far worse if I should tell you.

OEDIPUS   This fellow
  is bent on more delays, as it would seem.

HERDSMAN   O no, no! I have told you that I gave it.   1240

OEDIPUS   Where did you get this child from? Was it your own or
  did you get it from another?

HERDSMAN   Not
  my own at all; I had it from someone.

OEDIPUS   One of these citizens? or from what house?

HERDSMAN   O master, please—I beg you, master, please   1245
  don't ask me more.

OEDIPUS   You're a dead man if I
  ask you again.

HERDSMAN   It was one of the children
  of Laius.

OEDIPUS   A slave? Or born in wedlock?

HERDSMAN   O gods, I am on the brink of frightful speech.   1250

OEDIPUS   And I of frightful hearing. But I must hear.

HERDSMAN   The child was called his child; but she within,
  your wife would tell you best how all this was.

OEDIPUS   She gave it to you?

HERDSMAN   Yes, she did, my lord.

OEDIPUS   To do what with it?

HERDSMAN   Make away with it.   1255

OEDIPUS   She was so hard—its mother?

HERDSMAN   Aye, through fear
  of evil oracles.

OEDIPUS   Which?

HERDSMAN   They said that he
  should kill his parents.

OEDIPUS   How was it that you   1260 gave it away to this old man?

HERDSMAN   O master,
  I pitied it, and thought that I could send it
  off to another country and this man
  was from another country. But he saved it
  for the most terrible troubles. If you are   1265
  the man he says you are, you're bred to misery.

OEDIPUS   O, O, O, they will all come,
  all come out clearly! Light of the sun, let me
  look upon you no more after today!
  I who first saw the light bred of a match   1270
  accursed, and accursed in my living
  with them I lived with, cursed in my killing.

      [Exeunt all but the CHORUS.]

CHORUS
STROPHE   O generations of men, how I
  count you as equal with those who live
  not at all!   1275
  What man, what man on earth wins more
  of happiness than a seeming
  and after that turning away?
  Oedipus, you are my pattern of this,
  Oedipus, you and your fate!   1280
  Luckless Oedipus, whom of all men
  I envy not at all.

ANISTROPHE   In as much as he shot his bolt
  beyond the others and won the prize
  of happiness complete—   1285
  O Zeus—and killed and reduced to nought
  the hooked taloned maid of the riddling speech,
  standing a tower against death for my land:
  hence he was called my king and hence
  was honoured the highest of all   1290
  honours; and hence he ruled
  in the great city of Thebes.

STROPHE   But now whose tale is more miserable?
  Who is there lives with a savager fate?
  Whose troubles so reverse his life as his?   1295
  O Oedipus, the famous prince
  for whom a great haven
  the same both as father and son
  sufficed for generation,
  how, O how, have the furrows ploughed   1300
  by your father endured to bear you, poor wretch,
  and hold their peace so long?

ANTISTROPHE   Time who sees all has found you out
  against your will; judges your marriage accursed,
  begetter and begot at one in it.   1305
  O child of Laius,

would I had never seen you.
I weep for you and cry
a dirge of lamentation.
To speak directly, I drew my breath   1310
from you at the first and so now I lull
my mouth to sleep with your name.

          [*Enter a* SECOND MESSENGER.]

SECOND MESSENGER   O Princes always honoured by our country,
    what deeds you'll hear of and what horrors see,
    what grief you'll feel, if you as true-born Thebans   1315
    care for the house of Labdacus's sons.
    Phasis nor Ister[5] cannot purge this house,
    I think, with all their streams, such things
    it hides, such evils shortly will bring forth
    into the light, whether they will or not;   1320
    and troubles hurt the most
    when they prove self-inflicted.

CHORUS   What we had known before did not fall short
    of bitter groaning's worth; what's more to tell?

SECOND MESSENGER   Shortest to hear and tell—our glorious queen   1325
    Jocasta's dead.

CHORUS   Unhappy woman! How?

SECOND MESSENGER   By her own hand. The worst of what was done
    you cannot know. You did not see the sight.
    Yet in so far as I remember it
    You'll hear the end of our unlucky queen.   1330
    When she came raging into the house she went
    straight to her marriage bed, tearing her hair
    with both her hands, and crying upon Laius
    long dead—Do you remember, Laius,
    that night long past which bred a child for us   1335
    to send you to your death and leave
    a mother making children with her son?
    And then she groaned and cursed the bed in which
    she brought forth husband by her husband, children
    by her own child, an infamous double bond.   1340
    How after that she died I do not know,—
    for Oedipus distracted us from seeing.
    He burst upon us shouting and we looked
    to him as he paced frantically around,
    begging us always: Give me a sword, I say,   1345
    to find this wife no wife, this mother's womb,
    this field of double sowing whence I sprang
    and where I sowed my children! As he raved
    some god showed him the way—none of us there.
    Bellowing terribly and led by some   1350
    invisible guide he rushed on the two doors,—

---

5. Phasis is a large river in western Georgia; Ister is an ancient name for the Danube.

wrenching the hollow bolts out of their sockets,
he charged inside. There, there, we saw his wife
hanging, the twisted rope around her neck.
When he saw her, he cried out fearfully   1355
and cut the dangling noose. Then, as she lay,
poor woman, on the ground, what happened after,
was terrible to see. He tore the brooches—
the gold chased brooches fastening her robe—
away from her and lifting them up high   1360
dashed them on his own eyeballs, shrieking out
such things as: they will never see the crime
I have committed or had done upon me!
Dark eyes, now in the days to come look on
forbidden faces, do not recognize   1365
those whom you long for—with such imprecations
he struck his eyes again and yet again
with the brooches. And the bleeding eyeballs gushed
and stained his beard—no sluggish oozing drops
but a black rain and bloody hail poured down.   1370

So it has broken—and not on one head
but troubles mixed for husband and for wife.
The fortune of the days gone by was true
good fortune—but today groans and destruction
and death and shame—of all ills can be named   1375
not one is missing.

CHORUS   Is he now in any ease from pain?

SECOND MESSENGER   He shouts
for someone to unbar the doors and show him
to all the men of Thebes, his father's killer,
his mother's—no, I cannot say the word,   1380
it is unholy—for he'll cast himself
out of the land, he says, and not remain
to bring a curse upon his house, the curse
he called upon it in his proclamation. But
he wants for strength, aye, and someone to guide him;   1385
his sickness is too great to bear. You, too,
will be shown that. The bolts are opening.
Soon you will see a sight to waken pity
even in the horror of it.

          [Enter the blinded OEDIPUS.]

CHORUS   This is a terrible sight for men to see!   1390
I never found a worse!
Poor wretch, what madness came upon you!
What evil spirit leaped upon your life
to your ill-luck—a leap beyond man's strength!
Indeed I pity you, but I cannot   1395
look at you, though there's much I want to ask
and much to learn and much to see.

I shudder at the sight of you.

OEDIPUS O, O,
where am I going? Where is my voice 1400
borne on the wind to and fro?
Spirit, how far have you sprung?

CHORUS To a terrible place whereof men's ears
may not hear, nor their eyes behold it.

OEDIPUS Darkness! 1405
Horror of darkness enfolding, resistless, unspeakable visitant sped
   by an ill wind in haste!
madness and stabbing pain and memory
of evil deeds I have done!

CHORUS In such misfortunes it's no wonder 1410
if double weighs the burden of your grief.

OEDIPUS My friend,
you are the only one steadfast, the only one that attends on me;
you still stay nursing the blind man.
Your care is not unnoticed. I can know 1415
your voice, although this darkness is my world.

CHORUS Doer of dreadful deeds, how did you dare
so far to do despite to your own eyes?
what spirit urged you to it?

OEDIPUS It was Apollo, friends, Apollo, 1420
that brought this bitter bitterness, my sorrows to completion.
But the hand that struck me
was none but my own.
Why should I see
whose vision showed me nothing sweet to see? 1425

CHORUS These things are as you say.

OEDIPUS What can I see to love?
What greeting can touch my ears with joy?
Take me away, and haste—to a place out of the way!
Take me away, my friends, the greatly miserable, 1430
the most accursed, whom the gods too hate
above all men on earth!

CHORUS Unhappy in your mind and your misfortune,
would I had never known you!

OEDIPUS Curse on the man who took 1435
the cruel bonds from off my legs, as I lay in the field.
He stole me from death and saved me,
no kindly service.
Had I died then
I would not be so burdensome to friends. 1440

CHORUS I, too, could have wished it had been so.

OEDIPUS Then I would not have come
to kill my father and marry my mother infamously.
Now I am godless and child of impurity,
begetter in the same seed that created my wretched self. 1445
If there is any ill worse than ill,

that is the lot of Oedipus.

CHORUS   I cannot say your remedy was good;
you would be better dead than blind and living.

OEDIPUS   What I have done here was best done—don't tell me   1450
otherwise, do not give me further counsel.
I do not know with what eyes I could look
upon my father when I die and go
under the earth, nor yet my wretched mother—
those two to whom I have done things deserving   1455
worse punishment than hanging. Would the sight
of children, bred as mine are, gladden me?
No, not these eyes, never. And my city,
its towers and sacred places of the gods,
of these I robbed my miserable self   1460
when I commanded all to drive *him* out,
the criminal since proved by god impure
and of the race of Laius.
To this guilt I bore witness against myself—
with what eyes shall I look upon my people?   1465
No. If there were a means to choke the fountain
of hearing I would not have stayed my hand
from locking up my miserable carcase,
seeing and hearing nothing; it is sweet
to keep our thoughts out of the range of hurt.   1470

Cithaeron, why did you receive me? Why
having received me did you not kill me straight?
And so I had not shown to men my birth.

O Polybus and Corinth and the house,
the old house that I used to call my father's—   1475
what fairness you were nurse to, and what foulness
festered beneath! Now I am found to be
a sinner and a son of sinners. Crossroads,
and hidden glade, oak and the narrow way
at the crossroads, that drank my father's blood   1480
offered you by my hands, do you remember
still what I did as you looked on, and what
I did when I came here? O marriage, marriage!
you bred me and again when you had bred
bred children of your child and showed to men   1485
brides, wives and mothers and the foulest deeds
that can be in this world of ours.

Come—it's unfit to say what is unfit
to do.—I beg of you in god's name hide me
somewhere outside your country, yes, or kill me,   1490
or throw me into the sea, to be forever
out of your sight. Approach and deign to touch me

for all my wretchedness, and do not fear.
No man but I can bear my evil doom.

CHORUS   Here Creon comes in fit time to perform   1495
or give advice in what you ask of us.
Creon is left sole ruler in your stead.

OEDIPUS   Creon! Creon! What shall I say to him?
How can I justly hope that he will trust me?
In what is past I have been proved towards him   1500
an utter liar.

     [*Enter* CREON.]

CREON   Oedipus, I've come
not so that I might laugh at you nor taunt you
with evil of the past. But if you still
are without shame before the face of men   1505
reverence at least the flame that gives all life,
our Lord the Sun, and do not show unveiled
to him pollution such that neither land
nor holy rain nor light of day can welcome.

     [*To a servant.*]

Be quick and take him in. It is most decent   1510
that only kin should see and hear the troubles
of kin.

OEDIPUS   I beg you, since you've torn me from
my dreadful expectations and have come
in a most noble spirit to a man   1515
that has used you vilely—do a thing for me.
I shall speak for your own good, not for my own.

CREON   What do you need that you would ask of me?

OEDIPUS   Drive me from here with all the speed you can
to where I may not hear a human voice.   1520

CREON   Be sure, I would have done this had not I
wished first of all to learn from the god the course
of action I should follow.

OEDIPUS   But his word
has been quite clear to let the parricide,
the sinner, die.   1525

CREON   Yes, that indeed was said.
But in the present need we had best discover
what we should do.

OEDIPUS   And will you ask about
a man so wretched?

CREON   Now even you will trust
the god.   1530

OEDIPUS   So. I command you—and will beseech you—
to her that lies inside that house give burial
as you would have it; she is yours and rightly
you will perform the rites for her. For me—
never let this my father's city have me   1535
living a dweller in it. Leave me live

in the mountains where Cithaeron is, that's called
my mountain, which my mother and my father
while they were living would have made my tomb.
So I may die by their decree who sought   1540
indeed to kill me. Yet I know this much:
no sickness and no other thing will kill me.
I would not have been saved from death if not
for some strange evil fate. Well, let my fate
go where it will.   1545
          Creon, you need not care
about my sons; they're men and so wherever
they are, they will not lack a livelihood.
But my two girls—so sad and pitiful—
whose table never stood apart from mine,
and everything I touched they always shared—   1550
O Creon, have a thought for them! And most
I wish that you might suffer me to touch them
and sorrow with them.

    [*Enter* ANTIGONE *and* ISMENE, OEDIPUS' *two daughters.*]

    O my lord! O true noble Creon! Can I
really be touching them, as when I saw?   1555
What shall I say?
Yes, I can hear them sobbing—my two darlings!
and Creon has had pity and has sent me
what I loved most?
Am I right?   1560

CREON   You're right: it was I gave you this
because I knew from old days how you loved them
as I see now.

OEDIPUS   God bless you for it, Creon,
and may the god guard you better on your road
than he did me!   1565
O children,
where are you? Come here, come to my hands,
a brother's hands which turned your father's eyes,
those bright eyes you knew once, to what you see,
a father seeing nothing, knowing nothing,   1570
begetting you from his own source of life.
I weep for you—I cannot see your faces—
I weep when I think of the bitterness
there will be in your lives, how you must live
before the world. At what assemblages   1575
of citizens will you make one? to what
gay company will you go and not come home
in tears instead of sharing in the holiday?
And when you're ripe for marriage, who will he be,
the man who'll risk to take such infamy   1580
as shall cling to my children, to bring hurt
on them and those that marry with them? What

curse is not there? "Your father killed his father
and sowed the seed where he had sprung himself
and begot you out of the womb that held him." 1585
These insults you will hear. Then who will marry you?
No one, my children; clearly you are doomed
to waste away in barrenness unmarried.
Son of Menoeceus,[6] since you are all the father
left these two girls, and we, their parents, both 1590
are dead to them—do not allow them wander
like beggars, poor and husbandless.
They are of your own blood.
And do not make them equal with myself
in wretchedness; for you can see them now 1595
so young, so utterly alone, save for you only.
Touch my hand, noble Creon, and say yes.
If you were older, children, and were wiser,
there's much advice I'd give you. But as it is,
let this be what you pray: give me a life 1600
wherever there is opportunity
to live, and better life than was my father's.
CREON   Your tears have had enough of scope; now go within the house.
OEDIPUS   I must obey, though bitter of heart.
CREON   In season, all is good. 1605
OEDIPUS   Do you know on what conditions I obey?
CREON   You tell me them,
and I shall know them when I hear.
OEDIPUS   That you shall send me out
to live away from Thebes.
CREON   That gift you must ask of the god.
OEDIPUS   But I'm now hated by the gods.
CREON   So quickly you'll obtain your prayer.
OEDIPUS   You consent then?
CREON   What I do not mean, I do not use to say. 1610
OEDIPUS   Now lead me away from here.
CREON   Let go the children, then, and come.
OEDIPUS   Do not take them from me.
CREON   Do not seek to be master in everything,
for the things you mastered did not follow you throughout your life.

[As CREON and OEDIPUS go out.]

CHORUS   You that live in my ancestral Thebes, behold this Oedipus,— 1615
him who knew the famous riddles and was a man most masterful;
not a citizen who did not look with envy on his lot—
see him now and see the breakers of misfortune swallow him!
Look upon that last day always. Count no mortal happy till
he has passed the final limit of his life secure from pain. 1620

---

6. Creon is Menoeceus's son.

Antigone[1]

CHARACTERS

ANTIGONE, daughter of Oedipus
  (former king of Thebes)
ISMENE, daughter of Oedipus
CHORUS, fifteen aged noblemen of
  Thebes
KREON, king of Thebes, uncle and
  guardian of Antigone and Ismene

GUARD, an aged and lowly soldier
  under Kreon's command
HAIMON, son of Kreon
TEIRESIAS, an aged prophet
MESSENGER, an attendant of Kreon
EURYDIKE, wife of Kreon
Guards and attendants of Kreon,
  Teiresias, and Eurydike

[SETTING Outside the royal palace of Thebes. The scene shows the façade of the palace, which has a large central door. The time is just before dawn, on the morning following the successful defeat of Polyneices and his allies in their assault on Thebes.]

[*Enter* ANTIGONE *and* ISMENE *from the palace.*]

ANTIGONE   Ismene, my own sister, sharing the self-same blood,
of all the evils that descend from Oedipus
do you know one that Zeus does not fulfill for us,
the two still living? There is nothing—no!—no grief,
no doom, dishonor, or disgrace that I've not seen   5
counted among the evils that are yours and mine.
Now this! What is this proclamation that they say
the general has just made to all the city's people?
Have you heard anything? Or are you unaware
that evils due to enemies approach our friends?   10

ISMENE   To me no word of friends has come, Antigone,
sweet or distressing, since the time when you and I
were both deprived, we two, of our two brothers, both
struck dead by twofold hand within a single day;
and since the army of the Argives disappeared   15
during the night just past, I have learned nothing new—
whether my fortune has improved or I am doomed.

ANTIGONE   I knew it well. That's why I summoned you outside
the courtyard gates, for you to hear me by yourself.

ISMENE   What is it? You are clearly brooding on some news.   20

ANTIGONE   What? Has not Kreon honored only one of our
two brothers with a tomb, and dishonored the other?
Eteokles he has seen fit to treat with justice, so
they say, and lawfully concealed beneath
the ground, there to be honored by the dead below;   25
but as for Polyneices' miserable corpse,
they say the townsfolk have received a proclamation,

---

1. Translated by Ruby Blondell. This translation uses versions of names that are closer to the Greek, such as "Kreon" for "Creon."

that none may shroud him in a tomb or wail for him;
he must be left unwept, unburied, treasure sweet
for watching birds to feed on at their pleasure.   30
They say that this is what good Kreon has proclaimed
for you and me—yes, *me* as well!—and that he's coming
here to make his proclamation clear to those
who do not know; nor does he view the matter as
a trivial one: the penalty prescribed for doing   35
this is death from stoning by the city's people.
That's how things stand; soon you'll reveal if you're
by nature nobly born, or evil from good stock.

ISMENE   If that is how things are, unhappy one, what good
can *I* do, loosening or tightening the knot?   40

ANTIGONE   See if you'll join in laboring to do a deed.

ISMENE   What deed of danger? What can you be thinking of?

ANTIGONE   See if you'll join these hands of mine to lift the corpse.

ISMENE   What, bury him? When it's forbidden to the city?

ANTIGONE   Yes, bury my own brother—and yours too—if you're   45
not willing. *I* will not be caught in treachery.

ISMENE   Audacious one! Against Kreon's express command?

ANTIGONE   He has no business keeping me from what is mine.

ISMENE   Alas! Just think, my sister, of our father—how
he perished, hated and in ill-repute, for errors   50
he himself detected, after he himself
gouged out his twofold eyes with self-inflicting hand;[2]
next how his mother-wife—a twofold name in one—
blighted her life with woven strands of twisted rope;
third, our two brothers in a single day both killed   55
themselves in one another—wretched pair!—inflicting
one shared doom with two reciprocating hands;
look now in turn at us two, left here all alone—
our death will be the worst by far, if we defy
the law, and go beyond the power and vote of kings.   60
We must remember, first, that we two are by nature
women and not fit to fight with men; second,
that we are ruled by others stronger than ourselves,
and so must bow to this and even greater griefs.
So I for one shall beg those underneath the earth   65
to pardon me, since I am overpowered by force;
I shall obey those who are in authority,
for deeds that are excessive make no sense at all.

ANTIGONE   I would not urge you otherwise, nor would it bring
me pleasure if you did now wish to act with me.   70
You be as you think best, but I shall bury him.
To me it's fine to die performing such a deed.

---

2. Sophocles seems here to use the version of the myth in which Oedipus stays at Thebes
(rather than being exiled, as in *Oedipus the King*).

I'll lie there, dear to him, with my dear friend,[3] when I've
performed this crime of piety; for I must please
those down below a longer time than those up here,   75
since I shall lie there always. You, though, if you think
it best, dishonor what is honored by the gods.

ISMENE   I don't dishonor him; but it's impossible
for me by nature to defy the citizens.

ANTIGONE   Make your excuses! *I* shall go and heap up earth   80
into a tomb to bury him, my dearest brother.

ISMENE   Alas! How I am filled with dread for you, poor wretch!

ANTIGONE   Don't fear for *me*; guide your own destiny aright.

ISMENE   At least be sure that you reveal this deed to no
one else; conceal it secretly. I'll join in that.   85

ANTIGONE   Alas! Speak out! You'll be more hateful still if you
stay silent. No, proclaim my plan out loud to all!

ISMENE   You have a heart within you hot for chilling deeds.

ANTIGONE   I know that I am pleasing those I should please most.

ISMENE   Perhaps; but you're in love with the impossible.   90

ANTIGONE   Then when I've used up all my strength, I shall have done.

ISMENE   One should not hunt for the impossible at all.

ANTIGONE   If you speak so, you'll be a hateful enemy
to me, and justly hated by the dead man too.
Let me and the ill counsel that derives from me   95
suffer this awful fate; what I shall suffer will
be far less dire than dying an ignoble death!

ISMENE   Go, if you think it best; know that you're senseless to
be going, and yet rightly to your dear friends dear.

> [*Exit* ANTIGONE *along the side-entrance representing the path to the
> upland plain where the battle took place and Polyneices' body lies. Exit*
> ISMENE *into the palace. Enter the* CHORUS *of fifteen old, white-haired
> noblemen of Thebes, singing and dancing. They enter along the other
> side-entrance, which represents the road from the city of Thebes proper.*]

CHORUS   Oh bright beam of the sun,   100
loveliest light that ever shone   *Strophe A*
on seven-gated Thebes,
at last you have appeared,
oh eye of golden day,
rising on Dirce's streams,   105
stirring to headlong flight
with sharply piercing bit
the Argive,[4] shielded in white,
in all his panoply, gone.

---

3. The word translated by "dear" and "dear
friend" is *philos*, which connotes familial kind of
love and kinship.
4. I.e., the Athenians, who had allied them-

selves with Polyneices' rebels. "Dirce": river
west of Thebes, here used to symbolize the
city.

Polyneices, roused by a double-edged 110
dispute, led him to attack our land;
over our land he flew with a piercing
scream like an eagle, covering us with a
snow-white wing,
he with his numerous weapons and helmets 115
crested with horsehair.

> Over our halls he hovered, *Antistrophe A*
> maw gaping wide,
> murderous spears encircling
> our city's seven-mouthed gates,
> but was gone before he could glut 120
> his jaws with our streaming blood,
> or pine-fed Hephaistos could consume
> our crowning wreath of towers—
> such a crashing of Ares surged at their backs, 125
> tough task for the dragon who wrestled him.[5]

For Zeus exceedingly hates the boasts
of a mighty tongue. When he saw those men
coming on in a copious flood,
with the supercilious clanging of gold, 130
he struck one down with brandished fire
a man at his topmost goal,[6] who rushed
to raise up the victory cry.

> He teetered and fell to the resistant earth, *Strophe B*
> the fire-bringer who rushed madly on, 135
> breathing on us, in frenzied Bacchanal,[7]
> blasts of most hateful winds of enmity.
> But he failed in his attempt; mighty Ares,
> our right-hand trace-horse,[8] struck down hard,
> dispensing other deaths to other men. 140

Seven captains at seven gates,
seven matched with an equal number,
left bronze tribute for Zeus, battle-turner.
But that abhorrent pair of brothers,
born from a single father and mother, 145
fixed two powerful spears in each other,
and both have their share in a double death.

> But Victory of mighty name has come, *Antistrophe B*
> with joy responding to the joy

---

5. The "dragon" is the Thebans, who were supposed to have been born from dragon's teeth sowed in the ground. "Hephaistos": the blacksmith god, associated with fire. "Ares": god of war.
6. Kapaneus, ally of Polyneices, who boasted while scaling the city walls and was struck with a lightning bolt hurled by Zeus.

7. Bacchus/Dionysos is associated with frenzy or madness; Kapaneus is here compared to a worshipper of Bacchus.
8. On a four-horse racing chariot, the right front horse does the most work because it has to run fastest at the turns.

of many-charioted Thebes.   150
Now war is past, bring on forgetfulness!
Let us visit all the temples of the gods
with night-long dance and song!
May Bacchus, shaker of Thebes,[9] lead on!

But here comes Kreon, the son of Menoikeus,   155
king of the land, and our new ruler since
this new fortune has come from the gods.
What plan is he plying?
Why has he called for a special assembly
of elders to meet here,   160
sending a shared proclamation to all?

> [*Enter* KREON, *along the side-entrance leading from the battlefield. He
> may still be wearing armor, and is accompanied by armed men. The paro-
> dos ends, and the meter returns to the iambic trimeters used for spoken
> dialogue.*]

KREON   Oh men, the gods who tossed our city's ship on mighty
waves have safely righted it once more. And so
I sent my messengers to summon you to come
away from all the rest, because I know you always   165
did revere the power of Laios'[1] throne; so too
when it was Oedipus who steered the city right;
and when he perished, you remained still loyal to
their children, steadfast in your purpose and your thoughts.
So, since his sons have perished in a single day,   170
two brothers by a twofold fate, both striking and
struck down, hands foully stained with mutual fratricide,
it's I who now hold all the power and the throne,
through my close bond of kinship to the perished dead.

   It is impossible to learn in full the spirit   175
of a man, his purpose or his judgment, till
he's shown up by experience of rule and law.
For anyone who rules the city as a whole
and does not hold on to the counsels that are best,
but keeps a lock fixed on his tongue because of fear,   180
I think that man most evil, and I always have;
and he who counts a friend as more important than
his fatherland, he's nowhere in my reckoning.
For I—bear witness Zeus, who sees all things always!—
I'd not keep silent if I saw some doom instead   185
of safety moving on the people of this town;
nor would I ever count a man as my own friend
who felt ill will towards this land; I recognize
that this ship keeps us safe, and only when we sail
upon it upright can we make friends for ourselves.   190

---

9. Bacchus is the patron god of Thebes.   sor as king of Thebes.
1. Father of Oedipus and Oedipus's predeces-

Such are the laws with which I make this city great.
And brother to them is my proclamation to
the townsfolk in regard to Oedipus's sons.
Eteokles, who perished fighting for this city,
and did all deeds of greatness with his spear, will be   195
concealed within a tomb with all the offerings
that go down to the greatest of the dead below.
But his blood-kin, his brother—I mean Polyneices
who came back from exile with intent to burn
with fire from top to bottom his own fatherland   200
and his own family gods, intent to gorge himself
on blood he shared, and make his countrymen his slaves—
this city has received a proclamation, not
to honor him with funeral rites or wail for him,
but all must leave his body unentombed, to be   205
the food of birds and dogs, an outrage to behold.
Such is my purpose; never shall evil men be held
in higher honor than the just, at least by me;
but he who bears good will towards this city will
be honored by me equally in life and death.   210

CHORUS   It pleases you, Menoikeus' son, to treat like this
the man who shows ill-will towards this city and
the kindly one. You have the power to use what law
you like regarding both the dead and us who live.

KREON   See to it, then, that you watch over what I've said.   215

CHORUS   Assign this burden to some younger man to bear.

KREON   There are already watchers set to guard the corpse.

CHORUS   What else besides that would you order us to do?

KREON   Not to collaborate with those who disobey.

CHORUS   No one's so foolish as to be in love with death.   220

KREON   That is indeed the payment: death. But all the same,
profit destroys men often, through the hope of gain.

[*Enter* GUARD, *an old man dressed as a lowly soldier. He enters slowly and
hesitantly along the side-entrance leading from the battlefield.*]

GUARD   My lord, I really cannot say that I've arrived
here out of breath with speed or light and fleet of foot.
No, many times my anxious thoughts brought me up short,   225
and made me wheel round in the road to travel back.
My spirit spoke to me loquaciously, like this:
"Poor fool, why go where you will pay the penalty?"
"Stopping again, you wretch? If Kreon hears about
this from some other man, you're bound to suffer grief!"   230
These ruminations made my progress leisurely
and slow, until a short road turned into a long.
But in the end, the plan of coming to you won,
and if my words mean nothing, I'll speak anyway.
For I have come here holding firmly to the hope   235
that I can suffer nothing that is not my fate.

KREON   What is the reason for this apprehensiveness?

GUARD   I want to tell you my own situation first.
I did not do the deed, or see the one who did,
and it would be unjust for me to come to harm.   240

KREON   You're aiming well and building fences round the deed.
It's clear you've something unexpected to reveal.

GUARD   Great hesitation is induced by awful things.

KREON   Won't you speak out at last, and then get out of here?

GUARD   All right, I'm telling you. The corpse—someone just now   245
has buried it and gone; they sprinkled thirsty dust
upon its skin and carried out the proper rites.

KREON   What are you saying? What man dared to do this deed?

GUARD   I do not know. There was no mark from pickaxe blows,
no earth thrown up by mattocks; no, the ground was hard   250
and dry, not broken up or furrowed by the weight
of wagon wheels. The doer was one who left no sign.
When our first watcher for the day pointed this out,
uncomfortable amazement came upon us all.
The corpse had disappeared—not buried in a grave,   255
but covered with light dust as if to deflect a curse.
No sign was visible that any dog or savage
animal had been there tearing at the corpse.
Abusive words began to rumble back and forth,
with guard accusing guard, and in the end we would   260
have come to blows—no one was there to hinder it.
For each and every one of us had done the deed,
but no one clearly so, and all pled ignorance.
We were prepared to take up red-hot iron in
our hands, to walk through fire, to swear oaths by the gods   265
that we had not done this ourselves, and had no knowledge
of who else had planned or carried out the deed.
      When our inquiries got us nowhere, then at last
one man spoke up who made us all bow down our heads
towards the ground in fear; there was no way for us   270
either to contradict him or do as he said
and fare well from it. His advice was that this deed
should be reported to you rather than concealed.
This view won out, and I, ill-fated one, became
the one condemned by lot to win this fine reward.   275
I'm here against my will; against yours too, I know.
For no one likes a messenger who brings bad news.

CHORUS   My lord, my mind has been suggesting for some time
that possibly this deed was prompted by the gods.

KREON   Stop speaking now, before you stuff me full of rage,   280
or you'll be found to have no sense despite your age.
The words you speak are unendurable—to think
divinities might be concerned about this corpse!
Did they conceal his body to bestow a special
honor on a benefactor—he who came   285
to burn their pillared temples and their offerings,

to scatter into pieces their own land and laws?
Do you see gods bestowing honor on the evil?
It cannot be! No, there are men who chafe at me
within the city, rumbling at me secretly   290
for some time now, heads tossing, necks not justly held
beneath the yoke in due contentment with my rule.
I understand the situation well: the guards
were bribed by them with payment to perform this deed.
Money! No institution that's as evil ever   295
grew into existence for the human race.
This wipes out cities, forces men to leave their homes,
re-educates and warps the minds of mortals that
were good, inducing them to turn to shameful things,
shows human beings how to undertake all crimes,   300
and come to know impiety in every deed.
    Yet those who hired themselves for cash and did this deed
ensured that they would pay the penalty in time.
But by the reverence that Zeus receives from me,
know this full well—and I am speaking under oath: 305
if you guards do not find the one whose hand performed
this burial, and show him plainly to my eyes,
Hades[2] won't be enough for you; before you die
you'll hang alive until you make this outrage clear,
so that in future you may seize your plunder knowing   310
where to get your profits from, and learn that you
should not be fond of profiting from every source.
For you will see that after shameful takings the
majority of people end up doomed, not saved.

GUARD   Will you grant me a word, or shall I just turn and go?   315
KREON   Do you not know that even these words trouble me?
GUARD   But is their bite felt in your spirit or your ears?
KREON   Why try to pin down the location of my pain?
GUARD   The perpetrator pains your mind, but I your ears.
KREON   Oh what a natural chatterbox you are, it's clear!   320
GUARD   Perhaps; but I am not the one who did this deed.
KREON   You did the deed, and sold your life for money too.
GUARD   Ah!
How awful to believe when your beliefs are false!
KREON   Play with the word *belief*. But if you don't reveal
the perpetrators of this deed to me, then you'll   325
admit that profits basely won bring suffering.
        [*Exit* KREON, *into the palace.*]
GUARD   Above all else may he be found. But whether he
is caught or not—that is for fortune to decide—
there's no way that you'll see me coming here again.
On this occasion I've been saved beyond my hope   330
and judgment, so I owe the gods great gratitude.

2. God of the underworld; or, as here, the underworld itself.

[*Exit* GUARD, *along the same side-entrance by which he arrived.*]

CHORUS   Awesome wonders are many,[3]   *Strophe A*
   but none of them more awesome
   than the human race.
   This creature travels the grey sea   335
   before the stormy winter wind,
   pressing through surging waves that crest about him;
   the highest of gods he wears away,
   the tireless immortal Earth,
   turning her with the offspring of horses,   340
   as the plow runs to and fro from year to year.

   The tribe of light-headed birds,   *Antistrophe A*
   all kinds of savage beasts,
   and creatures born in the salty sea,
   he traps with his intricate coiling nets   345
   and leads away—ingenious man!
   With devices he overpowers
   the mountain-roaming beast
   that dwells in the wilderness,
   he breaks the shaggy-necked horse with a yoke   350
   on its neck, and the tireless mountain bull.

   Speech and wind-swift purpose,   *Strophe B*
   these has he taught himself,
   and the impulse to civic law,
   and how to escape the shafts   355
   of the inhospitable frosty sky
   and the harsh shafts of the rain—
   all-resourceful! Resourceless
   he meets nothing the future holds.
   Only from Hades will he fail   360
   to find escape; and yet escape
   from impossible sicknesses,
   this he has devised.

   By means of skilful contrivance,   *Antistrophe B*
   clever beyond hope,   365
   he comes to evil sometimes,
   sometimes to good.
   When he weaves in the laws of the earth,
   and the gods' sworn justice,
   he is high in his city; citiless   370
   is he whose daring makes him
   join with what is not fine.
   May he never share my hearth,

---

3. The Greek word translated by "awesome wonders," *deina*, has a range of meaning from "amazing" to "clever" to "dreadful."

may I never share his thinking,
he who would do such things.   375

> [*Enter* GUARD *leading Antigone, along the side-entrance by which he
> exited. Antigone's eyes are cast down.*]

My mind is divided! Is this a divine
portent? I know her! How can I argue that
this girl here is not Antigone?
Unhappy one, and child of an unhappy
father, of Oedipus! What does this mean?   380
Surely they are not leading you here,
found disobeying the laws of the king,
caught in an act of foolishness?

GUARD   This is the woman who performed the deed. We caught
her in the act of burial. But where is Kreon?   385

> [*Enter* KREON *from the palace, with attendants.*]

CHORUS   He's here, returning opportunely from the house.

KREON   What chance event makes my arrival opportune?

GUARD   My lord, there's nothing mortals should forswear, since sworn
resolve is falsified by second thoughts. Take me:
I was insisting I would not be back here in   390
a hurry, after being stormed at with your threats.
But joy that we have prayed for past all hope surpasses
every other pleasure in extent; and so
I've come—despite the oaths I swore that I would not—
leading this girl here, who was caught performing rites   395
of burial. This time there was no drawing lots;
this lucky find belongs to me, and no one else.
Now take her, lord, yourself, as is your wish; you can
interrogate her and convict her; but it's just
that I should leave here fully free from all these evils.   400

KREON   This woman that you bring, where did you catch her? How?

GUARD   We caught her burying that man; now you know all.

KREON   Do you know what you're saying? Do you speak aright?

GUARD   I saw her burying the corpse to which you had
forbidden burial. Are these words clear enough?   405

KREON   And how was she observed and taken in the act?

GUARD   What happened was like this. When we got back to our
position, subject to those awful threats of yours,
we brushed off all the dust that had been covering
the body, stripping bare the putrifying corpse,   410
and sat down on the hilltop with the wind behind
us, to escape from being stricken by the stench,
each man alert, and rousing one another with
loud taunts at any who might slacken from the task.
This lasted for the time it took the shining circle   415
of the sun to reach the center of the sky.
The heat was burning. Suddenly a whirlwind raised
a dusty column from the earth, a trouble high
as heaven, which filled up the plain, defacing all

the foliage of the trees, and choked the mighty sky.   420
We shut our eyes and bore the sickness sent by god.
     It took a long time for the storm to pass. And then
we saw this girl here wailing bitterly aloud,
in the piercing voice of a mother bird who sees her nest
is empty and her bed bereft of baby chicks.   425
Just so did she, on seeing that the corpse was bare,
cry out in lamentation, and call evil curses
down upon the ones who had performed this deed.
At once she gathered thirsty dust with her bare hands,
and lifting high a brazen pitcher, finely-wrought,   430
she crowned the corpse by pouring three libation-streams.[4]
     The instant that we saw her, we rushed forward and
hunted her down; she was completely unperturbed.
We charged her with the deeds of burial, both this
one and the first, and she did not deny a thing—   435
a fact that brought me grief and pleasure both at once:
it is most sweet to have escaped from evils for
oneself; and yet to bring a friend to evil is
distressing. But it's only natural that all
of this means less to me than my own safety.   440

KREON [to ANTIGONE]   You there! You, bowing down your head towards
     the ground!
Do you admit it or deny you did the deed?

ANTIGONE   I don't deny it; I admit the deed was mine.

KREON [to the GUARD]   You may now take yourself away, wherever you
     may wish, free and unburdened of this heavy charge.   445
          [He turns back to ANTIGONE.]
But as for you, tell me succinctly, not at length:
you knew a proclamation had forbidden this?

ANTIGONE   I knew. How could I not? It was a public fact.

KREON   And yet you had the daring to transgress these laws?

ANTIGONE   It was not Zeus who made this proclamation;   450
nor was it Justice dwelling with the gods below
who set in place such laws as these for humankind;
nor did I think your proclamations had such strength
that, mortal as you are, you could outrun those laws
that are the gods', unwritten and unshakable.   455
Their laws are not for now or yesterday, but live
forever; no one knows when first they came to light.
I was not going to pay the gods' just penalty
for breaking these, dreading the purposes of a
mere man. I knew that I must die—how could I not?—   460
regardless of the proclamation that you made.
But if I die before my time, I count that as
a profit. How can death not profit one who lives
surrounded by as many evils as myself?

---

4. Libations are liquid offerings poured to honor the gods or the dead.

For me, therefore, to meet this doom is equal to   465
no grief at all. But if I had endured the son
of my own mother to lie dead without a grave,
that would have brought me grief; but I'm not grieved by *this*.
And if you think my present deeds are foolishness,
perhaps the one who calls me foolish is the fool.   470

CHORUS   The child shows clearly her fierce father's fierceness; but
she does not understand the way to yield to evils.

KREON   Know well that over-rigid purposes most often
fall; the iron that is most powerful, that has
been baked in fire until it is extremely hard,   475
you'll see most often shattered into little bits;
a slender curb, I know, will school the spirit of
a raging-tempered horse; it is impossible
to harbor mighty thoughts when you are someone's slave.
This girl knew well how to commit an act of outrage   480
when she first transgressed against the published laws;
and here's a second outrage: after doing it
to boast of it and laugh, exulting in her deed.
It's clear enough that I'm no man, but she's the man,
if she can get away with holding power like this.   485
No, whether she's my sister's child, or tied to me
closer by blood than all my household under Zeus,
she won't escape from a most evil doom, nor will
her sister, her blood-kin, the other whom I hold
equally guilty in the planning of this tomb.   490
Call her. Just now I saw her in a frenzy in
the house, no longer in possession of her mind.
     [*Two of* KREON's *attendants exit into the palace.*]
The heart of those contriving in the dark what is
not right is often caught out in deceit before
they act. But this I also loathe—when someone caught   495
performing evil wants to glorify the deed.

ANTIGONE   Take me away and kill me. Do you want more than this?

KREON   No more. If I have that, then I have everything.

ANTIGONE   Then what's delaying you? For there is nothing in
your words that's pleasing to me—may there never be!   500
And naturally you disapprove of mine as well.
Yet how could I have won more glorious renown
than by the act of placing my own brother in
a tomb? These people here would say my action pleases
all of them, if fear did not lock up their tongues.   505
But this is one of kingship's many blessings—that
it can both act and speak just as it wishes to.

KREON   This view is yours alone of all these Kadmeans.[5]

ANTIGONE   It's their view too; because of you they curb their lips.

KREON   Aren't you ashamed of thinking differently from them?   510

_____

5. Kadmos (Cadmus) is the legendary founder of Thebes; hence "Kadmeans" are Thebans.

This painted limestone statue, discovered in Saqqara, Egypt, in 1850, depicts a scribe writing on a tablet. It dates from the third millennium B.C.E. Scribes were highly respected members of court in ancient literate societies; their work is the primary reason we have any sense of life in deep antiquity.

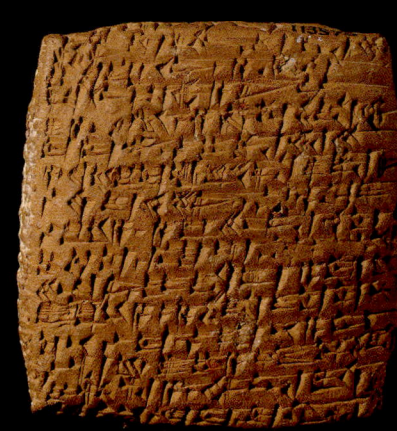

Clay tablets (right and top) and envelope (left) from central Turkey, dating from
ca. 1850 B.C.E. These objects contain a letter, written in cuneiform, from someone named
"Ashur-malik" to his brother "Ashur-idi" in which the former complains that his family
has been left in Ashur without food, fuel, or clothing over the winter. The letter writer
ran out of room on the large tablet and so had to continue his complaint on the little
supplemental tablet.

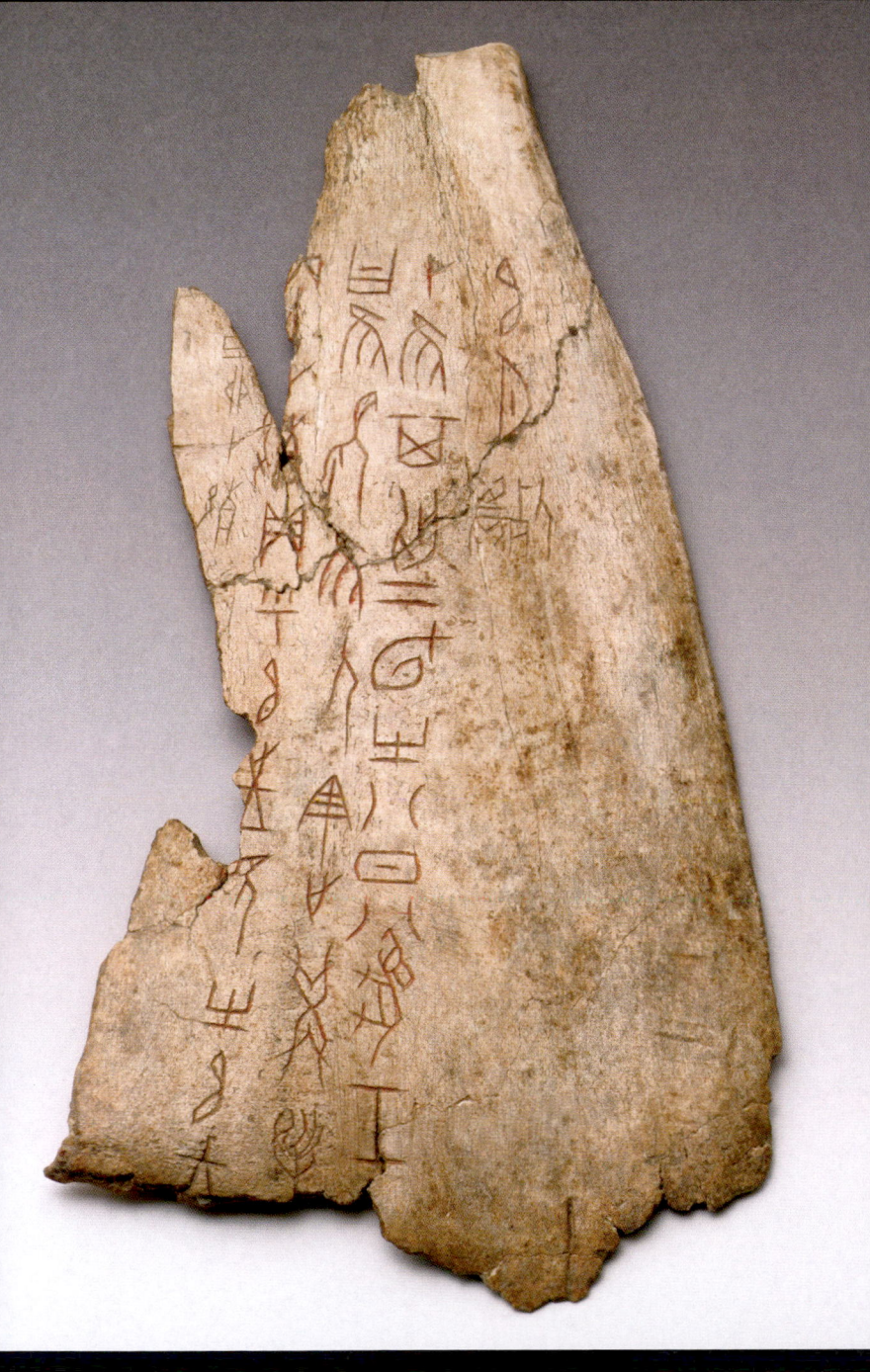

An "oracle bone," dating from the Shang Dynasty (2nd millennium B.C.E.) in China. Oracle bones were often made of ox scapula (shoulder blades) or tortoise belly-shells and were inscribed with divinations using a bronze pin or other carving implement. These bones represent the earliest significant gathering of Chinese writing.

Ancient Egyptians of aristocratic status were often buried with a specially commissioned papyrus manuscript of the *Book of the Dead* that pictured them making their way to the afterlife. The manuscript here, written in hieroglyphic script and with an image of the departed at the center, is the *Book of the Dead* for an Egyptian noble of Nubian origin named Maiherperi. It dates from the reign of the pharaoh Thutmose IV, ca. fourteenth century B.C.E.

One form of writing that was a basic part of citizenship in Athens during its classical period (the fifth and fourth centuries B.C.E.) was ballot-casting. The most common medium for casting votes was broken earthenware, on which citizens would write their selection. These shards, called *ostraka*, often record a vote on the question of whether or not to banish or exile someone. This term is the source of the English word *ostracism*.

This fragment, part of the 'sixth pillar edict' of King Aśoka (third century B.C.E.), shows the Brahmi script used during the Mauryan Dynasty in northern India. The Brahmi script is the ancestral source of all modern Indian scripts.

This Roman fresco painting, from a house in Pompeii whose details were preserved because of the eruption of Mount Vesuvius in 79 C.E., depicts a young woman holding a stylus and a wax tablet. Writing on wax tablets was a common means of taking notes and recording other ephemera in classical antiquity. The surface could be reused by warming and smoothing the wax to remove prior markings.

Beginning in Roman antiquity and continuing into medieval times, one of the highest-quality portable writing mediums was vellum. Made from the skin of domesticated mammals (calf, sheep, and goat skins were most common), vellum was smooth and durable and was generally reserved for special texts. Pictured here is a vellum manuscript of Homer's *Iliad* (called the *Ambrosian Iliad* or *Ilia Picta*) dating from the fifth century C.E. It is the only illustrated copy of Homer from classical antiquity to have survived.

ANTIGONE   I'm not ashamed of reverence for my flesh and blood.
KREON   Did he who died opposing him not share that blood?
ANTIGONE   He shared it, from one mother and one father too.
KREON   Then why give honor that's irreverent in his eyes?
ANTIGONE   The dead man's corpse will not bear witness to your words.   515
KREON   Yes, if you honor the irreverent equally.
ANTIGONE   No, for it was his brother, not some slave, who died.
KREON   Died trying to sack this land, the other in defense.
ANTIGONE   Despite that, Hades longs to see these laws fulfilled.
KREON   But good and bad should not share in them equally.   520
ANTIGONE   Who knows if this is not deemed faultless down below?
KREON   An enemy is not a friend, even in death.
ANTIGONE   My nature joins in friendship, not in enmity.
KREON   If you must show them friendship, go and do so down
   below! But while I live a woman shall not rule.   525
   [*The two attendants return from the palace leading* ISMENE. *She is
   distraught.*]
CHORUS   But here is Ismene in front of the gates,
   pouring the tears of a loving sister;
   a storm cloud is hanging over her brow,
   blighting her visage flushed with blood,
   wetting her lovely cheek with rain.   530
KREON   You there, who lurked inside the house, a viper sucking
   out my blood without my knowledge—I was not
   aware of nurturing two dooms to overthrow
   my throne—come, tell me, will you too admit you helped
   perform this burial, or swear your ignorance?   535
ISMENE   I did the deed—if she will join in saying so.
   I share in bearing the responsibility.
ANTIGONE: Justice will not allow this, since you did not want
   to do it, nor did I give you a share in it.
ISMENE   But in these evils I am not ashamed to make   540
   myself a fellow-sailor of your suffering.
ANTIGONE   Hades and those below know who can claim this deed;
   I do not like a friend who loves in word alone.
ISMENE   Don't, sister! Don't dishonor me by keeping me
   from joining in your death and rites for him who died.   545
ANTIGONE   Don't try to share this death with me. Don't claim as yours
   a deed you did not touch. My own death will suffice.
ISMENE   How can I long for life if you leave me behind?
ANTIGONE   Ask Kreon that; he is the one you care about.
ISMENE   Why give me pain like this, when it's no help to you?   550
ANTIGONE   If I do laugh at you then it's because of grief.
ISMENE   How then may I attempt to help you, even now?
ANTIGONE   Just save yourself; I don't begrudge you your escape.
ISMENE   Wretch that I am! Must I miss sharing in your doom?
ANTIGONE   You must; you made the choice to live, and I to die.   555
ISMENE   But not without me trying to talk you out of it.
ANTIGONE   One side approved your thinking and the other mine.

ISMENE   And yet the two of us are equally at fault.

ANTIGONE   Take heart! You are alive, but my soul has long since
been dead, that I might offer help to those who died.   560

KREON   One of these two, I say, has just been shown to be
quite senseless, and the other's been that way since birth.

ISMENE   Yes, lord; in evil fortune even people's inborn
sense does not remain within them, but departs

KREON   Like yours, when you chose evil deeds with evildoers.   565

ISMENE   How can I live my life without her, all alone?

KREON   Her—do not speak of her as someone still alive.

ISMENE   But will you really kill your own child's bride-to-be?[6]

KREON   Yes; there are other plots of land for him to plow.

ISMENE   Not like the harmony that fitted him to her.   570

KREON   I hate for sons of mine to marry evil women.

ISMENE   Oh dearest Haimon, how your father dishonors you!

KREON   You're paining me too much, you and your marriage bed.

ISMENE   Will you deprive him, your own offspring, of this girl?

KREON   It's Hades who will stop this marriage taking place.   575

ISMENE   It has been settled, so it seems, that she must die.

KREON   Settled—for you as well as me. No more delays!
Take them inside the house, attendants. From now on
they must be women and not wander unrestrained.
For even people who are bold will try to find   580
escape when they see Hades closing on their life.

> [*Attendants take* ANTIGONE *and* ISMENE *back into the palace.* KREON
> *remains on stage.*]

CHORUS   Blessed are they whose life has tasted no evil.   *Strophe A*
When a house is tossed by the gods,
no aspect of doom is lacking;
it spreads out over that family   585
like a surging wave of the salt sea
running over the surface
of murky darkness beneath;
blown by tempestuous Thracian blasts
it rolls black sand from the seabed,   590
and the wind-vexed headlands face
its blows with a groaning roar.

Ancient are the troubles I see   *Antistrophe A*
for the house of the Labdakids,[7]
heaped on the troubles of the dead;   595
no new generation frees the family,
but some god strikes them down
and they find no release.
Just now a light of hope shone forth

---

6. This is the first mention in the play of   7. Labdacus (Labdakos) was the father of
Haimon, Antigone's fiancé. Sophocles may have   Laius, father of Oedipus.
invented the engagement.

from the last root of Oedipus' house;   600
but in its turn it is cut down
by the bloody dust of the gods below,
by senseless words and a Fury in the mind.

What transgression of men,   *Strophe B*
oh Zeus, can constrain your power?   605
Sleep that conquers all
cannot defeat it; nor can
the tireless months of the years.
A potentate unaged by time,
you occupy the dazzling   610
splendor of Olympus.
Both now and through the future,
as through the past, this law will stand:
no vast thing moves into mortal lives without doom.

For widely wandering hope   *Antistrophe B*   615
benefits many men; but many
it cheats with light-headed passions.
it comes upon one who knows nothing
till he burns his foot in the hot fire.
It was some clever person   620
who declared this famous saying:
evil seems good, sooner or later,
to someone whose mind
a god leads towards doom;
he fares but the briefest of time without doom.   625
　　　　[*Enter* HAIMON, *along the side-entrance leading from the city proper.*]
Here is Haimon, the last and youngest-
born of your children. Has he arrived in
grief at the doom of his bride Antigone,
is he distraught to be cheated out of his
marriage-bed with his promised bride?   630
KREON　　We'll soon know better than a prophet could. My child,
　　have you come here in frenzy at your father, hearing
　　of my settled vote against your bride-to-be?
　　Or am I still your friend, whatever I may do?
HAIMON　　Father, I'm yours. Your judgments, being good ones, guide   635
　　my path aright, and I shall follow where they lead;
　　no marriage shall be reckoned by me as a prize
　　more valuable than having you as my good guide.
KREON　　Just so, my child; that's how your heart should be disposed:
　　to stand behind your father's judgment in all things.   640
　　This is the reason men pray to beget and keep
　　obedient offspring in their house—that they may pay
　　back evil to their father's enemies, and give
　　due honor to his friends, just as their father does.
　　But he who fathers children that provide no help,   645

what can you say he propagates but labors for
himself, and peals of laughter for his enemies?
So do not ever lose your senses, child, just out
of pleasure in a woman, knowing that an evil
woman as a bedmate in your house will make   650
a chilly armful to embrace; for what could be
a wound more serious than this, an evil friend?
So spit that girl away just like an enemy,
and let her marry someone else, in Hades' house.
For I have caught her disobeying openly,   655
this girl alone of all the city; and I shall
not falsify myself before the city, but
I'll kill her. Let her sing to Zeus of blood-kinship.
For if I raise my relatives by birth to be
disorderly, outsiders will be even worse.   660
For he who is a good man in his household will
be shown to be a just man in the city too.
I have full confidence that such a man would both
rule well, and serve well as a subject under rule,
and in a storm of spears stand firmly in his place,   665
a just man and a good one at his comrades' side.
But that transgressor who does violence to the law,—
or thinks to give commands to those who are in power,
whoever does this can receive no praise from me.
The one appointed by the city should be listened to,   670
in small things and in just things and the opposite.
There is no greater evil than unruliness.
It ruins cities and makes households desolate,
it breaks and turns to flight the ranks of allied spears.
But when the lives of mortals go aright, it is   675
obedience to rule that keeps most bodies safe.
Therefore we must defend the cause of order, and
by no means let a woman get the upper hand.
Better to fall, if we must do so, to a man;
then nobody could call us conquered by a woman.   680

CHORUS   To us, unless time's robbed us of our wits, you seem
to speak with sense about the things you're speaking of.

HAIMON   Father, the gods implant good sense in human beings,
the very best of everything that we possess.
I could not say—and may I never have the knowledge   685
to declare—that you're not right in what you say.
But things might also turn out well some other way.
It is my natural place to watch on your behalf,
at all that people say or do or criticize;
for awe at your expression hinders common men   690
from saying things that might displease you if you heard.
But I can hear, in dark obscurity, the things
the city says in lamention for this girl:
that she among all women least deserves to die

the evillest of deaths for deeds most glorious, 695
since she did not let her own brother, fallen in
the bloody slaughter, lie unburied or be torn
apart by fierce flesh-eating dogs or birds of prey.
Is golden honor not the lot that she deserves?
Such murky rumors are advancing secretly. 700
My father, no possession is more valuable
to me than your good fortune; for what greater treasure
can a child have than a father thriving in
renown, or can a father have than such a son?
Do not, then, clothe yourself in just one attitude— 705
that what you say, and only what you say, is right.
For those who think that they alone possess good sense,
or that no other has a tongue or spirit such
as theirs, when opened up expose their emptiness.
No, even if a man is clever, there's no shame 710
in learning many things and not straining too tight.
When trees beside a swollen winter torrent bend
and yield, you see how each twig is kept safe;
but those that strain against it perish root and branch.
And on a ship, if he who holds the power strains 715
the rigging tight and does not yield, he turns his rowing
benches over and completes his voyage upside down.
So come, yield from your rage; allow yourself to change.
If there is judgment even in a younger person
like myself, I say it's best by far for men 720
to be by nature full of knowledge in all things.
If not—since things are not inclined to be that way—
it's also fine to learn from others who speak well.

CHORUS   It's fitting, lord, if he says something timely, that
you learn, and you from him, since both have spoken well. 725

KREON   Are men of my age to be taught to have good sense
by someone who has only grown to this man's age?

HAIMON   Only in what is just. And even if I'm young,
you should not look at someone's age, but at his deeds.

KREON   Revering the disorderly—at deeds like that? 730

HAIMON   I'd never urge you to revere an evildoer.

KREON   And is this not the sickness *she's* afflicted with?

HAIMON   That's not what all the citizens of Thebes are saying.

KREON   And shall the city tell me what I should command?

HAIMON   You see how like a very young man that was said? 735

KREON   Am I to rule this land at someone else's whim?

HAIMON   There's no true city that belongs to just one man.

KREON   By law is not a city his who holds the power?

HAIMON   You'd do well ruling in a desert by yourself.

KREON   He's fighting as the woman's ally, so it seems. 740

HAIMON   If you're a woman; you're the one I care about.

KREON   Saying your father is unjust, most evil one?

HAIMON   Yes, since in justice I can see that you are wrong.

KREON   So I am wrong to show due reverence for my rule?

HAIMON   Irreverence, trampling on the honors of the gods.   745

KREON   Vile character, to give a woman precedence.

HAIMON   At least you will not catch me conquered by disgrace.

KREON   Yet all you say is spoken on behalf of *her*.

HAIMON   Of you and me as well, and of the lower gods.

KREON   There is no way that you will marry her alive!   750

HAIMON   Then she will die, in death destroying someone else!

KREON   Have you become so bold that you are threatening me?

HAIMON   What threat is it to speak against your empty judgments?

KREON   You'll weep for trying to teach me sense, when you have none.

HAIMON   If you were not my father, I'd say *you* lack sense.   755

KREON   Don't try to coax me with such words, you woman's slave.

HAIMON   You want to speak, yet hear no answer to your words?

KREON   What? By Olympus here above,[8] know well that you
   will soon regret abusing me with your complaints.
         [*He addresses his attendants.*]
   Bring out that loathsome creature, so that she may die   760
   at once, before her bridegroom's eyes, right at his side.
         [*Two attendants exit into the palace.*]

HAIMON   No! No! She shall not perish at my side—do not
   believe it! And you'll never see my face before
   your eyes again; so you may rave on madly with
   whatever friends still want to share your company!   765
         [HAIMON *rushes from the stage along the side-entrance leading to the
         plain.*]

CHORUS   My lord, the man has gone from us swift in his rage,
   and grief lies heavy on the mind of one so young.

KREON   Let him be gone to do, or think, things greater than
   a man; he will not free those two girls from their doom.

CHORUS   Is your mind really set on killing both of them?   770

KREON   Not her who had no part in it; your words are good.

CHORUS   By what doom do you plan to kill the other one?

KREON   I'll lead her to a place deserted by the steps
   of mortals, and conceal her, living, in a cave
   dug from the rock, with just a little food, enough   775
   to let the city as a whole escape pollution.
   And there perhaps by praying to the only god
   that she reveres—Hades—she may be spared from death;
   or else she'll come to recognize at last that to
   revere the realm of Hades is excessive labor.   780

CHORUS   Eros,[9] unconquered in battle!   *Strophe*
   Eros, you plunder possessions,
   you keep your night watch
   on a young girl's soft cheeks;
   you range over the sea   785

8. Mount Olympus, home of the gods, repre-   9. God of sexual desire.
sents divine power.

and through wild rural dwellings;
not one of the immortals can escape you,
not one of us human beings
whose lives are but a day;
and he who has you has madness.   790

You wrench aside minds to injustice,   *Antistrophe*
even of the just, to their ruin;
you have stirred up this quarrel too,
between men bound by blood;
radiant desire is the victor,   795
shining in the eyes of the bride
who graces the marriage bed;
this sits in rule by the mighty ordinances;
for the game-playing goddess
Aphrodite[1] is invincible in battle.   800
    [*Enter* ANTIGONE, *led by guards from the palace.*]

But now at this sight I myself am carried
away past the bounds of such ordinances,
I can no longer hold back the streams
of my tears, when I see Antigone pass
to the bridal chamber where all must sleep.   805

ANTIGONE   Look upon me, oh you citizens   *Strophe A*
of this my fatherland,
as I travel my last road,
gaze my last on the light of the sun,
and never again.   810
Hades who puts all to sleep
leads me still alive
to the shores of Akheron.[2]
No wedding hymn is my lot;
no marriage song sung for me;   815
no, I shall be Akheron's bride.

CHORUS   But are you not going with praise and renown
to the place where corpses lie concealed?
You were not struck by a wasting sickness
or given the wage that is paid by the sword;   820
you alone among mortals will go down
to Hades still living, a law to yourself.

ANTIGONE   I have heard that Tantalos's daughter,[3]   *Antistrophe A*
our guest who came from Phrygia,
perished most lamentably   825

---

1. Goddess of love, beauty, and sexuality.
2. River in the underworld.
3. Niobe, daughter of Tantalos, son of Zeus, who married Amphion, king of Thebes (hence "our guest"), boasted that she had more children than Leto, mother of Apollo and Artemis. Apollo and Artemis retaliated by killing all her children. She returned to Sipylos (in Ionia) and wept so continuously that she turned to a rock.

upon the peak of Sipylos;
like tenacious ivy the growth of rock
tamed her; as she wastes away
the pouring rains never leave her—
so men report—nor does the snow,   830
and under her tearful brow
her shoulder is wet with streams;
most like her a divinity puts me to sleep.

CHORUS   But she was a goddess and born from a god,
while we are mortals and human-born.   835
And yet it is great if people should say
when you perish that you have shared in the lot
of the godlike in life and again in death.

ANTIGONE   Alas, you laugh at me!   *Strophe B*
By my fathers' gods, why don't you save   840
this outrage until I have gone?
Why mock me in my presence?
Oh city! Oh city's wealthy men!
Oh springs of Dirce, sacred ground
of Thebes of the fine chariots,   845
you at least I call to witness
how I'm going, unwept by friends,
by what laws I go to the heaped-up prison
of my strange tomb. Unhappy me!
I have no home among mortals,   850
no home as a corpse among corpses,
with the living or with the dead.

CHORUS   Stepping forward to daring's very brink,
you stumbled with your foot, my child,
on the lofty pedestal of Justice.   855
You're paying for some ordeal of your father's.

ANTIGONE   You touch on the most distressing   *Antistrophe B*
of all my cares, the thrice-turned
lamentation for my father,
and for that whole destiny   860
allotted to us, the renowned
descendants of Labdacus.
Oh doom of a mother's bed,
ill-fated mother who slept
with her own son, my father!   865
Such was my unhappy birth.
To them I go thus cursed, unmarried,
to dwell without a home.
Oh my brother, the marriage you found
was ill-destined, dying   870
you slaughtered me, who still lived.

CHORUS   There's reverence in revering him;
but power—to those whom power concerns—
cannot permit transgression;

you're destroyed by your self-willed temper. 875

ANTIGONE   Unwept, unfriended, unaccompanied   *Epode*
by wedding song, I'm led away unhappily
along this road prepared for me.
No longer is it lawful for me,
wretch that I am, to look upon   880
the bright eye of this sacred torch;
no friend laments my unwept destiny.

KREON   Do you not know that no one would cease pouring forth
Songs of lament before their death, if that could help?
Lead her away as quickly as you can, and let   885
a covered tomb embrace her, as I said; then leave
her there alone, deserted, whether she desires
to die or live entombed beneath that kind of roof;
for we are pure as far as this girl is concerned;
but she shall be deprived of any home up here.   890

ANTIGONE   Oh grave! Oh marriage chamber! Oh you caverned dwelling-
place, eternal prison where I go to join
my own, who perished in such numbers and have been
received by Persephassa[4] with the dead below.
Now I am going down, the last of them, my death   895
the worst by far, before my life has reached its term.
Yet I still nurse the hope that when I get there I
shall come dear to my father, dearly loved by you
my mother, and to you, my own dear brother, dear.
For when you died, with my own hands I washed you and 900
laid out your bodies in due order, gave libations
to your graves. And now it is for tending your
corpse, Polyneices, that I'm reaping this reward.
    Yet, to those with sense I did well to honor you
for I would never have defied the citizens   905
to do this labor if the oozing corpse were that
of my own child, or if my husband lay there dead.
In satisfaction of what law do I say this?
My husband dead, I could have had another, and
a child from someone else, if I had lost the first; 910
but with my mother and my father both concealed
in Hades, no more brothers ever could be born.
By such a law as this I honored you, my own
dear brother, higher than them all; but Kreon thought
that I was doing wrong and daring awful deeds.   915
And now he has me in his hands; he leads me off
unbedded, unaccompanied by wedding song,
without a share in marriage or the nurturing
of children; thus deserted by my friends I go
alive, ill-fated, to the caverns of the dead.   920
What justice of divinities have I transgressed?

---

4. Another name for Persephone, queen of the underworld.

Why should I still, unhappy one, look to the gods?
What ally should I call on, when my reverent deed
has gained me condemnation for irreverence?
If this is viewed among the gods as something fine,   925
I'll find out, after suffering, that I was wrong;
but if these men are wrong, may what they suffer be
as evil as the unjust things they do to me.

CHORUS   Still the selfsame blasts of the selfsame winds
of the spirit are gripping this woman.   930

KREON   Therefore these men who are leading her off
will weep on account of their slowness.

ANTIGONE   Alas! That word has approached very close
to death!

KREON   I do not encourage her to take heart   935
in hope that this sentence won't be fulfilled.

ANTIGONE   Oh, my paternal town in the land of Thebes!
Oh, my ancestral gods!
Now I'm led off, there is no more delay.
Look on me, oh rulers of Thebes,   940
the last of your royal house who remains,
see what I suffer, from what kind of men,
for revering reverence.

> [ANTIGONE is led away by the guards along the side-entrance leading to
> the plain.]

CHORUS   Danae too endured to exchange   *Strophe A*
heaven's light for a bronze-bound dwelling.[5]   945
Concealed in a tomb-like bridal chamber,
she too was yoked.
Yet she was of honored family, child,
oh my child, and stored up the seed
of Zeus in a flow of gold.   950
Fate is awesome in its power.
Wealth cannot escape it,
nor Ares, nor towering walls,
nor black ships beaten by the salt sea.
And the son of Dryas,[6] quick to rage, was yoked,   *Antistrophe A*
king of the Edonians, imprisoned by Dionysos   956
in rocky bondage for his raging taunts.
Thus did the awful blossoming force
of his madness dwindle, drop by drop.
He did not recognize the god   960
until he attacked him in madness
with taunting tongue. He tried to stop

---

5. Danae's father was warned that he would
be killed by his daughter's son, so he shut her
up to prevent any man getting to her. But Zeus
impregnated her in the form of a golden shower,
and she gave birth to Perseus, who killed her

father.
6. Lycurgus, who resisted the arrival of Dionysus in Thrace and was driven mad by the
god, was finally imprisoned in a cave.

the women possessed by the god,
their fires and their cries of *Euoi!*
and provoked the flute-loving Muses.[7]   965

By the waters of the Dark Rocks,   *Strophe B*
and of the double sea,
are the shores of Bosporus,
and Thracian Salmydessus,
where neighboring Ares looked upon   970
the accursed blinding wound
dealt to Phineus's two sons
by his savage wife, a wound
that darkened the orbs of their eyes,
calling for vengeance, gouged out   975
by bloody hands and a sharp shuttle.[8]

Wasting away, that wretched pair,   *Antistrophe B*
they wept for their wretched fate,
offspring born of a mother
whose marriage was no marriage.   980
Her own seed made her queen
of the ancient-born Erekhthids;
she was nurtured in far-off caves,
among her father's storm-winds,
a horse-swift Boread over the steep hills,   985
a child of gods. Yet on her too
the long-lived Fates bore down, my child.

   [*Enter* TEIRESIAS, *a blind old prophet, by the side-entrance coming from
   Thebes proper; he is guided by a young boy.*]

TEIRESIAS   Oh lords of Thebes, we've come here by a road we shared,
two seeing through the eyes of one; for this is how
a blind man makes his way, with someone else to lead.   990
KREON   What is it, aged Teiresias? Do you have news?
TEIRESIAS   I'll tell you. You, believe the prophet and obey.
KREON   I've not departed from your thinking in the past.
TEIRESIAS   And that is why you've steered this city's course aright.
KREON   I can attest the benefits that I've received.   995
TEIRESIAS   Think now you stand again on fortune's razor-edge.
KREON   What is it? How I shudder at the words you speak!
TEIRESIAS   You'll find out when you hear the signs from my skilled craft.
   As I sat on the ancient seat where I perform
   my augury, a haven for all kinds of birds,[9]   1000
   I heard the birds give unknown voice, screeching

---

7. The Muses, goddesses of music and poetry,
are sometimes associated with Dionysos; *Euoi*
(*Evoi*) is the traditional cry in honor of the god.
8. Phineus, king of Salmydessus, married
Kleopatra, daughter of the wind-god Boreas and
granddaughter of Erekhtheus, mythical king of

Athens. She had two sons with him, but he
imprisoned her and married another wife, who
blinded the boys with a shuttle (needle used for
weaving) and had them also imprisoned.
9. Augury involved divining omens from the
behavior of birds.

in evil frenzy, babbling incoherently.
I sensed them tearing at each other with their bloody
claws—the whirring of their wings was a clear sign.
At once, in fear, I tried to make burnt-sacrifice   1005
upon an altar duly kindled; but Hephaistos
did not blaze forth from the offerings; instead
a putrid liquid from the thighs oozed out upon
the coals, and smoked and spattered, and the gall-bladder
exploded up into the air; the thighs, streaming   1010
with moisture, lay bared of their covering of lard.
I learned about these things—the failure of my rites
of prophecy, which gave no signs—from this boy here.
For just as I lead others onward, he leads me.
    And it's from *your* bad thinking that the city is   1015
so sick. Our public altars and our hearths have all
been tainted, every one, by dogs and birds with food
from the ill-fated fallen son of Oedipus.
And this is why the gods accept our sacrificial
prayers no more, nor flames from burning victims' thighs,   1020
nor do the birds scream cries that give me signs,
for they have eaten of a slain man's bloody fat.
    Think on this well, my child. To go wrong is a thing
shared by all humans. But when someone does go wrong,
that man's no longer foolish or unfortunate   1025
if he attempts to heal the evil he has fallen
into, and does not remain immovable.
Self-will is what incurs the charge of foolishness.
Yield to the dead and don't keep stabbing at a perished
man. What prowess is it to re-kill the dead?   1030
I think and speak for your own good; it is most sweet
to learn from one who speaks well, if it profits you.

KREON   Old man, you all keep shooting arrows at me, just
like archers at a target. Even your prophetic
skill is used against me. For a long time now   1035
I have been traded by your breed like merchandise.
Go, make your profits! Keep on trading silver-gold
from Sardis,[1] if you wish, and gold from India;
but you shall not conceal him in a tomb, not even
if the eagles, birds of Zeus, should wish to rend   1040
his flesh and take it up to Zeus's throne as food.
Not even then will I let him be buried out
of fear of this pollution. I know well no human
has the strength to bring pollution to the gods.
But mortals, even those with many awesome skills,   1045
fall shamefully, oh aged Teiresias, when they
speak finely shameful words for profit's sake.

TEIRESIAS   Ah!

---

1. Sardis in Lydia specialized in the production of electrum, an alloy of silver and gold.

Does any mortal know, or take into account . . .

KREON   What thing? What maxim shared by all is this you speak?

TEIRESIAS   . . . how far good counsel is the best thing to possess?   1050

KREON   As far, I think, as thoughtlessness does greatest harm.

TEIRESIAS   Yet this is just the sickness that is tainting you.

KREON   I'd rather not abuse a prophet in reply.

TEIRESIAS   You do so, when you say my prophecies are false.

KREON   They are! All prophets are a money-loving breed.   1055

TEIRESIAS   And kings a breed that loves to profit shamefully.

KREON   Do you not know that you are talking to a king?

TEIRESIAS   I know that it's through me you've kept this city safe.

KREON   You are a clever prophet, but you love injustice.

TEIRESIAS   You'll make me tell things still unmoved within my mind.   1060

KREON   Let them be moved! Just do not speak for profit's sake.

TEIRESIAS   Is that what I'm already doing, in your view?

KREON   Know that you'll never use my thinking for your trade!

TEIRESIAS   And you, know well you shall not live through many more
    swift-racing courses of the sun before you give   1065
    a child of your own flesh and blood in turn, a corpse
    to pay for corpses, since you've cast below a person
    who belongs above, making a living soul
    reside within a tomb dishonorably, and keep
    up here a corpse belonging to the gods below,   1070
    deprived of rites, of offerings, of piety.
    You have no business with such things; nor do the upper
    gods, but in this you're committing violence.
    Therefore the ruinous late-avenging Furies of
    the gods and Hades lie in wait for you, that you   1075
    may be caught up in these same evils in your turn.
    See if I'm saying this because I'm silver-plated!
    A little time will test my metal, showing forth
    both men's and women's wailing cries in your own house.
    Moreover all those cities have been shaken up   1080
    with enmity whose mangled flesh got funeral rites
    from dogs, or beasts, or flying birds that carried home
    the impious stench to every city and its hearths.

    In rage have I let fly these arrows, archer-like,
    against your heart, since you have pained me; they are sure,   1085
    and running will not help you to escape their fire.

    Come, child, lead me away to my own house, so that
    this man can let his rage fly forth at younger men,
    and learn to nurse a tongue that is more peaceable,
    a mind that's better than the thoughts he's thinking now.   1090

    [*Exit* TEIRESIAS, *led by his attendant, down the side-entrance into the city.*]

CHORUS   My lord, the man has gone from us with awful words
    of prophecy. And since the black hair on my head
    first turned to white, I know that he has never uttered
    to the city anything that turned out false.

KREON   I know it too, and I am shaken in my mind.   1095

To yield is awful; but, by standing firm, to strike
with ruin my proud heart—why, that is awful too.
CHORUS You need to take good counsel now, Menoikeus's son.
KREON What should I do then? Tell me, and I shall obey.
CHORUS Go, set the girl free from her rocky chamber, and   1100
construct a tomb for him who's lying there exposed.
KREON Is this what you advise? You think that I should yield?
CHORUS As quickly as you can, my lord. The gods' avenging
Harms, swift-footed, cut down those with evil thoughts.
KREON Alas! Reluctantly I leave my heart's resolve: 1105
I'll do it. There's no fighting with necessity.
CHORUS Go, then, and do it. Don't assign this task to others.
KREON I'll go at once. Go! Go, all my attendants, both
those present and those absent! Take up axes in
your hands, and rush towards the place—it's over there.   1110
And now that my opinion has reversed itself,
I shall be there to set her free, just as I was
the one who bound her. It is best, I fear, to live
until life's end preserving the established laws.

[*Exit* KREON *with attendants, along the side-entrance leading to the plain.*]

CHORUS Oh you of many names,   *Strophe A*
treasure of the Kadmean bride,   1116
child of deep-thundering Zeus,
who care for famous Italy,
and hold sway in Demeter's
folding hollows at Eleusis,   1120
a sanctuary shared by all,[2]
oh Bacchus, dwelling in Thebes,
the Bacchants' mother-city
by Ismenos's flowing stream,
at the sowing of the savage dragon's seed![3]   1125
The smoky flash of the torch   *Antistrophe A*
has seen you,
above the double-peaked rock,
where the Korycian Nymphs,
the Bacchants tread,   1130
and so has the stream of Kastalia.
The ivy-covered slopes
of Nysa's mountains[4] have sent you,
and the green shore clustered with grapes.
Immortal songs cry out *Euoi!* to you   1135
watching over the streets of Thebes.

2. Dionysos (i.e., Bacchus) was the child of
Zeus by Semele, daughter of Kadmos, founder of
Thebes. Dionysos was worshipped in southern
Italy, and at Eleusis, near Athens, alongside
Demeter, the fertility goddess.
3. Kadmos founded Thebes by sowing dragon's teeth, which sprouted up as the first men
of the city.
4. Mount Nysa, in Euboea, had an important
cult of Dionysos. The Korycian cave is on
Mount Parnassus, a few miles from Delphi;
the Kastalian stream flows from Parnassus to
Delphi.

You honor this city most highly, *Strophe B*
high above all the rest,
you along with your mother,
she who was struck by lightning.[5] 1140
Since all of the city's people
are gripped by a violent sickness,
come now too with purifying foot,
over the ridge of Parnassus,
or the groaning waters of the strait. 1145

Oh you who lead the chorus *Antistrophe B*
of stars that breathe forth fire,
you who watch over the voices
that cry out during the night,
offspring born of Zeus, 1150
appear to us, oh lord,
with your attendant Thyiads,[6]
who dance all night in madness
for bountiful Iakkhos!

[*Enter* MESSENGER, *along the side-entrance leading to the plain. He is an attendant of* KREON, *probably a slave.*]

MESSENGER   Neighbors of Kadmos and the house of Amphion,[7] 1155
there is no human life in any state that I
would ever praise or criticize as something fixed.
For fortune sets upright and fortune dashes down
whoever has good luck or bad at any time.
No prophet can tell mortals the established truth. 1160
Kreon was once a man to envy, in my view.
He saved this land of Kadmos from its enemies,
gained total power in the land and guided it,
sowed children's noble seed and throve in them.
Now all is gone. When even a man's pleasures let 1165
him down, then I no longer count him as alive—
I just consider him to be a living corpse.
Heap wealth within your house, if you so wish, and live
with royal show; and yet if joy is missing from
all this, I would not pay smoke's shadow to buy all 1170
the rest from any man, compared to pleasure.

CHORUS   What further weight of grief do you bring for our kings?

MESSENGER   They're dead. The living are responsible for death.

CHORUS   Who is the bloody murderer? Who lies dead? Speak!

MESSENGER   Haimon has perished, bloodied by one close to home. 1175

CHORUS   Was it his father's hand that did it, or his own?

MESSENGER   He killed himself, in wrath at blood his father shed.

---

5. Semele, mother of Dionysos, was struck by lightning when she insisted on seeing her lover, Zeus, in his true form.
6. Alternative name for the nymphs who accom-
pany Dionysos (i.e., Iakkhos, or Bacchus).
7. Mythical king of Thebes who built the walls of the city with magical lyre music.

CHORUS   How right, oh prophet, did you prove your words to be!
MESSENGER   That's how things stand; you may take counsel for the rest.
        [*Enter* EURYDIKE *from the palace, attended by maids.*]
CHORUS   But here is Kreon's wife, wretched Eurydike,   1180
    close by; I see her coming from the house. She must
    have heard about her son, or else she's here by chance.
EURYDIKE   Assembled townsfolk, I was starting to go out
    and overheard you. I was going to supplicate
    the goddess Pallas,[8] to address her with my prayers.   1185
    As I was loosening the bolts across the door
    to open it, a voice assailed my ears with words
    of evil to our house. I sank back, full of dread,
    upon my serving-maids, quite stricken from my wits.
    But speak again, whatever news you brought, and I   1190
    shall listen—I'm experienced in suffering.
MESSENGER   Dear mistress, I was there in person and I'll speak
    without omitting even one word of the truth.
    Why should I try to soothe you with soft words that will
    be shown as falsehoods later? Truth is always right.   1195
        I went, attending on your husband as his guide,
    up to the high part of the plain where Polyneices'
    corpse still lay unpitied, mangled by the dogs.
    We prayed first to the goddess of the road and Pluto[9]
    to restrain their rage and to be kind, and washed   1200
    him with the ritual washing, then with branches freshly
    plucked we burned the body—what was left of it—
    and built a lofty grave-mound from the earth that was
    his home, then made our way towards the prison of
    the girl, her bridal-cave of Hades, strewn with rock.   1205
    Near that unhallowed inner chamber someone heard
    a distant sound of high-pitched wailing cries, and came
    to tell our master Kreon of these signs. As he
    drew closer, miserable cries which gave no signs
    surrounded him; he moaned aloud and sent forth words   1210
    of bitter lamentation, "Ah, wretch that I am,
    am I a prophet? Am I moving down a path
    that's more unfortunate than any road I've walked
    before? My son's voice greets me. Servants, come,
    go closer quickly! Go up to the tomb and enter   1215
    by that gap where stones have been torn out, up to
    the grave's own mouth, and look to see if I detect
    the voice of Haimon, or the gods deceive my ears."
    At this command from our downhearted master we
    looked in; within the furthest recess of the tomb   1220
    we saw the maiden hanging by her neck, tied up
    there by a noose of finely woven cloth; the boy

8. Athena.
9. Pluto (Hades) is god of the underworld; the   goddess of the road is Hecate, associated with
    the underworld, witchcraft, and ghosts.

had flung himself around her waist in close embrace,
while he bemoaned his bridal bed now lost below,
his father's deeds and his unhappy marriage bed.   1225
When Kreon saw them, he moaned horribly and went
inside to him, and called out with a wailing cry:
"What deed is this you've done, bold wretch! What came into
your mind? By what disaster did you lose your wits?
Come out, my child, I beg you as a suppliant!"   1230
His son glared back at him with savage eyes, spat in
his face, said nothing in reply, and drew his two-
edged sword. His father rushed back to escape and Haimon
missed his aim. At once, ill-fated boy, in anger
at himself, he tensed himself upon his sword-   1235
point and drove half the blade into his side. Before
his wits departed he embraced the maiden with
a wilting arm; gasping, he spurted forth a sharp
swift stream of bloody drops upon the girl's white cheek.
He lies there, corpse embracing corpse. He has received   1240
his marriage rites at last—poor wretch—in Hades' house,
and demonstrated to the human race how far
ill-counsel is the greatest evil for a man.

    [Exit EURYDIKE *with her maids into the palace.]*

CHORUS   What do you think this means? The woman's gone again
without one word of good or evil from her lips.   1245

MESSENGER   I am astonished too. But I'm sustained by hope
that hearing of this grief for her own child she won't
think fit to make lament before the city, but
will set her maids to mourn this household woe inside.
She's too experienced in judgment to do wrong.   1250

CHORUS   I don't know; but I think that silence in excess
is just as weighty as extraordinary cries.

MESSENGER   I'll go inside the house, then I shall know if she
is really keeping something secretly concealed,
pent up within her raging heart. Your words are good: 1255
excessive silence also carries heavy weight.

    [Exit MESSENGER *into the palace. Enter* KREON *along the side-entrance
leading from the plain, carrying* HAIMON'S *corpse.]*

CHORUS   But here is our lord himself; he comes
with a clear-stamped monument held in his hands.
If it's lawful to say so, his doom wasn't caused
by any outsider—he did wrong himself.   1260

KREON   *Oh!*   *Strophe A*
The rigid wrongs, death-dealing,
of thoughtless wrongful thinking!
Oh you who here behold us,
kinsmen who killed and died!
Alas for my counsels' misfortune!   1265
Oh my son, too young
for your youthful doom!

Aiai! Aiai![1] You died, you departed,
through my ill counsel, not your own!

CHORUS   Alas! You seem now to see justice, but too late.   1270

KREON   *Alas!*
I have learned, wretch that I am! On my head
a god with a mighty weight struck down
at that moment, and tossed me in savage roads,
overthrew my joy—*alas!*—to be trampled.   1275
Ah! Ah! Oh alas for the labors,
the toilsome labors of mortals!

[*Enter* MESSENGER, *from the palace.*]

MESSENGER   You seem, my master, to have come with evils, yet
you have more still in store; the first you bear in your
own hands, but soon you will see others in the house.   1280

KREON   What greater evil follows evils such as these?

MESSENGER   Your wife is dead—in truth the mother of this corpse—
unhappy woman, killed just now by fresh-struck blows.

KREON   *Oh!*
Oh harbor of Hades, unpurifiable,   *Antistrophe A*
why, oh why are you destroying me?   1285
Oh herald of sorrow's evil tidings,
what word is this you utter?
Aiai! You've re-killed a man destroyed!
What are you telling me, boy?
What new slaughter do you say   1290
embraces me—*Aiai! Aiai!*—
on top of destruction a woman's doom?

[*The palace doors open to reveal the corpse of* EURYDIKE.[2]]

CHORUS   She can be seen. She is no longer shut indoors.

KREON   *Alas!*
Ah wretched me! I see this second evil!   1295
What destiny, what still awaits me?
I've just held my child in my hands,
wretch that I am, and now I see her,
another corpse before me.
Ah, ah, miserable mother! Ah my child!   1300

MESSENGER   There at the altar with a sharply whetted knife
she let her eyes close into darkness, after she
wailed first for dead Megareus's empty bed and then
for Haimon's. Last she sang out evil curses on
your head, because you were the killer of your sons.   1305

KREON   *Aiai! Aiai!*   *Strophe B*
My heart leaps with fear! Why does no one
strike my chest with a two-edged sword?
Wretched am I—*aiai!*—
dissolved in wretched anguish!   1310

---

1. Cry of grief.
2. The body would have been brought out on the *ekkuklema*, the trolley used in the theater to depict the inside of the building.

MESSENGER   Before she died, your wife denounced you as the one
    responsible for both the dooms of your two sons.
KREON   By just what form of bloody slaughter did she go?
MESSENGER   She struck with her own hand into her liver, when
    she heard of her son's death, so piercingly bewailed.   1315
KREON   *Alas! Alas!*
    To me, to no other mortal,
    this responsibility will cling forever.
    It was I who killed you, I, wretch that I am!
    It was I! I speak truly.   1320
    Oh, servants!
    Lead me as quick as you can,
    lead me out of the way,
    I who exist no more than nothing.
CHORUS   If any profit lies in evils, your advice   1325
    holds profit. Evils in our way are best when briefest.
KREON   Let it come, let it come!   *Antistrophe B*
    Let that finest of fates for me appear,
    bringing my final day,
    supremely best of fates!   1330
    Let it come, let it come,
    that I may never see another day!
CHORUS   That's in the future. Now we must perform what lies
    at hand. They care about these matters who should care.
KREON   My prayer encompassed all my passionate desires.   1335
CHORUS   Pray now no further. There is no deliverance
    for mortals from whatever is ordained for them.
KREON   Lead me away, a worthless man.
    I killed you, my son, without intending to,
    you too, my wife—ah, wretch that I am!   1340
    I cannot look towards either one.
    Nowhere can I lean for support.
    All in my hands is warped,
    and from outside
    a crushing destiny   1345
    has leapt down on my head.
    [KREON's *attendants lead him into the palace.*]
CHORUS   Sound thought is by far the foremost rule
    of happiness; when we deal with the gods
    we should never act with irreverence.
    Mighty words of boastful men   1350
    are paid for with mighty blows which teach
    sound thinking at last in old age.

EURIPIDES

ca. 480–406 B.C.E.

Euripides strikes many readers as the liveliest, funniest, and most provocative of the three great Athenian tragedians whose work survives. A younger contemporary of **Aeschylus** and **Sophocles**, Euripides lived through most of the cultural and political turmoil of the fifth century B.C.E., and was seen as one of the most influential voices for the revolutionary new ideas that were developing in this period. Controversial in his own time for his use of colloquial language and his depictions of unheroic heroes, sexually promiscuous women, and cruel, violent gods, Euripides has lost none of his power to shock, provoke, amuse, and engage his audiences.

LIFE AND TIMES

We know little of Euripides' personal life. He seems to have been married twice, and had three sons. He was a productive but only moderately successful tragedian: he wrote over ninety plays, but won first prize only four times. He specialized in unexpected plot twists and novel approaches to his mythological material: for instance, his play about Helen of Troy (*Helen*) makes her an entirely virtuous woman who never committed adultery or ran off with Paris. There are many moments of humor in Euripides, far more than in Aeschylus or Sophocles. At the same time, his vision is often very dark. His later plays about the Trojan War (such as *Hecuba* and *Trojan Women*) can be read as terrible indictments of the suffering caused to women, children, and families by the contemporary Peloponnesian War between Athens and Sparta.

He spent most of his life in Athens, but in his old age went to visit Macedon, where he died. It has often been suggested that he left Athens in outrage at the city's failure to appreciate him, but there is no evidence for this. Euripides was probably always popular with audiences, albeit less so with the judges of the dramatic competition, who perhaps felt an obligation to uphold civic ideals. Euripides continued to be widely read, quoted, and enjoyed for generations after his death.

Medea was first performed in the spring of 431 B.C.E., immediately before the outbreak of the Peloponnesian War. It was a time of prosperity for the city: the Greeks had defeated the Persians in the year of Euripides' birth, and now the Athenian Empire extended across the Mediterranean. Athens was deeply proud of the political, artistic, and intellectual achievements of the citizens.

It was also a time of new, antitraditional ideas, brought by the Sophists, men from other societies who came to Athens to teach "cleverness" or "wisdom"—*sophia*. The Sophists were seen by some as a mark of Athens' progressive openness to new modes of thought, but by others as a dangerous influence, liable to corrupt the city's young men. The tragedies of Euripides were associated by the comic dramatist Aristophanes, and probably many others, with the iconoclasm of the Sophists. Many contemporaries found the plays shocking and controversial. Euripides uses traditional myths, but he shifts attention away from the deeds of heroes toward domestic wrangling, and shows up moral and psychological weaknesses. Euripides was seen as a cynical realist about human nature: Sophocles said that while he showed people as they ought to be, Euripides showed them as they are.

Euripides put male heroes onstage in humiliated positions: they are bedraggled and dressed in rags, or are presented as obvious cowards, liars, or brutes. Euripides' outspoken, lustful, or violent, though often sympathetic, women were found particularly outrageous by his contemporaries. Lower-class characters and slaves were prominent, and sympathetically portrayed. In religious terms, too, his plays were challenging and controversial: his characters often question the old Greek myths about the gods, and the gods themselves often seem arbitrary or cruel in their dealings with humanity. Euripides also included vivid and realistic descriptions of violence, as in the messenger speech of the *Medea*, a horrifying account of how the princess Creusa's hair was burned up by her golden crown, while her poisoned dress corroded her skin and finally ripped the flesh from her bones.

THE WORK

Medea, like almost all Greek tragedies, is based on a traditional story. According to myth, the hero Jason was told by his uncle, Pelias, that he could not claim his rightful inheritance, the throne of Iolcus, unless he could perform a seemingly impossible quest: cross the Black Sea to the distant barbarian land of Colchis, ruled by the savage king Aeetes, and bring back to Greece the Golden Fleece, which was guarded by a dragon. Jason assembled a group of the finest Greek heroes, and built the world's first ship—the *Argo*—to take them to Colchis. Once they arrived, King Aeetes set Jason the task of plowing a field with a team of fire-breathing bulls. Luckily, the king's daughter, Medea, fell in love with Jason. She was skilled in magic, and enabled him to plow the field, lull the

dragon to sleep, steal the fleece, and escape back to Greece; she killed her own brother to distract the attention of their enraged Colchian pursuers. When they arrived in Iolcus, Pelias, going back on his word, tried to hang onto power. Medea got back at him by persuading Pelias' daughters that they could make their father immortal by boiling him alive—which was, of course, untrue. After the scandal was discovered, Jason and Medea were forced into exile. The couple had children, and eventually moved to Corinth. There, Jason decided to divorce Medea and marry a native Corinthian princess instead. With that, the action of *Medea* begins.

The most well-known part of the myth was the story of the quest of the Argonauts (sailors in the *Argo*) for the Golden Fleece. But Euripides focuses not on this heroic narrative but on its squalid aftermath, and he seems to have invented certain key aspects of the story. In previous versions, the children were either murdered by Creon's family or, according to another story, accidentally killed by Medea, when she tried to use magic to make them immortal. The shocking events at the end of this play would not have been anticipated by Euripides' audience.

Euripides' concentration on the domestic troubles in Corinth, rather than the heroic quest, allows him to present Jason in a disturbingly unheroic light: as a cad who struggles to muster unconvincing strategic and rhetorical arguments to justify his shabby treatment of his first wife. Although Jason tries to talk like a Sophist, it is Medea who is the real possessor of *sophia* in the play. The term *sophia* has negative and positive connotations: it can suggest deep understanding, but it can also imply mere cleverness. The play invites us to consider which character is the smartest: Jason, with his dodges and evasions, or Medea, with her unpredictable, cruel stratagems.

Medea is strongly marked as an outsider in three crucial ways: as a woman in a male-dominated world; as a foreigner or "barbarian" in a Greek city; and as a smart person surrounded by fools. On all these grounds, the play initially seems to invite us to side with Medea. She is obviously the wronged party in her relationship with Jason; and yet, even as she expresses her devastation at the betrayal, she never presents herself as a victim. Rather, she is fierce, "like a bull or a lioness," and highly articulate in her analysis of her situation. She claims even the male values of military honor for herself and for all women, suggesting in one famous passage that women who undergo the pain and danger of childbirth are far braver than men who fight in war: "I would rather face battle / three times than go through childbirth once." It is tempting to read these lines as proto-feminist, and to see Euripides, the clever poet, as sympathetic to his clever heroine, and as a defender of the rights and dignity of women and foreigners, before an audience of Athenian male citizens.

But as the play goes on, our vision of Medea is likely to change. We may begin to see her not as strong and brave, but as frighteningly violent; not as wise, but as too clever by half. This is a disturbing play that forces readers to revise their feelings several times. Is Medea sensible in her defense of her honor and her rights, or is she driven crazy by the gods of passion? Or should we see her as an agent of the gods, imposing divine justice on oath-breaking humans? Is Euripides challenging or confirming Greek male prejudices against foreigners and women? Is he recommending

new forms of wisdom, or warning against the false cleverness of upstarts and outsiders? And what does it say about the city of Athens that it is the Athenian king, Aegeus, who will welcome this terrifying figure into his community?

Thematically, the most important threads in the play include the opposition of order and chaos, and the idea of time, especially the reversal of time. The Nurse opens the play by wishing that history could be reversed, that the *Argo* had never set sail: the play begins with a desire to undo the beginning of the story. Medea is the granddaughter of a god, Helios, the Sun, which associates her closely with the regular passing of time, in the sun's rising and setting. Her violent revenge at the injustice done to her can be seen as an attempt to do the impossible: to undo, by violence, her life history ever since the sailing of the *Argo*, to regain her lost honor and resume her old self, an unmarried princess. It can also be seen as an attempt at justice, a restoration of order out of chaos—but at a terrible cost, and in violation of all moderation and humanity.

Medea is an endlessly fascinating play that seems strikingly modern in its examination of family life, infidelity, failed sexual relationships, the experience of immigrants in a foreign land, and how it feels to be an oppressed or marginalized member of society. It also points to the fear, felt by many people both ancient and modern, that the apparently weaker members of a community, such as women and resident aliens, may be smarter than their masters, and may, if pushed far enough, rise up to destroy their oppressors.

Medea[1]

Cast of Characters

Medea
Jason
Medea's nurse
Tutor of Medea and Jason's sons
Creon, King of Corinth

Aegeus, King of Athens
Messenger
Chorus of Corinthian women
Medea and Jason's two sons

SETTING   Corinth, in front of the house in which Medea and Jason have been living.

[*Enter* MEDEA'S NURSE *from inside the house.*]

NURSE   If only the *Argo*[2] had not slipped through
the dark Clashing Rocks[3] and landed at Colchis,
if only that pine tree had not been cut down
high on Mount Pelion and made into oars
for the heroes who went out for the Golden Fleece,   5
sent by King Pelias. Then my mistress Medea
would never have sailed to the towers of Iolcus,[4]
overwhelmed by her love for Jason.
She would not have talked the daughters of Pelias
into killing their father,[5] then fled here to Corinth[6]   10
with her husband and sons—where even in exile
she has charmed the citizens of her new home,
doing whatever she could to help out Jason.
That is the strongest safeguard there is:
when a wife always sides with her husband.   15
But now they're at odds, their bond is infected.
Deserting his children along with my mistress,
Jason has climbed into a royal bed,
with the daughter of Creon,[7] king of this land.
Poor Medea feels cruelly dishonored: 20
she keeps shouting about their oaths and bringing up
the solemn pledge of their joined right hands;
she keeps calling on the gods to witness
what kind of thanks she gets from Jason.
She stays in bed and won't eat; she hurts all over.   25

---

1. Translated by Sheila H. Murnaghan.
2. The first ship, constructed by Jason for his quest for the Golden Fleece.
3. Colchis, home of Medea, lay on the other side of the Black Sea from Corinth, past the rocks near the mouth of the Bosphorus.
4. Thessaly, in Greece.
5. Pelias, Jason's uncle, reneged on a promise to give Jason the throne of Iolchus if he

brought back the Golden Fleece. In revenge, Medea persuaded Pelias' daughters to boil him alive, believing that they would make him young again.
6. After the scandal of Pelias' murder, Jason and Medea had to go into exile, to Corinth.
7. Creon, king of Corinth, is not the same as the Creon (Kreon) of Thebes in Sophocles' Theban plays.

She's been weeping constantly since she heard
that she has been cast off by her husband.
She stares at the ground. When friends give advice,
she listens no more than a stone or the sea,
though sometimes she turns her pale neck away,   30
and sighs to herself about her dear father,
her homeland, her house—all those she betrayed
when she left with the man who now rejects her.
Poor thing, this disaster has made her learn
how hard it is to be cut off from home.   35
She hates her sons, gets no joy from seeing them.
I am afraid that she's planning something
[I know her: she's relentless and will not put up
with being mistreated. I can imagine
her sharpening a knife and stabbing someone,   40
sneaking into the house where the wedding bed's made,
to kill the king and his daughter's new bridegroom][8]
and will only cause herself more trouble.
She is fierce. If you get into a fight with her,
you won't come out singing a victory song.   45
        [*Enter the* TUTOR *with the two boys.*]
But here are the boys coming back from the track,
not thinking about their mother's problems—
young minds don't like to dwell on trouble.
TUTOR   Old servant of my mistress's house,
why do you stand here alone by the door,   50
pouring out your troubles to yourself?
Surely Medea doesn't want you to leave her?
NURSE   Old tutor of the sons of Jason,
when slaves are true-hearted, if their masters' luck
takes a turn for the worse, they suffer, too.   55
I felt so wretched about my mistress
that I craved the relief of coming out here
to tell her sad story to heaven and earth.
TUTOR   That poor woman has not stopped lamenting?
NURSE   If only! Her pain's still in its early stages.   60
TUTOR   What a fool, even if she is my mistress!
She still doesn't know her latest troubles.
NURSE   What is it, old man? Don't keep it to yourself.
TUTOR   No, nothing. I shouldn't have said what I did.
NURSE   Please don't leave a fellow slave in the dark.   65
If it really matters, I won't tell anyone.
TUTOR   I heard someone talking, though he didn't notice.
I was watching the old men playing checkers
there where they sit by the spring of Peirene.[9]

8. Words in brackets here and throughout are considered by most scholars to be later additions to the text, sometimes inserted by actors, sometimes by scholars and editors [translator's note].
9. A spring in Corinth.

He said that Creon, the king here in Corinth,   70
is planning to exile these boys from the city,
along with their mother. Whether this is true
I have no idea. I certainly hope not.
NURSE   Would Jason really put his sons through that,
even if he is on bad terms with their mother?   75
TUTOR   Old loyalties are trumped by new ones;
and that man is no friend to this household.
NURSE   We're done for, if we face a new wave of troubles
when we haven't bailed ourselves out from the last.
TUTOR   But now's not the right time for her to find out.   80
So you should keep quiet. Don't say a word.
NURSE   Children, do you hear how your father treats you?
He is my master: I can't curse him. But—
it's clear he's willing to hurt his own family.
TUTOR   And who isn't? It should be clear to you   85
that all people put themselves before others
[sometimes with good reason, sometimes for gain]
if this father prefers his new wife to his children.
NURSE   Go inside, boys. It will all be fine.
Now you, make sure they are kept by themselves,   90
not near their mother while she's so distraught.
She looks at them the way a mad bull would,
as if she's about to make some move.
She won't stop raging until she crushes someone—
better her enemies than people she loves.   95
MEDEA   [from inside]   It's too much, too much to bear!
I can't take any more. I want to die!
NURSE   Boys, see what I mean! Your mother
keeps stirring up her angry heart.
Quickly, quickly, into the house,   100
but don't go near her: stay out of view.
Don't get too close, be on the watch
for her vengeful heart and her self-willed,
savage temper.
Go on inside, quick as you can.   105
Her grief is like a thundercloud
which her mounting fury will ignite.
And then what will she do,
this proud-to-the-core, uncurbable spirit
stung by sorrows?   110
     [Exit the TUTOR and the boys into the house. Enter MEDEA]
MEDEA   I'm abused, I'm abused, that's why I cry.
Boys, you are cursed, your mother is loathsome.
You might as well die along with your father.
Let the whole house come down!
NURSE   No, no! I don't like the sound of that.   115
Why blame your sons for their father's
offenses? Why turn on them?

Children, I'm sick with fear for you.
Our rulers have frightening tempers;
rarely governed, always in charge,   120
they can't let go of their anger.
Better to stay on a level plain.
I'd rather grow old in safety
and not lead a life of grandeur.
"Moderation" is a fine motto,   125
and we do well to live by it.
Reaching for more never brings
any real advantage in human life—
only greater ruin when an angry god
comes down on a house.   130

[*Enter the* CHORUS *of Corinthian women.*]

CHORUS   I heard a voice! I heard the cry
of that poor Colchian woman!
Tell us, old nurse, has she still not calmed down?
I'm sure I could hear through the double doors
her wailing voice.   135
I get no joy from the grief in this house.
I consider myself a friend.

NURSE   There is no house. That's all gone.
The husband's possessed by a royal bed.
The wife wastes away in the innermost room,   140
and will not be comforted
by anything a friend can say.

MEDEA   Let it come! A thunderbolt
Straight through my head!
Why stay alive? In death   145
I can rest from a life I hate.

CHORUS   O Zeus, O Earth, O Light!
Do you hear the grief
in that girl's sad song?
Why this foolish lust   150
for a fatal resting place?
You want death to hurry up?
Do not ever ask for that.
So your husband adores someone else.
You should not rage at him.   155
Zeus will stand up for you.
Do not ruin yourself mourning that man.

MEDEA   Mighty Themis! Holy Artemis![1]
Do you see what I suffer—even after
I bound my hateful husband with solemn oaths?   160

---

1. Themis, whose name means "Right" or "Lawfulness," is a female Titan associated with order and keeping promises. Artemis, a daughter of Zeus, is a goddess who protects virgins and women in childbirth.

I'd gladly watch him and his new bride
being smashed to pieces with their whole house
for the huge wrong they have done to me.
My father! My city!—shamefully lost
when I killed my brother.[2]   165

NURSE   You can hear what gods she calls on:
unfailing Themis and great Zeus,
who oversees the oaths of mortals.
There is no way she'll end her anger
with just some empty gesture.   170

CHORUS   If she would meet us
        face-to-face
        and listen to our words,
she might let go of the rage in her heart,
and soften her harsh temper.   175
I am always eager
        to help a friend.
Go bring her out of the house.
        Tell her we're on her side.
        You have to act before she can hurt   180
        those boys in there: grief spurs her on.

NURSE   I doubt I can persuade her,
        but I'll do as you ask me to,
        and make one last attempt.
When we try to speak to her,   185
she glares at us like a bull
or a lioness with newborn cubs.
I have to say our ancestors
showed very little sense
when they invented melodies   190
for revels, festivals, and feasts,
the sweetest sounds in life,
but made no songs or harmonies
to soothe the bitter grief
that leads to death and devastation   195
and brings whole houses down.
A musical cure for that would be
worth having. Why should people sing
when they're gathered at a feast
and there's joy enough already   200
in the meal's abundance?

        [*Exit the* NURSE *into the house.*]

CHORUS   I hear the pain in her loud laments;
        she shouts out high and shrill,
        at the faithless husband who spurns her bed.

---

2. After the theft of the Golden Fleece, Jason and Medea were pursued by the outraged Colchians. To slow them down, Medea killed her brother, Aspyrtus, and threw his body parts behind her.

She calls on Themis to hear her wrongs, 205
  daughter of Zeus, upholder of oaths.
  Because of an oath, she crossed to Greece,
  sailing on the dark night waves
  of the Black Sea's watery gate.[3]

[*Enter* MEDEA *from the house, with attendants.*]

MEDEA Women of Corinth, I have left the house 210
to avoid offending you. With many people,
you know that they're proud whether they stay home
or go out. But others are seen as aloof
just because they choose to lead quiet lives.
People aren't fair when they judge with their eyes. 215
Not taking the trouble to look inside,
they hate someone on sight who's done them no harm.
So a stranger really has to fit in.
It's not good when even a self-willed native
is out of touch and rude to fellow citizens. 220
In my case, this unexpected calamity
has crushed my spirit. I am finished, friends,
done with life's joys. I wish I were dead.
My husband, who was everything to me,
is actually, I now see, the worst of men. 225
Of all living, breathing, thinking creatures,
women are the most absolutely wretched.
First, you have to pay an enormous sum
to buy a husband who, to make things worse,
gets to be the master of your body.[4] 230
And it's a gamble: you're as likely to get
a bad one as a good one. Divorce means disgrace
for women, and you can't say no to a husband.
Finding herself among strange laws and customs,
a wife needs to be clairvoyant; she has not 235
learned at home how to deal with her mate.
If we work hard at all these things,
and our husbands don't chafe at the yoke,
then that's an enviable life. Otherwise, we're better off dead.
A man who feels oppressed by the company at home, 240
goes out and gets relief for his low spirits
[turning to a friend or someone else his age],
but we can only look to that one other person.
They tell us that we enjoy a sheltered life,
staying at home while they are out fighting. 245
How wrong they are! I would rather face battle
three times than go through childbirth once.
But it isn't the same for you as for me.
This is your city. The houses you grew up in,

---

3. The "gate" is the Bosphorus Strait, connecting the Black Sea to the Mediterranean.

4. In ancient Greece, the bride's family had to pay a dowry to the husband.

all your daily pleasures, your friends, are here. 250
I am alone, without a city, disowned
by my husband, snatched from a foreign land.
I have no mother, brother, or other family
to shelter me now that disaster has struck.
So I have just one thing to ask of you: 255
if some plan or scheme occurs to me
by which I can get back at my husband
[and the king and his daughter, Jason's new wife],
say nothing. A woman is usually quite timid,
shying away from battles and weapons, 260
but if her marriage bed's dishonored,
no one has a deadlier heart.

CHORUS   I will do that. You are right to pay him back,
Medea. I can see why you're aggrieved.

     [Enter CREON.]

But here is Creon, ruler of this land, 265
coming to announce some new decision.

CREON   You, with your scowls and your spite for your husband,
Medea, I command you to leave this land.
Take your two sons and go into exile—
and no delaying. I have authority 270
over this decree, and I'm not going home
until I've placed you outside our borders.

MEDEA   Oh no! I am completely destroyed.
My enemies are spreading their sails to the wind,
and I can't disembark from disaster. 275
But bad as things are, I have to ask:
what's your reason, Creon, for throwing me out?

CREON   I'll come right out and say it: I'm afraid
that you'll do my daughter some incurable harm.
There are many signs that point to this. 280
You are clever and skilled at causing damage,
and you feel injured in your empty bed.
People have told me you're threatening us all:
the bride's father, the bridegroom, and the bride.
So I'm acting first to protect myself. 285
I would rather earn your hatred now
than regret later on that I was too lenient.

MEDEA   Not again!
Creon, the same thing keeps happening:
my reputation gets me into trouble. 290
No man who has his wits about him
would raise his sons to be too clever.
Not only will they be considered lazy,
they'll be resented by their fellow citizens.
When you propose a clever plan to dullards, 295
they see you as useless rather than clever;
and those who are thought to be sophisticated

are bothered when the people think you're smarter.
This is exactly what has happened to me.
I'm clever, so I'm envied by one group   300
[to some I'm idle, to some the reverse]
and annoy the rest—cleverness has limits.
I know you're afraid I'll do you some harm.
But why be worried? I am in no position
to go on the offensive against a king.   305
How have you wronged me? You gave your daughter
to the man you wanted to. The one I hate
is my husband. You were acting sensibly.
I don't blame you because you're doing well.
Marry her off! Best of luck to all! But—   310
just let me stay. I may have been mistreated,
but I'll keep quiet, yielding to my betters.

CREON Your words sound pleasing, but I am afraid
that you have some evil plan in your heart.
In fact, I trust you less than I did before.   315
A hot-tempered woman—or man—is easier
to guard against than a silent, clever one.
No, you have to leave at once. Enough talking.
It is decided: you are my enemy,
and none of your tricks can keep you here.   320

[MEDEA *kneels and grasps* CREON's *knees and hand in a gesture of ritual
supplication.*]

MEDEA No! By your knees! By your daughter the bride!
CREON Your words are wasted. You will never convince me.
MEDEA You're ignoring my prayers and driving me out?
CREON I care about my family, not about you.
MEDEA My lost home! I can't stop thinking about it.   325
CREON That's what means most to me, after my children.
MEDEA Oh, what a disaster to fall in love!
CREON That depends, I'd say, on the circumstances.
MEDEA Zeus, be sure to notice who's making me suffer.
CREON Don't be a fool! Go, and take my troubles with you.   330
MEDEA I have troubles too, far more than I need.
CREON My guards are preparing to throw you out.
MEDEA No, not that! Creon, I implore you.
CREON So you're determined to make this difficult.
MEDEA I will leave. I don't ask you to change that.   335
CREON Then why keep pressing me? Let go of my hand.
MEDEA Just let me stay here for one more day
so I can work out my plans for exile
and make some arrangements for my sons,
since their father is not inclined to help.   340
Show them some pity. You have children yourself;
It's only natural to wish these boys well.
I'm not worried about exile for myself
but I feel the hardship it brings my sons.

CREON   I'm really not a tyrant at heart: 345
   to my own cost, I have listened to others.
   Even though I know it's not a good idea,
   you get your wish. But I warn you,
   if tomorrow's sun finds you and your boys
   still inside the borders of this country,   350
   you will die. I say it, and I mean it.
   So stay on, if you must, for this one day;
   you won't have time to do the harm I fear.
        [*Exit* CREON. MEDEA *stands up.*]

CHORUS   Poor, poor woman,
   weighed down by troubles,   355
   where can you turn? What welcome,
   what house, what sheltering land
   [will you find]?
   Medea, some god has tossed you
     into a sea of constant trials.   360

MEDEA   It's bad all around. Who would deny that?
   But don't imagine that everything's settled.
   There are struggles ahead for the bridal pair,
   and many ordeals for the bride's father.
   Would I have fawned on him like that   365
   without something to gain or a secret plan?
   There wouldn't have been that talking and touching.
   But he is such a credulous fool:
   when he had a chance to throw me out
   and foil my plans, he gave me one more day   370
   to make corpses out of my three tormenters—
   the father, the daughter, and my own husband.
   I can think of many routes to their death;
   I'm not sure, friends, which one to try first,
   whether to set the newlyweds' house on fire,   375
   or stab someone's liver with a sharpened sword,
   silently entering the bridal bedroom.
   But there is a risk: if I am caught
   sneaking into the house, I will lose my life
   and give my enemies a chance to laugh.   380
   The safest course is the one I know best:
   to poison them with deadly drugs.
   That's it, then.
   But once they are dead—then what city
   will take me in? Where is the friend   385
   who will save my life by giving me shelter?
   Nowhere. So I will wait a little while,
   and if some tower of safety appears
   I will kill them with a hidden trick.
   But if I am forced to act in the open,   390
   I will strike with a sword. Ready to die,
   I will go to the very edge of daring.

By Hecate,[5] whom I most revere,
the goddess who is my chosen ally,
who haunts the darkest corners of my house,   395
they will not get away with causing this pain.
I will make sure they find their marriage bitter,
and bitter the tie with Creon, bitter my exile.
Now Medea, use everything you know;
you must plot and scheme as you approach   400
the dreadful act that will test your spirit.
Do you see what is being done to you?
Do not be mocked by this Sisyphean wedding;[6]
You spring from a noble father and Helios the sun.
You have the skill, and along with that   405
a woman's nature—useless for doing good
but just right for contriving evil.

CHORUS   Sacred streams are flowing backwards;
right and wrong are turned around.
It's men who do the shady scheming,   410
swear by the gods, then break their oaths.
News of this will bring us glory,
rightful honor for the female race;
women will at last be free
from the taint of ugly rumors.   415
Enough of ancient poets' legends
that tell of us as breaking faith!
The lord of song, divine Apollo,
did not grant the lyre's sweet music
for the speaking of our minds,   420
or I could have made an answer
to the stories spread by men.
Time's long record speaks on both sides.
Mad with love, you left your father.
Sailing through the briny border   425
of the double Clashing Rocks,[7]
you settled in a land of strangers.
Now your husband's left your bed;
so you're banished from this country,
a lonely exile without rights.   430

All over Greece, oaths prove hollow;
shame has melted into air.
And for you there's no safe harbor
in your lost paternal home,

5. Goddess associated with the moon and
with witchcraft.
6. I.e., in the spirit of Sisyphus, a legendary
Corinthian trickster, punished in Hades with the
eternal task of pushing a rock uphill only to have
it roll down again [translator's note].
7. The path between the cliffs is the Bosphorus Strait.

no escaping from your troubles,   435
as you watch a royal princess
take your marriage and your house.
    [*Enter* JASON.]

JASON   This is not the first time that I've observed
how impossible a stubborn person can be.
You had the chance to stay in this country,   440
going along with what your betters had planned,
but you're being thrown out for your pointless rants,
and there's nothing I can do. Fine! Don't stop
talking about "that disgusting Jason."
But for what you've said about the rulers—   445
you are lucky that it's only exile.
The king gets more and more angry. I've tried
to calm him down, hoping you could stay.
Yet you keep up this nonsense, raving on
against the king. So you're being thrown out.   450
Still, I am not one to abandon family.
I'm here now to look out for your interests,
so you and the boys don't leave without money
or other provisions. Exile's not easy.
Maybe you can't stop hating me,   455
but I'll always want what is best for you.

MEDEA   You really are disgusting! That sums up
what I have to say about your spinelessness.
You've really come here, when you are hated
[by me and the gods and everyone else]?   460
It's not some daring noble endeavor
to look friends in the face after you've wronged them,
but the lowest and sickest of human failings:
shamelessness. Still, it is good that you came.
If I name all your appalling actions,   465
I'll get some relief, and you'll feel much worse.
Let me start at the very beginning:
I saved you, as every Greek knows
who shipped out with you on the *Argo*,
when you had to bring the fire-breathing bulls   470
under a yoke and sow a deadly field.[8]
And that serpent, which never slept
and held the Golden Fleece in winding coils,
I killed it, bringing you the light of salvation.[9]
And as for me, I cheated my father   475
and followed you to Iolcus[1] and Mt. Pelion,

---

8. Jason was challenged by Medea's father, King Aeetes, to plow a field with a pair of fire-breathing bulls and sow it with dragon's teeth, which would instantly grow into armed men. With Medea's help, he succeeded.

9. The Golden Fleece had hung from a tree, around which coiled a fierce dragon; Medea succeeded in defeating the dragon.
1. Ancestral kingdom of Jason.

infatuated, not thinking straight.
I made Pelias die in the most gruesome way,
at his daughters' hands; I ruined his house.
All of this I did for you, you lowlife,   480
and you have deserted me for someone new
even though we have children. If we didn't,
you could be forgiven for wanting her.
Our oaths mean nothing to you. I can't tell
if you think those gods have lost their power,   485
or imagine that the rules have changed for mortals—
since you're well aware that you broke a promise.
My right hand here—to think I let you touch it,
and to clasp my knees.[2] I was abused
by a swindler, deceived by false hopes.   490
Still, let me ask you for some friendly advice.
[But why should I think you'd help me now?
Well, if I ask you, it'll make you look worse.]
So where should I go? To my father's house
which I betrayed when I ran off with you?   495
To the poor daughters of Pelias? I'm sure
I'd be welcome there, where I killed their father.
That is how it stands: my friends at home
hate me now, and those I should have treated well
I turned into enemies by helping you.   500
For what I did, you made me the envy
of all Greek women—with such a marvelous catch,
such a loyal husband that I'm being expelled,
a miserable outcast from this country,
without any friends, alone with my sons.   505
It doesn't look so good for the bridegroom—
children out begging with the woman who saved him.
Zeus, you should have given us a touchstone
for human nature as you did for gold!
We need a way to tell from someone's looks   510
whether or not he's base on the inside.

CHORUS There is a dreadful, incurable anger
when former lovers fall to fighting.

JASON It seems I'll have to be a skillful speaker,
and, like a careful pilot, reef in my sails   515
if I have any hope of outrunning
the surging onslaught of your angry words.
You make much of the help you gave me,
but I say that it was Aphrodite[3] alone
who assured the success of my venture.   520

---

2. Touching a person's right hand and knees
was a way of asking for a favor, assuming the
position of a supplicant. Medea is implying

that Jason has failed to pay her back for the
favors she did him.
3. Goddess of love, beauty, and sex.

You may be quick-witted, but like it or not,
I could tell how you were compelled
by Eros's sure arrows to save my life.[4]
But no need to tally this up exactly:
whatever you did was helpful enough.   525
Still, it's my view that you got much more
out of my being saved than I ever did.
First of all, you are living in Greece,
not some foreign country. Here you find justice
and the rule of law; force has no standing.   530
And all of Greece knows how clever you are;
you're famous. If you lived at the ends of the earth,
no one would ever have heard of you.
I see no point in a house full of gold,
or a gift for singing better than Orpheus,[5]   535
without the good fortune of being well known.
So—since you have turned this into a contest,
those are the things I accomplished for you.
Now, on this royal marriage that you dislike,
I can show you that I acted wisely,   540
soberly, and in the best interest
of you and the boys. Just stay calm for a moment.
When I moved here from the city of Iolcus,
I was dragged down by impossible problems.
What better solution could there be   545
for an exile like me than to marry the princess?
You are upset, but it's not what you think,
that I'm sick of you and smitten with this girl,
or want some prize for having lots of children;
I am satisfied with the ones we've got.   550
It's so we'll live well and won't be in need.
And that is important. I can tell you:
everyone steers clear of a penniless friend.
I will raise our sons as befits our family
and add some brothers to the boys you gave me.   555
Bringing them together in a single tribe,
I'll prosper. What are more children to you?
In my case, having new offspring benefits
the older ones. Is that such a bad plan?
You wouldn't say so if it weren't for the sex.   560
You women reach the point where you think
if all's well in the bedroom everything's fine;
but if some trouble arises there,
you insist on rejecting whatever's best.

4. I.e., Cupid, god of sex—the son of Aphrodite.
Eros shoots arrows that inspire desire.
5. Orpheus, son of the god Apollo and the
muse Calliope, was a poet-singer with semimag-
ical powers: even wild animals were enchanted
by his songs. Orpheus was famously devoted to
his wife, Eurydice; when she died, he traveled
down to the underworld to try to rescue her.

We should have some other way of getting children. 565
Then there would be no female race,
and mankind would be free from trouble.

CHORUS   Jason, you've put together a polished speech.
But, at the risk of disagreeing, I say
that you do wrong to desert your wife. 570

MEDEA   I'm clearly different from everyone else.
To me, a scoundrel who is good at speaking
should have to pay a special price for that.
Since he knows he can gloss over his crimes,
he'll try anything. But cleverness has limits. 575
That's what you are. So don't try to impress me
with clever words. A single point refutes you:
if you were so noble, you would have gotten
my consent to this marriage, not kept it secret.

JASON   Oh yes, I'm sure you would have agreed 580
if I had told you then, when even now
you can't help reacting with fury.

MEDEA   That wasn't it. You thought a foreign wife
would be an embarrassment in years to come.

JASON   You need to understand. It is not for the woman 585
that I'm taking on this royal marriage.
It's what I told you before. I only want
to give you protection and safeguard our children
by fathering royal siblings for them.

MEDEA   Spare me a life of shameful wealth 590
or a good situation that eats at my soul.

JASON   You know what you really need to pray for?
The sense not to see a good thing as shameful,
not to think you're suffering when you're doing fine.

MEDEA   Go on, be cruel. You have a safe home here, 595
while I'll be cast out with nowhere to go.

JASON   You chose that. Don't blame anyone else.

MEDEA   How? I betrayed you by marrying somebody?

JASON   By rudely cursing the royal family.

MEDEA   Well, I'll bring a curse to your house too. 600

JASON   I have had enough of squabbling with you,
but if you want some money from me
to provide for you and the boys in exile,
just say so. I want to be generous
and can contact friends who will treat you well. 605
You would be an idiot to turn me down.
You'll be better off if you forget your anger.

MEDEA   I want nothing to do with your friends.
I won't take anything you give. Don't bother.
No good comes from a bad man's gifts. 610

JASON   Well, the gods will witness how eager I am
to do what I can for you and the boys.
You are so stubborn that you reject what's good

and snub your friends. You will suffer all the more.

MEDEA   Just go! I'm sure that staying away this long   615
has left you longing for your new bride.
Go play the groom. And maybe I'm right to hope
you will have a marriage that makes you weep.

     [*Exit* JASON.]

CHORUS   Overwhelming love never leads to virtue,
     or a good reputation.   620
Just enough Aphrodite is the greatest blessing.
Goddess, don't aim at me with your golden bow
     and arrows dipped in desire.

I choose to be wooed by sober restraint—
     the best gift of the gods.   625
I won't have Aphrodite stirring up quarrels
by making me fall for a stranger. She should grant us
     harmonious marriages.

Beloved country! Beloved home!
May I never lose my city;   630
that is a life without hope,
the hardest of trials to bear.
Better, far better to die,
than ever come to that.
There is no deeper pain   635
than being cut off from home.

I have seen it for myself;
no one had to tell me.
For you have no city,
no friends who feel for you   640
in your bitter struggles.
Whoever doesn't honor friends
with an open heart,
deserves an awful death
and is no friend of mine.   645

     [*Enter* AEGEUS.][6]

AEGEUS   Hello, Medea! And all good wishes—
the warmest of greetings among true friends.

MEDEA   Good wishes to you, son of wise Pandion,
Aegeus! Where are you coming from?

AEGEUS   Straight from Apollo's ancient oracle.[7]   650

MEDEA   What took you there, to the center of the earth?[8]

AEGEUS   I wanted to know how I might have children.

6. This stage direction is a modern guess, though presumably the direction of Aegeus's entrance must differ from those of all previous entrances in the play—underscoring the unex-pectedness of his arrival.
7. Delphi.
8. At Delphi was a stone that was supposedly the navel of the Earth.

MEDEA	Goodness! Have you been childless all this time?
AEGEUS	Yes, childless—thanks, I am sure, to some god.
MEDEA	Do you have a wife, or do you sleep alone? 655
AEGEUS	I'm married; I have a wife who shares my bed.
MEDEA	And what did Apollo say about children?
AEGEUS	Subtler words than a man can make sense of.
MEDEA	Am I allowed to know what he said?
AEGEUS	Of course. I need the help of your clever mind. 660
MEDEA	Then if it's allowed, tell me what he said.
AEGEUS	Not to untie the foot of the wineskin . . .[9]
MEDEA	Before doing what? Or arriving where?
AEGEUS	Before I get back to my ancestral hearth.
MEDEA	And what's your reason for landing here? 665
AEGEUS	There's a man called Pittheus, king of Troezen.[1]
MEDEA	Son of Pelops,[2] said to be very pious.
AEGEUS	I want to ask him about the prophecy.
MEDEA	Yes, he's wise and knows about such things.
AEGEUS	And he's my most trusted comrade at war. 670
MEDEA	Well, good luck! I hope you get what you want.
AEGEUS	But why are you looking so red-eyed and pale?
MEDEA	It turns out I have the worst possible husband.
AEGEUS	What are you saying? Tell me what's upset you.
MEDEA	Jason mistreats me though I've given him no cause. 675
AEGEUS	What is he doing? Explain what you mean.
MEDEA	He put another woman in charge of our house.
AEGEUS	Would he do something so improper?
MEDEA	He would. So I, once prized, am now dismissed.
AEGEUS	Is he in love? Or has he fallen out with you? 680
MEDEA	So much in love that he's abandoned his family.
AEGEUS	Well, if he's that bad, forget about him.
MEDEA	He's in love with the thought of a royal match.
AEGEUS	Then tell me: who is the new wife's father?
MEDEA	Creon, who rules right here in Corinth. 685
AEGEUS	Well, I can see why you are angry.
MEDEA	Devastated. And I'm being expelled.
AEGEUS	From bad to worse! What's the reason for that?
MEDEA	Creon has declared me an exile from Corinth.
AEGEUS	And Jason accepts this? That's not right. 690
MEDEA	He protests now, but he'll gladly put up with it.

So I'm reaching out my hands to your face
and making myself your suppliant.
Take pity on me in my wretched state,

---

9. Wine was sometimes stored in animal skins, the leg being used as a spigot for dispensing drinks. The imagery suggests both "Don't get drunk" and "Don't have sex."
1. Pittheus will give his daughter Aethra to Aegeus, after getting him drunk; the Athenian hero Theseus will be conceived in this way.
2. Pelops, son of Tantalus, was served up as food to the gods by his father. The gods restored him to life, and he became the founder of the Peloponnese.

don't let me become a lonely outcast.   695
Take me into your country and your house.
Do this, and may the gods grant your wish.
May you live out the happy life you long for.
You don't know how lucky you are to find me:
I can take care of your lack of children.   700
I know the right drugs to make you a father.

AEGEUS   There are many reasons why I want to help.
First the gods, who favor suppliants,
and then the children you say I could have—
something where I'm really at a loss.   705
So, if you can get yourself to my land,
I will try to give you proper shelter.
[I should make one thing plain to you:
I'm not willing to take you away from here.]
If you leave this place on your own   710
and arrive at my house also on your own,
you will be safe. I will not hand you over.
But I can't offend my friends while I'm here.

MEDEA   Agreed. Now if you could make a formal pledge,
then I will feel you've treated me perfectly.   715

AEGEUS   You don't trust me? What's on your mind?

MEDEA   I trust you. But Pelias' family hates me,
and Creon, too. If you are bound by oaths,
you can't let them take me from your land.
If you just say yes and don't swear by the gods,   720
you might end up being gracious and giving in
to their demands. I'm completely powerless,
while they have wealth and status on their side.

AEGEUS   You clearly have this all figured out.
So if you think I should, I won't refuse.   725
This will put me in a stronger position,
with a good excuse to give your enemies,
and it helps you. Name the gods I should swear by.

MEDEA   Swear by the Earth and by the Sun, father
of my father,[3] and the entire race of gods.   730

AEGEUS   To do—or not to do—what? Say it.

MEDEA   Not ever to cast me out from your land,
and if some enemy tries to lead me away,
not to allow it while you live and breathe.

AEGEUS   I swear by the Earth and the light of the Sun,   735
and all the gods, I will do as you say.

MEDEA   Good. And the penalty if you break the oath?

AEGEUS   Whatever ungodly people have to suffer.

MEDEA   A good journey to you. All is in place.
I will come to your city as soon as I can,   740
once I have fulfilled my plans and desires.

3. Helios, the Sun, is father of Aeetes, king of Colchis, Medea's father.

CHORUS May Hermes,[4] guide of travelers,
　　　speed you to your home,
　　　and may you gain your heart's desire,
　　　for you are an honorable man, Aegeus,
　　　that is clear to me.　　　　　　　　　　　　745
　　　　　[*Exit* AEGEUS.]
MEDEA O Zeus, O Justice born of Zeus, O Sun!
　　　Now, friends, I know I am on the path
　　　to glorious victory over my enemies.
　　　Now I feel sure they will have to pay.　　　750
　　　I was at a loss, and then this man appeared,
　　　who will be a safe haven when my plots are done.
　　　I can fasten my mooring line to him
　　　when I have made my way to Athens.
　　　And now I will tell you what I have I mind;　　755
　　　listen to this, though I doubt you will like it.
　　　I will send a trusted servant to Jason
　　　who will ask him to meet me face to face.
　　　When he comes, I will give a soothing speech
　　　about how I agree with him and now believe　　760
　　　that his faithless marriage is a first-rate plan,
　　　advantageous and well thought through.
　　　Then I'll plead for the children to stay behind;
　　　not that I want to leave them in this hostile land
　　　[and have my children mistreated by enemies];　　765
　　　it's part of a trick to kill the king's daughter.
　　　I'll send them to her with gifts in their hands
　　　[for the bride, so they won't have to leave],
　　　a delicate robe and a golden crown.
　　　Once she takes this finery and puts it on,　　770
　　　she—and whoever touches her—will die
　　　because of poisons I will spread on the gifts.
　　　That's all there is to say on that subject.
　　　But the thought of what I have to do next
　　　fills me with grief: I need to kill the children,　　775
　　　no one should hope to spare them that.
　　　Once I've torn Jason's house apart, I'll leave
　　　and pay no price for the poor boys' death.
　　　I will bring myself to this unholy act
　　　because I cannot let my enemies laugh.　　780
　　　[So be it! Why should I live? I have no country,
　　　no home, no way of escaping my troubles.]
　　　It was a bad mistake to leave my home
　　　swayed by the words of a man from Greece,
　　　but with the gods' help I will punish him.　　785
　　　He won't see the children we had grow up

4. Hermes, the messenger god, was the child of Zeus by the nymph Maia.

and he won't be able to have any more
with his brand-new bride: no, she's doomed
to an agonizing death from my drugs.
No one should think I am meek and mild   790
or passive. I am quite the opposite:
harsh to enemies and loyal to friends,
the kind of person whose life has glory.

CHORUS   Now that you have shared this plan with me,
   I want to help you and to honor human law,   795
   and so I say to you: don't do this thing.

MEDEA   I see why you say that, but there's no other way;
   you haven't been through the troubles I have.

CHORUS   You would be able to kill your own children?

MEDEA   It is the surest way to wound my husband.   800

CHORUS   And to make yourself impossibly wretched.

MEDEA   So be it. We have done enough talking.

   [MEDEA *turns to her attendants.*]

   One of you servants, go bring Jason here.
   And you, the friends I trust with my closest secrets,
   if you respect me and have women's hearts,   805
   you will say nothing about my plan.

   [*Exit one of* MEDEA's *attendants.*]

CHORUS   The sons of Erechtheus,[5] long blessed with wealth,
   Athenian offspring of the Olympian gods,
   raised in a land untouched by war,
   nourished by the glorious arts,   810
   stride easily through the radiant air,
   where once, it's said, the holy Muses[6]
   gave birth to golden Harmony.

   I've heard that Aphrodite dips her cup
   in the streams of clear Cephisus,[7]   815
   and sends sweet breezes through the land.
   Crowned with a twining garland
   of fragrant, blooming roses,
   she sets Desire at Wisdom's side
   to foster all that's good.   820

   How can that land of sacred streams,
   that open-hearted city,
   be a fitting home for you,
   unholy woman,
   killer of children?   825

5. Athenians. Erechtheus was a legendary king
of Athens.
6. The Muses are the daughters of Zeus and
Mnemosyne (Memory). They inspire poetic

and musical creation, and their birthplace is
Pieria.
7. River in Athens.

Think what it is to strike a child!
Think who you are killing!
By every sacred thing
I beg of you:
spare those boys.   830

How can you find the will,
how can you steel your mind,
to lift your hand against your sons,
to do this awful thing?
How will you stop your tears,   835
when you see them dying?
They will huddle at your knees,
and you will not be able
to spill their blood
with a steady heart.   840
     [*Enter* JASON.]

JASON   You called me, so I've come. You may hate me,
but I won't let you down. I'm eager to hear
what you think you may need from me after all.

MEDEA   Jason, please overlook what I said before.
You should be willing to put up with my fits,   845
for the sake of the love that we once shared.
And I have been thinking all of this over
and berating myself for being obtuse.
Why turn on those who wish me well,
picking a fight with the country's rulers   850
and my husband, who serves us all
by marrying a princess and giving our sons
new royal brothers? Why be angry?
The gods will provide, so how can I lose?
Shouldn't I think of the boys? I can't forget   855
that I'm an exile and have no friends.
When I look at it that way, I can see
I've been confused and my rage was pointless.
I'm all for it now. I think you are wise
to arrange this connection. I'm the fool: 860
I should have thrown myself into these plans
and helped them along, tending the bed
and gladly serving your new bride.
It's just that women are . . . well, not quite wicked,
but anyway you shouldn't copy us   865
and get caught up in silly quarrels.
Please forgive me: I was wrong before
and now I understand much better.
Boys, boys! Come out of the house
to greet your father and talk to him.   870
     [*Enter the* TUTOR *and the two boys from the house.*]

End your anger towards one you should love
just as I, your mother, am doing.
We have made our peace, there is no more strife.
So take his hand. But oh, when I think
of all the trouble the future conceals!   875
My children, in your lives to come,
will you reach out a loving arm to me?
I am so quick to weep and full of fear.
I'm making up my quarrel with your father
but even so my eyes are filled with tears.   880

CHORUS   Tears are coming to my eyes as well.
I only hope there's nothing worse ahead.

JASON   I'm pleased with your present behavior, Medea,
and I forgive the past: of course a woman minds
if her husband decides to import a new wife.   885
But now your feelings have turned around,
and you recognize the better course at last.
That shows you are a sensible woman.
Now boys, don't think I've been a negligent father.
With the gods' help, I've secured your position.   890
I am quite sure that you will be leaders
here in Corinth, you and your new siblings.
Just be strong and stay well. I will do the rest,
along with whatever god's on our side.
I hope to see you turning into fine young men,   895
and towering over my enemies.
But you, why are your cheeks covered with tears?
Why do you look pale and turn away?
Aren't you happy with what I am saying?

MEDEA   It's nothing—just the thought of these children.   900

JASON   Don't worry. I will take care of everything.

MEDEA   You're right. I can rely on your promises.
It's just that women are made for tears.

JASON   But why are you so sad about the children?

MEDEA   I am their mother. And your hopes for their future   905
filled me with fear that those things won't happen.
Now some of what you are here to discuss
has been settled, so I'll move on to the rest:
since the rulers have decided to banish me
[and I really do see that it's for the best   910
so I won't be in your way, or theirs,
since I can't help seeming antagonistic],
I will comply and leave the country.
But the boys should stay here and be raised by you;
ask Creon to spare them this exile.   915

JASON   I may not convince him, but I will try.

MEDEA   You should get your bride to ask her father
to let the boys stay here in this country.

JASON   Good idea. She'll do it if I ask her:
    she is a woman like any other.   920
MEDEA   And I will be part of this effort, too.
    I will send her the most splendid gifts
    that can be found anywhere in the world
    [a delicate robe and a golden crown]
    and the boys will take them. Now servants,   925
    bring out the presents right away.
          [*Exit an attendant into the house.*]
    She will have many reasons to rejoice:
    In you she has the best of husbands
    and she will wear the ornaments
    that my grandfather Helios left to his heirs.   930
          [*Enter the attendant with the gifts.*]
    Take these wedding presents, boys,
    carry them to the happy royal bride.
    They will be perfect gifts for her.
JASON   That's ridiculous! Don't deprive yourself.
    Do you think the royal house needs dresses,   935
    or gold? You should hold on to these things.
    I am sure that her high regard for me
    will matter more than material objects.
MEDEA   No. They say even the gods are moved by gifts.
    For us, gold counts more than a million words.   940
    Her fortunes are high, she has a god on her side,
    she's young and has power. I'd give my life,
    and not just gold, to save the boys from exile.
    My sons, go into that fine rich house;
    appeal to your father's new wife, my mistress;   945
    ask for reprieve from a life of exile,
    and hand her the gifts. It is essential
    that she herself take them from you.
    Hurry! And bring back the good news
    that you have made your mother's wish come true.   950
          [*Exit* JASON, *the boys, and the* TUTOR.]
CHORUS   No more hoping that those children will live.
    No more, for they are on the road to murder.
    The bride will reach out for the golden chains,
    poor thing, she'll reach out for her doom.
    With her own hands she will place in her hair   955
    the finery of Death.

    Lured by their lovely unearthly glow
    she'll put on the dress and the wrought-gold crown
    and make her marriage in the world below.
    That is the trap into which she will fall,   960
    poor thing, she will follow her destiny,
    inescapable Death.

And you, unlucky groom,
new member of the royal house,
you are not able to see   965
that you're leading your boys to their life's end,
and bringing a hateful death to your bride.
You have no idea of your fate.

And you, poor mother of these boys,
I also grieve for you,   970
since you are set on making them die
because of the bed which your husband left.
He thoughtlessly abandoned you
and lives with another wife.
              [*Enter the boys and the* TUTOR.]
TUTOR   Mistress! The boys are spared the fate of exile!   975
The princess gladly accepted the gifts
with her own hands. She is on their side.
But . . .
why are you upset at this good fortune?
[Why have you turned your face away?   980
Why aren't you happy with what I'm saying?]
MEDEA   Oh no!
TUTOR   That doesn't fit with the news I brought.
MEDEA   Oh no, oh no!
TUTOR   What is it that I don't understand?   985
Was I wrong to think I was bringing good news?
MEDEA   You bring the news you bring. It's not your fault.
TUTOR   But why are you crying and turning away?
MEDEA   I can't help it, old friend. Terrible plans
have been devised by the gods—and by me.   990
TUTOR   The boys' good standing here will bring you back.
MEDEA   First I, in my grief, will bring others down.
TUTOR   Other mothers have been torn from their children.
You are mortal and must accept misfortune.
MEDEA   Yes, yes, I will. Now you go inside.   995
Take care of whatever the boys might need.
              [*Enter the* TUTOR *into the house.*]
O boys, boys, you still have a city,
and a home where, leaving me for good,
you will be cut off from your unhappy mother.
I will be an exile in a foreign land   1000
without the delight of watching you thrive,
without the joy of preparing your weddings,
tending the bath and the bed, lifting the torches.[8]
How much my own strong will has cost me!
I get nothing, boys, from raising you,   1005

8. Torches were an important feature of ancient weddings, which took place at night.

from running myself ragged with endless work.
The birth pangs I endured were pointless.
It pains me to think what hopes I had
that you would care for me in old age
and prepare me for burial when I die—   1010
the thing that everyone wants. But now
that happy dream is dead. Deprived of you,
I will live out my life in bitter grief.
And you will embark on a different life
with no more loving eyes for your mother.   1015
But why, why, boys, are you looking at me?
Why do you smile for this one last time?
Oh, what should I do? I lost heart, my friends,
as soon as I saw their beaming faces.
I can't do it. So much for my plans!   1020
I will take the boys away from here.
Why make them suffer to hurt their father
if it means I suffer twice as much myself?
I can't do that. So much for my plans!
But wait! Can I really bear to be laughed at   1025
and let my enemies go unpunished?
I have to steel myself. I can't be weak
and let those tender thoughts take over.
Children, into the house. And anyone
who is out of place at my sacrifice   1030
can stay away. I will not spare my hand.
But oh . . .
My angry heart, do not go through with this.
For all your pain, let the children live.
They can be with you and bring you joy.   1035
And yet—by the vengeful spirits of deepest Hades—[9]
there is no way I can allow my enemies
to seize my children and to mistreat them.
[It is certain that they have to die. And so
I should kill them, since I gave them life.]   1040
It is all in place: she cannot escape;
the crown is on her head; the royal bride
revels in her new dress. I heard it clearly.
Having set out myself on the darkest road
I will send my sons down one that's even darker.   1045
I will talk to them. Give me, my children,
give me, your mother, your hands to kiss.
Oh this hand! this mouth! this face!
Oh my dear ones, my noble sons!
Be happy—but there. Your father wrecked   1050
what we had here. Oh the joy of holding them,
of their tender skin, of their sweet breath.

9. The Furies.

Go in! Go in! I can no longer bear
to look at you. My grief is too strong.
I see the horror of what I am doing,   1055
but anger overwhelms my second thoughts—
anger, boundless source of evil.
        [*Exit the boys into the house.*]

CHORUS   I have often entered into
complicated trains of thought,
and pursued much deeper questions   1060
than women are supposed to tackle.
For there's a Muse that favors me
and confers the gift of wisdom,
not on all, but on a few—
[you'll find some women here and there]   1065
who are not strangers to that Muse.
So I can say that those who never
find themselves producing children
are more fortunate by far
than those who do.   1070
The childless never need to ask
whether children are in the end,
a curse or blessing in human life;
and since they have none of their own,
they are spared a world of trouble.   1075
Those parents who are blessed
with houses full of growing children
are constantly worn out by worry:
will they be able to raise them well
and leave behind enough to live on?   1080
And all along it isn't clear
whether after all this care
they'll turn out well or badly.
Then there is one final drawback,
the hardest thing of all to bear.   1085
When the parents find a way
to give their children what they need
to grow up strong and honest,
but then luck turns: death scoops them up
and carries their bodies down to Hades.   1090
What possible good can it do
for the gods to impose on us
this bitter, bitter sorrow
as the price of having children?

MEDEA   My friends, I have been waiting a long time now   1095
wondering how things would turn out in there.
But now I see one of Jason's servants
coming towards us. He is breathing hard,
and it's clear he has something grim to report.
        [*Enter the* MESSENGER.]

MESSENGER [Oh you have done a dreadful, lawless thing] 1100
  Run, Medea! Run! Make your escape—
  get away in a ship or overland in a carriage.
MEDEA And what has happened that means I should flee?
MESSENGER The royal princess has fallen down dead,
  along with her father, because of your poison. 1105
MEDEA You have brought the most wonderful news.
  I will always think of you as a true friend.
MESSENGER What are you saying? Are you out of your mind?
  You have desecrated the royal hearth,
  and you're glad? Not terrified at what you've done? 1110
MEDEA I have things to say in response to that.
  But please do not rush through your report.
  How exactly did they die? You will make me
  twice as happy if they died horribly.
MESSENGER When your boys and their father first arrived 1115
  at the new couple's house, there was much joy
  among the household slaves. We had been worried,
  but now a rumor was spreading through us
  that you and Jason had patched up your quarrel.
  One kissed their hands, another their golden heads, 1120
  and I in my happiness followed along
  into the women's rooms behind the children.
  The lady who had become our new mistress
  did not see at first that your sons were there;
  she just gazed adoringly at Jason. 1125
  But then suddenly she shut her eyes
  and turned her delicate face away,
  disgusted by the children's presence.
  But your husband mollified the girl,
  saying, "They are family, don't reject them, 1130
  let your anger go, look this way again;
  can't you treat your husband's kin as your own,
  accept their gifts, and ask your father
  to spare the boys from exile for my sake?"
  She relented when she saw those fine presents, 1135
  and granted him everything he asked.
  As soon as the boys and their father had left,
  she seized that elegant dress and put it on;
  she placed the golden crown on her head
  and arranged her hair in a shining mirror 1140
  smiling at her reflected features.
  Then she jumped up from her chair and ran
  all over the house on her little white feet,
  delighted with her presents; she kept looking down
  to see how the dress fell against her ankle. 1145
  But then we saw something truly horrible:
  her color changed; she staggered sideways
  on shaking legs; she nearly hit the ground

as she fell backwards into a chair.
An older woman, thinking at first 1150
that she was possessed by some god like Pan,[1]
raised a shout of joy. But then she saw
the foaming mouth, the skin drained of blood,
the eyeballs twisting in their sockets.
She countered that shout of joy with a shriek 1155
of woe. One slave girl rushed to the father's room;
another went straight to tell the husband
about his bride's collapse. The whole house rang
with the sound of their frantic footsteps.
In the time it would take a swift runner 1160
to cover the last lap of a footrace,
she came out of her speechless, sightless trance
with an awful, chilling cry of pain.
She was under a double assault:
the golden crown she had put in her hair 1165
spewed out a torrent of consuming flames,
while those fine robes she got from your children
were eating away at her pale flesh.
Burning in flames, she leapt up from her chair
and shook her head from side to side 1170
trying to throw off the crown. But the bands
held tight, and all of her shaking
only made the flames blaze twice as high.
She gave up the struggle and fell to the floor.
Only a parent would have known who she was. 1175
You really couldn't make out her eyes
or the shape of her face. From the top of her head
blood mixed with fire was streaming down;
the flesh flowed off her bones like pine sap,
loosened by the fangs of your unseen poison, 1180
a horrible sight. No one wanted to touch
the corpse. Her fate taught us caution.
But her poor father came in without warning;
he entered the room and found the body.
He began to wail and took it in his arms, 1185
kissed it, and spoke to it: "My poor child,
what god has destroyed you in this cruel way,
making me lose you when I'm at death's door?
All I want is to die with you, dear child."
When he stopped lamenting and tried to stand, 1190
he got tangled up in those silky robes,
like a laurel shoot encircled by ivy.
It was a horrible sort of wrestling match:
he kept struggling to get up on his legs
while she held him back. He pulled hard 1195

1. Half-man, half-goat, a pastoral god associated with wild, ecstatic behavior [translator's note].

but the flesh just came off his old bones.
In the end, he stopped fighting for his life,
worn out, no longer equal to the ordeal.
Two corpses lie there, the girl and her father
[nearby, a disaster that cries out for tears].   1200
I won't go into what this means for you;
you'll find out what penalty you have to pay.
The old truth comes home to me again:
human life is an empty shadow.
People who believe themselves to be   1205
the deepest thinkers are the biggest fools.
There isn't anyone who is truly blessed.
Rich people may be luckier than others
but I wouldn't really call them blessed.

     [*Exit the* MESSENGER.]

CHORUS   A god is giving Jason what he deserves: 1210
trouble after trouble in a single day.
[Poor girl, poor daughter of Creon,
I feel for you: you have been sent
to Hades to pay for Jason's marriage.]
MEDEA   Friends! My plan is clear: as fast as I can   1215
I will kill my sons and leave this land.
I cannot hold back and let those boys
be slaughtered by someone who loves them less.
They have to die, so it is only right
that I who gave them life should kill them.   1220
Arm yourself, my heart! Don't hesitate
to do the unavoidable awful thing.
I must pick up the sword and step across
the starting line of a painful course.
No weakening, no thoughts of the boys—   1225
how sweet they are, how you gave them birth.
Forget your children for this one day;
grieve afterwards. Even if you kill them,
they still are loved—by you, unlucky woman.

     [*Exit* MEDEA *into the house.*]

CHORUS   Look, Mother Earth and Radiant Sun,   1230
look at this deadly woman,
before she can raise her hand
to spill the blood of her children,
descendants of your golden line.
I dread to think of immortal blood   1235
shed by mortal hands!
Hold her back, Zeus-born light! Make her stop!
Get this miserable murderous Fury
out of the house!

All for nothing, your labor in childbirth,   1240
   all for nothing, your dearly loved children,

you who passed through the perilous border
of the dark-faced Clashing Rocks.
Why has relentless anger
settled in your heart,   1245
why this rage for death upon death?
The stain of kindred blood weighs heavy.
The gods send the killers evil pains
to echo evil crimes.

FIRST BOY (*in the house*)   No! No!   1250

CHORUS   Do you hear? Do you hear that child's cry?
Oh that wretched, ill-starred woman!

FIRST BOY   Help! How do I get away from our mother?

SECOND BOY   I don't know how. There's no escape.

CHORUS   Should I go in? I might prevent   1255
those boys from dying.

FIRST BOY   Yes, by the gods, yes! Help us now!

SECOND BOY   She has us cornered with her sword.

CHORUS   Wretched woman, made of stone, made of iron!
I see you really have it in you   1260
to turn your deadly hand
against the boys you bore yourself.

I have only heard of one other woman,
who raised her hand against her children:
Ino, driven wild by Zeus' wife[2]   1265
who made her wander far from home.
Poor woman, she plunged into the sea,
and dragged her children to unholy death.
Stepping over the seacliff's edge,
she died along with her two sons.   1270
Is any awful thing impossible now?
How much disaster has been caused
by the pain of women in marriage!

          [*Enter* JASON]

JASON   You women there beside the house,
is Medea inside, the perpetrator   1275
of these terrible crimes? Has she escaped?
Unless she burrows deep in the earth
or else grows wings and flies through the air,
the royal family will make her pay.
After she killed such powerful people,   1280
does she think she can get away scot-free?
Still, I'm mainly worried about the children.
Those she abused can do the same to her,

---

2. Ino, a daughter of Cadmus, king of Thebes, was driven mad by Dionysos to participate— along with Cadmus's mother—in the dismemberment of her nephew, Pentheus. Later, she was married to King Athamas and, driven mad by Hera, she leapt into the sea with one or more of their sons.

but I am here now to save my boys.
More suffering for me if Creon's kinsmen   1285
try to punish them for their mother's crime.

CHORUS   Poor man, you don't know all of your troubles,
or you would not have said what you just did.

JASON   What is it? Does she want to kill me too?

CHORUS   The boys are dead. Their mother killed them.   1290

JASON   What are you saying? Those words are death to me.

CHORUS   Don't think of your children as among the living.

JASON   She killed them . . . where? In the house or outside?

CHORUS   If you open the doors, you will see how they died.

JASON   Servants, draw back these bolts at once,   1295
open the doors, so I can see both evils:
the slain children and the woman I will punish.

[*Enter* MEDEA *in a winged chariot above the house, with the boys' bodies.*][3]

MEDEA   Why do you keep banging on the doors
to get at the boys and me who killed them?
Don't exert yourself. If you have something to say,   1300
I'm here, go ahead. But you'll never touch me.
This chariot from my grandfather the Sun
protects me from an enemy's hands.

JASON   You abomination, most hateful of women
to the gods, to me, to the whole human race.   1305
You were actually able to drive a sword
into sons you had borne; you've made me childless.
How can you live and see the light of the sun,
when you have committed this sacrilege
and ought to be dead? Now I see what I missed   1310
when I brought you from that barbarian place
into a Greek home. You are an evil being:
you betrayed your father and your native land.
The gods are crushing me for what you did
when you killed your brother at the family hearth   1315
before you boarded the beautiful *Argo*.
That's how you started. Then you married me,
you bore me children and you killed them
just because of some sexual grievance.
No Greek woman would ever do that.   1320
To think I bound myself to you instead
in a hateful, ruinous marriage
with an inhuman wife, a lioness
more savage than Etruscan Scylla.[4]
All the angry words I could hurl at you   1325
carry no sting, you are so brazen.

---

3. The stage mechanism used in the original production would have been the *mechane*, a crane typically used for divine appearances in Athenian tragedy.

4. Scylla is the sea monster near Etruria (modern-day Italy) who threatens Odysseus and his men in the *Odyssey*.

To hell with you, you filthy child-killer!
All that is left for me is to mourn my fate;
I have lost the joy of my new marriage;
the children that I fathered and brought up   1330
are gone. I'll never speak with them again.

MEDEA   I could refute your speech at length,
but Father Zeus already knows
how you were treated by me and what you did.
There is no way you could reject my bed   1335
and lead a happy life laughing at me,
you or the princess, no way that Creon
who arranged all this could throw me out
and not pay the price. So call me a lion,
or Scylla lurking on the Etruscan plain,   1340
I've done what I had to: I've pierced your heart.

JASON   But it hurts you too, you share in this pain.

MEDEA   The pain is worth it if it kills your laughter.

JASON   O children, what a vicious mother you had!

MEDEA   O boys, your father's disease destroyed you!   1345

JASON   It was not my hand that slaughtered them.

MEDEA   No, your arrogance and your brand-new marriage.

JASON   You really think sex was a reason to kill them?

MEDEA   You think being spurned is trivial for a woman?

JASON   Yes, if she's sensible. You resent everything.   1350

MEDEA   Well, they are gone, and that will bite deep.

JASON   Oh, but they will avenge themselves on you.

MEDEA   The gods know which of us started this trouble.

JASON   Yes, they know your mind and it disgusts them.

MEDEA   Hate all you want. I loathe the sound of your voice.   1355

JASON   And I loathe yours. We won't find it hard to part.

MEDEA   Then what's to be done? I too am eager for that.

JASON   Let me bury these bodies and weep for them.

MEDEA   Absolutely not. I will bury them myself
in the shrine of Hera of the Rocky Heights,   1360
where none of my enemies can get at them
or wreck their graves. Here in the land of Sisyphus[5]
I will institute a procession and sacred rites
as atonement for this unholy murder.[6]
Then I'll be off to the city of Erechtheus[7]   1365
to live with Aegeus, Pandion's son.
You will have a fitting death for a coward,
hit on the head by a piece of the *Argo*—
the bitter consequence of marrying me.

5. Corinth. Sisyphus was a notorious traitor, punished in the underworld for his deceitfulness by having to push a rock eternally up a hill, never managing to get it to the top without its rolling back down.
6. There was a sacred cult dedicated to "Hera of the rocky heights" at Corinth.
7. I.e., Athens.

JASON   Let a Fury rise up to avenge these boys,   1370
   and Justice that punishes bloodshed.

MEDEA   What god or spirit listens to you?
   You broke your oaths, you betrayed a friend!

JASON   Ha! Abomination! Child-killer!

MEDEA   Just go home and bury your wife.   1375

JASON   I am going, and without my children.

MEDEA   This grief is nothing. Wait till you're old.

JASON   O my children, so much loved!

MEDEA   By their mother, not by you.

JASON   And then you killed them?

MEDEA   To punish you.

JASON   Oh the misery! I just want to kiss them,   1380
   to hold them in my arms.

MEDEA   Now you want to hug them, talk to them,
   when before you shoved them aside.

JASON   By the gods,
   just let me touch their soft skin.

MEDEA   Not possible. Your words are useless.   1385

JASON   Zeus, do you hear? I am shut out,
   dismissed by this vicious animal,
   this lioness stained with children's blood.
   With all my being I grieve for them
   and summon the gods to witness   1390
   how you destroyed my children,
   and will not let me touch their bodies
   or bury them in proper tombs.
   I wish I had never fathered them
   to see them slaughtered by you.   1395

     [*Exit* MEDEA *in the chariot.*]

CHORUS   In all that Olympian Zeus watches over,
   Much is accomplished that we don't foresee.
   What we expect does not come about;
   the gods clear a path for the unexpected.
   That is how things happened here.   1400

ARISTOPHANES

ca. 450–385 B.C.E.

Aristophanes is the only comic poet from fifth-century B.C.E Athens whose writing has survived. His plays work on many levels: they combine the most basic kinds of humor (obscene sexual and scatalogical jokes, as well as physical comedy and farce) with sharp political and social satire, literary allusions and parodies, strange flights of fantasy (such as choruses of talking animals and topsy-turvy scenarios that turn the known world upside-down), and beautiful passages of poetry. His dramas, of which eleven survive complete, tell us a great deal about the attitudes of fifth-century Athenians and are still funny today.

LIFE AND TIMES

We know little about Aristophanes' life, beyond the fact that he was a prolific comic dramatist. In the small city-state of Athens, he was personally acquainted with the leading writers, thinkers, and politicians of his day, including those whom he satirized in his plays. Aristophanes was fairly successful in his own lifetime: he won first prize in several of the dramatic competitions at which his work was performed.

Most of Aristophanes' work dates from the years of the Peloponnesian War (431–404 B.C.E.). The war, in fact, is one of his main comic targets, as are the political demagogues, and newfangled thinkers and writers, whom Aristophanes presents as responsible for the decline in traditional moral values. Figures who are mocked repeatedly in these plays include Socrates, who is presented as a sophist with dangerous ideas that may corrupt the young and bring down traditional democratic Athens; **Euripides**, the tragedian, who is shown as

similarly corrupting in his depiction of loose women and blasphemous religious ideas; and Cleon, the demagogue, who supposedly misleads the common people and stirs them up for war. It is easy to see Aristophanes, throughtout, his career, as a conservative or traditionalist: someone who objected to the city's expensive military and imperial ambitions and spoke out against new ideas and styles of literature. But Aristophanes was also willing to mock the traditionalists and to suggest revolutionary ideas of his own. In Aristophanic comedy, the hero typically upsets the status quo to produce extraordinary results, including an ending in which dreams come true. For instance, in *Birds* (414 B.C.E.), two Athenians, tired of the war and taxes, go off to found a new city; they organize the birds, who cut off the smoke of sacrifice that the gods live on, and force Zeus to surrender the government of the universe to the birds. The audience may be left doubtful about how the crazy, utopian, or dystopian world of comic fantasy measures up against reality. How seriously can we take Aristophanes as a political writer? Were his plays meant to raise a laugh? Or were they designed to change the way Athenians thought, talked, and voted? These possibilities are not, of course, incompatible.

LYSISTRATA

Lysistrata has a particularly appealing premise: the women of Athens and Sparta decide to go on sex strike in order to stop the Peloponnesian War. When the play was first performed (in 411 B.C.E.), the Athenian fleet had recently been destroyed in the Sicilian Expedition (413 B.C.E.); many citizens lost their lives, while others were enslaved, and the economic as well as military consequences for the city were disastrous. Athenian victory now seemed unlikely, and public sentiment had begun to turn against the war. In this play the Athenian women, who have no political rights, seize the Acropolis, the repository of the city's treasury, and leave the men without sex or the money to carry on the war. They coordinate similar revolutions in all the Greek cities, including Sparta. The men are eventually "starved" into submission, and the Spartans come to Athens to end the war.

Aristophanes does not miss any of the comic possibilities inherent in his plot. Myrrhine's teasing game with her husband, Kinesias, for example, is classic theater, and the final appearance of the rigid Spartan ambassadors and their equally tense Athenian hosts is a visual and verbal climax of astonishing brilliance. But serious issues are also at stake. Lysistrata, whose name means "Disbander of Armies," is a true heroine, presented in entirely positive terms; it is hard not to feel that she is right to try to stop the Peloponnesian War.

Lysistrata makes us ask important questions not just about this war but about war in general. Why do the men insist on pursuing this "futile war," for which none of them can give a reasonable justification? To stop is "unthinkable," but nobody can explain why. Aristophanes suggests that the dirty secret of imperialism is that war and territorial aggression are a substitute for sex, and vice versa. The great expression of this diagnosis is the scene in which the Athenian and Spartan ambassadors divide up the naked body of Reconciliation, personified as a beautiful woman; they relate her various anatomical features to territories of Greece over which their cities were fighting. The concept is at once devastatingly accurate and, one could argue, an oversimplification. Such reductiveness is characteristic of comedy, which—in contrast to tragedy—offers us the reassurance that our craziest wishful fantasies can, somehow, come true.

The play raises similarly important questions about the social position of women. Ancient Athens was a particularly patriarchal society: elite women rarely left the house except for funerals or religious festivals, and women had no political rights—they were not citizens, and could not vote. *Lysistrata* seems to make the radical suggestion that things might go a lot better if women, not men, were in charge of the city. Lysistrata declares that "war shall be the business of womenfolk": it is too important a matter to be left to men, for women are its real victims. When asked what the women will do, she explains that they will treat politics just as they do wool in their household tasks: "unsnarling" it. The traditional tasks of women, including spinning and weaving, train one in the patient management of details, and this kind of skill, Lysistrata suggests, is precisely what is missing from the masculine headlong pursuit of war. Here and throughout the play, Aristophanes works with gender stereotypes, both inviting us to see the world through them and holding them up to good-natured ridicule. In her level-headed reasonableness and her common-sense commitment to peace, Lysistrata is the exception, not the norm. Most of the female characters in the play are obsessed with wine and sex. They are tricky and deceitful, always probing for men's weaknesses; they pose an obstacle to the conduct of serious political business. So men say, and the women in this play admit it. But trickery and deceit are here enlisted in the service of peace—in contrast to their destructive effects in, for example, Euripides' **Medea**. It is difficult to know how seriously we should take the play's apparent proto-feminism. Is Aristophanes really urging his male fellow citizens to let their wives take over the running of politics? Or is the idea of a government of women simply an argument ad absurdum: if men behave so crazily, could women do worse?

We do not know what the Athenians thought of the play. All we know is that they were not swayed by its serious undertone; the war continued for seven more exhausting years, until Athens's last fleet was defeated, the city was laid open to the enemy, and the empire was lost.

A NOTE ON THE TRANSLATION

The translation here is by the classical scholar Jeffrey Henderson. He renders Aristophanes' verse in a lively, colloquial prose. Aristophanes uses a lot of slang, and his language and imagery are sometimes crude, deliberately dirty, or shocking: it is therefore justifiable to render his Greek into vivid, slangy, and sometimes obscene English. Those who do not want to encounter bad language ought to steer clear of this play.

Lysistrata[1]

CHARACTERS

LYSISTRATA, an Athenian woman
KALONIKE, Lysistrata's friend
MYRRHINE, an Athenian wife
LAMPITO, a Spartan wife
MAGISTRATE, one of the ten Probouloi
OLD WOMEN (three), allies of Lysistrata

WIVES (four), Lysistrata's conspirators
KINESIAS, Myrrhine's husband
BABY, son of Kinesias and Myrrhine
SPARTAN HERALD
SPARTAN AMBASSADOR
ATHENIAN AMBASSADORS (two)

MUTE CHARACTERS

ATHENIAN WOMEN
ISMENIA, a Theban woman
KORINTHIAN WOMAN
SPARTAN WOMEN
SKYTHIAN GIRL, Lysistrata's slave
MAGISTRATE'S SLAVES
SKYTHIAN POLICEMEN
OLD WOMEN, allies of Lysistrata

MANES, Kinesias' slave
SPARTAN DELEGATES
SPARTAN SLAVES, with the
    Spartan delegation
ATHENIAN DELEGATES
RECONCILIATION
DOORKEEPER

CHORUS

OLD ATHENIAN MEN (twelve)

OLD ATHENIAN WOMEN (twelve)

Prologue

[SCENE: *A neighborhood street in Athens, after dawn. The stage-building has a large central door and two smaller, flanking doors. From one of these* LYSISTRATA *emerges and looks expectantly up and down the street.*]

LYSISTRATA   Now if someone had invited the women to a revel for Bacchos, or to Pan's shrine, or to Genetyllis's at Kolias,[2] they'd be jamming

---

1. Translated by Jeffrey Henderson. This translation uses names for people and places that are closer to the Greek, such as Korinth (Corinth) and Boiotia (Boeotia).
2. Promontory near Athens where stood a statue of Aphrodite, the goddess of beauty and carnal love. "Bacchos": also known as Dionysus, the god of wine. "Pan": goat-footed god of woods and pastures. "Genetyllis": protectress of childbirth (in some accounts, another name for Aphrodite; in others, her companion).

the streets with their tambourines. But now there's not a single woman here. [*The far door opens.*] Except for my own neighbor there. Good morning, Kalonike.[3]

KALONIKE   You too, Lysistrata.[4] What's bothering you? Don't frown, child. Knitted brows are no good for your looks.

LYSISTRATA   But my heart's on fire, Kalonike, and I'm terribly annoyed about us women. You know, according to the men we're capable of all sorts of mischief—

KALONIKE   And that we are, by Zeus![5]

LYSISTRATA   but when they're told to meet here to discuss something that really matters, they're sleeping in and don't show up!

KALONIKE   Honey, they'll be along. For wives to get out of the house is a lot of trouble, you know: we've got to look after the husband or wake up a slave or put the baby to bed, or give it a bath or feed it a snack.

LYSISTRATA   Sure, but there's other business they ought to take more seriously than that stuff.

KALONIKE   Well, Lysistrata dear, what exactly *is* this business you're calling us women together for? What's the deal? Is it a big one?

LYSISTRATA   Big!

KALONIKE   Not hard as well?

LYSISTRATA   It's big *and* hard, by Zeus.

KALONIKE   Then how come we're not all here?

LYSISTRATA   That's not what I meant! If it were, we'd all have shown up fast enough. No, it's something I've been thinking hard *about*, kicking it around, night after sleepless night.

KALONIKE   All those kicks must have made it really smart.

LYSISTRATA   Smart enough that the salvation of all Greece lies in the women's hands!

KALONIKE   In the *women's* hands? That's hardly reassuring!

LYSISTRATA   It's true: our country's future depends on *us*: whether the Peloponnesians[6] become extinct—

KALONIKE   Well, that would be just fine with me, by Zeus!

LYSISTRATA   and all the Boiotians[7] get annihilated—

KALONIKE   Not *all* of them, though: please spare the eels![8]

LYSISTRATA   I won't say anything like that about the Athenians, but you know what I *could* say. But if the women gather together here—the Boiotian women, the Peloponnesian women, and ourselves—together we'll be able to rescue Greece!

KALONIKE   But what can mere *women* do that's intelligent or noble? We sit around the house looking pretty, wearing saffron dresses and makeup and Kimberic[9] gowns and canoe-sized slippers.

---

3. A name meaning "beautiful victory."
4. A name meaning "disbander of armies."
5. King of the Greek gods.
6. Inhabitants of Peloponnesos, the peninsula that forms the southern Greek mainland, with whom Athens was at war; they were led by Sparta.

7. That is, the Thebans in Boiotia, northwest of Athens, its other main opponents in the Peloponnesian War.
8. A delicacy native to Boiotia.
9. Kimberic is presumably a reference to the style of dress of the ancient Germanic or Celtic tribes known as the Cimbri (Kimbri).

LYSISTRATA   Exactly! That's exactly what I think will rescue Greece: our fancy little dresses, our perfumes and our slippers, our rouge and our see-through underwear! 45

KALONIKE   How do you mean? I'm lost.

LYSISTRATA   They'll guarantee that not a single one of the men who are still alive will raise his spear against another—

KALONIKE   Then, by the Two Goddesses,[1] I'd better get my party dress 50 dyed saffron!

LYSISTRATA   nor hoist his shield—

KALONIKE   I'll wear a Kimberic gown!

LYSISTRATA   nor even pull a knife!

KALONIKE   I've got to buy some slippers! 55

LYSISTRATA   So shouldn't the women have gotten here by now?

KALONIKE   By *now*? My god, they should have taken wing and flown here ages ago!

LYSISTRATA   My friend, you'll see that they're typically Athenian: everything they do, they do too late. There isn't even a single woman here 60 from the Paralia, nor from Salamis.[2]

KALONIKE   Oh, them: I just *know* they've been up since dawn, straddling their mounts.

LYSISTRATA   And the women I reckoned would be here first, and counted on, the women from Acharnai,[3] they're not here either. 65

KALONIKE   Well, Theogenes' wife, for one, was set to make a fast getaway. [*Groups of women begin to enter from both sides.*] But look, here come some of your women now!

LYSISTRATA   And here come some others, over there!

KALONIKE   Phew! Where are *they* from? 70

LYSISTRATA   From Dungstown.

KALONIKE   It seems they've got some sticking to their shoes.

MYRRHINE   I hope we're not too late, Lysistrata. What do you say? Why don't you say something?

LYSISTRATA   Myrrhine,[4] I've got no medal for anyone who shows up late for important business. 75

MYRRHINE   Look, I couldn't find my girdle; it was dark. But now we're here, so tell us what's so important.

LYSISTRATA   No, let's wait a little while, until the women from Boiotia and the Peloponnesos come.

MYRRHINE   That's a much better plan. And look, there's Lampito coming 80 now!

[*Enter* LAMPITO, *accompanied by a group of other Spartan women, a Theban woman* (ISMENIA) *and a Korinthian woman.*]

---

1. Demeter, goddess of agriculture, and her daughter Persephone or Kore (the Maiden), queen of the underworld; both were associated with fertility and women.
2. Island in the Aegean Sea near Athens. "Paralia": a district on the coast of Attica, the

region in which Athens is located (literally, "seacoast").
3. A district near Athens.
4. A name meaning "myrtle," which was also a slang term for the vulva.

LYSISTRATA   Greetings, my very dear Spartan Lampito! My darling, how
dazzling is your beauty! What rosy cheeks, what firmness of physique!
You could choke a bull!

LAMPITO   Is true, I think, by Twain Gods. Much exercise, much leaping   85
to harden buttocks.[5]

KALONIKE   And what a beautiful pair of boobs you've got!

LAMPITO   Hey, you feel me up like sacrificial ox!

LYSISTRATA   And this other young lady here, where's *she* from?

LAMPITO   By Twain Gods, she come as representative of Boiotia.   90

MYRRHINE   She's certainly *like* Boiotia, by Zeus, with all her lush bottomland.

KALONIKE   Yes indeed, her bush has been most elegantly pruned.

LYSISTRATA   And who's this other girl?

LAMPITO   Lady of substance, by Twain Gods, from Korinth.[6]

KALONIKE   She's substantial all right, both frontside and backside.   95

LAMPITO   Who convenes this assembly of women here?

LYSISTRATA   I'm the one.

LAMPITO   Then please to tell what you want of us.

KALONIKE   That's right, dear lady, speak up. What's this important business of yours?   100

LYSISTRATA   I'm ready to tell you. But before I tell you, I want to ask you
a small question; it won't take long.

KALONIKE   Ask away.

LYSISTRATA   Don't you all pine for your children's fathers when they're
off at war? I'm sure that every one of you has a husband who's away.   105

KALONIKE   My husband's been away five months, my dear, at the Thracian front; he's guarding Eukrates.[7]

MYRRHINE   And *mine's* been at Pylos[8] *seven* whole months.

LAMPITO   And *mine*, soon as he come home from regiment, is strapping
on the shield and flying off.   110

KALONIKE   Even *lovers* have disappeared without a trace, and ever since
the Milesians[9] revolted from us, I haven't even seen a six-inch dildo,
which might have been a consolation, however small.

LYSISTRATA   Well, if I could devise a plan to end the war, would you be
ready to join me?   115

KALONIKE   By the Two Goddesses, I would, even if I had to pawn this
dress and on the very same day—drink up the proceeds!

MYRRHINE   And *I* think I would even cut myself in two like a flounder
and donate half to the cause!

LAMPITO   And I would climb up to summit of Taÿgeton,[1] if I'm able to   120
see where peace may be from there.

---

5. Spartan women, unlike their counterparts
in other polities, received an education similar
to that of men, including physical training.
Throughout, Aristophanes caricatures the
Doric dialect of the Spartans, which differed
notably from the Attic-Ionic Greek of the
Athenians. "Twain Gods": the twins Kastor and
Pollux, sons of Leda, Zeus, and Tyndareos,
king of Sparta, and patrons of the Spartans.
6. A city-state in the northern Peloponnesos;

like Sparta and Thebes, a rival of Athens.
7. An Athenian general; Thrace, a region in
northeastern Greece, was an ally of Athens, and
many battles were fought there during the war.
8. A district in the southern Peloponnesos,
occupied by the Athenians since 425 B.C.E.
9. The inhabitants of Miletus, a Greek city-
state on the coast of Asia Minor (present-day
Turkey) that revolted from Athens in 412 B.C.E.
1. A mountain range near Sparta.

LYSISTRATA   Here goes, then; no need to beat around the bush. Ladies, if we're going to force the men to make peace, we're going to have to give up—

KALONIKE   Give up what? Tell us.   125

LYSISTRATA   You'll do it, then?

KALONIKE   We'll do it, even if it means our death!

LYSISTRATA   All right. We're going to have to give up—cock. Why are you turning away from me? Where are you going? Why are you all pursing your lips and shaking your heads? What means thine altered color and 130 tearful droppings?[2] Will you do it or not? What are you waiting for?

KALONIKE   Count me out; let the war drag on.

MYRRHINE   Me too, by Zeus; let the war drag on.

LYSISTRATA   This from you, Ms. Flounder?[3] Weren't you saying just a moment ago that you'd cut yourself in half?   135

KALONIKE   Anything else you want, anything at all! I'm even ready to walk through fire; *that* rather than give up cock. There's nothing like it, Lysistrata dear.

LYSISTRATA   And what about you?

WOMAN   I'm ready to walk through fire, too.   140

LYSISTRATA   Oh what a low and horny race are we! No wonder men write tragedies about us: we're nothing but Poseidon and a bucket.[4] Dear Spartan, if you alone would side with me we might still salvage the plan; give me your vote!

LAMPITO   By Twain Gods, is difficult for females to sleep alone without 145 the hard-on. But anyway, I assent; is need for peace.

LYSISTRATA   You're an absolute dear, and the only real woman here!

KALONIKE   Well, what if we *did* abstain from, uh, what you say, which heaven forbid: would peace be likelier to come on account of *that*?

LYSISTRATA   Absolutely, by the Two Goddesses. If we sat around at home 150 all made up, and walked past them wearing only our see-through underwear and with our pubes plucked in a neat triangle, and our husbands got hard and hankered to ball us, but we didn't go near them and kept away, they'd sue for peace, and pretty quick, you can count on that!

LAMPITO   Like Menelaos! Soon as he peek at Helen's bare melons, he 155 throw his sword away, I think.[5]

KALONIKE   But what if our husbands pay us no attention?

LYSISTRATA   As Pherekrates said, skin the skinned dog.[6]

KALONIKE   Facsimiles are nothing but poppycock. And what if they grab us and drag us into the bedroom by force?   160

LYSISTRATA   Hold on to the door.

KALONIKE   And what if they beat us up?

---

2. The elevated language characteristic of tragedy is here (as often in Greek comedy) used for comic effect.

3. A flounder is a flat fish that looks as if it has been sliced in half.

4. An allusion to the myth of Tyro; after being seduced by Poseidon, god of the sea, she gave birth to twin boys whom she left in a tub by the edge of a river.

5. After the Greeks had captured Troy, Menelaos, king of Sparta, was about to kill his wife Helen for adultery when he was overcome by the beauty of her naked breasts.

6. That is, use a dildo. "Pherekrates": Athenian comic poet (slightly earlier than Aristophanes).

LYSISTRATA   Submit, but disagreeably: men get no pleasure in sex when
they have to force you. And make them suffer in other ways as well.
Don't worry, they'll soon give in. No husband can have a happy life if   165
his wife doesn't want him to.

KALONIKE   Well, if the two of you agree to this, then we agree as well.

LAMPITO   And we shall bring *our* menfolk round to making everyway fair
and honest peace. But how do you keep Athenian rabble from acting like
lunatics?   170

LYSISTRATA   Don't worry, we'll handle the persuasion on *our* side.

LAMPITO   Not so, as long as your battleships are afoot and your Goddess'
temple have bottomless fund of money.[7]

LYSISTRATA   In fact, that's also been well provided for: we're going to
occupy the Akropolis this very day. The older women are assigned that   175
part: while we're working out our agreement down here, they'll occupy
the Akropolis, pretending to be up there for a sacrifice.

LAMPITO   Sounds perfect, like rest of your proposals.

LYSISTRATA   Then why not ratify them immediately by taking an oath,
Lampito, so that the terms will be binding?   180

LAMPITO   Reveal an oath, then, and we all swear to it.

LYSISTRATA   Well said. Where's the Skythian[8] girl? [A SLAVE-GIRL *comes
out of the stage-building with a shield.*] What are you gawking at? Put
that shield down in front of us—no, the other way—and someone give
me the severings.   185

KALONIKE   Lysistrata, what kind of oath are you planning to make us
swear?

LYSISTRATA   What kind? The kind they say Aischylos once had people
swear: slaughtering an animal over a shield.[9]

KALONIKE   Lysistrata, you don't take an oath about peace over a shield!   190

LYSISTRATA   Then what kind of oath will it be?

KALONIKE   What if we got a white stallion somewhere and cut a piece off
him?[1]

LYSISTRATA   White stallion? Get serious.

KALONIKE   Well, how *are* we going to swear the oath?   195

LYSISTRATA   By Zeus, if you'd like to know, I can tell you. We put a big
black wine-bowl hollow-up right here, we slaughter a magnum of Thasian wine into it, and we swear not to pour any water into the bowl![2]

LAMPITO   Oh da, I cannot find words to praise that oath!

LYSISTRATA   Somebody go inside and fetch a bowl and a magnum. [*The*   200
SLAVE-GIRL *takes the shield inside and returns with a large wine-bowl
and a large cup.*]

MYRRHINE   Dearest ladies, what a conglomeration of pottery!

---

7. Athens' treasury—filled with tribute carried back by its navy—was in the Parthenon,
the temple of Athena on the Akropolis.
8. From Skythia, a vast region north and northeast of the Black Sea that was a source of slaves.
9. An allusion to Aeschylus's play *Seven
against Thebes* (467 B.C.E.).
1. A rare and costly sacrifice ("a piece" prob-

ably refers to the penis).
2. Greeks viewed drinking wine mixed with
water as a sign of refinement; the preference
of women for unadulterated wine was a comic
stereotype. "Thasian": from Thasos, an island
in the northern Aegean Sea that was famous
in antiquity for its apple-scented wine.

KALONIKE   [*Grabbing at the bowl*] Just touching this could make a person glad!

LYSISTRATA   Put it down! And join me in laying hands upon this boar.
[*All the women put a hand on the magnum.*] Mistress Persuasion and   205
Bowl of Fellowship, graciously receive this sacrifice from the women.
[*She opens the magnum and pours wine into the bowl.*]

KALONIKE   The blood's a good color and spurts out nicely.

LAMPITO   It smell good too, by Kastor!

MYRRHINE   Ladies, let me be the first to take the oath!

KALONIKE   Hold on, by Aphrodite! Not unless you draw the first lot!   210

LYSISTRATA   *All* of you lay your hands upon the bowl; you too, Lampito.
Now one of you, on behalf of you all, must repeat after me the terms of
the oath, and the rest of you will then swear to abide by them. No man
of any kind, lover or husband—

KALONIKE   No man of any kind, lover or husband—   215

LYSISTRATA   shall approach me with a hard-on. I can't hear you!

KALONIKE   shall approach me with a hard-on. Oh god, my knees are
buckling, Lysistrata!

LYSISTRATA   At home in celibacy shall I pass my life—

KALONIKE   At home in celibacy shall I pass my life—   220

LYSISTRATA   wearing a party-dress and makeup—

KALONIKE   wearing a party-dress and makeup—

LYSISTRATA   so that my husband will get as hot as a volcano for me—

KALONIKE   so that my husband will get as hot as a volcano for me—

LYSISTRATA   but never willingly shall I surrender to my husband.   225

KALONIKE   but never willingly shall I surrender to my husband.

LYSISTRATA   If he should use force to force me against my will—

KALONIKE   If he should use force to force me against my will—

LYSISTRATA   I will submit coldly and not move my hips.

KALONIKE   I will submit coldly and not move my hips.   230

LYSISTRATA   I will not raise my oriental slippers toward the ceiling.

KALONIKE   I will not raise my oriental slippers toward the ceiling.

LYSISTRATA   I won't crouch down like the lioness on a cheesegrater.[3]

KALONIKE   I won't crouch down like the lioness on a cheesegrater.

LYSISTRATA   If I live up to these vows, may I drink from this bowl.   235

KALONIKE   If I live up to these vows, may I drink from this bowl.

LYSISTRATA   But if I break them, may the bowl be full of water.

KALONIKE   But if I break them, may the bowl be full of water.

LYSISTRATA   So swear you one and all?

ALL   So swear we all!   240

LYSISTRATA   All right, then, I'll consecrate the bowl. [*She takes a long
drink.*]

KALONIKE   Only your share, my friend; let's make sure we're all on
friendly terms right from the start.

[*After they drink, a woman's joyful cry is heard offstage.*]

LAMPITO   What's that hurrah?

3. That is, to be mounted. The Greeks often made the handles of household utensils in the
shape of animals.

LYSISTRATA   It's just what I was telling you before: the women have occu-   245
pied the Akropolis and the Goddess' temple. Now, Lampito: you take off
and arrange things in Sparta, but leave these women here with us as
hostages.
[*Exit* LAMPITO.] Meanwhile, we'll go inside with the other women on
the Akropolis and bolt the gates behind us.   250

KALONIKE   But don't you think the men will launch a concerted attack
on us, and very soon?

LYSISTRATA   I'm not worried about *them*. They can't come against us with
enough threats or fire to get these gates open, except on the terms we've
agreed on.   255

KALONIKE   No they can't, by Aphrodite! Otherwise we women wouldn't
deserve to be called rascals you can't win a fight with!
[*All exit into the central door of the scene-building, which now represents
the Akropolis.*]

Parodos⁴

[*A semichorus composed of twelve old men, poorly dressed, slowly makes its way
along one of the wings into the orchestra. Each carries a pair of logs, an unlit
torch and a bucket of live coals.*]

MEN'S LEADER   Onward, Drakes, lead the way, even if your shoulder *is*
sore; you've got to keep toting that load of green olive-wood, no matter
how heavy it is.

MEN (*strophe*)
If you live long enough you'll get many surprises, yes sir!
Strymodoros: who in the world ever thought we'd hear   5
that women, the very creatures we've kept in our homes,
an obvious nuisance, now control the Sacred Image⁵
and occupy *my* Akropolis, and not only that,
they've locked the citadel gates with bolts and bars!

MEN'S LEADER   Let's hurry to the Akropolis, Philourgos, full speed ahead,   10
so we can lay these logs in a circle all around them, around all the
women who have instigated or abetted this business! We'll erect a single pyre and condemn them all with a single vote, then throw them on
top with our own hands, starting with Lykon's wife!

MEN (*antistrophe*)
By Demeter, while I still live they'll never laugh at me!   15
Not even Kleomenes,⁶ the first to occupy this place,
left here intact. No, for all he breathed the Spartan spirit,
he left without his weapons—surrendered to *me*!—
with only a little bitty jacket on his back, starving,
filthy, unshaven, and unwashed for six whole years.   20

MEN'S LEADER   That's the way I laid siege to *that* fellow—savagely! We
kept watch on these gates in ranks seventeen deep. So: am I to stand

---

4. Passage sung or recited when the chorus
enters the orchestra, the circular space in
front of the stage building.
5. A lifesize olive-wood statue of Athena,
housed in the Erechtheum on the Akropolis.
6. A Spartan king who, while attempting to
aid one Athenian faction, briefly occupied the
Akropolis in 508 B.C.E.

by *now* and do nothing to put down the effrontery of these *women*,
enemies of all the gods and of Euripides? If so, take down my trophy
that stands at Marathon![7]   25

MEN (*strophe*)

I'm almost at the end of my trek;
all that remains is the steep stretch
up to the Akropolis; can't wait to get there!
How in the world are we going to haul
these loads up there without a donkey?   30
This pair of logs is utterly crushing my shoulder!
But I've got to soldier on,
and keep my fire alight.
It mustn't go out on me before I've reached my goal.
    [*They blow into their buckets of coals.*]
Ouch, ugh! The smoke!   35

(*antistrophe*)

How terribly, Lord Herakles,[8] this smoke
jumped from the bucket and attacked me!
It bit both my eyes like a rabid bitch!
And as for this fire, it's Lemnian[9]
in every possible way; otherwise   40
it wouldn't have buried its teeth in my eyeballs that way!
Hurry forth to the citadel,
run to the Goddess' rescue!
If this isn't the time to help her, Laches, when will that time be?
    [*They blow on their buckets of coals again.*]
Ouch, ugh! The smoke!   50

MEN'S LEADER   Praise the gods, this fire's awake and plenty lively too.
Let's place our logs right here, then dip our torches into the buckets,
and when they're lighted we'll charge the gates like rams. If the women
don't unbolt the gates when we invite their surrender, we'll set the
portals afire and smoke them into submission. Very well, let's put the   55
logs down. Phew, that smoke! Damn! Would any of the generals at
Samos[1] care to help us with this wood? [*He laboriously wrestles his pair
of logs to the ground.*] They've finally stopped crushing my back! Now
it's *your* job, bucket, to rouse your coals to flame and thus supply me,
first of all, with a lighted torch! Lady Victory,[2] be our ally, help us win   60
a trophy over the women on the Akropolis and their present audacity!
    [*As the men crouch down to light their torches, the second semichorus
    enters on the run. It is composed of twelve old women, nicely dressed and
    carrying pitchers of water on their heads.*]

---

7. Plain about 25 miles northeast of Athens, where Athenians defeated a large invading Persian army in 490 B.C.E. "Euripides" (480–406 B.C.E.), tragedian typically portrayed by Aristophanes as a misogynist.
8. Son of Zeus, a demigod and the greatest of the classical heroes.
9. From Lemnos, a volcanic island sacred to Hephaestus, the blacksmith god, that was controlled by Athens (possibly alluding to the myth of the Lemnian women, who killed their husbands).
1. An island in the eastern Aegean that was serving as a critical Athenian military base.
2. Probably a reference to Athena Nike (Victory), whose temple also stood on the Akropolis.

WOMEN'S LEADER   I think I can see sparks and smoke, fellow women, as
  if a fire were ablaze. We must hurry all the faster!
WOMEN   (strophe)
  Fly, fly, Nikodike,
  before Kalyke and Kritylla are incinerated,   65
  blown from all directions
  by nasty winds and old men who mean death!
  I'm filled with dread: am I too late to help?
  I've just come from the well with my pitcher;
  it was hard to fill by the light of dawn,   70
  in the throng and crash and clatter of pots,
  fighting the elbows of housemaids and branded slaves.
  I hoisted it onto my head with zeal, and carry the water here
  to assist the women, my fellow citizens faced with burning.

(antistrophe)
  I've heard that some frantic old men   75
  are on the loose with three talents[3] of logs,
  like furnace-men at the public bathhouse.
  They're coming to the Akropolis, screaming
  the direst threats, that they mean to use their fire
  "to turn these abominable women into charcoal."   80
  Goddess, may I never see these women in flames;
  instead let them rescue Greece and her citizens from war and madness!
  O golden-crested Guardian of the citadel, that is why
  they occupy your shrine. I invite thee to be our ally, Tritogeneia,[4]
  defending it with water, should any man set it afire.   85
WOMEN'S LEADER   Hold on! Hey! What's this? Men! Awful, nasty men!
  No gentlemen, no god-fearing men would ever be caught doing this!
MEN'S LEADER   This here's a complication we didn't count on facing: this
  swarm of women outside the gates is here to help the others!
WOMEN'S LEADER   Fear and trembling, eh? Don't tell me we seem a lot to   90
  handle: you haven't even seen the tiniest fraction of our forces yet!
MEN'S LEADER   Phaidrias, are we going to let these women go on jabber-
  ing like this? Why hasn't somebody busted a log over their heads?
WOMEN'S LEADER   Let's ground our pitchers then; if anyone attacks us
  they won't get in our way.   95
MEN'S LEADER   By Zeus, if someone had socked them in the mouth a
  couple of times, like Boupalos,[5] they wouldn't still be talking!
WOMEN'S LEADER   Okay, here's my mouth; someone take a sock at it; I'll
  stand here and take it. But then I'm the bitch who gets to grab you by the
  balls!   100
MEN'S LEADER   If you don't shut up, I'll knock you right out of your old
  hide!

3. About 175 pounds.
4. An ancient name of Athena.
5. A sculptor (6th century B.C.E.), born on the
island of Chios, who was subjected to severe
satire and invective by the poet Hipponax.

WOMEN'S LEADER   Come over here and just touch Stratyllis with the tip of your finger.

MEN'S LEADER   What if I give you the one-two punch? Got anything   105
scary to counter with?

WOMEN'S LEADER   I'll rip out your lungs and your guts with my fangs.

MEN'S LEADER   There isn't a wiser poet than Euripides: no beast exists so
shameless as women!

WOMEN'S LEADER   Let's pick up our pitchers of water, Rhodippe.   110

MEN'S LEADER   Why did you bring water here, you witch?

WOMEN'S LEADER   And why have *you* got fire, you tomb? To burn yourself
up?

MEN'S LEADER   *I'm* here to build a pyre and burn up your friends.

WOMEN'S LEADER   And *I've* come to put it out with this.   115

MEN'S LEADER   *You're* going to put out *my* fire?

WOMEN'S LEADER   That's what you soon will see.

MEN'S LEADER   I think I might barbecue you with this torch of mine.

WOMEN'S LEADER   Got any soap with you? I'll give you a bath.

MEN'S LEADER   *You* give *me* a bath, you crone?   120

WOMEN'S LEADER   A bath fit for a bridegroom!

MEN'S LEADER   What insolence!

WOMEN'S LEADER   I'm a free woman!

MEN'S LEADER   I'll put a stop to your bellowing.

WOMEN'S LEADER   You're not on a jury now, you know.[6]   125

MEN'S LEADER   Torch her hair! [*The men advance.*]

WOMEN'S LEADER   Acheloos,[7] do your thing! [*The women douse them.*]

MEN'S LEADER   Oh! Damn!

WOMEN'S LEADER   It wasn't too hot, was it?

MEN'S LEADER   Hot? Stop it! What do you think you're doing?   130

WOMEN'S LEADER   I'm watering you, so you'll bloom.

MEN'S LEADER   But I'm already dried out from shivering!

WOMEN'S LEADER   You've got fire there; why not sit by it and get warm?

Episode[8]

[*Enter the* MAGISTRATE, *an irascible old man, accompanied by two slaves
carrying crowbars and four Skythian policemen.*]

MAGISTRATE   So the women's depravity bursts into flame again: beating
drums, chanting "Sabazios!," worshiping Adonis on the rooftops.[9] I
heard it all once before while sitting in Assembly. Demostratos[1] (bad
luck to him!) was moving that we send an armada to Sicily, while his
wife was dancing and yelling "Poor young Adonis!" Then Demostratos   5
moved that we sign up some Zakynthian[2] infantry, but his wife up on the

6. Paid jury duty provided old men with some financial support.
7. A large river in central Greece.
8. In ancient Greek drama, a scene of action between choral sections.
9. The cults of Sabazios and Adonis, which had come to Athens relatively recently from the East, were especially favored by women.
1. An Athenian orator and proponent of the expedition launched against Syracuse, on the island of Sicily, in 415 B.C.E.; the outcome was a disastrous loss for Athens.
2. From Zakynthos, an island in the Ionian Sea (west of the Peloponnesos) allied to Athens.

roof was getting drunk and going, "Beat your breast for Adonis!" But he
just went on making his motions, that godforsaken, disgusting Baron
Bluster! From women, I say, you get this kind of riotous extravagance!

MEN'S LEADER   [*Pointing to the* CHORUS OF WOMEN] Save your breath   10
till you hear about *their* atrocities! They've committed every kind, even
doused us with those pitchers. Now we get to shake water out of our
clothes as if we'd peed in them!

MAGISTRATE   By the salty sea-god it serves us right! When we ourselves are
accomplices in our wives' misbehavior and teach them profligacy, these   15
are the sort of schemes they bring to flower! Aren't *we* the ones who go to
the shops and say stuff like, "Goldsmith, about that necklace you made
me: my wife was having a ball the other night, and now the prong's
slipped out of its hole. Me, I've got to cruise over to Salamis. So if you've
got time, by all means visit her in the evening and fit a prong in her hole."   20
Another husband says this to a teenage shoemaker with a very grown-up
cock, "Shoemaker, my wife's pinky-toe hurts. It seems the top-strap is
cramping the bottom, where she's tender. So why don't you drop in on
her some lunchtime and loosen it up so there's more play down there?"
That's the sort of thing that's led to *this*, when I, a Magistrate, have lined   25
up timber for oars and now come to get the necessary funds, and find
myself standing at the gate, locked out by women! But I'm not going to
stand around. [*To the two slaves*] Bring the crowbars; I'll put a stop to
their arrogance. What are *you* gaping at, you sorry fool? And where are
you staring? I said crowbar, not winebar! Come on, put those crowbars   30
under the gates and start jimmying on that side; I'll help out on this side.

LYSISTRATA   [*Emerging from the gates*] Don't jimmy the gates; I'm coming out on my very own. Why do you need crowbars? It's not crowbars
you need; it's rather brains and sense.

MAGISTRATE   Really! You witch! Where's a policeman? Grab her and tie   35
both hands behind her back! [*One of the policemen advances on*
LYSISTRATA.]

LYSISTRATA   If he so much as touches me with his fingertip, by Artemis[3]
he'll go home crying, public servant or not! [*The policeman retreats.*]

MAGISTRATE   What, are you scared? [*To a second policeman*] You there,
help him out; grab her around the waist and tie her up, on the double!   40
[*A large* OLD WOMAN *emerges from the gates.*]

FIRST OLD WOMAN   If you so much as lay a hand on her, by Pandrosos[4]
I'll beat the shit out of you! [*Both policemen retreat.*]

MAGISTRATE   Beat the shit out of me! Where's another policeman? [*A
third policeman steps forward.*] Tie *her* up first, the one with the dirty
mouth!   45
[*A* SECOND OLD WOMAN *emerges from the gates.*]

SECOND OLD WOMAN   If you raise your fingertip to her, by our Lady of
Light[5] you'll be begging for an eye-cup! [*The third policeman retreats.*]

---

3. Virgin goddess of the hunt and the wilds,
twin sister of Apollo; she also brings release to
women in childbirth.
4. Daughter of the legendary first king of Ath-

ens; she was worshipped on the Akropolis.
5. This could be Hekate, goddess of the moon
and childbirth, or the alternative moon goddess, Artemis.

MAGISTRATE What's going on? Where's a policeman? [*The fourth police-man steps forward.*] Arrest her. I'll foil *one* of these sallies of yours!

[*A* THIRD OLD WOMAN *emerges from the gates.*]

THIRD OLD WOMAN If you come near her, by Eastern Artemis[6] I'll rip out   50
your hair till it screams! [*The fourth policeman retreats.*]

MAGISTRATE What a terrible setback! I'm out of policemen. But men
must never, ever be worsted by women! Skythians, let's charge them *en
masse*; form up ranks!

[*The four policemen prepare to charge.*]

LYSISTRATA By the Two Goddesses, you'll soon discover that we also   55
have four squadrons of fully armed combat-women, waiting inside!

MAGISTRATE Skythians, twist their arms behind their backs!

[*The policemen advance.*]

LYSISTRATA [*Calling into the Akropolis like a military commander*]
Women of the reserve, come out double-time! Forward, you spawn of
the marketplace, you soup and vegetable mongers! Forward, you land-
ladies, you hawkers of garlic and bread! [*Four squadrons of tough old*   60
*market-women rush out of the Akropolis and, together with the women
already onstage, attack the four policemen.*] Tackle them! Hit them!
Smash them! Call them names, the nastier the better! [*The policemen
run away howling.*] That's enough! Withdraw! Don't strip the bodies!

[*The women of the reserve go back into the Akropolis.*]

MAGISTRATE Terrible! What a calamity for my men!

LYSISTRATA Well, what did you expect? Did you think you were going up   65
against a bunch of slave-girls? Or did you think women lack gall?

MAGISTRATE They've got it aplenty, by Apollo, provided there's a wine-
shop nearby.

MEN'S LEADER You've little to show for all your talk, Magistrate of this
country! What's the point of fighting a battle of words with these   70
beasts? Don't you comprehend the kind of bath they've given us just
now—when we were still in our clothes, and without soap to boot?

WOMEN'S LEADER Well, sir, you shouldn't lift your hand against your
neighbors just anytime you feel like it. If you do, you're going to end up
with a black eye. I'd rather be sitting at home like a virtuous maiden,   75
making no trouble for anyone here, stirring not a single blade of grass.
But if anyone annoys me and rifles my nest, they'll find a wasp inside!

Onstage Debate

MEN (*strophe*)
Zeus, how in the world are we going to deal with these monsters?
They've gone beyond what I can bear! Now it's time for a trial:
together let's find out
what they thought they were doing
when they occupied Kranaos'[7] citadel   5

6. Artemis was worshipped throughout the
Greek world. To the east, in Tauris (the
present-day Crimean Peninsula), that worship
involved orgiastic rites.
7. A mythical king of Athens.

and the great crag of the Akropolis,
a restricted, holy place.

MEN'S LEADER   Question her and don't give in; cross-examine what she says.
It's scandalous to let this sort of behavior go unchallenged.

MAGISTRATE   Here's the first thing I'd like to know, by Zeus: what do you   10
mean by barricading our Akropolis?

LYSISTRATA   To keep the money safe and to keep *you* from using it to
finance the war.

MAGISTRATE   So we're at war on account of the money?

LYSISTRATA   Yes, and the money's why everything else got messed up,   15
too. Peisandros[8] and the others aiming to hold office were always
fomenting some kind of commotion so that they'd be able to steal it. So
let them keep fomenting to their hearts' content: they'll be withdrawing no more money from *this* place.

MAGISTRATE   But what do you plan to do?   20

LYSISTRATA   Don't you see? We'll manage it for you!

MAGISTRATE   *You'll* manage the money?

LYSISTRATA   What's so strange in that? Don't we manage the household
finances for you already?

MAGISTRATE   That's different!   25

LYSISTRATA   How so?

MAGISTRATE   These are *war* funds!

LYSISTRATA   But there shouldn't even *be* a war.

MAGISTRATE   How else are we to protect ourselves?

LYSISTRATA   We'll protect you.   30

MAGISTRATE   *You?*

LYSISTRATA   Yes, us.

MAGISTRATE   What brass!

LYSISTRATA   You'll be protected whether you like it or not!

MAGISTRATE   You're going too far!   35

LYSISTRATA   Angry, are you? We've got to do it anyway.

MAGISTRATE   By Demeter, you've got no right!

LYSISTRATA   You must be saved, dear fellow.

MAGISTRATE   Even if I don't ask to be?

LYSISTRATA   All the more so!   40

MAGISTRATE   And where do *you* get off taking an interest in war and
peace?

LYSISTRATA   We'll tell you.

MAGISTRATE   Well, make it snappy, unless you want to get hurt.

LYSISTRATA   Listen then, and try to control your fists.   45

MAGISTRATE   I can't; I'm so angry I can't keep my hands to myself.

FIRST OLD WOMAN   Then *you're* the one'll get hurt!

MAGISTRATE   Croak those curses at yourself, old bag! [*To* LYSISTRATA]
Start talking.

LYSISTRATA   Gladly. All along, being proper women, we used to suffer in   50
silence no matter what you men did, because you wouldn't let us make a

---

8. Athenian politician, often attacked in comedy for corruption. Soon after the first performance of *Lysistrata*, Peisandros joined an oligarchic faction that seized power, with widespread
violence and confiscations (by 410 B.C.E., democracy was restored).

sound. But you weren't exactly all we could ask for. No, we knew only too well what you were up to, and too many times we'd hear in our homes about a bad decision you'd made on some great issue of state. Then, masking the pain in our hearts, we'd put on a smile and ask you, "How did the Assembly go today? Any decision about a rider to the peace treaty?" And my husband would say, "What's that to you? Shut up!" And I'd shut up.

FIRST OLD WOMAN   I wouldn't have shut up!

MAGISTRATE   If you hadn't shut up you'd have got a beating!

LYSISTRATA   Well, that's why I *did* shut up. Later on we began to hear about even worse decisions you'd made, and then we would ask, "Husband, how come you're handling this so stupidly?" And right away he'd glare at me and tell me to get back to my sewing if I didn't want major damage to my head: "War shall be the business of menfolk,"[9] unquote.

MAGISTRATE   He was right on the mark, by Zeus.

LYSISTRATA   How could he be right, you sorry fool, when we were forbidden to offer advice even when your policy was *wrong*? But *then*—when we began to hear you in the streets openly crying, "There isn't a man left in the land," and someone else saying, "No, by Zeus, not a one"— after *that* we women decided to lose no more time and to band together to save Greece. What was the point of waiting any longer? So, if you're ready to take your turn at listening, we have some good advice, and if you shut up, as we used to, we can put you back on the right track.

MAGISTRATE   *You* put *us*—outrageous! I won't stand for it!

LYSISTRATA   Shut up!

MAGISTRATE   *Me* shut up for *you*? A damned woman, with a veil on your face too?[1] I'd rather die!

LYSISTRATA   If the veil's an obstacle, here, take mine, it's yours, put it on *your* face [*She removes her veil and puts it on the* MAGISTRATE's *head*], and *then* shut up!

FIRST OLD WOMAN   And take this sewing-basket too.

LYSISTRATA   Now hitch up your clothes and start sewing; chew some beans[2] while you work. War shall be the business of womenfolk!

WOMEN'S LEADER   Come away from your pitchers, women: it's our turn to pitch in with a little help for our friends!

WOMEN (*antistrophe*)
Oh yes! I'll dance with unflagging energy;
the effort won't weary my knees.
I'm ready to face anything
with women courageous as these:
they've got character, charm, and guts,
they've got intelligence and heart
that's both patriotic and smart!

WOMEN'S LEADER   Now, most valiant of prickly mommies and spikey grannies, attack furiously and don't let up: you're still running with the wind!

LYSISTRATA   If Eros of the sweet soul and Cyprian Aphrodite imbue our thighs and breasts with desire, and infect the men with sensuous rigidity

---

9. Words spoken by Hector to his wife, Andromache, in the *Iliad* (6.492).

1. Respectable women wore veils in public.

2. The ancient equivalent of gum chewing.

and club-cock, then I believe all Greece will one day call us Disbanders of Battles.[3]

MAGISTRATE What's your plan? 100

LYSISTRATA First of all, we can stop people going to the market fully armed and acting crazy.

FIRST OLD WOMAN Paphian[4] Aphrodite be praised!

LYSISTRATA At this very moment, all around the market, in the pottery shops and the grocery stalls, they're walking around in arms like Kory- 105
bantes![5]

MAGISTRATE By Zeus, a man's got to act like a man!

LYSISTRATA But it's totally ridiculous when he takes a shield with a Gorgon-blazon[6] to buy sardines!

FIRST OLD WOMAN Yes, by Zeus, I saw a long-haired fellow,[7] a cavalry 110
captain, on horseback, getting porridge from an old women and stick-
ing it into his brass hat. Another one, a Thracian, was shaking his shield and spear like Tereus;[8] he scared the fig-lady out of her wits and gulped down all the ripe ones!

MAGISTRATE So how will you women be able to put a stop to such a 115
complicated international mess, and sort it all out?

LYSISTRATA Very easily.

MAGISTRATE How? Show me.

[LYSISTRATA *uses the contents of the basket which the* MAGISTRATE *was given to illustrate her demonstration.*]

LYSISTRATA It's rather like a ball of yarn when it gets tangled up. We hold it this way, and carefully wind out the strands on our spindles, now this 120
way, now that way. That's how we'll wind up this war, if allowed, unsnarling it by sending embassies, now this way, now that way.

MAGISTRATE You really think your way with wool and yarnballs and spindles can stop a terrible crisis? How brainless!

LYSISTRATA I do think so, and if *you* had any brains you'd handle *all* the 125
polis' business the way we handle our wool!

MAGISTRATE Well, how then? I'm all ears.

LYSISTRATA Imagine the polis[9] as fleece just shorn. First, put it in a bath and wash out all the sheep-dung; spread it on a pallet and beat out the riff-raff with a stick and pluck out the thorns; as for those who clump 130
and knot themselves together to snag government positions, card them out and pluck off their heads. Next, card the wool into a basket of unity and goodwill, mixing in everyone. The resident aliens and any other for-

---

3. In Greek, *Lusimachas,* an allusion to Lysim-
ache (literally, "Battle Settler"), then priestess of Athena in Athens; possibly also a pun on the title character's name. "Eros": son of Aphrodite and, like his mother, a deity of carnal love. "Cyprian": of Cyprus, the island onto which the newly born Aphrodite emerged from the sea; also an important center of her cult.
4. Of Paphos, a city on Cyprus that was the site of a famous temple of Aphrodite.
5. Eastern worshippers of the Phrygian god-
dess Cybele, known for ecstatic dancing.
6. Emblem depicting one of the three snake-

haired sisters (common on warriors' shields); the sight of a Gorgon turned all who looked at her to stone.
7. That is, a Spartan; Spartan men tradition-
ally wore their hair long.
8. A mythical Thracian king whose story was told in a tragedy by Sophocles. He raped his sister-in-law Philomela and cut out her tongue, but his wife, Prokne, still learned of the deed and fed him their own son in revenge. All three were turned into birds.
9. The *polis* is the city-state.

eigner who's your friend, and anyone who owes money to the people's treasury, mix them in there, too. And by Zeus, don't forget the cities that are colonies of this land: they're like flocks of your fleece, each one separated from the others. So take all these flocks and bring them together here, joining them all and making one big bobbin. And from this weave a fine new cloak for the people! 135

MAGISTRATE   Isn't it awful how these women go like this with their sticks 140 and like this with their bobbins, when they share none of the war's burdens!

LYSISTRATA   None? You monster! We bear more than our fair share, first of all by giving birth to sons and sending them off to the army—

MAGISTRATE   Enough of that! Let's not open old wounds. 145

LYSISTRATA   Then, when we ought to be having fun and enjoying our bloom of youth, we sleep alone because of the campaigns. And to say no more about *our* case, it pains me to think of the maidens growing old in their rooms.

MAGISTRATE   Men grow old, too, don't they? 150

LYSISTRATA   That's quite a different story. When a man comes home he can quickly find a girl to marry, even if he's a greybeard. But a woman's prime is brief; if she doesn't seize it no one wants to marry her, and she sits at home looking for good omens.

MAGISTRATE   But any man who can still get a hard-on— 155

LYSISTRATA   Why don't you just drop dead? Here's a grave-site; buy a coffin; I'll start kneading you a honeycake.[1] [*Taking off her garland*] Use these as a wreath.

FIRST OLD WOMAN [*Handing him ribbons*]   You can have these from me.

SECOND OLD WOMAN   And this garland from me. 160

LYSISTRATA   All set? Need anything else? Get on the boat, then. Charon[2] is calling your name and you're holding him up!

MAGISTRATE   Isn't it shocking that I'm being treated like this? By Zeus, I'm going straight to the other magistrates to display myself just as I am![3]

LYSISTRATA [*As* MAGISTRATE *exits with his slaves*]   I hope you won't complain 165 about the funeral we gave you. I tell you what: the day after tomorrow, first thing in the morning, we'll perform the third-day offerings at your grave![4]

[*The* WOMEN *exit into the Akropolis.*]

Choral Debate

MEN'S LEADER   No free man should be asleep now! Let's strip for action, men, and meet this emergency! [*The* MEN *remove their jackets.*]

MEN (*strophe a*)
I think I smell much bigger trouble in this,
a definite whiff of Hippias[5] tyranny!
I'm terrified that certain men from Sparta 5

---

1. Traditionally given to the dead as an offering to Cerberus, the three-headed dog that guarded the entrance to the underworld.
2. The boatman who ferried dead souls across the river Styx to the underworld.
3. That is, dressed as both a woman and a corpse.
4. At dawn on the third day after death, the corpse was carried to its grave by a funeral procession, and family members made offerings.
5. A tyrant expelled from Athens in 510 B.C.E., with the help of the Spartan king Kleomenes.

have gathered at the house of Kleisthenes[6]
and scheme to stir up our godforsaken women
to seize the Treasury and my jury-pay,
my very livelihood.

MEN'S LEADER   It's shocking, you know, that they're lecturing the citizens   10
now, and running their mouths—mere women!—about brazen shields.
And to top it all off they're trying to make peace between us and the
men of Sparta, who are no more trustworthy than a starving wolf. Actually, this plot they weave against us, gentlemen, aims at tyranny! Well,
they'll never tyrannize over *me*: from now on I'll be on my guard, I'll   15
"carry my sword in a myrtle-branch" and go to market fully armed right
up beside Aristogeiton.[7] I'll stand beside him like this [*assuming the
posture of Aristogeiton's statue*]: that way I'll be ready to smack this godforsaken old hag right in the jaw! [*He advances on the* WOMEN'S LEADER
with fist raised.]

WOMEN'S LEADER   Just try it, and your own mommy won't recognize you   20
when you get home! Come on, fellow hags, let's start by putting *our*
jackets on the ground. [*The* WOMEN *remove their jackets.*]

WOMEN (*antistrophe a*)
Citizens of Athens, we want to start
by offering the polis some good advice,
and rightly, for she raised me in splendid luxury.   25
As soon as I turned seven I was an Arrephoros;
then I was a Grinder; when I was ten I shed
my saffron robe for the Foundress at the Brauronia.
And once, when I was a beautiful girl, I carried the Basket,
wearing a necklace of dried figs.[8]   30

WOMEN'S LEADER   Thus I *owe* it to the polis to offer some good advice.
And even if I *was* born a woman, don't hold it against me if I manage to
suggest something better than what we've got now. I have a stake in our
community: my contribution is *men*. You miserable geezers have *no*
stake, since you've squandered your paternal inheritance, won in the   35
Persian Wars,[9] and now pay no taxes in return. On the contrary, we're
all headed for bankruptcy on account of you! Have you anything to grunt
in rebuttal? Any more trouble from you and I'll clobber you with this
rawhide boot right in the jaw! [*She raises her foot at the* MEN'S LEADER.]

MEN (*strophe b*)
This behavior of theirs amounts to extreme hubris,   40
and I do believe it's getting aggravated.
No man with any balls can let it pass.

---

6. A contemporary of Aristophanes, frequently ridiculed in his plays as effeminate.
7. One of the assassins of Hipparchos (d. 514
B.C.E.), brother of Hippias; their statues stood
in the Agora, or marketplace. The Men's
Leader quotes a popular drinking song celebrating this killing.
8. This is a list of religious duties performed by
elite Greek girls. An Arrephoros was an acolyte
of Athena, seven to eleven years old; a Grinder

was a different kind of acolyte; Brauronia was
the location of a sanctuary of Artemis, involving
young girls at the age of the onset of menstrua-
tion. The final reference is to the yearly Athenian festival in honor of Athena, to whom girls
carried baskets of offerings. Figs symbolize fertility.
9. The conclusion of the wars with Persia, by
448 B.C.E., left Athens in control of an empire,
from which it exacted tribute.

MEN'S LEADER   Let's doff our shirts, 'cause a man's gotta smell like a
man from the word go and shouldn't be all wrapped up like souvlaki.
   [*The men remove their shirts.*]

MEN   Come on, Whitefeet!   45
We went against Leipsydrion[1]
when we still were something;
now we've got to rejuvenate, grow wings
all over, shake off these old skins of ours!

MEN'S LEADER   If any man among us gives these women the tiniest thing   50
to grab on to, there's no limit to what their nimble hands will do. Why,
they'll even be building frigates and launching naval attacks, cruising
against us like Artemisia.[2] And if they turn to horsemanship, you can
scratch our cavalry: there's nothing like a woman when it comes to
mounting and riding; even riding hard she won't slip off. Just look at   55
the Amazons in Mikon's[3] painting, riding chargers in battle against men.
Our duty is clear: grab each woman's neck and lock it in the wooden
stocks! [*He moves toward the* WOMEN'S LEADER.]

WOMEN   (*antistrophe b*)
By the Two Goddesses,[4] if you fire me up
I'll come at you like a wild sow and clip you bare,   60
and this very day you'll go bleating to your friends for help!

WOMEN'S LEADER   Quickly, women, let's also take off our tunics; a
woman's gotta smell like a woman, mad enough to bite! [*The women
remove their shirts.*]

WOMEN   All right now, someone attack me!
He'll eat no more garlic   65
and chew no more beans.
If you so much as curse at me, I boil over with such rage,
I'll be the beetle-midwife to your eagle's eggs.[5]

WOMEN'S LEADER   You men don't worry me a bit, not while my Lampito's
around and my Ismenia, the noble Theban girl. You'll have no power to   70
do anything about us, not even if you pass seven decrees: that's how
much every one hates you, you good-for-nothing, and especially our
neighbors. Why, just yesterday I threw a party for the girls in honor of
Hekate, and I invited my friend from next door, a fine girl who's very
special to me: an eel from Boiotia. But they said she couldn't come   75
because of *your* decrees. And you'll *never* stop passing these decrees
until someone grabs you by the leg and throws you away and breaks
your neck! [*She makes a grab for the* MEN'S LEADER's *leg.*]

---

1. A stronghold in northern Attica, used by those who sought unsuccessfully to overthrow the tyrant Hippias in 513 B.C.E.
2. Ruler of Caria (in present-day Turkey), an ally of the Persians; she led five ships against the Greeks at Salamis in 480 B.C.E.
3. Athenian sculptor and painter (5th century B.C.E.); his frescoes included one in the temple of Theseus that represented Athenians fighting Amazons, a nation of warrior women believed to live on the southeastern shore of the Black Sea.
4. Demeter and Persephone.
5. That is, testicles. In a fable by Aesop, a dung beetle avenges itself on an eagle by repeatedly breaking the bird's eggs.

Episode

[LYSISTRATA *comes out of the Akropolis and begins to pace.*]

WOMEN'S LEADER   O mistress of this venture and strategem,
  why com'st thou from thy halls so dour of mien?

LYSISTRATA   The deeds of ignoble women and the female heart
  do make me pace dispirited to and fro.

WOMEN'S LEADER   What say'st thou? What say'st thou?   5

LYSISTRATA   'Tis true, too true!

WOMEN'S LEADER   What dire thing? Pray tell it to thy friends.

LYSISTRATA   'Twere shame to say and grief to leave unsaid.

WOMEN'S LEADER   Hide not from me the damage we have taken.

LYSISTRATA   The story in briefest compass: we need to fuck!   10

WOMEN'S LEADER   Ah, Zeus!

LYSISTRATA   Why rend the air for Zeus? You see our plight.
  The truth is, I can't keep the wives away from their husbands any longer;
  they're running off in all directions. The first one I caught was over there
  by Pan's Grotto,[6] digging at her hole, and another was trying to escape   15
  by clambering down a pulley-cable. And yesterday another one mounted
  a sparrow and was about to fly off to Orsilochos' house when I pulled
  her off by her hair. They're coming up with every kind of excuse to go
  home. [*A wife comes out of the Akropolis, looks around, and begins to run
  offstage.*] Hey you! What's your hurry?   20

FIRST WIFE   I want to go home. I've got some Milesian wool in the house,
  and the moths are chomping it all up.

LYSISTRATA   Moths! Get back inside.

FIRST WIFE   By the Two Goddesses, I'll be right back; just let me spread
  it on the bed!   25

LYSISTRATA   You won't be spreading anything, nor be going anywhere.

FIRST WIFE   So I'm supposed to let my wool go to waste?

LYSISTRATA   If that's what it takes.

  [*As the first wife walks back toward* LYSISTRATA *a second runs out of
  the Akropolis.*]

SECOND WIFE   Oh my god, my god, the flax! I forgot to shuck it when I
  left the house!   30

LYSISTRATA   Here's another one off to shuck her flax. March right back here.

SECOND WIFE   By our Lady of Light,[7] I'll be back in a flash; just let me do
  a little shucking.

LYSISTRATA   No! No shucking! If *you* start doing it, some other wife will
  want to do the same.   35

  [*While the second wife walks back toward* LYSISTRATA *a third runs out
  of the Akropolis, holding her bulging belly.*]

THIRD WIFE   O Lady of Childbirth,[8] hold back the baby till I can get to a
  more profane spot![9]

LYSISTRATA   What are you raving about?

THIRD WIFE   I'm about to deliver a child!

---

6. A cave on the Akropolis containing a shrine
to Pan, goat-footed god of woods, pastures,
and wild places.
7. As at previous mention, this may be either

Artemis or Hecate.
8. Artemis, goddess of childbirth.
9. Sacred locations such as the Akropolis
would be polluted by birth or death.

LYSISTRATA   But you weren't pregnant yesterday.   40

THIRD WIFE   But today I am. Please, Lysistrata, send me home to the
midwife, and right away!

LYSISTRATA   What's the story? [*She feels the wife's belly.*] What's this? It's
hard.

THIRD WIFE   It's a boy.   45

LYSISTRATA [*Knocking on it*]   By Aphrodite, it's obvious you've got something metallic and hollow in there. Let's have a look. [*She lifts up the
wife's dress, exposing a large bronze helmet.*] Ridiculous girl! You're big
with the sacred helmet, not with child!

THIRD WIFE   But I *am* with child, by Zeus!   50

LYSISTRATA   Then what were you doing with this?

THIRD WIFE   Well, if I began to deliver here in the citadel, I could get
into the helmet and have my baby there, like a pigeon.

LYSISTRATA   What kind of story is that? Excuses! It's obvious what's going on.
You'll have to stay here till your—helmet has its naming-day.   55

THIRD WIFE   But I can't even *sleep* on the Akropolis, ever since I saw the
snake[1] that guards the temple.

FOURTH WIFE   And what about poor me—listening to the owls[2] go *woo
woo* all night is killing me!

LYSISTRATA   You nutty girls, enough of your horror stories! I guess you do   60
miss your husbands; but do you think they don't miss *you*? They're
spending some very rough nights, I assure you. Just be patient, good
ladies, and put up with this, just a little bit longer. There's an oracle
predicting victory for us, *if* we stick together. Here's the oracle right
here. [*She produces a scroll.*]   65

THIRD WIFE   Tell us what it says.

LYSISTRATA   Be quiet, then.
Yea, when the swallows hole up in a single home,
fleeing the hoopoes[3] and leaving the penis alone,
then are their problems solved, what's high is low: 70
so says high-thundering Zeus—

THIRD WIFE   You mean *we'll* be lying on top?

LYSISTRATA   But:
if the swallows begin to argue and fly away
down from the citadel holy, all will say,   75
no bird more disgustingly horny lives today!

THIRD WIFE   A pretty explicit oracle. Ye gods!

LYSISTRATA   So let's hear no more talk of caving in. Let's go inside. Dear
comrades, it would be a real shame if we betray the oracle. [*All enter
the Akropolis.*]

Choral Songs

MEN   (*strophe*)
I want to tell you all a tale
that once I heard when but a lad.

---

1. The snake sacred to Athena, believed to
live in the foundations of the Erechtheum,
had never been seen.

2. Birds sacred to Athena.
3. The bird into which Tereus was transformed, known for its erectile crest.

In olden times there lived a young man,
his name was Melanion.[4]
He fled from marriage until   5
he got to the wilderness.
And he lived in the mountains
and he had a dog,
and he wove traps and hunted rabbits,
but never went home again   10
because of his hatred.
That's how much *he* loathed women.
And, being wise, *we* loathe them just
as much as Melanion did.

MEN'S LEADER   How about a kiss, old bag?   15

WOMEN'S LEADER   Try it, and you've eaten your last onion!

MEN'S LEADER   How about I haul off and kick you? [*He kicks up his leg.*]

WOMEN'S LEADER [*Laughing*]   That's quite a bush you've got down there!

MEN'S LEADER   Well, Myronides too was rough down there,
and hairy-assed to all his enemies;   20
so too was Phormion.[5]

WOMEN (*antistrophe*)
I also want to tell you all a tale,
a reply to your Melanion.
There once was a drifter named Timon,
who fenced himself off with impregnable thorns,   25
as implacable as a Fury.[6]
So this Timon too
left home because of his hatred
<and lived in the mountains,>[7]
constantly cursing and railing   30
against the wickedness of men.
That's how much *he* loathed *you*,
wicked men, ever and always.
But he was a dear friend to women.

WOMEN'S LEADER   How would you like a punch in the mouth?   35

MEN'S LEADER   No way! You're really scaring me!

WOMEN'S LEADER   Then how about a good swift kick?

MEN'S LEADER   If you do you'll be flashing your twat!

WOMEN'S LEADER   Even so you'll never see
any hair down there on me: 40
I may be getting antiquated
but I keep myself well depilated.

---

4. In the myth featuring Melanion, the young man wins and marries Atalanta through a trick; she is the one fleeing marriage, having sworn to accept only the man who could defeat her in a footrace.
5. A successful Athenian general, as was Myronides (both 5th c. B.C.E.).
6. One of the Eumenides, monstrous female

personifications of vengeance. "Timon": a legendary misanthrope, depicted by Shakespeare in *Timon of Athens* (1607–8); nowhere else is he portrayed as a friend to women (see line 34, below).
7. The words inside angled brackets are supplied by the translator for a line missing in the Greek text.

[*The* WOMEN'S CHORUS *picks up their and the men's discarded clothing and both semichoruses withdraw from the center of the orchestra to sit along its edges; during the ensuing episode the women put their clothing back on.*]

Episode

[LYSISTRATA *appears on the roof of the stage-building, which represents the Akropolis ramparts, and walks to and fro, looking carefully in all directions; suddenly she stops and peers into the distance.*]

LYSISTRATA   All right! Yes! Ladies, come here, quick!

[MYRRHINE *and several other wives join* LYSISTRATA.]

WIFE   What is it? What's all the shouting?

LYSISTRATA   A man! I see a man coming this way, stricken, in the grip of Aphrodite's mysterious powers. Lady Aphrodite, mistress of Cyprus and Kythera[8] and Paphos, make thy journey straight and upright!   5

WIFE   Where is he, whoever he is?

LYSISTRATA   He's by Chloe's[9] shrine.

WIFE   By Zeus, I see him now! But who is he?

LYSISTRATA   Take a good look. Anyone recognize him?

MYRRHINE   Oh God, I do. He's my own husband Kinesias![1]   10

LYSISTRATA   All right, it's your job to roast him, to torture him, to bamboozle him, to love him and not to love him, and to give him anything he wants—except what you swore over the bowl not to.

MYRRHINE   Don't you worry, I'll do it!

LYSISTRATA   Great! I'll stick around here and help you bamboozle him   15
and roast him. Now everyone get out of sight!

[*All the wives go back inside except* LYSISTRATA. *Enter* KINESIAS, *wearing a huge erect phallus and accompanied by a male slave holding a baby. He is in obvious pain.*]

KINESIAS [*To himself*]   Oh, oh, evil fate! I've got terrible spasms and cramps. It's like I'm being broken on the rack!

LYSISTRATA [*Leaning down from the ramparts*]   Who's that who's standing up within our defense perimeter?   20

KINESIAS   Me.

LYSISTRATA   A man?

KINESIAS [*Brandishing his phallus*]   Of course a man!

LYSISTRATA   In that case please depart.

KINESIAS   And who are *you* to throw me out?   25

LYSISTRATA   The daytime guard.

KINESIAS   Then in the gods' name call Myrrhine out here to me.

LYSISTRATA   Listen to him, "call Myrrhine"! And who might *you* be?

KINESIAS   Her husband, Kinesias, from Paionidai.[2]

LYSISTRATA   Well, hello, dear chum! Among us *your* name is hardly   30
unknown or without celebrity. Your wife always has you on her lips; she'll be eating an egg or an apple and she'll say, "This one's for Kinesias."

---

8. The island, off the southern tip of the Peloponnesos, near which Aphrodite was born in the sea foam.

9. An epithet of the goddess Demeter (literally, "Verdant").

1. Common Greek name; in this play, also a sexual pun on the Greek verb *kinein*, "to move, to arouse."

2. A deme or village in Attica.

KINESIAS   Oh gods!

LYSISTRATA   Yes, by Aphrodite. And whenever the conversation turns to men, your wife speaks up forthwith and says, "Compared to Kinesias, everything else is trash!"   35

KINESIAS   Come on now, call her out!

LYSISTRATA   Well? Got anything for me?

KINESIAS [*Indicating his phallus*]   Indeed I do, if you want it. [LYSISTRATA *looks away.*] What about this? [*He tosses her a purse.*] It's all I've got,   40
and you're welcome to it.

LYSISTRATA   Okay then, I'll go in and call her for you. [*She leaves the ramparts.*]

KINESIAS   Make it quick, now! [*Alone*] I've had no joy or pleasure in my life since the day Myrrhine left the house. I go into the house and feel agony; everything looks empty to me; I get no pleasure from the food I   45
eat. Because I'm horny!

MYRRHINE [*Still out of sight, speaking to* LYSISTRATA]   I love that man, I love him! But he doesn't *want* my love. Please don't make me go out to him!

KINESIAS   Myrrhinikins, dearest, why are you doing this? Get down here!

MYRRHINE [*Appearing at the ramparts*] By Zeus, I'm not going down   50
there!

KINESIAS   You won't come down even when I ask you, Myrrhine?

MYRRHINE   You're asking me, but you don't want me at all.

KINESIAS   Me not want you? Why, I'm desolate!

MYRRHINE   I'm leaving.   55

KINESIAS   No, wait! At least listen to the baby! [*He grabs the baby from the slave and holds it up towards* MYRRHINE.] Come on you, yell for Mommy!

BABY   Mommy! Mommy! Mommy!

KINESIAS [*To* MYRRHINE]   Hey, what's wrong with you? Don't you feel   60
sorry for the baby, unwashed and unsuckled for six days now?

MYRRHINE   *Him* I feel sorry for. Too bad his *father* doesn't care about him!

KINESIAS: Get down here, you screwy woman, and see to your child!

MYRRHINE   How momentous is motherhood! I've got no choice but to go down there. [*She leaves the ramparts.* KINESIAS *returns the baby to the slave.*]

KINESIAS   <Absence really does make the heart grow fonder!> She seems   65
much younger than I remember, and she has a sexier look in her eyes. She acted prickly and very stuck-up too, but that just makes me want her even more!

[MYRRHINE *enters from the Akropolis gates and goes over to the baby, ignoring* KINESIAS.]

MYRRHINE   Poor sweetie pie, with such a lousy father, let me give you a kiss, Mommy's little dearest!   70

KINESIAS [*To* MYRRHINE's *back*]   What do you think you're doing, you naughty girl, listening to those other women and giving me a hard time and hurting yourself as well? [*He puts a hand on her shoulder.*]

MYRRHINE [*Wheeling around*] Don't you lay your hands on me!

KINESIAS   You know you've let our house, your things and mine, become   75
an utter mess?

MYRRHINE   It doesn't bother me.

KINESIAS   It doesn't bother you that the hens are pulling your woollens apart?

MYRRHINE   Not a bit.   80

KINESIAS   And what a long time it's been since you've celebrated Aphrodite's holy mysteries.[3] Won't you come home?

MYRRHINE   Not me, by Zeus; I'm going nowhere until you men agree to a settlement and stop the war.

KINESIAS   Well, if that's what's decided, then that's what we'll do.   85

MYRRHINE   Well, if that's what's decided, I'll be going home. But for the time being I've sworn to stay here.

KINESIAS   But at least lie down here with me; it's been so long.

MYRRHINE   No way. But I'm not saying I don't love you.

KINESIAS   Love me? So why won't you lie down, Myrrhine?   90

MYRRHINE   Right here in front of the baby? You must be joking!

KINESIAS   Zeus, no! Boy, take him home. [*Exit slave.*] There you are, the kid's out of our way. Now, why don't you just lie down?

MYRRHINE   Lie down *where*, you silly man?

KINESIAS [*Looking around*]   Where? Pan's Grotto will do fine.   95

MYRRHINE   But I need to be pure before I can go back up to the Akropolis.

KINESIAS   Very easily done: just wash off in the Klepsydra.[4]

MYRRHINE   You're telling me, dear, that I should go back on the oath I swore?

KINESIAS   Don't worry about any oath; let me take the consequences.   100

MYRRHINE   All right then, I'll get us a bed.

KINESIAS   No, don't; the ground's okay for us.

MYRRHINE   Apollo, no! I wouldn't dream of letting you lie on the ground, no matter what kind of man you are. [MYRRHINE *goes into one of the flanking doors, which represents Pan's Grotto.*]

KINESIAS   She really loves me, that's quite obvious!   105

MYRRHINE [*Returning with a cot*]   There you are! Lie right down while I undress. [KINESIAS *lies on the cot.*] But wait, I forgot, what is it, yes, a mattress! Got to get one.

KINESIAS   A mattress? Not for me, thanks.

MYRRHINE   By Artemis, it's shabby on cords.   110

KINESIAS   Well, give me a kiss.

MYRRHINE [*Kissing him*]   There. [*She returns to the Grotto.*]

KINESIAS   Oh lordy! Get the mattress quick!

MYRRHINE [*Returning with a mattress*]   There we are! Lie back down and I'll get my clothes off. But wait, what is it, a pillow, you haven't got a pillow!   115

KINESIAS   I don't need a pillow!

MYRRHINE   I do. [*She returns to the Grotto.*]

KINESIAS   Is this cock of mine supposed to be Herakles waiting for his dinner?[5]

MYRRHINE [*Returning with a pillow*] Lift up now, upsy-daisy. There, is that everything?   120

KINESIAS   Everything *I* need. Come here, my little treasure!

3. That is, had sexual intercourse.
4. A spring on the slope of the Akropolis.

5. The hero was routinely portrayed as having great appetites.

MYRRHINE   Just getting my breastband off. But remember: don't break
your promise about a peace-settlement.

KINESIAS   May lightning strike me, by Zeus!   125

MYRRHINE   You don't have a blanket.

KINESIAS   It's not a blanket I want—I want to fuck!

MYRRHINE   That's just what you're going to get. Back in a flash. [*She
returns to the Grotto.*]

KINESIAS   That woman drives me nuts with all her bedding!

MYRRHINE [*Returning with a blanket*]   Get up.   130

KINESIAS [*Pointing to his phallus*]   I've already got it up! [MYRRHINE *carefully arranges the blanket while* KINESIAS *fidgets.*]

MYRRHINE   Want some scent?

KINESIAS   Apollo,[6] no, none for me.

MYRRHINE   But *I* will, by Aphrodite, whether you like it or not.

KINESIAS [*As* MYRRHINE *returns to the Grotto*]   Then let the scent flow!   135
Lord Zeus!

MYRRHINE [*Returning with a round bottle of perfume*]   Hold out your
hand. Take some and rub it in.

KINESIAS   I don't like this scent, by Apollo; it takes a long time warming
up and it doesn't smell like conjugal pleasures.   140

MYRRHINE   Oh silly me, I brought the Rhodian[7] brand!

KINESIAS   No, wait, I like it! Let it go, you screwy woman!

MYRRHINE   What are you talking about? [*She returns to the Grotto.*]

KINESIAS   Goddamn the man who first decocted scent!

MYRRHINE   [*Returning with a long, cylindrical bottle*] Here, try this tube.   145

KINESIAS [*Pointing to his phallus*]   Got one already! Now lie down, you
slut, and don't bring me anything more.

MYRRHINE   By Artemis, I will. Just getting my shoes off. But remember,
darling, you're going to vote for peace. [*At this,* KINESIAS *averts his eyes
from* MYRRHINE *and fiddles with the blanket;* MYRRHINE *dashes off into
the Akropolis.*]

KINESIAS   I'll give it serious consideration. [*He looks up again, only to*   150
find MYRRHINE *gone.*] The woman's destroyed me, annihilated me! Not
only that: she's pumped me up and dropped me flat!

[*During the ensuing duet both semichoruses return to the center of the
orchestra; the women carry the shirts that the men had removed earlier.*]
Now what shall I do? Whom shall I screw?
I'm cheated of the sexiest girl I knew!
How will I raise and rear this orphaned cock?   155
Is Fox Dog[8] out there anywhere?
I need to rent a practical nurse!

MEN'S LEADER   Yea, frightful agony, thou wretch,
dost rack the soul of one so sore bediddled.
Sure I do feel for thee, alack!   160
What kidney could bear it,
what soul, what balls,

---

6. Greek god of prophecy, light, and healing.   8. Nickname of the famous pimp Philostratos.
7. From the Aegean island of Rhodes.

what loins, what crotch,
thus stretched on the rack
and deprived of a morning fuck?   165

KINESIAS   Ah Zeus! The cramps attack anew!

MEN'S LEADER   And *this* is what she's done to you, the detestable, revolting shrew!

WOMEN'S LEADER   No, she's totally sweet and dear!

MEN'S LEADER   Sweet, you say! She's wicked, wicked!   170

KINESIAS   You're right: wicked is what she is!
O Zeus, Zeus, raise up a great tornado,
with lightning bolts and all,
to sweep her up like a heap of grain
and twirl her into the sky,   175
and then let go and let her fall
back down to earth again,
and let her point of impact be
this dick of mine right here!

Episode

[*Enter a Spartan* HERALD, *both arms hidden beneath a long travelling cloak and pushing it out in front.*]

HERALD   [*To* KINESIAS] Where be the Senate of Athens or the Prytanies?[9] Have some news to tell them.

KINESIAS   And what might you be? Are you human? Or a Konisalos?[1]

HERALD   Am Herald, youngun, by the Twain, come from Sparta about settlement.   5

KINESIAS   And that's why you've come hiding a spear in your clothes?

HERALD   Not I, by Zeus, no spear!

KINESIAS   Why twist away from me? And why hold your coat out in front of you? You've got a swollen groin from the long ride, maybe?

HERALD   By Kastor, this guy crazy! [*He accidently reveals his erect phallus.*]   10

KINESIAS   Hey, that's hard-on, you rascal!

HERALD   No, by Zeus, is not! Don't be silly!

KINESIAS   Then what do you call *that*?

HERALD   Is Spartan walking-stick.

KINESIAS   [*Pointing to his own phallus*] Then *this* is a Spartan walking-stick too. Listen, I know what's up; you can level with me. How are things going in Sparta?   15

HERALD   All Sparta rise, also allies. All have hard-on. Need Pellana.[2]

KINESIAS   What caused this calamity to hit you? Was it Pan?

HERALD   Oh no. Was Lampito started it, yes, and then other women in Sparta, they all start together like in footrace, keep men away from their hair-pies.   20

KINESIAS   So how are you faring?

9. That portion of the Athenian council responsible for the day-to-day business of the state; its membership rotated.

1. A phallic fertility spirit associated with a

Spartan dance.

2. A city south of Sparta; here, the name appears to have obscure sexual connotations.

HERALD   Hard! Walk around town bent over, like men carrying oil-lamp
in wind. The women won't permit even to touch the pussy till all of us   25
unanimously agree to make peace-treaty with rest of Greeks.

KINESIAS   So this business is a global conspiracy by all the women! Now
I get it! Okay, get back to Sparta as quick as you can and arrange to
send ambassadors here with full powers to negotiate a treaty. And I'll
arrange for *our* Council to choose their own ambassadors; this cock of   30
mine will be Exhibit A.

HERALD   I fly away. You offer capital advice. [*He exits by the way he
entered;* KINESIAS *exits in the opposite direction.*]

MEN'S LEADER   A woman's harder to conquer than any beast, than fire,
and no panther is quite so ferocious.

WOMEN'S LEADER   You understand that, but then you still resist us? It's   35
possible, you rascal, to have our lasting friendship.

MEN'S LEADER   I'll never cease to loathe women!

WOMEN'S LEADER   Well, whenever you like. But meanwhile I'll not stand
for you to be undressed like that. Just look how ridiculous you are! I'm
coming over to put your shirt back on.   40
    [*She walks over and replaces his shirt, and the other women each follow
    suit for one of the men.*]

MEN'S LEADER   By god, that's no mean thing you've done for us. And
now I'm sorry I got mad and took it off.

WOMEN'S LEADER   And now you look like a man again, not so ridiculous.
And if you weren't so hostile I'd have removed
that bug in your eye, that's still in there, I see.   45

MEN'S LEADER   So *that's* what's been driving me nuts! Here, take my
ring;
please dig it out of my eye, then show it to me;
by god, it's been biting my eye for quite some time.

WOMEN'S LEADER   All right, I will, though you're a grumpy man.   50
    Great gods, what a humongous gnat you've got in there!
    There, take a look. Isn't it positively Trikorysian?[3]

MEN'S LEADER   By god, you've helped me; that thing's been digging wells,
and now it's out my eyes are streaming tears.

WOMEN'S LEADER   Then I'll wipe them away, though you're a genuine   55
rascal, and kiss you.

MEN'S LEADER   Don't kiss me!

WOMEN'S LEADER   I'll kiss you whether you like it or not!
    [*She does so, and the other women follow suit as before.*]

MEN'S LEADER   The worst of luck to you! You're born sweet-talkers.
The ancient adage gets it in a nutshell: 60
"Can't live *with* the pests or without 'em either."
But now I'll make peace, and promise nevermore
to mistreat you or to take mistreatment *from* you.
Let's get together, then, and start our song.
    [*The semichoruses become one and for the remainder of the play perform
    as a single chorus.*]

3. From Trikorythos, a marshy district in Attica.

CHORUS (*strophe*)
We don't intend to say anything   65
the least bit slanderous about
any citizen, you gentlemen out there,
but quite the opposite: to say and do
only what's nice, because the troubles
you've got already are more than enough.   70

So let every man and woman tell us
if they need to have a little cash,
say two or three minas;[4] we've got it at home
and we've got some purses for it, too.
And if peace should ever break out,   75
everyone that we lent money to
can forget to repay—if they got anything!

(*antistrophe*)
We're getting set to entertain
some visitors from Karystos[5] today;
they're fine and handsome gentlemen.   80
There'll be a special soup, and that piglet
of mine, I've sacrificed it on the grill,
and it's turning out to be fine and tender meat.
So come on over to my house today:
get up early and take a bath,   85
and bathe the kids, and walk right in.
You needn't ask anyone's permission,
just go straight on inside like it was yours,
because the door will be locked!

Episode

[*The* SPARTAN AMBASSADORS *enter, their clothes concealing conspicuous bulges. They are accompanied by slaves.*]

CHORUS-LEADER   Hey! Here come ambassadors from Sparta, dragging
long beards and wearing something around their waists that looks like
a pigpen. [*To the Spartans*] Gentlemen of Sparta: first, our greetings!
Then tell us how you all are doing?

SPARTAN AMBASSADOR   No use to waste a lot of time describing. Is best to   5
show how we're doing. [*The Spartans open their cloaks to reveal their erect phalli.*]

CHORUS-LEADER   Gosh! Your problem's grown very hard, and it seems to
be even more inflamed than before.

SPARTAN AMBASSADOR   Unspeakable! What can one say? We wish for
someone to come, make peace for us on any terms he like.   10

---

4. A substantial sum of money. "So let every man and woman tell us": a line unique in suggesting that women attended the perfor-

mances of ancient comedy.
5. A small town on the Aegean island of Euboea, north of Athens, that was an ally of Athens.

[ATHENIAN AMBASSADORS *enter from the opposite direction, with cloaks bulging.*]

CHORUS-LEADER   Look, I see a party of native sons approaching, like men wrestling, holding their clothes away from their bellies like that! Looks like a bad case of prickly heat.

FIRST ATHENIAN AMBASSADOR   [*To the* CHORUS-LEADER.] Who can tell us where Lysistrata is? The men are here, and we're . . . as you see. [*They   15 reveal their own erect phalli.*]

CHORUS-LEADER   *Their* syndrome seems to be the same as *theirs*. These spasms: do they seize you in the wee hours?

FIRST ATHENIAN AMBASSADOR   Yes, and what's worse, we're worn totally raw by being in this condition! If someone doesn't get us a treaty pretty soon, there's no way we won't be fucking Kleisthenes!   20

CHORUS-LEADER   If you've got any sense, you'll cover up there: you don't want one of the Herm-Dockers[6] to see you like this.

FIRST ATHENIAN AMBASSADOR   By god, that's good advice. [*The Athenians rearrange their cloaks to cover their phalli.*]

SPARTAN AMBASSADOR   By the Twain Gods, yes indeed. Come, put cloaks back on! [*The Spartans follow suit.*]   25

FIRST ATHENIAN AMBASSADOR   Greetings, Spartans! We've had an awful time.

SPARTAN AMBASSADOR   Dear colleague, we've had a *fearful* time, if those men saw us fiddling with ourselves.

FIRST ATHENIAN AMBASSADOR   Come on, then, Spartans, let's talk details. The reason for your visit?   30

SPARTAN AMBASSADOR   Are ambassadors, for settlement.

FIRST ATHENIAN AMBASSADOR   That's very good; us too. So why not invite Lysistrata to our meeting, since she's the only one who can settle our differences?

SPARTAN AMBASSADOR   Sure, by the Twain Gods, Lysistrata, and Lysistra-   35 tos[7] too if ye like!

[LYSISTRATA *emerges from the Akropolis gate.*]

FIRST ATHENIAN AMBASSADOR   It looks as if we don't have to invite her: she must have heard us, for here she comes herself.

CHORUS-LEADER   Hail, manliest of all women! Now is your time: be forceful and flexible, high-class and vulgar, haughty and sweet, a   40 woman for all seasons; because the head men of Greece, caught by your charms, have gathered together with all their mutual complaints and are turning them over to you for settlement.

LYSISTRATA   Well, it's an easy thing to do if you get them when they're hot for it and not testing each other for weaknesses. I'll soon know how ready   45 they are. Where's Reconciliation? [*A naked girl comes out of the Akropolis.*] Take hold of the Spartans first and bring them here; don't handle them with a rough or mean hand, or crudely, the way our husbands used to handle us, but use a wife's touch, like home sweet home. [*The* SPARTAN AMBASSADOR *refuses to give his hand.*] If he won't give you his hand, lead   50

6. The unknown individuals who, just before the great expedition was to leave for Sicily (in 415 B.C.E.), broke the erect phalluses off statues of Hermes. These representations of the messenger god, the patron of travelers, stood outside houses and public buildings throughout the city.
7. The masculine form of the name Lysistrata, perhaps also mocking the Spartans as homosexuals.

him by his weenie. [*The* SPARTAN AMBASSADOR *complies, and she leads him and his colleagues to* LYSISTRATA, *where they stand to her left.*] Now go and fetch those Athenians, too; take hold of whatever they give you and bring them here. [RECONCILIATION *escorts the Athenians to* LYSISTRATA'S *right.*] Spartans, move in closer to me, and you Athenians, too; I want you to listen to what I have to say. I *am* a woman, but still I've got a mind: I'm pretty intelligent in my own right, and because I've listened many a time to the conversations of my father and the older men I'm pretty well educated, too. Now that you're a captive audience I'm ready to give you the tongue-lashing you deserve—both of you. 55 60

    Don't both of you sprinkle altars from the same cup like kinsmen, at the Olympic Games, at Thermopylae, at Delphi,[8] and so many other places I could mention if I had to make a long list? Yet with plenty of enemies available with their barbarian armies, it's *Greek* men and *Greek* cities you're determined to destroy! That's the first point I wanted to make. 65

FIRST ATHENIAN AMBASSADOR   [*Gazing at* RECONCILIATION] My cock is bursting out of its skin and killing me!

LYSISTRATA   Next I'm going to turn to *you*, Spartans. Don't you remember the time when Perikleidas the Spartan came here on bended knee and sat at Athenian altars, white-faced in his scarlet uniform, begging for a military contingent? That time when Messenia was up in arms against you and the god was shaking you with an earthquake? And Kimon came with four thousand infantrymen and rescued all Lakedaemon?[9] And after that sort of treatment from the Athenians, you're now out to ravage their country, who've treated you so well? 70 75

FIRST ATHENIAN AMBASSADOR   By Zeus, they *are* guilty, Lysistrata!

SPARTAN AMBASSADOR   We're guilty—[*looking at* RECONCILIATION] but what an unspeakably fine ass!

LYSISTRATA   Do you Athenians think I'm going to let *you* off? Don't you remember the time when you were dressed in slaves' rags and the Spartans came in force and wiped out many Thessalian fighters, many friends and allies of Hippias?[1] That day when they were the only ones helping you to drive him out? How they liberated you, and replaced your slaves' rags with a warm cloak, as suits a free people? 80

SPARTAN AMBASSADOR   [*Still gazing at* RECONCILIATION] I never saw such a classy woman! 85

FIRST ATHENIAN AMBASSADOR   I've never seen a lovelier cunt!

LYSISTRATA   So after so many good deeds done, why are you at war? Why not stop this terrible behavior? Why not make peace? Come on, what's in the way? 90

---

8. Sites revered by all Greeks. At the Olympic Games, held quadrennially in Olympia, on the Peloponnesian Peninsula, a truce was observed; Thermopylae, in central Greece, was the site of the Spartans' heroic stand against the Persians in 480 B.C.E.; Delphi, in central Greece, was the site of the most important oracle of Apollo and of the Panhellenic games. 9. That is, Sparta. Kimon, an Athenian general and statesman, brought aid to the Spartans in 464 B.C.E. after a devastating earthquake was followed by a rebellion of their serfs. (Lysistrata refrains from adding that the Spartans abruptly sent the Athenians away, an affront to Athenian pride that resulted in Kimon's exile.)
1. The Spartans came to the aid of Athenian democrats and expelled the tyrant Hippias in 510 B.C.E. (Again, Lysistrata leaves out the acrimonious end of the story—the Spartans' later attempt to overthrow the democracy.) "Thessalian": from Thessaly, in northern Greece.

[*During the following negotiations* RECONCILIATION's *body serves as a map of Greece.*]

SPARTAN AMBASSADOR   We are ready, if they are ready to return to us this abutment.

LYSISTRATA   Which one, sir?

SPARTAN AMBASSADOR   Back Door[2] here, that we for long time count on having, and grope for.   95

FIRST ATHENIAN AMBASSADOR   By Poseidon, that you *won't* get!

LYSISTRATA   Give it to them, good sir.

FIRST ATHENIAN AMBASSADOR   Then who will *we* be able to harass?

LYSISTRATA   Just ask for some other place in return for that one.

FIRST ATHENIAN AMBASSADOR   Well, let's see now. First of all give us   100
Echinous here and the Malian Gulf behind it and both Legs.[3]

SPARTAN AMBASSADOR   By Twain Gods, we will not give *everything*, dear fellow!

LYSISTRATA   Let it go: don't be squabbling about legs.

FIRST ATHENIAN AMBASSADOR   Now I'm ready to strip down and do some   105
ploughing!

SPARTAN AMBASSADOR   Me first, by Twain Gods: before one ploughs one spreads manure!

LYSISTRATA   You may do that when you've ratified the settlement. If, after due deliberation, you do decide to settle, go back and confer with your allies.   110

FIRST ATHENIAN AMBASSADOR   *Allies*, dear lady? We're too hard up for that! Won't our allies, all of them, come to the same decision *we* have, namely, to fuck?

SPARTAN AMBASSADOR   *Ours* will, by Twain Gods!

FIRST ATHENIAN AMBASSADOR   And so will the Karystians,[4] by Zeus!   115

LYSISTRATA   You make a strong case. For the time being see to it you remain pure, so that we women can host you on the Akropolis with what we brought in our boxes. There you may exchange pledges of mutual trust, and after that each of you may reclaim his wife and go home.

FIRST ATHENIAN AMBASSADOR   What are we waiting for?   120

SPARTAN AMBASSADOR   [*To* LYSISTRATA]   Lead on wherever you wish.

FIRST ATHENIAN AMBASSADOR   By Zeus, yes, as quick as you can!

[LYSISTRATA *escorts* RECONCILIATION *inside, followed by the* SPARTAN *and* ATHENIAN AMBASSADORS; *the Spartans' slaves sit down outside the door, which is attended by a doorkeeper.*]

CHORUS   (*strophe*)
Intricate tapestries,
nice clothes and fine gowns
and gold jewellery: all that I own   125
is yours for the asking
for your sons and for your daughter, too,
when she's picked to march with the basket.[5]

---

2. Pylos; also a joke at the Spartans' supposed preference for anal sex.
3. Echinous is a town in Thessaly; the Malian Gulf is near Thermopylae; the "Legs" here are the walls that connected the city of Megara,

west of Athens, and its seaport, Nisaia.
4. The inhabitants of Karystos, a town on the island of Euboea.
5. That is, during a religious festival.

I declare my home open to everyone
to take anything you want.   130
Nothing is sealed up so tight
that you won't be able to break the seals
and take away what you find inside.
But you won't see anything
unless your eyes are sharper than mine.   135
(*antistrophe*)
    If anyone's out of bread
but has slaves and lots of little kids to feed,
you can get flour from my house:
puny grains, but a pound of them
grow up to be a loaf   140
that looks very hearty.
Any of you poor people are welcome
to come to my house with sacks and bags
to carry the flour away; my houseboy will load them up.
A warning though: don't knock at my door—   145
beware of the watchdog there!

Episode

FIRST ATHENIAN AMBASSADOR [*Still inside, knocking at the door and yelling
    to the doorkeeper*]   Open the door, you! [*He bursts through the door,
    sending the doorkeeper tumbling down the steps. He wears a garland and
    carries a torch, as from a drinking-party.*] You should have got out of the
    way. [*Other Athenians emerge, similarly equipped. To the slaves*] You
    there, why are you sitting around? Want me to singe you with this torch?
        What a stale routine! I refuse to do it. [*Encouragement from the*   5
    spectators.] Well, if it's absolutely necessary we'll go the extra mile,
    to do you all a favor. [*He begins to chase the slaves with his torch.*]
SECOND ATHENIAN AMBASSADOR   [*Joining the* FIRST] And we'll help you go
    that extra mile! [*To the slaves*] Get lost! You'll cry for your hair if you don't!
FIRST ATHENIAN AMBASSADOR   Yes, get lost, so the Spartans can come out   10
    after their banquet without being bothered. [*The slaves are chased off.*]
SECOND ATHENIAN AMBASSADOR   I've never been at a better party! The
    Spartans were really great guys, and we made wonderful company our-
    selves over the drinks.
FIRST ATHENIAN AMBASSADOR   Stands to reason: when we're sober we're not   15
    ourselves. If the Athenians will take my advice, from now on we'll do all our
    ambassadorial business drunk. As it is, whenever we go to Sparta sober, we
    start right in looking for ways to stir up trouble. When they say something
    we don't hear it, and when they don't say something we're convinced that
    they did say it, and we each return with completely different reports. But   20
    this time everything turned out fine. When somebody sang the Telamon
    Song when he should have been singing the Kleitagora Song,[6] everybody

6. Evidently songs of war and of love (Telamon was a legendary hero of the generation before
the Trojan War, and Kleitagora was a Spartan woman poet).

would applaud and even swear up and down what a fine choice it was. [*Some of the slaves approach the door again.*] Hey, those slaves are back! Get lost, you whip-fodder! [*They chase the slaves away.*]   25

SECOND ATHENIAN AMBASSADOR   Yes, by Zeus, here they come out of the door. [*The* SPARTAN AMBASSADORS *file out; their leader carries bagpipes.*]

SPARTAN AMBASSADOR [*To the stage-piper or to a piper who accompanies the Spartans*]   Take pipes, my good man, and I dance two-step and sing nice song for Athenians and ourselves.

FIRST ATHENIAN AMBASSADOR   God, yes, take the pipes: I love to watch   30
   you people dance!

SPARTAN AMBASSADOR   Memory, speed to this lad
   your own Muse, who knows
   about us and the Athenians,
   about that day at Artemision   35
   when *they* spread sail like gods
   against the armada
   and whipped the Medes,
   while Leonidas[7] led *us*,
   like wild boars we were, yes,   40
   gnashing our tusks, our jaws running
   streams of foam, and our legs, too.
   The enemy, the Persians,
   outnumbered the sand on the shore.

   Goddess of the Wilds, Virgin Beast-Killer,[8]   45
   come this way, this way to the treaty,
   and keep us together for a long long while.
   Now let friendship in abundance
   attend our agreement always,
   and may we ever abandon   50
   foxy stratagems.
   Come this way, this way,
   Virgin Huntress!

   [*A mute* LYSISTRATA *comes out of the Akropolis, followed by the Athenian and Spartan wives.*]

FIRST ATHENIAN AMBASSADOR   Well! Now that everything else has been wrapped up so nicely, it's time for you Spartans to reclaim these wives   55
of yours; and you Athenians, these here. Let's have husband stand by wife and wife by husband; then to celebrate our great good fortune let's have a dance for the gods. And let's be sure never again to make the same mistakes! [*The couples descend into the orchestra to dance to the* AMBASSADOR's *song; around them dance the members of the chorus, who are also paired in couples.*]
   Bring on the dance, include the Graces,   60
   and invite Artemis,

7. The Spartan king and general who led the small band against the Persians ("the Medes") at Thermopylae in 480 B.C.E.; at the same time, an indecisive naval battle took place nearby at

Cape Artemision. "Muse": a goddess of art and learning, conventionally invoked for inspiration.
8. Artemis.

and her twin brother, the benign Healer,[9]
and the Nysian whose eyes flash
bacchic among his maenads,
and Zeus alight with flame   65
and the thriving Lady his consort;[1]
and invite the divine powers
we would have as witnesses
to remember always
this humane peace,   70
which the goddess Kypris[2] has fashioned.
CHORUS   Alalai, yay Paian![3]
    Shake a leg, iai!
    Dance to victory, iai!
    Evoi evoi, evai evai![4]   75
FIRST ATHENIAN AMBASSADOR   Now, my dear Spartan, *you* give us some
    music: a new song to match the last one!
SPARTAN AMBASSADOR   Come back again from fair Taÿgetos,
    Spartan Muse, and distinguish this occasion
    with a hymn to the God of Amyklai[5]   80
    and Athena of the Brazen House[6]
    and Tyndareos' fine sons,
    who gallop beside the Eurotas.[7]
    Ho there, hop!
    Hey there, jump!   85
    Let's sing a hymn to Sparta,
    home of dance divine
    and stomping feet,
    where by the Eurotas's banks
    young girls frisk like fillies,   90
    raising dust-clouds underfoot
    and tossing their tresses
    like maenads waving their wands and playing,
    led by Leda's daughter,[8]
    their chorus-leader pure and pretty.   95

[*To the* CHORUS] Come on now, hold your hair in your hand, get your feet
hopping like a deer and start making some noise to spur the dance!
And sing for the goddess who's won a total victory, Athena of the Brazen House!

    [*All exit dancing, the* CHORUS *singing a traditional hymn to Athena.*]

9. Apollo. "Graces": the incarnations of beauty
and grace, daughters of Zeus.
1. The goddess Hera, sister and wife of Zeus.
"Maenads": the women who worship Dionysus, god of wine and of an emotional cult, who
was raised on Mount Nysa (the location of
which was a matter of dispute).
2. Aphrodite.
3. A title of Apollo ("Healer").

4. The ecstatic cry of worshippers of Dionysus.
5. Site south of Sparta of a major shrine to
Apollo.
6. Sparta's bronze-plated temple to Athena.
7. The river that runs by Sparta. "Tyndareos'
fine sons": Kastor and Pollux.
8. Helen, the daughter of Leda and Zeus; she
was worshipped as a goddess in Sparta.

PLATO

429–347 B.C.E.

It is often said that all later Western philosophical writings are mere "footnotes to Plato." Plato's dialogues have shaped how we think about politics, ethics, metaphysics, reason, education, truth, desire, God, and the soul. But Plato was not only a great thinker but also a great writer. The brilliance of his literary achievement was recognized in antiquity. The ancient critical work *On the Sublime* imagines Plato challenging **Homer** to a wrestling match; he is the only later writer, the author suggests, whose work could possibly rival the *Iliad* and the *Odyssey*. Plato's dialogues have the intellectual complexity of great philosophy, but also the comedy, pathos, and vivid evocations of people and places that we associate with great drama—or the novel.

LIFE AND TIMES

Plato came from a prominent and aristocratic Athenian family. In his youth, he was apparently interested mainly in poetry (we are told that he composed at least one tragedy), and in sports. *Plato* means "broad-shouldered" and is probably a nickname from his wrestling days; his real name was apparently Aristocles. But Plato's life was changed when, in his late teens or twenties, he encountered the most prominent of the Sophists ("wisdom teachers") in the city: Socrates.

Socrates, often seen as the world's first philosopher, wrote nothing. He must have been an extraordinary person, inspiring devotion in his followers—from all walks of Athenian society—as well as mistrust and controversy among those outside his intimate circle. Many of his acquaintances and students wrote dialogues featuring fictionalized portraits of the master. Plato and Xenophon are the only students of Socrates whose work survives in bulk, and they give us two very different versions of the ideal thinker, teacher, and moral hero. Xenophon's Socrates is a conventional teacher who recommends common-sense principles and who teaches in a fairly straightforward way: by telling people what to do and think. Plato's Socrates is a puzzling and fascinating figure, who claims not to be a teacher at all, and who works by means of questions, irony, and myth. It is impossible to know which of these literary characters comes closer to the historical Socrates. Moreover, Plato's depiction of Socrates varies enormously from one text to another. In some, Socrates professes total ignorance, and the result of all his questions is only to show that other people, too, have incomplete understanding of basic evaluative concepts like courage, pleasure, and holiness. In others, Plato's Socrates makes far more substantive philosophical claims. Perhaps Plato modulated the character of Socrates depending on the setting or genre of each dialogue. In any case, probably none of the dialogues reflects the real Socrates with any degree of precision; all are the literary and philosophical creation of Plato.

What is certain is that the life and, still more, the death of Socrates had a profound impact on Athenian society in general, and on Plato in particular. In 399 B.C.E., when Plato would have been thirty, Socrates was put on trial for inventing new deities, failing to believe in the gods of the city, and "corrupting the youth"; none of these things were infractions of specific laws, but Socrates was probably charged under the general law against "impiety."

Five years before Socrates' trial, Athens had lost the Peloponnesian War. In the aftermath of the war, Athenian democratic government failed: many citizens blamed democracy for the bad decisions the city had made during the long years of war. A repressive dictatorial regime, dominated by thirty Athenians of oligarchic sympathies, seized power in place of the rule of the people. "The Thirty," as they came to be known, were overthrown eight months later, and a democratic constitution was reinstituted. Some members of the Thirty, as well as other prominent Athenians who had or were suspected of antidemocratic leanings, were associates of Socrates; one, Critias, was Plato's uncle. The trial may well have been part of the reaction against the Thirty, especially since one of the main accusers, Anytus, was a leader of the restored democracy. Socrates was declared guilty and condemned to death. The means of execution was drinking poison (hemlock). Plato tells us that he himself was sick, and could not be present at the moment of his beloved teacher's death. But he wrote in the *Phaedo* a fictional account of the brave death of Socrates, surrounded by loving and intellectual followers, and maintaining his philosophical principles right up to the end.

After Socrates died, Plato became a writer, philosopher, and teacher. He featured Socrates as the principal speaker in philosophical dialogues that explored a variety of ethical and political problems; the *Republic*, an account of an ideal political and educational system, is the most famous. Plato's imagined city is not a democracy; indeed, democracy—the system under which Socrates was condemned—is roundly criticized as little better than tyranny, since, Plato's Socrates suggests here, it gives power to the ignorant many over the enlightened few. Ideally, this text suggests, rulers should become philosophers or philosophers, rulers: under such a system, it implies, a man like Socrates would not be a criminal condemned to death, but would be acknowledged as the leader he deserved to be.

Beyond writing, Plato made several other kinds of attempts to educate his contemporaries and change the society around him. He founded the Academy (from which we get the modern term *academics*), which was the earliest prototype for the modern university, the first-ever philosophical school with a permanent location. The Academy remained active as a center of philosophical training and research until it was suppressed by the Roman emperor Justinian in 529 C.E. Plato also made three trips to Sicily, trying to convert the tyrants of Syracuse into philosopher-kings. He failed; but, more important, he tried—despite the fact that the Sicilian court was hardly a safe environment for an interfering Athenian philosopher, and these trips could well have resulted in slavery or death. The attempt shows the depth of his commitment to trying to change the world and to be, like his beloved Socrates, not only a zealous idealistic philosopher but also a brave and good man. He devoted the last thirteen years of his life to teaching and writing at his Academy, where he died and was buried.

THE *SYMPOSIUM*

The *Symposium* (which means "Drinking Party") is deservedly one of Plato's best-loved works. Its subject—sexual love, for which the Greek term is *Eros*—is of universal interest and appeal. This dialogue has a wide range of vivid characters, all based on real historical figures whom Plato knew. These include the sentimental young tragic poet

Agathon; the pompously scientific doctor Eryximachus; the hiccuping, fantastical comedian Aristophanes; the sexy, drunken playboy Alcibiades; and, above all, the extraordinary figure of Socrates himself. The setting, at a party, gives us a memorable image of what elite Athenian nightlife might have been like: men lounging together on sofas, drinking wine (diluted with water, in the Greek fashion), being entertained by scantily dressed flute-girls, and enjoying conversation at all different levels—from highbrow philosophical and literary discussion to flirting, teasing, and drunken banter.

Plato probably wrote the *Symposium* between 384 and 379 B.C.E., some thirty years after the party that it describes. The historical setting is important, and we are made conscious of it from the beginning by the introductory "frame." Some Platonic dialogues open with the words of the first main speaker. Here, however, we begin with a conversation that precedes the main conversation and explains how what we are about to read came to be told. A follower of Socrates, Apollodorus, is accosted in the street by a friend, who begs to be told about the famous party at the house of Agathon. Apollodorus explains that the party was not a recent event, but took place several years earlier at the time of Agathon's first victory in the dramatic competition at the Great Dionysia (in 416 B.C.E.). Readers of the translation may well forget about the introductory frame as they read on; but the Greek text (in which there are distinctive syntactic forms for reported speech) constantly reminds us that we are overhearing an account of a conversation, not hearing the words of the speakers directly. There are many possible explanations for Plato's choice to introduce his dialogue in this way. On one level, the frame invites us to see the party of Agathon as a window into the past: the demoralized city that

limped to the end of the Peloponnesian War—and that would soon, in 399 B.C.E., execute Socrates—felt a nostalgia for the lost happiness of ten or fifteen years before. Perhaps, too, Plato is showing his readers that Socrates' activities and associates were less politically sinister than people might have suspected. Drinking parties were associated, in many people's minds, with clubs of antidemocratic, oligarchic aristocrats—such as Alcibiades. Athenian readers would have remembered that Alcibiades, who appears here as a drunken, devoted follower of Socrates, was disgraced and exiled from the city in 413 B.C.E. Far from plotting to overthrow the democracy, these friends just sit around talking about love—and so innocently that they neither have sex (with slave girls or each other) nor, for the most part, get drunk. On a thematic level, the frame introduces us to a central concern of the *Symposium*: the deep human desire for an absent, distant, perhaps unattainable object—whether that object is a long-gone drinking party, a sexy or puzzling person, or an abstract idea of beauty.

The *Symposium* develops into a series of speeches in praise of Eros. The themes of the speeches overlap, and each builds on what has gone before; but they are strikingly different in their approaches to the subject and in their style and tone, as each is carefully modulated to the individual speaker. First we have Phaedrus, a young follower of Socrates, who defines Eros as one of the most ancient of the gods, and emphasizes his central place in traditional mythology and poetry. Then comes the older Pausanias, the lover of Agathon, who discusses the moral, social, and legal status of sexual relationships in contemporary Athens, and distinguishes between good, "heavenly" love, which works for the education and betterment of both parties, and bad, "common" love, which is motivated only by the desire for physical pleasure. The speakers are lying on couches arranged in a circle, leaning on their elbows to sip their wine, and the next in order is Aristophanes. But he has hiccups, so the doctor, Eryximachus, speaks in his place, after giving the comic poet some useful advice about how to cure himself. Eryximachus reinterprets *eros* in terms of a confused and technical version of contemporary scientific theory: not merely does it apply to the desire of one person for another, but it becomes the physical force that drives all aspects of the universe to harmony, from the balance of elements in the human body to music and astronomy. Then Aristophanes, recovered from his hiccups, gives the most famous speech of the evening. He tells a fantastical story about how, long ago, humans were spherical creatures, some both male and female, others all male, others all female; since being split in two by the gods, each person is constantly searching for his or her "other half." The speech of Agathon—the tragic poet at whose house the party is taking place—takes us full circle back to the speech of Phaedrus: speaking in an elevated, poetic style that echoes trends in contemporary rhetoric, Agathon claims that Eros is not old, as Phaedrus claimed, but ever young and beautiful; Agathon insists that Eros can inspire even the untalented to produce inspired poetry.

Now it is Socrates' turn to speak, but he claims to be unable to perform as the others have done, since he knows nothing about the subject. So instead of giving a formal encomium (a speech of praise), he begins by cross-questioning Agathon, and gets him to admit that Eros is the desire for beauty, but is not itself beautiful. Then Socrates tells of an encounter he once had with a mysterious, probably fictional woman called Diotima, who taught him what love is. According to Diotima, Eros is not ultimately about the desire for beautiful bodies; it may begin with physical lust, but there is a "ladder of love" that we climb toward our ultimate desire: immortality and divine, eternal beauty.

At this point, the party is interrupted: the infamous young playboy and general, Alcibiades, turns up very drunk, and is half-carried inside by a flute-girl and some drunken friends. Instead of giving a speech in praise of Eros, Alcibiades gives a speech in praise—or condemnation—of Socrates. He tells how Socrates, extraordinarily by Athenian standards, practiced what we call Platonic love: although particularly appreciative of pretty young men, Socrates refused Alcibiades' sexual advances, even when they shared a blanket while out on a military campaign. In a reversal of the Athenian norm, Alcibiades, the younger man, tried to seduce the older Socrates; but Socrates remained unmoved. The relationship, or nonrelationship, of Alcibiades and Socrates forms the final test case through which we are asked to consider what we really want from one other. Does Alcibiades want the ugly old Socrates for his body, for his mind, for his wisdom, or for his beautiful soul? Is this apparently strange relationship really so different from other, more "normal" kinds of love? And what exactly does Socrates himself want?

Attitudes toward sex vary widely from one culture to another, and the *Symposium* is a vivid reminder of the fact that Athenian sexual norms were not quite like our own. All the speakers in the *Symposium* are male (with the exception of Diotima, the mysterious woman quoted by Socrates), and almost all of them (with a couple of interesting exceptions) assume that a discussion of *eros*—the whole set of emotions and behavior patterns that we might associate with falling in love—will apply primarily to men's love for younger males.

Modern readers may be tempted to apply modern categories to this kind of relationship: we call same-sex couples "homosexuals" and, depending on the age of the younger party, we might be anxious about child abuse. But these are not quite the right terms for the ancient Athenian social institution of pederasty ("boy love"). For one thing, we tend to think of homosexuality and heterosexuality as sexual identities, that is, as deep-seated, perhaps permanent inclinations; and we tend to assume that most people have either one or the other. By contrast, elite male Athenians seem to have assumed that most men will feel attraction both toward pretty boys and pretty women, and that in the normal course of events, a man in his early twenties will have highly public romantic relationships with adolescent boys before he settles down with a wife. The relationship evoked in the *Symposium* between Agathon and Pausanias is presented as unusual, in that it involves a lifelong commitment between same-sex partners, rather than a passing phase. This relationship is also unusual because it suggests some degree of equality. In a culture where women were hardly ever allowed out of the house, and where they received little or no education, it is perhaps not surprising that men mostly fell in love with one another. But it is striking, from a modern perspective, that the ideal pederastic relationship is imagined as fundamentally unequal: there must be an older man, the *erastes*, and an adolescent boy, the *eromenos*, who is courted. The "boy" may often have been as old as eighteen or nineteen, since puberty

came later in the ancient world; but presumably he may sometimes have been younger. One of the most interesting challenges of this text is to try to disentangle the sexual and social assumptions it reveals. This is a difficult task, because Plato is not, of course, reporting a real conversation, and we always have to wonder how much his version of Athenian sexuality might be slanted by his own highly individual point of view.

The *Symposium*'s vision of love and human desire is both alien and deeply familiar. Readers may feel a shock of recognition when they realize that the myth told by Aristophanes is the original source for the idea that true love is reuniting with one's "other half." And despite the strangeness of some of the sexual behaviors evoked here, Plato prompts us to ask questions that are relevant to all our lives, even beyond the realm of sexuality. What drives us to try to connect with one another? Are some sexual relationships better for us, morally or spiritually, than others? Can love be the path to truth or enlightenment? What is it that we really want from our friends and our lovers? Is sex just about pleasure, or the desire for physical closeness, or do we have a drive to get, through physical intimacy, to something nonphysical, such as understanding? If human beings long for beauty and wisdom, what are the best means of getting them? Can one person teach another to be a wiser or better person, and, if so, how? The *Symposium* provides food for deep reflection on all these issues, as well as combining, in a single text, both comic and serious drama.

Symposium[1]

PERSONS OF THE DIALOGUE.

APOLLODORUS, *who repeats to his companion the dialogue which he had heard from Aristodemus, and had already once narrated to Glaucon*

PHAEDRUS	AGATHON
PAUSANIAS	SOCRATES
ERYXIMACHUS	ALCIBIADES
ARISTOPHANES	A TROOP OF REVELLERS

SCENE:—The House of Agathon

Concerning the things about which you ask to be informed I believe that I am not ill-prepared with an answer.[2] For the day before yesterday I was coming from my own home at Phalerum[3] to the city, and one of my acquaintance, who had caught a sight of me from behind, calling out playfully in the distance, said: Apollodorus, O thou Phalerian man, halt! So I did as I was bid; and then he said, I was looking for you, Apollodorus, only just now, that I might ask you about the speeches in praise of love, which were delivered by Socrates, Alcibiades, and others, at Agathon's supper.[4] Phoenix, the son of Philip, told another person who told me of them; his narrative was very indistinct, but he said that you knew, and I wish that you would give me an account of them. Who, if not you, should be the reporter of the words of your friend? And first tell me, he said, were you present at this meeting?

Your informant, Glaucon,[5] I said, must have been very indistinct indeed, if you imagine that the occasion was recent; or that I could have been of the party.

Why, yes, he replied, I thought so.

Impossible, I said. Are you ignorant that for many years Agathon has not resided at Athens; and not three have elapsed since I became acquainted with Socrates, and have made it my daily business to know all that he says and does. There was a time when I was running about the world, fancying myself to be well employed, but I was really a most wretched being, no better than you are now. I thought that I ought to do anything rather than be a philosopher.

Well, he said, jesting apart, tell me when the meeting occurred.

In our boyhood, I replied, when Agathon won the prize with his first tragedy, on the day after that on which he and his chorus offered the sacrifice of victory.[6]

Then it must have been a long while ago, he said; and who told you—did Socrates?

No indeed, I replied, but the same person who told Phoenix;—he was a little fellow, who never wore any shoes, Aristodemus, of the deme of Cydathenaeum. He had been at Agathon's feast; and I think that in those days there was no one

---

1. Translated by Benjamin Jowett.
2. Apollodorus, a follower of Socrates, is speaking. He was present at Socrates' trial and death.
3. A port town near Athens.
4. Agathon was a tragedian. Alcibiades was a

notorious Athenian general. Both will appear later in the dialogue.
5. Probably Plato's brother, who was named Glaucon.
6. 416 B.C.E.

who was a more devoted admirer of Socrates.[7] Moreover, I have asked Socrates about the truth of some parts of his narrative, and he confirmed them. Then, said Glaucon, let us have the tale over again; is not the road to Athens just made for conversation? And so we walked, and talked of the discourses on love; and therefore, as I said at first, I am not ill-prepared to comply with your request, and will have another rehearsal of them if you like. For to speak or to hear others speak of philosophy always gives me the greatest pleasure, to say nothing of the profit. But when I hear another strain, especially that of you rich men and traders, such conversation displeases me; and I pity you who are my companions, because you think that you are doing something when in reality you are doing nothing. And I dare say that you pity me in return, whom you regard as an unhappy creature, and very probably you are right. But I certainly know of you what you only think of me—there is the difference.

COMPANION   I see, Apollodorus, that you are just the same—always speaking evil of yourself, and of others; and I do believe that you pity all mankind, with the exception of Socrates, yourself first of all, true in this to your old name, which, however deserved, I know not how you acquired, of Apollodorus the madman; for you are always raging against yourself and everybody but Socrates.

APOLLODORUS   Yes, friend, and the reason why I am said to be mad, and out of my wits, is just because I have these notions of myself and you; no other evidence is required.

COM   No more of that, Apollodorus; but let me renew my request that you would repeat the conversation.

APOLL   Well, the tale of love was on this wise:—But perhaps I had better begin at the beginning, and endeavour to give you the exact words of Aristodemus:

He said that he met Socrates fresh from the bath and sandalled; and as the sight of the sandals was unusual, he asked him whither he was going that he had been converted into such a beau:—

To a banquet at Agathon's, he replied, whose invitation to his sacrifice of victory I refused yesterday, fearing a crowd, but promising that I would come today instead; and so I have put on my finery, because he is such a fine man. What say you to going with me unasked?

I will do as you bid me, I replied.

Follow then, he said, and let us demolish the proverb:—

"To the feasts of inferior men the good unbidden go:"

instead of which our proverb will run:—

"To the feasts of the good the good unbidden go;"[8]

and this alteration may be supported by the authority of Homer himself, who not only demolishes but literally outrages the proverb. For, after picturing Agamemnon as the most valiant of men, he makes Menelaus, who is but a faint-hearted warrior, come unbidden to the banquet of Agamemnon, who is feasting and offering sacrifices, not the better to the worse, but the worse to the better.[9]

---

7. Literally, "was a lover [*erastes*] of Socrates."
8. The real proverb was "Good men go uninvited to an inferior man's feast." Socrates is punning on Agathon's name, which means "good."
9. The visit is in book 2 of the *Iliad*; Menelaus is

called a "limp spearman" in book 17. Agamemnon and Menelaus are brothers; Menelaus is the cuckolded husband of Helen, and Agamemnon is the leader of the forces who have gone to retrieve her and fight the Trojan War.

I rather fear, Socrates, said Aristodemus, lest this may still be my case; and that, like Menelaus in Homer, I shall be the inferior person, who

> "To the feasts of the wise unbidden goes."

But I shall say that I was bidden of you, and then you will have to make an excuse.

> "Two going together,"[1]

he replied, in Homeric fashion, one or other of them may invent an excuse by the way.

This was the style of their conversation as they went along. Socrates dropped behind in a fit of abstraction, and desired Aristodemus, who was waiting, to go on before him. When he reached the house of Agathon he found the doors wide open, and a comical thing happened. A servant coming out met him, and led him at once into the banqueting-hall in which the guests were reclining, for the banquet was about to begin. Welcome, Aristodemus, said Agathon, as soon as he appeared—you are just in time to sup with us; if you come on any other matter put it off, and make one of us, as I was looking for you yesterday and meant to have asked you, if I could have found you. But what have you done with Socrates?

I turned round, but Socrates was nowhere to be seen; and I had to explain that he had been with me a moment before, and that I came by his invitation to the supper.

You were quite right in coming, said Agathon; but where is he himself?

He was behind me just now, as I entered, he said, and I cannot think what has become of him.

Go and look for him, boy, said Agathon, and bring him in; and do you, Aristodemus, meanwhile take the place by Eryximachus.

The servant then assisted him to wash, and he lay down, and presently another servant came in and reported that our friend Socrates had retired into the portico of the neighbouring house. "There he is," said he, "and when I call to him he will not stir."

How strange, said Agathon; then you must call him again, and keep calling him.

Let him alone, said my informant; he has a way of stopping anywhere and losing himself without any reason. I believe that he will soon appear; do not therefore disturb him.

Well, if you think so, I will leave him, said Agathon. And then, turning to the servants, he added, "Let us have supper without waiting for him. Serve up whatever you please, for there is no one to give you orders; hitherto I have never left you to yourselves. But on this occasion imagine that you are our hosts, and that I and the company are your guests; treat us well, and then we shall commend you." After this, supper was served, but still no Socrates; and during the meal Agathon several times expressed a wish to send for him, but Aristodemus objected; and at last when the feast was about half over—for the fit, as usual, was not of long duration—Socrates entered. Agathon, who was reclining alone at the end of the table, begged that he would take the place

1. More partial quotations from the *Iliad* (10.224).

next to him; that "I may touch you," he said, "and have the benefit of that wise thought which came into your mind in the portico, and is now in your possession; for I am certain that you would not have come away until you had found what you sought."

How I wish, said Socrates, taking his place as he was desired, that wisdom could be infused by touch, out of the fuller into the emptier man, as water runs through wool out of a fuller cup into an emptier one; if that were so, how greatly should I value the privilege of reclining at your side! For you would have filled me full with a stream of wisdom plenteous and fair; whereas my own is of a very mean and questionable sort, no better than a dream. But yours is bright and full of promise, and was manifested forth in all the splendour of youth the day before yesterday, in the presence of more than thirty thousand Hellenes.[2]

You are mocking, Socrates, said Agathon, and ere long you and I will have to determine who bears off the palm of wisdom—of this Dionysus[3] shall be the judge; but at present you are better occupied with supper.

Socrates took his place on the couch, and supped with the rest; and then libations were offered, and after a hymn had been sung to the god, and there had been the usual ceremonies, they were about to commence drinking, when Pausanias said, And now, my friends, how can we drink with least injury to ourselves? I can assure you that I feel severely the effect of yesterday's potations, and must have time to recover; and I suspect that most of you are in the same predicament, for you were of the party yesterday. Consider then: How can the drinking be made easiest?

I entirely agree, said Aristophanes,[4] that we should, by all means, avoid hard drinking, for I was myself one of those who were yesterday drowned in drink.

I think that you are right, said Eryximachus, the son of Acumenus; but I should still like to hear one other person speak: Is Agathon able to drink hard?

I am not equal to it, said Agathon.

Then, said Eryximachus, the weak heads like myself, Aristodemus, Phaedrus,[5] and others who never can drink, are fortunate in finding that the stronger ones are not in a drinking mood. (I do not include Socrates, who is able either to drink or to abstain, and will not mind, whichever we do.) Well, as none of the company seem disposed to drink much, I may be forgiven for saying, as a physician, that drinking deep is a bad practice, which I never follow, if I can help, and certainly do not recommend to another, least of all to anyone who still feels the effects of yesterday's carouse.

2. The audiences of Agathon's plays. Hellenes are Greeks.
3. God of both wine and the theater.
4. The comic dramatist who was the author of, among other plays, *Lysistrata* and *Clouds*; the latter presents a hostile picture of Socrates as a Sophist, liable to talk nonsense and to

teach morally corrupting ideas to the young.
5. An associate of Socrates who appears in other Platonic dialogues, including *Phaedrus*. He was, like Alcibiades, among the group of oligarchic aristocrats exiled from Athens in 415 B.C.E. for profaning a religious ritual (the Eleusinian Mysteries).

I always do what you advise, and especially what you prescribe as a physician, rejoined Phaedrus the Myrrhinusian, and the rest of the company, if they are wise, will do the same.

It was agreed that drinking was not to be the order of the day, but that they were all to drink only so much as they pleased.

Then, said Eryximachus, as you are all agreed that drinking is to be voluntary, and that there is to be no compulsion, I move, in the next place, that the flute-girl, who has just made her appearance, be told to go away and play to herself, or, if she likes, to the women who are within. Today let us have conversation instead; and, if you will allow me, I will tell you what sort of conversation. This proposal having been accepted, Eryximachus proceeded as follows:—

I will begin, he said, after the manner of Melanippe in Euripides,

"Not mine the word"

which I am about to speak, but that of Phaedrus. For often he says to me in an indignant tone:—"What a strange thing it is, Eryximachus, that, whereas other gods have poems and hymns made in their honour, the great and glorious god, Love,[6] has no encomiast among all the poets who are so many. There are the worthy sophists too—the excellent Prodicus[7] for example, who have descanted in prose on the virtues of Heracles and other heroes; and, what is still more extraordinary, I have met with a philosophical work in which the utility of salt has been made the theme of an eloquent discourse; and many other like things have had a like honour bestowed upon them. And only to think that there should have been an eager interest created about them, and yet that to this day no one has ever dared worthily to hymn Love's praises! So entirely has this great deity been neglected." Now in this Phaedrus seems to me to be quite right, and therefore I want to offer him a contribution; also I think that at the present moment we who are here assembled cannot do better than honour the god Love. If you agree with me, there will be no lack of conversation; for I mean to propose that each of us in turn, going from left to right, shall make a speech in honour of Love. Let him give us the best which he can; and Phaedrus, because he is sitting first on the left hand, and because he is the father of the thought, shall begin.

No one will vote against you, Eryximachus, said Socrates. How can I oppose your motion, who profess to understand nothing but matters of love; nor, I presume, will Agathon and Pausanias; and there can be no doubt of Aristophanes, whose whole concern is with Dionysus and Aphrodite;[8] nor will any one disagree of those whom I see around me. The proposal, as I am aware, may seem rather hard upon us whose place is last; but we shall be contented if we hear some good speeches first. Let Phaedrus begin the praise of Love, and good luck to him. All the company expressed their assent, and desired him to do as Socrates bade him.

---

6. I.e., Eros.
7. Famous Sophist, or wisdom teacher; Socrates attended his lectures.

8. Aphrodite, goddess associated with sex and desire, is the mother of Eros (*eros* is Greek for "love" or "desire").

Aristodemus did not recollect all that was said, nor do I recollect all that he related to me; but I will tell you what I thought most worthy of remembrance, and what the chief speakers said.

Phaedrus began by affirming that Love is a mighty god, and wonderful among gods and men, but especially wonderful in his birth. For he is the eldest of the gods, which is an honour to him; and a proof of his claim to this honour is, that of his parents there is no memorial; neither poet nor prose-writer has ever affirmed that he had any. As Hesiod[9] says:—

> "First Chaos came, and then broad-bosomed Earth,
>   The everlasting seat of all that is,
>   And Love."

In other words, after Chaos, the Earth and Love, these two, came into being. Also Parmenides[1] sings of Generation:

> "First in the train of gods, he fashioned Love."

And Acusilaus[2] agrees with Hesiod. Thus numerous are the witnesses who acknowledge Love to be the eldest of the gods. And not only is he the eldest, he is also the source of the greatest benefits to us. For I know not any greater blessing to a young man who is beginning life than a virtuous lover, or to the lover than a beloved youth. For the principle which ought to be the guide of men who would nobly live—that principle, I say, neither kindred, nor honour, nor wealth, nor any other motive is able to implant so well as love. Of what am I speaking? Of the sense of honour and dishonour, without which neither states nor individuals ever do any good or great work. And I say that a lover who is detected in doing any dishonourable act, or submitting through cowardice when any dishonour is done to him by another, will be more pained at being detected by his beloved than at being seen by his father, or by his companions, or by anyone else. The beloved too, when he is found in any disgraceful situation, has the same feeling about his lover. And if there were only some way of contriving that a state or an army should be made up of lovers and their loves,[3] they would be the very best governors of their own city, abstaining from all dishonour, and emulating one another in honour; and when fighting at each other's side, although a mere handful, they would overcome the world. For what lover would not choose rather to be seen by all mankind than by his beloved, either when abandoning his post or throwing away his arms? He would be ready to die a thousand deaths rather than endure this. Or who would desert his beloved or fail him in the hour of danger? The veriest coward would become an inspired hero, equal to the bravest, at such a time; Love would inspire him. That courage which, as Homer says, the god breathes into the souls of some heroes, Love of his own nature infuses into the lover.

Love will make men dare to die for their beloved—love alone; and women as well as men. Of this, Alcestis, the daughter of Pelias, is a monument to all

---

9. Greek poet of about the 7th century B.C.E.; the quotation comes from his *Theogony* (116–20, with a line skipped).
1. Pre-Socratic (early 5th century B.C.E.) philosopher.

2. Early 5th-century genealogical writer.
3. The Greek city of Thebes did create such an army, the Sacred Band, in 379–378 B.C.E., probably a little after the composition of the *Symposium*.

Hellas;[4] for she was willing to lay down her life on behalf of her husband, when no one else would, although he had a father and mother; but the tenderness of her love so far exceeded theirs, that she made them seem to be strangers in blood to their own son, and in name only related to him; and so noble did this action of hers appear to the gods, as well as to men, that among the many who have done virtuously she is one of the very few to whom, in admiration of her noble action, they have granted the privilege of returning alive to earth; such exceeding honour is paid by the gods to the devotion and virtue of love. But Orpheus,[5] the son of Oeagrus, the harper, they sent empty away, and presented to him an apparition only of her whom he sought, but herself they would not give up, because he showed no spirit; he was only a harp-player, and did not dare like Alcestis to die for love, but was contriving how he might enter Hades alive; moreover, they afterwards caused him to suffer death at the hands of women, as the punishment of his cowardliness. Very different was the reward of the true love of Achilles[6] towards his lover Patroclus—his lover and not his love (the notion that Patroclus was the beloved one is a foolish error into which Aeschylus has fallen,[7] for Achilles was surely the fairer of the two, fairer also than all the other heroes; and, as Homer informs us, he was still beardless, and younger far). And greatly as the gods honour the virtue of love, still the return of love on the part of the beloved to the lover is more admired and valued and rewarded by them, for the lover is more divine; because he is inspired by God. Now Achilles was quite aware, for he had been told by his mother, that he might avoid death and return home, and live to a good old age, if he abstained from slaying Hector.[8] Nevertheless he gave his life to revenge his friend, and dared to die, not only in his defence, but after he was dead. Wherefore the gods honoured him even above Alcestis, and sent him to the Islands of the Blest.[9] These are my reasons for affirming that Love is the eldest and noblest and mightiest of the gods, and the chiefest author and giver of virtue in life, and of happiness after death.

This, or something like this, was the speech of Phaedrus; and some other speeches followed which Aristodemus did not remember; the next which he repeated was that of Pausanias. Phaedrus, he said, the argument has not been set before us, I think, quite in the right form;—we should not be called upon to praise Love in such an indiscriminate manner. If there were only one Love, then what you said would be well enough; but since there are more Loves than one, you should have begun by determining which of them was to be the theme of our praises. I will amend this defect; and first of all I will tell you which Love is deserving of praise, and then try to hymn the praiseworthy one in a manner worthy of him. For we all know that Love is inseparable from Aphrodite, and if

4. Greece. "Alcestis": in myth, when Admetus was fated to die, his wife Alcestis agreed to die in his stead. Euripides' *Alcestis* tells the story.
5. Mythical poet who tried to get his dead wife, Eurydice, back from the underworld, but failed, and was eventually torn apart by female worshippers of Dionysus (known as Maenads or Bacchantes).
6. Achilles was a Greek hero of the Trojan War, as recounted in Homer's *Iliad*.
7. In a lost tragedy, *Myrmidons*.

8. In the *Iliad*, Achilles knows that he is fated to die if he stays at Troy. He chooses to stay, to kill the Trojan hero Hector, who killed Achilles' beloved friend Patroclus. In Homer, Achilles and Patroclus share a tent and are devoted to each other, but they do not seem to be physical lovers; later Athenian tradition reinterpreted the relationship in more sexual terms.
9. In Greek mythology, a paradise for virtuous heroes.

there were only one Aphrodite there would be only one Love; but as there are two goddesses there must be two Loves. And am I not right in asserting that there are two goddesses? The elder one, having no mother, who is called the heavenly Aphrodite—she is the daughter of Uranus; the younger, who is the daughter of Zeus and Dione—her we call common; and the Love who is her fellow-worker is rightly named common, as the other love is called heavenly. All the gods ought to have praise given to them, but not without distinction of their natures; and therefore I must try to distinguish the characters of the two Loves. Now actions vary according to the manner of their performance. Take, for example, that which we are now doing, drinking, singing, and talking—these actions are not in themselves either good or evil, but they turn out in this or that way according to the mode of performing them; and when well done they are good, and when wrongly done they are evil; and in like manner not every love, but only that which has a noble purpose, is noble and worthy of praise. The Love who is the offspring of the common Aphrodite is essentially common, and has no discrimination, being such as the meaner sort of men feel, and is apt to be of women as well as of youths, and is of the body rather than of the soul—the most foolish beings are the objects of this love which desires only to gain an end, but never thinks of accomplishing the end nobly, and therefore does good and evil quite indiscriminately. The goddess who is his mother is far younger than the other, and she was born of the union of the male and female, and partakes of both. But the offspring of the heavenly Aphrodite is derived from a mother in whose birth the female has no part,—she is from the male only; this is that love which is of youths, and the goddess being older, there is nothing of wantonness in her. Those who are inspired by this love turn to the male, and delight in him who is the more valiant and intelligent nature; anyone may recognise the pure enthusiasts in the very character of their attachments. For they love not boys, but intelligent beings whose reason is beginning to be developed, much about the time at which their beards begin to grow.[1] And in choosing young men to be their companions, they mean to be faithful to them, and pass their whole life in company with them, not to take them in their inexperience, and deceive them, and play the fool with them, or run away from one to another of them. But the love of young boys should be forbidden by law, because their future is uncertain; they may turn out good or bad, either in body or soul, and much noble enthusiasm may be thrown away upon them; in this matter the good are a law to themselves, and the coarser sort of lovers ought to be restrained by force, as we restrain or attempt to restrain them from fixing their affections on women of free birth. These are the persons who bring a reproach on love; and some have been led to deny the lawfulness of such attachments because they see the impropriety and evil of them; for surely nothing that is decorously and lawfully done can justly be censured. Now here and in Lacedaemon[2] the rules about love are perplexing, but in most cities they are simple and easily intelligible; in Elis and Boeotia, and in countries having no gifts of eloquence, they are very straightforward; the law is simply in favour of these connexions, and no one, whether young or old, has anything to say to their discredit; the reason being, as I sup-

1. "Boys" does not mean small children but, rather, young teenagers. The physical signs of adolescence came later in the premodern world; beards often did not grow until a boy was about eighteen.

2. I.e., Sparta, a major Greek city-state and the enemy of Athens in the Peloponnesian War.

pose, that they are men of few words in those parts, and therefore the lovers do not like the trouble of pleading their suit. In Ionia and other places, and generally in countries which are subject to the barbarians, the custom is held to be dishonourable; loves of youths share the evil repute in which philosophy and gymnastics are held, because they are inimical to tyranny; for the interests of rulers require that their subjects should be poor in spirit, and that there should be no strong bond of friendship or society among them, which love, above all other motives, is likely to inspire, as our Athenian tyrants learned by experience; for the love of Aristogeiton and the constancy of Harmodius had a strength which undid their power.[3] And, therefore, the ill-repute into which these attachments have fallen is to be ascribed to the evil condition of those who make them to be ill-reputed; that is to say, to the self-seeking of the governors and the cowardice of the governed; on the other hand, the indiscriminate honour which is given to them in some countries is attributable to the laziness of those who hold this opinion of them. In our own country a far better principle prevails, but, as I was saying, the explanation of it is rather perplexing. For, observe that open loves are held to be more honourable than secret ones, and that the love of the noblest and highest, even if their persons are less beautiful than others, is especially honourable. Consider, too, how great is the encouragement which all the world gives to the lover; neither is he supposed to be doing anything dishonourable; but if he succeeds he is praised, and if he fail he is blamed. And in the pursuit of his love the custom of mankind allows him to do many strange things, which philosophy would bitterly censure if they were done from any motive of interest, or wish for office or power. He may pray, and entreat, and supplicate, and swear, and lie on a mat at the door, and endure a slavery worse than that of any slave—in any other case friends and enemies would be equally ready to prevent him, but now there is no friend who will be ashamed of him and admonish him, and no enemy will charge him with meanness or flattery; the actions of a lover have a grace which ennobles them; and custom has decided that they are highly commendable and that there is no loss of character in them; and, what is strangest of all, he only may swear and forswear himself (so men say), and the gods will forgive his transgression, for there is no such thing as a lover's oath. Such is the entire liberty which gods and men have allowed the lover, according to the custom which prevails in our part of the world. From this point of view a man fairly argues that in Athens to love and to be loved is held to be a very honourable thing. But when parents forbid their sons to talk with their lovers, and place them under a tutor's care,[4] who is appointed to see to these things, and their companions and equals cast in their teeth anything of the sort which they may observe, and their elders refuse to silence the reprovers and do not rebuke them—anyone who reflects on all this will, on the contrary, think that we hold these practices to be most disgraceful. But, as I was saying at first, the truth as I imagine is, that whether such practices are honourable or whether they are dishonourable is not a simple question; they are honourable to him who follows them honourably, dishonourable to him who follows them dishonourably. There is dishonour in yielding to the evil, or in an evil manner; but there is honour in yielding to the good, or in an honourable manner. Evil is the vulgar lover who

---

3. Athenian lovers who tried to overthrow the tyrant Hippias in 514 B.C.E.

4. Tutors were often slaves appointed to act as chaperones.

loves the body rather than the soul, inasmuch as he is not even stable, because he loves a thing which is in itself unstable, and therefore when the bloom of youth which he was desiring is over, he takes wing and flies away, in spite of all his words and promises; whereas the love of the noble disposition is lifelong, for it becomes one with the everlasting. The custom of our country would have both of them proven well and truly, and would have us yield to the one sort of lover and avoid the other, and therefore encourages some to pursue, and others to fly; testing both the lover and beloved in contests and trials, until they show to which of the two classes they respectively belong. And this is the reason why, in the first place, a hasty attachment is held to be dishonourable, because time is the true test of this as of most other things; and secondly there is a dishonour in being overcome by the love of money, or of wealth, or of political power, whether a man is frightened into surrender by the loss of them, or, having experienced the benefits of money and political corruption, is unable to rise above the seductions of them. For none of these things are of a permanent or lasting nature; not to mention that no generous friendship ever sprang from them. There remains, then, only one way of honourable attachment which custom allows in the beloved, and this is the way of virtue; for as we admitted that any service which the lover does to him is not to be accounted flattery or a dishonour to himself, so the beloved has one way only of voluntary service which is not dishonourable, and this is virtuous service.

For we have a custom, and according to our custom anyone who does service to another under the idea that he will be improved by him either in wisdom, or in some other particular of virtue—such a voluntary service, I say, is not to be regarded as a dishonour, and is not open to the charge of flattery. And these two customs, one the love of youth, and the other the practice of philosophy and virtue in general, ought to meet in one, and then the beloved may honourably indulge the lover. For when the lover and beloved come together, having each of them a law, and the lover thinks that he is right in doing any service which he can to his gracious loving one; and the other that he is right in showing any kindness which he can to him who is making him wise and good; the one capable of communicating wisdom and virtue, the other seeking to acquire them with a view to education and wisdom; when the two laws of love are fulfilled and meet in one—then, and then only, may the beloved yield with honour to the lover. Nor when love is of this disinterested sort is there any disgrace in being deceived, but in every other case there is equal disgrace in being or not being deceived. For he who is gracious to his lover under the impression that he is rich, and is disappointed of his gains because he turns out to be poor, is disgraced all the same: for he has done his best to show that he would give himself up to anyone's "uses base" for the sake of money; but this is not honourable. And on the same principle he who gives himself to a lover because he is a good man, and in the hope that he will be improved by his company, shows himself to be virtuous, even though the object of his affection turn out to be a villain, and to have no virtue; and if he is deceived he has committed a noble error. For he has proved that for his part he will do anything for anybody with a view to virtue and improvement, than which there can be nothing nobler. Thus noble in every case is the acceptance of another for the sake of virtue. This is that love which is the love of the heavenly goddess, and is heavenly, and of great price to individuals and cities, making the lover and the beloved alike eager in the work of their own improvement. But all other loves are the offspring of the other, who is the common goddess. To you, Phaedrus, I offer this my contribution in praise of love, which is as good as I could make extempore.

Pausanlas came to a pause—this is the balanced way in which I have been taught by the wise to speak; and Aristodemus said that the turn of Aristophanes was next, but either he had eaten too much, or from some other cause he had the hiccough, and was obliged to change turns with Eryximachus the physician, who was reclining on the couch below him. Eryximachus, he said, you ought either to stop my hiccough, or to speak in my turn until I have left off.

I will do both, said Eryximachus:[5] I will speak in your turn, and do you speak in mine; and while I am speaking let me recommend you to hold your breath, and if after you have done so for some time the hiccough is no better, then gargle with a little water; and if it still continues, tickle your nose with something and sneeze; and if you sneeze once or twice, even the most violent hiccough is sure to go. I will do as you prescribe, said Aristophanes, and now get on.

Eryximachus spoke as follows: Seeing that Pausanias made a fair beginning, and but a lame ending, I must endeavour to supply his deficiency. I think that he has rightly distinguished two kinds of love. But my art further informs me that the double love is not merely an affection of the soul of man towards the fair, or towards anything, but is to be found in the bodies of all animals and in productions of the earth, and I may say in all that is; such is the conclusion which I seem to have gathered from my own art of medicine, whence I learn how great and wonderful and universal is the deity of love, whose empire extends over all things, divine as well as human. And from medicine I will begin that I may do honour to my art. There are in the human body these two kinds of love, which are confessedly different and unlike, and being unlike, they have loves and desires which are unlike; and the desire of the healthy is one, and the desire of the diseased is another; and as Pausanias was just now saying that to indulge good men is honourable, and bad men dishonourable:— so too in the body the good and healthy elements are to be indulged, and the bad elements and the elements of disease are not to be indulged, but discouraged. And this is what the physician has to do, and in this the art of medicine consists: for medicine may be regarded generally as the knowledge of the loves and desires of the body, and how to satisfy them or not; and the best physician is he who is able to separate fair love from foul, or to convert one into the other; and he who knows how to eradicate and how to implant love, whichever is required, and can reconcile the most hostile elements in the constitution and make them loving friends, is a skilful practitioner. Now the most hostile are the most opposite, such as hot and cold, bitter and sweet, moist and dry, and the like. And my ancestor, Asclepius,[6] knowing how to implant friendship and accord in these elements, was the creator of our art, as our friends the poets

5. *Eryximachus* may mean "belch fighter"—an appropriate name for a man who can cure hiccups.
6. God of medicine.

here tell us, and I believe them; and not only medicine in every branch, but the arts of gymnastic and husbandry are under his dominion. Anyone who pays the least attention to the subject will also perceive that in music there is the same reconciliation of opposites; and I suppose that this must have been the meaning of Heracleitus,[7] although his words are not accurate; for he says that The One is united by disunion, like the harmony of the bow and the lyre. Now there is an absurdity in saying that harmony is discord or is composed of elements which are still in a state of discord. But what he probably meant was, that harmony is composed of differing notes of higher or lower pitch which disagreed once, but are now reconciled by the art of music; for if the higher and lower notes still disagreed, there could be no harmony,—clearly not. For harmony is a symphony, and symphony is an agreement; but an agreement of disagreements while they disagree there cannot be; you cannot harmonize that which disagrees. In like manner rhythm is compounded of elements short and long, once differing and now in accord; which accordance, as in the former instance, medicine, so in all these other cases, music implants, making love and unison to grow up among them; and thus music, too, is concerned with the principles of love in their application to harmony and rhythm. Again, in the essential nature of harmony and rhythm there is no difficulty in discerning love which has not yet become double. But when you want to use them in actual life, either in the composition of songs or in the correct performance of airs or metres composed already, which latter is called education, then the difficulty begins, and the good artist is needed. Then the old tale has to be repeated of fair and heavenly love—the love of Urania[8] the fair and heavenly muse, and of the duty of accepting the temperate, and those who are as yet intemperate only that they may become temperate, and of preserving their love; and again, of the vulgar Polyhymnia,[9] who must be used with circumspection that the pleasure be enjoyed, but may not generate licentiousness; just as in my own art it is a great matter so to regulate the desires of the epicure that he may gratify his tastes without the attendant evil of disease. Whence I infer that in music, in medicine, in all other things human as well as divine, both loves ought to be noted as far as may be, for they are both present.

The course of the seasons is also full of both these principles; and when, as I was saying, the elements of hot and cold, moist and dry, attain the harmonious love of one another and blend in temperance and harmony, they bring to men, animals, and plants health and plenty, and do them no harm; whereas the wanton love, getting the upper hand and affecting the seasons of the year, is very destructive and injurious, being the source of pestilence, and bringing many other kinds of diseases on animals and plants; for hoarfrost and hail and blight spring from the excesses and disorders of these elements of love, which to know in relation to the revolutions of the heavenly bodies and the seasons of the year is termed astronomy. Furthermore all sacrifices and the whole province of divination, which is the art of communion between gods and men—these, I say, are concerned only with the preservation of the good and the cure of the evil love. For all manner of impiety is likely to ensue if, instead of accepting and honouring and reverencing the harmonious love in

7. Pre-Socratic philosopher from Ephesus.
8. Muse of astronomy, often associated with universal love.
9. Muse of sacred poetry.

all his actions, a man honours the other love, whether in his feelings towards gods or parents, towards the living or the dead. Wherefore the business of divination is to see to these loves and to heal them, and divination is the peacemaker of gods and men, working by a knowledge of the religious or irreligious tendencies which exist in human loves. Such is the great and mighty, or rather omnipotent force of love in general. And the love, more especially, which is concerned with the good, and which is perfected in company with temperance and justice, whether among gods or men, has the greatest power, and is the source of all our happiness and harmony, and makes us friends with the gods who are above us, and with one another. I dare say that I too have omitted several things which might be said in praise of Love, but this was not intentional, and you, Aristophanes, may now supply the omission or take some other line of commendation; for I perceive that you are rid of the hiccough.

Yes, said Aristophanes, who followed, the hiccough is gone; not, however, until I applied the sneezing; and I wonder whether the harmony of the body has a love of such noises and ticklings, for I no sooner applied the sneezing than I was cured.

Eryximachus said: Beware, friend Aristophanes, although you are going to speak, you are making fun of me; and I shall have to watch and see whether I cannot have a laugh at your expense, when you might speak in peace.

You are quite right, said Aristophanes, laughing. I will unsay my words; but do you please not to watch me, as I fear that in the speech which I am about to make, instead of others laughing with me, which is to the manner born of our muse and would be all the better, I shall only be laughed at by them.

Do you expect to shoot your bolt and escape, Aristophanes? Well, perhaps if you are very careful and bear in mind that you will be called to account, I may be induced to let you off.

Aristophanes professed to open another vein of discourse; he had a mind to praise Love in another way, unlike that either of Pausanias or Eryximachus. Mankind, he said, judging by their neglect of him, have never, as I think, at all understood the power of Love. For if they had understood him they would surely have built noble temples and altars, and offered solemn sacrifices in his honour; but this is not done, and most certainly ought to be done: since of all the gods he is the best friend of men, the helper and the healer of the ills which are the great impediment to the happiness of the race. I will try to describe his power to you, and you shall teach the rest of the world what I am teaching you. In the first place, let me treat of the nature of man and what has happened to it; for the original human nature was not like the present, but different. The sexes were not two as they are now, but originally three in number; there was man, woman, and the union of the two, having a name corresponding to this double nature, which had once a real existence, but is now lost, and the word "Androgynous" is only preserved as a term of reproach. In the second place, the primeval man was round, his back and sides forming a circle; and he had four hands and four feet, one head with two faces, looking opposite ways, set on a round neck and precisely alike; also four ears, two privy members, and the remainder to correspond. He could walk upright as men now do, backwards or forwards as he pleased, and he could also roll over and over at a great pace, turning on his four hands and four feet, eight in all, like tumblers going over and over with their legs in the air; this was when he wanted to run fast. Now the sexes were three, and such as I have described them; because the sun, moon, and earth are three; and the man was originally the child of the sun, the woman of the earth, and the man-woman of the moon, which is made up of sun and earth, and they were all round and moved round and round like their parents. Terrible was their might and strength, and the thoughts of their hearts were great, and they made an attack upon the gods;[1] of them is told the tale of Otys and Ephialtes who, as Homer says, dared to scale heaven, and would have laid hands upon the gods. Doubt reigned in the celestial councils. Should they kill them and annihilate the race with thunderbolts, as they had done the giants, then there would be an end of the sacrifices and worship which men offered to them; but, on the other hand, the gods could not suffer their insolence to be unrestrained. At last, after a good deal of reflection, Zeus discovered a way. He said: "Methinks I have a plan which will humble their pride and improve their manners; men shall continue to exist, but I will cut them in two and then they will be diminished in strength and increased in numbers; this will have the advantage of making them more profitable to us. They shall walk upright on two legs, and if they continue insolent and will not be quiet, I will split them again and they shall hop about on a single leg." He spoke and cut men in two, like a sorb-apple which is halved for pickling, or as you might divide an egg with a hair; and as he cut them one after another, he bade Apollo give the face and the half of the neck a turn in order that the man might contemplate the section of himself: he would thus learn a lesson of humility. Apollo[2] was also bidden to heal their wounds and compose their forms. So he gave a turn to the face and pulled the skin from the sides all over that which in our language is called the belly, like the purses which draw in, and he made one mouth at the centre, which he fastened in a knot (the same which is called the navel); he also moulded the breast and took out most of the wrinkles, much as a shoemaker might smooth leather upon a last; he left a few, however, in the region of the belly and navel, as a memorial of the primeval state. After the division the two parts of man, each desiring his other half, came together, and throwing their arms about one another, entwined in mutual embraces, longing to grow into one, they were on the point of dying from hunger and self-neglect, because they did not like to do anything apart; and when one of the halves died and the other survived, the survivor sought another mate, man or woman as we call them,—being the sections of entire men or women,—and clung to that. They were being destroyed, when Zeus in pity of them invented a new plan: he turned the parts of generation round to the front, for this had not been always their position, and they sowed the seed no longer as hitherto like grasshoppers in the ground, but in one another; and after the transposition the male generated in the female in order that by the mutual embraces of man and woman they might breed, and the race might continue; or if man came to man they might be satisfied, and rest, and go their ways to the business of life: so ancient is the desire of one another which is implanted in us, reuniting our original nature, making one of two, and healing the state of man. Each of us when

---

1. In the *Odyssey* (11.308–21), the giants tried to pile mountains on top of each other to reach the gods.

2. God of light and also of medicine and healing.

separated, having one side only, like a flat fish, is but the indenture of a man, and he is always looking for his other half. Men who are a section of that double nature which was once called Androgynous are lovers of women; adulterers are generally of this breed, and also adulterous women who lust after men: the women who are a section of the woman do not care for men, but have female attachments; the female companions are of this sort. But they who are a section of the male follow the male, and while they are young, being slices of the original man, they hang about men and embrace them, and they are themselves the best of boys and youths, because they have the most manly nature. Some indeed assert that they are shameless, but this is not true; for they do not act thus from any want of shame, but because they are valiant and manly, and have a manly countenance, and they embrace that which is like them. And these when they grow up become our statesmen, and these only, which is a great proof of the truth of what I am saying. When they reach manhood they are lovers of youth, and are not naturally inclined to marry or beget children,—if at all, they do so only in obedience to the law; but they are satisfied if they may be allowed to live with one another unwedded; and such a nature is prone to love and ready to return love, always embracing that which is akin to him. And when one of them meets with his other half, the actual half of himself, whether he be a lover of youth or a lover of another sort, the pair are lost in an amazement of love and friendship and intimacy, and one will not be out of the other's sight, as I may say, even for a moment: these are the people who pass their whole lives together; yet they could not explain what they desire of one another. For the intense yearning which each of them has towards the other does not appear to be the desire of lover's intercourse, but of something else which the soul of either evidently desires and cannot tell, and of which she has only a dark and doubtful presentiment. Suppose Hephaestus,[3] with his instruments, to come to the pair who are lying side by side and to say to them, "What do you people want of one another?" they would be unable to explain. And suppose further, that when he saw their perplexity he said: "Do you desire to be wholly one; always day and night to be in one another's company? for if this is what you desire, I am ready to melt you into one and let you grow together, so that being two you shall become one, and while you live live a common life as if you were a single man, and after your death in the world below still be one departed soul instead of two—I ask whether this is what you lovingly desire, and whether you are satisfied to attain this?"—there is not a man of them who when he heard the proposal would deny or would not acknowledge that this meeting and melting into one another, this becoming one instead of two, was the very expression of his ancient need. And the reason is that human nature was originally one and we were a whole, and the desire and pursuit of the whole is called love. There was a time, I say, when we were one, but now because of the wickedness of mankind God has dispersed us, as the Arcadians were dispersed into villages by the Lacedaemonians.[4] And if we are not obedient to the gods, there is a danger that we shall be split up again and go about in basso-relievo, like the

3. God of fire and metalworking.
4. After the Arcadian city of Mantinea opposed Sparta, Sparta retaliated and prevented further insurgency by dividing the population, in

385 B.C.E. This reference is therefore anachronistic in terms of the dramatic date of the dialogue.

profile figures having only half a nose which are sculptured on monuments, and that we shall be like tallies. Wherefore let us exhort all men to piety, that we may avoid evil, and obtain the good, of which Love is to us the lord and minister; and let no one oppose him—he is the enemy of the gods who opposes him. For if we are friends of the god and at peace with him we shall find our own true loves, which rarely happens in this world at present. I am serious, and therefore I must beg Eryximachus not to make fun or to find any allusion in what I am saying to Pausanias and Agathon, who, as I suspect, are both of the manly nature, and belong to the class which I have been describing. But my words have a wider application—they include men and women everywhere; and I believe that if our loves were perfectly accomplished, and each one returning to his primeval nature had his original true love, then our race would be happy. And if this would be best of all, the best in the next degree and under present circumstances must be the nearest approach to such an union; and that will be the attainment of a congenial love. Wherefore, if we would praise him who has given to us the benefit, we must praise the god Love, who is our greatest benefactor, both leading us in this life back to our own nature, and giving us high hopes for the future, for he promises that if we are pious, he will restore us to our original state, and heal us and make us happy and blessed. This, Eryximachus, is my discourse of love, which, although different to yours, I must beg you to leave unassailed by the shafts of your ridicule, in order that each may have his turn; each, or rather either, for Agathon and Socrates are the only ones left.

Indeed, I am not going to attack you, said Eryximachus, for I thought your speech charming, and did I not know that Agathon and Socrates are masters in the art of love, I should be really afraid that they would have nothing to say, after the world of things which have been said already. But, for all that, I am not without hopes.

Socrates said: You played your part well, Eryximachus; but if you were as I am now, or rather as I shall be when Agathon has spoken, you would, indeed, be in a great strait.

You want to cast a spell over me, Socrates, said Agathon, in the hope that I may be disconcerted at the expectation raised among the audience that I shall speak well.

I should be strangely forgetful, Agathon, replied Socrates, of the courage and magnanimity which you showed when your own compositions were about to be exhibited, and you came upon the stage with the actors and faced the vast theatre altogether undismayed, if I thought that your nerves could be fluttered at a small party of friends.

Do you think, Socrates, said Agathon, that my head is so full of the theatre as not to know how much more formidable to a man of sense a few good judges are than many fools?

Nay, replied Socrates, I should be very wrong in attributing to you, Agathon, that or any other want of refinement. And I am quite aware that if you happened to meet with any whom you thought wise, you would care for their opinion much more than for that of the many. But then we, having been a part of the foolish many in the theatre, cannot be regarded as the select wise; though I know that if you chanced to be in the presence, not of one of ourselves, but of some really wise man, you would be ashamed of disgracing your-self before him—would you not?

Yes, said Agathon.

But before the many you would not be ashamed, if you thought that you were doing something disgraceful in their presence?

Here Phaedrus interrupted them, saying: Do not answer him, my dear Aga-thon; for if he can only get a partner with whom he can talk, especially a good-looking one, he will no longer care about the completion of our plan. Now I love to hear him talk; but just at present I must not forget the encomium on Love which I ought to receive from him and from everyone. When you and he have paid your tribute to the god, then you may talk.

Very good, Phaedrus, said Agathon; I see no reason why I should not pro-ceed with my speech, as I shall have many other opportunities of conversing with Socrates. Let me say first how I ought to speak, and then speak:—

The previous speakers, instead of praising the god Love, or unfolding his nature, appear to have congratulated mankind on the benefits which he con-fers upon them. But I would rather praise the god first, and then speak of his gifts; this is always the right way of praising everything. May I say without impiety or offence, that of all the blessed gods he is the most blessed because he is the fairest and best? And he is the fairest: for, in the first place, he is the youngest, and of his youth he is himself the witness, fleeing out of the way of age, who is swift enough, swifter truly than most of us like:—Love hates him and will not come near him; but youth and love live and move together—like to like, as the proverb says. Many things were said by Phaedrus about Love in which I agree with him; but I cannot agree that he is older than Iapetus and Kronos[5]:—not so; I maintain him to be the youngest of the gods, and youthful ever. The ancient doings among the gods of which Hesiod and Parmenides spoke, if the tradition of them be true, were done of Necessity and not of Love; had Love been in those days, there would have been no chaining or mutilation of the gods, or other violence, but peace and sweetness, as there is now in heaven, since the rule of Love began. Love is young and also tender; he ought to have a poet like Homer to describe his tenderness, as Homer says of Ate, that she is a goddess and tender:—

> "Her feet are tender, for she sets her steps,
> Not on the ground but on the heads of men:"[6]

herein is an excellent proof of her tenderness,—that she walks not upon the hard but upon the soft. Let us adduce a similar proof of the tenderness of Love; for he walks not upon the earth, nor yet upon the skulls of men, which are not so very soft, but in the hearts and souls of both gods and men, which are of all things the softest: in them he walks and dwells and makes his home. Not in every soul without exception, for where there is hardness he departs, where there is softness there he dwells; and nestling always with his feet and in all manner of ways in the softest of soft places, how can he be other than the softest of all things? Of a truth he is the tenderest as well as the youngest, and

5. Titans. Kronos was the father of Zeus; Iapetus was Kronos's brother. Zeus castrated, deposed, and imprisoned Kronos.
6. *Iliad* 19.92–93.

also he is of flexile form; for if he were hard and without flexure he could not enfold all things, or wind his way into and out of every soul of man undiscovered. And a proof of his flexibility and symmetry of form is his grace, which is universally admitted to be in an especial manner the attribute of Love; ungrace and love are always at war with one another. The fairness of his complexion is revealed by his habitation among the flowers; for he dwells not amid bloomless or fading beauties, whether of body or soul or aught else, but in the place of flowers and scents, there he sits and abides. Concerning the beauty of the god I have said enough; and yet there remains much more which I might say. Of his virtue I have now to speak: his greatest glory is that he can neither do nor suffer wrong to or from any god or any man; for he suffers not by force if he suffers; force comes not near him, neither when he acts does he act by force. For all men in all things serve him of their own free will, and where there is voluntary agreement, there, as the laws which are the lords of the city say, is justice. And not only is he just but exceedingly temperate, for Temperance[7] is the acknowledged ruler of the pleasures and desires, and no pleasure ever masters Love; he is their master and they are his servants; and if he conquers them he must be temperate indeed. As to courage, even the God of War is no match for him; he is the captive and Love is the lord, for love, the love of Aphrodite, masters him, as the tale runs;[8] and the master is stronger than the servant. And if he conquers the bravest of all others, he must be himself the bravest. Of his courage and justice and temperance I have spoken, but I have yet to speak of his wisdom; and according to the measure of my ability I must try to do my best. In the first place he is a poet (and here, like Eryximachus, I magnify my art), and he is also the source of poesy in others, which he could not be if he were not himself a poet. And at the touch of him everyone becomes a poet, "even though he had no music in him before";[9] this also is a proof that Love is a good poet and accomplished in all the fine arts; for no one can give to another that which he has not himself, or teach that of which he has no knowledge. Who will deny that the creation of the animals is his doing? Are they not all the works of his wisdom, born and begotten of him? And as to the artists, do we not know that he only of them whom love inspires has the light of fame?—he whom Love touches not walks in darkness. The arts of medicine and archery and divination were discovered by Apollo, under the guidance of love and desire; so that he too is a disciple of Love. Also the melody of the Muses, the metallurgy of Hephaestus, the weaving of Athene, the empire of Zeus over gods and men, are all due to Love, who was the inventor of them. And so Love set in order the empire of the gods—the love of beauty, as is evident, for with deformity Love has no concern. In the days of old, as I began by saying, dreadful deeds were done among the gods, for they were ruled by Necessity; but now since the birth of Love, and from the Love of the beautiful, has sprung every good in heaven and earth. Therefore, Phaedrus, I say of Love that he is the fairest and best in himself, and the cause of what is fairest and best in all other

---

7. "Temperance" is a translation of *sophrosyne*, which means "self-control" or "healthy-mindedness."
8. Ares and Aphrodite were adulterous lovers.

Hephaestus, Aphrodite's husband, caught them in bed and trapped them in a net.
9. Quotation from a fragment by Euripides.

things. And there comes into my mind a line of poetry in which he is said to be the god who

> "Gives peace on earth and calms the stormy deep,
> Who stills the winds and bids the sufferer sleep"

This is he who empties men of disaffection and fills them with affection, who makes them to meet together at banquets such as these: in sacrifices, feasts, dances, he is our lord—who sends courtesy and sends away discourtesy, who gives kindness ever and never gives unkindness; the friend of the good, the wonder of the wise, the amazement of the gods; desired by those who have no part in him, and precious to those who have the better part in him; parent of delicacy, luxury, desire, fondness, softness, grace; regardful of the good, regardless of the evil: in every word, work, wish, fear—saviour, pilot, comrade, helper; glory of gods and men, leader best and brightest: in whose footsteps let every man follow, sweetly singing in his honour and joining in that sweet strain with which love charms the souls of gods and men. Such is the speech, Phaedrus, half-playful, yet having a certain measure of seriousness, which, according to my ability, I dedicate to the god.

When Agathon had done speaking, Aristodemus said that there was a general cheer; the young man was thought to have spoken in a manner worthy of himself, and of the god. And Socrates, looking at Eryximachus, said: Tell me, son of Acumenus, was there not reason in my fears? and was I not a true prophet when I said that Agathon would make a wonderful oration, and that I should be in a strait?

The part of the prophecy which concerns Agathon, replied Eryximachus, appears to me to be true; but not the other part—that you will be in a strait.

Why, my dear friend, said Socrates, must not I or anyone be in a strait who has to speak after he has heard such a rich and varied discourse? I am especially struck with the beauty of the concluding words—who could listen to them without amazement? When I reflected on the immeasurable inferiority of my own powers, I was ready to run away for shame, if there had been a possibility of escape. For I was reminded of Gorgias,[1] and at the end of his speech I fancied that Agathon was shaking at me the Gorginian or Gorgonian[2] head of the great master of rhetoric, which was simply to turn me and my speech into stone, as Homer says, and strike me dumb. And then I perceived how foolish I had been in consenting to take my turn with you in praising love, and saying that I too was a master of the art, when I really had no conception how anything ought to be praised. For in my simplicity I imagined that the topics of praise should be true, and that this being presupposed, out of the true the speaker was to choose the best and set them forth in the best manner. And I felt quite proud, thinking that I knew the nature of true praise, and should speak well. Whereas I now see that the intention was to attribute to Love every species of greatness and glory, whether really belonging to him or not, without regard to truth or falsehood—that was no matter; for the original proposal seems to have been not that each of you should really praise Love, but only that you should appear to praise him. And so you attribute to Love every imag-

---

1. Sophist and orator (c. 485–c. 380 B.C.E.), known for his distinctively ornate style. 2. A pun. The monstrous Gorgon's head turned onlookers to stone.

inable form of praise which can be gathered anywhere; and you say that "he is all this," and "the cause of all that," making him appear the fairest and best of all to those who know him not, for you cannot impose upon those who know him. And a noble and solemn hymn of praise have you rehearsed. But as I misunderstood the nature of the praise when I said that I would take my turn, I must beg to be absolved from the promise which I made in ignorance, and which (as Euripides would say) was a promise of the lips and not of the mind.[3] Farewell then to such a strain: for I do not praise in that way; no, indeed, I cannot. But if you like to hear the truth about love, I am ready to speak in my own manner, though I will not make myself ridiculous by entering into any rivalry with you. Say then, Phaedrus, whether you would like to have the truth about love, spoken in any words and in any order which may happen to come into my mind at the time. Will that be agreeable to you?

Aristodemus said that Phaedrus and the company bid him speak in any manner which he thought best. Then, he added, let me have your permission first to ask Agathon a few more questions, in order that I may take his admissions as the premises of my discourse.

I grant the permission, said Phaedrus: put your questions. Socrates then proceeded as follows:—

In the magnificent oration which you have just uttered, I think that you were right, my dear Agathon, in proposing to speak of the nature of Love first and afterwards of his works—that is a way of beginning which I very much approve. And as you have spoken so eloquently of his nature, may I ask you further, Whether love is the love of something or of nothing? And here I must explain myself: I do not want you to say that love is the love of a father or the love of a mother—that would be ridiculous; but to answer as you would, if I asked is a father a father of something? to which you would find no difficulty in replying, of a son or daughter; and the answer would be right.

Very true, said Agathon.

And you would say the same of a mother?

He assented.

Yet let me ask you one more question in order to illustrate my meaning: Is not a brother to be regarded essentially as a brother of something?

Certainly, he replied.

That is, of a brother or sister?

Yes, he said.

And now, said Socrates, I will ask about Love:—Is Love of something or of nothing?

Of something, surely, he replied.

Keep in mind what this is, and tell me what I want to know—whether Love desires that of which love is.

Yes, surely.

And does he possess, or does he not possess, that which he loves and desires?

Probably not, I should say.

Nay, replied Socrates, I would have you consider whether "necessarily" is not rather the word. The inference that he who desires something is in want of

---

3. Allusion to a line in Euripides' play *Hippolytus*: "My tongue swore, not my mind."

something, and that he who desires nothing is in want of nothing, is in my judgment, Agathon, absolutely and necessarily true. What do you think?

I agree with you, said Agathon.

Very good. Would he who is great, desire to be great, or he who is strong, desire to be strong?

That would be inconsistent with our previous admissions.

True. For he who is anything cannot want to be that which he is?

Very true.

And yet, added Socrates, if a man being strong desired to be strong, or being swift desired to be swift, or being healthy desired to be healthy, in that case he might be thought to desire something which he already has or is. I give the example in order that we may avoid misconception. For the possessors of these qualities, Agathon, must be supposed to have their respective advantages at the time, whether they choose or not; and who can desire that which he has? Therefore, when a person says, I am well and wish to be well, or I am rich and wish to be rich, and I desire simply to have what I have—to him we shall reply: "You, my friend, having wealth and health and strength, want to have the continuance of them; for at this moment, whether you choose or no, you have them. And when you say, I desire that which I have and nothing else, is not your meaning that you want to have what you now have in the future?" He must agree with us—must he not?

He must, replied Agathon.

Then, said Socrates, he desires that what he has at present may be preserved to him in the future, which is equivalent to saying that he desires something which is nonexistent to him, and which as yet he has not got:

Very true, he said.

Then he and everyone who desires, desires that which he has not already, and which is future and not present, and which he has not, and is not, and of which he is in want;—these are the sort of things which love and desire seek?

Very true, he said.

Then now, said Socrates, let us recapitulate the argument. First, is not love of something, and of something too which is wanting to a man?

Yes, he replied.

Remember further what you said in your speech, or if you do not remember I will remind you: you said that the love of the beautiful set in order the empire of the gods, for that of deformed things there is no love—did you not say something of that kind?

Yes, said Agathon.

Yes, my friend, and the remark was a just one. And if this is true, Love is the love of beauty and not of deformity?

He assented.

And the admission has been already made that Love is of something which a man wants and has not?

True, he said.

Then Love wants and has not beauty?

Certainly, he replied.

And would you call that beautiful which wants and does not possess beauty?

Certainly not.

Then would you still say that love is beautiful?

Agathon replied: I fear that I did not understand what I was saying.

You made a very good speech, Agathon, replied Socrates; but there is yet one small question which I would fain ask:—Is not the good also the beautiful? Yes.

Then in wanting the beautiful, love wants also the good?

I cannot refute you, Socrates, said Agathon:—Let us assume that what you say is true.

Say rather, beloved Agathon, that you cannot refute the truth; for Socrates is easily refuted.

And now, taking my leave of you, I will rehearse a tale of love which I heard from Diotima of Mantineia,[4] a woman wise in this and in many other kinds of knowledge, who in the days of old, when the Athenians offered sacrifice before the coming of the plague, delayed the disease ten years. She was my instructress in the art of love, and I shall repeat to you what she said to me, beginning with the admissions made by Agathon, which are nearly if not quite the same which I made to the wise woman when she questioned me: I think that this will be the easiest way, and I shall take both parts myself as well as I can. As you, Agathon, suggested, I must speak first of the being and nature of Love, and then of his works. First I said to her in nearly the same words which he used to me, that Love was a mighty god, and likewise fair; and she proved to me as I proved to him that, by my own showing, Love was neither fair nor good. "What do you mean, Diotima," I said, "is love then evil and foul?" "Hush." she cried; "must that be foul which is not fair?" "Certainly," I said. "And is that which is not wise, ignorant? do you not see that there is a mean between wisdom and ignorance?" "And what may that be?" I said. "Right opinion," she replied; "which, as you know, being incapable of giving a reason, is not knowledge (for how can knowledge be devoid of reason? nor again, ignorance, for neither can ignorance attain the truth), but is clearly something which is a mean between ignorance and wisdom." "Quite true," I replied. "Do not then insist," she said, "that what is not fair is of necessity foul, or what is not good evil; or infer that because love is not fair and good he is therefore foul and evil; for he is in a mean between them." "Well," I said, "Love is surely admitted by all to be a great god." "By those who know or by those who do not know?" "By all." "And how, Socrates," she said with a smile, "can Love be acknowledged to be a great god by those who say that he is not a god at all?" "And who are they?" I said. "You and I are two of them," she replied. "How can that be?" I said. "It is quite intelligible," she replied; "for you yourself would acknowledge that the gods are happy and fair—of course you would—would you dare to say that any god was not?" "Certainly not," I replied. "And you mean by the happy, those who are the possessors of things good or fair?" "Yes." "And you admitted that Love, because he was in want, desires those good and fair things of which he is in want?" "Yes, I did." "But how can he be a god who has no portion in what is either good or fair?" "Impossible." "Then you see that you also deny the divinity of Love."

"What then is Love?" I asked; "Is he mortal?" "No" "What then?" "As in the former instance, he is neither mortal nor immortal, but in a mean between the two." "What is he, Diotima?" "He is a great spirit (daemon),[5] and like all

---

4. *Mantineia* suggests "place of prophecy." Diotima is presumably a fantasy figure.
5. A spirit, a notch down from the gods; this is

the word from which we get "demon," though it is positive here.

spirits he is intermediate between the divine and the mortal." "And what," I said, "is his power?" "He interprets" she replied, 'between gods and men, conveying and taking across to the gods the prayers and sacrifices of men, and to men the commands and replies of the gods; he is the mediator who spans the chasm which divides them, and therefore in him all is bound together, and through him the arts of the prophet and the priest, their sacrifices and mysteries and charms, and all prophecy and incantation, find their way. For God mingles not with man; but through Love all the intercourse and converse of God with man, whether awake or asleep, is carried on. The wisdom which understands this is spiritual; all other wisdom, such as that of arts and handicrafts, is mean and vulgar. Now these spirits or intermediate powers are many and diverse, and one of them is Love." "And who," I said, "was his father, and who his mother?" "The tale," she said, "will take time; nevertheless I will tell you. On the birthday of Aphrodite there was a feast of the gods, at which the god Poros or Plenty, who is the son of Metis or Discretion, was one of the guests. When the feast was over, Penia or Poverty, as the manner is on such occasions, came about the doors to beg. Now Plenty, who was the worse for nectar (there was no wine in those days), went into the garden of Zeus and fell into a heavy sleep; and Poverty considering her own straitened circumstances, plotted to have a child by him, and accordingly she lay down at his side and conceived Love, who partly because he is naturally a lover of the beautiful, and because Aphrodite is herself beautiful, and also because he was born on her birthday, is her follower and attendant. And as his parentage is, so also are his fortunes. In the first place he is always poor, and anything but tender and fair, as the many imagine him; and he is rough and squalid, and has no shoes, nor a house to dwell in; on the bare earth exposed he lies under the open heaven, in the streets, or at the doors of houses, taking his rest; and like his mother he is always in distress. Like his father too, whom he also partly resembles, he is always plotting against the fair and good; he is bold, enterprising, strong, a mighty hunter, always weaving some intrigue or other, keen in the pursuit of wisdom, fertile in resources; a philosopher at all times, terrible as an enchanter, sorcerer, sophist. He is by nature neither mortal nor immortal, but alive and flourishing at one moment when he is in plenty, and dead at another moment, and again alive by reason of his father's nature. But that which is always flowing in is always flowing out, and so he is never in want and never in wealth; and, further, he is in a mean between ignorance and knowledge. The truth of the matter is this: No god is a philosopher or seeker after wisdom, for he is wise already; nor does any man who is wise seek after wisdom. Neither do the ignorant seek after wisdom. For herein is the evil of ignorance, that he who is neither good nor wise is nevertheless satisfied with himself: he has no desire for that of which he feels no want." "But who then, Diotima," I said, "are the lovers of wisdom, if they are neither the wise nor the foolish?" "A child may answer that question," she replied; "they are those who are in a mean between the two; Love is one of them. For wisdom is a most beautiful thing, and Love is of the beautiful; and therefore Love is also a philosopher or lover of wisdom, and being a lover of wisdom is in a mean between the wise and the ignorant. And of this too his birth is the cause; for his father is wealthy and wise, and his mother poor and foolish. Such, my dear Socrates, is the nature of the spirit Love. The error in your conception of him was very natural, and as I imagine from what you say, has arisen out of a confusion of love and the beloved, which made you think that love was all beautiful. For the beloved is the truly beautiful, and delicate, and perfect, and blessed; but the principle of love is of another nature, and is such as I have described."

I said: "O thou stranger woman, thou sayest well; but, assuming Love to be such as you say, what is the use of him to men?" "That, Socrates," she replied, "I will attempt to unfold: of his nature and birth I have already spoken; and you acknowledge that love is of the beautiful. But someone will say: Of the beautiful in what, Socrates and Diotima?—or rather let me put the question more clearly, and ask: When a man loves the beautiful, what does he desire?" I answered her "That the beautiful may be his." "Still," she said, "the answer suggests a further question: What is given by the possession of beauty?" "To what you have asked," I replied, "I have no answer ready." "Then," she said, "let me put the word 'good' in the place of the beautiful, and repeat the question once more: If he who loves loves the good, what is it then that he loves?" "The possession of the good," I said. "And what does he gain who possesses the good?" "Happiness," I replied; "there is less difficulty in answering that question." "Yes," she said, "the happy are made happy by the acquisition of good things. Nor is there any need to ask why a man desires happiness; the answer is already final." "You are right," I said. "And is this wish and this desire common to all? and do all men always desire their own good, or only some men?—what say you?" "All men," I replied; "the desire is common to all." "Why, then," she rejoined, "are not all men, Socrates, said to love, but only some of them? whereas you say that all men are always loving the same things." "I myself wonder," I said, "why this is." "There is nothing to wonder at," she replied; "the reason is that one part of love is separated off and receives the name of the whole, but the other parts have other names." "Give an illustration," I said. She answered me as follows: "There is poetry, which, as you know, is complex and manifold.[6] All creation or passage of non-being into being is poetry or making, and the processes of all art are creative; and the masters of arts are all poets or makers." "Very true." "Still," she said, "you know that they are not called poets, but have other names; only that portion of the art which is separated off from the rest, and is concerned with music and metre, is termed poetry, and they who possess poetry in this sense of the word are called poets." "Very true," I said. "And the same holds of love. For you may say generally that all desire of good and happiness is only the great and subtle power of love; but they who are drawn towards him by any other path, whether the path of money-making or gymnastics or philosophy, are not called lovers—the name of the whole is appropriated to those whose affection takes one form only—they alone are said to love, or to be lovers." "I dare say," I replied, "that you are right." "Yes," she added, "and you hear people say that lovers are seeking for their other half; but I say that they are seeking neither for the half of themselves, nor for the whole, unless the half or the whole be also a good. And they will cut off their own hands and feet and cast them away, if they are evil; for they love not what is their own, unless perchance there be someone who calls

---

6. In Greek, *poesis*, from which the term "poetry" derives, covers any kind of making.

what belongs to him the good, and what belongs to another the evil. For there is nothing which men love but the good. Is there anything?" "Certainly, I should say, that there is nothing." "Then," she said, "the simple truth is, that men love the good." "Yes," I said. "To which must be added that they love the possession of the good?" "Yes, that must be added." "And not only the possession, but the everlasting possession of the good?" "That must be added too." "Then love," she said, "may be described generally as the love of the everlasting possession of the good?" "That is most true."

"Then if this be the nature of love, can you tell me further," she said, "what is the manner of the pursuit? what are they doing who show all this eagerness and heat which is called love? and what is the object which they have in view? Answer me." "Nay, Diotima," I replied, "if I had known, I should not have wondered at your wisdom, neither should I have come to learn from you about this very matter." "Well," she said, "I will teach you:—The object which they have in view is birth in beauty, whether of body or soul." "I do not understand you," I said; "the oracle requires an explanation." "I will make my meaning clearer," she replied. "I mean to say, that all men are bringing to the birth in their bodies and in their souls. There is a certain age at which human nature is desirous of procreation—procreation which must be in beauty and not in deformity; and this procreation is the union of man and woman, and is a divine thing; for conception and generation are an immortal principle in the mortal creature, and in the inharmonious they can never be. But the deformed is always inharmonious with the divine, and the beautiful harmonious. Beauty, then, is the destiny or goddess of parturition who presides at birth, and therefore, when approaching beauty, the conceiving power is propitious, and diffusive, and benign, and begets and bears fruit: at the sight of ugliness she frowns and contracts and has a sense of pain, and turns away, and shrivels up, and not without a pang refrains from conception. And this is the reason why, when the hour of conception arrives, and the teeming nature is full, there is such a flutter and ecstacy about beauty whose approach is the alleviation of the pain of travail. For love, Socrates, is not, as you imagine, the love of the beautiful only." "What then?" "The love of generation and of birth in beauty." "Yes," I said. "Yes, indeed," she replied. "But why of generation?" "Because to the mortal creature, generation is a sort of eternity and immortality," she replied; "and if, as has been already admitted, love is of the everlasting possession of the good, all men will necessarily desire immortality together with good: Wherefore love is of immortality."

All this she taught me at various times when she spoke of love. And I remember her once saying to me, "What is the cause, Socrates, of love, and the attendant desire? See you not how all animals, birds, as well as beasts, in their desire of procreation, are in agony when they take the infection of love, which begins with the desire of union; whereto is added the care of offspring, on whose behalf the weakest are ready to battle against the strongest even to the uttermost, and to die for them, and will let themselves be tormented with hunger or suffer anything in order to maintain their young. Man may be supposed to act thus from reason; but why should animals have these passionate feelings? Can you tell me why?" Again I replied that I did not know. She said to me: "And do you expect ever to become a master in the art of love, if you do not know this?" "But I have told you already, Diotima, that my ignorance is the reason why I come to you; for I am conscious that I want a teacher; tell me then the cause of this and of the other mysteries of love." "Marvel not," she said, "if you believe that love is of the immortal, as we have several times acknowledged; for here again, and on the same principle too, the mortal nature is seeking as far as is possible to be everlasting and immortal: and this is only to be attained by generation, because generation always leaves behind a new existence in the place of the old. Nay even in the life of the same individual there is succession and not absolute unity: a man is called the same, and yet in the short interval which elapses between youth and age, and in which every animal is said to have life and identity, he is undergoing a perpetual process of loss and reparation—hair, flesh, bones, blood, and the whole body are always changing. Which is true not only of the body, but also of the soul, whose habits, tempers, opinions, desires, pleasures, pains, fears, never remain the same in any one of us, but are always coming and going; and equally true of knowledge, and what is still more surprising to us mortals, not only do the sciences in general spring up and decay, so that in respect of them we are never the same; but each of them individually experiences a like change. For what is implied in the word 'recollection,' but the departure of knowledge, which is ever being forgotten, and is renewed and preserved by recollection, and appears to be the same although in reality new, according to that law of succession by which all mortal things are preserved, not absolutely the same, but by substitution, the old worn-out mortality leaving another new and similar existence behind—unlike the divine, which is always the same and not another? And in this way, Socrates, the mortal body, or mortal anything, partakes of immortality; but the immortal in another way. Marvel not then at the love which all men have of their offspring; for that universal love and interest is for the sake of immortality."

I was astonished at her words, and said: "Is this really true, O thou wise Diotima?" And she answered with all the authority of an accomplished sophist: "Of that, Socrates, you may be assured;—think only of the ambition of men, and you will wonder at the senselessness of their ways, unless you consider how they are stirred by the love of an immortality of fame. They are ready to run all risks greater far than they would have run for their children, and to spend money and undergo any sort of toil, and even to die, for the sake of leaving behind them a name which shall be eternal. Do you imagine that Alcestis would have died to save Admetus, or Achilles to avenge Patroclus, or your own Codrus in order to preserve the kingdom for his sons,[7] if they had not imagined that the memory of their virtues, which still survives among us, would be immortal? Nay," she said, "I am persuaded that all men do all things, and the better they are the more they do them, in hope of the glorious fame of immortal virtue; for they desire the immortal.

"Those who are pregnant in the body only, betake themselves to women and beget children—this is the character of their love; their offspring, as they hope, will preserve their memory and give them the blessedness and immortality which they desire in the future. But souls which are pregnant—for

7. Codrus was the legendary last king of Athens; he gave his life when it was prophesied that the city would defeat the invading Dorians only if the king was killed.

there certainly are men who are more creative in their souls than in their bodies—conceive that which is proper for the soul to conceive or contain. And what are these conceptions?—wisdom and virtue in general. And such creators are poets and all artists who are deserving of the name inventor. But the greatest and fairest sort of wisdom by far is that which is concerned with the ordering of states and families, and which is called temperance and justice. And he who in youth has the seed of these implanted in him and is himself inspired, when he comes to maturity desires to beget and generate. He wanders about seeking beauty that he may beget offspring—for in deformity he will beget nothing—and naturally embraces the beautiful rather than the deformed body; above all when he finds a fair and noble and well-nurtured soul, he embraces the two in one person, and to such an one he is full of speech about virtue and the nature and pursuits of a good man; and he tries to educate him; and at the touch of the beautiful which is ever present to his memory, even when absent, he brings forth that which he had conceived long before, and in company with him tends that which he brings forth; and they are married by a far nearer tie and have a closer friendship than those who beget mortal children, for the children who are their common offspring are fairer and more immortal. Who, when he thinks of Homer and Hesiod and other great poets, would not rather have their children than ordinary human ones? Who would not emulate them in the creation of children such as theirs, which have preserved their memory and given them everlasting glory? Or who would not have such children as Lycurgus[8] left behind him to be the saviours, not only of Lacedaemon, but of Hellas, as one may say? There is Solon,[9] too, who is the revered father of Athenian laws; and many others there are in many other places, both among Hellenes and barbarians, who have given to the world many noble works, and have been the parents of virtue of every kind; and many temples have been raised in their honour for the sake of children such as theirs; which were never raised in honour of anyone, for the sake of his mortal children.

"These are the lesser mysteries of love, into which even you, Socrates, may enter; to the greater and more hidden ones which are the crown of these, and to which, if you pursue them in a right spirit, they will lead, I know not whether you will be able to attain. But I will do my utmost to inform you, and do you follow if you can. For he who would proceed aright in this matter should begin in youth to visit beautiful forms; and first, if he be guided by his instructor aright, to love one such form only—out of that he should create fair thoughts; and soon he will of himself perceive that the beauty of one form is akin to the beauty of another; and then if beauty of form in general is his pursuit, how foolish would he be not to recognize that the beauty in every form is one and the same! And when he perceives this he will abate his violent love of the one, which he will despise and deem a small thing, and will become a lover of all beautiful forms; in the next stage he will consider that the beauty of the mind is more honourable than the beauty of the outward form. So that if a virtuous soul have but a little comeliness, he will be content to love and tend him, and

8. Legendary oligarchic lawgiver of Sparta.
9. Athenian lawmaker and statesman (ca. 638–ca. 558 B.C.E.).

will search out and bring to the birth thoughts which may improve the young, until he is compelled to contemplate and see the beauty of institutions and laws, and to understand that the beauty of them all is of one family, and that personal beauty is a trifle; and after laws and institutions he will go on to the sciences, that he may see their beauty, being not like a servant in love with the beauty of one youth or man or institution, himself a slave mean and narrow-minded, but drawing towards and contemplating the vast sea of beauty, he will create many fair and noble thoughts and notions in boundless love of wisdom;[1] until on that shore he grows and waxes strong, and at last the vision is revealed to him of a single science, which is the science of beauty everywhere. To this I will proceed; please to give me your very best attention:

"He who has been instructed thus far in the things of love, and who has learned to see the beautiful in due order and succession, when he comes toward the end will suddenly perceive a nature of wondrous beauty (and this, Socrates, is the final cause of all our former toils)—a nature which in the first place is everlasting, not growing and decaying, or waxing and waning; secondly, not fair in one point of view and foul in another, or at one time or in one relation or at one place fair, at another time or in another relation or at another place foul, as if fair to some and foul to others, or in the likeness of a face or hands or any other part of the bodily frame, or in any form of speech or knowledge, or existing in any other being, as for example, in an animal, or in heaven, or in earth, or in any other place; but beauty absolute, separate, simple, and everlasting, which without diminution and without increase, or any change, is imparted to the ever-growing and perishing beauties of all other things. He who from these ascending under the influence of true love, begins to perceive that beauty, is not far from the end. And the true order of going, or being led by another, to the things of love, is to begin from the beauties of earth and mount upwards for the sake of that other beauty, using these as steps only, and from one going on to two, and from two to all fair forms, and from fair forms to fair practices, and from fair practices to fair notions, until from fair notions he arrives at the notion of absolute beauty, and at last knows what the essence of beauty is. This, my dear Socrates," said the stranger of Mantineia, "is that life above all others which man should live, in the contemplation of beauty absolute; a beauty which if you once beheld, you would see not to be after the measure of gold, and garments, and fair boys and youths, whose presence now entrances you; and you and many a one would be content to live seeing them only and conversing with them without meat or drink, if that were possible—you only want to look at them and to be with them. But what if man had eyes to see the true beauty—the divine beauty, I mean, pure and clear and unalloyed, not clogged with the pollutions of mortality and all the colours and vanities of human life—thither looking, and holding converse with the true beauty simple and divine? Remember how in that communion only, beholding beauty with the eye of the mind, he will be enabled to bring forth, not images of beauty, but realities (for he has hold not of an image but of a reality), and bringing forth and nourishing true virtue to become the friend of God and be immortal, if mortal man may. Would that be an ignoble life?"

1. I.e., unstinting philosophy.

Such, Phaedrus—and I speak not only to you, but to all of you—were the words of Diotima; and I am persuaded of their truth. And being persuaded of them, I try to persuade others, that in the attainment of this end human nature will not easily find a helper better than love. And therefore, also, I say that every man ought to honour him as I myself honour him, and walk in his ways, and exhort others to do the same, and praise the power and spirit of love according to the measure of my ability now and ever.

The words which I have spoken, you, Phaedrus, may call an encomium of love, or anything else which you please.

When Socrates had done speaking, the company applauded, and Aristophanes was beginning to say something in answer to the allusion which Socrates had made to his own speech, when suddenly there was a great knocking at the door of the house, as of revellers, and the sound of a flute-girl was heard. Agathon told the attendants to go and see who were the intruders. "If they are friends of ours," he said, "invite them in, but if not, say that the drinking is over." A little while afterwards they heard the voice of Alcibiades resounding in the court; he was in a great state of intoxication, and kept roaring and shouting "Where is Agathon? Lead me to Agathon," and at length, supported by the flute-girl and some of his attendants, he found his way to them. "Hail, friends," he said, appearing at the door crowned with a massive garland of ivy and violets, his head flowing with ribands. "Will you have a very drunken man as a companion of your revels? Or shall I crown Agathon, which was my intention in coming, and go away? For I was unable to come yesterday, and therefore I am here today, carrying on my head these ribands, that taking them from my own head, I may crown the head of this fairest and wisest of men, as I may be allowed to call him. Will you laugh at me because I am drunk? Yet I know very well that I am speaking the truth, although you may laugh. But first tell me; if I come in shall we have the understanding of which I spoke? Will you drink with me or not?"

The company were vociferous in begging that he would take his place among them, and Agathon specially invited him. Thereupon he was led in by the people who were with him; and as he was being led, intending to crown Agathon, he took the ribands from his own head and held them in front of his eyes; he was thus prevented from seeing Socrates, who made way for him, and Alcibiades took the vacant place between Agathon and Socrates, and in taking the place he embraced Agathon and crowned him. Take off his sandals, said Agathon, and let him make a third on the same couch.

By all means; but who makes the third partner in our revels? said Alcibiades, turning round and starting up as he caught sight of Socrates. By Heracles, he said, what is this? here is Socrates always lying in wait for me, and always, as his way is, coming out at all sorts of unsuspected places: and now, what have you to say for yourself, and why are you lying here, where I perceive that you have contrived to find a place, not by a joker or lover of jokes, like Aristophanes, but by the fairest of the company?

Socrates turned to Agathon and said: I must ask you to protect me, Agathon; for the passion of this man has grown quite a serious matter to me. Since I became his admirer I have never been allowed to speak to any other fair one, or so much as to look at them. If I do, he goes wild with envy and jealousy, and not only abuses me but can hardly keep his hands off me, and at this moment he may do me some harm. Please to see to this, and either reconcile me to him, or, if he attempts violence, protect me, as I am in bodily fear of his mad and passionate attempts.

There can never be reconciliation between you and me, said Alcibiades; but for the present I will defer your chastisement. And I must beg you, Agathon, to give me back some of the ribands that I may crown the marvellous head of this universal despot—I would not have him complain of me for crowning you, and neglecting him, who in conversation is the conqueror of all mankind; and this not only once, as you were the day before yesterday, but always. Whereupon, taking some of the ribands, he crowned Socrates, and again reclined.

Then he said: You seem, my friends, to be sober, which is a thing not to be endured; you must drink—for that was the agreement under which I was admitted—and I elect myself master of the feast until you are well drunk. Let us have a large goblet, Agathon, or rather, he said, addressing the attendant, bring me that wine-cooler. The wine-cooler which had caught his eye was a vessel holding more than two quarts—this he filled and emptied, and bade the attendant fill it again for Socrates. Observe, my friends, said Alcibiades, that this ingenious trick of mine will have no effect on Socrates, for he can drink any quantity of wine and not be at all nearer being drunk. Socrates drank the cup which the attendant filled for him.

Eryximachus said: What is this, Alcibiades? Are we to have neither conversation nor singing over our cups; but simply to drink as if we were thirsty?

Alcibiades replied: Hail, worthy son of a most wise and worthy sire!

The same to you, said Eryximachus; but what shall we do?

That I leave to you, said Alcibiades.

"The wise physician skilled our wounds to heal"

shall prescribe and we will obey. What do you want?

Well, said Eryximachus, before you appeared we had passed a resolution that each one of us in turn should make a speech in praise of love, and as good a one as he could: the turn was passed round from left to right; and as all of us have spoken, and you have not spoken but have well drunken, you ought to speak, and then impose upon Socrates any task which you please, and he on his right-hand neighbour, and so on.

That is good, Eryximachus, said Alcibiades; and yet the comparison of a drunken man's speech with those of sober men is hardly fair; and I should like to know, sweet friend, whether you really believe what Socrates was just now saying; for I can assure you that the very reverse is the fact, and that if I praise anyone but himself in his presence, whether god or man, he will hardly keep his hands off me.

For shame, said Socrates.

Hold your tongue, said Alcibiades, for by Poseidon, there is no one else whom I will praise when you are of the company.

Well then, said Eryximachus, if you like praise Socrates.

What do you think, Eryximachus? said Alcibiades: shall I attack him and inflict the punishment before you all?

What are you about? said Socrates; are you going to raise a laugh at my expense? Is that the meaning of your praise?

I am going to speak the truth, if you will permit me.

I not only permit, but exhort you to speak the truth.

Then I will begin at once, said Alcibiades, and if I say anything which is not true, you may interrupt me if you will, and say "that is a lie," though my intention is to speak the truth. But you must not wonder if I speak anyhow as things come into my mind; for the fluent and orderly enumeration of all your singularities is not a task which is easy to a man in my condition.

And now, my boys, I shall praise Socrates in a figure which will appear to him to be a caricature, and yet I speak, not to make fun of him, but only for the truth's sake. I say, that he is exactly like the busts of Silenus,[2] which are set up in the statuaries' shops, holding pipes and flutes in their mouths; and they are made to open in the middle, and have images of gods inside them. I say also that he is like Marsyas[3] the satyr. You yourself will not deny, Socrates, that your face is like that of a satyr. Aye, and there is a resemblance in other points too. For example, you are a bully, as I can prove by witnesses, if you will not confess. And are you not a flute-player? That you are, and a performer far more wonderful than Marsyas. He indeed with instruments used to charm the souls of men by the power of his breath, and the players of his music do so still: for the melodies of Olympus[4] are derived from Marsyas who taught them, and these, whether they are played by a great master or by a miserable flute-girl, have a power which no others have; they alone possess the soul and reveal the wants of those who have need of gods and mysteries, because they are divine. But you produce the same effect with your words only, and do not require the flute: that is the difference between you and him. When we hear any other speaker, even a very good one, he produces absolutely no effect upon us, or not much, whereas the mere fragments of you and your words, even at secondhand, and however imperfectly repeated, amaze and possess the souls of every man, woman, and child who comes within hearing of them. And if I were not afraid that you would think me hopelessly drunk, I would have sworn as well as spoken to the influence which they have always had and still have over me. For my heart leaps within me more than that of any Corybantian[5] reveller, and my eyes rain tears when I hear them. And I observe that many others are affected in the same manner. I have heard Pericles[6] and other great orators, and I thought that they spoke well, but I never had any similar feeling; my soul was not stirred by them, nor was I angry at the thought of my own slavish state. But this Marsyas has often brought me to such a pass, that I have felt as if I could hardly endure the life which I am leading (this, Socrates, you will admit); and I am conscious that if I did not shut my ears against him, and fly as from the voice of the siren,[7] my fate would be like that of others,—he would transfix me, and I should grow old sitting at his feet. For he makes me confess that I ought not to live as I do, neglecting the wants of my own soul,

2. Drunken satyr—a mythical hairy, goatish creature, woodland follower of Dionysus, god of wine. Satyrs were often represented onstage and in art with large erections.
3. Marsyas competed with the god Apollo in music, and was flayed for his insolence.
4. Olympus was a legendary musician, loved by Marsyas.
5. Worshippers of the mother goddess, Cybele,

Corybantes achieved divine ecstasy through music and dance.
6. Famous Athenian general, statesman, and orator (ca. 495–429 B.C.E.).
7. Magical female birdlike creatures whose singing lured sailors to their doom. In book 12 of the *Odyssey*, Odysseus escaped their island by having his men tie him to the mast while they rowed to safety, their ears stopped with wax.

and busying myself with the concerns of the Athenians; therefore I hold my ears and tear myself away from him. And he is the only person who ever made me ashamed, which you might think not to be in my nature, and there is no one else who does the same. For I know that I cannot answer him or say that I ought not to do as he bids, but when I leave his presence the love of popularity gets the better of me. And therefore I run away and fly from him, and when I see him I am ashamed of what I have confessed to him. Many a time have I wished that he were dead, and yet I know that I should be much more sorry than glad, if he were to die: so that I am at my wit's end.

And this is what I and many others have suffered from the flute-playing of this satyr. Yet hear me once more while I show you how exact the image is, and how marvellous his power. For let me tell you; none of you know him; but I will reveal him to you; having begun, I must go on. See you how fond he is of the fair? He is always with them and is always being smitten by them, and then again he knows nothing and is ignorant of all things—such is the appearance which he puts on. Is he not like a Silenus in this? To be sure he is: his outer mask is the carved head of the Silenus; but, O my companions in drink, when he is opened, what temperance there is residing within! Know you that beauty and wealth and honour, at which the many wonder, are of no account with him, and are utterly despised by him: he regards not at all the persons who are gifted with them; mankind are nothing to him; all his life is spent in mocking and flouting at them. But when I opened him, and looked within at his serious purpose, I saw in him divine and golden images of such fascinating beauty that I was ready to do in a moment whatever Socrates commanded: they may have escaped the observation of others, but I saw them. Now I fancied that he was seriously enamoured of my beauty, and I thought that I should therefore have a grand opportunity of hearing him tell what he knew, for I had a wonderful opinion of the attractions of my youth. In the prosecution of this design, when I next went to him, I sent away the attendant who usually accompanied me (I will confess the whole truth, and beg you to listen; and if I speak falsely, do you, Socrates, expose the falsehood). Well, he and I were alone together, and I thought that when there was nobody with us, I should hear him speak the language which lovers use to their loves when they are by themselves, and I was delighted. Nothing of the sort; he conversed as usual, and spent the day with me and then went away. Afterwards I challenged him to the palaestra;[8] and he wrestled and closed with me several times when there was no one present; I fancied that I might succeed in this manner. Not a bit; I made no way with him. Lastly, as I had failed hitherto, I thought that I must take stronger measures and attack him boldly, and, as I had begun, not give him up, but see how matters stood between him and me. So I invited him to sup with me, just as if he were a fair youth, and I a designing lover. He was not easily persuaded to come; he did, however, after a while accept the invitation, and when he came the first time, he wanted to go away at once as soon as supper was over, and I had not the face to detain him. The second time, still in pursuance of my design, after we had supped, I went on conversing far into the night, and when he wanted to go away, I pretended that the hour was late and that he had much

8. Wrestling school; gymnasium.

better remain. So he lay down on the couch next to me, the same on which he had supped, and there was no one but ourselves sleeping in the apartment. All this may be told without shame to anyone. But what follows I could hardly tell you if I were sober. Yet as the proverb says, "In vino veritas,"[9] whether with boys, or without them; and therefore I must speak. Nor, again, should I be justified in concealing the lofty actions of Socrates when I come to praise him. Moreover I have felt the serpent's sting; and he who has suffered, as they say, is willing to tell his fellow-sufferers only, as they alone will be likely to understand him, and will not be extreme in judging of the sayings or doings which have been wrung from his agony. For I have been bitten by a more than viper's tooth; I have known in my soul, or in my heart, or in some other part, that worst of pangs, more violent in ingenuous youth than any serpent's tooth, the pang of philosophy, which will make a man say or do anything. And you whom I see around me, Phaedrus and Agathon and Eryximachus and Pausanias and Aristodemus and Aristophanes, all of you, and I need not say Socrates himself, have had experience of the same madness and passion in your longing after wisdom. Therefore listen and excuse my doings then and my sayings now. But let the attendants and other profane and unmannered persons close up the doors of their ears.

When the lamp was put out and the servants had gone away, I thought that I must be plain with him and have no more ambiguity. So I gave him a shake, and I said: "Socrates, are you asleep?" "No," he said. "Do you know what I am meditating?" "What are you meditating?" he said. "I think," I replied, "that of all the lovers whom I have ever had you are the only one who is worthy of me, and you appear to be too modest to speak. Now I feel that I should be a fool to refuse you this or any other favour, and therefore I come to lay at your feet all that I have and all that my friends have, in the hope that you will assist me in the way of virtue, which I desire above all things, and in which I believe that you can help me better than anyone else. And I should certainly have more reason to be ashamed of what wise men would say if I were to refuse a favour to such as you, than of what the world, who are mostly fools, would say of me if I granted it." To these words he replied in the ironical manner which is so characteristic of him:—"Alcibiades, my friend, you have indeed an elevated aim if what you say is true, and if there really is in me any power by which you may become better; truly you must see in me some rare beauty of a kind infinitely higher than any which I see in you. And therefore, if you mean to share with me and to exchange beauty for beauty, you will have greatly the advantage of me; you will gain true beauty in return for appearance—like Diomede, gold in exchange for brass.[1] But look again, sweet friend, and see whether you are not deceived in me. The mind begins to grow critical when the bodily eye fails, and it will be a long time before you get old." Hearing this, I said: "I have told you my purpose, which is quite serious, and do you consider what you think best for you and me." "That is good," he said; "at some other time then we will consider and act as seems best about this and about other matters." Whereupon, I

9. Literally, "truth in wine" (Latin); inebriation produces honesty.
1. Allusion to scene in the *Iliad* (6.232–36).

fancied that he was smitten, and that the words which I had uttered like arrows had wounded him, and so without waiting to hear more I got up, and throwing my coat about him crept under his threadbare cloak, as the time of year was winter, and there I lay during the whole night having this wonderful monster in my arms. This again, Socrates, will not be denied by you. And yet, notwithstanding all, he was so superior to my solicitations, so contemptuous and derisive and disdainful of my beauty—which really, as I fancied, had some attractions—hear, O judges; for judges you shall be of the haughty virtue of Socrates—nothing more happened, but in the morning when I awoke (let all the gods and goddesses be my witnesses) I arose as from the couch of a father or an elder brother.

What do you suppose must have been my feelings, after this rejection, at the thought of my own dishonour? And yet I could not help wondering at his natural temperance and self-restraint and manliness. I never imagined that I could have met with a man such as he is in wisdom and endurance. And therefore I could not be angry with him or renounce his company, any more than I could hope to win him. For I well knew that if Ajax[2] could not be wounded by steel, much less he by money; and my only chance of captivating him by my personal attractions had failed. So I was at my wit's end; no one was ever more hopelessly enslaved by another. All this happened before he and I went on the expedition to Potidaea;[3] there we messed together, and I had the opportunity of observing his extraordinary power of sustaining fatigue. His endurance was simply marvellous when, being cut off from our supplies, we were compelled to go without food—on such occasions, which often happen in time of war, he was superior not only to me but to everybody; there was no one to be compared to him. Yet at a festival he was the only person who had any real powers of enjoyment; though not willing to drink, he could if compelled beat us all at that,—wonderful to relate! no human being had ever seen Socrates drunk; and his powers, if I am not mistaken, will be tested before long. His fortitude in enduring cold was also surprising. There was a severe frost, for the winter in that region is really tremendous, and everybody else either remained indoors, or if they went out had on an amazing quantity of clothes, and were well shod, and had their feet swathed in felt and fleeces: in the midst of this, Socrates with his bare feet on the ice and in his ordinary dress marched better than the other soldiers who had shoes, and they looked daggers at him because he seemed to despise them.

I have told you one tale, and now I must tell you another, which is worth hearing,

"Of the doings and sufferings of the enduring man"[4]

while he was on the expedition. One morning he was thinking about something which he could not resolve; he would not give it up, but continued thinking from early dawn until noon—there he stood fixed in thought; and at noon attention was drawn to him, and the rumour ran through the wondering crowd

2. Mighty Greek hero of the Trojan War who carried a huge shield.
3. City besieged and defeated by Athens at the start of the Peloponnesian War.
4. Quotation from the *Odyssey* (4.242, 271).

that Socrates had been standing and thinking about something ever since the break of day. At last, in the evening after supper, some Ionians out of curiosity (I should explain that this was not in winter but in summer), brought out their mats and slept in the open air that they might watch him and see whether he would stand all night. There he stood until the following morning; and with the return of light he offered up a prayer to the sun, and went his way. I will also tell, if you please—and indeed I am bound to tell—of his courage in battle; for who but he saved my life? Now this was the engagement in which I received the prize of valour: for I was wounded and he would not leave me, but he rescued me and my arms; and he ought to have received the prize of valour which the generals wanted to confer on me partly on account of my rank, and I told them so (this, again, Socrates will not impeach or deny), but he was more eager than the generals that I and not he should have the prize. There was another occasion on which his behaviour was very remarkable—in the flight of the army after the battle of Delium,[5] where he served among the heavy-armed,—I had a better opportunity of seeing him than at Potidaea, for I was myself on horseback, and therefore comparatively out of danger. He and Laches[6] were retreating, for the troops were in flight, and I met them and told them not to be discouraged, and promised to remain with them; and there you might see him, Aristophanes, as you describe, just as he is in the streets of Athens, stalking like a pelican, and rolling his eyes,[7] calmly contemplating enemies as well as friends, and making very intelligible to anybody, even from a distance, that whoever attacked him would be likely to meet with a stout resistance; and in this way he and his companion escaped—for this is the sort of man who is never touched in war; those only are pursued who are running away headlong. I particularly observed how superior he was to Laches in presence of mind. Many are the marvels which I might narrate in praise of Socrates; most of his ways might perhaps be paralleled in another man, but his absolute unlikeness to any human being that is or ever has been is perfectly astonishing. You may imagine Brasidas and others to have been like Achilles; or you may imagine Nestor and Antenor[8] to have been like Pericles; and the same may be said of other famous men, but of this strange being you will never be able to find any likeness, however remote, either among men who now are or who ever have been—other than that which I have already suggested of Silenus and the satyrs; and they represent in a figure not only himself, but his words. For, although I forgot to mention this to you before, his words are like the images of Silenus which open; they are ridiculous when you first hear them; he clothes himself in language that is like the skin of the wanton satyr—for his talk is of pack-asses and smiths and cobblers and curriers, and he is always repeating the same things in the same words, so that any ignorant or inexperienced person might feel disposed to laugh at him; but he who opens the bust and sees what is within will find that they are the only words which have a meaning in

5. The Athenians were routed by the Boeotians at Delium, a Boeotian town, in 424 B.C.E.
6. Famous Athenian general (ca. 475–418 B.C.E.), who appears in an eponymous Platonic dialogue, on courage.
7. "Stalking like a pelican, and rolling his eyes"

is a quote from Aristophanes' *Clouds*, line 362.
8. Brasidas was a Spartan general in the Peloponnesian War. The mythical figures Nestor the Greek and Antenor the Trojan were counselors in the Trojan War.

them, and also the most divine, abounding in fair images of virtue, and of the widest comprehension, or rather extending to the whole duty of a good and honourable man.

This, friends, is my praise of Socrates. I have added my blame of him for his ill-treatment of me; and he has ill-treated not only me, but Charmides the son of Glaucon, and Euthydemus[9] the son of Diocles, and many others in the same way—beginning as their lover he has ended by making them pay their addresses to him. Wherefore I say to you, Agathon, "Be not deceived by him; learn from me and take warning, and do not be a fool and learn by experience, as the proverb says."

When Alcibiades had finished, there was a laugh at his outspokenness; for he seemed to be still in love with Socrates. You are sober, Alcibiades, said Socrates, or you would never have gone so far about to hide the purpose of your satyr's praises, for all this long story is only an ingenious circumlocution, of which the point comes in by the way at the end; you want to get up a quarrel between me and Agathon, and your notion is that I ought to love you and nobody else, and that you and you only ought to love Agathon. But the plot of this Satyric or Silenic drama has been detected, and you must not allow him, Agathon, to set us at variance.

I believe you are right, said Agathon, and I am disposed to think that his intention in placing himself between you and me was only to divide us; but he shall gain nothing by that move; for I will go and lie on the couch next to you.

Yes, yes, replied Socrates, by all means come here and lie on the couch below me.

Alas, said Alcibiades, how I am fooled by this man; he is determined to get the better of me at every turn. I do beseech you, allow Agathon to lie between us.

Certainly not, said Socrates; as you praised me, and I in turn ought to praise my neighbour on the right, he will be out of order in praising me again when he ought rather to be praised by me, and I must entreat you to consent to this, and not be jealous, for I have a great desire to praise the youth.

Hurrah! cried Agathon, I will rise instantly, that I may be praised by Socrates.

The usual way, said Alcibiades; where Socrates is, no one else has any chance with the fair; and now how readily has he invented a specious reason for attracting Agathon to himself.

Agathon arose in order that he might take his place on the couch by Socrates, when suddenly a band of revellers entered, and spoiled the order of the banquet. Someone who was going out having left the door open, they had found their way in, and made themselves at home; great confusion ensued, and everyone was compelled to drink large quantities of wine. Aristodemus said that Eryximachus, Phaedrus, and others went away—he himself fell asleep, and as the nights were long took a good rest: he was awakened towards daybreak by a crowing of cocks, and when he awoke, the others were either asleep, or had gone away; there remained only Socrates, Aristophanes, and Agathon, who were drinking out of a large goblet which they passed round, and Socrates was discoursing to them. Aristodemus was only half awake, and he did not

9. Real people who appear in other Platonic dialogues. Charmides was Plato's uncle.

hear the beginning of the discourse; the chief thing which he remembered was Socrates compelling the other two to acknowledge that the genius of comedy was the same with that of tragedy, and that the true artist in tragedy was an artist in comedy also.[1] To this they were constrained to assent, being drowsy, and not quite following the argument. And first of all Aristophanes dropped off, then, when the day was already dawning, Agathon. Socrates, having laid them to sleep, rose to depart; Aristodemus, as his manner was, following him. At the Lyceum[2] he took a bath, and passed the day as usual. In the evening he retired to rest at his own home.

1. This position would have sounded surprising to an ancient Athenian. Dramatists composed either comedy or tragedy, not both.

2. The Athenian Lyceum was an open-air gymnasium and meeting place.

TRAVEL AND CONQUEST

Travel, either voluntary or under compulsion, has been a constant in human life: throughout history, humans have moved from one country to another, and formed new communities in places far from their homes. The inhabitants of the ancient Mediterranean and Near East had little or no knowledge of the most distant parts of the world (such as the Americas). But the various societies of this part of the ancient world were far from insular. People were highly conscious of differences between their own culture and those of their neighbors, and curious about worlds beyond their own. Without Internet or television, the primary means of understanding cultural difference came through stories.

Storytelling and travel have always had a close connection with each other. Literature itself takes us on a journey to another world. Travel plays a central part even in our earliest surviving literary texts, and the storytellers' attitudes toward these journeys are often complex. The literary technique of telling the story of a journey can allow ancient writers to create an exciting, surprising

narrative, which includes elements that are far removed from the normal experience of most readers. Through a magical journey, a text may include a vision of the whole world. These texts can also use a literal journey as a way of representing psychological progress (as in the *Odyssey* and, later, Lucian's *True Story* and **Apuleius**'s *Golden Ass*). In these texts, the hero seems to learn and grow over the course of his journey. In studying literary narratives of spiritual journeys, we might also look forward to **Dante**'s *Divine Comedy* and John Bunyan's *Pilgrim's Progress*.

Ancient peoples were aware that travel broadens the mind. Travel in the ancient world could be undertaken willingly, by curious tourists or scholars hoping to learn or to teach. Customs of other places could make people pause to reflect on life at home: travel gave some people the freedom to think about and criticize the established order. More often, merchants and pirates traveled for economic gain. Archaeological evidence shows us that material objects (such as ceramic pots, beads, and, later, coinage) were often traded over large distances. With trade came cultural exchange; one culture often learned from another, in areas as disparate as building techniques, philosophy, science, mathematics, religion, and mythology. Ancient peoples could be quite capable of treating one another's cultures with respect.

But most often, people traveled against their will. Travel could be the

This unusual Babylonian tablet features a unique map of the Mesopotamian world, ca. 700–500 B.C.E. Babylon is shown at the center of the map. Other places, including Assyria and Elam, are also named. A body of water identified as the "Salt Sea" encircles the central area, and outside this ring of water lie eight "regions" that are described in the accompanying inscription.

result of political necessity: the Athenians expelled (or "ostracized") unpopular citizens, and Rome forced many elite figures (including the poet **Ovid** and the philosopher **Seneca**) into exile. People might also be forced to leave home by bad economic conditions. But as today, the most massive movements of people in antiquity were the result of war. Several cultures in the Mediterranean area tried to build an empire by invading and colonizing their neighbors, including the Babylonians, the Carthaginians, the Athenians, the Persians, the Macedonians, and, most successfully, the Romans. Often, those conquered and captured in war found themselves removed to the land of the victors, as slaves. Throughout antiquity, elite peoples lived with and depended on slaves, who were almost always nonnative people, captured in war or descended from captives. Since history is written by the winners, it can be difficult or impossible for us to recapture the experience of those who suffered in ancient wars, or to hear the voice of those enslaved and owned by the elite. Our vision of non-Egyptian, non-Greek, and non-Roman peoples is often filtered through sources that can only tell, at most, half the story. Sometimes literature—from **Homer's** *Iliad* onward—can seem to offer faint echoes of these lost voices, the peoples defeated and destroyed by war; but such texts are usually more illuminating about the mind-sets of the conquerors.

Like modern people, the ancients often felt the urge to define people from other cultures as essentially different from, and in some way less good than, themselves. Greeks, Romans, Hebrews, and Egyptians all defined their own cultures by contrasting themselves with the foreigners they encountered.

A common theme in Greek and Roman texts is the clash between Eastern and Western civilizations, in which easterners—such as the Persians or Egyptians—may be presented as more effeminate, weaker, or less trustworthy than the strong, masculine Athenians or Romans. We can sometimes see the authors of these texts struggling to present foreigners as different from themselves, even in cases where the barbarians were not easy to distinguish from the Greeks or Romans.

In the modern world, we do not have to travel in order to encounter peoples from other cultures; we can see people from many different ethnic backgrounds every day, in any large city of North America or Europe. Several ancient cultures were similarly cosmopolitan or multicultural and included peoples from a number of different ethnic and racial backgrounds. Multicultural societies were a common result of conquest and colonialism. For instance, from the fourth century B.C.E. onward (after Alexander the Great conquered Egypt in 332 B.C.E.), Greeks became the rulers of Egypt, creating a complex, multicultural society in the new city of Alexandria: it was in this period that the famous Rosetta Stone was produced, which helped nineteenth-century archaeologists decipher Egyptian hieroglyphics. The stone was inscribed with a bilingual tax decree in both Greek and Egyptian—a mark of a society in which people from different cultures, and speaking different languages, had to communicate with one another. Language—both in inscriptions and in literary texts—was an essential element in defining one culture against another, and in attempting to build bridges between them.

TALE OF THE SHIPWRECKED SAILOR

*T*ale of the Shipwrecked Sailor (ca. 1900 B.C.E.) is one of the oldest surviving fictional narratives from Egypt. It is an easy read and could appear at first sight like a folktale. A man consoles the returning leader of an expedition abroad, who is anxious about his reception at court. The speaker tells of his own failed journey to the Red Sea, which led to shipwreck and the loss of all his companions. He then encountered a giant snake that revealed itself to be a god, and we hear the snake tell its own story. The creature urges the sailor to practice self-control and to treasure his home and family. Despite the text's surface simplicity, it works on a number of different levels. The snake is not just an animal but also the Egyptian creator god, who existed as a snake in primeval times; this god emerges from the edge of the universe to address the man. The sailor promises to repay the snake with sacrifices, but it laughs at his presumption: the encounter seems to point to our failure to recognize the vast gulf between human and divine understanding. There is a surprising, perhaps humorous final twist in the tale: the man listening to the sailor entirely rejects his advice, sneering, "Don't act clever, my friend!" The ending of the story is a reminder that the ancients may not have been unquestioning in their attitudes toward their own "wisdom" literature. Should we conclude that travel, of all kinds, is undesirable, since there's no place like home? Or is some kind of journey necessary, if only to remind us of the value of home and the need for endurance? This engaging text offers a thought-provoking example of how stories may blur the lines between a geographic and a spiritual journey.

Tale of the Shipwrecked Sailor[1]

A clever Follower[2] speaks:
'May your heart be well, my Count!
Look, we have reached home,[3]
and the mallet is taken, the mooring post driven in,
and the prow-rope has been thrown on the ground;   5
praises are given and God is thanked,[4]
every man is embracing his fellow,
and our crew has come back safe,
with no loss to our expedition.

---

1. Translated by Richard B. Parkinson.
2. The Follower is a subordinate official, the tale's narrator and protagonist. The Count is a high-ranking official and the leader of the expedition that has just returned to Egypt.
3. "Home" is a translation of a characteristic term for the period meaning either "Egypt" or the royal residence.
4. No particular deity is specified. This widespread usage accommodates the many different deities people worshiped.

We've reached the very end of Wawat, and passed Biga![5] 10
Look, we have arrived in peace!
Our own land, we've reached it!

Listen to me, my Count!
I am free ⟨from⟩ exaggeration.
Wash yourself![6] Pour water on your hands! 15
So you may reply when you are addressed,
and speak to the king with self-possession,
and answer without stammering.
A man's utterance saves him.[7]
His speech turns anger away from him. 20
But you do as you wish!
It is tiresome to speak to you!

I shall tell you something similar,
which happened to me myself:
I had gone to the Mining Region[8] of the sovereign. 25
I had gone down to the Sea,
in a boat 120 cubits long,[9]
40 cubits broad,
in which there were 120 sailors from the choicest of Egypt.
They looked at the sea, they looked at the land, 30
and their hearts were stouter than lions'.

Before it came, they could foretell a gale,
a storm before it existed;
but a gale came up while we were at sea, before we had reached land.
The wind rose, and made an endless howling, 35
and with it a swell of eight cubits.
Only the mast broke it for me.
Then the boat died.[1]
Those in it—not one of them survived.
Then I was given up onto an island 40
by a wave of the sea.
With my heart as my only companion,
I spent three days alone.
I spent the nights inside
a shelter of wood, and embraced the shadows. 45
Then I stretched out my legs to learn what I could put in my mouth.

---

5. Biga, an island in the first cataract of the Nile, marked the beginning of Egypt. Wawat is Lower Nubia, immediately to the south. The expedition has been returning from Nubia.
6. One should purify oneself before going into the presence of the king. The narrator is encouraging the Count to prepare himself properly for his expected audience with the king.
7. Probably a proverb. A related one comes at the end of the tale.
8. Most likely southwestern Sinai, reached by ship on the Red Sea.
9. A cubit is 525 millimeters, about 20 inches. The boat is very large by ancient Egyptian standards.
1. The verb to die could be used for an inanimate thing, rather as ships are called "she" in English.

I found figs and grapes there, and every fine vegetable;
and there were sycomore figs there, and also ripened ones,[2]
and melons as if cultivated;
fish were there, and also fowl: 50
there was nothing which was not in it.
Then I ate my fill, and put aside
what was too much for my arms.
I took a fire drill, made fire,
and made a burnt offering to the Gods.[3]   55

Then I heard a noise of thunder; I thought it was a wave of the sea,
for the trees were splintering,
the earth shaking;
I uncovered my face and found it was a serpent coming.
There were 30 cubits of him.   60
His beard was bigger than two cubits,[4]
his flesh overlaid with gold,
and his eyebrows of true lapis lazuli.
He was rearing upwards.

He opened his mouth to me, while I was prostrate in front of him.[5]   65
He said to me, "Who brought you?[6]
Who brought you, young man?
Who brought you?
If you delay in telling me
who brought you to this island,   70
I will make you know yourself to be ashes,
turned into invisibility!"

"You speak to me, without me hearing.[7]
I am in front of you, and do not know myself,"
Then he put me in his mouth,   75
took me away to his dwelling place,
and laid me down without harming me.
I was safe, with no damage done to me.

He opened his mouth to me, while I was prostrate in front of him.[8]
Then he said to me: "Who brought you?   80
Who brought you, young man?

---

2. This shows that the island is cultivated, as is confirmed by the next line.

3. A fire drill is a stick spun against another piece of wood or a stone to produce a spark for lighting a fire. Burnt offerings were made to deities whose cult images were not present or who, like the sun god, were worshipped in their physical form.

4. The snake's beard shows that he has the form of a cult statue, as the precious materials mentioned in the next two lines also demonstrate.

5. The sailor has already identified that the snake is a god.

6. Probably a standard patronizing address to someone who seeks assistance. The snake then overawes the man with a threat that includes being consumed by his fiery breath.

7. The speaker shifts at this point. The absence of an indication of the change probably shows the sailor has lost consciousness from shock and on awaking cannot at first understand what is happening.

8. A gesture of supplication.

Who brought you to this island of the sea,
with water on all sides?"
Then I answered this to him, my arms bent in front of him.
I said to him, "It's because I was going down   85
to the Mining Region on a mission of the sovereign,
in a boat 120 cubits long,
40 cubits broad,
in which there were 120 sailors from the choicest of Egypt.
They looked at the sea, they looked at the land,   90
and their hearts were stouter than lions'.

Before it came, they could foretell a gale,
a storm before it existed;
each one of them—his heart was stouter,
his arm stronger, than his fellow's.   95
There was no fool among them.
And a gale came up while we were at sea, before we had reached land.
The wind rose, and made an endless howling,
and with it a swell of eight cubits.
Only the mast broke it for me.   100
Then the boat died.
Those in it—not one of them survived, except me.
And look, I am beside you.

Then I was brought to this island
by a wave of the sea."   105
And he said to me, "Fear not,
fear not, young man!
Do not be pale, for you have reached me!
Look, God has let you live,[9]
and has brought you to this island of the spirit;[1]   110
there is nothing which is not within it,
and it is full of every good thing.
Look, you will spend month upon month,
until you have completed four months in the interior of this island.
A ship will come from home,   115
with sailors in it whom you know,
and you will return home with them,
and die in your city.

How happy is he who can tell of his experience, so that the calamity
    passes![2]
I shall tell you something similar,   120
that happened on this island,
where I was with my kinsmen,
and with children amongst them.

---

9. The "God" evoked could also be understood
as "providence."
1. This may indicate that the island is imaginary.
2. This inverts a proverbial saying known in

various cultures. For example, Dante wrote,
"There is no greater pain than to recall a time
of happiness when in misery." The idea leads
the snake to tell his own tale.

With my offspring and my kinsmen, we were 75 serpents in all[3]—
I shall not evoke the little daughter,   125
whom I had wisely brought away.

Then a star fell,[4]
and because of it they went up in flames.
Now this happened when I wasn't with them;
they were burnt when I wasn't among them.   130
Then I died for them,[5] when I found them as a single heap of corpses.
If you are brave, master your heart,[6]
and you will fill your embrace with your children,
kiss your wife, and see your house!
This is better than anything.   135
You will reach home, and remain there,
amongst your kinsmen."
Stretched out prostrate was I,
and I touched the ground in front of him.

I said to him, "I shall tell your power to the sovereign.[7]   140
I shall cause him to comprehend your greatness.
I shall have them bring you laudanum and malabathrum,
terebinth and balsam,[8]
and the incense of the temple estates with which every God is content.
I shall tell what has happened to me, as what I have seen of
    your power.   145
They will thank God for you in the city
before the council of the entire land.

I shall slaughter bulls for you as a burnt offering.
I shall strangle fowls for you.
I shall have boats brought for you   150
laden with all the wealth of Egypt,
as is done for a God who loves mankind,
in a far land, unknown to mankind."

Then he laughed at me, at the things I had said,
which were folly to his heart.   155
He said to me, "Do you have much myrrh,
or all existing types of incense?
For I am the ruler of Punt;[9]

---

3. This number alludes to the 74 forms of the Egyptian sun god, perhaps with the addition of the snake himself. The "little daughter" is probably Maat ("Order"), known elsewhere as the sun god's daughter.

4. A falling star is known in other Egyptian sources as a portent. Here it strikes the group directly and annihilates them. This is probably a metaphor for the end of the world.

5. An extreme expression of grief.

6. The snake points out the moral the sailor should take from the cataclysm that he survived.

7. A deferential reference to the king of Egypt that is typical for this period.

8. The aromatics mentioned were all imported into Egypt, typically from the southwest, that is, the direction of the island where the man is.

9. A region reached from the Red Sea, probably on the latitude of modern Eritrea, from which Egypt imported aromatics and other African products. Punt also had a semimythical character as "God's Land" (the identity of the "God" is left open).

myrrh is mine;
that malabathrum you speak of bringing
is this island's plenty.
And once it happens that you have left this place,
you will never see this island again, which will have become water."[1]

Then that boat came,
as he had foretold previously.
Then I went and put myself up a tall tree,
and I recognized those inside it.
Then I went to report this,
and I found that he knew it.
Then he said to me, "Fare well,
fare well, young man,
to your house, and see your children!
Spread my renown in your city! Look, this is my due from you."[2]

Then I prostrated myself,
my arms bent in front of him.
Then he gave me a cargo
of myrrh and malabathrum,
terebinth and balsam,
camphor, *shaasekh*-spice, and eye-paint,
tails of giraffes,
a great mound of incense,
elephant tusks,
hounds and monkeys,
apes and all good riches.[3]

Then I loaded this onto the ship,
and it was then that I prostrated myself to thank God for him.
Then he said to me, "Look, you will arrive
within two months!
You will fill your embrace with your children.
You will grow young again at home, and be buried."
Then I went down to the shore nearby this ship.
Then I called to the expedition which was in this ship,
and I on the shore gave praises
to the lord of this island,
and those who were aboard did the same.[4]

We then sailed northwards,
to the Residence of the sovereign,
and we reached home
in two months, exactly as he had said.

160

165

170

175

180

185

190

195

---

1. The island exists only for the man's encounter with the snake and will vanish thereafter.
2. The god's desire to be known in Egypt mirrors hymns that extol the qualities of deities.
3. This list names products mentioned earlier, as well as various others that Egypt obtained

through trade. Not all of them can be identified with certainty.
4. The praise of the snake by the ship's crew parallels the thanks offered to God by the expedition at the beginning of the tale.

Then I entered before the sovereign, 200
and I presented him with this tribute
from the interior of this island.
Then he thanked God for me before the council of the entire land.
Then I was appointed as a Follower;
I was endowed with 200 persons.[5] 205
Look at me, after I have reached land, and have viewed my past
    experience!
Listen to my [speech]!
Look, it is good to listen to men.'
Then he said to me,[6] 'Don't act clever, my friend!
Who pours water [for] a goose, 210
when the day dawns for its slaughter on the morrow?'[7]
So it ends, from start to finish,[8]
as found in writing,
[as] a writing of the scribe with clever fingers,
Ameny son of Amenyaa (l.p.h.!).[9] 215

---

5. This gift of people would have made the narrator into a rich man.

6. The "me" is the sailor who has been the narrator all along, while "he" is the Count whom he has been addressing. The last three lines are the Count's response to the tale.

7. This appears to be a proverb, which may imply either that the narrator is the one preparing the Count for a bad reception from the king, or that it is pointless to console him with the example of his recovery from shipwreck when the Count has no future.

8. The text concludes with a short passage in red, known as a colophon, that gives an assurance of a good copy and the identity of the copyist.

9. "Life, prosperity, health!" is a wish appended typically to a king's name but also to that of a superior in a letter. In this case the scribe has been presumptuous, and perhaps humorous, by writing it after his own name.

SEMNA STELA OF SENWOSRET III

In ancient Egypt, military campaigns were an essential part of a successful king's role, ideally leading to an expansion of Egypt's frontiers. This inscription, from ca. 1830 B.C.E., commemorates such expansion and reflects on the duty of later generations to defend conquered territory. It is known from two copies, both carved on granite stelae—large round-topped stone slabs—that were set up in the fortresses of Uronarti and Semna, in today's northern Sudan. The king briefly recounts his achievements and praises his own valor, denigrates his Nubian enemies, and exhorts his successors to stand firm on the frontier. The text is part royal display and part exhortation to the occupying force in the fortresses; set up in an accessible place near a statue of Senwosret III, the stela would have provided a permanent inspiration for fortress personnel to honor the king and fight against his enemies.

Semna Stela of Senwosret III[1]

Horus: Divine of Forms;[2]
Two Ladies: Divine of Manifestations;
Dual King: Khakaure given life;
Golden Horus: Being;
Re's Bodily Son, whom he loves,   5
the Lord of the Two Lands: Senwosret,
given life, stability, power for all time!
Year 16, month 3 of Peret:[3]
his Person's making the southern boundary at Semna.

I have made my boundary, out-southing my forefathers.   10
I have exceeded what was handed down to me.
I am a king, whose speaking is acting;
what happens by my hand is what my heart plans;
one who is aggressive to capture,
swift to success;   15
who sleeps not with a matter (still) in his heart;
who takes thought for dependants, and stands by mercy;
who is unmerciful to the enemy that attacks him;
who attacks when attacked,
and is quiet when it is quiet;   20
who responds to a matter as it happens.
For he who is quiet after attack,
he is making the enemy's heart strong.
Aggression is bravery;
retreat is vile.   25
He who is driven from his boundary is a true back-turner,
since the Nubian only has to hear to fall at a word:[4]
answering him makes him retreat.
One is aggressive to him and he shows his back;
retreat and he becomes aggressive.   30
Not people to be respected—
they are wretches, broken-hearted!
My Person has seen it—it is not an untruth;
for I have plundered their women, and carried off their underlings,
gone to their wells,[5] driven off their bulls,   35
torn up their corn, and put fire to it.
As my father lives for me,[6]

1. Translated by Richard B. Parkinson.
2. The first seven lines of the text give the standard five-part titulary of Egyptian kings. "Horus" identifies the king as performing a divine role; the "Two Ladies" are the protective goddesses of the Two Lands (Upper and Lower Egypt); "Dual King" evokes two principal aspects of kingship; "Khakaure" means "the one who appears with the vital force of Re (the sun god)"; and "Lord of the Two Lands" precedes the king's birth name.
3. Peret is the middle of the three four-month

seasons in the Egyptian calendar.
4. This passage asserts that one needs only to confront the Nubians to defeat them, but the next one tells how the king has pursued a scorched-earth policy in their land.
5. The land of Upper Nubia, which Senwosret III states he has raided, is mostly desert, so that the inhabitants would rely on wells.
6. A standard form of oath, in which the oath taker swears by the life of a higher being. The king's "father" is a god, perhaps Amun, who is not named here.

I speak true;
here is no boastful phrase
which has come from my mouth.   40

Now, as for any son of mine who shall make firm this boundary
    my Person made,
he is my son, born of my Person;
the son who vindicates his father is a model,
making firm the boundary of his begetter.[7]
Now as for him who shall neglect it, shall not fight for it—   45
no son of mine, not born to me!
Now my Person has caused an image of my Person to be made,[8]
upon this boundary which my Person made,
so that you shall be firm for it, so that you shall fight for it.

7. The "son" evoked in this stanza is any successor of Senwosret III, and probably the
higher-ranking officers who served at the fortress as well. This line is a proverb that is also
known from literary instructions in wisdom.
8. This passage alludes to the statue set up
near the stela.

HERODOTUS

The Greek Herodotus (ca. 484–425
B.C.E.), who is known as the "father
of history," can also be seen as one of the
world's earliest anthropologists. Scholars
debate whether Herodotus actually traveled to all the places he describes, which
include Egypt, Persia, and India; some
of his accounts may well be based on
hearsay, or "oral history." But his *Histories* certainly show an intense interest in
trying to understand the diverse cultures
of non-Greek peoples, whom he calls
"barbarians." He is eager to incorporate
multiple points of view into his narrative, and to study the vast diversity of
human *nomos*—the Greek word for
"culture," "law," or "custom." Herodotus's *Histories* begin from the premise
that the west and the east have been at
war with each other since before the
time of the Trojan War. His goal is to
uncover the roots of the conflict, both
by tracing historical causes and by evoking cultural differences between, specifically, the Greeks, the Persians, and the
Egyptians. In his discussion of Egypt, he
acknowledges the great antiquity of
Egyptian culture, and the influence of
Egyptian thought on Greek myth, theology, and astronomy. The Persians, who
were for many years the military enemies of the Greeks, are presented as dis-
tinctly alien, but in some respects
superior, to the Greeks: for instance,
they value truthfulness, and Herodotus
expresses his approval of their law that
even a king cannot put a person to death
on the basis of just one charge.

From Histories[1]

From Book I

This is the publication of the research of Herodotus of Halicarnassus,[2] so that the actions of people shall not fade with time, so that the great and admirable monuments produced by both Greeks and barbarians shall not go unrenowned, and, among other things, to set forth the reasons why they waged war on each other.

Persian storytellers say that the Phoenicians[3] were the cause of the dispute, for they came from the so-called Red Sea to our sea,[4] inhabited the territory they now live in, and immediately set forth on long voyages. They shipped Egyptian and Assyrian merchandise to various places and they made a point of going to Argos. At that time, Argos was preeminent among the towns in the country which is now called Greece. Now, when the Phoenicians came to Argos, they laid out their cargo. On the fifth or sixth day after they arrived, when almost everything had been sold off, a large number of women—including the king's daughter—came down to the seashore. Her name (and the Greeks also agree in this) was Io, the daughter of Inachus.[5] While the women stood at the stern of the boat, buying the goods that appealed to them, the Phoenicians urged each other on and rushed them. Most of the women ran away, but Io was captured, along with some others. The Phoenicians put them in the boat and sailed away, bound for Egypt.

Although the Greeks do not agree, that is how the Persians say Io came to Egypt; and this act was the beginning of the violations of law. After this, they say that some Greeks, whose names I am unable to give you, though they would probably have been from Crete, put into port at Phoenician Tyre and abducted Europa,[6] the daughter of the king. This, though, was just a case of an eye for an eye, so the next crime, which the Greeks committed, was really the second in the series.

The Greeks sailed in a long warship to Colchian Aea, on the river Phasis.[7] After taking care of the business they had come about, they abducted Medea, the daughter of the king.[8] The Colchian king sent a messenger to Greece asking for his daughter back and demanding damages for the kidnapping. The

---

1. Translated by Walter Blanco.
2. "Research" is a translation of the Greek term *historia*, which literally means "investigation." Halicarnassus is a Greek city in Asia Minor, on the coast of modern Turkey.
3. Ancient Phoenicia was a maritime society known for its prominence in trade, located along the coast of modern Israel, Lebanon, and Syria. The main Phoenician cities were Tyre and Sidon.
4. The Red Sea, for the Greeks, covered the whole Indian Ocean, including what we now call the Red Sea, as well as the Persian Gulf. "Our sea" is the Mediterranean.
5. In Greek mythology, the god Zeus seduced Io and changed her into a heifer, so that he could have an affair with her in bull form,

without his wife Hera finding out. But Hera discovered the truth, and Io was forced to wander all over the world, finally escaping to Egypt, where she was restored to her human form. Herodotus assumes knowledge of this myth, but eliminates its fantastical elements.
6. Europa was a Phoenician girl, also abducted by Zeus when he was in the form of a bull. He carried her on his back to the island of Crete.
7. Colchis was the area south of the Caucasus Mountains, overlapping with modern Georgia; its river, the Phasis, is now called the Rion.
8. Medea helped the Greek hero Jason steal the Golden Fleece from her father, the king, and fled back to Corinth with him.

Greeks answered that since the Phoenicians had not given damages for the kidnapping of Io, the girl from Argos, they would not give anything, either.

They say that two generations after this event, Alexander,[9] the son of Priam, heard about it and hankered to abduct a Greek woman for himself, fully persuaded that he would not have to pay any penalty. After all, no one else had. After he kidnapped Helen, it seemed to the Greeks that the first thing to do was to send messengers asking for Helen back and demanding damages for the kidnapping. In the face of these demands, the Trojans brought up the kidnapping of Medea: the Greeks had given neither damages nor the girl when they had been asked, and now they wanted damages to be given to them by others!

So far, say the Persians, they had merely been stealing women from each other, but after this the Greeks were most greatly to blame because they began to lead armies into Asia before the Asians began to lead them into Europe. The Persians believe that raping women is the work of evil men, but that making a great to-do about vengeance after women have been raped is the work of fools. Prudent men are not concerned about women who have been raped, since it is perfectly plain that they could not be raped if they didn't really want to be.[1] The Persians say that they paid no attention to the abduction of their women from Asia, while the Greeks, for the sake of a Lacedaemonian woman, assembled a huge army and then invaded Asia and destroyed the power of Priam.[2] Because of this, the Persians have always considered the Greeks to be their enemies. You see, the Persians regard Asia and the barbarian people who live in it as their domain, while they think of Europe and the Greeks as separate.

That is how the Persians say it happened, and they trace the beginning of their hatred of the Greeks to the conquest of Troy. The Phoenicians, however, do not agree with the Persians about Io. They say that they did not have to resort to kidnapping to take her to Egypt, but that she had been having sex in Argos with the captain of the ship. When she found out that she was pregnant, she was so ashamed for the sake of her parents that she willingly sailed away with the Phoenicians to avoid discovery. That is what the Persians and the Phoenicians say.

I am not going to say that these events happened one way or the other. Rather, I will point out the man[3] who I know for a fact began the wrongdoing against the Greeks, and then proceed with my story while giving detailed accounts of cities both great and small. Many that were great in the past have become small, and many that used to be small have become great in my lifetime, so I will mention both alike because I know very well that human prosperity never remains in the same place.

* * *

These are the customs I know the Persians to observe. They are not allowed to build statues, temples, and altars, and in fact they accuse those who do of

9. Paris of Troy. The abduction of the Spartan king Menelaus's wife, Helen, by Paris (Alexander), started the Trojan War.
1. The translation "rape" is somewhat misleading. The word used here means "capture"; it is the same word translated in earlier paragraphs as "kidnap," and in the next sentence

as "abduction."
2. The Lacedaemonian (Spartan) woman is Helen. The invasion referred to is the Trojan War.
3. Croesus, ruler of Lydia, a kingdom adjacent to Persia.

silliness, in my opinion because unlike the Greeks, they don't think of the gods as having human form. It is their custom to climb to the mountaintops and sacrifice to Zeus, which is the name they give to the full circle of the sky. They sacrifice to the sun and the moon and the earth, as well as to fire, water, and air. At first, they sacrificed only to these, but they later learned to sacrifice to the Heavenly Aphrodite—they learned this from the Assyrians and the Arabians. The Assyrians call Aphrodite Mylitta, the Arabians call her Alilat, and the Persians call her Mitra.

This is the way the Persians sacrifice to the above-mentioned gods: they make no altars and light no fires when they are about to sacrifice. They don't pour libations or play the flute or wear garlands or sprinkle barley on their victims. Whenever someone wants to sacrifice to one of the gods, he leads the victim to a ritually pure place and invokes the god while wearing his turban wreathed, preferably, with myrtle. It is not allowed for the sacrificer to pray, in private, for good things for himself. Instead, he prays for the well-being of all the Persians and of the king, for the sacrificer, after all, is included among all the Persians. When he has cut up the sacrificial victim into pieces and then boiled the meat, he spreads out the tenderest grass—preferably clover—and then places all of the meat on top of it. When he has arranged the meat piece by piece, a Magus stands near and chants a hymn on the origin of the gods—anyway, that's the kind of hymn they say it is. It is not their custom to perform a sacrifice without a Magus. The sacrificer waits a little while, then carries away the meat and does whatever he wants with it.

The day of all days they celebrate the most is their own birthday. On that day, the right thing to do is to serve a bigger meal than on any other day. On that day, their rich people serve up oxen, horses, camels, and donkeys that have been roasted whole in ovens, while their poor people serve smaller cattle, like sheep and goats. They eat few main dishes, but lots of appetizers, one after another, and for this reason the Persians say that the Greeks eat a main course and then stop when they are still hungry since after dinner nothing worth mentioning is brought out, though they wouldn't stop eating if it was. They love wine, but they are not allowed to vomit or to urinate in front of someone else. But though they have to be careful about that, they are accustomed to deliberate about their most important affairs when they are drunk, and then, on the next day, when they are sober, the master of the house they have been deliberating in proposes the decision that pleased them most. If they like it even when they are sober, they adopt it, but if not, they let it go. If they ever come to a provisional decision while sober, though, they then get drunk and reconsider it.

This is how you can tell if people who happen to meet each other on the street are social equals: instead of a verbal greeting, they kiss each other on the lips. If one is of slightly lower rank, they kiss each other's cheeks. If one is of a much lower rank, though, he prostrates himself and pays homage to the other. After themselves, Persians have the highest respect for the people who live closest to them, and next highest for those next closest, and so on. In accordance with this principle, they have the least respect for those who live farthest away. They consider themselves to be the best of people by far and others to share worth proportionally, so the people who live the farthest away are the worst. Subject nations ruled each other even under Median rule. That is, the Medes[4] ruled over everything, but especially over those nearest to them, while those, in turn, ruled their neighbors, and so on. The Persians rank nations according to the same principle, by which each nation has a surrogate rule over the next one.

Nevertheless, the Persians are more inclined than other people to adopt foreign customs. For example, they wear Median clothes in the belief that they are more attractive than their own, and they wear Egyptian breastplates into war. They seek out and learn about all kinds of delights, and they even learned from the Greeks to have sex with boys. Each Persian man has many lawfully wedded wives, but many more mistresses.

Second only to being brave in battle, a man is considered manly if he has many sons to show for himself, and every year the king sends gifts to the man who shows off the most sons. They believe that there is strength in numbers. They educate their sons from the age of five to the age of twenty in only three things: horseback riding, archery, and telling the truth. The boy does not come into the presence of his father until he is five years old—until then he lives with the women. This is done so that if he should die while he is growing up he won't cause any grief to his father.

I approve of that custom, and I also approve of the one that forbids even the king to put someone to death on the basis of only one charge, and that forbids any Persian to do any of his household slaves any irreparable harm on the basis of one charge either. If, however, he finds on review that there are more and greater offenses than services, then he may give way to anger.

They say that no one has yet killed his own father or mother. It is inevitable, they say, that any such child who has ever been born will be found on investigation to have been either a changeling or a bastard. They say that it just isn't likely that a true parent will be killed by his own child.

Whatever they are not allowed to do, they are also not allowed to talk about. They consider lying to be the most disgraceful of all things. After that, it is owing money—for many reasons, but mostly, they say, because it is necessary for somebody who owes money to tell lies.

No citizen who is an albino or who has leprosy is allowed into the city or to mingle with other Persians. They say that he has committed some offense against the sun. Foreigners who catch these diseases are driven out of the country by posses. Even white doves are driven out, charged with the same offense.

They don't spit, urinate, or wash their hands in rivers, or allow anyone else to, for they especially revere rivers.

The Persians don't notice it, though we do, but this also happens to be true of them: their names, which refer to their physical characteristics or to their social importance, all end in the same letter, which the Dorians call san and which the Ionians call sigma. If you look into it, you will find that Persian names end in this letter—not some here and some there, but *all* of them.

I am able to say these things with certainty because I know them for a fact. There are things about the dead, though, which are concealed or referred to obliquely—for example that the corpse of a Persian man is not buried until it has been torn at by a bird or a dog. I know for sure, though, that the Magi

---

4. A people who lived in modern-day northwestern Iran, next to ancient Persia.

practice this—because they do it openly—and that the Persians cover a corpse with wax before putting it in the ground. The Magi are very different from other people, including the Egyptian priests. The Egyptian priests refrain from killing any living thing, except what they ritually sacrifice. The Magi, however, will kill everything but dogs and people with their own hands. In fact, they make a point of killing things, and go around killing ants and snakes and anything else that creeps, crawls, and flies. Well, that's how they've been practicing this custom since the beginning, so let it stay that way.

From Book II

As to the Egyptians, before Psammetichus[1] became king, they assumed that they were the very first people who ever existed. But when Psammetichus came to the throne, he wanted to know for sure who the first were, and ever since Psammetichus the Egyptians believe that the Phrygians preceded them, whereas they precede everybody else. Since Psammetichus could not find out who came first by asking questions, he devised this experiment: he gave two children chosen from the common people to a shepherd to raise among his sheep. He commanded that no one should make any sound in their presence, but that they should be kept to themselves in a solitary pen and should be brought she-goats from time to time, have their fill of milk, and be otherwise provided for. Psammetichus devised this experiment and gave this order because he wanted to find out—apart from meaningless babble—just what word first broke from the children.

And that's just what happened. After two years had gone by, this is what happened to the shepherd as he followed his routine: when he opened the door and went in, both children fell down before him and reached out their hands, saying "baakos!" The first time he heard this, the shepherd kept quiet about it, but since he heard the word every time he went there to do his chores, he mentioned it to his master and, at his master's command, led the children into his presence. When Psammetichus heard them for himself, he asked which people called something "baakos," and found out that it was what the Phrygians called bread. Calculating on the basis of this experiment, the Egyptians conceded that the Phrygians were older than they. I heard that is the way it was from the priests of the temple of Hephaestus in Memphis. (The Greeks talk a lot of nonsense, such as that Psammetichus cut out the tongues of some women and arranged for the children to live among these women.)

This is what they said about the upbringing of the children, but I heard other things in Memphis when I went there to confer with the priests of Hephaestus. I even went to Thebes and to Heliopolis since I wanted to know whether they would agree with the stories that came out of Memphis, because the Heliopolitans are said to be the most learned of all Egyptians when it comes to stories.

Now, I am not eager to relate what I heard about religion in these stories, except only for the names of the gods, since I believe that all men know the same things about gods, whatever they call them. If I do mention anything, it will be a necessary part of the story I am telling.

---

1. Ruler of Egypt from 663 to 609 B.C.E.

As to human affairs, however, all the priests agree about this: the Egyptians were the first of all mankind to discover the year, dividing the seasons into the twelve parts which make it up. They said that they figured this out from the stars. It seems to me that they went about this more intelligently than the Greeks, because the Greeks insert a month every other year on account of the seasons, whereas the Egyptians make up twelve thirty-day months and add five days to that number every year so that the circle of the seasons will come around to the same place every time. In addition, the priests said that the Egyptians were the first to regularly call the gods by twelve names, and that the Greeks adopted this practice from them. Furthermore, they were the first to assign altars and statues and temples to the gods, and to chisel pictures into stone. They outright proved to me that most of these things were so, but they merely asserted that the first human to rule Egypt was called Min.

AESCHYLUS

Aeschylus's *Persians* (472 B.C.E.) is our only surviving Greek tragedy with a real historical setting: it describes the wars between Greece and Persia, in which Aeschylus himself had fought. The play is set, surprisingly, in the Persian court, and represents an attempt to describe the war, which the Greeks won, from the other side. The Messenger Speech, included here, evokes the climactic battle of Salamis, presenting the event as a tragic disaster for Persia. It is noticeable that while the Persians are named and mourned as individuals, the Greeks are an undifferentiated mass. But it is also noteworthy that this supposedly Persian messenger presents the Greeks as fighters for freedom, one of whom cries out, "Forward, you sons of Hellas! Set your country free!" The destruction of the Persian Empire is the glory of democratic Athens. The play was clearly successful with its Athenian audience: it won first prize in the dramatic competition when it was first performed.

From Persians[1]

ATOSSA[2]   To those whose sons are with the army now, your words
  Bring fearful thoughts.
CHORUS   If I mistake not, you will soon

1. Translated by Philip Vellacott.
2. Queen of Persia, wife of the dead king Darius and mother of the current ruler, Xerxes.

Know the whole truth. That runner's undeniably
A Persian courier; good or bad, he'll bring us news.
    Enter a MESSENGER.
MESSENGER   O cities of wide Asia! O loved Persian earth,   5
Haven of ample wealth! One blow has overthrown
Your happy pride; the flower of all your youth is fallen.
To bring the first news of defeat's an evil fate;
Yet I must now unfold the whole disastrous truth:
Persians, our country's fleet and army are no more.   10
CHORUS   O grief, and grief again!
Weep, every heart that hears,
This cruel, unlooked-for pain.
MESSENGER   Yes; all that mighty armament is lost; and I
Still see the light, beyond all hope, and have come back.   15
CHORUS   Why have we lived so long?
The harvest of ripe years
Is new grief, sudden tears.
MESSENGER   Sirs, I was there; what I have told I saw myself;
I can recount each detail of the great defeat.   20
CHORUS   Lament and weep! In vain
Went forth our army, strong
In arrows, sabres, spears,
To Hellas' holy soil.[3]
MESSENGER   The shores of Salamis,[4] and all the neighbouring coasts,   25
Are strewn with bodies miserably done to death.
CHORUS   Weep and lament! Our dead
Are made the ocean's spoil,
Tossed on its restless bed,
Their folded cloaks spread wide   30
Over the drowning tide.
MESSENGER   Our bows and arrows were no help; there, overwhelmed
By crashing prows, we watched a nation sink and die.
CHORUS   Lament with loud despair
The cruel and crushing fate   35
Of those whom the gods' hate
Condemned to perish there.
MESSENGER   What name more hateful to our ears than Salamis?
Athens—a name of anguish in our memory!
CHORUS   Most hateful name of all—   40
Athens! Who can forget
Our Persian women's debt—
Innocent tears that fall
For husband lost, or son,
Long since at Marathon?[5]   45

---

3. Greece.
4. An island near Athens, the location of the climactic naval battle between Greece and the invading Persian army, in 480 B.C.E.

5. In its first invasion of Greece, the Persian army, led by Xerxes' father, Darius, was defeated at Marathon in 490 B.C.E.

ATOSSA   Good councillors, I have kept silence all this while
    Stunned with misfortune; this news is too terrible
    For narrative or question. Yet, being mortal, we
    Must endure grief when the gods send it. Therefore stand
    And tell the whole disaster, though your voice be choked   50
    With tears. Who is not dead? And whom have we to mourn
    Among our generals, whose post death leaves unmanned?
MESSENGER   Xerxes the king lives.
ATOSSA   Then the light of hope shines forth
    Like white dawn after blackest darkness, for my house.
MESSENGER   But Artembares, marshal of ten thousand horse,   55
    Floats, bruised by the hard rocks of the Silenian shore.
    A spear struck Dadaces, captain of a thousand men,
    And with an airy leap he hurtled from his ship.
    Tenagon, a true Bactrian born, first in their ranks,
    Now haunts the sea-worn fringe of Ajax' island home.[6]   60
    Three more, Lilaeus, Arsames, and Argestes,
    Struck down, were seen eddying round the Isle of Doves,[7]
    Butting the granite rocks. Metallus the Chrysean,
    Who led ten thousand foot and thirty thousand horse,
    Called the Black Cavalry—when he was killed, the hair   65
    Of his thick shaggy yellow beard was dyed blood-red,
    Dipped in the crimson sea. Magus the Arabian
    Is dead; and Bactrian Artames has stayed abroad,
    A settler in a rugged land; and Tharybis,
    Captain of five times fifty ships, a Lyrnean born,   70
    Is dead—his handsome face met an unhandsome end,
    Poor wretch, unburied. Syennesis, the bravest man
    In the whole army, leader of the Cilician troops,
    Who with his single arm destroyed more enemies
    Than any other, won great glory, and is dead.   75
    Such is the roll of officers who met their fate;
    Yet I have told but few of many thousand deaths.
ATOSSA   Alas! Here is the very crown of misery;
    For Persia, shame and loss and anguish of lament.
    But come, retrace your story now, and tell me this: 80
    What was the number of the Hellene ships, that they
    Dared to assault our fleet, and charge them prow to prow?
MESSENGER   Had Fortune favoured numbers, we would have won the day.
    Three hundred vessels made the total Hellene strength,
    Not counting ten picked warships. Xerxes had, I know,   85
    A thousand in command, of which two hundred and seven
    Were special fast ships. That was the proportion. Now,
    Do you say we entered battle with too weak a force?
    No. The result shows with what partial hands the gods

6. Salamis, supposedly the homeland of the   7. Salamis.
Homeric hero Ajax.

Weighed down the scale against us, and destroyed us all.   90
It is the gods who keep Athene's city[8] safe.
ATOSSA   What—safe? Is Athens then not ravaged after all?
MESSENGER   While she has men, a city's bulwarks stand unmoved.
ATOSSA   Now tell me how the two fleets fell to the attack.
Who first advanced, struck the first blow? Was it the Greeks,   95
Or my bold son, exultant with his countless ships?
MESSENGER   Neither, my queen. Some Fury, some malignant Power,
Appeared, and set in train the whole disastrous rout.
A Hellene[9] from the Athenian army came and told
Your son Xerxes this tale: that, once the shades of night   100
Set in, the Hellenes would not stay, but leap on board,
And, by whatever secret route offered escape,
Row for their lives. When Xerxes heard this, with no thought
Of the man's guile, or of the jealousy of gods,
He sent this word to all his captains: 'When the sun   105
No longer flames to warm the earth, and darkness holds
The court of heaven, range the main body of our fleet
Threefold, to guard the outlets and the choppy straits.'
Then he sent other ships to row right round the isle,
Threatening that if the Hellene ships found a way through   110
To save themselves from death, he would cut off the head
Of every Persian captain. By these words he showed
How ignorance of the gods' intent had dazed his mind.

     Our crews, then, in good order and obediently,
Were getting supper; then each oarsman looped his oar   115
To the smooth rowing-pin; and when the sun went down
And night came on, the rowers all embarked, and all
The heavy-armed soldiers; and from line to line they called,
Cheering each other on, rowing and keeping course
As they were ordered. All night long the captains kept   120
Their whole force cruising to and fro across the strait.
Now night was fading; still the Hellenes showed no sign
Of trying to sail out unnoticed; till at last
Over the earth shone the white horses of the day,
Filling the air with beauty. Then from the Hellene ships   125
Rose like a song of joy the piercing battle-cry,
And from the island crags echoed an answering shout.

     The Persians knew their error; fear gripped every man.
They were no fugitives who sang that terrifying
Paean, but Hellenes charging with courageous hearts   130
To battle. The loud trumpet flamed along their ranks.
At once their frothy oars moved with a single pulse,

---

8. Athens, whose patron goddess is Athena.   9. Greek.

Beating the salt waves to the bo'suns' chant; and soon
Their whole fleet hove clear into view; their right wing first,
In precise order, next their whole array came on, 135
And at that instant a great shout beat on our ears:
'Forward, you sons of Hellas! Set your country free!
Set free your sons, your wives, tombs of your ancestors,
And temples of your gods. All is at stake: now fight!'
Then from our side in answer rose the manifold 140
Clamour of Persian voices; and the hour had come.

At once ship into ship battered its brazen beak.
A Hellene ship charged first, and chopped off the whole stern
Of a Phoenician galley. Then charge followed charge
On every side. At first by its huge impetus 145
Our fleet withstood them. But soon, in that narrow space,
Our ships were jammed in hundreds; none could help another.
They rammed each other with their prows of bronze; and some
Were stripped of every oar. Meanwhile the enemy
Came round us in a ring and charged. Our vessels heeled 150
Over; the sea was hidden, carpeted with wrecks
And dead men; all the shores and reefs were full of dead.

Then every ship we had broke rank and rowed for life.
The Hellenes seized fragments of wrecks and broken oars
And hacked and stabbed at our men swimming in the sea 155
As fishermen kill tunnies or some netted haul.
The whole sea was one din of shrieks and dying groans,
Till night and darkness hid the scene. If I should speak
For ten days and ten nights, I could not tell you all
That day's agony. But know this: never before 160
In one day died so vast a company of men.

ATOSSA   Alas! How great an ocean of disaster has
Broken on Persia and on every eastern race!

MESSENGER   But there is more, and worse; my story is not half told.
Be sure, what follows twice outweighs what went before. 165

ATOSSA   What could be worse? What could our armament endure,
To outweigh all the sufferings already told?

MESSENGER   The flower of Persian chivalry and gentle blood,
The youth and valour of our choice nobility,
First in unmoved devotion to the king himself, 170
Are sunk into the mire of ignominious death.

ATOSSA   My friends, this evil news is more than I can bear.—
How do you say they died?

MESSENGER   Opposite Salamis
There is an island—small, useless for anchorage—
Where Pan the Dancer treads along the briny shore. 175
There Xerxes sent them, so that, when the enemy,
Flung from their ships, were struggling to the island beach,
The Persian force might without trouble cut them down,

And rescue Persian crews from drowning in the sea:
Fatal misjudgement! When in the sea-battle Heaven 180
Had given glory to the Hellenes, that same day
They came, armed with bronze shields and spears, leapt from their ships,
And made a ring round the whole island, that our men
Could not tell where to turn. First came a shower of blows
From stones slung with the hand; then from the drawn bowstring 185
Arrows leapt forth to slaughter; finally, with one
Fierce roar the Hellenes rushed at them, and cut and carved
Their limbs like butchers, till the last poor wretch lay dead.

This depth of horror Xerxes saw; close to the sea
On a high hill he sat, where he could clearly watch 190
His whole force both by sea and land. He wailed aloud,
And tore his clothes, weeping; and instantly dismissed
His army, hastening them to a disordered flight.
This, then, brings you new grief to mingle with the first.

ATOSSA   Oh, what malign Power so deceived our Persian hopes? 195
My son, marching to taste the sweetness of revenge
On Athens, found it bitter. Those who died before
At Marathon were not enough; Xerxes has won
For us not vengeance but a world of suffering.
But tell me now, what of those ships that have escaped? 200
Where did you leave them? Have you any certain news?

MESSENGER   The captains of surviving ships spread sail and fled
In swift disorder with a following wind. On land
The remnants of the army suffered fearful loss,
Tortured by hunger, thirst, exhaustion. Some of us 205
Struggled at last to Phocis and the Melian Gulf,
Where cool Spercheius wanders through the thirsty plain.
We came next to Achaea; then to Thessaly,
Half dead for want of food; and there great numbers died
Of thirst and hunger, for we suffered both. From there 210
We reached Magnesia, Macedonia, and the ford
Across the river Axius, and the reedy marsh
Of Bolbe, and Mount Pangaeus in Edonia.
That night some god woke Winter long before his time;
And holy Strymon was frost-bound. Men who before 215
Were unbelievers, then fell on their knees in worship
Of earth and heaven; and from the whole army rose
Innumerable prayers. Then over the firm ice
They made their way. Those of us who began to cross
Before the sun had shed abroad his sacred beams 220
Were saved. But soon his rays shone out like piercing flames,
Melting the ice in mid-stream. Helplessly they slipped,
Men heaped on men, into the water. He who died
Quickest, was luckiest. The handful who survived,

Suffering untold hardship, struggled on through Thrace   225
To safety, and now at last have reached their native earth.

    So, well may Persia's cities mourn their young men lost.
I have spoken truth; yet all I have told is but a part
Of all the evil God sent to strike Persia down.
CHORUS   O fatal Spirit of Destruction, cruelly   230
   You have attacked and trampled the whole Persian race.
ATOSSA   Our army is destroyed and gone. O bitter grief!
O vivid dream that lit the darkness of my sleep,
How clearly you forewarned me of calamity!
And, Councillors, how lightly you interpreted!   235
Yet, since you counselled me to pray, I am resolved
First to invoke the heavenly gods; then in my house
To prepare meal and oil and honey, and return
And offer them as gifts to Earth and to the dead.
What's done, I know, is done; yet I will sacrifice   240
In hope that time may bring about some better fate.
You meanwhile must take counsel on our present loss
With other faithful Councillors; and if my son
Returns while I am absent, comfort him, and bring him
Safe to the house, lest his despair heap grief on grief.   245
    Exit ATOSSA *with her attendants, and the* MESSENGER.
CHORUS   Thy hand, O Zeus our king, has swept from sight
   The boastful pride of Persia's vast array,
     And veiled the streets of Susa
     In gloomy mists of mourning.

AIRS, WATERS, PLACES

The author of the anonymous Greek Hippocratic text *Airs, Waters, Places* (late fifth century B.C.E.) provides a fascinating analysis of how national character might be affected by geographic and climatic conditions. The writer subscribes to some stereotypes about Asiatic peoples, but also tries to understand cultural difference and struggles with the important question of how physical environment and culture might inform one another. The word "Hippocratic" means that the text is part of a set of Greek medical writings associated with the famous doctor Hippocrates (ca. 460–370 B.C.E.), though probably not actually by him.

From Airs, Waters, Places[1]

I now want to show how different in all respects are Asia and Europe, and why races are dissimilar, showing individual physical characteristics. It would take too long to discuss this subject in its entirety but I will take what seem to me to be the most important points of difference.

Asia differs very much from Europe in the nature of everything that grows there, vegetable or human. Everything grows much bigger and finer in Asia, and the nature of the land is tamer, while the character of the inhabitants is milder and less passionate. The reason for this is the equable blending of the climate, for it lies in the midst of the sunrise facing the dawn. It is thus removed from extremes of heat and cold. Luxuriance and ease of cultivation are to be found most often when there are no violent extremes, but when a temperate climate prevails. All parts of Asia are not alike, but that which is centrally placed between the hot and the cold parts is the most fertile and well wooded; it has the best weather and the best water, both rain water and water from springs. It is not too much burnt up by the heat nor desiccated by parching drought; it is neither racked by cold nor drenched by frequent rains from the south or by snow. Crops are likely to be large, both those which are from seed and those which the earth produces of her own accord. But as the fruits of the latter are eaten by man, they have cultivated them by transplanting. The cattle raised there are most likely to do well, being most prolific and best at rearing their young. Likewise, the men are well made, large and with good physique. They differ little among themselves in size and physical development. Such a land resembles the spring time in its character and the mildness of the climate.

So much for the differences of constitution between the inhabitants of Asia and of Europe. The small variations of climate to which the Asiatics are subject, extremes both of heat and cold being avoided, account for their mental flabbiness and cowardice as well. They are less warlike than Europeans and tamer of spirit, for they are not subject to those physical changes and the mental stimulation which sharpen tempers and induce recklessness and hot-headedness. Instead they live under unvarying conditions. Where there are always changes, men's minds are roused so that they cannot stagnate. Such things appear to me to be the cause of the feebleness of the Asiatic race, but a contributory cause lies in their customs; for the greater part is under monarchical rule. When men do not govern themselves and are not their own masters they do not worry so much about warlike exercises as about not appearing warlike, for they do not run the same risks. The subjects of a monarchy are compelled to fight and to suffer and die for their masters, far from their wives, their children and friends. Deeds of prowess and valour redound to the advantage and advancement of their masters, while their own reward is danger and death. Moreover, such men lose their high-spiritedness through unfamiliarity with war and through sloth, so that even if a man be born brave and of stout heart, his character is ruined by this form of government. A good proof of this is that

1. Translated by J. Chadwick and W. N. Mann.

the most warlike men in Asia, whether Greeks or barbarians, are those who are not subject races but rule themselves and labour on their own behalf. Running risks only for themselves, they reap for themselves the rewards of bravery or the penalties of cowardice. You will also find that the Asiatics differ greatly among themselves, some being better and some worse. This follows from the variations of climate to which they are subject, as I explained before.

* * *

The remaining peoples of Europe differ widely among themselves both in size and appearance owing to the great and frequent climatic changes to which they are subject. Hot summers and hard winters, heavy rains followed by long periods of drought, all these occasion variations of every kind. It is reasonable that these changes should affect reproduction by variations in the coagulability of the semen so that its nature is different in summer and winter, in rainy weather and times of drought. I believe this to be the reason for the greater variation among individuals of the European races, even among the inhabitants of a single city, than is seen among Asiatics and also why they vary so much in size. When the weather changes often, abnormalities in the coagulation of the semen are more frequent than when the weather is constant. A variable climate produces a nature which is coupled with a fierce, hot-headed and discordant temperament, for frequent fears cause a fierce attitude of mind whereas quietness and calm dull the wits. Indeed, this is the reason why the inhabitants of Europe are more courageous than those of Asia. Conditions which change little lead to easy-going ways; variations to distress of body and mind. Calm and an easy-going way of living increase cowardice; distress and pain increase courage. That is one reason for the more warlike nature of Europeans. But another cause lies in their customs. They are not subjects of a monarchy as the Asiatics are and, as I have said before, men who are ruled by princes are the most cowardly. Their souls are enslaved and they are unwilling to risk their own lives for another's aggrandisement. On the other hand, those who govern themselves will willingly take risks because they do it for themselves. They are eager and willing to face even the worst of fates when theirs are the rewards of victory. It is clear, then, that the tradition of rule has no small influence on the courage of a people.

In general it may be said that these are the differences between Europe and Asia. There exist in Europe, then, people differing among themselves in size, appearance and courage, and the factors controlling those differences are those I have described. Let me summarize this plainly. When a race lives in a rough mountainous country, at a high elevation, and well watered, where great differences of climate accompany the various seasons, there the people will be of large physique, well-accustomed to hardihood and bravery, and with no small degree of fierceness and wildness in their character. On the other hand, in low-lying, stifling lands, full of meadows, getting a larger share of warm than cold winds, and where the water is warm, the people will be neither large nor slight, but rather broad in build, fleshy and black-haired. Their complexions are dark rather than fair and they are phlegmatic rather than bilious. Bravery and hardihood are not an integral part of their natural characters although these traits can be created by training. The people of a country where rivers drain the surface water and rain water have clear complexions and good health. But where there are no rivers and the drinking water is taken from lakes or marshes, the people will necessarily be more pot-bellied and splenetic. People who live in countries which are high, level, windswept and rainy tend to be of large stature and to show little variation among themselves. They are also of a less courageous and less wild disposition. In countries where there is a light waterless soil devoid of trees and where the seasons occasion but small changes in climate, the people usually have hard sinewy bodies, they are fair rather than dark and they are strong-willed and headstrong in temperament. Places where changes of weather are most frequent and of the greatest degree show the greatest individual differences in physique, temperament and disposition among the inhabitants.

The chief controlling factors, then, are the variability of the weather, the type of country and the sort of water which is drunk. You will find, as a general rule, that the constitutions and the habits of a people follow the nature of the land where they live. Where the soil is rich, soft and well-watered and where surface water is drunk, which is warm in summer and cold in winter, and where the seasons are favourable, you will find the people fleshy, their joints obscured, and they have watery constitutions. Such people are incapable of great effort. In addition, such a people are, for the most part, cowards. They are easy-going and sleepy, clumsy craftsmen and never keen or delicate. But if the land is bare, waterless and rough, swept by the winter gales and burnt by the summer sun, you will find there a people hard and spare, their joints showing, sinewy and hairy. They are by nature keen and fond of work, they are wakeful, headstrong and self-willed and inclined to fierceness rather than tame. They are keener at their crafts, more intelligent and better warriors. Other living things in such a land show a similar nature. These, then, are the most radically opposed types of character and physique. If you draw your deductions according to these principles, you will not go wrong.

HORACE

This ode by the Roman poet Horace (65–8 B.C.E.) deals with the defeat of the Roman general Antony and the Egyptian queen Cleopatra by Octavian (who would later become Augustus, the first Roman emperor). Horace makes use of a long tradition of Greek and Roman writers diminishing, and dismissing, their eastern, "barbarian" opponents, in order to justify Greco-Roman supremacy. In doing so, he covers up the fact that the battle in question was actually part of a civil war.

Ode 1.37[1]

Nunc est bibendum

Now we must drink, now we must
beat the earth with unfettered feet, now,
    my friends, is the time to load the couches
        of the gods with Salian feasts.[2]

Before this it was a sin to take the Caecuban[3]   5
down from its ancient racks, while the mad queen[4]
    with her contaminated flock of men
        diseased by vice was preparing

the ruin of the Capitol[5] and the destruction
of our power, crazed with hope   10
    unlimited and drunk
        with sweet fortune. But her madness

decreased when scarce a ship escaped the flames
and her mind, deranged by Mareotic wine,[6]
    was made to face real fears   15
        as she flew from Italy, and Caesar[7]

pressed on the oars (like a hawk
after gentle doves or a swift hunter
    after a hare on the snowy plains
        of Thrace) to put in chains   20

this monster sent by fate. But she looked
for a nobler death. She did not have a woman's fear
    of the sword, nor did she make
        for secret shores with her swift fleet.

Daring to gaze with face serene upon her ruined palace,   25
and brave enough to take deadly serpents
    in her hand, and let her body
        drink their black poison,

fiercer she was in the death she chose, as though
she did not wish to cease to be a queen, taken to Rome   30
    on the galleys of savage Liburnians,[8]
        to be a humble woman in a proud triumph.

---

1. Translated by David West. This poem has no title; West has used the first words of the Latin original as a title ("Now we must drink").
2. The Salii, priests of the war god Mars, were known for their energetic leaping, dancing, and feasting at their yearly festival, in March.
3. A type of wine.
4. Cleopatra, queen of Egypt, who aided her lover, the Roman general Antony, in his strug-gle against Octavian (later Augustus) in the last of the Roman civil wars. The poem celebrates Octavian's victory at Actium, in 31 B.C.E.
5. Hill in Rome, location of important Roman temples and center of Roman power.
6. A type of sweet wine.
7. Octavian.
8. Octavian used ships modeled on those of Liburnian pirates.

SENECA

Epistle 47 by the Roman philosopher Seneca (ca. 4 B.C.E.–65 C.E.), tutor to the emperor Nero, is a reminder of the brutality that many owners inflicted on their slaves. Seneca himself argues for a different approach: the slaveholder should insist on treating slaves "humanely," if only so that he can maintain his own psychological stability.

Epistle 47[1]

I'm glad to hear, from these people who've been visiting you,[2] that you live on friendly terms with your slaves. It is just what one expects of an enlightened, cultivated person like yourself. 'They're slaves,' people say. No. They're human beings. 'They're slaves.' But they share the same roof as ourselves. 'They're slaves.' No, they're friends, humble friends. 'They're slaves.' Strictly speaking they're our fellow-slaves, if you once reflect that fortune has as much power over us as over them.

This is why I laugh at those people who think it degrading for a man to eat with his slave. Why do they think it degrading? Only because the most arrogant of conventions has decreed that the master of the house be surrounded at his dinner by a crowd of slaves, who have to stand around while he eats more than he can hold, loading an already distended belly in his monstrous greed until it proves incapable any longer of performing the function of a belly, at which point he expends more effort in vomiting everything up than he did in forcing it down. And all this time the poor slaves are forbidden to move their lips to speak, let alone to eat. The slightest murmur is checked with a stick; not even accidental sounds like a cough, or a sneeze, or a hiccup are let off a beating. All night long they go on standing about, dumb and hungry, paying grievously for any interruption.

The result is that slaves who cannot talk before his face talk about him behind his back. The slaves of former days, however, whose mouths were not sealed up like this, who were able to make conversation not only in the presence of their master but actually with him, were ready to bare their necks to the executioner for him, to divert on to themselves any danger that threatened him; they talked at dinner but under torture they kept their mouths shut. It is just this high-handed treatment which is responsible for the frequently heard saying, 'You've as many enemies as you've slaves.' They are not our enemies when we acquire them; we make them so.

1. Translated by Robin Campbell.
2. Seneca's letters are addressed to a friend called Lucilius.

For the moment I pass over other instances of our harsh and inhuman behaviour, the way we abuse them as if they were beasts of burden instead of human beings, the way for example, from the time we take our places on the dinner couches, one of them mops up the spittle and another stationed at the foot of the couch collects up the 'leavings' of the drunken diners. Another carves the costly game birds, slicing off choice pieces from the breast and rump with the unerring strokes of a trained hand—unhappy man, to exist for the one and only purpose of carving a fat bird in the proper style—although the person who learns the technique from sheer necessity is not quite so much to be pitied as the person who gives demonstrations of it for pleasure's sake. Another, the one who serves the wine, is got up like a girl and engaged in a struggle with his years; he cannot get away from his boyhood, but is dragged back to it all the time; although he already has the figure of a soldier, he is kept free of hair by having it rubbed away or pulled out by the roots. His sleepless night is divided between his master's drunkenness and sexual pleasures, boy at the table, man in the bedroom. Another, who has the privilege of rating each guest's character, has to go on standing where he is, poor fellow, and watch to see whose powers of flattery and absence of restraint in appetite or speech are to secure them an invitation for the following day. Add to these the caterers with their highly developed knowledge of their master's palate, the men who know the flavours that will sharpen his appetite, know what will appeal to his eyes, what novelties can tempt his stomach when it is becoming queasy, what dishes he will push aside with the eventual coming of sheer satiety, what he will have a craving for on that particular day.

These are the people with whom a master cannot tolerate the thought of taking his dinner, assuming that to sit down at the same table with one of his slaves would seriously impair his dignity. 'The very idea!' he says. Yet have a look at the number of masters he has from the ranks of these very slaves.[3] Take Callistus' one-time master. I saw him once actually standing waiting at Callistus' door and refused admission while others were going inside, the very master who had attached a price-ticket to the man and put him up for sale along with other rejects from his household staff. There's a slave who has paid his master back—one who was pushed into the first lot, too, the batch on which the auctioneer is merely trying out his voice! Now it was the slave's turn to strike his master off his list, to decide that *he*'s not the sort of person he wants in *his* house. Callistus' master sold him, yes, and look how much it cost him!

How about reflecting that the person you call your slave traces his origin back to the same stock as yourself, has the same good sky above him, breathes as you do, lives as you do, dies as you do? It is as easy for you to see in him a free-born man as for him to see a slave in you. Remember the Varus disaster: many a man of the most distinguished ancestry, who was doing his military service as the first step on the road to a seat in the Senate, was brought low by fortune, condemned by her to look after a steading, for example, or a flock of sheep. Now think contemptuously of these people's lot in life, in whose very place, for all your contempt, you could suddenly find yourself.

---

3. Roman society allowed increasing numbers of slaves to gain their freedom and rise to high social positions.

I don't want to involve myself in an endless topic of debate by discussing the treatment of slaves, towards whom we Romans are exceptionally arrogant, harsh and insulting. But the essence of the advice I'd like to give is this: treat your inferiors in the way in which you would like to be treated by your own superiors. And whenever it strikes you how much power you have over your slave, let it also strike you that your own master has just as much power over you. 'I haven't got a master,' you say. You're young yet; there's always the chance that you'll have one. Have you forgotten the age at which Hecuba became a slave, or Croesus, or the mother of Darius, or Plato, or Diogenes?[4] Be kind and courteous in your dealings with a slave; bring him into your discussions and conversations and your company generally. And if at this point all those people who have been spoilt by luxury raise an outcry protesting, as they will, 'There couldn't be anything more degrading, anything more disgraceful,' let me just say that these are the very persons I will catch on occasion kissing the hand of someone else's slave.

Don't you notice, too, how our ancestors took away all odium from the master's position and all that seemed insulting or degrading in the lot of the slave by calling the master 'father of the household' and speaking of the slaves as 'members of the household' (something which survives to this day in the mime)? They instituted, too, a holiday on which master and slave were to eat together, not as the only day this could happen, of course, but as one on which it was always to happen. And in the household they allowed the slaves to hold official positions and to exercise some jurisdiction in it; in fact they regarded the household as a miniature republic.

'Do you mean to say,' comes the retort, 'that I'm to have each and every one of my slaves sitting at the table with me?' Not at all, any more than you're to invite to it everybody who isn't a slave. You're quite mistaken, though, if you imagine that I'd bar from the table certain slaves on the grounds of the relatively menial or dirty nature of their work—that muleteer, for example, or that cowhand. I propose to value them according to their character, not their jobs. Each man has a character of his own choosing; it is chance or fate that decides his choice of job. Have some of them dine with you because they deserve it, others in order to make them so deserving. For if there's anything typical of the slave about them as a result of the low company they're used to living in, it will be rubbed off through association with men of better breeding.

You needn't, my dear Lucilius, look for friends only in the City or the Senate; if you keep your eyes open, you'll find them in your own home. Good material often lies idle for want of someone to make use of it; just give it a trial. A man who examines the saddle and bridle and not the animal itself when he is out to buy a horse is a fool; similarly, only an absolute fool values a man according to his clothes, or according to his social position, which after all is only something that we wear like clothing.

---

4. All famous slaves. Hecuba, queen of Troy and wife of Priam, was enslaved when the Greeks captured the city. Croesus was the famously rich king of Lydia, who was eventually defeated and captured by Cyrus of Persia. Darius was emperor of Persia, who conducted an unsuccessful expedition against Greece. Plato, the philosopher, was about forty when he visited Sicily; he was deported by the tyrant of the country and sold into slavery. Diogenes, also a philosopher, was captured by pirates and enslaved.

'He's a slave.' But he may have the spirit of a free man. 'He's a slave.' But is that really to count against him? Show me a man who isn't a slave; one is a slave to sex, another to money, another to ambition; all are slaves to hope or fear. I could show you a man who has been a Consul who is a slave to his 'little old woman,' a millionaire who is the slave of a little girl in domestic service. I could show you some highly aristocratic young men who are utter slaves to stage artistes. And there's no state of slavery more disgraceful than one which is self-imposed. So you needn't allow yourself to be deterred by the snobbish people I've been talking about from showing good humour towards your slaves instead of adopting an attitude of arrogant superiority towards them. Have them respect you rather than fear you.

Here, just because I've said they 'should respect a master rather than fear him,' someone will tell us that I'm now inviting slaves to proclaim their freedom and bringing about their employers' overthrow. 'Are slaves to pay their "respects" like dependent followers or early morning callers? That's what he means, I suppose.' Anyone saying this forgets that what is enough for a god, in the shape of worship, cannot be too little for a master. To be really respected is to be loved; and love and fear will not mix. That's why I think you're absolutely right in not wishing to be feared by your slaves, and in confining your lashings to verbal ones; as instruments of correction, beatings are for animals only. Besides, what annoys us does not necessarily do us any harm; but we masters are apt to be robbed of our senses by mere passing fancies, to the point where our anger is called out by anything which fails to answer to our will. We assume the mental attitudes of tyrants. For they too forget their own strength and the helplessness of others and grow white-hot with fury as if they had received an injury, when all the time they are quite immune from any such danger through the sheer exaltedness of their position. Nor indeed are they unaware of this; but it does not stop them seizing an opportunity of finding fault with an inferior and maltreating him for it; they receive an injury by way of excuse to do one themselves.

But I won't keep you any longer; you don't need exhortation. It is a mark of a good way of life that, among other things, it satisfies and abides; bad behaviour, constantly changing, not for the better, simply into different forms, has none of this stability.

CATULLUS

ca. 84–ca. 54 B.C.E.

The poetry of Gaius Valerius Catullus conveys intense, and often conflicting, emotions. *Odi et amo*, he wrote: "I hate and love." These poems evoke the personal desires and enmities of a privileged but insecure and very young man: Catullus was only about thirty when he died. Reading Catullus, we feel in touch with raw feelings in a way that is rare in the literature of the ancient world. Catullus was also a technical master, who wrote in an impressive range of different verse patterns, and whose moods range from joy to grief, from vituperative obscenities to gentle teasing, and from self-pity to quiet nostalgia for lost and easier days. The pain, passion, lyricism, and humor in his poetry was a lasting inspiration for later love poets, both in ancient Rome and in modern times.

LIFE AND TIMES

Catullus was born in the northern Italian city of Verona, into a prominent aristocratic family (of the high social class called "equestrian"). He spent most of his life in Rome, making close friends and bitter enemies among his fellow Roman aristocrats. Perhaps he had an intense love affair (or several), which inspired the "Lesbia" poems. He does not seem to have married. Traditionally, Lesbia has been identified with Clodia Metella, an aristocratic, educated woman, whom Cicero cast as a sexual predator, a husband killer, and a drunk. But we have no contemporary evidence for the identification, and, of course, poets do not always base their love poems on real life. The name *Lesbia* is obviously designed to evoke literature as much as life: it alludes to the Greek poet **Sappho**, of Lesbos, who, like Catullus, wrote about the conflicting pains and pleasures of bittersweet love.

We know that in his late twenties, Catullus held a position in government that involved a trip to Bithynia, in Asia Minor; en route, he stopped at his brother's tomb, as he describes in a beautiful poem of quiet grief and farewell (poem 101). He died soon after his return to Rome; we do not know the cause.

Catullus lived out his short life in the last century of the Roman Republic. It was a time of conflict, especially between populist and aristocratic factions in Rome. Catullus lived to see the rise of the populist general Julius Caesar, who won extensive victories in Britain and Gaul, although the poet died before Caesar was assassinated (44 B.C.E.). Catullus sometimes satirizes Caesar and flaunts his lack of interest in Caesar's activities: "I am not too terribly anxious to please you, Caesar," he declares (poem 93). Catullus can be read as a deliberately antipolitical writer, who forms a novel and personal interpretation of conventional Roman public virtues. Masculinity, for Catullus, is defined not by military exploits like Caesar's but by sexual prowess and emotional control; even that most characterstic of Roman virtues, duty (*pietas* in Latin) is redefined, applied to Catullus's love for his treacherous girlfriend. Catullus makes use of the values and norms of his society, but he often turns them on their head.

POEMS

One hundred sixteen poems of Catullus survive, collected in a little book or "pamphlet." We do not know whether the arrangement as we have it represents Catullus's own authorial wishes. The poems are arranged by meter, not by subject, so that, for instance, the Lesbia poems do not all appear together. His poems are richly varied, including imitations of Greek poets, long poems on Greek mythological themes, personal and often obscene attacks on contemporaries ("I'll fuck the pair of you," one begins), lyrical celebrations of places and seasons, comic verse, and original love poems—some addressed to a woman, Lesbia, and a few to other love objects, such as the boy Juventius (poem 48).

The Lesbia poems are the most famous of Catullus's work. These poems present all the phases of a love affair, and their tone ranges from joy to torment to the depths of self-pity and back. Their direct and simple language seems to give readers immediate access to the poet's experience of desire and betrayal. Yet these are not diary entries but complex literary artifacts: it is one of the remarkable characteristics of Catullus's poetry that strong emotion and technical sophistication are not at odds with each other. Poem 51, for example, powerfully describes the physical symptoms of love in the speaker; but it is also a translation into Latin of one of Sappho's most passionate Greek lyrics (poem 31), which achieves the feat of also imitating Sappho's rhythms in Latin.

Catullus is a highly self-conscious poet who achieves a dynamic dialogue with his readers. The first poem of the collection asks: What kind of reader does Catullus want for his work? And will the reader be worthy of the poet's trust? How are we to interpret what we hear? Catullus often puts his readers in a tempting but awkward position, as if they were eavesdropping on a private conversation—either between Catullus and another person, or between Catullus and himself. In poem 83, for example, when Lesbia seems to abuse Catullus in the presence of her husband, the speaker interprets this as a sign of love for himself to which the husband is obtusely oblivious. But we may also wonder whether this is a wishful interpretation. Who really is the dupe? The reader never gets access to Lesbia's feelings; instead, the poems present the speaker himself constantly struggling to understand the mixed signals in their changing relationship. The poet subjects his own persona to deep and sometimes damaging analysis: we see his defensive constructions and deconstructions of his own masculine identity, and his unresolved tensions and self-deceptions. In the brilliant poem 8, for example, a dialogue the speaker has with himself at the time of a break-up, he resolves, over and over, to "hold out now, firmly," to be a man and get over his beloved; but the reader, overhearing, is aware of how far he is from the goal.

One of the major themes that runs through much of Catullus's work is the vast distance between one era and another, one moment and the next, as well as between one person and another, or even between one person and himself at different times. The Lesbia poems celebrate moments of connection, which can be violently ruptured by betrayal—like the flower brutally cut down in its prime by a plow that never notices its existence (poem 11). Even in the best of times, the joys of connectedness can be fragile, and may depend on delicate threads—a mortal sparrow (poems 2 and 3), a finite number of kisses (poems 5 and 7); the beautiful celebration of arrival and homecoming, poem 31, emphasizes that this place of relaxation and joy is a "peninsula," almost cut off from the mainland. Spring, in the lovely poem 46, is a time of "rich, sweltering fields," but also a time for friends to say goodbye. The longest poem included here, poem 64, is a celebration of the marriage of Thetis and Peleus, the parents of Achilles. On one level, the subject allows Catullus to challenge the writers of epic, to reinterpret the themes of the *Iliad* from an original angle: it is an "epyllion," a mini-epic. On another, the poem is a joyful and sometimes funny celebration of a magical wedding at sea. But this poem also has surprisingly dark elements: the story embroidered on the comforter to be used on the marriage bed depicts a scene of betrayal, of the Greek hero Theseus abandoning his bride, Ariadne, and leaving her crying alone on the island of Naxos. At a time when Rome was expanding into an enormous empire, but when internal factions threatened to destroy the city's stability, the poems of Catullus express a deep awareness of how quickly, and with what devastating consequences, everything can change.

Poems[1]

1

To whom will I give this sophisticated,
abrasively accomplished new collection?[2]
To you, Cornelius![3] You had the habit
of making much of my poetic little,
when you, the first in Italy, were boldly   5
unfolding all past ages in three volumes,
a monument of scholarship & labor!
And so it's yours; I hand this slim book over,
such as it is—for the sake of its patron
may it survive a century or better.   10

2

Sparrow, you darling pet of my beloved,
which she caresses, presses to her body
or teases with the tip of one sly finger
until you peck at it in tiny outrage!
—for there are times when my desired, shining   5
lady is moved to turn to you for comfort,
to find (as I imagine) ease for ardor,
solace, a little respite from her sorrow—

1. Translated by Charles Martin.
2. The original Latin suggests that the physical book has been polished "abrasively" with a pumice stone, to give it a pretty shine.
3. Cornelius Nepos, a contemporary of Catullus, who wrote a (lost) three-volume history, as well as biographies, other prose works, and poetry.

if I could only play with you as she does,
and be relieved of my tormenting passion!   10

3

Cry out lamenting, Venuses & Cupids,
and mortal men endowed with Love's refinement:
the sparrow of my lady lives no longer!
Sparrow, the darling pet of my beloved,
that was more precious to her than her eyes were;   5
it was her little honey, and it knew her
as well as any girl knows her own mother;
it would not ever leave my lady's bosom
but leapt up, fluttering from yon to hither,
chirruping always only to its mistress.   10
It now flits off on its way, goes, gloom-laden
down to where—word is—there is no returning.
Damn you, damned shades of Orcus[4] that devour
all mortal loveliness, for such a lovely
sparrow it was you've stolen from my keeping!   15
O hideous deed! O poor little sparrow!
It's your great fault that my lady goes weeping,
reddening, ruining her eyes from sorrow.

5

Lesbia, let us live only for loving,
and let us value at a single penny
all the loose flap of senile busybodies!
Suns when they set are capable of rising,
but at the setting of our own brief light   5
night is one sleep from which we never waken.
Give me a thousand kisses, then a hundred,
another thousand next, another hundred,
a thousand without pause & then a hundred,
until when we have run up our thousands   10
we will cry bankrupt, hiding our assets
from ourselves & any who would harm us,
knowing the volume of our trade in kisses.

7

My Lesbia, you ask how many kisses
would be enough to satisfy, to sate me!
—As many as the sandgrains in the desert
near Cyrene, where silphium is gathered,[5]
between the shrine of Jupiter the sultry   5

---

4. God of the underworld.
5. Silphium was a plant used in medicine and

seasoning grown in the North African city of
Cyrene (in modern Libya).

& the venerable sepulchre of Battus![6]
—As many as the stars in the tacit night
that watch as furtive lovers lie embracing:
only to kiss you with that many kisses
would satisfy, could sate your mad Catullus!   10
A sum to thwart the reckoning of gossips
& baffle the spell-casting tongues of envy.

8

Wretched Catullus! You have to stop this nonsense,
admit that what you see has ended is over!
Once there were days which shone for you with rare brightness,
when you would follow wherever your lady led you,
the one we once loved as we will love no other;   5
there was no end in those days to our pleasures,
when what you wished for was what she also wanted.
Yes, there were days which shone for you with rare brightness.
Now she no longer wishes; you mustn't want it,
you've got to stop chasing her now—cut your losses,   10
harden your heart & hold out firmly against her.
Goodbye now, lady. Catullus' heart is hardened,
he will not look to you nor call against your wishes—
how you'll regret it when nobody comes calling!
So much for you, bitch—your life is all behind you!   15
Now who will come to see you, thinking you lovely?
Whom will you love now, and whom will you belong to?
Whom will you kiss? And whose lips will you nibble?
But *you*, Catullus! *You* must hold out now, firmly!

11

Aurelius & Furius[7] true comrades,
whether Catullus penetrates to where in
outermost India booms the eastern ocean's
    wonderful thunder;

whether he stops with Arabs or Hyrcani,   5
Parthian bowmen or nomadic Sagae;[8]
or goes to Egypt, which the Nile so richly
    dyes, overflowing;

even if he should scale the lofty Alps, or
summon to mind the mightiness of Caesar[9]   10

6. The founder of Cyrene.
7. Marcus Furius Bibulus was a satirical poet, a contemporary of Catullus. Marcus Aurelius Cotta Maximus Messalinus, also a contemporary, was a Roman senator, poet, and orator.
8. The Sagae, or Scythians, were nomads in Persia. The Hyrcani are the inhabitants of the Caspian Sea region. Parthia was in modern-day Iran, and Parthians were famous for archery on horseback.
9. Julius Caesar (100–44 B.C.E.), who extended the Roman Empire northward to the Rhine and westward to the southern part of Britain.

viewing the Gallic Rhine, the dreadful Britons
   at the world's far end—

you're both prepared to share in my adventures,
and any others which the gods may send me.
Back to my girl then, carry her this bitter   15
   message, these spare words:

May she have joy & profit from her cocksmen,
go down embracing hundreds all together,
never with love, but without interruption
   wringing their balls dry;   20

nor look to my affection as she used to,
for she has left it broken, like a flower
at the edge of a field after the plowshare
   brushes it, passing.

16

I'll fuck the pair of you as you prefer it,
oral Aurelius, anal Furius,
who read my verses but misread their author:
you think that *I'm* effeminate, since *they* are!
Purity's proper in the godly poet,   5
but it's unnecessary in his verses,
which really should be saucy & seductive,
even salacious in a girlish manner
and capable of generating passion
not just in boys, but in old men who've noticed   10
getting a hard-on has been getting harder!
But you, because my poems beg for kisses,
thousands of kisses, you think I'm a fairy!
I'll fuck the pair of you as you prefer it.

31

None of the other islands & peninsulas
which Neptune[1] floats on sheets of untroubled water
or on the desolate face of the vast ocean
please me, delight me, dear Sirmio, as you do!
I still can't believe I've gotten back here safely   5
from Thynia, Bithynia—and stand before you!
What could be better? Every care dissolving,
shedding the burden of an exhausting journey,
back home among the gods of our own household
we find at last the couch, the rest we desired!   10
This alone repays us for our long labors.
How are you, sexy Sirmio! Rejoice with your master,

---

1. God of the sea.

and you too, bubbling lake of Lydian waters—
loose every last chortle of your locked-up laughter!

42

Up now, iambics[2]—get yourselves together,
all of you everywhere, however many!
—A flaming slut imagines that she'll mock me,
and now refuses to return the tablets
I write you verses down on—can you bear it?   5
Let's follow her & force her to return them.
Who're you after? *Her*—that one you see there,
shaking her ass & mouthing like a mimic,
the rabid bitch with the repulsive grimace!
Surround her now & force her to return them: 10
*"You wretched slut you give us back the tablets,
give us the tablets back you wretched slut you!"*
Doesn't that bother you? You filth, you flophouse,
you drain on even *my* profound invective!
—We mustn't think we've gotten satisfaction: 15
if nothing else, at least we can embarrass
the bitch & give her cheeks a little color.
Cry out once more, in unison & louder:
*"You wretched slut you give us back the tablets,
give us the tablets back you wretched slut you!"*   20
We're getting nowhere. Nothing seems to move her.
Maybe we ought to try another tactic
and see if it won't work a little better:
"Maiden most modest, give us back the tablets."

46

Spring fetches back the days of warming weather,
the equinoctial bluster of the heavens
is silenced by the Zephyr's[3] tender breezes.
It's time to leave the plains of Troy, Catullus,
and the rich, sweltering fields of Nicaea: 5
those glamourous Aegean cities beckon!
My mind is really anxious to be going,
my feet are dancing with anticipation!
So it's good-by now to those dear companions
who set out from a distant home together,   10
whom varied roads now carry back diversely.

48

Juventius, if I could play at kissing
your honeyed eyes as often as I wished to,

2. The original refers to "hendecasyllables,"   specialized.
an eleven-syllable meter in which Catullus   3. The west wind.

300,000 games would not exhaust me;
never could I be satisfied or sated,
although the total of our osculations   5
were greater than the ears of grain at harvest.

51[4]

To me that man seems like a god in heaven,
seems—may I say it?—greater than all gods are,
who sits by you & without interruption
         watches you, listens

to your light laughter, which casts such confusion   5
onto my senses, Lesbia, that when I
gaze at you merely, all of my well-chosen
         words are forgotten

as my tongue thickens & a subtle fire
runs through my body while my ears are deafened   10
by their own ringing & at once my eyes are
         covered in darkness!

Leisure, Catullus. More than just a nuisance,
leisure: you riot, overmuch enthusing.
Fabulous cities & their sometime kings have   15
         died of such leisure.

58

Lesbia, Caelius—yes, our darling,
yes, *Lesbia*, the Lesbia Catullus
once loved uniquely, more than any other!
—now on streetcorners & in wretched alleys
she shucks the offspring of greathearted Remus.[5]   5

64

They say it was pine sprung from the crown of Mount Pelion[6]
which swam clear across the perilous waters of Neptune
to the river Phasis in the realm of King Aeetes,[7]
back in those days when the best men the Argives could muster,
eager to carry the golden fleece out of Colchis,   5
dared to go racing their swift ship over the ocean
and stirred its cerulean surface with oars made of firwood.
Athena, who keeps the towers protecting the city,
she fashioned this hurtling carriage for those young men,

4. This poem, except for the last stanza, is a close imitation of Sappho 31; it uses Sappho's meter, sapphics.
5. Twin brother of Romulus; in Roman legend, together they built the walls of Rome.
6. Mountain in Thessaly, in central Greece.
7. The Greek hero Jason, with his crew of other heroes, was supposed to have made the first-ever sea journey when he sailed in the *Argo* from Greece to get the Golden Fleece from Colchis. "King Aeetes:" king of Colchis, on the Black Sea.

she joined the timbers of pine to the curve of the firm keel.   10
That ship, the Argo, first taught the seas about sailing.
And so, when its sharp beak plowed down through the wind-
          driven waters,
when it churned the billows white by the work of its oarblades,
incredulous sea nymphs came bobbing right up to the surface,
eager to catch just a glimpse of this unheard-of marvel!   15
If ever sailors were witness to wonders, those men were,
who saw with their very own eyes the Nereids rising,
barebreasted mermaids afloat on the whiteheaded ocean.
They say it was then that Peleus burned to have Thetis,
who raised no objection to taking a mortal husband,
and the Father himself judged that they ought to be married.[8]   20
O Heroes born in the happiest time of all ages,
the righteous offspring of gods & of mortal women,
I will not fail to celebrate you in my poem;
often I'll greet you, often your names will be mentioned,   25
and you especially, blessed beyond others in marriage,
Peleus, pillar of Thessaly, to whom the father
of heaven himself surrendered his very beloved!
Did Thetis enchant you—that loveliest of the Nereids?
Did Tethys give her consent to her granddaughter's marriage,   30
and Ocean, who cinches all of the world with his river?[9]
     And so at last, on the appointed day of the wedding,
the people of Thessaly throng to his palace together
in celebration, fillings its chambers completely,
gifts in their hands, expressions of joy on their faces.   35
Cieros is emptied, they pour from Phthiotic Tempe,
from the houses of Crannon & out through the gates of Larissa
they come to Pharsalus[1] & gather under its rooftops.
The land's left untilled, the backs of the oxen grow tender,
the curved rake no longer loosens the soil of the vineyard,   40
the young bull no longer breaks up the packed earth with the plowshare,
the dresser of vines no longer cuts back the branches of shade trees,
and a thin film of rust spreads over the idle equipment.
But in his opulent palace, great chambers receding
create a vista resplendent with glittering gold & silver;   45
ivory glows on the couch legs, the cups on the table gleam,
and all of that house is gay with the splendor of riches.
A couch fit for the goddess is set in the center,
one made of polished Indian ivory draped with a purple
coverlet steeped in the crimson dye of the sea conch.   50
     Embroidered with various figures of men from past ages,
its marvelous art reveals the great prowess of heroes.

---

8. Peleus, king of Aegina, married Thetis (one of the Nereids, or sea-goddesses); they were the parents of Achilles. "The Father" is Jupiter, father of the gods; according to myth, both Jupiter and Poseidon courted Thetis, but agreed to give her to the mortal Peleus, because it had been prophesied that her son would be greater than his father.
9. Tethys is another sea-goddess, the grandmother of Thetis and the wife of the sea-god Pontus (or Ocean).
1. Cieros, Tempe (in the region of Phthiotis), Crannon, Larissa, and Pharsalus are all Thessalian cities.

For there, staring out from the resonant seacoast of Dia,
Ariadne watches the swift fleet of Theseus leaving,[2]
and in her heart an unrestrainable fury arises,   55
for she still can't believe that she sees what she is seeing!
—no wonder, for sleep had deceived her: just now awakened,
she finds herself coolly abandoned there on the seashore.
Ungrateful, her lover flees, striking the waves with his oarblades,
leaving the storm winds to make good on his broken promise.   60
The weeping daughter of Minos stands still in the seaweed,
stands watching him in the distance: a Maenad in marble,[3]
rocked by the waves of her anguish, she stands there & watches;
her golden hair is no longer tied up in its headband,
the delicate veil no longer covers her torso,   65
her tender white breasts are no longer bound up in their halter;
all of her garments have slipped to her feet in confusion,
adrift in the salt tide that evenly scoured the coastline.
—Not that she noticed the headband or the veil floating
beside her, for it was you that she thought of, Theseus: 70
the wretched girl clung to you in complete desperation!
Venus of Eryx[4] had driven her crazy with sorrow,
sowing the seeds of that thorny grief in her spirit
much earlier, back in that time when the adamant hero
set out from the curved shore of the port at Piraeus[5]   75
and sailed to the Cretan quarters of the harsh King Minos.

  The story is that in those days the people of Athens
were forced by a plague to make restitution for slaying
one of the sons of King Minos by sending their finest
young men & maidens, a meal to the Minotaur's liking![6]   80
With these cares rocking the strait walls of his beloved city,
Theseus chose to offer himself as a victim,
rather than that any more of the living unliving
should be taken away from Athens to perish at Knossos.
So he set sail then, in a light boat, and favoring breezes   85
brought him to the tyrannous kingdom of greathearted Minos.
When she first caught sight of that handsome stranger, the royal
virgin (whose celibate couch still warmly enfolded
her in its maternal embraces, exuding the odors
of myrtle that grows on the banks of streams in Eurotas[7]   90
and the varied flowers that whispering spring engenders)
Ariadne kept her eyes fixed on him until they took fire,
until that fire had traveled the length of her body

2. Ariadne, daughter of Minos of Crete, helped the Greek hero Theseus get through the Labyrinth to kill the Minotaur. Theseus took her away with him but abandoned her on the island of Naxos (Dia) while she was taking a nap. The waking of abandoned Ariadne was a popular theme in ancient art.
3. Maenads are the wild female worshippers of Dionysos, god of wine; the term suggests frenzy or madness.
4. There was a temple to Venus, goddess of love and sexual desire, on Mount Eryx in Sicily.
5. Piraeus is the port of Athens. The "adamant hero" is Theseus.
6. The son of Minos, Androgeos, was sent by the king of Athens, Aegeus (father of Theseus), to fight a bull in Marathon; he was killed. Minos retaliated by demanding a yearly sacrifice of seven boys and seven girls from Athens to be transported to Knossos in Crete, fed to his monstrous half-bull stepson, the Minotaur.
7. River in southern Greece.

and made its way into even her innermost marrow!
O Cupid, you who arouse such extravagant passions, 95
forever mixing great joys & great sorrows together,
and you who rule upon Golgos & leafy Idalium,[8]
what were the waves like, on which you tossed the poor maiden's
passionate heart as she sighed for her fair-haired stranger?
How many times in exhaustion did she know terror, 100
and find herself turning even paler than gold,
while he impatiently waited to take on that savage
in a fight which would end either with death or with glory?
The gifts of incense she'd offered while praying to heaven
in fearful silence were neither unwelcome nor wasted. 105
Think of an oak, or a conebearing pine tree that oozes
with rosin, shaking its branches high up on Mount Taurus;[9]
one which a fierce storm, wrenching the grain of its timber
uproots & sends hurtling off to spread terrible havoc
for a great distance, until it lies prone in destruction: 110
then think of Theseus over the overcome monster
vainly tossing its horns in the unresisting breezes.
Unharmed—it had ended with glory—he felt his way back,
using a thin thread to guide his wandering footsteps,
or else, as he worked his way out of the labyrinth's windings, 115
its indiscernible maze would have left him bewildered.[1]

But why should I digress from my earliest subject,
and go on to tell how she turned from the face of her father
and the embrace of her sister, and lastly the mother
who grieved because she loved her daughter to distraction, 120
choosing the sweet love of Theseus over them all?
Or how she came to the foaming seacoast of Dia,
and how, when her eyes had been sealed up tightly in slumber,
her careless lover abandoned her & departed?
Often, they say, when her sorrow had turned into madness 125
that could not be silent, she uttered shrill cries of anguish,
and sadly worked her way up one of the steep mountains
to take a long look at the ocean's vast expanses:
then rushed abruptly down to plunge into the water,
lifting her clingy robe up over her bare leg; 130
and in her last moments of grief, in a voice broken
by sobs, she spoke, as chilly tears streamed down her face:
"So, you have torn me away from my family's altar
to leave me on this empty island, have you, Theseus?
—Gone off, ignoring the terrible justice of heaven, 135
sailing your god-damned cargo of lies back to Athens?
Could nothing, nothing at all, have turned that ferocious
mind of yours from this plan? Was there no tenderness lurking
within you, that might have urged you to offer me mercy?
For it wasn't *this* that you promised me ever so blandly, 140

8. City-states on the island of Cyprus.
9. In Asia Minor (modern-day Turkey).
1. Before Theseus entered the Labyrinth,
Ariadne provided him with a ball of thread to
unwind as he proceeded, thus leaving himself
a means of retracing his path and escaping.

it wasn't this at all that you led me to hope for
when you spoke of the happy marriage, the wedding we dreamt of—
words which the winds of heaven now tear into tatters!
Let no woman ever believe any oath that a man swears,
or ever expect him to keep faith with his fine speeches! 145
When they want something, when they are anxious to get it,
they take oaths without fear, and pour out their promises freely;
but just as soon as their hot desire is sated,
none of their lies & deceptions ever disturb them.
You know that when death whirled you around in confusion 150
I saved you, choosing to let my own brother perish,
rather than fail in my duty to you who've betrayed me!
And for my good service, I will be torn by birds & wild beasts
when my body lies here without any tomb to protect it.
What lion gave birth to you under a rock in the desert? 155
What sea conceived you, spewed you up out of its waters?
Or was it Syrtis, or Scylla, or dreadful Charybdis,[2]
that you repay the sweet gift of life in this fashion?
If, in your heart, you never intended our marriage
for fear of what your stern father had earlier told you, 160
nevertheless you could have brought me into your palace
as a servant, whose pleasure it would have been to humbly
attend you, bathing your white feet in clear water
and laying the purple coverlet out in your chamber.
But why should I cry out in vain to the ignorant air, 165
a woman maddened by suffering? The air is senseless,
unable to hear me, unable to make any answer.
By now he must be nearly half-done with his journey,
and no one at all appears on this bare stretch of seaweed.
In my final moments, fortune cruelly mocks me, 170
denying me those who would listen to my lamentations.
O God almighty, I wish that they had never
landed at Crete, those ships that came sailing from Athens,
that the lying sailor had never come with his dreadful
payment for the wild bull, or moored his ships in our harbor, 175
wickedly hiding his bloodthirsty plot under a pleasant
façade, while he stayed as an honored guest in the palace!
Where can I go? What hope shall I cling to, abandoned?
Shall I seek the mountains of Sidon?[3]—but a great gulf
of truculent water enforces my separation. 180
Or should I beg help from the father that I deserted
to follow a young man stained with the blood of my brother?[4]
Console myself with the trustworthy love of a husband
who flees me, bending inflexible oars in the water?
Here there is nothing but shoreline, an unpeopled island 185
with no way of crossing over the sea that surrounds it,
no means of fleeing, no hope at all—everywhere silence,

---

2. Syrtis is a quicksand; Scylla, a multi-headed monster, and Charybdis, a whirlpool goddess, are encountered by Odysseus in the *Odyssey*.

3. City on the coast of modern-day Lebanon.
4. Ariadne and the Minotaur had the same mother.

emptiness everywhere—terrible death shows his face here.
Nevertheless, before I sink down into darkness,
and before all feeling fades from my weary body,   190
I will implore the gods for justice to right my betrayal,
and beg the protection of heaven in my final moments.
O Furies,[5] charged with vengeance that punishes evil,
you whose bleak foreheads are girded with writhing serpents
which clearly display the outrage your cold hearts keep hidden,   195
come here to me quickly, listen to my lamentation,
which I deliver in pain from the depths of my passion,
unwillingly forced to, afire, blinded with madness!
—Since what I say is the truth, since I say it sincerely,
do not allow my lament to fade without issue: 200
but just as Theseus carelessly left me to die here,
may that same carelessness ruin him and his dearest!"
When she had emptied her heart of all of its sorrows,
anxiously seeking revenge for the way she'd been treated,
the ruler of heaven assented, majestically nodding,   205
and with that gesture the earth & the rough seas were shaken,
and the stars leapt in the firmament, quivering brightly.
But Theseus, in a dark mood which muddled his judgement,
let slip out of mind the instructions which he had clung to,
forgetting to raise the white sail which his father awaited,   210
the sweet sign that he was returning uninjured to Athens.
For they say that when Aegeus consigned his departing
son to the winds as his fleet left Athena's protection,
he first embraced the young man & then gave him these orders:
"My only son, dearer to me than even long life is,   215
whom I am forced to send off on a doubtful adventure,
although just restored to me at the end of my lifetime,
because my misfortune & your passionate courage
must take you away from me before my exhausted
eyes could have had their fill of your image before me,   220
I will not cheerfully let you leave here rejoicing,
or allow you to show any signs of fortune's good favor:
but first I will empty my heart of its wild lamentation,
soiling my white hairs with earth & a downpour of ashes,
and then hang dyed sails on your ship's swaying mastpole,   225
so that this grief of ours, this heart-wringing fire
will be proclaimed by sheets steeped in Iberian purple.
—Yet, if the goddess who dwells on sacred Itonus,
pledged to defend our people & the realm of Erechtheus,[6]
allows you to dabble your right hand in the bull's blood,   230
make certain that you remember these orders I give you
and keep them in mind no matter how long a time passes:
as soon as you catch your first glimpse of our hillside,
take every last vestige of mourning down from your yardarms
and set a white sail aloft in the twisted rigging,   235

---

5. Goddesses associated with vengeance.   Itonus founded a sanctuary of Athena.
6. Erechtheus is a legendary king of Athens;

so that the minute I see it, I'll understand—and gladly
welcome the fortunate hour of your reappearance!"
Theseus, at first, paid attention to these instructions,
but then they slipped from his mind, just as the wind-driven
clouds scatter from the snowy peak of a mountain.   240
His father, however, keeping vigil on the Acropolis,
wasting his eyes with tears that never stopped flowing,
when he first caught sight of those dark sails bellying outward
threw himself down from the rocky peak into the ocean,
believing that fate had cruelly taken Theseus.   245
So, when the hero entered his home, it was darkened
by mourning, and he received for himself as much sorrow
as he had thoughtlessly given the daughter of Minos,
who kept a sad watch as his ship sank into the distance,
dwelling on all of those cares with which she'd been wounded.   250

    But in another scene, flourishing Iacchus[7] swaggered,
surrounded by drunken Sileni & wanton young Satyrs;
burning with love, he was searching for you, Ariadne.
. . . .
and Maenads also, who raged all around in a rapture,   255
crying "*Euhoe! Euhoe!*"[8] as their heads crazily nodded.
Some of them whirled their weapons, spears tipped with vine-leaves;
some tossed about the limbs of a bull they'd dismembered,
and some were girding their bodies with writhing serpents
or worshipping ritual emblems kept hidden in baskets,   260
emblems which only initiates ever uncover.
Others with uplifted hands were beating their tambours
or shrilly clashing their hollow bronze cymbals together;
many of them had horns which were raucously blaring,
and the barbaric flute wailed out its hideous noises.   265
    Such were the figures which brightly adorned that rich hanging
whose ample folds lay over the couch of the goddess.
When the young Thessalians' desire to see it was sated
completely, they gave way to the gods descending from heaven;
you've seen the west wind rile the calm sea in the morning,   270
how it herds the steepening wavelets, sweeps them before it
as Dawn ascends to the gates of the journeying Sun;
those waves move slowly at first, urged on by a mild wind,
and advance with a muted sound of continuous laughter;
but after the wind has arisen, they run on together   275
and from a great distance they gleam with reflections of crimson:
so, moving out of the palace & out of its courtyard,
the mortal wedding guests drifted off in every direction.
After they left, the first to arrive from Mount Pelion's
summit was Chiron the Centaur[9] with pastoral presents;   280
for whatever grows wild in the fields or on the great mountains

---

7. Another name for Bacchus/Dionysos, god
of wine, who is accompanied by wild half-goat
men (Sileni and Satyrs). Dionysos swept Ariadne up after her abandonment and married

her; in some versions she became a goddess.
8. Ritual cry to Dionysos.
9. Chiron the Centaur (half-horse, half-
human) would later be the tutor of Achilles.

of Thessaly, whatever the mild Favonian breezes[1]
show in the way of flowers that grow beside rivers,
he brought along with him, all woven together unsorted,
and made the house laugh with odors that tickled the senses.   285
Directly came Peneus[2] next, from evergreen Tempe,
Tempe, completely encircled by ominous forests,
leaving the nymphs of the vale to continue their dancing;
not empty-handed, he fetched along elegant beech trees
plucked up by their dangling roots, and the straight-stemmed laurel   290
and nodding plane tree besides, and the pliant sister
of burnt-out Phaeton,[3] as well as the towering cypress:
he wove these together in a continuous pattern
to make a green curtain of branches surrounding the courtyard.
After him followed Prometheus,[4] known for invention,   295
still bearing the faded scars of that ancient atonement
which he had made while chained arm & leg to a mountain,
dizzily hanging from its precipitous summit.
Next came the father of gods[5] with his immortal children,
all except you, alone up in heaven, Apollo,   300
you & your sister who dwells on the mountains of Idrus;[6]
for she scorned Peleus too, even as you did,
and had no wish to honor the marriage of Thetis.

   After they'd settled themselves on the snowy white couches,
the tables before them were heaped with a various banquet.   305
Meanwhile, the Parcae[7] began to chant their prophetic
song, swaying their bodies as they moved about infirmly.
Their ancient limbs were covered in gleaming white garments
which fell to their ankles; their robes were bordered in crimson,
and their snowy white heads were encircled by crimson headbands: 310
their bony hands practiced the task they will practice forever.
The left hand held on to the distaff, wrapped up in soft wool,
and the right carefully drew the thread out, with the fingers
turned upward to shape it; then down went the thumb, and neatly
twirled the spindle poised on its circular flywheel;   315
and as they spun, they tugged the threads clean with their teeth:
bits of wool, which before had clung to the stuff they were working
now stuck to their poor withered lips in little dry tufts.
At their feet, baskets of plaited willow protected
soft bundles of gleaming fleece that lay ready for spinning.   320
And plucking the fibers, they chanted loudly & clearly,
uttered oracular speech in a sacred poem,
a poem no future age will condemn as untruthful:

1. Favonius was the Roman name for Zeph-
yrus, god of the west wind.
2. River god of Thessaly.
3. Phaeton, son of the sun god Helios, was
burnt when he tried to ride his father's chariot
across the sky. His sisters were so upset that
they turned into poplar trees, and their tears
turned into amber.
4. Titan who made humans and gave them
forbidden fire. As punishment he was chained

up and had his liver consumed by an eagle
every morning.
5. I.e., Jupiter (the Roman name for Zeus).
6. Apollo's sister is Diana. There must have
been a mythic explanation why these twins
boycotted the wedding, but it is unknown.
(Idrus is a region of Ionia where there was a
shrine to Diana.)
7. The three Fates, who spin the thread of
human lives.

"Heroic actions have made your name even more lustrous,
defender of Thessaly, dear to the ruler of heaven,   325
attend the true oracle which the three sisters deliver
on this festive day! As Destiny follows your motion,
run, spindles, run, drawing the threads that wait for the weaving.

Hesperus[8] will be here soon with those gifts which the newly
married all long for; the bride will follow him closely,   330
flooding your heart with love that will charm you completely
as she lies by you at night in the tenderest slumber,
asleep with her delicate arms clasping your strong neck.
Run, spindles, run, drawing the threads that wait for the weaving.

No house before this has sheltered such a great passion,   335
no love has ever linked lovers in any such union
as this one which joins Peleus & Thetis together.
Run, spindles, run, drawing the threads that wait for the weaving.

Your son will be dreadful Achilles, unknown to Panic,
whose enemies never will see him retreating from battle;   340
often he'll easily win in long-distance races,
outstripping even the deer who advances like fire.
Run, spindles, run, drawing the threads that wait for the weaving.

No hero will dare to confront him in hand-to-hand combat
when the Phrygian fields are drenched with the blood of Trojans,   345
and Agamemnon, the third heir of deceitful Pelops,[9]
tears down the walls of Troy when the long siege is over.
Run, spindles, run, drawing the threads that wait for the weaving.

Often the mothers of young sons about to be buried
will testify to his uncommon prowess in battle,   350
letting their unkempt hair fall loosely down to their shoulders
as they mar their withered breasts with their hands in bereavement.
Run, spindles, run, drawing the threads that wait for the weaving.

Just as a reaper hacks down the dense ears of ripe grain
under a burning sun, mowing the whole golden meadow,   355
Achilles will waste the young Trojans' limbs with his iron.
Run, spindles, run, drawing the threads that wait for the weaving.

The waves of Scamander will witness his heroic actions,
Scamander, which rushes into the stream of the Hellespont,[1]
whose neck he will narrow by flinging up great piles of corpses   360
until its deep flood runs warm & red from the slaughter.
Run, spindles, run, drawing the threads that wait for the weaving.

---

8. The evening star.
9. Grandfather of Agamemnon; Pelops won his
throne by cheating in a chariot race. "Phrygian
fields": Troy was located in Phrygia, a coastal

region of Asia Minor (modern-day Turkey).
1. Strait separating Europe from Asia Minor.
"Scamander": Trojan river, which flows with
blood in the *Iliad*.

But the last witness will be the gift given his spirit
in death, when the hero's high-heaped, circular mounded barrow
is graced with the snowy limbs of the sacrificed virgin.[2]   365
Run, spindles, run, drawing the threads that wait for the weaving.

As soon as chance gives the exhausted Achaians the power
to keep the chains which Neptune wove from keeping his city,[3]
that lofty tomb will be drenched with the blood of Polyxena,
struck down like a beast under the double-edged axeblade,   370
knees buckling as she pitches her headless corpse forward.
Run, spindles, run, drawing the threads that wait for the weaving.

Get going then, join those passions your hearts have desired;
now let the bridegroom take the goddess in fortunate union,
and let the bride be given right now to her eager new husband.   375
Run, spindles, run, drawing the threads that wait for the weaving.

The nurse who returns to attend her early tomorrow
will find that her neck can't be circled by yesterday's ribbon:[4]
run, spindles, run, drawing the threads that wait for the weaving;

the worried mother who fears that her daughter is lying   380
alone will learn that her hopes for an heir aren't groundless!
Run, spindles, run, drawing the threads that wait for the weaving."

    So, in a prophetic spirit announcing the future
joy of Peleus, the Parcae once chanted their poem.
For the gods would frequent the worshipful homes of heroes   385
and show themselves present wherever men were assembled
before contempt had become the response to religion.
Often Jove the father,[5] paying a regular visit
to one of his temples during the annual feast days,
would see a hundred bulls crash to earth in his honor.   390
And Liber[6] would rove on the peak of Parnassus, driving
his Maenads, who shook their wild hair & cried out *"Euhoe!"*
Then all of Delphi came pouring out of the city
to greet the young god with smoke wreathing their altars.
And often in deathbearing warfare, Mars, or Athena   395
the mistress of Triton, or Nemesis, Virgin of Rhamnus,[7]
would show themselves to encourage bands of armed men.
But after the earth had been imbued with hideous evil,
and men had abandoned all their desire for Justice,
when one brother had soaked his hands in the blood of another,   400
when children no longer wept at the deaths of their parents,

---

2. Polyxena, a daughter of King Priam of Troy,
was sacrificed on Achilles' tomb to satisfy the
ghost of the dead hero.
3. Neptune (Poseidon) and Apollo built the
walls of Troy. "Achaians": Greeks.
4. It was believed that loss of virginity thick-
ened a girl's neck.

5. I.e., Jupiter, king of the gods.
6. Another name for Dionysos ("Liberator").
7. Mars is god of war, and Athena is a warrior
goddess; Triton is a river in Boeotia; Nemesis
("Retribution") had a temple in Rhamnus, a
town near Athens.

when a father could wish for the death of his very own son,
for the new stepmother seems to have found him attractive;
when an unwitting young man lay with his impious mother,
who had no fear of the shades of her deified parents,   405
then good & evil were confused in criminal madness,
turning the righteous minds of the gods from our behavior.
So they no longer appear now when mortals assemble,
and shun the light of luminous day altogether.

70

My woman says there is no one whom she'd rather marry
    than me, not even Jupiter, if he came courting.
That's what she says—but what a woman says to a passionate lover
    ought to be scribbled on wind, on running water.

72

You used to say that you wished to know only Catullus,
    Lesbia, and wouldn't take even Jove before me!
I didn't regard you just as my mistress then: I cherished you
    as a father does his sons or his daughters' husbands.
Now that I know you, I burn for you even more fiercely,   5
    though I regard you as almost utterly worthless.
How can that be, you ask? It's because such cruelty forces
    lust to assume the shrunken place of affection.

75

To such a state have I been brought by your mischief, my Lesbia,
    and so completely ruined by my devotion,
that I couldn't think kindly of you if you did the best only,
    nor cease to love, even if you should do—everything.

76

If any pleasure can come to a man through recalling
    decent behavior in his relations with others,
not breaking his word, and never, in any agreement,
    deceiving men by abusing vows sworn to heaven,
then countless joys will await you in old age, Catullus,   5
    as a reward for this unrequited passion!
For all of those things which a man could possibly say or
    do have all been said & done by you already,
and none of them counted for anything, thanks to her vileness!
    Then why endure your self-torment any longer?   10
Why not abandon this wretched affair altogether,
    spare yourself pain the gods don't intend you to suffer!
It's hard to break off with someone you've loved such a long time:
    it's hard, but you have to do it, somehow or other.

Your only chance is to get out from under this sickness,　　　　15
　　no matter whether or not you think you're able.
O gods, if pity is yours, or if ever to any
　　who lay near death you offered the gift of your mercy,
look on my suffering: if my life seems to you decent,
　　then tear from within me this devouring cancer,　　　　20
this heavy dullness wasting the joints of my body,
　　completely driving every joy from my spirit!
Now I no longer ask that she love me as I love her,
　　or—even less likely—that she give up the others:
all that I ask for is health, an end to this foul sickness!　　　25
　　O gods, grant me this in exchange for my worship.

83

Lesbia hurls abuse at me in front of her husband:
　　that fatuous person finds it highly amusing!
Nothing gets through to you, jackass—for silence would signal
　　that she'd been cured of me, but her barking & bitching
show that not only haven't I not been forgotten,　　　　5
　　but that this burns her: and so she rants & rages.

85

I hate & love. And if you should ask how I can do both,
　　I couldn't say; but I feel it, and it shivers me.

92

Lesbia never avoids a good chance to abuse me
　　in public, yet I'll be damned if she doesn't love me!
How can I tell? Because I'm exactly the same: I malign her
　　always—yet I'll be damned if I don't really love her!

93

I am not too terribly anxious to please you, Caesar,[8]
　　nor even to learn the very first thing about you.

101

Driven across many nations, across many oceans,
　　I am here, my brother, for this final parting,
to offer at last those gifts which the dead are given
　　and to speak in vain to your unspeaking ashes,
since bitter fortune forbids you to hear me or answer,　　　　5
　　O my wretched brother, so abruptly taken!
But now I must celebrate grief with funeral tributes
　　offered the dead in the ancient way of the fathers;

8. I.e., Julius Caesar.

accept these presents, wet with my brotherly tears, and
   now & forever, my brother, hail & farewell.   10

107

If ever something which someone with no expectation
   desired should happen, we are rightly delighted!
And so this news is delightful—it's dearer than gold is:
   you have returned to me, Lesbia, my desired!
Desired, yet never expected—but you *have* come back   5
   to me! A holiday, a day of celebration!
What living man is luckier than I am? Or able
   to say that anything could possibly be better?

109

Darling, we'll both have equal shares in the sweet love you offer,
   and it will endure forever—you assure me.
O heaven, see to it that she can truly keep this promise,
   that it came from her heart & was sincerely given,
so that we may spend the rest of our days in this lifelong   5
   union, this undying compact of holy friendship.

VIRGIL

70–19 B.C.E.

Virgil's *Aeneid* is the greatest epic poem from ancient Rome. It has been one of the most profoundly influential works of all classical literature in the later Western cultural and literary tradition. The *Aeneid* can be described in ways that make it sound off-putting: as a work of nationalistic propaganda for a nation that no longer exists, or as a twelve-book poem about the importance of doing your duty. But such descriptions are entirely false to most readers' experience of this emotionally engaging and thought-provoking story. The *Aeneid* is an absorbing book, full of adventure, beauty, magic, dreams, love, loss, and violence. The characters make hard choices and have complex inner lives. The poem is also a profound meditation on the rights and wrongs of empire and colonialism that prompts us to ask whether civilizations, even the best of them, are ever founded without enormous personal and military cost.

LIFE AND TIMES

Virgil, whose full Roman name was Publius Vergilius Maro, was born near the peaceful northern Italian town of Mantua. His father probably owned land, and Virgil's poetry often shows a nostalgic appreciation for the quiet life of the Italian countryside. Before composing the *Aeneid*, Virgil wrote two books with a rural setting: the *Eclogues*, a set of ten poems featuring the songs and sorrows of fictional shepherds, and the *Georgics*, a four-book account of the struggles and triumphs of life on a farm. Ostensibly, neither of these texts has much to do with the subject of the *Aeneid*, which is about the quest to found an empire. But Virgil's poetic focus is surprisingly consistent throughout his career. Whether the setting is an empire or a village garden, he is interested in the value and pathos of the human struggle to build a home, even in hostile or near-impossible conditions. The farmer in the *Georgics*, whose hard work is washed away by a violent storm, is just as much a hero as the shipwrecked Trojans in the *Aeneid*.

When Virgil was young, the world beyond Mantua saw great political and military unrest. Rome, through its impressive military discipline, had already become the dominant power in the Mediterranean world; the city had defeated its main rival, the North African state of Carthage, some two generations before (in 146 B.C.E.). Now Rome was engaged in various further wars, struggling to expand the empire both eastward and westward. These wars generated greater glory for the nation, but also greater instability at home. In Virgil's childhood, Rome was still a Republic. No single man had control of the country; instead, government was divided among the people, the magistrates, and the Senate (an assembly of councilmen). But power was shifting away from the Senate and toward the military generals responsible for Rome's victories abroad. After a series of civil wars, Julius Caesar, one of these generals, became dictator of Rome. He was assassinated in 44 B.C.E., when Virgil was twenty-six. More civil wars followed, causing disruption both at home and abroad: many country landowners—including some around Mantua, though apparently not Virgil's family—were forced to leave their homes to make room for veterans returning from war. Finally, some twelve years after the assassination, Julius Caesar's adopted great-nephew Octavian defeated the joint forces of Antony and Cleopatra, and took control of Rome. In this volatile environment, Octavian was careful not to style himself "dictator," as Julius had done. Instead, he claimed to be restoring the old ways of the Republic. He named himself "Augustus" ("The Respected One"), the "Princeps" ("First Man"), and "Emperor Caesar." Throughout his rule, Augustus was interested in controlling his public image: he knew that careful manipulation of information was essential if he were to avoid the fate of his great-uncle. In this context, it is not surprising that the emperor had a close personal relationship with the writers of Rome, who would, as Augustus knew, play an important part in shaping his public image even after his death. Augustus hoped that Virgil would provide him with a great national epic to justify, glorify, and immortalize Augustan Roman power.

We do not know how happy Augustus was with the poem that Virgil actually produced, although apparently the poet read parts of it aloud to the emperor and his sister, to great emotional effect: the sister fainted. It is possible that Augustus had hoped for a more direct account of his own glorious deeds. But perhaps he was smart enough to realize that direct propaganda never has much of a shelf life. We also do not know whether Virgil himself was satisfied with his creation. He was apparently a quiet man, moderate in his ways; thanks to Augustus's favor, he was given an expensive villa in Rome, but he seems to have preferred the quiet life of the country. He never married. As a poet, he was a perfectionist, willing to spend many hours editing his work. We are told that he compared himself to a mother bear who licks her cubs into shape. This process shows in the complex rhythms and careful patterns of Virgil's poetic style. He died of a fever at the age of fifty-one, while returning from a trip to Greece. The

Aeneid was still incomplete, and apparently he gave orders from his deathbed for it to be burned. Fortunately for us, Augustus countermanded the orders, and saved the poem for posterity.

THE *AENEID*

Virgil's masterpiece is about Rome, but only indirectly. The story takes us back in time to a period well before the foundation of the city. It tells how one civilization mutates into another, finding the origins of Rome in the destruction of Troy. The poem follows the Trojan Aeneas as he escapes with his father, son, and a few companions from the smoking ruins of his home. On the journey to find a new home in the "western land," he has many adventures, including an affair with Dido, the beautiful queen of Carthage, and a trip down to the underworld, to meet his dead father. When he arrives in Italy, he struggles to establish a base in his new land—where some of the native inhabitants are far from welcoming.

The *Aeneid* deals with universal themes, including the basic human need to find, or create, a home. The story is accessible even to those who know nothing about ancient history. But readers will find it helpful to think carefully about how Virgil incorporates his own times into this mythical story. When Virgil was writing, Rome had only recently emerged from a long, terrifying period of civil war. Aeneas, like Augustus, must show strong leadership to a people traumatized by years of violence. Virgil's account of the sack of Troy, including the horrible slaughter of old king Priam before the eyes of his family, is vivid and harrowing—and many contemporary readers would have witnessed similar scenes with their own eyes. But the historical parallels in this poem are complex, and one cannot simply identify Aeneas with Augustus. The affair between Aeneas and Dido looks further back in history, to the Roman wars with Carthage. This episode also invites comparison with events of the more recent past. Like Augustus's military and political rival Antony, Aeneas falls in love with a beautiful African queen; in this interpretation, Dido foreshadows Cleopatra, who also ended up killing herself. Once Aeneas has arrived in Italy, there are further questions. Is Aeneas a foreign invader, pushing the boundaries of his empire into new lands—as Augustus did? Or are these battles between different Italian peoples more like a civil war? Virgil's evocation of historical parallels is rich and fascinating precisely because they are so hard to pin down. Moreover, temporal paradoxes are created by telling "history in the future tense": from the Roman reader's point of view, Carthage has already been defeated; but from Dido's perspective, her city has just begun to be built.

Virgil's use of literary antecedents is equally interesting. His poem combines the themes of the *Odyssey* (the wanderer in search of home) and the *Iliad* (the hero in battle). He borrows Homeric turns of phrase, similes, sentiments, and whole incidents; for instance, his Aeneas, like Odysseus, passes the land of the Cyclops, and descends alive to the world of the dead; like Achilles, he receives a new set of armor from his goddess mother, and kills in rage to avenge a dead friend. But Virgil is not playing a sterile game of copying **Homer**. Rather, Homeric parallels are part of how the poem generates meaning. Virgil often uses several Homeric allusions at the same time. For instance, Turnus—the Italian prince who is originally engaged to Lavinia, the woman who will become Aeneas's wife—is in some ways like one of the suitors in the *Odyssey*: the rival who must be defeated and killed. But on another level, Turnus is like Hector, the doomed Trojan hero of the *Iliad*, who dies defending his city and his people. From Turnus's perspective, Aeneas himself is more like the suitors of the *Odyssey*: he is a usurper in a place where he does not belong.

The *Aeneid*'s approach to storytelling is very different from that of the Homeric poems. Virgil often tells the parts of the story Homer left untold: for example, it is in Virgil, not Homer, that we get the full story of the Trojan Horse. On a more profound level, Virgil's presentation of war, peace, and human nature is quite unlike Homer's—it is both broader and deeper. Virgil is interested in communities that extend beyond the tribe or clan to the nation or the empire, and he evokes time that goes beyond the generations of a single family to the broad sweep of history. The characters, especially Aeneas, are more introspective and prone to ambivalent feelings than those in Homer; Virgil explores conflicts not just between one person and another but within an individual, between duty and the longings of the heart. In this way, Aeneas is a different kind of hero from any in Greek literature. The first time his name is mentioned, he is risking death by shipwreck and is overwhelmed by despair, wishing he could have died with his friends at Troy: he holds his hands to the sky and cries, "Three, four times blest, my comrades / lucky to die beneath the soaring walls of Troy." This is a close echo of the moment when Odysseus is shipwrecked after leaving Calypso's island and wishes he had died fighting at Troy instead of by drowning: "Those Greeks were lucky, three and four times over / who died upon the plain of Troy" (*Odyssey* 5.306–307). But the scenes are importantly different. Aeneas feels not only physical fear but also despair at being a survivor with no home to go to. We can contrast this sense of being totally lost with the first mention of Odysseus in the *Odyssey*: he longs for a home that still exists, whereas Aeneas's home has been destroyed. A little later, we see a different Aeneas when he talks to his men and tries to calm their fears, giving no hint of his own: "Call up your courage again,"

This detail from a black figure vase by the "Louvre Painter" (6th century B.C.E.) shows Aeneas carrying his father, Anchises, on his shoulders as they escape Troy.

he tells them; "dismiss your grief and fear." From the start of the poem, Aeneas will be put in situations where he cannot allow himself to show or act on his deepest feelings.

Virgil also seems to question the values of the Homeric warrior code. Aeneas is not, like Achilles, a man fighting for his personal honor, against even the leaders of his own side; rather, he is, and must be, a consensus builder, a team player. Odysseus (Romanized as *Ulysses*) is presented in the *Aeneid* as a cruel brute, lacking in the mercy for the defeated that Aeneas's father, Anchises, characterizes as an essential feature of the true Roman ("to spare the defeated, break the proud in war"). Moreover, Ulysses' cleverness—epitomized by the invention of the Trojan Horse—seems in this poem to be more like wicked dishonesty. Truthfulness is an essential element in the Roman code of honor: this is partly why Dido's accusation that Aeneas has deceived and betrayed her cuts so deeply.

Aeneas is often seen as the prototype of the ideal Roman ruler, devoted above all to *pietas*—a word from which we get *pity* and *piety*, and which covers both senses, though it is often translated as "duty." But whereas *duty* may suggest adherence to a set of abstract moral principles, the Latin word connotes devotion to particular people and entities: to the gods above all, but also to one's country, leaders, community, and family, especially father and sons. An iconic moment of Aeneas's *pietas* comes as he leaves his burning city, carrying his lame old father on his shoulders, holding the images of his household gods, and leading his little son by the hand. This scene reminds us that Aeneas is struggling to hold on to a community and create continuity even from the ruins of his old home. The *pietas* that holds families and cities together is contrasted in this poem with *furor* ("rage," "fury"), the wild passion that inspires bloodlust, both in Troy and on Italian shores.

But being good is not easy, and Virgil shows that Aeneas's repression of his own feelings for the sake of devotion comes at an enormous cost. Moreover, the poem seems to suggest that duty can even be harmful to other people. Aeneas, on the instructions of the gods, abandons the great passion of his life, his love for Dido, who had convinced herself that their relationship was equivalent to marriage. In despair, she kills herself. Virgil makes us admire and sympathize with Dido, and in doing so, we are forced to question whether Aeneas's mission is worthwhile. The *Aeneid* is not merely a celebration of Roman power; it is also an analysis of the costs of empire, both to the conquered and the conquerors. Moreover, we may wonder whether Rome itself—a city famously built by Romulus, who killed his brother Remus, a city defined by foreign and civil wars—is truly a civilization in which *pietas* is the defining value. This moral ambiguity continues up to the last lines of the poem, which many first-time readers will find shocking. We are left to wonder whether moderation or violence will be the truly defining quality of the future Roman Empire.

A NOTE ON THE TRANSLATION

Translation of this complex poem often reflects the ideological biases of the translator. Some versions make Virgil sound wholeheartedly enthusiastic about imperialism, eliminating much of his ambivalence; others make him sound unrelentingly gloomy about everything. Virgil's Latin is dignified, not colloquial, and has a beautiful, musical rhythm; but trying to reproduce this effect in modern English risks sounding merely pompous.

Several excellent recent translations have steered clear of these dangers and given us readable, fast-paced versions of the *Aeneid*. We have chosen Robert Fagles's translation, because it is particularly good at evoking the psychological depth of Virgil's characters, and it allows readers to experience the sheer narrative pleasure of reading the *Aeneid*.

From The Aeneid[1]

BOOK I

[Safe Haven after Storm]

Wars and a man I sing—an exile driven on by Fate,
he was the first to flee the coast of Troy,
destined to reach Lavinian[2] shores and Italian soil,
yet many blows he took on land and sea from the gods above—
thanks to cruel Juno's[3] relentless rage—and many losses   5
he bore in battle too, before he could found a city,
bring his gods to Latium, source of the Latin race,
the Alban lords and the high walls of Rome.[4]
                              Tell me,
Muse, how it all began. Why was Juno outraged?
What could wound the Queen of the Gods with all her power?   10
Why did she force a man, so famous for his devotion,[5]
to brave such rounds of hardship, bear such trials?
Can such rage inflame the immortals' hearts?

There was an ancient city held by Tyrian settlers,[6]
Carthage, facing Italy and the Tiber River's mouth[7]   15
but far away—a rich city trained and fierce in war.
Juno loved it, they say, beyond all other lands
in the world, even beloved Samos,[8] second best.
Here she kept her armor, here her chariot too,
and Carthage would rule the nations of the earth   20
if only the Fates were willing. This was Juno's goal
from the start, and so she nursed her city's strength.
But she heard a race of men, sprung of Trojan blood,
would one day topple down her Tyrian stronghold,

---

1. Translated by Robert Fagles.
2. Lavinium is the city founded in Italy by Aeneas, near the later city of Rome. It is named after his Latin wife, Lavinia. "Lavinian" here means "Italian."
3. Juno is queen of the gods, wife of Jupiter.
4. According to legend, after Aeneas died, his son Ascanius moved from Latium and founded the city of Alba Longa; from there came Romu-

lus and Remus, who built the walls of Rome.
5. The Latin word is *pietas*: "piety," "duty," "loyalty."
6. Tyre was the main city of the Phoenicians, an ancient seafaring merchant people.
7. The Tiber runs through Rome.
8. A Greek island famous for its cult of Hera (equivalent to the Roman Juno).

breed an arrogant people ruling far and wide,   25
proud in battle, destined to plunder Libya.
So the Fates were spinning out the future . . .[9]
This was Juno's fear
and the goddess never forgot the old campaign
that she had waged at Troy for her beloved Argos.[1]   30
No, not even now would the causes of her rage,
her bitter sorrows drop from the goddess' mind.
They festered deep within her, galled her still:
the judgment of Paris, the unjust slight to her beauty,
the Trojan stock she loathed, the honors showered on Ganymede   35
ravished to the skies.[2] Her fury inflamed by all this,
the daughter of Saturn[3] drove over endless oceans
Trojans left by the Greeks and brute Achilles.[4]
Juno kept them far from Latium, forced by the Fates
to wander round the seas of the world, year in, year out.   40
Such a long hard labor it was to found the Roman people.

　　Now, with the ridge of Sicily barely out of sight,
they spread sail for the open sea, their spirits buoyant,
their bronze beaks churning the waves to foam as Juno,
nursing deep in her heart the everlasting wound,   45
said to herself: "Defeated, am I? Give up the fight?
Powerless now to keep that Trojan king from Italy?
Ah but of course—the Fates bar my way.
And yet Minerva could burn the fleet to ash
and drown my Argive crews in the sea, and all for one,   50
one mad crime of a single man, Ajax, son of Oileus![5]
She hurled Jove's all-consuming bolt from the clouds,
she shattered a fleet and whipped the swells with gales.
And then as he gasped his last in flames from his riven chest
she swept him up in a cyclone, impaled the man on a crag.   55
But I who walk in majesty, I the Queen of the Gods,
the sister and wife of Jove[6]—I must wage a war,
year after year, on just one race of men!
Who will revere the power of Juno after this—
lay gifts on my altar, lift his hands in prayer?"   60

9. Refers to the Punic Wars of the third and second centuries B.C.E., in which Rome finally defeated Carthage; "Libya" is used as a generic term for the North African coast.
1. Argos is the homeland of Agamemnon and Menelaus; in the *Iliad*, Hera favors the Argives as they fight the Trojans and try to win back Helen, Menelaus's wife.
2. Paris, Prince of Troy, was asked to choose one of three goddesses: Hera, Athena (Minerva in Roman mythology), or Aphrodite (Venus to the Romans). He picked Aphrodite, and was rewarded with Helen, whom he took from her husband and led back to Troy. The second insult from the Trojans against Hera is that her husband, Zeus, once fell in love with

a Trojan boy, Ganymede, and brought him up to heaven to be his cupbearer.
3. Saturn, the Roman god of agriculture, was the father of both Jupiter and Juno.
4. The greatest Greek warrior. These survivors are the few Trojans whom Achilles has not killed.
5. In the aftermath of the Greek victory at Troy, one of the Greek soldiers, this Ajax (who is not the same as the strong hero Telemonian Ajax) raped the Trojan princess Cassandra in the temple of Minerva. The goddess took revenge by setting fire to the Greek fleet, and then overwhelming it with a storm.
6. Alternative name of Jupiter.

With such anger seething inside her fiery heart
the goddess reached Aeolia, breeding-ground of storms,
their home swarming with raging gusts from the South.
Here in a vast cave King Aeolus[7] rules the winds,
brawling to break free, howling in full gale force   65
as he chains them down in their dungeon, shackled fast.
They bluster in protest, roaring round their prison bars
with a mountain above them all, booming with their rage.
But high in his stronghold Aeolus wields his scepter,
soothing their passions, tempering their fury.   70
Should he fail, surely they'd blow the world away,
hurling the land and sea and deep sky through space.
Fearing this, the almighty Father banished the winds
to that black cavern, piled above them a mountain mass
and imposed on all a king empowered, by binding pact,   75
to rein them back on command or let them gallop free.

Now Juno made this plea to the Lord of Winds:
"Aeolus, the Father of Gods and King of Men gave you
the power to calm the waves or rouse them with your gales.
A race I loathe is crossing the Tuscan Sea,[8] transporting 80
Troy to Italy, bearing their conquered household gods—
thrash your winds to fury, sink their warships, overwhelm them
or break them apart, scatter their crews, drown them all!
I happen to have some sea-nymphs, fourteen beauties,
Deiopea the finest of all by far . . .   85
I'll join you in lasting marriage, call her yours
and for all her years to come she will live with you
and make you the proud father of handsome children.
Such service earns such gifts."
                                    Aeolus warmed
to Juno's offer: "Yours is the task, my queen,   90
to explore your heart's desires. Mine is the duty
to follow your commands. Yes, thanks to you
I rule this humble little kingdom of mine.
You won me the scepter, Jupiter's favors too,
and a couch to lounge on, set at the gods' feasts—   95
you made me Lord of the Stormwind, King of Cloudbursts."
With such thanks, swinging his spear around he strikes home
at the mountain's hollow flank and out charge the winds
through the breach he'd made, like armies on attack
in a blasting whirlwind tearing through the earth.   100
Down they crash on the sea, the Eastwind, Southwind,
all as one with the Southwest's squalls in hot pursuit,
heaving up from the ocean depths huge killer-breakers
rolling toward the beaches. The crews are shouting,
cables screeching—suddenly cloudbanks blotting out   105
the sky, the light of day from the Trojans' sight

7. Mythical king of the winds from the *Odyssey*.

8. Just west of central Italy; the Trojans have almost reached their destination.

as pitch-black night comes brooding down on the sea
with thunder crashing pole to pole, bolt on bolt
blazing across the heavens—death, everywhere
men facing instant death.   110
At once Aeneas, limbs limp in the chill of fear,
groans and lifting both his palms toward the stars
cries out: "Three, four times blest, my comrades
lucky to die beneath the soaring walls of Troy—
before their parents' eyes! If only I'd gone down   115
under your right hand—Diomedes, strongest Greek afield—
and poured out my life on the battle grounds of Troy!⁹
Where raging Hector lies, pierced by Achilles' spear,
where mighty Sarpedon lies, where the Simois River
swallows down and churns beneath its tides so many   120
shields and helmets and corpses of the brave!"¹

                                    Flinging cries
as a screaming gust of the Northwind pounds against his sail,
raising waves sky-high. The oars shatter, prow twists round,
taking the breakers broadside on and over Aeneas' decks
a mountain of water towers, massive, steep.   125
Some men hang on billowing crests, some as the sea
gapes, glimpse through the waves the bottom waiting,
a surge aswirl with sand.

                        Three ships the Southwind grips
and spins against those boulders lurking in mid-ocean—
rocks the Italians call the Altars, one great spine   130
breaking the surface—three the Eastwind sweeps
from open sea on the Syrtes'² reefs, a grim sight,
girding them round with walls of sand.

                                    One ship
that carried the Lycian³ units led by staunch Orontes—
before Aeneas' eyes a toppling summit of water   135
strikes the stern and hurls the helmsman overboard,
pitching him headfirst, twirling his ship three times,
right on the spot till the ravenous whirlpool gulps her down.
Here and there you can sight some sailors bobbing in heavy seas,
strewn in the welter now the weapons, men, stray spars   140
and treasures saved from Troy.

                                Now Ilioneus' sturdy ship,
now brave Achates', now the galley that carried Abas,
another, aged Aletes, yes, the storm routs them all,
down to the last craft the joints split, beams spring
and the lethal flood pours in.

                            All the while Neptune⁴   145

9. In the *Iliad*, Aeneas is wounded by the
Greek hero Diomedes, and is rescued by his
mother, Aphrodite.
1. Hector, the greatest Trojan hero, is killed
by Achilles in the *Iliad*. Sarpedon is another
fighter on the Trojan side, the favorite of Zeus,
who is killed by Achilles' friend Patroclus. The
Simois is the river at Troy, which in the *Iliad*

becomes thick with the blood and bodies of
those killed by Achilles.
2. A pair of shallow, sandy gulfs off the coast
of Libya.
3. Region in modern-day Turkey, allied with
Troy in the *Iliad*.
4. God of the sea (equivalent to the Greek
Poseidon).

sensed the furor above him, the roaring seas first and
the storm breaking next—his standing waters boiling up
from the sea-bed, churning back. And the mighty god,
stirred to his depths, lifts his head from the crests
and serene in power, gazing out over all his realm,   150
he sees Aeneas' squadrons scattered across the ocean,
Trojans overwhelmed by the surf and the wild crashing skies.
Nor did he miss his sister Juno's cunning wrath at work.
He summons the East- and Westwind, takes them to task:
"What insolence! Trusting so to your lofty birth?   155
You winds, you dare make heaven and earth a chaos,
raising such a riot of waves without my blessings.
You—what I won't do! But first I had better set
to rest the flood you ruffled so. Next time, trust me,
you will pay for your crimes with more than just a scolding.   160
Away with you, quick! And give your king this message:
Power over the sea and ruthless trident is mine,
not his—it's mine by lot, by destiny. His place,
Eastwind, is the rough rocks where you are all at home.
Let him bluster there and play the king in his court,   165
let Aeolus rule his bolted dungeon of the winds!"

Quicker than his command he calms the heaving seas,
putting the clouds to rout and bringing back the sun.
Struggling shoulder-to-shoulder, Triton and Cymothoë[5]
hoist and heave the ships from the jagged rocks   170
as the god himself whisks them up with his trident,
clearing a channel through the deadly reefs, his chariot
skimming over the cresting waves on spinning wheels
to set the seas to rest. Just as, all too often,
some huge crowd is seized by a vast uprising,   175
the rabble runs amok, all slaves to passion,
rocks, firebrands flying. Rage finds them arms
but then, if they chance to see a man among them,
one whose devotion and public service lend him weight,
they stand there, stock-still with their ears alert as   180
he rules their furor with his words and calms their passion.
So the crash of the breakers all fell silent once their Father,
gazing over his realm under clear skies, flicks his horses,
giving them free rein, and his eager chariot flies.

Now bone-weary, Aeneas' shipmates make a run   185
for the nearest landfall, wheeling prows around
they turn for Libya's coast. There is a haven shaped
by an island shielding the mouth of a long deep bay, its flanks
breaking the force of combers pounding in from the sea
while drawing them off into calm receding channels.   190
Both sides of the harbor, rock cliffs tower, crowned
by twin crags that menace the sky, overshadowing

5. Triton is a lesser sea god; Cymothoë is a sea nymph.

reaches of sheltered water, quiet and secure.
Over them as a backdrop looms a quivering wood,
above them rears a grove, bristling dark with shade, 195
and fronting the cliff, a cave under hanging rocks
with fresh water inside, seats cut in the native stone,
the home of nymphs. Never a need of cables here to moor
a weathered ship, no anchor with biting flukes to bind her fast.

Aeneas puts in here with a bare seven warships 200
saved from his whole fleet. How keen their longing
for dry land underfoot as the Trojans disembark,
taking hold of the earth, their last best hope,
and fling their brine-wracked bodies on the sand.
Achates is first to strike a spark from flint, 205
then works to keep it alive in dry leaves,
cups it around with kindling, feeds it chips
and briskly fans the tinder into flame.
Then, spent as they were from all their toil,
they set out food, the bounty of Ceres,[6] drenched 210
in sea-salt, Ceres' utensils too, her mills and troughs,
and bend to parch with fire the grain they had salvaged,
grind it fine on stones.
                                    While they see to their meal
Aeneas scales a crag, straining to scan the sea-reach
far and wide . . . is there any trace of Antheus now, 215
tossed by the gales, or his warships banked with oars?
Or Capys perhaps, or Caicus' stern adorned with shields?[7]
Not a ship in sight. But he does spot three stags
roaming the shore, an entire herd behind them
grazing down the glens in a long ranked line. 220
He halts, grasps his bow and his flying arrows,
the weapons his trusty aide Achates keeps at hand.
First the leaders, antlers branching over their high heads,
he brings them down, then turns on the herd, his shafts
stampeding the rest like rabble into the leafy groves. 225
Shaft on shaft, no stopping him till he stretches
seven hefty carcases on the ground—a triumph,
one for each of his ships—and makes for the cove,
divides the kill with his whole crew and then shares out
the wine that good Acestes,[8] princely man, had brimmed 230
in their casks the day they left Sicilian shores.

The commander's words relieve their stricken hearts:
"My comrades, hardly strangers to pain before now,
we all have weathered worse. Some god will grant us
an end to this as well. You've threaded the rocks 235
resounding with Scylla's howling rabid dogs,
and taken the brunt of the Cyclops' boulders, too.

6. Goddess of grain and harvest.
7. Names of lost Trojan leaders.

8. King in Sicily who gave the Trojans shelter
and extra supplies.

Call up your courage again. Dismiss your grief and fear.
A joy it will be one day, perhaps, to remember even this.
Through so many hard straits, so many twists and turns   240
our course holds firm for Latium.[9] There Fate holds out
a homeland, calm, at peace. There the gods decree
the kingdom of Troy will rise again. Bear up.
Save your strength for better times to come."

                                            Brave words.
Sick with mounting cares he assumes a look of hope   245
and keeps his anguish buried in his heart.
The men gird up for the game, the coming feast,
they skin the hide from the ribs, lay bare the meat.
Some cut it into quivering strips, impale it on skewers,
some set cauldrons along the beach and fire them to the boil.   250
Then they renew their strength with food, stretched out
on the beachgrass, fill themselves with seasoned wine
and venison rich and crisp. Their hunger sated,
the tables cleared away, they talk on for hours,
asking after their missing shipmates—wavering now   255
between hope and fear: what to believe about the rest?
Were the men still alive or just in the last throes,
forever lost to their comrades' farflung calls?
Aeneas most of all, devoted to his shipmates,
deep within himself he moans for the losses . . .   260
now for Orontes, hardy soldier, now for Amycus,
now for the brutal fate that Lycus may have met,
then Gyas and brave Cloanthus, hearts of oak.

    Their mourning was over now as Jove from high heaven,
gazing down on the sea, the whitecaps winged with sails,   265
the lands outspread, the coasts, the nations of the earth,
paused at the zenith of the sky and set his sights
on Libya, that proud kingdom. All at once,
as he took to heart the struggles he beheld,
Venus[1] approached in rare sorrow, tears abrim   270
in her sparkling eyes, and begged: "Oh you who rule
the lives of men and gods with your everlasting laws
and your lightning bolt of terror, what crime could my Aeneas
commit against you, what dire harm could the Trojans do
that after bearing so many losses, this wide world   275
is shut to them now? And all because of Italy.
Surely from them the Romans would arise one day
as the years roll on, and leaders would as well,
descended from Teucer's[2] blood brought back to life,
to rule all lands and seas with boundless power—   280
you promised! Father, what motive changed your mind?
With that, at least, I consoled myself for Troy's demise,
that heart-rending ruin—weighing fate against fate.

---

9. Region of central Italy, home of the Latin
race.

1. Aeneas's mother; goddess of love and sex.
2. Legendary first king of Troy.

But now after all my Trojans suffered, still
the same disastrous fortune drives them on and on.   285
What end, great king, do you set to their ordeals?

"Antenor[3] could slip out from under the Greek siege,
then make his passage through the Illyrian gulfs and,
safe through the inlands where the Liburnians rule,
he struggled past the Timavus River's source.[4]   290
There, through its nine mouths as the mountain caves
roar back, the river bursts out into full flood,
a thundering surf that overpowers the fields.
Reaching Italy, he erected a city for his people,
a Trojan home called Padua—gave them a Trojan name,   295
hung up their Trojan arms and there, after long wars,
he lingers on in serene and settled peace.
                                        "But we,
your own children, the ones you swore would hold
the battlements of heaven—now our ships are lost,
appalling! We are abandoned, thanks to the rage   300
of a single foe, cut off from Italy's shores.
Is this our reward for reverence,[5]
this the way you give us back our throne?"

    The Father of Men and Gods, smiling down on her
with the glance that clears the sky and calms the tempest,   305
lightly kissing his daughter on the lips, replied:
"Relieve yourself of fear, my lady of Cythera,[6]
the fate of your children stands unchanged, I swear.
You will see your promised city, see Lavinium's walls
and bear your great-hearted Aeneas up to the stars on high.   310
Nothing has changed my mind. No, your son, believe me—
since anguish is gnawing at you, I will tell you more,
unrolling the scroll of Fate
to reveal its darkest secrets. Aeneas will wage
a long, costly war in Italy, crush defiant tribes   315
and build high city walls for his people there
and found the rule of law. Only three summers
will see him govern Latium, three winters pass
in barracks after the Latins have been broken.
But his son Ascanius, now that he gains the name   320
of Iulus—Ilus he was, while Ilium ruled on high[7]—
will fill out with his own reign thirty sovereign years,
a giant cycle of months revolving round and round,
transferring his rule from its old Lavinian home

---

3. Trojan leader who escaped the city's sack
and settled in northern Italy.
4. Illyrium was a district, the Liburnians a
people, and Timavus a river on the coast of the
northern Adriatic sea.
5. *Pietas.*
6. Greek island where there was a cult of

Aphrodite.
7. *Ilium* is another name for Troy (hence the
title of Homer's epic poem: the *Iliad*). The
Julian family, which included Julius Caesar and
Augustus, claimed descent from Iulus (Julus),
originally name Ascanius.

to raise up Alba Longa's mighty ramparts.   325
There, in turn, for a full three hundred years
the dynasty of Hector will hold sway till Ilia,
a royal priestess great with the brood of Mars,
will bear the god twin sons.[8] Then one, Romulus,
reveling in the tawny pelt of a wolf that nursed him,   330
will inherit the line and build the walls of Mars
and after his own name, call his people Romans.[9]
On them I set no limits, space or time:
I have granted them power, empire without end.
Even furious Juno, now plaguing the land and sea and sky   335
with terror: she will mend her ways and hold dear with me
these Romans, lords of the earth, the race arrayed in togas.
This is my pleasure, my decree. Indeed, an age will come,
as the long years slip by, when Assaracus'[1] royal house
will quell Achilles' homeland, brilliant Mycenae too,   340
and enslave their people, rule defeated Argos.
From that noble blood will arise a Trojan Caesar,
his empire bound by the Ocean, his glory by the stars:
Julius, a name passed down from Iulus, his great forebear.
And you, in years to come, will welcome him to the skies,   345
you rest assured—laden with plunder of the East,
and he with Aeneas will be invoked in prayer.[2]
Then will the violent centuries, battles set aside,
grow gentle, kind. Vesta[3] and silver-haired Good Faith
and Romulus flanked by brother Remus will make the laws.   350
The terrible Gates of War with their welded iron bars
will stand bolted shut,[4] and locked inside, the Frenzy
of civil strife will crouch down on his savage weapons,
hands pinioned behind his back with a hundred brazen shackles,
monstrously roaring out from his bloody jaws."
                             So   355
he decrees and speeds the son of Maia[5] down the sky
to make the lands and the new stronghold, Carthage,
open in welcome to the Trojans, not let Dido,
unaware of fate, expel them from her borders.
Down through the vast clear air flies Mercury,   360
rowing his wings like oars and in a moment
stands on Libya's shores, obeys commands
and the will of god is done.

---

8. Ilia, also known as Rhea Silvia, was a priestess sworn to religious celibacy. She was raped
by Mars, the god of war, and gave birth to
twins, Romulus and Remus. Her brother, jealous of his own power, ordered that the babies
be killed; but instead, his servant abandoned
them in the wild, to be rescued by a wolf that
suckled them and raised them.
9. Virgil omits the fact that Romulus killed
his brother, Remus, to gain sole power over
the city.
1. An early king of Troy.

2. The "Trojan Caesar" is either Julius Caesar, who made Rome an empire, or Augustus
himself, who had plundered "the East" by
defeating the Egyptian queen Cleopatra.
3. Vesta is the goddess of the hearth, representative of home life.
4. There were real Gates of War in the temple
of Janus, which Augustus shut in 25 B.C.E.—the
first time they had been shut since 235 B.C.E.
5. A daughter of Atlas who was impregnated
by Jupiter and gave birth to Mercury (Roman
version of Hermes), the messenger god.

The Carthaginians calm their fiery temper
and Queen Dido, above all, takes to heart   365
a spirit of peace and warm good will to meet
the men of Troy.
                    But Aeneas, duty-bound,
his mind restless with worries all that night,
reached a firm resolve as the fresh day broke.
Out he goes to explore the strange terrain . . .   370
what coast had the stormwinds brought him to?
Who lives here? All he sees is wild, untilled—
what men, or what creatures? Then report the news
to all his comrades. So, concealing his ships
in the sheltered woody narrows overarched by rocks   375
and screened around by trees and trembling shade,
Aeneas moves out, with only Achates at his side,
two steel-tipped javelins balanced in his grip.
Suddenly, in the heart of the woods, his mother
crossed his path. She looked like a young girl,   380
a Spartan girl decked out in dress and gear
or Thracian Harpalyce tiring out her mares,
outracing the Hebrus River's rapid tides.[6]
Hung from a shoulder, a bow that fit her grip,
a huntress for all the world, she'd let her curls   385
go streaming free in the wind, her knees were bare,
her flowing skirts hitched up with a tight knot.

    She speaks out first: "You there, young soldiers,
did you by any chance see one of my sisters?
Which way did she go? Roaming the woods,   390
a quiver slung from her belt,
wearing a spotted lynx-skin, or in full cry,
hot on the track of some great frothing boar?"
So Venus asked and the son of Venus answered:
"Not one of your sisters have I seen or heard . . .   395
but how should I greet a young girl like you?
Your face, your features—hardly a mortal's looks
and the tone of your voice is hardly human either.
Oh a goddess, without a doubt! What, are you
Apollo's sister? Or one of the breed of Nymphs?   400
Be kind, whoever you are, relieve our troubled hearts.
Under what skies and onto what coasts of the world
have we been driven? Tell us, please. Castaways,
we know nothing, not the people, not the place—
lost, hurled here by the gales and heavy seas.   405
Many a victim will fall before your altars,
we'll slaughter them for you!"

6. The goddess Venus is dressed like a Spartan, a famously athletic and militaristic Greek
people, or Harpalyce, a girl who lived in the
wilds and devoted herself to hunting. The
Hebrus is a river in Thrace. In Greco-Roman
tradition, hunting was considered antithetical
to sex and marriage.

But Venus replied:
"Now there's an honor I really don't deserve.
It's just the style for Tyrian girls to sport
a quiver and high-laced hunting boots in crimson.   410
What you see is a Punic[7] kingdom, people of Tyre
and Agenor's town, but the border's held by Libyans
hard to break in war. Phoenician Dido is in command,
she sailed from Tyre, in flight from her own brother.
Oh it's a long tale of crime, long, twisting, dark,   415
but I'll try to trace the high points in their order . . .

  "Dido was married to Sychaeus, the richest man in Tyre,
and she, poor girl, was consumed with love for him.
Her father gave her away, wed for the first time,
a virgin still, and these her first solemn rites.   420
But her brother held power in Tyre—Pygmalion,
a monster, the vilest man alive.
A murderous feud broke out between both men.
Pygmalion, catching Sychaeus off guard at the altar,
slaughtered him in blood. That unholy man, so blind   425
in his lust for gold he ran him through with a sword,
then hid the crime for months, deaf to his sister's love,
her heartbreak. Still he mocked her with wicked lies,
with empty hopes. But she had a dream one night.
The true ghost of her husband, not yet buried,   430
came and lifting his face—ashen, awesome in death—
showed her the cruel altar, the wounds that pierced his chest
and exposed the secret horror that lurked within the house.
He urged her on: 'Take flight from our homeland, quick!'
And then he revealed an unknown ancient treasure,   435
an untold weight of silver and gold, a comrade
to speed her on her way.
                              "Driven by all this,
Dido plans her escape, collects her followers
fired by savage hate of the tyrant or bitter fear.
They seize some galleys set to sail, load them with gold—   440
the wealth Pygmalion craved—and they bear it overseas
and a woman leads them all. Reaching this haven here,
where now you will see the steep ramparts rising,
the new city of Carthage—the Tyrians purchased land as
large as a bull's-hide could enclose but cut in strips for size   445
and called it Byrsa, the Hide, for the spread they'd bought.
But you, who are you? What shores do you come from?
Where are you headed now?"
                              He answered her questions,
drawing a labored sigh from deep within his chest:
"Goddess, if I'd retrace our story to its start,   450
if you had time to hear the saga of our ordeals,
before I finished the Evening Star would close
the gates of Olympus, put the day to sleep . . .

7. I.e., Carthaginian.

From old Troy we come—Troy it's called, perhaps
you've heard the name—sailing over the world's seas   455
until, by chance, some whim of the winds, some tempest
drove us onto Libyan shores. I am Aeneas, duty-bound.
I carry aboard my ships the gods of house and home
we seized from enemy hands. My fame goes past the skies.
I seek my homeland—Italy—born as I am from highest Jove.   460
I launched out on the Phrygian sea with twenty ships,
my goddess mother marking the way, and followed hard
on the course the Fates had charted. A mere seven,
battered by wind and wave, survived the worst.
I myself am a stranger, utterly at a loss,   465
trekking over this wild Libyan wasteland,
forced from Europe, Asia too, an exile—"

    Venus could bear no more of his laments
and broke in on his tale of endless hardship:
"Whoever you are, I scarcely think the Powers hate you: 470
you enjoy the breath of life, you've reached a Tyrian city.
So off you go now. Take this path to the queen's gates.
I have good news. Your friends are restored to you,
your fleet's reclaimed. The winds swerved from the North
and drove them safe to port. True, unless my parents   475
taught me to read the flight of birds for nothing.
Look at those dozen swans triumphant in formation!
The eagle of Jove[8] had just swooped down on them all
from heaven's heights and scattered them into open sky,
but now you can see them flying trim in their long ranks,   480
landing or looking down where their friends have landed—
home, cavorting on ruffling wings and wheeling round
the sky in convoy, trumpeting in their glory.
So homeward bound, your ships and hardy shipmates
anchor in port now or approach the harbor's mouth,   485
full sail ahead. Now off you go, move on,
wherever the path leads you, steer your steps."
                                    At that,
as she turned away her neck shone with a rosy glow,
her mane of hair gave off an ambrosial fragrance,
her skirt flowed loose, rippling down to her feet   490
and her stride alone revealed her as a goddess.
He knew her at once—his mother—
and called after her now as she sped away:
"Why, you too, cruel as the rest? So often
you ridicule your son with your disguises!   495
Why can't we clasp hands, embrace each other,
speak out, and tell the truth?"

    Reproving her so, he makes his way toward town
but Venus screens the travelers off with a dense mist,

---

8. The eagle, king of the birds, was associated with Jupiter.

pouring round them a cloak of clouds with all her power,   500
so no one could see them, no one reach and hold them,
cause them to linger now or ask why they had come.
But she herself, lifting into the air, wings her way
toward Paphos,[9] racing with joy to reach her home again
where her temples stand and a hundred altars steam   505
with Arabian incense, redolent with the scent
of fresh-cut wreaths.
                Meanwhile the two men
are hurrying on their way as the path leads,
now climbing a steep hill arching over the city,
looking down on the facing walls and high towers.   510
Aeneas marvels at its mass—once a cluster of huts—
he marvels at gates and bustling hum and cobbled streets.
The Tyrians press on with the work, some aligning the walls,
struggling to raise the citadel, trundling stones up slopes;
some picking the building sites and plowing out their boundaries,   515
others drafting laws, electing judges, a senate held in awe.
Here they're dredging a harbor, there they lay foundations
deep for a theater, quarrying out of rock great columns
to form a fitting scene for stages still to come.
As hard at their tasks as bees in early summer,   520
working the blooming meadows under the sun
escorting a new brood out, young adults now,
or pressing oozing honey into the combs, the nectar
brimming the bulging cells, or gathering up the plunder
workers haul back in, or closing ranks like an army,   525
driving the drones, that lazy crew, from home.
The hive seethes with life, exhaling the scent
of honey sweet with thyme.
                "How lucky they are,"
Aeneas cries, gazing up at the city's heights,
"their walls are rising now!" And on he goes,   530
cloaked in cloud—remarkable—right in their midst
he blends in with the crowds, and no one sees him.

   Now deep in the heart of Carthage stood a grove,
lavish with shade, where the Tyrians, making landfall,
still shaken by wind and breakers, first unearthed that sign: 535
Queen Juno had led their way to the fiery stallion's head
that signaled power in war and ease in life for ages.
Here Dido of Tyre was building Juno a mighty temple,
rich with gifts and the goddess' aura of power.
Bronze the threshold crowning a flight of stairs,   540
the doorposts sheathed in bronze, and the bronze doors
groaned deep on their hinges.
                Here in this grove
a strange sight met his eyes and calmed his fears
for the first time. Here, for the first time,

---

9. Greek island where there was a cult center of Aphrodite.

Aeneas dared to hope he had found some haven,   545
for all his hard straits, to trust in better days.
For awaiting the queen, beneath the great temple now,
exploring its features one by one, amazed at it all,
the city's splendor, the work of rival workers' hands
and the vast scale of their labors—all at once he sees,   550
spread out from first to last, the battles fought at Troy,
the fame of the Trojan War now known throughout the world,
Atreus' sons and Priam—Achilles, savage to both at once.[1]
Aeneas came to a halt and wept, and "Oh Achates,"
he cried, "is there anywhere, any place on earth   555
not filled with our ordeals? There's Priam, look!
Even here, merit will have its true reward . . .
even here, the world is a world of tears
and the burdens of mortality touch the heart.
Dismiss your fears. Trust me, this fame of ours   560
will offer us some haven."

             So Aeneas says,
feeding his spirit on empty, lifeless pictures,
groaning low, the tears rivering down his face
as he sees once more the fighters circling Troy.
Here Greeks in flight, routed by Troy's young ranks,   565
there Trojans routed by plumed Achilles in his chariot.
Just in range are the snow-white canvas tents of Rhesus—
he knows them at once, and sobs—Rhesus' men betrayed
in their first slumber, droves of them slaughtered
by Diomedes splattered with their blood, lashing   570
back to the Greek camp their highstrung teams
before they could ever savor the grass of Troy
or drink at Xanthus' banks.[2]

             Next Aeneas sees
Troilus[3] in flight, his weapons flung aside,
unlucky boy, no match for Achilles' onslaught—   575
horses haul him on, tangled behind an empty warcar,
flat on his back, clinging still to the reins, his neck
and hair dragging along the ground, the butt of his javelin
scrawling zigzags in the dust.

             And here the Trojan women
are moving toward the temple of Pallas,[4] their deadly foe,   580
their hair unbound as they bear the robe, their offering,
suppliants grieving, palms beating their breasts
but Pallas turns away, staring at the ground.

             And Hector—
three times Achilles has hauled him round the walls of Troy
and now he's selling his lifeless body off for gold.   585

---

1. That is, Achilles was angry with Greeks as well as Trojans. *Atreus' sons*: Agamemnon and Menelaus, the Greek commanders in the Trojan War.
2. Rhesus, king of Thrace, came to help the Trojans, but was slaughtered by Odysseus and Diomedes in a night raid. An oracle had proclaimed that if Rhesus's horses ate Trojan grass and drank from the river Xanthus, Troy would not fall.
3. Troilus was a young son of King Priam of Troy.
4. Athena, who was hostile to Troy.

Aeneas gives a groan, heaving up from his depths,
he sees the plundered armor, the car, the corpse
of his great friend, and Priam reaching out
with helpless hands . . . [5]

           He even sees himself
swept up in the melee, clashing with Greek captains,   590
sees the troops of the dawn and swarthy Memnon's[6] arms.
And Penthesilea leading her Amazons bearing half-moon shields[7]—
she blazes with battle-fury out in front of her army,
cinching a golden breastband under her bared breast,
a girl, a warrior queen who dares to battle men.

                   And now   595
as Trojan Aeneas, gazing in awe at all the scenes of Troy,
stood there, spellbound, eyes fixed on the war alone,
the queen aglow with beauty approached the temple,
Dido, with massed escorts marching in her wake.
Like Diana urging her dancing troupes along   600
the Eurotas' banks or up Mount Cynthus' ridge[8]
as a thousand mountain-nymphs crowd in behind her,
left and right—with quiver slung from her shoulder,
taller than any other goddess as she goes striding on
and silent Latona[9] thrills with joy too deep for words.   605
Like Dido now, striding triumphant among her people,
spurring on the work of their kingdom still to come.
And then by Juno's doors beneath the vaulted dome,
flanked by an honor guard beside her lofty seat,
the queen assumed her throne. Here as she handed down   610
decrees and laws to her people, sharing labors fairly,
some by lot, some with her sense of justice, Aeneas
suddenly sees his men approaching through the crowds,
Antheus, Sergestus, gallant Cloanthus, other Trojans
the black gales had battered over the seas   615
and swept to far-flung coasts.

              Aeneas, Achates,
both were amazed, both struck with joy and fear.
They yearn to grasp their companions' hands in haste
but both men are unnerved by the mystery of it all.
So, cloaked in folds of mist, they hide their feelings,   620
waiting, hoping to see what luck their friends have found.
Where have they left their ships, what coast? Why have they come?
These picked men, still marching in from the whole armada,
pressing toward the temple amid the rising din
to plead for some goodwill.

5. Having killed Hector, Achilles dragged his corpse around the city behind his chariot, until Priam came to ransom his son's body.
6. King of the Ethiopians, who fought on the Trojan side.
7. The Amazons were a race of warrior women who fought for Troy.

8. Diana (Artemis in Greek mythology) is the virgin goddess associated with hunting. She was born on Delos, the island location of Mount Cynthus; Eurotas was a river in Sparta where she was worshipped.
9. Leto, Diana's mother.

Once they had entered,   625
allowed to appeal before the queen—the eldest,
Prince Ilioneus, calm, composed, spoke out:
"Your majesty, empowered by Jove to found
your new city here and curb rebellious tribes
with your sense of justice—we poor Trojans,   630
castaways, tossed by storms over all the seas;
we beg you: keep the cursed fire off our ships!
Pity us, god-fearing men! Look on us kindly,
see the state we are in. We have not come
to put your Libyan gods and homes to the sword,   635
loot them and haul our plunder toward the beach.
No, such pride, such violence has no place
in the hearts of beaten men.
               "There is a country—
the Greeks called it Hesperia, Land of the West,
an ancient land, mighty in war and rich in soil.   640
Oenotrians[1] settled it; now we hear their descendants
call their kingdom Italy, after their leader, Italus.
Italy-bound we were when, surging with sudden breakers
stormy Orion[2] drove us against blind shoals and from the South
came vicious gales to scatter us, whelmed by the sea,   645
across the murderous surf and rocky barrier reefs:
We few escaped and floated toward your coast.
What kind of men are these? What land is this,
that you can tolerate such barbaric ways?
We are denied the sailor's right to shore—   650
attacked, forbidden even a footing on your beach.
If you have no use for humankind and mortal armor,
at least respect the gods. They know right from wrong.
They don't forget.
               "We once had a king, Aeneas . . .
none more just, none more devoted to duty, none   655
more brave in arms. If Fate has saved that man,
if he still draws strength from the air we breathe,
if he's not laid low, not yet with the heartless shades,
fear not, nor will you once regret the first step
you take to compete with him in kindness.   660
We have cities too, in the land of Sicily,
arms and a king, Acestes, born of Trojan blood.
Permit us to haul our storm-racked ships ashore,
trim new oars, hew timbers out of your woods, so that,
if we are fated to sail for Italy—king and crews restored—   665
to Italy, to Latium we will sail with buoyant hearts.
But if we have lost our haven there, if Libyan waters
hold you now, my captain, best of the men of Troy,
and all our hopes for Iulus have been dashed,
at least we can cross back over Sicilian seas,   670

1. An ancient Italic people.
2. This constellation marks the approach of winter.

the straits we came from, homes ready and waiting,
and seek out great Acestes for our king."

So Ilioneus closed. And with one accord
the Trojans murmured Yes.
                        Her eyes lowered,
Dido replies with a few choice words of welcome: 675
"Cast fear to the winds, Trojans, free your minds.
Our kingdom is new. Our hard straits have forced me
to set defenses, station guards along our far frontiers.
Who has not heard of Aeneas' people, his city, Troy,
her men, her heroes, the flames of that horrendous war?   680
We are not so dull of mind, we Carthaginians here.
When he yokes his team, the Sun shines down on us as well.
Whatever you choose, great Hesperia—Saturn's fields—
or the shores of Eryx with Acestes as your king,[3]
I will provide safe passage, escorts and support   685
to speed you on your way. Or would you rather
settle here in my realm on equal terms with me?
This city I build—it's yours. Haul ships to shore.
Trojans, Tyrians: they will be all the same to me.
If only the storm that drove you drove your king   690
and Aeneas were here now! Indeed, I'll send out
trusty men to scour the coast of Libya far and wide.
Perhaps he's shipwrecked, lost in woods or towns."

    Spirits lifting at Dido's welcome, brave Achates
and captain Aeneas had long chafed to break free   695
of the mist, and now Achates spurs Aeneas on:
"Son of Venus, what feelings are rising in you now?
You see the coast is clear, our ships and friends restored.
Just one is lost. We saw him drown at sea ourselves.
All else is just as your mother promised."   700

    He'd barely ended when all at once the mist
around them parted, melting into the open air,
and there Aeneas stood, clear in the light of day,
his head, his shoulders, the man was like a god.
His own mother had breathed her beauty on her son,   705
a gloss on his flowing hair, and the ruddy glow of youth,
and radiant joy shone in his eyes. His beauty fine
as a craftsman's hand can add to ivory, or aglow
as silver or Parian marble[4] ringed in glinting gold.

    Suddenly, surprising all, he tells the queen: 710
"Here I am before you, the man you are looking for,
Aeneas the Trojan, plucked from Libya's heavy seas.
You alone have pitied the long ordeals of Troy—unspeakable—

---

3. Hesperia is "the western land," that is, Italy. established the Golden Age. *Eryx*: city in Sicily.
In Roman mythology, the Titan god Saturn, 4. That is, marble from the island of Paros; fa-
when driven out by Jupiter, fled to Italy and mous for its whiteness.

and here you would share your city and your home with us,
this remnant left by the Greeks. We who have drunk deep   715
of each and every disaster land and sea can offer.
Stripped of everything, now it's past our power
to reward you gift for gift, Dido, theirs as well,
whoever may survive of the Dardan[5] people still,
strewn over the wide world now. But may the gods,   720
if there are Powers who still respect the good and true,
if justice still exists on the face of the earth,
may they and their own sense of right and wrong
bring you your just rewards.
What age has been so blest to give you birth?   725
What noble parents produced so fine a daughter?
So long as rivers run to the sea, so long as shadows
travel the mountain slopes and the stars range the skies,
your honor, your name, your praise will live forever,
whatever lands may call me to their shores."
                                    With that,   730
he extends his right hand toward his friend Ilioneus,
greeting Serestus with his left, and then the others,
gallant Gyas, gallant Cloanthus.
                            Tyrian Dido marveled,
first at the sight of him, next at all he'd suffered,
then she said aloud: "Born of a goddess, even so   735
what destiny hunts you down through such ordeals?
What violence lands you on this frightful coast?
Are you that Aeneas whom loving Venus bore
to Dardan Anchises on the Simois' banks at Troy?
Well I remember . . . Teucer came to Sidon once,   740
banished from native ground, searching for new realms,
and my father Belus helped him.[6] Belus had sacked Cyprus,
plundered that rich island, ruled with a victor's hand.
From that day on I have known of Troy's disaster,
known your name, and all the kings of Greece.   745
Teucer, your enemy, often sang Troy's praises,
claiming his own descent from Teucer's ancient stock.
So come, young soldiers, welcome to our house.
My destiny, harrying me with trials hard as yours,
led me as well, at last, to anchor in this land.   750
Schooled in suffering, now I learn to comfort
those who suffer too."
                         With that greeting
she leads Aeneas into the royal halls, announcing
offerings in the gods' high temples as she goes.
Not forgetting to send his shipmates on the beaches   755
twenty bulls and a hundred huge, bristling razorbacks
and a hundred fatted lambs together with their mothers:
gifts to make this day a day of joy.

---

5. Dardanus founded the city of Dardania, just above Troy; hence the Dardans or Dardanians are the Trojans.

6. After the fall of Troy, Teucer (a Trojan archer who fought on the Greek side) was exiled and later founded Salamis, a city on the island of Cyprus. (This Teucer is not the legendary founder of Troy; see line 279.)

Within the palace
all is decked with adornments, lavish, regal splendor.
In the central hall they are setting out a banquet,   760
draping the gorgeous purple, intricately worked,
heaping the board with grand displays of silver
and gold engraved with her fathers' valiant deeds,
a long, unending series of captains and commands,
traced through a line of heroes since her country's birth.   765

Aeneas—a father's love would give the man no rest—
quickly sends Achates down to the ships to take
the news to Ascanius, bring him back to Carthage.
All his paternal care is focused on his son.
He tells Achates to fetch some gifts as well,   770
plucked from the ruins of Troy: a gown stiff
with figures stitched in gold, and a woven veil
with yellow sprays of acanthus round the border.
Helen's glory, gifts she carried out of Mycenae,
fleeing Argos for Troy to seal her wicked marriage—   775
the marvelous handiwork of Helen's mother, Leda.
Aeneas adds the scepter Ilione used to bear,
the eldest daughter of Priam; a necklace too,
strung with pearls, and a crown of double bands,
one studded with gems, the other, gold. Achates,   780
following orders, hurries toward the ships.

But now Venus is mulling over some new schemes,
new intrigues. Altered in face and figure, Cupid[7]
would go in place of the captivating Ascanius,
using his gifts to fire the queen to madness,   785
weaving a lover's ardor through her bones.
No doubt Venus fears that treacherous house
and the Tyrians' forked tongues,
and brutal Juno inflames her anguish too
and her cares keep coming back as night draws on.   790
So Venus makes an appeal to Love, her winged son:
"You, my son, are my strength, my greatest power—
you alone, my son, can scoff at the lightning bolts
the high and mighty Father hurled against Typhoeus.[8]
Help me, I beg you. I need all your immortal force.   795
Your brother Aeneas is tossed round every coast on earth,
thanks to Juno's ruthless hatred, as you well know,
and time and again you've grieved to see my grief.
But now Phoenician Dido has him in her clutches,
holding him back with smooth, seductive words,   800
and I fear the outcome of Juno's welcome here . . .
She won't sit tight while Fate is turning on its hinge.
So I plan to forestall her with ruses of my own

7. Cupid (whose name means "desire") is the
son of Venus and the god of sexual desire.
8. Jupiter hurled thunderbolts at the monster

Typhoeus (Typhon), and finally trapped him
under Mount Etna.

and besiege the queen with flames,
and no goddess will change her mood—she's mine,   805
my ally-in-arms in my great love for Aeneas.

   "Now how can you go about this? Hear my plan.
His dear father has just sent for the young prince—
he means the world to me—and he's bound for Carthage now,
bearing presents saved from the sea, the flames of Troy.   810
I'll lull him into a deep sleep and hide him far away
on Cythera's heights or high Idalium,[9] my shrines,
so he cannot learn of my trap or spring it open
while it's being set. And you with your cunning,
forge his appearance—just one night, no more—put on   815
the familiar features of the boy, boy that you are,
so when the wine flows free at the royal board
and Dido, lost in joy, cradles you in her lap,
caressing, kissing you gently, you can breathe
your secret fire into her, poison the queen   820
and she will never know."
                    Cupid leaps at once
to his loving mother's orders. Shedding his wings
he masquerades as Iulus, prancing with his stride.
But now Venus distils a deep, soothing sleep
into Iulus' limbs, and warming him in her breast   825
the goddess spirits him off to her high Idalian grove
where beds of marjoram breathe and embrace him with aromatic
flowers and rustling shade.
                  Now Cupid is on the move,
under her orders, bringing the Tyrians royal gifts,
his spirits high as Achates leads him on.   830
Arriving, he finds the queen already poised
on a golden throne beneath the sumptuous hangings,
commanding the very center of her palace. Now Aeneas,
the good captain, enters, then the Trojan soldiers,
taking their seats on couches draped in purple.   835
Servants pour them water to rinse their hands,
quickly serving them bread from baskets, spreading
their laps with linens, napkins clipped and smooth.
In the kitchens are fifty serving-maids assigned
to lay out foods in a long line, course by course,   840
and honor the household gods by building fires high.
A hundred other maids and a hundred men, all matched in age,
are spreading the feast on trestles, setting out the cups.
And Tyrians join them, bustling through the doors,
filling the hall with joy, to take invited seats   845
on brocaded couches. They admire Aeneas' gifts,
admire Iulus now—the glowing face of the god
and the god's dissembling words—and Helen's gown
and the veil adorned with a yellow acanthus border.

9. Another town with a temple of Venus, in Cyprus.

But above all, tragic Dido, doomed to a plague   850
about to strike, cannot feast her eyes enough,
thrilled both by the boy and gifts he brings
and the more she looks the more the fire grows.
But once he's embraced Aeneas, clung to his neck
to sate the deep love of his father, deluded father,   855
Cupid makes for the queen. Her gaze, her whole heart
is riveted on him now, and at times she even warms him
snugly in her breast, for how can she know, poor Dido,
what a mighty god is sinking into her, to her grief?
But he, recalling the wishes of his mother Venus,   860
blots out the memory of Sychaeus bit by bit,
trying to seize with a fresh, living love
a heart at rest for long—long numb to passion.

                                              Then,
with the first lull in the feast, the tables cleared away,
they set out massive bowls and crown the wine with wreaths.   865
A vast din swells in the palace, voices reverberating
through the echoing halls. They light the lamps,
hung from the coffered ceilings sheathed in gilt,
and blazing torches burn the night away.
The queen calls for a heavy golden bowl,   870
studded with jewels and brimmed with unmixed wine,
the bowl that Belus[1] and all of Belus' sons had brimmed,
and the hall falls hushed as Dido lifts a prayer:
"Jupiter, you, they say, are the god who grants
the laws of host and guest. May this day be one   875
of joy for Tyrians here and exiles come from Troy,
a day our sons will long remember. Bacchus,[2]
giver of bliss, and Juno, generous Juno,
bless us now. And come, my people, celebrate
with all goodwill this feast that makes us one!"   880

    With that prayer, she poured a libation to the gods,
tipping wine on the board, and tipping it, she was first
to take the bowl, brushing it lightly with her lips,
then gave it to Bitias—laughing, goading him on
and he took the plunge, draining the foaming bowl,   885
drenching himself in its brimming, overflowing gold,
and the other princes drank in turn. Then Iopas,
long-haired bard, strikes up his golden lyre
resounding through the halls. Giant Atlas[3]
had been his teacher once, and now he sings   890
the wandering moon and laboring sun eclipsed,
the roots of the human race and the wild beasts,
the source of storms and the lightning bolts on high,
Arcturus, the rainy Hyades and the Great and Little Bears,[4]

1. Dido's father.
2. God of wine (Dionysus in Greek mythology).
3. A Titan condemned for his defiance of

Jupiter to hold up the sky forever.
4. Stars and constellations.

and why the winter suns so rush to bathe themselves in the sea   895
and what slows down the nights to a long lingering crawl . . .
And time and again the Tyrians burst into applause
and the Trojans took their lead. So Dido, doomed,
was lengthening out the night by trading tales
as she drank long draughts of love—asking Aeneas   900
question on question, now about Priam, now Hector,
what armor Memnon, son of the Morning, wore at Troy,
how swift were the horses of Diomedes? How strong was Achilles?
"Wait, come, my guest," she urges, "tell us your own story,
start to finish—the ambush laid by the Greeks, the pain   905
your people suffered, the wanderings you have faced.
For now is the seventh summer that has borne you
wandering all the lands and seas on earth."

BOOK II

[The Final Hours of Troy]

Silence. All fell hushed, their eyes fixed on Aeneas now
as the founder of his people, high on a seat of honor,
set out on his story: "Sorrow, unspeakable sorrow,
my queen, you ask me to bring to life once more,
how the Greeks uprooted Troy in all her power,   5
our kingdom mourned forever. What horrors I saw,
a tragedy where I played a leading role myself.
Who could tell such things—not even a Myrmidon,
a Dolopian,[5] or comrade of iron-hearted Ulysses[6]—
and still refrain from tears? And now, too,   10
the dank night is sweeping down from the sky
and the setting stars incline our heads to sleep.
But if you long so deeply to know what we went through,
to hear, in brief, the last great agony of Troy,
much as I shudder at the memory of it all—   15
I shrank back in grief—I'll try to tell it now . . .

    "Ground down by the war and driven back by Fate,
the Greek captains had watched the years slip by
until, helped by Minerva's superhuman skill,
they built that mammoth horse, immense as a mountain,   20
lining its ribs with ship timbers hewn from pine.
An offering to secure safe passage home, or so
they pretend, and the story spreads through Troy.
But they pick by lot the best, most able-bodied men
and stealthily lock them into the horse's dark flanks   25
till the vast hold of the monster's womb is packed
with soldiers bristling weapons.
            "Just in sight of Troy
an island rises, Tenedos, famed in the old songs,

---

5. Myrmidons and Dolopians are companions   6. Roman name for Odysseus.
of Achilles.

powerful, rich, while Priam's realm stood fast.
Now it's only a bay, a treacherous cove for ships.   30
Well there they sail, hiding out on its lonely coast
while we thought—gone! Sped home on the winds to Greece.
So all Troy breathes free, relieved of her endless sorrow.
We fling open the gates and stream out, elated to see
the Greeks' abandoned camp, the deserted beachhead.   35
Here the Dolopians[7] formed ranks—
                                    "Here savage Achilles
pitched his tents—
                    "Over there the armada moored
and here the familiar killing-fields of battle.
Some gaze wonderstruck at the gift for Pallas,
the virgin never wed[8]—transfixed by the horse,   40
its looming mass, our doom. Thymoetes leads the way.
'Drag it inside the walls,' he urges, 'plant it high
on the city heights!' Inspired by treachery now
or the fate of Troy was moving toward this end.
But Capys with other saner heads who take his side,   45
suspecting a trap in any gift the Greeks might offer,
tells us: 'Fling it into the sea or torch the thing to ash
or bore into the depths of its womb where men can hide!'
The common people are split into warring factions.

    "But now, out in the lead with a troop of comrades,   50
down Laocoön[9] runs from the heights in full fury,
calling out from a distance: 'Poor doomed fools,
have you gone mad, you Trojans?
You really believe the enemy's sailed away?
Or any gift of the Greeks is free of guile?   55
Is that how well you know Ulysses? Trust me,
either the Greeks are hiding, shut inside those beams,
or the horse is a battle-engine geared to breach our walls,
spy on our homes, come down on our city, overwhelm us—
or some other deception's lurking deep inside it.   60
Trojans, never trust that horse. Whatever it is,
I fear the Greeks, especially bearing gifts.'

"In that spirit, with all his might he hurled
a huge spear straight into the monster's flanks,
the mortised timberwork of its swollen belly.   65
Quivering, there it stuck, and the stricken womb
came booming back from its depths with echoing groans.
If Fate and our own wits had not gone against us,
surely Laocoön would have driven us on, now,
to rip the Greek lair open with iron spears   70
and Troy would still be standing—
proud fortress of Priam, you would tower still!

---

7. From Dolopia, a region in Greece.   9. A Trojan priest of Neptune.
8. The goddess Athena was famously a virgin.

"Suddenly, in the thick of it all, a young soldier,
hands shackled behind his back, with much shouting
Trojan shepherds were hauling him toward the king.   75
They'd come on the man by chance, a total stranger.
He'd given himself up, with one goal in mind:
to open Troy to the Greeks and lay her waste.
He trusted to courage, nerved for either end,
to weave his lies or face his certain death.   80
Young Trojan recruits, keen to have a look,
came scurrying up from all sides, crowding round,
outdoing each other to make a mockery of the captive.
Now, hear the treachery of the Greeks and learn
from a single crime the nature of the beast . . .   85
Haggard, helpless, there in our midst he stood,
all eyes riveted on him now, and turning a wary glance
at the lines of Trojan troops he groaned and spoke:
'Where can I find some refuge, where on land, on sea?
What's left for me now? A man of so much misery!   90
Nothing among the Greeks, no place at all. And worse,
I see my Trojan enemies crying for my blood.'

        "His groans
convince us, cutting all our show of violence short.
We press him: 'Tell us where you were born, your family.
What news do you bring? Tell us what you trust to,   95
such a willing captive.'

       "'All of it, my king,
I'll tell you, come what may, the whole true story.
Greek I am, I don't deny it. No, that first.
Fortune may have made me a man of misery
but, wicked as she is,   100
she can't make Sinon a lying fraud as well.

        "'Now,
perhaps you've caught some rumor of Palamedes,[1]
Belus' son, and his shining fame that rings in song.
The Greeks charged him with treason, a trumped-up charge,
an innocent man, and just because he opposed the war   105
they put him to death, but once he's robbed of the light,
they mourn him sorely. Now I was his blood kin,
a youngster when my father, a poor man, sent me
off to the war at Troy as Palamedes' comrade.
Long as he kept his royal status, holding forth   110
in the councils of the kings, I had some standing too,
some pride of place. But once he left the land of the living,
thanks to the jealous, forked tongue of our Ulysses—
you're no stranger to *his* story—I was shattered,
I dragged out my life in the shadows, grieving,   115
seething alone, in silence . . .
outraged by my innocent friend's demise until

---

1. A Greek warrior who advised the Greeks to return home from Troy. Odysseus persuaded them that he was a traitor, and had him killed. He was descended from the Egyptian king Belus.

I burst out like a madman, swore if I ever returned
in triumph to our native Argos, ever got the chance
I'd take revenge, and my oath provoked a storm of hatred.   120
That was my first step on the slippery road to ruin.
From then on, Ulysses kept tormenting me, pressing
charge on charge; from then on, he bruited about
his two-edged rumors among the rank and file.
Driven by guilt, he looked for ways to kill me,   125
he never rested until, making Calchas[2] his henchman—
but why now? Why go over that unforgiving ground again?
Why waste words? If you think all Greeks are one,
if hearing the name *Greek* is enough for you,
it's high time you made me pay the price.   130
How that would please the man of Ithaca,[3]
how the sons of Atreus would repay you!'

                                          "Now, of course,
we burn to question him, urge him to explain—
blind to how false the cunning Greeks could be.
All atremble, he carries on with his tale,   135
lying from the cockles of his heart:

                                     "'Time and again
the Greeks had yearned to abandon Troy—bone-tired
from a long hard war—to put it far behind and
beat a clean retreat. Would to god they had.
But time and again, as they were setting sail,   140
the heavy seas would keep them confined to port
and the Southwind filled their hearts with dread
and worst of all, once this horse, this mass of timber
with locking planks, stood stationed here at last,
the thunderheads rumbled up and down the sky.   145
So, at our wit's end, we send Eurypylus off
to question Apollo's oracle now, and back
he comes from the god's shrine with these bleak words:
"With blood you appeased the winds, with a virgin's sacrifice
when you, you Greeks, first sought the shores of Troy.[4]   150
With blood you must seek fair winds to sail you home,
must sacrifice one more Greek life in return."

    "'As the word spread, the ranks were struck dumb
and icy fear sent shivers down their spines.
Whom did the god demand? Who'd meet his doom?   155
Just that moment the Ithacan hailed the prophet,
Calchas, into our midst—he'd twist it out of him,
what was the gods' will? The army rose in uproar.
Even then our soldiers sensed that I was the one,
the target of that Ulysses' vicious schemes—   160
they saw it coming, still they held their tongues.

2. Greek prophet.
3. Greek island ruled by Ulysses.
4. I phigeneia was sacrificed by her father,

Agamemnon, to allow the winds to blow the
fleet to Troy.

For ten days the seer, silent, closed off in his tent,
refused to say a word or betray a man to death.
But at last, goaded on by Ulysses' mounting threats
but in fact conniving in their plot, he breaks his silence   165
and dooms me to the altar. And the army gave consent.
The death that each man dreaded turned to the fate
of one poor soul: a burden they could bear.

  "'The day of infamy soon came . . .
the sacred rites were all performed for the victim,   170
the salted meal strewn, the bands tied round my head.
But I broke free of death, I tell you, burst my shackles,
yes, and hid all night in the reeds of a marshy lake,
waiting for them to sail—if only they would sail!
Well, no hope now of seeing the land where I was born   175
or my sweet children, the father I longed for all these years.
Maybe they'll wring from *them* the price for my escape,
avenge my guilt with my loved ones' blood, poor things.
I beg you, king, by the Powers who know the truth,
by any trust still uncorrupt in the world of men,   180
pity a man whose torment knows no bounds.
Pity me in my pain.
I know in my soul I don't deserve to suffer.'

  "He wept and won his life—our pity, too.
Priam takes command, has him freed from the ropes   185
and chains that bind him fast, and hails him warmly:
'Whoever you are, from now on, now you've lost the Greeks,
put them out of your mind and you'll be one of us.
But answer my questions. Tell me the whole truth.
Why did they raise up this giant, monstrous horse?   190
Who conceived it? What's it for? its purpose?
A gift to the gods? A great engine of battle?'

  "He broke off. Sinon, adept at deceit,
with all his Greek cunning lifted his hands,
just freed from their fetters, up to the stars   195
and prayed: 'Bear witness, you eternal fires of the sky
and you inviolate will of the gods! Bear witness,
altar and those infernal knives that I escaped
and the sacred bands I wore myself: the victim.
It's right to break my sworn oath to the Greeks,   200
it's right to detest those men and bring to light
all they're hiding now. No laws of my native land
can bind me here. Just keep your promise, Troy,
and if I can save you, you must save me too—
if I reveal the truth and pay you back in full.   205

  "'All the hopes of the Greeks, their firm faith
in a war they'd launched themselves
had always hinged on Pallas Athena's help.

But from the moment that godless Diomedes,
flanked by Ulysses, the mastermind of crime, 210
attacked and tore the fateful image of Pallas
out of her own hallowed shrine,[5] and cut down
the sentries ringing your city heights and seized
that holy image and even dared touch the sacred bands
on the virgin goddess' head with hands reeking blood— 215
from that hour on, the high hopes of the Greeks
had trickled away like a slow, ebbing tide . . .
They were broken, beaten men,
the will of the goddess dead set against them.
Omens of this she gave in no uncertain terms. 220
They'd hardly stood her image up in the Greek camp
when flickering fire shot from its glaring eyes
and salt sweat ran glistening down its limbs
and three times the goddess herself—a marvel—
blazed forth from the ground, shield clashing, spear brandished. 225
The prophet spurs them at once to risk escape by sea:
"You cannot root out Troy with your Greek spears unless
you seek new omens in Greece and bring the god back here"—
the image they'd borne across the sea in their curved ships.
So now they've sailed away on the wind for home shores, 230
just to rearm, recruit their gods as allies yet again,
then measure back their course on the high seas and
back they'll come to attack you all off guard.

 "'So Calchas read the omens. At his command
they raised this horse, this effigy, all to atone 235
for the violated image of Pallas, her wounded pride,
her power—and expiate the outrage they had done.
But he made them do the work on a grand scale,
a tremendous mass of interlocking timbers towering
toward the sky, so the horse could not be trundled 240
through your gates or hauled inside your walls
or guard your people if they revered it well
in the old, ancient way. For if your hands
should violate this great offering to Minerva,
a total disaster—if only god would turn it 245
against the seer himself!—will wheel down
on Priam's empire, Troy, and all your futures.
But if your hands will rear it up, into your city,
then all Asia in arms can invade Greece, can launch
an all-out war right up to the walls of Pelops.[6] 250
That's the doom that awaits our sons' sons.'

 "Trapped by his craft, that cunning liar Sinon,
we believed his story. His tears, his treachery seized

---

5. An oracle stated that Troy could not be
captured as long as the statue of Athena, the
Palladium (after one of Athena's titles, Pallas),
remained in place in her shrine.
6. Pelops was the grandfather of Agamemnon
and Menelaus; his walls are the walls of Argos.

the men whom neither Tydeus' son[7] nor Achilles could defeat,
nor ten long years of war, nor all the thousand ships.   255

   "But a new portent strikes our doomed people
now—a greater omen, far more terrible, fatal,
shakes our senses, blind to what was coming.
Laocoön, the priest of Neptune picked by lot,
was sacrificing a massive bull at the holy altar   260
when—I cringe to recall it now—look there!
Over the calm deep straits off Tenedos swim
twin, giant serpents, rearing in coils, breasting
the sea-swell side by side, plunging toward the shore,
their heads, their blood-red crests surging over the waves,   265
their bodies thrashing, backs rolling in coil on mammoth coil
and the wake behind them churns in a roar of foaming spray,
and now, their eyes glittering, shot with blood and fire,
flickering tongues licking their hissing maws, yes, now
they're about to land. We blanch at the sight, we scatter.   270
Like troops on attack they're heading straight for Laocoön—
first each serpent seizes one of his small young sons,
constricting, twisting around him, sinks its fangs
in the tortured limbs, and gorges. Next Laocoön
rushing quick to the rescue, clutching his sword—   275
they trap him, bind him in huge muscular whorls,
their scaly backs lashing around his midriff twice
and twice around his throat—their heads, their flaring necks
mounting over their victim writhing still, his hands
frantic to wrench apart their knotted trunks,   280
his priestly bands splattered in filth, black venom
and all the while his horrible screaming fills the skies,
bellowing like some wounded bull struggling to shrug
loose from his neck an axe that's struck awry,
to lumber clear of the altar . . .   285
Only the twin snakes escape, sliding off and away
to the heights of Troy where the ruthless goddess
holds her shrine, and there at her feet they hide,
vanishing under Minerva's great round shield.
                                                      "At once,
I tell you, a stranger fear runs through the harrowed crowd.   290
Laocoön deserved to pay for his outrage, so they say,
he desecrated the sacred timbers of the horse,
he hurled his wicked lance at the beast's back.
'Haul Minerva's effigy up to her house,' we shout,
'Offer up our prayers to the power of the goddess!'   295
We breach our own ramparts, fling our defenses open,
all pitch into the work. Smooth running rollers
we wheel beneath its hoofs, and heavy hempen ropes
we bind around its neck, and teeming with men-at-arms
the huge deadly engine climbs our city walls . . .   300

7. Diomedes.

And round it boys and unwed girls sing hymns,
thrilled to lay a hand on the dangling ropes
as on and on it comes, gliding into the city,
looming high over the city's heart.

                  "Oh my country!
Troy, home of the gods! You great walls of the Dardans   305
long renowned in war!

              "Four times it lurched to a halt
at the very brink of the gates—four times the armor
clashed out from its womb. But we, we forged ahead,
oblivious, blind, insane, we stationed the monster
fraught with doom on the hallowed heights of Troy.   310
Even now Cassandra[8] revealed the future, opening
lips the gods had ruled no Trojan would believe.
And we, poor fools—on this, our last day—we deck
the shrines of the gods with green holiday garlands
all throughout the city . . .

              "But all the while   315
the skies keep wheeling on and night comes sweeping in
from the Ocean Stream, in its mammoth shadow swallowing up
the earth, and the Pole Star, and the treachery of the Greeks.
Dead quiet. The Trojans slept on, strewn throughout
their fortress, weary bodies embraced by slumber.   320
But the Greek armada was under way now, crossing
over from Tenedos, ships in battle formation
under the moon's quiet light, their silent ally,
homing in on the berths they know by heart—
when the king's flagship sends up a signal flare,   325
the cue for Sinon, saved by the Fates' unjust decree,
and stealthily loosing the pine bolts of the horse,
he unleashes the Greeks shut up inside its womb.
The horse stands open wide, fighters in high spirits
pouring out of its timbered cavern into the fresh air: 330
the chiefs, Thessandrus, Sthenelus, ruthless Ulysses
rappeling down a rope they dropped from its side,
and Acamas, Thoas, Neoptolemus, son of Achilles,
captain Machaon, Menelaus, Epeus himself,
the man who built that masterpiece of fraud.   335
They steal on a city buried deep in sleep and wine,
they butcher the guards, fling wide the gates and hug
their cohorts poised to combine forces. Plot complete.

    "This was the hour when rest, that gift of the gods
most heaven-sent, first comes to beleaguered mortals,   340
creeping over us now . . . when there, look,
I dreamed I saw Prince Hector before my eyes,
my comrade haggard with sorrow, streaming tears,

---

8. Daughter of King Priam. Apollo fell in love
with her and gave her the gift of unerring prophecy; but when she refused him, he turned
the gift into a curse by ensuring that nobody
would ever believe her predictions.

just as he once was, when dragged behind the chariot,
black with blood and grime, thongs piercing his swollen feet—   345
what a harrowing sight! What a far cry from the old Hector
home from battle, decked in Achilles' arms[9]—his trophies—
or fresh from pitching Trojan fire at the Greek ships.
His beard matted now, his hair clotted with blood,
bearing the wounds, so many wounds he suffered   350
fighting round his native city's walls . . .
I dreamed I addressed him first, in tears myself
I forced my voice from the depths of all my grief:
'Oh light of the Trojans—last, best hope of Troy!
What's held you back so long? How long we've waited,   355
Hector, for you to come, and now from what far shores?
How glad we are to see you, we battle-weary men,
after so many deaths, your people dead and gone,
after your citizens, your city felt such pain.
But what outrage has mutilated your face   360
so clear and cloudless once? Why these wounds?'

   "Wasting no words, no time on empty questions,
heaving a deep groan from his heart he calls out:
'Escape, son of the goddess, tear yourself from the flames!
The enemy holds our walls. Troy is toppling from her heights.   365
You have paid your debt to our king and native land.
If one strong arm could have saved Troy, my arm
would have saved the city. Now, into your hands
she entrusts her holy things, her household gods.
Take them with you as comrades in your fortunes.   370
Seek a city for them, once you have roved the seas,
erect great walls at last to house the gods of Troy!'

   "Urging so, with his own hands he carries Vesta forth
from her inner shrine, her image clad in ribbons,
filled with her power, her everlasting fire.[1]

                              "But now,   375
chaos—the city begins to reel with cries of grief,
louder, stronger, even though father's palace
stood well back, screened off by trees, but still
the clash of arms rings clearer, horror on the attack.
I shake off sleep and scrambling up to the pitched roof   380
I stand there, ears alert, and I hear a roar like fire
assaulting a wheatfield, whipped by a Southwind's fury,
or mountain torrent in full spate, flattening crops,
leveling all the happy, thriving labor of oxen,
dragging whole trees headlong down in its wake—   385
and a shepherd perched on a sheer rock outcrop
hears the roar, lost in amazement, struck dumb.
No doubting the good faith of the Greeks now,
their treachery plain as day.

9. In the *Iliad*, Achilles' companion Patroclus
bears Achilles' arms (that is, his armor and
weapons) into battle and is killed by Hector,
who seizes them as trophies.
1. In the temple of Vesta, the hearth goddess,
was a fire that was never allowed to go out.

"Already, there,
the grand house of Deiphobus[2] stormed by fire,   390
crashing in ruins—
                    "Already his neighbor Ucalegon
up in flames—
                    "The Sigean straits[3] shimmering back the blaze,
the shouting of fighters soars, the clashing blare of trumpets.
Out of my wits, I seize my arms—what reason for arms?
Just my spirit burning to muster troops for battle,   395
rush with comrades up to the city's heights,
fury and rage driving me breakneck on
as it races through my mind
what a noble thing it is to die in arms!
                              "But now, look,
just slipped out from under the Greek barrage of spears,   400
Panthus, Othrys' son, a priest of Apollo's shrine
on the citadel—hands full of the holy things,
the images of our conquered gods—he's dragging along
his little grandson, making a wild dash for our doors.
'Panthus, where's our stronghold? our last stand?'—   405
words still on my lips as he groans in answer:
'The last *day* has come for the Trojan people,
no escaping this moment. Troy's no more.
Ilium, gone—our awesome Trojan glory.
Brutal Jupiter hands it all over to Greece,   410
Greeks are lording over our city up in flames.
The horse stands towering high in the heart of Troy,
disgorging its armed men, with Sinon in his glory,
gloating over us—Sinon fans the fires.
The immense double gates are flung wide open,   415
Greeks in their thousands mass there, all who ever
sailed from proud Mycenae. Others have choked
the cramped streets, weapons brandished now
in a battle line of naked, glinting steel
tense for the kill. Only the first guards   420
at the gates put up some show of resistance,
fighting blindly on.'

     "Spurred by Panthus' words and the gods' will,
into the blaze I dive, into the fray, wherever
the din of combat breaks and war cries fill the sky,   425
wherever the battle-fury drives me on and now
I'm joined by Rhipeus, Epytus mighty in armor,
rearing up in the moonlight—
Hypanis comes to my side, and Dymas too,
flanked by the young Coroebus, Mygdon's son.   430
Late in the day he'd chanced to come to Troy
incensed with a mad, burning love for Cassandra:
son-in-law to our king, *he* would rescue Troy. Poor man,
if only he'd marked his bride's inspired ravings!

2. A son of Priam.   the Sigeion promontory overlooking Troy.
3. Channel leading into the Aegean Sea, near

"Seeing their close-packed ranks, hot for battle,⁣   435
I spur them on their way: 'Men, brave hearts,
though bravery cannot save us—if you're bent on
following me and risking all to face the worst,
look around you, see how our chances stand.
The gods who shored our empire up have left us,   440
all have deserted their altars and their shrines.
You race to defend a city already lost in flames.
But let us die, go plunging into the thick of battle.
One hope saves the defeated: they know they can't be saved!'
That fired their hearts with the fury of despair.

                                        "Now   445
like a wolfpack out for blood on a foggy night,
driven blindly on by relentless, rabid hunger,
leaving cubs behind, waiting, jaws parched—
so through spears, through enemy ranks we plow
to certain death, striking into the city's heart,   450
the shielding wings of the darkness beating round us.
Who has words to capture that night's disaster,
tell that slaughter? What tears could match
our torments now? An ancient city is falling,
a power that ruled for ages, now in ruins.   455
Everywhere lie the motionless bodies of the dead,
strewn in her streets, her homes and the gods' shrines
we held in awe. And not only Trojans pay the price in blood—
at times the courage races back in their conquered hearts
and they cut their enemies down in all their triumph.   460
Everywhere, wrenching grief, everywhere, terror
and a thousand shapes of death.

                                        "And the first Greek
to cross our path? Androgeos leading a horde of troops
and taking *us* for allies on the march, the fool,
he even gives us a warm salute and calls out: 465
'Hurry up, men. Why holding back, why now,
why drag your heels? Troy's up in flames,
the rest are looting, sacking the city heights.
But you, have you just come from the tall ships?'
Suddenly, getting no password he can trust,   470
he sensed he'd stumbled into enemy ranks!
Stunned, he recoiled, swallowing back his words
like a man who threads his way through prickly brambles,
pressing his full weight on the ground, and blindly treads
on a lurking snake and back he shrinks in instant fear   475
as it rears in anger, puffs its blue-black neck.
Just so Androgeos, seeing us, cringes with fear,
recoiling, struggling to flee but we attack,
flinging a ring of steel around his cohorts—
panic takes the Greeks unsure of their ground   480
and we cut them all to pieces.
Fortune fills our sails in that first clash
and Coroebus, flushed, fired with such success,
exults: 'Comrades, wherever Fortune points the way,

wherever the first road to safety leads, let's soldier on. 485
Exchange shields with the Greeks and wear their emblems.
Call it cunning or courage: who would ask in war?
Our enemies will arm us to the hilt.'
        "With that he dons
Androgeos' crested helmet, his handsome blazoned shield
and straps a Greek sword to his hip, and comrades, 490
spirits rising, take his lead. Rhipeus, Dymas too
and our corps of young recruits—each fighter
arms himself in the loot that he just seized
and on we forge, blending in with the enemy,
battling time and again under strange gods, 495
fighting hand-to-hand in the blind dark
and many Greeks we send to the King of Death.
Some scatter back to their ships, making a run
for shore and safety. Others disgrace themselves,
so panicked they clamber back inside the monstrous horse, 500
burying into the womb they know so well.
        "But, oh
how wrong to rely on gods dead set against you!
Watch: the virgin daughter of Priam, Cassandra,
torn from the sacred depths of Minerva's shrine,
dragged by the hair, raising her burning eyes 505
to the heavens, just her eyes, so helpless,
shackles kept her from raising her gentle hands.
Coroebus could not bear the sight of it—mad with rage
he flung himself at the Greek lines and met his death.
Closing ranks we charge after him, into the thick of battle 510
and face our first disaster. Down from the temple roof
come showers of lances hurled by our own comrades there,
duped by the look of our Greek arms, our Greek crests
that launched this grisly slaughter. And worse still,
the Greeks roaring with anger—we had saved Cassandra— 515
attack us from all sides! Ajax, fiercest of all and
Atreus' two sons and the whole Dolopian army,
wild as a rampaging whirlwind, gusts clashing,
the West- and the South- and Eastwind riding high
on the rushing horses of the dawn, and the woods howl 520
and Nereus[4] thrashing his savage trident, churns up
the sea exploding in foam from its rocky depths.
And those Greeks we had put to rout, our ruse
in the murky night stampeding them headlong on
throughout the city—back they come, the first 525
to see that our shields and spears are naked lies,
to mark the words on our lips that jar with theirs.
In a flash, superior numbers overwhelm us.
Coroebus is first to go,
cut down by Peneleus' right hand he sprawls 530

4. An old sea god.

at Minerva's shrine, the goddess, power of armies.[5]
Rhipeus falls too, the most righteous man in Troy,
the most devoted to justice, true, but the gods
had other plans.
        "Hypanis, Dymas die as well,
run through by their own men—
                  "And you, Panthus,   535
not all your piety, all the sacred bands you wore
as Apollo's priest could save you as you fell.
Ashes of Ilium, last flames that engulfed my world—
I swear by you that in your last hour I never shrank
from the Greek spears, from any startling hazard of war—   540
if Fate had struck me down, my sword-arm earned it all.
Now we are swept away, Iphitus, Pelias with me,
one weighed down with age and the other slowed
by a wound Ulysses gave him—heading straight
for Priam's palace, driven there by the outcries.   545

    "And there, I tell you, a pitched battle flares!
You'd think no other battles could match its fury,
nowhere else in the city were people dying so.
Invincible Mars[6] rears up to meet us face to face
with waves of Greeks assaulting the roofs, we see them   550
choking the gateway, under a tortoise-shell of shields,[7]
and the scaling ladders cling to the steep ramparts—
just at the gates the raiders scramble up the rungs,
shields on their left arms thrust out for defense,
their right hands clutching the gables.   555
Over against them, Trojans ripping the tiles
and turrets from all their roofs—the end is near,
they can see it now, at the brink of death, desperate
for weapons, some defense, and these, these missiles they send
reeling down on the Greeks' heads—the gilded beams,   560
the inlaid glory of all our ancient fathers.
Comrades below, posted in close-packed ranks,
block the entries, swordpoints drawn and poised.
My courage renewed, I rush to relieve the palace,
brace the defenders, bring the defeated strength.   565

    "There was a secret door, a hidden passage
linking the wings of Priam's house—remote,
far to the rear. Long as our realm still stood,
Andromache, poor woman, would often go this way,
unattended, to Hector's parents, taking the boy   570
Astyanax[8] by the hand to see grandfather Priam.
I slipped through the door, up to the jutting roof
where the doomed Trojans were hurling futile spears.

5. Minerva was a warrior goddess, often depicted carrying weapons.
6. God of war (equivalent of the Greek Ares).
7. Position adopted by Roman soldiers: packed tightly together, they put their shields above their heads, making the army look like a tortoise.
8. Son of Hector and his wife, Andromache.

There was a tower soaring high at the peak toward the sky,
our favorite vantage point for surveying all of Troy   575
and the Greek fleet and camp. We attacked that tower
with iron crowbars, just where the upper-story planks
showed loosening joints—we rocked it, wrenched it free
of its deep moorings and all at once we heaved it toppling
down with a crash, trailing its wake of ruin to grind   580
the massed Greeks assaulting left and right. But on
came Greek reserves, no letup, the hail of rocks,
the missiles of every kind would never cease.

    "There at the very edge of the front gates
springs Pyrrhus, son of Achilles, prancing in arms,   585
aflash in his shimmering brazen sheath like a snake
buried the whole winter long under frozen turf,
swollen to bursting, fed full on poisonous weeds
and now it springs into light, sloughing its old skin
to glisten sleek in its newfound youth, its back slithering,   590
coiling, its proud chest rearing high to the sun,
its triple tongue flickering through its fangs.
Backing him now comes Periphas, giant fighter,
Automedon too, Achilles' henchman, charioteer
who bore the great man's armor—backing Pyrrhus,   595
the young fighters from Scyros raid the palace,
hurling firebrands at the roofs. Out in the lead,
Pyrrhus seizes a double-axe and batters the rocky sill
and ripping the bronze posts out of their sockets,
hacking the rugged oaken planks of the doors,   600
makes a breach, a gaping maw, and there, exposed,
the heart of the house, the sweep of the colonnades,
the palace depths of the old kings and Priam lie exposed
and they see the armed sentries bracing at the portals.

    "But all in the house is turmoil, misery, groans,   605
the echoing chambers ring with cries of women,
wails of mourning hit the golden stars.
Mothers scatter in panic down the palace halls
and embrace the pillars, cling to them, kiss them hard.
But on he comes, Pyrrhus with all his father's force,   610
no bolts, not even the guards can hold him back—
under the ram's repeated blows the doors cave in,
the doorposts, prised from their sockets, crash flat.
Force makes a breach and the Greeks come storming through,
butcher the sentries, flood the entire place with men-at-arms. 615
No river so wild, so frothing in spate, bursting its banks
to overpower the dikes, anything in its way, its cresting
tides stampeding in fury down on the fields to sweep
the flocks and stalls across the open plain.
I saw him myself, Pyrrhus crazed with carnage   620
and Atreus' two sons just at the threshold—

"I saw
Hecuba with her hundred daughters and daughters-in-law,[9]
saw Priam fouling with blood the altar fires
he himself had blessed.

"Those fifty bridal-chambers
filled with the hope of children's children still to come,   625
the pillars proud with trophies, gilded with Eastern gold,
they all come tumbling down—
and the Greeks hold what the raging fire spares.

   "Perhaps you wonder how Priam met his end.
When he saw his city stormed and seized, his gates   630
wrenched apart, the enemy camped in his palace depths,
the old man dons his armor long unused, he clamps it
round his shoulders shaking with age and, all for nothing,
straps his useless sword to his hip, then makes
for the thick of battle, out to meet his death.   635
At the heart of the house an ample altar stood,
naked under the skies,
an ancient laurel bending over the shrine,
embracing our household gods within its shade.
Here, flocking the altar, Hecuba and her daughters   640
huddled, blown headlong down like doves by a black storm—
clutching, all for nothing, the figures of their gods.
Seeing Priam decked in the arms he'd worn as a young man,
'Are you insane?' she cries, 'Poor husband, what impels you
to strap that sword on now? Where are you rushing?   645
Too late for such defense, such help. Not even
my own Hector, if *he* came to the rescue now . . .
Come to me, Priam. This altar will shield us all
or else you'll die with us.'

"With those words,
drawing him toward her there, she made a place   650
for the old man beside the holy shrine.

"Suddenly,
look, a son of Priam, Polites, just escaped
from slaughter at Pyrrhus' hands, comes racing in
through spears, through enemy fighters, fleeing down
the long arcades and deserted hallways—badly wounded,   655
Pyrrhus hot on his heels, a weapon poised for the kill,
about to seize him, about to run him through and pressing
home as Polites reached his parents and collapsed,
vomiting out his life blood before their eyes.
At that, Priam, trapped in the grip of death,   660
not holding back, not checking his words, his rage:
'You!' he cries, 'you and your vicious crimes!
If any power on high recoils at such an outrage,
let the gods repay you for all your reckless work,

9. Wife of Priam, king of Troy. He had fifty sons and fifty daughters—not all by Hecuba.

grant you the thanks, the rich reward you've earned.   665
You've made me see my son's death with my own eyes,
defiled a father's sight with a son's life blood.
You say you're Achilles' son? You lie! Achilles
never treated his enemy Priam so. No, he honored
a suppliant's rights, he blushed to betray my trust,   670
he restored my Hector's bloodless corpse for burial,
sent me safely home to the land I rule!'
                   "With that
and with all his might the old man flings his spear—
but too impotent now to pierce, it merely grazes
Pyrrhus' brazen shield that blocks its way   675
and clings there, dangling limp from the boss,
all for nothing. Pyrrhus shouts back: 'Well then,
down you go, a messenger to my father, Peleus' son![1]
Tell him about my vicious work, how Neoptolemus[2]
degrades his father's name—don't you forget.   680
Now—die!'
          "That said, he drags the old man
straight to the altar, quaking, slithering on through
slicks of his son's blood, and twisting Priam's hair
in his left hand, his right hand sweeping forth his sword—
a flash of steel—he buries it hilt-deep in the king's flank.   685

  "Such was the fate of Priam, his death, his lot on earth,
with Troy blazing before his eyes, her ramparts down,
the monarch who once had ruled in all his glory
the many lands of Asia, Asia's many tribes.
A powerful trunk is lying on the shore.[3]   690
The head wrenched from the shoulders.
A corpse without a name.
            "Then, for the first time
the full horror came home to me at last. I froze.
The thought of my own dear father filled my mind
when I saw the old king gasping out his life   695
with that raw wound—both men were the same age—
and the thought of my Creusa, alone, abandoned,
our house plundered, our little Iulus' fate.[4]
I look back—what forces still stood by me?
None. Totally spent in war, they'd all deserted,   700
down from the roofs they'd flung themselves to earth
or hurled their broken bodies in the flames.

---

1. Achilles was the son of Peleus. He was already dead, before the final storming of Troy killed by Paris with an arrow to the heel, his only vulnerability.
2. Literally, "New Warrior," another name for Pyrrhus, Achilles' son.
3. The detail that the body is left "on the shore"—which makes no narrative sense, since Priam is killed in the center of the city—is an allusion to the assassination of Pompey the Great. In the Roman civil war of 49–45 B.C.E., Pompey, representing the more aristocratic party, was defeated by the more populist Julius Caesar, and eventually assassinated; his body was famously abandoned on the beach of Egypt.
4. Creusa is Aeneas's wife; Iulus is his son.

["So,[5]
at just that moment I was the one man left
and then I saw her, clinging to Vesta's threshold,
hiding in silence, tucked away—Helen of Argos.   705
Glare of the fires lit my view as I looked down,
scanning the city left and right, and there she was . . .
terrified of the Trojans' hate, now Troy was overpowered,
terrified of the Greeks' revenge, her deserted husband's rage—
that universal Fury, a curse to Troy and her native land   710
and here she lurked, skulking, a thing of loathing
cowering at the altar: Helen. Out it flared,
the fire inside my soul, my rage ablaze to avenge
our fallen country—pay Helen back, crime for crime.

"'So, this woman,' it struck me now, 'safe and sound   715
she'll look once more on Sparta, her native Greece?
She'll ride like a queen in triumph with her trophies?
Feast her eyes on her husband, parents, children too?
Her retinue fawning round her, Phrygian[6] ladies, slaves?
That—with Priam put to the sword? And Troy up in flames?   720
And time and again our Dardan shores have sweated blood?
Not for all the world. No fame, no memory to be won
for punishing a woman: such victory reaps no praise
but to stamp this abomination out as she deserves,
to punish her now, they'll sing my praise for *that*.   725
What joy, to glut my heart with the fires of vengeance,
bring some peace to the ashes of my people!'

"Whirling words—I was swept away by fury now]
when all of a sudden there my loving mother[7] stood
before my eyes, but I had never seen her so clearly,   730
her pure radiance shining down upon me through the night,
the goddess in all her glory, just as the gods behold
her build, her awesome beauty. Grasping my hand
she held me back, adding this from her rose-red lips:
'My son, what grief could incite such blazing anger?   735
Why such fury? And the love you bore me once,
where has it all gone? Why don't you look first
where you left your father, Anchises, spent with age?
Do your wife, Creusa, and son Ascanius still survive?
The Greek battalions are swarming round them all,   740
and if my love had never rushed to the rescue,
flames would have swept them off by now or
enemy sword-blades would have drained their blood.
Think: it's not that beauty, Helen, you should hate,
not even Paris, the man that you should blame, no,   745

---

5. This passage is bracketed because many scholars believe it does not belong in the poem, since it is contradicted by a passage in book VI (573–623). The contradiction may be evidence of the *Aeneid*'s unfinished status at Virgil's death.
6. That is, Trojan. Phrygia was the region of modern-day Turkey that included Troy.
7. Venus.

it's the gods, the ruthless gods who are tearing down
the wealth of Troy, her toppling crown of towers.
Look around. I'll sweep it all away, the mist
so murky, dark, and swirling around you now,
it clouds your vision, dulls your mortal sight.   750
You are my son. Never fear my orders.
Never refuse to bow to my commands.
                                    "'There,
yes, where you see the massive ramparts shattered,
blocks wrenched from blocks, the billowing smoke and ash—
it's Neptune himself,[8] prising loose with his giant trident   755
the foundation-stones of Troy, he's making the walls quake,
ripping up the entire city by her roots.
                                    "'There's Juno,
cruelest in fury, first to commandeer the Scaean Gates,[9]
sword at her hip and mustering comrades, shock troops
streaming out of the ships.
                                    "'Already up on the heights—   760
turn around and look—there's Pallas holding the fortress,
flaming out of the clouds, her savage Gorgon glaring.[1]
Even Father himself, he's filling the Greek hearts
with courage, stamina—Jove in person spurring the gods
to fight the Trojan armies!
                                    "'Run for your life, my son.   765
Put an end to your labors. I will never leave you,
I will set you safe at your father's door.'

    "Parting words. She vanished into the dense night.
And now they all come looming up before me,
terrible shapes, the deadly foes of Troy,   770
the gods gigantic in power.
                                    "Then at last
I saw it all, all Ilium settling into her embers,
Neptune's Troy, toppling over now from her roots
like a proud, veteran ash on its mountain summit,
chopped by stroke after stroke of the iron axe as   775
woodsmen fight to bring it down, and over and
over it threatens to fall, its boughs shudder,
its leafy crown quakes and back and forth it sways
till overwhelmed by its wounds, with a long last groan
it goes—torn up from its heights it crashes down   780
in ruins from its ridge . . .
Venus leading, down from the roof I climb
and win my way through fires and massing foes.
The spears recede, the flames roll back before me.

---

8. The god of the sea and of earthquakes
(Poseidon in Greek mythology), who was hostile to the Trojans, since Laomedon, an early
king of Troy, failed to repay him for helping to
build the city walls.

9. The main entrance to Troy.
1. Pallas Athena's shield displays the head of
a Gorgon: the monster that turns those who
look at it to stone.

"At last, gaining the door of father's ancient house,   785
my first concern was to find the man, my first wish
to spirit him off, into the high mountain range,
but father, seeing Ilium razed from the earth,
refused to drag his life out now and suffer exile.
'You,' he argued, 'you in your prime, untouched by age,   790
your blood still coursing strong, you hearts of oak,
you are the ones to hurry your escape. Myself,
if the gods on high had wished me to live on,
they would have saved my palace for me here.
Enough—more than enough—that I have seen   795
one sack of my city, once survived its capture.²
Here I lie, here laid out for death. Come say
your parting salutes and leave my body so.
I will find my own death, sword in hand:
my enemies keen for spoils will be so kind.   800
Death without burial? A small price to pay.
For years now, I've lingered out my life,
despised by the gods, a dead weight to men,
ever since the Father of Gods and King of Mortals
stormed at me with his bolt and scorched me with its fire.'³   805

   "So he said, planted there. Nothing could shake him now.
But we dissolved in tears, my wife, Creusa, Ascanius,
the whole household, begging my father not to pull
our lives down with him, adding his own weight
to the fate that dragged us down.   810
He still refuses, holds to his resolve,
clings to the spot. And again I rush to arms,
desperate to die myself. Where could I turn?
What were our chances now, at this point?
'What!' I cried. 'Did you, my own father,   815
dream that I could run away and desert you here?
How could such an outrage slip from a father's lips?
If it please the gods that nothing of our great city
shall survive—if you are bent on adding your own death
to the deaths of Troy and of all your loved ones too,   820
the doors of the deaths you crave are spread wide open.
Pyrrhus will soon be here, bathed in Priam's blood,
Pyrrhus who butchers sons in their fathers' faces,
slaughters fathers at the altar. Was it for this,
my loving mother, you swept me clear of the weapons,   825
free of the flames? Just to see the enemy camped
in the very heart of our house, to see my son, Ascanius,
see my father, my wife, Creusa, with them, sacrificed,
massacred in each other's blood?

2. Troy had been sacked by Hercules, when
the previous king (Laomedon) cheated him.
3. When Anchises had his affair with Venus,
he was sworn to secrecy. He broke his word
and boasted about sleeping with the goddess,
so Jupiter hurled a thunderbolt at him as punishment, making him lame.

"'Arms, my comrades,
bring me arms! The last light calls the defeated.
Send me back to the Greeks, let me go back
to fight new battles. Not all of us here
will die today without revenge.'

                           "Now buckling on
my sword again and working my left arm through
the shieldstrap, grasping it tightly, just as I
was rushing out, right at the doors my wife, Creusa,
look, flung herself at my feet and hugged my knees
and raised our little Iulus up to his father.
'If you are going off to die,' she begged,
'then take us with you too,
to face the worst together. But if your battles
teach you to hope in arms, the arms you buckle on,
your first duty should be to guard our house.
Desert us, leave us now—to whom? Whom?
Little Iulus, your father and your wife,
so I once was called.'

                     "So Creusa cries,
her wails of anguish echoing through the house
when out of the blue an omen strikes—a marvel!
Now as we held our son between our hands
and both our grieving faces, a tongue of fire,
watch, flares up from the crown of Iulus' head,
a subtle flame licking his downy hair, feeding
around the boy's brow, and though it never harmed him,
panicked, we rush to shake the flame from his curls
and smother the holy fire, damp it down with water.
But Father Anchises lifts his eyes to the stars in joy
and stretching his hands toward the sky, sings out:
'Almighty Jove! If any prayer can persuade you now,
look down on us—that's all I ask—if our devotion
has earned it, grant us another omen, Father,
seal this first clear sign.'

                          "No sooner said
than an instant peal of thunder crashes on the left
and down from the sky a shooting star comes gliding,
trailing a flaming torch to irradiate the night
as it comes sweeping down. We watch it sailing
over the topmost palace roofs to bury itself,
still burning bright, in the forests of Mount Ida,[4]
blazing its path with light, leaving a broad furrow,
a fiery wake, and miles around the smoking sulfur fumes.
Won over at last, my father rises to his full height
and prays to the gods and reveres that holy star:
'No more delay, not now! You gods of my fathers,
now I follow wherever you lead me, I am with you.
Safeguard our house, safeguard my grandson Iulus!
This sign is yours: Troy rests in your power.

830

835

840

845

850

855

860

865

870

875

4. Mountain near Troy held sacred as the birthplace of Jupiter.

I give way, my son. No more refusals.
I will go with you, your comrade.'
                                    "So he yielded
but now the roar of flames grows louder all through Troy
and the seething floods of fire are rolling closer.
'So come, dear father, climb up onto my shoulders!   880
I will carry you on my back. This labor of love
will never wear me down. Whatever falls to us now,
we both will share one peril, one path to safety.
Little Iulus, walk beside me, and you, my wife,
follow me at a distance, in my footsteps.   885
Servants, listen closely . . .
Just past the city walls a gravemound lies
where an old shrine of forsaken Ceres⁵ stands
with an ancient cypress growing close beside it—
our fathers' reverence kept it green for years.   890
Coming by many routes, it's there we meet,
our rendezvous. And you, my father, carry
our hearthgods now, our fathers' sacred vessels.
I, just back from the war and fresh from slaughter,
I must not handle the holy things—it's wrong—   895
not till I cleanse myself in running springs.'
                                    "With that,
over my broad shoulders and round my neck I spread
a tawny lion's skin for a cloak, and bowing down,
I lift my burden up. Little Iulus, clutching
my right hand, keeps pace with tripping steps.   900
My wife trails on behind. And so we make our way
along the pitch-dark paths, and I who had never flinched
at the hurtling spears or swarming Greek assaults—
now every stir of wind, every whisper of sound
alarms me, anxious both for the child beside me   905
and burden on my back. And then, nearing the gates,
thinking we've all got safely through, I suddenly
seem to catch the steady tramp of marching feet
and father, peering out through the darkness, cries:
'Run for it now, my boy, you must. They're closing in,   910
I can see their glinting shields, their flashing bronze!'

    "Then in my panic something strange, some enemy power
robbed me of my senses. Lost, I was leaving behind
familiar paths, at a run down blind dead ends
when—
                "Oh dear god, my wife, Creusa—   915
torn from me by a brutal fate! What then,
did she stop in her tracks or lose her way?
Or exhausted, sink down to rest? Who knows?
I never set my eyes on her again.
I never looked back, she never crossed my mind—   920
Creusa, lost—not till we reached that barrow

---

5. Roman goddess of agriculture (equivalent to the Greek Demeter).

sacred to ancient Ceres where, with all our people
rallied at last, she alone was missing. Lost
to her friends, her son, her husband—gone forever.
Raving, I blamed them all, the gods, the human race—   925
what crueler blow did I feel the night that Troy went down?
Ascanius, father Anchises, and all the gods of Troy,
entrusting them to my friends, I hide them well away
in a valley's shelter, don my burnished gear
and back I go to Troy . . .   930
my mind steeled to relive the whole disaster,
retrace my route through the whole city now
and put my life in danger one more time.
                              "First then,
back to the looming walls, the shadowy rear gates
by which I'd left the city, back I go in my tracks,   935
retracing, straining to find my footsteps in the dark,
with terror at every turn, the very silence makes me cringe.
Then back to my house I go—if only, only she's gone there—
but the Greeks have flooded in, seized the entire place.
All over now. Devouring fire whipped by the winds   940
goes churning into the rooftops, flames surging
over them, scorching blasts raging up the sky.
On I go and again I see the palace of Priam
set on the heights, but there in colonnades
deserted now, in the sanctuary of Juno, there   945
stand the elite watchmen, Phoenix, ruthless Ulysses
guarding all their loot. All the treasures of Troy
hauled from the burning shrines—the sacramental tables,
bowls of solid gold and the holy robes they'd seized
from every quarter—Greeks, piling high the plunder.   950
Children and trembling mothers rounded up
in a long, endless line.
                              "Why, I even dared fling
my voice through the dark, my shouts filled the streets
as time and again, overcome with grief I called out
'Creusa!' Nothing, no reply, and again 'Creusa!'   955
But then as I madly rushed from house to house,
no end in sight, abruptly, right before my eyes
I saw her stricken ghost, my own Creusa's shade.
But larger than life, the life I'd known so well.
I froze. My hackles bristled, voice choked in my throat,   960
and my wife spoke out to ease me of my anguish:
'My dear husband, why so eager to give yourself
to such mad flights of grief? It's not without
the will of the gods these things have come to pass.
But the gods forbid you to take Creusa with you,   965
bound from Troy together. The king of lofty Olympus[6]
won't allow it. A long exile is your fate . . .

---

6. Jupiter, who rules from Mount Olympus, the highest mountain in Greece.

the vast plains of the sea are yours to plow
until you reach Hesperian land, where Lydian Tiber[7]
flows with its smooth march through rich and loamy fields,   970
a land of hardy people. There great joy and a kingdom
are yours to claim, and a queen to make your wife.
Dispel your tears for Creusa, whom you loved.
I will never behold the high and mighty pride
of their palaces, the Myrmidons, the Dolopians,   975
or go as a slave to some Greek matron, no, not I,
daughter of Dardanus that I am, the wife of Venus' son.
The Great Mother of Gods[8] detains me on these shores.
And now farewell. Hold dear the son we share,
we love together.'
                "These were her parting words   980
and for all my tears—I longed to say so much—
dissolving into the empty air she left me now.
Three times I tried to fling my arms around her neck,
three times I embraced—nothing . . . her phantom
sifting through my fingers,   985
light as wind, quick as a dream in flight.
                "Gone—
and at last the night was over. Back I went to my people
and I was amazed to see what throngs of new companions
had poured in to swell our numbers, mothers, men,
our forces gathered for exile, grieving masses.   990
They had come together from every quarter,
belongings, spirits ready for me to lead them
over the sea to whatever lands I'd choose.
And now the morning star was mounting above
the high crests of Ida, leading on the day.   995
The Greeks had taken the city, blocked off every gate.
No hope of rescue now. So I gave way at last and
lifting my father, headed toward the mountains."

Summary of Book III   *Aeneas and his fleet travel across the Mediterranean. Along their way, they meet the monstrous bird-women (Harpies) and visit Andromache, widow of Hector. Anchises dies, and the storm carries the Trojans to Carthage.*

---

7. "Hesperian" is literally "western." The River Tiber runs through Rome. "Lydian" is used as an alternative for "Etruscan," since the Etrus-cans were thought to come from Lydia in Asia Minor (modern-day Turkey).
8. Cybele is the mother goddess.

BOOK IV

[The Tragic Queen of Carthage]

But the queen—too long she has suffered the pain of love,
hour by hour nursing the wound with her lifeblood,
consumed by the fire buried in her heart.
The man's courage, the sheer pride of his line,
they all come pressing home to her, over and over.   5
His looks, his words, they pierce her heart and cling—
no peace, no rest for her body, love will give her none.

A new day's dawn was moving over the earth, Aurora's torch
cleansing the sky, burning away the dank shade of night
as the restless queen, beside herself, confides now   10
to the sister of her soul: "Dear Anna, the dreams
that haunt my quaking heart! Who is this stranger
just arrived to lodge in our house—our guest?
How noble his face, his courage, and what a soldier!
I'm sure—I know it's true—the man is born of the gods.   15
Fear exposes the lowborn man at once. But, oh, how tossed
he's been by the blows of fate. What a tale he's told,
what a bitter bowl of war he's drunk to the dregs.
If my heart had not been fixed, dead set against
embracing another man in the bonds of marriage—   20
ever since my first love deceived me, cheated me
by his death—if I were not as sick as I am
of the bridal bed and torch,[9] this, perhaps,
is my one lapse that might have brought me down.
I confess it, Anna, yes. Ever since my Sychaeus,   25
my poor husband met his fate, and my own brother
shed his blood and stained our household gods,[1]
this is the only man who's roused me deeply,
swayed my wavering heart . . .
The signs of the old flame, I know them well.   30
I pray that the earth gape deep enough to take me down
or the almighty Father blast me with one bolt to the shades,
the pale, glimmering shades in hell, the pit of night,
before I dishonor you, my conscience, break your laws.
He's carried my love away, the man who wed me first—   35
may he hold it tight, safeguard it in his grave."

She broke off, her voice choking with tears
that brimmed and wet her breast.
                              But Anna answered:
"Dear one, dearer than light to me, your sister,
would you waste away, grieving your youth away, alone,   40
never to know the joy of children, all the gifts of love?
Do you really believe that's what the dust desires,

9. Torches were used at weddings in antiquity.
1. Sychaeus, the husband of Dido and a priest
of Hercules, was murdered by her brother
Pygmalion, the king of Tyre (a Phoenician
city-state on the coast of modern-day Lebanon).
Dido then fled and eventually used Sychaeus'
wealth to found Carthage on the North African
coast.

the ghosts in their ashen tombs? Have it your way.
But granted that no one tempted you in the past,
not in your great grief,   45
no Libyan suitor, and none before in Tyre,
you scorned Iarbas[2] and other lords of Africa,
sons bred by this fertile earth in all their triumph:
why resist it now, this love that stirs your heart?
Don't you recall whose lands you settled here,   50
the men who press around you? On one side
the Gaetulian cities, fighters matchless in battle,
unbridled Numidians—Syrtes, the treacherous Sandbanks.
On the other side an endless desert, parched earth
where the wild Barcan marauders[3] range at will.   55
Why mention the war that's boiling up in Tyre,
your brother's deadly threats? I think, in fact,
the favor of all the gods and Juno's backing drove
these Trojan ships on the winds that sailed them here.
Think what a city you will see, my sister, what a kingdom   60
rising high if you marry such a man! With a Trojan army
marching at our side, think how the glory of Carthage
will tower to the clouds! Just ask the gods for pardon,
win them with offerings. Treat your guests like kings.
Weave together some pretext for delay, while winter   65
spends its rage and drenching Orion[4] whips the sea—
the ships still battered, weather still too wild."

These were the words that fanned her sister's fire,
turned her doubts to hopes and dissolved her sense of shame.
And first they visit the altars, make the rounds,   70
praying the gods for blessings, shrine by shrine.
They slaughter the pick of yearling sheep, the old way,
to Ceres, Giver of Laws, to Apollo, Bacchus who sets us free
and Juno above all, who guards the bonds of marriage.[5]
Dido aglow with beauty holds the bowl in her right hand,   75
pouring wine between the horns of a pure white cow
or gravely paces before the gods' fragrant altars,
under their statues' eyes refreshing her first gifts,
dawn to dusk. And when the victims' chests are splayed,
Dido, her lips parted, pores over their entrails,   80
throbbing still, for signs . . . [6]
But, oh, how little they know, the omniscient seers.
What good are prayers and shrines to a person mad with love?
The flame keeps gnawing into her tender marrow hour by hour
and deep in her heart the silent wound lives on.   85

---

2. King of the Berbers who granted Dido
the land on which to build her city; he then
demanded her hand in marriage, but she
refused him.
3. African groups living near Carthage.
4 Giant hunter said to stir the waves when he
walks or wades across the sea.
5. Ceres: goddess of grain and agriculture.

Apollo: god of the sun, associated with civilization. Bacchus: god of wine. Juno: queen of the
gods, goddess of marriage. All were associated
with the foundation of cities.
6. It was Roman custom to inspect the entrails
of the sacrificial victim and interpret any unusual
features as signs of the future.

Dido burns with love—the tragic queen.
She wanders in frenzy through her city streets
like a wounded doe caught all off guard by a hunter
stalking the woods of Crete, who strikes her from afar
and leaves his winging steel in her flesh, and he's unaware   90
but she veers in flight through Dicte's[7] woody glades,
fixed in her side the shaft that takes her life.
                                        And now
Dido leads her guest through the heart of Carthage,
displaying Phoenician power, the city readied for him.
She'd speak her heart but her voice chokes, mid-word.   95
Now at dusk she calls for the feast to start again,
madly begging to hear again the agony of Troy,
to hang on his lips again, savoring his story.
Then, with the guests gone, and the dimming moon
quenching its light in turn, and the setting stars   100
inclining heads to sleep—alone in the echoing hall,
distraught, she flings herself on the couch that he left empty.
Lost as he is, she's lost as well, she hears him, sees him
or she holds Ascanius back and dandles him on her lap,
bewitched by the boy's resemblance to his father,   105
trying to cheat the love she dare not tell.
The towers of Carthage, half built, rise no more,
and the young men quit their combat drills in arms.
The harbors, the battlements planned to block attack,
all work's suspended now, the huge, threatening walls   110
with the soaring cranes that sway across the sky.

Now, no sooner had Jove's dear wife perceived
that Dido was in the grip of such a scourge—
no thought of pride could stem her passion now—
than Juno approaches Venus and sets a cunning trap: 115
"What a glittering prize, a triumph you carry home!
You and your boy there, you grand and glorious Powers.
Just look, one woman crushed by the craft of two gods!
I am not blind, you know. For years you've looked askance
at the homes of rising Carthage, feared our ramparts.   120
But where will it end? What good is all our strife?
Come, why don't we labor now to live in peace?
Eternal peace, sealed with the bonds of marriage.
You have it all, whatever your heart desires—
Dido's ablaze with love,   125
drawing the frenzy deep into her bones. So,
let us rule this people in common: joint command.
And let her marry her Phrygian lover, be his slave
and give her Tyrians over to your control,
her dowry in your hands!"
                        Perceiving at once   130
that this was all pretense, a ruse to shift
the kingdom of Italy onto Libyan shores,
Venus countered Juno: "Now who'd be so insane

7. Mountain in Crete.

as to shun your offer and strive with you in war?
If only Fortune crowns your proposal with success!   135
But swayed by the Fates, I have my doubts. Would Jove
want one city to hold the Tyrians and the Trojan exiles?
Would he sanction the mingling of their peoples,
bless their binding pacts? You are his wife,
with every right to probe him with your prayers.   140
You lead the way. I'll follow."
                                        "The work is mine,"
imperious Juno carried on, "but how to begin
this pressing matter now and see it through?
I'll explain in a word or so. Listen closely.
Tomorrow Aeneas and lovesick Dido plan to hunt   145
the woods together, soon as the day's first light
climbs high and the Titan's[8] rays lay bare the earth.
But while the beaters scramble to ring the glens with nets,
I'll shower down a cloudburst, hail, black driving rain—
I'll shatter the vaulting sky with claps of thunder.   150
The huntsmen will scatter, swallowed up in the dark,
and Dido and Troy's commander will make their way
to the same cave for shelter. And I'll be there,
if I can count on your own good will in this—
I'll bind them in lasting marriage, make them one.   155
Their wedding it will be!"
                                        So Juno appealed
and Venus did not oppose her, nodding in assent
and smiling at all the guile she saw through . . .

Meanwhile Dawn rose up and left her Ocean bed
and soon as her rays have lit the sky, an elite band   160
of young huntsmen streams out through the gates,
bearing the nets, wide-meshed or tight for traps
and their hunting spears with broad iron heads,
troops of Massylian[9] horsemen galloping hard,
packs of powerful hounds, keen on the scent.   165
Yet the queen delays, lingering in her chamber
with Carthaginian chiefs expectant at her doors.
And there her proud, mettlesome charger prances
in gold and royal purple, pawing with thunder-hoofs,
champing a foam-flecked bit. At last she comes,   170
with a great retinue crowding round the queen
who wears a Tyrian cloak with rich embroidered fringe.
Her quiver is gold, her hair drawn up in a golden torque
and a golden buckle clasps her purple robe in folds.
Nor do her Trojan comrades tarry. Out they march,   175
young Iulus flushed with joy.
Aeneas in command, the handsomest of them all,
advancing as her companion joins his troop with hers.
So vivid. Think of Apollo leaving his Lycian haunts
and Xanthus in winter spate, he's out to visit Delos,   180

8. Hyperion, lord of the sun and one of the
Titans (pre-Olympian gods).

9. North African tribe.

his mother's isle,[1] and strike up the dance again
while round the altars swirls a growing throng
of Cretans, Dryopians, Agathyrsians with tattoos,
and a drumming roar goes up as the god himself
strides the Cynthian ridge,[2] his streaming hair   185
braided with pliant laurel leaves entwined
in twists of gold, and arrows clash on his shoulders.
So no less swiftly Aeneas strides forward now
and his face shines with a glory like the god's.

Once the huntsmen have reached the trackless lairs   190
aloft in the foothills, suddenly, look, some wild goats
flushed from a ridge come scampering down the slopes
and lower down a herd of stags goes bounding across
the open country, ranks massed in a cloud of dust,
fleeing the high ground. But young Ascanius,   195
deep in the valley, rides his eager mount
and relishing every stride, outstrips them all,
now goats, now stags, but his heart is racing, praying—
if only they'd send among this feeble, easy game
some frothing wild boar or a lion stalking down   200
from the heights and tawny in the sun.
                              Too late—
The skies have begun to rumble, peals of thunder first
and the storm breaking next, a cloudburst pelting hail
and the troops of hunters scatter up and down the plain,
Tyrian comrades, bands of Dardans, Venus' grandson Iulus   205
panicking, running for cover, quick, and down the mountain
gulleys erupt in torrents. Dido and Troy's commander
make their way to the same cave for shelter now.
Primordial Earth and Juno, Queen of Marriage,
give the signal and lightning torches flare   210
and the high sky bears witness to the wedding,
nymphs on the mountaintops wail out the wedding hymn.
This was the first day of her death, the first of grief,
the cause of it all. From now on, Dido cares no more
for appearances, nor for her reputation, either.   215
She no longer thinks to keep the affair a secret,
no, she calls it a marriage,
using the word to cloak her sense of guilt.

Straightway Rumor flies through Libya's great cities,
Rumor, swiftest of all the evils in the world.   220
She thrives on speed, stronger for every stride,
slight with fear at first, soon soaring into the air
she treads the ground and hides her head in the clouds.
She is the last, they say, our Mother Earth produced.
Bursting in rage against the gods, she bore a sister   225

---

1. The sun god Apollo is imagined leaving
Lycia when the river Xanthus floods, and going
to Delos, which was sacred to his mother, Leto.

2. Mount Cynthus was on Delos. Cretans and
Dryopians were Greek peoples; Agathyrsians
were a Scythian people.

for Coeus and Enceladus:[3] Rumor, quicksilver afoot
and swift on the wing, a monster, horrific, huge
and under every feather on her body—what a marvel—
an eye that never sleeps and as many tongues as eyes
and as many raucous mouths and ears pricked up for news.　230
By night she flies aloft, between the earth and sky,
whirring across the dark, never closing her lids
in soothing sleep. By day she keeps her watch,
crouched on a peaked roof or palace turret,
terrorizing the great cities, clinging as fast　235
to her twisted lies as she clings to words of truth.
Now Rumor is in her glory, filling Africa's ears
with tale on tale of intrigue, bruiting her song
of facts and falsehoods mingled . . .
"Here this Aeneas, born of Trojan blood,　240
has arrived in Carthage, and lovely Dido deigns
to join the man in wedlock. Even now they warm
the winter, long as it lasts, with obscene desire,
oblivious to their kingdoms, abject thralls of lust."

Such talk the sordid goddess spreads on the lips of men,　245
then swerves in her course and heading straight for King Iarbas,
stokes his heart with hearsay, piling fuel on his fire.

Iarbas—son of an African nymph whom Jove had raped—
raised the god a hundred splendid temples across
the king's wide realm, a hundred altars too,　250
consecrating the sacred fires
that never died, eternal sentinels of the gods.
The earth was rich with blood of slaughtered herds
and the temple doorways wreathed with riots of flowers.
This Iarbas, driven wild, set ablaze by the bitter rumor,　255
approached an altar, they say, as the gods hovered round,
and lifting a suppliant's hands, he poured out prayers to Jove:
"Almighty Jove! Now as the Moors[4] adore you, feasting away
on their gaudy couches, tipping wine in your honor—
do you see this? Or are we all fools, Father,　260
to dread the bolts you hurl? All aimless then,
your fires high in the clouds that terrify us so?
All empty noise, your peals of grumbling thunder?
That woman, that vagrant! Here in my own land
she founded her paltry city for a pittance.　265
We tossed her some beach to plow—on my terms—
and then she spurns our offer of marriage, she
embraces Aeneas as lord and master in her realm.
And now this second Paris . . .
leading his troupe of eunuchs, his hair oozing oil,　270
a Phrygian bonnet tucked up under his chin, he revels
in all that he has filched, while we keep bearing gifts

3. Titans, the first children of Earth.　　　4. A North African people.

to your temples—yes, yours—coddling your reputation,
all your hollow show!"

               So King Iarbas appealed,
his hand clutching the altar, and Jove Almighty heard   275
and turned his gaze on the royal walls of Carthage
and the lovers oblivious now to their good name.
He summons Mercury,[5] gives him marching orders:
"Quick, my son, away! Call up the Zephyrs,[6]
glide on wings of the wind. Find the Dardan captain   280
who now malingers long in Tyrian Carthage, look,
and pays no heed to the cities Fate decrees are his.
Take my commands through the racing winds and tell him
this is not the man his mother, the lovely goddess, promised,
not for *this* did she save him twice from Greek attacks.   285
Never. He would be the one to master an Italy
rife with leaders, shrill with the cries of war,
to sire a people sprung from Teucer's noble blood[7]
and bring the entire world beneath the rule of law.
If such a glorious destiny cannot fire his spirit,   290
if he will not shoulder the task for his own fame,
does the father of Ascanius grudge his son
the walls of Rome? What is he plotting now?
What hope can make him loiter among his foes,
lose sight of Italian offspring still to come   295
and all the Lavinian fields?[8] Let him set sail!
This is the sum of it. This must be our message."

Jove had spoken. Mercury made ready at once
to obey the great commands of his almighty father.
First he fastens under his feet the golden sandals,   300
winged to sweep him over the waves and earth alike
with the rush of gusting winds. Then he seizes the wand
that calls the pallid spirits up from the Underworld
and ushers others down to the grim dark depths,
the wand that lends us sleep or sends it away,   305
that unseals our eyes in death.[9] Equipped with this,
he spurs the winds and swims through billowing clouds
till in mid-flight he spies the summit and rugged flanks
of Atlas, whose long-enduring peak supports the skies.[1]
Atlas: his pine-covered crown is forever girded   310
round with black clouds, battered by wind and rain;
driving blizzards cloak his shoulders with snow,
torrents course down from the old Titan's chin
and shaggy beard that bristles stiff with ice.

---

5. The messenger god; Hermes in Greek
mythology.
6. Personified winds. Zephyr is usually the
gentle west wind.
7. Teucer was the first king of Troy.
8. Lavinium is the city Aeneas will found in
Italy.

9. Mercury is the god who guides the dead to
the underworld.
1. Atlas is a Titan who was condemned by
Zeus to stand holding up the sky. The Greeks
and later the Romans associated Atlas with
the mountains of North Africa.

Here the god of Cyllene[2] landed first,   315
banking down to a stop on balanced wings.
From there, headlong down with his full weight
he plunged to the sea as a seahawk skims the waves,
rounding the beaches, rounding cliffs to hunt for fish inshore.
So Mercury of Cyllene flew between the earth and sky   320
to gain the sandy coast of Libya, cutting the winds
that sweep down from his mother's father, Atlas.

                                   Soon
as his winged feet touched down on the first huts in sight,
he spots Aeneas founding the city fortifications,
building homes in Carthage. And his sword-hilt   325
is studded with tawny jasper stars, a cloak
of glowing Tyrian purple[3] drapes his shoulders,
a gift that the wealthy queen had made herself,
weaving into the weft a glinting mesh of gold.
Mercury lashes out at once: "You, so now you lay   330
foundation stones for the soaring walls of Carthage!
Building her gorgeous city, doting on your wife.
Blind to your own realm, oblivious to your fate!
The King of the Gods, whose power sways earth and sky—
he is the one who sends me down from brilliant Olympus,   335
bearing commands for you through the racing winds.
What are you plotting now?
Wasting time in Libya—what hope misleads you so?
If such a glorious destiny cannot fire your spirit,
[if you will not shoulder the task for your own fame,][4]   340
at least remember Ascanius rising into his prime,
the hopes you lodge in Iulus, your only heir—
you owe him Italy's realm, the land of Rome!"
This order still on his lips, the god vanished
from sight into empty air.

                          Then Aeneas   345
was truly overwhelmed by the vision, stunned,
his hackles bristle with fear, his voice chokes in his throat.
He yearns to be gone, to desert this land he loves,
thunderstruck by the warnings, Jupiter's command . . .
But what can he do? What can he dare say now   350
to the queen in all her fury and win her over?
Where to begin, what opening? Thoughts racing,
here, there, probing his options, turning
to this plan, that plan—torn in two until,
at his wits' end, this answer seems the best.   355
He summons Mnestheus, Sergestus, staunch Serestus,
gives them orders: "Fit out the fleet, but not a word.
Muster the crews on shore, all tackle set to sail,
but the cause for our new course, you keep it secret."

2. Mercury was born on Mount Cyllene, in
Greece.
3. Tyre was famed in the ancient world as the
source of a rare purple dye (made from snail

shells) often used to color royal vestments.
4. Bracketed because some editors believe
the line does not belong in the text.

Yet he himself, since Dido who means the world to him   360
knows nothing, never dreaming such a powerful love
could be uprooted—he will try to approach her,
find the moment to break the news gently,
a way to soften the blow that he must leave.
All shipmates snap to commands,   365
glad to do his orders.

                    True, but the queen—
who can delude a lover?—soon caught wind
of a plot afoot, the first to sense the Trojans
are on the move . . . She fears everything now,
even with all secure. Rumor, vicious as ever,   370
brings her word, already distraught, that Trojans
are rigging out their galleys, gearing to set sail.
She rages in helpless frenzy, blazing through
the entire city, raving like some Maenad[5]
driven wild when the women shake the sacred emblems,   375
when the cyclic orgy, shouts of "Bacchus!" fire her on
and Cithaeron echoes round with maddened midnight cries.

At last she assails Aeneas, before he's said a word:
"So, you traitor, you really believed you'd keep
this a secret, this great outrage?—steal away   380
in silence from my shores? Can nothing hold you back?
Not our love? Not the pledge once sealed with our right hands?
Not even the thought of Dido doomed to a cruel death?
Why labor to rig your fleet when the winter's raw,
to risk the deep when the Northwind's closing in?   385
You cruel, heartless—Even if you were not
pursuing alien fields and unknown homes,
even if ancient Troy were standing, still,
who'd sail for Troy across such heaving seas?
You're running away—from me? Oh, I pray you   390
by these tears, by the faith in your right hand—
what else have I left myself in all my pain?—
by our wedding vows, the marriage we began,
if I deserve some decency from you now,
if anything mine has ever won your heart,   395
pity a great house about to fall, I pray you,
if prayers have any place—reject this scheme of yours!
Thanks to you, the African tribes, Numidian warlords
hate me, even my own Tyrians rise against me.
Thanks to you, my sense of honor is gone,   400
my one and only pathway to the stars,
the renown I once held dear. In whose hands,
my guest, do you leave me here to meet my death?
'Guest'—that's all that remains of 'husband' now.
But why do I linger on? Until my brother Pygmalion   405
batters down my walls? Or Iarbas drags me off, his slave?

5. The Maenads (Bacchae) were female worshippers of Bacchus, who ran wild on Mount
Cithaeron in a ritual held every other year—as

depicted in Euripides' *Bacchae*, in which one
such god-frenzied woman kills her own son.

If only you'd left a baby in my arms—our child—
before you deserted me! Some little Aeneas
playing about our halls, whose features at least
would bring you back to me in spite of all,410
I would not feel so totally devastated,
so destroyed."

The queen stopped but he,
warned by Jupiter now, his gaze held steady,
fought to master the torment in his heart. At last
he ventured a few words: "I . . . you have done me415
so many kindnesses, and you could count them all.
I shall never deny what you deserve, my queen,
never regret my memories of Dido, not while I
can recall myself and draw the breath of life.
I'll state my case in a few words. I never dreamed420
I'd keep my flight a secret. Don't imagine that.
Nor did I once extend a bridegroom's torch
or enter into a marriage pact with you.
If the Fates had left me free to live my life,
to arrange my own affairs of my own free will,425
Troy is the city, first of all, that I'd safeguard,
Troy and all that's left of my people whom I cherish.
The grand palace of Priam would stand once more,
with my own hands I would fortify a second Troy
to house my Trojans in defeat. But not now.430
Grynean Apollo's oracle says that I must seize
on Italy's noble land, his Lycian lots say 'Italy!'⁶
There lies my love, there lies my homeland now.
If you, a Phoenician, fix your eyes on Carthage,
a Libyan stronghold, tell me, why do you grudge435
the Trojans their new homes on Italian soil?
What is the crime if *we* seek far-off kingdoms too?

"My father, Anchises, whenever the darkness shrouds
the earth in its dank shadows, whenever the stars
go flaming up the sky, my father's anxious ghost440
warns me in dreams and fills my heart with fear.
My son Ascanius . . . I feel the wrong I do
to one so dear, robbing him of his kingdom,
lands in the West, his fields decreed by Fate.
And now the messenger of the gods—I swear it,445
by your life and mine—dispatched by Jove himself
has brought me firm commands through the racing winds.
With my own eyes I saw him, clear, in broad daylight,
moving through your gates. With my own ears I drank
his message in. Come, stop inflaming us both450
with your appeals. I set sail for Italy—
all against my will."

Even from the start
of his declaration, she has glared at him askance,

6. Grynia was an Aeolian city sacred to Apollo. Lycia is another cult center of Apollo.

her eyes roving over him, head to foot, with a look
of stony silence . . . till abruptly she cries out   455
in a blaze of fury: "No goddess was your mother!
No Dardanus sired your line, you traitor, liar, no,
Mount Caucasus fathered you on its flinty, rugged flanks
and the tigers of Hyrcania gave you their dugs to suck![7]
Why hide it? Why hold back? To suffer greater blows?   460
Did *he* groan when *I* wept? Even look at me? Never!
Surrender a tear? Pity the one who loves him?
What can I say first? So much to say. Now—
neither mighty Juno nor Saturn's son, the Father,[8]
gazes down on this with just, impartial eyes.   465
There's no faith left on earth!
He was washed up on my shores, helpless, and I,
I took him in, like a maniac let him share my kingdom,
salvaged his lost fleet, plucked his crews from death.
Oh I am swept by the Furies, gales of fire![9] Now   470
it's Apollo the Prophet, Apollo's Lycian oracles:
they're his masters now, and now, to top it off,
the messenger of the gods, dispatched by Jove himself,
comes rushing down the winds with his grim-set commands.
Really! What work for the gods who live on high,   475
what a concern to ruffle their repose!
I won't hold you, I won't even refute you—go!—
strike out for Italy on the winds, your realm across the sea.
I hope, I pray, if the just gods still have any power,
wrecked on the rocks midsea you'll drink your bowl   480
of pain to the dregs, crying out the name of Dido
over and over, and worlds away I'll hound you then
with pitch-black flames, and when icy death has severed
my body from its breath, then my ghost will stalk you
through the world! You'll pay, you shameless, ruthless—   485
and I will hear of it, yes, the report will reach me
even among the deepest shades of Death!"

                                                                    She breaks off
in the midst of outbursts, desperate, flinging herself
from the light of day, sweeping out of his sight,
leaving him numb with doubt, with much to fear   490
and much he means to say.
Catching her as she faints away, her women
bear her back to her marble bridal chamber
and lay her body down upon her bed.

                                            But Aeneas
is driven by duty now. Strongly as he longs   495
to ease and allay her sorrow, speak to her,
turn away her anguish with reassurance, still,
moaning deeply, heart shattered by his great love,

---

7. Dardanus was the legendary founder of
Troy. The Caucasus mountains, between the
Black and Caspian Seas, and Hyrcania, south
of the Caspian, were notoriously wild, uncivi-
lized regions.
8. Jupiter was the son of Saturn.
9. The Furies are spirits of vengeance who
carry flaming torches.

in spite of all he obeys the gods' commands
and back he goes to his ships. 500
Then the Trojans throw themselves in the labor,
launching their tall vessels down along the beach
and the hull rubbed sleek with pitch floats high again.
So keen to be gone, the men drag down from the forest
untrimmed timbers and boughs still green for oars. 505
You can see them streaming out of the whole city,
men like ants that, wary of winter's onset, pillage
some huge pile of wheat to store away in their grange
and their army's long black line goes marching through the field,
trundling their spoils down some cramped, grassy track. 510
Some put shoulders to giant grains and thrust them on,
some dress the ranks, strictly marshal stragglers,
and the whole trail seethes with labor.

What did you feel then, Dido, seeing this?
How deep were the groans you uttered, gazing now 515
from the city heights to watch the broad beaches
seething with action, the bay a chaos of outcries
right before your eyes?
                    Love, you tyrant!
To what extremes won't you compel our hearts?
Again she resorts to tears, driven to move the man, 520
or try, with prayers—a suppliant kneeling, humbling
her pride to passion. So if die she must,
she'll leave no way untried.
                    "Anna, you see
the hurly-burly all across the beach, the crews
swarming from every quarter? The wind cries for canvas, 525
the buoyant oarsmen crown their sterns with wreaths.
This terrible sorrow: since I saw it coming, Anna,
I can endure it now. But even so, my sister,
carry out for me one great favor in my pain.
To you alone he used to listen, the traitor, 530
to you confide his secret feelings. You alone
know how and when to approach him, soothe his moods.
Go, my sister! Plead with my imperious enemy.
Remind him I was never at Aulis, never swore a pact
with the Greeks to rout the Trojan people from the earth![1] 535
I sent no fleet to Troy, I never uprooted the ashes
of his father, Anchises, never stirred his shade.
Why does he shut his pitiless ears to my appeals?
Where's he rushing now? If only he would offer
one last gift to the wretched queen who loves him: 540
to wait for fair winds, smooth sailing for his flight!
I no longer beg for the long-lost marriage he betrayed,
nor would I ask him now to desert his kingdom, no,

---

1. The Greek forces mustered at Aulis before sailing to Troy. It was here that Agamemnon killed his daughter to make the wind blow.

his lovely passion, Latium.[2] All I ask is time,
blank time: some rest from frenzy, breathing room   545
till my fate can teach my beaten spirit how to grieve.
I beg him—pity your sister, Anna—one last favor,
and if he grants it now, I'll pay him back,
with interest, when I die."

                      So Dido pleads and
so her desolate sister takes him the tale of tears   550
again and again. But no tears move Aeneas now.
He is deaf to all appeals. He won't relent.
The Fates bar the way
and heaven blocks his gentle, human ears.
As firm as a sturdy oak grown tough with age   555
when the Northwinds blasting off the Alps compete,
fighting left and right, to wrench it from the earth,
and the winds scream, the trunk shudders, its leafy crest
showers across the ground but it clings firm to its rock,
its roots stretching as deep into the dark world below   560
as its crown goes towering toward the gales of heaven—
so firm the hero stands: buffeted left and right
by storms of appeals, he takes the full force
of love and suffering deep in his great heart.
His will stands unmoved. The falling tears are futile.[3]

                            Then,   565
terrified by her fate, tragic Dido prays for death,
sickened to see the vaulting sky above her.
And to steel her new resolve to leave the light,
she sees, laying gifts on the altars steaming incense—
shudder to hear it now—the holy water going black   570
and the wine she pours congeals in bloody filth.[4]
She told no one what she saw, not even her sister.
Worse, there was a marble temple in her palace,
a shrine built for her long-lost love, Sychaeus.
Holding it dear she tended it—marvelous devotion—   575
draping the snow-white fleece and festal boughs.
Now from its depths she seemed to catch his voice,
the words of her dead husband calling out her name
while night enclosed the earth in its dark shroud,
and over and over a lonely owl perched on the rooftops   580
drew out its low, throaty call to a long wailing dirge.
And worse yet, the grim predictions of ancient seers
keep terrifying her now with frightful warnings.
Aeneas the hunter, savage in all her nightmares,
drives her mad with panic. She always feels alone,   585
abandoned, always wandering down some endless road,
not a friend in sight, seeking her own Phoenicians
in some godforsaken land. As frantic as Pentheus

2. Region of central Italy, land of the Latins.   three.
3. In the Latin, as here, it is unclear who is   4. Dido is trying to pour libations—liquid
crying; it could be Anna, Dido, Aeneas, or all   offerings to the gods.

seeing battalions of Furies, twin suns ablaze
and double cities of Thebes before his eyes.[5]
Or Agamemnon's Orestes hounded off the stage,   590
fleeing his mother armed with torches, black snakes,
while blocking the doorway coil her Furies of Revenge.[6]

So, driven by madness, beaten down by anguish,
Dido was fixed on dying, working out in her mind   595
the means, the moment. She approaches her grieving
sister, Anna—masking her plan with a brave face
aglow with hope, and says: "I've found a way,
dear heart—rejoice with your sister—either
to bring him back in love for me or free me   600
of love for him. Close to the bounds of Ocean,
west with the setting sun, lies Ethiopian land,
the end of the earth, where colossal Atlas turns
on his shoulder the heavens studded with flaming stars.
From there, I have heard, a Massylian priestess comes   605
who tended the temple held by Hesperian daughters.[7]
She'd safeguard the boughs in the sacred grove
and ply the dragon with morsels dripping loops
of oozing honey and poppies drowsy with slumber.
With her spells she vows to release the hearts   610
of those she likes, to inflict raw pain on others—
to stop the rivers in midstream, reverse the stars
in their courses, raise the souls of the dead at night
and make earth shudder and rumble underfoot—you'll see—
and send the ash trees marching down the mountains.   615
I swear by the gods, dear Anna, by your sweet life,
I arm myself with magic arts against my will.[8]

                              "Now go,
build me a pyre in secret, deep inside our courtyard
under the open sky. Pile it high with his arms—
he left them hanging within our bridal chamber—   620
the traitor, so devoted then! and all his clothes
and crowning it all, the bridal bed that brought my doom.
I must obliterate every trace of the man, the curse,
and the priestess shows the way!"

                              She says no more
and now as the queen falls silent, pallor sweeps her face.   625

---

5. Pentheus was the king of Thebes who, in Euripides' *Bacchae*, was driven mad so that he thought he saw two suns in the sky and was then killed by his own mother.

6. Agamemnon's son, Orestes, killed his mother in revenge for her killing his father. He was then driven mad by the Furies. The myth is the subject of Aeschylus's *Oresteia* and Euripides' *Orestes*.

7. The daughters of Hesperus, the Evening Star, tended a garden containing the golden apples that belonged to Hera. A never-sleeping dragon with a hundred heads also guarded the apples.

8. These allusions to witchcraft make Dido sound like Medea, the princess of Colchis with magical powers, who helped Jason steal the Golden Fleece from her father and escape back to Greece. Later, after several years of marriage, Jason abandoned Medea; she then, according to Euripides' *Medea*, took revenge by killing their children.

Still, Anna cannot imagine these outlandish rites
would mask her sister's death. She can't conceive
of such a fiery passion. She fears nothing graver
than Dido's grief at the death of her Sychaeus.
So she does as she is told.

           But now the queen,   630
as soon as the pyre was built beneath the open sky,
towering up with pitch-pine and cut logs of oak—
deep in the heart of her house—she drapes the court
with flowers, crowning the place with wreaths of death,
and to top it off she lays his arms and the sword he left   635
and an effigy of Aeneas, all on the bed they'd shared,
for well she knows the future. Altars ring the pyre.
Hair loose in the wind, the priestess thunders out
the names of her three hundred gods, Erebus, Chaos
and triple Hecate, Diana the three-faced virgin.[9]   640
She'd sprinkled water, simulating the springs of hell,
and gathered potent herbs, reaped with bronze sickles
under the moonlight, dripping their milky black poison,
and fetched a love-charm ripped from a foal's brow,
just born, before the mother could gnaw it off.   645
And Dido herself, standing before the altar,
holding the sacred grain in reverent hands—
with one foot free of its sandal, robes unbound[1]—
sworn now to die, she calls on the gods to witness,
calls on the stars who know her approaching fate.   650
And then to any Power above, mindful, evenhanded,
who watches over lovers bound by unequal passion,
Dido says her prayers.

            The dead of night,
and weary living creatures throughout the world
are enjoying peaceful sleep. The woods and savage seas   655
are calm, at rest, and the circling stars are gliding on
in their midnight courses, all the fields lie hushed
and the flocks and gay and gorgeous birds that haunt
the deep clear pools and the thorny country thickets
all lie quiet now, under the silent night, asleep.   660
But not the tragic queen . . .
torn in spirit, Dido will not dissolve
into sleep—her eyes, her mind won't yield to night.
Her torments multiply, over and over her passion
surges back into heaving waves of rage—   665
she keeps on brooding, obsessions roil her heart:
"And now, what shall I do? Make a mockery of myself,
go back to my old suitors, tempt them to try again?
Beg the Numidians, grovel, plead for a husband—
though time and again I scorned to wed their likes?   670
What then? Trail the Trojan ships, bend to the Trojans'
every last demand? So pleased, are they, with all the help,

---

9. Erebus is Darkness, son of Chaos. Hecate, sometimes identified with Diana the moon goddess, was the goddess of witchcraft.
1. All magical practices.

the relief I lent them once? And memory of my service past
stands firm in grateful minds! And even if I were willing,
would the Trojans allow me to board their proud ships— 675
a woman they hate? Poor lost fool, can't you sense it,
grasp it yet—the treachery of Laomedon's breed?[2]
What now? Do I take flight alone, consorting
with crews of Trojan oarsmen in their triumph?
Or follow them out with all my troops of Tyrians 680
thronging the decks? Yes, hard as it was to uproot
them once from Tyre! How can I force them back to sea
once more, command them to spread their sails to the winds?
No, no, die!
       You deserve it—
                    end your pain with the sword!
You, my sister, you were the first, won over by my tears, 685
to pile these sorrows on my shoulders, mad as I was,
to throw me into my enemy's arms. If only I'd been free
to live my life, untested in marriage, free of guilt
as some wild beast untouched by pangs like these!
I broke the faith I swore to the ashes of Sychaeus." 690

Such terrible grief kept breaking from her heart
as Aeneas slept in peace on his ship's high stern,
bent on departing now, all tackle set to sail.
And now in his dreams it came again—the god,
his phantom, the same features shining clear. 695
Like Mercury head to foot, the voice, the glow,
the golden hair, the bloom of youth on his limbs
and his voice rang out with warnings once again:
"Son of the goddess, how can you sleep so soundly
in such a crisis? Can't you see the dangers closing 700
around you now? Madman! Can't you hear the Westwind
ruffling to speed you on? That woman spawns her plots,
mulling over some desperate outrage in her heart,
lashing her surging rage, she's bent on death.
Why not flee headlong? 705
Flee headlong while you can! You'll soon see
the waves a chaos of ships, lethal torches flaring,
the whole coast ablaze, if now a new dawn breaks
and finds you still malingering on these shores.
Up with you now. Enough delay. Woman's a thing 710
that's always changing, shifting like the wind."
With that he vanished into the black night.

Then, terrified by the sudden phantom,
Aeneas, wrenching himself from sleep, leaps up
and rouses his crews and spurs them headlong on: 715
"Quick! Up and at it, shipmates, man the thwarts![3]
Spread canvas fast! A god's come down from the sky

---

2. Laomedon, father of Priam and previous
king of Troy, broke a promise to repay Apollo
and Neptune for building his city walls.
3. I.e., take up positions on the rowing benches.

once more—I've just seen him—urging us on
to sever our mooring cables, sail at once!
We follow you, blessed god, whoever you are—   720
glad at heart we obey your commands once more.
Now help us, stand beside us with all your kindness,
bring us favoring stars in the sky to blaze our way!"

Tearing sword from sheath like a lightning flash,
he hacks the mooring lines with a naked blade.   725
Gripped by the same desire, all hands pitch in,
they hoist and haul. The shore's deserted now,
the water's hidden under the fleet—they bend to it,
churn the spray and sweep the clear blue sea.
                                        By now
early Dawn had risen up from the saffron bed   730
of Tithonus,[4] scattering fresh light on the world.
But the queen from her high tower, catching sight
of the morning's white glare, the armada heading out
to sea with sails trimmed to the wind, and certain
the shore and port were empty, stripped of oarsmen—   735
three, four times over she beat her lovely breast,
she ripped at her golden hair and "Oh, by God,"
she cries, "will the stranger just sail off
and make a mockery of our realm? Will no one
rush to arms, come streaming out of the whole city,   740
hunt him down, race to the docks and launch the ships?
Go, quick—bring fire!
                        Hand out weapons!
                                        Bend to the oars!
What am I saying? Where am I? What insanity's this
that shifts my fixed resolve? Dido, oh poor fool,
is it only *now* your wicked work strikes home?   745
It should have then, when you offered him your scepter.
Look at his hand clasp, look at his good faith now—
that man who, they say, carries his fathers' gods,
who stooped to shoulder his father bent with age!
Couldn't I have seized him then, ripped him to pieces,   750
scattered them in the sea? Or slashed his men with steel,
butchered Ascanius, served him up as his father's feast?[5]
True, the luck of battle might have been at risk—
well, risk away! Whom did I have to fear?
I was about to die. I should have torched their camp   755
and flooded their decks with fire. The son, the father,
the whole Trojan line—I should have wiped them out,
then hurled myself on the pyre to crown it all!

---

4. The goddess Dawn had a human lover named Tithonus, whom she had made immortal (though not ageless) and brought to live with her.
5. These horrible possibilities have mythic precedents. Medea, when she eloped with Jason, ripped up her little brother's body and scattered the pieces on the sea, to distract their father as he tried to pursue the boat. Atreus, father of Agamemnon and Menelaus, killed his brother's children and served them to him at a feast.

"You, Sun, whose fires scan all works of the earth,[6]
and you, Juno, the witness, midwife to my agonies—   760
Hecate greeted by nightly shrieks at city crossroads—
and you, you avenging Furies and gods of dying Dido!
Hear me, turn your power my way, attend my sorrows—
I deserve your mercy—hear my prayers! If that curse
of the earth must reach his haven, labor on to landfall—   765
if Jove and the Fates command and the boundary stone is fixed,
still, let him be plagued in war by a nation proud in arms,
torn from his borders, wrenched from Iulus' embrace,
let him grovel for help and watch his people die
a shameful death! And then, once he has bowed down   770
to an unjust peace, may he never enjoy his realm
and the light he yearns for, never, let him die
before his day, unburied on some desolate beach![7]

"That is my prayer, my final cry—I pour it out
with my own lifeblood. And you, my Tyrians,   775
harry with hatred all his line, his race to come:
make that offering to my ashes, send it down below.
No love between our peoples, ever, no pacts of peace!
Come rising up from my bones, you avenger still unknown,
to stalk those Trojan settlers, hunt with fire and iron,   780
now or in time to come, whenever the power is yours.
Shore clash with shore, sea against sea and sword
against sword—this is my curse—war between all
our peoples, all their children, endless war!"

With that, her mind went veering back and forth—   785
what was the quickest way to break off from the light,
the life she loathed? And so with a few words
she turned to Barce, Sychaeus' old nurse—her own
was now black ashes deep in her homeland lost forever:
"Dear old nurse, send Anna my sister to me here.   790
Tell her to hurry, sprinkle herself with river water,
bring the victims marked for the sacrifice I must make.
So let her come. And wrap your brow with the holy bands.
These rites to Jove of the Styx that I have set in motion,
I yearn to consummate them, end the pain of love,   795
give that cursed Trojan's pyre to the flames."
The nurse bustled off with an old crone's zeal.

               But Dido,
trembling, desperate now with the monstrous thing afoot—
her bloodshot eyes rolling, quivering cheeks blotched
and pale with imminent death—goes bursting through   800
the doors to the inner courtyard, clambers in frenzy
up the soaring pyre and unsheathes a sword, a Trojan sword
she once sought as a gift, but not for such an end.

---

6. The sun (Helios) was sometimes personified as a god; he was the grandfather of Medea.
7. Another oblique refernce to the assassina-

tion of Pompey after he was defeated by Julius
Caesar in the civil war of 49–45 B.C.E (cf. book
II, line 690).

And next, catching sight of the Trojan's clothes
and the bed they knew by heart, delaying a moment   805
for tears, for memory's sake, the queen lay down
and spoke her final words: "Oh, dear relics,
dear as long as Fate and the gods allowed,
receive my spirit and set me free of pain.
I have lived a life. I've journeyed through   810
the course that Fortune charted for me. And now
I pass to the world below, my ghost in all its glory.
I have founded a noble city, seen my ramparts rise.
I have avenged my husband, punished my blood-brother,
our mortal foe. Happy, all too happy I would have been   815
if only the Trojan keels had never grazed our coast."
She presses her face in the bed and cries out:
"I shall die unavenged, but die I will! So—
so—I rejoice to make my way among the shades.
And may that heartless Dardan, far at sea,   820
drink down deep the sight of our fires here
and bear with him this omen of our death!"

All at once, in the midst of her last words,
her women see her doubled over the sword, the blood
foaming over the blade, her hands splattered red.   825
A scream goes stabbing up to the high roofs,
Rumor raves like a Maenad through the shocked city—
sobs, and grief, and the wails of women ringing out
through homes, and the heavens echo back the keening din—
for all the world as if enemies stormed the walls   830
and all of Carthage or old Tyre were toppling down
and flames in their fury, wave on mounting wave
were billowing over the roofs of men and gods.

Anna heard and, stunned, breathless with terror,
raced through the crowd, her nails clawing her face,   835
fists beating her breast, crying out to her sister now
at the edge of death: "Was it all for *this*, my sister?
You deceived me all along? Is this what your pyre
meant for me—this, your fires—this, your altars?
You deserted me—what shall I grieve for first?   840
Your friend, your sister, you scorn me now in death?
You should have called me on to the same fate.
The same agony, same sword, the one same hour
had borne us off together. Just to think I built
your pyre with my own hands, implored our fathers' gods   845
with my own voice, only to be cut off from you—
how very cruel—when you lay down to die . . .
You have destroyed your life, my sister, mine too,
your people, the lords of Sidon and your new city here.
Please, help me to bathe her wounds in water now,   850
and if any last, lingering breath still hovers,
let me catch it on my lips."

With those words
she had climbed the pyre's topmost steps and now,
clasping her dying sister to her breast, fondling her
she sobbed, stanching the dark blood with her own gown. 855
Dido, trying to raise her heavy eyes once more, failed—
deep in her heart the wound kept rasping, hissing on.
Three times she tried to struggle up on an elbow,
three times she fell back, writhing on her bed.
Her gaze wavering into the high skies, she looked 860
for a ray of light and when she glimpsed it, moaned.

Then Juno in all her power, filled with pity
for Dido's agonizing death, her labor long and hard,
sped Iris[8] down from Olympus to release her spirit
wrestling now in a deathlock with her limbs. 865
Since she was dying a death not fated or deserved,
no, tormented, before her day, in a blaze of passion—
Proserpina had yet to pluck a golden lock from her head
and commit her life to the Styx and the dark world below.[9]
So Iris, glistening dew, comes skimming down from the sky 870
on gilded wings, trailing showers of iridescence shimmering
into the sun, and hovering over Dido's head, declares:
"So commanded, I take this lock as a sacred gift
to the God of Death, and I release you from your body."

With that, she cut the lock with her hand and all at once 875
the warmth slipped away, the life dissolved in the winds.

Summary of Book V The Trojans see the flames of Dido's funeral pyre as they leave.
They sail back to Sicily, where they mark the death of Anchises with funeral rites and games.
The pilot of Aeneas' ship, Palinurus, is overwhelmed by sleep at the tiller, falls into the sea, and
drowns.

BOOK VI

[The Kingdom of the Dead]

So as he speaks in tears Aeneas gives the ships free rein
and at last they glide onto Euboean Cumae's beaches.[1]
Swinging their prows around to face the sea,
they moor the fleet with the anchors' biting grip
and the curved sterns edge the bay. Bands of sailors, 5
primed for action, leap out onto land—Hesperian land.[2]
Some strike seeds of fire buried in veins of flint,

8. Iris is the goddess who sometimes acts as
messenger between heaven and earth; she
appears as a rainbow (hence "iridescence").
9. Proserpina, queen of the underworld, would
normally have taken a lock of Dido's hair to
release her life; since her death is premature,
Iris does it instead.

1. Cumae, a Greek colony on the Italian coast
(in modern Campania, near Naples), was
founded by immigrants from the island of
Euboea. It was the seat of the Sibyl, a priestess
of Apollo, for many centuries.
2. "Hesperian" means "western"; Hesperia is
also a Greek name for Italy.

some strip the dense thickets, lairs of wild beasts,
and lighting on streams, are quick to point them out.
But devout Aeneas makes his way to the stronghold   10
that Apollo rules, throned on high, and set apart
is a vast cave, the awesome Sybil's secret haunt
where the Seer of Delos[3] breathes his mighty will,
his soul inspiring her to lay the future bare.
And now they approach Diana's[4] sacred grove   15
and walk beneath the golden roofs of god.

                           Daedalus,[5]
so the story's told, fleeing the realm of Minos,
daring to trust himself to the sky on beating wings,
floated up to the icy North, the first man to fly,
and hovered lightly on Cumae's heights at last.   20
Here, on first returning to earth, he hallowed
to you, Apollo, the oars of his rowing wings
and here he built your grand, imposing temple.
High on a gate he carved Androgeos' death[6]
and then the people of Athens, doomed—so cruel—   25
to pay with the lives of seven sons. Year in, year out,
the urn stands ready, the fateful lots are drawn.

    Balancing these on a facing gate, the land of Crete
comes rising from the sea. Here the cursed lust for the bull
and Pasiphaë spread beneath him, duping both her mates,   30
and here the mixed breed, part man, part beast, the Minotaur—
a warning against such monstrous passion. Here its lair,
that house of labor, the endless blinding maze,
but Daedalus, pitying royal Ariadne's love so deep,[7]
unraveled his own baffling labyrinth's winding paths,   35
guiding Theseus' groping steps with a trail of thread.
And you too, Icarus, what part you might have played
in a work that great, had Daedalus' grief allowed it.
Twice he tried to engrave your fall in gold and
twice his hands, a father's hands, fell useless.
                                 Yes,   40
and they would have kept on scanning scene by scene

3. Delos is the birthplace of Apollo, god of prophecy ("Seer").
4. Diana (equivalent to the Greek Artemis), sister of Apollo, was also worshipped at Cumae. She is identified in the original in her guise as Hecate, associated with witchcraft and ghosts.
5. Daedalus was the master craftsman of myth. When Pasiphaë, wife of King Minos of Crete, fell in love with a bull, Daedalus constructed an artificial cow for her to get inside, enabling her to have sex with the animal. She gave birth to the Minotaur, and Daedalus built a labyrinth to house him. He was fed on humans; the Athenians were forced to send fourteen young people a year to feed the monster. Daedalus later helped the Greek hero Theseus get

through the labyrinth and kill the Minotaur. He was punished with imprisonment, but managed to escape to Cumae on wings he had constructed himself. His son Icarus, who accompanied him, flew too close to the sun on his wax wings, which melted, and the boy drowned in what is still called the Icarian Sea (part of the Aegean Sea, near Samos).
6. Son of King Minos, Androgeos was killed by the Athenians; in recompense, Minos demanded a yearly tribute of seven boys and seven girls from Athens, to be fed to the Minotaur.
7. Ariadne, daughter of Minos, fell in love with Theseus; Daedalus told her how to help him, by bringing him a ball of thread with which to mark his path through the labyrinth.

if Achates, sent ahead, had not returned, bringing
Deiphobe, Glaucus' daughter, priestess of Phoebus
and Diana too, and the Sibyl tells the king:
"This is no time for gazing at the sights.   45
Better to slaughter seven bulls from a herd
unbroken by the yoke, as the old rite requires,
and as many head of teething yearling sheep."
Directing Aeneas so—and his men are quick
with the sacrifice she demands—   50
the Sibyl calls them into her lofty shrine.

　　Now carved out of the rocky flanks of Cumae
lies an enormous cavern pierced by a hundred tunnels,
a hundred mouths with as many voices rushing out,
the Sibyl's rapt replies. They had just gained   55
the sacred sill when the virgin cries aloud:
"Now is the time to ask your fate to speak!
The god, look, the god!"
　　　　　　　　　　　So she cries before
the entrance—suddenly all her features, all
her color changes, her braided hair flies loose   60
and her breast heaves, her heart bursts with frenzy,
she seems to rise in height, the ring of her voice no longer
human—the breath, the power of god comes closer, closer.
"Why so slow, Trojan Aeneas?" she shouts, "so slow
to pray, to swear your vows? Not until you do   65
will the great jaws of our spellbound house gape wide."
And with that command the prophetess fell silent.

　　An icy shiver runs through the Trojans' sturdy spines
and the king's prayers come pouring from his heart:
"Apollo, you always pitied the Trojans' heavy labors!   70
You guided the arrow of Paris, pierced Achilles' body.[8]
You led me through many seas, bordering endless coasts,
far-off Massylian tribes, and fields washed by the Syrtes,[9]
and now, at long last, Italy's shores, forever fading,
lie within our grasp. Let the doom of Troy pursue us   75
just this far, no more. You too, you gods and goddesses,
all who could never suffer Troy and Troy's high glory,
spare the people of Pergamum now,[1] it's only right.
And you, you blessed Sibyl who knows the future,
grant my prayer. I ask no more than the realm   80
my fate decrees: let the Trojans rest in Latium,
they and their roaming gods, their rootless powers!
Then I will build you a solid marble temple,
Apollo and Diana, establish hallowed days,

8. Paris, prince of Troy, guided by Apollo,
shot an arrow that pierced Achilles' only vulnerable spot, on his heel.
9. Quicksands off the coast of North Africa.
Massylian tribes: veiled references to Carthage,

since the Massylians lived adjacent to Carthage.
1. The Trojans. (Pergamum, or Pergamea, is
the city that Aeneas founded in Crete after
fleeing Troy.)

Apollo, in your name.[2] And Sibyl, for you too,   85
a magnificent sacred shrine awaits you in our kingdom.
There I will house your oracles, mystic revelations
made to our race, and ordain your chosen priests,
my gracious lady. Just don't commit your words
to the rustling, scattering leaves—   90
sport of the winds that whirl them all away.
Sing them yourself, I beg you!" There Aeneas stopped.

But the Sibyl, still not broken in by Apollo, storms
with a wild fury through her cave. And the more she tries
to pitch the great god off her breast, the more his bridle   95
exhausts her raving lips, overwhelming her untamed heart,
bending her to his will. Now the hundred immense
mouths of the house swing open, all on their own,
and bear the Sibyl's answers through the air:
"You who have braved the terrors of the sea,   100
though worse remain on land—you Trojans will reach
Lavinium's realm—lift that care from your hearts—
but you will rue your arrival. Wars, horrendous wars,
and the Tiber foaming with tides of blood, I see it all!
Simois, Xanthus, a Greek camp—you'll never lack them here.   105
Already a new Achilles[3] springs to life in Latium,
son of a goddess too! Nor will Juno ever fail
to harry the Trojan race, and all the while,
pleading, pressed by need—what tribes, what towns
of Italy won't you beg for help! And the cause of this,   110
this new Trojan grief? Again a stranger bride,
a marriage with a stranger once again.[4]
But never bow to suffering, go and face it,
all the bolder, wherever Fortune clears the way.
Your path to safety will open first from where   115
you least expect it—a city built by Greeks!"[5]
                                              Those words
re-echoing from her shrine, the Cumaean Sibyl chants
her riddling visions filled with dread, her cave resounds
as she shrouds the truth in darkness—Phoebus whips her on
in all her frenzy, twisting his spurs below her breast.   120
As soon as her fury dies and raving lips fall still,
the hero Aeneas launches in: "No trials, my lady,
can loom before me in any new, surprising form.
No, deep in my spirit I have known them all,
I've faced them all before. But grant one prayer.   125
Since here, they say, are the gates of Death's king
and the dark marsh where the Acheron[6] comes flooding up,

2. The Games to Apollo were established dur-
ing the Second Punic War (218–201 B.C.E.);
Augustus, Virgil's patron, built a temple to
Apollo on the Palatine.
3. Achilles: most important warrior in the *Iliad*.
Simois and Xanthus are rivers in Troy.

4. The first "stranger" or foreign bride was
Helen, for whom the Trojan War was fought
when she was taken from her husband by Paris.
5. Pallanteum, built by Arcadian Greeks and
the future site of Rome.
6. The river of grief in the Underworld.

please, allow me to go and see my beloved father,
meet him face to face.
Teach me the way, throw wide the sacred doors!   130
Through fires, a thousand menacing spears I swept him off
on these shoulders, saved him from our enemies' onslaught.
He shared all roads and he braved all seas with me,
all threats of the waves and skies—frail as he was
but graced with a strength beyond his years, his lot.   135
He was the one, in fact, who ordered, pressed me on
to reach your doors and seek you, beg you now.
Pity the son and father, I pray you, kindly lady!
All power is yours. Hecate[7] held back nothing,
put you in charge of Avernus' groves. If Orpheus   140
could summon up the ghost of his wife, trusting so
to his Thracian lyre and echoing strings; if Pollux
could ransom his brother and share his death by turns,
time and again traversing the same road up and down;
if Theseus, mighty Hercules—must I mention them?[8]   145
I too can trace my birth from Jove on high."

                              So he prayed,
grasping the altar while the Sibyl gave her answer:
"Born of the blood of gods, Anchises' son,
man of Troy, the descent to the Underworld is easy.
Night and day the gates of shadowy Death stand open wide,   150
but to retrace your steps, to climb back to the upper air—
there the struggle, there the labor lies. Only a few,
loved by impartial Jove or borne aloft to the sky
by their own fiery virtue—some sons of the gods
have made their way. The entire heartland here   155
is thick with woods, Cocytus glides around it,[9]
coiling dense and dark.
But if such a wild desire seizes on you—twice
to sail the Stygian marsh, to see black Tartarus twice—[1]
if you're so eager to give yourself to this, this mad ordeal,   160
then hear what you must accomplish first.

                              "Hidden
deep in a shady tree there grows a golden bough,
its leaves and its hardy, sinewy stem all gold,
held sacred to Juno of the Dead, Proserpina.[2]
The whole grove covers it over, dusky valleys   165
enfold it too, closing in around it. No one

---

7. Diana, in her guise as goddess of magic.
8. These lines cite four mythical heroes who have preceded Aeneas in journeying to the Underworld. The first is Orpheus, the master singer, who went in search of his dead wife and used his music to persuade Hades to give her back (though he lost her again on the way up when he turned to look at her). The second is Pollux, who shared immortality with his twin brother Castor, so that they each spent six months of the year in the Underworld. The third, Theseus, went to try to carry off Perse-phone, wife of Hades. The last, Heracles, had to bring back Cerberus, three-headed guard dog of Hades, as one of his Twelve Labors.
9. One of the rivers of the Underworld, the river of lamentation.
1. Tartarus is the abyss in Hades used as prison for the Titans; the Styx is another river of the Underworld (hence "Stygian").
2. Queen of the Underworld (hence, equivalent to Juno, Queen of the Upper World).

may pass below the secret places of earth before
he plucks the fruit, the golden foliage of that tree.
As her beauty's due, Proserpina decreed this bough
shall be offered up to her as her own hallowed gift.   170
When the first spray's torn away, another takes its place,
gold too, the metal breaks into leaf again, all gold.
Lift up your eyes and search, and once you find it,
duly pluck it off with your hand. Freely, easily,
all by itself it comes away, if Fate calls you on.   175
If not, no strength within you can overpower it,
no iron blade, however hard, can tear it off.

  "One thing more I must tell you.
A friend lies dead—oh, you could not know—
his body pollutes your entire fleet with death   180
while you search on for oracles, linger at our doors.
Bear him first to his place of rest, bury him in his tomb.
Lead black cattle there, first offerings of atonement.
Only then can you set eyes on the Stygian groves
and the realms no living man has ever trod."   185
Abruptly she fell silent, lips sealed tight.

    His eyes fixed on the ground, his face in tears,
Aeneas moves on, leaving the cavern, turning over
within his mind these strange, dark events.
His trusty comrade Achates keeps his pace   190
and the same cares weigh down his plodding steps.
They traded many questions, wondering, back and forth,
what dead friend did the Sibyl mean, whose body must be buried?
Suddenly, Misenus—out on the dry beach they see him,
reach him now, cut off by a death all undeserved.   195
Misenus, Aeolus'[3] son, a herald unsurpassed
at rallying troops with his trumpet's cry,
igniting the God of War with its shrill blare.
He had been mighty Hector's friend, by Hector's side
in the rush of battle, shining with spear and trumpet both.   200
But when triumphant Achilles stripped Hector's life,
the gallant hero joined forces with Dardan Aeneas,
followed a captain every bit as strong. But then,
chancing to make the ocean ring with his hollow shell,
the madman challenged the gods to match him blast for blast   205
and jealous Triton[4]—if we can believe the story—
snatched him up and drowned the man in the surf
that seethed between the rocks.
                                 So all his shipmates
gathered round his body and raised a loud lament,
devoted Aeneas in the lead. Then still in tears,   210
they rush to perform the Sibyl's orders, no delay,
they strive to pile up trees, to build an altar-pyre

---

3. Probably the god of the winds.   4. A sea god.

rising to the skies. Then into an ancient wood
and the hidden dens of beasts they make their way,
and down crash the pines, the ilex rings to the axe, 215
the trunks of ash and oak are split by the driving wedge,
and they roll huge rowans down the hilly slopes.

Aeneas spurs his men in the forefront of their labors,
geared with the same woodsmen's tools around his waist.
But the same anxiety keeps on churning in his heart 220
as he scans the endless woods and prays by chance:
"If only that golden bough would gleam before us now
on a tree in this dark grove! Since all the Sibyl
foretold of you was true, Misenus, all too true."

No sooner said than before his eyes, twin doves 225
chanced to come flying down the sky and lit
on the green grass at his feet. His mother's birds—
the great captain knew them and raised a prayer of joy:
"Be my guides! If there's a path, fly through the air,
set me a course to the grove where that rich branch 230
shades the good green earth. And you, goddess,
mother, don't fail me in this, my hour of doubt!"

With that he stopped in his tracks, watching keenly—
what sign would they offer? Where would they lead?
And on they flew, pausing to feed, then flying on 235
as far as a follower's eye could track their flight
and once they reached the foul-smelling gorge of Avernus,
up they veered, quickly, then slipped down through the clear air
to settle atop the longed-for goal, the twofold tree, its green
a foil for the breath of gold that glows along its branch. 240
As mistletoe in the dead of winter's icy forests
leafs with life on a tree that never gave it birth,
embracing the smooth trunk with its pale yellow bloom,
so glowed the golden foliage against the ilex evergreen,
so rustled the sheer gold leaf in the light breeze. 245
Aeneas grips it at once—the bough holds back—
he tears it off in his zeal
and bears it into the vatic Sibyl's shrine.

All the while
the Trojans along the shore keep weeping for Misenus,
paying his thankless ashes final rites. And first 250
they build an immense pyre of resinous pitch-pine
and oaken logs, weaving into its flanks dark leaves
and setting before it rows of funereal cypress,
crowning it all with the herald's gleaming arms.
Some heat water in cauldrons fired to boiling, 255
bathe and anoint the body chill with death.
The dirge rises up. Then, their weeping over,
they lay his corpse on a litter, swathe him round
in purple robes that form the well-known shroud.

Some hoisted up the enormous bier—sad service— 260
their eyes averted, after their fathers' ways of old,
and thrust the torch below. The piled offerings blazed,
frankincense, hallowed foods and brimming bowls of oil.
And after the coals sank in and the fires died down,
they washed his embers, thirsty remains, with wine. 265
Corynaeus sealed the bones he culled in a bronze urn,
then circling his comrades three times with pure water,
sprinkling light drops from a blooming olive spray,
he cleansed the men and voiced the last farewell.
But devout Aeneas mounds the tomb—an immense barrow 270
crowned with the man's own gear, his oar and trumpet—
under a steep headland, called after the herald now
and for all time to come it bears Misenus' name.[5]
                                    The rite
performed, Aeneas hurries to carry out the Sibyl's orders.
There was a vast cave deep in the gaping, jagged rock, 275
shielded well by a dusky lake and shadowed grove.
Over it no bird on earth could make its way unscathed,
such poisonous vapors steamed up from its dark throat
to cloud the arching sky. Here, as her first step,
the priestess steadies four black-backed calves, 280
she tips wine on their brows, then plucks some tufts
from the crown between their horns and casts them
over the altar fire, first offerings, crying out
to Hecate, mighty Queen of Heaven and Hell.
Attendants run knives under throats and catch 285
warm blood in bowls. Aeneas himself, sword drawn,
slaughters a black-fleeced lamb to the Furies' mother,
Night, and to her great sister, Earth, and to you,
Proserpina, kills a barren heifer. Then to the king
of the river Styx, he raises altars into the dark night 290
and over their fires lays whole carcasses of bulls
and pours fat oil over their entrails flaming up.
Then suddenly, look, at the break of day, first light,
the earth groans underfoot and the wooded heights quake
and across the gloom the hounds seem to howl 295
at the goddess coming closer.
                                    "Away, away!"
the Sibyl shrieks, "all you unhallowed ones—away
from this whole grove! But you launch out on your journey,
tear your sword from its sheath, Aeneas. Now for courage,
now the steady heart!" And the Sibyl says no more but 300
into the yawning cave she flings herself, possessed—
he follows her boldly, matching stride for stride.
                                    You gods
who govern the realm of ghosts, you voiceless shades and Chaos—
you, the River of Fire, you far-flung regions hushed in night—

5. The place is still called Capo Miseno (Cape of Misenus).

lend me the right to tell what I have heard, lend your power   305
to reveal the world immersed in the misty depths of earth.

On they went, those dim travelers under the lonely night,
through gloom and the empty halls of Death's ghostly realm,
like those who walk through woods by a grudging moon's
deceptive light when Jove has plunged the sky in dark   310
and the black night drains all color from the world.
There in the entryway, the gorge of hell itself,
Grief and the pangs of Conscience make their beds,
and fatal pale Disease lives there, and bleak Old Age,
Dread and Hunger, seductress to crime, and grinding Poverty,   315
all, terrible shapes to see—and Death and deadly Struggle
and Sleep, twin brother of Death, and twisted, wicked Joys
and facing them at the threshold, War, rife with death,
and the Furies' iron chambers, and mad, raging Strife
whose blood-stained headbands knot her snaky locks.   320

There in the midst, a giant shadowy elm tree spreads
her ancient branching arms, home, they say, to swarms
of false dreams, one clinging tight under each leaf.
And a throng of monsters too—what brutal forms
are stabled at the gates—Centaurs, mongrel Scyllas,   325
part women, part beasts, and hundred-handed Briareus
and the savage Hydra of Lerna, that hissing horror,
the Chimaera armed with torches—Gorgons, Harpies
and triple-bodied Geryon, his great ghost.[6] And here,
instantly struck with terror, Aeneas grips his sword   330
and offers its naked edge against them as they come,
and if his experienced comrade had not warned him
they are mere disembodied creatures, flimsy
will-o'-the-wisps that flit like living forms,
he would have rushed them all,   335
slashed through empty phantoms with his blade.

From there
the road leads down to the Acheron's Tartarean waves.
Here the enormous whirlpool gapes aswirl with filth,
seethes and spews out all its silt in the Wailing River.[7]
And here the dreaded ferryman guards the flood,   340
grisly in his squalor—Charon . . .
his scraggly beard a tangled mat of white, his eyes
fixed in a fiery stare, and his grimy rags hang down
from his shoulders by a knot. But all on his own
he punts his craft with a pole and hoists sail   345

6. Geryon was a terrifying giant. Centaurs are
half human, half horse. Scylla is a female sea
monster with several doglike heads, who features in the *Odyssey*. Briareus was one of three
sons of Sky and Earth (Uranus and Gaia), with
a hundred arms and fifty heads. The Hydra was
a multiple-headed snake, defeated by Heracles. The Chimaera was a fire-breathing hybrid
monster, usually imagined as a mix of lion,
goat, and snake. Gorgons are snakelike monsters; Harpies are female birdlike monsters.
7. Acheron, one of the Underworld rivers, led
into Cocytus, river of lamentation (Wailing
River).

as he ferries the dead souls in his rust-red skiff.
He's on in years, but a god's old age is hale and green.

A huge throng of the dead came streaming toward the banks:
mothers and grown men and ghosts of great-souled heroes,
their bodies stripped of life, and boys and unwed girls   350
and sons laid on the pyre before their parents' eyes.
As thick as leaves in autumn woods at the first frost
that slip and float to earth, or dense as flocks of birds
that wing from the heaving sea to shore when winter's chill
drives them over the waves to landfalls drenched in sunlight.   355
There they stood, pleading to be the first ones ferried over,
reaching out their hands in longing toward the farther shore.
But the grim ferryman ushers aboard now these, now those,
others he thrusts away, back from the water's edge.
                                                    Aeneas,
astonished, stirred by the tumult, calls out: "Tell me,   360
Sibyl, what does it mean, this thronging toward the river?
What do the dead souls want? What divides them all?
Some are turned away from the banks and others
scull the murky waters with their oars!"

        The aged priestess answered Aeneas briefly: 365
"Son of Anchises—born of the gods, no doubt—
what you see are Cocytus' pools and Styx's marsh,
Powers by which the gods swear oaths they dare not break.
And the great rout you see is helpless, still not buried.
That ferryman there is Charon. Those borne by the stream   370
have found their graves. And no spirits may be conveyed
across the horrendous banks and hoarse, roaring flood
until their bones are buried, and they rest in peace . . .
A hundred years they wander, hovering round these shores
till at last they may return and see once more the pools   375
they long to cross."
                        Anchises' son came to a halt
and stood there, pondering long, while pity filled his heart,
their lot so hard, unjust. And then he spots two men,
grief-stricken and robbed of death's last tribute:
Leucaspis and Orontes, the Lycian fleet's commander.   380
Together they sailed from Troy over windswept seas
and a Southern gale sprang up and
toppling breakers crushed their ships and crews.
                                              Look,
the pilot Palinurus was drifting toward him now,
fresh from the Libyan run where, watching the stars,   385
he plunged from his stern, pitched out in heavy seas.
Aeneas, barely sighting him grieving in the shadows,
hailed him first: "What god, Palinurus, snatched you
from our midst and drowned you in open waters?
Tell me, please. Apollo has never lied before.   390
This is his one reply that's played me false:

he swore you would cross the ocean safe and sound
and reach Italian shores.[8] Is *this* the end he promised?"

   But the pilot answered: "Captain, Anchises' son,
Apollo's prophetic cauldron has not failed you—   395
no god drowned me in open waters. No, the rudder
I clung to, holding us all on course—my charge—
some powerful force ripped it away by chance
and I dragged it down as I dropped headlong too.
By the cruel seas I swear I felt no fear for myself   400
to match my fear that your ship, stripped of her tiller,
steersman wrenched away, might founder in that great surge.
Three blustery winter nights the Southwind bore me wildly
over the endless waters, then at the fourth dawn, swept up
on a breaker's crest, I could almost sight it now—Italy!   405
Stroke by stroke I swam for land, safety was in my grasp,
weighed down by my sodden clothes, my fingers clawing
the jutting spurs of a cliff, when a band of brutes
came at me, ran me through with knives, the fools,
they took me for plunder worth the taking.   410
The tides hold me now
and the stormwinds roll my body down the shore.
By the sky's lovely light and the buoyant breeze I beg you,
by your father, your hopes for Iulus rising to his prime,
pluck me up from my pain, my undefeated captain!   415
Or throw some earth on my body—you know you can—
sail back to Velia's port.[9] Or if there's a way and
your goddess mother makes it clear—for not without
the will of the gods, I'm certain, do you strive
to cross these awesome streams and Stygian marsh— 420
give me your pledge, your hand, in all my torment!
Take me with you over the waves. At least in death
I'll find a peaceful haven."
                    So the pilot begged
and so the Sibyl cut him short: "How, Palinurus,
how can you harbor this mad desire of yours?   425
You think that you, unburied, can lay your eyes
on the Styx's flood, the Furies' ruthless stream,
and approach the banks unsummoned? Hope no more
the gods' decrees can be brushed aside by prayer.
Hold fast to my words and keep them well in mind   430
to comfort your hard lot. For neighboring people
living in cities near and far, compelled by signs
from the great gods on high, will appease your bones,
will build you a tomb and pay your tomb due rites
and the site will bear the name of Palinurus   435
now and always."
            That promise lifts his anguish,

---

8. No such promise is mentioned earlier in   9. A bay and later a city in southern Italy.
the poem.

drives, for a while, the grief from his sad heart.
He takes delight in the cape that bears his name.[1]

So now they press on with their journey under way
and at last approach the river. But once the ferryman,   440
still out in the Styx's currents, spied them moving
across the silent grove and turning toward the bank,
he greets them first with a rough abrupt rebuke:
"Stop, whoever you are at our river's edge,
in full armor too! Why have you come? Speak up,   445
from right where you are, not one step more! This
is the realm of shadows, sleep and drowsy night.
The law forbids me to carry living bodies across
in my Stygian boat. I'd little joy, believe me,
when Hercules came and I sailed the hero over,   450
or Theseus, Pirithous,[2] sons of gods as they were
with their high and mighty power. Hercules stole
our watchdog—chained him, the poor trembling creature,
dragged him away from our king's very throne! The others
tried to snatch our queen from the bridal bed of Death!"   455

But Apollo's seer broke in and countered Charon:
"There's no such treachery here—just calm down—
no threat of force in our weapons. The huge guard
at the gates can howl for eternity from his cave,
terrifying the bloodless shades, Persephone keep   460
her chastity safe at home behind her uncle's doors.
Aeneas of Troy, famous for his devotion, feats of arms,
goes down to the deepest shades of hell to see his father.
But if this image of devotion cannot move you, here,
this bough"—showing the bough enfolded in her robes—   465
"You know it well."
                    At this, the heaving rage
subsides in his chest. The Sibyl says no more.
The ferryman, marveling at the awesome gift,
the fateful branch unseen so many years,
swerves his dusky craft and approaches shore.   470
The souls already crouched at the long thwarts—
he brusquely thrusts them out, clearing the gangways,
quickly taking massive Aeneas aboard the little skiff.
Under his weight the boat groans and her stitched seams
gape as she ships great pools of water pouring in.   475
At last, the river crossed, the ferryman lands.
the seer and hero all unharmed in the marsh,
the repellent oozing slime and livid sedge.
                                        These
are the realms that monstrous Cerberus rocks with howls

1. There is still a Cape of Palinurus in southeastern Italy.
2. Thessalian king, descended from Zeus; he

was Theseus's best friend and accompanied
Theseus on his journey to the Underworld to
abduct Persephone.

braying out of his three throats,[3] his enormous bulk   480
squatting low in the cave that faced them there.
The Sibyl, seeing the serpents writhe around his neck,
tossed him a sop, slumbrous with honey and drugged seed,
and he, frothing with hunger, three jaws spread wide,
snapped it up where the Sibyl tossed it—gone.   485
His tremendous back relaxed, he sags to earth
and sprawls over all his cave, his giant hulk limp.
The watchdog buried now in sleep, Aeneas seizes
the way in, quickly clear of the river's edge,
the point of no return.

        At that moment, cries—   490
they could hear them now, a crescendo of wailing,
ghosts of infants weeping, robbed of their share
of this sweet life, at its very threshold too:
all, snatched from the breast on that black day
that swept them off and drowned them in bitter death.   495
Beside them were those condemned to die on a false charge.
But not without jury picked by lot, not without judge
are their places handed down. Not at all.
Minos the grand inquisitor stirs the urn,
he summons the silent jury of the dead,   500
he scans the lives of those accused, their charges.
The region next to them is held by those sad ghosts,
innocents all, who brought on death by their own hands;
despising the light, they threw their lives away.
How they would yearn, now, in the world above   505
to endure grim want and long hard labor!
But Fate bars the way. The grisly swamp
and its loveless, lethal waters bind them fast,
Styx with its nine huge coils holds them captive.

    Close to the spot, extending toward the horizon—   510
the Sibyl points them out—are the Fields of Mourning,
that is the name they bear. Here wait those souls
consumed by the harsh, wasting sickness, cruel love,
concealed on lonely paths, shrouded by myrtle bowers.
Not even in death do their torments leave them, ever.   515
Here he glimpses Phaedra, Procris, and Eriphyle grieving,
baring the wounds her heartless son had dealt her.[4]
Evadne, Pasiphaë, and Laodamia walking side by side,
and another, a young man once, a woman now, Caeneus,
turned back by Fate to the form she bore at first.[5]   520

3. Cerberus is the three-headed guard dog of
Hades.
4. Eriphyle was bribed with a necklace to persuade her husband to join the Argive war against
the Thebans, in which he was killed—their son
then killed her. Phaedra, wife of Theseus, fell in
love with her stepson Hippolytus and killed herself; Procris was jealous of her husband, who
accidentally killed her while she was spying on
him.

5. Caeneus was a woman who was changed
into a man by Neptune and was changed back
at death. Evadne was wife of the sacrilegious
Capaneus, who was struck dead by lightning;
she threw herself on his pyre. Pasiphaë was
wife of Minos and the queen of Crete who fell
in love with the bull and gave birth to the
Minotaur. Laodamia, wife of the first Greek
killed at Troy, chose to accompany him to the
Underworld.

And wandering there among them, wound still fresh,
Phoenician Dido drifted along the endless woods.
As the Trojan hero paused beside her, recognized her
through the shadows, a dim, misty figure—as one
when the month is young may see or seem to see   525
the new moon rising up through banks of clouds—
that moment Aeneas wept and approached the ghost
with tender words of love: "Tragic Dido,
so, was the story true that came my way?
I heard that you were dead . . .   530
you took the final measure with a sword.
Oh, dear god, was it I who caused your death?
I swear by the stars, by the Powers on high, whatever
faith one swears by here in the depths of earth,
I left your shores, my Queen, against my will. Yes,   535
the will of the gods, that drives me through the shadows now,
these moldering places so forlorn, this deep unfathomed night—
their decrees have forced me on. Nor did I ever dream
my leaving could have brought you so much grief.
Stay a moment. Don't withdraw from my sight.   540
Running away—from whom? This is the last word
that Fate allows me to say to you. The last."

    Aeneas, with such appeals, with welling tears,
tried to soothe her rage, her wild fiery glance.
But she, her eyes fixed on the ground, turned away,   545
her features no more moved by his pleas as he talked on
than if she were set in stony flint or Parian marble rock.
And at last she tears herself away, his enemy forever,
fleeing back to the shadowed forests where Sychaeus,
her husband long ago, answers all her anguish,   550
meets her love with love. But Aeneas, no less
struck by her unjust fate, escorts her from afar
with streaming tears and pities her as she passes.

    From there they labor along the charted path
and at last they gain the utmost outer fields   555
where throngs of the great war heroes live apart.
Here Tydeus comes to meet him, Parthenopaeus
shining in arms, and Adrastus' pallid phantom.[6] Here,
mourned in the world above and fallen dead in battle,
sons of Dardanus, chiefs arrayed in a long ranked line.   560
Seeing them all, he groaned—Glaucus, Medon, Thersilochus,
Antenor's three sons and the priest of Ceres, Polyboetes,
Idaeus too, still with chariot, still with gear in hand.[7]
Their spirits crowding around Aeneas, left and right,
beg him to linger longer—a glimpse is not enough—   565
to walk beside him and learn the reasons why he's come.

6. Three of the Argive leaders at Troy.   **7.** Names of Trojan warriors from the *Iliad*.

But the Greek commanders and Agamemnon's troops in phalanx,
spotting the hero and his armor glinting through the shadows—
blinding panic grips them, some turn tail and run
as they once ran back to the ships, some strain   570
to raise a battle cry, a thin wisp of a cry
that mocks their gaping jaws.

    And here he sees Deiphobus too, Priam's son
mutilated, his whole body, his face hacked to pieces—
Ah, so cruel—his face and both his hands, and his ears   575
ripped from his ravaged head, his nostrils slashed,
disgraceful wound. He can hardly recognize him,
a cowering shadow hiding his punishments so raw.
Aeneas, never pausing, hails the ghost at once
in an old familiar voice: "Mighty captain,   580
Deiphobus, sprung of the noble blood of Teucer,
who was bent on making you pay a price so harsh?
Who could maim you so? I heard on that last night
that you, exhausted from killing hordes of Greeks,
had fallen dead on a mangled pile of carnage.   585
So I was the one who raised your empty tomb
on Rhoeteum Cape and called out to your shade
three times with a ringing voice. Your name and armor
mark the site, my friend, but I could not find you,
could not bury your bones in native soil   590
when I set out to sea."

    "Nothing, my friend," Priam's son replies,
"you have left nothing undone. All that's owed
Deiphobus and his shadow you have paid in full.
My own fate and the deadly crimes of that Spartan whore[8]   595
have plunged me in this hell. Look at the souvenirs she left me!
And how we spent that last night, lost in deluded joys,
you know. Remember it we must, and all too well.
When the fatal horse mounted over our steep walls,
its weighted belly teeming with infantry in arms—   600
she led the Phrygian women round the city, feigning
the orgiastic rites of Bacchus,[9] dancing, shrieking
but in their midst she shook her monstrous torch,
a flare from the city heights, a signal to the Greeks.
While I in our cursed bridal chamber, there I lay,   605
bone-weary with anguish, buried deep in sleep,
peaceful, sweet, like the peace of death itself.
And all the while that matchless wife of mine
is removing all my weapons from the house,
even slipping my trusty sword from under my pillow.   610
She calls Menelaus in and flings the doors wide open,
hoping no doubt by this grand gift to him, her lover,

8. Helen.
9. Roman name for Dionysos, god of wine and frenzy.

to wipe the slate clean of her former wicked ways.
Why drag things out? They burst into the bedroom,
Ulysses, that rouser of outrage right beside them,   615
Aeolus' crafty heir.[1] You gods, if my lips are pure,
I pray for vengeance now—
deal such blows to the Greeks as they dealt *me*!
But come, tell me in turn what twist of fate
has brought you here alive? Forced by wanderings,   620
storm-tossed at sea, or prompted by the gods?
What destiny hounds you on to visit these,
these sunless homes of sorrow, harrowed lands?"

Trading words, as Dawn in her rose-red chariot
crossed in mid-career, high noon in the arching sky,   625
and they might have spent what time they had with tales
if the Sibyl next to Aeneas had not warned him tersely:
"Night comes on, Aeneas. We waste our time with tears.
This is the place where the road divides in two.
To the right it runs below the mighty walls of Death,   630
our path to Elysium, but the left-hand road torments
the wicked, leading down to Tartarus, path to doom."

"No anger, please, great priestess," begged Deiphobus.
"Back I go to the shades to fill the tally out.
Now go, our glory of Troy, go forth and enjoy   635
a better fate than mine." With his last words
he turned in his tracks and went his way.
                                            Aeneas
suddenly glances back and beneath a cliff to the left
he sees an enormous fortress ringed with triple walls
and raging around it all, a blazing flood of lava,   640
Tartarus' River of Fire, whirling thunderous boulders.
Before it rears a giant gate, its columns solid adamant,
so no power of man, not even the gods themselves
can root it out in war. An iron tower looms on high
where Tisiphone,[2] crouching with bloody shroud girt up,   645
never sleeping, keeps her watch at the entrance night and day.
Groans resound from the depths, the savage crack of the lash,
the grating creak of iron, the clank of dragging chains.
And Aeneas froze there, terrified, taking in the din:
"What are the crimes, what kinds? Tell me, Sibyl,   650
what are the punishments, why this scourging?
Why such wailing echoing in the air?"

The seer rose to the moment: "Famous captain of Troy,
no pure soul may set foot on that wicked threshold.

---

1. Reference to an alternative genealogy for
Ulysses (Odysseus), not as son of Laertes but
illegitimately fathered by Sisyphus, the infamous murderer and traitor, son of Aeolus.
2. One of the three Furies, divine figures of
vengeance.

But when Hecate put me in charge of Avernus' groves   655
she taught me all the punishments of the gods,
she led me through them all.
Here Cretan Rhadamanthus[3] rules with an iron hand,
censuring men, exposing fraud, forcing confessions
when anyone up above, reveling in his hidden crimes,   660
puts off his day of atonement till he dies, the fool,
too late. That very moment, vengeful Tisiphone, armed
with lashes, springs on the guilty, whips them till they quail,
with her left hand shaking all her twisting serpents,
summoning up her savage sisters, bands of Furies.   665
Then at last, screeching out on their grinding hinge
the infernal gates swing wide.
            "Can you see that sentry
crouched at the entrance? What a specter guards the threshold!
Fiercer still, the monstrous Hydra, fifty black maws gaping,
holds its lair inside.
            "Then the abyss, Tartarus itself   670
plunges headlong down through the darkness twice as far
as our gaze goes up to Olympus rising toward the skies.
Here the ancient line of the Earth, the Titans' spawn,
flung down by lightning, writhe in the deep pit.
There I saw the twin sons of Aloeus too,[4] giant bodies   675
that clawed the soaring sky with their hands to tear it down
and thrust great Jove from his kingdom high above.

"I saw Salmoneus[5] too, who paid a brutal price
for aping the flames of Jove and Olympus' thunder.
Sped by his four-horse chariot, flaunting torches,   680
right through the Greek tribes and Elis city's heart
he rode in triumph, claiming as *his* the honors of the gods.
The madman, trying to match the storm and matchless lightning
just by stamping on bronze with prancing horn-hoofed steeds!
The almighty Father hurled his bolt through the thunderheads—   685
no torches for him, no smoky flicker of pitch-pines, no,
he spun him headlong down in a raging whirlwind.
            "Tityus too:[6]
you could see that son of Earth, the mother of us all,
his giant body splayed out over nine whole acres,
a hideous vulture with hooked beak gorging down   690
his immortal liver and innards ever ripe for torture.
Deep in his chest it nestles, ripping into its feast
and the fibers, grown afresh, get no relief from pain.

3. Brother of Minos and, like Minos, a king of
Crete.
4. The Titans, who rebelled against Jupiter
(Jove) and were destroyed.
5. King of Elis, punished for impiety because

he pretended to Jupiter's might by using torches
to imitate lightning.
6. Tityos assaulted the goddess Latona and
was punished by being stretched out and forever devoured by a vulture.

"What need to tell of the Lapiths, Ixion, or Pirithous?[7]
Above them a black rock—now, now slipping, teetering,   695
watch, forever about to fall. While the golden posts
of high festal couches gleam, and a banquet spreads
before their eyes with luxury fit for kings . . .
but reclining just beside them, the oldest Fury
holds back their hands from even touching the food,   700
surging up with her brandished torch and deafening screams.

"Here those who hated their brothers, while alive,
or struck their fathers down
or embroiled clients in fraud, or brooded alone
over troves of gold they gained and never put aside   705
some share for their own kin—a great multitude, these—
then those killed for adultery, those who marched to the flag
of civil war and never shrank from breaking their pledge
to their lords and masters: all of them, walled up here,
wait to meet their doom.   "Don't hunger to know their doom,   710
what form of torture or twist of Fortune drags them down.
Some trundle enormous boulders, others dangle, racked
to the breaking point on the spokes of rolling wheels.
Doomed Theseus sits on his seat and there he will sit forever.
Phlegyas,[8] most in agony, sounds out his warning to all,   715
his piercing cries bear witness through the darkness:
'Learn to bow to justice. Never scorn the gods.
You all stand forewarned!'

"Here's one who bartered his native land for gold,
he saddled her with a tyrant, set up laws for a bribe,   720
for a bribe he struck them down. This one forced himself
on his daughter's bed and sealed a forbidden marriage.
All dared an outrageous crime and what they dared, they did.

"No, not if I had a hundred tongues and a hundred mouths
and a voice of iron too—I could never capture   725
all the crimes or run through all the torments,
doom by doom."
                      So Apollo's aged priestess
ended her answer, then she added: "Come,
press on with your journey. See it through,
this duty you've undertaken. We must hurry now.   730
I can just make out the ramparts forged by the Cyclops.[9]
There are the gates, facing us with their arch.

---

7. Pirithous, king of the Lapiths (known for their battle against the Centaurs) and friend of Theseus, tried to abduct Persephone and was chained up forever. Pirithous's father, Ixion, who assaulted Juno, was punished by being stretched on a wheel. (The punishments of the tottering rock and the food always out of reach are more normally associated with Tantalus.)
8. King of the Lapiths and father of Ixion; he was punished for setting fire to the temple of Apollo at Delphi.
9. The entrance to Elysium (the Fortunate Groves) was built by the god Vulcan, with help from the Cyclopes, famous for metalworking.

There our orders say to place our gifts."
                                    At that,
both of them march in step along the shadowed paths,
consuming the space between, and approach the doors.   735
Aeneas springs to the entryway and rinsing his limbs
with fresh pure water, there at the threshold,
just before them, stakes the golden bough.

   The rite complete at last,
their duty to the goddess performed in full,   740
they gained the land of joy, the fresh green fields,
the Fortunate Groves where the blessed make their homes.
Here a freer air, a dazzling radiance clothes the fields
and the spirits possess their own sun, their own stars.
Some flex their limbs in the grassy wrestling-rings,   745
contending in sport, they grapple on the golden sands.
Some beat out a dance with their feet and chant their songs.
And Orpheus himself, the Thracian priest with his long robes,[1]
keeps their rhythm strong with his lyre's seven ringing strings,
plucking now with his fingers, now with his ivory plectrum.   750

   Here is the ancient line of Teucer, noblest stock of all,
those great-hearted heroic sons born in better years,
Ilus, and Assaracus, and Dardanus, founder of Troy.
Far off, Aeneas gazes in awe—their arms, their chariots,
phantoms all, their lances fixed in the ground, their horses,   755
freed from harness, grazing the grasslands near and far.
The same joy they took in arms and chariots when alive,
in currying horses sleek and putting them to pasture,
follows them now they rest beneath the earth.
                                    Others, look,
he glimpses left and right in the meadows, feasting,   760
singing in joy a chorus raised to Healing Apollo,
deep in a redolent laurel grove where Eridanus River
rushes up, in full spate, and rolls through woods
in the high world above. And here are troops of men
who had suffered wounds, fighting to save their country,   765
and those who had been pure priests while still alive,
and the faithful poets whose songs were fit for Phoebus;
those who enriched our lives with the newfound arts they forged
and those we remember well for the good they did mankind.
And all, with snow-white headbands crowning their brows,   770
flow around the Sibyl as she addresses them there,
Musaeus[2] first, who holds the center of that huge throng,
his shoulders rearing high as they gaze up toward him:
"Tell us, happy spirits, and you, the best of poets,
what part of your world, what region holds Anchises?"   775

---

1. Orpheus, son of Apollo, is famous both for
his magical powers of song and also for his
association with Orphism, the set of religious

beliefs expounded by Anchises a little later in
this book (line 836 ff.).
2. Legendary poet and musician.

All for him we have come,
we've sailed across the mighty streams of hell."

    And at once the great soul made a brief reply:
"No one's home is fixed. We live in shady groves,
we settle on pillowed banks and meadows washed with brooks.   780
But you, if your heart compels you, climb this ridge
and I soon will set your steps on an easy path."

    So he said and walking on ahead, from high above
points out to them open country swept with light.
Down they come and leave the heights behind.   785

    Now father Anchises, deep in a valley's green recess,
was passing among the souls secluded there, reviewing them,
eagerly, on their way to the world of light above. By chance
he was counting over his own people, all his cherished heirs,
their fame and their fates, their values, acts of valor.   790
When he saw Aeneas striding toward him over the fields,
he reached out both his hands as his spirit lifted,
tears ran down his cheeks, a cry broke from his lips:
"You've come at last? Has the love your father hoped for
mastered the hardship of the journey? Let me look at your face,   795
my son, exchange some words, and hear your familiar voice.
So I dreamed, I knew you'd come, I counted the moments—
my longing has not betrayed me.
Over what lands, what seas have you been driven,
buffeted by what perils into my open arms, my son?   800
How I feared the realm of Libya³ might well do you harm!"

    "Your ghost, my father," he replied, "your grieving ghost,
so often it came and urged me to your threshold!
My ships are lying moored in the Tuscan sea.
Let me clasp your hand, my father, let me—   805
I beg you, don't withdraw from my embrace!"

    So Aeneas pleaded, his face streaming tears.
Three times he tried to fling his arms around his neck,
three times he embraced—nothing . . . the phantom
sifting through his fingers,   810
light as wind, quick as a dream in flight.

    And now Aeneas sees in the valley's depths
a sheltered grove and rustling wooded brakes
and the Lethe⁴ flowing past the homes of peace.
Around it hovered numberless races, nations of souls   815
like bees in meadowlands on a cloudless summer day
that settle on flowers, riots of color, swarming round
the lilies' lustrous sheen, and the whole field comes alive

---

3. Carthage.   4. River of forgetfulness.

with a humming murmur. Struck by the sudden sight,
Aeneas, all unknowing, wonders aloud, and asks: 820
"What is the river over there? And who are they
who crowd the banks in such a growing throng?"

   His father Anchises answers: "They are the spirits
owed a second body by the Fates. They drink deep
of the river Lethe's currents there, long drafts   825
that will set them free of cares, oblivious forever.
How long I have yearned to tell you, show them to you,
face to face, yes, as I count the tally out
of all my children's children. So all the more
you can rejoice with me in Italy, found at last."   830

   "What, Father, can we suppose that any spirits
rise from here to the world above, return once more
to the shackles of the body? Why this mad desire,
poor souls, for the light of life?"
                                        "I will tell you,
my son, not keep you in suspense," Anchises says,   835
and unfolds all things in order, one by one.
                                        "First,
the sky and the earth and the flowing fields of the sea,
the shining orb of the moon and the Titan sun, the stars:
an inner spirit feeds them, coursing through all their limbs,
mind stirs the mass and their fusion brings the world to birth.   840
From their union springs the human race and the wild beasts,
the winged lives of birds and the wondrous monsters bred
below the glistening surface of the sea. The seeds of life—
fiery is their force, divine their birth, but they
are weighed down by the bodies' ills or dulled   845
by earthly limbs and flesh that's born for death.
That is the source of all men's fears and longings,
joys and sorrows, nor can they see the heavens' light,
shut up in the body's tomb, a prison dark and deep.
                                        "True,
but even on that last day, when the light of life departs,   850
the wretches are not completely purged of all the taints,
nor are they wholly freed of all the body's plagues.
Down deep they harden fast—they must, so long engrained
in the flesh—in strange, uncanny ways. And so the souls
are drilled in punishments, they must pay for their old offenses.   855
Some are hung splayed out, exposed to the empty winds,
some are plunged in the rushing floods—their stains,
their crimes scoured off or scorched away by fire.
Each of us must suffer his own demanding ghost.
Then we are sent to Elysium's broad expanse,   860
a few of us even hold these fields of joy
till the long days, a cycle of time seen through,
cleanse our hard, inveterate stains and leave us clear
ethereal sense, the eternal breath of fire purged and pure.

But all the rest, once they have turned the wheel of time   865
for a thousand years: God calls them forth to the Lethe,
great armies of souls, their memories blank so that
they may revisit the overarching world once more
and begin to long to return to bodies yet again."

Anchises, silent a moment, drawing his son and Sibyl   870
with him into the midst of the vast murmuring throng,
took his stand on a rise of ground where he could scan
the long column marching toward him, soul by soul,
and recognize their features as they neared.
                                              "So come,
the glory that will follow the sons of Troy through time,   875
your children born of Italian stock who wait for life,
bright souls, future heirs of our name and our renown:
I will reveal them all and tell you of your fate.
                                              "There,
you see that youth who leans on a tipless spear of honor?
Assigned the nearest place to the world of light,   880
the first to rise to the air above, his blood
mixed with Italian blood, he bears an Alban name.[5]
Silvius, your son, your last-born, when late
in your old age your wife Lavinia brings him up,
deep in the woods—a king who fathers kings in turn,   885
he founds our race that rules in Alba Longa.
                                              "Nearby,
there's Procas, pride of the Trojan people, then come
Capys, Numitor, and the one who revives your name,
Silvius Aeneas, your equal in arms and duty,
famed, if he ever comes to rule the Alban throne.[6]   890
What brave young men! Look at the power they display
and the oakleaf civic crowns that shade their foreheads.
They will erect for you Nomentum, Gabii, Fidena town
and build Collatia's ramparts on the mountains,
Pometia too, and Inuis' fortress, Bola and Cora.   895
Famous names in the future, nameless places now.
                                              "Here,
a son of Mars, his grandsire Numitor's comrade—Romulus,
bred from Assaracus' blood by his mother, Ilia.[7]
See how the twin plumes stand joined on his helmet?
And the Father of Gods himself already marks him out   900
with his own bolts of honor. Under his auspices, watch,
my son, our brilliant Rome will extend her empire far
and wide as the earth, her spirit high as Olympus.
Within her single wall she will gird her seven hills,

5. Aeneas' son Ascanius is destined to found
the Italian kingdom of Alba Longa; his descendants will later found the city of Rome.
6. These are all kings of Alba Longa.
7. Numitor was a king of Alba Longa. His

daughter Ilia (also known as Rhea Silvia) was
raped by the war-god Mars and gave birth to
Romulus and Remus, who were raised by a
wolf. Assaracus is a Trojan ancestor.

blest in her breed of men: like the Berecynthian Mother[8]   905
crowned with her turrets, riding her victor's chariot
through the Phrygian cities, glad in her brood of gods,
embracing a hundred grandsons. All dwell in the heavens,
all command the heights.

               "Now turn your eyes this way
and behold these people, your own Roman people.   910
Here is Caesar[9] and all the line of Iulus
soon to venture under the sky's great arch.
Here is the man, he's here! Time and again
you've heard his coming promised—Caesar Augustus!
Son of a god, he will bring back the Age of Gold   915
to the Latian fields where Saturn once held sway,
expand his empire past the Garamants and the Indians[1]
to a land beyond the stars, beyond the wheel of the year,
the course of the sun itself, where Atlas bears the skies[2]
and turns on his shoulder the heavens studded with flaming stars.   920
Even now the Caspian and Maeotic kingdoms quake at his coming,[3]
oracles sound the alarm and the seven mouths of the Nile
churn with fear. Not even Hercules himself could cross
such a vast expanse of earth, though it's true he shot
the stag with its brazen hoofs, and brought peace   925
to the ravaged woods of Erymanthus, terrorized
the Hydra of Lerna with his bow.[4] Not even Bacchus
in all his glory, driving his team with vines for reins
and lashing his tigers down from Nysa's soaring ridge.[5]
Do we still flinch from turning our valor into deeds?   930
Or fear to make our home on Western soil?

                     "But look,
who is that over there, crowned with an olive wreath
and bearing sacred emblems? I know his snowy hair,
his beard—the first king to found our Rome on laws,
Numa,[6] sent from the poor town of Cures, paltry land,   935
to wield imperial power.

                "And after him comes Tullus
disrupting his country's peace to rouse a stagnant people,
armies stale to the taste of triumph, back to war again.
And just behind him, Ancus, full of the old bravado,
even now too swayed by the breeze of public favor.[7]

                         "Wait,   940
would you like to see the Tarquin kings, the overweening

---

8. Cybele, the mother goddess, was worshipped in the land of Troy and was depicted with a complicated diadem.

9. The emperor Augustus, Virgil's patron (63 B.C.E.–14 C.E.).

1. I.e., past Africa and India. Saturn (Saturnus) was an ancient Roman god associated with a lost Golden Age.

2. The Titan who holds up the sky.

3. Areas inhabited by the Scythians and Parthians, at the boundaries of the Roman Empire in Virgil's time.

4. Refers to three of the Labors of Heracles: killing the stag of Cerynaia, the boar of Erymanthus, and the Hydra.

5. Bacchus (Dionysos), a newcomer to the set of Olympian gods, traveled all over the world spreading his cult, including to India (Mount Nysa).

6. The second king of Rome, known for his piety.

7. Tullus and Ancus: the third and fourth legendary kings of Rome.

spirit of Brutus the Avenger, the fasces he reclaims?[8]
The first to hold a consul's power and ruthless axes,
then, when his sons foment rebellion against the city,
their father summons them to the executioner's block   945
in freedom's noble name, unfortunate man . . . [9]
however the future years will exalt his actions:
a patriot's love wins out, and boundless lust for praise.

                                     "Now,
the Decii and the Drusi—look over there—Torquatus too,
with his savage axe, Camillus bringing home the standards.[1]   950
But you see that pair of spirits? Gleaming in equal armor,
equals now at peace, while darkness pins them down,
but if they should reach the light of life, what war
they'll rouse between them! Battles, massacres—Caesar,[2]
the bride's father, marching down from his Alpine ramparts,   955
Fortress Monaco, Pompey her husband set to oppose him
with the armies of the East.
                          "No, my sons, never inure
yourselves to civil war, never turn your sturdy power
against your country's heart. You, Caesar,[3] you
be first in mercy—you trace your line from Olympus—   960
born of my blood, throw down your weapons now!

                                   "Mummius here,
he will conquer Corinth and, famed for killing Achaeans,
drive his victor's chariot up the Capitol's heights.
And there is Paullus,[4] and he will rout all Argos
and Agamemnon's own Mycenae and cut Perseus down—   965
the heir of Aeacus, born of Achilles' warrior blood—
and avenge his Trojan kin and Minerva's violated shrine.[5]

                                       "Who,
noble Cato, could pass you by in silence? Or you, Cossus?
Or the Gracchi and their kin? Or the two Scipios,
both thunderbolts of battle, Libya's scourge?   970
Or you, Fabricius, reared from poverty into power?
Or you, Serranus the Sower, seeding your furrow?
You Fabii, where do you rush me, all but spent?
And you, famous Maximus, you are the one man
whose delaying tactics save our Roman state.[6]   975

    "Others,[7] I have no doubt,
will forge the bronze to breathe with suppler lines,

---

8. The proud Tarquins, bad kings of early Rome, were expelled from the city by Brutus after Tarquinius Superbus raped Lucretia. This was, in legend, the end of Roman monarchy and the origin of the Roman Republic.
9. Brutus' sons tried to restore Tarquin to the throne and thus restore the monarchy; Brutus, in his capacity as consul, had them put to death.
1. All legendary Roman military heroes.
2. Julius Caesar, whose daughter married Pompey the Great. Pompey and Caesar fought each

other in the civil wars.
3. Augustus.
4. Aemelius Paullus defeated the king of Macedonia (168 B.C.E.); Mummius conquered Corinth in 146 B.C.E.
5. Refers to the rape of Cassandra by the Greek Ajax in the temple of Minerva (Athena) at Troy.
6. Famous historical Roman figures, all important for Rome's military success and rise to imperial power.
7. "Others" are Greeks.

draw from the block of marble features quick with life,
plead their cases better, chart with their rods the stars
that climb the sky and foretell the times they rise.
But you, Roman, remember, rule with all your power   980
the peoples of the earth—these will be your arts:
to put your stamp on the works and ways of peace,
to spare the defeated, break the proud in war."

    They were struck with awe as father Anchises paused,   985
then carried on: "Look there, Marcellus[8] marching toward us,
decked in splendid plunder he tore from a chief he killed,
victorious, towering over all. This man on horseback,
he will steady the Roman state when rocked by chaos,
mow the Carthaginians down in droves, the rebel Gauls.   990
He is only the third to offer up to Father Quirinus
the enemy's captured arms."
                        Aeneas broke in now,
for he saw a young man walking at Marcellus' side,[9]
handsome, striking, his armor burnished bright
but his face showed little joy, his eyes cast down.   995
"Who is that, Father, matching Marcellus stride for stride?
A son, or one of his son's descendants born of noble stock?
What acclaim from his comrades! What fine bearing,
the man himself! True, but around his head
a mournful shadow flutters black as night."
                            "My son,"   1000
his tears brimming, father Anchises started in,
"don't press to know your people's awesome grief.
Only a glimpse of him the Fates will grant the world,
not let him linger longer. Too mighty, the Roman race,
it seemed to You above, if this grand gift should last.   1005
Now what wails of men will the Field of Mars send up
to Mars' tremendous city! What a cortege you'll see,
old Tiber, flowing past the massive tomb just built!
No child of Troy will ever raise so high the hopes
of his Latin forebears, nor will the land of Romulus take   1010
such pride in a son she's borne. Mourn for his virtue!
Mourn for his honor forged of old, his sword arm
never conquered in battle. No enemy could ever
go against him in arms and leave unscathed,
whether he fought on foot or rode on horseback,   1015
digging spurs in his charger's lathered flanks.
Oh, child of heartbreak! If only you could burst
the stern decrees of Fate! You will be Marcellus.
Fill my arms with lilies, let me scatter flowers,
lustrous roses—piling high these gifts, at least,   1020
on our descendant's shade—and perform a futile rite."

8. Another military hero, successful in the Second Punic War.
9. The young man is the Marcellus who married Augustus' daughter Julia and would have been the heir to the empire, but died at the age of 19, in 23 B.C.E.

* * *

So they wander over the endless fields of air,
gazing at every region, viewing realm by realm.
Once Anchises has led his son through each new scene
and fired his soul with a love of glory still to come,   1025
he tells him next of the wars Aeneas still must wage,
he tells of Laurentine peoples, tells of Latinus' city,[1]
and how he should shun or shoulder each ordeal
that he must meet.
         There are twin Gates of Sleep.
One, they say, is called the Gate of Horn   1030
and it offers easy passage to all true shades.
The other glistens with ivory, radiant, flawless,
but through it the dead send false dreams up toward the sky.
And here Anchises, his vision told in full, escorts
his son and Sibyl both and shows them out now   1035
through the Ivory Gate.
         Aeneas cuts his way
to the waiting ships to see his crews again,
then sets a course straight on to Caieta's harbor.[2]
Anchors run from prows, the sterns line the shore.

Summary of books VII–VIII   Back in the upper world, Aeneas travels to the Trojan
exiles' promised land, Latium, in central Italy. In the capital city, Laurentum, he meets Latinus,
king of the Latin race, who has one daughter, Lavinia. An oracle has foretold that she must
marry a stranger, and the Latin people welcome Aeneas as their future king. But Amata, Latinus'
wife, had hoped her daughter would marry Turnus, leader of the rival Rutulian tribe. Juno, jealous of Trojan success, rouses the people to war and leads the native Italians against the invading
Trojans. Meanwhile, Aeneas has a vision of the god of the River Tiber, who tells him that his son
will found the city of Alba Longa, and that he should visit the Greek tribe of Arcadians, ruled by
Evander. Evander welcomes him, and shows him the future site of Rome. Evander sends his son,
Pallas, with troops of Arcadians and Etrurians, to fight with Aeneas. Meanwhile, Venus has had
her husband Vulcan forge a new set of armor for Aeneas, which she brings him as he and his
troops are resting, readying themselves for battle.

FROM BOOK VIII

[The Shield of Aeneas]

* * *

Down come captain Aeneas and all his fighters
picked for battle, water their horses well   715
and weary troops take rest.
         But the goddess Venus,
lustrous among the cloudbanks, bearing her gifts,
approached and when she spotted her son alone,
off in a glade's recess by the frigid stream,
she hailed him, suddenly there before him: "Look,   720

---

1. Latium, home of the "Laurentine peoples."   2. Modern-day Gaeta, on the west coast of Italy.

just forged to perfection by all my husband's skill:
the gifts I promised! There's no need now, my son,
to flinch from fighting swaggering Latin ranks
or challenging savage Turnus to a duel!"

    With that, Venus reached to embrace her son   725
and set the brilliant armor down before him
under a nearby oak.
                Aeneas takes delight
in the goddess' gifts and the honor of it all
as he runs his eyes across them piece by piece.
He cannot get enough of them, filled with wonder,   730
turning them over, now with his hands, now his arms,
the terrible crested helmet plumed and shooting fire,
the sword-blade honed to kill, the breastplate, solid bronze,
blood-red and immense, like a dark blue cloud enflamed
by the sun's rays and gleaming through the heavens.   735
Then the burnished greaves of electrum,[3] smelted gold,
the spear and the shield, the workmanship of the shield,
no words can tell its power . . .
                There is the story of Italy,
Rome in all her triumphs. There the fire-god forged them,
well aware of the seers and schooled in times to come,   740
all in order the generations born of Ascanius' stock
and all the wars they waged.
            And Vulcan forged them too,
the mother wolf stretched out in the green grotto of Mars,
twin boys at her dugs, who hung there, frisky, suckling
without a fear as she with her lithe neck bent back,   745
stroking each in turn, licked her wolf pups
into shape with a mother's tongue.[4]
             Not far from there
he had forged Rome as well and the Sabine women brutally
dragged from the crowded bowl when the Circus games were played
and abruptly war broke out afresh, the sons of Romulus   750
battling old King Tatius' hardened troops from Cures.[5]
Then when the same chiefs had set aside their strife,
they stood in full armor before Jove's holy altar,
lifting cups, and slaughtered a sow to bind their pacts.
                    Nearby,
two four-horse chariots, driven to left and right, had torn   755
Mettus apart—man of Alba, you should have kept your word—
and Tullus hauled the liar's viscera through the brush
as blood-drops dripped like dew from brakes of thorns.[6]
                        Porsenna,

---

3. Alloy of gold and silver.
4. Romulus and Remus, first builders of Rome's walls, who were suckled by the wolf.
5. At the first games in the Roman arena (the Circus), Roman men seized the Sabine women,
provoking their king, Tatius, to make war in revenge.
6. Mettus, king of Alba Longa, broke a promise to Tullus, third king of Rome, and was brutally punished.

there, commanding Romans to welcome banished Tarquin back,
mounted a massive siege to choke the city—Aeneas' heirs   760
rushing headlong against the steel in freedom's name.
See Porsenna to the life, his likeness menacing, raging,
and why? Cocles dared to rip the bridge down, Cloelia
burst her chains and swam the flood.[7]

                            Crowning the shield,
guarding the fort atop the Tarpeian Rock, Manlius   765
stood before the temple, held the Capitol's heights.
The new thatch bristled thick on Romulus' palace roof and
here the silver goose went ruffling through the gold arcades,
squawking its warning—Gauls attack the gates! Gauls
swarming the thickets, about to seize the fortress,   770
shielded by shadows, gift of the pitch-dark night.[8]
Gold their flowing hair, their war dress gold,
striped capes glinting, their milky necks ringed
with golden chokers, pairs of Alpine pikes in their hands,
flashing like fire, and long shields wrap their bodies.   775

   Here Vulcan pounded out the Salii, dancing priests of Mars,
the Luperci,[9] stripped, their peaked caps wound with wool,
bearing their body-shields that dropped from heaven,
and chaste matrons, riding in pillowed coaches,
led the sacred marches through the city.

                           Far apart   780
on the shield, what's more, he forged the homes of hell,
the high Gates of Death and the torments of the doomed,
with you, Catiline,[1] dangling from a beetling crag,
cringing before the Furies' open mouths.

                            And set apart,
the virtuous souls, with Cato[2] giving laws.

                           And amidst it all   785
the heaving sea ran far and wide, its likeness forged
in gold but the blue deep foamed in a sheen of white
and rounding it out in a huge ring swam the dolphins,
brilliant in silver, tails sweeping the crests
to cut the waves in two.

                       And here in the heart   790
of the shield: the bronze ships, the battle of Actium,[3]
you could see it all, the world drawn up for war,
Leucata Headland seething, the breakers molten gold.
On one flank, Caesar Augustus leading Italy into battle,

7. When the Etruscan tyrant Tarquin was banished from Rome, the Etruscan general Lars
Porsena attacked the city from a bridge, and
took a girl—Cloelia—hostage; but a Roman,
Cocles (better known as Horatius), tore down
the bridge, and rescued both girl and city.
8. In 390 B.C.E. Manlius defended Rome
against the invading Gauls; he was woken by
geese, who were the first to hear the attack.
9. Priests of Lupercus, the Roman equivalent

of Pan, the countryside god.
1. Conspirator who tried to overthrow the
Roman Republic in the first century B.C.E.
2. Cato the Younger, defender of the Republic, who killed himself after the victory of Julius
Caesar at Utica.
3. Site, on the northwestern Greek coast, of
a major naval engagement in which Octavian
(later called Augustus) defeated Antony and
Cleopatra in 31 B.C.E.

the Senate and People too, the gods of hearth and home   795
and the great gods themselves. High astern he stands,
the twin flames shoot forth from his lustrous brows and
rising from the peak of his head, his father's star.
On the other flank, Agrippa[4] stands tall as he steers
his ships in line, impelled by favoring winds and gods   800
and from his forehead glitter the beaks of ships
on the Naval Crown, proud ensign earned in war.

And opposing them comes Antony leading on
the riches of the Orient, troops of every stripe—
victor over the nations of the Dawn and blood-red shores   805
and in his retinue, Egypt, all the might of the East
and Bactra, the end of the earth, and trailing
in his wake, that outrage, that Egyptian wife![5]
All launch in as one, whipping the whole sea to foam
with tugging, thrashing oars and cleaving triple beaks   810
as they make a run for open sea. You'd think the Cyclades[6]
ripped up by the roots, afloat on the swells, or mountains
ramming against mountains, so immense the turrets astern
as sailors attack them, showering flaming tow and
hot bolts of flying steel, and the fresh blood running   815
red on Neptune's fields. And there in the thick of it all
the queen is mustering her armada, clacking her native rattles,
still not glimpsing the twin vipers hovering at her back,[7]
as Anubis[8] barks and the queen's chaos of monster gods
train their spears on Neptune, Venus, and great Minerva.   820
And there in the heart of battle Mars rampages on,
cast in iron, with grim Furies plunging down the sky
and Strife in triumph rushing in with her slashed robes
and Bellona[9] cracking her bloody lash in hot pursuit.
And scanning the melee, high on Actium's heights   825
Apollo bent his bow and terror struck them all,
Egypt and India, all the Arabians, all the Sabaeans
wheeled in their tracks and fled, and the queen herself—
you could see her calling, tempting the winds, her sails
spreading and now, now about to let her sheets run free.   830
Here in all this carnage the God of Fire forged her pale
with imminent death, sped on by the tides and Northwest Wind.
And rising up before her, the Nile immersed in mourning opens
every fold of his mighty body, all his rippling robes,
inviting into his deep blue lap and secret eddies   835
all his conquered people.
                     But Caesar[1] in triple triumph,

---

4. Son-in-law of Augustus, and admiral.
5. Although Actium was a battle between two
Roman factions in a civil war, it is presented
here as a conflict between the disciplined West
and the luxurious East. The "Egyptian wife"
is Cleopatra, queen of Egypt, with whom the
Roman general Antony was having an affair.

6. Greek islands.
7. Anticipating her death, since Cleopatra
poisoned herself with snakes.
8. Dog-headed Egyptian god.
9. Goddess of war.
1. Augustus, who took on the title "Caesar"

borne home through the walls of Rome, was paying
eternal vows of thanks to the gods of Italy:
three hundred imposing shrines throughout the city.
The roads resounded with joy, revelry, clapping hands,   840
with bands of matrons in every temple, altars in each
and the ground before them strewn with slaughtered steers.
Caesar himself, throned at brilliant Apollo's snow-white gates,
reviews the gifts brought on by the nations of the earth
and he mounts them high on the lofty temple doors   845
as the vanquished people move in a long slow file,
their dress, their arms as motley as their tongues.
Here Vulcan had forged the Nomad race, the Africans
with their trailing robes, here the Leleges, Carians,
Gelonian[2] archers bearing quivers, Euphrates flowing now   850
with a humbler tide, the Morini brought from the world's end,
the two-horned Rhine and the Dahae never conquered,
Araxes River bridling at his bridge.[3]
                                              Such vistas
the God of Fire forged across the shield
that Venus gives her son. He fills with wonder—   855
he knows nothing of these events but takes delight
in their likeness, lifting onto his shoulders now
the fame and fates of all his children's children.

Summary of Books IX–XI   *The war becomes bloody and violent. Jupiter orders a council
of the gods, reminding them that there was supposed to be peace between Trojans and Italians; but
he ends up renouncing responsibility: "the Fates will find the way," he declares. Pallas, son of
Evander, enters battle and is killed by Turnus. Aeneas longs to kill Turnus in revenge, but cannot
find him; Juno has spirited him away. Attempts at peace-making fail, and many are killed on both
sides, including a warrior princess named Camilla. Turnus insists on fighting Aeneas in single combat. Aeneas and King Latinus agree that if Turnus wins, the Trojans will leave, but if Turnus loses,
Aeneas will not enslave the native Italians, but will join with them on equal terms to form a new
nation. But the truce soon breaks, fighting starts again, and Aeneas is wounded. After Venus heals
him, he returns to battle in full armor, and eventually the Trojans and their allies attack Latium,
where Turnus has his stronghold. Turnus decides to fight him and again they agree to single combat;
everybody else draws back to leave space for the fight.*

FROM BOOK XII

[The Sword Decides All]

* * *

Latinus himself is struck that these two giant men,
sprung from opposing ends of the earth, have met,

2. The Lelegians and Carians were ancient
peoples of Asia Minor; the Gelonians were a
Scythian people of southern Russia.
3. Peoples and places indicating the vast extent
of the Roman Empire under Augustus: the
Euphrates is a river in Mesopotamia; the Morini

were a Gaulish tribe in modern-day Belgium,
beyond the Rhine River; the Dahae were a tribe
from east of the Caspian Sea; the Araxes River
(in modern-day Armenia) once had a bridge
built by Alexander that was swept away by
floods.

face to face, to let their swords decide.
                                       But they,
as soon as the battlefield lay clear and level,
charge at speed, rifling their spears at long range,   825
then rush to battle with shields and clanging bronze.
The earth groans as stroke after stroke they land
with naked swords: fortune and fortitude mix
in one assault. Charging like two hostile bulls
fighting up on Sila's woods or Taburnus' ridges,[4]   830
ramping in mortal combat, both brows bent for attack
and the herdsmen back away in fear and the whole herd
stands by, hushed, afraid, and the heifers wait and wonder,
who will lord it over the forest? who will lead the herd?—
while the bulls battle it out, horns butting, locking,   835
goring each other, necks and shoulders roped in blood
and the woods resound as they grunt and bellow out.
So they charge, Trojan Aeneas and Turnus, son of Daunus,[5]
shields clang and the huge din makes the heavens ring.
Jove himself lifts up his scales, balanced, trued,   840
and in them he sets the opposing fates of both . . .
Whom would the labor of battle doom? Whose life
would weigh him down to death?
                          Suddenly Turnus
flashes forward, certain he's in the clear and
raising his sword high, rearing to full stretch   845
strikes—as Trojans and anxious Latins shout out,
with the gaze of both armies riveted on the fighters.
But his treacherous blade breaks off, it fails Turnus
in mid-stroke—enraged, his one recourse, retreat,
and swifter than Eastwinds, Turnus flies as soon   850
as he sees that unfamiliar hilt in his hand,
no defense at all. They say the captain, rushing
headlong on to harness his team and board his car
to begin the duel, left his father's sword behind
and hastily grabbed his charioteer Metiscus' blade.   855
Long as the Trojan stragglers took to their heels and ran,
the weapon did its work, but once it came up against
the immortal armor forged by the God of Fire, Vulcan,
the mortal sword burst at a stroke, brittle as ice,
and glinting splinters gleamed on the tawny sand.   860
So raging Turnus runs for it, scours the field,
now here, now there, weaving in tangled circles
as Trojans crowd him hard, a dense ring of them
shutting him in, with a wild swamp to the left
and steep walls to the right.
                          Nor does Aeneas flag,   865
though slowed down by his wound, his knees unsteady,
cutting his pace at times but he's still in full fury,

---

4. Sila and Taburnus are mountainous, forested areas in southern Italy.   5. King of Apulia.

hot on his frantic quarry's tracks, stride for stride.
Alert as a hunting hound that lights on a trapped stag,
hemmed in by a river's bend or frightened back by the ropes   870
with blood-red feathers[6]—the hound barking, closing, fast
as the quarry, panicked by traps and the steep riverbanks,
runs off and back in a thousand ways but the Umbrian hound,[7]
keen for the kill, hangs on the trail, his jaws agape—
and now, now he's got him, thinks he's got him, yes   875
and his jaws clap shut, stymied, champing the empty air.
Then the shouts break loose, and the banks and rapids round
resound with the din, and the high sky thunders back. Turnus—
even in flight he rebukes his men as he races, calling
each by name, demanding his old familiar sword.   880
Aeneas, opposite, threatens death and doom at once
to anyone in his way, he threatens his harried foes
that he'll root their city out and, wounded as he is,
keeps closing for the kill. And five full circles
they run and reel as many back, around and back,   885
for it's no mean trophy they're sporting after now,
they race for the life and the lifeblood of Turnus.

    By chance a wild olive, green with its bitter leaves,
stood right here, sacred to Faunus,[8] revered by men
in the old days, sailors saved from shipwreck.   890
On it they always fixed their gifts to the local god
and they hung their votive clothes in thanks for rescue.
But the Trojans—no exceptions, hallowed tree that it was—
chopped down its trunk to clear the spot for combat.
Now here the spear of Aeneas had stuck, borne home   895
by its hurling force, and the tough roots held it fast.
He bent down over it, trying to wrench the iron loose and
track with a spear the kill he could not catch on foot.
Turnus, truly beside himself with terror—"Faunus!"
he cried, "I beg you, pity me! You, dear Earth,   900
hold fast to that spear! If I have always kept
your rites—a far cry from Aeneas' men
who stain your rites with war."
                So he appealed,
calling out for the god's help, and not for nothing.
Aeneas struggled long, wasting time on the tough stump,   905
no power of *his* could loose the timber's stubborn bite.
As he bravely heaves and hauls, the goddess Juturna,[9]
changing back again to the charioteer Metiscus,
rushes in and returns her brother's sword to Turnus.

---

6. Hunters used ropes and nets decorated with feathers.
7. A dog breed known for its skill in hunting. (Umbria is a region of northern Italy.)
8. An old Roman god associated with the countryside and forest.
9. A nymph of Italian lakes and springs, sister of Turnus; Jupiter made her immortal after he had an affair with her.

But Venus, incensed that the nymph has had her brazen way, 910
steps up and plucks Aeneas' spear from the clinging root.
So standing tall, with their arms and fighting hearts refreshed—
one who trusted all to his sword, the other looming fiercely
with his spear—confronting each other, both men breathless,
brace for the war-god's fray.

       Now at the same moment 915
Jove, the king of mighty Olympus, turns to Juno,
gazing down on the war from her golden cloud, and says:
"Where will it end, my queen? What is left at the last?
Aeneas the hero, god of the land: you know yourself,
you confess you know that he is heaven bound, 920
his fate will raise Aeneas to the stars.
What are you plotting? What hope can make you
cling to the chilly clouds? So, was it right
for a mortal hand to wound, to mortify a god?
Right to restore that mislaid sword to Turnus— 925
for without your power what could Juturna do?—
and lend the defeated strength? Have done at last.
Bow to my appeals. Don't let your corrosive grief
devour you in silence, or let your dire concerns come
pouring from your sweet lips and plaguing me forever. 930
We have reached the limit. To harass the Trojans
over land and sea, to ignite an unspeakable war,
degrade a royal house and blend the wedding hymn
with the dirge of grief: all that lay in your power.
But go no further. I forbid you now."

          Jove said no more. 935
And so, with head bent low, Saturn's daughter replied:
"Because I have known your will so well, great Jove,
against my *own* I deserted Turnus and the earth.
Or else you would never see me now, alone
on a windswept throne enduring right and wrong. 940
No, wrapped in flames I would be up on the front lines,
dragging the Trojan into mortal combat. Juturna?
I was the one, I admit, who spurred her on
to help her embattled brother, true, and blessed
whatever greater daring it took to save his life, 945
but never to shower arrows, never tense the bow.
I swear by the unappeasable fountainhead of the Styx,[1]
the one dread oath decreed for the gods on high.

               "So,
now I yield, Juno yields, and I leave this war I loathe.
But this—and there is no law of Fate to stop it now— 950
this I beg for Latium, for the glory of your people.
When, soon, they join in their happy wedding-bonds—
and wedded let them be—in pacts of peace at last,
never command the Latins, here on native soil,

---

1. River in the underworld; oaths sworn by the Styx could not be broken, even by the gods.

to exchange their age-old name, 955
to become Trojans, called the kin of Teucer,
alter their language, change their style of dress.
Let Latium endure. Let Alban kings hold sway for all time.
Let Roman stock grow strong with Italian strength.
Troy has fallen—and fallen let her stay— 960
with the very name of Troy!"

            Smiling down,
the creator of man and the wide world returned:
"Now there's my sister. Saturn's second child—
such tides of rage go churning through your heart.
Come, relax your anger. It started all for nothing. 965
I grant your wish. I surrender. Freely, gladly too.
Latium's sons will retain their fathers' words and ways.
Their name till now is the name that shall endure.
Mingling in stock alone, the Trojans will subside.
And I will add the rites and the forms of worship, 970
and make them Latins all, who speak one Latin tongue.
Mixed with Ausonian[2] blood, one race will spring from them,
and you will see them outstrip all men, outstrip all gods
in reverence. No nation on earth will match the honors
they shower down on you."

            Juno nodded assent to this, 975
her spirit reversed to joy. She departs the sky
and leaves her cloud behind.

            His task accomplished,
the Father turned his mind to another matter, set
to dismiss Juturna from her brother's battles.
They say there are twin Curses called the Furies . . . 980
Night had born them once in the dead of darkness,
one and the same spawn, and birthed infernal Megaera,[3]
wreathing all their heads with coiled serpents,
fitting them out with wings that race the wind.
They hover at Jove's throne, crouch at his gates 985
to serve that savage king
and whet the fears of afflicted men whenever
the king of gods lets loose horrific deaths and plagues
or panics towns that deserve the scourge of war.
Jove sped one of them down the sky, commanding: 990
"Cross Juturna's path as a wicked omen!"

   Down she swoops, hurled to earth by a whirlwind,
swift as a darting arrow whipped from a bowstring
through the clouds, a shaft armed by a Parthian,[4]
tipped with deadly poison, shot by a Parthian 995
or a Cretan archer—well past any cure—
hissing on unseen through the rushing dark.

2. Italian.
3. One of the Furies.

4. Parthia (a region in modern-day Iran) was
known for its skillful archers.

So raced this daughter of Night and sped to earth.
Soon as she spots the Trojan ranks and Turnus' lines
she quickly shrinks into that small bird that often,   1000
hunched at dusk on deserted tombs and rooftops, sings
its ominous song in shadows late at night. Shrunken so,
the demon flutters over and over again in Turnus' face,
screeching, drumming his shield with its whirring wings.
An eerie numbness unnerved him head to toe with dread,   1005
his hackles bristled in horror, voice choked in his throat.

Recognizing the Fury's ruffling wings at a distance,
wretched Juturna tears her hair, nails clawing her face,
fists beating her breast, and cries to her brother:
"How, Turnus, how can your sister help you now?   1010
What's left for me now, after all I have endured?
What skill do I have to lengthen out your life?
How can I fight against this dreadful omen?
At last, at last I leave the field of battle.
Afraid as I am, now frighten me no more,   1015
you obscene birds of night! Too well I know
the beat of your wings, the drumbeat of doom.
Nor do the proud commands of Jove escape me now,
our great, warm-hearted Jove. Are these his wages
for taking my virginity? Why did he grant me life   1020
eternal—rob me of our one privilege, death?
Then, for a fact, I now could end this agony,
keep my brother company down among the shades.
Doomed to live forever? Without you, my brother,
what do I have still mine that's sweet to taste?   1025
If only the earth gaped deep enough to take me down,
to plunge this goddess into the depths of hell!"
                                    With that,
shrouding her head with a gray-green veil and moaning low,
down to her own stream's bed the goddess sank away.

All hot pursuit, Aeneas brandishes high his spear,   1030
that tree of a spear, and shouts from a savage heart:
"More delay! Why now? Still in retreat, Turnus, why?
This is no foot-race. It's savagery, swordplay cut-and-thrust!
Change yourself into any shape you please, call up
whatever courage or skill you still have left.   1035
Pray to wing your way to the starry sky
or bury yourself in the earth's deep pits!"

Turnus shakes his head: "I don't fear you,
you and your blazing threats, my fierce friend.
It's the gods that frighten me—Jove, my mortal foe."   1040

No more words. Glancing around he spots a huge rock,
huge, ages old, and lying out in the field by chance,
placed as a boundary stone to settle border wars.

A dozen picked men could barely shoulder it up, men
of such physique as the earth brings forth these days,   1045
but he wrenched it up, hands trembling, tried to heave it
right at Aeneas, Turnus stretching to full height, the hero
at speed, at peak strength. Yet he's losing touch with himself,
racing, hoisting that massive rock in his hands and hurling,
true, but his knees buckle, blood's like ice in his veins   1050
and the rock he flings through the air, plummeting under
its own weight, cannot cover the space between them,
cannot strike full force . . .

               Just as in dreams
when the nightly spell of sleep falls heavy on our eyes
and we seem entranced by longing to keep on racing on,   1055
no use, in the midst of one last burst of speed
we sink down, consumed, our tongue won't work,
and tried and true, the power that filled our body
fails—we strain but the voice and words won't follow.
So with Turnus. Wherever he fought to force his way,   1060
no luck, the merciless Fury blocks his efforts.
A swirl of thoughts goes racing through his mind,
he glances toward his own Rutulians and their town,
he hangs back in dread, he quakes at death—it's here.
Where can he run? How can he strike out at the enemy?   1065
Where's his chariot? His charioteer, his sister? Vanished.

   As he hangs back, the fatal spear of Aeneas streaks on—
spotting a lucky opening he had flung from a distance,
all his might and main. Rocks heaved by a catapult
pounding city ramparts never storm so loudly, never   1070
such a shattering bolt of thunder crashing forth.
Like a black whirlwind churning on, that spear
flies on with its weight of iron death to pierce
the breastplate's lower edge and the outmost rim
of the round shield with its seven plies and right   1075
at the thick of Turnus' thigh it whizzes through,
it strikes home and the blow drops great Turnus
down to the ground, battered down on his bent knees.
The Rutulians spring up with a groan and the hillsides
round groan back and the tall groves far and wide   1080
resound with the long-drawn moan.

                       Turnus lowered
his eyes and reached with his right hand and begged,
a suppliant: "I deserve it all. No mercy, please,"
Turnus pleaded. "Seize your moment now. Or if
some care for a parent's grief can touch you still,   1085
I pray you—you had such a father, in old Anchises—
pity Daunus in his old age and send me back
to my own people, or if you would prefer,
send them my dead body stripped of life. Here,
the victor and vanquished, I stretch my hands to you,   1090
so the men of Latium have seen me in defeat.

Lavinia is your bride.
Go no further down the road of hatred."

Aeneas, ferocious in armor, stood there, still,
shifting his gaze, and held his sword-arm back,   1095
holding himself back too as Turnus' words began
to sway him more and more . . . when all at once
he caught sight of the fateful sword-belt of Pallas,[5]
swept over Turnus' shoulder, gleaming with shining studs
Aeneas knew by heart. Young Pallas, whom Turnus had overpowered,   1100
taken down with a wound, and now his shoulder flaunted
his enemy's battle-emblem like a trophy. Aeneas,
soon as his eyes drank in that plunder—keepsake
of his own savage grief—flaring up in fury,
terrible in his rage, he cries: "Decked in the spoils   1105
you stripped from one I loved—escape my clutches? Never—
Pallas strikes this blow, Pallas sacrifices you now,
makes you pay the price with your own guilty blood!"
In the same breath, blazing with wrath he plants
his iron sword hilt-deep in his enemy's heart.   1110
Turnus' limbs went limp in the chill of death.
His life breath fled with a groan of outrage
down to the shades below.[6]

---

5. Son of Evander, king of the Arcadians, who were allied with the Trojans.

6. The same lines are used in book XI for the death of the woman warrior, Camilla.

OVID

43 B.C.E.–17 C.E.

Ovid (whose full name was Publius Ovidius Naso) was one of the smartest, most prolific, and most consistently entertaining of the Roman poets. During his long and productive career, he wrote funny, perceptive poems about sex and relationships in contemporary Rome, as well as vivid retellings of ancient myths. His way of telling stories remains extraordinary for its subtlety and its depth of psychological understanding. His work had a massive influence on the poets and artists of the Middle Ages, the Renaissance, and beyond, and it is one of our most important and accessible sources for the rich mythology of ancient Greece and Rome.

LIFE AND TIMES

Ovid was born into an aristocratic ("equestrian") family, in the provincial Roman town of Sulmo, east of Rome. His father wanted him to become a lawyer, and therefore had him trained in rhetoric. Ovid's writing shows the influence of rhetorical technique, in its polished, witty style. But Ovid had no real interest in the law. He was a natural poet, and at the age of twenty, to his father's disappointment and disapproval, he quit his legal training. He held various minor governmental posts, but eventually became a full-time poet, with the financial aid of a rich patron called Messalla. Ovid became part of the literary circles of Rome: he knew the poets Propertius and **Horace**, and met **Virgil**, who was some twenty-seven years older.

Ovid married three times; he had been divorced twice before the age of thirty. His third wife seems to have had a daughter by a previous husband, but Ovid had no children of his own. Beyond that, we know little of Ovid's personal life. He wrote a great deal about extramarital sex, but emphasized that his poetic persona should not be taken as autobiography, declaring, "My Muse is slutty, but my life is chaste."

Ovid's work included various collections of poems on mythological topics, such as the *Fasti* (never finished), on the Roman calendar, and a set of poetic letters, the *Heroides*, from mythical heroines like Helen of Troy to their boyfriends. But most notorious, in his own time and later, were his two books about sex and relationships: the *Amores* and the *Ars Amatoria*. These used the tradition of Roman love elegy, which had begun with **Catullus** and had been developed by Ovid's friend Propertius, who evoked the desperate, abject longing of a man for a beloved and unreliable girlfriend. Ovid's love poetry focuses less on feelings than on behavior, and less on love than on sex, which he treats in a light, knowing tone. He gives, for example, a titillating account of some hot afternoon sex; tells anecdotes about his girlfriend's bad experiences with hair dye and about her attempted abortion; and offers advice about the best places to go and best lines to use for picking up a date.

All this was guaranteed to irritate the more conservative members of Roman society, who included—unfortunately for Ovid—the emperor, Augustus. Having seized power after winning the battle of Actium (in 31 B.C.E.), at the end of a long civil war, Augustus was eager to impose order on the fragmented society of Rome. A key element in his domestic strategy was to reform the morals and increase the population of the Roman elite, by promoting marriage and traditional family structures. New laws were imposed in 19–18 B.C.E. to encourage married couples to have children, and to punish adultery with exile. In this context, Ovid's *Ars Amatoria* seems deliberately calculated to enrage the emperor. The poem points up the hypocrisy of Roman sexual mores and suggests that, in fact, having lots of extramarital sex is far more traditional than Augustan family values, since the Romans have been doing it ever since the foundation of the city: it was through the rape of the Sabine women that the male inhabitants of the new city acquired wives and were able to supply Rome with future citizens.

Ovid seems to have gotten himself into even worse trouble by what he calls a mistake. We do not know exactly what happened; Ovid suggests that he saw something he should not have seen, perhaps involving the emperor's daughter, Julia, who was having an adulterous affair. Combined with the *Ars Amatoria* and Ovid's generally provocative stance toward Augustus, this mistake was the last straw; in 8 C.E., the emperor—acting, unusually, on his own initiative, without input from the Senate—condemned Ovid to permanent exile from Rome to Tomis, a remote town on the Black Sea, in modern Romania. He lived out the remaining eight years of his life in grim isolation, far from family and friends, in a cold, bleak place where, he claims, nobody even spoke Latin. Ovid wrote a series of poems from exile, mostly letters bewailing his sufferings and pleading—to friends, family, acquaintances, the general public, and to the emperor himself—to be forgiven and to be allowed back home. All were unsuccessful; Ovid died in Tomis, alone and unforgiven.

METAMORPHOSES

At the time of his exile in 8 C.E., Ovid was finishing his greatest work, the *Metamorphoses* (Greek for "changes"). It is less obviously provocative than Ovid's love poetry, but it, too, provides a radical challenge both to Augustan moral and political values and to traditional poetic norms. Virgil had written what Augustus wanted to be the official epic of the new order. For all its innovations, the *Aeneid* focused on the deeds of a single hero, and it treated its culture's dominant values (such as duty, imperial power, and military honor) with respect. The *Metamorphoses* is recognizably epic; it is the only poem Ovid wrote in the epic meter, dactylic hexameter. But it can be seen as a critical response to Virgil, even an anti-*Aeneid*. Ovid produced a series of miniature stories strung together into a long narrative of fifteen books. The transitions between them, and the connections drawn by the narrator, are often transparently contrived—perhaps in mockery of the idea of narrative unity. There is no single hero, and no moral values are presented without irony. There is, however, an element common to these stories: change; and despite its leisurely and roundabout course, the narrative has a discernible direction—as Ovid says in his introduction, "from the world's beginning to the present day." Starting with the creation of the world, the transformation of matter into living bodies (the first great metamorphosis), Ovid tells of human beings changed into animals, flowers, and trees. He proceeds through Greek myth to stories of early Rome and so to his own time, culminating in the ascension of the murdered Julius Caesar to the heavens in the form of a star and the divine promise that Augustus too, far in the future, will become a god; it is tempting to speculate that Ovid hoped—vainly—to improve his relationship with the emperor by means of these few lines. The last change of all is that of Ovid himself, who will, he declares, be transformed from a mortal man into his own immortal poem.

Change underlies both the narrative style and the vision of the world the poem projects. Virgil also told of a transformation, the new (Roman) order arising from the ruins of the old (Troy). But once the transformation was completed by the Augustan order, there was to be stability, permanence. Ovid tells of a world ceaselessly coming to be in a process that never ends. Augustan Rome is not the culminating point of history here, as it was in the *Aeneid*; indeed, the whole idea of a historical end or goal seems, in the *Metamorphoses*, impossible and absurd. Ovid's epic without a hero presents shifting perspectives and offers the reader no single point of view from which to judge his complex narratives. Against the forced imposition of political and moral unity he sets change itself.

Change is also central to the narrative manner of the *Metamorphoses*. Ovid constantly shifts his point of view, telling a story first from one character's perspective, and then from another's. One story is embedded in another, so that one narrative voice is piled on top of another, as when Venus tells Adonis the story of Atalanta. This story is set within the tale of Venus's love for Adonis and of his death, which is one of a series of stories sung by Orpheus in the poem's main narrative. In such cases, the immediate and the larger contexts give the same story different shades of meaning. And there are thematic connections between stories, so that motifs and images also change their meaning from one story to another, or over the course of a single story. Daphne and Syrinx are turned into plants (the laurel and the reed) that are henceforth attributes of the gods who tried to rape them, a form of appropriation that substitutes for sexual violence.

A common element of many stories in books I and II is the lust of male gods for female humans. On one level, the gods' desire is presented as ridiculous: when Jupiter turns himself into a bull, the narrator comments, "Majestic power and erotic love / do not get on together very well." But these stories are also focused on rape, and, at least some of the time, the narrator shows the terror and suffering of the human victim. These stories of rape may have political implications, for rape is the ultimate imposition of control. When powerful gods force themselves on defenseless women, the reader is invited to remember how easily authority can be abused.

But male gods are not the only sexual agents in the poem: women and goddesses, too, can be overwhelmed by desire, and can themselves become sexual predators. The stories selected here from later in the *Metamorphoses* bring out the complexity of Ovid's presentation of gender and sexuality. The story of Iphis and Ianthe suggests that social gender roles for women and men are more or less arbitrary: girls usually look different from boys, but their feelings may be exactly the same. That story has a happy ending, but the tales from book X show various ways in which desire causes pain, distorts our perceptions, and ends in disaster. The tale of Pygmalion may seem an exception, but we should remember that it begins with the artist's hatred of women for their loose morals, and that the story as a whole, whatever it may say about the power of art, can also be read as a fable of man's fabrication of woman—her person and her functions—according to his desires. These stories are narrated by Orpheus, the archetypal poet, after his failure to bring Eurydice back from the underworld. The pathology of desire is fundamental to Ovid's poem, since the lover hopes to stop time, to achieve permanent possession of the beloved; but all these stories show us how impossible such a dream is. The girl is always running from the god; the boy is always running from the goddess; Orpheus's wife cannot be brought back from the land of the dead. Reaching for the body of another, the lover's own body is transformed. The closest any of these characters can get to permanence is to be transformed into a growing (living, changing) plant that will always represent their unfulfilled longings.

The Italian baroque sculptor Giovanni Bernini carved statue groups of Apollo and Daphne and of Hades and Proserpina—stunning translations of Ovid's poetry into marble. **Milton** and **Dante** frequently alluded to the *Metamorphoses*, and both used Ovid's version of the Proserpina story: Milton in book 9 of *Paradise Lost*, as an image of death's entry into the world; Dante in the *Purgatorio*, to emphasize redemption from death. It was surely not only the fact that the *Metamorphoses* draws into itself most of the major classical myths (and a number of lesser-known stories as well) that has made the poem a source of subjects for artists and poets ever since but also the memorable ways these stories are told and their rich potential for meaning. The poem shows, again and again, the irresistible power of a well-told narrative to hold the attention and shape the imagination of those who read or listen to it.

Giovanni Bernini's seventeenth-century interpretation in marble of the rape of Proserpina.

From Metamorphoses[1]

FROM BOOK I

[Proem]

My mind leads me to speak now of forms changed
into new bodies: O gods above, inspire
this undertaking (which you've changed as well)
and guide my poem in its epic sweep
from the world's beginning to the present day.   5

1. Translated by Charles Martin.

[The Creation]

Before the seas and lands had been created,
before the sky that covers everything,
Nature displayed a single aspect only
throughout the cosmos; Chaos was its name,
a shapeless, unwrought mass of inert bulk   10
and nothing more, with the discordant seeds
of disconnected elements all heaped
together in anarchic disarray.

    The sun as yet did not light up the earth,
nor did the crescent moon renew her horns,   15
nor was the earth suspended in midair,
balanced by her own weight, nor did the ocean
extend her arms to the margins of the land.

    Although the land and sea and air were present,
land was unstable, the sea unfit for swimming,   20
and air lacked light; shapes shifted constantly,
and all things were at odds with one another,
for in a single mass cold strove with warm,
wet was opposed to dry and soft to hard,
and weightlessness to matter having weight.   25

    Some god (or kinder nature) settled this
dispute by separating earth from heaven,
and then by separating sea from earth
and fluid aether[2] from the denser air;
and after these were separated out   30
and liberated from the primal heap,
he bound the disentangled elements
each in its place and all in harmony.

    The fiery and weightless aether leapt
to heaven's vault and claimed its citadel;   35
the next in lightness to be placed was air;
the denser earth drew down gross elements
and was compressed by its own gravity;
encircling water lastly found its place,
encompassing the solid earth entire.[3]   40

    Now when that god (whichever one it was)
had given Chaos form, dividing it
in parts which he arranged, he molded earth
into the shape of an enormous globe,
so that it should be uniform throughout.   45

    And afterward he sent the waters streaming
in all directions, ordered waves to swell
under the sweeping winds, and sent the flood
to form new shores on the surrounded earth;
he added springs, great standing swamps and lakes,   50

2. A region of refined air, fiery in nature, believed to be above the "denser air" that was closer to the earth and composed the breathable atmosphere.

3. From Homer on, the ancients conceived of Ocean as a stream that surrounded the earth.

as well as sloping rivers fixed between
their narrow banks, whose plunging waters (all
in varied places, each in its own channel)
are partly taken back into the earth
and in part flow until they reach the sea, 55
when they—received into the larger field
of a freer flood—beat against shores, not banks.
He ordered open plains to spread themselves,
valleys to sink, the stony peaks to rise,
and forests to put on their coats of green. 60
 And as the vault of heaven is divided
by two zones on the right and two on the left,
with a central zone, much hotter, in between,
so, by the care of this creator god,
the mass that was enclosed now by the sky 65
was zoned in the same way, with the same lines
inscribed upon the surface of the earth.
Heat makes the middle zone unlivable,
and the two outer zones are deep in snow;
between these two extremes, he placed two others 70
of temperate climate, blending cold and warmth.[4]
 Air was suspended over all of this,
proportionately heavier than aether,
as earth is heavier than water is.
He ordered mists and clouds into position, 75
and thunder, to make test of our resolve,[5]
and winds creating thunderbolts and lightning.
 Nor did that world-creating god permit
the winds to roam ungoverned through the air;
for even now, with each of them in charge 80
of his own kingdom, and their blasts controlled,
they scarcely can be kept from shattering
the world, such is the discord between brothers.
 Eurus[6] went eastward, to the lands of Dawn,
the kingdoms of Arabia and Persia, 85
and to the mountain peaks that lie below
the morning's rays; and Zephyr took his place
on the western shores warmed by the setting sun.
The frozen north and Scythia were seized
by bristling Boreas; the lands opposite, 90
continually drenched by fog and rain,
are where the south wind, known as Auster, dwells.
Above these winds, he set the weightless aether,
a liquid free of every earthly toxin.
 No sooner had he separated all 95

4. The sky, that is, is divided into five horizontal zones, and therefore so is the earth beneath it. On either side of the earth's uninhabitable torrid region, over which the sun passes, lies a temperate zone, and the northern one contains the inhabited, civilized lands on earth (ancient writers were vague about what the southern temperate zone contained). The two outermost zones, farthest from the sun, were too cold to live in.
5. Thunder was considered an omen.
6. The east wind. Zephyr, Boreas, and Auster were the west, north, and south winds, respectively.

within defining limits, when the stars,
which formerly had been concealed in darkness,
began to blaze up all throughout the heavens;
and so that every region of the world
should have its own distinctive forms of life,   100
the constellations and the shapes of gods
occupied the lower part of heaven;
the seas gave shelter to the shining fishes,
earth received beasts, and flighty air, the birds.

   An animal more like the gods than these,   105
more intellectually capable
and able to control the other beasts,
had not as yet appeared: now man was born,
either because the framer of all things,
the fabricator of this better world,   110
created man out of his own divine
substance—or else because Prometheus[7]
took up a clod (so lately broken off
from lofty aether that it still contained
some elements in common with its kin),   115
and mixing it with water, molded it
into the shape of gods, who govern all.

   And even though all other animals
lean forward and look down toward the ground,
he gave to man a face that is uplifted,   120
and ordered him to stand erect and look
directly up into the vaulted heavens
and turn his countenance to meet the stars;
the earth, that was so lately rude and formless,
was changed by taking on the shapes of men.   125

* * *

[Apollo and Daphne]

Daphne,[8] the daughter of the river god
Peneus, was the first love of Apollo;
this happened not by chance, but by the cruel
outrage of Cupid; Phoebus, in the triumph   630
of his great victory against the Python,[9]
observed him bending back his bow and said,

   "What are *you* doing with such manly arms,
lascivious boy? That bow befits *our* brawn,[1]
wherewith we deal out wounds to savage beasts   635
and other mortal foes, unerringly:
just now with our innumerable arrows
we managed to lay low the mighty Python,
whose pestilential belly covered acres!   640

---

7. A god best known for stealing fire from the
gods and giving it to mortals. In some stories
he also created humans out of clay.
8. Literally, "Laurel" (Greek).

9. The enormous snake that Apollo (Phoebus)
had to kill in order to found his oracle at
Delphi. "Cupid": god of sexual desire.
1. The bow was one of Apollo's attributes.

Content yourself with kindling love affairs
with your wee torch—and don't claim *our* glory!"

The son of Venus[2] answered him with this:
"Your arrow, Phoebus, may strike everything:
mine will strike you: as animals to gods,   645
your glory is so much the less than mine!"

He spoke, and soaring upward through the air
on wings that thundered, in no time at all
had landed on Parnassus'[3] shaded height;
and from his quiver drew two arrows out   650
which operated at cross-purposes,
for one engendered flight, the other, love;
the latter has a polished tip of gold,
the former has a tip of dull, blunt lead;
with this one, Cupid struck Peneus' daughter,   655
while the other pierced Apollo to his marrow.

One is in love now, and the other one
won't hear of it, for Daphne calls it joy
to roam within the forest's deep seclusion,
where she, in emulation of the chaste   660
goddess Phoebe,[4] devotes herself to hunting;
one ribbon only bound her straying tresses.

Many men sought her, but she spurned her suitors,
loath to have anything to do with men,
and rambled through the wild and trackless groves   665
untroubled by a thought for love or marriage.

Often her father said, "You owe it to me,
child, to provide me with a son-in-law
and grandchildren!"

                    "Let me remain a virgin,
father most dear," she said, "as once before   670
Diana's father, Jove, gave her that gift."

Although Peneus yielded to you, Daphne,
your beauty kept your wish from coming true,
your comeliness conflicting with your vow:
at first sight, Phoebus loves her and desires   675
to sleep with her; desire turns to hope,
and his own prophecy deceives the god.

Now just as in a field the harvest stubble
is all burned off, or as hedges are set ablaze
when, if by chance, some careless traveler   680
should brush one with his torch or toss away
the still-smoldering brand at break of day—
just so the smitten god went up in flames
until his heart was utterly afire,
and hope sustained his unrequited passion.   685

He gazes on her hair without adornment:
"What if it were done up a bit?" he asks,

---

2. Goddess of love (Aphrodite in Greek).
3. Mountain in central Greece, near Delphi.

4. Diana (Artemis in Greek), Apollo's sister,
virgin goddess of the hunt.

and gazes on her eyes, as bright as stars,
and on that darling little mouth of hers,
though sight is not enough to satisfy;   690
he praises everything that he can see—
her fingers, hands, and arms, bare to her shoulders—
and what is hidden prizes even more.

   She flees more swiftly than the lightest breeze,
nor will she halt when he calls out to her: 695
"Daughter of Peneus, I pray, hold still,
hold still! I'm not a foe in grim pursuit!
Thus lamb flees wolf, thus dove from eagle flies
on trembling wings, thus deer from lioness,
thus any creature flees its enemy,   700
but I am stalking you because of love!

   "Wretch that I am: I'm fearful that you'll fall,
brambles will tear your flesh because of me!
The ground you're racing over's very rocky,
slow down, I beg you, restrain yourself in flight,   705
and I will follow at a lesser speed.

   "Just ask yourself who finds you so attractive!
I'm not a caveman, not some shepherd boy,
no shaggy guardian of flocks and herds—
you've no idea, rash girl, you've no idea   710
whom you are fleeing, that is why you flee!

   "Delphi, Claros, Tenedos are all mine,
I'm worshiped in the city of Patara![5]
Jove is my father, I alone reveal
what was, what is, and what will come to be!   715
The plucked strings answer my demand with song!

   "Although my aim is sure, another's arrow
proved even more so, and my careless heart
was badly wounded—the art of medicine
is my invention, by the way, the source   720
of my worldwide fame as a practitioner
of healing through the natural strength of herbs.

   "Alas, there is no herbal remedy
for the love that I must suffer, and the arts
that heal all others cannot heal their lord—"   725

   He had much more to say to her, but Daphne
pursued her fearful course and left him speechless,
though no less lovely fleeing him; indeed,
disheveled by the wind that bared her limbs
and pressed the blown robes to her straining body   730
even as it whipped up her hair behind her,
the maiden was more beautiful in flight!

   But the young god had no further interest
in wasting his fine words on her; admonished
by his own passion, he accelerates,   735
and runs as swiftly as a Gallic hound[6]

---

5. All centers of Apollo's cult.   6. A hunting breed famous for speed.

chasing a rabbit through an open field;
the one seeks shelter and the other, prey—
he clings to her, is just about to spring,
with his long muzzle straining at her heels, 740
while she, not knowing whether she's been caught,
in one swift burst, eludes those snapping jaws,
no longer the anticipated feast;
so he in hope and she in terror race.

 But her pursuer, driven by his passion, 745
outspeeds the girl, giving her no pause,
one step behind her, breathing down her neck;
her strength is gone; she blanches at the thought
of the effort of her swift flight overcome,
but at the sight of Peneus, she cries, 750
"Help me, dear father! If your waters hold
divinity, transform me and destroy
that beauty by which I have too well pleased!"

 Her prayer was scarcely finished when she feels
a torpor take possession of her limbs— 755
her supple trunk is girdled with a thin
layer of fine bark over her smooth skin;
her hair turns into foliage, her arms
grow into branches, sluggish roots adhere
to feet that were so recently so swift, 760
her head becomes the summit of a tree;
all that remains of her is a warm glow.

 Loving her still, the god puts his right hand
against the trunk, and even now can feel
her heart as it beats under the new bark; 765
he hugs her limbs as if they were still human,
and then he puts his lips against the wood,
which, even now, is adverse to his kiss.

 "Although you cannot be my bride," he says,
"you will assuredly be my own tree, 770
O Laurel, and will always find yourself
girding my locks, my lyre, and my quiver too—
you will adorn great Roman generals
when every voice cries out in joyful triumph
along the route up to the Capitol; 775
you will protect the portals of Augustus,
guarding, on either side, his crown of oak;[7]
and as I am—perpetually youthful,
my flowing locks unknown to the barber's shears—
so you will be an evergreen forever 780
bearing your brilliant foliage with glory!"

 Phoebus concluded. Laurel shook her branches
and seemed to nod her summit in assent.

---

7. The laurel tree, sacred to Apollo, was the symbol of victory not only in athletic contests but also in war; victorious Roman generals honored with a triumphal procession through the city to the Capitol wore a laurel wreath. The oak was sacred to Jupiter.

[*Jove and Io*]

There is a grove in Thessaly,[8] enclosed
on every side by high and wooded hills:
they call it Tempe. The river Peneus,   785
which rises deep within the Pindus range,
pours its turbulent waters through this gorge
and over a cataract that deafens all
its neighbors far and near, creating clouds   790
that drive a fine, cool mist along, until
it drips down through the summits of the trees.

    Here is the house, the seat, the inner chambers
of the great river; here Peneus holds court
in his rocky cavern and lays down the law   795
to water nymphs and tributary streams.

    First to assemble were the native rivers,
uncertain whether to congratulate,
or to commiserate with Daphne's father:
the Sperchios, whose banks are lined with poplars,   800
the ancient Apidanus and the mild
Aeas and Amprysus; others came later—
rivers who, by whatever course they take,
eventually bring their flowing streams,
weary of their meandering, to sea.   805

    Inachus[9] was the only river absent,
concealed in the recesses of his cave:
he added to his volume with the tears
he grimly wept for his lost daughter Io,
not knowing whether she still lived or not;   810
but since he couldn't find her anywhere,
assumed that she was nowhere to be found—
and in his heart, he feared a fate far worse.

    For Jupiter had seen the girl returning
from her father's banks and had accosted her: 815
"O maiden worthy of almighty Jove
and destined to delight some lucky fellow
(I know not whom) upon your wedding night,
come find some shade," he said, "in these deep woods—"
(showing her where the woods were *very* shady)   820
"while the sun blazes high above the earth!

    "But if you're worried about entering
the haunts of savage beasts all by yourself,
why, under the protection of a god
you will be safe within the deepest woods—   825
and no plebeian god, for I am he
who bears the celestial scepter in his hand,
I am he who hurls the roaming thunderbolt—
don't run from me!"

                 But run she did, through Lerna

---

8. A region of central Greece.
9. A river near Argos in the northeast Peloponnesus.

and Lyrcea,[1] until the god concealed   830
the land entirely beneath a dense
dark mist and seized her and dishonored her.
    Juno,[2] however, happened to look down
on Argos, where she noticed something odd:
swift-flying clouds had turned day into night   835
long before nighttime. She realized
that neither falling mist nor rising fog
could be the cause of this phenomenon,
and looked about at once to find her husband,
as one too well aware of the connivings   840
of a mate so often taken in the act.
    When he could not be found above, she said,
"Either I'm mad—or I am being had."
She glided down to earth from heaven's summit
immediately and dispersed the clouds.   845
    Having intuited his wife's approach,
Jove had already metamorphosed Io
into a gleaming heifer—a beauty still,
even as a cow. Despite herself,
Juno gave this illusion her approval,   850
and feigning ignorance, asked him whose herd
this heifer had come out of, and where from;
Jove, lying to forestall all inquiries
as to her origin and pedigree,
replied that she was born out of the earth.   855
Then Juno asked him for her as a gift.
    What could he do? Here is his beloved:
to hand her over is unnatural,
but not to do so would arouse suspicion;
shame urged him onward while love held him back.   860
Love surely would have triumphed over shame,
except that to deny so slight a gift
to one who was his wife and sister both
would make it seem that this was no mere cow!
    Her rival given up to her at last,   865
Juno feared Jove had more such tricks in mind,
and couldn't feel entirely secure
until she'd placed this heifer in the care
of Argus, the watchman with a hundred eyes:
in strict rotation, his eyes slept in pairs,   870
while those that were not sleeping stayed on guard.
No matter where he stood, he looked at Io,
even when he had turned his back on her.
    He let her graze in daylight; when the sun
set far beneath the earth, he penned her in   875
and placed a collar on her indignant neck.

---

1. A mountain on the border between Argos and Arcadia to the west. "Lerna": a marsh in the territory of Argos, near the coast.
2. Wife of Jupiter (Hera in Greek).

She fed on leaves from trees and bitter grasses,
and had no bed to sleep on, the poor thing,
but lay upon the ground, not always grassy,
and drank the muddy waters from the streams.   880

Having no arms, she could not stretch them out
in supplication to her warden, Argus;
and when she tried to utter a complaint
she only mooed—a sound which terrified her,
fearful as she now was of her own voice.   885

Io at last came to the riverbank
where she had often played; when she beheld
her own slack jaws and newly sprouted horns
in the clear water, she fled, terrified!

Neither her naiad sisters[3] nor her father   890
knew who this heifer was who followed them
and let herself be petted and admired.
Inachus fed her grasses from his hand;
she licked it and pressed kisses on his palm,
unable to restrain her flowing tears.   895

If words would just have come, she would have spoken,
telling them who she was, how this had happened,
and begging their assistance in her case;
but with her hoof, she drew lines in the dust,
and letters of the words she could not speak   900
told the sad story of her transformation.

"Oh, wretched me," cried Io's father, clinging
to the lowing calf's horns and snowy neck.
"Oh, wretched me!" he groaned. "Are you the child
for whom I searched the earth in every part?   905
Lost, you were less a grief than you are, found!

"You make no answer, unable to respond
to our speech in language of your own,
but from your breast come resonant deep sighs
and—all that you can manage now—you *moo*!   910

"But I—all unaware of this—was busy
arranging marriage for you, in the hopes
of having a son-in-law and grandchildren.
Now I must pick your husband from my herd,
and now must find your offspring there as well!   915

"Nor can I end this suffering by death;
it is a hurtful thing to be a god,
for the gates of death are firmly closed against me,
and our sorrows must go on forever."

And while the father mourned his daughter's loss,   920
Argus of the hundred eyes removed her
to pastures farther off and placed himself
high on a mountain peak, a vantage point
from which he could keep watch in all directions.

The ruler of the heavens cannot bear   925

3. River nymphs.

the sufferings of Io any longer,
and calls his son, born of the Pleiades,[4]
and orders him to do away with Argus.

Without delay, he takes his winged sandals,
his magic, sleep-inducing wand, and cap;   930
and so equipped, the son of father Jove
glides down from heaven's summit to the earth,
where he removes and leaves behind his cap
and winged sandals, but retains the wand;
and sets out as a shepherd, wandering   935
far from the beaten path, driving before him
a flock of goats he rounds up as he goes,
while playing tunes upon his pipe of reeds.

The guardian of Juno is quite taken
by this new sound: "Whoever you might be,   940
why not come sit with me upon this rock,"
said Argus, "for that flock of yours will find
the grass is nowhere greener, and you see
that there is shade here suitable for shepherds."

The grandson of great Atlas takes his seat   945
and whiles away the hours, chattering
of this and that—and playing on his pipes,
he tries to overcome the watchfulness
of Argus, struggling to stay awake;
even though Slumber closes down some eyes,   950
others stay vigilant. Argus inquired
how the reed pipes, so recently invented,
had come to be, and Mercury responded:

"On the idyllic mountains of Arcadia,[5]
among the hamadryads[6] of Nonacris,   955
one was renowned, and Syrinx[7] was her name.
Often she fled—successfully—from Satyrs,[8]
and deities of every kind as well,
those of the shady wood and fruited plain.

"In her pursuits and in virginity   960
Diana was her model, and she wore
her robe hitched up and girt above the knees
just as her goddess did; and if her bow
had been made out of gold, instead of horn,
anyone seeing her might well have thought   965
she *was* the goddess—as, indeed, some did.

"Wearing his crown of sharp pine needles, Pan[9]
saw her returning once from Mount Lycaeus,[1]

---

4. Mercury (Hermes in Greek) was the son of Maia, one of the Pleiades or daughters of Atlas. They were changed into stars when the hunter Orion was pursuing them along with their mother Pleione, whom he wanted to rape.
5. The rustic central region of the Peloponnesus. Nonacris was a town in its northern part.
6. Tree nymphs.

7. The name means "shepherd's pipe," a musical instrument made of reeds.
8. Woodland creatures—half man, half goat, bald, bearded, and highly sexed.
9. A god of the wild mountain pastures and woods, with goat's feet and horns. He was particularly associated with Arcadia.
1. A high mountain in Arcadia.

and began to say. . . ."

                There remained to tell
of how the maiden, having spurned his pleas,   970
fled through the trackless wilds until she came
to where the gently flowing Ladon stopped
her in her flight; how she begged the water nymphs
to change her shape, and how the god, assuming
that he had captured Syrinx, grasped instead   975
a handful of marsh reeds! And while he sighed,
the reeds in his hands, stirred by his own breath,
gave forth a similar, low-pitched complaint!

    The god, much taken by the sweet new voice
of an unprecedented instrument,   980
said this to her: "At least we may converse
with one another—I can have that much."

    That pipe of reeds, unequal in their lengths,
and joined together one-on-one with wax,
took the girl's name, and bears it to this day.   985

    Now Mercury was ready to continue
until he saw that Argus had succumbed,
for all his eyes had been closed down by sleep.
He silences himself and waves his wand
above those languid orbs to fix the spell.   990

    Without delay he grasps the nodding head
and where it joins the neck, he severs it
with his curved blade and flings it bleeding down
the steep rock face, staining it with gore.
O Argus, you are fallen, and the light   995
in all your lamps is utterly put out:
one hundred eyes, one darkness all the same!

    But Saturn's daughter[2] rescued them and set
those eyes upon the feathers of her bird,[3]
filling his tail with constellated gems.   1000

    Her rage demanded satisfaction, *now*:
the goddess set a horrifying Fury
before the eyes and the imagination
of her Grecian rival; and in her heart
she fixed a prod that goaded Io on,   1005
driving her in terror through the world
until at last, O Nile, you let her rest
from endless labor; having reached your banks,
she went down awkwardly upon her knees,
and with her neck bent backward, raised her face 1010
as only she could do it, to the stars;
and with her groans and tears and mournful mooing,
entreated Jove, it seemed, to put an end
to her great suffering.

                  Jove threw his arms
around the neck of Juno in embrace,   1015

2. Juno.   3. The peacock.

imploring her to end this punishment:
"In future," he said, "put your fears aside:
never again will you have cause to worry—
about *this* one." And swore upon the Styx.[4]

The goddess was now pacified, and Io   1020
at once began regaining her lost looks,
till she became what she had been before;
her body lost all of its bristling hair,
her horns shrank down, her eyes grew narrower,
her jaws contracted, arms and hands returned,   1025
and hooves divided themselves into nails;
nothing remained of her bovine nature,
unless it was the whiteness of her body.
She had some trouble getting her legs back,
and for a time feared speaking, lest she moo,   1030
and so quite timidly regained her speech.

She is a celebrated goddess now,
and worshiped by the linen-clad Egyptians.[5]
Her son, Epaphus, is believed to be
sprung from the potent seed of mighty Jove,   1035
and temples may be found in every city
wherein the boy is honored with his parent.

*   *   *

FROM BOOK II

[*Jove and Europa*]

When Mercury had punished her for these
impieties of thought and word,[6] he left
Athena's city, and on beating wings   1145
returned to heaven where his father Jove
took him aside and (without telling him
that his new passion was the reason) said:

"Dear son, who does my bidding faithfully,
do not delay, but with your usual   1150
swiftness fly down to earth and find the land
that looks up to your mother[7] on the left,
called Sidon[8] by the natives; there you will see
a herd of royal cattle some way off
upon a mountain; drive them down to shore."   1155

He spoke and it was done as he had ordered:
the cattle were immediately driven

---

4. One of the rivers of the underworld; the
gods swore solemn oaths by it.
5. Io was identified with Isis, at least by the
Greeks and Romans.
6. Mercury has been in Athens, where he tried
to have a love affair with Herse, daughter of
King Cecrops; promised help and then betrayed

by her sister Aglauros, he took his revenge on
Aglauros by turning her into a statue.
7. Maia, Mercury's mother, had been transformed into a star among the Pleiades in the
constellation Taurus.
8. One of the principal cities of Phoenicia (in
modern Lebanon).

down to a certain place along the shore
where the daughter of a great king used to play,
accompanied by maidens all of Tyre.[9]   1160

    Majestic power and erotic love
do not get on together very well,
nor do they linger long in the same place:
the father and the ruler of all gods,
who holds the lightning bolt in his right hand   1165
and shakes the world when he but nods his head,
now relinquishes authority and power,
assuming the appearance of a bull
to mingle with the other cattle, lowing
as gorgeously he strolls in the new grass.   1170

    He is as white as the untrampled snow
before the south wind turns it into slush.
The muscles stand out bulging on his neck,
and the dewlap[1] dangles on his ample chest;
his horns are crooked, but appear handmade,   1175
and flawless as a pair of matching gems.
His brow is quite unthreatening, his eye
excites no terror, and his countenance
is calm.

        The daughter of King Agenor[2]
admires him, astonished by the presence   1180
of peacefulness and beauty in the beast;
yet even though he seems a gentle creature,
at first she fears to get too close to him,
but soon approaching, reaches out her hand
and pushes flowers into his white mouth.   1185

    The lover, quite beside himself, rejoices,
and as a preview of delights to come,
kisses her fingers, getting so excited
that he can scarcely keep from doing it!

    Now he disports himself upon the grass,   1190
and lays his whiteness on the yellow sands;
and as she slowly overcomes her fear
he offers up his breast for her caresses
and lets her decorate his horns with flowers;
the princess dares to sit upon his back   1195
not knowing who it is that she has mounted,
and he begins to set out from dry land,
a few steps on false feet into the shallows,
then further out and further to the middle
of the great sea he carries off his booty;   1200
she trembles as she sees the shore receding
and holds the creature's horn in her right hand
and with the other clings to his broad back,
her garments streaming in the wind behind her.

---

9. Another city of Phoenicia, but here used of
Phoenicia itself.

1. A fold of loose skin hanging from the neck.
2. Europa. Agenor was the Phoenician king.

FROM BOOK V

[Ceres and Proserpina]

As the Muse spoke,[3] Minerva could hear wings
beating on air, and cries of greeting came
from high in the trees. She peered into the foliage,   430
attempting to discover where those sounds,
the speech of human beings to be sure,
were emanating from: why, from some birds!
Bewailing their sad fate, a flock of nine
magpies (which mimic anyone they wish to)   435
had settled in the branches overhead.
    Minerva having shown astonishment,
the Muse gave her a little goddess-chat:
"This lot has only recently been added
to the throngs of birds. Why? They lost a contest!   440
Their father was Pierus, lord of Pella,[4]
their mother was Evippe of Paeonia;
nine times she called upon Lucina's[5] aid
and nine times she delivered. Swollen up
with foolish pride because they were so many,   445
that crowd of simpleminded sisters went
through all Haemonia and through Achaea[6] too,
arriving here to challenge us in song:
    "'We'll show you girls just what real class is[7]
Give up tryin' to deceive the masses   450
Your rhymes are fake: accept our wager
Learn which of us is minor and which is major
There's nine of us here and there's nine of you
And you'll be nowhere long before we're through
Nothin's gonna save you 'cuz your songs are lame   455
And the way you sing 'em is really a shame
So stop with, "Well I *never*!" and "This *can't* be real!"
We're the newest New Thing and here is our deal
If we beat you, obsolete you, then you just get gone
From these classy haunts on Mount Helicon   460
We give you Macedonia—*if* we lose
An' that's an offer you just can't refuse
So take the wings off, sisters, get down and jam
And let the nymphs be the judges of our poetry slam!'
    "Shameful it was to strive against such creatures;   465
more shameful not to. Nymphs were picked as judges,

3. Minerva (Athena in Greek) has come to Mount Helicon in central Greece, the home of the nine Muses (daughters of Zeus and Memory, they are patronesses of poetry and the other arts). One of the Muses has told her of an attempt recently made to trap and rape them by the wicked Pyreneus.
4. City of Macedonia, in northern Greece. The Paeonians were a tribe living north of Macedonia.

5. Goddess of childbirth.
6. Regions of central Greece (*Haemonia* is another name for Thessaly). The sisters are traveling south toward Helicon.
7. Although there is no basis for it in the Latin text, the translator uses dialect and rhyme in the speeches and song of Pierus's daughters to show how they challenge, and partially deflate, the "high-culture" assumptions and language of the Muses.

sworn into service on their river banks,
and took their seats on benches made of tufa.
  "And then—not even drawing lots!—the one
who claimed to be their champion commenced;
she sang of war between the gods and Giants,   470
giving the latter credit more than due
and deprecating all that the great gods did;
how Typhoeus,[8] from earth's lowest depths,
struck fear in every celestial heart,
so that they all turned tail and fled, until,   475
exhausted, they found refuge down in Egypt,
where the Nile flows from seven distinct mouths;
she sang of how earthborn Typhoeus
pursued them even here and forced the gods
to hide themselves by taking fictive shapes:[9]   480
  "'In Libya the Giants told the gods to scram
The boss god they worship there has horns like a ram[1]
'Cuz Jupiter laid low as the leader of a flock
And Delius[2] his homey really got a shock
When the Giants left him with no place to go: 485
"Fuggedabout Apollo—make me a crow!"
And if you believe that Phoebus was a wuss
His sister Phoebe turned into a puss
Bacchus takes refuge in the skin of a goat
And Juno as a cow with a snow-white coat   490
Venus the queen of the downtown scene, yuh know what her wish is?
"Gimme a body just like a fish's"
Mercury takes on an ibis's shape
And that's how the mighty (cheep cheep) gods escape'   495
  "And then her song, accompanied on the lute,
came to an end, and it was our turn—
but possibly you haven't got the time
to listen to our song?"
                        "Oh, don't think that,"
Minerva said. "I want it word for word: 500
sing it for me just as you sang it then."
  The Muse replied: "We turned the contest over
to one of us, Calliope,[3] who rose,
and after binding up her hair in ivy
and lightly strumming a few plaintive chords,   505
she vigorously launched into her song:

  "'Ceres[4] was first to break up the soil with a curved plowshare,
the first to give us the earth's fruits and to nourish us gently,
and the first to give laws: every gift comes from Ceres.

---

8. Monstrous son of Earth. Like the Earth-born Giants, he challenged Jupiter and the Olympian gods and was defeated.
9. An "explanation" of the Egyptian gods' animal forms.
1. Ammon, the chief Egyptian god, identified by the Greeks and Romans with Zeus/Jupiter.

He had an important oracular cult in the Libyan desert (west of the Nile valley and part of Egypt under Roman rule).
2. Apollo, who was born on the island of Delos.
3. "Lovely Voice," the Muse of epic poetry.
4. Goddess of grain (Demeter).

The goddess must now be my subject. Would that I *could* sing 510
a hymn that is worthy of her, for she surely deserves it.
"'Vigorous Sicily sprawled across the gigantic body
of one who had dared aspire to rule in the heavens;
the island's weight held Typhoeus firmly beneath it.
Often exerting himself, he strives yet again to rise up, 515
but there in the north, his right hand is held down by Pelorus,
his left hand by you, Pachynus; off in the west, Lilybaeum[5]
weighs on his legs, while Mount Etna[6] presses his head, as
under it, raging Typhoeus coughs ashes and vomits up fire.
Often he struggles, attempting to shake off the earth's weight 520
and roll its cities and mountains away from his body.

"'This causes tremors and panics the Lord of the Silent,[7]
who fears that the earth's crust will crack and break open,
and daylight, let in, will frighten the trembling phantoms;
dreading disaster, the tyrant left his tenebrous kingdom; 525
borne in his chariot drawn by its team of black horses,
he crisscrossed Sicily, checking the island's foundation.

"'After his explorations had left him persuaded
that none of its parts were in imminent danger of falling,
his fears were forgotten, and Venus, there on Mount Eryx,[8] 530
observed him relaxing, and said, as she drew Cupid near her,
"My son, my sword, my strong right arm and source of my power,
take up that weapon by which all your victims are vanquished
and send your swift arrows into the breast of the deity
to whom the last part of the threefold realm[9] was allotted. 535
"'"You govern the gods and their ruler; you rule the defeated
gods of the ocean and govern the one who rules them, too;
why give up on the dead, when we can extend our empire
into their realm? A third part of the world is involved here!
And yet the celestial gods spurn our forbearance, 540
and the prestige of Love is diminished, even as mine is.
Do you not see how Athena and huntress Diana
have both taken leave of me?[1] The virgin daughter of Ceres
desires to do likewise—and will, if we let her!
But if you take pride in our alliance, advance it 545
by joining her to her uncle!"[2]
                              "'Venus ceased speaking and Cupid
loosened his quiver, and, just as his mother had ordered,
selected, from thousands of missiles, the one that was sharpest
and surest and paid his bow the closest attention,
and using one knee to bend its horn back almost double, 550
he pierces the heart of Dis with his barb-tipped arrow.

---

5. Mountains on the northeast, southeast, and western promontories of Sicily, respectively.
6. The large (and still active) volcano near the center of the east coast of Sicily.
7. Pluto or Hades, king of the dead.
8. Mountain in western Sicily with an important cult of Venus.

9. The underworld, ruled by Pluto. The other parts of the "threefold realm" are the sea (ruled by Neptune) and the sky or Mount Olympus (Jupiter).
1. Both were perpetual virgins.
2. Pluto (also called Dis) was the brother of Jupiter, the father by Ceres of Proserpina.

"'Near Henna's[3] walls stands a deep pool of water, called Pergus:
not even the river Cayster,[4] flowing serenely,
hears more songs from its swans; this pool is completely surrounded
by a ring of tall trees, whose foliage, just like an awning,   555
keeps out the sun and preserves the water's refreshing coolness;
the moist ground is covered with flowers of Tyrian purple;
here it is springtime forever. And here Proserpina
was playfully picking its white lilies and violets,
and, while competing to gather up more than her playmates,   560
filling her basket and stuffing the rest in her bosom,
Dis saw her, was smitten, seized her and carried her off;
his love was that hasty. The terrified goddess cried out
for her mother, her playmates—but for her mother most often,
since she had torn the uppermost seam of her garment,   565
and the gathered flowers rained down from her negligent tunic;
because of her tender years and her childish simplicity,
even this loss could move her to maidenly sorrow.
    "'Her abductor rushed off in his chariot, urging his horses,
calling each one by its name and flicking the somber,   570
rust-colored reins over their backs as they galloped
through the deep lakes and the sulphurous pools of Palike
that boil up through the ruptured earth, and where the Bacchiadae,
a race sprung from Corinth, that city between the two seas,
had raised their own walls between two unequal harbors.[5]   575
    "'There is a bay that is landlocked almost completely
between the two pools of Cyane and Pisaean Arethusa,
the residence of the most famous nymph in all Sicily,
Cyane, who gave her very own name to the fountain.
She showed herself now, emerged from her pool at waist level,   580
and recognizing the goddess, told Dis, "Go no further!
You cannot become the son-in-law of great Ceres
against her will: you should have asked and not taken!
If it is right for me to compare lesser with greater,
I accepted Anapis[6] when he desired to have me,   585
yielding to pleas and not—as in *this* case—to terror."
She spoke, and stretching her arms out in either direction,
kept him from passing. That son of Saturn could scarcely
hold back his anger; he urged on his frightening horses,
and then, with his strong right arm, he hurled his scepter   590
directly into the very base of the fountain;
the stricken earth opened a path to the underworld
and took in the chariot rushing down into its crater.
    "'Cyane, lamenting not just the goddess abducted,
but also the disrespect shown for *her* rights as a fountain,   595

---

3. A city in central Sicily.
4. River in Lydia in Asia Minor, famous for its many swans.
5. Syracuse, on the southeastern coast of Sicily, founded by Corinthian colonists in the 8th

century B.C.E. The Bacchiadae were a leading family who then ruled Corinth.
6. A river that empties into the sea near Syracuse.

tacitly nursed in her heart an inconsolable sorrow;
and she who had once been its presiding spirit,
reduced to tears, dissolved right into its substance.
You would have seen her members beginning to soften,
her bones and her fingertips starting to lose their old firmness;   600
her slenderest parts were the first to be turned into fluid:
her feet, her legs, her sea-dark tresses, her fingers
(for the parts with least flesh turn into liquid most quickly);
and after these, her shoulders and back and her bosom
and flanks completely vanished in trickling liquid;   605
and lastly the living blood in her veins is replaced by
springwater, and nothing remains that you could have seized on.
   "'Meanwhile, the terrified mother was pointlessly seeking
her daughter all over the earth and deep in the ocean.
Neither Aurora, appearing with dew-dampened tresses,   610
nor Hesperus[7] knew her to quit; igniting two torches
of pine from the fires of Etna, the care-ridden goddess
used them to illumine the wintery shadows of nighttime;
and when the dear day had once more dimmed out the bright stars,
she searched again for her daughter from sunrise to sunset.   615

   "'Worn out by her labors and suffering thirst, with no fountain
to wet her lips at, she happened upon a thatched hovel
and knocked at its humble door, from which there came forth
a crone who looked at the goddess, and, when asked for water,
gave her a sweet drink, sprinkled with toasted barley.   620
And, as she drank it, a boy with a sharp face and bold manner
stood right before her and mocked her and said she was greedy.
Angered by what he was saying, the goddess drenched him
with all she had not yet drunk of the barley mixture.
The boy's face thirstily drank up the spots as his arms were   625
turned into legs, and a tail was joined to his changed limbs;
so that he should now be harmless, the boy was diminished,
and he was transformed into a very small lizard.
Astonished, the old woman wept and reached out to touch him,
but the marvelous creature fled her, seeking a hideout.   630
He now has a name appropriate to his complexion,
Stellio, from the constellations spotting his body.
   "'To speak of the lands and seas the goddess mistakenly searched
would take far too long; the earth exhausted her seeking;
she came back to Sicily; and, as she once more traversed it,   635
arrived at Cyane, who would have told her the story
had she not herself been changed; but, though willing in spirit,
her mouth, tongue, and vocal apparatus were absent;
nevertheless, she gave proof that was clear to the mother:
Persephone's girdle (which happened by chance to have fallen   640
into the fountain) now lay exposed on its surface.
   "'Once recognizing it, the goddess knew that her daughter
had been taken, and tore her hair into utter disorder,

---

7. The evening star. "Aurora": goddess of the dawn.

and repeatedly struck her breasts with the palms of both hands.
With her daughter's location a mystery still, she reproaches 645
the whole earth as ungrateful, unworthy her gift of grain crops,
and Sicily more than the others, where she has discovered
the proof of her loss; and so it was here that her fierce hand
shattered the earth-turning plows, here that the farmers and cattle
perished alike, and here that she bade the plowed fields 650
default on their trust by blighting the seeds in their keeping.
Sicilian fertility, which had been everywhere famous,
was given the lie when the crops died as they sprouted,
now ruined by too much heat, and now by too heavy a rainfall;
stars and winds harmed them, and the greedy birds devoured 655
the seed as it was sown; the harvest of wheat was defeated
by thorns and darnels and unappeasable grasses.

"'Then Arethusa[8] lifted her head from the Elean waters
and swept her dripping hair back away from her forehead,
saying, "O Mother of Grain—and mother, too, of that virgin 660
sought through the whole world—here end your incessant labors,
lest your great anger should injure the earth you once trusted,
and which, unwillingly pillaged, has done nothing ignoble;
nor do I plead for my nation, since I am a guest here:
my nation is Pisa, I am descended from Elis, 665
and live as a stranger in Sicily—this land that delights me
more than all others on earth; here Arethusa
dwells with her household gods. Spare it, merciful goddess,
and when your cares and countenance both have been lightened,
there will come an opportune time to tell you the reason 670
why I was taken from home and borne off to Ortygia[9]
over a waste of waters. The earth gave me access,
showed me a path, and, swept on through underground caverns,
I raised my head here to an unfamiliar night sky.
But while gliding under the earth on a Stygian river, 675
I saw with my very own eyes your dear Proserpina;
grief and terror were still to be seen in her features,
yet she was nonetheless queen of that shadowy kingdom,
the all-powerful consort of the underworld's ruler."

"'The mother was petrified by the speech of the fountain, 680
and stood for a very long time as though she were senseless,
until her madness had been driven off by her outrage,
and then she set out in her chariot for the ethereal regions;
once there, with her face clouded over and hair all disheveled,
she planted herself before Jove and fiercely addressed him: 685
"Jupiter, I have come here as a suppliant, speaking
for my child—and yours: if you have no regard for her mother,
relent as her father—don't hold her unworthy, I beg you,
simply because *I* am the child's other parent!

---

8. A spring in Syracuse. Its waters are "Elean" because they were believed to originate in the district of Pisa in Elis, a region of the western Peloponnesus in mainland Greece.

9. The island on which Syracuse was originally built and on which the Arethusan spring was located.

The daughter I sought for so long is at last recovered,   690
if to recover means only to lose much more surely,
or if to recover means just to learn her location!
Her theft could be borne—if only he would return her!
Then let him do it, for surely *Jove's* daughter is worthy
of a mate who's no brigand, even if *my* daughter isn't."   695

"'Jupiter answered her, "She is indeed *our* daughter,
the pledge of our love and our common concern,
but if you will kindly agree to give things their right names,
this is not an injury requiring my retribution,
but an act of love by a son-in-law who won't shame you,   700
goddess, if you give approval; though much were lacking,
how much it is to be Jove's brother! But he lacks nothing,
and only yields to me that which the Fates have allotted.
Still, if you're so keen on parting them, your Proserpina
may come back to heaven—but only on one condition: 705
that she has not touched food, for so the Fates have required."

"'He spoke and Ceres was sure she would get back her daughter,
though the Fates were not, for the girl had already placated
her hunger while guilelessly roaming death's formal gardens,
where, from a low-hanging branch, she had plucked without thinking   710
a pomegranate, and peeling its pale bark off, devoured
seven of its seeds. No one saw her but Ascalaphus
(whom it is said that Orphne, a not undistinguished
nymph among those of Avernus, pregnant by Acheron,[1]
gave birth to there in the underworld's dark-shadowed forest);   715
he saw, and by his disclosure, kept her from returning.
"'Raging, the Queen of the Underworld turned that informer
into a bird of ill omen: sprinkling the waters
of Phlegethon[2] into the face of Ascalaphus,
she gave him a beak and plumage and eyes quite enormous.   720
Lost to himself, he is clad now in yellow-brown pinions,
his head increases in size and his nails turn to talons,
but the feathers that spring from his motionless arms scarcely flutter;
a filthy bird he's become, the grim announcer of mourning,
a slothful portent of evil to mortals—the owl.   725

"'That one, because of his tattling tongue, seems quite worthy
of punishment,—but you, daughters of Acheloüs,[3]
why do you have the plumage of birds and the faces of virgins?
Is it because while Proserpina gathered her flowers,
you, artful Sirens, were numbered among her companions?   730
No sooner had you scoured the whole earth in vain for her
than you desired the vast seas to feel your devotion,
and prayed to the gods, whom you found willing to help you,
that you might skim over the flood upon oars that were pinions,

1. Acheron ("Woe") is one of the rivers, and Avernus a lake, in the underworld. The name *Orphne* means "darkness" in Greek.
2. Fiery river of the underworld.

3. The Sirens, familiar from book 12 of the *Odyssey* and often associated with death in post-Homeric literature and art. Acheloüs is a large river in northwest Greece.

then saw your limbs turn suddenly golden with plumage.   735
And so that your tunefulness, which the ear finds so pleasing,
should not be lost, nor your gifts of vocal expression,
your maidenly faces remain, along with your voices.

"'But poised between his sorrowing sister and brother,
great Jove divided the year into two equal portions,   740
so now in two realms the shared goddess holds sway,
and as many months spent with her mother are spent with her husband.
She changed her mind then, and changed her expression to match it,
and now her fair face, which even Dis found depressing,
beams as the sun does, when, after having been hidden   745
before in dark clouds, at last it emerges in triumph.

"'Her daughter safely restored to her, kindhearted Ceres
wishes to hear *your* story now, Arethusa—
what did you flee from and what changed you into a fountain?
The splashing waters are stilled: the goddess raises   750
her head from their depths and wrings dry her virid tresses,
then tells the old tale of the river Alpheus'[4] passion.
"'"Once I was one of the nymphs who dwell in Achaea,"
she said, "and none had more zeal than I for traversing
the mountain pastures or setting out snares for small game.   755
But even though I did not seek to find fame as a beauty,
men called me that, my courage and strength notwithstanding;
nor was I pleased that my beauty was lauded so often,
and for my corporeal nature (which most other maidens
are wont to take pleasure in) I blushed like a rustic,   760
thinking it wrong to please men.
                              "'"Exhausted from hunting,
I was on my way back from the Stymphalian forest,[5]
and the fierce heat of the day was doubled by my exertions.
By chance I came on a stream, gently and silently flowing,
clear to the bottom, where you could count every pebble,   765
water so still you would scarcely believe it was moving.
Silvery willows and poplars, which the stream nourished,
artlessly shaded its banks as they sloped to the water.
"'"At once I approach and wiggle my toes in its wetness,
then wade in up to my knees—not satisfied wholly,   770
I strip off my garments and hang them up on a willow,
and, naked, merge with the waters. I strike and stroke them,
gliding below and thrashing about on the surface,
then hear a strange murmur that seems to come from the bottom,
which sends me scampering onto the near bank in terror: 775
'Why the great rush?' Alpheus cries from his waters,
then hoarsely repeating, 'Why the great rush, Arethusa?'
Just as I am, I flee without clothing (my garments
were on the bank opposite); aroused, Alpheus pursues me,

4. River that flows past Olympia in Elis.
5. The woods surrounding Lake Stymphalus in Arcadia.

my nakedness making me seem more ripe for the taking. 780

"'"Thus did I run, and thus did that fierce one press after,
as doves on trembling pinions flee from the kestrel,
as kestrels pursue the trembling doves and assault them.
To Orchomenus and past, to Psophis, Cyllene,
the folds of Maenalia, Erymanthus,[6] and Elis, 785
I continued to run, nor was he faster than I was;
but since Alpheus was so much stronger, I couldn't
outrun him for long, given his greater endurance.

"'"Nonetheless, I still managed to keep on running
across the wide fields, up wooded mountains, 790
on bare rocks, steep cliffs, in wastes wild and trackless;
with the sun at my back, I could see his shadow before me,
stretched out on the ground, unless my panic deceived me;
but surely I *did* hear those frightening footsteps behind me,
and felt his hot breath lifting the hair from my shoulders. 795

"'"Worn with exertion, I cried out, 'Help! Or I'm taken!
Aid your armoress, Diana—to whom you have often
entrusted your bow, along with your quiver of arrows!'
The goddess was moved by my plea and at once I was hidden
in a dense cloud of fine mist:[7] the river god, clueless, 800
circled around me, hidden in darkness, searching;
twice he unknowingly passed by the place where the goddess
had hidden me, and twice he called, 'Yo! Arethusa!'
How wretched was I? Why, even as the lamb is,
at hearing the howling of wolves around the sheepfold, 805
or as the rabbit in the briar patch who glimpses
the dog's fierce muzzle and feels too frightened to tremble.

"'"Alpheus remained there, for as he noticed no footprints
heading away from the cloud, he continued to watch it.
An icy sweat thoroughly drenched the limbs that he looked for, 810
and the dark drops poured from every part of my body;
wherever my foot had been, there was a puddle,
and my hair shed moisture. More swiftly than I can tell it,
I turned into liquid—even so, he recognized me,
his darling there in the water, and promptly discarded 815
the human form he had assumed for the occasion,
reverting to river, so that our fluids might mingle.
Diana shattered the earth's crust; I sank down,
and was swept on through sightless caverns, off to Ortygia,
so pleasing to me because it's the goddess's birthplace;[8] 820
and here I first rose up into the air as a fountain."

"'Here Arethusa concluded. The fruitful goddess summoned
her team of dragons and yoked them onto her chariot;
and guiding their heads with the reins, she was transported
up through the middle air that lies between earth and heaven 825

6. Towns and mountains of Arcadia.
7. Conventional means in ancient epic of making someone invisible.

8. The Ortygia where Arethusa ended up was in Syracuse, but Delos, the Aegean island where Diana was born, was also called Ortygia.

until she arrived in Athens, and, giving her carriage
to Triptolemus,[9] ordered him to go off and scatter
grain on the earth—some on land that had never been broken,
and some on land that had been a long time fallow.
   "'The young man was carried high up over Europe and Asia   830
until at last he came to the kingdom of Scythia.
Lyncus was king here; he brought him into his palace,
and asked him his name, his homeland, the cause of his journey,
and how he had come there.
                                        "'"My well-known homeland," he answered,
"is Athens; I am Triptolemus; neither by ship upon water   835
nor foot upon land have I come here; the air itself parted
to make me a path on which I coursed through the heavens.
I bear you the gifts of Ceres, which, sown in your broad fields,
will yield a bountiful harvest of nourishing produce."
   "'This the barbarian heard with great envy, and wishing   840
that he himself might be perceived as the donor,
took him in as a guest, and while the young man was sleeping,
approached with a sword, and as he attempted to stab him,
Ceres changed *Lyncus* to *lynx*, and ordered Triptolemus
to drive her sacred team through the air back to Athens.'   845

   "When our eldest sister had concluded
her superb performance, with one voice
the nymphs awarded victory to . . . the Muses!
   "And when the others, in defeat, reviled us,
I answered them: 'Since you display such nerve   850
in challenging the Muses, you deserve
chastisement—even more so since you've added
insult to outrage: our wise forbearance
is not without its limits, as you'll learn
when we get to the penalties, and vent   855
our righteous anger on your worthless selves.'
   "Then the Pierides[1] mock our threats,
and as they try to answer us by shouting
vulgarities and giving us the finger,
their fingers take on feathers and their arms   860
turn into pinions! Each one sees a beak
replace a sister's face, as a new bird
is added to the species of the forest;
and as they try to beat upon their breasts,
bewailing their new situation, they   865
all hang suspended, flapping in the air,
the forest's scandal—the P-Airides![2]
   "And even though they are all feathered now,
their speech remains as fluent as it was,
and they are famous for their noisiness   870
as well as for their love of argument."

9. Son of the king of Eleusis, the great cult
center of Demeter (Ceres) near Athens.

1. The daughters of Pierus.
2. The translator's pun on the name Pierides.

FROM BOOK IX

[Iphis and Isis]

Rumor might very well have spread the news 960
of this unprecedented transformation[3]
throughout the hundred towns of Crete, if they
had not just had a wonder of their own
to talk about—the change that came to Iphis.

For, once upon a time, there lived in Phaestus, 965
not far from the royal capital at Cnossus,
a freeborn plebeian named Ligdus, who
was otherwise unknown and undistinguished,
with no more property than fame or status,
and yet devout, and blameless in his life. 970

His wife was pregnant. When her time had come,
he gave her his instructions with these words:
"There are two things I pray to heaven for
on your account: an easy birth and a son.
The other fate is much too burdensome, 975
for daughters need what Fortune has denied us:
a dowry.
        "Therefore—and may God prevent
this happening, but if, by chance, it does
and you should be delivered of a girl,
unwillingly I order this, and beg 980
pardon for my impiety—*But let it die!*"
He spoke, and tears profusely bathed the cheeks
of the instructor and instructed both.
Telethusa continued to implore
her husband, praying him not to confine 985
their hopes so narrowly—to no avail,
for he would not be moved from his decision.

Now scarcely able to endure the weight
of her womb's burden, as she lay in bed
at midnight, a dream-vision came to her: 990
the goddess Io[4] stood (or seemed to stand)
before her troubled bed, accompanied
with solemn pomp by all her mysteries.
She wore her crescent horns upon her brow
and a garland made of gleaming sheaves of wheat, 995
and a queenly diadem; behind her stood
the dog-faced god Anubis, and divine
Bubastis (who defends the lives of cats),
and Apis as a bull clothed in a hide
of varied colors, with Harpocrates, 1000
the god whose fingers, pressed against his lips,
command our silence; and one often sought

3. The transformation of Byblis, who loved
her brother Caunus, into a fountain.
4. Identified with the Egyptian Isis, goddess
of fertility, marriage, and maternity, whose
cult was widespread in the Roman world.

by his devoted worshipers—Osiris;[5]
and the asp, so rich in sleep-inducing drops.
She seemed to wake, and saw them all quite clearly.   1005
    These were the words the goddess spoke to her:
"O Telethusa, faithful devotee,
put off your heavy cares! Disobey your spouse,
and do not hesitate, when Lucina
has lightened the burden of your labor,   1010
to raise this child, whatever it will be.
I am that goddess who, when asked, delivers,
and you will have no reason to complain
that honors you have paid me were in vain."
After instructing her, the goddess left.   1015
    The Cretan woman rose up joyfully,
lifted her hands up to the stars, and prayed
that her dream-vision would be ratified.
    Then going into labor, she brought forth
a daughter—though her husband did not know it.   1020
The mother (with intention to deceive)
told them *to feed the boy*. Deception prospered,
since no one knew the truth except the nurse.
    The father thanked the gods and named the child
for its grandfather, Iphis; since this name   1025
was given men and women both, his mother
was pleased, for she could use it honestly.
So from her pious lie, deception grew.
She dressed it as a boy—its face was such
that whether boy or girl, it was a beauty.   1030
    Meanwhile, the years went by, thirteen of them:
your father, Iphis, has arranged for you
a marriage to the golden-haired Ianthe,
the daughter of a Cretan named Telestes,
the maid most praised in Phaestus[6] for her beauty.   1035
The two were similar in age and looks,
and had been taught together from the first.
    First love came unexpected to both hearts
and wounded them both equally—and yet
their expectations were quite different: 1040
Ianthe can look forward to a time
of wedding torches and of wedding vows,
and trusts that one whom she believes a man
will be *her* man. Iphis, however, loves
with hopeless desperation, which increases   1045
in strict proportion to its hopelessness,
and burns—a maiden—for another maid!
    And scarcely holding back her tears, she cries,
"Oh, what will be the end reserved for Iphis,
gripped by a strange and monstrous passion known   1050

5. Husband of Isis, killed by his brother Set   of rebirth.
and restored to life by Isis; he is thus a figure 6. A city in Crete.

to no one else? If the gods had wished to spare me,
they should have; if they wanted to destroy me,
they should have given me a natural affliction.

  "Cows do not burn for cows, nor mares for mares;
the ram will have his sheep, the stag his does,   1055
and birds will do the same when they assemble;
there are no animals whose females lust
for other females! I wish that I were dead!

  "That Crete might bring forth monsters of all kinds.
Queen Pasiphaë[7] was taken by a bull,   1060
yet even *that* was male-and-female passion!
My love is much less rational than hers,
to tell the truth. At least she had the hope
of satisfaction, taking in the bull
through guile, and in the image of a cow,   1065
thereby deceiving the adulterer!

  "If every form of ingenuity
were gathered here from all around the world,
if Daedalus[8] flew back on waxen wings,
what could he do? Could all his learnèd arts   1070
transform me from a girl into a boy?
Or could *you* change into a boy, Ianthe?

  "But really, Iphis, pull yourself together,
be firm, cast off this stultifying passion:
accept your birth—unless you would deceive   1075
yourself as well as others—look for love
where it is proper to, as a woman should!
Hope both creates and nourishes such love;
reality deprives you of all hope.

  "No watchman keeps you from her dear embrace,   1080
no husband's ever-vigilant concern,
no father's fierceness, nor does she herself
deny the gifts that you would have from her.
And yet you are denied all happiness,
nor could it have been otherwise if all   1085
the gods and men had labored in your cause.

  "But the gods have not denied me anything;
agreeably, they've given what they could;
my father wishes for me what *I* wish,
she and her father both would have it be;   1090
but Nature, much more powerful than they are,
wishes it not—sole source of all my woe!

  "But look—the sun has risen and the day
of our longed-for nuptials dawns at last!
Ianthe will be mine—and yet not mine: 1095
we die of thirst here at the fountainside.

  "Why do you, Juno, guardian of brides,

---

7. Wife of King Minos of Crete, and mother
by a bull of the Minotaur.
8. Fabled craftsman who devised the heifer
disguise that enabled Pasiphaë to seduce the

bull and, later, built the labyrinth for the
Minotaur. Forced to flee Crete, he made wings
of feathers held together by wax, for himself
and his son, Icarus.

and you, O Hymen, god of marriage, come
to these rites, which cannot be rites at all,
for no one takes the bride, and both are veiled?"   1100

She said no more. Nor did her chosen burn
less fiercely as she prayed you swiftly come,
O god of marriage.

Fearing what you sought,
Telethusa postponed the marriage day
with one concocted pretext and another,   1105
a fictive illness or an evil omen.
But now she had no more excuses left,
and the wedding day was only one day off.

She tears the hair bands from her daughter's head
and from her own, and thus unbound, she prayed   1110
while desperately clinging to the altar:
"O holy Isis, who art pleased to dwell
and be worshiped at Paraetonium,
at Pharos, in the Mareotic fields,
and where the Nile splits into seven branches;   1115
deliver us, I pray you, from our fear!

"For I once saw thee and thy sacred emblems,
O goddess, and I recognized them all
and listened to the sound of brazen rattles[9]
and kept your orders in my memory.   1120

"And that my daughter still looks on the light,
and that I have not suffered punishment,
why, this is all your counsel and your gift;
now spare us both and offer us your aid."

Warm tears were in attendance on her words.   1125
The altar of the goddess seemed to move—
it *did* move, and the temple doors were shaken,
and the horns (her lunar emblem) glowed with light,
and the bronze rattles sounded.

Not yet secure,
but nonetheless delighted by this omen,   1130
the mother left with Iphis following,
as was her wont, but now with longer strides,
darker complexion, and with greater force,
a keener countenance, and with her hair
shorter than usual and unadorned,   1135
and with more vigor than a woman has.

And you who were so recently a girl
are now a boy! Bring gifts to the goddess!
Now boldly celebrate your faith in her!
They bring the goddess gifts and add to them   1140
a votive tablet with these lines inscribed:

GIFTS IPHIS PROMISED WHEN SHE WAS A MAID
TRANSFORMED INTO A BOY HE GLADLY PAID

9. Sistra, sacred rattles used in Isis's cult.

The next day's sun revealed the great wide world
with Venus, Juno, and Hymen all together   1145
gathered beneath the smoking nuptial torches,
and Iphis in possession of Ianthe.

FROM BOOK X[1]

[Pygmalion]

"Pygmalion observed how these women[2] lived lives of sordid
indecency, and, dismayed by the numerous defects
of character Nature had given the feminine spirit,
stayed as a bachelor, having no female companion.   315

    "During that time he created an ivory statue,
a work of most marvelous art, and gave it a figure
better than any living woman could boast of,
and promptly conceived a passion for his own creation.
You would have thought it alive, so like a real maiden   320
that only its natural modesty kept it from moving:
art concealed artfulness. Pygmalion gazed in amazement,
burning with love for what was in likeness a body.

    "Often he stretched forth a hand to touch his creation,
attempting to settle the issue: *was* it a body,   325
or was it—this he would not yet concede—a mere statue?
He gives it kisses, and they are returned, he imagines;
now he addresses and now he caresses it, feeling
his fingers sink into its warm, pliant flesh, and
fears he will leave blue bruises all over its body;   330
he seeks to win its affections with words and with presents
pleasing to girls, such as seashells and pebbles, tame birds,
armloads of flowers in thousands of different colors,
lilies, bright painted balls, curious insects in amber;
he dresses it up and puts diamond rings on its fingers,   335
gives it a necklace, a lacy brassiere and pearl earrings,
and even though all such adornments truly become her,
she does not seem to be any less beautiful naked.
He lays her down on a bed with a bright purple cover
and calls her his bedmate and slips a few soft, downy pillows   340
under her head as though she were able to feel them.

    "The holiday honoring Venus has come, and all Cyprus[3]
turns out to celebrate; heifers with gilded horns buckle
under the deathblow[4] and incense soars up in thick clouds;
having already brought his own gift to the altar,   345
Pygmalion stood by and offered this fainthearted prayer:

---

1. This selection of stories is part of the song sung by Orpheus, the legendary singer, after he has failed to redeem his wife, Eurydice, from the underworld. His theme, announced in the prologue of his song, is "young boys whom the gods have desired, / and . . . girls seized by forbidden and blameworthy passions."

2. Orpheus has just told of the Propoetides of Cyprus, who, as punishment for having denied Venus's divinity, became the first women to prostitute themselves.
3. Island in the eastern Mediterranean sacred to Venus.
4. I.e., as they are sacrificed.

'If you in heaven are able to give us whatever
we ask for, then I would like as my wife—' and not daring
to say, '—my ivory maiden,' said, '—one like my statue!'
Since golden Venus was present there at her altar,   350
she knew what he wanted to ask for, and as a good omen,
three times the flames soared and leapt right up to the heavens.

"Once home, he went straight to the replica of his sweetheart,
threw himself down on the couch and repeatedly kissed her;
she seemed to grow warm and so he repeated the action,   355
kissing her lips and exciting her breasts with both hands.
Aroused, the ivory softened and, losing its stiffness,
yielded, submitting to his caress as wax softens
when it is warmed by the sun, and handled by fingers,
takes on many forms, and by being used, becomes useful.   360
Amazed, he rejoices, then doubts, then fears he's mistaken,
while again and again he touches on what he has prayed for.
She is alive! And her veins leap under his fingers!

"You can believe that Pygmalion offered the goddess
his thanks in a torrent of speech, once again kissing   365
those lips that were not untrue; that she felt his kisses,
and timidly blushing, she opened her eyes to the sunlight,
and at the same time, first looked on her lover and heaven!
The goddess attended the wedding since she had arranged it,
and before the ninth moon had come to its crescent, a daughter   370
was born to them—Paphos,[5] who gave her own name to the island.

"She had a son named Cinyras, who would be regarded
as one of the blessèd, if he had only been childless.
I sing of dire events: depart from me, daughters,
depart from me, fathers; or, if you find my poems charming,   375
believe that I lie, believe these events never happened;
or, if you believe that they did, then believe they were punished.

"If Nature allows us to witness such impious misdeeds,
then I give my solemn thanks that the Thracian people
and the land itself are far away from those regions[6]   380
where evil like that was begotten: let fabled Panchaea[7]
be rich in balsam and cinnamon, costum and frankincense,
the sweat that drips down from the trees; let it bear incense
and flowers of every description: it also bears myrrh, and
too great a price was paid for that new creation.   385

"Cupid himself denies that his darts ever harmed you,
Myrrha, and swears that his torches likewise are guiltless;
one of the three sisters,[8] bearing a venomous hydra
and waving a Stygian firebrand, must have inspired your passion.
Hating a parent is wicked, but even more wicked   390
than hatred is this kind of love. Princes elected

---

5. One of the cities of Cyprus, whose name is
often used for the island as a whole.
6. A reminder that Orpheus is singing in
Thrace (the region stretching along the north
coast of the Aegean Sea).
7. An imaginary island near Arabia, rich in
spices.
8. The Furies.

from far and wide desire you, Myrrha; all Asia
sends its young men to compete for your hand in marriage:
choose from so many just one of these men for your husband,
so long as a certain one is not the one chosen.   395

    "She understood and struggled against her perversion,
asking herself, 'What have I begun? Where will it take me?
May heaven and piety and the sacred rights of fathers
restrain these unspeakable thoughts and repel my misfortune,
if this indeed *is* misfortune; yet piety chooses   400
not to condemn this love outright: without distinctions
animals copulate; it is no crime for the heifer
to bear the weight of her father upon her own back;
daughters are suitable wives in the kingdom of horses;
the billy goats enter the flocks that they themselves sire,   405
and birds are inseminated by those who conceive them:
blessed, the ones for whom such love is permitted!

    "'Human morality gives us such stifling precepts,
and makes indecent what Nature freely allows us!
But people say there are nations where sons and their mothers,   410
where fathers and daughters, may marry each other, increasing
the bonds of piety by their redoubled affections.
Wretched am I, who hadn't the luck to be born there,
injured by nothing more than mischance of location!

    "'Why do I obsess? Begone, forbidden desires;   415
of course he is worthy of love—but love for a father!
So, then, if I were not the daughter of great Cinyras,
I would be able to have intercourse with Cinyras:
though he is mine, he is not mine, and our nearness
ruins me: I would be better off as a stranger.   420

    "'It would be good for me to go far away from my country,
as long as I could escape from my wicked desires,
for what holds me here is the passion that I have to see him,
to touch and speak to Cinyras and give him my kisses—
if nothing more is permitted. You impious maiden,   425
what more can you imagine will ever be granted?
Are you aware how you confuse all rights and relations?
Would you be your mother's rival? The whore of your father?
Would you be called your son's sister? Your brother's own mother?
Do you not shudder to think of the serpent-coiffed sisters[9]   430
thrusting their bloodthirsty torches into the faces
of the guilty wretches that those three appear to and torture?

    "'But you, while your body is undefiled, keep your mind chaste,
and do not break Nature's law with incestuous pairing.
Think what you ask for: the very act is forbidden,   435
and he is devout and mindful of moral behavior—
ah, how I wish that he had a similar madness!'

    "She spoke and Cinyras, whom an abundance of worthy
suitors had left undecided, consulted his daughter,
ran their names by her and asked whom she wished for a husband;   440

9. Again, the Furies.

silent at first, she kept her eyes locked on her father,
seething until the hot tears spilled over her eyelids:
Cinyras, attributing this to the fears of a virgin,
bade her cease weeping, wiped off her cheeks, and kissed her;
Myrrha rejoiced overmuch at his gesture and answered   445
that she would marry a man 'just like you.' Misunderstanding
the words of his daughter, Cinyras approved them, replying,
'May you be this pious always.' Hearing that last word,
the virgin lowers her head, self-convicted of evil.

"Midnight: now sleep dissolves all the cares of the body;   450
Cinyras' daughter, however, lies tossing, consumed by
the fires of passion, repeating her prayers in a frenzy;
now she despairs, now she'll attempt it; now she is shamefaced,
now eager: uncertain: *What should she do now?* She wavers,
just like a tree that the axe blade has girdled completely,   455
when only the last blow remains to be struck, and the woodsman
cannot predict the direction it's going to fall in,
she, after so many blows to her spirit, now totters,
now leaning in one, and now in the other, direction,
nor is she able to find any rest from her passion   460
save but in death. Death pleases her, and she gets up,
determined to hang herself from a beam with her girdle:
'Farewell, dear Cinyras: may you understand why I do this!'
she said, as she fitted the noose around her pale neck.

"They say that, hearing her murmuring, her faithful old nurse   465
in the next chamber arose and entered her bedroom:
at sight of the grim preparations, she screams out, and striking
her breasts and tearing her garments, removes the noose from
around the girl's neck, and then, only then she collapses,
and weeping, embraces her, asking her why she would do it.   470

"Myrrha remained silent, expressionless, with her eyes downcast,
sorrowing only because her attempt was detected.
But the woman persists, baring her flat breasts and white hair,
and by the milk given when she was a babe in the cradle
beseeches her to entrust her old nurse with the cause of her sorrow. 475
The girl turns away with a groan; the nurse is determined
to learn her secret, and promises not just to keep it:

"'Speak and allow me to aid you,' she says, 'for in my old age,
I am not utterly useless: if you are dying of passion,
my charms and herbs will restore you; if someone wishes you evil, 480
my rites will break whatever spell you are under;
is some god wrathful? A sacrifice placates his anger.
What else could it be? I can't think of anything—Fortune
favors your family, everything's going quite smoothly,
both of your parents are living, your mother, your father—'   485
Myrrha sighed deeply, hearing her father referred to,
but not even then did the nurse grasp the terrible evil
in the girl's heart, although she felt that her darling
suffered a passion of some kind for some kind of lover.

"Nurse was unyielding and begged her to make known her secret,   490
whatever it was, pressing the tearful girl to her bosom;

and clasping her in an embrace that old age had enfeebled,
she said, 'You're in love—I am certain! I will be zealous
in aiding your cause, never you fear—and your father
will be none the wiser!'

                     "Myrrha in frenzy leapt up   495
and threw herself onto the bed, pressing her face in the pillows:
'Leave me, I beg you,' she said. 'Avoid my wretched dishonor;
leave me or cease to ask me the cause of my sorrow:
what you attempt to uncover is sinful and wicked!'

    "The old woman shuddered: extending the hands that now trembled   500
with fear and old age, she fell at the feet of her darling,
a suppliant, coaxing her now, and now attempting to scare her;
threatening now to disclose her attempted self-murder,
but pledging to aid her if she confesses her passion.

    "She lifted her head with her eyes full of tears spilling over   505
onto the breast of her nurse and repeatedly tried to
speak out, but repeatedly stopped herself short of confession,
hiding her shame-colored face in the folds of her garments,
until she finally yielded, blurting her secret:
'O mother,' she cried, 'so fortunate you with your husband!'   510
and said no more but groaned.

                    "The nurse, who now understood it,
felt a chill run through her veins, and her bones shook with tremor,
and her white hair stood up in stiff bristles. She said whatever
she could to dissuade the girl from her horrible passion,
and even though Myrrha knew the truth of her warning,   515
she had decided to die if she could not possess him.
'Live, then,' the other replied, 'and possess your—' Not daring
to use the word 'father,' she left her sentence unfinished,
but called upon heaven to stand by her earlier promise.

    "Now it was time for the annual feast days of Ceres;   520
the pious, and married women clad in white vestments,
thronged to the celebration, offering garlands
of wheat as firstfruits of the season; now for nine nights
the intimate touch of their men is considered forbidden.
Among these matrons was Cenchreïs, wife of Cinyras,   525
for her attendance during these rites was required.
And so, while the queen's place in his bed was left vacant,
the overly diligent nurse came to Cinyras,
finding him drunk, and spoke to him of a maiden
whose passion for him was real (although her name wasn't)   530
and praising her beauty; when asked the age of this virgin,
she said, 'the same age as Myrrha.' Commanded to fetch her,
nurse hastened home, and entering, cried to her darling,
'Rejoice, my dear, we have won!' The unlucky maiden
could not feel joy in her heart, but only grim sorrow,   535
yet still she rejoiced, so distorted were her emotions.

    "Now it is midnight, when all of creation is silent;
high in the heavens, between the two Bears, Boötes[1]

1. The Ox-herder, a constellation that was imagined as driving Ursa Major, the Great Bear.

had turned his wagon so that its shaft pointed downward;
Myrrha approaches her crime, which is fled by chaste Luna,[2]   540
while under black clouds the stars hide their scandalized faces;
Night lacks its usual fires; you, Icarus,[3] covered
your face and were followed at once by Erigone,
whose pious love of her father merited heaven.

"Thrice Myrrha stumbles and stops each time at the omen,   545
and thrice the funereal owl sings her his poem of endings;
nevertheless she continues, her shame lessened by shadows.
She holds the left hand of her nurse, and gropes with the other
blindly in darkness: now at the bedchamber's threshold,
and now she opens the door: and now she is led within,   550
where her knees fail her; she falters, nearly collapsing,
her color, her blood, her spirit all flee together.

"As she approaches the crime, her horror increases;
regretting her boldness, she wishes to turn back, unnoticed,
but even as she holds back, the old woman leads her   555
by the hand to the high bed, where she delivers her, saying,
'Take her, Cinyras—she's yours,' and unites the doomed couple.
The father accepts his own offspring in his indecent
bed and attempts to dispel the girl's apprehensions,
encouraging her not to be frightened of him, and   560
addressing her, as it happened, with a name befitting
her years: he called her 'daughter' while she called him 'father,'
so the right names were attached to their impious actions.

"Filled with the seed of her father, she left his bedchamber,
having already conceived, in a crime against nature   565
which she repeated the following night and thereafter,
until Cinyras, impatient to see his new lover
after so many encounters, brought a light in,
and in the same moment discovered his crime and his daughter;
grief left him speechless; he tore out his sword from the scabbard;   570
Myrrha sped off, and, thanks to night's shadowy darkness,
escaped from her death. She wandered the wide-open spaces,
leaving Arabia, so rich in palms, and Panchaea,
and after nine months, she came at last to Sabaea,[4]
where she found rest from the weariness that she suffered,   575
for she could scarcely carry her womb's heavy burden.

"Uncertain of what she should wish for, tired of living
but frightened of dying, she summed up her state in this prayer:
'O gods, if there should be any who hear my confession,
I do not turn away from the terrible sentence   580
that my misbehavior deserves; but lest I should outrage
the living by my survival, or the dead by my dying,
drive me from both of these kingdoms, transform me

---

2. The Moon, often associated with Diana, one of whose attributes was chastity.
3. More properly Icarius, a mythic Athenian. He received Dionysus into the city, and the god rewarded him with wine, which he shared with his countrymen. Feeling its effect, they thought they had been poisoned and killed him. His daughter Erigone hanged herself in grief, and both were changed into stars.
4. Arabia Felix, the southern tip of the Arabian Peninsula.

wholly, so that both life and death are denied me.'

"Some god *did* hear her confession, and heaven answered   585
her final prayer, for, even as she was still speaking,
the earth rose up over her legs, and from her toes burst
roots that spread widely to hold the tall trunk in position;
her bones put forth wood, and even though they were still hollow,
they now ran with sap and not blood; her arms became branches,   590
and those were now twigs that used to be called her fingers,
while her skin turned to hard bark. The tree kept on growing,
over her swollen belly, wrapping it tightly,
and growing over her breast and up to her neck; she
could bear no further delay, and, as the wood rose,   595
plunged her face down into the bark and was swallowed.

"Loss of her body has meant the loss of all feeling;
and yet she weeps, and the warm drops spill from her tree trunk;
those tears bring her honor: the distillate myrrh preserves and
will keep the name of its mistress down through the ages.   600

"But under the bark, the infant conceived in such baseness
continued to grow and now sought a way out of Myrrha;
the pregnant trunk bulged in the middle and its weighty burden
pressed on the mother, who could not cry out in her sorrow
nor summon Lucina with charms to aid those in childbirth.   605
So, like a woman exerting herself to deliver,
the tree groaned and bent over double, wet from its weeping.
Gentle Lucina stood by the sorrowing branches,
laid her hands onto the bark and recited the charms that
aid in delivery; the bark split open; a fissure   610
ran down the trunk of the tree and its burden spilled out,
a bawling boychild, whom naiads placed in soft grasses
and bathed in the tears of its mother. Not even Envy
could have found fault with his beauty, for he resembled
one of the naked cherubs depicted by artists,   615
and would have been taken as one, if you had provided
him with a quiver or else removed one from those others.

[*Venus and Adonis*]

"Time swiftly glides by in secret, escaping our notice,
and nothing goes faster than years do: the son of his sister
by his grandfather, the one so recently hidden   620
within a tree, so recently born, a most beautiful infant,
now is an adolescent and now a young man
even more beautiful than he was as a baby,
pleasing now even to Venus and soon the avenger
of passionate fires that brought his mother to ruin.   625

"For while her fond Cupid was giving a kiss to his mother,
he pricked her unwittingly, right in the breast, with an arrow
projecting out of his quiver; annoyed, the great goddess
swatted him off, but the wound had gone in more deeply
than it appeared to, and at the beginning deceived her.   630

"Under the spell of this fellow's beauty, the goddess

no longer takes any interest now in Cythera,[5]
nor does she return to her haunts on the island of Paphos,
or to fish-wealthy Cnidus or to ore-bearing Amathus;[6]
she avoids heaven as well, now—preferring Adonis,   635
and clings to him, his constant companion, ignoring
her former mode of unstrenuous self-indulgence,
when she shunned natural light for the parlors of beauty;
now she goes roaming with him through woods and up mountains
and over the scrubby rocks with her garments hitched up   640
and girded around her waist like a nymph of Diana,[7]
urging the hounds to pursue unendangering species,
hoppety hares or stags with wide-branching antlers,
or terrified does; but she avoids the fierce wild boars and
rapacious wolves and bears armed with sharp claws,   645
and shuns the lions, sated with slaughter of cattle.
    "And she warns you also to fear the wild beasts, Adonis,
if only her warning were heeded. 'Be bold with the timid,'
she said, 'but against the daring, daring is reckless.
Spare me, dear boy, the risk involved in your courage;   650
don't rile the beasts that Nature has armed with sharp weapons,
lest I should find the glory you gain much too costly!
For lions and bristling boars and other fierce creatures
look with indifferent eyes and minds upon beauty
and youth and other qualities Venus is moved by;   655
pitiless boars deal out thunderbolts with their curved tusks,
and none may withstand the frenzied assault of the lions,
whom I despise altogether.'
                        "And when he asked why,
she said, 'I will tell you this story which will amaze you,
with its retribution delivered for ancient wrongdoing.   660
    "'But this unaccustomed labor has left me exhausted—
look, though—a poplar entices with opportune shade, and
offers a soft bed of turf we may rest on together,
as I would like to.' And so she lay down on the grasses
and on her Adonis, and using his breast as a pillow,   665
she told this story, mixing her words with sweet kisses:

    "'Perhaps you'll have heard of a maiden able to vanquish
the swiftest of men in a footrace; this wasn't a fiction,
for she overcame all contestants; nor could you say whether
she deserved praise more for her speed or her beauty.   670
She asked some god about husbands. "A husband," he answered,
"is not for you, Atalanta: flee from a husband!
But you will not flee—and losing yourself, will live on!"
    "'Frightened by his grim prediction, she went to the forest
and lived there unmarried, escaping the large and persistent   675

***

5. Island south of the Peloponnesus, and like island of Cyprus, and Cnidus was a city in Asia
Cyprus sacred to Venus.   Minor.
6. All three were important centers of Venus's
cult: Paphos and Amathus were cities on the   7. As a virgin and huntress, the antithesis of
                                                 Venus.

throng of her suitors by setting out cruel conditions;
"You cannot have me," she said, "unless you outrun me;
come race against me! A bride and a bed for the winner,
death to the losers. Those are the rules of the contest."

"'Cruel? Indeed—but such was this young maiden's beauty   680
that a foolhardy throng of admirers took up the wager.
As a spectator, Hippomenes sat in the grandstand,
asking why anyone ever would risk such a danger,
just for a bride, and disparaging their headstrong passion.
However, as soon as he caught a glimpse of her beauty,   685
like mine or like yours would be if you were a woman,'
said Venus, 'her face and her body, both bared for the contest,
he threw up both hands and cried out, "I beg your pardons,
who only a moment ago disparaged your efforts,
but truly I had no idea of the trophy you strive for!"   690

"'Praises ignited the fires of passion and made him
hope that no young man proved to be faster than she was
and fear that one would be. Jealous, he asked himself why he
was leaving the outcome of this competition unventured:
"God helps those who improve their condition by daring,"   695
he said, addressing himself as the maiden flew by him.
Though she seemed no less swift than a Scythian arrow,
nevertheless, he more greatly admired her beauty,
and the grace of her running made her seem even more lovely;
the breezes blew back the wings attached to her ankles   700
while her loose hair streamed over her ivory shoulders
and her brightly edged knee straps fluttered lightly; a russet
glow fanned out evenly over her pale, girlish body,
as when a purple awning covers a white marble surface,
staining its artless candor with counterfeit shadow.   705

"'She crossed the finish line while he was taking it in, and
Atalanta, victorious, was given a crown and the glory;
the groaning losers were taken off: end of *their* story.
But the youth, undeterred by what had become of the vanquished,
stood on the track and fixed his gaze on the maiden: 710
"Why seek such an easy victory over these sluggards?
Contend with me," he said, "and if Fortune makes me the winner,
you will at least have been beaten by one not unworthy:
I am the son of Megareus, grandson of Neptune,
my great-grandfather; my valor is no less impressive   715
than is my descent; if you should happen to triumph,
you would be famous for having beaten Hippomenes."

"'And as he spoke, Atalanta's countenance softened:
she wondered whether she wished to win or to *be* won,
and asked herself which god, jealous of her suitor's beauty,   720
sought to destroy him by forcing him into this marriage:
"If *I* were judging, I wouldn't think I was worth it!
Nor am I moved by his beauty," she said, "though I could be,
but I *am* moved by his youth: his boyishness stirs me—
but what of his valor? His mind so utterly fearless?   725
What of his watery origins? His relation to Neptune?

What of the fact that he loves me and wishes to wed me,
and is willing to die if bitter Fortune denies him?

"'"Oh, flee from a bed that still reeks with the gore of past victims,
while you are able to, stranger; marrying *me* is   730
certain destruction! No one would wish to reject you,
and you may be chosen by a much wiser young lady!

"'"But why should I care for you—after so many have perished?
Now *he* will learn! Let him die then, since the great slaughter
of suitors has taught him nothing! He must be weary of living!   735
So—must he die then, because he wishes to wed me,
and is willing to pay the ultimate price for his passion?
He shouldn't have to! And even though it won't be *my* fault,
my victory surely will turn the people against me!

"'"If only you would just give it up, or if only,   740
since you're obsessed with it, you were a little bit faster!
How very girlish is the boy's facial expression!
O poor Hippomenes! I wish you never had seen me!
You're worthy of life, and if only *my* life had been better,
or if the harsh Fates had not prevented my marriage,   745
you would have been the one I'd have chosen to marry!"

"'She spoke, and, moved by desire that struck without warning,
loved without knowing what she was doing or feeling.
Her father and people were clamoring down at the racecourse,
when Neptune's descendent Hippomenes anxiously begged me: 750
"Cytherian Venus, I pray you preside at my venture,
aiding the fires that you yourself have ignited."
A well-meaning breeze brought me this prayer, so appealing
that, I confess, it aroused me and stirred me to action,
though I had scant time enough to bring off his rescue.   755

"'There is a field upon Cyprus, known as Tamasus,
famed for its wealth; in olden days it was given
to me and provides an endowment now for my temples;
and there in this field is a tree; its leaves and its branches
glisten and shimmer, reflecting the gold they are made of;   760
now, as it happened, I'd just gotten back from a visit,
carrying three golden apples that I had selected:
and showing myself there to Hippomenes only,
approached him and showed him how to use them to advantage.

"'Both of them crouched for the start; when horns gave the signal,   765
they took off together, their feet barely brushing the surface;
you would have thought they were able to keep their toes dry
while skimming over the waves, and could touch on the ripened
heads of wheat in the field without bending them under.

"'Cries of support and encouragement cheered on the young man;   770
"Now is the time," they screamed, "go for it, go for it, hurry,
Hippomenes, give it everything that you've got now!
Don't hold back! Victory!" And I am uncertain whether
these words were more pleasing to him or to his Atalanta,
for often, when she could have very easily passed him,   775
she lingered beside, her gaze full of desperate longing,
until she reluctantly sped ahead of his features.

"'And now Hippomenes, dry-mouthed, was breathlessly gasping,
the finish line far in the distance; he threw out an apple,
and the sight of that radiant fruit astounded the maiden,   780
who turned from her course and retrieved the glittering missile;
Hippomenes passed her: the crowd roared its approval.

"'A burst of speed now and Atalanta makes up for lost time:
once more overtaking the lad, she puts him behind her!
A second apple: again she falls back, but recovers,   785
now she's beside him, now passing him, only the finish
remains: "Now, O goddess," he cries, "my inspiration, be with me!"

"'With all the strength of his youth he flings the last apple
to the far side of the field: *this* will really delay her!
The maiden looked doubtful about its retrieval: I forced her   790
to get it and add on its weight to the burden she carried:
time lost and weight gained were equal obstructions: the maiden
(lest my account should prove longer than even the race was)
took second place: the trophy bride left with the victor.

"'But really, Adonis, wasn't I worthy of being   795
thanked for my troubles? Offered a gift of sweet incense?
Heedless of all I had done, he offered me neither!
Immediate outrage was followed by keen indignation;
and firmly resolving not to be spurned in the future,
I guarded against it by making this pair an example.   800

"'Now they were passing a temple deep in the forest,
built long ago by Echion to honor Cybele,[8]
Mother of Gods, and now the length of their journey
urged them to rest here, where unbridled desire
possessed Hippomenes, moved by the strength of my godhead.   805
There was a dim and cave-like recess near the temple,
hewn out of pumice, a shrine to the ancient religion,
wherein a priest of these old rites had set a great many
carved wooden idols. Hippomenes entered that place, and
by his forbidden behavior defiled it;[9] in horror,   810
the sacred images turned away from the act, and Cybele
prepared to plunge the guilty pair in Stygian waters,
but that seemed too easy; so now their elegant pale necks
are cloaked in tawny manes; curved claws are their fingers;
arms are now forelegs, and all the weight of their bodies   815
shifts to their torsos; and now their tails sweep the arena;
fierce now, their faces; growls supplant verbal expression;
the forest now is their bedroom; a terror to others,
meekly these lions champ at the bit of the harness
on either side of the yoke of Cybele's chariot.   820

"'My darling, you must avoid these and all other wild beasts,
who will not turn tail, but show off their boldness in battle;
flee them or else your courage will prove our ruin!'

8. A fertility goddess of Asia Minor known
as the Great Mother. She was often pictured
wearing a crown that resembled a city wall
with towers, and flanked by lions or riding in a
cart drawn by them.
9. It was considered sacrilege to have sexual
intercourse in the precinct of a temple.

"And after warning him, she went off on her journey,
carried aloft by her swans; but his courage resisted   825
her admonitions. It happened that as his dogs followed
a boar they were tracking, they roused it from where it was hidden,
and when it attempted to rush from the forest, Adonis
pierced it, but lightly, casting his spear from an angle;
with its long snout, it turned and knocked loose the weapon   830
stained with its own blood, then bore down upon our hero,
and, as he attempted to flee for his life in sheer terror,
it sank its tusks deep into the young fellow's privates,
and stretched him out on the yellow sands, where he lay dying.

"Aloft in her light, swan-driven chariot, Venus   835
had not yet gotten to Cyprus; from a great distance
she recognized the dying groans of Adonis
and turned her birds back to him; when she saw from midair
his body lying there, lifeless, stained with its own blood,
she beat her breasts and tore at her hair and her garments,   840
and leapt from her chariot, raging, to argue with grim Fate:

"'It will not be altogether as you would have it,'
she said. 'My grief for Adonis will be remembered
forever, and every year will see, reenacted
in ritual form, his death and my lamentation;   845
and the blood of the hero will be transformed to a flower.
Or were *you* not once allowed to change a young woman[1]
to fragrant mint, Persephone? Do you begrudge me
the transformation of my beloved Adonis?'

"And as she spoke, she sprinkled his blood with sweet nectar, 850
which made it swell up, like a transparent bubble
that rises from muck; and in no more than an hour
a flower sprang out of that soil, blood red in its color,
just like the flesh that lies underneath the tough rind
of the seed-hiding pomegranate. Brief is its season,   855
for the winds from which it takes its name, the anemone,
shake off those petals so lightly clinging and fated to perish."

---

1. Mentha, Hades' mistress, trampled by the jealous Persephone and transformed into the mint
(the meaning of her name).

SPEECH, WRITING, POETRY

Language is the most powerful tool possessed by human beings: it is our linguistic ability, more than anything else, that distinguishes us from animals. The development of writing was an enormously important development in the history of humanity, a leap second only to the development of language itself. Literacy allows for complex record keeping: a literate culture can have a far larger and more complex political and economic organization than is possible without writing. Through writing, we can communicate with people at a distance, over any expanse of space or time, and words can, in theory, be preserved forever. Moreover, written texts create the possibility of different kinds of communication, and even different kinds of thinking, from those available in an oral culture. Writing made way for the development of science and mathematics: it is impossible to solve a complex mathematical, scientific, or philosophical problem entirely in one's own head. It also allowed for new kinds of artistic composition—including history and other kinds of detailed narrative—that would be impossible to remember without the use of writing.

In the Mediterranean and Near East, the earliest people to develop systems of writing were the ancient Sumerians, who lived in the valley of Mesopotamia (between the Tigris and Euphrates rivers), and the ancient Egyptians. Sumerian cuneiform—"wedge-shape" markings inscribed on clay tablets—and Egyptian hieroglyphs both emerged in the latter half of the fourth millennium B.C.E. Variant writing systems were established by other ancient peoples much later in history: the Greeks invented their alphabet in the eighth century B.C.E., and their system was adapted by the Romans. Not surprisingly, ancient peoples were fully aware of the power of writing. The Sumerians showed legitimate pride in the fact that writing could be seen as their invention. In the poem *Enmerkar and the Lord of Aratta* (of which a section appears below), it is a Sumerian king who first molded clay and "put words on it," understanding that writing is a much more secure way to pass on an important message than merely telling your intentions to a messenger.

Both Sumer and Egypt were "scribal cultures," meaning that writing was an occupation for paid professionals, not something that everybody was expected to be able to do. Certain texts were used as models for novice scribes to copy, and some of these deal with the profession of the scribe itself—offering fascinating insight into how these early writers saw their task. These texts show how long and difficult a journey it was to become a proficient scribe—often with humor, as in descriptions of unpromising trainee scribes who fritter away their time drinking and partying, when they should be studying. But the texts also emphasize the value of the goal: the scribe was rewarded both

This detail from a red figure kylix (drinking cup) by the "Eretria Painter" (fifth century B.C.E.) shows the poet Lino instructing his student Mousaios.

financially and socially, as an honored member of society. The god Thoth, who was the patron of human scribes and himself scribe to the other gods, was one of the most powerful members of the Egyptian pantheon: he was, unlike other gods, self-created (through the power of language), and associated with knowledge, wisdom, healing, order, and correct judgment.

The complex relation between writing and social, political, and economic power is explored in our other Egyptian text, *The Tale of the Eloquent Peasant*. Here, a peasant goes to complain about the theft of his property to the magistrates, who record in writing his fluent but desperate, Job-like lament at the injustice he sees in his own life and in the world. The text seems to reflect an ambivalence toward writing. On the one hand, the poor man's words are conveyed through writing to the king, whose steward restores all the man's stolen property. On the other hand, the peasant's suffering is extended in order to provoke him to further eloquence and thereby generate more written literature. The text seems to suggest that writing can take on an aesthetic life of its own, and be valued—disturbingly enough—for reasons that may have nothing to do with morality.

Greek and Roman cultures were not primarily scribal: although people sometimes dictated to slaves (as a modern person might use a dictaphone), reading and writing were not seen as a specialty profession, and by the fifth century B.C.E., much of the elite male population could probably read and write, at least to some degree. But literacy did not, of course, become universal, and even those who could read encountered much of their "literature" orally, through recitation, singing, dramatic performance, and reading aloud; silent reading was almost unknown in the ancient world. Several Greek texts suggest anxiety about the transition from an oral to a literate culture. The only mention of writing in

A black granite sculpture from the fourteenth century B.C.E. depicting an Egyptian scribe.

the *Iliad*—a Greek poem based on an oral tradition—comes in book 6, in the story of Bellerophon, who is made to carry sinister "folded tablets" to a foreign king; unbeknown to the wronged hero, the tablets contain terrible lies against himself. The story depends on the fact that Bellerophon himself is presumably unable to read the tablets. In a culture where only a few can read and write, the power of marks on clay or papyrus can seem akin to magic. Indeed, in the Egyptian pantheon, Thoth was lord of magic, as well as of science and mathematics.

Greek and Roman authors often celebrated the quasi-magical power of writing to preserve words across space and time, even after the speaker's death. **Theognis**, a Greek lyric poet, trumpets his ability to bring immortality to his addressee: a poem can make the boy live forever. Theognis was probably composing at a time when few of his Greek contemporaries were literate (in the sixth century B.C.E.), and his metaphors hover in interesting ways between literate and oral models of language. The poet describes himself as singing (not writing), and, indeed, Theognis's poetry probably was sung mostly at drinking parties (known as *symposia*, "where men dine and pass the cup"); but Theognis also emphasizes that his poetry is infinitely repeatable, sung again and again by many different lips but always ascribed to the same author, because the work is "sealed"—like a written letter, or a written book of poetry. Later in the Greco-Roman tradition, once literacy was more widespread, poets began to emphasize the physicality of the book they were producing: **Callimachus** presents himself as inspired by the god Apollo, but not, like the archaic poet Hesiod, while he was out on the hillside, but at the first moment that he sat down to write, with "a writing tablet on my lap." **Horace** (in Ode 30) describes his poetic achievement in terms that are both physical and more than physical, since a book can be reproduced any number of times; the technology of writing allows the poet's work to defeat time and death ("I shall not wholly die"), and to last longer even than bronze or "the pyramids of kings."

But the power of writing could be seen as bad as well as good. In the *Phaedrus,* **Plato**'s Socrates tells a fable about an ancient king of Thebes who was offered writing as a new gift by the Egyptian god Thoth. Thoth claims that the art of writing would improve human memory; but the king adamantly rejects this view, claiming that it "will introduce forgetfulness into the soul." When thoughts are stored outside the mind, on the page, people will no longer bother to remember them for themselves. And once ideas are written down, we may give them credit for wisdom; but in fact, books are less, not more, truthful than living human minds, since

they are unable to change in response to new realizations. The possible disjunctions between literature and ethics, and between literature and truth, were of particular concern to the ancient Greeks, as we see in several texts collected here. Xenophanes criticizes the Homeric poems for misrepresenting the gods as setting a bad example to humanity. **Aristophanes**' comedy, *Frogs*, suggests that literature has an essential impact on the ethical and cultural life of a community: the premise of the play is that the city of Athens, in dire straits during its long war with Sparta, needs the help of a dead poet, who must be chosen and brought back to the world of the living by the theater god, Dionysus. Dionysus's choice comes down to the two tragedians, **Aeschylus** and **Euripides**, who represent two models for how a poet or writer might interact with society. Should literature inspire us to revere tradition, and rouse us to fight for our country—as Aeschylus's plays supposedly did? Or should it, rather, reflect people as they are, with all their flaws—even if, as some of Euripides' contemporaries claimed, the depiction of immoral behavior can inspire further wickedness? A version of this debate is still with us today.

One possible response is to claim that literature has nothing to do with morality, and to focus instead on the techniques that enable a work of literature to succeed or fail on its own terms. But good writing is not merely a matter of assembling correct words in the correct order: it also involves the heart. Even Horace's *Ars Poetica*, a work that stresses the concept of *decorum* ("appropriateness"), sometimes veers away from a purely technical account of good writing, as when he suggests that the poet must first feel for himself the emotions that he hopes to inspire in his reader. **Aristotle**'s *Poetics*, too, despite its emphasis on technique, suggests that poetry has a deep emotional and ethical function. Writing in response to Plato's criticisms of poetry and writing, Aristotle suggests that good poetry actually helps us become better people, by recalibrating or healing our emotional responses. The art of writing is, then, far less distant from the art of good living than Aristotle's teacher Plato had believed.

None of these texts are "literary criticism" in a modern sense. Instead of analyzing specific written works, their ancient authors are interested in discussing how, why, and whether a person should write. Technique is at the forefront in some of these texts, while others focus on broader ethical, political, and psychological issues. It is worthwhile to think hard about how ancient conceptions of speech, writing, and poetry differ from our own notions of "literature"—as well as about how these writers and thinkers laid the foundation on which modern literature studies could be built.

MESOPOTAMIA: ENMERKAR AND THE LORD OF ARATTA

This ancient Sumerian mythological story, composed perhaps around 2000 B.C.E., celebrates Sumer, and one of its major cities, Uruk, as the birthplace of writing. The goddess Inana (known as Ishtar in *The Epic of Gilgamesh*) permits Enmerkar, the king of the mighty city-state Uruk, to subjugate the people of Aratta—a mythical place rich in gold and jewels—and make them deliver tribute for her, to adorn her cult centers in Uruk. They resist, and after many exchanges of messengers, the Lord of Aratta proposes that the cities should each pick a champion, to fight it out. Enmerkar is willing to accept the challenge, on condition that the people of Aratta, if they lose, will pay even more tribute, or else face absolute destruction. At this point, the herald is overwhelmed and cannot remember the details of what he is to say. In response, Enmerkar invents writing, and sends the herald with clay tablets back to Aratta; this is the passage included here. The ending of the text is damaged and unclear, but it seems that the people of Aratta eventually submitted, sent tribute, and Enmerkar triumphed.

From Enmerkar and the Lord of Aratta[1]

From his throne he spoke to him like a raging torrent:[2]
"Messenger, when you speak to the lord of Aratta, say this:
"A cloth that is not black, a cloth that is not white,
"A cloth that is not brown, a cloth that is not red,
"A cloth that is not yellow, a cloth that is not pied—such a cloth
    I will give him!

5

---

1. Translated by Herman Vanstiphout.
2. The scene of the invention of writing by the king of Uruk opens with the king, Enmerkar, trying to instruct his messenger how to respond to the people of Aratta, who are not willing to pay tribute to Uruk.

"My dog is embraced by Enlil;[3] this dog I will send to him.
"My dog will wrangle with his dog
"So that the stronger one be known. Tell him that!
"Second, when you speak to him, say also this:
"He must now stop prevaricating and come to a decision   10
"Those of his city shall walk before him like sheep,
"And he, like a shepherd, shall follow them.
"At his coming, the holy mound of lapis lazuli
"Shall humble itself before him like a crushed reed.
"They shall amass shining gold and silver   15
"For Inana of the Eana
"In the courtyard of Aratta in great piles.[4]
"Third, when you speak to him, say also this:
"Beware lest I make (the people/Aratta) flee from their city like a dove
      from its tree,
"Lest I make them fly away like [a bird from its permanent nest].   20
"Lest I put a price on them [as on mere merchandise].
"[Lest I *make*] the wind carry them away!
"At his coming, when he holds the precious stones of the hills,
"He must build for me the shrines of Eridug, Abzu, and Enum;[5]
"He must adorn for me its architrave with a *slip of clay*;   25
"He must make it spread its shadow over the Land for me!
"When he speaks . . .
"Tell him this as a sign for him!"

> Thereupon the lord . . .
> on the throne dais, on the throne, the noble seed of princes,   30
> grown all alone.

His speech was very grand, its meaning very deep;
The messenger's mouth was too *heavy*, he could not repeat it.
Because the messenger's mouth was too *heavy*, and he could not repeat it,
The lord of Kulab[6] patted some clay and put the words on it as on a tablet.   35
Before that day, there had been no putting words on clay;
But now, when the sun rose on that day—so it was:
The lord of Kulab had put words as on a tablet—so it was!

> The messenger was like a bird flapping its wings.
Raging like a wolf chasing a kid   40
He crossed five, six, seven mountain ranges.
Lifting his head, he had reached Aratta.

Joyfully he stepped into the courtyard of Aratta
And proclaimed the preeminence of his king.
He spoke out what was in his heart   45
And transmitted it to the lord of Aratta:
"Your father, my king, has sent me;

---

3. One of the chief gods in the Mesopotamian pantheon. The messenger later calls Enmerkar a "son of Enlil."
4. The king of Uruk requests tribute paid in gold and silver from the Lord of Aratta for adorning the temple of Inana. Eana is the goddess's abode.
5. Other shrines to be built and adorned; Eridug was a city in southern Sumer.
6. Chancellor of King Enmerkar of Uruk.

"The lord of Unug; and Kulab[7] has sent me."
LORD OF ARATTA
"What is it to me what your king spoke, what he said?"
MESSENGER
"This is what my king spoke, what he said: 50
"My King is a tall MES-tree,[8] the son of Enlil.
"This tree has grown so tall that it links heaven and earth;
"Its crown reaches heaven;
"Its roots are set fast in the earth.
"He who has manifested lordship and kingship,   55
"Enmerkar, son of the Sun, gave me this tablet.
"O lord of Aratta, when you have read this tablet, learned the gist of
      the message,
"When you will have replied to me whatever you want,
"To the scion of the one with the gleaming beard,
"To him whom the mighty cow bore on the hill of the lustrous power,   60
"To him who grew up on the soil of Aratta,
"To him who was suckled by the rear of the true cow,
"To him, suited for office in Kulab, mountain of the great powers,
"To Enmerkar, son of the Sun,
"I will speak that word as glad tidings in the shrine Eana.   65
"In his Gipar, bearing fruit like a young MES-tree,
"I shall repeat it to my king, the lord of Kulab."

      This having been said,
The lord of Arratta took from the messenger
The tablet (and held it) next to a brazier.   70
The lord of Aratta inspected the tablet.
The spoken words were mere wedges[9]—his brow darkened.
The lord of Aratta kept looking at the tablet (in the light of) the brazier.

7. Kulab was part of the city of Uruk, probably a temple quarter. *Unug*: Sumerian name for "Uruk," the city-state ruled by King Enmerkar.
8. Silvery tree of great worth.
9. The Sumerian *gag* ("nail, wedge") is not the technical term for the wedge-shaped cuneiform writing. Thus, the passage is written from the perspective of the stunned Lord Aratta, who does not understand that the incisions on the clay tablet are spoken words recorded in the newly invented medium of writing.

EGYPT: THE TALE OF THE ELOQUENT PEASANT

Composed around 1850 B.C.E. during the Middle Kingdom, the classical age of Egyptian literature, this text is one of the longest Egyptian literary tales to survive complete. It tells the story of a poor merchant from an oasis near the Nile Delta, who is robbed and pleads for justice to the king's high steward. The steward recognizes the peasant's extraordinary gift for fine speech and detains him until he has declaimed nine extensive petitions that center on the theme of justice. Suspense in the tale rises with each round of declamation, since the peasant does not know that he has already won his case. The steward remains silent, thus goading the peasant into ever greater eloquence, which ranges from flattery to abuse and despair. At one point the steward even commands that the peasant be beaten, in order to stimulate him to yet higher flights of eloquence. The text is a complex meditation on the relation—or disjunction—of moral order and fine speech, as transcribed into fine writing.

From The Tale of the Eloquent Peasant[1]

And this peasant came to petition
the High Steward Meru's son Rensi,
and said, 'High Steward, my lord!
Great of the great,
leader of all that is not and all that is! 5

If you go down to the Sea of Truth,[2]
you will sail on it with true fair wind;
the bunt will not strip off your sails, nor your boat delay;
nor will misfortune come upon your mast, nor your yards break;
you will not go headlong, and be grounded; 10
nor will the flood carry you off;
nor will you taste the river's evil, nor stare in the face of fear.
But to you the fish will come caught;
you will catch fatted fowl.

For you are a father to the orphan[3] 15
and a husband to the widow,

---

1. Translated by Richard B. Parkinson.
2. A pun on the Sea of Maat, a waterway known from texts about the next world. The Egyptian for "truth," "justice," and "order" is *maat*, a different word from the name of the next-worldly stretch of water.
3. These lines give standard phrases describing the righteous behavior of high officials.

a brother to the divorced,
an apron to the motherless.
Let me make your name in this land, with every good law:
Leader free from selfishness!   20
Great one free from baseness!
Destroyer of Falsehood! Creator of Truth!
Who comes at the voice of the caller!

I speak so that you will hear.
Do Truth, praised one whom the praised praise!   25
Drive off my need—look, I am weighed down!
Examine me—look, I am at a loss!'

Now this peasant made this speech
in the reign of the Majesty of the Dual King Nebkaure, the justified.[4]
The High Steward Meru's son Rensi   30
then went before his Majesty
and said, 'My lord, I have found one of the peasants,
whose speech is truly perfect, and whose goods have been stolen.
And, look, he has come to me to appeal about it.'

And his Majesty said, 'As you wish to see me in health   35
you shall delay him here,
without answering anything he says!
For the sake of his speaking, be quiet!
Then we shall be brought it in writing, and we shall hear it.
But provide sustenance for his wife and children!   40
Look, one of these peasants only comes
to Egypt when his house is all but empty.
Also, provide sustenance for this peasant himself!
You shall have the provisions given to him
without letting him know that you are giving him them!'   45

And he was given ten loaves of bread,[5]
and two jars of beer daily.
The High Steward Meru's son
Rensi gave them—
gave them to his friend, and his friend gave them to him.   50
Then the High Steward Meru's son Rensi sent
to the mayor of the Wadi Natrun
about making provisions for this peasant's wife,
three gallons daily.

                          *   *   *

And this peasant came to appeal to him a third time   55
and said, 'High Steward, my lord!
You are a Sungod, lord of heaven, with your entourage.

---

4. A king of the tenth dynasty of Heracleopolis, ca. 2050 B.C.E. "The justified" is a standard epithet of the deceased.

5. A generous but not excessive ration. Rensi routes the provisions indirectly so that the peasant should not know who sent them.

Everyone's portion is with you, like a flood.
You are a Nileflood who revives the water-meadows, and restores
   the ravaged mounds.
Punisher of the robber, protector of the poor—   60
become not a torrent against the appealer!

Take heed of eternity's approach! Wish to endure,[6]
as is said, "Doing Truth is the breath of life."
Deal punishment to the punishable!
May your standard never be equalled!   65
Do the scales wander?
Is the balance partial?
And is Thoth lenient?[7] If so, then you should do evil!
You should bestow yourself as the twin of these three!
If the three are lenient, then you can be lenient.   70
Do not answer good with bad!
Do not put one thing in another's place!
Or speech will grow, even more than weeds,
to reach the smeller with its answer.
The man who waters evil to make deception grow—   75
this is three times to make him act.

Steer according to the sail!
Remove the torrent to do Truth!
Beware turning back while at the tiller!
Maintaining earth's rightness is doing Truth.   80
Speak not falsehood, for you are great!
Be not light, for you are weighty!
Speak not falsehood, you are the scales!
Stray not, you are the standard!
Look, you yourself are the very scales: 85
if they tilt, then you can tilt.
Drift not, but steer!
Rescue with the tiller rope!
Seize not, but act against the seizer!
A selfish great one is not truly great.   90
But your tongue is the plummet;
your heart is the weight;
your lips are its arms.
So if you disregard the fierce, who will beat off wretchedness?

Look, you are a wretched washerman,[8]   95
a selfish one who destroys friendship,
and forsakes his faithful companion for his client—
anyone who comes and supplies him is his brother.
Look, you are a ferryman who ferries only fareholders,

---

6. In order to survive into the next life, Rensi
should act justly.
7. Thoth, the assessor of the balance in judgment after death, is incorruptible and so not

lenient.
8. The next stanza denigrates Rensi, whose
role as a high official should include care for
the indigent.

a doer of right whose righteousness is flawed. 100
Look, you are a storehouse keeper,
who does not let someone in penury escape a debt.

Look, you are a hawk to the folk,[9]
who lives on the wretched birds.
Look, you are a butcher 105
whose joy is slaughter, without feeling any of the carnage.
Look, you are a shepherd—
is it not a wrong for me that you cannot reckon?
If not, then you can create loss—a predatory crocodile,
a shelter which has abandoned the harbour of the whole land! 110

Hearer, you do not hear!
So why do you not hear?
Is it because the predator has today already been beaten off for me?
The crocodile retreats?
What use for you is this? 115
The mystery of Truth will be found, and Falsehood cast
    down on the ground!
Do not plan tomorrow before it comes; the evil in it cannot be known!'

Now the peasant spoke this speech
⟨to⟩ the High Steward Meru's son Rensi
at the entrance of the office.[1] 120
Then he set two attendants on him with whips.
Then they beat all his limbs with them.[2]

* * *

And this peasant came to appeal to him a ninth time,[3]
and said, 'High Steward, my lord!
The tongue of men is their balance; 125
and scales are what detect deficiency,
dealing punishment to the punishable: let the standard be like you!

Even when its portion exists, Falsehood [sallies forth],
but Truth turns back to confront it;
Truth is the property of Falsehood,
which lets it flourish, but Falsehood has never been gathered in.[4] 130
If Falsehood sets out, it strays;
it cannot cross in a ferry, and has not altered its course.

---

9. A perversion of an image of the king as a
defender of his people.
1. The peasant never enters Rensi's office.
Petitions are heard at doorways or other places
of transition.
2. This passage takes the text forward; without it, the peasant would have exhausted his
possibilities for recourse against Nemtinakht

through Rensi. In the next stanza, not included
here, the peasant accuses Rensi of abusing all
the roles that he holds and exploiting them for
his own ends.
3. This is the the peasant's final petition.
4. A metaphor of harvest that says that Truth
is under the control of Falsehood, whose growth
in an imperfect world cannot be checked.

He who is rich with it has no children,[5]
and no heirs on earth.
And he who sails with it cannot touch land,
his boat cannot moor in its harbour.

Be heavy no more, you have not yet been light!
Delay no more, you have not yet been swift!
Be not partial! Do not listen to the heart!
Do not disregard one you know!
Do not blind yourself against one who looks to you! Do not fend
   off a supplicator!

You should abandon this negligence, so that your sentence
   will be renowned!
Act for him who acts for you[6]
and listen to none against him,
so that a man will be summoned according to his true right!
There is no yesterday for the negligent,
no friend for him who is deaf to Truth,
no holiday for the selfish.
The accuser becomes wretched,[7]
more wretched than when a pleader,
and the opponent becomes a murderer.
Look, I am pleading to you, and you do not hear—
I will go and plead about you to Anubis.'[8]

And the High Steward Meru's son Rensi
sent two attendants to turn him back.
And this peasant was afraid, thinking this was done
to punish him for the speech he had made.
And this peasant said, 'The thirsty man
approaching water,
the nurseling reaching his mouth
for milk—they die,
while for him who longs to see it come,
death comes slowly.'
And the High Steward Meru's son Rensi said,
'Don't be afraid, peasant!
Look, you will be dealing with me.'
And this peasant swore an oath,
'So, shall I live on your bread,[9]
and drink your beer for ever?'
And the High Steward Meru's son Rensi said,

135

140

145

150

155

160

165

170

'Now wait here and hear your petitions!'
And he caused every petition to be read out
from a fresh roll according to [its] content.
And the High Steward Meru's son Rensi had them presented   175
before the Majesty of the Dual King Nebkaure, the justified.
And they seemed more perfect to his heart
than anything in this entire land.
And his Majesty said, 'Judge yourself, Meru's son!'

And the High Steward Meru's son Rensi   180
sent two attendants to [bring this Nemtinakht].
Then he was brought, and an inventory made [of his household].
Then he found six persons, as well as [his . . .],
his barley, his emmer,
his donkeys, his swine,[1] and his flocks.   185
And this Nemtinakht [was given] to this peasant,
[with all his property, all his] ser[vants],
[and all the belongings] of this Nemtinakht.

So it ends, [from start to finish,
as found in writing].

---

1. Pigs were commonly raised in ancient Egypt, but were subject to some sort of taboo and are almost absent from the pictorial and literary record. This is a rare exception.

EGYPT: TEXTS ON THE SCRIBAL PROFESSION

These texts on the scribal profession, composed in late New Kingdom Egypt (ca. 1300–1100 B.C.E.), were used by apprentice scribes as they practiced their writing skills. Many Egyptian literary texts exalted the calling of the scribe as administrator, rather than as magician, a characterization prominent in fictional tales. The texts selected here praise the life of the scribe, and mock students of writing who fail to concentrate on their studies. The texts also describe the hardships experienced by people who make their living in other ways. The scribe does not suffer as they do, and he may be the one who orders others to suffer when their dues are collected, generally in the form of rents. The last example is a prayer to Thot (or Thoth), the Egyptian god of scribes.

Reminder of the Scribe's Superior Status[1]

The overseer of the record-keepers of the treasury of Pharaoh, l.p.h.,[2] Amunemone speaks to the scribe Pentawere. This letter is brought to you saying: I have been told that you have abandoned writing and that you reel about in pleasures, that you have given your attention to work in the fields, and that you have turned your back on hieroglyphs. Do you not remember the condition of the field hand in the face of the registration of the harvest-tax, the snake having taken away half of the grain and the hippopotamus having eaten the remainder? The mice are numerous in the field, the locust descends, and the cattle eat. The sparrows bring want to the field hand. The remainder which is (on) the threshing floor is finished, and it is for the thieves. Its 'value in copper' is lost, and the yoke of oxen is dead from threshing and ploughing. The scribe has moored (at) the riverbank.[3] He reckons the tax, with the attendants bearing staffs and the Nubians[4] rods of palm. They [say]: Give the grain! There is none. They beat [him] vigorously. He is bound and cast into the well. They beat [him], drowning [him] head first, while his wife is bound in his presence. His children are manacled; his neighbors have abandoned them and fled. Their grain is gathered. But a scribe, he is the taskmaster of everyone. There is (no) taxing of the work of the scribe. He does not have dues. So take note of this.

Advice to the Youthful Scribe

O scribe, do not be idle, do not be idle, or you shall be curbed straight way. Do not give your heart to pleasures, or you shall fail. Write with your hand, recite with your mouth, and converse with those more knowledgeable than you. Exercise the office of magistrate, and then you will find it [advantageous] in old age. Fortunate is a scribe skilled in his office, the possessor of (a good) upbringing. Persevere in action daily, and you will gain mastery over them. Do not spend a day of idleness or you shall be beaten. The youth has a back and he hearkens to the beating of him.[1] Pay attention. Hearken to what I have said. You will find it advantageous. One teaches apes (to) dance, and one tames horses.[2] One can place a kite in a nest, and a falcon can be caught by the wings. Persevere in conversation. Do not be idle. Write. Do not feel distaste.

---

1. All selections translated by William Simpson.
2. In this period the living king was normally referred to by the name of the institution "Pharaoh" (literally "Great Estate"); l.p.h. is an abbreviation for "life, prosperity, health," a stereotyped wish formula written after a word for the king in documents and inscriptions.
3. Unlike the field hand, the scribe is brought by boat, so that he does not have to walk.
4. Nubians were widely employed in the police and the military.
1. The dull student learns by being beaten. A stronger form of this idea is to say that a pupil's ear is on his back.
2. If animals can learn, even a pupil scribe must be able to do so.

Prayer to Thot for Skill in Writing

Come to me, Thot, O noble Ibis, O god who longs for Khmun, O dispatch-writer of the Ennead, the great one of Unn.[1] Come to me that you may give advice and make me skillful in your office. Better is your profession than all professions. It makes (men) great. He who is skilled in it is found (fit) to exercise (the office of) magistrate. I have 'seen' many for whom you have acted, and they are in the Council of the Thirty,[2] they being strong and powerful through what you have done. You are the one who has given advice. You are the one who has given advice to the motherless man.[3] Shay and Renenwetet[4] are with you. Come to me that you may advise me. I am the servant of your house. Let me relate your prowess in whatever land I am. Then the multitude of men shall say: How great are the things that Thot has done. Then they shall come with their children to brand[5] them with your profession, a calling good to the lord of victory. Joyful is the one who has exercised it.

1. The ibis is the sacred bird of Thot (also spelled Thoth). Khmun (Hermopolis) is his sacred city, also known as Unu. Thot is the scribe of the gods, of whom the Ennead (group of nine) are the most important.
2. A legal and administrative body.

3. In addition to protecting scribes, Thot cares for the helpless.
4. The deities of fate and fortune.
5. This evokes the metaphor of human beings as the "cattle of the god."

XENOPHANES

Xenophanes[1] (ca. 570–475 B.C.E.), who came from the Greek city of Colophon on the Ionian coast (overlapping with modern Turkey), was a poet and philosopher whose work has survived only through quotation in later authors. He satirized the idea that gods are like human beings and criticized, on moral grounds, the representations of gods in the poetry of **Hesiod** and **Homer**.

[The myths of the theologians and poets] are full of every impiety; hence Xenophanes, criticizing Homer and Hesiod, says:
   Homer and Hesiod attributed to the gods everything
   which among men is shameful and blameworthy—
   theft and adultery and mutual deception.
   —Sextus Empiricus, *Against the Mathematicians* IX

1. The work of Xenophanes does not survive, but we have quotations from him in other, much later authors. Here, the parts in regular font are summaries of his views, and the parts in italics are thought to be exact quotations. Translated by Jonathan Barnes.

Homer and Hesiod, according to Xenophanes of Colophon,
> *recounted many lawless deeds of the gods—*
> *theft and adultery and mutual deception.*

For Cronus, under whom they say was the golden age, castrated his father and ate his children. . . .

—Sextus Empiricus, Against the Mathematicians I

Xenophanes of Colophon, teaching that god is one and incorporeal, rightly says:
> *There is one god, greatest among gods and men,*
> *similar to mortals neither in shape nor in thought.*

And again:
> *But mortals think that gods are born,*
> *and have clothes and speech and shape like their own.*

And again:
> *But if cows and horses or lions had hands*
> *and drew with their hands and made the things men make,*
> *then horses would draw the forms of gods like horses, cows like cows,*
> *and each would make their bodies*
> *similar in shape to their own.*

—Clement, Miscellanies 5.14

THEOGNIS

Theognis, who lived sometime in the sixth century B.C.E., was a Greek poet from the isthmus of Corinth. The collection that survives under his name includes many maxims, poems, and poem fragments, some of which are not by Theognis: some may have been composed one or two hundred years after his death. The poetry in this collection was probably sung at drinking parties for aristocratic young men and idealizes eloquence; it shows intense hostility to "the common man," and celebrates the love between an upper-class speaker and his beautiful boyfriend, Kyrnos.

From Elegies[1]

O Lord, the son of Leto, child of Zeus,[2]
I won't forget you now or at the end.
I'll sing you first and last and in between,
You, listen, and be favourable to me.

---

1. Translated by Dorothea Wender.
2. The god Apollo, who was associated with poetry.

I seal my words of wisdom with your name,[3]   5
Kurnos; no man can steal them now, nor try
To slip his trash in with my excellence,
And every man will say, 'This is a song
That great Theognis, the Megarian, sang.'

* * *

I give you wings. You'll soon be lifted up   10
Across the land, across the boundless crests
Of ocean; where men dine and pass the cup,
You'll light there, on the lips of all the guests,
Where lithe, appealing lads will praise you, swelling
Their song to match the piper's sweet, shrill tone.   15
At length, my boy, you'll enter Hades' dwelling,
That black hole where departed spirits moan,
But even then your glory will not cease,
Your well-loved name will stay alive, unworn;
You'll skim across the mainland, over Greece,   20
Over the islands and the sea, not borne
By horses, Kurnos; you'll be whirled along
By violet-crowned maids, the Muses; yours
Will be each practised singer's finest song,
As long as light exists and earth endures.   25
I give you this, for what? To be reviled—
To be betrayed and lied to, like a child.

3. The "seal" may be the title written on the scroll.

ARISTOPHANES

First performed in Athens in 405 B.C.E., *Frogs* is a comedy about the god Dionysus (associated with wine and theater) descending to the underworld to recover a dead tragic poet to save the city at a time of crisis in the war against Sparta. The choice comes down to two: the older, more traditional **Aeschylus**, author of *Agamemnon*, who claims to be able to inspire his audience with patriotic, military fervor, but whose writing style is represented as pompous, wordy, and (literally) heavy; or the younger, more entertaining **Euripides**, author of *Medea*, who writes in a more colloquial style and represents morally dubious behavior with realism and zing.

From Frogs[1]

EURIPIDES   Don't anyone dare tell me to let go of this chair.[2]
   With me—in the art of poetry—there's no one to compare.
DIONYSUS   Aeschylus, you say nothing.
   Don't you hear what this man's claiming?
EURIPIDES   As always, he's being aloof—like his tragedies.   5
DIONYSUS   That's a bit much, friend. Don't exaggerate.
EURIPIDES   I've had this fellow's number for a long time.
   The most boring primitives is what he likes to create:
   unlettered, unfettered, unruly, uncouth, they froth at the mouth
   in a flood of bombastical—diarrheical foam.   10
AESCHYLUS   Really? You son of a vegetable-selling bitch?
   This coming from you, you bleeding-burst-bubble-piece-of-bosh!
   You beggermonger with an avocation to stitch
   old sacks, you'll be sorry you said that.
DIONYSUS   Hold on, Aeschylus. "Heap not the fuel on your fiery gall."[3]   15
AESCHYLUS   No, I won't hold on. Not till I've laid bare
   the impudence of this creator of spastics here.
DIONYSUS   Hey, boys, a lamb, bring on a black lamb.[4]
   I can see what's heading our way—a storm.
AESCHYLUS   [*continuing his tirade against* EURIPIDES]
   You connoisseur of dirty Cretan songs   20
   fouling our art with incestuous intercourse.
DIONYSUS   That's enough, illustrious Aeschylus,
   and you, Euripides, poor fellow, it would be wise
   to move out of range of this storm of hail.
   He's so angry he might break your skull   25
   with a crushing retort and your *Telephus*[5] would come to naught.
   And you, Aeschylus,
   do try to keep calm and free your repartee
   from rancor and abuse.
   It's simply not done for two well-known literary men   30
   to wrangle like fishwives or go up in a blaze
   like an oak tree on fire.
EURIPIDES   I am ready to take him on if *he* is.
   I'm not backing down.
   He can have the first go in this verbal bout   35
   and pick away at the entire
   gamut and guts of my songs and tragedies.

1. Translated by Paul Roche. This scene takes place in Hades, the underworld; Pluto, god of the underworld, is sitting onstage, on his throne. Dionysus, god of wine and theater, has come to take a dead tragic poet back up with him to Athens to save the city in its time of crisis at the end of the Peloponnesian War. He has to decide between Aeschylus and Euripides, so a competition is organized; the winner will be taken back to the upper world.
2. Euripides apparently grabs the place of honor, to the right of Pluto, the king.
3. Presumably a quotation from Aeschylus.
4. Apparently a good sacrifice for defense against bad weather.
5. A lost tragedy by Euripides.

I don't care which: my *Peleus*, my *Aeolus*,
my *Meleager*—yes, and even my *Telephus*.

DIONYSUS   And, Aeschylus, what about you? Speak out.   40

AESCHYLUS   I could have wished avoiding this altercation.
The odds are so uneven.

DIONYSUS   How d'you mean?

AESCHYLUS   My poetry hasn't died with me—
it's still alive up there,   45
whereas his is as moribund as he.
    Still, if that's what you want, I don't care.

DIONYSUS   Will someone go and get the incense and the fire
and I'll begin this display of supererogation with a prayer
that my decisions in this contest will be fair.   50
    Meanwhile will the Chorus invoke the Muses with a hymn.

MEN AND WOMEN
    Come, you holy maidens of Zeus,
    You Muses nine, who activate the decisions and the minds
    Of men along wonderfully clear and luminous lines
    When they are pitted against each other in tough and abstruse   55
    Debate, we invite you to come and admire the vigor and prowess
    Of this couple of speakers, each of which is a master
    Of handling enormous slabs of verb
    As well as piddling chips of syllable. Look and observe
    The mighty minds that are about to commence.   60

DIONYSUS   Both of you now offer up a prayer before you say your piece.

AESCHYLUS   Great Demeter, who sustains my faculties, let me be worthy of
    your Mysteries.[6]

DIONYSUS   You now, Euripides.
Present your incense, make your prayer.   65

EURIPIDES   Thanks, but I pray to a different set of deities.

DIONYSUS   Your own personal ones? Brand-new, of course?

EURIPIDES   Sure.

DIONYSUS   Go on then. Have recourse to those personal gods of yours.

EURIPIDES   Ether—you, my grazing pastures   70
        As well as Nous and Nosey Parker[7]
        Arm me with the words for argument.

Strophe[8]

MEN   Now we're all agog to hear
        Two literary geniuses at work
        Who have decided to go to war   75
        In a duel of words.

---

6. Demeter, goddess of harvest and fertility, was celebrated in a secret mystery cult at Eleusis.
7. Ether is the personification of the upper part of the sky; Nous is mind, which the phi-losopher Anaxagoras had claimed was the primary force in the physical world.
8. The first part of a choral ode, in a different meter from the dialogue in the original. It is echoed, metrically, by the antistrophe.

The tongues of both will go berserk.
Their spirits are not short of valor
Nor are their minds short of vigor.
So we may safely assume that soon   80
One will utter something smart,
Whetted, and keen,
The other score with a brilliant thrust
And reasons torn up by the roots
Scattering words in a cloud of dust.   85

LEADER   Very well, begin your speechifying at once.
   Don't fail to make it clever, but not pretentious
   or commonplace with silly riddles.
EURIPIDES   Good, but before I tell you the kind of creative writer I am
   let me make clear what an impostor and sham my adversary is.   90
      What he did was set himself up to diddle
   the audiences he inherited from Phrynichus,[9]
   Who were already pretty far gone in imbecility.
      His Prologues always begin with some solitary soul,
   an Achilles, say, or a Niobe,[1]   95
   all muffled up so you can't see their faces
   and not uttering a syllable.
      Quite a travesty, I'd say, of dramatic tragedy.
DIONYSUS   Yes, you've got it exactly.
EURIPIDES   And while they sit there mute as dummies,   100
   the Chorus lets go in a litany
   of nonstop choral baloney.
DIONYSUS   All the same, I quite enjoyed his silences.
   They weren't as bad as today's babbling histrionics.
EURIPIDES   That's because you're easily taken in.   105
DIONYSUS   Perhaps you're right, but how else could he have written?
EURIPIDES   Nevertheless, it's sheer chicanery.
      He wants the audience to sit there interminably,
   all ears cocked for the moment Niobe
   utters a whimper. Meanwhile the play drags on.   110
DIONYSUS   The rascal, he took me in!
   Aeschylus, I'll thank you to stop fidgeting.
EURIPIDES   It's because I'm showing him up. . . .
      Then after he's bumbled along like this till the play's almost done,
   he lets fly with a volley of words   115
   as formidable as a beribboned bull
   flaunting crests and a shaggy scowl,

---

9. A tragedian who was a little older than
Aeschylus; his work is lost.
1. Achilles was the greatest Greek hero at
Troy; Niobe was a woman whose fourteen
children were all killed by Apollo and Artemis,
in punishment for her pride. Each was featured in lost tragedies by Aeschylus.

which is followed by a whole string of scarecrow weirdies
designed to make your flesh crawl.
AESCHYLUS   How cruel!   120
EURIPIDES   And never does he utter a word that makes sense.
DIONYSUS   Aeschylus, do stop grinding your molars.
EURIPIDES   It's all river-Scamanders,[2]
    fosses and bronze-bossed bucklers
    emblazoned with eagle-griffins   125
    and great rough-hewn declarations
    for which there are never explanations.
DIONYSUS   Don't I know it!
    "I've lain awake all through the long leviathan of the night,[3] trying to tell
    what is meant by a swooping hippocockerell.[4]   130
AESCHYLUS   It's the figurehead painted on our ships at Troy, you cretin.
DIONYSUS   And I was imagining it to be Eryxis,[5] son of Philoxenus.
EURIPIDES   But honestly
    do we really have to have cockerells in high tragedy?
AESCHYLUS   All right, you god-detested,   135
    in what sort of themes have you invested?
EURIPIDES   Well, for a start,
    no hippocockerells and not a single stag crossed with a goat,
    the kind of freak you might expect to see
    on a strip of Persian tapestry.   140
        None of that!
    When you passed on to me the tragic art
    the poor thing was loaded to the ground with bombast and fat.
        Immediately, I put her on a diet
    and got her weight down by a course of long walks   145
    and little mouthfuls of syllables in fricassee.
        I also fed her chopped repartee
    and a concoction of verbal juice pressed out of books.
        Then as a pick-me-up I dosed her with a tincture
    of monodies from Cephisophon.[6]   150
        I never shambled along like you
    with the first thing that entered my noggin,
    or plunged ahead leaving the audience in a stew.
        The first character to walk on
    explained the nature of the play and—   155
AESCHYLUS   A better nature than yours, any day!
EURIPIDES   [ignoring the interruption] . . . from the opening lines
    I got all the characters going:
    wife speaking, servant speaking,

---

2. The river in Troy.
3. Parodic quotation from a line in Euripides'
Hippolytus.
4. Apparently a word used in a lost play by

Aeschylus.
5. Famously ugly man.
6. A friend of Euripides and fellow poet.

and of course the boss and young girl,   160
not to mention the old crone.

AESCHYLUS   Such vulgarity! It calls for the death penalty.

EURIPIDES   Not so. It's straightforward democracy.

DIONYSUS   Be that as it may, pal,
but that's a topic I'd keep off if I were you.   165

EURIPIDES   [*gesturing to the audience*] And I taught you people
the art of conversation and—

AESCHYLUS   I'll say you did, and in my view
you should have been sliced down the middle.

EURIPIDES   . . . some of the nicer subtleties   170
like how to make words tell;
how to think and observe and decide;
how to be quick off the mark and shrewd;
how to expect the worst and face reality in the round—

AESCHYLUS   I'll say you did!   175

EURIPIDES   . . . by re-creating the workaday world we know
and things that are part of our living,
things I couldn't sham without being shown up as a fraud
because they're common knowledge. So
I never tried to bamboozle them by fibbing   180
or by bombast and persiflage.
    I never tried to frighten them with brutes like your Cycnus and
    your Memnon[7]
careering about in chariots with bells clanging.
    And just look at the difference between his devotees and mine;   185
he's got Pussy-Beard Phormisius and Sidekick Megaenetus[8]
rip-'em-uppers-treetrunk-twisters
and bushy-bearded-bugle-blowing lancers
whereas I've got Cleitophon and the clever Theramenes.[9]

DIONYSUS   Theramenes? Yes, he's supersmart,   190
surmounts every crisis and on the brink of disaster
always manages to land on his feet.
    Whatever the fix, he always throws a six.

EURIPIDES   That's exactly what I meant,
Teaching people how to think,   195
Putting logic into art
And making it a rational thing
Which enables them to grasp
And manage almost everything
Better than they've ever done,   200
Especially matters in the home,
Asking "Is everything all right?"

---

7. Trojan warriors, killed by Achilles; they apparently featured in a lost work of Aeschylus.
8. Athenian contemporaries, a politician and a soldier, respectively.
9. Two other Athenians, both prominent in politics.

"What happened to this?" "Oh, damn!
Who the deuce went off with that?"

DIONYSUS   Ye gods, you're right!   205
When an Athenian comes home now
He starts to bawl the servants out:
"What's happened to that cooking pot?"
"Who bit the head off that sprat?"
"The basin I bought last year is shot."   210
"Where's the garlic? Do you know?"
"Who's been getting at the olives?" . . .
Whereas before Euripides
They sat like gawking dummies half alive.

Antistrophe

WOMEN   "Renowned Achilles, do you behold this?"[1]   215
How will you respond to it?
Will you lose that famous temper?
Do take care
And not go running amok.
His gibes certainly are no joke,   220
So, good sir, do take care.
Do not be consumed with bile,
Furl the canvas, slacken sheets,
Shorten sail.
Slowly, slowly cruise along   225
Till the breeze blows soft and strong
And bears you steadily along.

LEADER   [to AESCHYLUS] You, first of Greeks to raise pinnacles of
praise to adorn all tragic waffle, open up your throttle.

AESCHYLUS   I'm furious matters have come to this. My stomach turns   230
that I have to demean myself by arguing with this man's
pretensions, but I must because otherwise
he'll say that I'm reduced to silence. . . . So tell me this:
What are the attributes that make a poet famous?

EURIPIDES   Skill and common sense, by which we are able to make   235
ordinary people better members of the State.

AESCHYLUS   And say you've done the opposite—made honest folk
into libertines—what punishment would you merit?

DIONYSUS   Don't ask him—death.

AESCHYLUS   Just give a thought to what they were like   240
when they came from my hand:
six-foot heroes all of them who never shirked,
unlike your loafers and your useless jerks,

1. This was the first line of Aeschylus's lost play *Myrmidons*, about Achilles (the Myrmidons were his companions in war).

these latter-day washouts we have now.

Those others were men of spears, men of darts, the very breath   245
of white-plumed helmets waving and ox-hide hearts.

DIONYSUS   Heavens, it's helmets now! He'll wear me out.

EURIPIDES   What method did you use to make them so elite?

DIONYSUS   Come on, Aeschylus, lay off being aloof.

AESCHYLUS   I did it by shoving Ares into everything.   250

DIONYSUS   Exactly how?

AESCHYLUS   In my *Seven Against Thebes* . . . I contrived
to make every male who saw it hot for war.

DIONYSUS   Not very nice to have connived
in making Thebans braver in battle than us Athenians![2]   255
You ought to be chastised.

AESCHYLUS   I think not.
You Athenians could have had the same training
but you didn't think it worth it. . . .

Then, when I produced my *Persians*,[3] it sent them raving   260
to annihilate the enemy. So you see,
in the end I didn't come off too badly.

DIONYSUS   I love the part when they heard that Darius[4] was no more,
and they couldn't celebrate enough, clapping their hands and shouting,
"Hurrah! Hurrah!"   265

AESCHYLUS   This is the sort of thing that poets should celebrate,
and this, you may remember, is what one finds
among the best of poets from earliest times.

Orpheus revealed to us the mysteries,
and also taught us to abhor murder as a crime.   270

Musaeus made us aware of things like clairvoyance
and also how to cure diseases.[5]

Hesiod taught us how to work the land, when to plow,
when to sow; and as to Homer, the divine,
did he not earn his fame and undying renown   275
by giving us lessons on how to esteem
military training, armory, and the discipline of men?

DIONYSUS   That may be so but all the same
he did pretty dismally with that airhead Pantacles[6]
who only yesterday made a fool of himself on parade   280
trying to fix the plumes of his helmet while he had it on his head.

AESCHYLUS   I know, but surely he did inspire other brave men,
for instance, the indomitable Lamachus,[7]
who was for me the role model in courage, like Patroclus

---

2. Thebes was on the Spartan side, against
Athens, in the Peloponnesian War.
3. The only extant historical tragedy, based on
the Athenian victory against the Persians in
480 B.C.E.
4. Darius was the emperor of Persia. In
Aeschylus's play, he appears as a ghost.

5. Orpheus was a legendary poet whose name
became associated with a mysterious religious
cult (Orphism). Musaeus was another legendary poet.
6. Unknown figure.
7. Athenian general.

and the lion-hearted Teucer[8]—the role model for all of us,   285
inspiring valor and giving us courage to emulate them whenever
the bugle for battle blew. . . . I never did create
strumpets like Phaedra or Stheneboea, like you.[9]
    You'll never find anywhere in anything I wrote
a lascivious bitch.   290
EURIPIDES   Don't I know it! You left poor Aphrodite[1] out.
AESCHYLUS   I should think so, whereas you
have let her squash you and your whole household flat.
DIONYSUS   He's got you there, Euripides, for you've been hit by the
same fate you invented for other people's wives.[2]   295
EURIPIDES   [ignoring the insult] You tiresome man,
what harm to the community was ever done
by my Stheneboea?
AESCHYLUS   You put decent women married to decent men
in a situation like that of Bellerephon   300
that drives them to suicide.
EURIPIDES   All right, but I didn't invent the plot of Phaedra.
AESCHYLUS   Worse luck, no! But the poet shouldn't side
with what is evil and display it on the stage like a demonstration.
    Children may have teachers but adults have the poet   305
and the poet ought to keep things on a higher plane.
EURIPIDES   [sarcastically] As high as Mount Lycabettus, no doubt, or lofty
Parnassus, and they're to be our instructors in the good?
My word! Can't you do your teaching in the language of men?
AESCHYLUS   Listen, you miserable heel, the lofty thought and the high ideal   310
call for a language to match,
and if the deities are clothed in rare attire
their language, too, should be out of the ordinary.
    This is where I blazed a trail,
which you've managed to undermine.   315
EURIPIDES   How have I?
AESCHYLUS   For a start, by the way you dress your royalty.
    They're all in rags like any pitiful wretch.
EURIPIDES   But whom do I hurt by that?
AESCHYLUS   Well, to begin with,   320
it tempts the rich to shirk their responsibility:
a wealthy tycoon evades the funding of a warship
by dressing up in rags and whimpering about his poverty.[3]
DIONYSUS   Yes, underneath the rags, by Demeter,
he's in lovely fleecy underwear   325
and you see him splashing out on fish in the market square.

8. Patroclus was Achilles' closest friend;
Teucer was the best Greek archer at Troy.
9. Phaedra fell in love with her stepson, Hippolytus; Stheneboea, a married woman, tried
to seduce the young hero Bellerophon, and
when rejected, accused him of rape. Euripides
wrote notorious tragedies about them, including Stheneboea (which is lost), and Hippolytus

(which survives).
1. Goddess of sex.
2. Apparently there was a rumor that Euripides' wife was having an affair.
3. Rich Athenian citizens had an obligation to
contribute to public works—for instance, by
equipping warships.

AESCHYLUS   What's more, you've taught people to prattle and gab,
   emptying the wrestling schools and turning the young men's
      bottoms into flab
   as they prattle away—and you've encouraged the crew   330
   of the *Paralus*[4] to answer their officers back.
      But in the old days when I was alive all they knew
   was how to clamor for their grub
   and shout "Ship ahoy" and "Heave-to."

DIONYSUS   That's exactly it, by Apollo.   335
   Now they fart in the bottom bencher's face,
   shit on their messmates and go off with people's clothes when on shore.
      What's more,
   they give lip to their commanders and refuse to row,
   so the ship goes drifting to and fro.   340

AESCHYLUS   What bad behavior is he not responsible for?
      Showing us a woman acting as a pander,
      Or producing a baby in the very temple,
      And others even coupling with their brothers
      And saying that "something living's not alive,"[5]   345
      The consequences naturally are simple:
      A society swamped by lawyers' clerks
      And buffoons lying their heads off to the people,
      And, because nobody takes any exercise,
      When it comes to running with a torch, no one tries.   350

DIONYSUS   You couldn't be righter. I almost doubled up
      At the Panathenaea[6] laughing when
      A slow coach of a booby thumped along,
      Stooped, white as a sheet, fat.
      And when he got to the Gates by the potter's field   355
      People whacked him on his belly and butt
      And ribs and sides and all his miserable hide.
      As he scurried along he began to fart
      With gas enough to keep his torch alight.

Strophe

MEN   Great is the struggle, grand the tussle,   360
      The war's now under way.
      One of them lands a hefty biff.
      The other ducks with a swing
      In counterattack. It's hard to say
      Which of them will win. . . .   365

---

4. Ship used for official Athenian missions.
5. All events in plays by Euripides. The nurse
in *Hippolytus* acts as a pander, trying to get
Phaedra and her stepson together; Auge, in
the lost *Auge*, had a baby in a temple; Canace

had sex with her brother in the lost *Aeolus*.
The source and significance of the quotation
is unclear.
6. A huge citywide festival.

Hey, you two, you've not fought enough,
Many more buffetings are due
And plenty of cerebral stuff.
Whatever it is you're fighting about
Go at it hard and argue it out.   370
Flense the old and strip for the new.
Get down to the nitty-gritty
And something erudite.

Antistrophe

WOMEN   And if you're afraid that people won't know
     What it is all about   375
And have no inkling, are unable to follow
     The twists of an argument,
Don't give it a thought; as a matter of fact
Things are different today.
Everyone's an expert now   380
And knows his book of rules by heart
     And every nicety
Is fully briefed and clever as well,
And sharply honed, as we all know,
So that's not something to worry about.   385
Don't be afraid—enjoy it all.
People are primed to the hilt.[7]

---

7. The competition continues for some time, and includes a contest in which each poet weighs his words against the other's words on a big set of scales. In the end, Dionysus pronounces Aeschylus the winner.

PLATO

C omposed around 370 B.C.E. by the brilliant Greek philosopher Plato, *Phaedrus* is a dialogue about love, passion, madness, and rhetoric, which features Plato's teacher, Socrates, and Socrates' young friend Phaedrus. The last passage of the text focuses on the arts of writing and of rhetoric, which Socrates claims are quite different from true wisdom.

From Phaedrus[1]

SOCRATES Well, do you know how best to please god when you either use words or discuss them in general?

PHAEDRUS Not at all. Do you?

SOCRATES I can tell you what I've heard the ancients said, though they alone know the truth. However, if we could discover that ourselves, would we still care about the speculations of other people?

PHAEDRUS That's a silly question. Still, tell me what you say you've heard.

SOCRATES Well, this is what I've heard. Among the ancient gods of Naucratis[2] in Egypt there was one to whom the bird called the ibis is sacred. The name of that divinity was Theuth,[3] and it was he who first discovered number and calculation, geometry and astronomy, as well as the games of checkers and dice, and, above all else, writing.

Now the king of all Egypt at that time was Thamus, who lived in the great city in the upper region that the Greeks call Egyptian Thebes; Thamus is what they call Ammon.[4] Theuth came to exhibit his arts to him and urged him to disseminate them to all the Egyptians. Thamus asked him about the usefulness of each art, and while Theuth was explaining it, Thamus praised him for whatever he thought was right in his explanations and criticized him for whatever he thought was wrong.

The story goes that Thamus said much to Theuth, both for and against each art, which it would take too long to repeat. But when they came to writing, Theuth said: "O King, here is something that, once learned, will make the Egyptians wiser and will improve their memory; I have discovered a potion[5] for memory and for wisdom." Thamus, however, replied: "O most expert Theuth, one man can give birth to the elements of an art, but only another can judge how they can benefit or harm those who will use them. And now, since you are the father of writing, your affection for it has made you describe its effects as the opposite of what they really are. In fact, it will introduce forgetfulness into the soul of those who learn it: they will not practice using their memory because they will put their trust in writing, which is external and depends on signs that belong to others, instead of trying to remember from the inside, completely on their own. You have not discovered a potion for remembering, but for reminding; you provide your students with the appearance of wisdom, not with its reality. Your invention will enable them to hear many things without being properly taught, and they will imagine that they have come to know much while for the most part they will know nothing. And they will be difficult to get along with, since they will merely appear to be wise instead of really being so."

---

1. Translated by Alexander Nehamas and Paul Woodruff. The philosopher Socrates and a young friend called Phaedrus have gone for a walk outside the city of Athens, eager to discuss a speech Phaedrus has just heard by the famous orator Lysias. After a discussion of rhetoric, in which Socrates questions the value of Lysias's work on the grounds that it is more about impressive appearances than truth, the conversation turns to writing.
2. A Greek trading colony.
3. The Egyptian god of writing, measurement, and calculation; also spelled Thot or Thoth.
4. Ammon is the king of the Egyptian gods.
5. The word for potion, *pharmakon*, can mean "drug," "medicine," "poison," or "cure."

PHAEDRUS   Socrates, you're very good at making up stories from Egypt or wherever else you want!

SOCRATES   But, my friend, the priests of the temple of Zeus at Dodona say that the first prophecies were the words of an oak. Everyone who lived at that time, not being as wise as you young ones are today, found it rewarding enough in their simplicity to listen to an oak or even a stone, so long as it was telling the truth, while it seems to make a difference to you, Phaedrus, who is speaking and where he comes from. Why, though, don't you just consider whether what he says is right or wrong?

PHAEDRUS   I deserved that, Socrates. And I agree that the Theban king was correct about writing.

SOCRATES   Well, then, those who think they can leave written instructions for an art, as well as those who accept them, thinking that writing can yield results that are clear or certain, must be quite naive and truly ignorant of Ammon's prophetic judgment: otherwise, how could they possibly think that words that have been written down can do more than remind those who already know what the writing is about?

PHAEDRUS   Quite right.

SOCRATES   You know, Phaedrus, writing shares a strange feature with painting. The offspring of painting stand there as if they are alive, but if anyone asks them anything, they remain most solemnly silent. The same is true of written words. You'd think they were speaking as if they had some understanding, but if you question anything that has been said because you want to learn more, it continues to signify just that very same thing forever. When it has once been written down, every discourse roams about everywhere, reaching indiscriminately those with understanding no less than those who have no business with it, and it doesn't know to whom it should speak and to whom it should not. And when it is faulted and attacked unfairly, it always needs its father's support; alone, it can neither defend itself nor come to its own support.

PHAEDRUS   You are absolutely right about that, too.

SOCRATES   Now tell me, can we discern another kind of discourse, a legitimate brother of this one? Can we say how it comes about, and how it is by nature better and more capable?

PHAEDRUS   Which one is that? How do you think it comes about?

SOCRATES   It is a discourse that is written down, with knowledge, in the soul of the listener; it can defend itself, and it knows for whom it should speak and for whom it should remain silent.

PHAEDRUS   You mean the living, breathing discourse of the man who knows, of which the written one can be fairly called an image.

SOCRATES   Absolutely right. And tell me this. Would a sensible farmer, who cared about his seeds and wanted them to yield fruit, plant them in all seriousness in the gardens of Adonis in the middle of the summer and enjoy watching them bear fruit within seven days? Or would he do this as an amusement and in honor of the holiday, if he did it at all? Wouldn't he use his knowledge of farming to plant the seeds he cared for when it was appropriate and be content if they bore fruit seven months later?

PHAEDRUS   That's how he would handle those he was serious about, Socrates, quite differently from the others, as you say.

SOCRATES   Now what about the man who knows what is just, noble, and good? Shall we say that he is less sensible with his seeds than the farmer is with his?

PHAEDRUS   Certainly not.

SOCRATES   Therefore, he won't be serious about writing them in ink, sowing them, through a pen, with words that are as incapable of speaking in their own defense as they are of teaching the truth adequately.

PHAEDRUS   That wouldn't be likely.

SOCRATES   Certainly not. When he writes, it's likely he will sow gardens of letters for the sake of amusing himself, storing up reminders for himself "when he reaches forgetful old age" and for everyone who wants to follow in his footsteps, and will enjoy seeing them sweetly blooming. And when others turn to different amusements, watering themselves with drinking parties and everything else that goes along with them, he will rather spend his time amusing himself with the things I have just described.

PHAEDRUS   Socrates, you are contrasting a vulgar amusement with the very noblest—with the amusement of a man who can while away his time telling stories of justice and the other matters you mentioned.

SOCRATES   That's just how it is, Phaedrus. But it is much nobler to be serious about these matters, and use the art of dialectic. The dialectician chooses a proper soul and plants and sows within it discourse accompanied by knowledge—discourse capable of helping itself as well as the man who planted it, which is not barren but produces a seed from which more discourse grows in the character of others. Such discourse makes the seed forever immortal and renders the man who has it as happy as any human being can be.

PHAEDRUS   What you describe is really much nobler still.

SOCRATES   And now that we have agreed about this, Phaedrus, we are finally able to decide the issue.

PHAEDRUS   What issue is that?

SOCRATES   The issue which brought us to this point in the first place: We wanted to examine the attack made on Lysias on account of his writing speeches, and to ask which speeches are written artfully and which not. Now, I think that we have answered that question clearly enough.

PHAEDRUS   So it seemed; but remind me again how we did it.

SOCRATES   First, you must know the truth concerning everything you are speaking or writing about; you must learn how to define each thing in itself; and, having defined it, you must know how to divide it into kinds until you reach something indivisible. Second, you must understand the nature of the soul, along the same lines; you must determine which kind of speech is appropriate to each kind of soul, prepare and arrange your speech accordingly, and offer a complex and elaborate speech to a complex soul and a simple speech to a simple one. Then, and only then, will you be able to use speech artfully, to the extent that its nature allows it to be used that way, either in order to teach or in order to persuade. This is the whole point of the argument we have been making.

PHAEDRUS   Absolutely. That is exactly how it seemed to us.

SOCRATES   Now how about whether it's noble or shameful to give or write a speech—when it could be fairly said to be grounds for reproach, and when not? Didn't what we said just a little while ago make it clear—

PHAEDRUS   What was that?

SOCRATES   That if Lysias or anybody else ever did or ever does write—privately or for the public, in the course of proposing some law—a political document which he believes to embody clear knowledge of lasting importance, then this writer deserves reproach, whether anyone says so or not. For to be unaware of the difference between a dream-image and the reality of what is just and unjust, good and bad, must truly be grounds for reproach even if the crowd praises it with one voice.

PHAEDRUS   It certainly must be.

SOCRATES   On the other hand, take a man who thinks that a written discourse on any subject can only be a great amusement, that no discourse worth serious attention has ever been written in verse or prose, and that those that are recited in public without questioning and explanation, in the manner of the rhapsodes[6] are given only in order to produce conviction. He believes that at their very best these can only serve as reminders to those who already know. And he also thinks that only what is said for the sake of understanding and learning, what is truly written in the soul concerning what is just, noble, and good can be clear, perfect, and worth serious attention: Such discourses should be called his own legitimate children, first the discourse he may have discovered already within himself and then its sons and brothers who may have grown naturally in other souls insofar as these are worthy; to the rest, he turns his back. Such a man, Phaedrus, would be just what you and I both would pray to become.

PHAEDRUS   I wish and pray for things to be just as you say.

SOCRATES   Well, then: our playful amusement regarding discourse is complete. Now you go and tell Lysias that we came to the spring which is sacred to the Nymphs and heard words charging us to deliver a message to Lysias and anyone else who composes speeches, as well as to Homer and anyone else who has composed poetry either spoken or sung, and third, to Solon[7] and anyone else who writes political documents that he calls laws: If any one of you has composed these things with a knowledge of the truth, if you can defend your writing when you are challenged, and if you can yourself make the argument that your writing is of little worth, then you must be called by a name derived not from these writings but rather from those things that you are seriously pursuing.

PHAEDRUS   What name, then, would you give such a man?

SOCRATES   To call him wise, Phaedrus, seems to me too much, and proper only for a god. To call him wisdom's lover—a philosopher—or something similar would fit him better and be more seemly.

PHAEDRUS   That would be quite appropriate.

SOCRATES   On the other hand, if a man has nothing more valuable than what he has composed or written, spending long hours twisting it around, pasting parts together and taking them apart—wouldn't you be right to call him a poet or a speech writer or an author of laws?

6. Performers who recited portions of poetry   7. Famous Athenian lawmaker.
from memory for entertainment.

PHAEDRUS   Of course.

SOCRATES   Tell that, then, to your friend.

PHAEDRUS   And what about you? What shall you do? We must surely not forget your own friend.

SOCRATES   Whom do you mean?

PHAEDRUS   The beautiful Isocrates.[8] What are you going to tell him, Socrates? What shall we say he is?

SOCRATES   Isocrates is still young, Phaedrus. But I want to tell you what I foresee for him.

PHAEDRUS   What is that?

SOCRATES   It seems to me that by his nature he can outdo anything that Lysias has accomplished in his speeches; and he also has a nobler character. So I wouldn't be at all surprised if, as he gets older and continues writing speeches of the sort he is composing now, he makes everyone who has ever attempted to compose a speech seem like a child in comparison. Even more so if such work no longer satisfies him and a higher, divine impulse leads him to more important things. For nature, my friend, has placed the love of wisdom in his mind.

That is the message I will carry to my beloved, Isocrates, from the gods of this place; and you have your own message for your Lysias.

PHAEDRUS   So it shall be. But let's be off, since the heat has died down a bit.

SOCRATES   Shouldn't we offer a prayer to the gods here before we leave?

PHAEDRUS   Of course.

SOCRATES   O dear Pan[9] and all the other gods of this place, grant that I may be beautiful inside. Let all my external possessions be in friendly harmony with what is within. May I consider the wise man rich. As for gold, let me have as much as a moderate man could bear and carry with him.

Do we need anything else, Phaedrus? I believe my prayer is enough for me.

PHAEDRUS   Make it a prayer for me as well. Friends have everything in common.

SOCRATES   Let's be off.

---

8. Athenian teacher and orator.   9. God of the countryside.

ARISTOTLE

The Greek philosopher Aristotle (384–322 B.C.E.), a pupil of Plato's, founded a school of his own, and wrote on an enormous range of subjects, from ethics and politics to zoology, metaphysics, physics, logic, and mathematics. His extant works, unlike those of **Plato**, are based on lecture notes, and are therefore written in a somewhat dry style. His study of poetry (*Poetics*, one of his shorter treatises) focuses on the component features of the best tragedy, and offers a defense of good dramatic poetry against the Platonic charge that it can be morally and emotionally corrupting.

From Poetics[1]

* * * Thus, Tragedy is an imitation of an action that is serious, complete, and possessing magnitude; in embellished language, each kind of which is used separately in the different parts; in the mode of action and not narrated; and effecting through pity and fear [what we call] the *catharsis*[2] of such emotions. By "embellished language" I mean language having rhythm and melody, and by "separately in different parts" I mean that some parts of a play are carried on solely in metrical speech while others again are sung.

The constituent parts of tragedy. Since the imitation is carried out in the dramatic mode by the personages themselves, it necessarily follows, first, that the arrangement of Spectacle will be a part of tragedy, and next, that Melody and Language will be parts, since these are the media in which they effect the imitation. By "language" I mean precisely the composition of the verses, by "melody" only that which is perfectly obvious. And since tragedy is the imitation of an action and is enacted by men in action, these persons must necessarily possess certain qualities of Character and Thought, since these are the basis for our ascribing qualities to the actions themselves—character and thought are two natural causes of actions—and it is in their actions that men universally meet with success or failure. The imitation of the action is the Plot. By plot I here mean the combination of the events; Character is that in virtue of which we say that the personages are of such and such a quality; and Thought is present in everything in their utterances that aims to prove a point or that expresses an opinion. Necessarily, therefore, there are in tragedy as a whole, considered as a special form, six constituent elements, viz. Plot, Character, Language, Thought, Spectacle, and Melody. Of these elements, two [Language and Melody] are the

---

1. Translated by James Hutton, who has added bracketed text for clarity.
2. *Catharsis* is used elsewhere in Aristotle as a medical term, meaning "purgation." Tragedy "purges" the spectators' emotions. Aristotle does not explain exactly what this means.

media in which they effect the imitation, one [Spectacle] is the *manner*, and three [Plot, Character, Thought] are the *objects* they imitate; and besides these there are no other parts. So then they employ these six forms, not just some of them so to speak; for every drama has spectacle, character, plot, language, melody, and thought in the same sense, but the most important of them is the organization of the events [the plot].

Plot and character. For tragedy is not an imitation of men but of actions and of life. It is in action that happiness and unhappiness are found, and the end[3] we aim at is a kind of activity, not a quality; in accordance with their characters men are of such and such a quality, in accordance with their actions they are fortunate or the reverse. Consequently, it is not for the purpose of presenting their characters that the agents engage in action, but rather it is for the sake of their actions that they take on the characters they have. Thus, what happens— that is, the plot—is the end for which a tragedy exists, and the end or purpose is the most important thing of all. What is more, without action there could not be a tragedy, but there could be without characterization. * * *

Now that the parts are established, let us next discuss what qualities the plot should have, since plot is the primary and most important part of tragedy. I have posited that tragedy is an imitation of an action that is a whole and com- plete in itself and of a certain magnitude—for a thing may be a whole, and yet have no magnitude to speak of. Now a thing is a whole if it has a beginning, a middle, and an end. A beginning is that which does not come necessarily after something else, but after which it is natural for another thing to exist or come to be. An end, on the contrary, is that which naturally comes after something else, either as its necessary sequel or as its usual [and hence probable] sequel, but itself has nothing after it. A middle is that which both comes after some- thing else and has another thing following it. A well-constructed plot, there- fore, will neither begin at some chance point nor end at some chance point, but will observe the principles here stated. * * *

Contrary to what some people think, a plot is not ipso facto a unity if it revolves about one man. Many things, indeed an endless number of things, happen to any one man some of which do not go together to form a unity, and similarly among the actions one man performs there are many that do not go together to produce a single unified action. Those poets seem all to have erred, therefore, who have composed a *Heracleid*, a *Theseid*, and other such poems, it being their idea evidently that since Heracles was one man, their plot was bound to be unified. * * *

From what has already been said, it will be evident that the poet's function is not to report things that have happened, but rather to tell of such things as might happen, things that are possibilities by virtue of being in themselves inevitable or probable. Thus the difference between the historian and the poet is not that the historian employs prose and the poet verse—the work of Herod- otus[4] could be put into verse, and it would be no less a history with verses than without them; rather the difference is that the one tells of things that have been and the other of such things as might be. Poetry, therefore, is a more

3. Purpose.
4. Historian of the Persian Wars (ca. 480–430/425? B.C.E.).

philosophical and a higher thing than history, in that poetry tends rather to express the universal, history rather the particular fact. A universal is: The sort of thing that (in the circumstances) a certain kind of person will say or do either probably or necessarily, which in fact is the universal that poetry aims for (with the addition of names for the persons); a particular, on the other hand is: What Alcibiades[5] did or had done to him. * * *

Among plots and actions of the simple type, the episodic form is the worst. I call episodic a plot in which the episodes follow one another in no probable or inevitable sequence. Plots of this kind are constructed by bad poets on their own account, and by good poets on account of the actors; since they are composing entries for a competitive exhibition, they stretch the plot beyond what it can bear and are often compelled, therefore, to dislocate the natural order. * * *

Some plots are simple, others complex; indeed the actions of which the plots are imitation are at once so differentiated to begin with. Assuming the action to be continuous and unified, as already defined, I call that action simple in which the change of fortune takes place without a reversal or recognition, and that action complex in which the change of fortune involves a recognition or a reversal or both. These events [recognitions and reversals] ought to be so rooted in the very structure of the plot that they follow from the preceding events as their inevitable or probable outcome; for there is a vast difference between following from and merely following after. * * *

Reversal (Peripety) is, as aforesaid, a change from one state of affairs to its exact opposite, and this, too, as I say, should be in conformance with probability or necessity. For example, in *Oedipus*, the messenger[6] comes to cheer Oedipus by relieving him of fear with regard to his mother, but by revealing his true identity, does just the opposite of this. * * *

Recognition, as the word itself indicates, is a change from ignorance to knowledge, leading either to friendship or to hostility on the part of those persons who are marked for good fortune or bad. The best form of recognition is that which is accompanied by a reversal, as in the example from *Oedipus*. * * *

Next in order after the points I have just dealt with, it would seem necessary to specify what one should aim at and what avoid in the construction of plots, and what it is that will produce the effect proper to tragedy.

Now since in the finest kind of tragedy the structure should be complex and not simple, and since it should also be a representation of terrible and piteous events (that being the special mark of this type of imitation), in the first place, it is evident that good men ought not to be shown passing from prosperity to misfortune, for this does not inspire either pity or fear, but only revulsion; nor evil men rising from ill fortune to prosperity, for this is the most untragic plot of all—it lacks every requirement, in that it neither elicits human sympathy nor stirs pity or fear. And again, neither should an extremely wicked man be seen falling from prosperity into misfortune, for a plot so constructed might indeed call forth human sympathy, but would not excite pity or fear, since the first is felt for a person whose misfortune is undeserved and the second for someone like ourselves—pity for the man suffering undeservedly, fear for the man like ourselves—and hence neither pity nor fear would be aroused in this case. We are

---

5. A brilliant but unscrupulous Athenian statesman (ca. 450–404 B.C.E.).

6. The Corinthian herdsman in Sophocles' *Oedipus the King*.

left with the man whose place is between these extremes. Such is the man who on the one hand is not pre-eminent in virtue and justice, and yet on the other hand does not fall into misfortune through vice or depravity, but falls because of some mistake;[7] one among the number of the highly renowned and prosperous, such as Oedipus and Thyestes[8] and other famous men from families like theirs.

It follows that the plot which achieves excellence will necessarily be single in outcome and not, as some contend, double, and will consist in a change of fortune, not from misfortune to prosperity, but the opposite from prosperity to misfortune, occasioned not by depravity, but by some great mistake on the part of one who is either such as I have described or better than this rather than worse. (What actually has taken place confirms this; for though at first the poets accepted whatever myths came to hand, today the finest tragedies are founded upon the stories of only a few houses, being concerned, for example, with Alcmeon, Oedipus, Orestes, Meleager, Thyestes, Telephus, and such others as have chanced to suffer terrible things or to do them.) So, then, tragedy having this construction is the finest kind of tragedy from an artistic point of view. And consequently, those persons fall into the same error who bring it as a charge against Euripides that this is what he does in his tragedies and that most of his plays have unhappy endings. For this is in fact the right procedure, as I have said; and the best proof is that on the stage and in the dramatic contests, plays of this kind seem the most tragic, provided they are successfully worked out, and Euripides, even if in everything else his management is faulty, seems at any rate the most tragic of the poets. * * *

In the characters and the plot construction alike, one must strive for that which is either necessary or probable, so that whatever a character of any kind says or does may be the sort of thing such a character will inevitably or probably say or do and the events of the plot may follow one after another either inevitably or with probability. (Obviously, then, the denouement of the plot should arise from the plot itself and not be brought about "from the machine," as it is in *Medea* and in the embarkation scene in the *Iliad*.[9] The machine is to be used for matters lying outside the drama, either antecedents of the action which a human being cannot know, or things subsequent to the action that have to be prophesied and announced; for we accept it that the gods see everything. Within the events of the plot itself, however, there should be nothing unreasonable, or if there is, it should be kept outside the play proper, as is done in the *Oedipus* of Sophocles.) * * *

---

7. The Greek word is *hamartia*. It has sometimes been translated as "flaw" (hence the expression "tragic flaw") and thought of as a moral defect, but comparison with Aristotle's use of the word in other contexts suggests strongly that he means by it "mistake" or "error" (of judgment).

8. Brother of Atreus and his rival over the kingship of Argos. Pretending to be reconciled, Atreus gave a feast at which he served Thyestes' own sons to their father. Thyestes' only surviving son, Aegisthus, later helped murder Atreus's son Agamemnon.

9. The reference is to an incident in the second book of the *Iliad*: an attempt of the Greek rank and file to return home and abandon the siege is arrested by the intervention of Athena. If it were a drama, she would appear literally as the *deus ex machina* ("god from the machine"), the pulley that was employed in the theater to show the gods flying in space. It has come to mean any implausible way of solving complications of the plot. In Euripides' play, Medea escapes from Corinth on the machine, in her magic chariot.

The chorus in tragedy. The chorus ought to be regarded as one of the actors, and as being part of the whole and integrated into performance, not in Euripides' way but in that of Sophocles. In the other poets, the choral songs have no more relevance to the plot than if they belonged to some other play. And so nowadays, following the practice introduced by Agathon,[1] the chorus merely sings interludes. But what difference is there between the singing of interludes and taking a speech or even an entire episode from one play and inserting it into another?

1. A younger contemporary of Euripides; most of his plays were produced in the 4th century B.C.E.

CALLIMACHUS

The hyperlearned poet and librarian Callimachus (third century B.C.E.) was a Greek born in Libya who spent most of his life in the cosmopolitan Greek-Egyptian city of Alexandria. *Aetia* ("Causes")—a poem of which only part survives—was originally four books long, and told the mythical stories of the origins of various cults and traditions. The beginning, included here, is a poetic manifesto outlining Callimachus's commitment to short, careful, precise compositions over long, unwieldy, and derivative forms of poetry.

From Aetia[1]

The Telchines,[2] who know nothing
of poetry and hate the Muses, often
snipe at me, because it's not a monotonous
uninterrupted poem featuring kings
and heroes in thousands of verses   5
that I've produced, driving my song instead
for little stretches, like a child,
though the tale of my years
is not brief.
      Well, here's what I say
to the Telchines:
        'Born eaters
of your own hearts, [the Coan poet][3]   10
was not, admittedly, a man of few verses

1. Translated by Frank Nisetich. Only parts of this poem survive.
2. Mythical monsters; the name is applied here to Callimachus's critics.

3. Philitas, a scholar-poet a generation older than Callimachus. Apparently, he and Mimnermus (below) wrote both long and shorter works; these have not survived.

but all the same his bountiful Demeter far
outweighs the woman he celebrated
at length.
       And of the two books   15
Mimnermus[4] wrote, not the one that tells
of the big woman, but the one composed
with a delicate touch, displays
the poet at his sweetest.
            Let the crane
who revels in the blood of Pygmies fly   20
far from Egypt, and the Massagetai
shoot at the Mede long range:[5] nightingales
are sweeter like this.
           To hell with you, then,
spiteful brood of Jealousy: from now on
we'll judge poetry by the art,   25
not by the mile. And don't expect a song
to rush from my lips with a roar:
it's Zeus' job, not mine, to thunder.'
   The very first time I sat down and put
a writing tablet on my lap, my own   30
Lykian[6] Apollo said to me:
            'Make your sacrifice
as fat as you can, poet, but keep
your Muse on slender rations. And see that you go
where no hackneys plod: avoid the ruts
carved in the boulevard, even if it means   35
driving along a narrower path.'
           And so I sing for those
who love the shrill cicada's cry, and hate
the clamour of asses. Let someone else,
loud as any long-eared brute, bray
for their amusement. As for me,   40
I would be small and winged—yes,
even so, to sing
with dew upon my lips, the food
of morning culled from air divine, shedding
the years that weigh on me   45
like Sicily on Enkelados.[7]
         The Muses
won't repulse in grey old age
the man on whom they smiled in his youth.

---

4. Greek elegiac poet from the 7th century
B.C.E.
5. The Pygmies were a legendary race of tiny
people who made war against cranes. The
Massagetai were a northern race famous for
their archery; the Mede were also known for

skill in archery.
6. The epithet may suggest either "wolf killer"
or "god of light." Apollo is the god of poetry.
7. Zeus threw the island of Sicily on top of
the giant Enkelados.

HORACE

The Roman poet Horace (65–8 B.C.E.) was roughly contemporary with Virgil (whom he knew), and was the most prominent lyric poet during the time of Emperor Augustus. He was from a modest background (son of a freed slave) but made his way up the social ladder through education and talent. His *Odes* were a virtuosic technical achievement, transferring complex Greek meters into Latin. In the last poem (Ode 30) in the third book, he celebrates his own achievement, presenting poetry—usually written on papyrus scrolls—as more glorious and permanent than inscriptions on bronze tablets, which would have included legal and administrative documents. His *Ars Poetica* ("art of poetry") is a treatise in verse on the norms for successful poetry.

Ode 30[1]

[*Exegi Monumentum*]

I have built a monument more lasting than bronze
and set higher than the pyramids of kings.
It cannot be destroyed by gnawing rain
or wild north wind, by the procession

of unnumbered years or by the flight of time.   5
I shall not wholly die. A great part of me
will escape Libitina.[2] My fame will grow,
ever-renewed in time to come, as long as

the priest climbs the Capitol with the silent Virgin.[3]
I shall be spoken of where fierce Aufidus thunders   10
and where Daunus, poor in water,
rules the country people.[4] From humble beginnings

I was able to be the first to bring Aeolian song
to Italian measures.[5] Take the proud honour
well-deserved, Melpomene, and be pleased   15
to circle my hair with the laurel of Delphi.[6]

---

1. Translated by David West. The *Odes* have no titles: the translator has used the first two words of the Latin original ("I have built a monument") as a title.
2. Goddess of death.
3. Alludes to the religious rituals of Rome, which often involved a climb up the Capitoline hill, to the temple at the top, by the chief priest and the Vestal Virgins (holy girls vowed to religious chastity).

4. Aufidus is a river in Apulia, near Horace's home; Daunus is a legendary early king of the area.
5. Horace was the first Roman poet to adapt the Greek ("Aeolian") choral meters of Sappho and Alcaeus into Latin.
6. Melpomene is the name of the tragic muse, here used for any muse. Delphi and the laurel tree are sacred to Apollo, god of poetry.

From Ars Poetica[1]

Suppose a painter decided to set a human head
on a horse's neck, and to cover the body with coloured feathers,
combining limbs so that the top of a lovely woman
came to a horrid end in the tail of an inky fish—
when invited to view the piece, my friends, could you stifle your   5
     laughter?
Well, dear Pisos,[2] I hope you'll agree that a book containing
fantastic ideas, like those conceived by delirious patients,
where top and bottom never combine to form a whole,
is exactly like that picture.   'Painters and poets alike
have always enjoyed the right to take what risks they please.'   10
I know; I grant that freedom and claim the same in return,
but not to the point of allowing wild to couple with tame,
or showing a snake and a bird, or a lamb and tiger, as partners.

Often you'll find a serious work of large pretensions
with here and there a purple patch that is sewn on   15
to give a vivid and striking effect—lines describing
Diana's grove and altar,[3] or a stream which winds and hurries
along its beauteous vale, or the river Rhine, or a rainbow.
But here they are out of place. Perhaps you can draw a cypress;
what good is that, if the subject you've been engaged to paint   20
is a shipwrecked sailor swimming for his life? The job began
as a wine-jar; why as the wheel revolves does it end as a jug?
So make what you like, provided the thing is a unified whole.
Poets in the main (I'm speaking to a father and his excellent sons)
are baffled by the outer form of what's right. I strive to be brief,   25
and become obscure; I try for smoothness, and instantly lose
muscle and spirit; to aim at grandeur invites inflation;
excessive caution or fear of the wind induces grovelling.
The man who brings in marvels to vary a simple theme
is painting a dolphin among the trees, a boar in the billows.   30
Avoiding a fault will lead to error if art is missing.

Any smith in the area round Aemilius' school[4]
will render nails in bronze and imitate wavy hair;
the final effect eludes him because he doesn't know how
to shape a whole. If I wanted to do a piece of sculpture,   35
I'd no more copy him than I'd welcome a broken nose,
when my jet black eyes and jet black hair had won admiration.

You writers must pick a subject that suits your powers,
giving lengthy thought to what your shoulders are built for
and what they aren't. If your choice of theme is within your scope,   40

---

1. Translated by Niall Rudd.
2. Roman noblemen, a father and two sons; apparently patrons of Horace's.
3. Diana (Artemis in Greek) is the goddess associated with the countryside, hunting, and the moon.
4. A school for gladiators, near which craftsmen and artists worked.

you won't have to seek for fluent speech or lucid arrangement.
Arrangement's virtue and value reside, if I'm not mistaken,
in this: to say right now what has to be said right now,
postponing and leaving out a great deal for the present.

The writer pledged to produce a poem must also be subtle   45
and careful in linking words, preferring this to that.
When a skilful collocation renews a familiar word,
that is distinguished writing. If novel terms are demanded
to introduce obscure material, then you will have the
chance to invent words which the apron-wearing Cethegi[5]   50
never heard; such a right will be given, if it's not abused.
New and freshly created words are also acceptable
when channelled from Greek, provided the trickle is small. For why
should Romans refuse to Virgil and Varius what they've allowed
to Caecilius and Plautus?[6] And why should they grumble if I succeed 55
in bringing a little in, when the diction of Ennius and Cato[7]
showered wealth on our fathers' language and gave us unheard of
names for things? We have always enjoyed and always will
the right to produce terms which are marked with the current stamp.
Just as the woods change their leaves as year follows year   60
(the earliest fall, *and others spring up to take their place*)
so the old generation of words passes away,
and the newly arrived bloom and flourish like human children.
We and our works are owed to death, whether our navy
is screened from the northern gales by Neptune[8] welcomed ashore—   65
a royal feat—or a barren swamp which knew the oar
feeds neighbouring cities and feels the weight of the plough,
or a river which used to damage the crops has altered its course
and learned a better way. Man's structures will crumble;
so how can the glory and charm of speech remain for ever?   70
Many a word long dead will be born again, and others
which now enjoy prestige will fade, if Usage requires it.
She controls the laws and rules and standards of language.

The feats of kings and captains and the grim battles they fought—
the proper metre for such achievements was shown by Homer.   75
The couplet of longer and shorter lines provided a framework,
first for lament, then for acknowledging a prayer's fulfilment.
Scholars, however, dispute the name of the first poet
to compose small elegiacs; the case is still undecided.
Fury gave Archilochus[9] her own missile—the iambus.   80

5. An ancient Roman family who would have worn wraparound skirts rather than the togas worn by aristocrats in Horace's day.
6. Virgil (author of the *Aeneid*) and Varius were both writers contemporary with Horace; Caecilius and Plautus were older Roman writers, from the 2nd century B.C.E.
7. Ennius was an early Roman epic poet. Cato the Elder, a politician and moralist from the 3rd century B.C.E., is cited as an upholder of traditional Latin and of traditional Roman morality.
8. God of the sea.
9. Greek satirical poet (7th century B.C.E.), who wrote in iambic meter. The iamb ("iambus") is a metrical unit, or "foot."

The foot was found to fit the sock and the stately buskin,[1]
because it conveyed the give and take of dialogue; also
it drowned the noise of the pit and was naturally suited to action.
The lyre received from the Muse the right to celebrate gods[2]
and their sons, victorious boxers, horses first in the race,   85
the ache of a lover's heart, and uninhibited drinking.
If, through lack of knowledge or talent, I fail to observe
the established genres and styles, then why am I hailed as a poet?
And why, from misplaced shyness, do I shrink from learning the trade?

A comic subject will not be presented in tragic metres.   90
Likewise Thyestes' banquet is far too grand a tale
for verse of an everyday kind which is more akin to the sock.[3]
Everything has its appropriate place, and it ought to stay there.
Sometimes, however, even Comedy raises her voice,
as angry Chremes[4] storms along in orotund phrases;   95
and sometimes a tragic actor grieves in ordinary language—
Peleus and Telephus (one an exile, the other a beggar)[5]
both abandon their bombast and words of a foot and a half
when they hope to touch the listener's heart with their sad appeals.

Correctness is not enough in a poem; it must be attractive,   100
leading the listener's emotions in whatever way it wishes.
When a person smiles, people's faces smile in return;
when he weeps, they show concern. Before you can move me to tears,
you must grieve yourself. Only then will your woes distress me,
Peleus or Telephus. If what you say is out of character,   105
I'll either doze or laugh. Sad words are required
by a sorrowful face; threats come from one that is angry,
jokes from one that is jolly, serious words from the solemn.
Nature adjusts our inner feelings to every variety
of fortune, giving us joy, goading us on to anger,   110
making us sink to the ground under a load of suffering.
Then, with the tongue as her medium, she utters the heart's emotions.

1. Iambic meter was also, later, used for drama. The "sock" means comedy, the "stately buskin" means tragedy—particular types of footwear were characteristic of the two genres.
2. Lyric meters were used for hymns.
3. Thyestes was tricked by his brother into eating his own children. This story was treated in tragedy; Horace is arguing that it is not appropriate for comedy ("the sock").
4. A stock old-man character from comedy.
5. Characters from tragedy. Peleus was exiled after killing his brother; Telephus was wounded by Achilles and, in Euripides' version of the story, dressed as a beggar when he went to ask Clytemnestra for help.

II

India's Ancient Epics and Tales

T he Indian subcontinent stretches from the borders of Iran and Afghanistan to those of Myanmar, and from the edges of Tibet and China to the Indian Ocean; also called South Asia, it covers an area as large as western Europe. From about the fifth century B.C.E. onward, the ancient Greeks knew this region as *Indos*, a term adapted from the Persians; after the seventh century C.E., Muslim societies came to refer to it as *al-Hind*. For much of its long history, the subcontinent has not been politically united, but it has been remarkably cohesive in its social and cultural practices: it has evolved as a distinct "cultural zone" within Asia, very different in language, religion, art, population, and ways of life from the comparable cultural zones of China and the Middle East.

THE PREHISTORIC ORIGINS OF INDIAN LITERATURE

The kinds of stories ancient Indian literature tells, the forms they take, and the themes they explore are connected to the subcontinent's past before the appearance of historical records. The earliest settled society in South Asia organized on a significant scale was that of the Indus Valley and Harappa

Kṛṣṇa battles the horse demon, Keshi. From a fifth-century C.E. terra-cotta carving.

(ca. 2600–1900 B.C.E.), which established a far-flung network of small towns and ports across what are now Pakistan and western India. This civilization had extensive contacts with Mesopotamia during the period in which the epic *Gilgamesh* was being composed in Sumerian. The Indus-Harappan people had a writing system of their own, but it remains undeciphered, even though we know a great deal about their material culture. Conquered or gradually displaced by the Indo-Aryans, or overcome by economic, political, or natural disasters, this population receded from the subcontinent's prehistory by about 1900 B.C.E., some segments perhaps surviving among the aboriginal and other ancient groups dispersed across the Indian peninsula down to modern times.

The Indo-Aryan people may have begun to arrive on the Indian subconti-

nent as early as 2000 B.C.E., and to create a new settled society over the next few centuries in what are now northern Pakistan and India. Originally a nomadic pastoral people who moved with vast herds of cattle in search of grazing land, the Indo-Aryans branched off from the Indo-Iranian people, who probably migrated from the Caucasus Mountains region (modern Chechnya) to the plateau of Iran late in the third millennium B.C.E. The Indo-Iranians were themselves one of the major groups of the Indo-European people, who spread in many stages from their Caucasian homeland westward into Europe and eastward into Asia. One western Indo-European group, roughly contemporaneous with the earliest Indo-Iranians and Indo-Aryans, migrated to the Mediterranean region also around 2000 B.C.E., initially establishing the Mycenaean civilization and

An eighteenth-century watercolor depicting Kṛṣṇa protecting cowherds and cows during a fire.

subsequently emerging in history as the ancient Greeks and Romans.

When the Indo-Aryans started settling in Punjab (now divided between India and Pakistan) in the second millennium B.C.E., they established an organized agrarian village society distinct from the urban society of their Indus-Harappan predecessors, who had focused on trade. This Indo-Aryan innovation, with its economic basis in agriculture (on small family farms) and animal husbandry (mainly of the domesticated cow), has proven to be the subcontinent's enduring social form of the past 3,500 years. In the mid-twentieth century, when it still had nearly 750,000 such villages, Mahatma Gandhi famously characterized India as a "land of villages"; and, in our own times, we still invoke the "holy cow"—an image that the Indo-Aryans created in their earliest poems on the subcontinent.

The Indo-Aryans brought with them the language that eventually became Sanskrit, the medium of the largest body of Indian literature, produced continuously from approximately 1200 B.C.E. to 1800 C.E. Sanskrit is intimately related to Greek and Latin: these languages share much of their grammar, use similar sentence structures, and draw on hundreds of common roots for their vocabularies. All three languages, along with ancient Persian, may therefore have evolved from a single source called proto-Indo-European, a language (lost since antiquity) presumably used by the ancestors of the Greeks, Romans, Indo-Iranians, and Indo-Aryans a few thousand years earlier.

But the connections among these scattered peoples are not merely linguistic. When they settled at the end of their respective migrations, they began to worship pantheons of gods, establish social hierarchies, practice rituals and customs, and adopt political models that strongly resembled one another. Most important, their songs, tales, and cycles of myths seemed to invoke a common stock of older memories, images, and narratives. By the first millennium B.C.E., Greek, Sanskrit, and Latin were highly differentiated from one another, and their emerging literatures—from, respectively, **Homer** (ca. eighth century B.C.E.); **Vālmīki** (ca. sixth century B.C.E.), the author of the original *Rāmāyaṇa*; and **Virgil** (first century B.C.E.) onward—developed along independent trajectories. But they still contained remarkable echoes of one another that we cannot fully explain.

ORALITY AND WRITING IN INDIA

The first works on the subcontinent were hymns and ritual formulas (*mantras*) composed in Sanskrit, which were gathered with commentary and other theological material in four large groupings of discourse called the Vedas; these gave rise to an extensive, interconnected body of philosophy and mystical speculation called the Upaniṣads, fifty-two of which are important. Developed between approximately 1200 and 700 B.C.E., much of this literature was classified as scripture (*śruti*, revelation that is heard) and revealed knowledge (*veda*). Although the Vedic hymns are in verse, and some of them are poetry of the highest order, and even though the visionaries (*ṛṣis*) who "received them from the gods" are called *kavis* (poets), the texts themselves are not classified as *kāvya* (poetry): from this perspective, *mantras* are of divine origin and hence sacred, whereas poetry—no matter how beautiful and profound—is made by human authors and hence always mundane. Since divine revelation and knowledge need to be explained to human audiences, the

Vedas and the Upaniṣads engendered many works of authoritative and specialized commentary (*śāstras*) as well as numerous compendiums and rule books (*sūtras*), which, by the latter half of the first millennium B.C.E., became part of the canon of Vedic religion and, centuries later, of classical Hinduism, one of the most important cultural forces on the subcontinent.

Although some of the essential commentaries and rule books were prepared after a writing system became available, the Hindu canon as a whole was transmitted orally throughout the ancient period. In this method of oral transmission, which is still practiced in our times, specialist priests and scholars belonging to the *brāhmaṇa* caste are trained from early childhood to memorize an entire work in multiple forms: by phoneme (sound unit), word, verse, chapter, and book; by mnemonic summaries of the whole work, and by its "indexed" words; and even by the reverse order of its verses. Taught orally for a dozen years, a good Vedic priest who specializes in the *Ṛg-veda* (ca. 1000 B.C.E.), for example, can recite all 1,028 hymns in its ten books, can confirm their correct order, can reproduce any individual verse at will, and can orally list every occurrence of a given word in the text. Unlike a bard, a Vedic reciter communicates divine revelation, and hence is not free to invent, embellish, or err. In post-Vedic times (starting ca. 500 B.C.E.), this method was extended to other kinds of composition in Sanskrit. In the classical period (ca. 400–1100 C.E.), for instance, poets and literary scholars memorized entire bodies of *kāvya*, so that their literature was always at hand— a practice that also continued well into the twentieth century.

Knowledge of the early writing system of the Indus-Harappan people did not survive the end of their civilization, around 1900 B.C.E. A new system of indigenous writing most likely reappeared around 500 B.C.E., and acquired its canonical form some 250 years later. This was the Brahmi script system, in which writing proceeds from left to right and uses alphabetical letters and diacritical marks to represent syllables (whole sounds), and hence is classified as an alpha-syllabary system, as distinct from the Greek and Latin scripts, which are strictly alphabetical. Brahmi migrated rapidly across South Asia after 250 B.C.E., spawning what would eventually become, over the next 1,500 years or so, the dozen distinct script systems in which most of the languages of the region are recorded. These include Sanskrit, Bengali, Hindi, Marathi, Kannada, and Tamil, among other languages, Urdu being among the few exceptions written in a modified Persian-Arabic script, which arrived from outside the subcontinent. During the same period, Brahmi also migrated out of India and became a transnational phenomenon of world importance: it engendered the scripts of Tibetan (Tibet), Burmese (Myanmar), Thai (Thailand), Javanese and Sumatran (Indonesia), Cham (Vietnam), and Tagalog (the Philippines), and hence launched literacy and literature across a wide swath of Asia.

By the beginning of the Common Era, professional scribes had begun to produce manuscripts with a metal stylus on prepared sheets of bark or palm leaves, tied together with string. Paper and ink first became common on the Indian subcontinent in the thirteenth century C.E.; until then, for more than a millennium, the principal form of a Sanskrit book was a palm-leaf manuscript: though highly perishable, it succeeded in recording an enormous quantity of literature, disseminating Indian epics, lyrics, stories, and plays all over the subcontinent, and well beyond its boundaries.

SOCIETY, POLITICS, AND RELIGION

The first Vedic hymns (ca. 1200 B.C.E.), and the first collection of hymns, the Ṛg-veda saṃhitā (ca. 1000 B.C.E.), were most likely composed in Punjab, "the land of five rivers" that are the tributaries of the Indus. Over the next few centuries, the Indo-Aryans pushed farther east, settling on the wider and equally fertile plains surrounding the Ganges river system, up to modern Bihar and Bengal. By the seventh century B.C.E., the expansion of agriculture and cattle breeding produced enough prosperity to support the first towns and cities across northern India, such as Banaras and Ayodhyā (which still flourish today). With this emerged the first recognizable political form in India: the small republic centered around an urban capital, not unlike a city-state, ruled by a lineage of hereditary monarchs. This became both the historical context and the narrative setting of the first Sanskrit epic, the Rāmāyaṇa, begun in the sixth century B.C.E. and composed on the central Gangetic plains.

A couple of centuries later, the small republics started to give way to bigger kingdoms that could garner sufficient surpluses from the land to maintain large armies, and control territories of several hundred square miles. Shortly after Alexander the Great invaded western and northern India, reaching Punjab in 327 B.C.E. and leaving behind a Greek colony in Gandhara (today's Peshawar and Swat Valley region, in Pakistan), the Maurya dynasty established the subcontinent's first empire—which stretched from Afghanistan to Bengal, and from the Himalayan foothills to the Deccan Plateau. Situated imaginatively in the transitional period between small republics and a vast empire, the other ancient Sanskrit epic, the Mahabharata (ca. 400 B.C.E.–400 C.E.), represents a world of powerful monarchies and many medium-sized kingdoms, from which the older republican ideal was beginning to fade.

This evolving world was shaped by the religion we now call Hinduism. As we see from the Rāmāyaṇa and the Mahabharata, one of the most influential ideas in Hinduism is that the universe, as it exists, is fashioned in a vast process of self-generation, in which all the primordial substance out of which it is made is godhead itself. Godhead, or "the god beyond god," is the absolute and undifferentiated original matter of the universe, and it divides itself into everything that exists; it is eternal and indestructible, and hence has no beginning or end in time. God in this view is not a creator god, or an anthropomorphic father, or a wrathful or vengeful deity; godhead is unknowable, unimaginable, and indescribable. Since everything that exists is made out of godhead (and there is no other elemental matter in the universe), god is everywhere and in everything—a view that constitutes pantheism. In some Vedic hymns, this all-pervading godhead is called Puruṣa, "spirit" (in the masculine gender); in the Upaniṣads, it is renamed Brahman (not to be confused with either brāhmaṇa, the priestly caste-group, or Brahmā, the later, anthropomorphic "god of creation"). The soul, spirit, or "self" (ātman) that animates every living creature is nothing but a piece of Puruṣa or Brahman, so it, too, is eternal and indestructible. The universe as we know it has a beginning in cosmic time, and therefore also comes to an end; since godhead cyclically differentiates itself into a particular universe, all its indestructible substance must return to it at the end of a cycle and be reintegrated into its primordial state. Any life-form's ultimate goal therefore is to be reunited with absolute godhead; for an individual soul or ātman, such a

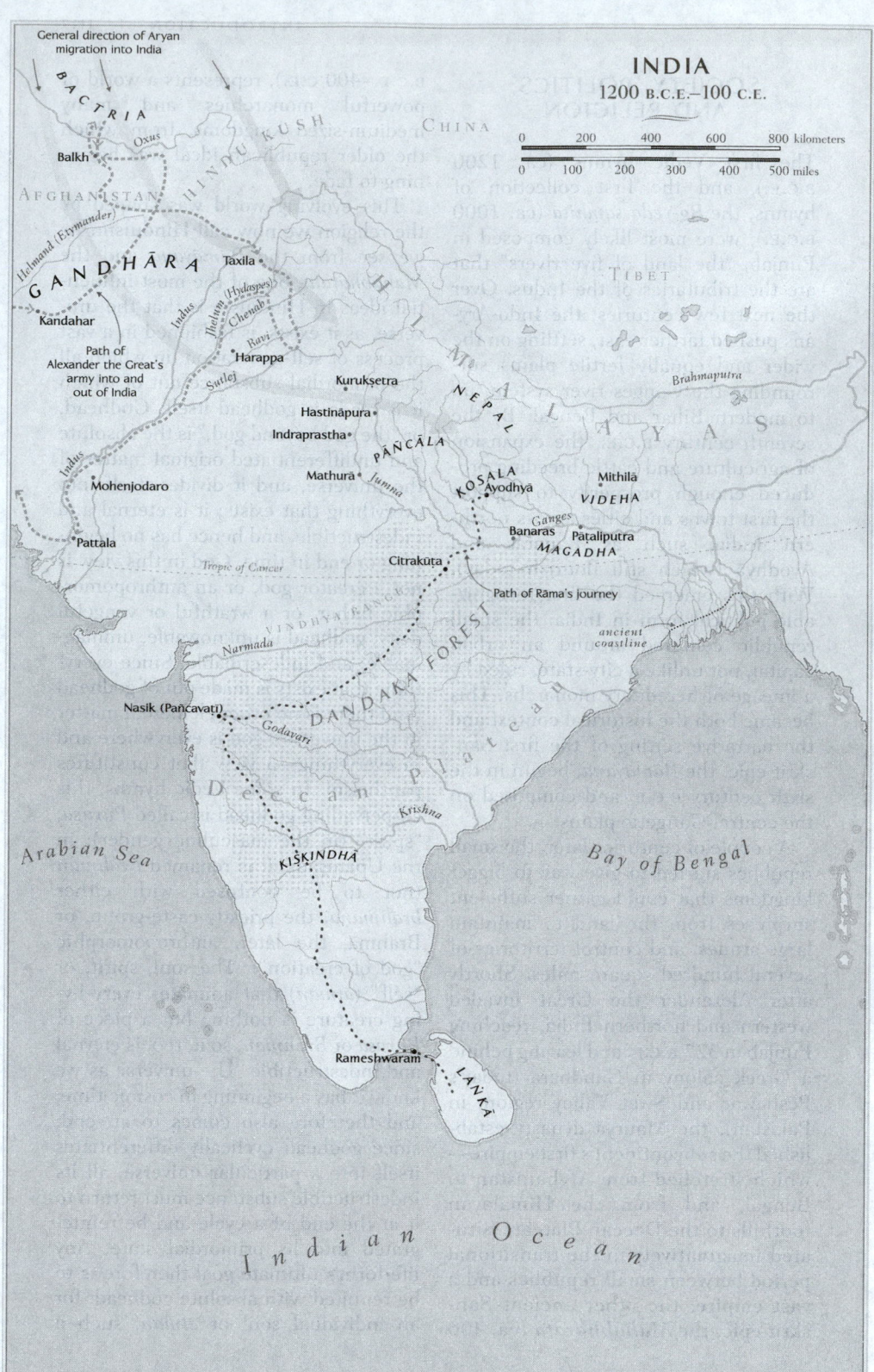

General direction of Aryan
migration into India

B A C T R I A

H I N D U   K U S H

CHINA

Balkh

Oxus

AFGHANISTAN

Ilmand (Etymander)

GANDHĀRA

Taxila

Kandahar

Path of
Alexander the Great's
army into and
out of India

Indus

Jhelum (Hydaspes)

Chenab

Ravi

Harappa

Sutlej

Mohenjodaro

Indus

Pattala

Tropic of Cancer

H I M A L A Y A S

TIBET

Brahmaputra

NEPAL

Kurukṣetra

Hastināpura

Indraprastha

PĀÑCĀLA

Mathurā

Jumna

KOSALA

Ayodhyā

Mithilā

VIDEHA

Ganges

Banaras

Pāṭaliputra

MAGADHA

Citrakūṭa

Path of Rāma's journey

Narmada

V I N D H Y A   R A N G E

DANDAKA FOREST

ancient
coastline

Nasik (Pañcavati)

Godavari

D e c c a n   P l a t e a u

Krishna

Arabian Sea

KIṢKINDHĀ

Bay of Bengal

Rameshwaram

LANKA

I n d i a n   O c e a n

0   200   400   600   800 kilometers
0 100 200 300 400 500 miles

A sandstone sculpture at the Temple of Śiva, Elephanta (ca. seventh–eighth centuries C.E.), depicting the "Trimurti" of Hinduism: Śiva, Viṣṇu, and Brahmā.

union with the elemental stuff of the universe is possible only if it can achieve *mokṣa*, or "liberation," from its differentiated existence.

Works such as the *Rāmāyaṇa* and the *Mahabharata* further show us that many of Hinduism's characteristic doctrines follow from this theology of *Brahman* and *ātman*. Each of the popular gods in its pantheon becomes an aspect or a manifestation of godhead in an anthropomorphic or concrete form, which is especially useful in making divinity accessible to humans. The great gods Viṣṇu and Śiva are manifestations of godhead in equal measure; though Viṣṇu is often characterized as the god of preservation, and Śiva is distinguished as the god of destruction, each performs all the functions of creation, preservation, and destruction that only pure godhead can perform. The same is true of the anthropomorphic Brahmā, usually called the god of creation; and, by extension—because Hinduism, in the final analysis, does not attribute gender to godhead—it is equally true of the goddesses Lakṣmī, Pārvatī, and Sarasvatī (the consorts of Viṣṇu, Śiva, and Brahmā, respectively), each of whom also is a complete embodiment of godhead. Since godhead can thus take on countless forms, there cannot be any one true representation of divinity; from its earliest phase, Hinduism therefore consistently commits itself to polytheism, the belief that there are many gods. As a result, from its very beginnings in agrarian Indo-Aryan society in northern India, Hinduism emerges as a fundamentally pluralistic religion, tolerant (in principle) of the worship of many different gods in many different ways, and of the pursuit of divergent ways of life, each of which has the potential to discover a path to *mokṣa* for an individual *ātman*.

THE RELIGIOUS CONTEXTS OF EPIC AND TALE

Within this broad matrix, India's early epics and narrative traditions develop along specific religious lines, but also in keeping with the social world shaped by Hinduism. Vālmīki's *Rāmāyaṇa*, composed and transmitted orally at the outset, is classified as the first poem in Sanskrit because it emphasizes imaginative and aesthetic excellence outside a religious context; but it also takes the mythology of Viṣṇu and the practices of Hindu society for granted. In this framework, Viṣṇu is the "supreme god" who manifests all aspects of godhead; and Vedic rituals are essential for pleasing various gods and ensuring that individuals can pursue mokṣa. At the same time, the epic depicts a hierarchical society divided into four main caste-groups by birth: brāhmaṇas (priests), kṣatriyas (warriors), vaiśyas (traders), and śūdras (servants and cultivators). Theologically, this separation of castes is part of the primary differentiation of godhead into distinct categories of existence, and hence is divinely ordained and immutable; in most circumstances, an individual therefore cannot migrate from one caste to another on the basis of, say, talent or accomplishment. This structure is maintained by a system of endogamous marriage, in which legitimate spouses must belong to the same caste-group, so that their children are also born into their social category; in such a world, marriage is irrevocable, and miscegenation and adultery across castes can deeply destabilize not only the human order, but the cosmic moral order as well. The Rāmāyaṇa also depicts a society of villages and small republics, in which dynasties of kings do not yet pursue imperial ambitions: their role here is to preserve the divine order of things, in both the mundane world and the cosmos at large, which is populated by human beings, animal, plants, and inanimate things as well as demons, celestial beings, and gods.

In the Mahābhārata, composed a little later, village society coexists with a more complex urban world: the land is now divided into many sizable dynastic kingdoms on the verge of imperial formations. The four caste-groups (varṇas) have separated into five, with the addition of "untouchables" and foreigners (such as the Greeks left behind by Alexander's army); and each caste-group is differentiated into numerous specific castes (jātīs). While the Rāmāyaṇa upholds the ideal of monogamous marriage within caste boundaries, the Mahābhārata explores multiple marriages and reproductive relationships, overlaying polygamy with polyandry and complicating issues of legitimacy, illegitimacy, and legacy by birth. Whereas the earlier epic distinguishes sharply between good and evil, the later poem adopts more complex and varying views on how action (karma) can accord with divine law (dharma); as the laws revealed by the gods in the Vedas and explained in later authoritative discourse (such as the śāstras and sūtras) are intricate, many judgments regarding the rightness and wrongness of particular actions founder in uncertainty. The **Bhagavad-gītā**, which is part of the Mahabharata, tackles the dilemmas of karma in the most difficult of situations: when is war just, how can violence and killing ever be justified, and under what circumstances can human beings even conceive of taking up arms against family and loved ones? The philosophical and theological arguments about the human and the divine, and about social and political organization, launched by the Indo-Aryans toward the end of the second millennium B.C.E., thus reach a poetic culmination in the encyclopedic structure of the Mahabharata a thousand years later.

By the sixth century B.C.E.— the likely date of Vālmīki's original Rāmāyaṇa—several indigenous responses to the Hindu theology of Brahman and ātman had already found historical expression. The strongest criticism and rejection came from two near contemporaries of Vālmīki: Mahāvīra, the last of Jainism's founders, and Siddhartha-Gautama Buddha, who launched

Buddhism. Adopting a severe form of philosophical skepticism and atheism, Buddhism argued that there is no god beyond god (as postulated in Hinduism), no creation by differentiation, and that the universe therefore has no substantial reality. If *Brahman* does not exist, then living creatures have no eternal and indestructible *ātmans*; our perception that we possess an enduring self is therefore an illusion, and the only end of life can be a "snuffing out" or extinction of illusory identity. Such a snuffing out—the literal meaning of *nirvāṇa*—is the exact opposite of what the Hindus call *mokṣa*, the liberation of a substantial *ātman* from a material body for reunification with the ultimate, primordial substance, *Brahman*. And yet, perhaps paradoxically, Buddhism accepts the reality of karma and rebirth: even an illusory self is reborn numerous times, because it is deluded into believing that it has a persistent identity. This delusion ends only when the self reaches Enlightenment (the condition of being a Buddha), understands that it is not a substantial entity, and hence acquires the power to extinguish itself, attaining *nirvāṇa*. Such a rejection of Hinduism finds a narrative exposition in the *Jātaka* tales (ca. fourth century B.C.E.), which are part of the canon of Theravada Buddhism in the Pali language. The *Jātaka*'s vision, especially the playful irreverence and philosophical dissidence in a series of its short tales, offers us a profound cultural alternative to the heroic Hindu worlds of the *Rāmāyaṇa*, the *Mahabharata*, and the *Bhagavad-gītā*.

As this historical overview suggests, for most of the ancient period the Indian subcontinent was not politically united. This pattern was to continue in the Common Era, down to modern times; since the end of British colonial rule (1757–1947), South Asia has come to be divided into seven nations, and its total population is now nearly 1.6 billion people, about three-fourths of whom live in contemporary India. The ancient period also witnessed internal religious division, with Jainism and Buddhism dissenting from Hinduism— a process that was repeated later with the arrival of other faiths, such as Zoroastrianism (ca. eleventh century) and Christianity, and the rise of Sikhism (both sixteenth century). Nevertheless, for the more than three millennia since the establishment of agrarian Indo-Aryan village society, the subcontinent has functioned as a cohesive cultural zone characterized by diversity and pluralism, which define the distinctive context of its early epics and tales.

THE RĀMĀYAṆA OF VĀLMĪKI

ca. 550 B.C.E.

The *Rāmāyaṇa* is many things to many people. It is a tale of adventure across a vast land, from palace to forest to sea; and a love story about an ideal prince and an ideal woman, whose relationship falters late in their marriage. It is a heroic epic about injustice and war, abduction and disinheritance, but also a wondrous tale involving gods, humans, animals, and demons with supernatural powers. It is a religious epic that explains the ways of the gods to human beings, and offers a model of justice and prosperity on earth. Moreover, it is great entertainment: like a roller coaster, it takes us up and down through many facets of human experience, from goodness, beauty, and romance to fear and tragedy.

CONTEXT

All we know about Vālmīki is the little he tells us about himself in his poem. He was an ascetic spiritual practitioner who had renounced normal life in human society, and lived in a small ashram, a hermit's enclave, on the banks of a river. One day he saw a pair of birds making love to each other, but a moment later a hunter shot and killed the male bird with an arrow. Incensed with this violent intrusion into a scene of great natural tenderness and beauty, Vālmīki pronounced an irrevocable curse on the hunter. Reflecting on what he had just uttered, the poet realized that he had spontaneously composed a *śloka*, an unrhymed metrical verse like a couplet, which fully

expressed his compassionate grief for the slaughtered bird. Realizing that this verse form would be a perfect vehicle for story as well as song, Vālmīki set about using the *śloka* to compose the heroic and romantic tale of Rāma and Sītā, whose twin sons, Lava and Kuśa—by a twist of events—were then being raised in his ashram. Thus, the poet's life and character are fully integrated with the heroic world he creates and the tale he chooses to narrate. In the version of the epic we have inherited, and in the tradition since Vālmīki's time, he is celebrated as "the first poet," and his *Rāmāyaṇa* is known as "the inaugural poem" in Indian literature.

Vālmīki's epic tale—nearly one-and-a-half times the combined length of the **Iliad** and the **Odyssey**—was originally composed in Sanskrit around the sixth century B.C.E. By that time, a settled society had been in place in northern India for at least a thousand years. Agriculture had become the principal economic activity on the fertile plains around the Indus and Ganges rivers, and it supported a network of prosperous villages, towns, and cities. Society was organized by caste, with priests (*brāhmaṇas*), warriors (*kṣatriyas*), and traders (*vaiśyas*) comprising the three main groups, and the large populace that served them (*śūdras*) constituting the fourth category in the hierarchy. The caste structure was maintained primarily by a system of arranged marriage, in which, ideally, the bridegroom and the bride belonged to the same caste but not the same clan. Each caste-group had its own laws and moral codes (*dharma*), which defined its members' duties and obligations, but it also had to obey laws that applied to all of society. These laws were not made by human beings: they were given by the gods, and were contained in scripture.

Hinduism, which was central to upholding this social order, had been established in its early form several centuries before Vālmīki; its scriptural canon included ritual texts (the Vedas) as well as philosophy and theology (the Upaniṣads). In this system of beliefs, human beings could find "salvation" only if they accumulated "good karma" by propitiating the gods and following *dharma* precisely. But moral laws and codes of conduct are always complex and subtle, and hence easy to violate; numerous rituals are therefore necessary to keep the gods happy, maintain the moral and social orders, and make up for ethical lapses.

The world of the *Rāmāyaṇa* is structured in a similar way, but it also contains many gods, among whom three are the most important: Brahmā, primarily a benign and paternalistic god of creation; Śiva, chiefly an angry and retributive god who engenders cycles of creation and destruction; and Viṣṇu, mainly a benevolent god who preserves the moral balance of the universe. Much of the flux and dynamism of the universe is due to the perpetual struggle for supremacy between Śiva and Viṣṇu. Śiva intervenes in the human world directly, in his multifaceted anthropomorphic form; Viṣṇu, in contrast, "comes down on earth" in a series of distinct avatars or incarnations, living temporarily among mortal creatures each time for the purpose of destroying a particular source of evil. A vital feature of the *Rāmāyaṇa* is that it tells the story of Lord Viṣṇu's seventh incarnation, when he embodied himself as prince Rāma, in order to end the demonic king Rāvaṇa's reign of terror on earth and beyond.

The mundane world that Vālmīki's characters inhabit is also a deeply political one, where the two upper caste-groups, the *brāhmaṇas* (priests) and the *kṣatriyas* (warriors and rulers), dominate society. The land is divided into small, autonomous republics with prosperous cities for their capitals. The king belongs to a dynasty of warriors, but is not an absolute monarch; his power is mediated by court priests and scholarly *brāhmaṇas*. He is defined as a "protector of *dharma*," and his ideal role is to ensure that he and his subjects follow all laws. He is also fully answerable to his subjects; as their moral caretaker, he is obliged to pay attention to their needs, their voices of affirmation and protest. Moreover, the king is further constrained by life in his palace: he is usually polygamous, and has several queens; he is therefore the head of an extended family whose members participate actively in affairs of state. The warrior-dynasties in these republics follow the law of primogeniture, so that the eldest son ascends the throne in the next generation; but the inheritance of the kingdom can be complicated by the protodemocratic politics of the royal family as well as of public opinion, or by the inability of the king and his queens to beget a son. All these aspects of early Indian society, religion, and politics come into play in the dramatic narrative of the *Rāmāyaṇa*.

WORK

While Vālmīki probably composed his poem around 550 B.C.E., it was expanded and polished anonymously by others over the next five or six hundred years. Since writing systems did not exist in his society, he must have composed the epic orally, using a large repertoire of formulaic expressions. During its first few centuries, the *Rāmāyaṇa* must have been transmitted with the sophisticated methods of memorization, preservation, and reproduction already used for Hindu scripture. In its modern canonical form, the Sanskrit *Rāmāyaṇa* contains about 24,000 couplets (*ślokas*) and is divided into seven books (*kāṇḍas*), each subdivided into a large number of chapters (*sargas*), most of which contain between twenty and fifty couplets. The first and last books seem to have been added later; they explicitly interpret Rāma as an avatar of Viṣṇu, and provide a multilayered narrative frame for the five books in the middle.

The English version of the *Rāmāyaṇa* reproduced here is not a translation but an adaptation and retelling of Vālmīki's poem. For the most part, it condenses the narrative of each chapter in a style that appeals to modern readers; but, in select passages, especially with important pieces of dialogue, its rendering is closer to the original. Our selection consists of excerpts from books 2 through 6 that capture the key moments of the tale; together, they convey the epic's essential story as Vālmīki probably imagined it.

To understand our selection, it is necessary to know what happens in book 1, *Bāla* ("Childhood"), which is not represented here. In that book, Rāvaṇa, the brilliant and highly accomplished king of Laṅkā (an island in the south, modern Sri Laṅkā), has become invincible, demonic, and evil. Lord Viṣṇu therefore has to descend to earth in a human form and destroy him, and so takes birth as Rāma, the eldest son of Daśaratha, king of Kosala, and his principal queen, Kausalyā. Daśaratha also has two other queens, who bear him sons (Rāma's half-brothers): Kaikeyī is the mother of Bharata, whereas Sumitrā has twins, Lakṣmaṇa and Śatrughna. All four boys are

trained as warriors and future rulers; Rāma and Lakṣmaṇa, inseparable since childhood, become the pupils of the sage Viśvāmitra. As teenagers, they travel with Viśvāmitra to the neighboring Videha, where Rāma wins a suitors' contest for Sītā, the foster-daughter of that republic's king but actually a child of the goddess Earth.

Our selection begins with book 2, *Ayodhyā*, where Daśaratha follows the code of primogeniture and proclaims Rāma as heir apparent to Kosala's throne, and the republic's citizens celebrate the decision enthusiastically. But following an intrigue in the extended family, Daśaratha gives in to the demand that his second son, Bharata, be made king, and that Rāma be exiled for fourteen years. We then see how Rāma responds to this development, and what decisions he, Sītā, Lakṣmaṇa, and Bharata make under the circumstances. The chapters in this book are composed in a realistic style on the whole, and they give us vivid glimpses into the thoughts and feelings of the characters involved in the struggle for power.

The excerpts from the next four books focus on Rāma, Sītā, and Lakṣmaṇa's fourteen-year exile together, and the narrative now has the atmosphere of fairy tale and fantasy. In book 3, *Āraṇya* ("The Forest"), the trio pushes deeper into the vast Daṇḍaka forest, south of the River Ganges, whose only inhabitants are animals, ascetics, and demons. We discover how they learn to survive under hostile conditions, and what kinds of dangers and temptations they encounter. While the three are living peacefully in the Pañcavaṭī woodlands (in central India), Rāma and Lakṣmaṇa unwittingly initiate a conflict with Śūrpaṇakhā and her brother Rāvaṇa, the demonic king of Laṅkā. Enraged by their provocation, Rāvaṇa decides to destroy Rāma by abducting Sītā; how he

A "Mughal"-style illustration from the *Rāmāyaṇa* dating from ca. 1600 C.E. shows Rāma chasing a golden deer.

carries out his plan constitutes a pivotal moment in the epic. When Rāma realizes that Sītā is gone, he virtually goes mad with grief.

While searching desperately for Sītā, in book 4, *Kiṣkindhā* ("The Kingdom of the Monkeys"), Rāma and Lakṣmaṇa encounter a tribe of monkeys, whose citadel is at Kiṣkindhā (in southern India). Intervening in the political quarrels among their factions, the princes persuade the monkeys, and one of their powerful leaders, Hanumān, to help them look for her. In book 5, *Sundara* ("The Sundara Hill" [in Laṅkā]), Hanumān spies on Rāvaṇa's capital, and discovers where Sītā is held captive. But she refuses to escape with Hanumān for reasons that deepen the moral dimension of the story, and that leave him in a quandary. Hanumān then sets fire to Rāvaṇa's city as a warning of impending war, and returns to apprise Rāma of the situation.

In book 6, *Yuddha* ("The War"), the monkeys build a bridge or causeway across the straits to Laṅkā with remarkable inventiveness. One of Rāvaṇa's brothers betrays him and joins the princes, helping them with their battle plans. After a lengthy conflict, in which Rāvaṇa's other brothers are killed and Lakṣmaṇa is wounded, Rāma finally confronts the demon king in single combat. When he recovers Sītā, however, he finds himself deeply troubled by the question of whether she has been faithful to him during her long captivity. Resolving his dilemma with a dramatic test of fidelity, Rāma returns to Ayodhyā with Sītā and Lakṣmaṇa, and is crowned king. His reign brings peace, prosperity, and justice to the republic of Kosala, and represents the ideal of kingship.

Our selection ends on this happy note, but the canonical version of Vālmīki's epic continues further. In book 7, *Uttara* ("The Final Book"), not included here, Rāma seems set to rule happily for the rest of his days; but people soon begin to gossip viciously about Sītā's probable infidelity with Rāvaṇa. In a misguided attempt to be morally answerable to his subjects, Rāma banishes Sītā, even though he knows that the rumors are false and that she is pregnant. Sītā takes refuge in the sage Vālmīki's ashram, where she gives birth to twin boys, Lava and Kuśa. Vālmīki composes a long poem about the life of Rāma; he trains the twins as bards, and teaches them to sing his epic beautifully. One day they sing the tale before the king, who does not know that they are his sons; when he recognizes them, he sends for his beloved queen. Overwhelmed by her suffering by then, however, Sītā asks her mother, the Earth, to take her back; the ground opens beneath her feet, and she disappears forever. Heartbroken, Rāma divides his kingdom between his sons, gives up his life on earth, and returns to heaven in his divine form as Viṣṇu, his task of destroying Rāvaṇa's evil accomplished.

Vālmīki's style in the original varies according to narrative mode. Many important events are narrated directly from an omniscient point of view; in contrast, when characters in the story tell a tale or engage in dialogue, the verse is adapted to capture their voices and personalities. In book 2, when the action is situated in the palace, the descriptions are frequently realistic; in books 3 through 5, when the action is set in the forest and focuses on animals, demons, and fantastic events—Rāvaṇa changing his form, Hanumān flying over the sea—the atmosphere and effect are often fantastic. Even in the forest scenes, however, dream-like passages can be interspersed with flashes of realism, indicating how carefully the text is crafted throughout.

Vālmīki's poem articulates a strong moral vision. It offers us the ideals of Rāma as a son, husband, and king who is serene, courageous, and circumspect; Sītā as a vibrant, thoughtful, and selfless wife and mother; Lakṣmaṇa as a brother and brother-in-law whose first thought is always for his extended family; and Hanumān as a loyal devotee. All these characters are larger than life, but each of them is also flawed or suffers great injustice. Moreover, in a polygamous society, Vālmīki's epic proposes the norm of monogamous marriage based on mutual love between husband and wife; in a world of political conflict, it portrays republics that build alliances for peace, and rulers and subjects who live by the law, aiming for social harmony. It explicitly promotes justice, goodness, balance, and morality in forms that remain valid today, even though we may not always agree on the details from a modern perspective.

As a literary narrative with scripture-like religious authority, the story of Rāma is special because it is fully integrated into the annual Hindu calendar, the way the story of Christ and the rituals of Christmas, Good Friday, and Easter are woven into the Christian calendar. Every year, in the weeks following the autumnal equinox, the public festivals of Dusehrā and Divālī mark the anniversaries, respectively, of Rāma's victory over Rāvaṇa and Rāma's return to Ayodhyā. Over the nine nights preceding Dusehrā, thousands of local Hindu communities throughout India perform the Rāma-līlā, "the play of Rāma"; in each community, children, teenagers, and adults enact the full story of Rāma in nightly installments on an amateur stage, culminating in a ritual burning of gigantic effigies representing Rāvaṇa and his brothers. On the next night of the new moon (usually in late October), every Indian village, town, and city celebrates Divālī, the festival of lights, a symbolic affirmation of Rāma's coronation as king and the cyclical restoration of goodness and justice in the world.

During the past two millennia, Vālmīki's Rāmāyaṇa has spread astonishingly far. In India, hundreds of translations, imitations, adaptations, and retellings have appeared in the dozens of languages that gradually replaced Sanskrit after the first millennium C.E. Many of these local and regional versions of the epic—such as Kamban's Īrāmavatāram (Tamil, twelfth century) and Tulsīdās's Rāmacaritamānasa (Avadhi/Hindi, sixteenth century)—have become literary and religious classics in their own right; and many of them are transmitted orally, in a form called the Rāma-kathā ("the story of Rāma"), in public readings and recitations by professional performers sponsored annually by local communities. Outside India, the Rāmāyaṇa has migrated to the Persian, Arabic, and Chinese worlds; the central character of the Monkey King in *Journey to the West*, one of the four major classical novels in Chinese, is modeled on Hanumān. The epic has also reached every part of Southeast Asia, from Malaysia and Indonesia to the Philippines. Vālmīki's tale (originally a Hindu work) reappears with variations in the Thai Rāmakien (thirteenth century), the national epic of Thailand; in the relief sculptures at Angkor Wat, the Hindu temple complex in Cambodia (twelfth century onward); in Balinese classical and folk dance, dance drama, and pantomime; and in the spectacular puppet and shadow-puppet theaters of Malaysia and Indonesia (Muslim-majority societies) and Thailand and Cambodia (Buddhist-majority societies). The characters and stories of Rāma and Sītā, Lakṣmaṇa and Hanumāna and Rāvaṇa, are among the best known for almost half the world's population today.

The Rāmāyaṇa of Vālmīki[1]

From Book 2

Ayodhyā

AYODHYĀ 15–16

The brāhmaṇas[2] had got everything ready for the coronation ceremonies. Gold pots of holy water from all the sacred rivers, most of them gathered at their very source, were ready. All the paraphernalia like the umbrella, the chowries,[3] an elephant and a white horse, were ready, too.

But, the king did not emerge, though the sun had risen and the auspicious hour was fast approaching. The priests and the people wondered: "Who can awaken the king, and inform him that he had better hurry up!" At that moment, Sumantra[4] emerged from the palace. Seeing them, he told them: "Under the king's orders I am going to fetch Rāma." But, on second thought, knowing that the preceptors and the priests commanded even the king's respect, he returned to the king's presence to announce that they were awaiting him. Standing near the king, Sumantra sang: "Arise, O king! Night has flown. Arise and do what should be done." The weary king asked: "I ordered you to fetch Rāma, and I am not asleep. Why do you not do as you are told to do?" This time, Sumantra hurried out of the palace and sped to Rāma's palace.

Entering the palace and proceeding unobstructed through the gates and entrances of the palace, Sumantra beheld the divine Rāma, and said to him: "Rāma, the king who is in the company of queen Kaikeyī desires to see you at once." Immediately, Rāma turned to Sītā and announced: "Surely, the king and mother Kaikeyī wish to discuss with me some important details in connection with the coronation ceremony. I shall go and return soon." Sītā, for her part, offered a heartfelt prayer to the gods: "May I have the blessing of humbly serving you during the auspicious coronation ceremony!"

As Rāma emerged from his palace there was great cheer among the people who hailed and applauded him. Ascending his swift chariot he proceeded to the king's palace, followed by the regalia. Women standing at the windows of their houses and richly adorned to express their joy, showered flowers on Rāma. They praised Kausalyā, the mother of Rāma; they praised Sītā, Rāma's consort: "Obviously she must have done great penance to get him as her husband." The people rejoiced as if they themselves were being installed on the throne. They said to one another: "Rāma's coronation is truly a blessing to all the people. While he rules, and he will rule for a long time, no one will even have an unpleasant experience, or ever suffer." Rāma too was happy to see the huge crowds of people, the elephants and the horses—indicating that people had come to Ayodhyā from afar to witness the coronation.

---

1. Translated by Swami Venkatesananda.
2. Priests, members of the highest caste.
3. Yak-tail fans used to ward off flies; kings were attended by fan bearers.

4. King Daśaratha's charioteer and chief bard. The charioteer/bard (*sūta*) composed and narrated ancient epics and sagas.

AYODHYĀ 17–18

As Rāma proceeded in his radiant chariot towards his father's palace, the people were saying to one another: "We shall be supremely happy hereafter, now that Rāma will be king. But, who cares for all this happiness? When we behold Rāma on the throne, we shall attain eternal beatitude!" Rāma heard all this praise and the people's worshipful homage to him, with utter indifference as he drove along the royal road.[5] The chariot entered the first gate to the palace. From there on Rāma went on foot and respectfully entered the king's apartments. The people who had accompanied him eagerly waited outside.

Rushing eagerly and respectfully to his father's presence, Rāma bowed to the feet of his father and then devoutly touched the feet of his mother Kaikeyī, too. "O Rāma!" said the king: he could not say anything more, because he was choked with tears and grief. He could neither see nor speak to Rāma. Rāma sensed great danger: as if he had trodden on a most poisonous serpent. Turning to Kaikeyī, Rāma asked her: "How is it that today the king does not speak kindly to me? Have I offended him in any way? Is he not well? Have I offended prince Bharata or any of my mothers? Oh, it is agonizing: and incurring his displeasure I cannot live even for an hour. Kindly reveal the truth to me."

In a calm, measured and harsh tone, Kaikeyī now said to Rāma: "The king is neither sick nor angry with you. What he must tell you he does not wish to, for fear of displeasing you. He granted me two boons. When I named them, he recoiled. How can a truthful man, a righteous king, go back on his own word? Yet that is his predicament at the moment. I shall reveal the truth to you if you assure me that you will honor your father's promise." For the first time Rāma was distressed: "Ah, shame! Please do not say such things to me! For the sake of my father I can jump into fire. And, I assure you, Rāma does not indulge in double talk. Hence, tell me what the king wants to be done."

Kaikeyī lost no time. She said: "Long ago I rendered him a great service, and he granted me two boons. I claimed them now: and he promised. I asked for these boons: that Bharata should be crowned, and that you should go away to Daṇḍaka forest now. If you wish to establish that both you and your father are devoted to truth, let Bharata be crowned with the same paraphernalia that have been got ready for you, and go away to the forest for fourteen years. Do this, O best of men, for that is the word of your father; and thus would you redeem the king."

AYODHYĀ 19–20

Promptly and without the least sign of the slightest displeasure, Rāma said: "So be it! I shall immediately proceed to the forest, to dwell there clad in bark and animal skin.[6] But why does not the king speak to me, nor feel happy in my presence? Please do not misunderstand me; I shall go, and I myself will gladly give away to my brother Bharata the kingdom, wealth, Sītā and even my own life, and it is easier when all this is done in obedience to my father's command. Let

---

5. Rāma is an equanimous hero, one who is not affected by praise or blame.
6. Hermits and ascetics who lived in forests had to wear tree bark and animal skins. Queen Kaikeyī's demands included requiring Rāma to live the austere life of a hermit.

Bharata be immediately requested to come. But it breaks my heart to see that father does not say a word to me directly."

Kaikeyī said sternly: "I shall attend to all that, and send for Bharata. I think, however, that you should not delay your departure from Ayodhyā even for a moment. Even the consideration that the father does not say so himself, should not stop you. Till you leave this city, he will neither bathe nor eat." Hearing this, the king groaned, and wailed aloud: "Alas, alas!" and became unconscious again. Rāma decided to leave at once and he said to Kaikeyī: "I am not fond of wealth and pleasure: but even as the sages are, I am devoted to truth. Even if father had not commanded me, and you had asked me to go to the forest I would have done so! I shall presently let my mother and also Sītā know of the position and immediately leave for the forest."

Rāma was not affected at all by this sudden turn of events. As he emerged from the palace, with Lakṣmaṇa, the people tried to hold the royal umbrella over him: but he brushed them aside. Still talking pleasantly and sweetly with the people, he entered his mother's apartment. Delighted to see him, Kausalyā began to glorify and bless him and asked him to sit on a royal seat. Rāma did not, but calmly said to her: "Mother, the king has decided to crown Bharata as the yuvarāja[7] and I am to go to the forest and live there as a hermit for fourteen years." When she heard this, the queen fell down unconscious and grief-stricken. In a voice choked with grief, she said: "If I had been barren, I would have been unhappy; but I would not have had to endure this terrible agony. I have not known a happy day throughout my life. I have had to endure the taunts and the insults of the other wives of the king. Nay, even he did not treat me with kindness or consideration: I have always been treated with less affection and respect than Kaikeyī's servants were treated. I thought that after your birth, and after your coronation my luck would change. My hopes have been shattered. Even death seems to spurn me. Surely, my heart is hard as it does not break into pieces at this moment of the greatest misfortune and sorrow. Life is not worth living without you; so if you have to go to the forest, I shall follow you."

AYODHYĀ 21

Lakṣmaṇa said: "I think Rāma should not go to the forest. The king has lost his mind, overpowered as he is by senility and lust. Rāma is innocent. And, no righteous man in his senses would forsake his innocent son. A prince with the least knowledge of statesmanship should ignore the childish command of a king who has lost his senses." Turning to Rāma, he said: "Rāma, here I stand, devoted to you, dedicated to your cause. I am ready to kill anyone who would interfere with your coronation—even if it is the king! Let the coronation proceed without delay."

Kausalyā said: "You have heard Lakṣmaṇa's view. You cannot go to the forest because Kaikeyī wants you to. If, as you say, you are devoted to dharma, then it is your duty to stay here and serve me, your mother. I, as your mother, am as much worthy of your devotion and service as your father is: and I do not give you permission to go to the forest. If you disobey me in this, terrible will be

7. Crown prince.

your suffering in hell. I cannot live here without you. If you leave, I shall fast unto death."

Rāma, devoted as he was to dharma, spoke: "Among our ancestors were renowned kings who earned fame and heaven by doing their father's bidding. Mother, I am but following their noble example." To Lakṣmaṇa he said: "Lakṣmaṇa, I know your devotion to me, love for me, your prowess and your strength. The universe rests on truth: and I am devoted to truth. Mother has not understood my view of truth, and hence suffers. But I am unable to give up my resolve. Abandon your resolve based on the principle of might; resort to dharma;[8] let not your intellect become aggressive. Dharma, prosperity and pleasure are the pursuit of mankind here;[9] and prosperity and pleasure surely follow dharma: even as pleasure and the birth of a son follow a dutiful wife's service of her husband. One should turn away from that action or mode of life which does not ensure the attainment of all the three goals of life, particularly of dharma; for hate springs from wealth and the pursuit of pleasure is not praiseworthy. The commands of the guru, the king, and one's aged father, whether uttered in anger, cheerfully, or out of lust, should be obeyed by one who is not of despicable behavior, with a view to the promotion of dharma. Hence, I cannot swerve from the path of dharma which demands that I should implicitly obey our father. It is not right for you, mother, to abandon father and follow me to the forest, as if you are a widow. Therefore, bless me, mother, so that I may have a pleasant and successful term in the forest."

AYODHYĀ 22—23

Rāma addressed Lakṣmaṇa again: "Let there be no delay, Lakṣmaṇa. Get rid of these articles assembled for the coronation. And with equal expedition make preparations for my leaving the kingdom immediately. Only thus can we ensure that mother Kaikeyī attains peace of mind. Otherwise she might be worried that her wishes may not be fulfilled! Let father's promise be fulfilled. Yet, so long as the two objects of Kaikeyī's desire are not obtained, there is bound to be confusion in everyone's mind. I must immediately leave for the forest; then Kaikeyī will get Bharata here and have him installed on the throne. This is obviously the divine will and I must honor it without delay. My banishment from the kingdom as well as my return are all the fruits of my own doing (kṛtānta: end of action). Otherwise, how could such an unworthy thought enter the heart of noble Kaikeyī? I have never made any distinction between her and my mother; nor has she ever shown the least disaffection for me so far. The 'end' (reaction) of one's own action cannot be foreseen: and this which we call 'daiva' (providence or divine will) cannot be known and cannot be avoided by anyone. Pleasure, pain, fear, anger, gain, loss, life and death—all these are brought about by 'daiva.' Even sages and great ascetics are prompted by the divine will to give up their self-control and are subjected to lust and anger. It is

8. The religious and moral law, code of righteousness.
9. The phrase "dharma, prosperity and pleasure" refers to the first three goals of life for

Hindu householders: "religious acts, wealth and public life, and sexual love and family life."

unforeseen and inviolable. Hence, let there be no hostility towards Kaikeyī; she is not to blame. All this is not her doing, but the will of the divine."

Lakṣmaṇa listened to all this with mixed feelings: anger at the turn events had taken, and admiration for Rāma's attitude. Yet, he could not reconcile himself to the situation as Rāma had done. In great fury, he burst forth: "Your sense of duty is misdirected, O Rāma. Even so is your estimation of the divine will. How is it, Rāma, that being a shrewd statesman, you do not see that there are self-righteous people who merely pretend to be good for achieving their selfish and fraudulent ends? If all these boons and promises be true, they could have been asked for and given long ago! Why did they have to wait for the eve of coronation to enact this farce? You ignore this aspect and bring in your argument of the divine will! Only cowards and weak people believe in an unseen divine will: heroes and those who are endowed with a strong mind do not believe in the divine will. Ah, people will see today how my determination and strong action set aside any decrees of the divine will which may be involved in this unrighteous plot. Whoever planned your exile will go into exile! And you will be crowned today. These arms, Rāma, are not handsome limbs, nor are these weapons worn by me ornaments: they are for your service."

AYODHYĀ 24–25

Kausalyā said again: "How can Rāma born of me and the mighty emperor Daśaratha live on food obtained by picking up grains and vegetables and fruits that have been discarded? He whose servants eat dainties and delicacies—how will he subsist on roots and fruits? Without you, Rāma, the fire of separation from you will soon burn me to death. Nay, take me with you, too, if you must go."

Rāma replied: "Mother, that would be extreme cruelty towards father. So long as father lives, please serve him: this is the eternal religion. To a woman her husband is verily god himself. I have no doubt that the noble Bharata will be very kind to you and serve you as I serve you. I am anxious that when I am gone, you should console the king so that he does not feel my separation at all. Even a pious woman who is otherwise righteous, if she does not serve her husband, is deemed to be sinner. On the other hand, she who serves her husband attains blessedness even if she does not worship the gods, perform the rituals or honor the holy men."

Seeing that Rāma was inflexible in his resolve, Kausalyā regained her composure and blessed him. "I shall eagerly await your return to Ayodhyā, after your fourteen years in the forest," said Kausalyā.

Quickly gathering the articles necessary, she performed a sacred rite to propitiate the deities and thus to ensure the health, safety, happy sojourn and quick return of Rāma. "May dharma which you have protected so zealously protect you always," said Kausalyā to Rāma. "May those to whom you bow along the roads and the shrines protect you! Even so, let the missiles which the sage Viśvāmitra[1] gave you ensure your safety. May all the birds and beasts of

---

1. "Missiles" (astra) are magical weapons bestowed on worthy heroes by gods and sages. The sage Viśvāmitra had presented the young Rāma and Lakṣmaṇa with such missiles when they protected his sacrificial rites in the forest from attacks by demons (book 1, Bāla).

the forest, celestial beings and gods, the mountains and the oceans, and the deities presiding over the lunar mansions, natural phenomena and the seasons be propitious to you. May the same blessedness be with you that Indra enjoyed on the destruction of his enemy Vṛtra, that Vinatā bestowed upon her son Garuḍa, that Aditi pronounced upon her son Indra when he was fighting the demons, and that Viṣṇu enjoyed while he measured the heaven and earth.[2] May the sages, the oceans, the continents, the Vedas and the heavens be propitious to you."[3]

As Rāma bent low to touch her feet, Kausalyā fondly embraced him and kissed his forehead, and then respectfully went round him before giving him leave to go.

AYODHYĀ 26–27

Taking leave of his mother, Rāma sought the presence of his beloved wife, Sītā. For her part, Sītā who had observed all the injunctions and prohibitions connected with the eve of the coronation and was getting ready to witness the auspicious event itself, perceived her divine spouse enter the palace and with a heart swelling with joy and pride, went forward to receive him. His demeanor, however, puzzled her: his countenance reflected sorrow and anxiety. Shrewd as she was she realized that something was amiss, and hence asked Rāma: "The auspicious hour is at hand; and yet what do I see! Lord, why are you not accompanied by the regalia, by men holding the ceremonial umbrella, by the royal elephant and the horses, by priests chanting the Vedas, by bards singing your glories? How is it that your countenance is shadowed by sorrow?"

Without losing time and without mincing words, Rāma announced: "Sītā, the king has decided to install Bharata on the throne and to send me to the forest for fourteen years. I am actually on my way to the forest and have come to say good-bye to you. Now that Bharata is the yuvarāja, nay king, please behave appropriately towards him. Remember: people who are in power do not put up with those who sing others' glories in their presence: hence do not glorify me in the presence of Bharata. It is better not to sing my praises even in the presence of your companions. Be devoted to your religious observances and serve my father, my three mothers and my brothers. Bharata and Śatrughna should be treated as your own brothers or sons. Take great care to see that you do not give the least offense to Bharata, the king. Kings reject even their own sons if they are hostile, and are favorable to even strangers who may be friendly. This is my counsel."

Sītā feigned anger, though in fact she was amused. She replied to Rāma: "Your advice that I should stay here in the palace while you go to live in the forest is unworthy of a heroic prince like you, Lord. Whereas one's father,

2. The narrative of the heroic god Indra's victory over the dragonlike demon Vṛtra is an important myth in the *Ṛg-veda*, the oldest of the Hindu scriptures. Aditi is the mother of the gods. The eagle Garuḍa is the mount of Viṣṇu, the god of preservation. In the fifth of his ten incarnations, Viṣṇu took the form of a dwarf (Vāmana), who subsequently grew into the gigantic figure Trivikrama ("the god of three strides"), spanned earth and sky with two strides, then crushed the demon Bali with his third step.

3. The four Vedas are the ancient scriptures of the Hindus. The oceans, continents, and heavens of the Hindu universe are held to have sacred powers.

mother, brother, son and daughter-in-law enjoy their own good or misfortune, the wife alone shares the life of her husband. To a woman, neither father nor son nor mother nor friends but the husband alone is her sole refuge here in this world and in the other world, too. Hence I shall accompany you to the forest. I shall go ahead of you, clearing a path for you in the forest. Life with the husband is incomparably superior to life in a palace, or an aerial mansion, or a trip to heaven! I have had detailed instructions from my parents on how to conduct myself in Ayodhyā! But I shall not stay here. I assure you, I shall not be a burden, an impediment, to you in the forest. Nor will I regard life in the forest as exile or as suffering. With you it will be more than heaven to me. It will not be the least hardship to me; without you, even heaven is hell."

AYODHYĀ 28–29

Thinking of the great hardships they would have to endure in the forest, however, Rāma tried to dissuade Sītā in the following words: "Sītā, you come of a very wealthy family dedicated to righteousness. It is therefore proper that you should stay behind and serve my people here. Thus, by avoiding the hardships of the forest and by lovingly serving my people here, would you gladden my heart. The forest is not a place for a princess like you. It is full of great dangers. Lions dwell in the caves; and it is frightening to hear their roar. These wild beasts are not used to seeing human beings; the way they attack human beings is horrifying even to think about. Even the paths are thorny and it is hard to walk on them. The food is a few fruits which might have fallen on their own accord from the trees: living on them, one has to be contented all day. Our garments will be bark and animal skins: and the hair will have to be matted and gathered on the top of the head. Anger and greed have to be given up, the mind must be directed towards austerity and one should overcome fear even where it is natural. Totally exposed to the inclemencies of nature, surrounded by wild animals, serpents and so on, the forest is full of untold hardships. It is not a place for you, my dear."

This reiteration on the part of Rāma moved Sītā to tears. "Your gracious solicitude for my happiness only makes my love for you more ardent, and my determination to follow you more firm. You mentioned animals: they will never come anywhere near me while you are there. You mentioned the righteousness of serving your people: but, your father's command that you should go to the forest demands I should go, too; I am your half: and because of this, again I cannot live without you. In fact you have often declared that a righteous wife will not be able to live separated from her husband. And listen! This is not new to me: for even when I was in my father's house, long before we were married, wise astrologers had rightly predicted that I would live in a forest for some time. If you remember, I have been longing to spend some time in the forest, for I have trained myself for that eventuality. Lord, I feel actually delighted at the very thought that I shall at last go to the forest, to serve you constantly. Serving you, I shall not incur the sin of leaving your parents: thus have I heard from those who are well-versed in the Vedas and other scriptures, that a devoted wife remains united with her husband even after they leave this earth-plane. There is therefore no valid reason why you should wish to leave me here and go. If you still refuse to take me with you, I have no alternative but to lay down my life."

AYODHYĀ 30–31

To the further persuasive talk of Rāma, Sītā responded with a show of annoyance, courage and firmness. She even taunted Rāma in the following words: "While choosing you as his son-in-law, did my father Janaka realize that you were a woman at heart with a male body? Why, then, are you, full of valor and courage, afraid even on my account? If you do not take me with you I shall surely die; but instead of waiting for such an event, I prefer to die in your presence. If you do not change your mind now, I shall take poison and die." In sheer anguish, the pitch of her voice rose higher and higher, and her eyes released a torrent of hot tears.

Rāma folded her in his arms and spoke to her lovingly, with great delight: "Sītā, I could not fathom your mind and therefore I tried to dissuade you from coming with me. Come, follow me. Of course I cannot drop the idea of going to the forest, even for your sake. I cannot live having disregarded the command of my parents. Indeed, I wonder how one could adore the unmanifest god, if one were unwilling to obey the commands of his parents and his guru whom he can see here. No religious activity nor even moral excellence can equal service of one's parents in bestowing supreme felicity on one. Whatever one desires, and whatever region one desires to ascend to after leaving this earth-plane, all this is secured by the service of parents. Hence I shall do as commanded by father; and this is the eternal dharma. And you have rightly resolved, to follow me to the forest. Come, and get ready soon. Give away generous gifts to the brāhmaṇas and distribute the rest of your possessions to the servants and others."

Lakṣmaṇa now spoke to Rāma: "If you are determined to go, then I shall go ahead of you." Rāma, however, tried to dissuade him: "Indeed, I know that you are my precious and best companion. Yet, I am anxious that you should stay behind and look after our mothers. Kaikeyī may not treat them well. By thus serving our mothers, you will prove your devotion to me." But Lakṣmaṇa replied quickly: "I am confident, Rāma, that Bharata will look after all the mothers, inspired by your spirit of renunciation and your adherence to dharma. If this does not prove to be the case, I can exterminate all of them in no time. Indeed, Kausalyā is great and powerful enough to look after herself: she gave birth to you! My place is near you; my duty to serve you."

Delighted to hear this, Rāma said: "Then let us all go. Before leaving I wish to give away in charity all that I possess to the holy brāhmaṇas. Please get them all together. Take leave of your friends and get our weapons ready, too."

* * *

From Book 3

Āraṇya

ĀRAṆYA 14–15

Rāma, Lakṣmaṇa and Sītā were proceeding towards Pañcavaṭī.[4] On the way they saw a huge vulture. Rāma's first thought was that it was a demon in disguise. The vulture said: "I am your father's friend!" Trusting the vulture's words, Rāma asked for details of its birth and ancestry.

The vulture said: "You know that Dakṣa Prajāpati[5] had sixty daughters and the sage Kaśyapa married eight of them. One day Kaśyapa said to his wives: 'You will give birth to offspring who will be foremost in the three worlds.' Aditi, Diti, Danu and Kālaka listened attentively; the others were indifferent. As a result, the former four gave birth to powerful offspring who were superhuman. Aditi gave birth to thirty-three gods. Diti gave birth to demons. Danu gave birth to Aśvagrīva. And, Kālaka had Naraka and Kālikā. Of the others, men were born of Manu, and the sub-human species from the other wives of Kaśyapa. Tāmra's daughter was Sukī whose granddaughter was Vinatā who had two sons, Garuḍa and Aruṇa. My brother Sampāti and I are the sons of Aruṇa. I offer my services to you, O Rāma. If you will be pleased to accept them, I shall guard Sītā when you and Lakṣmaṇa may be away from your hermitage. As you have seen, this formidable forest is full of wild animals and demons, too."

Rāma accepted this new friendship. All of them now proceeded towards Pañcavaṭī in search of a suitable place for building a hermitage. Having arrived at Pañcavaṭī, identified by Rāma by the description which the sage Agastya had given, Rāma said to Lakṣmaṇa: "Pray, select a suitable place here for building the hermitage. It should have a charming forest, good water, firewood, flowers and holy grass." Lakṣmaṇa submitted: "Even if we live together for a hundred years, I shall continue to be your servant. Hence, Lord, you select the place and I shall do the needful." Rejoicing at Lakṣmaṇa's attitude, Rāma pointed to a suitable place, which satisfied all the requisites of a hermitage. Rāma said: "This is holy ground; this is charming; it is frequented by beasts and birds. We shall dwell here." Immediately Lakṣmaṇa set about building a hermitage for all of them to live in.

Rāma warmly embraced Lakṣmaṇa and said: "I am delighted by your good work and devoted service: and I embrace you in token of such admiration. Brother, you divine the wish of my heart, you are full of gratitude, you know dharma; with such a man as his son, father is not dead but is eternally alive."

Entering that hermitage, Rāma, Lakṣmaṇa and Sītā dwelt in it with great joy and happiness.

ĀRAṆYA 16

Time rolled on. One day Lakṣmaṇa sought the presence of Rāma early in the morning and described what he had seen outside the hermitage. He said: "Winter, the season which you love most, has arrived, O Rāma. There is dry

---

4. "Five banyan trees," a grove in western India, toward which Rāma has been directed by the sage Agastya.

5. A progenitor god in ancient Hindu mythology.

cold everywhere; the earth is covered with foodgrains. Water is uninviting; and fire is pleasant. The first fruits of the harvest have been brought in; and the agriculturists have duly offered some of it to the gods and the manes, and thus reaffirmed their indebtedness to them. The farmer who thus offers the first fruits to gods and manes is freed from sin.

"The sun moves in the southern hemisphere; and the north looks lusterless. Himālaya, the abode of snow, looks even more so! It is pleasant to take a walk even at noon. The shade of a tree which we loved in summer is unpleasant now. Early in the morning the earth, with its rich wheat and barley fields, is enveloped by mist. Even so, the rice crop. The sun, even when it rises, looks soft and cool like the moon. Even the elephants which approach the water, touch it with their trunk but pull the trunk quickly away on account of the coldness of the water.

"Rāma, my mind naturally thinks of our beloved brother Bharata. Even in this cold winter, he who could command the luxury of a king, prefers to sleep on the floor and live an ascetic life. Surely, he, too, would have got up early in the morning and has perhaps had a cold bath in the river Sarayū. What a noble man! I can even now picture him in front of me: with eyes like the petals of a lotus, dark brown in color, slim and without an abdomen, as it were. He knows what dharma is. He speaks the truth. He is modest and self-controlled, always speaks pleasantly, is sweet-natured, with long arms and with all his enemies fully subdued.[6] That noble Bharata has given up all his pleasures and is devoted to you. He has already won his place in heaven, Rāma. Though he lives in the city; yet, he has adopted the ascetic mode of life and follows you in spirit.

"We have heard it said that a son takes after his mother in nature: but in the case of Bharata this has proved false. I wonder how Kaikeyī, in spite of having our father as her husband, and Bharata as her son, has turned out to be so cruel."

When Lakṣmaṇa said this, Rāma stopped him, saying: "Do not speak ill of our mother Kaikeyī, Lakṣmaṇa. Talk only of our beloved Bharata. Even though I try not to think of Ayodhyā and our people there, when I think of Bharata, I wish to see him."

ĀRAṆYA 17–18

After their bath and morning prayers, Rāma, Lakṣmaṇa and Sītā returned to their hermitage. As they were seated in their hut, there arrived upon the scene a dreadful demoness. She looked at Rāma and immediately fell in love with him! He had a handsome face; she had an ugly face. He had a slender waist; she had a huge abdomen. He had lovely large eyes; she had hideous eyes. He had lovely soft hair; she had red hair. He had a lovable form; she had a terrible form. He had a sweet voice; hers resembled the barking of a dog. He was young; she was haughty. He was able; her speech was crooked. He was of noble conduct; she was of evil conduct. He was beloved; she had a forbidding appearance. Such a demoness spoke to Rāma: "Who are you, young men; and what are both of you doing in this forest, with this lady?"

6. A list of the conventional attributes of a handsome, brave, and virtuous warrior.

Rāma told her the whole truth about himself, Lakṣmaṇa and Sītā, about his banishment from the kingdom, etc. Then Rāma asked her: "O charming lady,[7] now tell me who you are." At once the demoness replied: "Ah, Rāma! I shall tell you all about myself immediately. I am Śūrpaṇakhā, the sister of Rāvaṇa. I am sure you have heard of him. He has two other brothers, Kumbhakarṇa and Vibhīṣaṇa.[8] Two other brothers Khara and Dūṣaṇa live in the neighborhood here. The moment I saw you, I fell in love with you. What have you to do with this ugly, emaciated Sītā? Marry me. Both of us shall roam about this forest. Do not worry about Sītā or Lakṣmaṇa: I shall swallow them in a moment." But, Rāma smilingly said to her: "You see I have my wife with me here. Why do you not propose to my brother Lakṣmaṇa who has no wife here?" Śūrpaṇakhā did not mind that suggestion. She turned to Lakṣmaṇa and said: "It is all right. You please marry me and we shall roam about happily." She was tormented by passion.

Lakṣmaṇa said in a teasing mood: "O lady, you see that I am only the slave of Rāma and Sītā. Why do you choose to be the wife of a slave? You will only become a servant-maid. Persuade Rāma to send away that ugly wife of his and marry you." Śūpaṇakhā turned to Rāma again. She said: "Unable to give up this wife of yours, Sītā, you turn down my offer. See, I shall at once swallow her. When she is gone you will marry me; and we shall roam about in this forest happily." So saying, she actually rushed towards Sītā. Rāma stopped her in time, and said to Lakṣmaṇa: "What are you doing, Lakṣmaṇa? It is not right to jest with cruel and unworthy people. Look at the plight of Sītā. She barely escaped with her life. Come, quickly deform this demoness and send her away."

Lakṣmaṇa drew his sword and quickly cut off the nose and the ears of Śūpaṇakhā. Weeping and bleeding she ran away. She went to her brother Khara and fell down in front of him.

* * *

Summary   Distraught and furious, Śūrpaṇakhā asks her brothers Khara and Dūṣaṇa, who live in nearby Janasthāna, to avenge her insult by killing Rāma and Lakṣmaṇa. However, Rāma and Lakṣmaṇa kill the brothers and all their troops.

ĀRAṆYA 32–33

Śūrpaṇakhā witnessed the wholesale destruction of the demons of Janasthāna,[9] including their supreme leader Khara. Stricken with terror, she ran to Laṅkā. There she saw her brother Rāvaṇa, the ruler of Laṅkā, seated with his ministers in a palace whose roof scraped the sky.[1] Rāvaṇa had twenty arms, ten heads, was broad-chested and endowed with all the physical qualifications of a monarch. He had previously fought with the gods, even with their chief Indra. He was well versed in the science of warfare and knew the use of the celestial missiles in battle. He had been hit by the gods, even by the discus[2] of lord Viṣṇu,

---

7. This formulaic phrase used in addressing a lady is meant ironically here.
8. The names of the demons are suggestive: Śūrpaṇakhā means "woman with nails as large as winnowing baskets" and Kumbhakarṇa

means "pot ear." Vibhīṣaṇa means "terrifying."
9. A region near Pañcavaṭī.
1. A conventional description of a palace or mansion.
2. A wheel with sharp points, Viṣṇu's weapon.

but he did not die. For, he had performed breathtaking austerities for a period of ten thousand years, and offered his own heads in worship to Brahmā the creator and earned from him the boon that he would not be killed by any superhuman or subhuman agency (except by man). Emboldened by this boon, the demon had tormented the gods and particularly the sages.

Śūrpaṇakhā entered Rāvaṇa's presence, clearly displaying the physical deformity which Lakṣmaṇa had caused to her. She shouted at Rāvaṇa in open assembly: "Brother, you have become so thoroughly infatuated and addicted to sense-pleasure that you are unfit to be a king any longer. The people lose all respect for the king who is only interested in his own pleasure and neglects his royal duties. People turn away from the king who has no spies, who has lost touch with the people and whom they cannot see, and who is unable to do what is good for them. It is the employment of spies that makes the king 'far-sighted' for through these spies he sees quite far. You have failed to appoint proper spies to collect intelligence for you. Therefore, you do not know that fourteen thousand of your people have been slaughtered by a human being. Even Khara and Dūṣaṇa have been killed by Rāma. And, Rāma has assured the ascetics of Janasthāna which is your territory, that the demons shall not do them any harm. They are now protected by him. Yet, here you are; reveling in little pleasures!

"O brother, even a piece of wood, a clod of earth or just dust, has some use; but when a king falls from his position he is utterly useless. But that monarch who is vigilant, who has knowledge of everything, through his spies, who is self-controlled, who is full of gratitude and whose conduct is righteous—he rules for a long time. Wake up and act before you lose your sovereignty."

This made Rāvaṇa reflect.

ĀRANYA 34–35

And, Rāvaṇa's anger was roused. He asked Śūrpaṇakhā: "Tell me, who is it that disfigured you thus? What do you think of Rāma? Why has he come to Daṇḍaka forest?"

Śūrpaṇakhā gave an exact and colorful description of the physical appearance of Rāma. She said: "Rāma is equal in charm to Cupid himself. At the same time, he is a formidable warrior. When he was fighting the demons of Janasthāna, I could not see what he was doing; I only saw the demons falling dead on the field. You can easily understand when I tell you that within an hour and a half he had killed fourteen thousand demons. He spared me, perhaps because he did not want to kill a woman. He has a brother called Lakṣmaṇa who is equally powerful. He is Rāma's right-hand man and alter ego; Rāma's own life-force moving outside his body. Oh, you must see Sītā, Rāma's wife. I have not seen even a celestial nymph who could match her in beauty. He who has her for his wife, whom she fondly embraces, he shall indeed be the ruler of gods. She is a fit bride for you; and you are indeed the most suitable suitor for her. In fact, I wanted to bring that beautiful Sītā here so that you could marry her: but Lakṣmaṇa intervened and cruelly mutilated my body. If you could only look at her for a moment, you would immediately fall in love with her. If this proposal appeals to you, take some action quickly and get her here."

Rāvaṇa was instantly tempted. Immediately he ordered his flying chariot to be got ready. This vehicle which was richly adorned with gold, could move freely wherever its owner willed. Its front part resembled mules with fiendish heads. Rāvaṇa took his seat in this vehicle and moved towards the seacoast. The coastline of Laṅkā was dotted with hermitages inhabited by sages and also celestial and semi-divine beings. It was also the pleasure resort of celestials and nymphs who went there to sport and to enjoy themselves. Driving at great speed through them, Rāvaṇa passed through caravan parks scattered with the chariots of the celestials. He also drove through dense forests of sandal trees, banana plantations and cocoanut palm groves. In those forests there were also spices and aromatic plants. Along the coast lay pearls and precious stones. He passed through cities which had an air of opulence.

Rāvaṇa crossed the ocean in his flying chariot and reached the hermitage where Mārīca[3] was living in ascetic garb, subsisting on a disciplined diet. Mārīca welcomed Rāvaṇa and questioned him about the purpose of his visit.

ĀRAṆYA 36–37

Rāvaṇa said to Mārīca: "Listen, Mārīca. You know that fourteen thousand demons, including my brother Khara and the great warrior Triśira, have been mercilessly killed by Rāma and Lakṣmaṇa who have now promised their protection to the ascetics of Daṇḍaka forest, thus flouting our authority. Driven out of his country by his angry father, obviously for a disgraceful action, this unrighteous and hard-hearted prince Rāma has killed the demons without any justification. And, they have even dared to disfigure my beloved sister Śūrpaṇakhā. I must immediately take some action to avenge the death of my brother and to restore our prestige and our authority. I need your help; kindly do not refuse this time.

"Disguising yourself as a golden deer of great beauty, roam near the hermitage of Rāma. Sītā would surely be attracted, and she would ask Rāma and Lakṣmaṇa to capture you. When they go after you, leaving Sītā alone in the hermitage, I shall easily abduct Sītā." Even as Rāvaṇa was unfolding this plot, Mārīca's mouth became dry and parched with fear. Trembling with fear, Mārīca said to Rāvaṇa:

"O king, one can easily get in this world a counselor who tells you what is pleasing to you; but hard it is to find a wise counselor who tells you the unpleasant truth which is good for you—and harder it is to find one who heeds such advice. Surely, your intelligence machine is faulty and therefore you have no idea of the prowess of Rāma. Else, you would not talk of abducting Sītā. I wonder: perhaps Sītā has come into this world to end your life, or perhaps there is to be great sorrow on account of Sītā, or perhaps maddened by lust, you are going to destroy yourself and the demons and Laṅkā itself. Oh, no, you were wrong in your estimation of Rāma. He is not wicked; he is righteousness incarnate. He is not cruel-hearted; he is generous to a fault. He has not been disgraced and exiled from the kingdom. He is here to honor the promise his father had given his mother Kaikeyī, after joyously renouncing his kingdom.

"O king, when you entertain ideas of abducting Sītā you are surely playing with fire. Please remember: when you stand facing Rāma, you are standing face to face with your own death. Sītā is the beloved wife of Rāma, who is

---

3. An uncle of Rāvaṇa, expert in sorcery.

extremely powerful. Nay, give up this foolish idea. What will you gain by thus gambling with your sovereignty over the demons, and with your life itself? Please consult the noble Vibhīṣaṇa and your virtuous ministers before embarking upon such unwise projects. They will surely advise you against them."

* * *

ĀRAṆYA 42

Rāvaṇa was determined, and Mārīca knew that there was no use arguing with him. Hence, after the last-minute attempt to avert the catastrophe, Mārīca said to Rāvaṇa: "What can I do when you are so wicked? I am ready to go to Rāma's āśrama.[4] God help you!" Not minding the taunt, Rāvaṇa expressed his unabashed delight at Mārīca's consent. He applauded Mārīca and said: "That is the spirit, my friend: you are now the same old Mārīca that I knew. I guess you had been possessed by some evil spirit a few minutes ago, on account of which you had begun to preach a different gospel. Let us swiftly get into this vehicle and proceed to our destination. As soon as you have accomplished the purpose, you are free to go and to do what you please!"

Both of them got into the flying chariot and quickly left the hermitage of Mārīca. Once again they passed forests, hills, rivers and cities: and soon they reached the neighborhood of the hermitage of Rāma. They got down from that chariot which had been embellished with gold. Holding Mārīca by the hand, Rāvaṇa said to him: "Over there is the hermitage of Rāma, surrounded by banana plantations. Well, now, get going with the work for which we have come here." Immediately Mārīca transformed himself into an attractive deer. It was extraordinary, totally unlike any deer that inhabited the forest. It was unique. It dazzled like a huge gem stone. Each part of its body had a different color. The colors had an unearthly brilliance and charm. Thus embellished by the colors of all the precious stones, the deer which was the demon Mārīca in disguise, roamed about near the hermitage of Rāma, nibbling at the grass now and then. At one time it came close to Sītā; then it ran away and joined the other deer grazing at a distance. It was very playful, jumping about and chasing its tail and spinning around. Sītā went out to gather flowers. She cast a glance at that extraordinary and unusual deer. As she did so, the deer too, sensing the accomplishment of the mission, came closer to her. Then it ran away, pretending to be afraid. Sītā marveled at the very appearance of this unusual deer the like of which she had not seen before and which had the hue of jewels.

ĀRAṆYA 43

From where she was gathering flowers, Sītā, filled with wonder to see that unusual deer, called out to Rāma: "Come quick and see, O Lord; come with your brother. Look at this extraordinary creature. I have never seen such a beautiful deer before." Rāma and Lakṣmaṇa looked at the deer, and Lakṣmaṇa's suspicions were aroused: "I am suspicious; I think it is the same demon Mārīca

4. Hermitage.

in disguise. I have heard that Mārīca could assume any form at will, and through such tricks he had brought death and destruction to many ascetics in this forest. Surely, this deer is not real: no one has heard of a deer with rainbow colors, each one of its limbs shining resplendent with the color of a different gem! That itself should enable us to understand that it is a demon, not an animal."

Sītā interrupted Lakṣmaṇa's talk, and said: "Never mind, one thing is certain; this deer has captivated my mind. It is such a dear. I have not seen such an animal near our hermitage! There are many types of deer which roam about near the hermitage; this is just an extraordinary and unusual deer. It is superlative in all respects: its color is lovely, its texture is lovely, and even its voice sounds delightful. It would be a wonderful feat if it could be caught alive. We could use it as a pet, to divert our minds. Later we could take it to Ayodhyā: and I am sure all your brothers and mothers would just adore it. If it is not possible to capture it alive, O Lord, then it can be killed, and I would love to have its skin. I know I am not behaving myself towards both of you: but I am helpless; I have lost my heart to that deer. I am terribly curious."

In fact, Rāma was curious, too! And so, he took Sītā's side and said to Lakṣmaṇa: "It is beautiful, Lakṣmaṇa. It is unusual. I have never seen a creature like this. And, princes do hunt animals and cherish their skins.[5] By sporting and hunting kings acquire great wealth! People say that that is real wealth which one pursues without premeditation. So, let us try to get the deer or its skin. If, as you say, it is a demon in disguise, then surely it ought to be killed by me, just as Vātāpi who was tormenting and destroying sages and ascetics was justly killed by the sage Agastya.[6] Vātāpi fooled the ascetics till he met the sage Agastya. This Mārīca, too, has fooled the ascetics so far: till coming to me today! The very beauty of his hide is his doom. And, you, Lakṣmaṇa, please guard Sītā with great vigilance, till I kill this deer with just one shot and bring the hide along with me."

ĀRANYA 44–45

Rāma took his weapons and went after the strange deer. As soon as the deer saw him pursuing it, it started to run away. Now it disappeared, now it appeared to be very near, now it ran fast, now it seemed confused—thus it led Rāma far away from his hermitage. Rāma was fatigued, and needed to rest. As he was standing under a tree, intrigued by the actions of the mysterious deer, it came along with other deer and began to graze not far from him. When Rāma once again went for it, it ran away. Not wishing to go farther nor to waste more time, Rāma took his weapon and fitted the missile of Brahmā[7] to it and fired. This missile pierced the illusory deer-mask and into the very heart of the demon.

5. Hermits are required to take a vow of nonviolence, but Rāma, a warrior prince, is allowed to carry arms and to hunt.
6. The demon Vātāpi killed ascetics by tricking them. Disguising himself, he would invite innocent wayfarers to a meal. He would magically conceal himself in the food, thus entering his guests' bellies; he would then kill the men by splitting open their stomachs. The sage Agastya outwitted and killed Vātāpi by digesting his meal, and with it, the demon himself, before he could tear the sage's stomach open.
7. The creator god in the triad of Hindu great gods.

Mārīca uttered a loud cry, leapt high into the sky and then dropped dead onto the ground. As he fell, however, he remembered Rāvaṇa's instructions and assuming the voice of Rāma cried aloud: "Hey, Sītā; hey, Lakṣmaṇa."

Rāma saw the dreadful body of the demon. He knew now that Lakṣmaṇa was right. And, he was even more puzzled by the way in which the demon wailed aloud before dying. He was full of apprehension. He hastened towards the hermitage.

In the hermitage, both Sītā and Lakṣmaṇa heard the cry. Sītā believed it was Rāma's voice. She was panic-stricken. She said to Lakṣmaṇa: "Go, go quickly: your brother is in danger. And, I cannot live without him. My breath and my heart are both violently disturbed." Lakṣmaṇa remembered Rāma's admonition that he should stay with Sītā and not leave her alone. He said to her: "Pray, be not worried." Sītā grew suspicious and furious. She said to him: "Ah, I see the plot now! You have a wicked eye on me and so have been waiting for this to happen. What a terrible enemy of Rāma you are, pretending to be his brother!" Distressed to hear these words, Lakṣmaṇa replied: "No one in the three worlds can overpower Rāma, blessed lady! It was not his voice at all. These demons in the forest are capable of simulating the voice of anyone. Having killed that demon disguised as a deer, Rāma will soon be here. Fear not." His calmness even more annoyed Sītā, who literally flew into a rage. She said again: "Surely, you are the worst enemy that Rāma could have had. I know now that you have been following us, cleverly pretending to be Rāma's brother and friend. I know now that your real motive for doing so is either to get me or you are Bharata's accomplice. Ah, but you will not succeed. Presently, I shall give up my life. For I cannot live without Rāma." Cut to the quick by these terrible words, Lakṣmaṇa said: "You are worshipful to me: hence I cannot answer back. It is not surprising that women should behave in this manner: for they are easily led away from dharma; they are fickle and sharp-tongued. I cannot endure what you said just now. I shall go. The gods are witness to what took place here. May those gods protect you. But I doubt if when Rāma and I return, we shall find you." Bowing to her, Lakṣmaṇa left.

ĀRAṆYA 46

Rāvaṇa was looking for this golden opportunity. He disguised himself as an ascetic, clad in ocher robes, carrying a shell water-pot, a staff and an umbrella, and approached Sītā who was still standing outside the cottage eagerly looking for Rāma's return. His very presence in that forest was inauspicious: and even the trees and the waters of the rivers were frightened of him, as it were. In a holy disguise, Rāvaṇa stood before Sītā: a deep well covered with grass; a death-trap.

Gazing at the noble Sītā, who had now withdrawn into the cottage and whose eyes were raining tears, Rāvaṇa came near her, and though his heart was filled with lust, he was chanting Vedic hymns. He said to Sītā in a soft, tender and affectionate tone: "O young lady! Pray, tell me, are you the goddess of fortune or the goddess of modesty, or the consort of Cupid himself?" Then Rāvaṇa described her incomparable beauty in utterly immodest terms, unworthy of an anchorite whose form he had assumed. He continued: "O charming lady! You have robbed me of my heart. I have not seen such a beautiful lady, neither a divine or a semi-divine being. Your extraordinary form and your youthfulness, and your living in this forest, all these together agitate my mind. It is not right that you should live in this forest. You should stay in palaces. In the forest monkeys, lions, tigers and other wild animals live. The forest is the natural habitat of demons who roam freely. You are living alone in this dreadful forest: are you not afraid, O fair lady? Pray, tell me, why are you living in this forest?"

Rāvaṇa was in the disguise of a brāhmaṇa. Therefore, Sītā offered him the worship and the hospitality that it was her duty to offer a brāhmaṇa. She made him sit down; she gave him water to wash his feet and his hands. Then she placed food in front of him.

Whatever she did only aggravated his lust and his desire to abduct her and take her away to Laṅkā.

ĀRAṆYA 47–48

Sītā, then, proceeded to answer his enquiry concerning herself. He appeared to be a brāhmaṇa; and if his enquiry was not answered, he might get angry and curse her.[8] Sītā said: "I am a daughter of the noble king Janaka; Sītā is my name. I am the beloved consort of Rāma. After our marriage, Rāma and I lived in the palace of Ayodhyā for twelve years." She then truthfully narrated all that took place just prior to Rāma's exile to the forest. She continued: "And so, when Rāma was twenty-five and I was eighteen, we left the palace and sought the forest-life.[9] And so the three of us dwell in this forest. My husband, Rāma, will soon return to the hermitage gathering various animals and also wild fruits. Pray, tell me who you are, O brāhmaṇa, and what you are doing in this forest roaming all alone."

Rāvaṇa lost no time in revealing his true identity. He said: "I am not a brāhmaṇa, O Sītā: I am the lord of demons, Rāvaṇa. My very name strikes terror in the hearts of gods and men. The moment I saw you, I lost my heart to you; and I derive no pleasure from the company of my wives. Come with me, and be my queen, O Sītā. You will love Laṅkā. Laṅkā is my capital, it is surrounded by the ocean and it is situated on the top of a hill. There we shall live together, and you will enjoy your life, and never even once think of this wretched forest-life."

Sītā was furious to hear this. She said: "O demon-king! I have firmly resolved to follow Rāma who is equal to the god of gods, who is mighty and charming, and who is devoted to righteousness.[1] If you entertain a desire for me, his wife, it is like tying yourself with a big stone and trying to swim across the ocean: you are doomed. Where are you and where is he: there is no comparison. You are like a jackal; he the lion.[2] You are like base metal; he gold."

8. Priestly *brāhmaṇas* and sages have the power to curse people as well as to bestow boons.
9. Rāma must have been thirteen and Sītā six years old when they were married. The practice of "child marriage" continued in India until very recently.

1. A special epithet of Rāma. "God of gods": an epithet used for warriors, kings, and heroes. It is a reference to Indra, king of heaven and all the gods.
2. King of animals, the lion represents regal majesty and courage, while the jackal is the embodiment of cunning and deceit.

But Rāvaṇa would not give up his desire. He repeated: "Even the gods dare not stand before me, O Sītā! For fear of me even Kubera the god of wealth abandoned his chariot and ran away to Kailāsa. If the gods, headed by Indra, even sense I am angry, they flee. Even the forces of nature obey me. Laṅkā is enclosed by a strong wall; the houses are built of gold with gates of precious stones. Forget this Rāma, who lives like an ascetic, and come with me. He is not as strong as my little finger!" Sītā was terribly angered: "Surely you seek the destruction of all the demons, by behaving like this, O Rāvaṇa. It cannot be otherwise since they have such an unworthy king with no self-control. You may live after abducting Indra's wife, but not after abducting me, Rāma's wife."

ĀRAṆYA 49–50

Rāvaṇa made his body enormously big and said to Sītā: "You do not realize what a mighty person I am. I can step out into space, and lift up the earth with my arms; I can drink up the waters of the oceans; and I can kill death itself. I can shoot a missile and bring the sun down. Look at the size of my body." As he expanded his form, Sītā turned her face away from him. He resumed his original form with ten heads and twenty arms. Again he spoke to Sītā: "Would you not like to be renowned in the three worlds? Then marry me. And, I promise I shall do nothing to displease you. Give up all thoughts of that mortal and unsuccessful Rāma."

Rāvaṇa did not wait for an answer. Seizing Sītā by her hair and lifting her up with his arm, he left the hermitage. Instantly the golden chariot appeared in front of him. He ascended it, along with Sītā. Sītā cried aloud: "O Rāma." As she was being carried away, she wailed aloud: "O Lakṣmaṇa, who is ever devoted to the elder brother, do you not know that I am being carried away by Rāvaṇa?" To Rāvaṇa, she said: "O vile demon, surely you will reap the fruits of your evil action: but they do not manifest immediately." She said as if to herself: "Surely, Kaikeyī would be happy today." She said to the trees, to the river Godāvarī, to the deities dwelling in the forest, to the animals and birds: "Pray, tell Rāma that I have been carried away by the wicked Rāvaṇa." She saw Jaṭāyu and cried aloud: "O Jaṭāyu! See, Rāvaṇa is carrying me away."

Hearing that cry, Jaṭāyu woke up. Jaṭāyu introduced himself to Rāvaṇa: "O Rāvaṇa, I am the king of vultures, Jaṭāyu. Pray, desist from this action unworthy of a king. Rāma, too, is a king; and his consort is worthy of our protection. A wise man should not indulge in such action as would disgrace him in the eyes of others. And, another's wife is as worthy of protection as one's own. The cultured and the common people often copy the behavior of the king. If the king himself is guilty of unworthy behavior what becomes of the people? If you persist in your wickedness, even the prosperity you enjoy will leave you soon.

"Therefore, let Sītā go. One should not get hold of a greater load than one can carry; one should not eat what he cannot digest. Who will indulge in an action which is painful and which does not promote righteousness, fame or permanent glory? I am sixty thousand years old and you are young. I warn you. If you do not give up Sītā, you will not be able to carry her away while I am alive and able to restrain you! I shall dash you down along with that chariot."

ĀRAŅYA 51

Rāvaņa could not brook this insult: he turned towards Jaṭāyu in great anger. Jaṭāyu hit the chariot and Rāvaņa; Rāvaņa hit Jaṭāyu back with terrible ferocity. This aerial combat between Rāvaņa and Jaṭāyu looked like the collision of two mountains endowed with wings. Rāvaņa used all the conventional missiles, the Nālikas, the Nārācas and the Vikarņis. The powerful eagle shrugged them off. Jaṭāyu tore open the canopy of the chariot and inflicted wounds on Rāvaņa himself.

In great anger, Jaṭāyu grabbed Rāvaņa's weapon (a cannon) and broke it with his claws. Rāvaņa took up a more formidable weapon which literally sent a shower of missiles. Against these Jaṭāyu used his own wings as an effective shield. Pouncing upon this weapon, too, Jaṭāyu destroyed it with his claws. Jaṭāyu also tore open Rāvaņa's armor. Nay, Jaṭāyu even damaged the gold-plated propellers of Rāvaņa's flying chariot, which had the appearance of demons, and thus crippled the craft which would take its occupant wherever he desired and which emitted fire. With his powerful beak, Jaṭāyu broke the neck of Rāvaņa's pilot.

With the chariot thus rendered temporarily useless, Rāvaņa jumped out of it, still holding Sītā with his powerful arm. While Rāvaņa was still above the ground, Jaṭāyu again challenged him: "O wicked one, even now you are unwilling to turn away from evil. Surely, you have resolved to bring about the destruction of the entire race of demons. Unknowingly or wantonly, you are swallowing poison which would certainly kill you and your relations. Rāma and Lakṣmaņa will not tolerate this sinful act of yours: and you cannot stand before them on the battle-field. The manner in which you are doing this unworthy act is despicable: you are behaving like a thief not like a hero." Jaṭāyu swooped on Rāvaņa and violently tore at his body.

Then there ensued a hand-to-hand fight between the two. Rāvaņa hit Jaṭāyu with his fist; but Jaṭāyu tore Rāvaņa's arms away. However, new ones sprang up instantly. Rāvaņa hit Jaṭāyu and kicked him. After some time, Rāvaņa drew his sword and cut off the wings of Jaṭāyu. When the wings were thus cut, Jaṭāyu fell, dying. Looking at the fallen Jaṭāyu, Sītā ran towards him in great anguish, as she would to the side of a fallen relation. In inconsolable grief, Sītā began to wail aloud.

ĀRAŅYA 52–53

As Sītā was thus wailing near the body of Jaṭāyu, Rāvaņa came towards her. Looking at him with utter contempt, Sītā said: "I see dreadful omens, O Rāvaņa. Dreams as also the sight and the cries of birds and beasts are clear indicators of the shape of things to come.[3] But you do not notice them! Alas, here is Jaṭāyu, my father-in-law's friend who is dying on my account. O Rāma, O Lakṣmaņa, save me, protect me!"

Once again Rāvaņa grabbed her and got into the chariot which had been made airworthy again. The Creator, the gods and the celestials who witnessed

---

3. See the description of Trijaṭā's dream, below (p. 1173). Dreams and omens play a comparable role in the culture of the Greeks and Romans.

this, exclaimed: "Bravo, our purpose is surely accomplished."[4] Even the sages of the Daṇḍaka forest inwardly felt happy at the thought, "Now that Sītā has been touched by this wicked demon, the end of Rāvaṇa and all the demons is near." As she was carried away by Rāvaṇa, Sītā was wailing aloud: "O Rāma, O Lakṣmaṇa."

Placed on the lap of Rāvaṇa, Sītā was utterly miserable. Her countenance was full of sorrow and anguish. The petals of the flowers that dropped from her head fell and covered the body of Rāvaṇa for a while. She was of beautiful golden complexion; and he was of dark color. Her being seated on his lap looked like an elephant wearing a golden sash, or the moon shining in the midst of a dark cloud, or a streak of lightning seen in a dense dark cloud.

The chariot streaked through the sky as fast as a meteor would. On the earth below, trees shook as if to reassure Sītā: "Do not be afraid," the waterfalls looked as if mountains were shedding tears, and people said to one another, "Surely, dharma has come to an end, as Rāvaṇa is carrying Sītā away."

Once again Sītā rebuked Rāvaṇa: "You ought to feel ashamed of yourself, O Rāvaṇa. You boast of your prowess; but you are stealing me away! You have not won me in a duel, which would be considered heroic. Alas, for a long, long time to come, people will recount your ignominy, and this unworthy and unrighteous act of yours will be remembered by the people. You are taking me and flying at such speed: hence no one can do anything to stop you. If only you had the courage to stop for a few moments, you would find yourself dead. My lord Rāma and his brother Lakṣmaṇa will not spare you. Leave me alone, O demon! But, you are in no mood to listen to what is good for your own welfare. Even as, one who has reached death's door loves only harmful objects. Rāma will soon find out where I am and ere long you will be transported to the world of the dead."

Rāvaṇa flew along, though now and then he trembled in fear.

ĀRAŅYA 54–55

The chariot was flying over hills and forests and was approaching the ocean. At that time, Sītā beheld on the ground below, five strong vānaras[5] seated and watching the craft with curiosity. Quickly, Sītā took off the stole she had around her shoulders and, removing all her jewels and putting them in that stole, bundled them all up and threw the bundle into the midst of the vānaras, in the hope that should Rāma chance to come there they would give him a clue to her whereabouts.

Rāvaṇa did not notice this but flew on. And now the craft, which shot through space at great speed, was over the ocean; a little while after that, Rāvaṇa entered Laṅkā along with his captive Sītā. Entering his own apartments, Rāvaṇa placed Sītā in them, entrusting her care to some of his chief female attendants. He said to them: "Take great care of Sītā. Let no male approach these apartments without my express permission. And, take great care to let Sītā have whatever she wants and asks for. Any neglect on your part means instant death."

---

4. We are reminded here that Viṣṇu incarnated himself as Rāma at the request of the gods, who wished Rāvaṇa to be killed.
5. Some scholars have suggested that *vānaras*, usually translated as "monkeys" or "apes," refers to tribal people or apelike human beings. This translator has left the word untranslated.

Rāvaņa was returning to his own apartments: on the way he was still considering what more could be done to ensure the fulfilment of his ambition. He sent for eight of the most ferocious demons and instructed them thus: "Proceed at once to Janasthāna. It was ruled by my brother Khara; but it has now been devastated by Rāma. I am filled with rage to think that a mere human being could thus kill Khara, Dūṣaṇa and all their forces. Never mind: I shall put an end to Rāma soon. Keep an eye on him and keep me informed of his movements. You are free to bring about the destruction of Rāma." And, the demons immediately left.

Rāvaņa returned to where Sītā was and compelled her to inspect the apartments. The palace stood on pillars of ivory, gold, crystal and silver and was studded with diamonds. The floor, the walls, the stairways—everything was made of gold and diamonds. Then again he said to Sītā: "Here at this place there are over a thousand demons ever ready to do my bidding. Their services and the entire Laṅkā I place at your feet. My life I offer to you; you are to me more valuable than my life. You will have under your command even the many good women whom I have married. Be my wife. Laṅkā is surrounded by the ocean, eight hundred miles on all sides. It is unapproachable to anybody; least of all to Rāma. Forget the weakling Rāma. Do not worry about the scriptural definitions of righteousness: we shall also get married in accordance with demoniacal wedding procedure. Youth is fleeting. Let us get married soon and enjoy life."

ĀRAŅYA 56

Placing a blade of grass between Rāvaņa and herself,[6] Sītā said: "O demon! Rāma, the son of king Daśaratha, is my lord, the only one I adore. He and his brother Lakṣmaṇa will surely put an end to your life. If they had seen you lay your hands on me, they would have killed you on the spot, even as they laid Khara to eternal rest. It may be that you cannot be killed by demons and gods; but you cannot escape being killed at the hands of Rāma and Lakṣmaṇa. Rāvaņa, you are doomed, beyond doubt. You have already lost your life, your good fortune, your very soul and your senses, and on account of your evil deeds Laṅkā has attained widowhood.[7] Though you do not perceive this, death is knocking at your door, O Rāvaņa. O sinner, you cannot under any circumstances lay your hands on me. You may bind this body, or you may destroy it: it is after all insentient matter, and I do not consider it worth preserving, nor even life worth living—not in order to live a life which will earn disrepute for me."

Rāvaņa found himself helpless. Hence, he resorted to threat. He said: "I warn you, Sītā. I give you twelve months in which to make up your mind to accept me as your husband. If within that time you do not so decide, my cooks will cut you up easily for my breakfast." He had nothing more to say to her. He turned to the female attendants surrounding her and ordered them: "Take this Sītā away to the Aśoka grove. Keep her there. Use every method of persuasion that you know of to make her yield to my desire. Guard her vigilantly. Take her and break her will as you would tame a wild elephant."

6. The magical power of Sītā's virtue allows her to use even a blade of grass as an effective barrier between herself and her abductor.
7. The ancient Indian king was considered to be the husband of the land he ruled, and kingdoms were often personified as a goddess (e.g., Laṅkā, pp. 1163–64).

The demonesses thereupon took Sītā away and confined her to the Aśoka grove, over which they themselves mounted guard day and night. Sītā did not find any peace of mind there, and stricken with fear and grief, she constantly thought of Rāma and Lakṣmaṇa.

It is said that at the same time, the creator Brahmā felt perturbed at the plight of Sītā. He spoke to Indra, the chief of gods: "Sītā is in the Aśoka grove. Pining for her husband, she may kill herself. Hence, go reassure her, and give her the celestial food to sustain herself till Rāma arrives in Laṅkā." Indra, thereupon, appeared before Sītā. In order to assure her of his identity he showed that his feet did not touch the ground and his eyes did not wink.[8] He gave her the celestial food, saying: "Eat this, and you will never feel hunger or thirst, nor will fatigue overpower you." While Indra was thus talking to Sītā, the goddess of sleep (Nidrā) had overpowered the demonesses.

ĀRAṆYA 57–58

Mārīca, the demon who had disguised himself as a unique deer, had been slain. But Rāma was intrigued and puzzled by the way in which Mārīca died, after crying: "O Sītā, O Lakṣmaṇa." Rāma sensed a deep and vicious plot. Hence he made haste to return to his hermitage. At the same time, he saw many evil omens. This aggravated his anxiety. He thought: "If Lakṣmaṇa heard that voice, he might rush to my aid, leaving Sītā alone. The demons surely wish to harm Sītā; and this might well have been a plot to achieve that purpose."

As he was thus brooding and proceeding towards his hermitage, he saw Lakṣmaṇa coming towards him. The distressed Rāma met the distressed Lakṣmaṇa; the sorrowing Rāma saw the sorrowful Lakṣmaṇa. Rāma caught hold of Lakṣmaṇa's arm and asked him, in an urgent tone: "O Lakṣmaṇa, why have you left Sītā alone and come? My mind is full of anxiety and terrible apprehension. When I see all these evil omens around us, I fear that something terrible has happened to Sītā. Surely Sītā has been stolen, killed or abducted."

Lakṣmaṇa's silence and grief-stricken countenance added fuel to the fire of anxiety in Rāma's heart. He asked again: "Is all well with Sītā? Where is my Sītā, the life of my life, without whom I cannot live even for an hour? Oh, what has happened to her? Alas, Kaikeyī's desire has been fulfilled today. If I am deprived of Sītā, I shall surely die. What more could Kaikeyī wish for? If, when I enter my hermitage, I do not find Sītā alive, how shall I live? Tell me, Lakṣmaṇa; speak. Surely, when that demon cried: 'O Lakṣmaṇa' in my voice, you were afraid that something had happened to me. Surely, Sītā also heard that cry and in a state of terrible mental agony, sent you to me. It is a painful thing that thus Sītā has been left alone; the demons who were waiting for an opportunity to hit back have been given that opportunity. The demons were sore distressed by my killing of the demon Khara. I am sure that they have done some great harm to Sītā, in the absence of both of us. What can I do now? How can I face this terrible calamity?"

Still, Lakṣmaṇa could not utter a word concerning what had happened. Both of them arrived near their hermitage. Everything that they saw reminded them of Sītā.

8. Attributes of the immortals.

ĀRANYA 59–60

And, once again before actually reaching the hermitage, and full of apprehension on account of Sītā, Rāma said to Lakṣmaṇa: "Lakṣmaṇa, you should not have come away like this, leaving Sītā alone in the hermitage. I had entrusted her to your care." When Rāma said this again and again, Lakṣmaṇa replied: "I have not come to you, leaving Sītā alone, just because I heard the demon Mārīca cry: 'O Lakṣmaṇa, O Sītā' in your voice. I did so only upon being literally driven by Sītā to do so. When she heard the cry, she immediately felt distressed and asked me to go to your help. I tried to calm her saying: 'It is not Rāma's voice; it is unthinkable that Rāma, who is capable of protecting even the gods, would utter the words, 'save me.' She, however, misunderstood my attitude. She said something very harsh, something very strange, something which I hate even to repeat. She said: 'Either you are an agent of Bharata or you have unworthy intentions towards me and therefore you are happy that Rāma is in distress and do not rush to his help.' It is only then that I had to leave."

In his anxiety for Sītā, Rāma was unimpressed by this argument. He said to Lakṣmaṇa: "Swayed by an angry woman's words, you failed to carry out my words; I am not highly pleased with what you have done, O Lakṣmaṇa."

Rāma rushed into their hermitage. But he could find no trace of Sītā in it. Confused and distressed beyond measure, Rāma said to himself, as he continued to search for Sītā: "Where is Sītā? Alas, she could have been eaten by the demons. Or, taken away by someone. Or, she is hidden somewhere. Or, she has gone to the forest." The search was fruitless. His anguish broke its bounds. Not finding her, he was completely overcome by grief and he began to behave as if he were mad.[9]

Unable to restrain himself, he asked the trees and the birds and the animals of the forest; "Where is my beloved Sītā?" The eyes of the deer, the trunk of the elephant, the boughs of trees, the flowers—all these reminded Rāma of Sītā. "Surely, you know where my beloved Sītā is. Surely, you have a message from her. Won't you tell me? Won't you assuage the pain in my heart?" Thus Rāma wailed. He thought he saw Sītā at a distance and going up to 'her,' he said: "My beloved, do not run away. Why are you hiding yourself behind those trees? Will you not speak to me?" Then he said to himself: "Surely it was not Sītā. Ah, she has been eaten by the demons. Did I leave her alone in the hermitage only to be eaten by the demons?" Thus lamenting, Rāma roamed awhile and ran around awhile.

ĀRANYA 61–62

Again Rāma returned to the hermitage, and, seeing it empty, gave way to grief again. He asked Lakṣmaṇa: "Where has my beloved Sītā gone, O Lakṣmaṇa? Or, has she actually been carried away by someone?" Again, imagining that it

9. The description of the lover maddened by grief, searching for his beloved, is a theme in many literary traditions: examples include the Greek myth of Orpheus's search for Eurydice and the Persian story of Majnun ("the mad lover"), who wanders in the wilderness looking for Laila.

was all fun and a big joke which Sītā was playing, he said: "Enough of this fun, Sītā; come out. See, even the deer are stricken with grief because they do not see you." Turning to Lakṣmaṇa again, he said: "Lakṣmaṇa, I cannot live without my Sītā. I shall soon join my father in the other world. But, he may be annoyed with me and say: 'I told you to live in the forest for fourteen years; how have you come here before that period?' Ah Sītā, do not forsake me."

Lakṣmaṇa tried to console him: "Grieve not, O Rāma. Surely, you know that Sītā is fond of the forest and the caves on the mountainside. She must have gone to these caves. Let us look for her in the forest. That is the proper thing to do; not to grieve."

These brave words took Rāma's grief away. Filled with zeal and eagerness, Rāma along with Lakṣmaṇa, began to comb the forest. Rāma was distressed: "Lakṣmaṇa, this is strange; I do not find Sītā anywhere." But Lakṣmaṇa continued to console Rāma: "Fear not, brother; you will surely recover the noble Sītā soon."

But this time, these words were less meaningful to Rāma. He was overcome by grief, and he lamented: "Where shall we find Sītā, O Lakṣmaṇa, and when? We have looked for her everywhere in the forest and on the hills, but we do not find her." Lamenting thus, stricken with grief, with his intelligence and his heart robbed by the loss of Sītā, Rāma frequently sighed in anguish, muttering: "Ah my beloved."

Suddenly, he thought he saw her, hiding herself behind the banana trees, and now behind the karnikara trees. And, he said to 'her': "My beloved, I see you behind the banana trees! Ah, now I see you behind the karnikara tree: my dear, enough, enough of this play: for your fun aggravates my anguish. I know you are fond of such play; but pray, stop this and come to me now."

When Rāma realized that it was only his hallucination, he turned to Lakṣmaṇa once more and lamented: "I am certain now that some demon has killed my beloved Sītā. How can I return to Ayodhyā without Sītā? How can I face Janaka, her father? Oh, no: Lakṣmaṇa, even heaven is useless without Sītā; I shall continue to stay in the forest; you can return to Ayodhyā. And you can tell Bharata that he should continue to rule the country."

ĀRAŅYA 63–64

Rāma was inconsolable and even infected the brave Lakṣmaṇa. Shedding tears profusely, Rāma continued to speak to Lakṣmaṇa who had also fallen a prey to grief by this time: "No one in this whole world is guilty of as many misdeeds as I am, O Lakṣmaṇa: and that is why I am being visited by sorrow upon sorrow, grief upon grief, breaking my heart and dementing me. I lost my kingdom, and I was torn away from my relations and friends. I got reconciled to this misfortune. But then I lost my father. I was separated from my mother. Coming to this hermitage, I was getting reconciled to that misfortune. But I could not remain at peace with myself for long. Now this terrible misfortune, the worst of all, has visited me.

"Alas, how bitterly Sītā would have cried while she was carried away by some demon. May be she was injured; may be her lovely body was covered with blood. Why is it that when she was subjected to such suffering, my body did not split into pieces? I fear that the demon must have cut open Sītā's neck and drunk her blood. How terribly she must have suffered when she was dragged by the demons.

"Lakṣmaṇa, this river Godāvarī was her favorite resort. Do you remember how she used to come and sitting on this slab of stone talk to us and laugh? Probably she came to the river Godāvarī in order to gather lotuses? But, no: she would never go alone to these places.

"O sun! You know what people do and what people do not do. You know what is true and what is false. You are a witness to all these. Pray, tell me, where has my beloved Sītā gone. For, I have been robbed of everything by this grief. O wind! You know everything in this world, for you are everywhere. Pray, tell me, in which direction did Sītā go?"

Rāma said: "See, Lakṣmaṇa, if Sītā is somewhere near the river Godāvarī." Lakṣmaṇa came back and reported that he could not find her. Rāma himself went to the river and asked the river: "O Godāvarī, pray tell me, where has my beloved Sītā gone?" But the river did not reply. It was as if, afraid of the anger of Rāvaṇa, Godāvarī kept silent.

Rāma was disappointed. He asked the deer and the other animals of the forest: "Where is Sītā? Pray, tell me in which direction has Sītā been taken away." He then observed the deer and the animals; all of them turned southwards and some of them even moved southwards. Rāma then said to Lakṣmaṇa: "O Lakṣmaṇa, see, they are all indicating that Sītā has been taken in a southerly direction."

ĀRAṆYA 64

Lakṣmaṇa, too, saw the animals' behavior as sure signs indicating that Sītā had been borne away in a southerly direction, and suggested to Rāma that they should also proceed in that direction. As they were thus proceeding, they saw petals of flowers fallen on the ground. Rāma recognized them and said to Lakṣmaṇa: "Look here, Lakṣmaṇa, these are petals from the flowers that I had given to Sītā. Surely, in their eagerness to please me, the sun, the wind and the earth, have contrived to keep these flowers fresh."

They walked further on. Rāma saw footprints on the ground. Two of them he immediately recognized as those of Sītā. The other two were big—obviously the footprints of a demon. Bits and pieces of gold were strewn on the ground. Lo and behold, Rāma also saw blood which he concluded was Sītā's blood: he wailed again: "Alas, at this spot, the demon killed Sītā to eat her flesh." He also saw evidence of a fight: and he said: "Perhaps there were two demons fighting for the flesh of Sītā."

Rāma saw on the ground pieces of a broken weapon, an armor of gold, a broken canopy, and the propellers and other parts of a flying chariot. He also saw lying dead, one who had the appearance of the pilot of the craft. From these he concluded that two demons had fought for the flesh of Sītā, before one carried her away. He said to Lakṣmaṇa: "The demons have earned my unquenchable hate and wrath. I shall destroy all of them. Nay, I shall destroy all the powers that be who refuse to return Sītā to me. Look at the irony of fate, Lakṣmaṇa: we adhere to dharma, but dharma could not protect Sītā who has been abducted in this forest! When these powers that govern the universe witness Sītā being eaten by the demons, without doing anything to stop it, who is there to do what is pleasing to us? I think our meekness is misunderstood to be weakness. We are full of self-control, compassion and devoted to the welfare of all beings: and yet these virtues have become as good as vices in us now. I shall set aside all these virtues and the universe shall witness my supreme glory which will bring about the destruction of all creatures, including the demons. If Sītā is not immediately brought back to me, I shall destroy the three worlds—the gods, the demons and other creatures will perish, becoming targets of my most powerful missiles. When I take up my weapon in anger, O Lakṣmaṇa, no one can confront me, even as no one can evade old age and death."

ĀRAṆYA 65–66

Seeing the world-destroying mood of Rāma, Lakṣmaṇa endeavored to console him. He said to Rāma:

"Rāma, pray, do not go against your nature. Charm in the moon, brilliance in the sun, motion in the air, and endurance in the earth—these are their essential nature: in you all these are found and in addition, eternal glory. Your nature cannot desert you; even the sun, the moon and the earth cannot abandon their nature! Moreover, being king, you cannot punish all the created beings for the sin of one person. Gentle and peaceful monarchs match punishment to crime: and, over and above this, you are the refuge of all beings and their goal. I shall without fail find out the real criminal who has abducted Sītā; I shall find out whose armor and weapons these are. And you shall mete out just punishment to the sinner. Oh, no, no god will seek to displease you, O Rāma: Nor these trees, mountains and rivers. I am sure they will all eagerly aid us in our search for Sītā. Of course, if Sītā cannot be recovered through peaceful means, we shall consider other means.

"Whom does not misfortune visit in this world, O Rāma? And, misfortune departs from man as quickly as it visits him. Hence, pray, regain your composure. If you who are endowed with divine intelligence betray lack of endurance in the face of this misfortune, what will others do in similar circumstances?

"King Nahuṣa, who was as powerful as Indra, was beset with misfortune.[1] The sage Vasiṣṭha, our family preceptor, had a hundred sons and lost all of them on one day! Earth is tormented by volcanic eruptions, and earthquakes. The sun and the moon are afflicted by eclipses. Misfortune strikes the great ones and even the gods.

"For, in this world people perform actions whose results are not obvious; and these actions which may be good or evil, bear their own fruits. Of course, these fruits are evanescent. People who are endowed with enlightened intelligence know what is good and what is not good. People like you do not grieve over misfortunes and do not get deluded by them.

"Why am I telling you all this, O Rāma? Who in this world is wiser than you? However, since, as is natural, grief seems to veil wisdom, I am saying all this.

---

1. King Nahuṣa, an ancestor of Rāma, became so powerful that he claimed the throne of Indra, king of gods, but an arrogant act soon effected his fall from his exalted position.

All this I learnt only from you: I am only repeating what you yourself taught me earlier. Therefore, O Rāma, know your enemy and fight him."

ĀRAṆYA 67–68

Rāma then asked Lakṣmaṇa: "O Lakṣmaṇa, tell me, what should we do now?" Lakṣmaṇa replied: "Surely, we should search this forest for Sītā."

This advice appealed to Rāma. Immediately he fixed the bayonet to his weapon and with a look of anger on his face, set out to search for Sītā. Within a very short time and distance, both Rāma and Lakṣmaṇa chanced upon Jaṭāyu, seriously and mortally wounded and heavily bleeding. Seeing that enormous vulture lying on the ground, Rāma's first thought was: "Surely, this is the one that has swallowed Sītā." He rushed forward with fixed bayonet.

Looking at Rāma thus rushing towards him, and rightly inferring Rāma's mood, Jaṭāyu said in a feeble voice: "Sītā has been taken away by Rāvaṇa. I tried to intervene. I battled with the mighty Rāvaṇa. I broke his armor, his canopy, the propellers and some parts of his chariot. I killed his pilot. I even inflicted injuries on his person. But he cut off my wings and thus grounded me." When Rāma heard that the vulture had news of Sītā, he threw his weapon away and kneeling down near the vulture embraced it.

Rāma said to Lakṣmaṇa: "An additional calamity to endure, O Lakṣmaṇa. Is there really no end to my misfortune? My misfortune plagues even this noble creature, a friend of my father's." Rāma requested more information from Jaṭāyu concerning Sītā, and also concerning Rāvaṇa. Jaṭāyu replied: "Taking Sītā with him, the demon flew away in his craft, leaving a mysterious storm and cloud behind him. I was mortally wounded by him. Ah, my senses are growing dim. I feel life ebbing away, Rāma. Yet, I assure you, you will recover Sītā." Soon Jaṭāyu lay lifeless. Nay, it was his body, for he himself ascended to heaven. Grief-stricken afresh, Rāma said to Lakṣmaṇa: "Jaṭāyu lived a very long life; and yet has had to lay down his life today. Death, no one in this world can escape. And what a noble end! What a great service this noble vulture has rendered to me! Pious and noble souls are found even amongst subhuman creatures, O Lakṣmaṇa. Today I have forgotten all my previous misfortunes: I am extremely tormented by the loss of this dear friend who has sacrificed his life for my sake. I shall myself cremate it, so that it may reach the highest realms."

Rāma himself performed the funeral rites, reciting those Vedic mantras[2] which one recites during the cremation of one's own close relations. After this, Rāma and Lakṣmaṇa proceeded on their journey in search of Sītā.

* * *

Summary   The monkey hordes sent to search for Sītā in the southern direction by Sugrīva, king of the monkeys, are disheartened and take refuge in a cave near the southern ocean to discuss their course of action.

2. Sacred chants, usually from the scriptures.

From Book 4

Kiṣkindhā

KIṢKINDHĀ 56, 57, 58

The sound, the gust of wind and dust preceded the arrival near the cave of a huge vulture. The vānaras who were seated on a flat surface outside the cave saw the vulture perched on a big rock. The vulture was known as Sampāti and was the brother of Jaṭāyu. It said to itself: "Surely, unseen providence is in control of the whole world. By that benign providence it has been decreed that my food should thus arrive at my very door, as it were. As and when each one of these vānaras dies I shall eat the flesh." The vānaras, however, heard this and were greatly disturbed.

With a mind agitated by intense fear, Aṅgada[3] said to Hanumān: "Death has come to us, disguised as a vulture. But, then, did not the noble Jaṭāyu give up his life in the service of Rāma. Even so we shall die in his service. Jaṭāyu suffered martyrdom while actually trying to help Sītā; but we, unfortunately, have not been able to find where she is."

Sampāti heard this. His mind was now disturbed. He asked: "Who is there who mentioned the name of my dearly beloved brother Jaṭāyu? I have not heard from him or of him for a very long time. Hearing of his murder my whole being is shaken. How did it happen?"

Even after this, the vānaras were skeptical: however, they helped Sampāti get down from the rock. Aṅgada then related the whole story of Rāma, including his friendship with Sugrīva and the killing of Vāli. He concluded: "We were sent in search of Sītā. We cannot find her. And the time-limit set by Sugrīva has expired. Afraid to face him, we have decided to fast unto death, lying here."

Sampāti said: "Jaṭāyu was my brother. Both of us flew to the abode of Indra when the latter had killed the demon Vṛtra. Jaṭāyu was about to faint, while we were near the sun. And I shielded him. By the heat of the sun my wings were burnt and I fell down here.[4] Though wingless and powerless, I shall help you in my own way, O vānaras, for the sake of Rāma. Some time ago, I saw a beautiful lady being carried away by Rāvaṇa: she was crying: 'O Rāma, O Lakṣmaṇa.' He dwells in Laṅkā, an island eight hundred miles from here. There, I can actually see Rāvaṇa and also Sītā living in Laṅkā, on account of the strength of my vision. I can also see through intuition that you will find Sītā before returning to Kiṣkindhā. Now, take me to the seaside so that I can offer libations for the peace of my brother's soul." The vānaras gladly obliged Sampāti.

KIṢKINDHĀ 59–60

Jāmbavān who heard Sampāti mention that he had seen Sītā, approached Sampāti and asked: "Pray, tell me in detail where Sītā is and who has seen her?" Sampāti replied:

"Indeed, my son Supārśva had an even more direct encounter with Rāvaṇa and Sītā than I had. I shall narrate the story to you in detail. Please listen.

---

3. Son of Vāli, brother of Sugrīva, king of the monkeys.
4. This narrative is similar to the Greek myth of

Icarus. Endowed with wings made by his father, Daedalus, Icarus flew too close to the sun; his wings melted, and he plunged to his death.

"I told you that in a foolhardy attempt to fly to the sun, my wings got burnt. I fell down wingless on this mountain. Just as the celestials are excessively lustful, snakes possess terrible anger, deer are easily frightened, and we vultures are voracious eaters. How could I appease insatiable hunger when I had no wings? My son Supārśva volunteered to supply me with food regularly. One day, recently, he failed to appear at the usual time, and I was tormented by hunger. When I took him to task for that lapse, he narrated what had happened that day. He said: 'I was looking for some meat to bring to you for your meal. At that time I saw a big demon flying away with a lady in his arms. I stopped him wishing to bring both of them for your meal today. But he begged of me to let him go: who could deny such a request? So I let him go. Later, some of the sages in the region exclaimed: "By sheer luck has Sītā escaped alive today." After they had flown away, I went on looking in that direction for a considerable time, and I saw that lady dropping ornaments on the hills. I was delayed by all this, O father!' It was from my son Supārśva that I heard about the abduction of Sītā in the first place. I could not challenge and kill Rāvaṇa, because I had neither wings nor the strength for it. But I shall render service to Rāma in my own way.

"There lived on this mountain a great sage named Niśākara. On the day that Jaṭāyu and I flew towards the sun and on which my wings had been completely burnt, I fell down here. I remained unconscious for some time. Later I regained consciousness. With great difficulty I reached the hermitage of the sage, as I was eager to see him. After some time I saw him coming to the hermitage, surrounded by bears, deer, tigers, lions and snakes! When he entered the hermitage, they returned to the forest. He merely greeted me and went in. But soon he came back to where I was and said: 'Are you not Sampāti? Was not Jaṭāyu your brother? Both of you used to come here in human forms, to salute me. Ah, I recognize you. But tell me: who has burnt your wings and why have they been burnt?'"

KIṢKINDHĀ 61, 62, 63

Sampāti continued: "My physical condition and the loss of wings and vitality prevented me from giving a complete account of our misadventure. However, I said to the sage: 'Determined to pursue the sun, we flew towards it. We soared high into the sky. From there we looked at the earth: the cities looked like cartwheels! We heard strange noises in the space. The mountains on earth looked like pebbles; the rivers looked like strings which bound the earth! The Himālaya and the Vindhya[5] appeared to be elephants bathing in a pond. And our sense of sight was playing tricks with us. It looked as if the earth were on fire. We then concentrated on the sun to get our bearings right. It looked as big as the earth. Jaṭāyu decided to return. I followed him. I tried to shield him against the fierce rays of the sun; and my wings were burnt. Jaṭāyu fell in Janasthāna, I think. I am here on the Vindhya.[6] What shall I do now? I have lost everything. My heart seeks death which I shall meet by jumping off a peak.'

5. The Himalaya mountain range spans the northern and northeastern borders of the Indian subcontinent. The Vindhya Mountains are located in the northern part of central India.
6. The location of Sampāti's cave in the

"Vindhya" is problematic since soon after the monkeys meet the old vulture, they reach the shore of the southern ocean, across which Hanumān leaps to the island of Laṅkā.

"The sage, however, contemplated for a while and said: 'Do not despair. You will get back your wings, sight, life force and strength. A prediction have I heard: soon the earth will be ruled by king Daśaratha whose son Rāma will go to the forest in obedience to his father's will, and there Rāma will lose his wife Sītā in search of whom he will send vānaras. When you inform the vānaras where Sītā is kept in captivity, you will gain new wings. In fact, I can make your wings grow now: but it is better you get them after rendering a great service to Rāma.' Soon afterwards, the sage left this world.

"I have impatiently been waiting for you all, all these hundreds of years. I have often thought of committing suicide; but I have abandoned the idea every time, knowing that I have an important mission in life. I even scolded my son the other day for his having let Rāvaṇa get away with Sītā; but I myself could not pursue Rāvaṇa."

As Sampāti was speaking thus, new wings sprouted from his sides, even as the vānaras were looking on. The vānaras were delighted. Sampāti continued: "It is by the grace of the sage Niśākara that I have regained these wings, O vānaras. And, the sprouting of these wings is positive proof that you will be successful in finding Sītā."

Sampāti flew away, in an attempt to see if he could still fly! The vānaras had abandoned the idea of fasting unto death. They had regained their enthusiasm and their morale. They set out once again in search of Sītā.

KIŚKINDHĀ 64–65

Sampāti's words inspired confidence in the vānaras, but that enthusiasm lasted only till they actually faced the ocean itself. They reached the northern shore of the southern ocean, and stopped there. When they saw the extent of the ocean, their hearts sank. All of them wailed with one voice: "How can we get beyond this and search for Sītā?"

Aṅgada said to them: "Do not despair, O vānaras! He who yields to despondency is robbed of his strength and valor, and he does not reach his goal." Upon hearing this, all the vānaras surrounded Aṅgada, awaiting his plan. He continued: "Who can cross this ocean? Who will fulfill the wish of Sugrīva? Surely, it is by the grace of that vānara who is able to cross this ocean that we shall all be able to return home and behold our wives and children: it is by his grace that Rāma and Lakṣmaṇa can experience great joy." No one answered. Aṅgada said again: "Surely, you know that you have immeasurable strength. No one can obstruct your path. Come on, speak up. Let me hear how far each one of you can go."

One by one the mightiest amongst the vānaras answered: "I can go eighty miles." "I can go double that distance." "I can cover treble that distance." And so on till Jāmbavān's turn[7] came. He said: "In days of yore I had great strength and I could easily have gone across and returned. But on account of my great age I have grown weak. Once upon a time when lord Viṣṇu assumed the gigantic form (to measure the whole earth with one foot, and the sky with the other) I went round him. But now, alas, I am incapable of crossing this little ocean."

---

7. Jāmbavān is a ṛkṣa, a word usually translated as "bear."

Aṅgada himself declared: "I can surely cross this ocean and go to Laṅkā. But I am not sure if I can make the return journey. And, if I do not return, my going to Laṅkā would have been in vain." But Jambavān intervened and said: "Oh, no: you should not undertake this task. When an expedition is organized the commander himself should not participate in it. You are the very root of this whole expedition. And, the wise say that one should always protect the root; for so long as the root is preserved one can always expect to reap the harvest. You are our respected leader, and you should therefore not risk your own life in this venture."

Aṅgada said: "If no one else can cross the ocean and I should not, then we are all doomed to die here. What shall we do?" Jambavān, however, had other ideas: he said: "O prince, there is someone amongst us who can do this."

KIṢKINDHĀ 66–67

Jāmbavān said to Hanumān: "What about you, O mighty hero? Why don't you speak up? Your might is equal to that of Sugrīva, nay even to that of Rāma and Lakṣmaṇa; and yet you are quiet.

"I shall remind you of your birth and your ancestry. There once was a nymph called Puñjikasthalā. She was once cursed by a sage as a result of which she was reborn as Añjanā, the daughter of a vānara chief called Kuñjara. Añjanā married Kesari. This nymph who had the body of a human woman was once resting on the top of a hill. It is said that the wind-god, by whom her clothes had been blown up revealing her attractive legs, fell in love with her. Her body was, as it were, embraced by the wind-god. But she was furious and exclaimed: 'Who dares to violate my chastity?' The wind-god replied: 'Nay, I shall not violate you, O vānara lady! However, since as wind I have entered your body, you will bear a child who will vie with me in power.'

"Añjanā gave birth to you, O Hanumān! When you were a baby, you once saw the sun in the sky. You thought it was a fruit, and jumped up to pluck it from the sky. But, Indra struck you down with his thunderbolt and you fell down.[8] Your left chin was broken; and hence you came to be known as hanu-man. It is said that when you were thus injured, the wind-god was angered; there was no movement of wind in the world. The frightened gods propitiated the wind-god; and Brahmā the creator then gave you the boon of invincibility in battle. When Indra came to know that you did not die on being hit by the thunderbolt, he conferred a boon on you, that you will die only when you wish to.

"There is no one equal to you in strength or in the ability to cross this ocean, nay, an ocean far wider than this. All others are despondent; the mission surely depends upon you."

When his glory was thus sung and he was reminded of his own power, Hanumān grew in stature, as it were. Seeing him thus filled with enthusiasm, the other vānaras jumped for joy. Hanumān grew in size; and shook his tail in great delight. He said: "Of course I can cross this ocean! With the strength of my arms I can push this ocean away. Stirred by my legs, the ocean will overflow its bounds. I can break up mountains. I can leap into the sky and sail along. I am equal to the wind-god in strength and valor. No one is equal to me other

---

8. A thunderbolt-wielding king of the gods, Indra is the Indian counterpart of the Greek god Zeus.

than Garuḍa of divine origin. I can even lift up the island of Laṅkā and carry it away."

Greatly inspired by Hanumān's words, the vānaras exclaimed with one voice: "Bravo, O Hanumān. You have saved us all. We shall pray for the success of your mission, standing on one leg till you return." Hanumān ascended the mountain, ready to leap.

From Book 5

Sundara

Hanumān was preparing to jump across the ocean and to cross the ocean to go to Laṅkā. Before undertaking this momentous and vital adventure, he offered prayers to the sun-god, to Indra, to the wind-god, to the Creator and to the elements. He turned to the east and offered his salutations to the wind-god, his own divine parent. He turned his face now to the south, in order to proceed on his great mission.

As he stood there, with his whole being swelling with enthusiasm, fervor and determination, and as he pressed his foot on the mountain before taking off from there, the whole mountain shook. And the shock caused the trees to shed their flowers, birds and beasts to leave their sheltered abodes, subterranean water to gush forth, and even the pleasure-loving celestials and the peace-loving ascetics to leave the mountain resorts, to fly into the sky and watch Hanumān's adventure from there. Giving proof of their scientific skill and knowledge, these celestials and sages remained hovering over the hill, eager to witness Hanumān's departure to Laṅkā. They said to one another: "This mighty Hanumān who is the god-child of the wind-god himself, will swiftly cross this ocean; for he desires to cross the ocean in order to achieve the mission of Rāma and the mission of the vānaras."

Hanumān crouched on the mountain, ready to go. He tensed his body in an effort to muster all the energy that he had. He held his breath in his heart and thus charged himself with even more energy.

He said to the vānaras who surrounded him: "I shall proceed to Laṅkā with the speed of the missile discharged by Rāma. If I do not find Sītā there, I shall with the same speed go to the heaven to search for her. And, if I do not see her even there, I shall get hold of Rāvaṇa, bind him and bring him over to the presence of Rāma. I shall definitely return with success. If it is difficult to bind Rāvaṇa and bring him, I shall uproot Laṅkā itself and bring it to Rāma."

After thus reassuring the vānaras, Hanumān took to the sky. The big trees that stood on the mountain were violently drawn into the slip-stream. Some of these trees flew behind Hanumān; others fell into the ocean; and yet others shed their blossoms on the hill tops, where they lay as a colorful carpet, and on the surface of the ocean where they looked like stars in the blue sky.

SUNDARA I

The mighty Hanumān was on his way to Laṅkā. He flew in the southerly direction, with his arms outstretched. One moment it looked as if he would soon drink the ocean; at another as if he desired to drink the blue sky itself. He followed the course of wind, his eyes blazing like fire, like lightning.

Hanumān flying in the air with his tail coiled up behind looked like a meteor with its tail flying from north to the south. His shadow was cast on the surface of the ocean: this made it appear as if there were a big ship on the ocean. As he flew over the surface of the ocean, the wind generated by his motion greatly agitated the ocean. He actually dashed the surface of the ocean with his powerful chest. Thus the sea was churned by him as he flew over it. Huge waves arose in his wake with water billowing high into fine spray which looked like clouds. Flying thus in the sky, without any visible support, Hanumān appeared to be a winged mountain.

Hanumān was engaged in the mission of Rāma: hence the sun did not scorch him. Rāma was a descendant of the solar dynasty. The sages who were present there in their ethereal forms showered their blessings upon him.

Sāgara, the deity presiding over the ocean, bethought to himself: "In days of yore, Rāma's ancestors the sons of king Sagara, rendered an invaluable service to me.[9] And it therefore behoves me to render some service to this messenger of Rāma who is engaged in the service of Rāma. I should see that Hanumān does not tire himself and thus fail in his mission. I should arrange for him to have some rest before he proceeds further."

Thus resolved, Sāgara summoned the deity presiding over the mountain named Maināka which had been submerged in the ocean, and said to Maināka: "O Maināka, Indra the chief of gods has established you here in order to prevent the denizens from the subterranean regions from coming up. You have the power to extend yourself on all sides. Pray, rise up and offer a seat to Hanumān who is engaged on an important mission on behalf of Rāma, so that he can refresh himself before proceeding further."

SUNDARA 1

Readily agreeing to this request, the mountain Maināka rose from the bed of the ocean. As Hanumān flew towards Laṅkā he saw this mountain actually emerge from the ocean and come into his view. However, he considered that it was an obstacle to his progress towards Laṅkā, an obstruction on his path, to be quickly overcome. Hanumān actually flew almost touching the peak of the mountain and by the force of the motion, the peak was actually broken.

Assuming a human-form the deity presiding over the Maināka mountain addressed Hanumān who was still flying: "O Hanumān, pray accept my hospitality. Rest a while on my peak. Refresh yourself. The ocean was extended by the sons of king Sagara, an ancestor of Rāma. Hence the deity presiding over the ocean wishes to return the service as a token of gratitude: thus to show one's gratitude is the eternal dharma. With this end in view, the ocean-god has commanded me to rise to the surface and offer you a resting place. It is our tradition to welcome and to honor guests, even if they are ordinary men: how much more important it is that we should thus honor men like you! There is yet another reason why I plead that you should accept my hospitality! In ancient times, all the mountains were endowed with wings. They used to fly

9. Looking for the horse that was stolen from their father's royal sacrifice, the 60,000 sons of Rāma's ancestor Sagara dug up the entire earth and its surrounding continents and seas, thus expanding the ocean's domain.

around and land where they liked; thus, they terrorized sages and other beings. In answer to their prayer, Indra the chief of gods, wielded his thunderbolt and clipped off the wings of the mountains. As Indra was about to strike me, the wind-god bore me violently away and hid me in the ocean—so that I escaped Indra's wrath. I owe a debt of gratitude to the wind-god who is your god-father. Pray, allow me to discharge that debt by entertaining you."

Hanumān replied politely: "Indeed, I accept your hospitality, in spirit. Time is passing; and I am on an urgent mission. Moreover, I have promised not to rest till my task is accomplished. Hence, forgive my rudeness and discourtesy: I have to be on my way." As a token acceptance of Maināka's hospitality, Hanumān touched the mountain with his hand and was soon on his way. The gods and the sages who witnessed this scene were greatly impressed with Maināka's gesture of goodwill and Hanumān's unflagging zeal and determination. Indra, highly pleased with the Maināka mountain, conferred upon it the boon of fearlessness.

SUNDARA I

The gods and the sages overseeing Hanumān's flight to Laṅkā had witnessed his first feat of strength when he took off from the Mahendra mountain, and his second feat of strength and enthusiasm when he declined even to rest and insisted on the accomplishment of the mission. They were eager to assure themselves still more conclusively of his ability to fulfill the task he had undertaken.

The gods and the sages now approached Surasā (mother of the Nāgas)[1] and said to her: "Here is Hanumān, the god-child of the wind-god, who is flying across the ocean. Pray, obstruct his path just a short while. Assume a terrible demoniacal form, with the body as big as a mountain, with terrible looking teeth and eyes, and mouth as wide as space. We wish to ascertain Hanumān's strength. And we therefore wish to see whether when he is confronted by you, he triumphs over you or becomes despondent."

In obedience to their command, Surasā assumed a terrible form and confronted Hanumān with her mouth wide open. She said to him, as he approached her mouth while flying in the air: "Ah, fate has decreed that you should serve as my food today! Enter my mouth and I shall eat you up."

Hanumān replied: "O lady, I am on an important mission. Rāma, the son of king Daśaratha, came to the forest to honor his father's promise. While he was in the forest with his wife, Sītā, and his brother, Sītā was abducted by Rāvaṇa, the ruler of Laṅkā. I am going to Laṅkā to find her whereabouts. Do not obstruct my path now. Let me go. If the gods have ordained that I should enter your mouth, I promise that as soon as I discover Sītā and inform Rāma of her whereabouts, I shall come back and enter your mouth."

But, Surasā could not be put off. She repeated: "No one can escape me; and it has been decreed that you shall enter my mouth." She opened her mouth wide. Hanumān, by his yogic power, made himself minute, quickly entered her mouth and as quickly got out! He then said to her: "O lady, let me now proceed. I have fulfilled your wish and honored the gods' decree: I have entered your mouth! Salutations to you! I shall go to where Sītā is kept in captivity."

1. A class of serpents or demigods.

Surasā abandoned her demoniacal form and resumed her own form which was pleasant to look at. She blessed Hanumān: "Go! You will surely find Sītā and re-unite her with Rāma." The gods and the sages were thrilled to witness this third triumph of Hanumān.

SUNDARA 1

Hanumān continued to fly towards Laṅkā, along the aerial route which contains rain-bearing clouds, along which birds course, where the masters of music[2] move about, and along which aerial cars which resemble lions, elephants, tigers, birds and snakes, fly—the sky which is also the abode of holy men and women with an abundant store of meritorious deeds, which serves as a canopy created by the creator Brahmā to protect living beings on earth, and which is adorned with planets, the moon, the sun and the stars.

As he flew onwards, he left behind him a black trail which resembled black clouds, and also trails which were red, yellow and white. He often flew through cloud-formations.

A demoness called Simhikā saw Hanumān flying fearlessly in the sky and made up her mind to attack him. She said to herself: "I am hungry. Today I shall swallow this big creature and shall appease my hunger for some time." She caught hold of the shadow cast by Hanumān on the surface of the ocean. Immediately, Hanumān's progress was arrested and he was violently pulled down. He wondered: "How is it that suddenly I am dragged down helplessly?" He looked around and saw the ugly demoness Simhikā. He remembered the description which Sugrīva had given of her and knew it was Simhikā without doubt.

Hanumān stretched his body and the demoness opened her mouth wide. He saw her mouth and her inner vital organs through it. In the twinkling of an eye, he reduced himself to a minute size and dropped into her mouth. He disappeared into that wide mouth. The gods and the sages witnessing this were horrified. But with his adamantine nails he tore open the vital parts of the demoness and quickly emerged from her body. Thus, with the help of good luck, firmness and dexterity Hanumān triumphed over this demoness. The gods applauded this feat and said: "He in whom are found (as in you) these four virtues (firmness, vision, wisdom and dexterity) does not despair in any undertaking."

Hanumān had nearly covered the eight hundred miles, to his destination. At a short distance he saw the shore of Laṅkā. He saw thick forests. He saw the mountains known as Lamba. And he saw the capital city Laṅkā built on the mountains. Not wishing to arouse suspicion, he softly landed on the Lamba mountains which were rich in groves of Ketaka, Uddalaka and cocoanut trees.

SUNDARA 2

Though Hanumān had crossed the sea, covering a distance of eight hundred miles, he felt not the least fatigue nor exhaustion. Having landed on the mountain range close to the shore of the ocean, Hanumān roamed the forests for some time. In them he saw trees of various kinds, bearing flowers and fruits.

2. *Gandharvas*, a class of demigods.

He saw the city of Laṅkā situated on the top of a hill, surrounded by wide moats and guarded by security forces of demons. He approached the northern gate to the city and quietly surveyed it. That gate was guarded by the most ferocious looking demons armed to the teeth with the most powerful weapons. Standing there, he thought of Rāvaṇa, the abductor of Sītā.

Hanumān thought: "Even if the vānara forces do come here, of what use would that be? For Rāvaṇa's Laṅkā cannot be conquered even by the gods. Only four of us can cross the ocean and come here—Aṅgada, Nīla, Sugrīva and myself. And that is totally useless. One cannot negotiate with these demons and win them over by peaceful means. Anyhow, I shall first find out if Sītā is alive or not, and only then consider the next step."

In order to find out where Sītā was kept in captivity, he had to enter Laṅkā. The wise Hanumān considered that aspect of his mission. He thought: "Surely, I must be very careful, cautious and vigilant. If I am not, I might ruin the whole mission. An undertaking even after it has been carefully deliberated and decided upon will fail if it is mishandled by an ignorant or inefficient messenger. Therefore I should consider well what should be done and with due regard to all the pros and cons, I should vigilantly ensure that I do nothing which ought not to be done. I should enter the city in such a way that my presence and my movements are not detected; and I see that Rāvaṇa's security forces are so very efficient that it will not be easy to escape detection."

Thus resolved, Hanumān reduced himself to a small size, to the size of a cat as it were, and when darkness had fallen, proceeded towards the city. Even from a distance he could see the affluence that the city enjoyed. It had buildings of many stories. It had archways made of gold. It was brilliantly lit and tastefully decorated. The city was of unimaginable beauty and glory. When Hanumān saw it, he was filled with a mixture of feelings, feelings of despondence, and joy—joy at the prospect of seeing Sītā, and despondency at the thought of the difficulty involved in it.

Unnoticed by the guards, Hanumān entered the gateway.

SUNDARA 3

Hanumān was still contemplating the difficulties of the imminent campaign for the recovery of Sītā. Conquering Laṅkā by force seemed to him to be out of the question. He thought: "Possibly only Kumuda, Aṅgada, Suṣena, Mainda, Dvivida, Sugrīva, Kuśaparva, Jāmbavān and myself may be in a position to cross the ocean and come here. However, in spite of the heavy odds against such a campaign, there is the immeasurable prowess of Rāma and Lakṣmaṇa: surely they can destroy the demons without any difficulty whatsoever."

As he was entering the city, he was intercepted by Laṅkā, the guardian of the city. She questioned him: "Who are you, O vānara? This city of Laṅkā cannot be entered by you!" Hanumān was in no mood to reveal his identity: and he questioned her, in his turn: "Who are you, O lady? And why do you obstruct my path?" Laṅkā replied: "At the command of the mighty Rāvaṇa, I guard this city. No one can ignore me and enter this city: and you, O vānara, will soon enter into eternal sleep, slain at my hands!"

Hanumān said to her: "I have come as a visitor to this city, to see what is to be seen here. When I have seen what I wish to see, I shall duly return to where

I have come from. Pray, let me proceed." But Laṅkā continued to say: "You cannot enter without overpowering me or winning my permission," and actually hit Hanumān on his chest with her hand.

Hanumān's anger was aroused. Yet, he controlled himself: for he did not consider it right to kill a woman! He clenched his fist and struck Laṅkā. She fell down, and then revealed: "Compose yourself, O vānara! Do not kill me. The truly strong ones do not violate the code of chivalry, and they do not kill a woman. I am Laṅkā, and he who has conquered me has conquered Laṅkā. That was what Brahmā the creator once said: 'When a vānara overpowers you, know that then the demons have cause for great fear.' I am sure that this prophecy refers to you, O vānara! I realize now that the inevitable destruction of the demons of Laṅkā has entered the territory in the form of Sītā who has been forcibly brought here by Rāvaṇa. Go, enter the city: and surely you will find Sītā and accomplish all that you desire to accomplish."

SUNDARA 4–5

Hanumān did not enter the city through the heavily guarded main gate, but climbed over the wall. Then he came to the main road and proceeded towards his destination—the abode of Rāvaṇa. On the way Hanumān saw the beautiful mansions from which issued the sound of music, and the sound of the citizens' rejoicing. He saw, too, prosperous-looking mansions of different designs calculated to bring happiness and greater prosperity to the owners of the mansions. He heard the shouts of wrestling champions. Here and there he heard bards and others singing the glories of Rāvaṇa, and he noticed that these bards were surrounded by citizens in large numbers, blocking the road.

Right in the heart of the city, Hanumān saw in the main square numerous spies of Rāvaṇa: and these spies looked like holy men, with matted hair, or with shaven heads, clad in the hides of cows or in nothing at all. In their hands they carried all sorts of weapons, right from a few blades of grass to maces and sticks. They were of different shapes and sizes and of different appearance and complexions. Hanumān also saw the garrison with a hundred thousand soldiers right in front of the inner apartments of Rāvaṇa.

Hanumān approached the palace of Rāvaṇa himself. This was a truly heavenly abode. Within the compound of the palace and around the building there were numerous horses, chariots, and also flying chariots. The palace was built of solid and pure gold and the inside was decorated with many precious stones, fragrant with incense and sandalwood which had been sprinkled everywhere: Hanumān entered the palace.

It was nearly midnight. The moon shone brilliantly overhead. From the palace wafted the strains of stringed musical instruments; good-natured women were asleep with their husbands; the violent night-stalkers[3] also emerged from their dwellings to amuse themselves. In some quarters, Hanumān noticed wrestlers training themselves. In some others, women were applying various cosmetic articles to themselves. Some other women were sporting with their husbands. Others whose husbands were away looked unhappy and pale, though they were still beautiful. Hanumān saw all these: but he did not see Sītā anywhere.

---

3. A class of demons. The word is also used more generally for "demons."

Not seeing Sītā, the beloved wife of Rāma, Hanumān felt greatly distressed and unhappy and he became moody and dejected.

SUNDARA 6, 7, 8

Hanumān was greatly impressed by the beauty and the grandeur of Rāvaṇa's palace which he considered to be the crowning glory of Laṅkā itself. He did not all at once enter Rāvaṇa's inner apartments. First he surveyed the palaces of the other members of the royal family and the leaders of the demons, like Prahasta. He surveyed the palaces of Rāvaṇa's brothers Kumbhakarṇa and Vibhīṣaṇa, as also that of Rāvaṇa's son Indrajīt. He was greatly impressed by the unmistakable signs of prosperity that greeted him everywhere. After thus looking at the palaces of all these heroes, Hanumān reached the abode of Rāvaṇa himself.

Rāvaṇa's own inner apartments were guarded by terrible-looking demons, holding the most powerful weapons in their hands. Rāvaṇa's own private palace was surrounded by more armed forces; and even these garrisons were embellished by gold and diamonds. Hanumān entered the palace and saw within it palanquins, couches, gardens and art galleries, special chambers for enjoying sexual pleasures and others for indulging in other pastimes during the day. There were also special altars for the performance of sacred rituals. The whole palace was resplendent on account of the light emitted by precious stones which were found everywhere. Everywhere the couches, the seats and the dining vessels were of gold; and the floor of the whole palace was fragrant with the smell of wine and liquor. In fact Hanumān thought that the palace looked like heaven on earth, resplendent with the wealth of precious gems, and fragrant with the scent of a variety of flowers which covered its dome making it look like a flower-covered hill.

There were swimming pools with lotuses and lilies. In one of them there was the carved figure of a lordly elephant offering worship to Lakṣmī, the goddess of wealth.

Right in the center of the palace stood the best of all flying chariots, known as Puṣpaka. It had been painted with many colors and provided with numerous precious gems. It was decorated with lovely figures of snakes, birds, and horses fashioned of gems, silver and coral. Every part of that flying chariot had been carefully engineered, only the very best materials had been used, and it had special features which even the vehicles of the gods did not have—in fact, in it had been brought together only special features! Rāvaṇa had acquired it after great austerities and effort.

Hanumān saw all this. But, he did not see Sītā anywhere!

SUNDARA 9

Hanumān ascended the chariot Puṣpaka from which he could easily look into the inner apartments of Rāvaṇa! As he stood on the chariot, he smelled the extraordinary odor emanating from Rāvaṇa's dining room—the odor of wines and liquors, the smell of excellent food. The smell was appetizing and Hanumān thought the food should be nourishing. And, he saw at the same time the beautiful hall of Rāvaṇa which had crystal floors, with inlaid figures made of ivory, pearls, diamonds, corals, silver and gold. The hall was resplendent with pillars of gems. There was on the floor, a carpet of extraordinary beauty and design. On the walls were murals of several countries' landscapes. This hall thus provided all the five senses with the objects for their utmost gratification! A soft light illumined this hall.

On the carpet beautiful women lay asleep. With their mouths and their eyes closed, they had fallen asleep, after drinking and dancing, and from their bodies issued the sweet fragrance of lotuses. Rāvaṇa, sleeping there surrounded by these beautiful women, looked like the moon surrounded by the stars in the night sky. They were all asleep in beautiful disorder. Some were using their own arms as the pillow, others used the different parts of yet others' bodies as their pillow. Their hair was in disarray. Their dress was in disarray, too. But none of these conditions diminished the beauty of their forms. From the breath of all the women there issued the smell of liquor.

These women had come from different grades of society. Some of them were the daughters of royal sages, others those of brāhmaṇas, yet others were the daughters of gandharvas (celestial artists), and, of course, some were the daughters of demons: and all of them had voluntarily sought Rāvaṇa, for they loved him. Some he had won by his valor; others had become infatuated with him. None of these women had been carried away by Rāvaṇa against their wish. None of them had been married before. None of them had desire for another man. Rāvaṇa had never before abducted any woman, except Sītā.

Hanumān thought for a moment: Rāvaṇa would indeed have been a good man if he had thus got Sītā too, to be his wife: that is, before she had married Rāma and if he had been able to win her by his valor or by his charm. But, Hanumān contemplated further: by abducting the wife of Rāma, Rāvaṇa had certainly committed a highly unworthy action.

SUNDARA 10—11

In the center of that hall, Hanumān saw the most beautiful and the most luxurious bed: it was celestial in its appearance, built entirely of crystal and decked with gems. The lord of the demons, Rāvaṇa himself was asleep on it. The sight of this demon was at first revolting to Hanumān; so he turned his face away from Rāvaṇa. But then he turned his gaze again to Rāvaṇa. He saw that the two arms of Rāvaṇa were strong and powerful, and they were adorned with resplendent jewelry. His face, his chest, in fact his whole body was strong and radiant. His limbs shone like the lightning.

Around this bed were others on which the consorts of Rāvaṇa were asleep. Many of them had obviously been entertaining the demon with their music; and they had fallen asleep with the musical instruments in their arms. On yet another bed was asleep the most charming of all the women in that hall: she surpassed all the others in beauty, in youth and in adornment. For a moment Hanumān thought it was Sītā: and the very thought that he had seen Sītā delighted him.

But that thought did not last long. Hanumān realized: "It cannot be. For, separated from Rāma, Sītā will not sleep, nor will she enjoy herself, adorn herself or drink anything. Nor will Sītā ever dwell with another man, even if he be a celestial: for truly there is none equal to Rāma." He turned away from the hall, since he did not see Sītā there.

Next, Hanumān searched the dining hall and the kitchen: there he saw varieties of meats and other delicacies, condiments and a variety of drinks. The dining hall floor had been strewn with drinking vessels, fruits and even anklets and armlets which had obviously fallen from their wearers as they were drinking and getting intoxicated.

While he was thus inspecting the palace and searching for Sītā, a thought flashed in Hanumān's mind: was he guilty of transgressing the bounds of morality, in as much as he was gazing at the wives of others, while they were asleep with their ornaments and clothes in disarray? But, he consoled himself with the thought: "True, I have seen all these women in Rāvaṇa's apartment. But, no lustful thought has entered my mind! The mind alone is the cause of good and evil actions performed by the senses; but my mind is devoted to and established in righteousness. Where else can I look for Sītā, except among the womenfolk in Rāvaṇa's palace: shall I look for a lost woman among a herd of deer? I have looked for Sītā in this place with a pure mind; but she is not to be seen."

SUNDARA 12–13

Hanumān had searched the whole palace of Rāvaṇa. But he could not find Sītā. He reflected: "I shall not yield to despair. For, it has been well said that perseverance alone is the secret of prosperity and great happiness; perseverance alone keeps all things going, and crowns all activities with success. I shall search those places which I have not yet searched." He then began to search for Sītā in other parts of the palace. He saw many, many other women, but not Sītā.

Hanumān then searched for Sītā outside the palace. Yet, he could not find her. Once again dejection gripped him. He thought: "Sītā is to be found nowhere; yet Sampāti did say that he saw Rāvaṇa and he saw Sītā, too. Perhaps it was mistaken identity. It may be that slipping from the control of Rāvaṇa, Sītā dropped her body into the sea. Or, it may be she died of shock. Or, perhaps when she did not yield to him, Rāvaṇa killed her and ate her flesh. But it is impossible that she had consented to be Rāvaṇa's consort. Whether she is lost, or she has perished or has died, how can I inform Rāma about it? On the other hand, to inform Rāma and not to inform Rāma—both these appear to be objectionable. What shall I do now?" He also reflected on the consequence of his returning to Kiṣkindhā with no news of Sītā. He felt certain that: "When Rāma hears the bad news from me, he will give up his life. So will Lakṣmaṇa. And then their brothers and mothers in Ayodhyā. Nor could Sugrīva live after Rāma departs from this world. He will be followed to the other world by all the vānaras of Kiṣkindhā. What a terrible calamity will strike Ayodhyā and Kiṣkindhā if I return without news of Sītā's safety!" He resolved: "It is good that I should not return to Kiṣkindhā. Like an ascetic I shall live under a tree here. Or, I can commit suicide by jumping into the sea. However, the wise ones say that suicide is the root of many evils, and that if one lives one is sure to find what one seeks."

The consciousness of his extraordinary strength suddenly seized Hanumān! He sprang up and said to himself: "I shall at once kill this demon Rāvaṇa. Even if I cannot find Sītā, I shall have avenged her abduction by killing her abductor. Or, I shall kidnap him and take him to Rāma." Then he thought of a few places in Laṅkā he had not yet searched: one of them was Aśoka-grove. He resolved to go there. Before doing so, he offered a prayer: "Salutations to Rāma and Lakṣmaṇa; salutations to Sītā, the daughter of Janaka. Salutations to Rudra, Indra, Yama, the wind-god, to the moon, fire, and the Maruts." He turned round in all directions and invoked the blessings of all. He knew he needed them for he felt that demons of superhuman strength were guarding the Aśoka-grove.

SUNDARA 14–15

Hanumān then climbed the palace wall and jumped into the Aśoka-grove. It was most beautiful and enchanting, with trees and creepers of innumerable types.

In that grove, Hanumān also saw the bird sanctuary, the ponds and artificial swimming pools hemmed by flights of steps which had been paved with expensive precious and semi-precious stones. He also saw a hill with a waterfall flowing from its side. Not far from there, he saw a unique Aśoka or Siṁśapā tree which was golden in its appearance. The area around this tree was covered with trees which had golden leaves and blossoms, giving the appearance that they were ablaze.

Climbing up that unique Siṁśapā tree, Hanumān felt certain that he would soon see Sītā. He reasoned: "Sītā was fond of the forests and groves, according to Rāma. Hence, she will doubtless come to this yonder lotus-pond. Rāma did say that she was fond of roaming the forest: surely, then, she would wish to roam this grove, too. It is almost certain that the grief-stricken Sītā would come here to offer her evening prayers. If she is still alive, I shall surely see her today."

Seated on that Aśoka or Siṁśapā tree, Hanumān surveyed the whole of the grove. He was enthralled by the beauty of the grove, of the trees, and of the blossoms which were so colorful that it appeared as if the whole place were afire. There were numerous other trees, too, all of which were delightful to look at. While he was thus surveying the scene, he saw a magnificent temple, not far from him. This temple had a hall of a thousand pillars, and looked like the Kailāsa.[4] The temple had been painted white. It had steps carved out of coral. And its platforms were all made of pure gold.

And, then, Hanumān saw a radiant woman with an ascetic appearance. She was surrounded by demonesses who were apparently guarding her. She was radiant though her garments were soiled. She was beautiful in form, though emaciated through sorrow, hunger and austerity. Hanumān felt certain that it was Sītā, and that it was the same lady whom he had momentarily seen over the Ṛsymūka hill. She was seated on the ground. And, she was frequently sighing, surely on account of her separation from Rāma. With great difficulty, Hanumān recognized her as Sītā: and in this he was helped only by the graphic and vivid description that Rāma had given him.

Looking at her, thus pining for Rāma, and recollecting Rāma's love for her, Hanumān marveled at the patience of Rāma in that he could live without Sītā even for a short while.

4. The Himalayan peak on which the god Śiva dwells.

SUNDARA 16–17

Hanumān contemplated the divine form of Sītā for a few minutes; and he once again gave way to dejection. He reflected: "If even Sītā who is highly esteemed by the noble and humble Lakṣmaṇa, and who is the beloved of Rāma himself, could be subjected to such sorrow, indeed one should conclude that Time is all-powerful. Surely, Sītā is utterly confident in the ability of Rāma and Lakṣmaṇa to rescue her; and hence she is tranquil even in this misfortune. Only Rāma deserves to be her husband, and she to be Rāma's consort." How great was Rāma's love for Sītā! And, what an extraordinary person Sītā was! Hanumān continued to "weigh" her in his own mind's balance: "It was for the sake of Sītā that thousands of demons in the Daṇḍaka forest were killed by Rāma. It was for her sake alone that Rāma killed Vāli and Kabandha. Khara, Dūṣaṇa, Triśira—so many of these demons met their end because of her. And, why not: she is such a special person that if, for her sake, Rāma turned the whole world upside down it would be proper. For, she was of extraordinary birth, she is of extraordinary beauty and she is of extraordinary character. She is unexcelled in every way. And, what an extraordinary love she has for Rāma, in that she patiently endures all sorts of hardships living, as she does, as a captive in Laṅkā. Again, Rāma pines for her and is eagerly waiting to see her, to regain her. Here she is, constantly thinking of Rāma: she does not see either these demonesses guarding her, nor the trees, flowers or fruits, but with her heart centered in Rāma, she sees him alone constantly." He was now certain that that lady was in fact Sītā.

The moon had risen. The sky was clear and the moonlight enabled Hanumān to see Sītā clearly. He saw the demonesses guarding Sītā. They were hideous-looking and deformed in various parts of their bodies. Their lips, breasts and bellies were disproportionately large and hanging. Some were very tall; others were very short. They were mostly dark-complexioned. Some of them had ears, etc., that made them look like animals. They were querulous, noisy, and fond of flesh and liquor. They had smeared their bodies with meat and blood; and they ate meat and blood. Their very sight was revolting and frightening. There in their midst was Sītā.

Sītā's dress and her appearance reflected her grief. At the foot of the tree whose name, Aśoka, meant free of sorrow, was seated Sītā immersed in an ocean of sorrow, surrounded by these terrible demonesses! It was only her confidence in the prowess and the valor of her lord Rāma that sustained her life. Hanumān mentally prostrated to Rāma, to Lakṣmaṇa and to Sītā and hid himself among the branches of the tree.

SUNDARA 18, 19, 20

Night was drawing to a close. In his palace, Rāvaṇa was being awakened by the Vedic recitation of brāhmaṇa-demons who were well versed in the Vedas and other scriptural texts, and also by musicians and bards who sang his praises. Even before he had time to adorn himself properly, Rāvaṇa thought of Sītā and longed intensely to see her. Quickly adorning himself with the best of ornaments and clad in splendid garments, he entered the Aśoka-grove, accompanied by a hundred chosen women who carried golden torches, fans, cushions and other articles. They were still under the influence of alcohol: and Rāvaṇa, though mighty and powerful, was under the influence of passion for Sītā.

Hanumān recognized the person he had seen asleep in the palace the previous night.

Seeing him coming in her direction, the frightened Sītā shielded her torso with her legs and hands, and began to weep bitterly. Pining for Rāma, distressed on account of her separation from him and stricken with grief, the most beautiful and radiant Sītā resembled eclipsed fame, neglected faith, enfeebled understanding, forlorn hope, ruined prospect, disregarded command, and obstructed worship; eclipsed moon, decimated army, fuelless flame, river in drought. She was constantly engaged in the prayer that Rāma might soon triumph over Rāvaṇa and rescue her.

Rāvaṇa appeared to be chivalrous in his approach to Sītā, and his words were meaningful and sweet: he said to Sītā, "Pray, do not be afraid of me, O charming lady! It is natural for a demon to enjoy others' wives and abduct them forcibly; it is the demon's own dharma. But, I shall not violate you against your wishes. For, I want to win your love; I want to win your esteem. I have enough strength to restrain myself. Yet, it breaks my heart to see you suffer like this; to see you, a princess, dressed like this in tattered and dirty garments. You are born to apply the most delightful cosmetic articles, to wear royal attire, and to adorn yourself with the most expensive jewels. You are young, youthful: this is the time to enjoy yourself, for youth is passing. There is none in the three worlds who is as beautiful as you are, O princess: for, having fashioned you, the Creator has retired. You are so beautiful that no one in the three worlds—not even Brahamā the creator—could but be overcome by passion. When you accept me, all that I have will become yours. Even my chief wives will become your servants. Let me warn you: no one in the three worlds is my match in strength and valor. Rāma, even if he is alive, does not even know where you are: he has no hope of regaining you. Give up this foolish idea of yours. Let me behold you appropriately dressed and adorned. And, let us enjoy life to your heart's content."

SUNDARA 21–22

Rāvaṇa's words were extremely painful to the grief-stricken Sītā. She placed a blade of grass in front of her, unwilling even to speak to Rāvaṇa directly, and said: "You cannot aspire for me any more than a sinful man can aspire for perfection! I will not do what is unworthy in the eyes of a chaste wife. Surely, you do not know dharma, nor do you obviously listen to the advice of wise counselors. Set an example to your subjects, O demon: and consort with your own wives; desire for others' wives will lead to infamy. The world rejoices at the death of a wicked man: even so it will, soon, on your death. But do not desire for me. You cannot win me by offering me power or wealth: for I am inseparable from Rāma even as light from the sun. He is the abode of righteousness, of dharma; take me back to him and beg his pardon. He loves those who seek his refuge. If you do not, you will surely come to grief: for no power on earth can save you from Rāma's weapon. His missiles will surely destroy the entire Laṅkā. In fact, if you had not stolen me in the absence of Rāma and Lakṣmaṇa, you would not be alive today: you could not face them, you coward!"

Rāvaṇa's anger was roused, and he replied: "Normally, women respond to a pleasant approach by a man. But you seem to be different, O Sītā. You rouse my anger; but my desire for you subdues that anger. My love for you prevents me from killing you straight away; though you deserve to be executed, for all the insulting and impudent words you utter. Well, I had fixed one year as the time-limit for you to make up your mind. Ten months have elapsed since then. You have two more months in which to decide to accede to my wish. If you fail to do so, my cooks will prepare a nice meal of your flesh for me to eat."

But, Sītā remained unmoved. She said to Rāvaṇa: "You are prattling, O wicked demon: I can by my own spiritual energy reduce you to ashes: but I do not do so on account of the fact that I have not been so ordered by Rāma and I do not want to waste my own spiritual powers."

The terrible demon was greatly enraged by these words of Sītā. He threatened her: "Wait, I shall destroy you just now." But he did not do so. However, he said to the demonesses guarding Sītā: "Use all your powers to persuade Sītā to consent to my proposal." Immediately, Rāvaṇa's consorts embraced him and pleaded: "Why don't you enjoy our company, giving up your desire for Sītā? For, a man who seeks the company of one who has no love for him comes to grief, and he who seeks the company of one who loves him enjoys life." Hearing this and laughing aloud, Rāvaṇa walked away.

SUNDARA 23–24

After Rāvaṇa had left the grove, the demonesses said: "How is it that you do not value Rāvaṇa's hand? Perhaps you do not know who he is. Of the six Prajāpatis who were the sons of the creator himself, Pulastya is the fourth; of Pulastya was the sage Viśrava born, and he was equal to Pulastya himself in glory. And this Rāvaṇa is the son of Viśrava. He is known as Rāvaṇa because he makes his enemies cry.[5] It is a great honor to accept his proposal. Moreover, this Rāvaṇa worsted in battle the thirty-three deities presiding over the universe. Hence he is superior even to the gods. And, what is most important: he surely loves you so much that he is prepared to abandon his own favorite wives and give you all his love."

Sītā was deeply pained by these words uttered by the demonesses. She said: "Enough of this vulgar and sinful advice. A human being should not become the wife of a demon. But, even that is irrelevant. I shall not under any circumstance abandon my husband and seek another." The demonesses were enraged and began to threaten Sītā. And, Hanumān was witnessing all this.

The demonesses said again: "You have shown enough affection to the unworthy Rāma. Excess of anything is undesirable and leads to undesirable result. You have so far conformed to the human rules of conduct. It is high time that you abandoned that code, abandoned the human Rāma and consented to be Rāvaṇa's wife. We have so far put up with the rude and harsh words you have uttered; and we have so far offered you loving and wholesome advice, intent as we are on your welfare. But you seem to be too stupid to see the truth. You have been brought here by Rāvaṇa; you have crossed the ocean. Others cannot cross the ocean and come to your rescue. We tell you this, O Sītā: even Indra cannot rescue you from here. Therefore, please do as we tell you, in your interest. Enough of your weeping. Give up this sorrow which is destructive.

5. *Rāvaṇa*, from the verb *ru*, "to roar," "to cry."

Abandon this wretched life. Attain love and pleasure. Make haste, O Sītā: for youth, especially of women, is but momentary and passes quickly. Make up your mind to become Rāvaṇa's wife. If, however, you are obstinate, we shall ourselves tear your body and eat your heart."

Other demonesses took up the cue and began to threaten Sītā. They said: "When I first saw this lovely woman brought into Laṅkā by Rāvaṇa the desire arose in me that I should eat her liver and spleen, her breasts and her heart. I am waiting for that day. . . . What is the delay? Let us report to the king that she died and he will surely ask us to eat her flesh! . . . We should divide her flesh equally and eat it, there should be no quarrel amongst us. . . . After the meal, we shall dance in front of the goddess Bhadrakāli."

SUNDARA 25–26

In utter despair, Sītā gave vent to her grief by thinking aloud: "The wise ones have rightly said that untimely death is not attained here either by man or a woman. Hence though I am suffering intolerable anguish on account of my separation from my beloved husband, I am unable to give up my life. This grief is slowly eating me. I can neither live nor can I die. Surely, this is the bitter fruit of some dreadful sin committed in a past birth. I am surrounded by these demonesses: and how can Rāma reach me here? Fie upon human birth, and fie upon the state of dependence upon others, as a result of which I cannot even give up my life.

"What a terrible misfortune it was that even though I was living under the protection of Rāma and Lakṣmaṇa, I was abducted by Rāvaṇa, in their absence. Even more terrible it is that having been separated from my beloved husband I am confined here surrounded by these terrible demonesses. And, the worst part of it is: in spite of all these misfortunes, my heart does not burst with anguish thus letting me die. Of course, I shall never allow Rāvaṇa to touch me, so long as I am alive.

"I wonder why Rāma has not taken steps to come to my aid. For my sake he killed thousands of demons while we were in the forest. True I am on an island; but Rāma's missiles have no difficulty crossing oceans and finding their target. Surely, he does not know where I am. Alas, even Jaṭāyu who could have informed Rāma of what had happened was killed by Rāvaṇa. If only he knew I was here, Rāma would have destroyed Laṅkā and dried up the ocean with his missiles. All the demonesses of Laṅkā would weep then, as I am weeping now; all the demons would be killed by Rāma. Laṅkā would be one huge crematorium.

"I see all sorts of evil portents. I shall be re-united with Rāma. He will come. He will destroy all these demons. If only Rāma comes to know where I am, Laṅkā will be turned desolate by him, burnt by his terrible missiles. On the other hand, the time is fast running out: the time limit that Rāvaṇa had fixed for me to decide. Two more months: and I shall be cut into pieces for Rāvaṇa's meal. May it be that Rāma himself is no more, having succumbed to grief on account of my separation? Or, may it be that he has turned an ascetic? Usually, people who love each other forget each other when they are separated: but not so Rāma whose love is eternal. Blessed indeed are the holy sages who have reached enlightenment and to whom the pleasant and the unpleasant are non-different. I salute the holy ones. And, fallen into this terrible misfortune, I shall presently give up my life."

SUNDARA 27

Hearing the words of Sītā, some of the demonesses grew terribly angry. They threatened: "We shall go and report all this to Rāvaṇa; and then we shall be able to eat you at once." Another demoness named Trijaṭā just then woke up from her slumber and announced: "Forget all this talk about eating Sītā, O foolish ones! I have just now dreamt a dream which forewarns that a terrible calamity awaits all of you." The demonesses asked: "Tell us what the dream was."

Trijaṭā narrated her dream in great detail: "I saw in my dream Rāma and Lakṣmaṇa, riding a white chariot. Sītā was sitting on a white mountain, clad in shining white robes. Rāma and Sītā were re-united. Rāma and Lakṣmaṇa then got on a huge elephant which Sītā, too, mounted. Sītā held out her arms and her hands touched the sun and the moon. Rāma, Lakṣmaṇa and Sītā later mounted the Puṣpaka chariot and flew away in a northerly direction. From all these I conclude that Rāma is divine and invincible.

"Listen to me further. In another dream I saw Rāvaṇa. His head had been shaven. He was covered with oil. He wore crimson clothes. He was drunk. He had fallen from the Puṣpaka chariot. Later, I saw him dressed in black but smeared in a red pigment and dragged by a woman riding a vehicle drawn by donkeys. He fell down from the donkey. He was prattling like a mad man. Then he entered a place which was terribly dark and foul-smelling. Later a dark woman with body covered in mud bound Rāvaṇa's neck and dragged him away in a southerly direction.[6] I saw Kumbhakarṇa as also the sons of Rāvaṇa in that dream; all of them undergoing the same or similar treatment. Only Vibhīṣaṇa's luck was different. He was clad in a white garment, with white garlands, and had a royal white umbrella held over his head.[7]

"I also saw in that dream that the whole of Laṅkā had been pushed into the sea, utterly destroyed and ruined. I also saw a rather strange dream. I saw Laṅkā burning furiously: though Laṅkā is protected by Rāvaṇa who is mighty and powerful, a vānara was able to set Laṅkā ablaze, because the vānara was a servant of Rāma.

"I see a clear warning in these dreams, O foolish women! Enough of your cruelty to Sītā; I think it is better to please her and win her favor. I am convinced that Sītā will surely achieve her purpose and her desire to be re-united with Rāma."

Hearing this, Sītā felt happy and said: "If this comes true, I shall certainly protect all of you."

SUNDARA 28, 29, 30

But, the demonesses did not pay heed to Trijaṭā. And, Sītā thought:

"Truly have the wise ones declared that death never comes to a person before the appointed time. My time has come. Rāvaṇa has said definitely that if I do not agree to him I will be put to death. Since I can never, never love him, it is certain that I shall be executed. Hence, I am condemned already. I shall, therefore, incur no blame if I voluntarily end my life today. O Rāma! O Lakṣmaṇa!

---

6. The south is the direction of misfortune, the ancestors, and death.

7. In this context, the color white symbolizes virtue, purity, and sovereignty.

O Sumitrā! O Kausalyā! O Mother! Caught helplessly and brought to this dreadful place, I am about to perish. Surely it was my own 'bad-time' that approached me in the form of that golden deer, and I, a foolish woman sent the two princes in search of it. Maybe, they were killed by some demon. Or, maybe they are alive and do not know where I am.

"Alas, whatever virtue I practiced and the devotion with which I served my own lord and husband, all these have come to naught; I shall presently abandon this ill-fated life of mine. O Rāma, after you complete the fourteen-year term of exile, you will return to Ayodhyā and enjoy life with the queens you might marry. But, I who loved you and whose heart is forever fastened to you, shall soon be no more.

"How shall I end this life? I have no weapon; nor will anyone here give me a weapon or poison to end my life. Ah, I shall use this string with which my hair has been tied and hang myself from this tree."

Thinking aloud in this manner, Sītā contemplated the feet of Rāma and got ready to execute herself. At the same time, however, she noticed many auspicious omens which dissuaded her from her wish to end her life. Her left eye, left arm and left thigh throbbed.[8] Her heart was gladdened, her sorrow left her for the moment, her despair abated, and she became calm and radiant once again.

Hanumān, sitting on the tree, watched all this. He thought: "If I meet Sītā in the midst of these demonesses, it would be disastrous. In fact, she might get frightened and cry and before I could make the announcement concerning Rāma, I might be caught. I can fight all the demons here; but then I might be too weak to fly back. I could speak to her in the dialect of the brāhmaņa; but she might suspect a vānara speaking Sanskrit to be Rāvaņa himself![9] To speak to Sītā now seems to be risky; yet, if I do not, she might commit suicide. If one does not act with due regard to place and time, the contrary results ensue. I shall sing the glories of Rāma softly and thus win Sītā's confidence. Then I shall deliver Rāma's message to her in a manner which will evoke her confidence."

SUNDARA 31, 32, 33

After deep deliberation, Hanumān decided upon the safest and the wisest course! Softly, sweetly, clearly and in cultured accents, he narrated the story of Rāma. He said: "A descendant of the noble Ikșvāku was the emperor Daśaratha, who was a royal sage in as much as he was devoted to asceticism and righteousness, while yet ruling his kingdom. His eldest son Rāma was equally powerful, glorious and righteous. To honor his father's promise to his step-mother, Rāma went to the Daņḍaka forest along with his brother Lakṣmaņa, and his wife Sītā. There, Rāma killed thousands of demons. A demon disguised as a deer tricked Rāma and Lakṣmaņa away, and at that time, the wicked Rāvaņa abducted Sītā. Rāma went searching for her; and while so wandering the forest cultivated the friendship of the vānara Sugrīva. Sugrīva commissioned millions

8. In the case of men, the throbbing of the right eye, arm, or thigh signifies good fortune.
9. Women in all castes and men in castes lower than those of the *brāhmaņas* and the *kṣatriyas* often spoke languages or dialects other than Sanskrit. Sītā can speak Sanskrit because she has been educated as a princess of the *kṣatriya* caste-group.

of vānaras to search for Sītā. Endowed with extraordinary energy, I crossed the ocean; and blessed I am that I am able to behold that Sītā."

Sītā was supremely delighted to hear that speech. She looked up and down, around and everywhere, and saw the vānara Hanumān. But, seeing the vānara seated on the tree, Sītā was frightened and suspicious. She cried aloud. "O Rāma, O Lakṣmaṇa." She was terror-stricken as the vānara approached her; but she was pleasantly surprised to see that he came humbly and worshipfully. She thought: "Am I dreaming? I hope not; it forebodes ill to dream of a vānara. Nay, I am not dreaming. Maybe, this is hallucination. I have constantly been thinking of Rāma. I have constantly uttered his name, and talked about him. Since my whole being is absorbed in him, I am imagining all this. But, I have reasoned out all this carefully within myself; yet, this being here is not only clearly seen by me, but it talks to me, too! I pray to the gods, may what I have just heard be true."

With his palms joined together in salutation over his head, Hanumān humbly approached Sītā and asked: "Who are you, O lady? Are you indeed the wife of that blessed Rāma?"

Highly pleased with this question, Sītā thereupon related her whole story: "I am the daughter-in-law of king Daśaratha, and the daughter of king Janaka. I am the wife of Rāma. We lived happily in Ayodhyā for twelve years. But when Rāma was about to be crowned, his step-mother Kaikeyī demanded the boon from her husband that Rāma should be banished to the forest. The king swooned on hearing this; but Rāma took it upon himself to fulfill that promise. I followed him; and Lakṣmaṇa, too, came with us. One day when they were away, Rāvaṇa forcibly carried me and brought me here. He has given me two more months to live; after which I shall meet my end."

SUNDARA 34–35

Once again bowing down to Sītā, Hanumān said to her: "O divine lady, I am a messenger sent by Rāma. He, as also his brother Lakṣmaṇa, send their greetings and hope that you are alive and well." Sītā rejoiced and thought to herself: "Surely, there is a lot of truth in the old adage: 'Happiness is bound to come to the man who lives, even though after a long time.'" But, as Hanumān came near her, she grew suspicious and would not even look at him: she thought, and said to him: "O Rāvaṇa! Previously you assumed the disguise of a mendicant and abducted me. Now, you have come to torment me in the guise of a vānara! Pray, leave me alone." But, on the other hand, she reasoned to herself: "No this cannot be; for on seeing this vānara, my heart rejoices."

Hanumān, however, reassured her: "O blessed Sītā, I am a messenger sent by Rāma who will very soon kill these demons and rescue you from their captivity. Rāma and Lakṣmaṇa constantly think of you. So does king Sugrīva whose minister Hanumān, I am. Endowed with extraordinary energy I crossed the sea. I am not what you suspect me to be!"

At her request, Hanumān recounted the glories of Rāma:[1] "Rāma is equal to the gods in beauty, charm and wisdom. He is the protector of all living beings,

1. In the description that follows, Hanumān reiterates many of the qualities and attributes ascribed to Rāma throughout the epic. This conventional portrait of the ideal man blends physical characteristics and character traits.

of his own people, of his work and of his dharma; he is the protector of people of different occupations, of good conduct, and he himself adheres to good conduct and makes others do so, too. He is mighty, friendly, well-versed in scriptures and devoted to the holy ones. He is endowed with all the characteristics of the best among men, which are: broad shoulders, strong arms, powerful neck, lovely face, reddish eyes, deep voice, dark-brown colored skin; he has firm chest, wrist and fist; he has long eyebrows, arms and scrotum; he has symmetrical locks, testicles and knees; he has strong bulging chest, abdomen and rim of the navel; reddish in the corner of his eyes, nails, palms and soles; he is soft in his glans, the lines of his feet and hair; he has deep voice, gait and navel; three folds adorn the skin of his neck and his abdomen; the arch of his feet, the lines on his soles, and the nipples are deep; he has short generative organ, neck, back and shanks; three spirals adorn the hair on his head; there are four lines at the root of his thumb; and four lines on his forehead; he is four cubits tall; the four pairs of his limbs (cheeks, arms, shanks and knees) are symmetrical; even so the other fourteen pairs of limbs; his limbs are long. He is excellent in every way. Lakṣmaṇa, Rāma's brother, is also full of charm and excellences."

SUNDARA 35–36

Hanumān then narrated in great detail all that had happened. He mentioned in particular how Rāma was moved to tears when Hanumān showed him the pieces of jewelry that Sītā had dropped on the hill. He concluded that narrative by affirming: "I shall certainly attain the glory of having seen you first; and Rāma too will soon come here to take you back." He also revealed to Sītā his own identity: "Kesari, my father, lived on the mountain known as Malayavān. Once he went to the Gokarṇa mountain at the command of the sages to fight and to kill a demon named Sāmbasadana who tormented the people. I was born of the wind-god and my mother Añjanā. I tell you again, O divine lady, that I am a vānara, and I am a messenger sent by Rāma; here, behold the ring which has been inscribed with the name of Rāma. Whatever might have been the cause of your suffering captivity, it has almost come to an end."

When she saw the signet ring, Sītā felt the presence of Rāma himself; she was filled with joy. Her attitude to Hanumān, too, immediately and dramatically changed. She exclaimed: "You are heroic, capable, and wise, too, O best among vānaras. What a remarkable feat you have accomplished by crossing this vast ocean, a distance of eight hundred miles.[2] Surely, you are not an ordinary vānara in that you are not afraid of even Rāvaṇa. I am delighted to hear that Rāma and Lakṣmaṇa are well. But why has he not rescued me yet: he could dry up the ocean, in fact he could even destroy the whole earth with his missiles if he wanted to. Perhaps, they had to wait for the propitious moment, and that moment which would mean the end of my suffering has not yet arrived.

"O Hanumān, tell me more about Rāma. Does he continue to rely on both self-effort and divine agency in all that he undertakes? Tell me, O Hanumān, does he still love me as before? And, I also hope that, pining for me, he does not waste away. And also tell me: how will Rāma rescue me from here. Will

2. Not a realistic estimate of the distance between Laṅkā and the southern tip of India, which is much shorter than this.

Bharata send an army? When he renounced the throne and when he took me to the forest, he displayed extraordinary firmness: is he still as firm in his resolves? Oh, I know that he loves me more than anyone else in this world."

Hanumān replied: "You will soon behold Rāma, O Sītā! Stricken with grief on account of his separation from you, Rāma does not eat meat, nor drink wine; he does not even wish to ward off flies and mosquitoes that assail him. He thinks of you constantly. He hardly sleeps; and if he does, he wakes up calling out 'Ah Sītā.' When he sees a fruit or flower, he thinks of you." Hearing the glories of Rāma, Sītā was rid of sorrow; hearing of his grief, Sītā grew equally sorrowful.

SUNDARA 37

Sītā replied to Hanumān: "Your description of Rāma's love for me comes to me like nectar mixed with poison. In whatever condition one may be, whether one is enjoying unlimited power and prosperity or one is in dreadful misery, the end of one's action drags a man as if he were tied with a rope. Look at the way in which Rāma, Lakṣmaṇa and I have been subjected to sorrow: surely, no one can overcome destiny. I wonder when the time will come when I shall be united with Rāma once again. Rāvaṇa gave me one year, of which ten months have passed and only two are left. At the end of those two months, Rāvaṇa will surely kill me. There is no alternative. For, he does not fancy the thought of taking me back to Rāma. In fact, such a course was suggested by Rāvaṇa's own brother Vibhīṣaṇa: so his own daughter Kalā told me. But Rāvaṇa turns a deaf ear upon such wise counsel."

Hanumān said to Sītā: "I am sure that Rāma will soon arrive here, with an army of forest-dwellers and other tribes, as soon as I inform him of your where-abouts. But, O divine lady, I have another idea. You can rejoin your husband this very day. I can enable you to end this sorrow instantly. Pray, do not hesi-tate; get on my back, and seek union (yogam) with Rāma now. I have the power to carry you, or even Laṅkā, Rāvaṇa and everything in it! No one will be able to pursue me or to overcome me. What a great triumph it will be if I return to Kiṣkindhā with you on my back!"

For a moment Sītā was thrilled at this prospect. But she remarked almost in jest: "You are speaking truly like a vānara, an ignorant tribesman. You are so small: and you think you can carry me over the ocean!" Hanumān, thereupon, showed Sītā his real form. Seeing him stand like a mountain in front of her, Sītā felt sure that his confidence was justified, but said to him: "O mighty Hanumān, I am convinced that you can do as you say. But I do not think it is proper for me to go with you. You may proceed at great speed; but I may slip and fall into the ocean. If I go with you, the demons will suspect our relation-ship and give it an immoral twist. Moreover, many demons will pursue you: how will you, unarmed as you are, deal with them and at the same time pro-tect me? I might once again fall into their hands. I agree you have the power to fight them: but if you kill them all, it will rob Rāma of the glory of killing them and rescuing me. Surely, when Rāma and Lakṣmaṇa come here with you, they will destroy the demons and liberate me. I am devoted to Rāma: and I will not of my own accord touch the body of another man. There-fore, O Hanumān, enable Rāma and Lakṣmaṇa to come here with greatest expedition."

SUNDARA 38

Hanumān, the wise vānara, was highly impressed and thoroughly convinced of the propriety of Sītā's arguments. He applauded them, and prayed: "If you feel you should not come, pray, give me a token which I might take back with me and which Rāma might recognize."

This suggestion revived old memories and moved Sītā to tears. She said to Hanumān: "I shall give you the best token. Please remind my glorious husband of a delightful episode in our forest-life which only he and I know. This happened when we were living near Citrakooṭa hill. We had finished our bath; and we had had a lot of fun playing in water, Rāma was sitting on my lap. A crow began to worry me. I kept it away threatening it with stones. It hid itself. When I was getting dressed and when my skirt slipped a little, the crow attacked me again: but I defended myself angrily. Looking at this Rāma laughed, while sweetly pacifying me.

"Both of us were tired. I slept on Rāma's lap for sometime. Later Rāma slept with his head resting on my lap. The crow (who was Indra's son in disguise) attacked me again and began to inflict wounds on my body. A few drops of blood trickled from my chest and fell on Rāma who awoke. Seeing the vicious crow perched on a nearby tree, Rāma picked up the missile named after the creator and hurled it at the crow. That crow flew round to the three worlds but found no asylum anywhere else.

"Eventually it sought refuge with Rāma himself. Rāma was instantly pacified. Yet, the missile could not be neutralized. The crow sacrificed its right eye and saved its life." As she was narrating the story, Sītā felt the presence of Rāma and addressed him: "O Rāma, you were ready to use the Brahmā-missile towards a mere crow for my sake; why do you suffer my abduction with patience? Though I have you as my lord and master, yet I live here like a destitute! Have you no compassion for me: it was from you I learnt that compassion is the greatest virtue!" She said to Hanumān again: "No power on earth can confront Rāma. It is only my ill-luck that prevents them from coming to my rescue."

Hanumān explained: "It was only ignorance of your whereabouts that has caused this delay, O divine lady. Now that we know where you are, the destruction of the demons is at hand." Sītā said: "The fulfillment of this mission depends upon you; with your aid, Rāma will surely succeed in his mission. But, please tell Rāma that I shall be alive only for a month more." Then as a further token, Sītā took off a precious jewel from her person and gave it to Hanumān. Receiving that jewel, and with Sītā's blessings Hanumān was ready to depart.

* * *

From Book 6

Yuddha

YUDDHA 109, 110, 111

When Rāma and Rāvaņa began to fight, their armies stood stupefied, watching them! Rāma was determined to win; Rāvaņa was sure he would die: knowing this, they fought with all their might. Rāvaņa attacked the standard on Rāma's car: and Rāma similarly shot the standard on Rāvaņa's car. While Rāvaņa's standard fell; Rāma's did not. Rāvana next aimed at the "horses" of Rāma's car: even though he attacked them with all his might, they remained unaffected.

Both of them discharged thousands of missiles: these illumined the skies and created a new heaven, as it were! They were accurate in their aim and their missiles unfailingly hit the target. With unflagging zeal they fought each other, without the least trace of fatigue. What one did the other did in retaliation.

Rāvana shot at Mātali[3] who remained unaffected by it. Then Rāvana sent a shower of maces and mallets at Rāma. Their very sound agitated the oceans and tormented the aquatic creatures. The celestials and the holy brāhmanas witnessing the scene prayed: "May auspiciousness attend to all the living beings, and may the worlds endure forever. May Rāma conquer Rāvana." Astounded at the way in which Rāma and Rāvana fought with each other, the sages said to one another: "Sky is like sky, ocean is like ocean; the fight between Rāma and Rāvana is like Rāma and Rāvana—incomparable."

Taking up a powerful missile, Rāma correctly aimed at the head of Rāvana; it fell. But another head appeared in its place. Every time Rāma cut off Rāvana's head, another appeared! Rāma was puzzled. Mātali, Rāma's driver, said to Rāma: "Why do you fight like an ordinary warrior, O Rāma? Use the Brahmā-missile; the hour of the demon's death is at hand."

Rāma remembered the Brahmā-missile which the sage Agastya had given him. It had the power of the wind-god for its "feathers"; the power of fire and sun at its head; the whole space was its body; and it had the weight of a mountain. It shone like the sun or the fire of nemesis. As Rāma took it in his hands, the earth shook and all living beings were terrified. Infallible in its destructive power, this ultimate weapon of destruction shattered the chest of Rāvana, and entered deep into the earth.

Rāvana fell dead. And the surviving demons fled, pursued by the vānaras. The vānaras shouted in great jubilation. The air resounded with the drums of the celestials. The gods praised Rāma. The earth became steady, the wind blew softly and the sun was resplendent as before. Rāma was surrounded by mighty heroes and gods who were all joyously felicitating him on the victory.

YUDDHA 112, 113

Seeing Rāvana lying dead on the battlefield, Vibhīsana burst into tears. Overcome by brotherly affection, he lamented thus: "Alas, what I had predicted has come true: and my advice was not relished by you, overcome as you were by lust and delusion. Now that you have departed, the glory of Lankā has departed. You were like a tree firmly established in heroism with asceticism for its strength, spreading out firmness in all aspects of your life: yet you have been cut down. You were like an elephant with splendor, noble ancestry, indignation, and pleasant nature for parts: yet you have been killed. You, who were like blazing fire have been extinguished by Rāma."

Rāma approached the grief-stricken Vibhīsana and gently and lovingly said to him: "It is not right that you should thus grieve, O Vibhīsana, for a mighty warrior fallen on the battlefield. Victory is the monopoly of none: a hero is either slain in battle or he kills his opponent. Hence our ancients decreed that

3. Indra, king of the gods, has sent his own charioteer, Mātali, to drive Rāma's chariot in battle.

the warrior who is killed in combat should not be mourned. Get up and consider what should be done next."

Vibhīṣaṇa regained his composure and said to Rāma: "This Rāvaṇa used to give a lot in charity to ascetics; he enjoyed life; he maintained his servants well; he shared his wealth with his friends, and he destroyed his enemies. He was regular in his religious observances; learned he was in the scriptures. By your grace, O Rāma, I wish to perform his funeral in accordance with the scriptures, for his welfare in the other world." Rāma was delighted and said to Vibhīṣaṇa: "Hostility ends at death. Take steps for the due performance of the funeral rites. He is your brother as he is mine, too."

The womenfolk of Rāvaṇa's court, and his wives, hearing of his end, rushed out of the palace, and, arriving at the battlefield, rolled on the ground in sheer anguish. Overcome by grief they gave vent to their feelings in diverse heart-rending ways. They wailed: "Alas, he who could not be killed by the gods and demons, has been killed in battle by a man standing on earth. Our beloved lord! Surely when you abducted Sītā and brought her to Laṅkā, you invited your own death! Surely it was because death was close at hand that you did not listen to the wise counsel of your own brother Vibhīṣaṇa, and you ill-treated him and exiled him. Even later if you had restored Sītā to Rāma, this evil fate would not have overtaken you. However, it is surely not because you did what you liked, because you were driven by lust, that you lie dead now: God's will makes people do diverse deeds. He who is killed by the divine will dies. No one can flout the divine will, and no one can buy the divine will nor bribe it."

* * *

YUDDHA 115, 116

Rāma returned to the camp where the vānara troops had been stationed. He turned to Lakṣmaṇa and said: "O Lakṣmaṇa, install Vibhīṣaṇa on the throne of Laṅkā and consecrate him as the king of Laṅkā. He has rendered invaluable service to me and I wish to behold him on the throne of Laṅkā at once."

Without the least loss of time, Lakṣmaṇa made the necessary preparations and with the waters of the ocean consecrated Vibhīṣaṇa as king of Laṅkā, in strict accordance with scriptural ordinance. Rāma, Lakṣmaṇa and the others were delighted. The demon-leaders brought their tributes and offered them to Vibhīṣaṇa who in turn placed them all at Rāma's feet.

Rāma said to Hanumān: "Please go, with the permission of king Vibhīṣaṇa, to Sītā and inform her of the death of Rāvaṇa and the welfare of both myself and Lakṣmaṇa." Immediately Hanumān left for the Aśoka-grove. The grief-stricken Sītā was happy to behold him. With joined palms Hanumān submitted Rāma's message and added: "Rāma desires me to inform you that you can shed fear, for you are in your own home as it were, now that Vibhīṣaṇa is king of Laṅkā." Sītā was speechless for a moment and then said: "I am delighted by the message you have brought, O Hanumān; and I am rendered speechless by it. I only regret that I have nothing now with which to reward you; nor is any gift equal in value to the most joyous tidings you have brought me." Hanumān submitted: "O lady, the very words you have uttered are more precious than all the jewels of the world! I consider myself supremely blessed to have witnessed Rāma's victory and Rāvaṇa's destruction." Sītā was even more delighted: she said, "Only you can utter such sweet words, O Hanumān, endowed as you are with manifold excellences. Truly you are an abode of virtues."

Hanumān said: "Pray, give me leave to kill all these demonesses who have been tormenting you so long." Sītā replied: "Nay, Hanumān, they are not responsible for their actions, for they were but obeying their master's commands. And, surely, it was my own evil destiny that made me suffer at their hands. Hence, I forgive them. A noble man does not recognize the harm done to him by others: and he never retaliates, for he is the embodiment of goodness. One should be compassionate towards all, the good and the wicked, nay even towards those who are fit to be killed: who is free from sin?" Hanumān was thrilled to hear these words of Sītā, and said: "Indeed you are the noble consort of Rāma and his peer in virtue and nobility. Pray, give me a message to take back to Rāma." Sītā replied: "Please tell him that I am eager to behold his face." Assuring Sītā that she would see Rāma that very day, Hanumān returned to Rāma.

YUDDHA 117, 118, 119

Hanumān conveyed Sītā's message to Rāma who turned to king Vibhīṣaṇa and said: "Please bring Sītā to me soon, after she has had a bath and has adorned herself." Immediately Vibhīṣaṇa went to Sītā and compelled her to proceed seated in a palanquin, to where Rāma was. Vānaras and demons had gathered around her, eager to look at Sītā. And Vibhīṣaṇa, in accordance with the tradition, wished to ensure that Sītā was not seen by these and rebuked them to go away. Restraining him, Rāma said: "Why do you rebuke them, O Vibhīṣaṇa? Neither houses nor clothes nor walls constitute a veil for a woman; her character alone is her veil. Let her descend from the palanquin and walk up to me." So she did.

Rāma said sternly: "My purpose has been accomplished, O Sītā. My prowess has been witnessed by all. I have fulfilled my pledge. Rāvaṇa's wickedness has been punished. The extraordinary feat performed by Hanumān in crossing the ocean and burning Laṅkā[4] has borne fruit. Vibhīṣaṇa's devotion has been rewarded." Rāma's heart was in a state of conflict, afraid as he was of public ridicule. Hence, he continued: "I wish to let you know that all this was done not for your sake, but for the sake of preserving my honor. Your conduct is open to suspicion, hence even your sight is displeasing to me. Your body was touched by Rāvaṇa: how then can I, claiming to belong to a noble family, accept you? Hence I permit you to go where you like and live with whom you like—either Lakṣmaṇa, Bharata, Śatrughna, Sugrīva or even Vibhīṣaṇa. It is difficult for me to believe that Rāvaṇa, who was so fond of you, would have been able to keep away from you for such a long time."

Sītā was shocked. Rāma's words wounded her heart. Tears streamed down her face. Wiping them, she replied: "O Rāma, you are speaking to me in the language of a common and vulgar man speaking to a common woman. That which was under my control, my heart, has always been yours; how could I

---

4. When Hanumān destroys the groves of Laṅkā, Rāvaṇa's henchmen capture him and set his tail on fire. Hanumān sets fire to Laṅkā's mansions with his fiery tail and himself escapes unhurt.

prevent my body from being touched when I was helpless and under another person's control? Ah, if only you had conveyed your suspicion through Hanumān when he came to meet me, I would have killed myself then and saved you all this trouble and the risk involved in the war." Turning to Lakṣmaṇa, she said: "Kindle the fire, O Lakṣmaṇa: that is the only remedy. I shall not live to endure this false calumny." Lakṣmaṇa looked at Rāma and with his approval kindled the fire. Sītā prayed: "Even as my heart is ever devoted to Rāma, may the fire protect me. If I have been faithful to Rāma in thought, word or deed, may the fire protect me. The sun, the moon, the wind, earth and others are witness to my purity; may the fire protect me." Then she entered into the fire, even as an oblation poured into the fire would. Gods and sages witnessed this. The women who saw this screamed.

YUDDHA 120, 121

Rāma was moved to tears by the heart-rending cries of all those women who witnessed the self-immolation of Sītā. At the same time, all the gods, including the trinity—the Creator, the Preserver, and the Redeemer (or Transformer)[5]— arrived upon the scene in their personal forms. Saluting Rāma, they said: "You are the foremost among the gods, and yet you treat Sītā as if you were a common human being!"

Rāma replied to these divinities: "I consider myself a human being, Rāma the son of Daśaratha. Who I am, and whence I am, may you tell me!"

Brahmā the creator said: "You are verily lord Nārāyaṇa.[6] You are the imperishable cosmic being. You are the truth. You are eternal. You are the supreme dharma of the worlds. You are the father even of the chief of the gods, Indra. You are the sole refuge of perfected beings and holy men. You are the Om,[7] and you are the spirit of sacrifice. You are that cosmic being with infinite heads, hands and eyes.[8] You are the support of the whole universe. The whole universe is your body. Sītā is Lakṣmī[9] and you are lord Viṣṇu, who is of a dark hue, and who is the creator of all beings. For the sake of the destruction of Rāvaṇa you entered into a human body. This mission of ours has been fully accomplished by you. Blessed it is to be in your presence; blessed it is to sing your glories; they are truly blessed who are devoted to you, for their life will be attended with success."

As soon as Brahmā finished saying this, the god of fire emerged from the fire in his personal form, holding up Sītā in his hands. Sītā shone in all her radiance. The god of fire who is the witness of everything that takes place in the world, said to Rāma: "Here is your Sītā, Rāma. I find no fault in her. She has not erred in thought, word or deed. Even during the long period of her detention in the abode of Rāvaṇa, she did not even think of him, as her

---

5. The triad of the three great gods, Brahmā (Creator), Viṣṇu (Preserver), and Śiva (Redeemer or Transformer).

6. Viṣṇu in his primeval cosmic form.

7. A sacred chant (mantra) of the Vedas.

8. The cosmic being described here is Puruṣa,

or "Man," a primeval being with innumerable heads, arms, and eyes who was offered as the sacrificial victim by the gods and sages in the first sacrifice, described in a hymn of the Ṛg-veda.

9. Goddess-consort of Viṣṇu.

heart was set on you. Accept her: and I command you not to treat her harshly."

Rāma was highly pleased at this turn of events. He said: "Indeed, I was fully aware of Sītā's purity. Even the mighty and wicked Rāvaṇa could not lay his hands upon her with evil intention. Yet, this baptism by fire was necessary, to avoid public calumny and ridicule, for though she was pure, she lived in Laṅkā for a long time. I knew, too, that Sītā would never be unfaithful to me: for we are non-different from each other even as the sun and its rays are. It is therefore impossible for me to renounce her."

After saying so, Rāma was joyously reunited with Sītā.

YUDDHA 122, 123

Lord Śiva then said to Rāma: "You have fulfilled a most difficult task. Now behold your father, the illustrious king Daśaratha who appears in the firmament to bless you and to greet you."

Rāma along with Lakṣmaṇa saw that great monarch, their father clad in a raiment of purity and shining by his own luster. Still seated in his celestial vehicle, Daśaratha lifted up Rāma and placing him on his lap, warmly embraced him and said: "Neither heaven nor even the homage of the gods is as pleasing to me as to behold you, Rāma. I am delighted to see that you have successfully completed the period of your exile and that you have destroyed all your enemies. Even now the cruel words of Kaikeyī haunt my heart; but seeing you and embracing you, I am rid of that sorrow, O Rāma. You have redeemed my word and thus I have been saved by you. It is only now that I recognize you to be the supreme person incarnated as a human being in this world in order to kill Rāvaṇa."

Rāma said: "You remember that you said to Kaikeyī, 'I renounce you and your son'? Pray, take back that curse and may it not afflict Kaikeyī and Bharata." Daśaratha agreed to it and then said to Lakṣmaṇa: "I am pleased with you, my son, and you have earned great merit by the faithful service you have rendered to Rāma."

Lastly, king Daśaratha said to Sītā: "My dear daughter, do not take to heart the fire ordeal that Rāma forced you to undergo: it was necessary to reveal to the world your absolute purity. By your conduct you have exalted yourself above all women." Having thus spoken to them, Daśaratha ascended to heaven.

Before taking leave of Rāma, Indra prayed: "Our visit to you should not be fruitless, O Rāma. Command me, what may I do for you?" Rāma replied: "If you are really pleased with me, then I pray that all those vānaras who laid down their lives for my sake may come back to life. I wish to see them hale and hearty as before. I also wish to see the whole world fruitful and prosperous." Indra replied: "This indeed is an extremely difficult task. Yet, I do not go back on my word, hence I grant it. All the vānaras will come back to life and be restored to their original form, with all their wounds healed. Even as you had asked, the world will be fruitful and prosperous."

Instantly, all the vānaras arose from the dead and bowed to Rāma. The others who witnessed this marveled and the gods beheld Rāma who had all his wishes fulfilled. The gods returned to their abodes.

* * *

Summary   After crowning Vibhīṣaṇa king of Laṅkā, Rāma, Lakṣmaṇa and Sītā fly to Ayodhyā in Rāvaṇa's flying chariot, accompanied by Vibhīṣaṇa, Sugrīva, Hanumān, and the monkey hordes.

YUDDHA 130

Bharata immediately made the reception arrangements. He instructed Śatrughna: "Let prayers be offered to the gods in all temples and houses of worship with fragrant flowers and musical instruments."

Śatrughna immediately gave orders that the roads along which the royal procession would wend its way to the palace should be leveled and sprinkled with water, and kept clear by hundreds of policemen cordoning them. Soon all the ministers, and thousands of elephants and men on horse-back and in cars went out to greet Rāma. The royal reception party, seated in palanquins,[1] was led by the queen-mother Kausalyā herself; Kaikeyī and the other members of the royal household followed—and all of them reached Nandigrāma.[2]

From there Bharata headed the procession with the sandals of Rāma placed on his head, with the white royal umbrella and the other regalia.[3] Bharata was the very picture of an ascetic though he radiated the joy that filled his heart at the very thought of Rāma's return to the kingdom.

Bharata anxiously looked around but saw no signs of Rāma's return! But, Hanumān reassured him: "Listen, O Bharata, you can see the cloud of dust raised by the vānaras rushing towards Ayodhyā. You can now hear the roar of the Puṣpaka flying chariot."

"Rāma has come!"—these words were uttered by thousands of people at the same time. Even before the Puṣpaka landed, Bharata humbly saluted Rāma who was standing on the front side of the chariot. The Puṣpaka landed. As Bharata approached it, Rāma lifted him up and placed him on his lap. Bharata bowed down to Rāma and also to Sītā and greeted Lakṣmaṇa. And he embraced Sugrīva, Jāmbavān, Aṅgada, Vibhīṣaṇa and others. He said to Sugrīva: "We are four brothers, and with you we are five. Good deeds promote friendship, and evil is a sign of enmity."

Rāma bowed to his mother who had become emaciated through sorrow, and brought great joy to her heart. Then he also bowed to Sumitrā and Kaikeyī. All the people thereupon said to Rāma: "Welcome, welcome back, O Lord."

Bharata placed the sandals in front of Rāma, and said: "Rāma, here is your kingdom which I held in trust for you during your absence. I consider myself supremely blessed in being able to behold your return to Ayodhyā. By your grace, the treasury has been enriched tenfold by me, as also the storehouses and the strength of the nation." Rāma felt delighted. When the entire party

1. Litters in which people were carried by bearers.
2. The village outside the city of Ayodhyā, from which Bharata ruled the kingdom on behalf of Rāma.

3. By carrying Rāma's sandals on his head, Bharata indicates his subservience to and reverence for Rāma as his sovereign, elder brother, and teacher.

had disembarked, he instructed that the Puṣpaka be returned to its original owner, Kubera.[4]

YUDDHA 131

The coronation proceedings were immediately initiated by Bharata. Skilled barbers removed the matted locks of Rāma. He had a ceremonial bath and he was dressed in magnificent robes and royal jewels. Kausalyā herself helped the vānara ladies to dress themselves in royal robes; all the queens dressed Sītā appropriately for the occasion. The royal chariot was brought; duly ascending it, Rāma, Lakṣmaṇa and Sītā went in a procession to Ayodhyā, Bharata himself driving the chariot. When he had reached the court, Rāma gave his ministers and counselors a brief account of the events during his exile, particularly the alliance with the vānara chief Sugrīva, and the exploits of Hanumān. He also informed them of his alliance with Vibhīṣaṇa.

At Bharata's request, Sugrīva despatched the best of the vānaras to fetch water from the four oceans, and all the sacred rivers of the world. The aged sage Vasiṣṭha thereupon commenced the ceremony in connection with the coronation of Rāma. Rāma and Sītā were seated on a seat made entirely of precious stones. The foremost among the sages thereupon consecrated Rāma with the appropriate Vedic chants. First the brāhmaṇas, then the virgins, then the ministers and warriors, and later the businessmen poured the holy waters on Rāma.[5] After that the sage Vasiṣṭha placed Rāma on the throne made of gold and studded with precious stones, and placed on his head the dazzling crown which had been made by Brahmā the creator himself. The gods and others paid their homage to Rāma by bestowing gifts upon him. Rāma also gave away rich presents to the brāhmaṇas and others, including the vānara chiefs like Sugrīva. Rāma then gave to Sītā a necklace of pearls and said: "You may give it to whom you like, Sītā." And, immediately Sītā bestowed that gift upon Hanumān.

After witnessing the coronation of Rāma, the vānaras returned to Kiṣkindhā. So did Vibhīṣaṇa return to Laṅkā. Rāma looked fondly at Lakṣmaṇa and expressed the wish that he should reign as the prince regent. Lakṣmaṇa did not reply: he did not want it. Rāma appointed Bharata as prince regent. Rāma thereafter ruled the earth for a very long time.

During the period of Rāma's reign, there was no poverty, no crime, no fear, and no unrighteousness in the kingdom. All the people constantly spoke of Rāma; the whole world had been transformed into Rāma. Everyone was devoted to dharma. And Rāma was highly devoted to dharma, too. He ruled for eleven thousand years.

YUDDHA 131

Rāma's rule of the kingdom was characterized by the effortless and spontaneous prevalence of dharma. People were free from fear of any sort. There were

4. God of wealth.
5. The *brāhmaṇas*, ministers and warriors, and businessmen represent the three highest caste-groups in Hindu society.

no widows in the land: people were not molested by beasts and snakes, nor did they suffer from diseases. There was no theft, no robbery nor any violence. Young people did not die, making older people perform funeral services for them. Everyone was happy and everyone was devoted to dharma; beholding Rāma alone, no one harmed another. People lived long and had many children. They were healthy and they were free from sorrow. Everywhere people were speaking all the time about Rāma; the entire world appeared to be the form of Rāma. The trees were endowed with undying roots, and they were in fruition all the time and they flowered throughout the year. Rain fell whenever it was needed. There was a pleasant breeze always. The brāhmaṇas (priests), the warriors, the farmers and businessmen, as also the members of the servant class, were entirely free from greed, and were joyously devoted to their own dharma and functions in society. There was no falsehood in the life of the people who were all righteous. People were endowed with all auspicious characteristics and all of them had dharma as their guiding light. Thus did Rāma rule the world for eleven thousand years, surrounded by his brothers.

This holy epic Rāmāyaṇa composed by the sage Vālmīki, promotes dharma, fame, long life and in the case of a king, victory. He who listens to it always is freed from all sins. He who desires sons gets them, and he who desires wealth becomes wealthy, by listening to the story of the coronation of Rāma. The king conquers the whole world, after overcoming his enemies. Women who listen to this story will be blessed with children like Rāma and his brothers. And they, too, will be blessed with long life, after listening to the Rāmāyaṇa. He who listens to or reads this Rāmāyaṇa propitiates Rāma by this; Rāma is pleased with him; and he indeed is the eternal lord Viṣṇu.

LAVA AND KUŚA said: Such is the glorious epic, Rāmāyaṇa. May all recite it and thus augment the glory of dharma, of lord Viṣṇu. Righteous men should regularly listen to this story of Rāma, which increases health, long life, love, wisdom and vitality.

THE MAHABHARATA

ca. 400 B.C.E.–400 C.E.

The *Mahabharata*, composed in Sanskrit about 2000 years ago, is the longest poem in the world, about eight times the combined length of the *Iliad* and the *Odyssey*. It is one of the oldest compositions in world literature to offer us a sustained reflection on the possibilities of a just war and a harmonious society, and it does so by telling the story of a dynasty of kings in northern India deeply divided by the pursuit of power and wealth. The division leads to a tragic conflict on an epic scale. The *Mahabharata* seeks to explain these events by mapping out their place within ancient India as a whole, and by reflecting on the nature of law, right action, and political power, and on the intricate connections between power, violence, and good and evil. It has a cast of hundreds, and in addition to its central narrative, there are very many stories told by one character to another by way of instruction or consolation. The *Mahabharata* brings to life the full range of human emotion—love, envy, anger, sorrow, spiritual aspiration, joy, humor, and much more besides. It says of itself, "What is found in this poem . . . may be found elsewhere. But anything it does not contain is found nowhere."

CONTEXT

The *Mahabharata* attributes its own authorship to a sage called Vyasa who is also a participant in the action. But the epic as it now exists, in the most accurate scholarly edition, may well have been composed over several generations. It has always been the source of retellings in various forms and has been translated into all the major Indian languages. Every Hindu is familiar with at least the outline of the narrative and with the main subsidiary stories. And the *Bhagavada-gītā*, which sits at the heart of the epic, is probably the most revered text within Hinduism. The story starts with Vyasa being asked by a descendant of the ruling dynasty to narrate the history of his ancestors, and particularly to explain the great war that had divided and devastated his family a few generations earlier. Vyasa has composed his tale as a long poem and taught it to a disciple, who becomes the main narrator in the text of the epic.

Many aspects of the society depicted in the *Mahabharata* resemble the world in which it was composed. Large parts of the plains surrounding the River Ganges have been cleared of forests, and their indigenous inhabitants displaced, to make room for a multifac-

eted, settled society. While the majority of people live in small villages in the countryside, cultivating the land, a sizable urban population has emerged in towns and cities that serve as market and administrative centers. Capital cities are large and prosperous; the palaces of the kings are imposing, and royal households contain hundreds of occupants.

In the place and time of the *Mahabharata*, both inside and outside the story, Indian society is highly differentiated. The four main social classes (*varnas*)—consisting of the brahmins (priests), *kshatriyas* (warriors), *vaishyas* (traders), and *shudras* (peasants and those who serve the three higher groups)—are overlaid onto numerous specific and local categories. Each of these smaller groups, containing many lineages and clans, tends to have its own distinctive occupation, rituals, codes of conduct, marriage customs, dress, and dietary rules. In addition, three other groups are visible in this society: the so-called untouchables, a fifth social category that has been clearly separated from the others; various aboriginal tribes, who live in particular regions and have distinct identities; and groups of foreign origin, who have migrated to specific parts of the country. To an important degree, these divisions persist in India to this day. The story of Ekalavya, which features in the first of the extracts that follow, is still an iconic tale for socially marginalized groups.

The *Mahabharata* is much preoccupied with the maintenance of social distinctions, seeing them as the basis of the moral order. Karna's treatment, a consequence of his supposedly lowly birth, is an important and tragic element in the narrative. Yet, ironically, almost none of the main characters has straightforward parentage, being fathered by gods, or born from pots, deer or even blades of grass! We encounter polygamous as well as poly-androus families, warriors who have become scholars, and priests who have become warriors.

In the world surrounding the epic tale, but also present within it, the priestly and warrior classes have joined forces to constitute a distinct ruling elite. The brahmins here are scholars and spiritual practitioners, but some are also worldly participants in court poli-tics, at home in statecraft and expert in the arts of war—notably Drona, the brahmin teacher of weaponry to the Bharata cousins.

As members of a composite class pur-suing power and wealth, these *kshatriyas* and brahmins are fully engaged with war and conquest, with extending their king-doms, and with establishing long-term dynastic rule. Two or more branches of a common lineage sometimes compete—often violently and unscrupulously—for territory and dominance. That is the case with the Bharata clan.

In a dynamic and unstable political order of this sort, in which the material and practical stakes are high, the cen-tral problems often revolve around the nature of the law. What constitutes right and wrong, good and evil, justice and injustice, legitimacy and illegiti-macy? How can, or should, power and violence be constrained, and by whom, and why? When are war and violence justified? The *Mahabharata* narrates its long tale in the context of these questions, focusing on the concept of *dharma*, which refers at once to law (as given by the spiritual authorities), to the moral and ethical basis of order in the universe as well as in the human world, and to the duties and obliga-tions of an individual acting and making choices in their specific circumstances within everyday society. In this world-view, an individual or a society practic-ing *dharma* is good, and one violating it is evil. But *dharma* is subtle; law, spe-cific moral and ethical codes, and prac-tical rules of conduct are confusing and even inconsistent. Following them is never easy, and the probability of breaking them—and hence of perpetrat-ing evil—is high.

One striking aspect of *dharma* is the relation between speech and events. A vow, a blessing, or a prediction, once uttered, has to be fulfilled, otherwise dishonor accrues to the speaker. It is as if anything that intervenes between an utterance and its realization is the responsibility of the speaker, rather than of fate, or of any circumstances that life might throw up. Persons of great spiri-tual power can deliver curses or boons, and these are always fulfilled.

Responding to the world inside and outside his poem, Vyasa suggests that human beings on their own cannot resolve the moral dilemmas of *dharma*; they need the intervention of the gods. His epic therefore represents a time when Vishnu, the god who preserves the moral order of the universe, descends on earth as Lord Krishna, in order to destroy evil. Within Hinduism, Krishna is commonly seen as Vishnu's eighth avatar, just as Rama in the *Rāmāyaṇa* is the seventh (in a series of ten major incarnations). Krishna is a prince of a kingdom in western India, and he enters the story as a friend and political ally of its heroes.

THE EPIC

The *Mahabharata*'s main events center around the long-established Bharata dynasty, at a point when the burden of governing the kingdom falls upon two brothers, Dhritarashtra and Pandu. The eldest, Dhritarashtra, is born blind, and so is thought unfit to rule; Pandu, sec-ond in line, becomes the king.

Difficulties of succession to the throne arise with the next generation because Pandu is cursed to die the moment he touches either of his queens with sexual desire, and hence he cannot father any children. His two wives are able to draw upon a special divine power bestowed on Kunti, the elder wife, when she was very young. She gives birth to three sons, and Madri, the younger wife, has twins, each supernaturally engendered by a god. These five "surrogate" sons of Pandu are the Pandavas, the heroes of the epic: Yudhishthira, begotten by Dharma (the god of righteousness); Bhima, begotten by the Wind; Arjuna, begotten by Indra (the king of the gods, the Indian equivalent of Zeus); and Nakula and Sahadeva, begotten by the twin gods, the Ashvins.

In the meantime, Pandu's blind elder brother, Dhritarashtra, also has children; his wife, Gandhari, bears him one hundred sons (and one daughter), collectively called the Kauravas—the eldest of whom is Duryodhana. He is the epic's "villain." However, part of what makes the *Mahabharata* great is that those on the "wrong" side are capable of virtuous acts, while the heroes (even Krishna himself) sometimes engage in morally dubious behavior.

Duryodhana is born on the same day as his cousin Bhima, and hence is younger than Yudhishthira. By the law of primogeniture, Yudhishthira, the eldest in his generation among the Bharatas, ought to be the next king. But Dhritarashtra is the eldest son in the previous generation (and hence the original inheritor of the kingdom), and his eldest son, Duryodhana, encouraged by his father, therefore feels that he has a claim to the throne. The irresolvable conflict between these two applications of the *dharma* of succession creates lifelong tensions between the Pandavas and the Kauravas. When the conflict intensifies, the realm is divided, and the Pandavas create their own kingdom, centered on the beautiful city of Indraprastha, from which Yudhishthira becomes increasingly powerful, eventually being consecrated "king of kings."

The story could perhaps have ended there. But Duryodhana's envy will not allow him to rest until the Pandavas are destroyed. In this, he is supported by his weak father, Dhritarashtra. The epic follows the conflict between the two sets of cousins, through dramatic events, heroic struggles, the intervention of the gods, and tragic loss, until it arrives at the final resolution. Along the way, the human condition in all its grandeur, its courage, and its frailty is imaginatively explored.

As in other ancient epics, male honor and military prowess are central to the narrative. But one of the distinctive features of the *Mahabharata* is the importance of strong, resourceful, and articulate women—notably Draupadi (wife to the five Pandavas) and Kunti (Pandu's elder wife). In this, it differs from the Homeric epics, for instance, where women are far more peripheral.

The style and narrative structure of the *Mahabharata* stand in contrast to those of the *Rāmāyaṇa*. The *Rāmāyaṇa* is stylistically more uniform, linguistically more poetic, and more linear in its narrative progression (in spite of its many tales within tales). Although it is not immediately apparent from the extracts which follow, the structure of the *Mahabharata* is like a nest of Chinese boxes, with narratives framed within narratives and a multiplicity of narrators.

Largely because of their many-sided significance, the stories of the *Mahabharata* have traveled widely across Asia over the past sixteen hundred years, becoming an integral part of folklore, literature, and performance traditions from Indonesia and Malaysia to the Philippines. In particular, the *Bhagavad-gītā*—Krishna's teaching to Arjuna on the field of battle—has been translated into all the major languages of the world and has become an indispensable part of world literature. Its application to the dilemmas of a well-lived life continues to be exhaustively explored and drawn upon, within the Hindu religious tradition, and beyond.

From the time of its composition to this day, the *Mahabharata* has been a constant reference point in Indian culture. With its numerous stories, involving several hundred major and minor characters, the epic has served as a general reservoir of tales to live by. Individual episodes illustrate situations that we typically encounter, mirror many of the ethical dilemmas we ourselves face, and offer solutions that we can apply to our own lives. Many of the poem's characters and events are memorable and entertaining. Bhima, the impetuous strongman among the Pandavas, is a perennial children's favorite, as is Hanuman in the *Rāmāyaṇa* (who, like Bhima, is fathered by the Wind). Karna, Duryodhana's unfortunate friend, is a byword for tragic self-

sacrifice. The *Mahabharata* provides its audiences with a comprehensive education in politics, ethics, and morality. And, above all, it is an exciting, terrifying, moving, tragic, and sometimes humorous story on an enormous scale.

Since almost the only complete English translation to date (by K. M. Ganguli, available online) runs to around 5000 closely packed pages of nineteenth century prose, any version of the epic aimed at the general reader is bound to be an abridgement. The passages selected here come from a verse retelling of the *Mahabharata* by Carole Satyamurti. The verse form of the Sanskrit original would be impossible to reproduce in contemporary English, so the form chosen is blank verse, which, arguably, occupies a position in the English literary tradition comparable to the *shloka* form in Sanskrit.

The Mahabharata[1]

From *Book 1: The Book of the Beginning*

Summary   The Bharata cousins grow up together at Hastinapura and are taught the skills of battle by Drona, a distinguished weapons master.

LEARNING THE ARTS OF WAR

* * *

Drona gathered the royal youths together
and addressed them: "I have a driving passion
gnawing my heart, a task that will stab at me
until it's done. Will you give me your word
that, when the time is right, when you have mastered   5
all the skills with weapons I can teach you,
you will help me carry out this task?"
The Kauravas shifted uneasily
and stayed silent, but brave Arjuna,
ambidextrous third-born son of Pandu,   10

---

1. In her selections from the *Mahabharata* as well as in the headnote, the translator, Carol Satyamurti, presents Sanskrit terms without the diacritical marks used elsewhere in this anthology.

promised without hesitation. Drona
embraced him warmly, and shed tears of joy.

•

Drona was a most exacting master,
demanding discipline from all his pupils.
The hundred Kauravas, five Pandavas   15
and Ashvatthaman, the stern teacher's son,
were treated all alike in principle—
though now and then, Drona devised ways
of giving his son a little extra time;
and since Arjuna was exceptional   20
in his dedication, he became
the favorite among all Drona's pupils,
cherished even more than his own son.

As was to be expected from their birth,
almost all the youths were competent,   25
or excelled, at one weapon or another.
They mastered the basic skills of archery,
of fighting with sword and javelin, with the spear,
dagger, mace, and the small hand-thrown dart.
They learned to fight on horseback and on foot,   30
and how to steer a chariot; they learned
every earthly weapon, and a few,
according to their inner aptitude,
were taught astras[2]—for the proper use
of these occult weapons was dependent   35
on the depth of spiritual maturity
attained by the man who would summon them.

Drona arranged frequent competitions
so each boy knew exactly how he ranked
on the scale of skill, for every weapon.   40
Through this strategy, each prince possessed
something to aspire to, someone to beat.

Ashvatthaman, being his father's son,
had outstanding knowledge of the lore
and mantras of the god-given astras.   45
Yudhishthira was the best charioteer—
no one could outmaneuver him at speed.
Bhima and Duryodhana, both stronger
by far than any of the others, shone
at wielding the spike-encrusted mace,   50
swinging its colossal weight with ease.

2. Supernatural weapons of great power, invoked by specific incantations—mantras.

The twins, Sahadeva and Nakula,
were outstanding swordsmen, and they moved,
elegant as dancers, round each other,
perfectly matched.

But it was Arjuna,   55
tall, quick-moving, perfectly proportioned,
who was the best all-round kshatriya:
accomplished at each single form of combat,
and better by far at the art of archery
than all the others. You only had to see   60
his natural poise—the way he moved and stood,
his one-pointed attention as he drew
back the bowstring, letting the arrow fly
at just the right moment, and no other—
to know that this youth was extraordinary.   65
In him, natural genius was harnessed
to a fanatical determination.

A master can only teach a pupil
those things he is ready to receive.
Young Arjuna was like a water jug   70
thirsty for water. He learned everything
from Drona, sometimes indirectly.

One night,
the lesson went on hour after hour until
it grew quite dark. As Arjuna was eating
his late meal, a sudden gust of wind   75
blew out the taper light, and yet his hand
found its way to each dish in front of him
unerringly. Suddenly, he rose—
and running out into the moonless night
he flexed his bow, nocked an arrow, let fly,   80
although the target was invisible;
then, feeling his way through the inky darkness,
he found each arrow clinched into the place
he had intended.

Now he had understood
what it means to aim, but without straining.   85
He had a glimpse of how one may become
a channel for the world's natural forces
to play themselves out. How, without striving,
without attachment to the end result,
abandoning desire and memory,   90
an arrow can be loosed, and find its home.
This he learned that night. It was a lesson
he would have to learn anew in great anguish,
years from now.

For hours each day, he practiced.
Even Drona, not easily impressed,   95
was awed by him, and told him privately,
"Arjuna, I shall do all in my power
to see that you become the greatest archer
in the whole world—this I promise you."
The young man swelled with joy and, in time,   100
came to feel this honor was his right.

•

One day, Drona held a competition
in archery. He had a small wooden bird
placed high in a tree, and asked each pupil
to shoot it in the head with a single arrow.   105
One by one they stepped up to the mark.
"Tell me everything you see," said Drona.
Some mentioned the tree, some the topmost limbs,
others the bird itself. Some got distracted
by trying to identify the species   110
and wondering if it was real. Drona
dismissed each one before he could take aim.
Then Arjuna stepped up. "What do you see?"
"I see the bird's head."
"What else?"   115
"Nothing, master."
"Then loose your arrow, son."
                              Calmly, Arjuna
took aim, released. The tiny bird splintered,
its head shattered, and the painted fragments
floated to earth. Drona praised him warmly.   120
"When the time comes, Arjuna, you will give
my lost friend Drupada[3] what he deserves!"

Another time, the young Bharata princes
went swimming in the Ganga[4] with their master
who, standing in the shallows, offered up   125
prayers to the gods, and for his ancestors.
Suddenly, one of the rough-hewn logs
that floated by the bank stirred into life—
a gigantic crocodile! Its cruel jaws
gaped hugely, then locked fast round Drona's leg.   130
It began to drag him into deeper water.
Almost instantaneously, it seemed,
yet without haste, Arjuna raised his bow
and a stream of well-aimed arrows found their mark
in the monster's eye and neck. Its vicious grip   135

---

3. Drona's former friend, now mortal enemy.
4. The Ganges, India's most important and sacred river.

slackened; it sank, bloodying the water.
Not a thought had ruffled Arjuna's mind.
He had simply acted. For this feat,
Drona bestowed on him the *Brahma Head*,[5]
a weapon so deadly it could not be used   140
against mere mortals without burning up
the whole world; it was to be reserved
for fighting supernatural enemies.

Ashvatthaman, jealous that his father
had favored Arjuna above himself,   145
pestered Drona for the supreme weapon,
nagging, wheedling until Drona, worn down,
taught him the mantra he had shown Arjuna,
the mantra that would summon the *Brahma Head*.
But in doing so Drona was uneasy,   150
suspecting as he did that Ashvatthaman
desired the weapon for ignoble reasons.

•

To be the favored pupil of one's master
is what each disciple longs for, strives for.
But it may not be the blessing it appears.   155
Envy feeds the flames of enmity,
and when they heard Drona repeatedly
extolling Arjuna, the Kauravas
choked with resentment; to Duryodhana,
every word of praise for Arjuna   160
was bitterest wormwood. Great praise may also
lead to great pride, and young Arjuna
was not immune to that.

                              Drona's renown
as a preceptor in the princely arts
spread throughout the kingdom, and beyond.   165
There was no finer weapons school than his,
and kshatriya boys traveled from near and far
to learn from him. There was a boy called Karna,
son of a driver, whom other boys despised
but feared as well. He was tall, aquiline,   170
and was distinguished by his gold cuirass
and golden earrings—features he was born with.
Wary of rebuff, he made no friends;
only Duryodhana was kind to him.
He was an archer of exceptional skill.   175
Seeing that Arjuna was the star pupil,
Karna sought to rival him in all things

5. A supernatural weapon.

and was painfully jealous of his prowess.
Arjuna scorned him, treating him with contempt.

Gathering his nerve, he went to Drona.   180
"Master, please teach me the *Brahma* weapon."
"That ultimate weapon can only be learned,"
said Drona, "by a brahmin of stringent vows,
or a kshatriya who has undertaken
great austerities[6]: no one else at all."   185
Karna saw that Drona would never teach
the higher mysteries of a warrior's skill
to one who was of lowly origin.
Angry and sad, he gathered his possessions
determined to seek out another teacher,   190
vowing that, one day, he would be back;
he would prove himself greater than Arjuna!
He left the city, passing through the gate
unremarked, and was soon forgotten.

                                    •

One night, as he was walking in his garden,   195
Drona was startled by a rustling sound—
a boy leapt from the bushes and threw himself
at the guru's feet. He turned his dark face
upward in adoration, and begged Drona
to accept him as one of his disciples.   200
He was a nishada, a forest tribal,
called Ekalavya, younger than the princes,
lithe, with a strange accent.
                                    Drona sighed,
"I have to disappoint you—I only teach
youths who come from highborn families.   205
You're a nishada. It just wouldn't do."
Ekalavya bowed his head and, springing up,
was gone.
                    He ran, sure-footed, through the forest.
In a moonlit clearing at its heart,
lush with vigorous vines, there was a pool   210
lovely with lotuses. The boy scooped up
clay from the water's edge and carefully
modeled a life-size figure of his master.
It took him many days and nights of work,
work informed by pure-hearted commitment.   215

When the likeness was complete, Ekalavya
slept. Then he rose, gathered perfumed flowers
and made a garland for his master's neck.
"Bless me, Guruji."[7] And having touched

6. Acts of severe self-denial and self-discipline. *Brahmin*: member of the highest (priestly) caste.
7. Honorific meaning "Revered Teacher."

earth with his brow, he began to practice   220
with faith, devotion, and pure discipline.

Time passed.

      One sparkling afternoon in winter,
the Pandavas rode out into the forest
to hunt wild boar. Their prized dog was with them
snuffling, bounding off ahead of them.   225
Suddenly they heard it growl, and then
a frenzy of barks, making birds fly upward
in alarm. Then stifled whines. The hound
slunk from the bushes, bleeding and subdued,
and the princes found it had been silenced   230
by seven evenly spaced arrows clamping
its muzzle shut. They were amazed—surely,
at the first wound, the dog would have bolted.
These arrows must have flown from the bowstring
in unimaginably quick succession.   235
And so precisely! Even Arjuna
could never have accomplished such a feat.

Following the track the dog had taken
they came upon a clearing in the wood
where a dark-skinned youth, his crude bow raised,   240
was shooting a cascade of arrows, calmly,
gracefully, and with such dazzling skill
the brothers were astounded.

        "Who are you?
And where could you have learned to shoot like that?"
The youth replied, "My name is Ekalavya,   245
my father is the chief of the nishadas,
and I owe my skill to the great Drona,
my master."

      Soberly, the brothers rode
back to the city. Pale with jealousy,
Arjuna took Drona to one side.   250
"Did you not promise me, not long ago,
that I would be the world's greatest archer?
How, then, can you be teaching, secretly,
that lowborn boy—an archer so accomplished
he makes me look like a mere beginner!"   255
Drona was mystified, then called to mind
the forest boy he had refused to teach.

With Arjuna, he set off for the forest
and there they came across Ekalavya
calmly practicing, his rough-hewn arrows   260

clustering in a line of perfect circles
on a straw target.

         He fell at Drona's feet,
surprise and joy lighting his dark face
at seeing his master. Drona, for his part,
had never witnessed such unearthly skill—   265
he could understand Arjuna's despair.
He framed what he must say. "Ekalavya,
if I am your teacher, you should now
give me my fee."

         "Name it—anything!"
the boy cried, flooded with happiness   270
that he had been acknowledged by his guru.
"There is no gift I shall withhold from you."
"Then," said Drona, "give me your right thumb."

Ekalavya's smile did not falter.
With an arrow's single downward slash   275
he sliced off his right thumb, and placed it, dripping,
at Drona's feet. From now on, he would never
shoot with such breathtaking speed. And Drona's
words would not be falsified—Arjuna
would be the greatest archer in the world.   280

The Pandava glowed with confidence restored.
Without a word, the two then strode away
and out of Ekalavya's small story.

But we may imagine this: Ekalavya
bound the throbbing socket of his thumb   285
with herbs and soothing leaves, then sat in thought.
Sunlight left the forest canopy,
dusk came, then darkness. Still he sat alone.
He listened to the creatures of the night
as they went about their earnest purposes   290
constrained, and free.

         In the dawn light, he rose
and bathed, then stood in front of Drona's statue.
In respect, he touched its feet. Then, straightening,
he took his bow, began again to practice.

THE TOURNAMENT

    *   *   *

Imagine an enormous amphitheater.
To build it, on the outskirts of the city,
hundreds of laborers had toiled for months.

For Drona had decided the young princes
had now learned from him everything they could,   5
and all their years of effort would be crowned
by a grand demonstration of their skills.
Hastinapura[8] had never seen the like.

Word had traveled fast throughout the kingdom.
Excited crowds had gathered from small towns,   10
from villages, from fishing settlements;
even ascetics in their forest ashrams
had heard the news and come for the spectacle.
People camped outside the city walls
on land that gently sloped down to the river,   15
and near the forest's edge, where they could gather
brushwood for cooking. Even before first light,
fragrant woodsmoke from a thousand fires
was already rising, flames leaping
as if impatient, like the jostling people   20
anxious for the great day to begin.
A crowd formed, pressing toward the gate
which opened when the sun began to rise
above the pinnacles of the king's palace.

How glorious the arena was, far bigger   25
than anything ever seen, even in dreams:
oval-shaped, and lined with ranks of seats
steeply banked, rising, tier on tier,
and shaded from the sun by colored awnings.

While people waited, drummers and trumpeters   30
made joyful, stirring music. Crafty tinkers
touted their wares—bangles, lamps, ornaments,
gaudy trinkets that children pestered for—
and snack sellers worked the narrow aisles.

Just as people started to get restless,   35
deep triumphal notes sounded from conches
positioned all around the stadium.
There was a stir, up at the far end.
All heads turned toward the royal enclosure
splendid with its patterns in gold leaf,   40
its lattices, its jeweled canopy.
A walkway linked the arena to the palace
and now, emerging into the bright sunlight,
King Dhritarashtra came with careful steps,
guided by the arm of Vidura.   45
His queen walked beside him, led by Kunti,

8. City in northern India that was the capital of the Kauravas; most of the incidents in the
Mahabharata take place here.

then Kripa, and then grandfather Bhishma[9]
with other court notables, all resplendent
in brilliant silks and jewels. And at last
came Drona, the master, dressed in purest white—   50
white sacred thread, white hair, white beard, white garlands,
white sandal paste smeared across his body.
A roar went up, a salvo of applause:
whatever skills the young princes possessed,
whatever feats they were about to show,   55
they owed to him.

•

           And now the performance starts.
First the princes each take up a bow
in order of age, led by Yudhishthira
and, mounted on horses, canter round the ring,
then wheel in an elaborate formation,   60
well-fitting breastplates glittering, dazzling.
They perform amazing feats of archery,
taking aim at a revolving target
hung in the center, shooting, galloping
faster and faster, while not a single arrow   65
misses its goal. The display only stops
when the bristling target is crammed with arrows.

Next, there are races. The best charioteers
among the princes line up to compete—
which of them will drive his gleaming vehicle   70
fastest round ten laps of the arena?
One by one, they weave a complex course
round obstacles, cutting through twists and bends
hugging them close, hauling their horses round
without the wheels grazing. Each chariot   75
is freshly painted and adorned with flowers.
Each one is drawn by four glossy horses
bred for this, superbly schooled, manes braided,
and in each, the driver stands, erect,
magnificent, dressed in burnished armor.   80

Now, Drona announces a mock fight.
One hundred and five princes brandish weapons
and seem about to slaughter one another
so savage are their shouts, so fierce they look,
their swords and daggers flashing as they thrust,   85
feint, dance around each other. The huge crowd

---

9. Vidura is the brother of Pandu and Dhritarashtra. He is known for his wisdom, but
because his mother was low-born, he has lower
status than his brothers. Kunti is the mother of
three of the Pandavas. Kripa is the princes'
first weapons teacher. Bhishma is the celibate
patriarch of the Bharata clan.

is on its feet, shouting the princes' names,
more anxious than encouraging—and yet,
at a slight sign from Drona, it all stops;
not a single drop of blood has been spilled.   90

In the royal enclosure, Vidura
is describing everything that happens
to Dhritarashtra, and Kunti to Gandhari.[1]
"On a day like this," sighs Dhritarashtra,
"I envy hopelessly those who can see,   95
who now are witnessing my young sons' triumph."

Now Bhima, built like a colossal boulder,
and the strong and nimble Duryodhana
fight with maces. Drona emphasizes
that this, too, is a mock fight—though quite soon   100
it is clear they are serious. They will inflict
as much harm as they can, swinging their clubs
with the huge momentum of their powerful arms,
roaring like two rutting elephants,
sparks leaping as the weapons clash, rebound.   105
The crowd screams support, some for one,
some for the other, starting to trade blows
between themselves. Drona stops the contest,
fearing a bloody riot in the stands.
Each cousin has suffered wounds. Grim-faced, silent,   110
they stalk off. This has seemed like a rehearsal
for a deadly fight that is to come, one day.

There is loud grumbling on the terraces
at the violent and exciting duel
being cut short. But Drona raises his voice: 115
"I now present to you Prince Arjuna,
son of Indra,[2] greatest of all archers,
whom I love even more than my own son."

Conches blare, drums beat out a tattoo
in a joyful musical explosion.   120
The cry goes up—*Ar-ju-na! Ar-ju-na!*
The crowd yearns for the legendary warrior;
they stamp their feet, chanting in ecstasy.
He, above all, is the prince they wish to see.

Wild anticipation often leads   125
only to disappointment. Not today!
Muscular, graceful, shining hair unbound,
Arjuna steps forward, bows to Drona.

1. Dhritarashtra's wife, mother of the Kauravas. For all her life, she wears a blindfold so as
to have no advantage over her blind husband.
2. King of the gods; Indian equivalent of Zeus.

Completely focused, with no hint of strain
he raises his bow, draws back his left arm
and then—   130
              and then the miracles begin!

First he sends an effortless stream of arrows
into the mouth of a tiny wooden boar
so far off it is almost out of sight.
Not one misses. The crowd roars in delight.   135
Then he does the same again, blindfolded,
then with his back turned. It looks impossible,
and yet it seems tame when you see what follows.
He stands with his eyes closed, his lips moving
in a silent mantra. He shoots an arrow   140
straight into the sky. Slowly it rises,
then begins to glow, then blazes, then
the sky is on fire over the arena.
The crowd cringes in terror but, next moment,
a stream of flashing silver arcs upward   145
and instantly the sky becomes a sea,
an upside-down ocean, quenching the flames.
These are truly weapons of the gods!

More marvels follow. Arjuna moves swiftly
with the panache and poise of a great dancer,   150
master of his body, never doubting
that he can transcend nature's normal laws.
He changes size at will. He conjures mountains.
He shoots an arrow into the sand, making
the ground split wide open in front of him,   155
and close when he has walked inside—and then,
when people start to worry, a yawning crack
opens up before the royal stand—
Arjuna steps out and bows to his uncle!

The crowd erupts, delighted and relieved.   160
They shriek themselves hoarse, blow whistles, stamp their feet
until they are sore. This is the day's climax;
what they have seen will never be surpassed.

                               •

When at last the uproar had died down,
and people were preparing to go home,   165
they became aware of a strange sound,
like thunder, coming from beside the gate.
Someone said, "That sound is a challenge,
some hero is slapping his arms boastfully."

The crowd was hushed, looking toward the gate.   170
A man strode forward, an imposing figure,

beautiful, tall as a kadamba[3] tree.
A shining gold cuirass encased his body
and in his ears, there sparkled golden earrings,
like two drops of sunlight. He looked forbidding—   175
serious, remote, stern even, as if
his life had been hard. Anyone could tell
from his bearing, the authority
with which he walked into the arena
holding his bow as though it were a scepter,   180
that this man was a very great warrior.

He inclined his head to Dhritarashtra,
nodded to Drona, then turned to Arjuna
and, although he did not raise his voice,
his words were heard all over the stadium.   185
"Pandava, you seem to take great pride
in the facile feats you've just displayed to us.
With the master's permission, I, Karna,
will now match every easy act of yours,
each paltry trick. So don't be too puffed up."   190

Drona gave consent, probably curious
to see what his former pupil had become
since he left Hastinapura as a boy.
Surely this man would not outdo Arjuna.
The crowd was humming with curiosity.   195
Who could this be? There was complete silence.
Then, effortlessly, Karna emulated
every feat Arjuna had performed.
Some people thought them even better done,
and felt like fools that they themselves had been   200
so easily impressed before. As one,
like a surging wave, the crowd rose, cheering.
Karna raised his arms triumphantly.

Drona seemed shocked. Arjuna looked tense
and angry; he considered himself insulted.   205
But Duryodhana joyfully embraced
Karna. "Welcome to you, strong-armed hero!
Hastinapura is honored by your presence.
You certainly know how to humble pride!
From today, the kingdom of the Bharatas   210
is home to you; ask of me what you will."
"I choose two things to ask of you," said Karna,
"your friendship, and a duel with Arjuna."

Arjuna addressed the towering Karna:
"How dare you barge in here uninvited!   215

---

3. A beautiful evergreen tree native to South Asia.

Karna, I swear to you, when I have killed you
you will sink to the realm reserved for those
who indulge in empty boastful prattling!"

Karna smiled. "This place is open to all.   220
Strength is what matters here, not whimpering words,
not half-baked insults. A truly great warrior
will rise to any challenge. I, Karna,
challenge you to a contest—no mere display,
but a duel to the death between archers.
I shall behead you in your teacher's presence—   225
or will you admit I have the greater skill?'

"I'll send you to hell first!" cried Arjuna.

•

As he spoke, the sky grew dark—Indra,
bringer of storms, was gathering his forces
as if to bless his son. But the next moment   230
a shaft of brilliant sunlight pierced the clouds,
making a golden circle around Karna.[4]

In the royal box, Kunti fainted.
She had realized who Karna was
and was overcome, remembering   235
the lovely golden infant she had sent
floating down the river, to take his chance.
Now her heart hammered with fear—her sons
fighting to the death! But she said nothing.

Kripa, expert in the etiquette   240
of dueling, spoke now: "Here stands Arjuna,
third-born son of Pandu of this royal house,
youngest offspring of Kunti, his wife.
It is known that no prince will condescend
to duel with a man of lesser lineage   245
than his own. You must tell us, hero,
who your father is. Who is your mother?
To what royal clan do you belong?"

Like a drooping flower drenched with rain,
Karna hung his head. Arjuna waited.   250
Then Duryodhana spoke up forcefully:
"This rigmarole is just old-fashioned nonsense!
But if Arjuna is too punctilious
to fight with anyone except a prince
I have the solution. Our vassal state,   255

4. Karna is a foundling, raised in the family of a driver, but really the child of Kunti and the sun
god, Surya.

Anga, lacks a ruler. Here and now
I propose that this outstanding man
shall be consecrated king of Anga.
Then there will be no excuse for Arjuna
to dodge away from dueling with him."   260

Dhritarashtra gave his blessing; brahmins
were summoned, bringing all the ritual objects
needed for consecration—flowers, gold,
roasted rice grains, water from the Ganga,
a white silk parasol, emblem of a king—   265
and, in the presence of the cheering crowd,
Karna was installed as king of Anga.

He turned to Duryodhana. "How can I
ever repay you for this priceless gift?"
The prince smiled with pleasure. "All I want   270
from you, Karna, is your lifelong friendship.
I know, together, we shall do great things."
Karna's face lit up. "Here is my promise—
as long as I shall live, while these two arms
have strength and skill in them, I shall defend you.   275
Your future will be mine, your interests, mine.
All that my head and heart can give are yours."

An old man tottered forward from the crowd
sweating and trembling, leaning on a stick.
The man was Karna's father, Adhiratha.[5]   280
Seeing him, Karna went over to him
and, in reverence, touched the old man's feet
with his head, still wet from the anointing.
Adhiratha's face was bright with love.
"My son!" he cried, his eyes moist with tears.   285

The Pandavas laughed. "This man's a wagoner,"
jeered Bhima, "and you're his son! Off with you,
off to the stables—go and muck out horses.
That's where you belong!" Karna breathed hard
and fixed his gaze on the sun, low in the sky.   290

Immediately, up sprang Duryodhana
and, in a white-hot rage, he said to Bhima,
"Wolf-belly,[6] your rudeness and crass ignorance
are hardly worthy of the kshatriya
you claim to be. The learned texts distinguish   295
three kinds of king—one of a royal line,
the leader of an army, and a hero.
This man, by his heroic skill, his courage,

5. Karna's adoptive father.
6. Bhima's nickname, a reference to his huge appetite.

has proved himself equal to any of us.
Prowess counts most for a kshatriya.   300

"As for lineage—just think about it.
It's not unknown for sons of kshatriya mothers
to become Brahmins. Drona here was born
from a water pot, Kripa from reeds.
Arjuna calls himself a son of Pandu   305
but in fact, as we all know, his origins
are murky—and the same goes for his brothers.
Think of Pandu himself, and my father,
and Uncle Vidura—we respect them
and yet their birth was by no means straightforward.[7]   310

"The most powerful forces in the world
are often born in darkness. Think of fire,
the molten fire that sleeps beneath the ocean
but will erupt at the apocalypse
to engulf the earth. The mightiest rivers   315
have unimpressive origins; their greatness
grows as they make their journey through the world
joining with others, broadening, deepening,
meeting barriers, overcoming them.
That's how it is with the noblest warriors.   320
But, of course, a deer can't sire a tiger
and this man is a tiger—so I would guess
his mysterious birth must hold a clue
to his greatness. Karna deserves—hear me out—
our deep respect and, in my eyes at least,   325
he is a king.

                    "Now, tell your little brother
to gather his scattered wits, pick up his bow
and fight the king of Anga—if he dares!"

At this, the audience murmured its approval.
But night had fallen, it was too late to fight.   330
The crowd drifted away, talking of Karna.

7. Dhritarashtra, Pandu, and Vidura were all fathered by Vyasa.

DRAUPADI'S BRIDEGROOM CHOICE

Summary   Following an attempt on their lives—a fire planned by Duryodhana—the Pandavas, together with their mother, Kunti, are living in disguise. They have been told that a competition is to take place in Kampilya for the hand of Draupadi, the beautiful daughter of Drupada. They decide to go there.

* * *

Kampilya was buzzing with preparation.
The Pandavas, still disguised as brahmins,
smeared with ash, barefoot, with heavy beards,
were lodging with a potter's family.
Every day, they walked around the city   5
with their begging bowls, separately, alert
for searching looks. But they noticed none.
Young brahmins, even with a proud demeanor,
attracted no attention—crowds of brahmins
had come to Kampilya, drawn by the prospect   10
of rich presents. Every evening, Kunti
shared out what the brothers had been given.

The city streets were jostling with strangers
from far and near. In every public space,
entertainers—jugglers, contortionists,   15
conjurors, dancers, all kinds of musicians—
scrambled for the most strategic pitch.

Gossip was rife. Who was the lucky suitor
who would prove brave and skilled enough to win
the dazzling Draupadi? Some imagined   20
a warrior of godlike looks and strength
sweeping down in a bejeweled chariot
to win his bride and carry her away.

At last, the auspicious day. The sky was brilliant.
Brahmins had consecrated the event.   25
Crowds of spectators, fizzing with excitement,
were pressing forward into the arena
where Draupadi's future would be decided.
Surrounded by tall mansions, glistening
white as the sunlit snows of the Himalaya,[8]   30
and lavishly adorned with costly hangings,
the amphitheater was an impressive sight.

Now, from the massive entrance to the palace,
Draupadi, with her brother, Drishtadyumna,
walked slowly to the dais, head slightly bowed.   35
She was dressed in scarlet silk; her ornaments
were of the finest jewel-encrusted gold.
Her beauty made those who had never seen her

8. The world's highest mountain range, extending over a vast region of central Asia, including parts of northern India.

gasp—her skin with the sheen of a black pearl,
her lovely face, lustrous wavy hair,   40
her perfect body, fragrant as blue lotus;
while in her eyes, in her calm expression,
there was something that engendered awe.
Surely she was nervous? So much depended
on these few hours.

                Prince Dhrishtadyumna spoke.   45
"Warriors who are gathered here today
hoping to win the hand of Draupadi,
the task is this: a bow has been provided
together with five arrows. Overhead
is a revolving wheel and, higher still,   50
a small target. You have to string the bow,
and hit the target with each of the arrows,
aiming through the wheel. My sister, Draupadi,
will choose her husband from those who succeed."

The task had been devised by Drupada.   55
He was hoping, against all the odds,
that Arjuna might have survived the fire
and could be among the assembled warriors.
King Drupada had witnessed at first hand
what Arjuna could do. Still, he had kept   60
his great wish to himself. Now, he waited.

Dhrishtadyumna announced the contestants
by name and pedigree. Duryodhana
was here with Karna and Duhshasana
and several more of Dhritarashtra's sons;   65
Shalya, king of the Madras, with his sons;
Drona's son Ashvatthaman, Shakuni,
Shishupala, known as the Bull of Chedi;
Satyaki, and dozens of other champions
from the Vrishni clan—in sum, there were scores   70
of royal heroes. Under an ample awning
they sat in silence. Tension was palpable.

Inconspicuous among the brahmins,
the Pandavas were staring at Draupadi,
mesmerized. At a distance, Krishna,   75
prince of the Vrishnis, turned to Balarama,
his older brother; "Look at those brahmins—there."
Balarama looked; and smiled at Krishna.
Neither of them would compete that day.
Krishna knew why the Panchala princess   80
had come into the world—the same reason
as he himself: to be an instrument
for the deliverance of the suffering earth.
To carry out their part in the gods' design.

The first contestant stepped up to the mark.   85
The bow provided had been specially made
for this occasion, crafted like bows of old
when men were men, and kshatriyas, demigods.
It was so stiff and heavy, few could lift it,
let alone string it and take aim with it.   90
Prince after prince made the attempt, but failed.
As they tried to bend the bow, it sprang back
flinging them to the ground, smashing their limbs.
They limped away, sore, angry, and ashamed,
desire for Draupadi evaporated.   95
Duryodhana tried, so did his brothers,
but none could even begin to bend the bow.
Shishupala, a formidable warrior,
and his powerful friend Jarasandha
each made the attempt, but each of them   100
was flung onto his knees, humiliated.

Karna stepped forward. He, if anyone,
would have the necessary strength and, yes,
he grasped and bent the bow into a circle
and was about to string it, when he heard   105
Draupadi exclaim in a clear voice,
"I will not choose a suta[9] for my husband!"
Karna laughed bitterly, laid down the bow
and, glancing at the sun, walked to his place.

Now you could hear a stirring in the stands,   110
a frisson of surprise. A young brahmin
was striding forward. Some people were scornful;
others said, "Nothing is impossible
to a brahmin of strict vows—and, besides,
that one has the stature of a god!"   115

Almost casually, as though the task
were child's play to him, the young man raised the bow,
strung it, and shot five arrows through the wheel.
They clustered close around the target's center;
with the fifth, the target fell to earth.   120
The contest was over. The crowd cheered and stamped.
A rain of flowers fell on the hero's head.

Draupadi took up the ritual garland
of white flowers, and walked toward the victor.
Smiling, she draped the garland round his neck.   125

Most spectators were happy that the princess
had such a worthy husband, even though

9. A driver, hence a person of a low caste.

he was not the prince they naturally expected.
But there was uproar from the kshatriyas—
angry shouting from the Kauravas   130
and many others: "Drupada has cheated!
He has treated us with complete contempt
and broken the rules. The law is very clear—
only a kshatriya should have his daughter.
He should die!" Several of them surged forward   135
to kill the king. But Bhima and Arjuna
rushed to defend him. Bhima snatched up a tree,
stripped off the leaves and, swinging it like a club,
lunged like Death himself at furious Shalya,
king of the Madras. The assembled brahmins,   140
shaking their deerskins, banging their water pots,
were all for joining in, but Arjuna
waved them back, and drawing the mighty bow
with which he had won Draupadi, he entered
into the affray.

        "So, we were right,"   145
said Krishna to his brother Balarama.
"Those brahmins are, indeed, the Pandavas."
"Oh, what a joy," exclaimed Balarama,
"that the sons of Kunti, our father's sister,
are alive after all!"

        Meanwhile, the mayhem   150
continued. The uneventful brahmin life
the Pandavas had led for so many months
had left them hungry for action. Arjuna
found himself fighting against Karna,
Karna not recognizing his opponent.   155
Arjuna rejoiced to have the chance
to test his warrior's skill against the man
who had caused him shame at the tournament.

They fought like gods. All the other warriors
dropped their weapons so they could observe   160
the well-matched pair, the lightning exchange
of arrows, the whirling bodies, dancing feet.
This was a duel, but also an expression
of the highest art, and each great archer
was exhilarated by the other's skill.   165
"Are you the Art of Archery incarnate?"
asked Karna. "I am not," replied Arjuna,
"I am a brahmin, adept at the astras,
master of the divine *Brahma* weapon,
and I shall defeat you. Fight on, hero!"   170

But Karna withdrew, unwilling to oppose
brahminic power. The brawl started up again—

Bhima against Shalya, pounding each other
like two great elephants in rut. The battle
was starting to turn ugly. And then Krishna   175
intervened with diplomatic words:
"The bride was righteously and fairly won;
this fighting is unseemly." Reluctantly,
still unappeased, the kshatriyas turned away
and set out on the journey to their kingdoms.   180

Kunti had stayed at home, restless, enduring,
hour after hour, that dull anxiety
so familiar to mothers everywhere.
She thought of everything that was at stake,
and of the dangers. At last, she heard her sons'   185
voices in the yard. "Mother! Mother!
we have brought back largesse!"
                          "Then, my dears,
you will share it equitably between you,"
called Kunti. Then they walked in with Draupadi!

Kunti was startled; then she was overjoyed   190
and she and Draupadi embraced each other.
But then she wrung her hands. "Oh! I just said
you must share whatever you were bringing.
But how can you share Draupadi without
breaching dharma? Yet, if you don't, my words   195
will be a lie." The brothers became silent.
Their mother's word was always absolute—
what could they do? They talked into the night,
and as they talked, glancing at Draupadi,
all five brothers fell in love with her.   200

Suddenly, Yudhishthira remembered
the story told them by the wise Vyasa.[1]
Of course—to avoid making their mother
a liar, they should *all* marry Draupadi.
A heaven-sent solution! Up to now,   205
nothing had come between the Pandavas;
the marriage of one could have bred jealousy
among the rest. And though Arjuna had won
the Panchala princess, he should not marry
before Yudhishthira, his eldest brother.   210
When Draupadi looked at these five heroes,
each wonderful in his own way, she knew
the gods had given her a fivefold blessing.

                          •

Krishna and Balarama came to see them
(the first time the cousins had met each other)   215
and wished them all good fortune. The young men

1. A story about a girl who made a wish for a husband five times.

were delighted. "But how did you know us,"
asked Yudhishthira, "disguised as we are?"
Krishna smiled. "Who but the Pandavas
would look so powerful and so dignified?   220
But we should not stay now." And they took their leave.
Dhrishtadyumna, watching secretly,
was now convinced that the brothers were, indeed,
the Pandavas, and went to tell his father.
The king rejoiced. His hopes had been fulfilled: 225
the brave young brahmin really was Arjuna!

Next day, Drupada sent a splendid chariot
to bring the Pandavas to the royal palace
where they declared their true identities.
He asked the brothers how they had escaped   230
the dreadful fire, and what had happened since.
The story took some time. Drupada smiled.
"Now you need have no worries—all my wealth
and my fine army is at your disposal.
You will certainly regain your kingdom.   235
The Kauravas will not oppose you, now
our dynasties are to be joined by marriage."

But five husbands! There he drew the line.
A kshatriya could marry several wives,
that was normal, but he had never heard   240
of one woman having many husbands.
It was not right. It was at odds with dharma.
Yudhishthira referred to well-known stories
where rishis[2]—not offenders against dharma,
but holy men—had shared the same woman.   245
"That may be well for brahmins," said Drupada,
"but not for us. How can I give my daughter,
my dark flower, princess of Panchala,
to *five* husbands, and still preserve her honor?"

At this point, Vyasa was announced,   250
timely as ever. Drupada turned to him,
"Muni,[3] knower of minds, I need your wisdom,"
and he told Vyasa of the strange proposal.
Vyasa took the king to a private room.
"Drupada," said Vyasa, "it is true   255
that such a thing is rare in recent times.
But in a nobler age, it was quite common.
And the marriage of your fire-born daughter
to these five brothers, was long ago ordained
by Shiva."

Then Vyasa told the story: 260

2. In Hinduism, sages or saints of great, spiritual attainment.
3. A term of respect.

"The gods were once performing a sacrifice in the Naimisha Forest. Yama, god of death, was fully occupied with sacrificial duties, and had no time to attend to the death of creatures. So human beings lived on and on, and the earth was becoming overcrowded. The immortal gods went to Brahma[4] and complained that nothing now distinguished them from men.

"'Rest assured,' said Brahma, 'that as soon as the sacrifice is over, Yama will resume normal activity and people will die as they always have.'

"The gods returned to the sacrifice, and Indra, chief of gods, noticed a woman washing herself in the Ganga. She was weeping and, as she wept, each tear became a golden lotus that floated on the water.

"'Who are you,' he asked, 'and why are you weeping?'

"'I will show you—come with me,' she said. She led him to a nearby place where a youth was sitting playing dice, so utterly engrossed in the game that he took no notice when Indra spoke to him.

"'Pay attention when I speak to you!' said Indra, 'Don't you know that I am the chief of gods?'

"The youth smiled and glanced at Indra who became paralyzed immediately for the youth was none other than the great lord Shiva.[5] When he had finished his game, he told the woman to touch Indra, who collapsed on the ground.

"'You need to be taught a lesson for your overweening pride,' said Shiva. 'Move that great boulder to one side and enter the cave that you will find behind it.' Trembling with fear, Indra did so and, imprisoned in the cave, he found four other Indras exactly like himself.

"The five Indras begged Shiva to set them free. 'You will recover your celestial status,' said Shiva, 'but only after you have been born in the world of mortals.' The Indras asked that they should at least have gods as their fathers. 'Let the gods Dharma, Vayu, Indra, and the Ashvins be our begetters.' Shiva agreed to this, and so it was that five remarkable sons were born to Pandu. Shiva also decreed that Shri, goddess of royal fortune, would be their shared wife in the world of men.

"Supreme Vishnu[6] approved this arrangement. He plucked from his own head one white hair and one black hair, and placed them in human wombs. These were born as Krishna and Balarama.

"So, you see," said Vyasa to Drupada,
"what seems to you contrary to dharma
is, in fact, celestially ordained."
Drupada gave in. "If the great Shiva
himself has blessed this marriage, my clear duty   5
is to make it possible." So it was
that Draupadi became the willing bride
of all five brothers. On successive days,
in order of their age, they married her.
And it is said that, for each one of them,   10
she came as a virgin to the bridal bed.

•

---

4. God of created beings; one of the principal gods of the ancient Vedic religion of the *Mahabharata*.
5. God of destruction and transformation;

another of the principal Vedic gods.
6. God of protection, preservation of the good, and restoration of dharma; another of the principal Vedic deities.

Drupada, having overcome his scruples,
exulted in the fortune that had brought him
five great sons-in-law instead of one.
He gave them all spacious living quarters   15
and every luxury and entertainment.
Krishna and Balarama spent time with them
and the cousins became deeply attached.
Krishna and Arjuna, in particular,
developed a profound friendship.

                           The brothers   20
were happy in Kampilya. But very often
their thoughts would travel to Hastinapura.
Sitting together in the cool of evening
they wondered what Duryodhana was planning.
They knew their cousin, knew only too well   25
his vengeful, proud, and avaricious nature.
But they had found safety with Drupada
and, though it could not last, although they felt
they would grow slack without the discipline
and challenges that came with their heritage,   30
they gave themselves, for now, to the delight
of family, of friendship, and of love.

From *Book 2: The Book of the Assembly Hall*

Summary   The Bharata kingdom has been divided, and the Pandavas have prospered in their part of it, based at Indraprastha. Full of envy, Duryodhana and his uncle, Shakuni, conceive a plot: Yudhishthira will be invited by Dhritarashtra to a dice game. He has no skill at dice, but he is honor-bound to accept the invitation. Unbeknownst to the Pandavas, Shakuni has magic dice that follow his will.

THE DICE GAME

Yudhishthira, along with his entourage—
his brothers, wife, servants, many brahmins—
arrived at Hastinapura, and was welcomed
by blind Dhritarashtra and his queen.
The women of the court were not best pleased   5
by the sight of Draupadi's priceless jewels.

The next day, Yudhishthira and his brothers
were taken to the newly built pavilion.
The whole court had assembled for the game—
gamblers, court officials, nobles, princes.   10
There was an air of nervous expectation,
though the king described it as "a friendly match,
for the pleasure and amusement of our guests."

"Welcome to all present—let play commence!"
cried Duryodhana with false bonhomie.   15

"Shakuni will play on my behalf;
I put my entire wealth at his disposal."

"Gambling by proxy," said Yudhishthira,
"seems contrary to honorable practice.
However, if you insist, I shall accept.   20
Gambling is not a noble pastime,
unlike honest victory in war.
There is no kshatriya valor in it.
Dicing involves deceit—Shakuni,
I exhort you not to win by trickery."   25

"When a Vedic scholar[7] competes with one
who has no Vedic knowledge, it is deceit,
though no one calls it so," said Shakuni.
"In any sport involving competition,
the effort to defeat one's adversary   30
could be called ignoble, though it never is.
In playing dice, the stronger player tries
to defeat the weaker—that is the game.
If you are afraid, refuse the challenge."
"I have vowed never to refuse a challenge,"   35
said the Pandava. "Let the game begin.
We all are in the hands of destiny."

Yudhishthira was the first to name his stake—
"This pearl necklace, richly worked with gold"—
matched by Shakuni. He cast his dice.   40

Shakuni cast, his supple hands flashing
like lightning. He smiled slightly, "I have won."

Yudhishthira protested, "You confused me
with a trick. But very well, Shakuni,
let us continue. My store of gold: 45
a hundred finely fashioned silver jars,
each containing one thousand gold pieces."
He threw his dice.

                So did clever Shakuni:
"I have won."

              Yudhishthira grew angry.
"My beautiful and swift royal chariot,   50
the one that brought us here—it stands outside
hung with bells, furnished with tiger skins—
drawn by eight noble purebred horses
white as moonbeams, all this is my stake."
Again he threw, closing his eyes until   55

7. The Vedas are the most ancient Hindu scriptures, the province mainly of brahmins.

he heard Shakuni's voice,
                    "Look, I have won."

It was as if the world shrank to a script
Yudhishthira must follow. He could not see
how Shakuni was managing to win,
he could not track the other's sinuous moves.   60
He was consumed by furious desire,
a rage to triumph over his tormenter
and recoup his losses. Nothing else mattered.
"I have a thousand rutting elephants,
well trained, powerful, huge as monsoon clouds;   65
fit for a king, each one a fearless fighter
with terrible tusks, caparisoned in gold."

"Look, I have won."

                  "A hundred thousand slave girls,
beautiful and finely dressed, accomplished
in all the courtly arts, especially dancing   70
and singing; used to waiting on celestials,
brahmins, kings—I stake them all." He threw.

"Look, I have won." Shakuni's silken voice
was steady, not a trace of exultation.
Dhritarashtra, though, was feverish,   75
agog to know each new development,
asking repeatedly, "Has my son won?"

"I have thousands of serving men, well trained
in all the domestic skills, indoors and out."

"All these, I have won," smiled Shakuni.   80

"Thousands of fine horses, and the same number
of warriors, well trained, well kitted-out,
each with a thousand coins as monthly pay
whether he fights or not. All this I stake."

Shakuni performed his graceful throw   85
effortlessly. "Look, I have won it all."

"Celestial horses, pretty as partridges,
given to Arjuna by the gandharvas.[8]
I stake them."

                  Shakuni murmured, "I have won."

"Innumerable chariots, sturdy carts   90
and their handlers. I hereby stake them all!"

8. Celestial beings, frequent allies of the Pandavas.

"Won," said Shakuni.

        "Four hundred chests
bursting with pure gold!" cried Yudhishthira.

"I have won them all," said Shakuni.

        •

The heat was rising in the assembly hall.   95
Yudhishthira's four brothers had turned ashen.
Duryodhana was shaking with excitement.
Vidura approached the king quietly:
"O wise king, I beg you—reconsider
what you have set in train. Do you remember   100
when Duryodhana was born he cried aloud
like a jackal, an ill-omened howling
that echoed through the palace; echoes still.
I urged you then to sacrifice your son—
one son, for the sake of the whole family.   105
I told you he was sure to bring destruction
to the Bharatas. You would not listen.
Now, see what he is doing.

            "Don't let your son
bring ruin to the blameless Pandavas.
Let the ambidextrous archer, Arjuna,   110
remove him, for the good of the Bharatas.
I see you in raptures every time he wins.
But really—he is losing. The consequence
of this, for all of us, will be unspeakable.
And to what end are you allowing it?   115

"There is a story of a foolish hunter
who captured forest birds which spat pure gold
and kept them in his house. He became rich
but, not content with what the birds produced,
he cut them open and, for instant gain,   120
destroyed the birds on which he could have lived
forever. You have enormous wealth yourself,
far more than you can use. Better to keep
the friendship of the virtuous Pandavas
than to win all they own."

        Duryodhana,   125
overhearing, sneered at Vidura,
"You've always been partial to the Pandavas.
And yet you stay around here, like a cat
scratching spitefully at those who feed it.
You should get lost, old man, we do not need   130
your gloomy notions." Vidura replied,
"It is never hard to find a toady

who tells you what you want to hear. Far harder
to find an impartial, honest truth-teller."

Meanwhile, Yudhishthira had staked, and lost,   135
the vast contents of his treasury,
his palaces, lands, his great assembly hall,
the heaven-inspired city of Indraprastha,
his entire kingdom. Each time he threw,
although he well knew the odds were against him,   140
he hoped, against reason, for a miracle.
Glassy-eyed, he sat in slumped silence.

"Have you nothing more?" murmured Shakuni.
"Surely your luck will turn—you could win back
everything you've lost."

                  The Pandavas,   145
silenced by respect for protocol,
willed Yudhishthira to walk away.
But in a voice not like his own at all,
as if half drunk, or mesmerized, he said,
"My brother Nakula, who is wealth to me,   150
my young lion with the mighty arms,
I stake him now." A disbelieving gasp
ran through the hall. Shakuni, impassive,
threw his dice.

              "Look, I have won Nakula."

"My brother Sahadeva, wise and just,   155
learned in the matters of this world;
even though the last thing he deserves
is to be staked like this—I stake him now."

"Look, I have won your brother Sahadeva.
It seems these youngest two are dispensable,   160
unlike your brothers Arjuna and Bhima."

"Wretch!" cried Yudhishthira, face drained of blood,
"Never try to put a knife blade between us.
The five of us are of one heart and soul.
He that is the world's greatest warrior,   165
victorious over every enemy,
the prince who is the hero of the world,
my brother Arjuna—I stake him now!"

"Look, I have won him too," Shakuni smiled.
"Why not stake the last wealth you have left?"   170

"The strongest mace-bearer that ever lived,
my great-souled prince, massive as a bull,
fearless in war, kindest of sons and brothers,

who would spend his last ounce of strength for us—
how little he deserves this. I stake Bhima."   175

"Look, I have won!"

                  The horrified spectators
might have thought that now that the four brothers
were passing into slavery, the dice game
was over. They were wrong.

                      "O Pandava,"
said Shakuni, "have you nothing left to stake?"   180

"Only I myself," said Yudhishthira,
"am still unwon, still free to leave this hall
and travel where I will. Yet how can I,
having stripped my brothers of their liberty,
count my freedom more valuable than theirs?   185
I hereby stake myself!"

                 "Look, I have won,"
smiled Shakuni. "But in staking your own self
while you still had property, you have done wrong.
There still remains an asset dear to you,
your wife, Draupadi, the dark princess   190
of Panchala, she of outstanding beauty.
By staking her, you could win back yourself."

"She who is perfect," whispered Yudhishthira,
"neither too tall nor too short, whose eyes
sparkle with love, whose care for us is boundless,   195
our matchless Draupadi—yes, I stake her!"

At once, there was agitation in the hall.
Nobles, elders, members of the court
were deeply shocked at this turn of events.
Vidura slumped down, wringing his hands.
Drona and Bhishma were silent, bathed in sweat.   200
Some people fainted. Only Duryodhana
and his friends laughed aloud, and Dhritarashtra,
excited, asked repeatedly, "Is she won?"

"Look," cried Shakuni, "I have won her!   205
I have won the Panchala princess!"

"Go, retainer," said Duryodhana
to Vidura, "fetch Draupadi from her rooms.
They're too good for her now—let her sweep the floor.
Let her move to the slave women's quarters."   210

"Wretched prince," said Vidura, "don't you know
that by today's vile and unworthy actions

you are tying a cord round your own neck
and dangling above a dreadful chasm?
In any case, Draupadi is not a slave—   215
the king staked her when he had lost himself."
"A curse on you!" shouted Duryodhana.
He turned to a lowborn page: "You go and fetch her
to serve the household of the Kauravas."

Trembling, and with reluctant steps,   220
the messenger approached Draupadi's door.
"O queen, you are summoned to the hall.
King Yudhishthira has lost his reason
and gambled every one of his possessions—
city, wealth, his kingdom and then, madam,   225
his brothers, and himself, and, madam . . . you.
So Prince Duryodhana has ordered me
to escort you to his servants' quarters
where you will be put to menial work."

Draupadi was distraught and deeply shocked   230
but found the words to say to the page, "Go back,
and ask my husband if he gambled me
before he lost himself, or afterward.
Then come and tell me."

                     The messenger obeyed   90
but could get no answer from Yudhishthira,   235
almost demented with despair and guilt.
"Let her be brought to the assembly hall,"
said Duryodhana. "She can ask her question
for herself." And again he sent the page
to Draupadi. "I will not come," she said.   240
"But say that I am willing to respect
what the venerable men in the assembly
may definitely tell me."

                     Seeing the page
quaking with dread, this time Duryodhana
sent Duhshasana, his closest brother,   245
bloodthirsty and coarse, to fetch Draupadi.

"Come, my fine girl, you've been lost at dice
and are nothing but a slave. We own you now.
You'll have to learn to love the Kauravas
and show us how you've made our cousins happy!   250
I'm here to fetch you, you've no choice. Be quick."
She tried to run, hoping to find protection
in the women's quarters. Duhshasana
followed, grabbed her, pushed her, dragging her
by the hair toward the assembly hall.   255
She whispered that it was her time of the month

when she should not be seen, when she was wearing
a single garment, but he laughed lewdly.
"Let everybody see you have your period—
wear what you like, or come to us stark naked.   260
Slave! You can't be so particular.
Call on the gods until your voice is hoarse—
'Nara, Narayana . . .'⁹ They won't rescue you!"

Soon she was flung in front of the assembly,
her long hair loose, her garment torn, disheveled   265
and stained with blood. Every decent man
lowered his eyes in shame, but none of them—
not the elders, and not her five husbands—
uttered a word of protest. They were silenced,
for to speak out would have been disrespectful   270
to Dhritarashtra; and some of those present
feared falling out with Duryodhana.

Draupadi stood upright in their midst,
glowing with anger. She glanced scornfully
at her husbands, and that one glance hurt them   275
more than the loss of everything they owned.
She addressed Duhshasana, "It is an outrage
for you to drag me here—a virtuous woman—
to a hall of men! I see before me
many elders well versed in propriety   280
and in dharma—yet not one of them
raises his voice at this disgraceful insult.
Do they lack courage? Or do they condone
your vile behavior? A curse on you!
My husbands will not pardon this offense!"   285

"Slave! Slave!" jeered Duhshasana, rubbing his hands.
Karna laughed, thinking of how Draupadi
had scorned him at her bridal tournament,
and Shakuni and Duryodhana cheered.
But everybody else was choked with shame   290
and sorrow, and stayed dumb.

                    Draupadi spoke.
"My noble husband is the son of Dharma
and follows dharma. Let no word of mine
be heard as blaming him in any way.
I wish to hear an answer to my question."   295

Bhishma said, "Dharma is a subtle matter.
The answer to your question is not obvious.
One without property has nothing to stake
but, on the other hand, it is accepted

9. Names for the god Vishnu and his companion.

that wives are the chattels of their husbands.   300
Shakuni is an unsurpassed dice-player;
your husband played him of his own free will.
He himself has not accused Shakuni
of cheating."

      Draupadi replied at once,
"Great-spirited Yudhishthira was summoned   305
to this hall and, having no real choice,
was challenged to a shoddy gambling match
despite the fact that, as is widely known,
he has no skill at dice. Then his opponent,
Shakuni, took vile advantage of him—   310
how then could he be said to have lost?
My lord was caught up in low exploitation—
only possible because he cleaves
to principle. As I understand it,
when he put me up as his last stake   315
he had already gambled himself away
into slavery—is that not so?"
Draupadi again looked to Bhishma,
master of every nuance of the law,
for a clear reply. No answer came.   320

Seeing Draupadi weeping piteously,
Bhima, unable to contain himself,
leapt to his feet, his eyes blood-red with rage,
and shouted wildly at Yudhishthira,
"I never heard of a gambler who staked   325
even the life of a common prostitute,
let alone that of his *wife*! Oh! Shame on you!"
He made as if he would attack his brother,
but Arjuna restrained him. "Wolf-belly!
Never have you uttered such an insult   330
to our brother. In playing against his will
when invited by a respected elder,
he acted as a kshatriya should act.
You, though, by this rash outburst, are falling
away from the highest dharma; you're matching   335
our enemies' dishonor and wickedness."

Then Vikarna, one of the younger sons
of Dhritarashtra, addressed the assembled elders,
urging those present to express a view.
There was silence, so he spoke himself.   340
"It's deeply shameful for her to be dragged here.
Yudhishthira was under the influence
of an addiction; he had lost control
of his own actions, so should not be seen
as properly responsible. Furthermore,   345
it was not his own idea, but Shakuni's

to stake his wife—this despite the fact
that Yudhishthira is not her sole husband.
In any case, it's clear that the Pandava
could not lose his wife if he had lost himself,   350
since slaves can have no right to property.
Draupadi is no slave—it stands to reason."
There were sounds of approbation in the hall.

Karna answered him contemptuously,
"You notice none of the elders speaks for her;   355
only you, you green, impulsive youth,
are swayed by sentiment. The fact remains,
we clearly heard Yudhishthira stake all,
all his possessions. That includes Draupadi.
As for her being brought into this hall   360
scantily dressed—if that's what's upsetting you—
that is not an act of impropriety.
Even to strip her naked would be no sin
since she has joined herself to five husbands,
flouting every law of decency,   365
and therefore is undoubtedly a whore
in the eyes of gods and men. Duhshasana—
make the Pandavas take off their clothes,
and strip this woman."
                           At this, the Pandavas
removed their upper garments and flung them down.   370
Duhshasana then grabbed at the loose end
of Draupadi's robe, and began to pull . . .

                                     . . . Draupadi
closed her eyes in silent concentration.
Duhshasana brayed with triumphant laughter
as he twirled her round, unraveling   375
yard upon yard of cloth which pooled and pooled
on the marble floor, more and more of it.
His gleeful smile began to fade, as minutes
passed and more minutes, and the garment
covered her as securely as before,   380
though a stream of silk, a multicolored river,
shimmered and snaked around the assembly hall.
Everyone cried out in utter wonder,
and glowered at the sons of Dhritarashtra.
Duhshasana gave up, tired and angry.   385

Bull-like Bhima roared, his voice like thunder,
"As the gods are my witnesses, I vow
that, before I enter the halls of Death,
I will tear open this man's wicked breast
and drink his blood, as a lion savages   390
a helpless deer, its eyes pleading in vain.

If I do not, then let me never reach
the pure and blessed realm of my ancestors!"

All who heard him shivered. The tide of feeling
was now increasingly behind the Pandavas,   395
and against the weak-willed Dhritarashtra
who was sitting, mute, stroking his chin.
Vidura addressed the gathering:
"Learned men, it is not right that Draupadi
stands here, with no answer to her question.   400
I urge you to speak." But there was silence.
"Take this slave girl away," ordered Karna.
But as Duhshasana was dragging her,
Draupadi cried, "Stop! I have a duty
which I neglected to perform before   405
through no fault of mine—to greet the elders
in this assembly in the proper fashion.
My lords, I do not deserve this treatment—
to be forced to stand before this court in shame
by you, members of the honored family   410
that is now mine. Since my svayamvara,[1]
I have never been paraded in this way
for men to scrutinize. Lords of the earth,
where is honor in this hall? Where is dharma?
Time must be out of joint when such outrages   415
can be enacted unprovoked, unchallenged.
I am the wife of great Yudhishthira,
equal to him in rank. I am the daughter
of King Drupada, and the friend of Krishna.
I ask again for an answer to my question—   420
am I won, or not? Am I a lowly slave,
or am I a queen in a distinguished line?
You surely know the law. I will accept
whatever you decide."

        Bhishma answered,
"As I've already said, the law is subtle,   425
so obscure that even Drona slumps
with his head bowed. But this much is certain—
you are blameless. What has been done today
will bring disaster on the Bharatas."

Duryodhana spoke: "This doom-mongering   430
is so much old man's talk. Stick to the point.
Draupadi, the answer to your question
lies with your husbands—the four younger ones.
If they disown Yudhishthira and declare
that he is not your lord, then you go free."   435
Duryodhana's cronies applauded him,

1. The traditional bridegroom choice ceremony.

while others shed tears at the Pandavas'
cruel predicament. But strong-armed Bhima,
quite clear on this, said, "Do you really think
that if high-souled and just Yudhishthira   440
were not our unquestioned lord, your ugly head
would still be sitting on your shoulders? Only
because I bow to his authority,
and because Arjuna tightly holds me back,
do I sit quiet, rather than littering   445
the floor of this assembly with the corpses
of you and your friends, killed with my bare hands!"

"Dark-skinned Draupadi," said Karna, "notice—
no one here is speaking up to say
you have not been won. In fact Yudhishthira   450
had lost you when he lost himself. Accept it,
you are a slave's wife—or, rather, former wife,
since slaves own nothing.
                          Go now to the quarters
of the king's relatives; the Kauravas,
and not Kunti's sons, are your masters now.   455
Choose another husband, one who will not
gamble you away—or shall we share you?
In slaves, a willing, sensual disposition
is always welcome. Show us what you can do."

Duryodhana laughed, and bared his hairy thigh   460
obscenely to the weeping Draupadi.
At this, Bhima's eyes blazed scarlet, "I swear
the day will come when I will break that thigh
in a great battle, and you will plummet then
into the deepest, darkest pit of Death!"   465

Duryodhana turned again to the Pandavas:
"Come, reply. I'll abide by your decision."

Arjuna said, "Our brother was our master
when he staked us. But when Yudhishthira
had lost himself, then whose master was he?   470
No one's master—not even Draupadi's.
It follows, then, he had no right to stake her."
He turned to the assembly, "Now acknowledge
that the blameless Draupadi retains
her freedom, and her status, as before."   475
Many agreed with Arjuna's solution.

Just then, a jackal began to howl loudly
somewhere in the palace; asses squealed,
and frightful birds croaked. King Dhritarashtra
found the courage to address his son: 480
"Duryodhana, you have gone too far.

This blameless princess of the Panchalas
has endured the most grievous insults.
Virtuous Draupadi, ask me for a boon
and you shall have it."   485
                    "My lord," said Draupadi,
"free the dutiful Yudhishthira
from servitude, so that his son and mine
can never be taunted with the name of slave."
"Let it be so," conceded Dhritarashtra.
"And now let me grant you a second boon."   490
"Then, my lord, let my other husbands go,
together with their weapons and chariots."
"It shall be as you say," said Dhritrashtra,
"Now, ask again."
                    "My lord," said Draupadi,
"greed is a threat to virtue. These two boons   495
are enough for me. My noble husbands
will make their own way, through their own good acts."
"This is remarkable," said haughty Karna.
"In Draupadi, the Pandavas have a boat
ferrying them across to their salvation."   500

Bhima now leapt to his feet, on fire
to unleash on the Kauravas the fury
he had suppressed before. But Yudhishthira
forbade it and, approaching Dhritarashtra,
affirmed his loyalty. "Go now in peace,"   505
said the king, "and bear no grudge against us.
Look with indulgence on your old, blind uncle.
All you lost, I hereby return to you."

With that, the Pandavas, somber and relieved,
mounted their splendid chariots, and left,   510
setting out on the road to Indraprastha.

                          * * *

You can imagine Duryodhana's rage
when he heard the king dismantling
everything he and Shakuni had achieved.
He and his uncle formed a simple plan.
He held his peace until the dust had settled   5
in the wake of the departing chariot wheels,
then went to Dhritarashtra.

                          "Do you think
that by restoring all their wealth and assets
to my cousins, all can be as before?
How wrong you are! The Pandavas will never   10
forget how Draupadi was insulted.
As we speak, the angry sons of Pandu,
before they have even reached Indraprastha,

are planning their revenge—Arjuna flexing
his bow, *Gandiva*,[2] Bhima whirling his mace,   15
the others urging on their horses, eager
to gather an invincible fighting force,
summoning their allies from far and near
to march on Hastinapura.

       "Remember,
a wise ruler deals with his enemies   20
before they grow in strength. Listen, Father,
our hope lies in the saintly Yudhishthira.
If you summon him to play another
game of dice, his honor won't allow him
to refuse you. He's bound to lose again.   25
This time round, we will propose new terms:
just one throw each, and let the stake be this—
that whoever loses will relinquish
his kingdom to the other. For twelve years
that loser will be exiled in the forest;   30
the thirteenth year must be spent in public,
incognito. If he is recognized,
then another thirteen years of exile
must begin. But if he succeeds in hiding
his identity, then his former kingdom   35
will be returned to him. Those will be the terms
of the wager. But in fact, by then,
we will have used his absence to assemble
a huge and loyal army, and to garner
powerful allies; so, if it comes to war,   40
we will easily defeat the Pandavas."

Ignoring the advice of wise counselors,
the king, fearing the vengeance of his nephews,
prepared to send after Yudhishthira
with this renewed summons. Queen Gandhari   45
came and pleaded with him. She loved her son
but she feared the portents, and knew disaster
dwelt in the person of Duryodhana.
"I understand, my lord, why, at his birth,
you could not bring yourself to kill our son,   50
a helpless infant—despite the prophecy
and worthy Vidura's advice. But now
you must oppose him. Surely it is fathers
who should dictate to sons, not the reverse.
The great-hearted Pandavas agree to peace.   55
You must lead Duryodhana by example
before he brings down ruin on us all."

"If fate decrees the ruin of our race,"
said Dhritarashtra, "I cannot oppose it.

2. The mighty bow created by Brahma.

Let the Pandavas return. Let our son   60
gamble once more with Yudhishthira."

A messenger pursued the Pandavas
and caught up with them on the road to home.
They were shocked and angry, but Yudhishthira
felt unable to refuse the summons.   65
"What happens to us, good and bad, depends
on what's ordained. Whether I accept
or refuse, in the end it makes no difference."

Sorrowful, head bowed, Yudhishthira
seated himself before the gaming table,   70
flanked by his four brothers, oppressed by fate.
In the tense silence before play began
his eyes happened to fall on Karna's feet.
They struck him as familiar. Then he forgot.
Opposite, Shakuni smiled unctuously.   75
He explained the new terms of the game,
what was at stake. Yudhishthira's face was blank.
He threw. Shakuni threw, and "Look," he said,
"Look, I have won!"

          •

       At once, the Pandavas
prepared for exile, shedding their princely clothes,   80
wrapping themselves in crudely cured deerskins,
Draupadi still wearing her bloodstained robe.
Duhshasana could not contain his glee
and danced around the brothers, taunting them.
"These sons of Pandu are no men, they're eunuchs!   85
All this time they have been puffed up with pride,
contemptuous of the sons of Dhritarashtra,
but now they are brought crashing to the earth.
Choose a different husband, Draupadi—
the Pandavas are nothing now, mere husks   90
without substance."

       As they left the hall,
Duryodhana did a grotesque imitation
of Bhima's leonine walk. "You stupid fool,"
said Wolf-belly, "your idiotic antics
will come back to haunt you when I tear you   95
limb from limb, and break that thigh of yours,
and when I rip open Duhshasana's chest
and drink his blood."

          "Be sure," said Arjuna
"that Bhima's words are true." He turned to Karna.
"More certain than the sun's brightness, more certain   100
than the moon's coldness is this vow of mine:

that thirteen years from now, I will dispatch you,
son of Radha[3] to the realm of Death
if, on that day, our kingdom is not returned."

Yudhishthira said farewell to Bhishma   105
who blessed him. "Son, by your worthy actions
you have surpassed even your ancestors.
Go well. I shall look to your return."

Vidura proposed to Yudhishthira
that Kunti, being frail with age, should stay   110
in Hastinapura, with him, and not face
the rigors of the forest. Pale, sobbing,
Kunti said goodbye to her mighty sons.
Taking Draupadi aside, she said,
"My dear one, I know you are strong and brave.   115
You will come through this. Please keep special watch
on Sahadeva, my youngest, favorite son.
Help him to guard against despondency.
Oh, why has this disaster befallen you?
It must be due to my own ill fortune.   120
If I had known my family would wander
the pathless forest, having lost everything,
I never would have brought my growing sons
to Hastinapura after Pandu's death.
Pandu, I now think, was most fortunate   125
only to know our sons in times of joy;
he never dreamed of sorrow such as this."

As the Pandavas walked through the city
Yudhishthira draped his shawl across his face
lest his furious glance should cast the evil eye.   130
Bhima strode with his massive arms outspread
to strike fear in the hearts of his opponents.
Arjuna scattered sand as he walked along,
each grain standing for an enemy
he would one day strike down with his arrows.   135
Sahadeva had covered up his face,
while Nakula, lest women should weep for him,
had smeared himself with dust from head to foot.

Draupadi said, "As I am stained with blood,
so, thirteen years from now, Kaurava women   140
will be smeared with the blood of their slaughtered sons
and offer up oblations for their dead."

Crowds of grieving people lined the streets.
Then the Pandavas passed through the city gate
accompanied by devoted brahmins   145
led by Dhaumya, their household priest,

---

3. Karna's adoptive mother.

holding sacrificial kusa grass,[4]
intoning the most somber Vedic verses.

•

Shortly after the unfortunate exiles,
no longer visible to straining eyes,   150
had disappeared among the forest trees,
the sky became green, and grew strangely dark
as if the forces of the night were coveting
the brilliance of day. There were other portents
and premonitions, dreams and appearances,   155
so that dread, rather than joy, soon pervaded
Dhritarashtra's court. The seer Narada
appeared and addressed the Kauravas: "Take heed!
In thirteen years, you misguided princes
who hear my words now will die violently   160
through Duryodhana's actions, and through the might
of the Pandavas." And, having spoken,
the seer strode up into the sky and vanished.

Duryodhana, Karna, and Duhshasana
were horrified, and appealed to Drona   165
to protect them from the wrath to come.
"The Pandavas are sons of gods," said Drona,
"and it is said that they cannot be killed.
Nevertheless, when the time comes, I shall not
abandon those who ask for my protection,   170
even though I know my life is forfeit.
Dhrishtadyumna, prince of the Panchalas,
has sworn to kill me, to avenge his father.[5]
He will surely succeed on the battlefield.

Dhritarashtra, listening, said, "Vidura,   175
bring back the Pandavas. Or, if it's too late,
at least send them our blessings." And he sat
wringing his hands. His attendant, Sanjaya,
questioned him. "Why do you fret and groan—
you have obtained vast wealth, and the whole kingdom."   180
"Ah," said Dhritarashtra, "I can only think
of the future, and its terrible punishment."
"My lord, that is your doing," said Sanjaya.
"You would not listen to the words of wisdom
offered by Vidura, nor to the portents.   185
Through his wickedness, your foolish son
will be the death of all the Kauravas."

"It is the work of fate," sighed Dhritarashtra.
"I always try to make the best decisions,

---

4. Also known as Halfa grass, an Old World
perennial grass used in medicine and religious
ceremonies since ancient times.

5. Dhrishtadyumna's father, Drupada, and
Drona are old enemies.

but when the gods intend someone's defeat   190
they first make him mad, so that the wrong course
seems to him the right one. The power of fate
can be simply this twisted view of things.
All else follows. The Pandavas will never
forgive the way Draupadi was insulted.   195
Knowing their strength, and aware that Krishna
is their ally, I have never wanted
conflict with them. Yet my foolishness,
my great love for my son, will bring about
the all-consuming tragedy of war."   200

From *Book 5: The Book of Perseverence*

KRISHNA'S MISSION

Summary   After thirteen years in exile, the Pandavas are entitled, under the terms of the dice game, to have their kingdom returned to them. But Duryodhana refuses. There are various unsuccessful efforts to avert war. Eventually, Krishna, with an entourage, travels to Hastinapura on a final diplomatic mission.

* * *

In their chariots, flanked by foot soldiers,
they traveled in procession through the streets
of Hastinapura, past crowds thronging,
jostling to catch a glimpse of Krishna,
cheering in ecstasy. Dark-skinned Krishna,   5
swathed in a robe of yellow silk, resembled
a sapphire in a setting of bright gold.

The council was assembled. Also present
were kings and generals of the allied armies,
splendid in their sumptuous robes and jewels.   10
As Krishna entered, all rose to their feet,
and he noticed, hovering in the sky,
several seers, headed by Narada.
At Krishna's prompting, Bhishma welcomed them,
offering them fine seats and worthy guest gifts.   15
Now, in this assembly of the powerful,
after the usual formalities,
addressing Dhritarashtra, Kirshna spoke
His voice was like a deep and resonant drum,
reaching the furthest corners of the chamber.   20

"Sir, I bring greetings from Yudhishthira.
He sends respects, and prays for your good health.
He wishes me to say he bears no grudge
for what he and his family have suffered
up to now.

         "But you know why I stand here.   25
The house of Bharata has been renowned,

always, for its honor and probity,
for its courageous following of dharma,
which has brought it riches and acclaim.
But now your sons, led by Duryodhana,   30
have brought your great house into disrepute
by straying into greed, and cruelly
stripping your nephews of their patrimony.
This is shameful, king. If you do not check
your wayward son, catastrophe will follow—   35
a war so terrible, the entire clan
together with their allies on both sides
will be strewn, lifeless, on the field of battle,
with no one left to light their funeral pyres.
I have come here wishing to benefit   40
both the Kauravas and the Pandavas.
If you now follow the righteous course
it will be for your good as well as theirs."

After Krishna had finished his address,
the eminent seers—Rama Jamadagnya,   45
Narada, and Kanva—also spoke,
making the same point through parables,
stories of pride punished by the gods,
designed to change Duryodhana's resolve.
He sat, stony-faced, quite unmoved.   50
Dhritarashtra murmured, "You are right,
all of you, but I cannot act alone.
I am powerless—speak to my son."

Krishna turned to Duryodhana,
sitting at his ease, next to Karna,   55
and spoke kindly to him. "Best of Bharatas,
listen to the wisdom of your father,
and of the elders, not to your misguided
and malevolent advisers. They may say
that you can win a glorious victory.   60
It is not so. What man on earth but you
would make enemies of your virtuous cousins—
and for what? For slaughter and destruction.
Look at your brothers here, your sons, your allies—
don't make them die for you. For die they will.   65
You could live in peace with the Pandavas,
each in your own domain, each enhancing
the power and prosperity of the other.
Together, you could be invincible."

The king and all the elders lent their voices   70
to Krishna's plea. They summoned up a prospect
of peaceful times, certain that Yudhishthira
was sincere in his expressed intention
to put past cruelties out of his mind.

"When Krishna returns to Upaplavya,[6]   75
why not go with him, son," suggested Bhishma.
"Let Yudhishthira take you by the hands,
and his brothers welcome you with affection."

But when Duryodhana stood up to speak,
his angry breath hissing between his teeth,   80
it was clear that nothing he had heard
had had the least effect. "Long-haired Krishna,
you are reviling me because you favor
the Pandavas. You always have. These elders
are also hostile to me. The fact is   85
I have done nothing wrong. Yudhishthira
came freely to the gambling hall, and lost.
He paid; and now he wants us to return
Indraprastha to him.

                    "But I maintain
that the hasty carve-up of the kingdom,   90
long ago, was an ill-judged mistake.
It never should have happened. I was young
and could not prevent it. In recent years
I have ruled the entire kingdom as proxy
for my father here. He is the king.   95
I am his eldest son, his heir apparent.
That is how it will stay. The Pandavas
will not receive a speck of Bharata land,
not while I'm alive! I'm ready to fight.
Manliness consists in making efforts—   100
striving, never giving in to pressure.
A kshatriya can have no greater honor
than to die in the glorious heat of battle.
If it comes to death, then heaven awaits me."

Krishna's dark eyes shone with mockery.   105
"You shall have your wish. You'll find a hero's bed
for certain! There is not a single warrior
who will see his home again once he rides out
to battle with the mighty Arjuna,
unvanquishable even by the gods!   110
'Nothing wrong'? Don't think it is forgotten
how you tried to burn the Pandavas alive,
how you entrapped them in the gambling hall,
how you subjected virtuous Draupadi
to utter humiliation. And you claim   115
that you've done nothing wrong? Shame, Duryodhana!

6. City in northern India where the Pandavas have camped in anticipation of war with the
Kauravas.

"You say I am partial to the Pandavas
but I seek what is best for them *and* you.
Not one of the wise elders in this hall—
not Bhishma, Drona, Kripa, Vidura,
not even your own father—takes your part   120
in your intransigent malevolence.
If you act against the best advice
you will put yourself in the gravest danger."

Duhshasana spoke to Duryodhana   125
"Brother, if you don't agree to peace
it seems to me that Bhishma and Drona here
will capture you—and me and Karna too—
and hand you over to Yudhishthira."
Duryodhana, black with rage, sprang to his feet   130
and disrespectfully strode from the hall,
followed by his friends.

              Krishna turned toward
Bhishma, Drona, and the other elders.
"I call on you now to act—it is your duty.
Act now, while there is time. A while ago,   135
in the prosperous kingdom of the Bhojas,
I removed an upstart prince, Kamsa,
who had usurped the throne while his father lived.
There was civil war. By eliminating
that one prince, the kingdom was returned   140
to peace, prosperity, and lawfulness.
I urge you, revered elders—do the same.
Bind the perverse prince and his friends, before
they bring disaster on an unknown scale.
Sacrifice the few to save the many."   145

Silence. Dhritarashtra, as though deaf,
made no answer, but sent for Gandhari
hoping his son would listen to his mother.
"Dhritarashtra, you are much to blame,"
said Gandhari. "Out of misplaced love   150
you have allowed your son to have his way,
and now he is past control. I'll speak to him."

Flanked by his friends, his face dark with resentment,
Duryodhana was brought back to the hall
and stood, shifting sulkily, barely listening   155
while his mother made familiar arguments.
"This kingdom has always been ruled according
to the law of succession. Yudhishthira,
as the eldest of the Bharata princes,
is generally acknowledged heir apparent.   160
We all know about the obsessive hatred
you have always harbored for your cousins

and, because you have your father's ear—
a father incapable of saying no—
you have engaged in all kinds of deceit   165
and trickery to seize the throne yourself.

"But the fact remains—the true succession
rests with Yudhishthira. He is generous,
only claiming that half of the kingdom
he ruled before he was tricked out of it.   170
Yet, gripped by greed, you stubbornly refuse
to give up even this. I blame your father.
If Dhritarashtra had performed his duty,
and restrained you years ago, would you, my son,
be the stubborn fool who stands here now,   175
bringing ruin on the Bharatas?"

Again, the prince swept out of the assembly,
followed by loyal Karna and Shakuni.
Together they devised a daring plot:
seeing that Krishna could not be appeased,   180
and perceiving him as unprotected,
Duryodhana proposed to take him hostage,
keep him prisoner until the Pandavas
agreed to give up all claim to the kingdom.

But observant Satyaki[7] got wind of it   185
and went to tell Krishna and the elders
in the assembly. Once more, Duryodhana
was forced to listen to their reprimands:
Dhritarashtra said, "You must be deranged!
Do you not grasp the measure of Krishna's power?   190
If you attempted such a hare-brained scheme,
that would be your final act on earth;
you would be like a moth attacking fire.
Just as no human hand can stop the wind,
or reach the moon, as no man can lift the earth,   195
so there is no force that can capture Krishna."

Krishna turned his gaze on Duryodhana.
"Half-witted prince, just try to use force on me
and Yudhishthira's problem will be over.
I will capture you and your crass friends   200
and hand you over to the Pandavas.
You think I am just one man, easy prey,
but with me, on this spot, stand the great seers,
the Pandavas, and all our mighty allies."

He laughed a thunderous laugh and, instantly,   205
he was surrounded by a blinding light.

7. Krishna's kinsman.

His body blazed fire, and from his many arms
sprang thumb-sized Pandavas and countless warriors,
Narada and the other holy seers,
Indra, the Ashvins, and many other gods.   210
From his mouth and nostrils flickered flames.
Conches, discuses, and other weapons
shone around him, held in his many hands.[8]

Dazzled, those assembled shrank away
and covered up their eyes in utter terror.   215
Only the wisest—Bhishma, Vidura,
Drona, Sanjaya—looked on in wonder.
Krishna resumed his human shape, and walked
out of the hall. The king called after him,
"You've seen what power I hold over my son!   220
Make sure my nephews know I wish them well.
If Duryodhana stays on this wicked path
there's nothing I can do."

                                            "You are indeed
powerless," said Krishna ironically.

He left the hall, bound for Upaplavya.   225
But before setting out, there were two more
people he must see, to complete his mission.

THE TEMPTATION OF KARNA

Krishna went first to Kunti's residence.
He bent and touched her feet in deep respect.
"Kunti, mother of heroes, I am leaving."
He talked about his unsuccessful mission:
"I and the elders all spoke with one voice   5
but Duryodhana is immovable.
The whole family is in thrall to him,
heading for the abyss. Now, please tell me,
what should I say to your sons on your behalf?"

"Remind them," said Kunti, "they are kshatriyas.   10
Tell them to have regard for their dharma—
which is to fight, to protect the people,
to wield authority. Tell Yudhishthira
this is what his father and I prayed for,
not for a son who would gabble the Vedas   15
parrot-fashion, and pass his time with rishis.
Remind him that a king is the creator
of the times he lives in, not the reverse.

---

8. As with other Hindu deities, Krishna's multiple supernatural powers sometimes appear as
multiple arms, each hand holding a specific
symbolic object, such as a discus or a mace.

Ashvins: twin gods often represented as the
horsemen of the sunrise and the sunset, bringing good fortune.

"Tell him this ancient story:

"There was once a woman of the kshatriya class, famously strong-willed, whose son, defeated in a battle with the Sindhus,[9] lay about all day in gloom and apathy. His mother came to him in his apartments, where he was dallying with his concubines.

"The mother said, 'Whose son are you? Not mine, that's for sure! Are you too cowardly to rouse your anger, too feeble even to cling to a low branch with your fingernails? Have some self-respect! You look like a man, but you behave like a eunuch. Wallow in self-pity if you want to waste the rest of your life.

"'Get up, coward! You have no pride at all. Your enemies are most delighted with you and think you have forgiven them. Have you? Are you going to grow old like a dog, or are you going to rouse yourself and fight back, even if it means your early death? It is far more honorable to blaze up for an instant than to smolder like a pile of damp chaff. Effort is what counts.'

"The son said, 'Your heart is made of iron, relentless, pitiless, warmongering mother. You can't love me, speaking without compassion as you do.'

"The mother said, 'I was born into a great family, highly honored while your father was alive. Now I am pitied, stripped of wealth, ashamed that I can't give to brahmins as before. Your wife is suffering, your little sons long to have a father they can be proud of. We are at sea—be a harbor to us! We are drowning—be a raft to save us! Stand up tall, find your dignity. Better to break in the middle than to bend. You have it in you to be a heroic king. Unknown to you, we have a hidden treasury which you can draw on to raise an army. Stiffen your spine, rise up, defend yourself, be a terror to your enemies. Why don't you answer me?'

"The son said: 'I have kept silent because I wanted to listen to your every word, mother. Now I have found my manhood! I shall fight and, whether I win victory or not, I shall have lived like a kshatriya!'

"Tell my sons that story, Krishna," said Kunti,
"to remind them where their duty lies."

As Krishna left the city, he called on Karna
and asked him to ride with him a little way
in his chariot. Seriously, he addressed him.   5
"Karna, you are well versed in the Vedas.[1]
You know, then, that a child born to a woman
out of wedlock becomes her husband's child
when she marries. That is the case with you.
You are the first-born son of Kunti, conceived   10
by Surya, the sun god—in law, therefore,
you are the eldest of the Pandavas,
a Bharata on your father's side, my cousin
on your mother's." Krishna explained to him
the detailed circumstances of his birth.   15

---

9. The ancient Indian kingdom of Sindhu flourished along the Indus River in what is now Pakistan.

1. The most ancient Indian sacred scriptures, dating to the second millennium B.C.E.

"Recognize then with joy, son of Kunti,
that you are the rightful heir to the kingdom.
Come with me today, my dear cousin,
to Upaplavya. Greet the Pandavas
as your true brothers. They will be overjoyed.   20
Yudhishthira will gladly renounce his claim
in your favor. Of all the sons of Pandu
it is you whose skill and temperament,
combining truthfulness with martial zeal,
most fits him to govern a great kingdom.   25
Your nephews will fall down and clasp your feet,
and you will share Draupadi as your wife.

"You are not the son of a wagoner,
you are a kshatriya. This very day,
you can be crowned. Brahmins will officiate,   30
I myself shall perform your consecration.
You will be king, with Yudhishthira
as your younger deputy. Bhima will hold
the shining parasol over your head.
Today, let the Pandavas be united!"   35

Karna had been staring at him, amazed,
as this glorious future was laid before him.
Moments passed. Karna remained silent.
Then he spoke.
                    "Krishna, I have no doubt
you speak out of friendship for me. I believe   40
what you have just told me. It makes clear
what, all my life, has been a mystery.
I have always felt that I was born to fight.
I am never more at ease within myself
than when I raise my bow, and test my skill   45
against overpowering odds.

                    "So, Krishna,
under the law I am a kshatriya
and, from what you say, a Pandava.
But this revelation comes too late.
Kunti abandoned me. She cast me out   50
like rubbish, as if I had been stillborn,
left me to the caprices of the river.
Adhiratha found me, and he and Radha
loved me from the first. Out of love for me
Radha's breasts poured forth milk immediately.   55
Out of love she cleaned up my excrement.
Adhiratha performed the birth rites for me
as a suta.[2] He taught me all he knew.

2. Mixed-caste offspring of a kshatriya father and a brahmin mother; in the *Mahabharata*, charioteers are often sutas.

I love him and respect him as my father.
When I came of age, he found wives for me.   60
I have sons and daughters—sutas, Krishna.
My heart is tied to them with bonds of love.
Do you think I would disown them now?

"Furthermore, nothing—not gold, not offers
of all the kingdoms in the world, not fear,   65
not lust for power—could make me break my word.
And I have promised Duryodhana
that I will be his bosom friend till death.
Duryodhana has raised armies and prepared
for war because I have encouraged him,   70
and I have vowed to defeat Arjuna
single-handed. Only one of us
will live to walk away.

                          "I know full well
that, with your help, the Pandavas will win.
I can see it now—all their great warriors   75
in their chariots, banners flying, ranged
on the field of Kurukshetra. It will be
the greatest war sacrifice that the world
has ever seen, with you as the chief priest.
I see the Terrifier,[3] with monkey standard   80
fluttering boldly above his chariot.
Gandiva will be the ladle, men's courage
the sacrificial ghee.[4] The divine missiles
will be invocations uttered by Arjuna,
and men's blood will be the oblation, Krishna.   85
So much blood.

                   "I want you to promise
not to tell the Pandavas what you have said.
If Yudhishthira knew I am his brother
he would resign his kingdom to me at once;
and I would give it to Duryodhana,   90
to whom I owe whatever wealth and honor
I have enjoyed. But I know the kingdom
would best belong to him who has Lord Krishna
as his friend and guide—that is, Yudhishthira.
I regret the insults I have flung   95
at the Pandavas, to please Duryodhana.
You can tell them that, when the time is right."

Krishna smiled. Then he laughed, and said,
"Can my offer really not persuade you?
Not even when you know that Duryodhana   100
would probably give up all thought of war

3. An epithet for Arjuna.
4. Clarified butter, a staple of Indian cuisine and, since ancient times, a common religious offering.

if you changed sides, knowing he could not win?
Not even when I am offering you the earth?
Not even when I tell you that this war
will involve unprecedented carnage?   105
There will be no more lucky throws at dice.
Arjuna's *Gandiva* throws blazing iron."

"I know it all already," Karna said.
"I had a dream—Yudhishthira ascending
steps to a huge palace, with his brothers.   110
All wore resplendent robes and white turbans
and Yudhishthira was eating rice and ghee
which you had served him, from a golden platter;
I knew that he was swallowing the earth.
Then I saw the armies of Duryodhana,   115
all in red turbans, except for Ashvatthaman,
Kripa, and Kritavarman, turbaned in white.
There were open tumbrils drawn by camels,
and Bhishma, Drona, and the rest of us
were being carried off to Yama's realm.[5]   120

"So I have no illusions. But my honor
is more precious to me than life itself.
I know the dreadful bloodbath that is coming
has been caused by me and my associates
encouraging the folly of Duryodhana.   125
But it is too late. I will not betray
those I love, or the Kaurava for whom
I have pledged to die, if die I must."

"Then," said Krishna, "the last hope is gone.
I have seen my mission fail completely.   130
Tell the elders this month is propitious—
not too hot or cold, plenty of fodder
and fuel in the fields. In seven days
it will be New Moon, the Day of Indra.
Tell them that is the day war should begin."   135

Karna embraced Krishna long and hard.
"When we next meet," he said, "it will be in heaven."

                            •

Vidura was in torment. He could not sleep.
He saw all too clearly what was coming,
as in a nightmare from which one cannot wake.   140
He spoke to Kunti to relieve his feelings
and she, sick with anxiety herself,
wondered what she could do—and thought of Karna.
"Surely," she thought, "when he knows the truth

5. Yama is the god of Death.

he will obey me as his mother, and stand   145
with his brothers against Duryodhana.
That way, war may be prevented, even now."

She rose early, and went to look for Karna,
finding him where he stood every morning—
on the riverbank, stripped to the waist,   150
chanting his praises to the god of light.
She waited by a tree, taking shelter
from the sun's already oppressive heat,
until Karna had finished his devotions.

He turned and, seeing her, he bowed, hands joined.   155
"I, the son of Radha and Adhiratha,
greet you, my lady. How may I be of service?"

She blurted out, "Karna, I have to tell you—
you are *my* son, not the son of Radha
and Adhiratha. The sun god is your father."   160
And Kunti told the story of Karna's birth,
asking him, as Krishna had before her,
to join his brothers as a true Pandava.
Immediately, Karna heard a voice
that came from the sun: *Kunti speaks the truth;*   165
obey your mother and you will benefit.

But Karna's mind was steady as he replied,
"Noble lady, I hear what you say.
But you did me irreparable wrong
when you cast me on the river. By that act   170
you robbed me of the honor and respect
I should have had as a kshatriya.
What enemy could ever have harmed me more
than you have? All these years, you have witnessed me
slighted and abused within the court,   175
heard me sneered at, called 'the suta's son,'
only the king's sons befriending me.
Yet you said nothing. You have never acted
as my mother—you only speak up now
in your own interest, to protect your sons.   180

"For all the men who live in comfort here,
enjoying the bounty of the Bharatas,
the time has come to repay what they owe.
For Drona, Bhishma, Ashvatthaman, Kripa,
and for me as well, honor demands   185
that we be true to our salt. Duryodhana
is entitled to my love and loyalty
and he shall have them—I shall strain every sinew
to defeat the sons of Pandu."
                              Then, softening,

"But here is my word—only Arjuna,   190
not his brothers, will meet death at my hands.
In that way, when the terrible war ends,
you will still have five sons."
                                        Kunti sobbed
in anguish, knowing Karna spoke the truth.
There being neither time nor space for pity,   195
Karna bowed, and they went their separate ways.

                            •

That night, Duryodhana sent for his brahmins
and asked them to foretell what was to come.
They shook their heads, "The planets are at odds,
the stars are angry, and hostile animals—   200
jackals, wolves—prowl the far horizon.
We see meteors falling on your armies
and vultures circling the city. Dumb horses
are seen to weep and lie down in the fields
and foul diseases rake the population."   205

Duryodhana quaked within, but shrugged it off.
The prince would not be turned from his fatal path.

From *Book 7: The Book of Drona*

THE DEATH OF ABHIMANYU

Summary   The war has been going on for several days, with huge loss of life on both sides.
Drona is now in charge of the Kaurava forces. The Trigartas, allies of Duryodhana, have sworn
to defeat Arjuna, or die in the attempt, a challenge which he cannot honorably ignore, even
though it means that he is drawn away from the main action on the battlefield. Krishna is acting
as Arjuna's charioteer.

Sanjaya[6] continued:
Morning broke over the dismal plain.
From the vast carnage of the days before,
the jumbled bodies, limbs and carcasses,
too numerous now to be attended to,   5
littered the field as far as the eye could see.

Reviewing the events of the previous day,
Duryodhana concealed his boiling rage
as he addressed Drona before the troops.
"Drona," he said, "you made me a promise   10
which, it seems, you conveniently forgot,
since you failed to seize Yudhishthira.
He was within your grasp; you did not grasp him.
I am wondering whose side you support."

---

6. The entire account of the war is in the   been given divine sight in order that he can
voice of Dhritarashtra's aide, Sanjaya, who has   report to the king on the events as they unfold.

Despite the fact that he had made every effort,   15
Drona was ashamed. "I promise you:
before the sun sinks on another day
I will put in place a battle formation
so large, so tight, so intricately designed
that no man will escape—a trap for heroes!   20
And I swear to kill a prominent warrior
from among the Pandavas. But, once again,
you have to entice Arjuna away
from the main action. He is invincible."

That thirteenth morning, there was no eagerness   25
for what was coming. For the weary troops,
despite brave words and boastful declarations,
endurance was the order of the day,
not confidence.

          The hot-blooded Trigartas,
as had been planned, challenged Arjuna   30
to fight them in the southern part of the field.
Drona directed ten thousand of his men
into the wheel formation, a rotating,
winding, circular shape, impossible
to penetrate, save by a very few.   35
This was a hand-picked and experienced force
who had solemnly sworn never to break ranks.
They had smeared themselves with sandal paste
and, terrible to see, all wore red robes
with gold ornaments, and scarlet banners.   40
Ten thousand trained, courageous warriors,
yet they advanced as one, shoulder to shoulder,
shields edge to edge, standards overlapping—
a sight to strike fear in all who witnessed it.

At the front rode Drona, and behind him   45
were proud Jayadratha[7] with Ashvatthaman.
Duryodhana, shaded by his parasol,
was flanked by his greatest chariot warriors—
Karna, Kripa, Duhshasana among them.

The Pandavas met Drona's force head on.   50
A fierce battle followed, with many hundreds
massacred or wounded mortally.
The wheel was unassailable, and from it
a storm of missiles rained on the Pandavas
who could make no headway, but instead   55
time and again took dreadful punishment.
Yudhishthira drew Abhimanyu[8] aside.

---

7. The husband of Dhritarashtra and Gand-   8. Arjuna's young son by his second wife,
hari's only daughter.   Krishna's sister, Subhadra.

He was still a boy, but in accomplishment
and in beauty he rivaled his great father.
All the virtues, all the martial skills   60
of the five sons of Pandu, and of Krishna,
were united in him. Abhimanyu
was admired and loved by all who knew him.

Yudhishthira addressed him. "With your father
engaged elsewhere, you are the only one   65
who knows how to break into the wheel.
Child, for the sake of all of us you must try
to penetrate what Drona has constructed
or else, when Arjuna returns, he'll blame us."
Abhimanyu was fired up with zeal.   70
"Today, the world will witness my great feats;
I shall slaughter all who challenge me
or I'll not call myself Arjuna's son!
Only—my father taught me how to enter
the wheel, but not how to come out again."   75
"Once you have broken in," said Yudhishthira,
"you will force a path for us to follow.
Never fear, we shall be close behind you
and we can smash it open from within."
"Then," said Abhimanyu, "I will fly   80
like a mad moth into a searing fire!"

Hearing what Abhimanyu had in mind,
his charioteer was woebegone, fearful
that the task was far too dangerous.
"You have scant experience of war;   85
Drona with all his skill will surely crush you."
But Abhimanyu, full of cheerfulness,
said, "Oh, Sumitra! It will be glorious!
Who is Drona? Is he omnipotent?
Even if I were to face my father   90
or my uncle on the battlefield
I should not be afraid. Now, driver—drive!"

Thus Abhimanyu, dressed in flashing armor,
tall and beautiful as a flowering tree,
standard flying over his splendid chariot,   95
urged his driver on. The Kauravas
rejoiced to see him coming to the trap.
The Pandavas followed closely in his wake.

Mocking catcalls, whistles, ululations
reached him from the jeering Kauravas   100
but Abhimanyu was the first to strike
hard and precisely, like a human scythe
shearing a field of grass. First, he lopped off
arms by the hundred still grasping spears and bows.

Then Kaurava heads were rolling on the ground.   105
surprised by death, fine turbans still intact
adorned with precious jewels. Single-handed,
the boy brought chaos to his adversaries.

Duryodhana advanced to engage with him.
At once, at Drona's urging, the best warriors   110
moved forward to protect your noble son,
courageous as he was, and Abhimanyu
was forced to back off, roaring like a lion
whose prey has been denied him. Savagely,
he hurtled through your son's brigades, dispatching   115
countless men with his swift-flying arrows,
feats so dazzling that even the Kauravas
shouted in admiration.

                Fighting free
of this initial skirmish, Abhimanyu
managed to break open the wheel formation   120
and entered. At once, he was surrounded.
The Pandavas were following hard behind
but, before they could enter, they were blocked
by Jayadratha. Violent and rapacious,
the powerful king of Sindhu had long harbored   125
bitter hatred toward the Pandavas,
ever since Bhima had prevented him
from abducting Draupadi in the forest,
and savagely humiliated him.
After he had engaged in austerities   130
great lord Shiva had granted him a boon—
that at the crucial time he would have the power
to hold in check the might of the Pandavas.

Now, that time had come. The Pandavas,
try as they might, could not penetrate the wheel.   135
Jayadratha held them off with ease,
smashing their weapons in their helpless hands.
Soon, the route by which Abhimanyu entered
closed again, as elephants, troops, and chariots
rearranged themselves. The young prince stood   140
quite alone, surrounded, unprotected
before the legions of the Kauravas.

O majesty, what followed will be sung
as deathless legend, generations hence.
The young hero gathered his resources   145
and demonstrated his unearthly skill
and courage. Many great Kaurava warriors,
the best there were, died at his hands that day.
Beautiful as a flame in a dark place,
it was as if this were a delightful game.   150

A kind of joyful calm pervaded him.
He crowed in exultation as he aimed
unfailingly with arrows and with spear,
with sword and mace—with every kind of weapon,
earthly and celestial.

            He received   155
many painful wounds, and still he fought,
inflicting thousands more on his opponents.
He fought like a young god, and all who saw him
would remember it to their dying day.
Drona rejoiced that his favorite pupil   160
had passed on all his prowess to his son.

He killed Karna's brother, and he slew
Lakshmana, Duryodhana's cherished son.
He caused many strong, courageous fighters
to fall back. Wave after wave of warriors   165
rushed at him; and he repulsed them all,
slicing off hands, arms, ears, so that the ground
was an altar sluiced with sacrificial blood.
And yet, because of his respect for kindred,
Abhimanyu battled with restraint;   170
as Drona remarked, he often chose to wound
rather than kill. "Ah," sneered Duryodhana,
"our Drona has a soft spot for the princeling;
if he wanted, he could finish him,
master that he is; yet he does not do it."   175

For hours, Abhimanyu appeared tireless.
Although the Pandavas could not reach him,
they saw his amazing deeds and cheered him on
until the dust of battle hid him from them.

               •

How could it not end in tragedy   180
when no help was at hand for Abhimanyu?
One by one, his weapons were destroyed,
his bow broken, his chariot smashed, his spear
splintered. Finally he fought on foot,
only a mace to defend himself, for now   185
he was the target more than the attacker.
As cowardly wolves prefer to hunt in packs,
six of the most powerful Kauravas—
Drona, Karna, Kripa, Kritavarman,
Ashvatthaman, and Duhshasana's son—   190
set upon the exhausted Abhimanyu.
These were great warriors; they knew full well
that a mob attack on a lone opponent
was contrary to dharma. Yet they did it.
Duhshasana's son delivered the final blow   195
with a mace, smashing the young hero's head

as, already down, he tried to rise.
Abhimanyu, Arjuna's best beloved,
beautiful in death as he was in life,
fell to earth, and did not move again.   200
It was as though the full and luminous moon
had fallen from the sky to the black earth.
The Kauravas, a much depleted army,
whooped with delirious joy.

           It was dusk.
The last fiery filaments of the sun   205
streaked the sky over the western hill.
The warriors surveyed the devastation,
the battlefield resembling a sacked city.
Scavengers were gathering already
to feast on the abundant human flesh: 210
crows and ravens, jackals, kanka birds[9]
ripping at the frail skin of the fallen
to drink their fat, lick marrow from their bones,
guzzle their blood.

           These were fallen comrades,
brothers, sons, fathers reduced to this   215
welter of mere matter, food for birds.
Unable to perform the proper rites,
the living felt defiled, grief unresolved.
The somber troops slouched silently to their tents.

The Pandavas were overwhelmed with sorrow   220
for Abhimanyu. Yudhishthira could see
that his men had lost all zest for battle.
"We must not grieve," he told them, "we should rather
follow Abhimanyu's great example.
Today, he slaughtered countless Kauravas.   225
That hero is in heaven; if we stand firm,
we shall defeat our enemies for sure."

But privately, Yudhishthira was crushed
by grief for his brave and beloved nephew.
He sat in his tent, weeping bitter tears,   230
blaming himself entirely. "Oh, Abhimanyu!
It was for me that you risked everything.
For me you battled with such bravery.
Eager for victory, I urged you on.
How shall I face Arjuna? How will Subhadra   235
bear to live without her precious son?
And Krishna—how will he find consolation
now that his nephew, little more than a child,
has left the earth?"

---

9. Herons (Sanskrit); often depicted as carrion birds that haunt battlefields.

At this point, Vyasa
appeared, to give comfort. For Yudhishthira   240
in the face of this catastrophe,
it was as if the fact of death had struck him
for the first time. "What does it mean," he said,
"that men are born, are nourished by their mothers,
nurtured with care, have rich experience,   245
learn the ways of human intercourse,
love, create, take pleasure in the world,
acquire a warrior's skills, respect dharma—
what does it mean that such men can ride out
in the morning, courageous, full of hope,   250
and by evening are mere carrion
for crows to feast on? Why? What is death?"

"Death takes everything that lives," said Vyasa,
"there is no exception." And he told
the story of the lady Death herself,   255
and how Brahma, creator of the worlds,
sent her out to achieve his purposes,
so his created worlds would not become
overburdened. "For creatures—even for gods—
death is part of life, that is the law,   260
and everything that lives carries the germ
of its own destruction. Understanding this,
a wise person does not grieve, Yudhishthira."
Yudhishthira took comfort from this story,
and Vyasa told him many other tales   265
of kings whose sons were taken away by Death.

Vyasa said to him, "Abhimanyu
lived his life fully, although he was so young.
He will be in heaven; and those who taste heaven
never prefer this world to that bliss."   270

·

Arjuna had won a splendid victory
over the forces that had sworn to kill him,
but at nightfall, riding back with Krishna,
he was seized with a dreadful premonition.
The camp was silent; no one greeted them.   275
He had heard of Drona's wheel deployment
and, knowing that Abhimanyu had not learned
how to exit it, he hoped and prayed
that his brave son had not been entrapped.
On every side, he noticed ashen faces.   280

Hearing the truth, he thought he would die of grief.
He sank down, sighing, face awash with tears.
"Krishna, Subhadra will not survive this news.
Oh, my beloved boy, I remember
how I and your mother held you in our arms.   285

My glorious son, the joy of all who knew you,
witty, courageous, generous, and kind—
if I will never see your face again
how can I live? In that dreadful wheel,
standing alone, you must have thought that soon   290
your father would arrive to rescue you.
But no, you would have focused on the fight
and nothing else—a hero to the end."

Arjuna was gripped by deep despair.
Krishna gently spoke to him. "My friend,   295
bear this with fortitude. You are not the first,
nor will you be the last to lose a loved one.
Abhimanyu has gone to the realm for those
who meet death courageously in battle,
with a cheerful heart. We are warriors;   300
for us, this is how it has always been."

"How did it happen?" asked Arjuna, grim-faced.
"Tell me exactly. How could Abhimanyu
die with my great brothers to protect him?
Sons of Pandu, sons of Drupada,   305
what were you doing!? Do you carry weapons
merely as ornaments? Did you cowards watch
while my brave boy fought overwhelming odds?"

When he heard the facts, grief turned to rage
at wicked Jayadratha. He swore an oath: 310
"Before darkness falls tomorrow night,
I will cut off Jayadratha's head,
unless he comes and begs on his knees for mercy.
If I do not, may I never enter heaven,
but may I meet the hideous fate of those   315
who kill their parents, who cuckold their teachers,
defile women, betray the innocent trust
of those who depend on them. If I do not,
if, tomorrow night, Jayadratha
still struts the earth, breathing our common air,   320
I shall enter a blazing fire and die!"

•

In the opposing camp, the Kauravas
picked up a chilling sound on the night breeze,
faint at first, then swelling ever louder,
a sound to shake the world to its foundations: 325
Devadatta, Arjuna's great conch,
sounding out a challenge and a threat,
followed by furious shouts from the Pandavas.

Jayadratha knew it was meant for him.
Gripped by fear, he had a sense that death   330

was rushing to meet him. "Ah! What can I do?
Shall I escape at once, fly home to Sindhu?"
"Take heart, calm your fear," said Duryodhana.
"Who could harm you, when you will be surrounded
by our bravest, most accomplished warriors?   335
And you yourself are a tiger among fighters."
His spies had told him about Arjuna's oath
and, craftily, he thought if Jayadratha
could be protected until the sun went down
Arjuna would fail and, bound by honor,   340
he would have to immolate himself.

Slightly reassured, Jayadratha
went to Drona's tent, and knelt before him.
"Master, will you tell me Arjuna's secret,
how his arrows fly so fast, so far, so deep?"   345
"Son," said Drona, "Arjuna's skill has been
honed in the crucible of suffering.
No one can defeat him. But take heart,
I will protect you. You should fight tomorrow;
be true, follow your kshatriya dharma."   350

                    •

Through spies, the Pandavas were given news
of the elaborate arrangments planned
to guard the Sindhu king. Krishna, concerned,
wished that Arjuna had been less hasty
in uttering his vow. But the Terrifier   355
was scornful. "I assure you, Jayadratha
is already on his way to Yama's realm.
Tomorrow, he and his ill-fated friends
will have cause bitterly to regret the day
they wallowed in the sin of child murder!"   360

At Arjuna's request, Krishna visited
Abhimanyu's mother, Krishna's sister,
who was with Draupadi and Uttaraa,
the young hero's even younger wife.
Krishna told them of Abhimanyu's feats,   365
assuring them he was certainly in heaven.
"Alas!" cried Subhadra, "O my child,
my beautiful one, deserving of the best
this earth can give, how can you be sleeping
now on the cold ground, your lovely body   370
punctured by arrows! O son, O sinless one,
this world is desolate without you in it!
My little boy, my arms ache to hold you,
I long for the smell of your skin, your hair.
Oh, I am hungry for the sight of you.   375
That you could die with Krishna to protect you
is proof of fate's unfathomable ways."

Uttaraa and Draupadi, Abhimanyu's
second mother, paced wildly in their grief,
weeping without cease, inconsolable.   380
Krishna told them of Arjuna's vow, and how
Abhimanyu's death would be avenged,
but still they wept; the most extreme vengeance
could not restore to them their beloved boy.

Krishna returned to camp in sorrow. That night   385
no one slept well. They thought of tomorrow
and what had to be done to bring success.
What if Arjuna should fail? What then?
What if he were killed? How could Yudhishthira
pursue this war without him? What would he do?   390
Throughout the Pandava army, every man
prayed that Arjuna's mission would succeed.

Before he retired to rest, long-haired Krishna
walked out onto a small rise in the land
and sprinkled it with water. Immediately   395
lush grass covered it, and fresh-sprung flowers.
He laid out objects for the night offering
to the gods, and Arjuna came to join him.
Learned priests consecrated the Pandava
and Arjuna felt his heart become lighter.   400
He hung fragrant garlands round Krishna's neck
and gave him the ritual night-offering.

At the darkest hour, Krishna left his tent
and sought out Daruka, his charioteer.
"Tomorrow, we have the greatest challenge yet.   405
Arjuna swore this oath impulsively
without consulting me. I fear the worst.
Even the son of Kunti cannot kill
a man whom Drona has promised to protect.
Duryodhana will summon every means   410
to thwart Arjuna's intentions. I want you
to bring my chariot and all my weapons
and follow us, so I can support him
if things go wrong. Oh, Daruka, Arjuna
is more dear to me than all the world.   415
I could not bear this life if he were dead."

Restless on his bed, Arjuna wondered
how he would be able to keep his vow
if Jayadratha skulked behind a stockade
of chariots assembled by the Kauravas.   420

He slept at last, a sleep riven by nightmares.
Then he dreamed Krishna came to comfort him
and told him not to despair. "All that exists

rests in the lap of time. Despair is the foe
that robs you of the energy to act.   425
You must obtain the weapon, *Pashupata*,[1]
from Lord Shiva. Fasten your mind's eye
on him. When you have found him, be silent.
Then honor him, devote yourself to him
and, by his grace, he will give you *Pashupata*."   430

Arjuna sat down in meditation
and it seemed he was traveling through the sky
with Krishna, over beautiful terrain,
over the snowy slopes of Himavat,
over the remotest mountain regions,   435
over the pleasure gardens of Kubera,
over groves where apsarases[2] played.
They paused on a mountain peak to view the earth
shimmering gold beneath them, with its cities
and lakes scattered like the loveliest flowers.   440

At last, they reached the home of Lord Shiva.
The god was sitting, huge and awe-inspiring,
glowing with his own fire, trident in hand.
Parvati, his wife, was by his side.
Arjuna and Krishna bowed before him   445
and sang a hymn of praise, "O Lord Shiva,
to you who are the soul of the universe;
to you the unconquered, the all-merciful;
to you who have a thousand thousand eyes;
to you whose name is Death, lord of creatures,   450
all-powerful, and all-compassionate,
we join our hands in homage and devotion."

"Welcome, Nara and Narayana,"
said the god, smiling. "Tell me what you desire
and I will grant it." Arjuna looked deeply   455
into the flame that is the mighty god
and saw there the ritual night-offering
he had given Krishna earlier.

Shiva granted them the powerful weapon,
showed them where to find it, and how to use it.   460
Thus, for the second time, the son of Kunti
received the terrifying *Pashupata*.
Joyfully, the heroes worshiped Shiva
and returned to earth, and blissful sleep.

1. Supernatural weapon of invincible power.   Himavat: god of the mountains, a personifica-
2. Celestial nymphs. Kubera: god of wealth.   tion of the Himalayan mountains.

IN PURSUIT OF JAYADRATHA

"Tell me, Sanjaya," said Dhritarashtra,
"after they had slaughtered Abhimanyu
so contrary to dharma, so unfairly,
how could our warriors hold up their heads?
And when they heard the great conch *Devadatta*,   5
how could they march out to face Arjuna,
grim as all-destroying Death himself?
I fear what you will tell me. Oh, my friend,
I wish we had made peace with the Pandavas.
If only we had taken heed when Krishna   10
came as their envoy. But Duryodhana
was foolish and stubborn, and this holocaust
is the result."

        "You should blame yourself,"
said Sanjaya. "You had a hundred chances
to guide your son with a restraining hand.   15
You pandered to his greed—your lamentations
are like the hollow clank of empty vessels,
and come too late. What is done is done.
If you had set your son on the right path,
if you had heeded wiser heads than yours,   20
this disaster never would have happened.
O king, prepare yourself—your misery
has only just begun. Now I shall tell you
what happened on the fourteenth day of war."

                      •

Arjuna woke refreshed and confident.   25
He took his bath and performed his devotions.
Yudhishthira was woken by the sound
of his musicians welcoming the dawn.
After his morning rituals were over
he held a meeting of his greatest warriors.   30
Turning to Krishna in deep respect, he begged
that he would do all he could for Arjuna.
Krishna reassured him. "Arjuna
will certainly fulfill his vow this day."
Arjuna, worried for Yudhishthira,   35
asked Satyaki, that undefeated warrior,
to make all efforts to protect the king.

Everything that could be done was done:
horses fed and harnessed, the chariots
and weapons checked and blessed, well-fitting armor   40
carefully tied on. Last, the great standard
bearing the emblem of the divine monkey
was fixed in its socket. With a last embrace
between the brothers, the fighting day began,
a day of make-or-break, a day of truth.   45

The blare of conches, the relentless beat
of numberless war drums struck the Kauravas
like a summons to eternity.
More than any of them, Jayadratha
was trembling with terror and dismay.   50
But as Drona laid out his battle plan,
and as he blew his conch with confidence,
the Sindhu king started to take heart.
Drona had mobilized his divisions
into a complex wheeled-cart formation;   55
behind it, an impenetrable lotus
and, inside that, a strong needle array.
All these forces, well trained and determined,
stood between Jayadratha and his fate.

Arjuna, at the vanguard of his army,   60
where the densest arrow showers would fall,
was imposing—tall, muscular, and graceful,
with shining eyes. Driven by dark-skinned Krishna,
he stood high on his gleaming chariot
upright, his black hair streaming out behind him.   65
His armor glittered. He was garlanded,
and on his head was the dazzling diadem
given to him by his father, Indra.
His jeweled earrings sparkled in the sun.
Relaxed, alert, he grasped his bow *Gandiva*,   70
while, above him, the great ape on his standard
bared its teeth and snarled at the enemy.

Battle began. Arjuna's whole effort
must be to penetrate the Kaurava force
to reach Jayadratha. He told Krishna   75
to drive at your son Durmashana, the prince
positioned in the vanguard of your army.
The onslaught was devastating, and broke up
the front ranks of the Kauravas, who fled
under the fury of his attack. Heads   80
by the hundred were severed in a flash
of well-aimed arrows, and tumbled to the ground
like heavy fruit, while, for a short moment,
headless trunks fought on before they fell.
Duhshasana's strong elephant division   85
joined the battle then, but did no better
and retreated, bristling with arrows.

Now, Arjuna formally approached Drona.
He joined his hands in respect. "Master," he said,
"as your pupil, I claim your protection.
Look upon me as if I were your son.   90
Allow me to put the Sindhu king to death

as he deserves, and as I have sworn to do.
Help me keep my word."

                Drona smiled slightly.
"If you want Jayadratha, take me first!"   95
and he pelted Arjuna with arrows,
wounding his horses, severing his bowstring.
Arjuna fought back, volley for volley,
weapon for weapon, white horses against red.
This was a contest between the most skilled warriors,   100
a demonstration of most dazzling prowess.
But as the sun climbed higher in the sky,
Krishna urged Arjuna to leave the duel
and keep his mind fixed on the main objective.
"What?" cried Drona, "Are you giving up   105
on an opponent who is not yet beaten?"
"You are not my opponent," said Arjuna,
turning away from him, "but my dear master."

Mounting an assault on Drona's forces,
Arjuna released a thousand arrows   110
in the time a normal fighter would fire ten.
Kauravas fell by the hundred. Pandavas
also suffered losses. And Arjuna
was knocked senseless by a well-aimed lance
flung by Shrutayus.[3] Quickly recovering,   115
he invoked the *Shakra* weapon, which spewed out
many thousands of straight and speedy arrows,
and the Kauravas were washed glistening red
as bloody fountains sprang from elephants,
horses and men, splashing to the ground.   120
Gaining, yard by yard, Krishna drove forward
until at last they broke through Drona's lines
and shattered the well-planned lotus formation
as the Kauravas scattered in disarray.

                   •

Horrified, Duryodhana rushed over   125
to where Drona stood. "It's a disaster!
Arjuna is scorching our infantry
like a raging fire consuming tinder.
It is as if my troops were feeble children!
How long have you eaten at my table?   130
I have pampered you in every way,
yet I know your heart is with the Pandavas—
I was a fool to trust you!" Drona sighed.
He was expecting this; Duryodhana
could not bear things not to go his way   135
and had to find somewhere to pin the blame.

---

3. Warrior-king of the Kalingas, allies of the Kauravas.

The tantrum soon passed. "Forgive me, Drona—
put it down to rage and disappointment.
We must at all costs guard Jayadratha.
What hinders you?"

                "It's the sheer speed," said Drona.   140
"Those horses are the finest in the world,
and Krishna drives with supernatural skill,
swerving, dodging through the smallest gaps.
I am not young, pace is not my strength.
I propose that you protect Jayadratha,   145
block the Pandava from getting near him,
while I attempt to seize Yudhishthira."

"But how can I do that," groaned Duryodhana,
"when even you have failed? The gods themselves
couldn't stop him."

                "I have a solution,"   150
said Drona; and he gave Duryodhana
a gleaming, finely wrought golden breastplate
and fastened it on, chanting secret mantras,
tying it with sacred *Brahma* strings.
Pausing only to receive Drona's blessings,   155
Duryodhana, restored to confidence
and followed by the hosts of the Trigartas,
set out to do battle with Arjuna.

           •

Bent on capturing Yudhishthira,
Drona turned to the front of the array   160
where he sought to hold back Dhrishtadyumna.[4]
advancing at the head of a vast force.
Drupada's son aimed to divide and conquer.
Drona tried to stop him, but repeatedly
the Kauravas were split in three. One part   165
gravitated toward Kritavarman,
hotly harassed by Yudhishthira;
another coalesced round Jalasandha,[5]
chased by mace-wielding Bhima; while a third,
harried by the brilliant Dhrishtadyumna,   170
gathered around Drona. Fighting was fierce;
shafts of sunlight struggling through clouds of dust
made seeing difficult, but showers of arrows,
loosed with no special target, found a mark
in man and beast alike.

                Dhrishtadyumna   175
urged his charioteer, "Quickly! Approach

---

4. Commander in chief of the Pandavas.   leader of the Yadavas, were allied with the
5. King of Magadha; he and Kritavarman,   Kauravas.

Drona, that boastful warrior, that great teacher,
that brahmin traitor to his natural calling!"
Then the two accomplished fighters clashed.
It was a spectacle—all around them   180
other fighting stopped, so men could watch
the consummate display of archery,
the two well matched, making little headway
against each other. Then Drishtadyumna
rashly leapt up onto Drona's chariot,   185
poised on the backs of his rust-red horses
to fight him hand to hand. It was a feat
to remember. But Drona knocked away
his sword, wounding him in many places
and, if Satyaki had not rescued him,   190
and himself taken on the fight with Drona,
it could have been the end for Dhrishtadyumna.

Satyaki and Drona fought like gods—
fiercely, but with finesse and self-possession.
The sky grew overcast as clouds of arrows   195
blotted out the sun, and soon they both
ran with blood. Each hoped for victory,
and other warriors stood around, watching,
gripped by such astounding mastery.
(At heart, Drona, too, applauded Satyaki,   200
noting that he had learned from Arjuna
skills Drona himself had taught the Pandava.)
Both were masters of celestial weapons,
and each of them could neutralize the other.
Neither won. Eventually, Yudhishthira   205
called his troops to arms, and general battle
was resumed.

                              •

              Now the white sun had started
on its inexorable downward course
toward the outline of the Asta hills.
Krishna and Arjuna, with their divisions,   210
forced a passage through the Kaurava ranks,
their sights set steadfastly on Jayadratha.
Arjuna, with his limitless supply
of iron-tipped arrows, inflicted dreadful harm,
but the Kauravas had too much at stake   215
to slacken their resolve.

                     So did Arjuna.
The going was hard. The chariot maintained
enormous speed, and still the Terrifier
was killing men a league ahead of him.
No chariot had moved as fast before.   220
It moved with the speed of imagination,
the speed of thought, the speed of rapt desire.

But the horses were becoming tired.
Krishna was concerned. "We must unyoke them,
remove their arrows, give them time to breathe.   225
And they need to drink, but there is no water."
Arjuna shot an arrow at the ground
and at once a sparkling lake appeared,
with water birds and dense, shade-giving trees.
Then he made a shelter out of arrows   230
and, while he held back the Kauravas,
Krishna led the horses under it
and calmly unyoking them from the chariot,
rubbed and stroked them with an expert touch
so they revived from their fatigue and wounds.   235
To unyoke horses in the midst of battle!
Such a thing had never been done before.

Seeing this, at first the Kaurava troops
roared in triumph; surely now they had him,
heroic Arjuna, on foot and alone!   240
But calm and focused, the great Pandava
raked your forces with his powerful weapons.
"Just our luck!" groaned some of them. "Duryodhana
has set us up as sacrificial sheep.
He doesn't seem to understand that no one   245
can defeat Arjuna. King Jayadratha
is a dead man already. Duryodhana
should make arrangements for his funeral rites."

Now, with the horses rested, Krishna drove
furiously forward, sweeping aside   250
all attempts to block their headlong progress.
The two heroes shone like twin dazzling suns.

At last, they caught a glimpse of Jayadratha
with Duryodhana protecting him.
Joy seized them. Now Arjuna roared in rage   255
and exultation. "Even Indra himself
with all the celestials could not save him now!"
They advanced all the faster, hooves thundering,
terrible ape banner striking terror
into the heart of the cowering Sindhu king.   260

"Attack Duryodhana!" shouted Krishna.
"It's time to kill that wicked ill-wisher,
that greedy villain!"
                    "Drive on!" cried Arjuna,
remembering his cousin's many wrongs.

Duryodhana jeered, "Come on, son of Pandu,   265
fight me if you dare! Show everyone
if this great prowess people talk about

is real heroism, or empty talk!"
Arjuna took aim and loosed his arrows
at Duryodhana, who stood there, laughing   270
as the shafts bounced harmlessly off his armor
time after time. Krishna was astonished.
Arjuna realized: "The villain's armor
must have been tied onto him by Drona.
But I know a mantra that will make him   275
vulnerable again, a powerful weapon."
He invoked that weapon, but before
it reached Duryodhana, it was deflected
by Drona, from a distance. If Arjuna
had invoked the weapon a second time   280
it would have killed his own troops, and himself.
Instead, he used his ordinary skill
to kill Duryodhana's charioteer and horses
and smash his chariot. He then shot off
your son's leather gauntlets, and pierced his hands.   285
Krishna blew his conch *Panchajanya,*
Arjuna gave a blast on *Devadatta,*
and the Kaurava forces stood stupefied.

* * *

"Satyaki is approaching," said Krishna.
"Yudhishthira must have ordered him   290
to join you; as he comes, he is dispatching
Kauravas by the hundred. Satyaki,
your friend and disciple, is truly great."
Arjuna was not pleased. "My instructions
were to guard Yudhishthira. Now Drona,   295
like a circling hawk, will swoop on him.

"And look—you can see Satyaki's in trouble:
he is tired, his weapons all but spent,
and now he is being attacked by Bhurishravas,[6]
that formidable fighter! This is too much!   300
Yudhishthira was wrong to send him here.
Now I have to worry about him
and about Yudhishthira, *and* somehow
slaughter Jayadratha before sunset!"

Bhurishravas, strong and menacing,   305
advanced on Satyaki. "Today, my friend,
prepare to die. The wives of all those heroes
whom you have killed will rejoice, I promise you."
"Save your breath," scoffed Satyaki. "Stop boasting,
you bag of wind!" With that, they launched themselves   310
with great energy, wounding each other
with showers of arrows, so that their blood flowed.

6. A prince of Bahlika and one of eleven Kaurava commanders.

They ended up on foot, circling each other
with naked swords, grasping their bull-hide shields.
They roared and grunted like two elephants,   315
sometimes thrusting, sometimes head-butting,
rolling on the ground, wrestling, no holds barred.

Bhurishravas looked likely to be victor
since Satyaki, who had never known defeat,
was exhausted and was lacking weapons.   320
Sooner than see Satyaki broken now,
Arjuna chose a razor-headed arrow
and sliced off the arm of Bhurishravas,
the sword still in its hand. The warrior
cried to him in wrath. "Oh, Arjuna,   325
this is a sinful act, cruel and heartless—
I was not fighting you. Were you not taught
the rules of righteous conduct? Shame on you!
You have been keeping sinful company;
no doubt that's why you've left the path of virtue."   330

"Self-defense is not a sin," said Arjuna,
"and Satyaki is like a part of me—
my dear disciple and my honored kinsman.
You had your sword poised to cut his throat—
it would have been a sin just to stand by."   335

Bhurishravas, now useless as a warrior,
vowed to die by fasting unto death,
and sat meditating upon mantras,
senses withdrawn, in great tranquillity.
But Satyaki still wanted to dispatch him,   340
remembering the pain he had inflicted
in killing Satyaki's beloved sons
earlier in the war. He raised his sword
and, with one blow, beheaded his enemy.
"Alas! Shame! Shame!" cried the Kauravas.   345
Satyaki snapped back, "What's your complaint?
This man has been killed in the press of battle.
Wicked Kauravas! Where was your sense of shame
when you set upon an unprotected boy
like a pack of slavering hyenas?   350
Where was *shame* then? I see you do not answer!

"I have it on reputable authority
that men should always act to accomplish that
which gives the most grief to their enemies—
even women were killed in the old days.   355
In killing this man, I acted lawfully."

No one there applauded him, however,
neither Kaurava nor Pandava.

Time moved relentlessly, marked by the sun
indifferently sailing through the heavens,   360
dropping westward. No earthly thing would make it
slow its course, however high the stake,
even if Arjuna should lose his life
for want of a few extra, dawdling, minutes.
The Pandava was desperate. "Speed on!   365
Speed on the horses, Krishna, outstrip the sun!
Make my vow true!"

       Duryodhana was tense;
the Pandava chariot was approaching fast.
"Karna, take up arms against Arjuna.
Look at the sun! We only have to stop him   370
briefly and the world will belong to us.
Without him, the Pandavas are finished."
Karna, in great pain from his fight with Bhima,
said, "Fate will decide, but I will do my best."

For this last-ditch defense, the Kauravas   375
mobilized their most accomplished fighters:
Ashvatthaman, Kripa, Duhshasana,
Karna and his son Vrishasena,
Shalya the Madra king, Duryodhana . . .
But even as they grouped themselves for battle   380
in a cordon around the Sindhu king,
and as the sun was throwing streaks of flame
across the sky, Arjuna was already
laying waste to the Kaurava defense.

Then followed the most fierce and bitter fighting   385
of the whole war so far. Great Arjuna,
whose thoughts were never far from Abhimanyu,
massacred by the men before him now,
fought like a god. A hundred of his arrows
pierced Karna, bathing him in blood. Karna   390
in return pelted him with arrows;
Arjuna cut them all off in mid-flight,
then sent a special shaft—which Ashvatthaman
intercepted, knocking it to earth.
Arjuna killed Karna's four fine horses   395
and his charioteer. Ashvatthaman
hauled Karna up onto his own chariot
and the fight continued, others weighing in.

Such was the damage dealt by Arjuna
that the Kaurava troops began to falter   400
as they stumbled over the mangled bodies
of their comrades, who formed a jumbled mound
at least three deep. Strewn with dead elephants,

with horses missing heads or hooves, with men
whose wounds were like gaping mouths, gushing blood,   405
some moving still, some screaming and pleading,
the scene was a truly horrifying hell.

The chariot was mud-caked and obstructed
but Krishna, with preternatural skill, managed
to steer a course nearer, ever nearer   410
to Jayadratha. Suddenly it was clear
that between the Sindhu king and death
stood only a handful of exhausted troops,
defeated and disorganized.

                  But look!
Only the barest sliver of the sun   415
could still be seen above the Asta hill
and Jayadratha himself, fresh and rested,
fought Arjuna, with everything to gain.
To and fro went the advantage. Kaurava
warriors rallied now to Jayadratha   420
and surrounded him. "Arjuna," said Krishna,
"I will resort to yoga to make it seem
as if the sun has set. Do not yourself
be deceived. Thinking he's safe, Jayadratha
will relax his guard—and you can finish him."   425

The sky grew dusky. The Kauravas sent up
a cheer of relief, and dropped their vigilance.
"Arjuna!" cried Krishna, "Now is the moment!
But be careful. The Sindhu king carries
a dangerous protection. Whoever causes   430
his severed head to fall upon the ground,
that person's own head will disintegrate
into a hundred pieces. The time has come
for you to invoke the marvelous *Pashupata*."

Arjuna, with the mantras he had learned,   435
aimed *Pashupata* at Jayadratha.
His head flew off and, carried by the weapon,
traveled to where the Sindhu king's old father
was sitting in profound meditation.
Down fell Jayadratha's head, landing   440
in the lap of his own father. Oblivious,
old Sindhu did not notice and, when he rose,
it fell onto the ground, and his own head
exploded in a cloud of fragments.

                  "Shame!"
cried the outraged Kauravas. "What wickedness!   445
Arjuna has flown in the face of dharma
and killed the Sindhu king when day was over."

"The dust got in your eyes, that's all," said Krishna.
"Rub them and look again—it's not yet sunset."
And now, gazing at the western sky,   450
everyone could see the crimson segment.
It was still only late afternoon.

"I still cannot grasp," said Dhritarashtra,
"how we could fail against the Pandavas
when our forces are so well prepared,   455
so numerous. What can it be but fate?"

"Perhaps," said Sanjaya, "our forces know
the cause they are supporting is unrighteous.
The kings who make up Duryodhana's army
are his vassals—they are obliged to fight.   460
Perhaps the allies of the Pandavas
are fighting from conviction, confident
that their cause is just."

                              "How can we know?"
said the blind king. "Destiny plays with us;
it will always have the final word.   465

                    * * *

From *Book 8: The Book of Karna*

Summary   Finally, after years of enmity, Arjuna and Karna meet on the battlefield. Shalya,
himself a king, is acting as Karna's charioteer.

TRAGIC KARNA

                    * * *

The time had come. This would be the duel
that would decide the outcome of the war.
It struck onlookers that the two combatants
looked surprisingly alike: both tall,
broad-chested, well-proportioned, beautiful,   5
both god-like in their energy and strength.
Among the demons and celestial beings,
some supported Arjuna, some Karna.
The sky was for Karna, the earth for Arjuna.
Vaishyas, shudras, and those of mixed descent   10
cheered for Karna, while Arjuna was the hope
of the higher orders.[7]

---

7. In ancient Indian society, *vaishyas* were
traders and landholders who formed the third-
ranking *varna*, or caste; *shudras* were peasant
laborers born into the fourth-ranking and lowest *varna*. The "higher orders" were, first, the
priestly *brahmins*, and second the *kshatriyas*, or
warriors.

The gods themselves
were divided between the two heroes.
Indra supported his son, Arjuna,
while Surya[8] sought victory for Karna.   15

Karna asked Shalya, "Tell me, if I am killed
what will you do then?" Shalya replied,
"I will myself kill Krishna and Arjuna."
Arjuna asked Krishna the same question.
"Arjuna," said Krishna, smiling, "the earth   20
will split into a thousand jagged fragments
before Karna will succeed in killing you!
If it did happen, it would be a sign—
the last days of the world would be approaching,
and I would kill both Karna and Shalya   25
with my bare hands!" Arjuna was joyful.
"Today I shall grind Karna in the dust,
and make sorrowing widows of his wives.
Today, Abhimanyu's grieving mother
will receive some comfort, and today   30
Kunti will receive the news she longs for."

To the deafening sound of drums and conches,
the two great heroes closed on one another
like two clashing banks of rain-filled cloud,
or like two maddened elephants in season.   35

Although each warrior was supremely skilled
at cutting the other's arrows in mid-flight,
soon blood was flowing freely on both sides.
Bhima, thinking Karna was doing better,
squeezed his hands in rage. "Come on, Arjuna,   40
how can you let your arrows miss their mark!
Think how this wretched man insulted us!"
And Krishna, too, reproached him. "Arjuna,
the Kauravas are cheering as though they think
Karna has won. Take *Sudarshana*,   45
my razor-headed discus, and separate
Karna's head from his contemptible body!"

Arjuna braced himself for greater effort.
He invoked the lethal *Brahma* weapon,
but Karna, smiling, baffled it in mid-flight,   50
rendering it harmless. Arjuna
called up other celestial weapons, able
to inflict huge damage. So did Karna.
He fought with such panache, such superb skill,
it looked as if he would certainly prevail   55

8. God of the sun.

as arrows poured in torrents from his bow.
The watching Kauravas yelled with delight.

But the battle was not over. The fine bodies
of both great warriors were slick with blood
but both had plentiful reserves of strength,   60
courage, and energy. Karna released
five arrows like snakes, piercing Krishna
and passing through him to sink into the earth.
In fact, these were snakes indeed, related
to one Arjuna had killed at Khandava.[9]   65
Incensed, Arjuna cut up these arrows,
and sent them winging back with such force
that Karna, deeply wounded, trembled in pain.
Then Arjuna sprayed the surrounding Kauravas
with such a dense onslaught of darts and arrows   70
that the sky turned black. They fled in terror.
Unsupported, Karna felt no fear
but rushed at Arjuna with a joyful heart.

O king, never before has there been seen
a duel between such transcendent warriors.   75
Having many weapons of different kinds
at their disposal, the two fighters displayed
miraculous and beautiful maneuvers;
and the celestials, watching from the sky,
shouted in admiration, sprinkling   80
the heroes with cool, perfumed sandal-water.[1]

Ashvasena, Arjuna's snake enemy,
managed to insinuate himself
into Karna's quiver, where he took shape
as a blazing arrow. Nocked on the bowstring,   85
he caused the sky to shimmer with evil portents—
thunderbolts and fiery meteors.
"Use another arrow," shouted Shalya,
"that one will not have the effect you want."
But Karna rejected the advice, and loosed   90
the awe-inspiring arrow. It seemed to carve
a channel in the firmament as it flew
straight for Arjuna's head. Calmly, easily,
Krishna pressed down the chariot with his feet,
causing it to sink. In this way, the arrow   95
did not behead Arjuna, but merely knocked
his lovely jeweled diadem to the ground.
The Pandava bound his hair with a white cloth.

---

9. In an incident years before, Arjuna and
Krishna helped Indra to clear the Khandava
Forest of its inhabitants, snakes among them.

1. That is, water steeped in fragrant sandalwood.

The snake hissed at Karna, "When you shot me
you did not aim with care. That is why   100
I was unable to decapitate him."
"Who are you?" asked Karna.
                              "I am a hater
of Arjuna, my mother's murderer.
Shoot me again, and you will quickly see
his head knocked from his shoulders." Karna said,   105
"Karna will not win through another's power;
and I will not shoot an arrow a second time."
"As you please," hissed the snake, and he aimed himself
straight at Arjuna—who sliced him up
in mid-flight, and sent him writhing, spinning   110
to earth.

          Krishna righted the chariot
and, as he did so, Karna attacked.
Arjuna, with several well-judged shots,
penetrated Karna's armor; exultant,
Karna struck him back, laughing aloud.   115
Arjuna, with preternatural skill,
stripped Karna of his beautiful gold headdress,
his jeweled earrings, and his shining armor,
then wounded him so deeply and severely
that Karna gasped, staggered, streamed with blood.   120

The driver's son set down his bow and quiver,
thus signaling a respite. Arjuna,
observant of the rules, let fall his bow,
but Krishna urged him on. "Don't let up now!
Karna is your hate-filled enemy.   125
Kill him while you can—as Indra did
when he slaughtered the demon Namuchi."[2]

Arjuna obeyed, and soon Karna
was spiked with arrows all over his body.
But, rallying, he snatched up his fine bow   130
and pelted Arjuna with fiery shafts.
Now he struggled to recall the words
of the mantra for the highest *Brahma* weapon,
but his mind was blurred; he could not grasp them.[3]
His inner light was wavering in him.   135

The hour of Karna's death was fast approaching.
Time itself, whispering in his ear,
told him that earth was starting to devour

2. Indra slew Namuchi after assuring him he
would not.
3. Many years before, Karna had been cursed

by his weapons teacher that he would forget
the mantra at the moment when he most
needed it.

his chariot wheel. The chariot lurched, tilted
and stuck fast in the ground. His lovely bow   140
fell from his hand. Mortally wounded now,
wringing his hands in despair, Karna cried,
"I have followed dharma, but righteousness,
after all, does not protect the righteous.
Instead, righteousness is destroying me!"   145

As Krishna and Arjuna closed in on him
Karna climbed down from his chariot
and struggled to release his mud-bound wheel.
"Hold off!" he cried. "Only a coward strikes
when his opponent has laid down his arms.   150
Arjuna, you are a man of principle,
you observe dharma—do what you know is right!"

Krishna shouted, "It is well and good
for you to plead dharma when you're in trouble.
Where was dharma when you outraged Draupadi?   155
Where was it when you helped Duryodhana
to plot the murder of the Pandavas?
And where, when you connived in their exile?
And when young Abhimanyu was outnumbered,
where was dharma then?"

                          Karna bowed his head.   160
He picked up his bow. Then Arjuna destroyed
Karna's glittering bejeweled standard,
symbol of Duryodhana's ardent hopes.
Seeing that, a shocked lament arose
from all the watching Kauravas. Arjuna   165
took out his hefty arrow *Anjalika*
with blade as broad as two hands joined together
and, placing it in his bow *Gandiva*,
he prayed that it would find its rightful mark.
And aimed. *Anjalika,* flaming like a comet,   170
flew with unearthly speed, straight and true,
and struck off Karna's head. It fell to earth
as the red disc of the sun drops at sunset.
It was afternoon.

                          As Karna's head and trunk
fell, still lovely, glistening with blood,   175
the light that always seemed to shine from him
left his body, and rising through the sky,
traveled to the sun, and merged with it.
Everyone saw that. Karna's fallen head
lay like a quenched fire after a sacrifice,   180
or like a boulder loosed from a mountainside
by a violent storm.

When Karna fell,
the rivers ceased to flow, the sun turned pale,
the planet Mercury seemed to change its course
and the earth trembled.

•

It is said by some   185
that as Karna's spirit left his body,
he saw a brahmin (Krishna in disguise)
who asked him for gold. Having none to give,
with a stone, Karna knocked out his own teeth,
with their gold caps, washed them, and offered them.   190
Then Krishna granted him the supreme vision
of his divine self, riding on Garuda,[4]
and promised him whatever boon he wished.
Karna considered choosing victory
for Duryodhana. But he asked, rather,   195
that Kunti should be brought news of his death.
He knew she would then come to the battlefield
and tell his brothers who he really was.
He asked a second boon. In his life,
he had been unable to gain the merit   200
of feeding others, since no one would want
hospitality from a driver's son.
He asked Krishna that in his next birth
he should have that chance. Krishna blessed him
and granted his wish.

•

Sanjaya went on: 205
When Karna fell, the fighting was suspended
and warriors of both sides gathered round
in disbelief. Some of them were awestruck,
some were fearful, others sorrowful,
sobbing in grief, according to their natures.   210

The Pandavas were wild with exultation.
They blew their conches, shouted, waved their arms,
and flapped their garments, dancing in delight.
Bhima roared and slapped his arms in triumph.
Arjuna, his vow fulfilled, relinquished   215
hostility for Karna. Yudhishthira
felt he had been reborn, and had to look
and look again at the body of the man
he had so long feared. "What good fortune,"
he exclaimed, "has today delivered   220
victory! Krishna, today I have become
king of the earth, together with my brothers,
and it is thanks to you."

4. The celestial eagle.

Duryodhana's troops,
in disarray, milled around aimlessly
like horses without riders, or like boats   225
bobbing directionless on a choppy sea.
Grim, sorrowful, Shalya drove Karna's chariot,
now freely moving, away from the scene of death.
Duryodhana was shocked past all expressing.
Tears poured from his eyes. But seeing his men   230
leaderless, he gathered his resolve
and rallied them. Then, for a little while,
battle resumed between the two armies.
Many of the warriors fled the field.
Duryodhana fought bravely, and attempted   235
to bring them back. "What is the use of running?
The Pandavas will pursue you everywhere.
Better to fight bravely and die with honor."
Reluctantly, with faces pale as ash,
the men turned, and obeyed your son's command.   240

Shalya turned Duryodhana's attention
to the hideous sights of the battlefield:
the bloody corpses of men and animals,
the chaos of war's paraphernalia.
"You yourself are the cause of all this horror.   245
The sun is hanging low over the hills;
let the troops retire for the night."

Later, Duryodhana gave way to grief.
"Alas, Karna! Alas!" he cried, and stood
weeping beside his friend, who lay surrounded   250
by hundreds of gently glowing oil-filled lamps.

From: *Books 17 and 18: The Books of the Final Journey and the Ascent to Heaven*

THE FINAL JOURNEY

Summary   The war ends in death for the main Kauravas and victory for the Pandavas. Yudhishthira becomes king and rules wisely for thirty-six years. At the end of that time, Krishna dies, and the Pandavas decide that it is time for them to leave the earth. Yudhishthira makes Parikshit, Arjuna's grandson, his heir.

* * *

When the people heard of the king's decision
they were distressed and tried to change his mind,
but he was firm, and managed to convince them
that it was for the best. Then he turned his thoughts
to departure. On the appointed day,   5
the five Pandavas and Draupadi,
clothed in garments of bark, and having fasted,
left Hastinapura. They were reminded

of the time so many years before
when they had left the city in bark clothing   10
after the defeat in the gambling hall.
Then, they were entering miserable exile;
now, quitting Hastinapura forever,
they were at peace, feeling only joy.
Some citizens escorted them on their way,   15
still hoping to persuade them to return.
But failing, and bidding them a last farewell,
they turned back to the city, and their new king.[5]
Only a stray dog stayed with the Pandavas,
trotting along behind them, keeping pace.   20

Traveling on foot, for many months
they circumambulated the whole land
of Bharatavarsha,[6] through varied terrain.
Living austerely, they first turned eastward
toward the rising sun and the eastern mountains,   25
following the course of the mighty Ganga
to where its waters flow into the sea.
Arjuna still carried his bow *Gandiva*,
and his quivers, once inexhaustible.
They were useless to him now, but still   30
he was attached to them, as to old friends.

As they approached the coast, a tall figure
appeared in front of them. "I am the fire god,
Agni," he said. "It was I who burned
the Khandava Forest all those years ago.   35
Arjuna, I gave you *Gandiva* then,
procured from Varuna, the god of waters,
and now it is time to give it back to him.
It will return to earth in another era.
Like Krishna's discus, it will be taken up   40
to benefit the world." Then Arjuna,
standing on a rock, threw his weapons
out into the ocean, where they sank.

The Pandavas went on toward the south
following the shore by the Eastern Ghats.[7]   45
Next, they went west and north through many kingdoms
that once had owed them fealty, unnoticed
and unrecognized. Eventually,
they reached the coast where Dvaraka[8] once stood,
radiant jewel of the western sea   50
now submerged beneath its crashing surf.

5. Parikshit, Arjuna's grandson.   7. Mountain range along India's east coast.
6. The land of the Bharatas.   8. Krishna's city.

The travelers turned inland, heading northeast,
and still the scruffy dog was at their heels.
At last, they sighted the majestic outline
of snowy Himavat,[9] the king of mountains   55
dazzling in the sun, known as the source
of the sacred Sarasvati.[1] They climbed upward,
ever higher, through the sparkling air.
In the distance, they could hear the roar
of rivers tumbling down over the rocks   60
through deep ravines. During their twelve-year exile,
when they had spent time in the high mountains
consoled by the peace and beauty of the place,
Yudhishthira had promised to return
at his life's end, as a penitent.   65
Now, as they walked in a state of meditation
they passed through groves of flowering plants, surrounded
by the singing of innumerable birds.

But they did not stay. Steadfastly they journeyed
onward toward the pure land of Mount Meru,[2]   70
greatest of mountains, home to the mightiest gods.

Then, as they walked in single file, Draupadi
fell down, lifeless. "Brother," exclaimed Bhima,
"why has she died now, she who was blameless,
who never did a sinful act?" Yudhishthira   75
thought, then said, "She was wife to all of us,
but she has always favored Arjuna.
Perhaps that was her sin."

                    They traveled on
and, after some time, Sahadeva fell.
"Why?" asked Bhima.   80
                    "Perhaps he was too proud
of his wisdom," said Yudhishthira.

Nakula fell next. "He was righteous
and intelligent," said Yudhishthira,
"but he thought that none could rival him
in beauty. I suppose that is the reason   85
why he has fallen now."

                    Then Arjuna
fell to the ground and gave up the breath of life.
"Why Arjuna?" asked Bhima. "I cannot think
of any time when he spoke untruthfully,

---

9. Part of the Himalayan range visible from the south (in India).
1. Indian river with headwaters in the Himalayas.

2. Mythical mountain said to be the center of the cosmos and the entrance to heaven from earth.

even as a joke."

"He was too proud,"   90
replied Yudhishthira. "You remember—
he boasted that he would defeat our foes
in a single day. He was contemptuous
of other archers. That is why he has fallen."

Then Bhima fell to the ground. "Why me?" he cried.   95
"I want to know." Yudhishthira replied,
"You were a glutton; you failed to attend
to the wants of others. And you were a boaster,
proud of your mighty arms. But for all of us,
our death is preordained." And he walked on   100
without looking back, accompanied
only by the dog.

     After Yudhishthira
had trudged on through the snow for many days,
his gaze fixed steadily upon Mount Meru,
he was exhausted. There was a rushing wind   105
and Indra appeared to him on a fine chariot.
"Climb on," he said, "and come with me to heaven."
But Yudhishthira stayed where he stood,
looking back down the mountain. "My brothers
and Draupadi must go with me," he said.   110
"I do not want to be in heaven without them."
"Do not grieve for them, Bharata," said Indra.
"They have all reached heaven ahead of you,
having cast off their bodies. It is ordained
that you should reach heaven in bodily form."   115

"This dog must come with me," said Yudhishthira.
"Through our entire journey, he has walked
beside me loyally, sharing all hardships."
"Impossible. Heaven is no place for dogs,"
said Indra. "You have won the supreme reward   120
by your virtuous life—there is no sin
in abandoning the dog."

     "I cannot do it,"
said Yudhishthira. "It would be wicked
to cast aside one who is so devoted
from a selfish desire for the joys of heaven."   125
"But you have renounced all other ties,"
said the god. "You left your wife and brothers
lying on the ground. Why is this dog different?"
"They were already dead. There was nothing more
I could do for them. This dog is alive.   130
To abandon him would be equivalent
to the worst sins—slaughtering a woman,
theft from a brahmin, injuring a friend.
I have never done such a sinful deed,

and I never will, so long as I have breath.   135
Indra, I cannot, and I will not do it."

Suddenly, the animal was transformed
into the god of righteousness himself:
Dharma, father of Yudhishthira.
He was delighted with his virtuous son.   140
"This compassion is a supreme example
of your righteous mode of life. There is no one
in all the worlds more virtuous than you."

Yudhishthira was taken up to heaven
by Indra, accompanied by other gods   145
and celestial beings. The seer Narada
was one of many there who welcomed him.
He told Yudhishthira that no one else
had ever had the privilege of earning
heaven while they were in their earthly body.   150

Yudhishthira thanked the gods. "But now," he said,
"I wish to go to that realm where my brothers
and Draupadi have gone. I want to join them."

"You have earned a special place," said Indra.
"Why do you still cling to your old attachments?   155
Your four brothers and Draupadi have reached
happiness. You should stay here with us—
enjoy your great success."

                    But Yudhishthira
insisted that he wanted to be only
where his brothers and his wife had gone.   160

"Open your eyes, Yudhishthira," said Indra.
Yudhishthira looked around—and what he saw
was Duryodhana! The Kaurava
was seated on a splendid throne, surrounded
by gods and many heavenly attendants,   165
together with the other Kauravas.
Yudhishthira, shocked and outraged, turned his back.
"How can this be! This wicked cousin of ours,
this man, driven by greed and bitter envy,
was responsible for the deaths of millions   170
and the desolation of millions more.
It was due to him that the blameless Draupadi
was humiliated; due to him
that we endured those thirteen years of exile,
suffering privation—yet here he sits   175
enjoying the rewards of Indra's heaven!
I do not even want to look at him.
Let me go to where my brothers are."

"This response is wrong, Yudhishthira,"
said Narada. "Heaven knows no enmity. 180
You should put all these concerns behind you.
I know Duryodhana behaved wrongly
to the Pandavas, but by the sacrifice
of his body on the field of battle,
and by his courage, he has pleased the gods. 185
He never ceased to follow kshatriya dharma.
He never fought unfairly. You should approach him
in a spirit of goodwill."

             Yudhishthira
looked away. "I do not see my brothers,
or any of the heroes who fought with us; 190
nor do I see Karna. Ever since
my mother told me that he was our brother
I have longed for him, both night and day.
When I noticed, in the gaming hall,
that Karna's feet so much resembled Kunti's, 195
I should have realized. I should have spoken.
I wish to go to him, and to the others,
my other brothers and faithful Draupadi.
Where my loved ones are—that is heaven.
For me, this place is not heaven at all." 200

The gods ordered a celestial messenger
to escort Yudhishthira to his kinsfolk.
The messenger went first, to show the way
over rough terrain. It was treacherous,
mushy with flesh and blood, bones, hair, 205
and stinking of the cadavers that lay
all around, swarming with flies and maggots
gorging on the decomposing bodies.
The way was lined with fire, and it was jostling
with crows and other scavengers, their beaks 210
iron-hard and cruel. Dark spirits lurked there
with needle-sharp incisors and hideous claws.
They passed a river, boiling and foul-smelling,
and a stand of trees whose every leaf
cut like the keenest blade. Worst of all, 215
people on every side were enduring
the most dreadful torture imaginable.

"How much further?" asked Yudhishthira.
"What is this place? And where are my brothers?"

The messenger stopped. "My instructions are 220
that I should come this far only. If you wish,
you may return with me." Yudhishthira
was suffocated by the dreadful stench
and stifling heat. His courage was failing him.

He turned round to follow the messenger.   225
But then he heard piteous voices, calling out,
"Son of Dharma! Royal sage! Great Bharata!
Pity us! As long as you are here
a fragrant breeze is bringing us relief.
Please stay, even for a little while."   230

"Ah, how terrible!" exclaimed Yudhishthira.
The voices seemed familiar. "Who are you?"
he called to them. He heard the voices answer,
clamorous with pain—
"I am Karna!"   235
"I am Bhima!"
"I am Arjuna!"
"I am Nakula!"
"I am Sahadeva!"
"I am Draupadi!"   240
"I am Dhrishtadyumna!"
"We are the sons of Draupadi!"

Yudhishthira, horrified and bewildered,
could not understand. It seemed to him
that everything he knew, and had believed   245
throughout his life, had been turned upside down.
"What madness is this?" he asked himself.
"What have these beloved people done
that they should be consigned to hell like this?
It makes no sense at all that Duryodhana   250
should be enjoying every luxury
while these dear ones, who have been most scrupulous
in observing dharma—and all these months
have been steadfast in yoga[3]—are suffering.
Am I dreaming, perhaps? Is this delusion?"   255
Yudhishthira began to blaze with anger.
"What kind of beings are the gods we worship
with such devotion? What is dharma worth
if these good souls can be so cruelly treated?"

He spoke to the messenger. "I shall stay here.   260
How could I enjoy gross privilege
in heaven, having seen what you have shown me?
My presence here seems to bring some relief
to these dear people. Therefore, I shall remain
to comfort them. This is where I belong."   265

The messenger went away. But in no time
the gods appeared, with Indra at their head,
and, among them, the lord of righteousness.
Immediately, the scene changed completely.
Dark became light. The dreadful sights and smells   270

3. Spiritual discipline.

disappeared. A gentle, fragrant breeze
blew all around. There were no tortured beings,
no rotting corpses, no lacerating trees.

"Yudhishthira," said Indra, "do not be angry.
You will suffer no more of these illusions.   275
Hell has to be witnessed by every king.
Whoever first encounters heaven will afterward
experience hell. He who endures hell first
will afterward see heaven. Sinful people
enjoy the fruits of their good actions first,   280
spending some time in heaven before hell.
For those whose lives were mainly virtuous
it is the opposite. Because you tricked Drona[4]
by letting him believe his son was dead,
you, through a trick, had to spend time in hell.   285
It was the same for your brothers. Illusion
caused them to suffer, just for a short time.
Now that is at an end. Shed grief and anger.
Your brothers and your kinsfolk have now gone
to those realms where they enjoy happiness."   290

Lord Dharma spoke. "My son, I am highly pleased.
You have passed all the tests I set for you.
By the Dvaita lake, you answered my riddles.
You showed loyalty even to a dog.
And here, out of compassion, you chose to share   295
the suffering of others. There is no one
in all the worlds more virtuous than you.
You must now bathe in the celestial Ganga[5]
where you will cast off your human body."

This Yudhishthira did. And, with his body,   300
all resentment, grief, hostility
also fell away. Then the gods took him
to the place where everyone he loved,
as well as all the sons of Dhritarashtra,
were enjoying bliss. There he saw Krishna   305
in his divine form; and each of his brothers
transformed by splendor, yet recognizable,
associating with the gods, their fathers.
He saw Karna, with Surya, the sun god.
He saw Draupadi, radiant with light,   310
accompanied by all her royal sons.
He saw Abhimanyu. He saw Pandu
reunited with Kunti and Madri.
He saw Bhishma, Drona . . . so many heroes
it would take an eon to name them all.   315

4. During the war, Yudhishthira tricked Drona   man, had been killed.
by letting him believe that his son, Ashvattha-   5. The River Ganges.

THE BHAGAVAD-GĪTĀ

ca. fourth century B.C.E.–fourth century C.E.

The *Bhagavad-gītā* asks the most difficult of questions. What is a just war, and when can the use of armed conflict to resolve a political stalemate be justified? Under what circumstances is it possible to engage in a violent conflict with family members, clansmen, teachers, and friends—the very people who have nurtured us since infancy—and claim a victory that is morally right? What is such a victory worth if, in the name of life, wealth, or truth, it destroys what we love? As a philosophical poem, the *Bhagavad-gītā* does not provide simple answers but offers explanations that are appropriately difficult because they involve dilemmas that cannot be resolved once and for all.

CONTEXT

During the past two centuries, it has become commonplace to treat the *Bhagavad-gītā* as an independent poem, which can be read and understood by itself for its philosophical message as a meditation on universal issues. But the work is actually an integral part of the *Mahabharata*, and was originally composed as the sixty-third minor book of that epic, and included in its sixth major book, *Bhīṣma*. Since it is a poem within a poem, the *Bhagavad-gītā* is best interpreted in relation to the epic's larger narrative, setting, and background.

The *Mahabharata* is attributed to a single poet or compiler named Kṛṣṇa Dvaipāyana, but it was composed collaboratively by many generations of poets in Sanskrit between about 400 B.C.E. and 400 C.E. Its main story concerns a protracted conflict between two branches of a royal dynasty in northern India, over the inheritance of a kingdom and the succession to its throne. The embattled groups are the Kauravas and the Pāṇḍavas, who are paternal cousins; the Kauravas are one hundred brothers, led by their eldest, Duryodhana, whereas the Pāṇḍavas are five half brothers, the three eldest being Yudhiṣṭhira, Bhīma, and Arjuna. Both branches have strong and legitimate claims to the kingdom, and one possible settlement is a division of the dominion, so that each set of cousins can rule its own territory without conflict. But Duryodhana and his brothers, the Kauravas, resist such a solution; using a variety of strategies, they deny the Pāṇḍavas' claim, and send the five brothers and their shared wife (in a polyandrous marriage) into a thirteen-year exile, with the promise to restore their share of territory if they meet several conditions. The Pāṇḍavas complete their exile as required, but when they return to Duryodhana's court, he refuses to honor his word.

At this point in the main narrative, Lord Kṛṣṇa—a human avatar of Viṣṇu, the god who primarily preserves the moral order of the universe—intervenes on behalf of the Pāṇḍavas. In the course of his life in human form, Kṛṣṇa became a close friend of the third Pāṇḍava, Arjuna, in his youth; now, many years later, when Arjuna and his half brothers find themselves in an impossible situation with their cousins, Kṛṣṇa agrees to serve as their ambassador to Duryodhana. Even though Kṛṣṇa (whose divinity is evident to the other characters in the epic) offers the Kauravas a peaceable solution in accordance with *dharma* (law, morality, duty, obligation), Duryodhana refuses to give the Pāṇḍavas even five small villages as their share of the kingdom. In consultation with Kṛṣṇa, the Pāṇḍavas decide that the only way in which they can now assert their legitimate claim to the kingdom is by going to war with the Kauravas. This is a just war because their claim is based strictly on the *dharma* of succession and inheritance; and it is a justifiable war because they have exhausted every possibility of a peaceful resolution of the stalemate with the Kauravas.

The Kauravas and Pāṇḍavas then prepare for armed conflict, and their respective armies gather on the battlefield of Kurukṣetra (about sixty-five miles north of modern Delhi). Arjuna, the most skilled and feared archer of his times, enters the battlefield on a chariot, with Kṛṣṇa serving as his charioteer. But in the moments just before the battle begins, Arjuna looks at the forces arrayed on the enemy side, and sees in their midst all his cousins as well as many people he grew up with— teachers, friends, and members of his clan, people he has known and loved much of his life. Faced with the prospect of shedding their blood, he throws down his weapons and refuses to fight: he cannot imagine how any such war could possibly be good or right. But, in doing so, he immediately places himself in moral jeopardy as a warrior, because *dharma* requires that a *kṣatriya* be prepared to wage war whenever necessary, and in this case his cause is just. Caught between his fundamental duty as a warrior and his equally powerful obligation to preserve the lives of those he loves, Arjuna turns to Kṛṣṇa—his friend, aide, and counselor—and asks for his divine advice under the circumstances. The *Bhagavad-gītā* is the poetic record of that moment of crisis in Arjuna's mind, and of the conversation he has with God on the brink of war.

WORK

The *Bhagavad-gītā* is divided into eighteen chapters or cantos composed in verse, and its total length runs to seven hundred couplets. In the translation from which our selection of passages is drawn, each canto is called a "chapter"; it contains, in part, Kṛṣṇa's instruction to Arjuna about what is involved in war, violence, duty, courage, life, and death (among other things), and why it is essential to fight a just war, even if it means destroying precious lives.

The structure of the *Bhagavad-gītā* as a whole has two layers of interspersed dialogue: one between Sañjaya and Dhṛtarāṣṭra, which defines the outer frame of the book, and the other between Arjuna and Kṛṣṇa, which occurs in an inner frame. Dhṛtarāṣṭra is the father of the Kauravas and the current head of the dynasty; he is blind and old, and cannot participate in or even observe the battle. He sits in his chariot on the edge of the battlefield with his chari-oteer, a youth named Sañjaya; on the eve of the war, Dvaipāyana, the original author of the *Mahabharata*, grants Sañjaya "celestial vision," so that he can omnisciently observe everything in the past, present, and future, and everything that happens on the battlefield, in public and in private; throughout the eighteen days of the war, Sanjaya tells the blind Dhṛtarāṣṭra what happens in the war, and we, the readers, also witness the entire conflict through Sañjaya's "visionary eye." Our excerpts here mostly omit the dialogue between Sañjaya and Dhṛtarāṣṭra in the various cantos; the main exception is the passage from Chapter Eleven, which ends with a portion of Sañjaya's narrative.

In the excerpt from Chapter One we hear Arjuna's voice, explaining to Kṛṣṇa at length why he is unable to take up arms against his blood relatives, mentors, and friends. In the segments from Chapter Two, Kṛṣṇa begins his response to Arjuna's dilemma by explaining the nature of the imperishable self or soul embodied in every human being. In the portions reproduced from Chapter Three, Arjuna raises fresh questions about human action in relation to the inner self and to evil, and Kṛṣṇa teaches him the yoga or discipline of action, especially as it should be practiced by a warrior. In the next excerpt, which jumps ahead to Chapter Six, Kṛṣṇa then explains what self-discipline in general is, and what a man who establishes complete control over himself can accomplish. In the final passage, drawn from Chapter Eleven, Arjuna achieves a comprehensive, new understanding of his task as a warrior, and asks Kṛṣṇa to reveal his full divine form; Kṛṣṇa does so, but the vision is so intense that a merely human eye cannot experience it. The narrator Sanjaya, talking to King Dhṛtarāṣṭra, therefore intercedes with his extraordinary visual capacity, and reports, in part, what Kṛṣṇa reveals to Arjuna.

The passages from the *Bhagavad-gītā* reproduced here cover only a small portion of Lord Kṛṣṇa's advice to Arjuna on the battlefield of Kurukṣetra. In the course of the eighteen cantos of the book, Kṛṣṇa constructs a long argument, containing many strands, about the justification for violence in the context of a war that is morally right and in complete accordance with all applicable aspects of *dharma*. Especially when encountered in excerpts, this argument can be, and often has been, easily misunderstood. Kṛṣṇa emphatically does *not* offer a general justification for violence under all circumstances; the use of violence to settle a major dispute can be justified only when every possible option for a peaceful resolution has been explored within the full scope of the law, and all such options have failed. Moreover, in a just war, only the thoroughly trained and disciplined warrior can use violence, and even he can do so only when he is in complete control of himself, and selflessly pursues his duty as defined by *dharma*.

From The Bhagavad-gītā[1]

CHAPTER ONE[2]

* * *

20   "Now Monkey-Bannered Arjuna,[3]
     seeing his foes drawn up for war,
     raised his bow, that Son of Pandu,
     as the weapons began to clash.

21   "Then he said these words to Krishna:[4]
     'Lord of the Earth, Unshaken One,
     bring my chariot to a halt
     between the two adverse armies,

---

1. Translated by Gavin Flood and Charles Martin. Verse numbers run to the left of the text.
2. Most of the *Bhagavad-gītā* is narrated by Sañjaya; the double quotation marks throughout these excerpts represent Sanjaya's direct speech, addressed to Dhṛtarāṣṭra. For an explanation of these two characters, who define the outer narra-

tive frame of the poem, see the "Work" section of the headnote. The single quotation marks represent the dialogue between Arjuna and Kṛṣṇa, which takes place within Sanjaya's narrative.
3. The third of the five sons of Pāṇḍu.
4. An incarnation of Viṣṇu, the preserver god.

22 'so I may see these men, arrayed
   here for the battle they desire,
   whom I am soon to undertake
   a warrior's delight in fighting!

23 'I see those who have assembled,
   the warriors prepared to fight,
   eager to perform in battle
   for Dhritarashtra's evil son!'[5]

24 "When Arjuna had spoken so
   to Krishna, O Bharata,[6]
   he, having brought their chariot
   to a halt between the armies,

25 "in the face of Bhishma, Drona,[7]
   and the other Lords of the Earth,[8]
   said, 'Behold, O Son of Pritha,[9]
   how these Kurus[1] have assembled!'

26 "And there the son of Pritha saw
   rows of grandfathers and grandsons;
   sons and fathers, uncles, in-laws;
   teachers, brothers and companions,

27 "all relatives and friends of his
   in both of the assembled armies.
   And seeing them arrayed for war,
   Arjuna, the Son of Kunti,

28 "felt for them a great compassion,
   as well as great despair, and said,
   'O Krishna, now that I have seen
   my relatives so keen for war,

29 'I am unstrung: my limbs collapse
   beneath me, and my mouth is dry,
   there is a trembling in my body,
   and my hair rises, bristling;

30 'Gandiva, my immortal bow,[2]
   drops from my hand and my skin burns,
   I cannot stand upon my feet,
   my mind rambles in confusion—

5. Duryodhana, the leader of the Kauravas, who is the eldest son of Dhrtarāstra.
6. An alternate name or epithet for Dhrtarāstra, who, like his brother Pāndu and their respective sons, is a descendant of Bhārata, the founder of their dynasty of kings.
7. Drona was the teacher or guru of both the Kauravas and the Pāndavas; Bhīsma is the granduncle of both these branches of the family.
8. "Lord of the earth" is a common epithet for a king in epic Sanskrit.
9. Another name for Kuntī, the mother of Arjuna and the Pāndavas.
1. Another name for the Kauravas.
2. A powerful celestial bow of great antiquity and renown that Arjuna won from the fire god, Agni.

31 'All inauspicious are the signs
that I see, O Handsome-Haired One![3]
I foresee no good resulting
from slaughtering my kin in war!

32 'I have no wish for victory,
nor for kingship and its pleasures!
O Krishna, what good is kingship?
What good even life and pleasure?

33 'Those for whose sake we desire
kingship, pleasures and enjoyments,
are now drawn up in battle lines,
their lives and riches now abandoned:

34 'fathers, grandfathers; sons, grandsons;
my mother's brothers and the men
who taught me in my youth; brothers-
and fathers-in-law: kinsmen all!

35 'Though they are prepared to slay us,
I do not wish to murder them,
not even to rule the three worlds—
how much less one earthly kingdom?

36 'What joy for us in murdering
Dhritarashtra's sons, O Krishna?
for if we killed these murderers,
evil like theirs would cling to us!

37 'So we cannot in justice slay
our kinsmen, Dhritarashtra's sons,
for, having killed our people, how
could we be pleased, O Madhava?[4]

38 'Even if they, mastered by greed,
are blind to the consequences
of the family's destruction,
of friendships lost to treachery,

39 'how are we not to comprehend
that we must turn back from evil?
The wrong done by this destruction
is evident, O Shaker of Men.

40 'For with the family destroyed,
its eternal laws must perish;

3. Kṛṣṇa is often depicted with long, flowing hair.
4. One of Viṣṇu's 1,008 names in Hindu ritual and mythology, meaning "the one sweet as honey."

and when they perish, lawlessness
overwhelms the whole family.

41 'Whelmed by lawlessness, the women
of the family are corrupted;
from corrupted women comes
the intermingling of classes.[5]

42 'Such intermingling sends to hell
the family and its destroyers:
their ancestors fall then, deprived
of rice and water offerings.[6]

43 'Those who destroy the family,
who institute class-mingling,
cause the laws of the family
and laws of caste to be abolished.

44 'Men whose familial laws have been
obliterated, O Krishna,
are damned to dwell eternally
in hell, as we have often heard.

45 'It grieves me that as we intend
to murder our relatives
in our greed for pleasures, kingdoms,
we are fixed on doing evil!

46 'If the sons of Dhritarashtra,
armed as they are, should murder me
weaponless and unresisting,
I would know greater happiness!'

47 "And having spoken, Arjuna
collapsed into his chariot,
his bow and arrows clattering,
and his mind overcome with grief."

5. "Intermingling" here refers to miscegenation, and "classes" to caste-groups. The caste
system is based on endogamy, or marriage
within a caste-group (*varṇa*) or caste (*jātī*);
only if both partners come from the same
social category can that category be reproduced in the next generation. Here Kṛṣṇa
affirms that if two spouses belong to different
social categories (*varṇa* or *jātī*), then their children do not belong to the same category as
their parents, and hence undermine the "laws
of caste."
6. Hindus are required to make these ritual
offerings to their ancestors.

CHAPTER TWO

* * *

"The Lord[7] said:

11 'Although you seem to speak wisely,
you have mourned those not to be mourned:
the wise do not grieve for those gone
or for those who are not yet gone.

12 'There was no time when I was not,
nor you, nor these lords around us,
and there will never be a time
henceforth when we shall not exist.

13 'The embodied one passes through
childhood, youth, and then old age,
then attains another body;
in this the wise are undeceived.[8]

14 'Contacts with matter by which we
feel heat and cold, pleasure and pain,
are transitory, come and go:
these you must manage to endure.

15 'Such contacts do not agitate
a wise man, O Bull among Men,
to whom pleasure and pain are one.
He is fit for immortality.

16 'Non-being cannot come to be,
nor can what is come to be not.
The certainty of these sayings
is known by seers of the truth.

17 'Know it as indestructible,
that by which all is pervaded;
no one may cause the destruction
of the imperishable one.

18 'Bodies of the embodied one,
eternal, boundless, all-enduring,
are said to die; the one cannot:
therefore, take arms, O Bharata!

19 'This man believes the one may kill;
That man believes it may be killed;

---

7. Lord Kṛṣṇa, who now addresses Arjuna.
8. Here Kṛṣṇa explains the process of reincarnation, emphasizing the identity of the seemingly finite embodied soul (*ātman*) with the infinite and imperishable universal spirit or godhead (*Brahman*).

both of them lack understanding:
it can neither kill nor *be* killed.

20 'It is not born, nor is it ever mortal,
and having been, will not pass from existence;
ancient, unborn, eternally existing,
it does not die when the body perishes.

21 'How can a man who knows the one
to be eternal (both unborn
and without end) murder or cause
another to? Whom does he kill?

22 'Someone who has abandoned worn-out garments
sets out to clothe himself in brand-new raiment;
just so, when it has cast off worn-out bodies,
the embodied one will encounter others.

23 'This may not be pierced by weapons,
nor can this be consumed by flames;
flowing waters cannot drench this,
nor blowing winds desiccate this.

24 'Not to be pierced, not to be burned,
neither drenched nor desiccated—
eternal, all-pervading, firm,
unmoving, everlasting this!

25 'This has been called unmanifest,
unthinkable and unchanging;
therefore, because you know this now,
you should not lament, Arjuna.

26 'But even if you think that this
is born and dies time after time,
forever, O great warrior,
not even then should you mourn this.

27 'Death is assured to all those born,
and birth assured to all the dead;
you should not mourn what is merely
inevitable consequence.

28 'Beginnings are unmanifest,
but manifest the middle-state,
and ends unmanifest again;
so what is your complaint about?

29 'Somebody looks upon this as a marvel,
and likewise someone tells about this marvel,
and yet another hears about this marvel,
but even having heard it, no one knows it.

30　'The one cannot ever perish
　　in a body it inhabits,
　　O Descendent of Bharata;
　　and so no being should be mourned.

31　'Nor should you tremble to perceive
　　your duty as a warrior;
　　for him there is nothing better
　　than a battle that is righteous.

32　'And if by chance they will have gained
　　the wide open gate of heaven,
　　O Son of Pritha, warriors
　　rejoice in fighting such as that!

33　'If you turn from righteous warfare,
　　your behavior will be evil,
　　for you will have abandoned both
　　your duty and your honored name.

34　'People will speak of your disgrace
　　forever, and an honored man
　　who falls from honor into shame
　　suffers a fate much worse than death.

* * *

47　"'Your concern should be with action,
　　never with an action's fruits;
　　these should never motivate you,
　　nor attachment to inaction.

48　'Established in this practice, act
　　without attachment, Arjuna,
　　unmoved by failure or success!
　　Equanimity is yoga.

49　'Action is far inferior
　　to the practice of higher mind;
　　seek refuge there, for pitiful
　　are those moved by fruit of action!

50　'One disciplined by higher mind
　　here casts off good and bad actions;
　　therefore, be yoked to discipline;
　　discipline is skill in actions.

51　'Having left the fruit of action,
　　the wise ones yoked to higher mind
　　are freed from the bonds of rebirth,
　　and go where no corruption is.

52　'When your higher mind has crossed
　　over the thicket of delusion,

you will become disenchanted
with what is heard in the *Vedas*.[9]

53 'When, unvexed by revelation,
your higher mind is motionless
and stands fixed in meditation,
then you will attain discipline.'

"Arjuna asked,

54 'Tell me, Krishna, how may I know
the man steady in his wisdom,
who abides in meditation?
How should that one sit, speak and move?'

"The Blessed Lord replied,

55 'When he renounces all desires
entering his mind, Arjuna,
and his self rests within the Self,[1]
then his wisdom is called steady.

56 'He who is not agitated
by suffering or by desires,
freed from anger, fear and passions,
is called a sage of steady mind.

57 'Who is wholly unimpassioned,
not rejoicing in the pleasant,
nor rejecting the unpleasant,
is established in his wisdom.

58 'And when this one wholly withdraws
all his senses from their objects,
as a tortoise draws in its limbs,
his wisdom is well-established.'"

* * *

CHAPTER THREE

"Arjuna said:

1 'If you regard the intellect
as superior to action,
why urge me, O Handsome-Haired One,
into actions so appalling?

9. Krṣṇa suggests here that the older ritualistic knowledge embodied in the Vedas is useless for the liberation of the individual self or soul from the bondage of karma.
1. This is a play on the word *ātman*, which means both "the self" (soul) and "oneself." Krṣṇa now begins to describe the techniques for and effects of "withdrawing" one's senses from interaction with the external world and focusing them instead on the interior self.

2   'By your equivocating speech,
     my mind is, as it were, confused.
     Tell me this one thing, and clearly:
     By what means may I reach the best?'

          "The Blessed Lord said:

3   'As I have previously taught,
     there are two paths, O Blameless One:
     there is the discipline of knowledge
     and the discipline of action.

4   'Not by not acting in this world
     does one become free from action,
     nor does one approach perfection
     by renunciation only.

5   'Not even for a moment does
     someone exist without acting.
     Even against one's will, one acts
     by the nature-born qualities.[2]

6   'He who has restrained his senses,
     but sits and summons back to mind
     the sense-objects, is said to be
     a self-deluding hypocrite.

7   'But he whose mind controls his senses,
     who undertakes the discipline
     of action by the action-organs,
     without attachment, is renowned.

8   'You must act as bid, for action
     is better than non-action is:
     not even functions of the body
     could be sustained by non-action.

9   'This world is bound by action, save
     for action which is sacrifice;
     therefore, O Son of Kunti, act
     without attachment to your deeds.

10   'When Prajapati brought forth life,
     he brought forth sacrifice as well,
     saying, "By this may you produce,
     may this be your wish-fulfilling cow."[3]

2. There are three such primary qualities: *sat-tva* (purity, light), *rajas* (passion, heat), and *tamas* (inertia, darkness).
3. In Vedic religion, Prajapati is the god (creator) of all mortal creatures. In Hindu mythology generally, *kāmadhenu* is a celestial cow who has the power to fulfill the wishes of any-

one who worships her. Here Prajāpatī suggests that the act of sacrificing is itself like a wish-granting *kāmadhenu*. In the Vedic worldview, the preservation of the universe depends on the sacrifices made to the gods, and such ritual was at the center of the religion.

11   'Nourish the gods with sacrifice,
and they will nourish you as well.
By nourishing each other, you
will realize the highest good.

12   'Nourished by sacrifice, the gods
will give the pleasures you desire.
One who enjoys such gifts without
repaying them is just a thief.

13   'The good, who eat of the remains
from sacrifice, rise up faultless.
But the wicked, who cook only
for their own sakes, eat their own filth.

14   'Beings come to exist by food,
which emanates from the rain god,
who comes to be by sacrifice,
which arises out of action.

15   'Know that action comes from Brahman,
Brahman comes from the eternal;
so the all-pervading Brahman
is based in sacrifice forever.

16   'One who in this world does not turn
the wheel, thus setting it in motion,
lives uselessly, O Son of Pritha,
a sensual, malicious life.

17   'But the man whose only pleasure
and satisfaction is the self,
which is his sole contentment too,
has no task he must accomplish.

18   'That man finds no significance
in what has, or has not, been done;
moreover, he does not depend
on any being whatsoever.

19   'Therefore, act without attachment
in whatever situation,
for by the practice of detached
action, one attains the highest.

20   'Only by action Janaka[4]
and the others reached perfection.
In order to maintain the world,
your obligation is to act.

4. Celebrated character in the dialogues of the *Bṛhadāraṇyaka Upaniṣad*; an exemplar of the warrior-king who is also a man of discipline (a yogi).

21 'Whatever the best leader does
the rank and file will also do;
everyone will fall in behind
the standard such a leader sets.

22 'O Son of Pritha, there is nought
that I need do in the three worlds,[5]
nor anything I might attain;
and yet I take part in action.

23 'For if I were not always to
engage in action ceaselessly,
men everywhere would soon follow
in my path, O Son of Pritha.

24 'Should I not engage in action,
these worlds would perish, utterly;
I would cause a great confusion,
and destroy all living beings.

25 'The unwise are attached to action
even as they act, Arjuna;
so, for the welfare of the world,
the wise should act with detachment.'"

* * *

"Arjuna said:

36 'Say what impels a man to do
such evil, Krishna, what great force
urges him, forces him into it,
even if he is unwilling?'

"The Blessed Lord said:

37 'Know that the enemy is this:
desire, anger, whose origins
are in the quality of passion,
all consuming, greatly harmful.

38 'As fire is obscured by smoke,
or by dust, a mirror's surface,
or an embryo by its membrane,
so this is covered up by that.

39 'Knowledge is constantly obscured
by this enemy of the wise,
by this insatiable fire
whose form, Arjuna, is desire.

---

5. Heaven, earth, and the underworld.

40   'The senses, mind, and intellect
are its abode, as it is said.
Having obscured knowledge with these,
it deludes the embodied one.

41   'When you have subdued your senses,
then, O Bull of the Bharatas,
kill this demon, the destroyer
of all knowledge and discernment.

42   'Senses are said to be important,
but mind is higher than they are,
and intellect is above mind;
but Self is greater than all these.

43   'So knowing it to be supreme,
and sustaining the self with Self,
slay the foe whose form is desire,
so hard to conquer, Arjuna.'"

CHAPTER SIX

*   *   *

10   "'The yogi should be self-subdued
always, and stand in solitude,
alone, controlled in thought and self,
without desires or possessions.

11   'Having established for himself
a steady seat in a pure place,
neither too high nor yet too low,
covered with grass, deer hide and cloth,

12   'with his mind sharpened to one point,
with thought and senses both subdued,
there he should sit, doing yoga
so as to purify the self,

13   'keeping his head, neck and body
aligned, erect and motionless,
gaze fixed on the tip of his nose,
not looking off distractedly,

14   'now fearless and with tranquil self,
firm in avowed celibacy,
with his thought focused on myself,
he should sit, devoted to me.

15   'Thus always chastening himself
the yogi's mind, subdued, knows peace,
whose farthest point is cessation;
thereafter, he abides in me.

16 'Yoga is not for the greedy,
nor yet for the abstemious;
not for one too used to sleeping,
nor for the sleepless, Arjuna.

17 'Yoga destroys the pain of one
temperate in his behavior,
in his food and recreation,
and in his sleep and waking too.

18 'After his thought has been subdued,
and abides only in the Self,
free from all longing and desire,
then he is said to be steadfast.

19 '"Like a lamp in a windless place
unflickering," is the likeness
of the yogi subdued in thought,
performing yoga of the Self.

20 'Where all thought comes to cease, restrained
by the discipline of yoga,
where, by the self, the Self is seen,
one is satisfied in the Self.

21 'When he knows that eternal joy
grasped only by the intellect,
beyond the senses where he dwells,
he does not deviate from truth;

22 'having attained it, he believes
there is no gain superior;
abiding there, he is unmoved
even by profound suffering.

23 'Let him know that the dissolving
of the union with suffering
is called yoga, to be practiced
with persistence, mind undaunted.

24 'Having abandoned all desires
born to satisfy intentions,
and having utterly restrained
the many senses by the mind,

25 'Gradually let him find rest,
his intellect under control,
his mind established in the Self,
not thinking about anything.

26 'Having subdued the unsteady
mind in motion, he should lead it
back from wherever it strays to,
into the domain of the Self.

27 'Supreme joy comes to the yogi
of calm mind and tranquil passion,
who has become one with Brahman
and is wholly free of evil.

28 'Constantly controlling himself,
the yogi, freed from evil now,
swiftly attains perpetual
joy of contact here with Brahman.

29 'He whose self is yoked by yoga
and who perceives sameness always,
will see the Self in all beings
and see all beings in the Self.

30 'I am not lost for someone who
perceives my presence everywhere,
and everything perceives in me,
nor is that person lost for me.

31 'The yogi firmly set in oneness
who worships me in all beings,
whatever the path that he takes,
will nonetheless abide in me.

32 'The yogi who sees all the same
analogous to his own Self
in happiness or suffering
is thought supreme, O Arjuna.'"

Summary   In Chapters Seven through Ten, Krishna explains diverse aspects of the nature of the infinite spirit, gradually unveiling the mystery of his own identity as the highest manifestation of that universal spirit and thus leading up to the revelation of his cosmic form in Chapter Eleven.

CHAPTER ELEVEN

"Arjuna said,

1   'As a result of your kindness
in speaking of that greatest secret
recognized as the Supreme Self,
I have been left undeluded.

2   'I have, in detail, heard you speak
Of creatures' origins and ends,
and of your eternal greatness,
O One of Lotus-Petal-Eyes.

3   'This is just as you have spoken
about yourself, O Supreme Lord.
I desire to behold your
lordly form, O Supreme Spirit.

4   'If you think it is possible
     for me to see this, then, O God,
     O Lord of Yoga, allow me
     to behold your eternal Self!'

     "The Blessed Lord said,

5   'O Son of Pritha, look upon
     my hundredfold, no, thousandfold
     forms various and celestial,
     forms of diverse shapes and colors!

6   'Behold the *Adityas* and *Vasus*,
     the *Rudras*, *Ashvins* and *Maruts*,[6]
     many unseen previously!
     Behold these wonders, Arjuna!

7   'Here behold all the universe,
     beings moving and motionless,
     standing as one in my body,
     and all else that you wish to see!

8   'Because you are unable to
     behold me with your mortal eye,
     I give you one that is divine:
     Behold my majestic power!'"

     Sanjaya[7] said,

9   "And after saying this, O King,
     Vishnu, the great Lord of Yoga,
     revealed his supreme, majestic
     form to him, the Son of Pritha.

10   "That form has many eyes and mouths,
     and many wonders visible,
     with many sacred ornaments,
     and many sacred weapons raised.

11   "Clothed in sacred wreaths and garments,
     with many sacred fragrances,
     and comprising every wonder,
     the infinite, omniscient god!

12   "If in the sky a thousand suns
     should have risen all together,
     the brilliance of it would be like
     the brilliance of that Great-Souled One.

---

6. Groups of Hindu deities: Adityas are sun gods; Vasus are elemental deities; Rudras are wind gods; the Ashvins are twin gods of sunrise and sunset; and the Maruts are storm gods.
7. The bard who is narrating the events of the battle to King Dhṛtarāṣṭra.

13 "And then the Son of Pandu saw
the universe standing as one,
divided up in diverse ways,
embodied in the god of gods."

* * *

"Arjuna said:

43 'Father of all the world, the still and moving,
you are what it worships and its teacher;
with none your match, how could there be one greater
in the three worlds, O Power-Without-Equal?

44 'Making obeisance, lying in prostration,
I beg your indulgence, praiseworthy ruler;
as father to son, as one friend to another,
as lover to beloved, show your mercy!

45 'I am pleased to have seen what never has been
seen before, yet my mind quakes in its terror:
show me, O God, your human form; have mercy,
O Lord of Gods, abode of all the cosmos!

46 'I wish to see you even as I did once,
wearing a diadem, with mace and discus;
assume that form now wherein you have four arms,
O thousand-armed, of every form the master!'

"The Blessed Lord said,

47 'For you, Arjuna, by my grace and favor,
this highest form is brought forth by my power,
of splendor made, universal, endless, primal,
and never seen before by any other.

48 'Not Vedic sacrifice nor recitation,
gifts, rituals, strenuous austerities,
will let this form of mine be seen by any
mortal but you, O Hero of the Kurus!

49 'You should not tremble, nor dwell in confusion
at seeing such a terrible appearance.
With your fears banished and your mind now cheerful,
look once again upon my form, Arjuna.'

Sanjaya said,

50 "So Krishna, having spoken to Arjuna,
stood before him once more in his own aspect;
having resumed again a gentle body,
the Great Soul calmed the one who had been frightened.

"Arjuna said,

51 'Seeing once again your gentle,
human form now, I am composed,
O Agitator of Mankind;
my mind is restored to normal.'

"The Blessed Lord said,

52 'It is difficult to see this
aspect of me that you have seen;
even the gods are forever
desirous of seeing it.

53 'Not by studying the *Vedas*,
nor even by austerities,
and not by gifts or sacrifice,
may I be seen as you saw me;

54 'but by devotion undisturbed
can I be truly seen and known,
and entered into, Arjuna,
O Scorcher of the Enemy!

55 'Who acts for me, depends on me,
devoutly, without attachment
or hatred for another being,
comes to me, O Son of Pandu!'"

THE JĀTAKA

fourth century B.C.E.

In the fable of the goose with golden eggs, a farmer finds that one of his geese lays a golden egg each day; wanting to get rich faster, he kills the bird for all the gold inside it, but finds nothing, and hence loses even his daily income. This story comes to us from one of **Aesop**'s fables in ancient Greece, but it also has an astonishing parallel in the *Jātaka* tale "The Golden Goose," told by Buddhists in ancient India. Greeks and Indians seem to have invented a narrative with the same ideas (a goose, an unlimited supply of gold) and the same moral (greed undoes itself), at almost the same time—the middle of the first millennium B.C.E., before they had any direct contact with each other in historical times.

CONTEXT

The *Jātaka*, a set of 547 tales, is one of the books in the canon of Buddhist scripture. The canon of Theravada Buddhism, composed in Pali, and known as the

Tipiṭaka, is divided into three main parts: Vinaya (texts concerning discipline, for monks and nuns), Sutta (texts of sermons or sayings, mostly of Siddhartha-Gautama Buddha), and Abhidhamma (texts of speculative philosophy or "higher teaching"). The *Jātaka* is included in the Sutta, because it is believed to be a record of the Buddha's actions in the world in his previous lives. Like other texts in the canon, it is an anonymous work of collective authorship, composed over several generations after the Buddha's death (fifth century B.C.E.).

Theravada Buddhists use Pali as the uniform language of their scripture and its accompanying commentary. Pali emerged in the first millennium B.C.E. as one of several distinct Prakrits ("natural languages"), which are closely related to refined Sanskrit but much simpler than it; unlike Sanskrit, which was not usually spoken, except by priests, scholars, and courtiers under special circumstances, the Prakrits were the common spoken languages of the ancient period. Pali could therefore be used to preach to ordinary people, and it became central to the egalitarian mission of Theravada Buddhism as a "way of life" that can be adopted by anybody. As narratives recorded in a colloquial medium, the *Jātaka* tales have performed several essential functions in this context. They have been used in sermons to engage audiences, much like the parables from the life of Jesus in Christianity, and they have been the objects of meditation as well as philosophical analysis. They have also enabled the Buddha's common followers to commemorate and reflect on his exemplary life (or many lives), even as they have circulated like popular folktales and fables, bringing his message to the populace at large.

The *Jātaka* tales take it for granted that living creatures transmigrate from one life to another, as a consequence of the law of karma. According to this law, every act that a human being performs in the world "bears fruit," or has a good or bad moral effect; the cumulative good and evil from a person's lifetime of deeds supposedly attach to his or her *ātman*, inner self or soul. If, at the moment of physical death, the sum of a person's good deeds outweighs the sum of evil actions, the self is ready for "salvation"; but if evil exceeds goodness, the self is reborn in the world in a new body (and, possibly, as a different life-form), with an opportunity to perform good and earn salvation over a whole new lifetime.

When a self is reborn—or transmigrates into another life—it carries with it all the residual good and evil from the previous life; the reborn person therefore has to do enough good in the new life not only to exceed the evil that he or she will inevitably do in the present, but also to wipe out the excess of evil from the preceding lifetime. So, even as a new lifetime offers an opportunity to do good and achieve salvation, it also substantially increases the chances of failure, because it is notoriously difficult to do good in the world even without a backlog of evil to overcome. Most human selves in the world therefore are likely to be reborn again and again, trapped in their karma. But, as "The Hare's Self-Sacrifice" tells us below, whether human selves do or do not break free of transmigration, their existence is determined "according to their deeds."

WORK

The *Jātaka* tales consistently adopt the view that all living creatures seek liberation from the cycle of lifetimes by pursuing goodness. To this purpose, it depicts the Buddha (Siddhartha-Gautama) in numerous human and animal forms in his lifetimes before he finally attained Enlightenment (a state of complete understanding of the nature of reality, the created universe, and human life), which gave him the means to break through the "bondage" of karma and rebirth. In the first story reproduced here, he is born as a *brāhmaṇa* and then reborn as a golden goose; in the second story, he is a hare; in the third, a monkey; and, in each case, the form he takes is "endowed with consciousness of its former existences." Each tale is then about the goodness that the Buddha conscientiously accumulated in a particular form and life, preparatory to the lifetime in which he became the Enlightened One.

As represented in our selection, the *Jātaka* tales vary in their narrative organization, imaginative effect, and cultural complexity. "The Golden Goose," perhaps the simplest of the stories, resembles an animal fable, in which the Buddha (as a goose) gives his golden feathers, one by one, to his widow and daughters from a former life, who have been living on the charity of neighbors and friends since his death (as a human). The story can be understood as a cautionary tale against greed; but, in a Buddhist context, it can also be interpreted as a reminder of the necessity of detachment from, and ultimately renunciation of, family.

The other two stories are more complicated in their structure as well as message. "The Hare's Self-Sacrifice" involves not only the Buddha, reborn as a hare, and three other animals in the wild—a monkey, a jackal, and an otter—with whom he tries to live in harmony. It also involves the Hindu god Indra (called Sakka in the Pali canon), a symbolic competition between him and the Buddha for moral authority over the universe, and a victory for the Buddha, who lets out "a cry of exultation like a lion roaring." At the same time, the tale suggests that the spots we see on the moon every night are daubed in the shape of a hare, in order to commemorate this lifetime of the Buddha

and his victory over Indra. "The Monkey's Heroic Self-Sacrifice" then takes us deeper into the natural world and the world of animals, to show us how the Buddha, reborn as a monkey who leads eighty thousand of his fellow creatures, selflessly gives up his life for them while helping them escape from avaricious humans. It also creates a myth about how human beings discovered the delicious fruit called the mango, and offers a parable about a king's responsibilities to his subjects.

In all three tales, the Buddha (then still a *bodhisattva*, one who has the potential for enlightenment but has not yet attained it) makes an elemental sacrifice, risking his own life and limb for the benefit of others. In each case, he maintains the right "mindfulness," keeping his intentions clear of selfish considerations; and his will is focused on the accumulation of goodness across many lifetimes, without which he cannot be ready for Enlightenment. These tales therefore are much more than entertaining stories, or even fables with moral lessons that can be summed up in a phrase or two; they are narratives whose meanings cannot be deciphered only at the level of "story," or only in an aesthetic context.

The tradition of Indian animal fables that grow out of the *Jātaka* tales in later centuries, as in the **Pañcatantra** and the *Hitopdeśa*, shifts toward practical wisdom and common sense in everyday life. The *Jātaka* tales resist this tendency; they remain tied closely to the ideal of a *bodhisattva*'s "six perfections": selfless giving to others; moral clarity and firmness; patience or forbearance; unstinting effort in the pursuit of the right goals; meditation; and wisdom. The tales thus become a means not only to entertain a storyteller's audience, but also to educate children and common people (who may not have access to literacy), and to communicate the abstract message of a scriptural canon.

The Golden Goose[1]

Once upon a time when Brahmadatta[2] was reigning in Benares,[3] the Bodhisatta[4] was born a brahmin,[5] and growing up was married to a bride of his own rank, who bore him three daughters named Nandā, Nandavatī and Sundarinandā. The Bodhisatta dying, they were taken in by neighbours and friends, whilst he was born again into the world as a golden goose endowed with consciousness of its former existences.[6] Growing up, the bird viewed his own magnificent size and golden plumage, and remembered that previously he had been a human being. Discovering that his wife and daughters were living on the charity of others, the goose bethought him of his plumage like hammered and beaten gold and how by giving them a golden feather at a time he could enable his wife and daughters to live in comfort. So away he flew to where they dwelt and alighted on the top of the central beam of the roof. Seeing the Bodhisatta, the wife and girls asked where he had come from; and he told them that he was their father who had died and been born a golden goose, and that he had come to visit them and put an end to their miserable necessity of working for hire. "You shall have my feathers," said he, "one by one, and they will sell for enough to keep you all in ease and comfort." So saying, he gave them one of his feathers and departed. And from time to time he returned to give them another feather, and with the proceeds of their sale these brahmin-women grew prosperous and quite well-to-do. But one day the mother said to her daughters, "There's no trusting animals, my children. Who's to say your father might not go away one of these days and never come back again? Let us use our time and pluck him clean next time he comes, so as to make sure of all his feathers." Thinking this would pain him, the daughters refused. The mother in her greed called the golden goose to her one day when he came, and then took him with both hands and plucked him. Now the Bodhisatta's feathers had this property that if they were plucked out against his wish, they ceased to be golden and became like a crane's feathers. And now the poor bird, though he stretched his wings, could not fly, and the woman flung him into a barrel and gave him food there. As time went on his feathers grew again (though they were plain white ones now), and he flew away to his own abode and never came back again.

1. Translated by H. T. Francis and E. J. Thomas.
2. A mythical king; many *Jātaka* tales begin with the formulaic phrase "Once upon a time."
3. Modern Banaras or Varanasi, also called Kashi; oldest and most famous holy city in India, on the River Ganges. Banaras is associated mainly with Hinduism and its major god, Śiva; but it is also vital to Buddhism, because the Buddha preached his first sermon in its deer park.
4. Pali term, equivalent to Sanskrit *bodhisattva*; used for "a being on the path to enlightenment" or a Buddha-to-be. Since the *Jātaka* tells stories about Siddhartha-Gautama's lives previous to the one in which he attained enlightenment, they refer to him as a Bodhisatta rather than as the Buddha.
5. A member of the Hindu caste-group of hereditary priests and scholars.
6. In both Hinduism and Buddhism, an individual "self" or soul that is reborn due to a net accumulation of "bad karma" in previous lives carries forward memories of those actions into its current life. Such memories enable it to seek liberation by aiming for a net accumulation of "good karma."

The Hare's Self-Sacrifice[1]

Once upon a time when Brahmadatta was reigning in Benares, the Bodhisatta came to life as a young hare and lived in a wood. On one side of this wood was the foot of a mountain, on another side a river, and on the third side a border-village. The hare had three friends—a monkey, a jackal and an otter. These four wise creatures lived together and each of them got his food on his own hunting-ground, and in the evening they again came together. The hare in his wisdom by way of admonition preached the Truth[2] to his three companions, teaching that alms are to be given, the moral law to be observed, and holy days to be kept. They accepted his admonition and went each to his own part of the jungle and dwelt there.

And so in the course of time the Bodhisatta one day observing the sky, and looking at the moon knew that the next day would be a fast-day,[3] and address-ing his three companions he said, "To-morrow is a fast-day. Let all three of you take upon you the moral precepts, and observe the holy day. To one that stands fast in moral practice, almsgiving brings a great reward. Therefore feed any beggars[4] that come to you by giving them food from your own table." They readily assented, and abode each in his own place of dwelling.

On the morrow quite early in the morning, the otter sallied forth to seek his prey and went down to the bank of the Ganges. Now it came to pass that a fisherman had landed seven red fish, and stringing them together on a withe, he had taken and buried them in the sand on the river's bank. And then he dropped down the stream, catching more fish. The otter, scenting the buried fish, dug up the sand till he came upon them, and pulling them out cried thrice, "Does anyone own these fish?" And not seeing any owner he took hold of the withe with his teeth and laid the fish in the jungle where he dwelt, intending to eat them at a fitting time. And then he lay down, thinking how virtuous he was! The jackal too sallied forth in quest of food and found in the hut of a field-watcher two spits, a lizard and a pot of milk-curd. And after thrice crying aloud, "To whom do these belong?" and not finding an owner, he put on his neck the rope for lifting the pot, and grasping the spits and the lizard with his teeth, he brought and laid them in his own lair, thinking, "In due season I will devour them," and so lay down, reflecting how virtuous he had been.

The monkey also entered the clump of trees, and gathering a bunch of mangoes laid them up in his part of the jungle, meaning to eat them in due season, and then lay down, thinking how virtuous he was. But the Bodhisatta in due time came out, intending to browse on the kusa-grass,[5] and as he lay in the jungle, the thought occurred to him, "It is impossible for me to offer grass to any beggars that may chance to appear, and I have no sesame, rice,

---

1. Translated by H. T. Francis and E. J. Thomas.
2. Most likely an early version of the moral law that the Buddha systematized in his doc-trine of Four Noble Truths.
3. In the lunisolar calendar followed by Bud-dhism, Hinduism, and Jainism, some days,

corresponding to particular phases of the moon, are set aside for keeping fasts.
4. Begging is part of the vow of poverty observed by Buddhist monks and many Hindu ascetics.
5. Used in Hindu rituals.

and such like. If any beggar shall appeal to me, I shall have to give him my own flesh to eat." At this splendid display of virtue, Sakka's[6] white marble throne manifested signs of heat. Sakka on reflection discovered the cause and resolved to put this royal hare to the test. First of all he went and stood by the otter's dwelling-place, disguised as a brahmin, and being asked why he stood there, he replied, "Wise Sir, if I could get something to eat, after keeping the fast, I would perform all my ascetic duties." The otter replied, "Very well, I will give you some food," and as he conversed with him he repeated the first stanza:[7]

> Seven red fish I safely brought to land from Ganges flood,
> O brahmin, eat thy fill, I pray, and stay within this wood.

The brahmin said, "Let be till to-morrow. I will see to it by and by." Next he went to the jackal, and when asked by him why he stood there, he made the same answer. The jackal, too, readily promised him some food, and in talking with him repeated the second stanza:

> A lizard and a jar of curds, the keeper's evening meal,
> Two spits of roasted flesh withal I wrongfully did steal:
> Such as I have I give to thee: O brahmin, eat, I pray,
> If thou shouldst deign within this wood a while with us to stay.

Said the brahmin, "Let be till to-morrow. I will see to it by and by." Then he went to the monkey, and when asked what he meant by standing there, he answered just as before. The monkey readily offered him some food, and in conversing with him gave utterance to the third stanza:

> An icy stream, a mango ripe, and pleasant greenwood shade,
> Tis thine to enjoy, if thou canst dwell content in forest glade.

Said the brahmin, "Let be till to-morrow. I will see to it by and by." And he went to the wise hare, and on being asked by him why he stood there, he made the same reply. The Bodhisatta on hearing what he wanted was highly delighted, and said, "Brahmin, you have done well in coming to me for food. This day will I grant you a boon that I have never granted before, but you shall not break the moral law by taking animal life.[8] Go, friend, and when you have piled together logs of wood, and kindled a fire, come and let me know, and I will sacrifice myself by falling into the midst of the flames, and when my body is roasted, you shall eat my flesh and fulfil all your ascetic duties." And in thus addressing him the hare uttered the fourth stanza:

---

6. Indra, king of gods, who rewards those who display extraordinary virtue.
7. The traditional stanza known as *gāthā*. The formula by which the stanzas are introduced shows that they were meant to be memorized. The Pali stanzas in the *Jātaka* tales are very old, stylistically more archaic than the stanzas

of the Hindu epics, and seem to have been used by monks as keys to memorize and summarize the tales.
8. According to the Buddha, the taking of life results in evil karma; therefore, he stressed extreme nonviolence.

> Nor sesame, nor beans, nor rice have I as food to give,
> But roast with fire my flesh I yield, if thou with us wouldst live.

Sakka, on hearing what he said, by his miraculous power caused a heap of burning coals to appear, and came and told the Bodhisatta. Rising from his bed of kusa-grass and coming to the place, he thrice shook himself that if there were any insects within his coat, they might escape death. Then offering his whole body as a free gift he sprang up, and like a royal swan, alighting on a cluster of lotuses, in an ecstasy of joy he fell on the heap of live coals. But the flame failed even to heat the pores of the hair on the body of the Bodhisatta, and it was as if he had entered a region of frost. Then he addressed Sakka in these words: "Brahmin, the fire you have kindled is icy-cold: it fails to heat even the pores of the hair on my body. What is the meaning of this?" "Wise Sir," he replied, "I am no brahmin. I am Sakka, and I have come to put your virtue to the test." The Bodhisatta said, "If not only thou, Sakka, but all the inhabitants of the world were to try me in this matter of almsgiving, they would not find in me any unwillingness to give," and with this the Bodhisatta uttered a cry of exultation like a lion roaring. Then said Sakka to the Bodhisatta, "O wise hare, be thy virtue known throughout a whole aeon."[9] And squeezing the mountain, with the essence thus extracted, he daubed the sign of a hare on the orb of the moon.[1] And after depositing the hare on a bed of young kusa-grass, in the same wooded part of the jungle, Sakka returned to his own place in heaven. And these four wise creatures dwelt happily and harmoniously together, fulfilling the moral law and observing holy days, till they departed to fare according to their deeds.

The Monkey's Heroic Self-Sacrifice[1]

Once upon a time when Brahmadatta was reigning in Benares, the Bodhisatta was born as a monkey.[2] When he grew up and attained stature and stoutness, he was strong and vigorous, and lived in the Himalaya with a retinue of eighty thousand[3] monkeys. Near the Ganges bank there was a mango tree (others say it was a banyan), with branches and forks, having a deep shade and thick leaves, like a mountain-top.[4] Its sweet fruits, of divine fragrance and flavour, were as large as water-pots: from one branch the fruits

---

9. A unit of cosmic time, consisting of a thousand cycles of four ages.
1. Throughout India the markings on the moon are recognized as being in the shape of a hare, and this *Jātaka* is one of the tales that explains its origin. Folklorists have discovered legends about a hare on the moon among other peoples, including the Kalmuks, the Hottentots, and some Native American groups.
1. Translated by H. T. Francis and E. J. Thomas.
2. As demonstrated by the role of Hanumān,

Rāma's monkey helper in the *Rāmāyaṇa*, monkeys are beloved characters in Indian folklore; there are several *Jātakas* about the Bodhisatta's births as a monkey.
3. A large number or a multitude.
4. The tree is gigantic. A banyan tree (a kind of fig tree with spreading aerial roots) of that size would have made a suitable home for a large monkey troop, but its fruit hardly compares with the sweet mango, the allure of which is a crucial point in this tale.

fell on the ground, from one into the Ganges water, from two into the main trunk of the tree. The Bodhisatta, while eating the fruit with a troop of monkeys, thought, "Someday danger will come upon us owing to the fruit of this tree falling on the water"; and so, not to leave one fruit on the branch which grew over the water, he made them eat or throw down the flowers at their season from the time they were of the size of a chick-pea. But notwithstanding, one ripe fruit, unseen by the eighty thousand monkeys, hidden by an ant's nest, fell into the river, and stuck in the net above the king of Benares who was bathing for amusement with a net above him and another below. When the king had amused himself all day and was going away in the evening, the fishermen, who were drawing the net, saw the fruit and not knowing what it was, shewed it to the king. The king asked, "What is this fruit?" "We do not know, sire." "Who will know?" "The foresters, sire." He had the foresters called, and learning from them that it was a mango, he cut it with a knife, and first making the foresters eat of it, he ate of it himself and had some of it given to his seraglio and his ministers. The flavour of the ripe mango remained, pervading the king's whole body. Possessed by desire[5] of the flavour, he asked the foresters where that tree stood, and hearing that it was on a river bank in the Himalaya quarter, he had many rafts joined together and sailed upstream by the route shewn by the foresters. The exact account of days is not given. In due course they came to the place, and the foresters said to the king, "Sire, there is the tree." The king stopped the rafts and went on foot with a great retinue, and having a bed prepared at the foot of the tree, he lay down after eating the mango fruit and enjoying the various excellent flavours. At every side they set a guard and made a fire. When the men had fallen asleep, the Bodhisatta came at midnight with his retinue. Eighty thousand monkeys moving from branch to branch ate the mangoes. The king, waking and seeing the herd of monkeys, roused his men and calling his archers said, "Surround these monkeys that eat the mangoes so that they may not escape, and shoot them: to-morrow we will eat mangoes with monkey's flesh." The archers obeyed, saying, "Very well," and surrounding the tree stood with arrows ready. The monkeys seeing them and fearing death, as they could not escape, came to the Bodhisatta and said, "Sire, the archers stand round the tree, saying, 'We will shoot those vagrant monkeys': what are we to do?" and so stood shivering. The Bodhisatta said, "Do not fear, I will give you life"; and so comforting the herd of monkeys, he ascended a branch that rose up straight, went along another branch that stretched towards the Ganges, and springing from the end of it, he passed a hundred bow-lengths and lighted on a bush on the bank. Coming down, he marked the distance, saying, "That will be the distance I have come": and cutting a bamboo shoot at the root and stripping it, he said, "So much will be fastened to the tree, and so much will stay in the air," and so reckoned the two lengths, forgetting the part fastened on his own waist. Taking the shoot he fastened one end of it to the tree on the Ganges bank and the other to his own waist, and then cleared the space of a hundred bow-lengths with a speed of a cloud torn by

5. Identified as the root cause of existential suffering.

the wind. From not reckoning the part fastened to his waist, he failed to reach the tree: so seizing a branch firmly with both hands he gave signal to the troop of monkeys, "Go quickly with good luck, treading on my back along the bamboo shoot." The eighty thousand monkeys escaped thus, after saluting the Bodhisatta and getting his leave. Devadatta[6] was then a monkey and among that herd: he said, "This is a chance for me to see the last of my enemy," so climbing up a branch he made a spring and fell on the Bodhisatta's back. The Bodhisatta's back broke and great pain came on him. Devadatta having caused that maddening pain went away: and the Bodhisatta was alone. The king being awake saw all that was done by the monkeys and the Bodhisatta: and he lay down thinking, "This animal, not reckoning his own life, has caused the safety of his troop." When day broke, being pleased with the Bodhisatta, he thought, "It is not right to destroy this king of the monkeys: I will bring him down by some means and take care of him": So turning the raft down the Ganges and building a platform there, he made the Bodhisatta come down gently, and had him clothed with a yellow robe on his back and washed in Ganges water, made him drink sugared water, and had his body cleansed and anointed with oil refined a thousand times; then he put an oiled skin on a bed and making him lie there, he set himself, on a low seat, and spoke the first stanza:

> You made yourself a bridge for them to pass in safety through:
> What are you then to them, monkey, and what are they to you?

Hearing him, the Bodhisatta instructing the king spoke the other stanzas:

> Victorious king, I guard the herd, I am their lord and chief,
> When they were filled with fear of thee and stricken sore with grief.
>
> I leapt a hundred times the length of bow outstretched that lies,
> When I had bound a bamboo-shoot firmly around my thighs:
>
> I reached the tree like thunder-cloud sped by the tempest's blast;
> I lost my strength, but reached a bough: with hands I held it fast.
>
> And as I hung extended there held fast by shoot and bough,
> My monkeys passed across my back and are in safety now.
>
> Therefore I fear no pain of death, bonds do not give me pain,
> The happiness of those was won o'er whom I used to reign.
>
> A parable for thee, O king, if thou the truth would'st read:
> The happiness of kingdom and of army and of steed
> And city must be dear to thee, if thou would'st rule indeed.

The Bodhisatta, thus instructing and teaching the king, died. The king, calling his ministers, gave orders that the monkey-king should have obsequies like a king, and he sent to the seraglio, saying, "Come to the cemetery, as retinue for the monkey-king, with red garments, and dishevelled hair, and torches

---

6. Gautama Buddha's evil cousin, who appears in many *Jātakas*.

in your hands." The ministers made a funeral pile with a hundred waggon loads of timber. Having prepared the Bodhisatta's obsequies in a royal manner, they took his skull, and came to the king. The king caused a shrine to be built at the Bodhisatta's burial-place, torches to be burnt there and offerings of incense and flowers to be made; he had the skull inlaid with gold, and put in front raised on a spearpoint: honouring it with incense and flowers, he put it at the king's gate when he came to Benares, and having the whole city decked out he paid honour to it for seven days. Then taking it as a relic and raising a shrine, he honoured it with incense and garlands all his life; and established in the Bodhisatta's teaching he did alms and other good deeds, and ruling his kingdom righteously became destined for heaven.

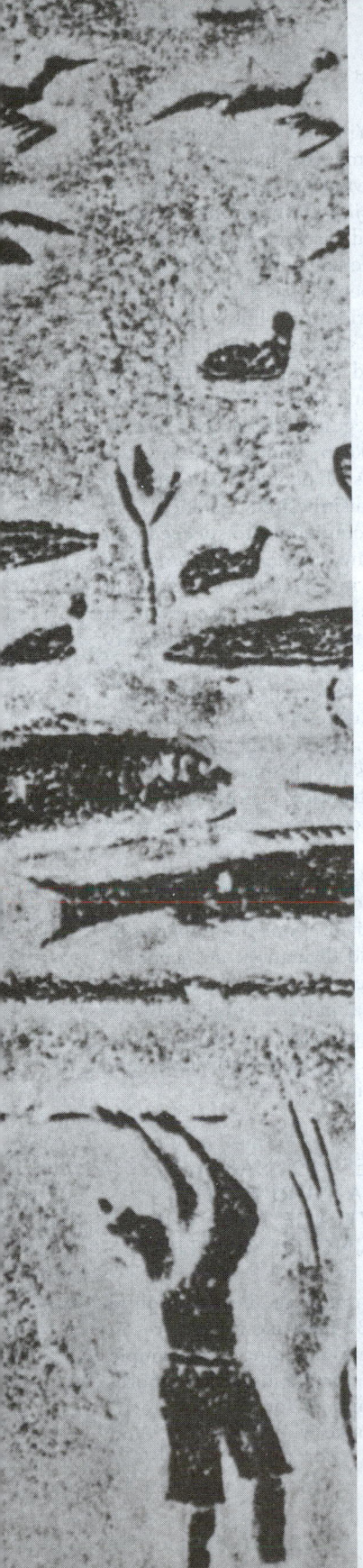

III

Early Chinese Literature and Thought

Many great civilizations have perished with little consequence. What we know of them comes from the imaginative reconstructions of scholars, from inscriptions, and from the accounts of early travelers. Civilizations like those of ancient Egypt and Mesopotamia left extensive written records that were swept aside by other civilizations; the very names by which we refer to them—Egypt and Mesopotamia—are Greek. This is not the case with China, the oldest surviving civilization, whose literary tradition stretches over more than three thousand years. Its earliest literature set patterns and posed questions that shaped the actions and values of the Chinese people for thousands of years, serving as the connective tissue that gave its civilization a sense of unity and continuity.

Throughout China's long history, its territories, ruling classes, capitals, religions, and customs kept changing with the rise and fall of ruling dynasties; and its peoples have spoken a great number of widely divergent Chinese dialects as well as many non-Chinese languages from the Turkic, Mongolian, and even Indo-European language families. Thus, China might easily have become fragmented

A contemporary rubbing made from a Han Dynasty (206 B.C.E.–220 C.E.) earthenware tile that depicts scenes of hunting and harvesting.

by regional interests and linguistic differences like Europe after the fall of the Roman Empire. But whereas Rome was truly a conquest empire, a political center that ruled over many peoples, each with its own sense of distinct ethnic identity, traditional China was an idea tied to cultural values and the power of the written word. Certainly, Chinese emperors did at certain times in history conquer territories as remote as Korea, Vietnam, Tibet, and Taiwan. But China could survive periods of turmoil and even rule by non-Chinese conquerors such as the Mongols and the Manchus because peoples on the margins of the ancient heartland had for centuries been adopting China's writing, cultural values, and institutions, and had thus become "Chinese." Many times in China's history, regional identity has become subordinate to a belief in cultural and political unity.

BEGINNINGS: EARLY SAGE RULERS

Although China has always been in contact with western parts of the Eurasian landmass, it developed independently from the earlier Mesopotamian, Egyptian, and Indus Valley city civilizations. By the third millennium B.C.E. at least a dozen Neolithic (New Stone Age) cultures flourished along the Yellow River in the north and the Yangtze River in the south. By the second millennium B.C.E. most settlements had defensive walls made of rammed earth, a sign of the increasing influence of military elites, who defended the populace against other rising city-states. Later Chinese historians placed into this early period a lineage of sage rulers who laid the foundations for Chinese civilization. Fu Xi reputedly taught people how to raise silkworms. He also invented the eight trigrams, symbols consisting of three broken or

unbroken (Yin and Yang) lines each, which became the basis for China's canonical divination text, the *Classic of Changes (Yijing)*. Shennong invented the plow and instructed people in the use of medicinal herbs. Huangdi, the "Yellow Emperor," was a patron of medicine and agriculture. His scribe, Cang Jie, invented writing by creating graphs that imitated the articulate tracks of birds, realizing that the new technology "could regulate the various professions and keep under scrutiny the various kinds of people." A later sage ruler, Yao, disinherited his inept son and chose a commoner to succeed him on the throne, thus establishing the principle of virtue and merit over blood lineage. This commoner, Shun, was an ideal ruler and a model of filial piety (he remained true to his parents despite their repeated attempts to kill him). His successor, the Great Yu, showed exemplary dedication to the welfare of his people and invented irrigation, constructing channels to tame the Great Flood that occurred during his reign.

Encapsulated in this lineage of legendary rulers are fundamental values of Chinese civilization: the importance of writing and divination; an economy based on intensive agriculture and silk production; a political philosophy of virtue that emphasizes fixed social roles; and practices of self-cultivation and herbal medicine.

EARLIEST DYNASTIES: CHINA DURING THE BRONZE AGE AND THE BEGINNING OF WRITING

China's Bronze Age began around 2000 B.C.E. By 1200 B.C.E., cultures in several regions of China made ample use of bronze for the molding of more-effective weapons, for the new technology of spoke-wheel chariots, and

This tortoiseshell, inscribed with writing dating from ca. 1200 B.C.E., was used for ceremonial divination.

for the production of ritual bronze vessels used in ceremonies honoring gods and ancestors. A small area in the Yellow River basin of north-central China is the best known of these Bronze Age cultures: thanks to the groundbreaking archaeological discovery of inscriptions on tortoiseshells and cattle bones in 1898, this area could be identified as the so-called second dynasty—the Shang (ca. 1500–1045 B.C.E.). The first dynasty is traditionally identified as the Xia, whose name and list of kings are recorded in later texts, but whose existence hasn't been linked to any of the known Bronze Age archaeological sites.

The Shang was a loose confederation of city-states with a complex state system, large settlements, and, most important, a common writing system. Although it remains unclear when the Chinese script began to be developed, it appeared as a fully functional writing system during the later period of the Shang dynasty. To date, more than 48,000 fragments of inscribed shells and bones have been found. These so-

called oracle bone inscriptions are usually short records of divination rituals. Ritual specialists and the Shang kings would apply heat to the bones and use the resulting cracks to interpret or predict events: determining weather, harvest, floods, or tribute payments; divining the outcome of imminent war or the birth of male offspring; or even finding the causes for the toothache of a royal family member. Thus, writing was part of ritual practices that guided political decision making and harmonized the relation between human beings and the world of unpredictable spiritual forces in the cosmos. Its use was a prerogative of the Shang king and his elites.

From the inscriptions we can see that the Shang kings paid meticulous attention to the veneration of their dead ancestors and various gods, including the highest god, Di, who also commanded rain and thunder. They used war captives as slaves and sacrificial victims and employed conscript workers for monumental labor projects. For example, the sumptuous grave site of Lady Hao, one

Among the many objects fashioned out of bronze during the Shang Dynasty were "fangding," ritual vessels for cooking and presenting food. This fangding is the only extant example that is decorated with a human face.

of the prominent Shang king Wu Ding's many wives, contained hundreds of bronze objects.

THE ZHOU CONQUEST AND THE "MANDATE OF HEAVEN"

Around 1045 B.C.E. the Zhou people overthrew the Shang. The Zhou were an agrarian people and former allies of the Shang. Their justification of the conquest set the model for subsequent dynastic shifts in Chinese history. Texts recorded during the first centuries of Zhou rule claimed that a new power, "Heaven," transferred the mandate to rule to the Zhou, because the moral worth of the Shang had declined and the last Shang rulers were decadent tyrants without regard for the people. In turn, the first rulers of the Zhou, King Wen (the "cultured" or "civilized" king) and his son King Wu (the "martial" king), who completed the conquest, were praised as paragons of virtue and "sons of Heaven" deserving of the mandate. After the Zhou conquest, the claim to power in China depended on the claim to virtuous rule, which in large measure meant holding to the statutes and models of the earliest sage rulers and the virtuous early Zhou kings.

THE DECLINE OF THE EASTERN ZHOU AND THE AGE OF CHINA'S PHILOSOPHICAL MASTERS

After their conquest, the early Zhou kings rewarded their allies with gifts of land. But initially strong personal ties between the Zhou kings and their allies weakened over the centuries, and in 771 B.C.E. some vassals joined forces with nomadic tribesmen and killed the king. The Zhou court fled and moved the capital to the east. Historians thus distin-

guish between the Western Zhou (1045–771 B.C.E.) and the Eastern Zhou (770–256 B.C.E.) periods. The Zhou kings never regained full control over their vassals. Although its kings continued to rule for another five centuries, the Eastern Zhou Dynasty lacked strong central authority, allowing its former vassals to build up their domains into belligerent independent states. On the southern and western borders of the old Zhou domain, powerful new states arose: Chu, Wu, and Yue in the south and Qin in the west. Although many of these new kingdoms had their distinct traditions, they gradually absorbed Zhou culture, and their rulers often sought to trace their descent either from the Zhou royal house or from more ancient, northern Chinese ancestors. Just before the defeat of the Western Zhou, there were around two hundred lords with domains of varying size, all under the titular rule of the Zhou king. By the third century B.C.E., only seven powerful states were left in the struggle over supremacy, and in 256 B.C.E. the last Zhou king was killed.

The Eastern Zhou Period was one of the most formative periods in Chinese history. The Eastern Zhou rulers built new institutions, and among its vassal states a lively interstate diplomacy unfolded; new military technology revolutionized warfare, and the old aristocracy was gradually dismantled and replaced by a new class of advisers and strategists. During the earlier part of the Eastern Zhou Period, the so-called Spring and Autumn Annals Period (722–481 B.C.E., named after the court chronicle of Confucius's home state of Lu in eastern China), the old aristocracy in their chariots were still central to combat, and an honor code of military conduct was respected. Battles started with an agreement on both sides, states that were in mourning for their rulers were not attacked, and, if a state was defeated, the conqueror respectfully continued the ancestral sacrifices for the vanquished ruling lineage. This changed dramatically during the latter half of the Eastern Zhou, the so-called Warring States Period (403–221 B.C.E., named after a collection of stories about political intrigues between the Zhou states): mass infantry armies built on coercive drafts replaced the old aristocracy; raw power politics and strategic deception became the norm; the newly invented crossbow allowed soldiers to kill their enemies at greater distance, not in noble close combat; and rulers of the larger Zhou states started to call themselves kings, indicating that they not only defied the authority of the Zhou king but also intended to replace him as ruler over all of China.

It was in this climate that **Confucius**, and the philosophical masters who followed in his wake, formulated visions of how to live and govern well in a corrupt world. Chinese call this the period when "a hundred schools of thought bloomed." The Eastern Zhou Period coincides with the period when the religions and philosophies of ancient India, Greece, Persia, and Israel took shape, and scholars have compared the social and political conditions facilitating this flourishing in these different civilizations. In China, rulers of the feudal states employed able advisers, or "masters," to help them gain more resources, territory, and power, and the Chinese masters often moved between states in search for employment and patronage.

ZHOU CHINA DURING
CONFUCIUS'S TIME
6TH–5TH C. B.C.E.

THE EMERGENCE OF UNIFIED CHINA
350–221 B.C.E.

Chinese call the texts written by masters or compiled by their disciples "Masters Literature." This name derives from scenes that show a charismatic master in vivid conversation with disciples, rulers, or other contemporaries. Masters Literature flourished from the time of Confucius through the Han Dynasty (206 B.C.E.–220 C.E.). This rich corpus of texts, represented in this anthology by selections from the *Analects*, and from *Laozi* and *Zhuangzi*, reveals the broad spectrum of opinions on fundamental questions: How can we create social order in a society that is incessantly at war? How can we become exemplary, fulfilled human beings in a less-than-ideal society? How can we make use of history and existing precedents to create a better future? How should we use words, and what impact can words and ideas have on social reality?

Later Chinese texts divided the masters and their followers into schools of thought, although the boundaries between their positions were often more fluid than the labels suggest. The most prominent schools were the Confucians, the Mohists (named after their master, Mozi), the Daoists, the Logicians, the Legalists, and the Yin-Yang Masters, each advocating its own programs, adopting different styles of argument, and engaging the rival camps in polemical disputes. The schools had varied degrees of success: while Confucianism and Daoism became the intellectual and religious backbone of traditional China (joined by Buddhism after it reached China from India around the Common Era), the Mohists and Logicians died out, the Yin-Yang Masters produced specialists in divination and calendrical science, and the Legalists, who advocated authoritarian rule through harsh laws, became the black sheep of early Chinese thought. They were openly decried as tyrannical and inhuman, but many of their ideas and methods were used by the architects of the Chinese empire throughout the centuries.

Confucius, the first and most exemplary master whose sayings are preserved in the *Analects*, believed that a return to the values of the virtuous early Zhou kings, a respect for social hierarchies, self-cultivation through proper ritual behavior, and the study of ancient texts could bring order. The most radical opponents of Confucius and his followers were thinkers who advocated passivity and following of the natural "way," or *dao*. The Daoists had a deep mistrust of human-made things: conscious effort, artifice, and words. *Laozi*, a collection of poems and the foundational text of Daoism, proposed passivity as a means of ultimately prevailing over one's opponents and gaining spiritual and political control. By contrast, many passages in *Zhuangzi*, the second most important Daoist text of Masters Literature, renounce any claim to societal influence and celebrate the joy of an unharmed life devoted to reflecting on the workings of the mind and on the relativity of perception and values.

Apart from the philosophical masters, there were other people who put their lament about the corruptness of the age into writing. Qu Yuan (ca. 340–278 B.C.E.), an aristocrat of the southern state of Chu, tirelessly advised the king of Chu to beware of the militaristic ambitions of the northern state of Qin. When his advice fell increasingly on deaf ears and he was badmouthed by his envious colleagues, he decided to commit suicide, not without describing his frustrated quest for appreciation and his disenchantment with the world in a long and plaintive poem, "**Encountering Sorrow**." What Qu Yuan had tried to prevent at all cost—the militaristic ascent of Qin—reached its pinnacle in 221 B.C.E., when the first Chinese empire was founded.

FOUNDATIONS OF IMPERIAL CHINA: THE QIN AND THE HAN

The state of Qin, which had a reputation for ruthlessness and untrustworthiness, but whose armies were well disciplined and well supplied, destroyed the Zhou royal domain in 256 B.C.E. and conquered the last of the independent states in 221 B.C.E. That year is one of the most important dates in Chinese history. Conscious of the historical moment's weight, the king of Qin conferred the title "First Emperor of Qin" upon himself to mark the novelty of his achievement. Although the Qin was a short-lived dynasty, many of its measures—designed to create a new type of state with a strong centralized bureaucracy—were adopted and adapted by the rulers of the subsequent Han Dynasty (206 B.C.E.–220 C.E.). With the Qin unification, China was finally an empire. Imperial China, with its upheavals, dynastic shifts, and momentous changes, would last another 2,100 years—until the Republican Revolution of 1911.

Some scholars credit the Qin Dynasty's policy reforms with the success of the Chinese empire. Since the fourth century B.C.E., ministers associated with the Legalist school advised the kings of Qin to reduce the power of the old nobility and to base governance on a direct connection between ruler and bureaucrats controlled by the strict rule of written law codes and policies. In the decades before the Qin unification, the Legalist thinker Han Feizi (d. ca. 233 B.C.E.) had found particular favor with the king of Qin. Although Han Feizi was ultimately forced into suicide by the slander of suspicious colleagues, his vision of governance was adopted for the new empire.

The First Emperor's megalomania became legendary in later Chinese history, exerting as much fascination as horror. Though much of his statecraft

Perhaps the most illustrative symbol of the First Emperor's megalomania and imperial ambitions is the vast terra-cotta army, unearthed in 1974, that the emperor had buried with him. Over 7,000 life-size sculptures fill the burial site.

was subtle, many of his most famous policies had a chilling simplicity. Some, such as unifying the currency, the various scripts, and the weights and measures used in different states, deserve credit. But his solution to intellectual disagreement was the suppression of scholars and the burning of all books except for practical manuals of medicine, agriculture, and divination and for the historical records of Qin. The "Qin Burning of the Books," of 213 B.C.E., was one of the most traumatic events in Chinese history.

After the death of the First Emperor, rebellions broke out. Many of the rebels tried to restore the old pre-Qin states, but the final winner, a simple commoner named Liu Bang, became the first emperor of the Han Dynasty and continued the centralized govern-ment strategy of the Qin, while eliminating its unpopular features, loosening some particularly cruel laws, cutting taxes, and refraining from the constant labor mobilizations that the Qin emperor had forced on his people.

The Han Dynasty lasted more than four hundred years. The Han was the crucial phase of imperial consolidation that set patterns for future Chinese dynasties. During this period China expanded its boundaries into Central Asia and parts of modern Korea and Vietnam. Han emperors learned to deal with the challenging threat of northern frontier tribes, developing strategies that proved effective for subsequent empires: fight them, pay them off, or appease them with marriage alliances, offering Chinese princesses as brides to the tribal chieftains.

THE HAN EMPIRE
ca. 50 B.C.E.

Qin Empire (to 207 B.C.E.)

Han expansion (to 9 C.E.) with dates of annexation 59 B.C.E.

Han protectorate (59 B.C.E.–23 C.E.)

Former Han imperial capital ⊡
Qin imperial capital ☐   Later Han imperial capital ⊞
defensive wall ⌐⌐   trade route – –

eastern limit of Roman occupation (117 C.E.)

Lake Baikal

MONGOLIA

Aral Sea
Lake Balkash
TIAN SHAN
Turfan
Silk Road
Xiongnu tribes
Gobi Desert
106 B.C.E.
KOREA
Sea of Japan

Caspian Sea
Samarkand
Wulei
Taklamakan Desert
Dunhuang
115 B.C.E.
Yellow R.
Linzi
Yellow Sea
approximate ancient coastline

Oxus
Kashgar
Bactra
KUNLUN SHAN
Liangzhou
Luoyang
Chang'an

PARTHIA
HINDUKUSH
Khotan
Taxila
Shu
Yangtze
110 B.C.E.
Changsha
100 B.C.E.
Minjiang

Kandahar
KUSHANA
HIMALAYAS
Ba
136–82 B.C.E.
Nanhai

Indus
ARABIA
Pāṭaliputra
Tropic of Cancer
border of Nanyue independent kingdom (206–113 B.C.E.)
Nanyue
Hainan
South China Sea

Arabian Sea
INDIA
Bay of Bengal
VIETNAM

0   400   800   1200   1600   2000 kilometers
0   200   400   600   800   1000   1200 miles

The most influential Han ruler was Emperor Wu, whose long reign lasted from 141 to 87 B.C.E. He undertook costly campaigns to expand the empire and established government monopolies on the production of iron, salt, and liquor to finance them. He was a generous patron of the arts, of music, and of scholarship. Although he was intrigued by immortality techniques, portents, and the occult, he was the first emperor to privilege Confucian scholars, founding a state academy for the education of government officials and setting up positions for professors to teach the so-called Five Classics: the *Classic of Changes*, used for divination; the *Classic of Documents*, a collection of proclamations by early sage kings and ministers; the **Classic of Poetry**, a collection of poetry including hymns to the Zhou ancestors and ballads recounting the history of the Zhou; the *Spring and Autumn Annals*, a historical chronicle; and the *Record of Rites*, the

most important of several works on ritual. During Emperor Wu's reign the first comprehensive history of China was written, by a court historian and his son, Sima Qian (ca. 145–86 B.C.E.), who suffered the punishment of castration for a minor disagreement with Emperor Wu but persisted in finishing his monumental history, which became the model for subsequent dynastic histories of China into the twentieth century.

Early China was a groundbreaking period of enduring influence on all subsequent periods of Chinese history. These first 1,500 years of Chinese history, from the Shang Dynasty to the end of the Han Dynasty, saw the emergence of enduring political institutions and ideologies, of moral standards and social manners. The literature produced during this period encapsulates these values and formative patterns and is still the canonical foundation of Chinese civilization.

CLASSIC OF POETRY

ca. 1000–600 B.C.E.

Standing at the beginning of China's three-millennia-long literary tradition, the *Classic of Poetry* (also known as *Book of Songs* or *Book of Odes*) is the oldest poetry collection of East Asia. Its poems reflect the breadth of early Chinese society. Some poems convey the history and values of the earlier part of the Zhou Dynasty (ca. 1045–256 B.C.E.), whose founding kings set a standard of ideal governance for later generations. Others treat themes familiar from folk ballads: courtship, marriage and love, birth and death, and the stages of the agricultural cycle such as planting and harvesting. Filled with images of nature and the plain life of an agricultural society, the *Classic of Poetry* offers a distinctive, fresh simplicity. Because of the collection's canonical status, centuries of commentary and interpretation have accrued around it, adding to its meaning and significance and endowing the simple scenes in the poems with moral or political purpose. The anthology has had a profound impact on the literatures of Korea, Japan, and Vietnam and was an important element of the traditional curriculum throughout East Asia until the beginning of the twentieth century.

THE ANTHOLOGY AND ITS SIGNIFICANCE

While other ancient literary traditions were founded on epics about gods and heroes, or sprawling legends about the origins of the cosmos, the *Classic of Poetry* provided a different sort of foundation for Chinese literature, made up of the compact and evocative form of lyric poetry. Because Chinese literature originated with the *Classic of Poetry*, short verse gained a degree of political, social, and pedagogical importance in East Asia that it has not enjoyed anywhere else in the world.

The *Classic of Poetry* contains 305 poems and consists of three parts, the "Airs of the Domains" (*Guofeng*, 160 poems), the "Odes/Elegances" (*Ya*, 105 poems), and the "Hymns" (*Song*, 40 poems). The "Hymns" are the oldest part and contain songs used in ritual performances to celebrate the Zhou royal house. Next are the "Odes," narrative ballads about memorable historical events. The youngest poems are the "Airs of the Domains," based on folk ballads from some fifteen domains of the Zhou kingdom. (The early Zhou kings gave lands to their loyal vassals and gradually built a multistate system of "domains" extending from modern-day Beijing far beyond the Yangtze River in the south.) Tradition credited **Confucius**, the most important of the early philosophical masters, with the compilation of the *Classic of Poetry*. He allegedly selected the poems in the collection from three thousand poems he found in the archives of the Zhou kingdom. Therefore, the choice and arrangement of the poems were seen as an expression of Confucius's philosophy. Confucius believed that political order depended on the ability of individuals in society to cultivate their moral virtue and thus contribute to social order. We know from the *Analects*, a collection containing Confucius's sayings, that Confucius thought highly of the *Classic of Poetry*. He advised his own son to study the *Clas-*

sic of Poetry to enhance his ability to express his opinions, he praised disciples who quoted passages from the Classic of Poetry to make a particular point, and he saw a comprehensive educational program in the anthology: "The Classic of Poetry can provide you with stimulation and with observation, with a capacity for communion, and with a vehicle for grief. At home, they [the poems] enable you to serve your father, and abroad, to serve your lord. Also, you will learn there the names of many birds, animals, plants, and trees." Confucius's high opinion of the Classic of Poetry led to its inclusion in the canon of "Confucian Classics." The other classics are the Classic of Changes, used for divination; the Classic of Documents, a collection of sayings by early kings and ministers; the Spring and Autumn Annals, a historical chronicle of Confucius's home state of Lu; and the Record of Rites, the most important of a few books on ritual. The Confucian Classics became the curriculum of the state academy that Emperor Wu of the Han Dynasty founded in 124 B.C.E.

As a further sign of the Classic of Poetry's canonization during the Han Dynasty, a **"Great Preface"** written for the anthology became the single most fundamental statement about the nature and function of poetry in East Asia. Written more than half a millennium after the anthology's compilation, the "Great Preface" claimed that there were "six principles" (liu yi) of poetry: the three categories in which the poems were placed ("Airs of the Domains," "Odes," and "Hymns") and the three rhetorical devices of "enumeration" (fu), "comparison" (bi), and "evocative image" (xing). Scholars and poets have debated the usefulness and precise meaning of these principles for the last two millennia, but on a basic level the principles illuminate rhetorical patterns that distinguish the Classic of Poetry and even later Chinese poetry. The concept

of feng is a good case in point: it refers to the "Airs of the Domains" section of the anthology, but it also contains a rich web of associations that grew up around its literal meaning, "wind": Like wind that causes grass to sway, the ruler can "influence" (feng) his people and instill virtuous behavior in them through poetry. For their part, his subjects can express their dissatisfaction with their ruler through "criticism" (feng). In reality, most poems in the anthology contain at best indirect criticism. But the idea that poetry and song can bridge the gulf between social classes, that they can serve as a tool for mutual "influence" and "criticism" and give the people a voice, helping them keep bad rulers in check, was central to the Confucian understanding of poetry and society. Poetry made room for social critique and created the institution of "remonstration," the duty of officials in the bureaucracy to speak out against abuses of power.

THE POEMS

Our selections come from the "Odes" section ("She Bore the Folk") and the "Airs" section (all other poems), and conclude with the "Great Preface." Although almost all poems in the Classic of Poetry are anonymous, they give voice to many different players in Zhou society, such as kings, aristocrats and peasants, men and women in love, and, collectively, to communities as they celebrate harvest or worship their ancestors. Poems put into the mouths of peasants or soldiers show considerable literary skill, which suggests that a member of the educated elite at the courts of the Zhou domains must have given them their final shape.

The constraints imposed by society and the conflict between individual desire and social expectations are important themes in the "Airs" section. Marriage is often praised as a sanctioned form of sexual relation, but some poems also celebrate the pleasures of transgression. "Boat of Cypress" is a remarkable outcry of a heart that refuses to bend to society's wishes. Unlike the virtuous Zhou Dynasty, the domain of Zheng and its music were associated with sensual pleasures: "Zhen and Wei," for example, depicts a festival scene along two rivers. Although its frolicking man and woman do not go beyond politely exchanging flowers as courtship gifts, the scene is highly charged with eroticism.

The protagonists in the romantic plots that appear in the poems of the "Airs of the Domains" could be from any culture past or present, but the extensive tradition of commentaries endowed these poems with specific moral and historical significance. According to the canonical "Mao commentary," "Fishhawk," the first poem of the *Classic of Poetry*, in which a young man is tormented by his desire for a girl, is not a simple romantic folk song. Instead, the commentary claims that the poem praises the consort of King Wen for being free from jealousy when her husband takes a new consort, a typical situation in traditional Chinese society, where men could have several wives. This counterintuitive reading of the poem established "Fishhawk" as a model of exemplary female behavior for all times and embedded it in the history of the early Zhou kings.

The central stylistic device of the *Classic of Poetry* is repetition with variation. Many of the poems consist of three rhyming stanzas of four or six lines with four syllables each. The stanza format encourages line repetitions, which give the poems melodic rhythm and, with the introduction of small variations, additional meaning. In "Plums Are Falling," the fruits become fewer with each repetition until the woman has finally decided whom among her suitors she wants to marry. In "Peach Tree Soft and Tender," the peach tree goes through the natural cycle of bearing blossoms, fruits, and leaves while a new bride, who

it is hoped will bear many descendants for the family line, is introduced into the household. Far from being a simplistic rhetorical device, repetition with variation gives compelling shape to a suitor's intrusive desire and his lover's fear of scandal in "Zhongzi, Please." As the insolent Zhongzi systematically advances stanza by stanza from the village wall to the family's fence and through the garden towards his lover's bedchamber, the helpless woman, fearing her parents' and brothers' reproach and society's disapproval, fends her lover off by promising to keep him in her thoughts.

Among the rhetorical devices listed in the "Great Preface" to the *Classic of Poetry*, "exposition" (*fu*) and "affective image" (*xing*) are particularly interesting. Exposition, the enumeration of sequences of events in straightforward narrative fashion, structures longer odes like "She Bore the Folk," a poem on the miraculous birth of Lord Millet, the inventor of agriculture and legendary ancestor of the Zhou people. Lord Millet's birth to a resourceful mother who steps into a god's footprint and his subsequent development into the Zhous' ancestor and cultural hero are recounted through vivid enumeration. The ritual acts that the Zhou people perform to celebrate the harvest and commemorate their ancestor are also related through "exposition." Poems from the "Airs" section, by contrast, mostly employ "comparisons" (*bi*) and "affective images." Comparisons are like similes: "Huge Rat" compares an exploitative lord directly to a voracious rodent. Affective images are much more elusive and do not easily translate into any rhetorical trope in the Western tradition. *Xing*, the term rendered as "affective image," literally means "stimulus" or "excitement." *Xing* brings natural images into suggestive resonance with human situations, stimulating the imagination and pushing perception beyond a simple comparison of one thing to another. Often, the animals or plants used to evoke human situations appear in the same scene with the human protagonists, but the relation between the animals or plants and the humans is mysterious. For example, in "Dead Roe Deer" the reader sees a landscape in which a girl, a "maiden white as marble," who has just been seduced by a man, hovers next to a dead deer "wrapped in white rushes."

The resonant, elusive imagery of the *Classic of Poetry* has enticed readers through the ages. The poet and critic Ezra Pound (1885–1972), attracted to and inspired by the use of imagery in Chinese poetry, spearheaded the new movement of "imagism" in the 1910s, experimenting with the poetic power that sparse juxtaposition of images whose relation remains obscure can produce. His adoption of such poetic techniques in turn profoundly influenced modernist writers such as T. S. Eliot and James Joyce. Although Pound did not know Chinese, he eventually produced a poetic rendering of the *Classic of Poetry* in collaboration with the Harvard sinologist Achilles Fang. Because of their diver-

gence from the wording of the originals, Pound's versions might better be conceived as English poems in their own right than translations. Yet they can come close to the Chinese originals in other ways. In Pound's version, the second stanza of "Dead Roe Deer" reads, "Where the scrub elm skirts the wood, be it not in white mat bound, as a jewel flawless found, dead as doe is maidenhood." Death hovers ominously over the deer, the woman, and her maidenhood. Here we see the drama of the distinctive Chinese trope of *xing* in full play, transposed into the English language.

The *Classic of Poetry* has left deep traces in the literary cultures of East Asia into the modern period. Because its compilation was attributed to Confucius and its traditional interpretations emphasized Confucian values, it was part and parcel of the education of political elites. Yet, despite the dominant moralizing interpretations, the poems of the *Classic of Poetry* have retained their pristine simplicity and have lost nothing of their evocative power to voice fundamental human emotions and challenges.

CLASSIC OF POETRY[1]

I. Fishhawk

The fishhawks sing *guan guan*
on sandbars of the stream.
Gentle maiden, pure and fair,
fit pair for a prince.

Watercress grows here and there,   5
right and left we gather it.
Gentle maiden, pure and fair,
wanted waking and asleep.

Wanting, sought her, had her not,
waking, sleeping, thought of her,   10

1. Translated by Stephen Owen.

on and on he thought of her,
he tossed from one side to another.

Watercress grows here and there,
right and left we pull it.
Gentle maiden, pure and fair,   15
with harps we bring her company.

Watercress grows here and there,
right and left we pick it out.
Gentle maiden, pure and fair,
with bells and drums do her delight.   20

VI. Peach Tree Soft and Tender

Peach tree soft and tender,
how your blossoms glow!
The bride is going to her home,
she well befits this house.

Peach tree soft and tender,   5
plump, the ripening fruit.
The bride is going to her home,
she well befits this house.

Peach tree soft and tender,
its leaves spread thick and full.   10
The bride is going to her home,
she well befits these folk.

XX. Plums Are Falling

Plums are falling,
seven are the fruits;
many men want me,
let me have a fine one.

Plums are falling,   5
three are the fruits;
many men want me,
let me have a steady one.

Plums are falling,
catch them in the basket;   10
many men want me,
let me be bride of one.

XXIII. Dead Roe Deer

A roe deer dead in the meadow,
all wrapped in white rushes.
The maiden's heart was filled with spring;
a gentleman led her astray.

Undergrowth in forest,   5
dead deer in the meadow,
all wound with white rushes,
a maiden white as marble.

Softly now, and gently, gently,
do not touch my apron, sir,   10
and don't set the cur to barking.

XXVI. Boat of Cypress

That boat of cypress drifts along,
it drifts upon the stream.
Restless am I, I cannot sleep,
as though in torment and troubled.
Nor am I lacking wine   5
to ease my mind and let me roam.

This heart of mine is no mirror,
it cannot take in all.
Yes, I do have brothers,
but brothers will not be my stay.   10
I went and told them of my grief
and met only with their rage.

This heart of mine is no stone;
you cannot turn it where you will.
This heart of mine is no mat;   15
I cannot roll it up within.
I have behaved with dignity,
in this no man can fault me.

My heart is uneasy and restless,
I am reproached by little men.   20
Many are the woes I've met,
and taken slights more than a few.
I think on it in the quiet,
and waking pound my breast.

Oh Sun! and you Moon!   25
Why do you each grow dim in turn?
These troubles of the heart

are like unwashed clothes.
I think on it in the quiet,
I cannot spread wings to fly away.   30

XLII. Gentle Girl

A gentle girl and fair
awaits by the crook of the wall;
in shadows I don't see her;
I pace and scratch my hair.

A gentle girl and comely   5
gave me a scarlet pipe;
scarlet pipe that gleams—
in your beauty I find delight.

Then she brought me a reed from the pastures,
it was truly beautiful and rare.   10
Reed—the beauty is not yours—
you are but beauty's gift.

LXIV. Quince

She cast a quince to me,
a costly garnet I returned;
it was no equal return,
but by this love will last.

She cast a peach to me,   5
costly opal I returned;
it was no equal return,
but by this love will last.

She cast a plum to me,
a costly ruby I returned;   10
it was no equal return,
but by this love will last.

LXXVI. Zhongzi, Please

Zhongzi, please
don't cross my village wall,
don't break the willows planted there.
It's not that I care so much for them,
but I dread my father and mother;   5

Zhongzi may be in my thoughts,
but what my father and mother said—
that too may be held in dread.

Zhongzi, please
don't cross my fence,   10
don't break the mulberries planted there.
It's not that I care so much for them,
but I dread my brothers;
Zhongzi may be in my thoughts,
but what my brothers said—   15
that too may be held in dread.

Zhongzi, please
don't cross into my garden,
don't break the sandalwood planted there.
It's not that I care so much for them,   20
but I dread others will talk much;
Zhongzi may be in my thoughts,
but when people talk too much—
that too may be held in dread.

XCV. Zhen and Wei

O Zhen and Wei together,
swollen now they flow.
Men and maids together,
chrysanthemums in hand.
The maid says, "Have you looked?"   5
The man says, "I have gone."
"Let's go then look across the Wei,
it is truly a place for our pleasure."
Man and maid together
each frolicked with the other   10
and gave as gift the peony.

O Zhen and Wei together,
flowing deep and clear.
Men and maids together,
teeming everywhere.   15
The maid says, "Have you looked?"
The man says, "I have gone."
"Let's go then look across the Wei,
it is truly a place for our pleasure."
Man and maid together   20
each will frolic with the other
and give as gift the peony.

CXIII. Huge Rat

Huge rat, huge rat,
eat my millet no more,
for three years I've fed you,
yet you pay me no heed.

I swear that I will leave you   5
and go to a happier land.
A happy land, a happy land,
and there I will find my place.

Huge rat, huge rat,
eat my wheat no more,   10
for three years I've fed you
and you show no gratitude.

I swear that I will leave you
and go to a happier realm.
A happy realm, a happy realm,   15
there I will find what I deserve.

Huge rat, huge rat,
eat my sprouts no more,
for three years I have fed you,
and you won't reward my toil.   20

I swear that I will leave you
and go to happy meadows.
Happy meadows, happy meadows
where none need wail and cry.

CCXLV. She Bore the Folk

She who first bore the folk—
Jiang it was, First Parent.
How was it she bore the folk?—
she knew the rite and sacrifice.
To rid herself of sonlessness   5
she trod the god's toeprint
    and she was glad.
She was made great, on her luck settled,
the seed stirred, it was quick.
She gave birth, she gave suck,   10
and this was Lord Millet.

When her months had come to term,
her firstborn sprang up.
Not splitting, not rending,

working no hurt, no harm.   15
He showed his godhead glorious,
the high god was greatly soothed.
He took great joy in those rites
and easily she bore her son.

She set him in a narrow lane,   20
but sheep and cattle warded him.
She set him in the wooded plain,
he met with those who logged the plain.
She set him on cold ice,
birds sheltered him with wings.   25
Then the birds left him
and Lord Millet wailed.
This was long and this was loud;
his voice was a mighty one.

And then he crept and crawled,   30
he stood upright, he stood straight.
He sought to feed his mouth,
and planted there the great beans.
The great beans' leaves were fluttering,
the rows of grain were bristling.   35
Hemp and barley dense and dark,
the melons, plump and round.

Lord Millet in his farming
had a way to help things grow:
He rid the land of thick grass,   40
he planted there a glorious growth.
It was in squares, it was leafy,
it was planted, it grew tall.
It came forth, it formed ears,
it was hard, it was good.   45
Its tassels bent, it was full,
he had his household there in Dai.

He passed us down these wondrous grains:
our black millets, of one and two kernels,
millets whose leaves sprout red or white,   50
he spread the whole land with black millet,
and reaped it and counted the acres,
spread it with millet sprouting red or white,
hefted on shoulders, loaded on backs,
he took it home and began this rite.   55

And how goes this rite we have?—
at times we hull, at times we scoop,
at times we winnow, at times we stomp,
we hear it slosh as we wash it,
we hear it puff as we steam it.   60

Then we reckon, then we consider,
take artemisia, offer fat.
We take a ram for the flaying,
then we roast it, then we sear it,
to rouse up the following year.   65

We heap the wooden trenchers full,
wooden trenchers, earthenware platters.
And as the scent first rises
the high god is peaceful and glad.
This great odor is good indeed,   70
for Lord Millet began the rite,
and hopefully free from failing or fault,
it has lasted until now.

The Great Preface

"Fishhawk" is the virtue of the Queen Consort and the beginning of the "Airs"
[*Feng*, the first large section of the *Classic of Poetry*].[1] It is the means by which
the world is influenced (*feng*) and by which the relations between husband and
wife are made correct. Thus it is used in smaller communities, and it is used in
larger domains. "Airs" (*Feng*) are "Influence" (*feng*); it is to teach. By influence
it stirs them; by teaching it transforms them.[2]

The poem is that to which what is intently on the mind (*zhi*) goes. In the
mind, it is "being intent" (*zhi*); coming out in language, it is a "poem."

The affections are stirred within and take on form in words. If words alone
are inadequate, we speak it out in sighs. If sighing is inadequate, we sing it. If
singing is inadequate, unconsciously our hands dance it and our feet tap it.[3]

Feelings emerge in sounds; when those sounds have patterning, they are
called "tones." The tones of a well-managed age are at rest and happy: its government is balanced. The tones of an age of turmoil are bitter and full of anger:
its government is perverse. The tones of a ruined state are filled with lament
and brooding: its people are in difficulty.[4]

Thus to correctly present achievements and failures, to move Heaven and
Earth, to stir the gods and spirits, there is nothing more appropriate than poetry.
By it the former kings managed the relations between husbands and wives, per-

1. "The Great Preface" is attached to "Fishhawk," the first poem of the *Classic of Poetry*.
In traditional Confucian interpretations, the
poem was understood as celebrating the virtue
of the queen consort of King Wen of the Zhou
Dynasty.
2. *Feng*, a central term of "The Great Preface,"
literally means "wind." By extension, it means
"influence" (like wind bending the grasses) and
"Airs," the poetry in the first part of the *Classic
of Poetry* that was understood as a means to
positively influence people's behavior.

3. Although *qi*, "vital breath," is not directly
mentioned, the psychology of poetic composition described here relies on the notion that a
release of vital breath results in ever stronger
forms of outward expression: words, sighs,
songs, or dance.
4. Since the poems in the *Classic of Poetry*
were performed to music, the "tones" that
reveal the social and political conditions under
which the poems were composed became
manifest in both the words and the music.

fected the respect due to parents and superiors, gave depth to human relations, beautifully taught and transformed the people, and changed local customs.

Thus there are six principles in the poems: (1) Airs (*Feng*); (2) "exposition" (*fu*); (3) "comparison" (*bi*); (4) "affective image" (*xing*); (5) Odes (*Ya*); (6) Hymns (*song*).[5]

By *feng*, those above transform those below; also by *feng*, those below criticize those above. When an admonition is given that is governed by patterning, the one who speaks it has no culpability, yet it remains adequate to warn those who hear it. In this we have *feng*.[6]

When the Way of the Kings declined, rites and moral principles were abandoned; the power of government to teach failed; the government of the domains changed; the customs of the family were altered. And at this point the changed *Feng* ("Airs") and the changed *Ya* ("Odes") were written. The historians of the domains understood clearly the marks of success and failure; they were pained by the abandonment of proper human relations and lamented the severity of punishments and governance. They sang their feelings to criticize (*feng*) those above, understanding the changes that had taken place and thinking about former customs. Thus the changed *Feng* emerge from the affections, but they go no further than rites and moral principles. That they should emerge from the affections is human nature; that they go no further than rites and moral principles is the beneficent influence of the former kings.

Thus the affairs of a single state, rooted in the experience of a single person, are called *Feng*. To speak of the affairs of the whole world and to describe customs (*feng*) common to all places is called *Ya*. *Ya* means "proper." These show the source of either flourishing or ruin in the royal government. Government has its greater and lesser aspects: thus we have a "Greater *Ya*" and a "Lesser *Ya*." The "Hymns" give the outward shapes of praising full virtue, and they inform the spirits about the accomplishment of great deeds. These are called the "Four Beginnings" and are the ultimate perfection of the Poems.

---

5. The "six principles" consist of the three main parts of the *Classic of Poetry* (the "Airs," "Odes," and "Hymns") and three modes of expression ("exposition," "comparison," and "affective image"). "Exposition" describes poems with a longer narrative of events, "comparison" describes poems that use similes, and "affective image" describes poems that use natural imagery that parallels a human situation and should stir the emotions. The "six principles" became staple terms in discussions of poetry in East Asia.

6. A last addition to the many meanings of *feng*: ministers or simple people can "criticize" their rulers or superiors through this kind of poetry.

CONFUCIUS

551–479 B.C.E.

To this day there is virtually no aspect of East Asia on which Confucius and his ideas have not had some impact. When Confucius died in 479 B.C.E., he was a relatively little-known figure, having failed to find a ruler willing to implement his philosophical vision. Although he had attracted quite a few followers and had even established a school toward the end of his life, nobody could have anticipated then how this man's legacy would shape the destiny of China, East Asia, and the world. About 350 years later, Confucian values were not only widely known and revered but had also become the basis for official Chinese state ideology during the Han Dynasty (206 B.C.E.– 220 C.E.). Twenty-five hundred years later, Confucius is a national icon for China's venerable past, although Confucianism, the system of beliefs and practices that developed on the basis of Confucius's ideas, took a severe beating in mainland China during much of the twentieth century.

LIFE AND TIMES

Confucius was born in the northeastern state of Lu in today's Shandong Province. Confucius came from the lower ranks of hereditary nobility. Like other masters during the fifth to the third centuries B.C.E., a period of heated intellectual debates comparable to the contemporary flourishing of Greek philosophy, he was eager to put his talents at the disposal of an able ruler who would implement his ideas. But the rulers of Lu were often at the mercy of powerful clans whose arrogance scandalized Confucius. For example, Confucius took offence when one of the great local clans

in Lu used eight rows of dancers for the ceremonies at their ancestral temple, a lavish number that only the Zhou king had the prerogative to use. In Confucius's mind, this was not a simple breach of superficial protocol but a blatant symptom of the rottenness of the political system. Disgusted with the situation in his home state, Confucius left Lu and spent many years wandering from court to court, in search of a ruler who would appreciate his talents and political vision. He finally returned to Lu and lived out his life as a teacher, gathering a considerable following.

THE ZHOU HERITAGE AND CONFUCIUS'S INNOVATION

Confucius's philosophical vision brims with admiration for the values of the early Zhou rulers. The Zhou Dynasty (ca. 1045–256 B.C.E.), by Confucius's time already five centuries old, began with two exemplary rulers, King Wen and King Wu. King Wu had destroyed the last remnants of the reputedly despised Shang Dynasty in the eleventh century B.C.E., and instituted a new government that took pride in showing concern for the people and enforcing wise policies. After King Wu's death his brother, the Duke of Zhou, conducted government affairs for the duke's young nephew, King Cheng, who was still a child. Besides King Wen, the Duke of Zhou had particular importance for Confucius, not just because he was the ancestor of the ducal family of Confucius's home state. The Duke of Zhou also protected his nephew from rebellions and challenges to the newly founded dynasty and was an exemplary regent, with an eye on the welfare of the dynasty, not on his personal ambitions. But the splendor of the dynastic founders vanished over the next half millennium, as the Zhou kings increasingly lost control over the feudal lords, who had started out as their allies in the war against the Shang. By Confucius's time the Zhou kings had only nominal power and China consisted of rival states, whose rulers competed for territory and power. In the *Analects* Confucius often sharply criticizes the irreverent behavior of the feudal lords toward the Zhou king and showcases their corruption to explain his vision of proper government.

Although Confucius claims in the *Analects* that he is merely the "transmitter" of Zhou values and not an "innovator," he actually built a new tradition. Confucius's conviction that the political chaos he perceived around him could be avoided by returning to the moral values of the venerable founders of the Zhou Dynasty, Kings Wu and Wen and the Duke of Zhou, paid homage to tradition but was also visionary, even revolutionary. His emphasis on the importance of social roles and rituals could reinforce existing hierarchies, but at the same time it allowed individuals to develop their inner potential and find a meaningful place in society. His pedagogical program, which promoted the reading of a group of texts, later called "Confucian Classics," and their application to life's challenges, could lead to mindless memorization designed merely for career advancement, but it also enabled people to better understand and take control of their lives by following the moral models, historical precedents, and words of wisdom contained in these canonical texts.

DIVERSITY AND CORE VALUES IN THE *ANALECTS*

Confucius's vision has been extraordinarily influential over the past two and a half millennia and has profoundly shaped the societies not just of China but also of Korea, Japan, and Vietnam. The *Analects*, best translated as "Collected Sayings," convey the power of Confucius's vision. A collection of brief quotations, conversations, and anecdotes from the life of Confucius, the *Analects* were not written by the master himself, but compiled by later generations of disciples. They probably reached their current form only during the second century B.C.E., when Confucius's ideas were gaining influence and it became necessary to create a representative collection of his sayings out of the vast body of Confucius lore that circulated in various other books. Later it became the key text to understanding the great master's character and ideas. The *Analects* throw light on people, concrete situations, and above all the exemplary model of Confucius himself, instead of supplying systematic expositions of his ideas or abstract definitions of moral philosophy. When commenting on central concepts such as "goodness" or "humanity" (*ren*), "ritual" (*li*), and "respect for one's parents" (*xiao*), Confucius might utter different, even contradictory maxims: sometimes he claims that anybody who wants to can become "humane" in a moment, but at other times he turns the concept into a distant ideal. He also explains that his answers sometimes differ, because an overeager disciple needs to be held back, while a timid one needs to be encouraged. Another explanation for the widely divergent pieces of advice to be found in the *Analects* is that it was compiled over several centuries and thus includes the changing opinions of the compilers.

RITUAL

Despite the diversity of views expounded in the *Analects*, it is possible to identify a core set of values. First, there is Confucius's emphasis on ritual. Everything we do in life is a ritual, whether we greet each other with a handshake or mark life's important moments, such as birth and death, with special observances. Although Confucius briefly refers to earlier notions of the powers of Heaven and declares that he respects the gods and spirits, his concern is with our world, the world of human society. Rituals are thus used not to communicate with divine powers, but instead to make social life meaningful. One learns and perfects these rituals in one's community through continuous practice and self-cultivation. The person who has perfected himself in this manner is the *junzi*—the "superior person," or "gentleman." The word referred originally to a prince of aristocratic birth, but Confucius boldly applies it to moral, not hereditary, superiority. Although Confucius at times denies having reached the stage of *junzi* himself, he makes clear that anybody can become a *junzi*, and that everyone should strive to reach that ideal. The *Analects* also idealize historical figures whom Confucius considers models of exemplary moral conduct. Even before the sage rulers of the Zhou, there were the sage emperors of highest antiquity, including Emperor Shun, whose moral charisma was so overwhelming that it sufficed for him to sit in proper ritual position on his throne to induce spontaneous order in his empire. In Confucianism, models of proper ritual behavior are crucial to guiding one's moral self-cultivation, and book 10 of the *Analects* enshrines the master himself as such a model actor: it is the only book in which the master does not speak, but is simply shown in silent ritual action. That the compilers of the *Analects* placed this book at the heart of the *Analects*' twenty books shows that they admired Confucius not just for what he said, but for his exemplary conduct throughout his life.

SOCIAL ROLES

A second recurrent concern in the *Analects* is Confucius's attention to social roles. In his words humans owe each other "goodness" or "humanity" (*ren*)—that is, empathy and reciprocal concern, mutual respect and obligation. Some later Confucians, such as Mencius (ca. 372–289 B.C.E.), believed that this natural ability for empathy was even more important than ritual. The natural and spontaneous basis for respect is the relation between child and parent. From this experience, respect is extended to other figures, such as elder siblings, seniors, and rulers.

Although Confucius endorses social hierarchies, he abhorred any form of force and coercion. Because Confucianism and its canonical texts became the basis for the recruitment of bureaucrats and part of the ideology of government in imperial China, it is sometimes portrayed as a philosophy that, in contrast to Daoism, puts social duty over natural desires. Yet the stance of Confucius in the *Analects* is much more complex. He often navigates between the instincts of inborn nature and the need for cultivation, the power of spontaneous action and the importance of patient learning, the pleasures of a life in harmony with one's wishes and the duties of a life devoted to political service. In book 18 we see Confucius attracted to recluses, dropouts who reject life in society; another time Confucius praises the view of a disciple who values ritual celebration and joyful singing with friends over petty state service. At yet another point Confucius recommends avoiding government service unless a virtuous ruler is on the throne.

EFFICIENT ACTION

Goodness, ritual, and attention to social roles create order in society; efficient action, another major Confucian concern, helps to maintain it and to effect change in the world. One of Confucius's most attractive ideas is his promise that it is possible to harmonize one's natural impulses with social norms and thus become an efficient, harmonious agent in society. He himself apparently reached this balance only in old age: "At seventy I follow all the desires of my heart without breaking any rule." Throughout the *Analects*, Confucius is fascinated with various kinds of efficiency. Emperor Shun, facing south on his throne and thereby creating order in the world, is the prime incarnation of minimalist action put to great effect. The notion that the moral charisma of a sage ruler can be so powerful that there is no need to resort to lowly means of war and violence became the basis of the traditional Chinese view of rulership. Confucius's admiration for efficient thinking is best exemplified by his praise of his favorite disciple Yan Hui: "When he is told one thing he understands ten." The master of efficient speech, Confucius himself seems always to know more than he says: his utterances can be so short that they verge on the obscure. Sometimes he even speaks of his desire to reject language altogether.

THE IMPORTANCE OF CANONICAL TEXTS IN CONFUCIANISM

Confucius and his followers, called *Ru*, or "traditionalist scholars," considered the study of the ancient texts that contained the legacy of the Zhou as paramount to self-cultivation. Confucius is traditionally associated with the composition of the **Classic of Poetry, Classic of History, Record of Ritual, Spring and Autumn Annals**, and *Classic of Changes*, which were later called the "Confucian Classics." Today hardly anybody believes that they were written or compiled by Confucius. These books became the curriculum in the first Chinese state university, founded in 124 B.C.E. by Emperor Wu of the Han Dynasty. Later the Confucian Classics and other canonical Confucian texts such as the *Analects* formed the basis for the all-important civil service examination system, which allowed hundreds of thousands of individuals to attain office in the expansive bureaucracy of the Chinese empire. For more than two millennia these texts were the backbone of the training of political and cultural elites throughout East Asia and Confucius was venerated in temples as "the foremost teacher," a deity of moral perfection and learning.

Throughout its long history, Confucianism has served many political, social, and religious causes, and it has therefore also met with strident criticism. Already in the late fifth century B.C.E., Mozi, the first forceful critic of Confucius, wrote a devastating piece, "Against the Confucians," in which he parodied Confucians as "beggars, greedy hamsters, and staring he-goats who puff themselves up like wild boars." Their clothes, cries Mozi, are hopelessly old-fashioned, and they cling to the importance of ritual only because they hope to get a good meal out of the sacrificial food prepared for the occasion.

In the twentieth century, Chinese intellectuals and the Communist Party waged mass campaigns against Confucianism, considering it the utmost evil and blaming it for everything that supposedly went wrong with China's modernization. Yet many public intellectuals in Taiwan and the United States have been propagating "Neo-Confucianism" and are convinced that it can help renew humanistic values in today's harsh and cynical world. Since the 1990s the Confucius temples in mainland China have been rebuilt. Confucius is now discussed on television talk shows in China, and the Chinese government uses his name to represent China in the world. References to Confucius hovered over the Beijing Olympics of 2008, and in the first decade of the twenty-first century the government founded several hundred "Confucius Institutes" around the world, thus using the old sage as an icon for the propagation of Chinese language and culture. The future of Confucius's legacy is as bright as ever.

From Analects[1]

From *Book I*

1.1. The Master said: "To learn something and then to put it into practice at the right time: is this not a joy? To have friends coming from afar: is this not a delight? Not to be upset when one's merits are ignored: is this not the mark of a gentleman?"

1.4. Master Zeng said: "I examine myself three times a day. When dealing on behalf of others, have I been trustworthy? In intercourse with my friends, have I been faithful? Have I practiced what I was taught?"

1.11. The Master said: "When the father is alive, watch the son's aspirations. When the father is dead, watch the son's actions. If three years later, the son has not veered from the father's way, he may be called a dutiful son indeed."

1.15. Zigong said: "'Poor without servility; rich without arrogance.' How is that?" The Master said: "Not bad, but better still: 'Poor, yet cheerful; rich, yet considerate.'" Zigong said: "In the *Poems*, it is said: 'Like carving horn, like sculpting ivory, like cutting jade, like polishing stone.' Is this not the same idea?" The Master said: "Ah, one can really begin to discuss the *Poems* with you! I tell you one thing, and you can figure out the rest."

From *Book II*

2.1. The Master said: "He who rules by virtue is like the polestar, which remains unmoving in its mansion while all the other stars revolve respectfully around it."

2.2. The Master said: "The three hundred *Poems*[2] are summed up in one single phrase: 'Think no evil.'"

2.4. The Master said: "At fifteen, I set my mind upon learning. At thirty, I took my stand. At forty, I had no doubts. At fifty, I knew the will of Heaven. At sixty, my ear was attuned. At seventy, I follow all the desires of my heart without breaking any rule."

2.7. Ziyou asked about filial piety. The Master said: "Nowadays people think they are dutiful sons when they feed their parents. Yet they also feed their dogs and horses. Unless there is respect, where is the difference?"

1. Translated by Simon Leys.   **2.** Another name for the *Classic of Poetry*.

2.11. The Master said: "He who by revising the old knows the new, is fit to be a teacher."

2.19. Duke Ai[3] asked: "What should I do to win the hearts of the people?" Confucius replied: "Raise the straight and set them above the crooked, and you will win the hearts of the people. If you raise the crooked and set them above the straight, the people will deny you their support."

From *Book III*

3.5. The Master said: "Barbarians who have rulers are inferior to the various nations of China who are without."

3.21. Duke Ai asked Zai Yu which wood should be used for the local totem. Zai Yu replied: "The men of Xia used pine; the men of Yin used cypress; the men of Zhou used *fir*, for (they said) the people should *fear*."[4]

   The Master heard of this; he said: "What is done is done, it is all past; there would be no point in arguing."

3.24. The officer in charge of the border at Yi requested an interview with Confucius. He said: "Whenever a gentleman comes to these parts, I always ask to see him." The disciples arranged an interview. When it was over, the officer said to them: "Gentlemen, do not worry about his dismissal. The world has been without the Way for a long while. Heaven is going to use your master to ring the tocsin."

From *Book IV*

4.8. The Master said: "In the morning hear the Way; in the evening die content."

4.15. The Master said: "Shen, my doctrine has one single thread running through it." Master Zeng Shen replied: "Indeed."

   The Master left. The other disciples asked: "What did he mean?" Master Zeng said: "The doctrine of the Master is: Loyalty and reciprocity, and that's all."

From *Book V*

5.9. The Master asked Zigong: "Which is the better, you or Yan Hui?"[5]— "How could I compare myself with Yan Hui? From one thing he learns, he deduces ten; from one thing I learn, I only deduce two." The Master said: "Indeed, you are not his equal, and neither am I."

---

3. Ruler of the dukedom of Lu, Confucius's home state.
4. Zai Yu, one of Confucius's disciples, replies to the duke with a pun: in the original text the chestnut tree (*li*), translated here as "fir," puns on "fear" (*li*).
5. Confucius's most beloved disciple.

5.10. Zai Yu was sleeping during the day. The Master said: "Rotten wood cannot be carved; dung walls cannot be troweled. What is the use of scolding him?"

The Master said: "There was a time when I used to listen to what people said and trusted that they would act accordingly, but now I listen to what they say and watch what they do. It is Zai Yu who made me change."

5.20. Lord Ji Wen[6] always thought thrice before acting. Hearing this, the Master said: "Twice is enough."

5.26. Yan Hui and Zilu were in attendance. The Master said: "How about telling me your private wishes?"

Zilu said: "I wish I could share my carriages, horses, clothes, and furs with my friends without being upset when they damage them."

Yan Hui said. "I wish I would never boast of my good qualities or call attention to my good deeds."

Zilu said: "May we ask what are our Master's private wishes?"

The Master said: "I wish the old may enjoy peace, friends may enjoy trust, and the young may enjoy affection."

From *Book VI*

6.3. Duke Ai asked: "Which of the disciples has a love of learning?" Confucius replied: "There was Yan Hui who loved learning; he never vented his frustrations upon others; he never made the same mistake twice. Alas, his allotted span of life was short; he is dead. Now, for all I know, there is no one with such a love of learning."

6.12. Ran Qiu said: "It is not that I do not enjoy the Master's way, but I do not have the strength to follow it." The Master said: "He who does not have the strength can always give up halfway. But you have given up before starting."

6.13. The Master said to Zixia: "Be a noble scholar, not a vulgar pedant."

6.18. The Master said: "When nature prevails over culture, you get a savage; when culture prevails over nature, you get a pedant. When nature and culture are in balance, you get a gentleman."

6.20. The Master said: "To know something is not as good as loving it; to love something is not as good as rejoicing in it."

6.22. Fan Chi asked about wisdom. The Master said: "Secure the rights of the people; respect ghosts and gods, but keep them at a distance—this is wisdom indeed."

Fan Chi asked about goodness. The Master said: "A good man's trials bear fruit—this is goodness indeed."

---

6. Grand officer of the state of Lu, who lived before Confucius's time.

6.23. The Master said: "The wise find joy on the water, the good find joy in the mountains. The wise are active, the good are quiet. The wise are joyful, the good live long."

From *Book VII*

7.1. The Master said: "I transmit, I invent nothing. I trust and love the past. In this, I dare to compare myself to our venerable Peng."[7]

7.3. The Master said: "Failure to cultivate moral power, failure to explore what I have learned, incapacity to stand by what I know to be right, incapacity to reform what is not good—these are my worries."

7.5. The Master said: "I am getting dreadfully old. It has been a long time since I last saw in a dream the Duke of Zhou."[8]

7.16. The Master said: "Even though you have only coarse grain for food, water for drink, and your bent arm for a pillow, you may still be happy. Riches and honors without justice are to me as fleeting clouds."

7.21. The Master never talked of: miracles; violence; disorders; spirits.

From *Book VIII*

8.5. Master Zeng said: "Competent, yet willing to listen to the incompetent; talented, yet willing to listen to the talentless; having, yet seeming not to have; full, yet seeming empty; swallowing insults without taking offense—long ago, I had a friend who practiced these things."

8.8. The Master said: "Draw inspiration from the *Poems*; steady your course with the ritual; find your fulfillment in music."

8.13. The Master said: "Uphold the faith, love learning, defend the good Way with your life. Enter not a country that is unstable: dwell not in a country that is in turmoil. Shine in a world that follows the Way; hide when the world loses the Way. In a country where the Way prevails, it is shameful to remain poor and obscure; in a country which has lost the Way, it is shameful to become rich and honored."

8.17. The Master said: "Learning is like a chase in which, as you fail to catch up, you fear to lose what you have already gained."

---

7. Identifications of this figure vary, but venerable Peng might have been a virtuous official of the Shang Dynasty (ca. 1500–1045 B.C.E.).
8. Son of King Wen, who together with King Wu founded the Zhou Dynasty (1045–256

B.C.E.). He laid the groundwork for basic institutions of the Zhou Dynasty and is the founding ancestor of the state of Lu, Confucius's home state.

From *Book IX*

9.5. The Master was trapped in Kuang. He said: "King Wen is dead: is civilization not resting now on me? If Heaven intends civilization to be destroyed, why was it vested in me? If Heaven does not intend civilization to be destroyed, what should I fear from the people of Kuang?"[9]

9.6. The Grand Chamberlain asked Zigong: "Is your Master not a saint? But then, why should he also possess so many particular aptitudes?" Zigong replied: "Heaven indeed made him a saint; but he also happens to have many aptitudes."

Hearing of this, the Master said: "The Grand Chamberlain truly knows me. In my youth, I was poor; therefore, I had to become adept at a variety of lowly skills. Does such versatility befit a gentleman? No, it does not."

9.12. The Master was very ill. Zilu organized the disciples in a retinue, as if they were the retainers of a lord. During a remission of his illness, the Master said: "Zilu, this farce has lasted long enough. Whom can I deceive with these sham retainers? Can I deceive Heaven? Rather than die amidst retainers, I prefer to die in the arms of my disciples. I may not receive a state funeral, but still I shall not die by the wayside."

9.14. The Master wanted to settle among the nine barbarian tribes of the East. Someone said: "It is wild in those parts. How would you cope?" The Master said: "How could it be wild, once a gentleman has settled there?"

9.17. The Master stood by a river and said: "Everything flows like this, without ceasing, day and night."

9.23. The Master said: "One should regard the young with awe: how do you know that the next generation will not equal the present one? If, however, by the age of forty or fifty, a man has not made a name for himself, he no longer deserves to be taken seriously."

From *Book X*

10.2. At court, when conversing with the under ministers, he was affable; when conversing with the upper ministers, he was respectful. In front of the ruler, he was humble yet composed.

10.4. When entering the gate of the Duke's palace, he walked in discreetly. He never stood in the middle of the passage, nor did he tread on the threshold.

When he passed in front of the throne, he adopted an expression of gravity, hastened his step, and became as if speechless. When ascending the steps of the audience hall, he lifted up the hem of his gown and bowed, as if short of

---

9. Kuang was a border town where Confucius nearly fell into the hands of a lynch mob who mistook him for an adventurer who had ransacked the region. Confucius uses a pun in making his point: the name of King Wen, the founder of the Zhou Dynasty, also means "civilization" (*wen*).

breath; on coming out, after descending the first step, he expressed relief and contentment.

At the bottom of the steps, he moved swiftly, as if on wings. On regaining his place, he resumed his humble countenance.

From *Book XI*

11.9. Yan Hui died. The Master said: "Alas! Heaven is destroying me. Heaven is destroying me!"

11.10. Yan Hui died. The Master wailed wildly. His followers said: "Master, such grief is not proper." The Master said: "In mourning such a man, what sort of grief would be proper?"

11.26. Zilu, Zeng Dian, Ran Qiu, and Gongxi Chi were sitting with the Master. The Master said: "Forget for one moment that I am your elder. You often say: 'The world does not recognize our merits.' But, given the opportunity, what would you wish to do?"

Zilu rushed to reply first: "Give me a country not too small,[1] but squeezed between powerful neighbors; it is under attack and in the grip of a famine. Put me in charge: within three years, I would revive the spirits of the people and set them back on their feet."

The Master smiled. "Ran Qiu, what about you?"

The other replied: "Give me a domain of sixty to seventy—or, say, fifty to sixty leagues; within three years I would secure the prosperity of its people. As regards their spiritual well-being, however, this would naturally have to wait for the intervention of a true gentleman."

"Gongxi Chi, what about you?"

"I don't say that I would be able to do this, but I would like to learn: in the ceremonies of the Ancestral Temple, such as a diplomatic conference for instance, wearing chasuble and cap, I would like to play the part of a junior assistant."

"And what about you, Zeng Dian?"

Zeng Dian, who had been softly playing his zithern, plucked one last chord and pushed his instrument aside. He replied: "I am afraid my wish is not up to those of my three companions." The Master said: "There is no harm in that! After all, each is simply confiding his personal aspirations."

"In late spring, after the making of the spring clothes has been completed, together with five or six companions and six or seven boys, I would like to bathe in the River Yi, and then enjoy the breeze on the Rain Dance Terrace, and go home singing." The Master heaved a deep sigh and said: "I am with Dian!"

The three others left; Zeng Dian remained behind and said: "What did you think of their wishes?" The Master said: "Each simply confided his personal aspirations."

"Why did you smile at Zilu?"

---

1. Literally "a country of a thousand chariots."

"One should govern a state through ritual restraint; yet his words were full of swagger."

"As for Ran Qiu, wasn't he in fact talking about a full-fledged state?"

"Indeed; have you ever heard of 'a domain of sixty to seventy, or fifty to sixty leagues'?"

"And Gongxi Chi? Wasn't he also talking about a state?"

"A diplomatic conference in the Ancestral Temple! What could it be, if not an international gathering? And if Gongxi Chi were there merely to play the part of a junior assistant, who would qualify for the main role?"

From *Book XII*

12.2.   Ran Yong asked about humanity. The Master said: "When abroad, behave as if in front of an important guest. Lead the people as if performing a great ceremony. What you do not wish for yourself, do not impose upon others. Let no resentment enter public affairs; let no resentment enter private affairs."

Ran Yong said: "I may not be clever, but with your permission I shall endeavor to do as you have said."

12.5.   Sima Niu was grieving: "All men have brothers; I alone have none." Zixia said: "I have heard this: life and death are decreed by fate, riches and honors are allotted by Heaven. Since a gentleman behaves with reverence and diligence, treating people with deference and courtesy, all within the Four Seas are his brothers. How could a gentleman ever complain that he has no brothers?"

12.7.   Zigong asked about government. The Master said: "Sufficient food, sufficient weapons, and the trust of the people." Zigong said: "If you had to do without one of these three, which would you give up?"—"Weapons."—"If you had to do without one of the remaining two, which would you give up?"— "Food; after all, everyone has to die eventually. But without the trust of the people, no government can stand."

12.11.   Duke Jing of Qi asked Confucius about government. Confucius replied: "Let the lord be a lord; the subject a subject; the father a father; the son a son." The Duke said: "Excellent! If indeed the lord is not a lord, the subject not a subject, the father not a father, the son not a son, I could be sure of nothing anymore—not even of my daily food."

12.18.   Lord Ji Kang was troubled by burglars. He consulted with Confucius. Confucius replied: "If you yourself were not covetous, they would not rob you, even if you paid them to."

12.19.   Lord Ji Kang asked Confucius about government, saying: "Suppose I were to kill the bad to help the good: how about that?" Confucius replied: "You are here to govern, what need is there to kill? If you desire what is good, the people will be good. The moral power of the gentleman is wind, the moral power of the common man is grass. Under the wind, the grass must bend."

From *Book XIII*

13.1. Zilu asked about government. The Master said: "Guide them. Encourage them." Zilu asked him to develop these precepts. The Master said: "Untiringly."

13.3. Zilu asked: "If the ruler of Wei were to entrust you with the government of the country, what would be your first initiative?" The Master said: "It would certainly be to rectify the names." Zilu said: "Really? Isn't this a little farfetched? What is this rectification for?" The Master said: "How boorish can you get! Whereupon a gentleman is incompetent, thereupon he should remain silent. If the names are not correct, language is without an object. When language is without an object, no affair can be effected. When no affair can be effected, rites and music wither. When rites and music wither, punishments and penalties miss their target. When punishments and penalties miss their target, the people do not know where they stand. Therefore, whatever a gentleman conceives of, he must be able to say; and whatever he says, he must be able to do. In the matter of language, a gentleman leaves nothing to chance."

13.10. The Master said: "If a ruler could employ me, in one year I would make things work, and in three years the results would show."

13.11. The Master said: "'When good men have been running the country for a hundred years, cruelty can be overcome, and murder extirpated.' How true is this saying!"

13.12. The Master said: "Even with a true king, it would certainly take one generation for humanity to prevail."

13.20. Zigong asked: "How does one deserve to be called a gentleman?" The Master said: "He who behaves with honor, and, being sent on a mission to the four corners of the world, does not bring disgrace to his lord, deserves to be called a gentleman."

"And next to that, if I may ask?"

"His relatives praise his filial piety and the people of his village praise the way he respects the elders."

"And next to that, if I may ask?"

"His word can be trusted; whatever he undertakes, he brings to completion. In this, he may merely show the obstinacy of a vulgar man; still, he should probably qualify as a gentleman of lower category."

"In this respect, how would you rate our present politicians?"

"Alas! These puny creatures are not even worth mentioning!"

From *Book XIV*

14.24. The Master said: "In the old days, people studied to improve themselves. Now they study in order to impress others."

14.35. The Master said: "No one understands me!" Zigong said: "Why is it that no one understands you?" The Master said: "I do not accuse Heaven, nor do I blame men; here below I am learning, and there above I am being heard. If I am understood, it must be by Heaven."

14.38. Zilu stayed for the night at the Stone Gate. The gatekeeper said: "Where are you from?" Zilu said: "I am from Confucius's household."—"Oh, is that the one who keeps pursuing what he knows is impossible?"

14.43. Yuan Rang sat waiting, with his legs spread wide. The Master said: "A youth who does not respect his elders will achieve nothing when he grows up, and will even try to shirk death when he reaches old age: he is a parasite." And he struck him across the shin with his stick.

From *Book XV*

15.3. The Master said: "Zigong, do you think that I am someone who learns a lot of things and then stores them all up?"—"Indeed; is it not so?" The Master said: "No. I have one single thread on which to string them all."

15.5. The Master said: "Shun[2] was certainly one of those who knew how to govern by inactivity. How did he do it? He sat reverently on the throne, facing south—and that was all."

15.7. The Master said: "How straight Shi Yu was! Under a good government, he was straight as an arrow: under a bad government, he was straight as an arrow. What a gentleman was Qu Boyu![3] Under a good government, he displayed his talents. Under a bad government, he folded them up in his heart."

15.31. The Master said: "In an attempt to meditate, I once spent a whole day without food and a whole night without sleep: it was no use. It is better to study."

From *Book XVII*

17.4. The Master went to Wucheng, where Ziyou was governor. He heard the sound of stringed instruments and hymns. He was amused and said with a smile: "Why use an ox-cleaver to kill a chicken?" Ziyou replied: "Master, in the past I have heard you say: 'The gentleman who cultivates the Way loves all men; the small people who cultivate the Way are easy to govern.'" The Master said: "My friends, Ziyou is right. I was just joking."

17.9. The Master said: "Little ones, why don't you study the *Poems*? The *Poems* can provide you with stimulation and with observation, with a capacity for communion, and with a vehicle for grief. At home, they enable you to serve your father, and abroad, to serve your lord. Also, you will learn there the names of many birds, animals, plants, and trees."

17.19. The Master said: "I wish to speak no more." Zigong said: "Master, if you do not speak, how would little ones like us still be able to hand down any teachings?" The Master said: "Does Heaven speak? Yet the four seasons follow their course and the hundred creatures continue to be born. Does Heaven speak?"

---

2. Emperor of high antiquity known for his exemplary virtue. The throne usually faced south.

3. Shi Yu and Qu Boyu were both high officials in the state of Wei. Confucius was once hosted by Qu Boyu.

17.21. Zai Yu asked: "Three years mourning for one's parents—this is quite long. If a gentleman stops all ritual practices for three years, the practices will decay; if he stops all musical performances for three years, music will be lost. As the old crop is consumed, a new crop grows up, and for lighting the fire, a new lighter is used with each season. One year of mourning should be enough." The Master said: "If after only one year, you were again to eat white rice and to wear silk, would you feel at ease?"—"Absolutely."—"In that case, go ahead! The reason a gentleman prolongs his mourning is simply that, since fine food seems tasteless to him, and music offers him no enjoyment, and the comfort of his house makes him uneasy, he prefers to do without all these pleasures. But now, if you can enjoy them, go ahead!"

Zai Yu left. The Master said: "Zai Yu is devoid of humanity. After a child is born, for the first three years of his life, he does not leave his parents' bosom. Three years mourning is a custom that is observed everywhere in the world. Did Zai Yu never enjoy the love of his parents, even for three years?"

From *Book XVIII*

18.5. Jieyu, the Madman of Chu, went past Confucius, singing:

> Phoenix, oh Phoenix!
> The past cannot be retrieved,
> But the future still holds a chance
> Give up, give up!
> The days of those in office are numbered!

Confucius stopped his chariot, for he wanted to speak with him, but the other hurried away and disappeared. Confucius did not succeed in speaking to him.

18.6. Changju and Jieni were ploughing together. Confucius, who was passing by, sent Zilu to ask where the ford was. Changju said: "Who is in the chariot?" Zilu said: "It is Confucius." "The Confucius from Lu?" "Himself."— "Then he already knows where the ford is."

Zilu then asked Jieni, who replied: "Who are you?"—"I am Zilu."—"The disciple of Confucius, from Lu?"—"Yes."—"The whole universe is swept along by the same flood; who can reverse its flow? Instead of following a gentleman who keeps running from one patron to the next, would it not be better to follow a gentleman who has forsaken the world?" All the while he kept on tilling his field.

Zilu came back and reported to Confucius. Rapt in thought, the Master sighed: "One cannot associate with birds and beasts. With whom should I keep company, if not with my own kind? If the world were following the Way, I would not have to reform it."

DAODEJING / LAOZI

sixth–third centuries B.C.E.

Attributed to a master called Laozi, the *Daodejing* ("The Classic of the Way and Its Virtue") is the most often translated early Chinese text. It is also the most paradoxical, because it uses logical contradictions to articulate its vision. The *Daodejing* exhorts its readers in pithy, simple language to return to the natural way of things, to reject the corruptions of human civilization, and to adopt a productive passiveness, a stance of "nonaction," that promises unexpected success. It claims that those who understand it will preserve their lives in a dangerous world, reach their goals, and gain political power. The *Daodejing* declares at one point that its message is easy to understand, but the fact that more than seven hundred commentaries have been written on the *Daodejing* over the past 2,200 years shows that it is hardly self-explanatory. The lack of agreement among readers about the *Daodejing*'s message has only increased its popularity. It has become familiar to readers around the world thanks to the great number of translations, which sometimes differ so considerably that readers wonder whether they are all reading the same source text.

The *Daodejing* contains eighty-one short chapters written in rhythmic verse. It is divided into two main parts: one part on the "Way" (*dao*) and one part on "Virtue" (*de*). The Way refers to a natural, uncorrupted way of being that pervades everything in heaven and earth, from all beings in the cosmos to humans. Virtue is the power inherent in each thing in its natural state and the force that allows humans to reach their full potential. Both concepts were central to the intense philosophical debates initi-ated by **Confucius** (551–479 B.C.E.), and they remained important during the so-called Warring States Period (403–221 B.C.E.), when China was divided into small rival states. During this time thinkers traveled from state to state to offer political advice to rulers hungry for territory and power. The rich corpus of so-called Masters Literature, philosoph-ical texts centered around charismatic master figures, allows us to follow these masters' arguments in great detail. Much of the debate focused on how rul-ers should govern their states, and how individuals can live the best possible life. Although the thinkers of the Warring States Period did not agree about the meaning of the Way and of Virtue, they all considered these concepts impor-tant, and they discussed and debated them at length. Yet the *Daodejing* placed so much emphasis on the con-cept of *dao* that, together with **Zhuangzi**, it became the foundational text of Dao-ism, the "School of the Way." Recent excavations that produced copies of the *Daodejing* from a tomb datable to around 300 B.C.E. confirm that the text existed by that time in its more or less finished form, though the order of chap-ters differs.

Many Masters Texts argue for good government and a good life by referring to memorable historical events and peo-ple. But the *Daodejing* boldly projects its message beyond any specific time and place. Instead, it evokes cosmic cat-egories such as the Way and relies on the power not of history but of universal natural imagery: the "uncarved block," the "spirit of the valley," the "gateway of the manifold secrets," or "the mysteri-ous female." There is no identifiable speaker, except for an indefinite "I" that delivers words of wisdom as if talking from the "cosmic void." Claiming that the Way cannot be named or explained, many chapters define it negatively. They criticize conventional wisdom and elevate the values that contradict it. The *Daodejing* teaches that weakness, softness, and passivity, not force, rigidity, and assertive action, are qualities key to surviving in a dangerous world. It preaches that emptiness, not fullness; the female, not the male principle; and counterintuitive, not conventional wisdom are needed to succeed. Unlike most early Chinese texts that hurl their attacks directly against their opponents, the *Daodejing* cleverly abstains from naming rival schools of thought and thus places itself above the heated intellectual strife that surrounds it. It does not mention Confucius by name, but its polemical attack on Confucian values such as moral virtue, positive action, and refinement through education, which leads away from the state of nature, leaves no doubt that the *Daodejing* was partly written as a refutation of Confucius and his followers.

Despite its praise of weakness and nonaction, the *Daodejing* contains a powerful political philosophy and provides recipes of how to "win the empire" and how to succeed in a world of political competition and intrigue. This aspect of its message is addressed to those aspiring to become both sages and rulers: they should preserve their power by keeping the populace ignorant and manipulating them imperceptibly from above, giving the impression of not interfering but ultimately exercising absolute power.

In traditional China, the *Daodejing* was attractive because it provided a radical alternative to the Confucian vision of human morality and cultivation and was couched in poignant paradoxical formulations. Instead of arguing against the Confucian vision, it built an alternative universe that seemed to transcend the intellectual disputes of the centuries during which it was written. Although its political teachings appear abstract to the point of becoming impractical, the *Daodejing* has lost nothing of its influence. It is present in ever new editions on bookshelves around the world and variously praised as a manual of self-actualization, professional success, and leadership training in a postindustrial world.

Daodejing[1]

I

The way that can be spoken of
Is not the constant way;
The name that can be named
Is not the constant name.
The nameless was the beginning of heaven
    and earth;
The named was the mother of the myriad creatures.
Hence always rid yourself of desires in order to
    observe its secrets;
But always allow yourself to have desires in order
    to observe its manifestations.

1. Translated by D. C. Lau.

These two are the same
But diverge in name as they issue forth.   10
Being the same they are called mysteries,
Mystery upon mystery—
The gateway of the manifold secrets.

II

The whole world recognizes the beautiful as the beautiful, yet this is
    only the ugly; the whole world recognizes the good as the good,
    yet this is only the bad.
Thus Something and Nothing produce each other;
The difficult and the easy complement each other;
The long and the short off-set each other;
The high and the low incline towards each other;   5
Note and sound harmonize with each other;
Before and after follow each other.
Therefore the sage keeps to the deed that consists in taking no action
    and practises the teaching that uses no words.
The myriad creatures rise from it yet it claims no authority;
It gives them life yet claims no possession;   10
It benefits them yet exacts no gratitude;
It accomplishes its task yet lays claim to no merit.
It is because it lays claim to no merit
That its merit never deserts it.

III

Not to honor men of worth will keep the people from contention; not to
    value goods which are hard to come by will keep them from theft; not
    to display what is desirable will keep them from being unsettled of
    mind.
Therefore in governing the people, the sage empties their minds but fills
    their bellies, weakens their wills but strengthens their bones. He
    always keeps them innocent of knowledge and free from desire, and
    ensures that the clever never dare to act.
Do that which consists in taking no action, and order will prevail.

IV

The way is empty, yet use will not drain it.
Deep, it is like the ancestor of the myriad creatures.
Blunt the sharpness;
Untangle the knots;
Soften the glare;   5
Let your wheels move only along old ruts.
Darkly visible, it only seems as if it were there.
I know not whose son it is.
It images the forefather of God.

V

Heaven and earth are ruthless, and treat the myriad creatures as straw
    dogs;[2] the sage is ruthless, and treats the people as straw dogs.
Is not the space between heaven and earth like a bellows?
It is empty without being exhausted:
The more it works the more comes out.
Much speech leads inevitably to silence.   5
Better to hold fast to the void.

VI

The spirit of the valley never dies.
This is called the mysterious female.
The gateway of the mysterious female
Is called the root of heaven and earth.
Dimly visible, it seems as if it were there,   5
Yet use will never drain it.

VII

Heaven and earth are enduring. The reason why heaven and earth can be
    enduring is that they do not give themselves life. Hence they are able
    to be long-lived.
Therefore the sage puts his person last and it comes first,
Treats it as extraneous to himself and it is preserved.
Is it not because he is without thought of self that he is able to accomplish
    his private ends?

VIII

Highest good is like water. Because water excels in benefiting the myriad
    creatures without contending with them and settles where none would
    like to be, it comes close to the way.
In a home it is the site that matters;
In quality of mind it is depth that matters;
In an ally it is benevolence that matters;
In speech it is good faith that matters;   5
In government it is order that matters;
In affairs it is ability that matters;
In action it is timeliness that matters.
It is because it does not contend that it is never at fault.

XI

Thirty spokes
Share one hub.
Adapt the nothing therein to the purpose in hand, and you will have the
    use of the cart. Knead clay in order to make a vessel. Adapt the

---

2. Straw dogs were sometimes used in rituals. They were treated with great respect during the
ceremony, only to be trampled on and discarded afterward.

nothing therein to the purpose in hand, and you will have the use of
the vessel. Cut out doors and windows in order to make a room. Adapt
the nothing[3] therein to the purpose in hand, and you will have the use
of the room.

Thus what we gain is Something, yet it is by virtue of Nothing that this can
be put to use.

XII

The five colors make man's eyes blind;
The five notes make his ears deaf;
The five tastes injure his palate;
Riding and hunting
Make his mind go wild with excitement;   5
Goods hard to come by
Serve to hinder his progress.
Hence the sage is
For the belly
Not for the eye.   10
Therefore he discards the one and takes the other.

XVI

I do my utmost to attain emptiness;
I hold firmly to stillness.
The myriad creatures all rise together
And I watch their return.
The teeming creatures   5
All return to their separate roots.
Returning to one's roots is known as stillness.
This is what is meant by returning to one's destiny.
Returning to one's destiny is known as the constant.
Knowledge of the constant is known as discernment.   10
Woe to him who wilfully innovates
While ignorant of the constant,
But should one act from knowledge of the constant
One's action will lead to impartiality,
Impartiality to kingliness,   15
Kingliness to heaven,
Heaven to the way,
The way to perpetuity,
And to the end of one's days one will meet with no danger.

XVII

The best of all rulers is but a shadowy presence to his subjects.
Next comes the ruler they love and praise;
Next comes one they fear;
Next comes one with whom they take liberties.

---

3. "Nothing" in these instances refers to the empty spaces of wheels, vessels, and rooms.

When there is not enough faith, there is lack of good faith.   5
Hesitant, he does not utter words lightly.
When his task is accomplished and his work done
The people all say, 'It happened to us naturally.'

XVIII

When the great way falls into disuse
There are benevolence and rectitude;
When cleverness emerges
There is great hypocrisy;
When the six relations[4] are at variance   5
There are filial children;
When the state is benighted
There are loyal ministers.

XIX

Exterminate the sage, discard the wise,
And the people will benefit a hundredfold;
Exterminate benevolence, discard rectitude,
And the people will again be filial;
Exterminate ingenuity, discard profit,   5
And there will be no more thieves and bandits.
These three, being false adornments, are not enough
And the people must have something to which they
    can attach themselves:
Exhibit the unadorned and embrace the uncarved
    block,
Have little thought of self and as few desires as
    possible.   10

XX

Exterminate learning and there will no longer be worries.
Between yea and nay
How much difference is there?
Between good and evil
How great is the distance?   5
What others fear
One must also fear.
And wax without having reached the limit.
The multitude are joyous

4. One commentator takes them as the rela-   brother, and husband and wife.
tion between father and son, elder and younger

As if partaking of the *tai lao*[5] offering   10
Or going up to a terrace in spring.
I alone am inactive and reveal no signs,
Like a baby that has not yet learned to smile,
Listless as though with no home to go back to.
The multitude all have more than enough.   15
I alone seem to be in want.
My mind is that of a fool—how blank!
Vulgar people are clear.
I alone am drowsy.
Vulgar people are alert.   20
I alone am muddled.
Calm like the sea:
Like a high wind that never ceases.
The multitude all have a purpose.
I alone am foolish and uncouth.   25
I alone am different from others
And value being fed by the mother.

XXV

There is a thing confusedly formed,
Born before heaven and earth.
Silent and void
It stands alone and does not change,
Goes round and does not weary.   5
It is capable of being the mother of the world.
I know not its name
So I style it 'the way'.
I give it the makeshift name of 'the great'.
Being great, it is further described as receding,   10
Receding, it is described as far away,
Being far away, it is described as turning back.
Hence the way is great; heaven is great; earth is great; and the king is also
     great. Within the realm there are four things that are great, and the
     king counts as one.
Man models himself on earth,
Earth on heaven,   15
Heaven on the way,
And the way on that which is naturally so.

XXVIII

Know the male
But keep to the role of the female
And be a ravine to the empire.
If you are a ravine to the empire,

---

5. A ritual feast, where three kinds of animals—ox, sheep, and pig—were sacrificed.

Then the constant virtue will not desert you   5
And you will again return to being a babe.
Know the white
But keep to the role of the black
And be a model to the empire.
If you are a model to the empire,   10
Then the constant virtue will not be wanting
And you will return to the infinite.
Know honor
But keep to the role of the disgraced
And be a valley to the empire.   15
If you are a valley to the empire,
Then the constant virtue will be sufficient
And you will return to being the uncarved block.
When the uncarved block shatters it becomes vessels.
The sage makes use of these and becomes the lord
    over the officials.   20
Hence the greatest cutting
Does not sever.

XXXVII

The way never acts yet nothing is left undone.
Should lords and princes be able to hold fast to it,
The myriad creatures will be transformed of their
    own accord.
After they are transformed, should desire raise its
    head,
I shall press it down with the weight of the nameless
    uncarved block.   5
The nameless uncarved block
Is but freedom from desire,
And if I cease to desire and remain still,
The empire will be at peace of its own accord.

XXXVIII

A man of the highest virtue does not keep to virtue and that is why he has
    virtue. A man of the lowest virtue never strays from virtue and that is
    why he is without virtue. The former never acts yet leaves nothing
    undone. The latter acts but there are things left undone. A man of the
    highest benevolence acts, but from no ulterior motive. A man of the
    highest rectitude acts, but from ulterior motive. A man most
    conversant in the rites acts, but when no one responds rolls up his
    sleeves and resorts to persuasion by force.
Hence when the way was lost there was virtue; when virtue was lost there
    was benevolence; when benevolence was lost there was rectitude;
    when rectitude was lost there were the rites.
The rites are the wearing thin of loyalty and good faith
And the beginning of disorder;

Foreknowledge is the flowery embellishment of the way   5
And the beginning of folly.
Hence the man of large mind abides in the thick not in the thin, in the fruit
    not in the flower.
Therefore he discards the one and takes the other.

XLII

The way begets one; one begets two; two begets three; three begets the
    myriad creatures.
The myriad creatures carry on their backs the *yin* and embrace in their
    arms the *yang* and are the blending of the generative forces of the two.
There are no words which men detest more than 'solitary', 'desolate', and
    'hapless', yet lords and princes use these to refer to themselves.
Thus a thing is sometimes added to by being diminished and diminished by
    being added to.
What others teach I also teach. 'The violent will not come to a natural end.'
    I shall take this as my precept.   5

XLVIII

In the pursuit of learning one knows more every day; in the pursuit of the
    way one does less every day. One does less and less until one does
    nothing at all, and when one does nothing at all there is nothing that is
    undone.
It is always through not meddling that the empire is won. Should you
    meddle, then you are not equal to the task of winning the empire.

LXIV

It is easy to maintain a situation while it is still
    secure;
It is easy to deal with a situation before symptoms
    develop;
It is easy to break a thing when it is yet brittle;
It is easy to dissolve a thing when it is yet minute.
Deal with a thing while it is still nothing;   5
Keep a thing in order before disorder sets in.
A tree that can fill the span of a man's arms
Grows from a downy tip;
A terrace nine storeys high
Rises from hodfuls of earth;   10
A journey of a thousand miles
Starts from beneath one's feet.
Whoever does anything to it will ruin it; whoever lays hold of it will
    lose it.
Therefore the sage, because he does nothing, never ruins anything; and,
    because he does not lay hold of anything, loses nothing.
In their enterprises the people   15
Always ruin them when on the verge of success.

Be as careful at the end as at the beginning
And there will be no ruined enterprises.
Therefore the sage desires not to desire
And does not value goods which are hard to come by;   20
Learns to be without learning
And makes good the mistakes of the multitude
In order to help the myriad creatures to be natural
    and to refrain from daring to act.

LXX

My words are very easy to understand and very easy to put into practice, yet no
    one in the world can understand them or put them into practice.
Words have an ancestor and affairs have a sovereign. It is because people are
    ignorant that they fail to understand me.
Those who understand me are few;
Those who imitate me are honoured.
Therefore the sage, while clad in homespun, conceals on his person a
    priceless piece of jade.   5

LXXVI

A man is supple and weak when living, but hard and stiff when dead. Grass and
    trees are pliant and fragile when living, but dried and shrivelled when dead.
    Thus the hard and the strong are the comrades of death; the supple and
    the weak are the comrades of life.
Therefore a weapon that is strong will not vanquish;
A tree that is strong will suffer the axe.
The strong and big takes the lower position,
The supple and weak takes the higher position.   5

LXXXI

Truthful words are not beautiful; beautiful words are not truthful. Good words
    are not persuasive; persuasive words are not good. He who knows has no
    wide learning; he who has wide learning does not know.
The sage does not hoard.
Having bestowed all he has on others, he has yet more;
Having given all he has to others, he is richer still.
The way of heaven benefits and does not harm; the way of the sage is bountiful
    and does not contend.   5

SONGS OF THE SOUTH

ca. fourth century B.C.E.–second century C.E.

Whether in language or landscape, temperament or culture, the regional differences between north and south in today's China are significant. Although this north-south dynamic has taken different forms over the last three millennia, its earliest manifestation in literature is the poetry anthology *Songs of the South* (literally called *Chuci* or *Lyrics of Chu*). This collection contains a genre of poetry that flourished from the Warring States Period (403–221 B.C.E.) to the Han Dynasty (206 B.C.E.–220 C.E.) in the region of Chu, a powerful southern state on the margins of the territory controlled by the Zhou Dynasty (ca. 1045–256 B.C.E.), whose center of power was located in the north. The early Chinese dynasties developed along the Yellow River in the north: China's earliest poetry anthology, the **Classic of Poetry** (ca. 600 B.C.E.), contained hymns in praise of the early rulers of the Zhou Dynasty, and interpretations of this classic emphasized Confucian values of moral virtue and wise statecraft. Although the state of Chu had close links to the north, the *Songs of the South* are remarkably distinct from the northern tradition of poetry. In contrast to the unadorned, earthy poems of the *Classic of Poetry*, the *Songs of the South* seduce the reader into a mythical realm where shamans, gods, and rulers of high antiquity mingle freely, surrounded by exotic flora or flying through the air on dragons with floating rainbow banners, unencumbered by gravity or historical chronology. The poetic geography of the *Songs of the South* gave southern China a lush and vibrant face for ages to come.

While the poems in the *Classic of Poetry* are anonymous, the central poems of the *Songs of the South* have been attributed to the tragic hero Qu Yuan (ca. 340–278 B.C.E.). He is considered the first lyric poet of China. Eight of the seventeen poetry cycles included in the *Songs of the South* are attributed to this aristocratic statesman, who was slandered by envious rivals. He lost the favor of King Huai, was banished under Huai's successor, and ultimately drowned himself in the Miluo River in despair.

Our knowledge of Qu Yuan is based on two wildly different accounts. We have the historian Sima Qian's (ca. 145–85 B.C.E.) biography of Qu Yuan, which portrays Qu Yuan as a loyal minister with political foresight, someone entangled in the unification conquests launched by the state of Qin. Qu Yuan understands the military ambitions of Qin and predicts Chu's downfall. The kings of Chu ignore Qu Yuan's repeated warnings against Qin's aggressive militarism, but half a century after Qu Yuan's death his prophecy comes true: Qin completes the conquest of the remaining Zhou feudal states, and establishes an unprecedented autocratic regime.

But there is also the image of Qu Yuan that can be derived from "Encountering Sorrow," the longest poem in the *Songs of the South*. Here, Qu Yuan is a superhuman being who moves smoothly through time and space: he expounds on his moral worth (expressed for example in the fragrance of flowers), revels in spirit travel through the cosmos, and, in the end, abruptly announces his wish to die. The intensely lyric lament of "Encountering

Sorrow" lacks a historical or political setting. Its urgent expression of despair comes from the voice of a human, but the methods of this voice's attempt to gain recognition in a corrupt world are supernatural and allegorical. Comparing the Qu Yuan in the poem "Encountering Sorrow" and the Qu Yuan in Sima Qian's historical biography gives insight into the remarkable life of one extraordinary person—both historical and supernatural. It also shows the emergence of the figure of the unsuccessful, loyal scholar-official, who suffers injustice and uses writing as an alternative means to gain immortality. This figure became tremendously successful in Chinese history and resonates still today with intellectuals who feel at odds with Chinese society.

Qu Yuan lived in the waning days of the Zhou Dynasty, when seven larger states, which were only nominally subservient to the weak Zhou kings, engaged in constant warfare with mass armies that grew ever more technologically advanced. The southern state of Chu became one of the largest and most powerful among them. But it was ultimately unable to resist the militaristic northern state of Qin, which managed to conquer all other Chinese states by 221 B.C.E., leading to the foundation of the first unified Chinese empire. Although the state of Chu was thus integrated into the Qin and Han empires, it remained a distinctive cultural force, and the southern princely courts became a lively stage for thinkers and poets as well as for adepts of Daoism. By the second century C.E., a certain Wang Yi (d. 158 C.E.), who had access to the Han imperial library, compiled the poems attributed to Qu Yuan and his later followers into the *Songs of the South*. He also added a detailed commentary and included his own poetry at the end of the anthology, as a closure to four centuries of poetic production in the style of Qu Yuan.

No one will ever fully understand the nature and origin of the oldest pieces in the *Songs of the South,* and the debates about Qu Yuan's historical identity and his relation to the poems in the anthology are not likely to reach any firm conclusions. It is best to think of the poems as part of a dramatic repertoire, which grew out of liturgical songs performed at shamanistic rituals. The main elements of the Qu Yuan narrative correspond to the stages of the relationship between a shaman-lover and a deity: the lover laments being neglected by the deity, makes a case for his beauty and worth, and then goes on a spirit quest through the cosmos. The oldest works in the *Songs of the South,* the "Nine Songs" (three are represented in our selections), portray ritual celebrations, whose speakers perform the role of deities or take a shamanistic mediator role to communicate with deities. Many plot elements from the "Nine Songs" resurface in "Encountering Sorrow." Flowers feature in the "Nine Songs" as adornments of deities or as decoration used during ritual celebrations; cosmic travels of (or in pursuit of) the beloved play an important role, as do tantalizing erotic encounters with a deity who turns his back on the anxious lover.

"Encountering Sorrow" is an idiosyncratic and seductive poem that puts considerable strains on its readers. Although the speaker tells of his plight with captivating intimacy, "Encountering Sorrow" does not have a unified voice. We can only make sense of this plaintive monologue once we discern the multiple personalities inhabiting its voice: there is the humiliated aristocrat, who seeks employment and recognition by a worthy ruler—this voice resonates with Sima Qian's historical account of Qu Yuan. But there is also the spirit traveler who is able to hitch dragons to tour the heavens and meet sage rulers who lived many centuries ago—this voice is closer to the fantastic portrait of deities in the "Nine Songs." Also, the speaker alternates between pursuing worthy rulers and beautiful women. He speaks as a passionate gardener, real and metaphorical: the Qu Yuan of "Encountering Sorrow" with his aristocratic pride is linked to notions of fragrance and purity. He plants exquisite flowers like orchids and sweet angelica, feeds on petals of chrysanthemums, wears waterlily robes, and even uses lotus as tissue paper to wipe his tears. (The plant names are translated for poetic flavor rather than botanical precision, since much of the early Chinese flora has no correlative in literary English.) The speaker claims to possess a sort of "moral perfume," which he contrasts with the stinky vulgarity of envious weeds and treacherous plants, kennings for his enemies at court. Thus, what is considered the first individual lyric voice of the Chinese literary tradition is, ironically, a polyphony of identities, some of them not even human.

It is hard to overstate the importance of the *Songs of the South*. They furnished themes, styles, and imagery for China's oldest properly literary genre,

the rhapsody. They provided religious metaphors for immortality techniques, propagated by Daoists who promised the possibility of physical transformation into winged immortals through a combination of bodily control, alchemy, and diet; and they profoundly shaped the way later poetry and landscape writing translated visual imagination into text.

The *Songs of the South* are enthrallingly visual. Over the last few decades, the traditional literary image of Chu has been complemented in unexpected ways by thousands of objects dating to the Warring States Period and Han Dynasty that archaeologists have unearthed in the region of the ancient state of Chu. The mysterious mythological scenes and entangled patterns of plants and fabled animals—dragons, phoenixes, tigers, serpent-shaped deities—are reminiscent of Qu Yuan's entourage on his travel through the cosmos. Although they do not solve the many riddles of this complex text, these newly discovered remainders of Chu culture confirm the strong cultural identity conveyed by the extraordinary *Songs of the South*.

From The Nine Songs[1]

Lord in the Clouds

In orchid baths bathed,   hair washed in blooms' scent,
our robes are resplendent,   with lavender flowers.
The holy one writhes,   he lingers within her,
she glows with a nimbus,   his light is unbounded.
He shall be here transfixed   in the Temple of Life,   5
He whose rays are the equal   of sun and the moon;
in his dragon-drawn cart,   the garb of the god,
he soars in his circles   around and around.

1. Translated by and with notes adapted from Stephen Owen.

The holy one glistens,   for he has come down;
he lifts up in a gust,   afar into clouds.   10
He scans all the heartland   and far off beyond,
across seas on each side;   where does he end?
We yearn for our Lord   and heave a great sigh,
hearts greatly troubled,   and fretful within.

The Lord of the East

"I glow coming forth   in the eastlands,
I shine on my porch   by the tree Fusang,[2]
then slapping my steeds   to a steady gallop,
the night is lit up,   and the day breaks.

My dragon team hitched,   I ride on the thunder,   5
bearing banners of cloud   streaming behind.
But I heave a great sigh   on the point of ascending;
there the heart falters,   I look back with care:
for the sounds and beauty   so give a man joy
those who watch are transfixed   and forget to go.   10

Harps tightly strung,   the drums alternating,
bells being rung,   chime frames shaking,
fifes sing out,   pipes are blown;
those who act holy ones,   wholesome and comely,
hover here winging,   suddenly mount,   15
reciting the lyrics   joining in dance.

Catching the pitch,   matching the rhythms,
the holy ones come,   they cover the sun.
In gown of green cloud   and white rainbow mantle,
I raise the long arrow,   I shoot Heaven's Wolf,   20
with yew-bow in hand   I now sink back under,
and seize the North Dipper   to pour cinnamon wine,
then clutching my reins,   I rush soaring high,
    off far through darkness   voyaging east."

The Hill Wraith

It seemed there was someone   in the cleft of the hills,
her mantle was hanging moss,   she was girded with ivy,
her eyes glanced upon me,   her mouth formed a smile;
"You who yearn for me,   who am so comely—

I ride the red leopard,   striped lynxes attend me,   5
with magnolia-wood wagon,   my flags, plaited cassia,
my cloak is stone-orchid,   my sash is asarum,
I snap the sweet fragrance,   gift for him that I love."

---

2. The sun rose from the Fusang tree in the east.

She dwells in bamboo's darkness,   she never sees sky;
the way was steep and hard,   late she came and alone.   10

Alone she stands forth,   high on the hill,
with clouds' rolling billows   there down below her;
it grows dim and blacker,   daylight turns dark,
and in gustings of east wind   the goddess rains.
I remain for the holy one,   transfixed, forget going,   15
the year has grown late,   who will clothe me in flowers?

I picked three-bloom asphodel   out in the hills,
on slopes rough and rocky,   through tangles of vines;
reproaching the Lady,   I in grief forget going,
for though she may love me,   she does not find time.   20

In the hills there is someone,   sweet smell of lavender,
she drinks from the stone-springs   in shadow of pines

and though she may love me,   she holds back unsure.
The sky shakes in thunder,   with darkness comes rain,
the apes are all wailing,   in the night monkeys moan;   25
the whistling of winds   that howl through the trees;
I long for the Lady,   fruitless torment I find.

Encountering Sorrow[1]

1

Of the god-king Gaoyang   I am the far offspring,[2]
my late honored sire   bore the name of Boyong.
The *sheti* stars[3] aimed   to the year's first month;
gengyin was the day   that I came down.[4]

2

He scanned and he delved   into my first measure,   5
from the portents my sire   gave these noble names:
The name that he gave me   was Upright Standard;
and my title of honor   was Godly Poise.[5]

---

1. Translated by and with notes adapted from Stephen Owen.
2. Gaoyang was one of the mythic emperors of high antiquity, from whom the Chu royal house claimed ancestry. Though not the ruling family, Qu Yuan's clan, the Qu, was one of the three royal clans of Chu and descended from Gaoyang.
3. A constellation by whose position early astronomers determined the beginning of the year.
4. *Gengyin* is the precise day in the sixty-day cycle, which the Chinese used to count time.
5. To choose a name, the father reads his son's "measure," based either on astronomical conjunctions of his birth or on his physiognomy. These "noble names" are not usually associated with Qu Yuan.

3

Such bounty I had   of beauty within,
and to this was added   fair countenance.   10
I wore mantles of river rush   and remote angelica,
strung autumn orchids   to hang from my sash.

4

They fled swiftly from me,   I could not catch them—
I feared the years passing   would keep me no company.
At dawn I would pluck   magnolia on bluffs,   15
in the twilight on isles   I called undying herbs.

5

Days and months sped past,   they did not long linger,
springtimes and autumns   altered in turn.
I thought on things growing,   on the fall of their leaves,
and feared for the Fairest,   her drawing toward dark.[6]   20

6

Cling to your prime,   forsake what is rotting—
why not change   from this measure of yours?
Mount a fine steed,   go off at a gallop—
I will now take the lead,   ride ahead on the road.

7

The Three Kings of old   were pure and unblemished,[7]   25
all things of sweet scent   indeed were theirs.
Shen's pepper was there,   together with cassia,
white angelica, sweet clover   were not strung alone.

8

Such shining grandeur   had Kings Yao and Shun;
they went the true way,   they held to the path.   30
But sloven and scruffy   were Kings Jie and Zhou;
they walked at hazard   on twisted trails.[8]

---

6. The "fairest" is the Chu king in the figure of
a beautiful woman. Thus Qu Yuan's later quest
for a mate is taken as a search for a prince who
will appreciate his worth and employ him.
7. This might refer to three earlier kings of
Chu, although interpretations vary.
8. Yao and Shun were two sage kings of high
antiquity much revered in northern China. In
the southern Chu tradition they play a quasi-
religious role. The speaker later goes to visit
Shun, or Zhonghua, who was supposedly buried at Cangwu in Chu (stanza 47), in order to
lodge his plaint. Yao's two daughters married
Shun and became river goddesses after Shun's
death. Jie and Zhou were the last kings of two
early dynasties and known as exemplarily bad
rulers.

9

Those men of faction   had ill-gotten pleasures,
their paths went in shadow,   narrow, unsafe.
Not for myself   came this dread of doom—   35
I feared my king's chariot   soon would be tipped.

10

In haste I went dashing   in front and behind,
till I came to the tracks   of our kings before.
Lord Iris[9] did not fathom   my nature within,
he believed ill words,   he glowered in rage.   40

11

I knew well my bluntness   had brought me these woes,
yet I bore through them,   I could not forswear.
I pointed to Heaven   to serve as my warrant,
it was all for the cause   of the Holy One.

12

To me at first   firm word had been given,   45
she regretted it later,   felt otherwise.
I made no grievance   at this break between us,
but was hurt that the Holy One   so often changed.

13

I watered my orchids   in all their nine tracts,
and planted sweet clover   in one hundred rods;   50
I made plots for peonies   and for the wintergreen,
mixed with asarum   and sweet angelica.

14

I wished stalks and leaves   would stand high and flourish,
I looked toward the season   when I might reap.
If they withered and dried,   it would cause me no hurt,   55
I would grieve if such sweetness   went rotting in weeds.

15

Throngs thrust themselves forward   in craving and want,
they never are sated   in things that they seek.
They show mercy to self,   by this measure others,
in them the heart stirs   to malice and spite.   60

9. Kenning for the king, now figured as a male deity.

16

Such a headlong horse race,   each hot in pursuit,
is not a thing   that thrills my own heart.
Old age comes on steadily,   soon will be here,
I fear my fair name   will not be fixed firmly.

17

At dawn I drank dew   that dropped on magnolia,   65
in twilight ate blooms   from chrysanthemums shed.
If my nature be truly comely,   washed utterly pure,
what hurt can I have   in long wanness from hunger?

18

I plucked tendrils of trees   to knot white angelica,
pierced fallen pistils   of flowering ivy.   70
I reached high to cassia   for stringing sweet clover,
and corded the coilings   of the rope vine.

19

Yes, I took as my rule   those fair men before me,
it was not the garb worn   in the ways of our age.
Though it did not agree   with men of these days,   75
I would rest in the pattern   left by Peng and by Xian.[1]

20

Long did I sigh   and wipe away tears,
sad that men's lives   lay in such peril.
Though love of the fair   was the halter that guided me,
at dawn I was damned   and by twilight, undone.   80

21

Yes, I was undone   for sash hung with sweet clover,
then I added to it   the angelica and orchid.
Still my heart   will find goodness in these—
though I die many times,   I will never regret.

22

I reproach the Holy One's   unbridled rashness,   85
never discerning   what lies in men's hearts.

---

1. Peng and Xian were two legendary shaman ancestors. Here and in the poem's last line traditional commentators often took them as a single name. Peng Xian, a worthy adviser to a king of the Shang Dynasty (ca. 1500–1045 B.C.E.), drowned himself in despair, thus suffering a fate similar to Qu Yuan's.

Women-throngs envied   my delicate brows,
they made scurrilous songs,   they said I loved lewdness.

23

Of these times the firm folkways: to be skillful in guile;
facing compass and square,   they would alter the borehole.   90
They forswear the straight line,   go chasing the crooked;
rivals for false faces,   such is their measure.

24

A woe wells within me,   to be so hapless,
alone at an impasse   in times such as these.
Best to die promptly,   to vanish away,   95
for I cannot bear   to show myself thus.

25

The great bird of prey   does not go in flocks,
so it has been   from times long ago.
The square and the circle   can never be matched,
what man can find peace   on a way not his own?   100

26

Bending one's heart,   quelling one's will,
abiding faults found,   submitting to shame,
embracing pure white,   death for the right—
these indeed were esteemed   by wise men before us.

27

I regretted my course   was not well discerned,   105
long I stood staring,   about to go back.
I turned my coach round   along the same path—
it was not yet too far   I had strayed in my going.

28

I let horses walk   through meadows of orchids,
to a hill of pepper trees I raced,   there rested the while,   110
I drew close, did not reach him,   I met with fault-finding,
I withdrew to restore   that garb I first wore.

29

Waterlilies I fashioned   to serve as my robe,
I gathered the lotus   to serve as my skirt.
Let it be over then,   no man knows me,   115
my nature in truth   has a scent sweet and steadfast.

30

High was my hat,   above me it loomed,
well strung, the pendants   that swung from my sash.
Sweet scent and stench   were all intermingled,
this gleaming flesh only   suffered no dwindling.   120

31

All at once I looked back,   and I let my eyes roam,
I would go off to view   the wild lands around.
Pendants in bunches,   I was richly adorned,
their sweet fragrance spread,   ever more striking.

32

Each man has a thing   in which he finds joy:
I alone love the fair,   in that I abide.   125
Though my limbs be cut from me,   I still will not change,
for how could my heart   be made to cower?

33

Then came the Sister,   tender and distressed,[2]
mild of manner   she upbraided me thus,   130
she said: "Gun was unyielding,   he fled into hiding,
at last died untimely   on moors of Mount Yu.[3]

34

"Why such wide culling,   such love of the fair,
in you alone bounty   of beautiful raiment?
Haystacks of stinkweed   are heaped in their rooms;   135
you alone stand aloof   and refuse such attire.

35

"No swaying the throngs   person by person;
None says: 'Come, discern   this my nature within!'
Now men rise together,   each favors his friends,
why do you stand alone—why not listen to me?"   140

36

I trust sages before us   for moderate judgment,
my heart swelled in torment,   it had come now to this,

---

2. Although "Sister" was often interpreted as
Qu Yuan's actual sister, it might be a title rather
than a proper name. It is unclear whether to
read this in the literal or figurative sense.
3. Gun, here a figure of fatal stubbornness,

was a son of Gao Yang, who was charged by the
sage-king Yao with controlling the great flood.
When he failed, he was executed and his body
abandoned on Mount Yu.

I crossed Xiang and Yuan,   faring on southward,
reached Zhonghua, King Shun,   to state him my case:

37

"King Qi had Nine Stanzas   and the Nine Songs—   145
extreme in wild pleasures,   he did as he pleased.
He was heedless of troubles,   made no plans for the morrow,
whereby the five sons   brought strife to his house.[4]

38

"Yi recklessly ventured,   he was lavish in hunts,
he also loved shooting   the great foxes.   150
Such turbulent wickedness   rarely ends well:
and Han Zhuo was lusting   to seize his bride.[5]

39

"Guo Ao garbed himself   in the stiffened leather;
he followed his wants,   he failed to forbear.
He lost himself daily   in wild pleasures,   155
whereby his own head   was toppled and fell.[6]

40

"Xia's Jie was steadfast   in his misdeeds,
in pursuit of these   he met with his doom.
Shang's Zhow, the Lord Xin,   minced men to stew,
whereby Yin's great lineage   could not last long.[7]   160

41

"Yu the Mighty was stern,   respectful and godly;[8]
the right way was Zhou's norm,   it thus did not err.
They raised men of worth,   rewarded the able,
they kept the straight line,   they did not veer.

42

"Sovereign Heaven is slanted   in favor of none;   165
it discerns a man's virtues,   puts helpers beside him.

4. King Qi was the son of Gun's son, the Great Yu, who finally tamed the great flood and founded the Xia Dynasty. He brought back the "Nine Songs" from Heaven.

5. Yi the Archer seized the kingship after King Qi's death, but was subsequently killed by his retainer Han Zhuo.

6. Yet a further step in the genealogy of the Xia Dynasty: Guo Ao was a son of Han Zhuo and Yi the Archer's stolen bride. He was killed by Shao Gang, who restored the Xia Dynasty.

7. Jie was the last ruler of the Xia Dynasty and notorious for his misrule. Zhow was the depraved last ruler of the subsequent dynasty, the Shang (also called Yin).

8. The speaker returns to the Great Yu, Gun's son and founder of the Xia Dynasty.

When wisdom and sense   do deeds that are splendid,
they may then act their will   in this land down below.

43

"I scanned times before us,   looked to times yet to come,
read the measures of men,   and the ends of their plans: 170
who found wanting in virtue   may be put to use?
who found wanting in good   may be still retained?

44

"By the brink stands my body,   I am in death's peril,
I discern my first nature   and still regret not.
Not judging the drillhole,   they squared the peg: 175
indeed, fair men of old   came to mince in a stew.

45

"Sighs come from me often,   the heart swells within,
sad that I and these times   never will be matched.
I plucked sage and lotus   to wipe away tears,
that soak my gown's folds   in their streaming."   180

46

I knelt with robes open,   thus stated my case,
having grasped so clearly   what is central and right,
I teamed jade white dragons,   rode the Bird that Hides Sky,
waiting on winds   to fleetly fare upward.

47

At dawn I loosed wheel-block   there by Cangwu   185
and by twilight I reached   the Gardens of Air.[9]
I wished to bide a while   by the windows of gods,
but swift was the sun   and it soon would be dusk.

48

I bade sun-driver Xihe,   to pause in her pace,
to stand off from Yanzi   and not to draw nigh.[1]   190
On and on stretched my road,   long it was and far,
I would go high and go low   in this search that I made.

9. Cangwu was the mountain where the sage-king Shun was buried. Shun was the successor of the sage-king Yao, who had employed Gun to fight the great flood. On his cosmic travels Qu Yuan had just visited Shun (also called Zhonghua) in the preceding ten stanzas to state his case. The "Gardens of Air" were a section of the Kunlun Mountain Range in western China, a region associated with immortals.
1. Xihe is the goddess who drives the sun's chariot across the sky. Mount Yanzi is located in the extreme west, where the sun goes down; thus, the poet is ordering the sun not to set.

49

I watered my horses   in the Pools of Xian,
and twisted the reins   on the tree Fusang,
snapped a branch of the Ruo Tree   to block out the sun,   195
I roamed freely the while   and lingered there.[2]

50

Ahead went Wang Shu   to speed on before me,
behind came Fei Lian,   he dashed in my train.[3]
Phoenix went first   and warned of my coming,
Thunder Master told me   that all was not set.   200

51

I bade my phoenixes   mount up in flight,
to continue their going   both by day and by night.
Then the whirlwinds massed,   drawing together,
they marshaled cloud-rainbows,   came to withstand me.

52

A bewildering tumult,   first apart, then agreeing,   205
and they streamed flashing colors,   high and then low.
I bade the God's gatekeeper   open the bar;
he stood blocking gateway   and stared at me.

53

The moment grew dimmer,   light soon would be done,
I tied signs in orchids,   standing there long.   210
An age foul and murky   cannot tell things apart;
it loves to block beauty   from malice and spite.

54

At dawn I set to fare   across the White Waters,
I climbed Mount Langfeng,   there tethered my horses.[4]
All at once I looked back,   my tears were streaming,   215
sad that the high hill   lacked any woman.

55

At once I went roaming   to the Palace of Spring,
I broke sprays of garnet   to add to my pendants.

2. When rising the sun is bathed in the Pools of
Xian and comes out at the base of the Fusang
tree. The Ruo tree is at the opposite side of the
world, where the sun sets.

3. Wang Shu was the driver of the moon, Fei
Lian the god of winds.
4. White Waters and Mount Langfeng are
sections of the Kunlun Range.

Before the blooms' glory   had fallen away,
I would seek a woman below   to whom I might give them.[5]   220

56

Feng Long I bade   to go riding the clouds,
to seek out Fufei   down where she dwells.[6]
I took pendant-sash,   I tied there a message,
and bade Lady Mumbler   act as my envoy.

57

A bewildering tumult,   first apart, then agreeing,   225
she suddenly balked,   she could not be swayed.
She went twilights to lodge   at Farthest-of-Rocks,
and at dawn bathed her hair   in Weiban Stream.[7]

58

She presumed on her beauty,   she was scornful and proud,
in wild pleasures daily   she wantonly strayed.   230
Though beautiful truly,   she lacked right behavior—
I let her go then,   I sought for another.

59

I let my gaze sweep   over all the world's ends,
I roamed throughout Sky,   then I came down.
I viewed the surging crest   of a terrace of onyx,   235
there saw a rare woman,   the You-Song's daughter.[8]

60

I bade the venom-owl   make match between us,
and the venom-owl told me   she was not fair.
Early summer's dove-cock   went away singing,
and I still loathe   its petty wiles.   240

61

My heart then faltered,   doubts overcame me,
I wanted to go myself;   it was not allowed.

5. "Woman below" probably refers here to Fufei as a river goddess.
6. Feng Long was the god of clouds and thunder, Fufei the goddess of the river Luo, near Luoyang in the northeast, the capital of the Zhou Dynasty (ca. 1045–256 B.C.E.), during which Qu Yuan lived.

7. The goddess has apparently wandered to the far west, to the Weiban Stream next to the Ruo Stream, where the sun sets.
8. The mother of the ancestor of the royal house of the Shang Dynasty. She was a gift from the You-Song, the main clan of the Song tribes, to Gao Xin.

Already the phoenix   had given my troth gifts,
still I feared that Gao Xin   had come before me.[9]

62

I wanted to alight far away,   there was no place to halt,   245
so I drifted the while   and roamed at my ease.
If still not yet married   to Shaokang the Prince,
there remained the two Yao girls   of the clan You-Yu.[1]

63

My envoy was feeble,   my matchmaker bumbling;
I feared words to charm them   would not hold fast.   250
An age foul and murky,   it spites a man's worth,
it loves to block beauty,   it acclaims what is ill.

64

Remote and far   are the chambers of women;
and the wise king also   is not yet aware.
I keep feelings within me,   do not bring them forth,   255
yet how can I bear   that it be thus forever?

65

I sought stalks of milfoil,   and slips to cast lots,
and bade Holy Fen   to divine the thing for me.
I said:
"Two lovely beings   must surely be matched;   260
whose fairness is steadfast   that I may adore her?

66

"Consider the wide sweep   of these Nine Domains—
can it be only here   that a woman be found?"
He said:
"Undertake to fare far,   be not full of doubts;   265
none who seeks beauty   would let you slip by.

67

"Is there any place lacking   in plants of sweet fragrance?
why must you cherish   your former abode?
This age is a dark one,   eyes are dazzled and blinded,
no man can discern   our good or our bad.   270

9. Gao Xin married the woman from the Song tribes. The speaker's courtship of "You-Song's daughter" fails because, in high antiquity long before Qu Yuan's time, she married Gao Xin.

1. Ousted by a rival, Shaokang, rightful heir to the Xia throne, fled to the You-Yu, the main clan of the Yu tribes, whose ruler gave him his two daughters in marriage.

68

"What men love and loathe   is never the same—
only these men of faction   alone stand apart.
Each person wears mugwort,   stuffed in their waists,
they declare that the orchid   may never be strung.

69

"If in judgment of plants   they still cannot grasp it,   275
can they ever be right   on the beauty of gems?
They seek shit and mire   to stuff their sachets,
and say that Shen's pepper   lacks any sweet smell."

70

I wished to follow Holy Fen's   lot of good fortune,
yet still my heart faltered,   doubts overcame me.
The Shaman Xian   would descend in the twilight,[2]   280
I clasped pepper and rice   to beseech him.

71

The gods blotted sky,   their full hosts descending,
spirit vassals of Many Doubts   joined to go greet them.[3]
In a light-burst the Sovereign   sent forth his spirit,   285
giving me word   of a lucky outcome.

72

He said:
"Undertake to fare high   and then to fare low,
find one who agrees   with the yardstick and square.
Yu the Mighty was stern,   he sought one who matched him,   290
he held to Gao Yao   as one able to suit him.[4]

73

"If one's nature within   loves what is fair,
what need to make use   of matchmaker or envoy?
Yue held an earth-ram   upon Fu's cliff;
Wuding employed him   and did not doubt.[5]   295

74

"Once there was Lü Wang   who swung a butcher's knife,
yet he met Zhou's King Wen   and he was raised up.

2. The Shaman Xian mentioned in stanza 19.
3. "Many Doubts" (literally "Nine Doubts") was the mountain range in the south where the sage-king Shun was supposedly buried.
4. Again, the Great Yu, who tamed the flood and founded the Xia Dynasty. Gao Yao was a worthy minister of the Great Yu.
5. King Wuding of the Shang Dynasty found a labor convict named Yue on Fu Cliff and recruited him as minister.

And there was Ning Qi,   a singer of songs;
Huan of Qi heard him;   he served as the helper.[6]

75

"Yet act now before   the year grows too late,   300
now while the season   has not yet passed.
I fear only cries early   from summer's nightjar,
making all plants   lose their sweet scent."

76

My pendants of garnet,   how they dangle down from me—
yet the throngs would dim them,   cover them up.   305
These men of faction   are wanting in faith,
I fear their malice,   that they will break them.

77

The times are in tumult,   ever transforming—
how then may a man   linger here long?
Orchid, angelica change,   they become sweet no more;   310
Iris, sweet clover alter,   they turn into straw.

78

These plants that smelled sweet   in days gone by
have now become nothing   but stinking weeds.
Can there be any reason   other than this?—
the harm that is worked   by no love for the fair.   315

79

I once thought that orchid   could be steadfast:
it bore me no fruit,   it was all show.
Forsaking its beauty,   it followed the common;
it wrongly is ranked   in the hosts of sweet scent.

80

Pepper is master of fawning,   it is swaggering, reckless,   320
only mock-pepper stuffs   sachets hung from waists.
It pressed hard to advance,   it struggled for favor,
what sweet scent remains   that is able to spread?

6. Like Yue these are figures of worthy officials recruited in unexpected places. Lü Wang was first a butcher, then a fisherman before being discovered by a king of the Zhou Dynasty in old age and made a minister. Ning Qi was a petty merchant who would perform songs as he rapped the horns of his buffalo. Duke Huan of Qi heard of his worth and made him his aide.

81

Truly, ways of these times⠀⠀are willful and loose,
who now is able⠀⠀to avoid being changed?⠀⠀⠀⠀⠀325
Look on orchid and pepper,⠀⠀see them like this—
will less be true⠀⠀of river rush and wintergreen?

82

Only these my own pendants⠀⠀are still to be prized;
forsaken is loveliness,⠀⠀and I come to this.
Yet their sweet scent spreads,⠀⠀it is not diminished,⠀⠀330
an aroma that even now⠀⠀has still not abated.

83

In their blending's balance⠀⠀I take my delight,
I will drift and will roam,⠀⠀seeking the woman.
And while such adornment⠀⠀is still in its glory,
I will range widely looking,⠀⠀both high and low.⠀⠀⠀335

84

Since Holy Fen told me⠀⠀my fortunate lot,
I will choose a luck-day,⠀⠀and I will set out.
I snap sprays of garnet⠀⠀to serve as my viands,
fine garnet meal⠀⠀will serve as my fare.

85

For me have been hitched⠀⠀those dragons that fly,⠀⠀⠀340
mixed onyx and ivory⠀⠀serve as my coach.
How can a mind set apart⠀⠀be ever like others?
I will go away far,⠀⠀keep myself removed.

86

I bent my way round⠀⠀at Kunlun Mountain,
long and far was the road,⠀⠀there I ranged widely.⠀⠀345
I raised my cloud-rainbows,⠀⠀dimming and darkening,
jade phoenix chimes rang⠀⠀with a jingling voice.

87

At dawn I loosed the wheel-block⠀⠀at Ford-of-the-Sky,[7]
by twilight I came⠀⠀to the ends of the west.
Phoenix spread its wings,⠀⠀and bore up my banners,⠀⠀350
high aloft it soared,⠀⠀its wingbeats were steady.

7. The narrowest point in the Milky Way.

88

All at once I was facing   across Drifting Sands,
I went down the Red Waters,   there took my ease.[8]
I signaled the dragons   to make me a bridge,
I called to West's Sovereign   to take me across.   355

89

Long and far was the road,   it was filled with perils,
I passed word to my hosts: drive straight and attend me.
I made way to Mount Buzhou,   there turned to the left,
toward the Sea of the West,   my appointed goal.[9]

90

Then I massed all my chariots,   a thousand strong,   360
jade hubs lined even,   we galloped together.
I hitched my eight dragons,   heaving and coiling,
and bore my cloud banners   streaming behind.

91

I then quelled my will   and paused in my pace;
the gods galloped high   far to the distance,   365
they were playing "Nine Songs"   and dancing "the Shao,"[1]
making use of this day   to take their delight.

92

I was mounting aloft   to such dazzling splendor—
all at once I glanced down   to my homeland of old.
My driver grew sad,   my horses felt care,   370
they flexed looking backward   and would not go on.

The Ending Song

It is done now forever!
in all the kingdom there is no man,   no man who knows me,
then why should I care   for that city, my home?
Since no one can join me   in making good rule,   375
I will go off to seek   where Peng and Xian dwell.[2]

---

8. "Drifting Sands" is a general term for the
imagined terrors of China's northwestern deserts. The Red Waters flowed off to the Kunlun
Range in the far west.
9. Mount Buzhou is a mythical mountain in
the far west.
1. Ancient ceremonial music and dance. These

"Nine Songs" are a legendary repertoire and not
the shamanistic hymns given earlier in this
poem.
2. As in stanza 19, this refers either to Peng and
Xian, two legendary shamans, or to Peng Xian, a
worthy adviser to a king of the Shang Dynasty.

ZHUANGZI

fourth–second centuries B.C.E

The *Zhuangzi*, a text attributed to a figure called Zhuangzi (ca. 369–286 B.C.E), is the most iridescent example of early Chinese Masters Literature. Conveying wisdom about how to live a good life in a world filled with violence and conceit, the rich philosophical genre of Masters Literature flourished for half a millennium, beginning at the time of **Confucius** (551–479 B.C.E). Next to the *Daodejing* ("The Classic of the Way and Its Virtue," attributed to a master called **Laozi**), the *Zhuangzi* is considered the second most foundational text of Daoist philosophy. For Zhuangzi the good life was one of freedom from societal bounds, spent far away from political obligation, in blissful accordance with the *dao,* the "natural Way." As Zhuangzi claims at one point, he preferred happily "dragging his tail in the mud" like a giant tortoise to getting involved in current affairs. Zhuangzi's wit and literary versatility is playful, while always giving his readers the sense that something fundamental is being said, and this makes the *Zhuangzi* fresh and thought provoking even today.

Little is known about the philosopher Zhuangzi beyond what we hear about him in *Zhuangzi*. Many masters of his time traveled from state to state and offered political advice to rulers during the contentious Warring States Period (fourth–third centuries B.C.E), which preceded the unification of China under the Qin Dynasty (221 B.C.E.). They relied on the patronage of these fickle rulers in return. Zhuangzi did not seek patronage or office, but seemed content to tell his stories and write. He did, however, gather admir-ers: only the first seven of the *Zhuangzi*'s thirty-three chapters are attributed to him, while the remaining chapters were probably written over several centuries by later followers.

The *Zhuangzi* is written in a prose of constantly changing styles, with embedded verse passages. It moves from wise jokes and funny parables to moments of passionate seriousness and tight philosophical arguments that turn imperceptibly into parodies. It hovers between hilarious anecdotes and complex philosophical treatises, between deriding and celebrating the power of language, between humiliating proponents of clever logic and brilliantly mobilizing their tools against them, and between rhetorical pyrotechnics and gestures toward some grand truth. This grand truth is often conveyed by fantastic creatures, such as monstrous birds, ocean spirits, or remarkable trees, that populate a gigantic universe that dwarfs our human world and teaches—and laughs at—the ultimate relativity of our perspective. The structure of the first seven chapters is intricate: what seems at first to be a discontinuous series of parables gradually reveals itself as an echoing interplay of themes, sometimes bending a thought in a new direction or standing an earlier argument on its head.

This changeable form of narrative and argument allows Zhuangzi to unmask our lack of understanding and to ask fundamental questions about human life. Humans, he claims, do not understand what is really useful: in one parable, Huizi, a clever proponent of the contemporary school of logicians and both a dear friend of Zhuangzi and a frequent target of his parodic jibes, destroys a large gourd because he finds it useless as a water container, but lacks the imagination to make it into a boat that would allow him to leisurely roam the lakes and rivers. Similarly, people do not understand the usefulness of the physical deformity of "Crippled Shu," another character Zhuangzi introduces to make his point: the deformity protects him from being drafted for war and secures him social-welfare grain payments. But most people fail to understand that preserving one's life is more precious than serving in office or acquiring fame in society. And they fail to understand that death is a liberating pleasure. In *Zhuangzi* we see repeatedly how those with deeper understanding of the world rejoice over a beloved's passing, to the outrage of everybody else. One master muses at his friend's deathbed about the wonderful schemes of the creator of the universe and asks enthusiastically, "Where is he going to send you? Will he make you into a rat's liver? Will he make you into a bug's arm?" In another chapter a speaking skull lying by the wayside instructs Zhuangzi that death and liberation from the world are better than a king's life. Sometimes, existence itself becomes a puzzling miracle. In one episode Zhuangzi awakes from a dream in which he was a butterfly and comes to wonder whether he is Zhuangzi dreaming of being a butterfly or a butterfly dreaming of being Zhuangzi. Life is full of pleasures, says Zhuangzi, but so is death because it liberates us from our earthly cares in this life. Moreover, it allows us to return to the flow of the *dao* and become somebody—or more often something—new and exciting in the grander scheme of the "Ten Thousand Things" that make up the cosmos.

For Zhuangzi the greatest sources of misunderstanding are words. Words acquire meaning through human convention and are therefore limited to a

human scale and human problems. In chapter 2 he moves into a logical argument on the relativity of the terms *this* and *that* as well as *right* and *wrong*. The argument is intricate and stylized, and at some point readers begin to suspect that they are reading the parody of an argument, a suspicion confirmed when Zhuangzi's grand summation culminates in a joke. But then again, this is perhaps the only proper conclusion for an argument against the absolute validity of arguments and of the meaning of words. In another chapter a wheelwright named Pian teaches his lord the radical emptiness of words, something he has learned from his profession. When Pian dares to point out that the book his lord is reading contains only "chaff and dregs of the men of old," his lord gets so angry that he demands the wheelwright defend his claim or face execution. The eloquent wheelwright explains quickly that supreme skill and wisdom cannot be transmitted in words but die with the person who has acquired them through intuition, training, and insight. Just as he cannot teach his art of wheel making to his sons, books are merely the empty traces of their writers' wisdom: their meaning has left them and they have no lessons to teach.

That Zhuangzi chooses a lowly artisan to teach his arrogant lord a lesson is no coincidence. Figures of authority and conventional wisdom, such as Confucius, appear as either fools or humble disciples aspiring to some grasp of Zhuangzian wisdom. Criminals and freaks, artisans and animals, and other outsiders embody and understand the *dao*; they constitute a colorful group of countermasters. Gigantic animals allow Zhuangzi to remind his readers that proportions, like values and words, are linked to a particular viewpoint: many anecdotes set their happy protagonists flying, riding the clouds, or sailing the oceans and winds. In chapter 1, "Free and Easy Wandering," he begins with a monstrous sea creature, whose name is Kun ("Fish Eggs"). Kun is transformed into the Peng, a bird that is so large its wings hang over the sky to both horizons. The Peng flies so high that when it looks down all it sees is blue. Suddenly the focus shifts to a tiny hollow in a floor to explain how the Peng can fly at all. Then a little quail twitters jealously, "Where does he think *he's* going?" In dizzying sequence Zhuangzi shifts scales and observers, exercising the readers' imaginations to break down their habitual perspectives.

Alongside the *Daodejing,* the *Zhuangzi* is one of the foundational texts of Daoist philosophy. While these two texts share a general outlook—a rejection of conventional wisdom, a pleasure in paradox, a call to return to a natural Way, and a polemical stance against Confucianism—their visions diverge on crucial points. Zhuangzi's happy abstention from any will to rule is foreign to the *Daodejing*'s advice on how to gain power and become a successful ruler. His joyful embrace of death contrasts with the notion in the *Daodejing* that death is a state of alienation and rigidity, and runs completely counter to the pursuit of immortality through bodily practices and drugs in later Daoism. Most important, while the

Daodejing repeats its pithy paradoxes in short verse over and over again, Zhuangzi revels in the pleasure of storytelling, sometimes adding narrative flesh to the abstract cosmic arguments of the *Daodejing,* and sometimes varying or contradicting them.

In the intellectual world of China and beyond, the *Zhuangzi* is unique: its anecdotes and parables shimmer with comic playfulness and wear their weighty philosophical themes with unbearable lightness. The uncertainty of whether Zhuangzi is the butterfly or the butterfly is Zhuangzi does not create the intellectual pessimism or existential angst of a radical skeptic who solemnly doubts everything in the world. Rather, there is an exuberant joy in being part of the "great transformation of things." With this philosophical style, his sophisticated reflection on language, and his whiff of iconoclasm, Zhuangzi has been popular with ancients and moderns alike: Oscar Wilde, the famous Irish wit, was attracted to the text and reviewed one of its early translations into English in 1889. For all his readers, nobody can quite pin Zhuangzi down. As his earliest followers said: "Above he wandered with the Creator, below he made friends with those who had gone beyond life and death. . . . So veiled and arcane! He has never been completely comprehended."

Zhuangzi[1]

CHAPTER I

Free and Easy Wandering

In the northern darkness there is a fish and his name is Kun.[2] The Kun is so huge I don't know how many thousand li[3] he measures. He changes and becomes a bird whose name is Peng. The back of the Peng measures I don't know how many thousand li across and, when he rises up and flies off, his

1. The followings selections are translated by and with notes adapted from Burton Watson.
2. Kun means fish roe, a figure for something

tiny.
3. A unit of distance; in this period it was roughly a quarter of a mile.

wings are like clouds all over the sky. When the sea begins to move, this bird sets off for the southern darkness, which is the Lake of Heaven.

The *Universal Harmony*[4] records various wonders, and it says: "When the Peng journeys to the southern darkness, the waters are roiled for three thousand li. He beats the whirlwind and rises ninety thousand li, setting off on the sixth-month gale." Wavering heat, bits of dust, living things blowing each other about—the sky looks very blue. Is that its real color, or is it because it is so far away and has no end? When the bird looks down, all he sees is blue too.

If water is not piled up deep enough, it won't have the strength to bear up a big boat. Pour a cup of water into a hollow in the floor and bits of trash will sail on it like boats. But set the cup there and it will stick fast, for the water is too shallow and the boat too large. If wind is not piled up deep enough, it won't have the strength to bear up great wings. Therefore when the Peng rises ninety thousand li, he must have the wind under him like that. Only then can he mount on the back of the wind, shoulder the blue sky, and nothing can hinder or block him. Only then can he set his eyes to the south.

The cicada and the little dove laugh at this, saying, "When we make an effort and fly up, we can get as far as the elm or the sapanwood tree, but sometimes we don't make it and just fall down on the ground. Now how is anyone going to go ninety thousand li to the south!"

If you go off to the green woods nearby, you can take along food for three meals and come back with your stomach as full as ever. If you are going a hundred li, you must grind your grain the night before; and if you are going a thousand li, you must start getting the provisions together three months in advance. What do these two creatures understand? Little understanding cannot come up to great understanding; the short-lived cannot come up to the long-lived.

How do I know this is so? The morning mushroom knows nothing of twilight and dawn; the summer cicada knows nothing of spring and autumn. They are the short-lived. South of Chu there is a caterpillar which counts five hundred years as one spring and five hundred years as one autumn. Long, long ago there was a great rose of Sharon that counted eight thousand years as one spring and eight thousand years as one autumn. They are the long-lived. Yet Pengzu alone is famous today for having lived a long time, and everybody tries to ape him. Isn't it pitiful!

Among the questions of Tang to Qi we find the same thing. In the bald and barren north, there is a dark sea, the Lake of Heaven. In it is a fish which is several thousand li across, and no one knows how long. His name is Kun. There is also a bird there, named Peng with a back like Mount Tai and wings like clouds filling the sky. He beats the whirlwind, leaps into the air, and rises up ninety thousand li, cutting through the clouds and mist, shouldering the blue sky, and then he turns his eyes south and prepares to journey to the southern darkness.

The little quail laughs at him, saying, "Where does he think *he's* going? I give a great leap and fly up, but I never get more than ten or twelve yards before I come down fluttering among the weeds and brambles. And that's the best kind

---

4. Identified variously as the name of a man or the name of a book. Probably Zhuangzi intended it as the latter, and is poking fun at the philosophers of other schools who cite ancient texts to prove their assertions.

of flying anyway! Where does he think *he's* going?" Such is the difference between big and little.

Therefore a man who has wisdom enough to fill one office effectively, good conduct enough to impress one community, virtue enough to please one ruler, or talent enough to be called into service in one state, has the same kind of self-pride as these little creatures. Song Rongzi[5] would certainly burst out laughing at such a man. The whole world could praise Song Rongzi and it wouldn't make him exert himself; the whole world could condemn him and it wouldn't make him mope. He drew a clear line between the internal and the external, and recognized the boundaries of true glory and disgrace. But that was all. As far as the world went, he didn't fret and worry, but there was still ground he left unturned.

Liezi[6] could ride the wind and go soaring around with cool and breezy skill, but after fifteen days he came back to earth. As far as the search for good fortune went, he didn't fret and worry. He escaped the trouble of walking, but he still had to depend on something to get around. If he had only mounted on the truth of Heaven and Earth, ridden the changes of the six breaths, and thus wandered through the boundless, then what would he have had to depend on?

Therefore I say, the Perfect Man has no self; the Holy Man has no merit; the Sage has no fame.

Yao wanted to cede the empire to Xu You.[7] "When the sun and moon have already come out," he said, "it's a waste of light to go on burning the torches, isn't it? When the seasonal rains are falling, it's a waste of water to go on irrigating the fields. If you took the throne, the world would be well ordered. I go on occupying it, but all I can see are my failings. I beg to turn over the world to you."

Xu You said, "You govern the world and the world is already well governed. Now if I take your place, will I be doing it for a name? But name is only the guest of reality—will I be doing it so I can play the part of a guest? When the tailor-bird builds her nest in the deep wood, she uses no more than one branch. When the mole drinks at the river, he takes no more than a bellyful. Go home and forget the matter, my lord. I have no use for the rulership of the world! Though the cook may not run his kitchen properly, the priest and the impersonator of the dead at the sacrifice do not leap over the wine casks and sacrificial stands and go take his place."

Jian Wu said to Lian Shu, "I was listening to Jie Yu's talk—big and nothing to back it up, going on and on without turning around. I was completely dumbfounded at his words—no more end than the Milky Way, wild and wide of the mark, never coming near human affairs!"

"What were his words like?" asked Lian Shu.

"He said that there is a Holy Man living on faraway Gushe Mountain, with skin like ice or snow, and gentle and shy like a young girl. He doesn't eat the

---

5. He taught a doctrine of social harmony, frugality, and the rejection of conventional standards of honor and disgrace.
6. A Daoist sage who appears frequently in the *Zhuangzi*. A book attributed to him was compiled around the 3rd or 4th century C.E.
7. A famous hermit. Yao was a legendary sage-king of great antiquity.

five grains, but sucks the wind, drinks the dew, climbs up on the clouds and mist, rides a flying dragon, and wanders beyond the four seas. By concentrating his spirit, he can protect creatures from sickness and plague and make the harvest plentiful. I thought this was all insane and refused to believe it."

"You would!" said Lian Shu. "We can't expect a blind man to appreciate beautiful patterns or a deaf man to listen to bells and drums. And blindness and deafness are not confined to the body alone—the understanding has them too, as your words just now have shown. This man, with this virtue of his, is about to embrace the ten thousand things and roll them into one. Though the age calls for reform, why should he wear himself out over the affairs of the world? There is nothing that can harm this man. Though flood waters pile up to the sky, he will not drown. Though a great drought melts metal and stone and scorches the earth and hills, he will not be burned. From his dust and leavings alone you could mold a Yao or a Shun![8] Why should he consent to bother about mere things?"

A man of Song who sold ceremonial hats made a trip to Yue, but the Yue people cut their hair short and tattoo their bodies and had no use for such things. Yao brought order to the people of the world and directed the government of all within the seas. But he went to see the Four Masters of the faraway Gushe Mountain, [and when he got home] north of the Fen River, he was dazed and had forgotten his kingdom there.

Huizi[9] said to Zhuangzi, "The king of Wei gave me some seeds of a huge gourd. I planted them, and when they grew up, the fruit was big enough to hold five piculs.[1] I tried using it for a water container, but it was so heavy I couldn't lift it. I split it in half to make dippers, but they were so large and unwieldly that I couldn't dip them into anything. It's not that the gourds weren't fantastically big—but I decided they were no use and so I smashed them to pieces."

Zhuangzi said, "You certainly are dense when it comes to using big things! In Song there was a man who was skilled at making a salve to prevent chapped hands, and generation after generation his family made a living by bleaching silk in water. A traveler heard about the salve and offered to buy the prescription for a hundred measures of gold. The man called everyone to a family council. 'For generations we've been bleaching silk and we've never made more than a few measures of gold,' he said. 'Now, if we sell our secret, we can make a hundred measures in one morning. Let's let him have it!' The traveler got the salve and introduced it to the king of Wu, who was having trouble with the state of Yue. The king put the man in charge of his troops, and that winter they fought a naval battle with the men of Yue and gave them a bad beating.[2] A portion of the conquered territory was awarded to the man as a fief. The salve had the power to prevent chapped hands in either case; but one man used it to get a fief, while the other one never got beyond silk bleaching—because they used it in different ways. Now you had a gourd big enough to hold five piculs. Why

---

8. Another legendary sage-king of great antiquity.
9. A famous logician, who often appears as an interlocutor in dialogues with Chuang Chou.

1. A picul is a measure of volume.
2. Because the salve, by preventing the soldiers' hands from chapping, made it easier for them to handle their weapons.

didn't you think of making it into a great tub so you could go floating around the rivers and lakes, instead of worrying because it was too big and unwieldly to dip into things! Obviously you still have a lot of underbrush in your head!"

Huizi said to Zhuangzi, "I have a big tree of the kind men call *shu*. Its trunk is too gnarled and bumpy to apply a measuring line to, its branches too bent and twisty to match up to a compass or square. You could stand it by the road and no carpenter would look at it twice. Your words, too, are big and useless, and so everyone alike spurns them!"

Zhuangzi said, "Maybe you've never seen a wildcat or a weasel. It crouches down and hides, watching for something to come along. It leaps and races east and west, not hesitating to go high or low—until it falls into the trap and dies in the net. Then again there's the yak, big as a cloud covering the sky. It certainly knows how to be big, though it doesn't know how to catch rats. Now you have this big tree and you're distressed because it's useless. Why don't you plant it in Not-Even-Anything Village, or the field of Broad-and-Boundless, relax and do nothing by its side, or lie down for a free and easy sleep under it? Axes will never shorten its life, nothing can ever harm it. If there's no use for it, how can it come to grief or pain?"

CHAPTER 2
Discussion on Making All Things Equal

Ziqi of south wall sat leaning on his armrest, staring up at the sky and breathing—vacant and far away, as though he'd lost his companion.[3] Yan Cheng Ziyou, who was standing by his side in attendance, said, "What is this? Can you really make the body like a withered tree and the mind like dead ashes? The man leaning on the armrest now is not the one who leaned on it before!"

Ziqi said, "You do well to ask the question, Yan. Now I have lost myself. Do you understand that? You hear the piping of men, but you haven't heard the piping of earth. Or if you've heard the piping of earth, you haven't heard the piping of Heaven!"

Ziyou said, "May I venture to ask what this means?"

Ziqi said, "The Great Clod[4] belches out breath and its name is wind. So long as it doesn't come forth, nothing happens. But when it does, then ten thousand hollows begin crying wildly. Can't you hear them, long drawn out? In the mountain forests that lash and sway, there are huge trees a hundred spans around with hollows and openings like noses, like mouths, like ears, like jugs, like cups, like mortars, like rifts, like ruts. They roar like waves, whistle like arrows, screech, gasp, cry, wail, moan, and howl, those in the lead calling out *yeee!*, those behind calling out *yuuu!* In a gentle breeze they answer faintly, but in a full gale the chorus is gigantic. And when the fierce wind has passed on, then all the hollows are empty again. Have you never seen the tossing and trembling that goes on?"

---

3. Interpreted variously to mean his associates, his wife, or his own body.
4. The earth.

Ziyou said, "By the piping of earth, then, you mean simply [the sound of] these hollows, and by the piping of man [the sound of] flutes and whistles. But may I ask about the piping of Heaven?"

Ziqi said, "Blowing on the ten thousand things in a different way, so that each can be itself—all take what they want for themselves, but who does the sounding?"

Great understanding is broad and unhurried; little understanding is cramped and busy. Great words are clear and limpid; little words are shrill and quarrelsome. In sleep, men's spirits go visiting; in waking hours, their bodies hustle. With everything they meet they become entangled. Day after day they use their minds in strife, sometimes grandiose, sometimes sly, sometimes petty. Their little fears are mean and trembly; their great fears are stunned and overwhelming. They bound off like an arrow or a crossbow pellet, certain that they are the arbiters of right and wrong. They cling to their position as though they had sworn before the gods, sure that they are holding on to victory. They fade like fall and winter—such is the way they dwindle day by day. They drown in what they do—you cannot make them turn back. They grow dark, as though sealed with seals—such are the excesses of their old age. And when their minds draw near to death, nothing can restore them to the light.

Joy, anger, grief, delight, worry, regret, fickleness, inflexibility, modesty, willfulness, candor, insolence—music from empty holes, mushrooms springing up in dampness, day and night replacing each other before us, and no one knows where they sprout from. Let it be! Let it be! [It is enough that] morning and evening we have them, and they are the means by which we live. Without them we would not exist; without us they would have nothing to take hold of. This comes close to the matter. But I do not know what makes them the way they are. It would seem as though they have some True Master, and yet I find no trace of him. He can act—that is certain. Yet I cannot see his form. He has identity but no form.

The hundred joints, the nine openings, the six organs, all come together and exist here [as my body]. But which part should I feel closest to? I should delight in all parts, you say? But there must be one I ought to favor more. If not, are they all of them mere servants? But if they are all servants, then how can they keep order among themselves? Or do they take turns being lord and servant? It would seem as though there must be some True Lord among them. But whether I succeed in discovering his identity or not, it neither adds to nor detracts from his Truth.

Once a man receives this fixed bodily form, he holds on to it, waiting for the end. Sometimes clashing with things, sometimes bending before them, he runs his course like a galloping steed, and nothing can stop him. Is he not pathetic? Sweating and laboring to the end of his days and never seeing his accomplishment, utterly exhausting himself and never knowing where to look for rest—can you help pitying him? I'm not dead yet! he says, but what good is that? His body decays, his mind follows it—can you deny that this is a great sorrow? Man's life has always been a muddle like this. How could I be the only muddled one, and other men not muddled?

If a man follows the mind given him and makes it his teacher, then who can be without a teacher? Why must you comprehend the process of change and form your mind on that basis before you can have a teacher? Even an idiot has his teacher. But to fail to abide by this mind and still insist upon your rights and wrongs—this is like saying that you set off for Yue today and got there yesterday.[5] This is to claim that what doesn't exist exists. If you claim that what doesn't exist exists, then even the holy sage Yu couldn't understand you, much less a person like me!

Words are not just wind. Words have something to say. But if what they have to say is not fixed, then do they really say something? Or do they say nothing? People suppose that words are different from the peeps of baby birds, but is there any difference, or isn't there? What does the Way rely upon, that we have true and false? What do words rely upon, that we have right and wrong? How can the Way go away and not exist? How can words exist and not be acceptable? When the Way relies on little accomplishments and words rely on vain show, then we have the rights and wrongs of the Confucians and the Mo-ists.[6] What one calls right the other calls wrong; what one calls wrong the other calls right. But if we want to right their wrongs and wrong their rights, then the best thing to use is clarity.

Everything has its "that," everything has its "this." From the point of view of "that" you cannot see it, but through understanding you can know it. So I say, "that" comes out of "this" and "this" depends on "that"—which is to say that "this" and "that" give birth to each other. But where there is birth there must be death; where there is death there must be birth. Where there is acceptability there must be unacceptability; where there is unacceptability there must be acceptability. Where there is recognition of right there must be recognition of wrong; where there is recognition of wrong there must be recognition of right. Therefore the sage does not proceed in such a way, but illuminates all in the light of Heaven.[7] He too recognizes a "this," but a "this" which is also "that," a "that" which is also "this." His "that" has both a right and a wrong in it; his "this" too has both a right and a wrong in it. So, in fact, does he still have a "this" and "that"? Or does he in fact no longer have a "this" and "that"? A state in which "this" and "that" no longer find their opposites is called the hinge of the Way. When the hinge is fitted into the socket, it can respond endlessly. Its right then is a single endlessness and its wrong too is a single endlessness. So, I say, the best thing to use is clarity.

To use an attribute to show that attributes are not attributes is not as good as using a nonattribute to show that attributes are not attributes. To use a horse to show that a horse is not a horse is not as good as using a non-horse to show that a horse is not a horse.[8] Heaven and earth are one attribute; the ten thousand things are one horse.

What is acceptable we call acceptable; what is unacceptable we call unacceptable. A road is made by people walking on it; things are so because they are called so. What makes them so? Making them so makes them so. What makes them not so? Making them not so makes them not so. Things all must have that which is so; things all must have that which is acceptable. There is nothing that is not so, nothing that is not acceptable.

---

5. A typical paradox of the logician Huizi.
6. Followers of a utilitarian philosophical school who opposed the traditional ceremonies that the Confucians saw as essential to a good society.

7. Nature or the Way.
8. Zhuangzi pokes fun at the logician Gongsun Long and his treatises "A White Horse Is Not a Horse" and "Attributes Are Not Attributes in and of Themselves."

For this reason, whether you point to a little stalk or a great pillar, a leper or the beautiful Xishi, things ribald and shady or things grotesque and strange, the Way makes them all into one. Their dividedness is their completeness; their completeness is their impairment. No thing is either complete or impaired, but all are made into one again. Only the man of far-reaching vision knows how to make them into one. So he has no use [for categories], but relegates all to the constant. The constant is the useful; the useful is the passable; the passable is the successful; and with success, all is accomplished. He relies upon this alone, relies upon it and does not know he is doing so. This is called the Way.

But to wear out your brain trying to make things into one without realizing that they are all the same—this is called "three in the morning." What do I mean by "three in the morning"? When the monkey trainer was handing out acorns, he said, "You get three in the morning and four at night." This made all the monkeys furious. "Well, then," he said, "you get four in the morning and three at night." The monkeys were all delighted. There was no change in the reality behind the words, and yet the monkeys responded with joy and anger. Let them, if they want to. So the sage harmonizes with both right and wrong and rests in Heaven the Equalizer. This is called walking two roads.

The understanding of the men of ancient times went a long way. How far did it go? To the point where some of them believed that things have never existed—so far, to the end, where nothing can be added. Those at the next stage thought that things exist but recognized no boundaries among them. Those at the next stage thought there were boundaries but recognized no right and wrong. Because right and wrong appeared, the Way was injured, and because the Way was injured, love became complete. But do such things as completion and injury really exist, or do they not?

There is such a thing as completion and injury—Mr. Zhao playing the lute is an example. There is such a thing as no completion and no injury—Mr. Zhao not playing the lute is an example.[9] Zhao Wen played the lute; Music Master Kuang waved his baton; Huizi leaned on his desk. The knowledge of these three was close to perfection. All were masters, and therefore their names have been handed down to later ages. Only in their likes they were different from him [the true sage]. What they liked, they tried to make clear. What he is not clear about, they tried to make clear, and so they ended in the foolishness of "hard" and "white."[1] Their sons, too, devoted all their lives to their fathers' theories, but till their death never reached any completion. Can these men be said to have attained completion? If so, then so have all the rest of us. Or can they not be said to have attained completion? If so, then neither we nor anything else have ever attained it.

---

9. Zhao Wen was a famous lute (*qin*) player. But the best music he could play (i.e., complete) was only a pale and partial reflection of the ideal music, which was thereby injured and impaired, just as the unity of the Way was injured by the appearance of love—i.e., someone's likes and dislikes. Hence, when Mr.

Zhao refrained from playing the lute, there was neither completion nor injury.
1. The logicians Huizi and Gongsun Long spent much time discussing paradoxes involving the relation between attributes such as "hard" and "white" and the things to which they pertain.

The torch of chaos and doubt—this is what the sage steers by. So he does not use things but relegates all to the constant. This is what it means to use clarity.

Now I am going to make a statement here. I don't know whether it fits into the category of other people's statements or not. But whether it fits into their category or whether it doesn't, it obviously fits into some category. So in that respect it is no different from their statements. However, let me try making my statement.

There is a beginning. There is not yet beginning to be a beginning. There is a not yet beginning to be a not yet beginning to be a beginning. There is being. There is nonbeing. There is a not yet beginning to be nonbeing. There is a not yet beginning to be a not yet beginning to be nonbeing. Suddenly there is nonbeing. But I do not know, when it comes to nonbeing, which is really being and which is nonbeing. Now I have just said something. But I don't know whether what I have said has really said something or whether it hasn't said something.

There is nothing in the world bigger than the tip of an autumn hair,[2] and Mount Tai is tiny. No one has lived longer than a dead child, and Pengzu died young. Heaven and earth were born at the same time I was, and the ten thousand things are one with me.

We have already become one, so how can I say anything? But I have just *said* that we are one, so how can I not be saying something? The one and what I said about it make two, and two and the original one make three. If we go on this way, then even the cleverest mathematician can't tell where we'll end, much less an ordinary man. If by moving from nonbeing to being we get to three, how far will we get if we move from being to being? Better not to move, but to let things be!

The Way has never known boundaries; speech has no constancy. But because of [the recognition of a] "this," there came to be boundaries. Let me tell you what the boundaries are. There is left, there is right, there are theories, there are debates, there are divisions, there are discriminations, there are emulations, and there are contentions. These are called the Eight Virtues. As to what is beyond the Six Realms,[3] the sage admits its existence but does not theorize. As to what is within the Six Realms, he theorizes but does not debate. In the case of the *Spring and Autumn*,[4] the record of the former kings of past ages, the sage debates but does not discriminate. So [I say,] those who divide fail to divide; those who discriminate fail to discriminate. What does this mean, you ask? The sage embraces things. Ordinary men discriminate among them and parade their discriminations before others. So I say, those who discriminate fail to see.

The Great Way is not named; Great Discriminations are not spoken; Great Benevolence is not benevolent; Great Modesty is not humble; Great Daring does not attack. If the Way is made clear, it is not the Way. If discriminations are put into words, they do not suffice. If benevolence has a constant object, it

2. Figure for something extremely tiny. The strands of animal fur were believed to grow particularly fine in autumn.
3. The universe: heaven, earth, and the four directions.
4. Probably a reference to the *Spring and Autumn Annals*, a history of the state of Lu said to have been compiled by Confucius.

cannot be universal. If modesty is fastidious, it cannot be trusted. If daring attacks, it cannot be complete. These five are all round, but they tend toward the square.[5]

Therefore understanding that rests in what it does not understand is the finest. Who can understand discriminations that are not spoken, the Way that is not a way? If he can understand this, he may be called the Reservoir of Heaven. Pour into it and it is never full, dip from it and it never runs dry, and yet it does not know where the supply comes from. This is called the Shaded Light.

So it is that long ago Yao said to Shun, "I want to attack the rulers of Zong Kuai and Xu'ao. Even as I sit on my throne, this thought nags at me. Why is this?"

Shun replied, "These three rulers are only little dwellers in the weeds and brush. Why this nagging desire? Long ago, ten suns came out all at once and the ten thousand things were all lighted up. And how much greater is virtue than these suns!"[6]

Nie Que asked Wang Ni, "Do you know what all things agree in calling right?"

"How would I know that?" said Wang Ni.

"Do you know that you don't know it?"

"How would I know that?"

"Then do things know nothing?"

"How would I know that? However, suppose I try saying something. What way do I have of knowing that if I say I know something I don't really not know it? Or what way do I have of knowing that if I say I don't know something I don't really in fact know it? Now let me ask *you* some questions. If a man sleeps in a damp place, his back aches and he ends up half paralyzed, but is this true of a loach? If he lives in a tree, he is terrified and shakes with fright, but is this true of a monkey? Of these three creatures, then, which one knows the proper place to live? Men eat the flesh of grass-fed and grain-fed animals, deer eat grass, centipedes find snakes tasty, and hawks and falcons relish mice. Of these four, which knows how food ought to taste? Monkeys pair with monkeys, deer go out with deer, and fish play around with fish. Men claim that Maoqiang and Lady Li were beautiful, but if fish saw them they would dive to the bottom of the stream, if birds saw them they would fly away, and if deer saw them they would break into a run. Of these four, which knows how to fix the standard of beauty for the world? The way I see it, the rules of benevolence and righteousness and the paths of right and wrong are all hopelessly snarled and jumbled. How could I know anything about such discriminations?"

Nie Que said, "If you don't know what is profitable or harmful, then does the Perfect Man likewise know nothing of such things?"

Wang Ni replied, "The Perfect Man is godlike. Though the great swamps blaze, they cannot burn him; though the great rivers freeze, they cannot chill him; though swift lightning splits the hills and howling gales shake the sea,

5. All are originally perfect, but may become "squared"—i.e., impaired by the misuses mentioned.

6. Here virtue is to be understood in a positive sense, as the power of the Way.

they cannot frighten him. A man like this rides the clouds and mist, straddles the sun and moon, and wanders beyond the four seas. Even life and death have no effect on him, much less the rules of profit and loss!"

Ju Quezi said to Zhang Wuzi, "I have heard Confucius say that the sage does not work at anything, does not pursue profit, does not dodge harm, does not enjoy being sought after, does not follow the Way, says nothing yet says something, says something yet says nothing, and wanders beyond the dust and grime. Confucius himself regarded these as wild and flippant words, though I believe they describe the working of the mysterious Way. What do you think of them?"

Zhang Wuzi said, "Even the Yellow Emperor would be confused if he heard such words, so how could you expect Confucius to understand them? What's more, you're too hasty in your own appraisal. You see an egg and demand a crowing cock, see a crossbow pellet and demand a roast dove. I'm going to try speaking some reckless words and I want you to listen to them recklessly. How will that be? The sage leans on the sun and moon, tucks the universe under his arm, merges himself with things, leaves the confusion and muddle as it is, and looks on slaves as exalted. Ordinary men strain and struggle; the sage is stupid and blockish. He takes part in ten thousand ages and achieves simplicity in oneness. For him, all the ten thousand things are what they are, and thus they enfold each other.

"How do I know that loving life is not a delusion? How do I know that in hating death I am not like a man who, having left home in his youth, has forgotten the way back?

"Lady Li was the daughter of the border guard of Ai.[7] When she was first taken captive and brought to the state of Jin, she wept until her tears drenched the collar of her robe. But later, when she went to live in the palace of the ruler, shared his couch with him, and ate the delicious meats of his table, she wondered why she had ever wept. How do I know that the dead do not wonder why they ever longed for life?

"He who dreams of drinking wine may weep when morning comes; he who dreams of weeping may in the morning go off to hunt. While he is dreaming he does not know it is a dream, and in his dream he may even try to interpret a dream. Only after he wakes does he know it was a dream. And someday there will be a great awakening when we know that this is all a great dream. Yet the stupid believe they are awake, busily and brightly assuming they understand things, calling this man ruler, that one herdsman—how dense! Confucius and you are both dreaming! And when I say you are dreaming, I am dreaming, too. Words like these will be labeled the Supreme Swindle. Yet, after ten thousand generations, a great sage may appear who will know their meaning, and it will still be as though he appeared with astonishing speed.

"Suppose you and I have had an argument. If you have beaten me instead of my beating you, then are you necessarily right and am I necessarily wrong? If I have beaten you instead of your beating me, then am I necessarily right and

---

7. She was taken captive by Duke Xian of Jin in 671 B.C.E., and later became his consort.

are you necessarily wrong? Is one of us right and the other wrong? Are both of us right or are both of us wrong? If you and I don't know the answer, then other people are bound to be even more in the dark. Whom shall we get to decide what is right? Shall we get someone who agrees with you to decide? But if he already agrees with you, how can he decide fairly? Shall we get someone who agrees with me? But if he already agrees with me, how can he decide? Shall we get someone who disagrees with both of us? But if he already disagrees with both of us, how can he decide? Obviously, then, neither you nor I nor anyone else can decide for each other. Shall we wait for still another person?

"But waiting for one shifting voice [to pass judgment on] another is the same as waiting for none of them. Harmonize them all with the Heavenly Equality, leave them to their endless changes, and so live out your years. What do I mean by harmonizing them with the Heavenly Equality? Right is not right; so is not so. If right were really right, it would differ so clearly from not right that there would be no need for argument. If so were really so, it would differ so clearly from not so that there would be no need for argument. Forget the years; forget distinctions. Leap into the boundless and make it your home!"

Penumbra said to Shadow, "A little while ago you were walking and now you're standing still; a little while ago you were sitting and now you're standing up. Why this lack of independent action?"

Shadow said, "Do I have to wait for something before I can be like this? Does what I wait for also have to wait for something before it can be like this? Am I waiting for the scales of a snake or the wings of a cicada? How do I know why it is so? How do I know why it isn't so?"

Once Zhuang Zhou dreamt he was a butterfly, a butterfly flitting and fluttering around, happy with himself and doing as he pleased. He didn't know he was Zhuang Zhou. Suddenly he woke up and there he was, solid and unmistakable Zhuang Zhou. But he didn't know if he was Zhuang Zhou who had dreamt he was a butterfly, or a butterfly dreaming he was Zhuang Zhou. Between Zhuang Zhou and a butterfly there must be *some* distinction! This is called the Transformation of Things.

CHAPTER 3
The Secret of Caring for Life

Your life has a limit but knowledge has none. If you use what is limited to pursue what has no limit, you will be in danger. If you understand this and still strive for knowledge, you will be in danger for certain! If you do good, stay away from fame. If you do evil, stay away from punishments. Follow the middle; go by what is constant, and you can stay in one piece, keep yourself alive, look after your parents, and live out your years.

Cook Ding was cutting up an ox for Lord Wenhui. At every touch of his hand, every heave of his shoulder, every move of his feet, every thrust of his knee—zip! zoop! He slithered the knife along with a zing, and all was in perfect rhythm, as though he were performing the dance of the Mulberry Grove or keeping time to the Jingshou music.[8]

"Ah, this is marvelous!" said Lord Wenhui. "Imagine skill reaching such heights!"

Cook Ding laid down his knife and replied, "What I care about is the Way, which goes beyond skill. When I first began cutting up oxen, all I could see was the ox itself. After three years I no longer saw the whole ox. And now—now I go at it by spirit and don't look with my eyes. Perception and understanding have come to a stop and spirit moves where it wants. I go along with the natural makeup, strike in the big hollows, guide the knife through the big openings, and follow things as they are. So I never touch the smallest ligament or tendon, much less a main joint.

"A good cook changes his knife once a year—because he cuts. A mediocre cook changes his knife once a month—because he hacks. I've had this knife of mine for nineteen years and I've cut up thousands of oxen with it, and yet the blade is as good as though it had just come from the grindstone. There are spaces between the joints, and the blade of the knife has really no thickness. If you insert what has no thickness into such spaces, then there's plenty of room—more than enough for the blade to play about it. That's why after nineteen years the blade of my knife is still as good as when it first came from the grindstone.

"However, whenever I come to a complicated place, I size up the difficulties, tell myself to watch out and be careful, keep my eyes on what I'm doing, work very slowly, and move the knife with the greatest subtlety, until—flop! the whole thing comes apart like a clod of earth crumbling to the ground. I stand there holding the knife and look all around me, completely satisfied and reluctant to move on, and then I wipe off the knife and put it away."

"Excellent!" said Lord Wenhui. "I have heard the words of Cook Ding and learned how to care for life!"

When Gongwen Xuan saw the Commander of the Right,[9] he was startled and said, "What kind of man is this? How did he come to be footless? Was it Heaven? Or was it man?"

"It was Heaven, not man," said the commander. "When Heaven gave me life, it saw to it that I would be one-footed. Men's looks are given to them. So I know this was the work of Heaven and not of man. The swamp pheasant has to walk ten paces for one peck and a hundred paces for one drink, but it doesn't want to be kept in a cage. Though you treat it like a king, its spirit won't be content."

When Lao Dan[1] died, Qin Shi went to mourn for him; but after giving three cries, he left the room.

"Weren't you a friend of the Master?" asked Laozi's disciples.

---

8. The Mulberry Grove is identified as a rain dance from the time of King Tang of the Shang Dynasty, and the Jingshou music as part of a longer composition from the time of the sage-king Yao.
9. Probably the ex–Commander of the Right, since he has been punished by having one foot amputated, a common penalty in ancient China.
1. Laozi, the reputed author of the *Daodejing*. In Zhuangzi he appears as a contemporary of Confucius.

"Yes."

"And you think it's all right to mourn him this way?"

"Yes," said Qin Shi. "At first I took him for a real man, but now I know he wasn't. A little while ago, when I went in to mourn, I found old men weeping for him as though they were weeping for a son, and young men weeping for him as though they were weeping for a mother. To have gathered a group like *that*, he must have done something to make them talk about him, though he didn't ask them to talk, or make them weep for him, though he didn't ask them to weep. This is to hide from Heaven, turn your back on the true state of affairs, and forget what you were born with. In the old days this was called the crime of hiding from Heaven. Your master happened to come because it was his time, and he happened to leave because things follow along. If you are content with the time and willing to follow along, then grief and joy have no way to enter in. In the old days, this was called being freed from the bonds of God.

"Though the grease burns out of the torch, the fire passes on, and no one knows where it ends."

FROM CHAPTER 4

In the World of Men

Carpenter Shi went to Qi and, when he got to Crooked Shaft, he saw a serrate oak standing by the village shrine. It was broad enough to shelter several thousand oxen and measured a hundred spans around, towering above the hills. The lowest branches were eighty feet from the ground, and a dozen or so of them could have been made into boats. There were so many sightseers that the place looked like a fair, but the carpenter didn't even glance around and went on his way without stopping. His apprentice stood staring for a long time and then ran after Carpenter Shi and said, "Since I first took up my ax and followed you, Master, I have never seen timber as beautiful as this. But you don't even bother to look, and go right on without stopping. Why is that?"

"Forget it—say no more!" said the carpenter. "It's a worthless tree! Make boats out of it and they'd sink; make coffins and they'd rot in no time; make vessels and they'd break at once. Use it for doors and it would sweat sap like pine; use it for posts and the worms would eat them up. It's not a timber tree—there's nothing it can be used for. That's how it got to be that old!"

After Carpenter Shi had returned home, the oak tree appeared to him in a dream and said, "What are you comparing me with? Are you comparing me with those useful trees? The cherry apple, the pear, the orange, the citron, the rest of those fructiferous trees and shrubs—as soon as their fruit is ripe, they are torn apart and subjected to abuse. Their big limbs are broken off, their little limbs are yanked around. Their utility makes life miserable for them, and so they don't get to finish out the years Heaven gave them, but are cut off in midjourney. They bring it on themselves—the pulling and tearing of the common mob. And it's the same way with all other things.

"As for me, I've been trying a long time to be of no use, and though I almost died, I've finally got it. This is of great use to me. If I had been of some use, would I ever have grown this large? Moreover you and I are both of us things. What's the point of this—things condemning things? You, a worthless man about to die—how do you know I'm a worthless tree?"

When Carpenter Shi woke up, he reported his dream. His apprentice said, "If it's so intent on being of no use, what's it doing there at the village shrine?"[2]

"Shhh! Say no more! It's only *resting* there. If we carp and criticize, it will merely conclude that we don't understand it. Even if it weren't at the shrine, do you suppose it would be cut down? It protects itself in a different way from ordinary people. If you try to judge it by conventional standards, you'll be way off!"

* * *

There's Crippled Shu—chin stuck down in his navel, shoulders up above his head, pigtail pointing at the sky, his five organs on the top, his two thighs pressing his ribs. By sewing and washing, he gets enough to fill his mouth; by handling a winnow and sifting out the good grain, he makes enough to feed ten people. When the authorities call out the troops, he stands in the crowd waving good-by; when they get up a big work party, they pass him over because he's a chronic invalid. And when they are doling out grain to the ailing, he gets three big measures and ten bundles of firewood. With a crippled body, he's still able to look after himself and finish out the years Heaven gave him. How much better, then, if he had crippled virtue!

When Confucius visited Chu, Jie Yu, the madman of Chu, wandered by his gate crying, "Phoenix, phoenix, how his virtue failed! The future you cannot wait for; the past you cannot pursue. When the world has the Way, the sage succeeds; when the world is without the Way, the sage survives. In times like the present, we do well to escape penalty. Good fortune is light as a feather, but nobody knows how to hold it up. Misfortune is heavy as the earth, but nobody knows how to stay out of its way. Leave off, leave off—this teaching men virtue! Dangerous, dangerous—to mark off the ground and run! Fool, fool—don't spoil my walking! I walk a crooked way—don't step on my feet. The mountain trees do themselves harm; the grease in the torch burns itself up. The cinnamon can be eaten and so it gets cut down; the lacquer tree can be used and so it gets hacked apart. All men know the use of the useful, but nobody knows the use of the useless!"

FROM CHAPTER 6
The Great and Venerable Teacher

Master Si, Master Yu, Master Li, and Master Lai were all four talking together. "Who can look upon nonbeing as his head, on life as his back, and on death as his rump?" they said. "Who knows that life and death, existence and annihilation, are all a single body? I will be his friend!"

The four men looked at each other and smiled. There was no disagreement in their hearts and so the four of them became friends.

All at once Master Yu fell ill. Master Si went to ask how he was. "Amazing!" said Master Yu. "The Creator is making me all crookedly like this! My back

---

2. The shrine, or altar of the soil, was always situated in a grove of beautiful trees. The oak was therefore serving a purpose by lending an air of sanctity to the spot.

sticks up like a hunchback and my vital organs are on top of me. My chin is hidden in my navel, my shoulders are up above my head, and my pigtail points at the sky. It must be some dislocation of the yin and yang!"[3]

Yet he seemed calm at heart and unconcerned. Dragging himself haltingly to the well, he looked at his reflection and said, "My, my! So the Creator is making me all crookedy like this!"

"Do you resent it?" asked Master Si.

"Why no, what would I resent? If the process continues, perhaps in time he'll transform my left arm into a rooster. In that case I'll keep watch on the night. Or perhaps in time he'll transform my right arm into a crossbow pellet and I'll shoot down an owl for roasting. Or perhaps in time he'll transform my buttocks into cartwheels. Then, with my spirit for a horse, I'll climb up and go for a ride. What need will I ever have for a carriage again?

"I received life because the time had come; I will lose it because the order of things passes on. Be content with this time and dwell in this order and then neither sorrow nor joy can touch you. In ancient times this was called the 'freeing of the bound.' There are those who cannot free themselves, because they are bound by things. But nothing can ever win against Heaven—that's the way it's always been. What would I have to resent?"

Suddenly Master Lai grew ill. Gasping and wheezing, he lay at the point of death. His wife and children gathered round in a circle and began to cry. Master Li, who had come to ask how he was, said, "Shoo! Get back! Don't disturb the process of change!"

Then he leaned against the doorway and talked to Master Lai. "How marvelous the Creator is! What is he going to make of you next? Where is he going to send you? Will he make you into a rat's liver? Will he make you into a bug's arm?"

Master Lai said, "A child, obeying his father and mother, goes wherever he is told, east or west, south or north. And the yin and yang—how much more are they to a man than father or mother! Now that they have brought me to the verge of death, if I should refuse to obey them, how perverse I would be! What fault is it of theirs? The Great Clod burdens me with form, labors me with life, eases me in old age, and rests me in death. So if I think well of my life, for the same reason I must think well of my death. When a skilled smith is casting metal, if the metal should leap up and say, 'I insist upon being made into a Moye!'[4] he would surely regard it as very inauspicious metal indeed. Now, having had the audacity to take on human form once, if I should say, 'I don't want to be anything but a man! Nothing but a man!', the Creator would surely regard me as a most inauspicious sort of person. So now I think of heaven and earth as a great furnace, and the Creator as a skilled smith. Where could he send me that would not be all right? I will go off to sleep peacefully, and then with a start I will wake up."

Master Sanghu, Mengzi Fan, and Master Qinzhang, three friends, said to each other, "Who can join with others without joining with others? Who can do with others without doing with others? Who can climb up to heaven and

---

3. The female and male principles, respectively; darkness and light, the duality by which all things function. Medical disorders were often described as imbalances of the yin and yang.

4. A famous sword of King Helü (ruled 514–496 B.C.E.) of the southern state of Wu.

wander in the mists, roam the infinite, and forget life forever and forever?" The three men looked at each other and smiled. There was no disagreement in their hearts and so they became friends.

After some time had passed without event, Master Sanghu died. He had not yet been buried when Confucius, hearing of his death, sent Zigong[5] to assist at the funeral. When Zigong arrived, he found one of the dead man's friends weaving frames for silkworms, while the other strummed a lute. Joining their voices, they sang this song:

> Ah, Sanghu!
> Ah, Sanghu!
> You have gone back to your true form
> While we remain as men, O!

Zigong hastened forward and said, "May I be so bold as to ask what sort of ceremony this is—singing in the very presence of the corpse?"

The two men looked at each other and laughed. "What does this man know of the meaning of ceremony?" they said.

Zigong returned and reported to Confucius what had happened. "What sort of men are they anyway?" he asked. "They pay no attention to proper behavior, disregard their personal appearance and, without so much as changing the expression on their faces, sing in the very presence of the corpse! I can think of no name for them! What sort of men are they?"

"Such men as they," said Confucius, "wander beyond the realm; men like me wander within it. Beyond and within can never meet. It was stupid of me to send you to offer condolences. Even now they have joined with the Creator as men to wander in the single breath of heaven and earth. They look upon life as a swelling tumor, a protruding wen, and upon death as the draining of a sore or the bursting of a boil. To men such as these, how could there be any question of putting life first or death last? They borrow the forms of different creatures and house them in the same body. They forget liver and gall, cast aside ears and eyes, turning and revolving, ending and beginning again, unaware of where they start or finish. Idly they roam beyond the dust and dirt; they wander free and easy in the service of inaction. Why should they fret and fuss about the ceremonies of the vulgar world and make a display for the ears and eyes of the common herd?"

Zigong said, "Well then, Master, what is this 'realm' that you stick to?"

Confucius said, "I am one of those men punished by Heaven. Nevertheless, I will share with you what I have."

"Then may I ask about the realm?"[6] said Zigong.

Confucius said, "Fish thrive in water, man thrives in the Way. For those that thrive in water, dig a pond and they will find nourishment enough. For those that thrive in the Way, don't bother about them and their lives will be secure. So it is said, the fish forget each other in the rivers and lakes, and men forget each other in the arts of the Way."

Zigong said, "May I ask about the singular man?"

---

5. One of Confucius's disciples.
6. The word *fang*, translated here as "realm," may also mean "method" or "procedure," and

Confucius's answer seems to stress this latter meaning.

"The singular man is singular in comparison to other men, but a companion of Heaven. So it is said, the petty man of Heaven is a gentleman among men; the gentleman among men is the petty man of Heaven."

Yan Hui said to Confucius, "When Mengsun Cai's mother died, he wailed without shedding any tears, he did not grieve in his heart, and he conducted the funeral without any look of sorrow. He fell down on these three counts, and yet he is known all over the state of Lu for the excellent way he managed the funeral. Is it really possible to gain such a reputation when there are no facts to support it? I find it very peculiar indeed!"

Confucius said, "Mengsun did all there was to do. He was advanced beyond ordinary understanding and he would have simplified things even more, but that wasn't practical. However, there is still a lot that he simplified. Mengsun doesn't know why he lives and doesn't know why he dies. He doesn't know why he should go ahead; he doesn't know why he should fall behind. In the process of change, he has become a thing [among other things], and he is merely waiting for some other change that he doesn't yet know about. Moreover, when he is changing, how does he know that he is really changing? And when he is not changing, how does he know that he hasn't already changed? You and I, now—we are dreaming and haven't waked up yet. But in his case, though something may startle his body, it won't injure his mind; though something may alarm the house [his spirit lives in], his emotions will suffer no death. Mengsun alone has waked up. Men wail and so he wails, too—that's the reason he acts like this.

"What's more, we go around telling each other, I do this, I do that—but how do we know that this 'I' we talk about has any 'I' to it? You dream you're a bird and soar up into the sky; you dream you're a fish and dive down in the pool. But now when you tell me about it, I don't know whether you are awake or whether you are dreaming. Running around accusing others is not as good as laughing, and enjoying a good laugh is not as good as going along with things. Be content to go along and forget about change and then you can enter the mysterious oneness of Heaven."

FROM CHAPTER 7

Fit for Emperors and Kings

The emperor of the South Sea was called Shu [Brief], the emperor of the North Sea was called Hu [Sudden], and the emperor of the central region was called Hundun [Chaos]. Shu and Hu from time to time came together for a meeting in the territory of Hundun, and Hundun treated them very generously. Shu and Hu discussed how they could repay his kindness. "All men," they said, "have seven openings so they can see, hear, eat, and breathe. But Hundun alone doesn't have any. Let's trying boring him some!"

Every day they bored another hole, and on the seventh day Hundun died.

FROM CHAPTER 12

Heaven and Earth

Zigong traveled south to Chu, and on his way back through Jin, as he passed along the south bank of the Han, he saw an old man preparing his fields for planting. He had hollowed out an opening by which he entered the well and from which he emerged, lugging a pitcher, which he carried out to water the fields. Grunting and puffing, he used up a great deal of energy and produced very little result.

"There is a machine for this sort of thing," said Zigong. "In one day it can water a hundred fields, demanding very little effort and producing excellent results. Wouldn't you like one?"

The gardener raised his head and looked at Zigong. "How does it work?"

"It's a contraption made by shaping a piece of wood. The back end is heavy and the front end light and it raises the water as though it were pouring it out, so fast that it seems to boil right over! It's called a well sweep."

The gardener flushed with anger and then said with a laugh, "I've heard my teacher say, where there are machines, there are bound to be machine worries; where there are machine worries, there are bound to be machine hearts. With a machine heart in your breast, you've spoiled what was pure and simple; and without the pure and simple, the life of the spirit knows no rest. Where the life of the spirit knows no rest, the Way will cease to buoy you up. It's not that I don't know about your machine—I would be ashamed to use it!"

Zigong blushed with chagrin, looked down, and made no reply. After a while, the gardener said, "Who are you, anyway?"

"A disciple of Kong Qiu."[7]

"Oh—then you must be one of those who broaden their learning in order to ape the sages, heaping absurd nonsense on the crowd, plucking the strings and singing sad songs all by yourself in hopes of buying fame in the world! You would do best to forget your spirit and breath, break up your body and limbs—then you might be able to get somewhere. You don't even know how to look after your own body—how do you have any time to think about looking after the world! On your way now! Don't interfere with my work!"

Zigong frowned and the color drained from his face. Dazed and rattled, he couldn't seem to pull himself together, and it was only after he had walked on for some thirty li that he began to recover.

One of his disciples said, "Who was that man just now? Why did you change your expression and lose your color like that, Master, so that it took you all day to get back to normal?"

"I used to think there was only one real man in the world," said Zigong. "I didn't know there was this other one. I have heard Confucius say that in affairs you aim for what is right, and in undertakings you aim for success. To spend little effort and achieve big results—that is the Way of the sage. Now it seems that this isn't so. He who holds fast to the Way is complete in Virtue; being complete in Virtue, he is complete in body; being complete in body, he is complete in spirit; and to be complete in spirit is the Way of the sage. He is content to live among the people, to walk by their side, and never know where he is going. Witless, his purity is complete. Achievement, profit, machines, skill—they have no place in this man's mind! A man like this will not go where he has no will to go, will not do what he has no mind to do. Though the world might praise him and say he had really found something, he would look unconcerned and never turn his head; though the world might condemn him and say he had lost something, he would look serene and pay no heed. The praise and blame

7. Confucius.

of the world are no loss or gain to him. He may be called a man of Complete Virtue. I—I am a man of the wind-blown waves."

When Zigong got back to Lu, he reported the incident to Confucius. Confucius said, "He is one of those bogus practitioners of the arts of Mr. Chaos. He knows the first thing but doesn't understand the second. He looks after what is on the inside but doesn't look after what is on the outside. A man of true brightness and purity who can enter into simplicity, who can return to the primitive through inaction, give body to his inborn nature, and embrace his spirit, and in this way wander through the everyday world—if you had met one like that, you would have had real cause for astonishment. As for the arts of Mr. Chaos, you and I need not bother to find out about them."

FROM CHAPTER 13[8]

The Way of Heaven

Duke Huan was reading in his hall. Wheelwright Pian, who was cutting a wheel just outside the hall, put aside his hammer and chisel and went in. There he asked Duke Huan, "What do those books you are reading say?" The duke answered, "These are the words of the Sages." The wheelwright said, "Are the Sages still around?" And the duke answered, "They're dead." Then the wheelwright said, "Well, what you're reading then is no more than the dregs of the ancients." The duke: "When I, a prince, read, how is it that a wheelwright dares come and dispute with me? If you have an explanation, fine. If you don't have an explanation, *you* die!" Then Wheelwright Pian said, "I tend to look at it in terms of my own work: when you cut a wheel, if you go too slowly, it slides and doesn't stick fast; if you go too quickly, it jumps and doesn't go in. Neither too slowly nor too quickly—you achieve it in your hands, and those respond to the mind. I can't put it into words, but there is some fixed principle there. I can't teach it to my son, and my son can't get instruction in it from me. I've gone on this way for seventy years and have grown old in cutting wheels. The ancients have died, and along with them, that which cannot be transmitted. Therefore what you are reading is nothing more than the dregs of the ancients."

* * *

FROM CHAPTER 17[9]

Autumn Floods

Once, when Zhuangzi was fishing in the Pu River, the king of Chu sent two officials to go and announce to him: "I would like to trouble you with the administration of my realm."

Zhuangzi held on to the fishing pole and, without turning his head, said, "I have heard that there is a sacred tortoise in Chu that has been dead for three thousand years. The king keeps it wrapped in cloth and boxed, and stores it in

---

8. Translated by Stephen Owen.   and with notes adapted from Burton Watson.
9. The following selections are translated by

the ancestral temple. Now would this tortoise rather be dead and have its bones left behind and honored? Or would it rather be alive and dragging its tail in the mud?"

"It would rather be alive and dragging its tail in the mud," said the two officials.

Zhuangzi said, "Go away! I'll drag my tail in the mud!"

When Huizi was prime minister of Liang, Zhuangzi set off to visit him. Someone said to Huizi, "Zhuangzi is coming because he wants to replace you as prime minister!" With this Huizi was filled with alarm and searched all over the state for three days and three nights trying to find Zhuangzi. Zhuangzi then came to see him and said, "In the south there is a bird called the Yuanchu—I wonder if you've ever heard of it? The Yuanchu rises up from the South Sea and flies to the North Sea, and it will rest on nothing but the Wutong tree, eat nothing but the fruit of the Lian and drink only from springs of sweet water. Once there was an owl who had gotten hold of a half-rotten old rat, and as the Yuanchu passed by, it raised its head, looked up at the Yuanchu, and said, 'Shoo!' Now that you have this Liang state of yours, are you trying to shoo me?"

Zhuangzi and Huizi were strolling along the dam of the Hao River when Zhuangzi said, "See how the minnows come out and dart around where they please! That's what fish really enjoy!"

Huizi said, "You're not a fish—how do you know what fish enjoy?"

Zhuangzi said, "You're not I, so how do you know I don't know what fish enjoy?"

Huizi said, "I'm not you, so I certainly don't know what you know. On the other hand, you're certainly not a fish—so that still proves you don't know what fish enjoy!"

Zhuangzi said, "Let's go back to your original question, please. You asked me *how* I know what fish enjoy—so you already knew I knew it when you asked the question. I know it by standing here beside the Hao."

FROM CHAPTER 18
Perfect Happiness

When Zhuangzi went to Chu, he saw an old skull, all dry and parched. He poked it with his carriage whip and then asked, "Sir, were you greedy for life and forgetful of reason, and so came to this? Was your state overthrown and did you bow beneath the ax, and so came to this? Did you do some evil deed and were you ashamed to bring disgrace upon your parents and family, and so came to this? Was it through the pangs of cold and hunger that you came to this? Or did your springs and autumns pile up until they brought you to this?"

When he had finished speaking, he dragged the skull over and, using it for a pillow, lay down to sleep.

In the middle of the night, the skull came to him in a dream and said, "You chatter like a rhetorician and all your words betray the entanglements of a living man. The dead know nothing of these! Would you like to hear a lecture on the dead?"

"Indeed," said Zhuangzi.

The skull said, "Among the dead there are no rulers above, no subjects below, and no chores of the four seasons. With nothing to do, our springs and autumns are as endless as heaven and earth. A king facing south on his throne could have no more happiness than this!"

Zhuangzi couldn't believe this and said, "If I got the Arbiter of Fate to give you a body again, make you some bones and flesh, return you to your parents and family and your old home and friends, you would want that, wouldn't you?"

The skull frowned severely, wrinkling up its brow. "Why would I throw away more happiness than that of a king on a throne and take on the troubles of a human being again?" it said.

FROM CHAPTER 20

The Mountain Tree

Zhuang Zhou was wandering in the park at Diaoling when he saw a peculiar kind of magpie that came flying along from the south. It had a wingspread of seven feet and its eyes were a good inch in diameter. It brushed against Zhuang Zhou's forehead and then settled down in a grove of chestnut trees. "What kind of bird is that!" exclaimed Zhuang Zhou. "Its wings are enormous but they get it nowhere; its eyes are huge but it can't even see where it's going!" Then he hitched up his robe, strode forward, cocked his crossbow and prepared to take aim. As he did so, he spied a cicada that had found a lovely spot of shade and had forgotten all about [the possibility of danger to] its body. Behind it, a praying mantis, stretching forth its claws, prepared to snatch the cicada, and it too had forgotten about its own form as it eyed its prize. The peculiar magpie was close behind, ready to make off with the praying mantis, forgetting its own true self as it fixed its eyes on the prospect of gain. Zhuang Zhou, shuddering at the sight, said, "Ah!—things do nothing but make trouble for each other—one creature calling down disaster on another!" He threw down his crossbow, turned about, and hurried from the park, but the park keeper [taking him for a poacher] raced after him with shouts of accusation.

Zhuang Zhou returned home and for three months looked unhappy. Lin Ju, in the course of tending to his master's needs, questioned him, saying, "Master, why is it that you are so unhappy these days?"

Zhuang Zhou said, "In clinging to outward form I have forgotten my own body. Staring at muddy water, I have been misled into taking it for a clear pool. Moreover, I have heard my Master say, 'When you go among the vulgar, follow their rules!' I went wandering at Diaoling and forgot my body. A peculiar magpie brushed against my forehead, wandered off to the chestnut grove, and there forgot its true self. And the keeper of the chestnut grove, to my great shame, took me for a trespasser! That is why I am unhappy."

Yangzi, on his way to Song, stopped for the night at an inn. The innkeeper had two concubines, one beautiful, the other ugly. But the ugly one was treated as a lady of rank, while the beautiful one was treated as a menial. When Yangzi asked the reason, a young boy of the inn replied, "The beautiful one is only too aware of her beauty, and so we don't think of her as beautiful. The ugly one is only too aware of her ugliness, and so we don't think of her as ugly."

Yangzi said, "Remember that, my students! If you act worthily but rid yourself of the awareness that you are acting worthily, then where can you go that you will not be loved?"

FROM CHAPTER 22
Knowledge Wandered North

Master Dongguo asked Zhuangzi, "This thing called the Way—where does it exist?"

Zhuangzi said, "There's no place it doesn't exist."

"Come," said Master Dongguo, "you must be more specific!"

"It is in the ant."

"As low a thing as that?"

"It is in the panic grass."

"But that's lower still!"

"It is in the tiles and shards."

"How can it be so low?"

"It is in the piss and shit!"

Master Dongguo made no reply.

Zhuangzi said, "Sir, your questions simply don't get at the substance of the matter. When Inspector Huo asked the superintendent of the market how to test the fatness of a pig by pressing it with the foot, he was told that the lower down on the pig you press, the nearer you come to the truth. But you must not expect to find the Way in any particular place—there is no thing that escapes its presence! Such is the Perfect Way, and so too are the truly great words. 'Complete,' 'universal,' 'all-inclusive'—these three are different words with the same meaning. All point to a single reality.

"Why don't you try wandering with me to the Palace of Not-Even-Anything—identity and concord will be the basis of our discussions and they will never come to an end, never reach exhaustion. Why not join with me in inaction, in tranquil quietude, in hushed purity, in harmony and leisure? Already my will is vacant and blank. I go nowhere and don't know how far I've gotten. I go and come and don't know where to stop. I've already been there and back, and I don't know when the journey is done. I ramble and relax in unbordered vastness; Great Knowledge enters in, and I don't know where it will ever end.

"That which treats things as things is not limited by things. Things have their limits—the so-called limits of things. The unlimited moves to the realm of limits; the limited moves to the unlimited realm. We speak of the filling and emptying, the withering and decay of things. [The Way] makes them full and empty without itself filling or emptying; it makes them wither and decay without itself withering or decaying. It establishes root and branch but knows no root and branch itself; it determines when to store up or scatter but knows no storing or scattering itself."

FROM CHAPTER 26

Outer Things[1]

Traditionalists[2] break into tombs using the *Poems*[3] and Ceremony.

The chief Traditionalist deigned to convey these words, "It beginneth to grow light in the east. How's it going?"

The subordinate Traditionalist responded, "I haven't got the skirt and jacket off yet, but there's a pearl in his mouth."

The high Traditionalist: "Verily it is even as the *Poems* say:

> Green, green groweth grain
> upon the slopes of the mound.
> The man ungenerous alive,
> in death his mouth will hold no pearl.[4]

I'll grab the whiskers and pull down on the beard; you take a metal bar, break through his cheeks, and slowly part his jaws, but don't damage the pearl in his mouth."

CHAPTER 30

Of Swords

A long time ago King Wen of Zhao took great pleasure in swordplay, and over three thousand men thronged his gates to receive his patronage as swordsmen. In his presence they would hack at each other day and night, and every year more than a hundred died of their wounds. But the king loved it dearly and never tired of it. It went on like this for three years, and as the kingdom's fortunes slid into decline, the nobility debated what to do about it.

Crown Prince Kui was appalled by the situation, and summoned his entourage. "I will offer a reward of a thousand pieces of gold to anyone who can dissuade the king from this mania of his and put a stop to these swordsmen."

Members of his entourage said, "Zhuangzi can certainly do it."

The crown prince then sent a messenger with a thousand pieces of gold to offer to Zhuangzi. But Zhuangzi refused to accept the gold and went back with the messenger to see the crown prince. "What is it that the Crown Prince wants of me, presenting me a thousand pieces of gold?"

The crown prince said, "I have heard of your sagely understanding, and out of respect I offered you a thousand pieces of gold so that you could distribute it to your followers. Since you have refused to accept it, what more can I say?"

Zhuangzi said, "I have heard of the purpose for which you want to employ me, which is to put an end to the king's amusements. Now let us suppose, on the one hand, that I try to persuade the king and in doing so, offend him, thus not satisfying you; in that case, I will be executed. What would I do with gold then? On the other hand, let us suppose that I persuade the king and do satisfy you. In that case, I could have anything I wanted in the Kingdom of Zhao."

1. Translated by Stephen Owen.
2. Confucian scholars well versed in the Classics.
3. *Classic of Poetry*.

4. Because these verses are not included in the current version of the *Classic of Poetry*, they were probably invented here to parody the behavior of Confucian scholars.

The crown prince said, "True. However, our king will see only swordsmen."

Zhuangzi: "Understood. But I am rather good with the sword."

The crown prince: "Be that as it may, the swordsmen that our king sees all have messy hair with bristling locks and slouched caps, plain, rough cap-strings, robes hitched up in the back, bulging eyes, and stumbling speech. This is the sort the king prefers. Since you will no doubt visit the king wearing your scholar's clothes, the whole thing will inevitably be a complete failure."

Zhuangzi: "Would you please have a swordsman's clothes prepared for me?"

Three days later, after the swordsman's clothes had been prepared, he met with the crown prince, and the crown prince presented him to the king, who waited for him with a bare blade drawn. Zhuangzi entered the gate of the great hall without hurrying; and when he saw the king, he did not bow.

The king, "Now that you have had the Crown Prince put you forward, what do you expect to do for me?"

"I've heard that the king enjoys swordplay, so I've come to see the king by way of swordplay."

The king said, "How can that sword of yours defend you?"

"If I had an opponent every ten paces, I could go a thousand leagues without pausing."

The king liked that very much. "Then there's no match for you in the whole world."

Zhuangzi said, "In swordplay one

> displays himself as vacant,
> initiates by advantage,
> is the second to swing the blow,
> is the first to strike home.

And I wish to have the chance to put this to the test."

The king said, "Stop now. Go to your lodgings and await my bidding. I'll invite you when I have arranged a contest to the death."

Then the king tried his swordsmen against one another for seven days, during which over sixty died of their wounds. Of these he got five or six men, whom he had bring their swords into the great hall. Then he summoned Zhuangzi.

"Today I'm going to have my men match swords."

Zhuangzi: "I've been looking forward to this for a long time."

The king: "Which would you use as your weapon, the long or the short?"

"For my own use, anything is fine. However, I have three swords that may be used only by a king. Let me tell you about these first, and then we will have the trial."

The king said, "Tell me about these three swords."

"There is an Emperor's sword, a sword of the great nobility, and the sword of an ordinary man."

The king said, "What is the Emperor's sword like?"

Zhuangzi said, "The sword of an Emperor:

> has as its point Yan Valley and Mount Stonewall,
> has as its blade Tai Mountain in Qi,
> has its blunt edge in the kingdoms of Jin and Wei,

has as its guard the kingdoms Zhou and Song,
has as its hilt the kingdoms Han and Wei;
its wrappings are the barbarians that surround us,
its sheath is the four seasons,
it is wound about by the Sea of Bo,
Mount Heng is the sash from which it hangs,
it is governed by the five phases,
it makes judgments of punishment or virtue;
it is brought forth through Dark and Light,
it is held through spring and summer,
and is used in autumn and winter.
This sword, when held straight, has nothing before it,
pointed up, has nothing above it,
pressed downward, has nothing below it,
and swung, has nothing around it.
It slashes the clouds that drift above,
it cuts to Earth's axis below.
Use this sword but once,
and the nobility will all be brought in line,
and the whole world will yield—
for this is the sword of an Emperor."

As if in a daze, King Wen was completely absorbed. He said, "What is the sword of the great nobility like?"

Zhuangzi said, "The sword of the great nobility:

has as its point shrewd and valiant gentlemen,
has as its blade honest and unassuming gentlemen,
has its blunt edge in good and worthy gentlemen,
has as its guard loyal and wise gentlemen,
has as its hilt daring and outstanding gentlemen.
And this sword too, when held straight, has nothing before it,
pointed up, has nothing above it,
pressed downward, has nothing below it,
and swung, has nothing around it.
It takes model from the roundness of Heaven above,
whereby it moves with sun, moon, and stars.
It takes model from the squareness of Earth below,
whereby it moves with the four seasons.
From the center it knows the people's will,
by which it brings peace to lands all around.
Use this sword but once,
and it is like a rumbling quake of thunder.
Within the boundaries all around,
there is no man but yields to it
and obeys the bidding of their lord.
This is a sword of the great nobility."

The king then asked, "And what is the sword of the ordinary man like?"

Zhuangzi said, "The sword of the ordinary man belongs to one with messy hair, with bristling locks and slouched cap, plain, rough cap-strings, robes hitched up in the back, bulging eyes, and stumbling speech, men who hack at each other in front of you. A high hack will chop off a neck, and a low one cuts liver or lungs. This is the sword of the ordinary man, and it is no different from cockfighting, with a life cut off in a single morning. It has no use at all in the workings of a kingdom. We have here a king, to whom belongs the position of an Emperor, and yet who is in love with the sword of the ordinary man. And for this king's sake I have taken the liberty of disparaging it."

The king then drew him up into the hall where the Master of the Kitchens was having food set out. The king kept circling the table, until Zhuangzi said, "Sit calmly and settle your spirit. I have finished my expostulation on swords." Thereafter the king did not leave his palace for three months, and his swordsmen all perished on their own swordpoints in their places.

Selected Bibliographies

I. Ancient Mediterranean and Near Eastern Literature

On the early history of writing, an excellent starting point is Walter Ong, *Orality and Literacy: Technologizing of the Word* (1982), which teases out the cultural and psychological implications of the shift from an oral to a literate culture. Those with a particular interest in Near Eastern cultures can begin with James Pritchard's classic anthology of texts in translation, containing many illustrations: *The Ancient Near East: An Anthology of Texts and Pictures* (reissued 2010). A good illustrated survey of Greek and Roman culture by a number of different specialists is John Boardman, Jasper Griffin, and Oswyn Murray, *The Oxford History of the Classical World* (1986). Introductory texts that combine discussion of Greek, Roman, and Near Eastern cultures include *An Introduction to the Ancient World* (2008), by Lukas de Blois and R. J. van der Spek, and the less scholarly but lively *The History of the Ancient World: From the Earliest Accounts to the Fall of Rome*, by Susan Wise Bauer (2007). Reliable general introductions to Greek and Roman literature include Albin Lesky, *Greek Literature* (reissued 1996), and G. B. Conte, *Latin Literature: A History* (reissued 1999). For more information about the ancient world, including images of ancient art, architecture, and artifacts, as well as ancient Greek and Roman texts, a wonderful resource is Tufts University's website *Perseus* (www.perseus.tufts.edu).

Aeschylus
Simon Goldhill, *Aeschylus: The Oresteia* (1992), is a clearly written introduction to the whole trilogy and includes both discussion of metaphor and other literary techniques, and an account of the political and social background. There is more on Aeschylus's staging in an older but still useful study, Oliver Taplin, *The Stagecraft of Aeschylus: The Dramatic Use of Entrances and Exits in Greek Tragedy* (1977). Further discussion of Aeschylus's literary techniques appears in D. J. Conacher, *Aeschylus' Oresteia: A Literary Commentary* (1987). A good recent collection of important essays is Michael Lloyd, ed., *Aeschylus* (2007).

Aesop
The introduction to Laura Gibb, trans., *Aesop's Fables* (2008), draws attention to the complex tradition by which these fables came to be written down, in many different forms. The ancient, anonymous *Life of Aesop* appears in Lloyd Daly, trans., *Anthology of Greek Popular Literature* (1998). The Loeb edition of Babrius, reputed author of a set of fables in Greek verse, from the first century C.E., and Phaedrus, a Macedonian slave who wrote Latin verse fables in the first century C.E., in English translation, includes a survey of parallels between the Aesopic fable and the traditions of ancient Mesopotamia (1965). A useful scholarly survey of the genre is Gert-Jan van Dijk, *Ainoi, Logoi, Mythoi: Fables in Archaic, Classical, and Hellenistic Greek Literature: With a Study of the Theory and Terminology of the Genre* (1997).

Ancient Athenian Drama
A good introduction to the genre of Athenian tragedy, which includes discussions of all the

extant plays and is particularly strong on social context, is Edith Hall, *Greek Tragedy: Suffering under the Sun* (2010). Marianne McDonald and J. Michael Walton, eds., *Cambridge Companion to Greek and Roman Theatre* (2007), includes essays on both tragedy and comedy, and also has some discussion of staging. Another fine collection of introductory essays, on tragedy, comedy, and satyr plays, is Ian C. Storey and Arlene Allan, *A Guide to Ancient Greek Drama* (2005). Further information on performance contexts, in the fifth century and also in modern revivals, can be found in David Wiles, *Mask and Performance in Greek Tragedy: From Ancient Festival to Modern Experimentation* (2007). Many pieces of visual evidence of Greek theater, including vase paintings, statues, and photographs of remaining theater sites, are collected in Richard Green and Eric Handley, *Images of the Greek Theater* (1995).

Ancient Egyptian Literature

The material and cultural background to ancient Egyptian civilization is presented in John Baines and Jaromir Malek, *Cultural Atlas of Ancient Egypt* (2000). Ian Shaw, ed., *The Oxford History of Ancient Egypt* (2000), is a useful treatment with broad cultural coverage for some periods. Marc van de Mieroop, *A History of Ancient Egypt* (2011), is the most up-to-date and reliable history. Alan K. Bowman, *Egypt after the Pharaohs, 332 BC–AD 642: From Alexander to the Arab Conquest* (1996), is an excellent presentation of the post-Pharaonic period. Two reliable surveys of Egyptian religion are Byron E. Shafer, ed., *Religion in Ancient Egypt: Gods, Myths, and Personal Practice* (1991), and Stephen Quirke, *Ancient Egyptian Religion* (1995). Donald B. Redford, ed., *The Oxford Encyclopedia of Ancient Egypt*, 3 vols. (2001), has articles on most major topics relating to ancient Egypt. The *UCLA Encyclopedia of Egyptology* (www.uee.ucla.edu) is an online resource that will gradually supersede print materials in its area.

There is no broad, general study of all periods of ancient Egyptian literature, but the works detailed in this paragraph have introductions setting the ancient works in context, in addition to prefatory remarks and notes on the individual texts. The largest and richest collection of translations is Miriam Lichtheim, *Ancient Egyptian Literature: A Book of Readings* (1973–80; reprinted with new foreword, 2006), 3 vols. A one-volume work that concentrates on fictional texts is William Kelly Simpson, ed., *The Literature of Ancient Egypt* (3rd ed., 2003). R. B. Parkinson, *Voices from Ancient Egypt* (1991), gives an excellent, more diverse selection from the Middle Kingdom. Parkinson has also provided an outstanding full translation of Middle Kingdom texts, The Tale of Sinuhe *and Other Ancient Egyptian Poems, 1940–1640 BC* (1998), and his *Reading Ancient Egyptian Poetry: Among Other Histories* (2009) is a detailed study of the context and background of the principal Middle Kingdom tales and includes questions of performance and new translations of the oldest surviving manuscripts.

For those wishing to explore Egyptian literature in relation to other Near Eastern literatures, William W. Hallo and K. Lawson Younger, eds., *The Context of Scripture: Canonical Compositions, Monumental Inscriptions, and Archival Documents from the Biblical World* (2003), 3 vols., is a rich resource. Susan Walker and Peter Higgs, eds., *Cleopatra of Egypt: From History to Myth* (2001), places *Stela of Taimhotep* in the context of the art and religion of its period (184–87).

Aristophanes

A prose translation of *Lysistrata*, along with Aristophanes' two other comedies about women, appears in Jeffrey Henderson, trans. and ed., *Three Plays by Aristophanes: Staging Women* (1996, 2010); this collection has a useful introduction to the plays and to Athenian comedy in general. A good general introduction to Aristophanes is D. M. MacDowell, *Aristophanes and Athens: An Introduction to the Plays* (1995). More on the genre can be found in Gregory Dobrov, ed., *Brill's Companion to the Study of Greek Comedy* (2010). The political context of the plays is discussed in Keith C. Sidwell, *Aristophanes the Democrat: The Politics of Satirical Comedy during the Peloponnesian War* (2009). A good discussion of staging is Martin Revermann, *Comic Business: Theatricality, Dramatic Technique and Performance Contexts of Aristophanic Comedy* (2006).

Catullus

A good general literary introduction is Charles Martin, *Catullus* (1992). An important study of Catullus's masculine, macho persona is David Wray, *Catullus and the Poetics of Roman Manhood* (2001). To know more about Clodia, on whom Lesbia may have been based, read Cicero's *Pro Caelio, which is* included in Michael Grant, trans., *Selected Political Speeches* (1977). Maria Wyke, *The Roman Mistress: Ancient and Modern Representations* (2002), mostly focuses on authors later than Catullus, but has important implications for interpretation of the Lesbia poems; Wyke reads the poet's girlfriend as a literary creation and stresses that she need not be based on any real person.

Creation and the Cosmos
A useful survey of ancient Near Eastern literature is J. M. Sasson, *Civilizations of the Ancient Near East* (1995), vol. 4, a large part of which is dedicated to the literatures of Egypt. In Markham J. Geller and Mineke Schipper, eds., *Imagining Creation* (2008), W. G. Lambert's article "Mesopotamian Creation Stories" (15–59) includes a general survey of Mesopotamian creation myths and a new translation of the *Enuma Elish.* Introductions to Sumerian and Akkadian literature can also be found in J. Black et al., *The Literature of Ancient Sumer* (2004), and B. R. Foster, *Before the Muses* (2005). Martin West's introduction to his prose translation of *Theogony and Works and Days* (1999), draws useful parallels between Hesiodic and Near Eastern myths. Jenny Strauss Clay, *Hesiod's Cosmos* (2003), is an intelligent literary account of Greek myth. Catherine Osborne, *Presocratic Philosophy: A Very Short Introduction* (2004), gives a good overview of Thales and the other pre-Socratics and points the reader to further secondary sources. Stuart Gillespie and Philip Hardie, eds., *The Cambridge Companion to Lucretius* (2007), contains essays by prominent Lucretius scholars on both literary and philosophical questions.

Euripides
A good collection of scholarly essays on Euripides is Judith Mossman, ed., *Euripides* (2003). For representations of "barbarians" in tragedy, including in *Medea,* see Edith Hall, *Inventing the Barbarian: Greek Self-Definition through Tragedy* (1989). Ruby Blondell, ed., *Women on the Edge: Four Plays* (1999), includes a translation of *Medea* and three other Euripides plays focused on women, as well as a useful introduction that discusses representations of gender in these plays. A good general introduction to Euripides, with

brief discussions of all nineteen extant plays and a focus on their reception after ancient times is Michael Walton, *Euripides Our Contemporary* (2010). William Allan, *Euripides: Medea* (2002), surveys the most important literary themes of the play.

Gilgamesh
The most recent scholarly translations of *The Epic of Gilgamesh* are Stephanie Delany, *Myths from Mesopotamia: Creation, the Flood, Gilgamesh, and Others* (1989); Maureen Kovacs, *The Epic of Gilgamesh* (1989); Andrew George, *The Epic of Gilgamesh: The Babylonian Epic Poem and Other Texts in Akkadian and Sumerian* (1999) and *The Babylonian Gilgamesh Epic: Introduction, Critical Edition, and Cuneiform Texts* (2003); and Benjamin Foster, *The Epic of Gilgamesh* (2001). They contain ample commentary and important introductory articles that aid in the interpretation of the epic. The poet Stephen Mitchell's *Gilgamesh: A New English Version* (2004) is a smooth verse retelling of the epic. David Ferry, *Gilgamesh: A New Rendering into English Verse* (1992) is also recommended. For a study of the evolution of the story over time, see Geffrey Tigay, *The Evolution of the Gilgamesh Epic* (1982). Alexander Heidel shows the importance of *Gilgamesh* for biblical studies in *The Gilgamesh Epic and Old Testament Parallels* (1963). Rivkah Harris, *Gender and Aging in Mesopotamia: The Gilgamesh Epic and Other Ancient Literature* (2000), discusses the gender dynamic in the epic in the light of other ancient texts. John Maier, *Gilgamesh: A Reader* (1997), contains seminal articles on *Gilgamesh* and an extensive bibliography. David Damrosch, *The Buried Book: The Loss and Rediscovery of the Great Epic of Gilgamesh* (2007), tells the story of the colonial adventurers, scholars, and contemporary writers involved in the rediscovery of *Gilgamesh.*

For those wishing to discover the riches of Mesopotamian literature beyond *Gilgamesh,* Benjamin Foster's voluminous *Before the Muses: An Anthology of Akkadian Literature* (1993, 2005) and *From Distant Days: Myths, Tales, and Poetry of Ancient Mesopotamia* (1995) contain a wealth of material. Jack Sasson et al., *Civilizations of the Ancient Near East* (1995), vol. 4, is devoted to languages and literatures of the region. For vivid presentations of Mesopotamian civilization, see Jean Bottéro, *Mesopotamia: Writing, Reasoning, and the Gods* (1992); J. N. Postgate, *Early Mesopotamia: Society and Econ-*

omy at the Dawn of History (1992); and Benjamin Foster and Karen Polinger Foster, *Civilizations of Ancient Iraq* (2009).

The Hebrew Bible

Richard Elliott Friedman, *Who Wrote the Bible?* (1987), is a clear introduction to the idea that each of the first books of the Bible is composed from several narrative strands (the "documentary hypothesis"). The *Anchor Bible*, in multiple volumes, has useful introductions and notes to each book of the Bible, including historical information. More on the historicity of the Bible can be found in Ronald Hendel, *Remembering Abraham: Culture, History and Memory in Ancient Israel* (2004). Robert Alter and Frank Kermode, eds., *The Literary Guide to the Bible* (1987), has useful essays on approaching the stylistic and narrative structures of the Bible. James L. Crenshaw, *Defending God: Biblical Responses to the Problem of Evil* (2005), is an interesting attempt to grapple with the central moral problems raised by the Hebrew Bible.

Homer

The first chapter of Erich Auerbach's *Mimesis: The Representation of Reality in Western Literature* (1953), trans. Willard Trask, gives a stimulating account of how Homeric narrative technique might differ from that of the Hebrew Bible. Essential works on the relation of the Homeric poems to the Greek oral tradition include Albert Lord, *The Singer of Tales* (1960), and Milman Parry, *The Making of Homeric Verse* (1973). Jenny Strauss Clay, *The Wrath of Athena: Gods and Men in the Odyssey* (1983), provides a useful overview of the gods in the epic. Female characters, human and divine, are discussed in Beth Cohen, ed., *The Distaff Side: Representing the Female in Homer's* Odyssey (1995). A good collection of classic essays on the *Odyssey* is Seth Schein, ed., *Reading the* Odyssey: *Selected Interpretative Essays* (1996). Those interested in the history of Homeric Greece will find useful information in M. I. Finley, *Early Greece: The Bronze and Archaic Ages* (1981). James Tatum, *The Mourner's Song: War and Remembrance from the* Iliad *to Vietnam* (2003), is a moving account of the *Iliad* in the context of later representations of war. Sheila Murnaghan's introductory essays to Stanley Lombardo's

translations of the *Odyssey* (2000) and the *Iliad* (1997) provide rich interpretations of important literary themes, such as disguise, hospitality, heroism, and death.

Ovid

Sarah Mack, *Ovid* (1988), is a good general introduction, with a long chapter on the *Metamorphoses*. Philip Hardie, *Ovid's Poetics of Illusion* (2002), is an important guide to Ovid's poetic technique; metapoetic aspects are also discussed in R. A. Smith, *Poetic Allusion and Poetic Embrace in Ovid and Virgil* (1997), which includes a fine reading of the Pygmalion episode. Garth Tissol, *The Face of Nature* (1997), provides a useful close reading of the poem, including discussion of Ovid's puns, and looks in particular at the Myrrha episode. Charles Martindale, *Ovid Renewed: Ovidian Influences on Literature and Art from the Middle Ages to the Twentieth Century* (1988), gives some idea of the importance of Ovid for later literature.

Plato

An interesting collection of scholarly essays on both philosophical and literary themes, with some discussion of postclassical reception, is J. H. Lesher, Debra Nails, and Frisbee C. C. Sheffield, eds., *Plato's Symposium: Issues in Interpretation and Reception* (2006). A good introduction to themes in the text is Richard Hunter, *Plato's Symposium* (2004). Those interested in studying Plato more broadly can find pointers in Julia Annas, *Plato: A Very Short Introduction* (2003). A provocative philosophical discussion of Plato's use of the dialogue form can be found in Charles Kahn, *Plato and the Socratic Dialogue: The Philosophical Use of a Literary Form* (1996). The extensive scholarly and theoretical work on Athenian sexuality includes David M. Halperin, John J. Winkler, and Froma I. Zeitlin, eds., *Before Sexuality: The Construction of Erotic Experience in the Ancient Greek World* (1990), which explores sexuality as a cultural construct; Kenneth Dover's introduction to his edition of the *Symposium* (1980) and his *Greek Homosexuality* (1989), which assumes, controversially, that the term "*homosexuality*" can be applied back to the Greeks; and the equally controversial work of James Davidson, *The Greeks and Greek Love* (2009).

Sappho

A useful collection of scholarly essays is Ellen Greene, ed., *Reading Sappho: Contemporary Approaches* (1996). Marguerite Johnson, *Sappho* (2007), is a clear, short introduction to some important literary themes in the poet's work. Sappho is read alongside two male, contemporary lyric poets in A. P. Burnett, *Three Archaic Poets: Archilochus, Alcaeus, Sappho* (1983). The reception of Sappho is particularly interesting; Margaret Reynolds, ed., *The Sappho Companion* (2000), is a collection of translations, imitations, and adaptations of Sappho's poems by postclassical poets and writers.

Sophocles

A good literary introduction to Sophocles, which draws on psychoanalytic and anthropological ideas to emphasize pairs of concepts (such as civilization versus wildness) is Charles Segal, *Tragedy and Civilization: An Interpretation of Sophocles* (1981). Important essays by various scholars on *Oedipus the King,* including a classic article by E. R. Dodds on common student misinterpretations of the play, are collected in Michael O'Brien, ed., *Twentieth-Century Interpretations of* Oedipus Rex (1968). Mary Blundell, *Helping Friends and Harming Enemies* (1989), reads Sophocles through the maxim of Greek popular morality alluded to in its title; one chapter is devoted to *Antigone.* The city of Thebes in Greek tragedy in general, and in these plays in particular, is discussed by Froma Zeitlin in her essay in Zeitlin and John J. Winkler, eds., *Nothing to Do with Dionysos?* (1990). In two editions of the plays in Greek, scholars have written introductions that are accessible and useful even to the nonspecialist reader: R. D. Dawe on *Oedipus Tyrannos,* and Mark Griffith on *Antigone* (1982 and 1999 respectively). The political dimensions of the plays are particularly difficult for modern readers to grasp; an interesting attempt to apply the specifics of Athenian political history to the plays is Michael Vickers, *Sophocles and Alcibiades: Athenian Politics in Ancient Greek Literature* (2008). Both plays have been adapted in many different ways for the modern stage; one important example is Seamus Heaney's version of *Antigone,* set in Northern Ireland, *The Burial at Thebes* (2004).

Speech, Writing, Poetry

Walter Ong, *Orality and Literacy: The Technologizing of the Word* (2002), is essential reading. On the social contexts of scribal life in Mesopotamia, see L. E. Pearce, "The Scribes and Scholars of Ancient Mesopotamia," in J. M. Sasson et al., eds., *Civilizations of the Ancient Near East* (1995). More ancient Greek and Roman texts expressing ideas about speech, literacy, and literature can be found in D. Russell and M. Winterbottom, eds. and trans., *Ancient Literary Criticism* (1972). An important close reading of Aristotle's *Poetics* is S. Halliwell, *Aristotle's Poetics* (1986); see also his translation with commentary (1987). An introduction to the *Ars Poetica* is Bernard Frischer, *Shifting Paradigms: New Approaches to Horace's* Ars poetica (1991). Andrew Ford, *The Origins of Criticism* (2002), is an important account of how literary criticism came into being. A groundbreaking discussion of ancient modes of reading, including the importance of allegorical reading, is Peter Struck, *Birth of the Symbol* (2004). A. Richard Hunter, *Critical Moments in Classical Literature: Studies in the Ancient View of Literature and Its Uses* (2009), also offers insights into how the ancient Greeks and Romans imagined their literature.

Travel and Conquest

Two controversial accounts of racial identity and power in the ancient world, and in modern understandings of the ancient world, are Martin Bernal, *Black Athena: The Afroasiatic Roots of Classical Civilization* (1987), which emphasizes Egyptian influence on Greek myth and culture; and Edward Said, *Orientalism* (1978), which traces modern "occidentalist" bias back to the ancient Greeks and includes a reading of Aeschylus's *Persians.* A more recent, also controversial account is Benjamin Isaac, *The Invention of Racism in Classical Antiquity* (2004). A good collection of essays on Herodotus can be found in the *Cambridge Companion to Herodotus* (2006). Page DuBois, *Slavery: Antiquity and Its Legacy* (2009), juxtaposes ancient and modern experiences of slavery. The introduction to Sandra R. Joshel and Sheila Murnaghan, eds., *Women and Slaves in Greco-Roman Culture: Differential Equations* (1998), gives good insights into how we might look at these nonelite groups in classical cultures. Carol Doherty, *The Poetics of Colonization* (1993), is an interesting attempt to read archaic Greek poetry in the light of ancient experiences of colonization.

Amanda Podany, *Brotherhood of Kings: How International Relations Shaped the Ancient Near East* (2010), provides a broad vista of intercultural and diplomatic contacts in the Ancient Near East. Muzhou Pu (or Mu-chou Poo), *Enemies of Civilization: Attitudes toward Foreigners in Ancient Mesopotamia, Egypt, and China* (2005), compares how three of the world's most ancient civilizations defined themselves against their neighbors.

To read more tales from the Middle Kingdom like *The Tale of the Shipwrecked Sailor*, Richard B. Parkinson, The Tale of Sinuhe *and Other Ancient Egyptian Poems, 1940–1640 BC* (1997), contains outstanding full translations. John H. Taylor, *Egypt and Nubia* (1991), further explores relations between Egypt and Nubia. On royal inscriptions and their relation to other Egyptian literary genres, see Christopher Eyre, "The Semna Stelae: Quotation, Genre and Functions of Literature," in Sarah Israelit-Groll, ed., *Studies in Egyptology Presented to Miriam Lichtheim*, vol. 1 (1990).

Virgil
The structure of the whole poem is discussed in David O. Ross, *Virgil's* Aeneid: *A Reader's Guide* (2007). S. Harrison, ed., *Oxford Readings in Virgil's* Aeneid (1990) has useful articles on many aspects of the poem. A good literary introduction to the whole poem is Michael C. J. Putnam, *Virgil's Aeneid: Interpretation and Influence* (1995). Yasmin Syed, *Virgil's* Aeneid *and the Roman Self* (2005), gives an interesting account of how the poem participated in, and formed, Roman cultural values. A good short discussion of Virgilian allusion to earlier literature, why it works and why it matters, is R. O. A. M. Lyne, *Further Voices in Virgil's* Aeneid (1987). S. Quinn, ed., *Why Virgil?* (2000), includes literary essays and some examples of modern literature imitating or responding to Virgil. David Quint, *Epic and Empire* (1993), provides an important model for reading Virgil and later epics in terms of the losers and winners of history.

II. India's Ancient Epics and Tales

Burton Stein, *A History of India* (1998), and Stanley Wolpert, *A New History of India* (2008), offer good, complementary historical overviews of ancient India; Upinder Singh, *A History of Ancient and Early Medieval India* (2009), provides a more detailed, up-to-date account. Romila Thapar, *Cultural Pasts: Essays in Early Indian History* (2000), contains the best critical analyses of specific aspects of the ancient period. Thomas R. Trautmann, *The Aryan Debate* (2005), surveys recent controversies on India's prehistory, and includes a selection of important texts from the eighteenth century onward. Patrick Olivelle, *Upaniṣads* (1996), provides an excellent overview of Vedic religion, with translations of some canonical texts; Gavin Flood, *An Introduction to Hinduism* (1996), explains both early and later forms of the religion. Peter Harvey, *An Introduction to Buddhism* (1990), covers history, doctrine, and practice, with a focus on Mahayana Buddhism; Joseph M. Kitagawa and Mark D. Cummings, *Buddhism and Asian History* (1989), offers greater depth as well as a broader sweep, with specialist essays by many scholars.

The Bhagavad-Gītā
Among the world's canonical religious texts, the *Bhagavad-gītā* is second only to the Bible in the number of times it has been translated, and the range of languages into which it has been rendered. Of the many modern translations available in English, Barbara Stoler Miller, *The* Bhagavad-gītā: *Krishna's Counsel in Time of War* (1986), is one of the most reliable and accessible. R. C. Zaehner, *The Bhagavad-gītā* (1969), includes the original Sanskrit text in English transcription, along with a literal rendering, a more polished version, and a commentary on each verse. The most useful Indian translation into English is S. Radhakrishnan's older *The Bhagavad-gītā*—1948 and later editions. For a discussion of Indian interpretations of the poem, see Robert Minor, *Modern Interpreters of the* Bhagavadgītā (1986); and for an account of its reception in the West, consult Eric Sharpe, *The Universal Gītā: Western Images of the* Bhagavad Gītā, *a Bicentennial Survey* (1985).

The Jātaka

A complete English translation is available in E. B. Cowell, *The Jātaka: Or Stories of the Buddha's Former Births*, 6 vols. (1981). A good selection is provided in H. T. Francis and E. J. Thomas, eds., *Jātaka Tales* (1956). On the wide influence of this work from Afghanistan to China, see M. Cummings, *The Lives of the Buddha in the Art and Literature of Asia* (1982). The fascinating story of the *Jātaka's* transmission to Europe is recounted in T. W. Rhys David's introduction to *Buddhist Birth Stories* (1880). An excellent translation of the canonical Sanskrit version of this work is offered in Peter Khoroche, *Once the Buddha Was a Monkey: Aryasura's Jātakamala* (1989).

The Mahabharata

The best condensed version of the epic in English, which enables readers to grasp it as a whole and also to become familiar with many of its details, is C. V. Narasimhan, *Mahābhārata: An English Version Based on Selected Verses* (1965). A complete rendering of the poem that is still useful is Manmatha Nath Dutt, *A Prose English Translation of the* Mahābhārata (1895–1905), in six volumes. A full scholarly translation of the first five major books of the epic, with notes and critical commentary, is available in the three volumes of J. A. B. Van Buitenen, *The Mahābhārata* (1975–). Important modern Indian interpretations include V. S. Sukhtankar, *The Meaning of the* Mahā bhārata (1957), and Irawati Karve, *Yuganta: The End of an Epoch* (1971).

The Rāmāyaṇa of Vālmīki

The Rāmāyaṇa of Vālmīki: An Epic of Ancient India (1984–), translated, annotated, and introduced by various scholars led by Robert Goldman, is the best recent version in English; five volumes, representing books 1 through 5, have appeared so far. Swami Venkatesanand, *The Concise Rāmāyaṇa* (1988), the source of our text, is a condensed prose version, which emphasizes the religious message of Vālmīki's epic, interpreted from a conservative modern perspective. A particularly readable literary prose rendering of Kamban's twelfth-century Tamil version of the poem appears in R. K. Narayan, *The Rāmā yaṇa* (1972). Important scholarly essays on most aspects of "the story of Rāma" are collected in Paula Richman, *Many Rāmāyaṇas: The Diversity of a Narrative Tradition in South Asia* (1991).

III. Early Chinese Literature and Thought

Jacques Gernet, *A History of Chinese Civilization* (1982), is a commanding survey history of China. Patricia Ebrey, Anne Walthall, and James Palais, *Pre-Modern East Asia to 1800: A Cultural, Social and Political History* (2009), is an excellent shorter account of Chinese history in the broader context of East Asia. Michael Loewe and Edward Shaughnessy, eds., *The Cambridge History of Ancient China* (1999), is a comprehensive reference work for early Chinese history and culture. For a vivid account of thought and society in early imperial China, see Mark Lewis, *The Early Chinese Empires: Qin and Han* (2007). For a comprehensive history of Chinese Literature refer to Kang-i Sun Chang and Stephen Owen, eds., *The Cambridge History of Chinese Literature* (2010). Wiebke Denecke, Wai-yee Li, and Xiaofei Tian, eds., *The Oxford Handbook of Classical Chinese Literature (1000 BCE–900 CE)* (2017) gives a comprehensive thematic, topical, and cross-cultural overview of Chinese literature during its first two millennia.

For those wishing to explore more early Chinese texts, Stephen Owen, *Anthology of Chinese Literature, Beginnings to 1911* (1996), presents a rich selection of Chinese literature with ample introductory material and commentary. Cyril Birch, *Anthology of Chinese Literature* (1965), and Victor Mair, *The Columbia Anthology of Traditional Chinese Literature* (1994), which is organized by genre and not chronology, are also recommended. For early Chinese thought and religion, see William Theodore de Bary, *Sources of Chinese Tradition* (2nd ed. 1999), a two-volume anthology covering a broad variety of original texts in translation from the beginnings to the modern period.

For broader explorations of Chinese Masters Literature, see Benjamin Schwartz, *The World of Thought in Ancient China* (1985); A. C. Graham, *Disputers of the Tao: Philosophical Argument in Ancient China* (1989); Chad Hansen, *A Daoist Theory of Chinese Thought: A Philosophical Interpretation* (1992); and Wiebke Denecke, *The Dynamics of Masters Literature: Early Chinese Thought from Confucius to Han Feizi* (2010). To explore comparisons between Ancient Greece and China, see Lisa Raphals, *Knowing Words: Wisdom and Cunning in the Classical Traditions of China and Greece* (1992), and Steven Shankman and Stephen Durrant, *The Siren and the Sage: Knowledge and Wisdom in Ancient Greece and China* (2000).

Classic of Poetry

Other translations for comparison include Arthur Waley, *The Book of Songs* (1937), and Ezra Pound, *The Classic Anthology Defined by Confucius* (1954). Anecdotes by the Han Dynasty scholar Han Ying (fl. 150 B.C.E.) that show how poems from the *Classic of Poetry* were applied to concrete situations and moral questions can be found in James R. Hightower, *Han Shih Wai Chuan: Han Ying's Illustrations of the Didactic Application of the* Classic of Songs (1952). For stimulating studies of the anthology and its interpretation, see Steven Van Zoeren, *Poetry and Personality: Reading, Exegesis and Hermeneutics in Traditional China* (1991), and Haun Saussy, *The Problem of a Chinese Aesthetic* (1993). Pauline Yu, *The Reading of Imagery in the Chinese Poetic Tradition* (1987), is a compelling study of imagery in the *Classic of Poetry* and other Chinese texts. For the "Great Preface" of the *Classic of Poetry* and Chinese poetics in general, Stephen Owen's *Readings in Chinese Literary Thought* (1992) gives a captivating introduction to major works of Chinese literary thought and provides a bilingual translation of the original texts with detailed commentary. James Liu's *Chinese Theories of Literature* (1975) sketches major Chinese paradigms of the concept of literature. To explore literary thought in more recent times, see *Modern Chinese Literary Thought: Writings on Literature, 1893–1945*, ed. Kirk Denton (1996). For scholarly essays on Chinese literary criticism in general, see *Chinese Aesthetics and Literature: A Reader,* ed. Corinne H. Dale (2004). For a broader exploration of literary interpretation in Chinese and Western literatures, see Longxi Zhang's *The Tao and the Logos: Literary Hermeneutics, East and West* (1992).

Confucius

There are many translations of the *Analects.* The selections in this anthology are from Simon Leys's complete translation, *The Analects of Confucius* (1997). Arthur Waley's resonant translation of 1938 has recently been reprinted with an explanatory introduction by Sarah Allan (2000). D. C. Lau, *Analects* (1979), is a solid translation and contains a lucid introduction to Confucius and his ideas. Roger T. Ames and Henry Rosemont, *The Analects of Confucius: A Philosophical Translation* (1998), provides the classical Chinese text alongside an English version. For an overview of early Chinese philosophy and thought, read A. C. Graham, *Disputers of the Tao: Philosophical Argument in Ancient China* (1989), and Wiebke Denecke, *The Dynamics of Masters Literature. Early Chinese Thought from Confucius to Hanfeizi* (2011). Herbert Fingarette, *Confucius—The Secular as Sacred* (1972), remains one of the most persuasive accounts of the appeal of the *Analects.* David L. Hall and Roger T. Ames, *Thinking through Confucius* (1987), is an innovative reading of the *Analects* inspired by American pragmatic philosophy. John Makeham, *Transmitters and Creators: Chinese Commentators and Commentaries on the* Analects (2003), gives insight into later commentators' understanding of the *Analects.* For a compelling account of early Confucianism, see Robert Eno, *The Confucian Creation of Heaven: Philosophy and the Defense of Ritual Mastery* (1990). Thomas A. Wilson, *On Sacred Grounds: Culture, Society, Politics, and the Formation of the Cult of Confucius* (2002), is a collection of articles about the religious dimensions of Confucianism and the Confucius cult. Lionel Jensen, *Manufacturing Confucianism: Chinese Traditions and Universal Civilization* (1997), discusses how the image of Confucianism created by European missionaries working in China during the sixteenth and seventeenth centuries has influenced modern understandings. John Makeham, *Lost Soul: "Confucianism" in Contemporary Chinese Academic Discourse* (2008), surveys the significance of Confucianism in today's intellectual debates.

Daodejing

Among the many translations of the *Daodejing*, D. C. Lau, *Tao Te Ching* (1963); Roger Ames and David L. Hall, Daodejing—*Making This Life Significant—A Philosophical Translation* (2003); and Red Pine, *Lao-tzu's Taoteching: With Selected Commentaries of the Past 2000 Years* (1997), are especially recommended. Robert G. Henricks, *Lao-Tzu's Tao Te Ching: A New Translation Based on the Recently Discovered Ma-wang-tui Texts* (1989) and *Lao Tzu's Tao Te Ching: A Translation of the Startling New Documents Found at Guodian* (2000), are based on excavated manuscripts of the *Daodejing* and are interesting to compare to the received text. For an overview of early Chinese philosophy and thought, read A. C. Graham, *Disputers of the Tao: Philosophical Argument in Ancient China* (1989), and Wiebke Denecke, *The Dynamics of Masters Literature. Early Chinese Thought from Confucius to Hanfeizi* (2011).

For a broader view on the *Daodejing* within the context of Early Chinese intellectual debates, see the chapters on the *Daodejing* in the books on Chinese Masters Literature indicated in the regional introduction to "Early Chinese Thought and Literature." Arthur Waley, *The Way and Its Power: A Study of the Tao Te Ching and Its Place in Chinese Thought* (1958), is still a classic study of the *Daodejing*. Michael LaFargue, *Tao and Method: A Reasoned Approach to the Tao Te Ching* (1994), is a compelling reconstruction of what the text might have meant to its earliest readers. For interpretations of one of the most influential commentators of the *Daodejing*, see Rudolf Wagner, *The Craft of the Chinese Commentator: Wang Bi on the Laozi* (2000) and *A Chinese Reading of the Daodejing: Wang Bi's Commentary on the Laozi with Critical Text and Translation* (2003). For views on the *Daodejing* and its relation to the *Laozi* and Daoism, see Livia Kohn and Michael LaFargue, *Lao-tzu and the Tao-te-ching* (1998), and Mark Csikszentmihalyi and Philip J. Ivanhoe, *Religious and Philosophical Aspects of the Laozi* (1999).

Songs of the South

David Hawkes, *The Songs of the South: An Anthology of Poems by Qu Yuan and Other Poets* (1985), contains a complete translation with a detailed introduction. You can compare the translation to Hsien-yi Yang and Gladys Yang, *Li sao, and Other Poems of Qu Yuan* (1955). Zong-Qi Cai, ed., *How To Read Chinese Poetry: A Guided Anthology* (2008), contains an annotated bilingual translation of parts of the "Nine Songs" and of "Encountering Sorrow." On the "Nine Songs," see Arthur Waley's classic work *The Nine Songs: A Study of Shamanism in Ancient China* (1973). On the allegorical interpretation of the *Songs of Chu*, see Geoffrey R. Waters, *Three Elegies of Ch'u: An Introduction to the Traditional Interpretation of the 'Ch'u Tz'u'* (1985), and the relevant chapter in Pauline Yu's *The Reading of Imagery in the Chinese Poetic Tradition* (1987). The essays in Constance Cook and John S. Major, *Defining Chu: Image and Reality in Ancient China* (1999), portray the culture of Chu in the light of the recent archaeological discoveries.

Zhuangzi

There are a number of good English translations, including Burton Watson, *The Complete Works of Chuang Tzu* (1968); A. C. Graham, *Chuang-tzu: The Inner Chapters* (1981); Sam Hamill and J. P. Seaton, *The Essential Chuang Tzu* (1998); and Brook Ziporyn, *Zhuangzi: The Essential Writings with Selections from Traditional Commentaries* (2009). For an overview of early Chinese philosophy and thought, read A. C. Graham, *Disputers of the Tao: Philosophical Argument in Ancient China* (1989), and Wiebke Denecke, *The Dynamics of Masters Literature. Early Chinese Thought from Confucius to Hanfeizi* (2011). For situating *Zhuangzi* in the context of early Chinese intellectual debates see the chapters on *Zhuangzi* in the books on Chinese Masters Literature indicated in the regional introduction to "Early Chinese thought and literature." *Zhuangzi* has inspired many interpretive essays and personal reflections, some of which can be found in Roger T. Ames, *Wandering at Ease in the Zhuangzi* (1998); Paul Kjellberg and Philip J. Ivanhoe, *Essays on Skepticism, Relativism and Ethics in the Zhuangzi* (1996); and Victor H. Mair, *Experimental Essays on Chuang-tzu* (1983).

Timeline

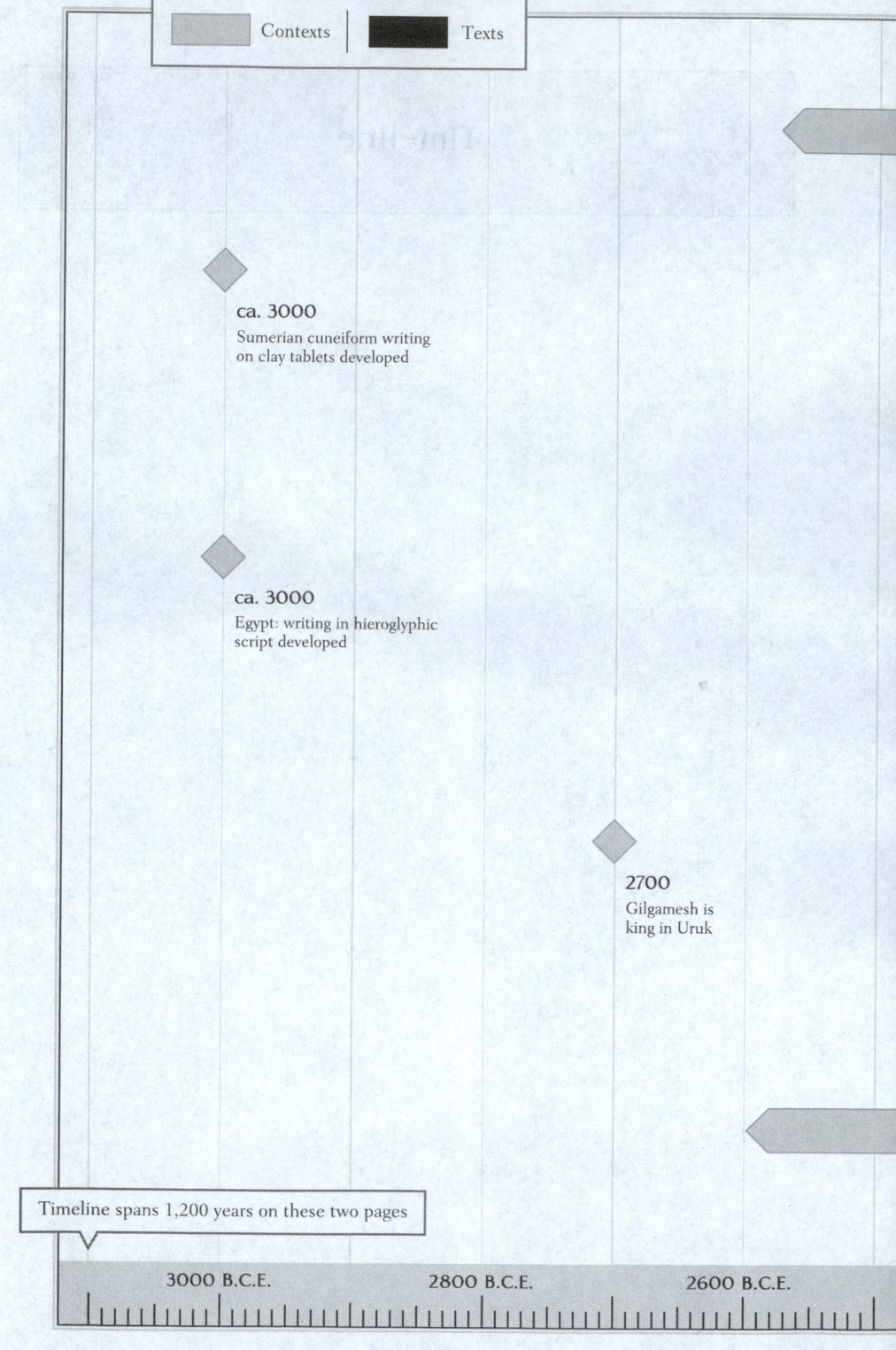

Contexts | Texts

ca. 3000
Sumerian cuneiform writing
on clay tablets developed

ca. 3000
Egypt: writing in hieroglyphic
script developed

2700
Gilgamesh is
king in Uruk

Timeline spans 1,200 years on these two pages

3000 B.C.E.   2800 B.C.E.   2600 B.C.E.

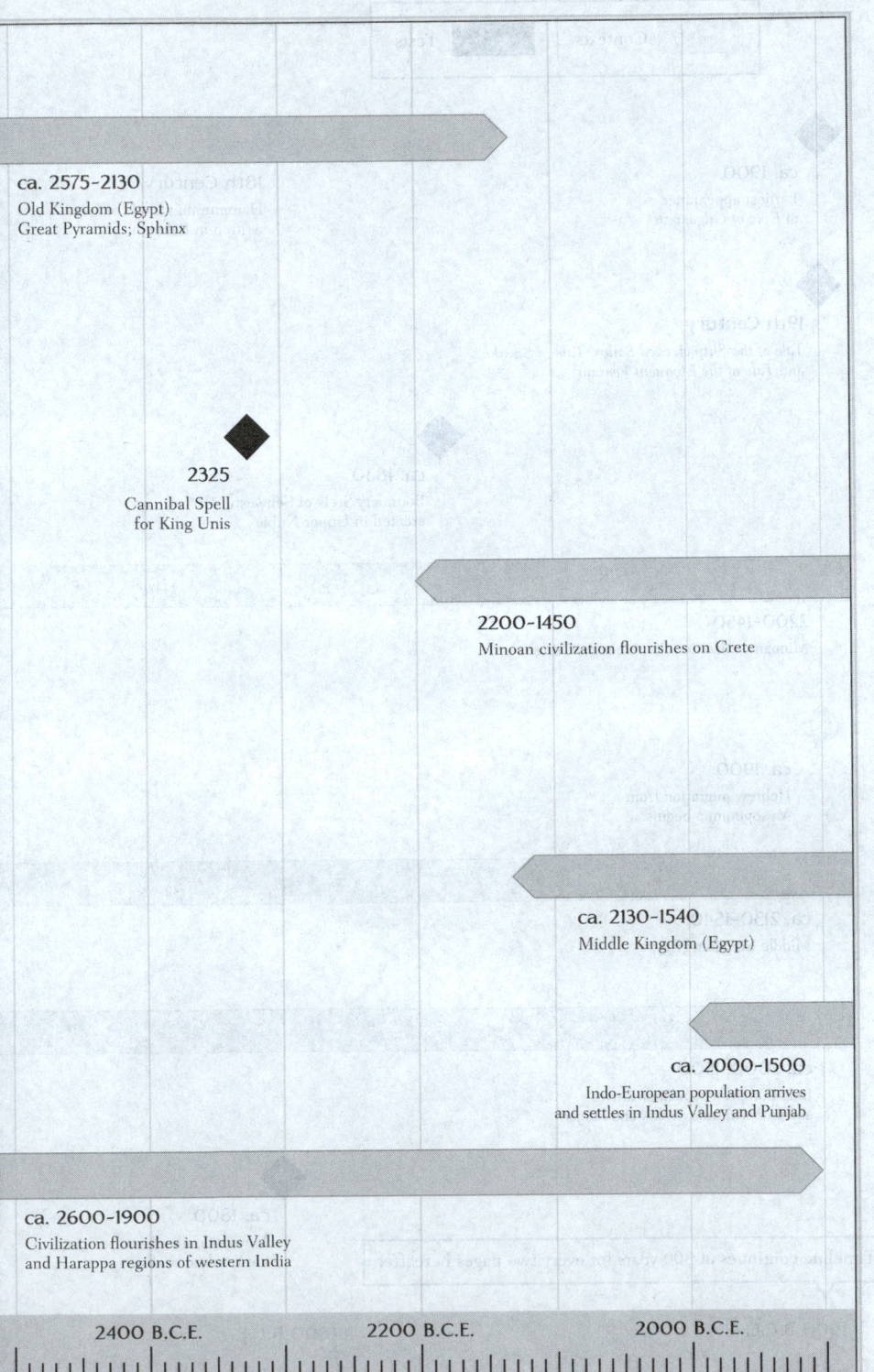

ca. 2575–2130
Old Kingdom (Egypt)
Great Pyramids; Sphinx

2325
Cannibal Spell
for King Unis

2200–1450
Minoan civilization flourishes on Crete

ca. 2130–1540
Middle Kingdom (Egypt)

ca. 2000–1500
Indo-European population arrives
and settles in Indus Valley and Punjab

ca. 2600–1900
Civilization flourishes in Indus Valley
and Harappa regions of western India

2400 B.C.E.   2200 B.C.E.   2000 B.C.E.

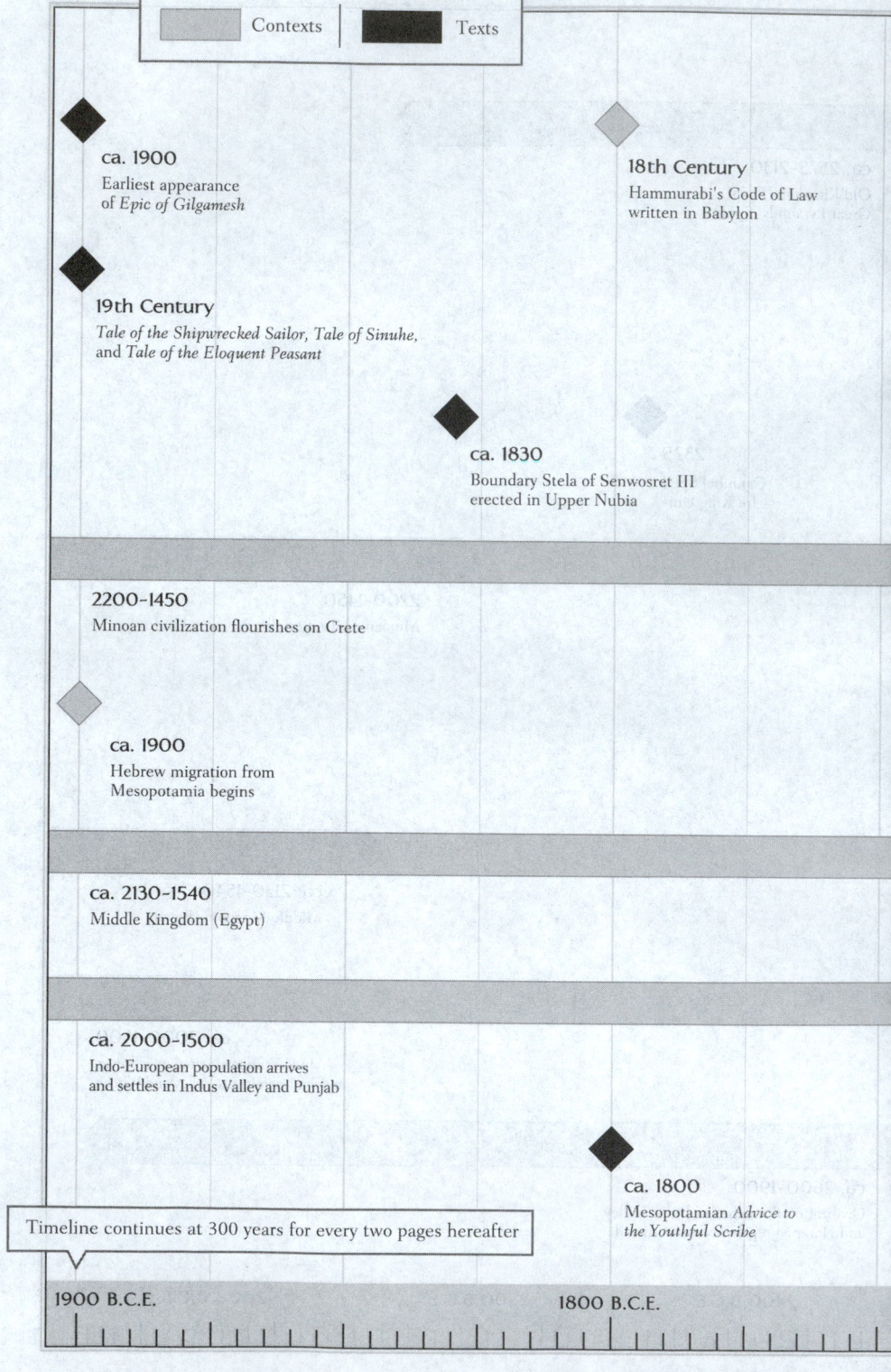

Contexts | Texts

ca. 1900
Earliest appearance
of *Epic of Gilgamesh*

18th Century
Hammurabi's Code of Law
written in Babylon

19th Century
Tale of the Shipwrecked Sailor, Tale of Sinuhe,
and *Tale of the Eloquent Peasant*

ca. 1830
Boundary Stela of Senwosret III
erected in Upper Nubia

2200-1450
Minoan civilization flourishes on Crete

ca. 1900
Hebrew migration from
Mesopotamia begins

ca. 2130-1540
Middle Kingdom (Egypt)

ca. 2000-1500
Indo-European population arrives
and settles in Indus Valley and Punjab

ca. 1800
Mesopotamian *Advice to
the Youthful Scribe*

Timeline continues at 300 years for every two pages hereafter

1900 B.C.E.   1800 B.C.E.

1700 B.C.E.

1600 B.C.E.

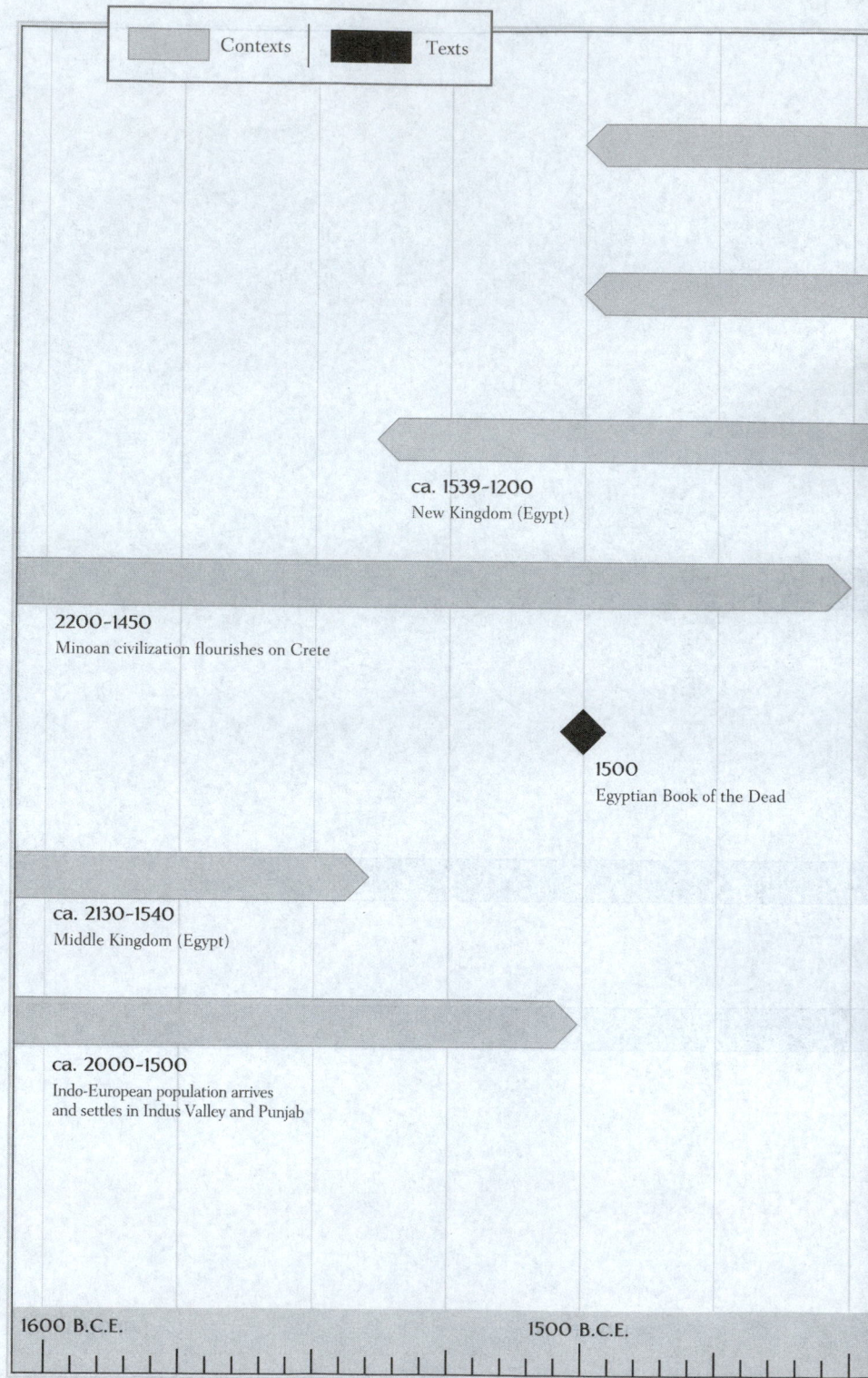

Contexts | Texts

ca. 1539–1200
New Kingdom (Egypt)

2200–1450
Minoan civilization flourishes on Crete

1500
Egyptian Book of the Dead

ca. 2130–1540
Middle Kingdom (Egypt)

ca. 2000–1500
Indo-European population arrives
and settles in Indus Valley and Punjab

1600 B.C.E.   1500 B.C.E.

ca. 1500-1200
Earliest form of Sanskrit developed

ca. 1500-1200
Indo-European settlers establish agrarian
village society in northwestern India

ca. 1350
Akhenaten's *Great
Hymn to Aten*

ca. 1450
Mycenaeans from mainland
Greece occupy Crete

ca. 1375-1354
Egyptian king Akhenaten dedicates
his capital to Aten, the sun god

1400 B.C.E.

1300 B.C.E.

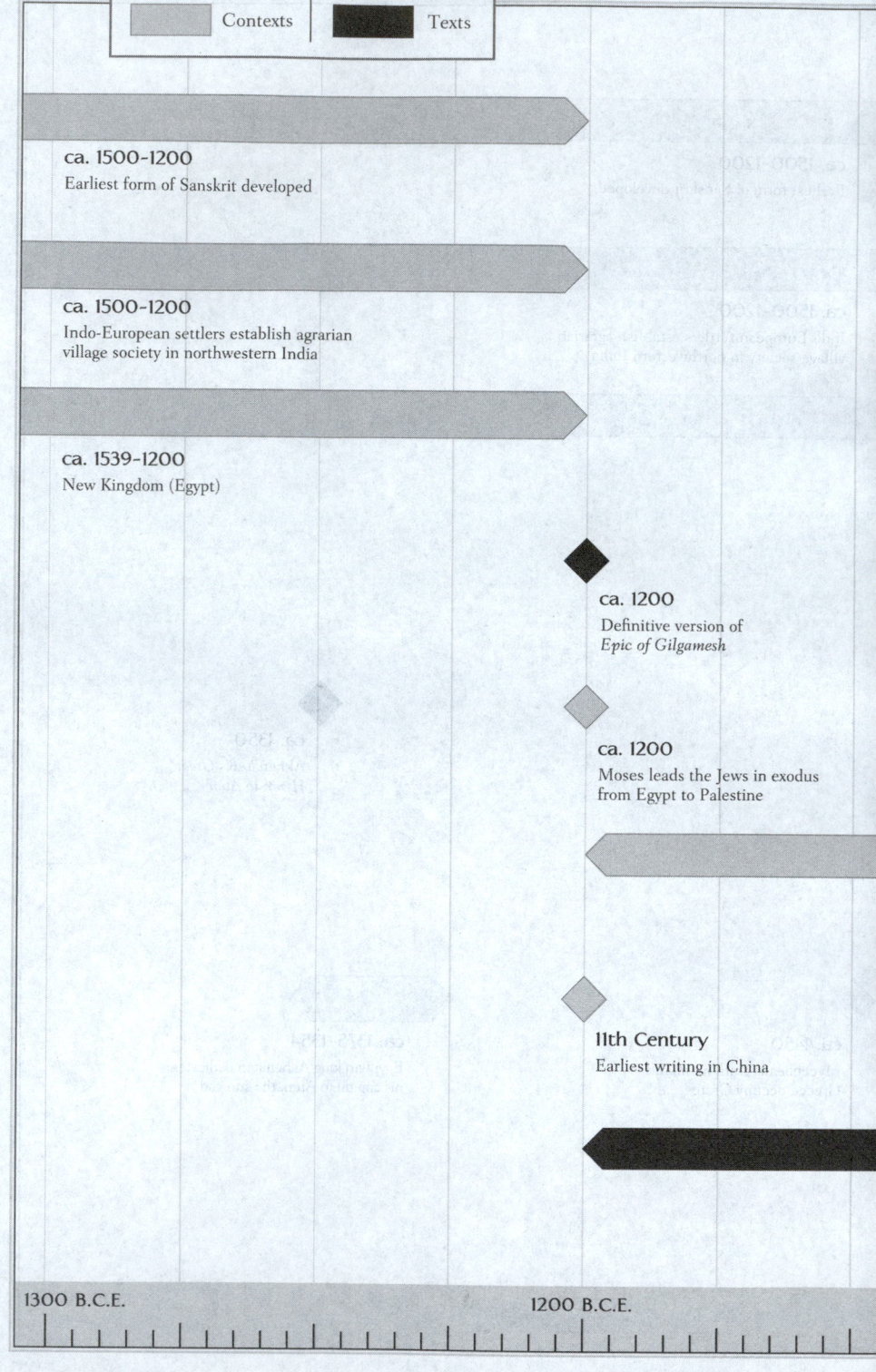

Contexts | Texts

ca. 1500-1200
Earliest form of Sanskrit developed

ca. 1500-1200
Indo-European settlers establish agrarian
village society in northwestern India

ca. 1539-1200
New Kingdom (Egypt)

ca. 1200
Definitive version of
Epic of Gilgamesh

ca. 1200
Moses leads the Jews in exodus
from Egypt to Palestine

11th Century
Earliest writing in China

1300 B.C.E.

1200 B.C.E.

1045
King Wen and King Wu
found the Zhou Dynasty
in China

ca. 1200-900
Emergence of Hindu beliefs and
rituals in India. Caste system develops

ca. 1200-700
The Vedas (Hindu scripture) and early Upaniṣads (philosophical
and mystical texts) composed in the Punjab region of India

1100 B.C.E.   1000 B.C.E.

Contexts | Texts

ca. 1000
Parts of the Hebrew Bible assembled

1000–925
David, then Solomon,
king in Israel

ca. 1000–600
Poems in *Classic of Poetry* composed

ca. 1200–900
Emergence of Hindu beliefs and
rituals in India. Caste system develops

ca. 1200–700
The Vedas (Hindu scripture) and early Upaniṣads (philosophical
and mystical texts) composed in the Punjab region of India

1000 B.C.E.   900 B.C.E.

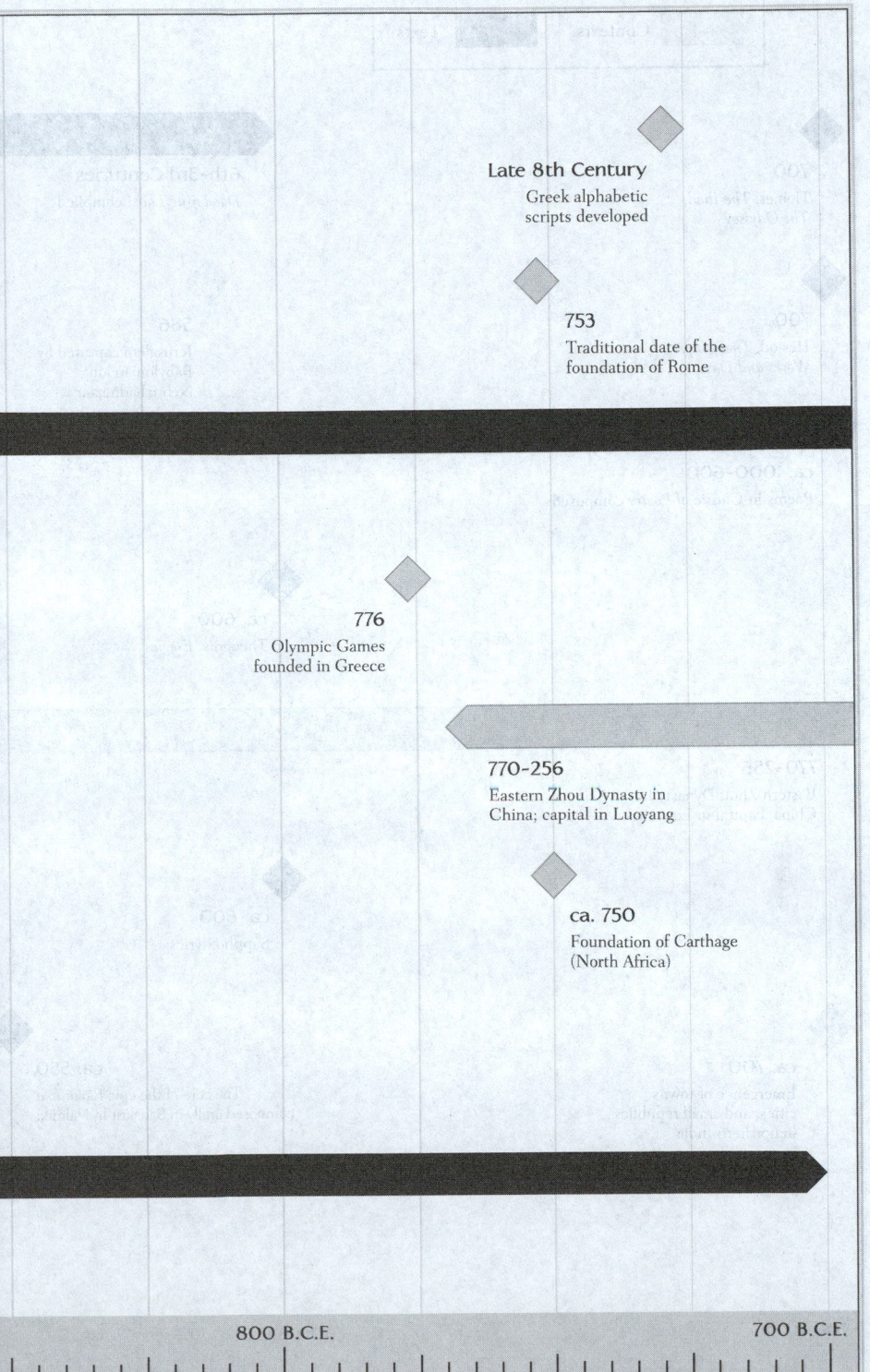

Late 8th Century
Greek alphabetic
scripts developed

753
Traditional date of the
foundation of Rome

776
Olympic Games
founded in Greece

770–256
Eastern Zhou Dynasty in
China; capital in Luoyang

ca. 750
Foundation of Carthage
(North Africa)

800 B.C.E.   700 B.C.E.

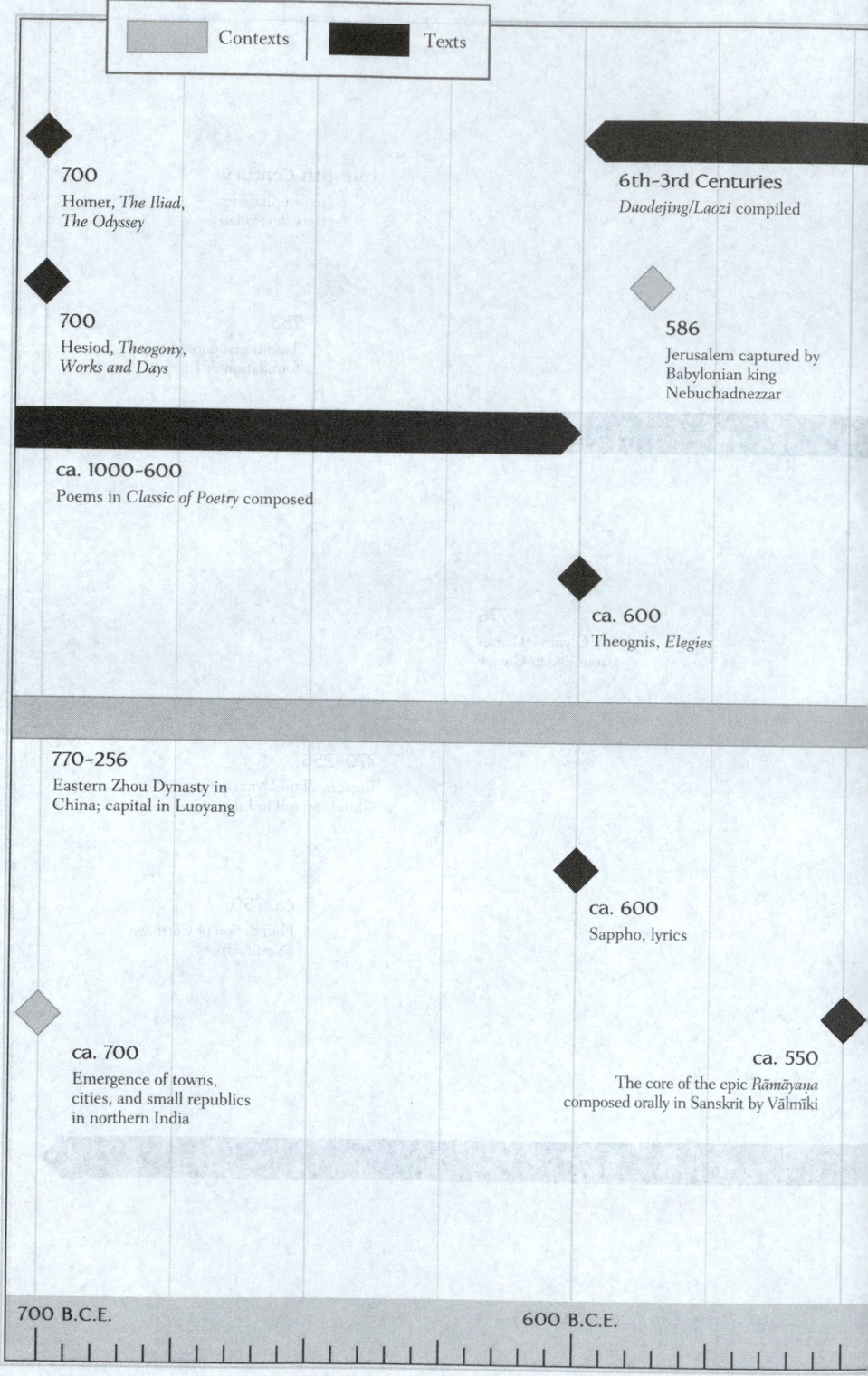

Contexts   Texts

700
Homer, *The Iliad,*
The Odyssey

700
Hesiod, *Theogony,*
Works and Days

ca. 1000–600
Poems in *Classic of Poetry* composed

770–256
Eastern Zhou Dynasty in
China; capital in Luoyang

ca. 700
Emergence of towns,
cities, and small republics
in northern India

6th–3rd Centuries
Daodejing/Laozi compiled

586
Jerusalem captured by
Babylonian king
Nebuchadnezzar

ca. 600
Theognis, *Elegies*

ca. 600
Sappho, lyrics

ca. 550
The core of the epic *Rāmāyaṇa*
composed orally in Sanskrit by Vālmīki

700 B.C.E.   600 B.C.E.

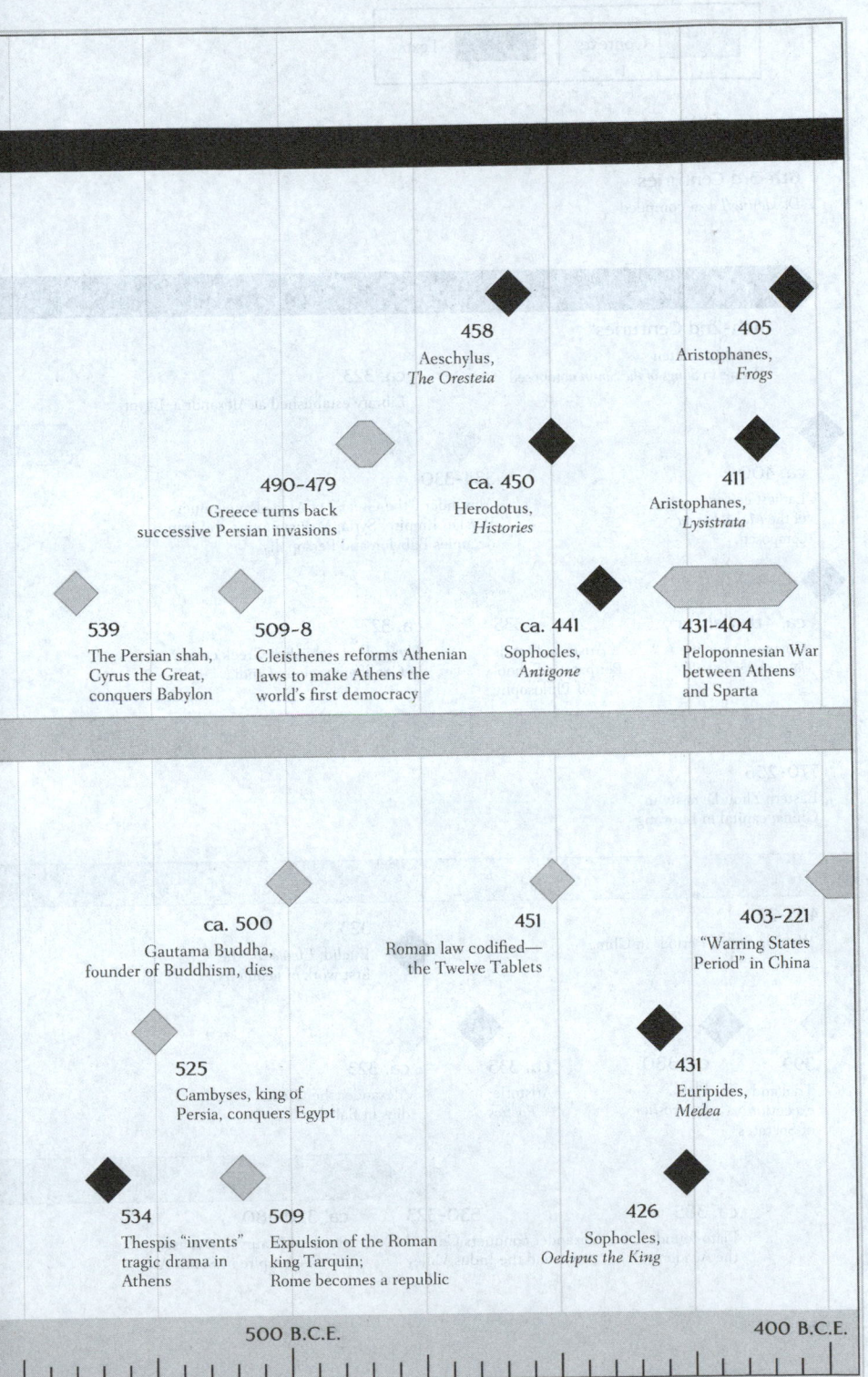

458
Aeschylus,
The Oresteia

405
Aristophanes,
Frogs

490–479
Greece turns back
successive Persian invasions

ca. 450
Herodotus,
Histories

411
Aristophanes,
Lysistrata

539
The Persian shah,
Cyrus the Great,
conquers Babylon

509-8
Cleisthenes reforms Athenian
laws to make Athens the
world's first democracy

ca. 441
Sophocles,
Antigone

431–404
Peloponnesian War
between Athens
and Sparta

ca. 500
Gautama Buddha,
founder of Buddhism, dies

451
Roman law codified—
the Twelve Tablets

403–221
"Warring States
Period" in China

525
Cambyses, king of
Persia, conquers Egypt

431
Euripides,
Medea

534
Thespis "invents"
tragic drama in
Athens

509
Expulsion of the Roman
king Tarquin;
Rome becomes a republic

426
Sophocles,
Oedipus the King

500 B.C.E.

400 B.C.E.

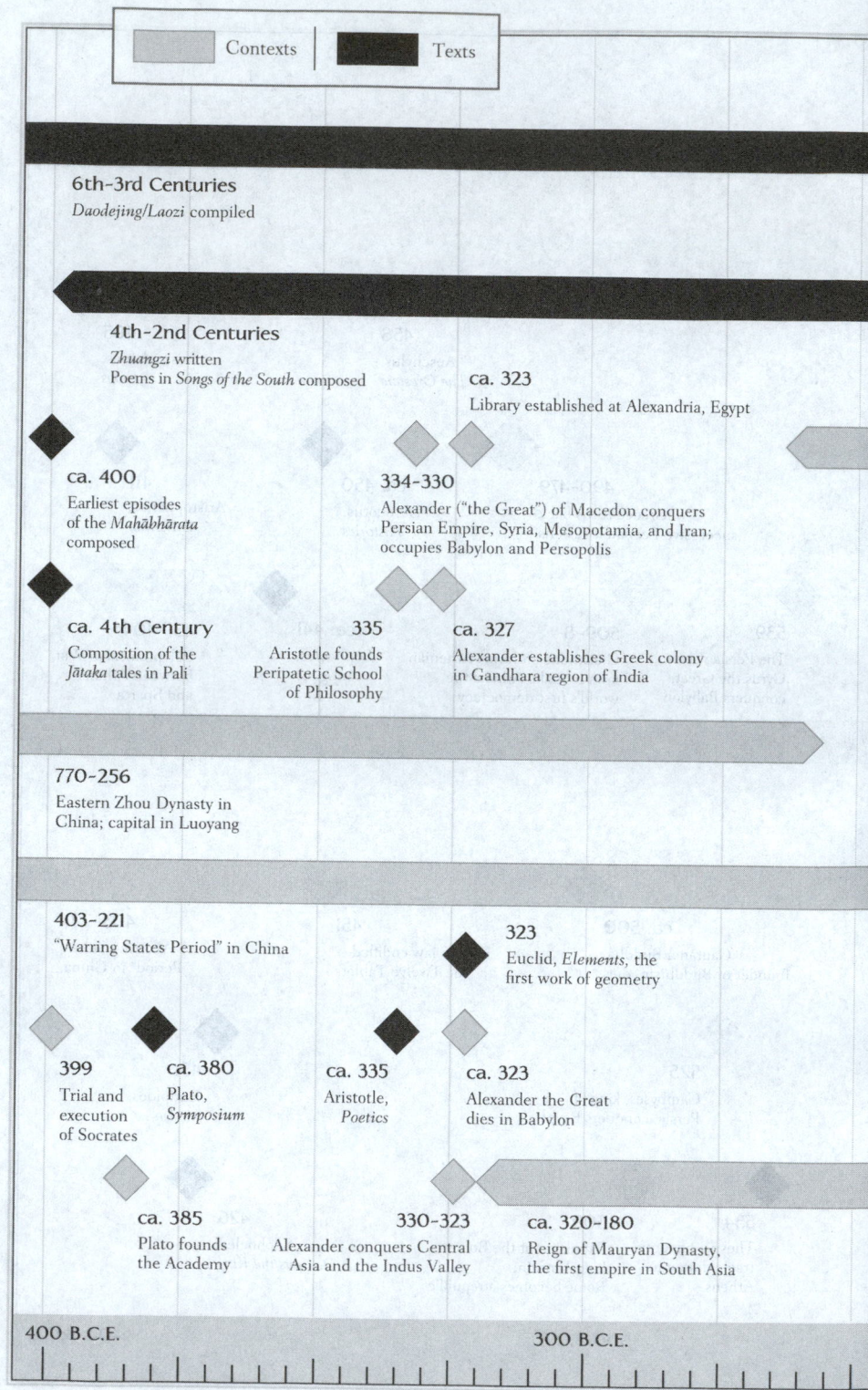

Contexts | Texts

6th-3rd Centuries
Daodejing/Laozi compiled

4th-2nd Centuries
Zhuangzi written
Poems in *Songs of the South* composed

ca. 323
Library established at Alexandria, Egypt

ca. 400
Earliest episodes
of the *Mahābhārata*
composed

334-330
Alexander ("the Great") of Macedon conquers
Persian Empire, Syria, Mesopotamia, and Iran;
occupies Babylon and Persopolis

ca. 4th Century
Composition of the
Jātaka tales in Pali

335
Aristotle founds
Peripatetic School
of Philosophy

ca. 327
Alexander establishes Greek colony
in Gandhara region of India

770-256
Eastern Zhou Dynasty in
China; capital in Luoyang

403-221
"Warring States Period" in China

323
Euclid, *Elements*, the
first work of geometry

399
Trial and
execution
of Socrates

ca. 380
Plato,
Symposium

ca. 335
Aristotle,
Poetics

ca. 323
Alexander the Great
dies in Babylon

ca. 385
Plato founds
the Academy

330-323
Alexander conquers Central
Asia and the Indus Valley

ca. 320-180
Reign of Mauryan Dynasty,
the first empire in South Asia

400 B.C.E.   300 B.C.E.

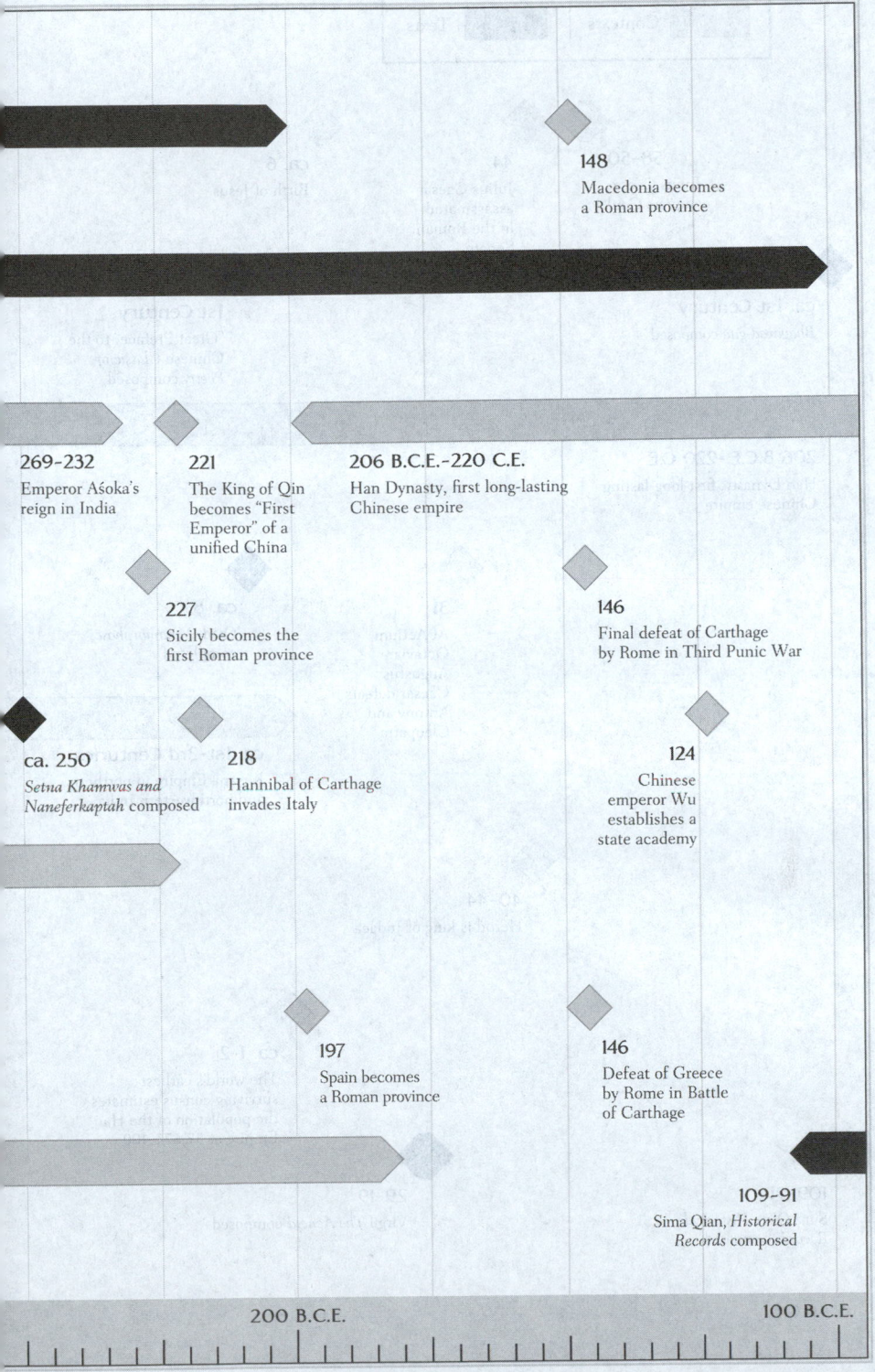

148
Macedonia becomes
a Roman province

269-232
Emperor Aśoka's
reign in India

221
The King of Qin
becomes "First
Emperor" of a
unified China

206 B.C.E.–220 C.E.
Han Dynasty, first long-lasting
Chinese empire

227
Sicily becomes the
first Roman province

146
Final defeat of Carthage
by Rome in Third Punic War

ca. 250
Setna Khamwas and
Naneferkaptah composed

218
Hannibal of Carthage
invades Italy

124
Chinese
emperor Wu
establishes a
state academy

197
Spain becomes
a Roman province

146
Defeat of Greece
by Rome in Battle
of Carthage

109-91
Sima Qian, *Historical*
Records composed

200 B.C.E.   100 B.C.E.

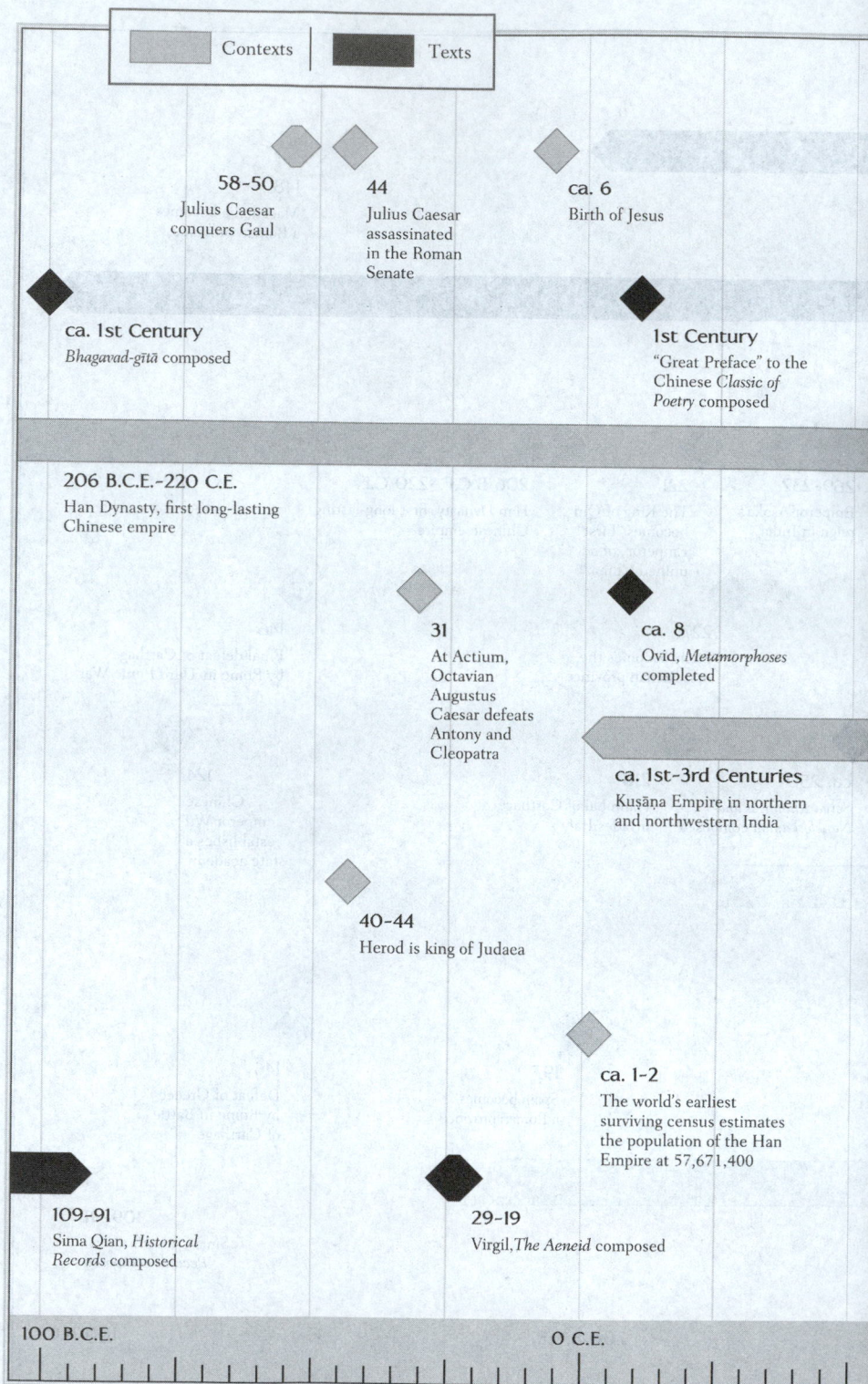

Contexts | Texts

58–50
Julius Caesar conquers Gaul

44
Julius Caesar assassinated in the Roman Senate

ca. 6
Birth of Jesus

ca. 1st Century
Bhagavad-gītā composed

1st Century
"Great Preface" to the Chinese *Classic of Poetry* composed

206 B.C.E.–220 C.E.
Han Dynasty, first long-lasting Chinese empire

31
At Actium, Octavian Augustus Caesar defeats Antony and Cleopatra

ca. 8
Ovid, *Metamorphoses* completed

ca. 1st–3rd Centuries
Kuṣāṇa Empire in northern and northwestern India

40–44
Herod is king of Judaea

ca. 1–2
The world's earliest surviving census estimates the population of the Han Empire at 57,671,400

109–91
Sima Qian, *Historical Records* composed

29–19
Virgil, *The Aeneid* composed

100 B.C.E.   0 C.E.

57

Japan sends diplomatic envoys
to the Han court in China

ca. 2nd Century

Completion of the canonical
Sanskrit version of the *Rāmāyaṇa*

ca. 100

Earliest introduction of
Buddhism into China

105

Earliest paper
made in China

100 C.E.   200 C.E.

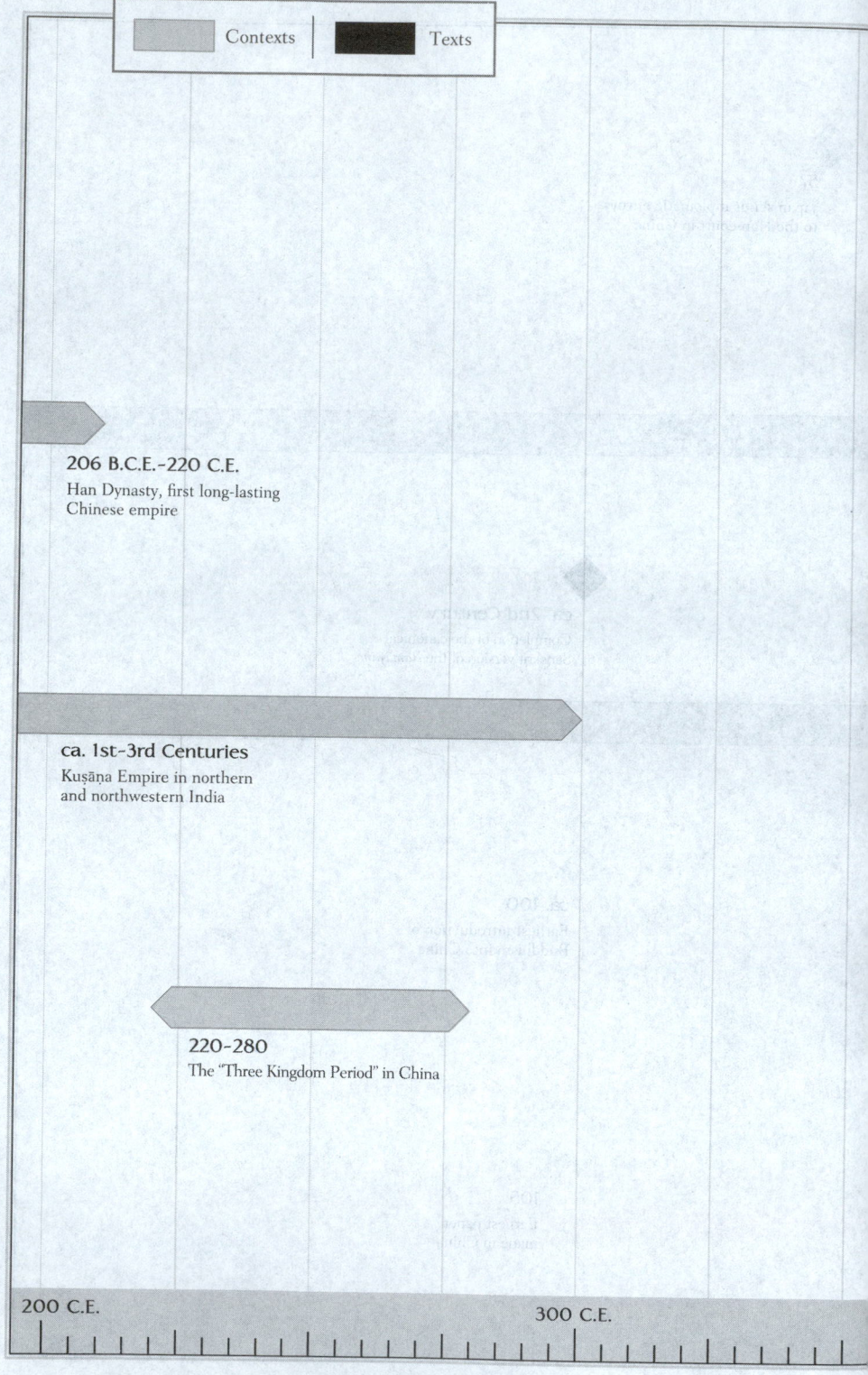

Contexts | Texts

206 B.C.E.–220 C.E.
Han Dynasty, first long-lasting
Chinese empire

ca. 1st–3rd Centuries
Kuṣāṇa Empire in northern
and northwestern India

220–280
The "Three Kingdom Period" in China

200 C.E.   300 C.E.

◆

ca. 400
Completion of the canonical Sanskrit
version of the *Mahābhārata*

Permissions Acknowledgments

Index